THE COLLECTED WORKS OF
SAMUEL TAYLOR COLERIDGE 12

MARGINALIA

General Editor: KATHLEEN COBURN

THE COLLECTED WORKS

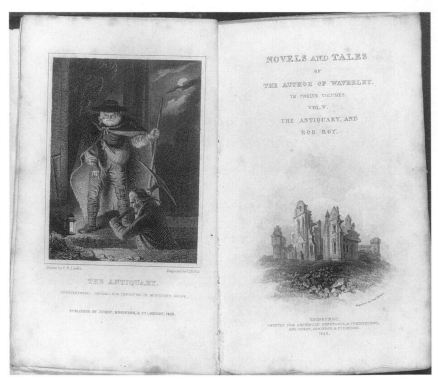

1. The frontispiece and title-page to Vol v of Sir Walter Scott's *Novels and Tales*
(12 vols Edinburgh 1823). Coleridge understood the portrait of the bearded
Dr Dousterswivel to have been modelled on himself.
See Walter SCOTT COPY A headnote
The British Library; reproduced by kind permission

Samuel Taylor Coleridge

Marginalia

IV

Pamphlets to Shakespeare

EDITED BY

H. J. Jackson and
George Whalley

✣ BOLLINGEN SERIES LXXV
PRINCETON UNIVERSITY PRESS

This edition of the text by Samuel Taylor Coleridge is
copyright © 1998 by Princeton University Press

The Collected Works, sponsored by Bollingen Foundation, is published in
the United States of America by Princeton University Press,
41 William Street, Princeton, New Jersey 08540
All rights reserved
ISBN 0-691-09957-X
LCC 87-104402

Library of Congress Cataloging-in-Publication Data
Coleridge, Samuel Taylor, 1772–1834.
Marginalia.
(Bollingen series; 75) (The Collected Works
of Samuel Taylor Coleridge; 12)
Includes bibliographical references.
Contents: I. Abbt to Byfield—2. Camden to
Hutton—3. Irving to Oxlee.
I. Whalley, George, 1915–1983. II. Title. III. Series. IV. Series: Coleridge,
Samuel Taylor, 1772–1834. Works. 1969; 12.
PR4470.F69 vol. 12 [PR4480] 87-104402
ISBN 0-691-09879-4 (Princeton University Press: v. 1)
ISBN 0-691-09889-1 (Princeton University Press: v. 2)
ISBN 0-691-09954-5 (Princeton University Press: v. 3)

The Collected Works constitutes
the seventy-fifth publication in Bollingen Series

The present work, number 12 of the Collected Works,
is in 6 volumes, this being 12: IV

Princeton University Press books are printed on acid-free paper and meet
the guidelines for permanence and durability of the Committee on
Production Guidelines for Book Longevity of the Council on Library Resources

Printed in the United States of America
1 3 5 7 9 10 8 6 4 2

THIS EDITION
OF THE WORKS OF
SAMUEL TAYLOR COLERIDGE
IS DEDICATED
IN GRATITUDE TO
THE FAMILY EDITORS
IN EACH GENERATION

CONTENTS

━━━━━━━━ IV ━━━━━━━━

Marginalia

[† designates a "Lost Book"—a book reported to contain marginal notes in C's hand but which the editor has not been able to find and for which no transcript of marginalia is known to exist.]

vii

Contents

LIST OF ILLUSTRATIONS

FOREWORD

Now THAT THIS EDITION is moving steadily toward completion, it is time for a review of some of the changes in policy or practice that have been introduced during its piecemeal publication, and for some anticipation of the final stages while they are still open to advice from readers. As I write this foreword to the fourth volume of the *Marginalia*, I await public scholarly reaction to the third. Informal and private responses seem to indicate that readers were scarcely aware of the change of editors, so that, as we had hoped, continuity was preserved in the presentation of the text as it had been in the change from one printing house to another in Volume Two. Nevertheless, changes have occurred as the circumstances of production were altered and as users began to report difficulties or make suggestions. Although the general statement of editorial policy in I xxiii–xxxii remains authoritative, readers may notice some divergence in practice, as the editors had to wrestle with the special requirements of particular cases and weigh the demands of a given textual situation against the dream of absolute consistency. One significant change introduced in Volume Three has to do with the representation and position of Coleridge's marginal marks—daggers, crosses, stars and the like, all standardised by convention as asterisks: whereas the earlier volumes occasionally set them off by using a single square bracket at the left-hand end of a line so as approximately to reproduce the point marked in the margin of the book (as in BLANCO WHITE 1), it was found that in the process of transmission from manuscript to transcription and then to type and print the symbol was liable to have strayed a long way from its original position, and so the asterisk is now located (without a bracket) within the text at the point at which Coleridge seems to have been moved to make his quick mark in the margin—that is, in the line that he marked and at the point in the line that he apparently meant to take note of. (Furthermore, when the textus is not in English, Coleridge's internal markings are printed in colour in the translation as well as in the textus, for the benefit of readers using the English versions only.) Readers ought to be aware of the element of editorial judgment and regularisation in these cases, as in the more commonplace conventions of standardised valedictions, paragraphing, and the use of italic type instead of underlining.

Other, minor changes to the textual policies announced in Volume One are the representation of Coleridge's "paragraph mark" (∫∫) as §, since it turns out that he used it to stand for "section" as well as for "paragraph" and that both editors had at one time or another found themselves obliged to violate the stated policy; and the restoration of the ampersand & (for *et* "and") in Latin passages as they appeared in the original works. In printing extracts from plays, we have normalised the format so that all speakers' names are given in small capitals however they were presented in the various editions that Coleridge read.

In addition to annotated texts from Sherlock to Zwick, Volumes Five and Six are expected to include addenda as well as a comprehensive index to the *Marginalia*. In case readers may know of the existence of annotated texts that I am not aware of, or of better texts of works already in print in this edition (e.g. holograph, where we have had to publish from transcripts or printed versions), I shall give here a short-title list of the current Table of Contents for Volumes Five and Six, and I invite corrections or additions. The annotated works we intend to publish are these, "lost" titles being omitted: William Sherlock *A Vindication of the . . . Trinity* (1690); Algernon Sidney *Works* (1772); Sir Philip Sidney *Arcadia* (1638); Philip Skelton *Complete Works* (1824); Charles Smith *Seven Letters on National Religion* (1833); John Smith *Select Discourses* (1660); Karl Wilhelm Ferdinand Solger *Philosophische Gespräche* (1817); Robert Southey *The Doctor* (1834), *History of Brazil* (1810–19), *Joan of Arc* (1796), *Life of Wesley* (1820), *Lives of the British Admirals* (1833–7); Friedrich Spee *Trutz Nachtigall* (1817); Benedict Spinoza *Opera quae supersunt omnia* (1802–3); Thomas Stanley *The History of Philosophy* (1701); Mariana Starke *Travels on the Continent* (1820); William Steele *Mr Recorder's Speech* (1833); Heinrich Steffens *Anthropologie* (1822), *Beyträge zur innern Naturgeschichte der Erde* (1801), *Caricaturen des Heiligsten* (1819–21), *Die gegenwärtige Zeit* (1817), *Geognostisch-geologische Aufsätze* (1810), *Grundzüge der philosophischen Naturwissenschaft* (1806), *Ueber die Idee der Universitäten* (1809); [John Sterling] *Arthur Coningsby* (1833); Sir William Stewart *Outlines of a Plan for the General Reform of the British Land Forces* (1806); Edward Stillingfleet *Origines Sacrae* (1675); John Strype *The History of the Life . . . [of] Edward Grindal* (1710), *Memorials of . . . Thomas Cranmer* (1694); Johann Caspar Suicerus *Thesaurus ecclesiasticus* (1682); Emanuel Swedenborg *De coelo et ejus mirabilibus et inferno* (1758), *De cultu et amore dei* (1745), *De equo albo* (1758), *Oeconomia regni animalis* (1740–1), *Prodromus philosophiae* (1734), *Regnum animale* (1744–5), *True Christian Religion* (1819), *The Wisdom of Angels* (1816); Jonathan Swift *Works* (1768); Thomas Swinburne *A Letter to* . . . *Robert Peel* (1827); Isaac Taylor *Natural History of Enthusiasm* (1829); Jeremy Taylor *A Course of Sermons* (1678), *Holy Living and Holy Dying* (1676), *Holy Living and Holy Dying* (1710), *The Worthy Communicant* (1674), *Polemicall Discourses* (1674); John Taylor *An Essay on Money* (1830); Esias Tegnér *Der Frithiofs-Sage* (1826); W. G. Tennemann *Geschichte der Philosophie* (1798–1819); Alfred, Lord Tennyson *Poems, Chiefly Lyrical* (1830); St Teresa *Works* (1675); Johann Nicolaus Tetens *Philosophische Versuche* (1777); Jean de Thévenot *Travels into the Levant* (1687); Ludwig Tieck *The Old Man of the Mountain* (1831); Charles Tennyson Turner *Sonnets and Fugitive Pieces* (1830); L. K. Valckenaer *Diatribe de Aristobulo Judaeo* (1806); Sir Harry Vane *A Healing Question* (1660); Robert Vaughan *The Life and Opinions of John de Wycliffe* (1828); William Vincent *The Greek Verb Analysed* (1795); "Vindex" *The Conduct of the British Government* (1831); Virgil *Georgica hexaglotta* (1827); F. M. A. de Voltaire *A Treatise on Toleration* (1779); G. Voss *Poeticarum institutionum* (1647); Edward Gibbon Wakefield *A Letter from Sydney* (1829); John Walker *A Dictionary of the English Language* (1775); William Wall *Conference about Infant Baptism* (1809?); John Benn Walsh *On the Present Balance of Parties* (1832); *Popular Opinions on Parliamentary Reform* (1831); Daniel Waterland *The Importance of the Doctrine of the Holy Trinity* (1734), *A Vindication of Christ's Divinity* (1719); Alaric A. Watts *Poetical Sketches* (1823); John Webster *The Displaying of Supposed Witchcraft* (1677); Adam Weishaupt *Apologie des Misvergnügens und Uebels* (1790), *Ueber Wahrheit und sittliche Volkommenheit* (1793–7); William Charles Wells *Two Essays* (1818); Benjamin Wheeler *Theological Lectures* (1819); John Whitaker *The Origin of Arianism Disclosed* (1791); Gilbert White *Works, in Natural History* (1802); Thomas Whitfield *A Discourse on the Liberty of Conscience* (1649); Christoph Martin Wieland *Comische Erzählungen* (1785?), *Idris* (1785), *Neueste Gedichte* (1780); Edward Williams *Poems, Lyric and Pastoral* (1794); Walter Wilson *Memoirs of the Life and Times of Daniel De Foe* (1830); Johann Christoff Wolf *Curae philologicae et criticae* (1735); Christian von Wolff *Logic* (1770); Christopher Wordsworth *Six Letters to Granville Sharp* (1802), *"Who Wrote ΕΙΚΩΝ ΒΑΣΙΛΙΚΗ?" Considered* (1828); William Wordsworth "Benjamin the Waggoner", *The Excursion* (1814), "The Prelude" MS B, translation of Virgil *Aeneid*; Francis Wrangham *Life of Dr Richard Bentley* (1816), *Scraps* (1816); Xenophon *Memoirs of Socrates* (1767); *Zeitschrift für spekulative Physik* ed F. W. J. von Schelling (1800–1); Henry Augustus Zwick *Calmuc Tartary* (1831).

The addenda will include the following: Thomas Amory *Life of John Buncle* (1756); Edwin Atherstone *The Last Days of Herculaneum* (1821); an additional note to John and Michael Banim *Tales by the O'Hara Family* (1826); additional notes to Richard Baxter *Reliquiae Baxterianae* (1696); *La danse des morts* (1789); *Declaration of Principles* (n.d.); Viscount Dillon *The Life and Opinions of Sir Richard Maltravers* (1822); William Godwin "Abbas King of Persia"; John Haslam *Medical Jurisprudence* (1817); J. G. Herder *Metacritique* (1799); Horace *Opera*; Immanuel Kant "Der Streit der Fakultäten" in *Vermischte Schriften* (1799); Pietro Metastasio *Opere* (1782–3). There will also be an Appendix of "Ghosts", i.e. of works reported as having contained notes by Coleridge which, upon examination, proved not to. For a convenient list of works said to have been annotated by Coleridge but now lost, see articles by George Whalley in *Book Collector* xvi (1968) 428–42 and xviii (1969) 223; although the list now stands in need of correction, thanks largely to Professor Whalley's own later work, it is still a useful working guide.

ACKNOWLEDGMENTS

The edition continues to make large financial demands on its supporters. In the four years or so since the last volume went in, I have been generously assisted by the Princeton University Press, which both maintains the Coleridge Office in Toronto and enables me to escape from it now and then; by the Social Sciences and Humanities Research Council of Canada, which has paid for released time, for computer equipment, and for invaluable student assistance; by the Cassidy Fund of Trinity College, which allowed me to make a flying visit to libraries in New York and to hire some surprisingly keen undergraduates as proofreaders; and by the Humanities and Social Sciences Committee of the University of Toronto, which made funds available for an out-of-season trip to libraries in London and Oxford.

As to the libraries themselves, the headnotes to individual titles in this volume will reveal the locations of the annotated volumes and suggest how important the cooperation of all the institutions concerned has been. The extent of my demands on the patience and resourcefulness of the staff involved has not always been in proportion to the amount of material held, however, and I must make special mention of the library staff of Victoria College, Trinity College, and the Fisher Rare Books Library in the University of Toronto; of the Houghton Library at Harvard; and of the literally wonderful British Library. Other libraries that do not actually hold Coleridge books included in this volume have dealt with me or my enquiries with great civility, notably the Wellcome Library, the library of the Royal Institution of Engineers, the Public Record Office, and the library of the National Maritime Museum, all in London; the Bodleian Library in Oxford; and the University Library in Cambridge. Of the private collectors who have given me access to their valuable books and papers, I am particularly grateful to Denise Coleridge of Axminster, and to Paul Betz of Washington DC.

The University of Toronto continues to be an ideal spot for an editor, especially for an editor of Coleridge. Size has a lot to do with it, but size isn't everything. The institution has an honourable history of support for ambitious scholarly projects like the *Collected Works*; the English Department, more than twenty years ago now, founded an annual Conference on Editorial Problems that has built up an extraordinary international network for advice (though it has to be admitted that the advice very often is, Don't do it); and I have been able to count on the sympathetic understanding of the current head of the department, Tom Adamowski. The human and intellectual resources of my own and other departments have always been available, so I thank particularly, for their solutions to some of the problems in the *Marginalia*, Timothy Barnes, Chris McDonough, and John Warden, in Classics; John Beattie, in History and Criminology; Alan Bewell, Alexander Leggatt, Jane Millgate, and Peter Heyworth, in English; Trevor Levere, in History of Science; Dennis McAuliffe, in Italian; Colin Proudman and Douglas Fox, in Divinity; E. J. Revell, in Near Eastern Studies; Brian Stock, in Comparative Literature; and David Townsend, in Medieval Studies.

Besides my dependence on their published volumes, which will be apparent in the footnotes, I have often called on the editors of other titles in the series for assistance, and always met a ready response. In this volume as before, I have had substantial help from Anthony Harding, John Beer, James Engell, and R. A. Foakes; but I hope I will be excused for saying that in this group the absolute paragon is my husband, J. R. de J. Jackson, who puts up with Coleridge conundrums even before breakfast and after bedtime. Raimonda Modiano has been an invaluable collaborator in the German texts, and the role of the Classical Editor, Lorna Arnold, goes far beyond the notice that she is given as a coeditor for several titles here: on top of everything else, she read this whole volume in a draft version and made hundreds of constructive suggestions. She is and has for many years been the unsung heroine of the edition as a whole.

Finally, much of the technical side of this edition, from the supplying of translations to the checking of references and the seemingly endless proofreading, has been accomplished by undergraduate, graduate, and post-graduate students—notably, for the German texts, by Nicholas Halmi, Royce Nickel, and Thomas Wagenbaer—without whose labour this volume might never have appeared. To Nicholas Halmi, who has Coleridgean breadth of learning combined with un-Coleridgean scholarly scrupulosity, I am particularly indebted. And in the Coleridge Office, at the centre of it all, somehow keeping track, is Rea Wilmshurst, the *sine qua non*.

Toronto, January 1994   H. J. JACKSON

POSTSCRIPT. While this volume was in production, the unthinkable happened: Rea Wilmshurst was stricken with cancer and died—peacefully in the end, but after a stubborn fight and not until she had put things in order one last time. She introduced Marion Filipiuk to the Coleridge Project as her successor so that business here could continue as usual. For Rea's generosity and professionalism, and for Marion's calm in catastrophic circumstances, we cannot be grateful enough.

EDITORIAL PRACTICE: A BRIEF GUIDE

F OR the definition of "marginalia", "textus", and "submarginalia" see *CM* I xxiii–xxvi. For special terms such as "fly-pages", "annex", "ms transcript", "quasi-marginalia", "lost book", and "marked book" see I xxx–xxxii.

All marginalia are transcribed literatim from the original mss, whenever these were available to the editor: cancelled words and phrases are restored; idiosyncratic spellings and obvious misspellings are reproduced without comment; slips of the pen and accidental repetitions are also reproduced normally with explanation in a textual note. See I xxiii. (When C's notes are published from a transcript in another hand, slips of the pen and cancellations are normally ignored.) A second parenthesis or quotation mark omitted by oversight is supplied by the editor without comment unless the placing of the mark is in doubt. Illegible deletions are omitted.

The annotated books are entered in alphabetical order by author, and within an author-entry in alphabetical order by title. Reference to annotated books within this edition is made by short title (identifiable from the running headlines) to which the serial number of a particular annotation can be attached: e.g. DONNE *Sermons* COPY B **57**. (Bold figures are used only for serial numbers of marginalia.) Editorial footnotes are identified by attaching the number of the footnote indicator to the abbreviated title of the book: e.g. DONNE *Sermons* COPY B **57** n 2. See also I xxix–xxx.

CONVENTIONS USED IN TRANSCRIPTION

[wild]	A reading supplied by the editor when the word has been lost from the ms by cropping or physical damage
[not][a]	A word inserted by the editor to supply an unintentional omission on Coleridge's part, or to clarify the sense of an elliptical or ambiguous phrase. The accompanying textual note [a] accounts for the insertion
[? wild]	An uncertain reading
[? wild/world]	Possible alternative readings
[. . .]	An illegible word or phrase
[. . . . .]	A passage of undetermined extent illegible through rubbing or offsetting, or lost by cropping or other physical damage

xix

⟨ ⟩   A word or passage inserted between the lines, or marked for inser-
                    tion from another part of the page (in which case a textual note is
                    provided). An inserted word or passage is not so marked when it
                    follows immediately upon a cancellation in the ms

ABBREVIATIONS

This list reflects the use of abbreviations in this volume only; for a complete list
covering the whole set of *Marginalia* see Volume VI. Place of publication is London, unless otherwise noted. Special abbreviations that apply only to certain au-
thor-entries or book-entries are given in the appropriate headnote.

Altick   Richard D. Altick *The Shows of London* (Cambridge MA & Lon-
                    don 1978)

AR (1825)   S. T. Coleridge *Aids to Reflection* (1825)

AR (*CC*)   S. T. Coleridge *Aids to Reflection* ed John Beer (London & Prince-
                    ton 1993) – *CC* IX

AV   The "Authorised Version"—or "King James Version"—of the
                    Bible, in modern orthography

BCP   *The Book of Common Prayer and Administration of the Sacraments
                    and Other Rites and Ceremonies of the Church According to the
                    Use of the Church of England*

BL   S. T. Coleridge *Biographia Literaria; or Biographical Sketches of
                    My Literary Life and Opinions*

BL (1847)   S. T. Coleridge *Biographia Literaria* ed H. N. and Sara Coleridge
                    (2 vols 1847)

BL (*CC*)   S. T. Coleridge *Biographia Literaria* ed James Engell and W.
                    Jackson Bate (2 vols London & Princeton 1983) = *CC* VII

BM   British Library, Reference Division, formerly "British Museum
                    Library"

B Works   George Berkeley *Works* ed A. A. Luce and T. E. Jessop (9 vols
                    1948–57)

C   Samuel Taylor Coleridge

C&S   S. T. Coleridge *On the Constitution of the Church and State,
                    According to the Idea of Each* (2nd ed 1830)

C&S (*CC*)   S. T. Coleridge *On the Constitution of the Church and State*
                    ed John Colmer (London & Princeton 1976) = *CC* X

CC   *The Collected Works of Samuel Taylor Coleridge* general ed
                    Kathleen Coburn (London & Princeton 1969–)

CCD   J. Robert Barth, S. J. *Coleridge and Christian Doctrine* (Cambridge
                    MA 1969)

C d r V	See Kant *C d r V*
CL	Charles Lamb
CL	*Collected Letters of Samuel Taylor Coleridge* ed Earl Leslie Griggs (6 vols Oxford & New York 1956–71)
CM (CC)	S. T. Coleridge *Marginalia* ed George Whalley and H. J. Jackson (London & Princeton 1980–) = *CC* xii
CN	*The Notebooks of Samuel Taylor Coleridge* ed Kathleen Coburn (New York, Princeton & London 1957–)
Coffman	Ralph J. Coffman *Coleridge's Library: A Bibliography of Books Owned or Read by Samuel Taylor Coleridge* (Boston 1987)
CRB	*Henry Crabb Robinson on Books and Their Writers* ed Edith J. Morley (3 vols 1938)
col(s)	column(s)
DC	Derwent Coleridge
DC SC (1888)	*The Philological Library of . . . Derwent Coleridge* (Sotheby Jul 1888). Marked copy: BM SC S 956(1)
De Q	Thomas De Quincey
De Q Works	*The Collected Writings of Thomas De Quincey* ed David Masson (14 vols Edinburgh 1889–90)
DNB	*Dictionary of National Biography* (1885–)
DW	Dorothy Wordsworth
D Works	René Descartes *Philosophical Works* tr E. S. Haldane and G. T. Ross (2 vols Cambridge 1911)
EC	*The English Catalogue of Books (including the original "London" Catalogue* [of 1786 for 1700–86]) . . . *Issued in the United Kingdom . . . 1801–1836* ed R. A. Peddie and Q. Waddington (1914)
Ed Rev	*The Edinburgh Review* (Edinburgh & London 1802–1929)
EHC	Ernest Hartley Coleridge
EOT (CC)	S. T. Coleridge *Essays on His Times in "The Morning Post" and "The Courier"* ed David V. Erdman (3 vols London & Princeton 1978) = *CC* iii
Friend (CC)	S. T. Coleridge *The Friend* ed Barbara E. Rooke (2 vols London & Princeton 1969) = *CC* iv
Gillman SC (1843)	*Catalogue of a Valuable Collection of Books, Including the Library of James Gillman, Esq* (Henry Southgate 1843). Marked copies: BM SC Sg 64 (2) and Sg a 53. The Gillman lots were 303–466, 468–501, 504–34: *CM (CC)* i clxi n 1

G Mag	*The Gentleman's Magazine* (1731–1907)
Green SC (1880)	*Catalogue of the Library of Joseph Henry Green . . . Sold by Auction* (Sotheby Jul 1880). Marked copy: BM SC S 805 (1)
Green SC (1884)	*Catalogue of Scarce and Valuable Books, Including a Remarkable Collection of Coleridgeiana* (Scribner & Welford, New York 1884)
Hansard	*The Parliamentary Debates from the Year 1803 to the Present Time* ed T. C. Hansard (41 vols 1812–20)
HC	Hartley Coleridge
HCR	Henry Crabb Robinson
HD	Humphry Davy
HLQ	*Huntington Library Quarterly* (1937–)
HNC	Henry Nelson Coleridge
JHG	Joseph Henry Green
Kant *C d r V*	Immanuel Kant *Critik der reinen Vernunft*
Kant *C d r V* B	Immanuel Kant *Critik der reinen Vernunft* 2nd ed (1787)
Kant *VS*	Immanuel Kant *Vermischte Schriften* (4 vols Halle & Königsberg 1799–1807)
Kemp Smith	*Immanuel Kant's Critique of Pure Reason* tr Norman Kemp Smith (rev ed 1933)
LCL	Loeb Classical Library
Lects 1795 (CC)	S. T. Coleridge *Lectures 1795: On Politics and Religion* ed Lewis Patton and Peter Mann (London & Princeton 1971) = *CC* I
Lects 1808–1819	S. T. Coleridge *Lectures 1808–1819: On Literature* ed Reginald A. Foakes (2 vols London & Princeton 1987) = *CC* v
Levere	Trevor H. Levere *Poetry Realized in Nature: Samuel Taylor Coleridge and Early Nineteenth-Century Science* (Cambridge 1981)
lit	literally
LL (M)	*The Letters of Charles and Mary Anne Lamb* ed Edwin W. Marrs, Jr (3 vols Ithaca NY 1975–8)
L Works (1903)	*The Works of Charles and Mary Lamb* ed E. V. Lucas (5 vols 1903)
Logic (CC)	S. T. Coleridge *Logic* ed J. R. de J. Jackson (London & Princeton 1981) = *CC* XIII
Lost List	A handlist prepared by George Whalley of books known to have been annotated by C but not located at the time this edi-

	tion went to press. An incomplete version was published in *Book Collector* xvii (1968) 428–42 and xviii (1969) 223
LR	*The Literary Remains of Samuel Taylor Coleridge* ed H. N. Coleridge (4 vols 1836–9)
LS (CC)	S. T. Coleridge *Lay Sermons* [being *The Statesman's Manual* and *A Lay Sermon*] ed R. J. White (London & Princeton 1972) = *CC* vi
Method	*S. T. Coleridge's Treatise on Method as Published in the Encyclopaedia Metropolitana* ed Alice D. Snyder (1934)
N	Notebook of Samuel Taylor Coleridge (numbered or lettered) in ms. References are given by folio
N&Q	*Notes and Queries* (1849–)
NTP	*Notes, Theological, Political and Miscellaneous* ed Derwent Coleridge (1853)
NYPL	New York Public Library
ODCC	*The Oxford Dictionary of the Christian Church* ed F. L. Cross (1971)
OED	*The Oxford English Dictionary* (12 vols Oxford 1970) and *Supplement* (4 vols Oxford 1987)
Op Max	"Opus Maximum" MSS in the Huntington Library, San Marino CA; and in VCL
p-d	paste-down. See "Editorial Practice" *CM* i xxx
Phil Trans RS	*The Philosophical Transactions of the Royal Society* (1665–1821)
P Lects (1949)	*The Philosophical Lectures of Samuel Taylor Coleridge* ed Kathleen Coburn (London & New York 1949)
PW (CC)	*Poetical Works* ed J. C. C. Mays (3 vols London & Princeton in preparation) – *CC* xvi
PW (EHC)	*The Complete Poetical Works of Samuel Taylor Coleridge* ed E. H. Coleridge (2 vols Oxford 1912)
QR	*The Quarterly Review* (1809–1952)
Rees	*Cyclopaedia* ed Abraham Rees (39 vols 1809–19)
RES	*Review of English Studies* (1925–)
RS	Robert Southey
SC	Sara Coleridge (daughter of C, and wife of HNC)
SC Memoir	*Memoir and Letters of Sara Coleridge* [ed Edith Coleridge] (2 vols 1873)
SH	Sara Hutchinson

Sh (Arden)	The Arden Edition of the Works of William Shakespeare (London 1899–) (for editorial details see SHAKESPEARE General Note)
Sh (Reed)	*The Plays of William Shakespeare* ed Isaac Reed (21 vols 1803)
SM (*CC*)	S. T. Coleridge *The Statesman's Manual* in *Lay Sermons* ed R. J. White (London & Princeton 1972) = *CC* VI
Southey SC (1844)	*Catalogue of the Valuable Library of the Late Robert Southey* (Sotheby, May 1844). Marked copy: BM S-C S 252 (1)
SW	F. W. J. von Schelling *Sämmtliche Werke* ed K. F. A. Schelling (14 vols Stuttgart 1856–61)
SW & F (*CC*)	S. T. Coleridge *Shorter Works and Fragments* ed H. J. Jackson and J. R. de J. Jackson (2 vols London & Princeton 1995) = *CC* XI
TL	S. T. Coleridge *Hints Towards the Formation of a More Comprehensive Theory of Life*. Pub *SW & F* (*CC*) 481–557
Tooke	John Horne Tooke Ἔπεα Πτεροεντα, *or, The Diversions of Purley* (Vol I 1786, repr 1798; Vol II 1805)
TT (*CC*)	*Table Talk of Samuel Taylor Coleridge* ed Carl R. Woodring (London & Princeton 1990) = *CC* XIV
var	*variatim* "variously": used to indicate minor differences from the original in a quoted text
VCL	Victoria College Library, University of Toronto
VS	See Kant *VS*
WL (*M* 2)	*Letters of William and Dorothy Wordsworth; the Middle Years* ed Ernest de Selincourt, rev Mary Moorman (2 vols Oxford 1969–70)
W Library	Chester L. Shaver and Alice C. Shaver *Wordsworth's Library. A Catalogue Including a List of Books Housed by Wordsworth for Coleridge from c. 1810 to c. 1830* (New York & London 1979)
W Prose	*The Prose Works of William Wordsworth* ed W. J. B. Owen and Jane Worthington Smyser (3 vols Oxford 1974)
WPW	*The Poetical Works of William Wordsworth* ed Ernest de Selincourt and Helen Darbishire (5 vols Oxford 1940–9)
WW	William Wordsworth

MARGINALIA

"PAMPHLETS—DIVINITY"

[A made-up volume of eight works, bound together after C's death.]
1824–33. 8°.

British Library C 126 h 2

Monogram "C" of John Duke Coleridge on ⁻4. Works are listed in alphabetical
order by authors' names rather than in the order in which they are bound together.
Where the author's name is given in small caps (as BAINES) it means that the
work contains notes by C and has its own full entry elsewhere in *CM* (*CC*).

CONTENTS.

Peter Augustine BAINES. *Faith, Hope, and Charity. The Substance of a
Sermon Preached at the Dedication of the Catholic Chapel at Brad-
ford, in the County of York, on Wednesday, July 27, 1825.* 2nd ed 1827.

Richard Cattermole. *A Sermon, the Substance of which was Preached at
St. Matthew's Church, Brixton, Surrey, in January, 1831.* 1831. Presentation copy inscribed by the author, unopened. "S. T. C." label on
title-page verso.

William Ellery CHANNING. *A Discourse Delivered at the Installation of
the Rev. Mellish Irving Motte, as Pastor of the South Congregational
Society in Boston, May 21, 1828.* Boston, rpt London 1828.

Alexander Charles Louis D'ARBLAY. *The Vanity of All Earthly Greatness. A Funeral Sermon on His Majesty, George the Fourth, Preached
in Camden Chapel, St. Pancras, on Sunday, July XVIII, MDCCCXXX.*
2nd ed rev 1830. Presentation copy inscribed by the author.

Joseph Fletcher. *The Constitution of the Bible Society Defended. In a Letter to the Hon. and Rev. Gerard T. Noel.* 1831. Presentation copy, inscribed by the author; unopened beyond p 9 (of 64 pp).

Thomas Griffith. *Life a Pilgrimage. A Sermon, Preached in Ram's
Chapel, Homerton, on New Year's Day, 1833.* [1833]. Presentation
copy, inscribed by the author; unopened after p 9 (of 24 pp).

Joseph HUGHES. *The Believer's Prospect and Preparation, Described in
a Discourse Delivered in Broadmead Meeting House, Bristol, on Sunday Morning, March 6, 1831, on Occasion of the Death of the Rev.
Robert Hall . . . To Which is Annexed, the Address Delivered at the In-
terment, on the Previous Wednesday, by the Rev. T. S. Crisp.* 1831.

James RELLY. *The Believer's Treasury; or, the Union, Consanguinity, and Affinity, of Christ and His Church, Illustrated in the Light of Scripture . . . to which is Added, an Essay on the Apostolic Manner of Preaching the Gospel.* Rev ed 1824.

"PAMPHLETS—MISCELLANEOUS"

[A made-up volume of 12 works.] 1814–33. 8°.

British Library C 126 h 3

Monogram "C" of John Duke Coleridge on p ⁻4; pasted onto the same page a partial list of the contents, in the hand of EHC. As in the preceding entry, works are listed in alphabetical order.

CONTENTS.

John Abernethy. *Reflections on Gall and Spurzheim's System of Physiognomy and Phrenology. Addressed to the Court of Assistants of the Royal College of Surgeons, in London, in June, 1821.* 1821. Presentation copy inscribed by the author; "S. T. C." label on verso of title-page.

Joseph Adams. *An Illustration of M^r. Hunter's Doctrine, Particularly Concerning the Life of the Blood, in Answer to the Edinburgh Review of Mr. Abernethy's Lectures.* 1814. Presentation copy inscribed by the author.

Alphabeta linguarum praecipuarum hodiernarum sequuntur; scilicet hebraïcae et chaldaïcae, cum litteris rabbinicis; samaritanae, syriacae, cum litteris nestorianis et antiquis estrangelis; arabicae, persicae, aethiopicae, armeniacae, coptae sive aegyptiacae, illyricae, dalmaticae, georgianae, et gothicae; cum specimene characterum chinensium [n.d.]. Pencilled note on title-page, perhaps by EHC: "[? With] S T Coleridge".

William Lisle Bowles. *Two Letters to the Right Honorable Lord Byron, in Answer to His Lordship's Letter to **** ******, on the Rev. W. L. Bowles's Strictures on the Life and Writings of Pope: More Particularly on the Question, Whether Poetry be More Immediately Indebted to What is Sublime or Beautiful in the Works of Nature, or the Works of Art?* 2nd ed rev 1821. Presentation copy inscribed by the author. Unopened pp 57–60, 61–4 (of 67 pages).

[William Ellery Channing]. *Remarks on the Character and Writings of John Milton; Occasioned by the Publication of His Lately Discovered "Treatise on Christian Doctrine." From the* Christian Examiner, *Vol. III. No. I.* 2nd ed rev Boston 1826. Presentation copy inscribed by the author. Correction p 47, apparently by Channing.

"PAMPHLETS ON THE SLAVE TRADE"

[A made-up volume of three tracts, labelled on the spine "Pamphlets on the Slave Trade".] 1821–33. 8°.

British Library C 126 h 14 (1–3)

As in the preceding entries, works are listed in alphabetical order.

CONTENTS.

ANALYSIS *of the Report of a Committee of the House of Commons on the Extinction of Slavery. With Notes by the Editor. 1833.*

Foreign Slave Trade. Abstract of the Information Recently Laid on the Table of the House of Commons on the Subject of the Slave Trade; Being a Report Made by a Committee Specially Appointed for the Purpose, to the Directors of the African Institution on the 8th of May, 1821, and by Them Ordered to be Printed, as a Supplement to the Annual Report of the Present Year. 1821. "S. T. C." label on verso of title-page; C's name written on the paper cover (not by C). Unopened pp 77–88, 109–48, 161–76 (of 180 pp).

Sir Henry George GREY. *Corrected Report of the Speech of Viscount Howick, in the House of Commons, May 14, 1833, on Colonial Slavery, with an Appendix, Containing a Plan for the Abolition of Slavery.* 1833.

8

JOHN JAMES PARK
1795–1833

Conservative Reform. A letter addressed to Sir William Betham . . . .
London 1832. 8°.

British Library C 126 h 15(4), bound as "Pamphlets on the Reform Bill"

MS TRANSCRIPT. VCL LT 15; wm J. GREEN & SON 1830. In an unidentified
hand, but with one correction in C's hand.

DATE. After Oct 1832 (the date of the Preface).

1   pp +1–15 (15 being the last printed page), pencil

We are all, the best of us, imperfect Mortals, more or less laden with Sins,
and sin-begotten infirmities. If we deemed no one worthy the name and
duties of a Friend, but one who in no part of his conduct and character
gave reasons for regret or for blame, Friendship could have no existence
on earth, nor any occasion for displaying itself.

Now as a poor self-condemned Creature, who yet in any moment, in
which I was myself, would hesitate at no sacrifice for the interest of those,
I have professed to love, I require three things in the person who has asked
me to call him my FRIEND.

First, a charitable if not a tender Consideration of the circumstances; a
pitying allowance for the temptations, that have been resisted, in coun-
terpoised[a] of those, under which I have fallen.

Second—& notwithstanding the former, a prompt & unsparing Openness. To have seen or suspected should be instantly followed by the reproof or the question.

Thirdly, and the holiest office of Friendship, *Hope* even against Hope
for the sustentation[1] of Hope in our poor self-condemning Friend. O try
to save him from despairing of himself. In the Duck-and-Drake projection across the stream of Error and Misery let the Friend be as the elastic
force of the Water, giving a new bound to the Stone, & preventing its

---

[a] For "counterpoise" presumably

[1] At this point in the MS TRANSCRIPT, C inserted an explanatory phrase, "susten- tation or the sustenance or supporting". The word appears also in AR (CC) 247.

touch of the stream from being its submersion.[2]—O how much can Hope
& the Infusion of Hope from a kind Friend effect for a right-principled
Soul, groaning under the sense even more bitterly than under the consequences of its error & frailty. My Disease is—Impatient Cowardice of
Pain & the desperation of outwearied Hope.[3]   S. T. Coleridge

[1][2] The game of skimming or skipping flat stones over water is sometimes called "ducks and drakes", and the stone itself a "drakestone".

[1][3] With the same context of opium-in-duced weakness, C echoed the phrase used here in a letter of 1832 to JHG: *CL* vi 894. The TRANSCRIPT was probably made for Green, who habitually used paper with the "Green" wm in notes and correspondence.

The Dogmas of the Constitution. Four lectures, being the first, tenth, eleventh, & thirteenth of a course on the theory & practice of the constitution, delivered at King's College, London, in the commencement term of that institution. London 1832. 8°.

Not located; marginalia pub from MS TRANSCRIPT.

MS TRANSCRIPT. University of Texas (Humanities Research Center): transcript by SC used for *NTP* 223–8. The original volume probably belonged to HNC, who was a lawyer; **2** is addressed to "Henry". The transcript labels textus "P" for "Park" and notes "STC"; these initials have been omitted here. A pencilled note by SC identifies "STC Notes on Savigny (by Hayward) and on Park's *Dogmas of the Constitution*"; a neat little note in ink reads "Copied *S. D.*"

DATE. Probably Apr–May 1832, shortly after publication (the Preface is dated 31 Mar 1832); the Reform Bill, to which C refers as still under discussion, received the royal assent 7 Jun 1832; C discussed Park's work with HNC 20 or 21 May (*TT—CC*—I 296–7 and nn 1, 2), and wrote to JHG about it 18 May (*CL* VI 909). Park's lectures had been influenced by *C&S*, to which he alludes p 130.

1   p vi | Preface

If, as it seems now to be admitted, the word has gone forth that this country is to return to the Constitution it had before the Revolution,—a Constitution of independent estates—who are to struggle for power as chances shall bring them uppermost, and to play the game of "which is the justice, which is the thief," according as the tide of events shall enable the one—or the other—party in the state to proclaim its "*fiat justitia, ruat coelum* [let justice be done, though the heavens fall];"—the writer is not so vain or so ignorant as to suppose that the addition of one little pamphlet to those that have preceded, can create a single *eddy* of public opinion against the tide.

If the ~~three pound~~ 3ˢ 10ᵈ rent clause pass, far worse, I fear;[1] and the legislative mind might recall the two last lines of the charm for the cramp, which we had great faith in, at Christ's Hospital.

---

[1] The constitution, C thinks, will be *worse* than it was before 1688 if the Reform Bill passes with the clause that extends the franchise to (male) householders paying at least £10 p.a. in rent, i.e. a weekly rent of three shillings and tenpence.

Charm for the Cramp.
The Devil is tying a knot in my leg:
Mark! Luke! and John! unloose it, I beg,
Crosses three we make to ease us,
Two for the Thieves and one for Christ Jesus.[2]

2 p xi

If the *theory* of the Constitution turn out, upon close examination, to be fraught with the most invincible absurdities, and if, notwithstanding, those absurdities have not been practically felt, the question must be by what means they have been escaped from; and the answer can only be this,—by a constant practical violation of the theory itself, although without an open or avowed renunciation of it, and with the cautious preservation of most of its *forms*.

The *Theory* of the Constitution? Why, the Constitution itself is the Idea, ultimate aim and as such the moral actuating and plastic *Law* of the *Government*.[1] But even a theory of the *Government* (Government used *sensu latissimo*[2])—where, Mr Devil! is it to be found? In the dreams of Blackstone or De Lolme or the yet shallower Locke?[3] A Theory = θεωρία—*contemplatio*, i.e. such a subjective (= mental) arrangement of all the parts or particulars, as far as they have hitherto been known, which appear to constitute a given thing, as enables us to reflect on that complex thing, as a unity of interdependents.[4] Now Laws, Rules, and Customs of Parliament are the *subjects* of the synopsis, not its materials. The resolution of the Lower House read at the opening of every Session, I believe,

1[2] This schoolboy's charm appears in *TT* in an expanded form derived not from these marginalia but from C's notes on Asgill: *TT* (*CC*) I 301 n 9, II 172 and n 1. C's emphasis on "Two for the Thieves" responds to Park's quotation from *King Lear* IV vi 153–4, "which is the justice, which is the thief?"

2[1] This definition is elaborated in *C&S* (*CC*) 18–20.

2[2] "In the widest sense".

2[3] C dismisses the standard authorities, John Locke's *Two Treatises of Government* (1690), Jean Louis de Lolme's *The Constitution of England* (1775, an enlarged translation of *La Constitution de l'Angleterre*, 1771), and the general introduction to Sir William Blackstone's *Commentaries on the Laws of England* (1765–9). A series of notebook entries of May 1810 (*CN* III 3829–36, 3839–44) records a careful reading of parts of Blackstone, including a slighting reference to Locke (q *CN* III 3835n); but by Mar 1815, C was saying, "Neither Blackstone or De Lolme have truly given the Theory of our Constitution" (*CL* IV 554). C also attacks Locke's theory of government in *LS* (*CC*) 108–10. Park himself refers to Blackstone and De Lolme in **7** textus below.

2[4] In the twelfth of his philosophical lectures, delivered 15 Mar 1819, C gave a similar definition of theory and went on, using illustrations from science, to distinguish theory from hypothesis and law, and to show how one might be related to another: *P Lects* (1949) 359–61.

against interference of Peers in Elections is and was a mere asinine fling out of the Commons, that never had, and never could have, (i.e. since the polyarchy of the feudal Lords was sufficiently represt to allow the existence of a House of Commons) any practical meaning.[5] But Burke in his criminatory letter to the Duke of Portland against M[r] Fox, exposed this answer—.[6] Do beware, Henry! of confounding the terms, theory and principle—theory and idea—theory and law. A theory is ordinarily a mere piece-toy for the benefit of the memory—a μνημόνικον τεκνικον,[7] made like squibs & crackers, to be exploded by the first spark of a new fact or *term*. Of course mathematical theorems are (for this very reason) an exception. But in all real knowledge the account of the terms is as below—Hypopoiēsis = Suf*fiction*. ex. gr. Des Cartes' Vortices. Hypothesis = a Supposition, ex. gr. Oxyg: + Hydr = Water. Theory = [a] ex. Orrery, Walker's Eidouranion. Law = objectivè ens et agens.[8]

2[a] A word may have been omitted here, perhaps something illegible—or in Greek—that the transcriber could not make out

2[5] By a standing order of 1701, a resolution against the interference of peers in elections was read out annually at the opening session of the House of Commons. The order was observed throughout C's lifetime and on into the twentieth century, but seems to have been altogether futile, and was eventually abandoned.

2[6] SC's transcript reads "answer (argument?)", but the parenthetical alternative is plainly hers and not C's, and it has been omitted here. *A Letter . . . to his Grace the Duke of Portland, on the Conduct of the Minority in Parliament. Containing Fifty-four Articles of Impeachment against the Rt. Hon. C. J. Fox* (1797) constituted a public announcement of the breach between Burke and Fox. Opposing Fox's campaign for parliamentary reform, and contradicting his charge that peers interfere in elections, Burke wrote, "Mr. Fox and the Friends of the People are not so ignorant as not to know, that Peers do not interfere in Elections as Peers, but as men of property— They well know that the House of Lords . . . [without the support of the Crown and the House of Commons] could not exist a single year. They know, that all these parts of our Constitution, whilst they are balanced as opposing interests, are also connected as

friends . . ." (69–70).

2[7] "A technical device to aid the memory".

2[8] In this cluster of terms C has used both Greek words and the Latin equivalents, in order to clarify etymological distinctions. The group is hierarchically arranged from the product of fancy, the "suffiction" or "*making* under", through the more reliable products of the understanding (drawing attention to literal meanings, C defines "hypothesis" in *CN* III 3587 as "the placing of one known fact under others as their *ground* or foundation"), to the absolute reality of a law apprehended by the reason. For these distinctions see also *Friend (CC)* I 476–80, *TT (CC)* I 393–4, ARGENS 6 n 2, and *BL (CC)* I 102. According to C, Descartes' speculation about the formation of the universe from the circular movements of material particles and their accumulation in vortices or eddies differs from the chemical analysis of water in being based upon no known fact. "Walker's Eidouranion", invented about 1781, was essentially an enlarged orrery (a model of the solar system, with movable parts) used for popular astronomical exhibitions: see Altick 80–2. *Objectivè ens et agens*, i.e. "objectively being and acting".

3 p xi | Continuing **2** textus

The whole argument of the conservative party in the House of Commons, talented as it has been in some respects, has involved one grand and fatal error in logic.

Unluckily partial Mr Park appears to this vile barbarous vocable![1] why not shillinged, farthinged, tenpenced, &c.? The formation of a participle passive from a noun is a license, that requires some peculiar felicity to excuse it.[2]

4 p xv

Now either the theoretic right of the people to "a full and fair representation," in other words, to an exclusive occupation of the House of Commons by their own representatives, is a real right, or it is not; while Lord Erskine, in effect admitting it to be so, treats it in the same breath like the toy of a child, to be given out or withheld for the day, according as he is ill or well behaved. A Constitution which cannot weather an occasional fit of bad humour, must surely be a very faulty one!

Excellent! But the Whig principle like the Devil "a liar from the beginning".[1] Even its essence is a contradiction under the form or notion of a compromise. And as the Devil is *per se* a mere *ens non verè ens*,[2] that can *appear* only in coexistence with the product of the Logos or God-fiat— so Whiggism only by virtue of Toryism or republicanism with a symbol of unity.

5 pp xvi–xvii

It will be seen from the following pages that the writer is neither Whig nor Tory,—that neither "Reformer" nor "Anti-Reformer" would define his school of politics,—but that he is a disciple, or promotor, whichever the reader may choose, of the nascent school of *inductive politics*, or *observational* political science; a science, which, leaving on the right hand and on the left all conventional principles which have hitherto been accredited, to be ultimately adopted, or rejected, as scientific judgment and

---

3[1] The TRANSCRIPT reads ". . . vocable. ('talented')", clarifying the sense. Examples in the *OED* suggest that using "talented" in this sense was a very recent innovation; one of the authors quoted is RS.

3[2] This remark reappears in *TT* under 8 Jul 1832, although there is no entry for that date in the ms; presumably HNC used these notes, addressed to him, in making up the work: *TT* (*CC*) I 303 n 4, II 174. Cf Johnson's similar objection to the adjectival use of the past participle formed from a noun: "Gray" *Lives of the Poets* ed G. Birkbeck Hill (3 vols Oxford 1905) III 434.

4[1] John 8.44 var.

4[2] "A being not truly a being".

resolution alone shall decide, seeks first, and above all things, to elevate the vague and notional element of political philosophy to the rank of the certain sciences, or, as they are felicitously *denominated by French authors, "les sciences d'observation."

!!! I.e. no *sciences* at all. It grieves me to find this passage in a man of such very superior intellect and soundness of principle as Mr Park so evidently is. I boldly affirm that my philosophy is the true *inductive* logic. The *science d'observation* of the Celtic Anthropöid is, if anything, *deductive*.

* O for an Act of Parliament for the transportation to America or Van Dæmon's Land of this vile infelicissimous[1] "felicitously"!

6 pp xxi–xxii

The general and long-continued prevalence of *excess* in the force or influence of the Crown, or Government, as the constituent evil of the political world, (an evil which, under various modal varieties, this country has been struggling with, with few interventions, from the period of the Norman Conquest, and which struggle has given a colour and character to the whole literature, language, and mental material of the nation,) has wrought as perfect an example, probably, as the world can afford, of the fact in mental philosophy above adverted to . . .

Has not Mr Park in this instance confounded the evils of the Baronial Polyarchy, and the grinding insolence of a conquering race, aggravating that Polyarchy, with the excess of the Royal Power? Did the Norman Kings do more than enact the tyrannies of the Norman Barons on a somewhat larger scale?

7 p 6 | Lecture 1

The propositive or theoretic constitution of Great Britain (if it ever existed in a pure state, which is very doubtful) has ceased to have any existence for upwards of a century and a half—has, for upwards of a century and a half, been superseded by a totally different machinery; but the fact has never been PUBLICLY recognised or recorded,—the substituted constitution has never been formally reduced to a proposition; no De Lolme, or Blackstone, has descanted upon *its* virtues, or pointed out *its* defects . . .

5[1] Probably a deliberate punning, not a misspelling of Van Diemen's Land (*CL* vi 631 has a more orthodox spelling): C would like to send the word to the devil. "Infelicissimous", "most unfortunate", C coining an English word from a Latin superlative.

Very *doubtful?* Yes, as it is very doubtful, that the Moon is made of green cheese, and that the spirits of virtuous Welshmen made perfect are transplanted thither in the shape of Mites! Blackstone's was the age of shallow Law. Monarchy, Aristocracy & Democracy, as *such*, exclude each the other; but if the elements are to interpenetrate, how absurd to call a lump of Sugar Hydrogen, Oxygen, & Carbon! Nay, to take three lumps and call the first Hydr. the second Oxyg. and the third Carbon![1]

8   p 8

The real government of this country unquestionably is, or has been, a commixture, or contribution, or combination, of the three elements of the constitution in the Commons' house of parliament, as the arena of government . . .

Never! at no period.

9   p 9

I intend . . . to follow out the evidences of this tacit or undeclared constitution; and, at the same time, to contrast them with the instances in which the forms of the accredited constitution have been scrupulously preserved.

More truly, nonsensically *blaired.*[1]

10   p 10

We shall be told, in the language of Paley, that "the balance of power in the constitution consists in this: that there is no power possessed by one part of the legislature, the abuse or excess of which is not checked by some antagonist power residing in another part; and, that the power of the two houses of parliament to frame laws is checked by the king's negative;" and yet we should find so accomplished a constitutional writer as Mr. Hallam, describing that exercise of prerogative as one "which no ordinary circumstances can reconcile either with prudence, or *with a constitutional administration of government."*—(Hallam, Const. Hist. iii. 202.)

7[1] HNC incorporated this note in *TT* 21 May 1832, but see *TT* (*CC*) ɪ 296–7 n 2. For Blackstone see **2** n 3 above.

9[1] Possibly from the Scots "blaer" or "blair" or "blare" meaning "to dull the edge" of a knife or cutting tool (*Scottish National Dictionary*); possibly, however, a transcriber's error, perhaps for "blared" (uttered loudly).

Nevertheless the Royal Veto is and remains an essential part of the Constitution. That, in the spirit of compromise characteristic of England, it acts virtually and by prevention, does not evacuate the power itself.

11 p 12

Besides, the public *will* have notions, *will* have ideas,* on all subjects, and *will* act upon them; and, if you trouble not yourself to give them materials for accurate notions, they *will* take up ideal* ones . . .

* Lax terminology is a grievous impediment to clear reasoning.[1]

12 p 13

It will be my endeavour to avoid both the defects which are here so forcibly pointed out, and, while I refresh your memories, and, I trust, add to your stores, on the facts of the constitution, to exhibit them in such a light as shall lead you to perceive their true philosophy . . .

I cannot flatter myself that Mr Park can have done more than merely *looked* at my Essay on the Constitution.[1]

11[1] C campaigned for philosophically precise use of terms, esp for the differentiation of ideas from conceptions (e.g. *C&S*— *CC*—12–13) and notions (e.g. LACUNZA **17** n 1) and other related words.

12[1] I.e. *C&S*, which Park refers to p 130.

PARLIAMENTARY DEBATES

The Parliamentary Debates from the Year 1803 to the Present Time: forming a continuation of the work entituled "The parliamentary history of England from the earliest period to the year 1803." Published under the superintendence of T. C. Hansard. Vol xxxvi. Comprising the period from the twenty-eighth day of April, to the twelfth day of July, 1817. 1817. 8°.

New York Public Library (Berg Collection)

The leaves are opened only for cols 103–242, 295–522, 599–682, 691–818, 847–90, 1375–1418, 1423–34, 1439–50.

DATE. Mid–Jul 1817? C's active interest in the issue of Catholic Emancipation, from essays in the *Morning Post* in 1800 to *C&S* in 1829, is outlined in *C&S* (*CC*) xlii–li. Although it seems most likely that he read these reports when they first appeared, the campaign for emancipation was not very active in 1817—no bill was actually before the House (**12** n 2), and the supporters of emancipation were themselves divided—and it is possible that C took up this work at a later stage of the history of the campaign. The Catholic Relief Bill was passed in 1829.

1   cols 339–41 | 9 May 1817: Roman Catholic Question

The great difficulty he [Mr Yorke] had always found in the way of bringing this question to a satisfactory result, was *the foreign influence*; *and no consideration could possibly induce him to yield in any material degree to the petitions of the Roman Catholics, but the prospect of security to the Protestant establishment from such an influence.

* Strange, that after having heard such a Speech as Leslie Foster's[1] any man of common sense should think *foreign* influence the main evil of Irish Hierocracy!—If any thing, it is rather likely to act as a *palliative*.

---

[1] The motion before the House was simply to form a committee to review the laws relating to the Roman Catholics; it was eventually defeated by 245 to 221 votes. John Leslie Foster (c 1781–1842), whose speech is reported in cols 304–39, argued against the extension of political power for Roman Catholics by describing the status quo in Ireland as being already an "*imperium in imperio*" by virtue of the great influence of a "body of ecclesiastics . . . totally unconnected with the state, studiously independent of it" (col 307) but entirely subservient to their own bishops. Foster was an Irishman, though at the time M.P. for Yarmouth, in the Isle of Wight.

2   p ⁺1, pencil, referring to col 368 | Mr Webber's speech, beginning at col 352

Will that illustrious person [the Prince Regent] do, in his royal father's name, what his royal father [George III] has declared would be a violation of his coronation oath? . . . Should that royal mind be restored to your daily prayers, shall he wake to reign under a new constitution, and over . . . a different people? Will his son . . . say, this, sire, I have done in your name? In your name, I have repealed the principle which placed our family on the throne. It will no longer continue there by an hereditary right qualified by Protestantism, but on the proud democratic principle of election.

P. 368
   No danger in ~~deriving~~ placing *hereditary* Right ~~from~~ on the ground of greater evil from disturbing the indisputed in any given instance than the evils threatened by that instance, as long as no higher ground is pretended for *elective* Right in the contingency of the converse— namely, the overbalance of the evil threatened us by James II.—Hence the philosophic precision as well as political Wisdom of our ancestors 1688 in combining both—hereditary Right & the exception, thus at once admitting & qualifying both—[1]

3   cols 369–70

One ground only remains for sophistical evasion to make a stand on. I have heard it asserted, that the oath does not apply to legislative function—wretched casuistry! Is not that peculiarly within the voluntary acts of prerogative? Executive acts belong to the responsibility of ministers; but assent or dissent being an act of the mind, must be determined within itself—does not belong to the responsibility of ministers, but belongs to the responsibility of the mind that exercises it . . .

This is going too far, & unnecessarily. All, the argument required, was that *certain* Assents and Dissents had been raised by the Constitution above ministerial responsibility—that these had been particularized in the Coronation Oath[1]—& that the existing Securities against Popery was over.

2[1] The Act of Settlement of 1689 debarred Roman Catholics or persons marrying Roman Catholics from the English throne, thereby ensuring a succession based on heredity as long as heredity produced a Protestant heir.

3[1] For the Coronation Oath see **4** n 1 following.

4   p $^+$1, pencil, referring to col 369

The contradiction effected by the frantic Hatred of the Tories, whether Jacobites, or *non*-Jacobites on a thorough *Romish* principle, viz. that no principle but must yield to that of *the* Church—the contr., I say, effected by the Test Acts of Queen Anne—See Webster's speech p. 369.[1]

The Romish Apostacy—Antichrist—.[2] Now unless the Laudites[3] expect a man or incarnate Devil as a personal Antichrist, I demand what Antichrist could do, that the Romish Hier.[4] has not done, & is not now doing?—In Spain? in Ireland?

Of Persecution—& the contemptuous overly Spirit of Canning[5] who from the Quakers, Seceders &c believe that Persecution alone in all cases can make a religious Body act according to their religious principles—the utter inapplic. to the Pseudo-Catholic—

Why Christianity could not be *persecuted away*—no more than Gravitation or the Newtonian System—because Xt did not consist in *a* Church.[6]

5   pp $^+$1–$^+$2, pencil, ending on a narrow strip of paper pasted to $^+$3

The limits of ministerial responsibility the commence⟨ment⟩ of the Royal Personality & personal response to God—Assent to the Catholic Bill clearly such—How could the Ministers be punished for an act of Parliament?—extra-legally—[? Right]—& so might the King—Here again the Wisdom of 1688[1]—in setling the Dispute between [? Apis]

6   cols 381–2

His right [a man's], in a state of society, is not to govern, but to be well governed.* To contend the contrary, is the very essence of Jacobinism,

---

4[1] Not "Webster" but Daniel Webb Webber (c 1757–1847), whose speech surveyed the history of legislation against the Roman Catholics and opposed the motion on the ground that concessions to the Roman Catholics would entail a violation of the Coronation Oath, in which the monarch swears to defend the Protestant reformed religion. (The relevant section of the Oath is q *C&S* [*CC*] xxxvi n 1.) The Test Act excluding Roman Catholics from public office was passed—as Webber says—in 1673, in the reign of Charles II and not of Queen Anne, though it remained in force until 1829.

4[2] "Antichrist" is not Webber's term but C's, as in *C&S* (*CC*) 129–45; it may have been prompted by Webber's lurid account (col 374) of the organisation and power of the Roman Catholic Church.

4[3] Followers of William Laud and the High-Church party; not in *OED*. For C's opinion of Laud see e.g. QUARTERLY REVIEW **9** below; also HACKET *Scrinia* **2** and n 1.

4[4] The Romish hierocracy, as **1**.

4[5] Webber does not refer to George Canning (1770–1827), the eminent Tory statesman, and C appears to be invoking the name chiefly to identify a tone associated with Canning's celebrated rhetoric.

4[6] Cf C's distinction between the Church of Christ and the National Church in *C&S* (*CC*) 111–28.

5[1] As **2** n 1.

the fundamental principle of which is, the application of the theories drawn from the visionary state of nature, to the institutions of civil society.

* Sounds big; but means little; and concludes nothing. The Whig will reply—The Right to a Thing implies the Right to its necessary means—but in order to be well-governed the People must have a share in the Government as the only known security.

7   cols 399–400 | Lord Castlereagh's speech

Never would he believe that any existing danger could be aggravated by the introduction into parliament of a few noble Catholic peers, or of a few generous Catholic commoners.*

* Who rests the Objection on this basis? Who fears the danger from this quarter? The Obj. is—You will yourself establish an irresistible *Right* to be the Established Church in Ireland for the Catholic Hierarchy—and increase the Zeal for Proselytism a 100 fold.—

8   cols 413–14 | Mr Peel's speech

* We might have proscribed the religion of the Roman Catholics, and reduced them, by the severity of penal statutes, to a state of degradation. This policy we have pursued, and, be the consequences what they may, I never can regret that it has been abandoned. To revert to this policy is impossible.

* Alas! in this very expression lies the weakness and misery of the Age! Not the religion of the Roman Catholics; but the Roman-catholicism, i.e. the soul-&-state-blighting *Ir*religion, of so many of our Fellow-Citizens!—[1]

9   cols 419–22

Why do you call upon him [the Roman Catholic] to renounce such doctrines ["the worst principles and doctrines that his most bigotted enemies in any age have imputed to him"]? Do you suspect that he entertains them? If you do, you should disqualify him, not from being a member of parliament, but from being a member of society:* if you do not, why do you humiliate him by requiring a disclaimer?

8[1] In C's view, the essential points of their religion were common to all Christians; not the religion, but the faulty emphases of the Roman Church establishment were to be condemned. In *C&S* (*CC*) 129–45, C bluntly identifies the Church of Rome as the Church of Antichrist.

* So it is! The most zealous defenders of Protestantism betray the strongholds of their cause in their anxiety to proved[a] their own Liberality and *Gentlemanly* Feelings. Either they *do* tend to disqualify the Papists from being safe and unharming Members of Society—or they disqualify him from nothing—and from political direct Power only to strait-waistcoat their evil tendency toward Society.

---

10 cols 427–8 | Mr Grattan's speech

A right hon. gentleman (who I regret was not more attended to by the House) observed in the course of his speech, that this was a Protestant constitution. That right hon. gentleman may baptize the constitution as he will; but originally it was Catholic.* It was founded by Catholics. All the great laws to which the people owe their rights and liberties were the works of Catholics.

* This is the πρωτον ψευδος, the ground-error, of the Philo-Romanists—. Catholics if you please; but not Roman-Catholics.

---

11 cols 615–18 | House of Lords 16 May 1817: The Bishop of Llandaff [Dr Herbert Marsh] speaks, beginning at col 614

* This Speech is so like the Man—a genuine Flower of the indigenous growth of Marsh-land! The Premise ingenious & the more plausible as appearing to be a Concession—and the deduction immediate and legitimate. Yet the whole a quaking Patch over a Hollow—a piece of Bog-land. The premise is false—it is not *comparative* worth & capacity that is to ~~determine~~ direct a *Legislature*, ⌀in the determination of eligibility; but *sufficient* capacity, *sufficient* worth. The *comparative* belongs to the Electors. ~~in the g~~[a] [b]general permission of eligibility; but *sufficient* worth, *sufficient* capacity. The comparison between A and B, both having *sufficient*, belongs to the Electors in the particular case.—[1]   S. T. C.[c]

9[a] A slip for "prove"
11[a] The deleted words are faintly written and smeared
11[b-c] Without deleting his original wording, C added the second version at the top of the page

11[1] Herbert Marsh (1757–1839), in academic and political circles one of the most important churchmen of his time, argued against the extension of Roman Catholic rights on purely civil grounds, asserting that as essentially subjects of "a foreign prince", Roman Catholics are comparatively deficient in the political requirements of "*civil capacity* and *civil worth*" (cols 617–18).

12　pp ⁻2–⁻1 (half-title), referring to cols 616–17

May 16, 1817.

MARSH ✳ [1] Rom. Cath.—p. 616, 617.[2]

To the Legislature belongs the ~~right and duty~~ of determining the general Eligibility. And as the [? ~~general~~] ~~prohibition to elect~~ [? ~~upon~~] ~~every particular instance the Custom where Nature & the universal~~ Denial of this privilege to persons not previously ineligible by Nature or Universal Custom, as Children, Women, Ideots &c, is presumptively an evil, both to the Candidate ~~so~~ disqualified, and to the electors, whose right of suffrage is narrowed, an equal presumption ought to exist, on the other side, in order to legitimate such prohibitions.—In other words, Nature, or universal Custom, [? ~~or~~] ha~~ve~~s rendered certain persons or classes ineligible—Women, for instance, and Children. Where the Law goes farther, ~~there~~ it must proceed on the warrantable presumption, that ~~the Citizens cause~~ the disqualified persons[a] stand in the same predicament with Women & Children—namely, that they are defective in one or more of the qualities or conditions, indispensable to the right ~~performance of the Duties~~ exercise of the Functions, with which they are to be entrusted. On this principle the absence of the presumptive *signs* ⟨& pledges⟩ of Independence, (Lands or known Income) disqualifies for ~~standing a Candidate~~ being elected for the H. of Commons—and manifest Dependence (as in the case of menial Servants, Placemen during pleasure &c) disqualifies for being an Elector.—

Still the principle holds good, that by virtue of the British Constitution (for I have nothing to do with rights of Man or rights of Nature) Eligibility to the Legislature, ~~is a Right,~~ in the absence of all known or fairly presumable Reason to the contrary, ⟨is a Right.⟩ Now ~~the only~~ no other Reason can be imagined but insufficiency for the due performance of the Senatorial Functions and Duties. And as the Laws regulating the right of Eligibility are of course past without reference to this or that Individual, of whom the Legislature is not supposed to know any thing, there must be found in the circumstances and relations, the enumeration of which constitutes the *class* or *sort* which the Legislature has in contemplation, good reason for supposing that a person belonging to this class will not possess *sufficient* loyalty, sufficient independence, *sufficient* impartiality in all the questions & interests, on which he will have to decide, to make

---

12[a] Originally "persons disqualified", but marked for transposition

12[1] "Opposed to".　　　　　　　　　**12**[2] The argument is summarised in **11** n 1.

him a safe & fit *Mean* to the proposed End.—

  Thus, then!

The simple eligibility of Classes of Men it belongs to the Legislature to determine; and this it does on grounds of sufficiency. Insufficiency may be defined ⟨generally, &⟩ before hand, ~~not~~ without ⟨the⟩ knowlege of individual character, which is requisite in estimating the *merits*, ⟨& still more in estimating the⟩ comparative merit, of particular Persons. But in what way shall the Law pre-define the *absence* of *excellence*, or the exact quantum *over* and *above* what is sufficient for the purpose—on which the eligibility is to be ~~given~~ allowed or denied?—The ~~preferability of this or that eligible Individual~~ more or less eligibility of *persons*, or the comparative sufficiency of the Candidates, it belongs to the Electors to determine. [? ~~So~~] ~~therefore~~ In ~~my~~ the present state of my convictions, I should vote with Bishop Marsh; but so far from voting on the same grounds with him, I should be disposed to admit a something less than compleat *Sufficiency* in the Romish Catholics themselves, in the persuasion that ~~it~~ the deficience of the Few would be compensated by the more than sufficiency of the great majority of the Legislators—and the opposite & counteractive character of their prejudices. It would be hard, indeed, if there were not as many *High* Church Men, and zealots of Protestant Ascendancy, as Catholics—so that the result would be, the one would neutralize the other—& the question left for the moderate men to decide—

The Law ~~does~~ is not so properly said to disqualify certain sorts or classes of persons, as to declare the disqualifying causes.

  In the preceding remarks I suppose the question to turn on the fitness or expediency of permitting Romanist Men of Property to sit in both Houses. In this point of view I should not, I think, oppose the Catholic Bill.—But this is not *my* ground of Objection. Not the Bill, but the Principles set forth in the Preamble of the Bill,[3] and the (ως εμοιγε δοκεῖ)[4] inevitable Consequences of the legislative solemn Sanction of these Principles—these are *my* terror!—

12[3] While it is possible that C read and annotated these speeches a decade after they were delivered, and that he refers to a late version of the Catholic Relief Bill, it is more likely that he construed Grattan's motion for a committee as an attempt to revive the Bill of 1813, which began with a Preamble recognising the permanent and inviolable establishment of the Protestant succession and the Protestant churches of England, Ireland and Scotland, but asserting that "it would tend to promote the interest of the same, and strengthen our free constitution, of which they are an essential part, if the civil and military disqualifications, under which his Majesty's Roman Catholic subjects now labour, were removed". C fears that the emancipation of the Roman Catholics would tend to undermine rather than to strengthen the constitution.

12[4] "As it seems to me, at least".

WILLIAM PARNELL

d 1821

An Historical Apology for the Irish Catholics. Dublin 1807. 8°.

State Library of Victoria, Melbourne, Australia

Inscribed p ⁻3 (p-d): "Thoˢ. Poole." C has corrected a typo on p 3.

MS TRANSCRIPT. VCL LT 32, in an unknown hand.

DATE. Probably Jun–Sept 1807, while C was staying with Poole and using his library. Notes based upon this work appear in *CN* II 3205.

1 p ⁻2

One among the very best political Essays, that have fallen to my perusal. Yet because in addition to numerous well-chosen, well-stated and undeniable Facts, and to conclusions deduced from them with the strictest as well as clearest logic, the work abounds with the eloquence of vivid fancy kindled by vivid feelings, I should not be surprized to hear some *SCOTCHman (Review-scribe, or State-pharisee) *hint* his distrust of the Author's *Judgment*; and support his opinion by a quotation from the PRO-FOUND †Essay on the Human Understanding by the GREAT LOCK, who therein magisterially informs us, that all eloquence, all power of imagination, & the similar accompaniedments of justly, tho' highly excited

* Mem. so to sound the first syllable; as to render the disgraceful fact conveyed in the second as little audible as possible.

† carefully sounded in all its depths by me, S. T. C., and found at the deepest ancle-deephigh relatively to ‡Des Cartes; but very muddy: Ergo, profound—for what better proof of ⟨its⟩ Depth thaɤn that no one can see to the bottom of it?—

‡ from whom & his immediate disciples all that is true or ingenious in the Essay is stolen.[1]

---

[1]¹ C's claim since 1801, when he put this case in letters to the Wedgwoods, copies of which were made for Poole: *CL* II 677–703; cf 708–10.

25

passion ~~is~~ are, if employed in *reasoning*, a *trick*, a *cheat*; & the writers or orators to be considered as Impostors & Mountebanks.[2]   S. T. C.

[1][2] C mocks the *Edinburgh* reviewers and their veneration for Locke, who wrote against rhetoric in *Essay* bk 3 ch 10 sect 34: "But yet, if we would speak of Things as they are, we must allow, that all the Art of Rhetorick, besides Order and Clearness, all the artificial and figurative applications of Words Eloquence hath invented, are for nothing else but to insinuate wrong *Ideas*, move the Passions, and thereby mislead the Judgment; and so indeed are perfect cheat . . .".

SAMUEL PARR

1747–1825

A Spital Sermon preached at Christ Church, upon Easter Tuesday, April 15, 1800; to which are added notes, &c. [What edition C used is not known; in the absence of evidence, the first edition (London 1801, 4°) has been used.]

Not located; marginalia pub "J. M. G.", i.e. John Matthew Gutch, *N&Q* 1st ser VII (1853) 280. Parr's sermon, his best-known work, involved him in controversy with William Godwin, whose *Thoughts Occasioned by the Perusal of Dr. Parr's Spital Sermon* (1801) C also annotated.

DATE. 1814–15? Although C knew about Parr's sermon in Jun 1801 (*CL* II 736) and may have read it by then, this sustained note on atheism and education seems to belong to a later period, possibly 1814–15 when C was living near Bristol and was in regular contact with Gutch over the publication of *BL*.

1   pp 100–1 | Parr's Note to p 13, line 28

"Knight Errant of Atheism":] . . . Upon the various effects of Superstition, where it has spread widely, and thriven long, we can reason from *facts*. But in the original frame of the human mind, and in the operations of all those moral causes which regulate our conduct, or affect our happiness, there seems to be a most active, constant, and invincible principle of *resistance* to the encroachments of Atheism. "All nature cries aloud" against them, "through all her works," not in speculation only, but in practice.

I never had even a doubt in *my being* concerning the supreme Mind; but understand too sufficiently the difficulty of any intellectual demonstration of his existence, and see too plainly how inevitably the principles of many pious men (Locke, Priestley, Hartley, even Archbishop King)[1]

1[1] C had admired the works of Locke, Priestley and Hartley as a young man, before he became convinced that their materialist principles had atheistical consequences. The name of William King (1650–1729), abp of Dublin, probably occurred to him as a link between Locke and Hartley, for King's *Ori-gin of Evil*, originally pub in Latin in 1702, was written on Lockean principles, and Hartley declared his indebtedness to an essay prefixed to the 1731 English translation of it in his *Observations on Man* (1791) I [iii].

would lead to atheism by fair production of consequences, not to feel in perfect charity with all good men, atheist or theist; and, let me add, though I now seem to feel firm ground of *reason* under my belief in God, not gratefully to attribute my uniform past *theism* more to general feeling than to depth of understanding. Within this purpose I hope that, without offence, I may declare my conviction, that in the French Revolution atheism was an effect, not a cause; that the same wicked men, under other circumstances and fashions, would have done the same things as Anabaptists within Munster, or as Inquisitors among the South American Indians;[2] and that atheism from conviction, and as a ruling motive and impulse (in which case only can it be fairly compared with superstition) is a quiescent state, and *per se* harmless to all but the atheist himself. Rather is it that overwhelming preference of experimental philosophy, which, by smothering over more delicate perceptions, and debilitating often to impotence the faculty of going into ourselves, leads to atheism as a conscious creed, and in its extreme is atheism in its essence. This rather is, I should deem, the more perilous, and a plainer and better object for philosophical attack. O! bring back *Jack the Giant Killer* and the *Arabian Nights* to our children, and Plato and his followers to new men, and let us have chemistry as we have watchmakers or surgeons (I select purposely honourable and useful callings), as a *division* of human labour, as a worthy profession for a few, not as a glittering master-feature of the education of men, women, and children.—[3]   S. T. C.

1[2] In 1533–5 a group of Anabaptists took over Münster as the first stage in the conquest of the world. While the town was besieged for over a year by forces supporting its expelled bishop, the Anabaptists legalised polygamy and condoned some barbaric acts of violence. The Spanish Inquisition was active in South America—between 1581 and 1776, there are said to have been 59 heretics burned at Lima—but its victims were not Indians, but Europeans; perhaps C intended a more general reference to the cruel treatment of the South Americans by the Spaniards, documented for his generation by such works as Sheridan's *Pizarro* (1799) and RS's *History of Brazil* (1810–19).

1[3] The characterisation of the age as one in which philosophy, education and science systematically suppress spiritual values is a major theme in C's work: see, e.g., the characteristic letter to Lord Liverpool, *CL* IV 757–63. C's recommendation of works of fantasy for children, in the face of a fashion for realism and didacticism, appears also e.g. in HOMER *Works* 1 and n 5, MILLER 4 and n 7.

ABRAHAM PARSONS

d 1785

Travels in Asia and Africa; including a journey from Scanderoon to Aleppo, and over the desert to Bagdad and Bussora; a voyage from Bussora to Bombay, and along the western coast of India; a voyage from Bombay to Mocha and Suez in the Red Sea; and a journey from Suez to Cairo and Rosetta, in Egypt. [Ed John Paine Berjew.] London 1808. 4°.

Collection of Richard Wordsworth

Inscribed in RS's hand at the foot of the title-page: "R Southey. Aug: 31. 1811.. Liverpool." Inscribed in pencil on p ⁻3: "See pages 204 & 307 for notes by S. T. C. also 14 & 214. D. W." Also inscribed in ink on the same page: "W. Wordsworth Belonged to Rydal Mount Library in [? Ivy] Room. handed down to M. L. Mair (née Wordsworth) 1883 White Moss. Rydal Mere." In a "Cottonian" binding (made by the women of the household out of old dresses) of dark blue with an overall pattern of small yellow globes and black flowers.

DATE. Feb–Mar 1812, when C was staying at Greta Hall.

1   p 14 | Ch 1

Whenever the eastern mountains begin to be capp'd, that is, over top'd with a cloud, a ragea is expected; it does not seem to blow horizontally like other winds, but is seen to gush like torrents of rain down the chasms of the mountains, which are immensely high, and as the ships go very near, they feel the whole effect of its fury, shifting so very suddenly three or four points one way, then back again, that each great cleft, or chasm, in the mountains, seems to send down a separate wind; yet those winds are seldom or never felt six leagues down the gulph with any degree of violence.

The same phænomenon occurs often from Crossfell in Westmoreland, & from the cloudy Cap is called Helm (= helmet) wind. It seems electrical & akin to the Water-spout at Sea/—

2   p 204 | Ch 10

It sometimes happens that a man will bring up three or four hundred oysters in a day, and not find as many pearls as are worth five shillings; as

29

there are more which have not any, than those that have; and of these many have only small pearls, some of them so very diminutive as to be incapable of being bored; these are what the English call seed pearls.

This seems to ⟨me⟩ a strong presumption in favour of my hypothesis: viz: that the Pearl originates in some minute particle of an angular shape which the oyster by accident, more or less common according to the soil of the Bed and perhaps the organization of the Shell itself, has taken in— that this irritating the fleshy part the animal gradually coats it by means of the same secretion, which[a] & possibly from the same stimulus, it in every case coats the interior of its shell.—Were it (as a very intelligent E India Purser thought) a natural part of the fish, it would be found in all Oysters of the same kind, & not at all in other kinds. Whereas the contrary is true in both cases.[1]   S. T. C.

3   p 214

* Bombay, was first called so by the Portuguese, literally in English, Goodbay, which it is in all respects; being so very capacious, as to be capable of receiving any number of ships of any size or draft of water, with room sufficient to moor clear of each other in safety.

>   * Harbour'd from Toil *here* did th' Adventurers Gay
>   Squat down at ease, and nam'd it hence *Bum*-Bay.[1]

4   p 215

. . . large ships use much of it [i.e. "the external fibres of the cocoa-nut"], made into cables, hawsers, and smaller ropes; it is called k<u>yah</u>.

Coir[1]

5   p 307 | Ch 14

In the outskirts of the city [Cairo], and the villages adjacent, are many public ovens for hatching chickens. . . . It is observed that these chicken

2[a] For "with which"?

2[1] There was still disagreement among scientists about the formation of pearls—as C's remarks indicate—but the essentially correct solution proposed by C had been put forward by Réaumur in the early eighteenth century. C recorded his debate with the Purser—Adam Wilson, "a well-informed and intelligent young man"—in letters of Feb 1812: *CL* III 368, 372–4.

3[1] Not in *PW* (EHC). The name of the city appears actually to have been derived from a name of the goddess Parvati.

4[1] C gives the correct English term for coconut fibre, standard in this form for only about thirty years when he wrote, and yet unfixed in Parsons' time.

are not so large as those hatched by the hen, and that the greater part of them are defective in their claws, wanting one or more. This they account for, from the smallest eggs being picked out for the ovens, and their being so closely compressed.

It is observed, that Hens thus reared, from the eggs of Hens likewise so reared, lose the instinct of brooding & hatching. This fact confirms my hypothesis of Instinct—viz—Memoria corporea, seu in organizatâ materiâ vitali immanens, et inde una cum corpore per generationem fœtui transmissibilis[1]—Μνήμη ὑλοζωϊκὸς = hylozoic Memory.[2]   S. T. C.

5[1] "Bodily memory, or [memory] immanent in organised living matter, whence along with bodily form it can be transmitted in the process of reproduction to the foetus."

5[2] C translates his own Greek. The view of instinct outlined here is more systematically developed in *AR* (*CC*) 242–50.

BLAISE PASCAL

1623–1662

Les Provinciales ou lettres escrittes par Louis de Montalte, à un provincial de ses amis & aux RR. PP. Jesuites, sur la morale & la politique de ces Pères: traduites en Latin par Guillaume Wendrock . . . en Espagnol par le S^r. Gratien Cordero . . . et en Italien par le S^r. Cosimo Brunetti, &c. Cologne 1684. 8°.

Victoria College Library (Coleridge Collection)

Inscribed on p ⁻5 (p-d) in two different hands: "Ce livre m'a été donné en 1739 Par" and "Cha: Rambouïllet 1728." Inscribed "S. T. C—" on the title-page, not in C's hand. Marked "Green Bequest". A leaf, originally between the present pp ⁺1 and ⁺2, has been cut out leaving a stub: it may have had a note written on it. There is a note of two words in ink on p 42, probably by the previous owner, written before cropping, and a pencilled cross on p 27 which may be C's: see ANNEX.

DATE. 21 Sept 1803 and perhaps a few days following: *CL* II 994. C "seized" upon this book when he found it in RS's library, and evidently took it to London and then to Malta in 1804: *CN* II 2133n.

1   p ⁻5 (p-d)

Pacchiaretti[1]

2   p 21, pencil, at the end of Letter 1

Admirable Letter

3   p 41, pencil, at the end of Letter 2

At least equal to the first / what Life is given even to a Theological Controversy by the introduction of Character & Drama!

4   p ⁺5

G. Fricker 120, Goswell S^t/[1]

[1][1] The name of a sweet Spanish wine, Pajarete, to which C was introduced in Germany in 1798: *CL* I 439; cf *BL (CC)* II 183 and *CN* I 371.

[4][1] Evidently a London address for C's brother-in-law, George Fricker, for whom C tried to find a job before he left for Malta in Apr: *CL* II 1064, 1067, 1085, 1118, 1121, 1123–4.

5   p $^+6$ (p-d)

There can be no doubt, that the Jesuits only *accomodated* their doctrines to the manners & opinions of the Catholics—this indeed Paschal confesses—these horrid opinions therefore & their utter subversion of moral feelings & notions must have been the fruit of the essentials of the Catholic Church / yes! & truly is so at this very day. Other orders may not have *written* as openly as the Jesuits; but they really *act* on the same principles.—⟨This I *know*.⟩   S. T. C.—

Annex

There is a pencilled cross—apparently C's—against a paragraph on p 27. The text is printed in four columns across two pages, to accommodate the four languages—French, Latin, Spanish and Italian respectively. C's mark is next to the Italian version, but since the four vary considerably, and it is difficult to be sure what language he read the passage in, all four are reproduced here. The translation is from the French.

(1) Elle est bien satisfaite de leur complaisance. Elle n'exige pas qu'ils nient la necessité de la grace efficace: ce seroit trop les presser: il ne faut pas tyranniser ses amis: les Jesuites ont assez gagné. Car le monde se paye de paroles: peu approfondissent les choses; & ainsi le nom de *grace suffisante* estant reccu des deux costez, quoy qu'avec divers sens, il n'y a personne, hors les plus fins Theologiens, qui ne pense que la chose que ce mot signifie soit tenuë aussi bien par les Jacobins que par les Jesuites.

(2) *Ergo hoc ipsorum obsequio Jesuitae contenti, non adurgent ut gratiam efficacem abdicent. Durius istud omnino, nec imponendum statim amicis servitium. Pro tempore bene rem gessere Jesuitae. Etenim sic sunt homines: verbis lactantur, de re ipsa parum laborant. Quotumquemque censes quaestionum interiora rimari? Ita* sufficientis gratiae *voce utrinque recepta, vario licet sensu, si acutissimos Theologos excipias, vix invenias qui rem voce notatam non aeque putet a Dominicanis admitti, atque à Jesuitis: in quo non stultissimos istos fuisse, temporis progressu probabitur.*

(3) Esta la Compañia muy satisfecha y gustosa del agasajo que la hazen. No pide que los Dominicanos nieguen absolutamente la necessidad de la gracia eficaz: esso seria apretar mucho: No es menester tiranizar sus amigos. Harto ganaron con esso los Jesuitas, porque los hombres sè pagan de palabras: pocos son los que ahondan, y que van al alma del sentido; con que siendo bien recebido el termino de *gracia suficiente* y aceptado de entrambas partes, aunque en differente sentido, ninguno ay, exceptos los mas sutiles Theologos, que no piense que los Dominicanos llevan la misma dotrina que los Jesuitas y que estàn conformes en el sentido desse termino; y por lo que le sigue se verá que los Jesuitas no son los mas lerdos.

(4) *Ell' è più che sodisfatta del lor consenso; la non cerca di fargli negar la necessità della grazia efficace: sarebbe un troppo affollarla: non bisogna tyranneggiare gli amici. I Gesuiti hanno guadagnato abbastanza, perch' il mondo si paga di parole, pochi ricercan le cose al fondo; E cosi il nome* di grazia sufficiente *essendo ricevuto d'ambe le parti, benche con diversi sensi, non v'è nessuno dai più sottili Teologi in fuori, che non creda che quel che questa parola significa, sia tenuto tanto dai Domenicani che dai Gesuiti.*

[It [the Society of Jesus] was well pleased by their [the Dominicans'] cooperation. It did not demand that they deny the necessity of efficient grace: that would be asking too much; you must not tyrannise over your friends, and the Jesuits had won enough. Words are the currency of the world; few go deeply into things; and so since the phrase "sufficient grace" was accepted by both sides—though with different meanings—none but the subtlest theologians doubted that the thing signified by the phrase was just as much a doctrine of the Jacobins [other versions read "Dominicans"] as of the Jesuits.]

GIUSEPPE LUCA PASINI
1687–1770

Vocabolario Italiano-Latino per uso degli studiosi di belle lettere nelle regie scuole di Torino, in cui si contengono le frasi più eleganti e difficili, i modi di dire, proverbi ec. dell'una e l'altra lingua; con in fine le favole, e i nomi delle principali città, castella, mari, fiumi, monti, ec. Venice 1794. 4°.

Victoria College Library (Coleridge Collection)

Inscribed by C in ink in a very large hand on p ⁻2: "Sara Hutchinson | S. T. Coleridge", the first name crossed out in ink but still legible. Below this in pencil, also in C's hand: "S. Hutchinson | S. T. Coleridge | Jan 23, 1805."

DATE. **1** may have been written in Malta 23 Jan 1805, when the work was inscribed. The connection with SH is obscure, and C may have written her name simply for the pleasure of linking it with his. The etymological note **2** seems to be later: see **2** nn 1, 2.

1 p ⁻3

I know no *good* Lexicon or Dictionary relative to the *Ideal* of one, except Adelung's German Wörterbuch, which tho of course far enough from perfect, is yet cast in the mould of the Just Ideal, & agrees with it sufficiently to give Adelung a claim to *Wonder*, which yet will become *sane Admiration*, without loss of Size or Vividness.[1]—O that *we* had such a work, instead of our entertaining *Quotation-book*, but most contemptible, *Dictionary*, Johnson's[2]—The glory of Adelung is, that supposing an enlightened Prince, every 30 or 40 years might send forth new knowlege in a new Edition, so *recipient* of excellence is the admirable plan of Adelung.

[1] C used and probably acquired J. C. Adelung's *Versuch eines vollständigen grammatisch-kritischen Wörterbuches der hochdeutschen Mundart* (4 vols 1774–86; 2nd ed 1793–1801) in Germany in 1799: *CN* I 378n; cf *CN* II 2354n. He habitually referred to Adelung with admiration: in *BL* ch 10 (*CC*) I 211, he is "the first of Lexicographers". His dictionary is distinguished by including examples of ordinary usage (as opposed to Johnson's literary illustrations) and equivalent words in other languages, both features appealing to C.

[2] As habitually as he praised Adelung, C dismissed Samuel Johnson's *Dictionary of the English Language* (1755): e.g. *BL* ch 12 (*CC*) I 237n–8n.

Of Dictionaries on the ordinary plan this is either the best, or *one* of the very best, I have seen.   S. T. Coleridge.

2   pp ⁻2–⁻1

1. ₤ Εις¹ = is = this: αυτοσι ανηρ² = myself or speaking of himself [in]ᵃ the third Person, as little Children do & the Savages, & even as the French, & German, still do, in the phrase *One* he̶ eats heartily after exercise—*Man* esst gerne &c—

1. Εις = this man.

2. Δυο And thou—two—tu & thence Δεω to join, & by another mood of sense & feeling Δαω to divide³ / Thence Δε, τε, πε, σε, all originally signifying "and"⁴ / thence (by which I always meanʃ *in* this), a Polypus of the same Sisterhood, each being his own ⟨mother &⟩ father, and the B̶r̶o̶t̶h̶e̶r̶ Sister & Brother of his own children—"Δε, τε, πε, σε, da,⁵ add, and &c &c.["]—

1. Εις. This man, pointing with inverted finger at my own breast.

2. Δυο—& thou.

2ᵃ Page torn; word supplied by editor

2¹ C suggests, with a disregard for accents and breathings that was widespread in his day, that εἱς (*heis*, "one"), is the same as the Latin pronoun *is* ("this man", "he"); he may also be suggesting an association with the verb εἱναι, "to be". In this note, C speculates about the etymological origins of the Greek numbers from one to ten, tracing them to primitive counting on the fingers. This material is repeated in a condensed form in *CN* IV 4693 (1820) and in *SW & F* (*CC*) 1345–53, a note of 17 Sept 1827, where in both cases it follows a more elaborate and derivative linguistic exercise as a scheme of C's own. No single source has been discovered for it, but if it belongs, as it appears to do, to the period of especially active etymologising about the turn of the century, then Adelung (see **1** n 1 above) may have started it off: his entry for *fünf*, "five", includes the observation that the word was commonly believed to be derived from *Finger*, reflecting the practice of counting on the fingers.

2² "This man". Using this phrase before 1804 in KANT *Anthropologie* COPY A **1**, C comments on Kant's observation that children begin by referring to themselves in the third person.

2³ The hypothetical verb δάω is mentioned in Johan Daniel van Lennep *Etymologicum linguae graecae* rev ed Everhard Scheid (2 vols Utrecht 1790) under δαίω, δὲ, and δέω; according to Lennep both verbs meant "divide" or "separate", but his editor Scheid preferred another meaning of δέω, "I bind" or "I connect". For C's acquaintance with Lennep see EICHHORN *Alte Testament* **10** n 1.

2⁴ For δέ, its meaning and derivation, see also QUARTERLY JOURNAL **3** n 3; δέ and τε were both very common words in ancient Greek; π may be substituted for τ in the Aeolic, and τ for σ in the Attic dialect, but πε and σε meaning "and" are not recorded. Both δέ and τε follow, not precede, the words to which they apply, and there is no trace of any of these syllables being used as a prefix in the sense C requires.

2⁵ Latin, "give", imperative.

3. Τρεις. Τερ εις.[6] Thrice one—but τερ = he, or and he. τε ερ. The ερ = he remains in the Teutonic Dialect of the Gothic, and peeps out in the ετερος[7] of the Cadmæan & Attic or Greek.[8]

4. Τετταρος = τε ετερος = and another

5. Πεντε = πε εν τε = and one yet from πε (the Eolic for τε). ⟨our ~~pint~~ Pint, tho' now the 4th of the half gallon⟩

6. Εξ. Non liquet[9]—The Division.[10]—i.e. The first number to be counted over again, or on the Thumb of the other Hand/ Pollex = εξ πολεων— the dividing of numbers.[11] N.B. What connection has Polliceor with Pollex?[12]

7. Επτα = επειτα = επ' αυτα = then, next to these.

8. [? Οκτω] ογδ[. . .] [? the Eolic or that][b] more ancient dialect of Magna Grecia, the mother of the Latin,[13] must have been o with a digamma = Hog or Og, the Latin ⟨Hoc.⟩—.[14] Ογδοα is τουτο δαεω / hoc alligo.[15]

9. εννεα = yet a new one.

2[b] Words obscured by the heavy deletion of "Sara Hutchinson" on the other side of the leaf

2[6] I.e. "treis" may be expanded to *ter* (Latin "thrice") and *heis* ("one").

2[7] [*H*]*eteros*, "other".

2[8] C here seems to side with the supporters of Gothic as the original Japetic language. He divided the Japetic race into two main branches, Greco-Roman and Gothic, in the lecture of 30 Jan 1818 (*Lects 1808– 1819—CC*—II 70–1), and he usually appears to give the priority to Greek. The Phoenician Cadmus was the legendary bringer to Greece of the alphabet, the Samothracian mysteries, and (according to some theories) of the language itself.

2[9] "Six. It is not clear."

2[10] The fact that C had been taught to ignore diacritical marks in Greek meant that he could treat ἔξ (*hex*, six) as the same word as ἐξ (*ex*, out of, away from), hence marking the "division" between one hand and the other as you cross over to count the sixth thing. Scheid in Lennep I 279–80 (cited in n 3) makes the same suggestion, without mentioning *pollex*, the thumb. C discusses *ex* and *pollex* also in *CN* III 4436.

2[11] "Out of many": in Homeric Greek, πολεων is the epic form of the genitive plural of πολυς, and this phrase is used e.g. in *Iliad* 15.680.

2[12] I.e. "I promise" (or hold forth) with "the thumb". Modern etymologists would deny that there is any connection.

2[13] It was then still believed, as by the Greeks and Romans themselves, that Latin was an early form of the Greek Aeolic dialect. It is now classed as belonging to a different and earlier branch of the Indo-European family. Magna Graecia was the collective name for the Greek colonies in Italy.

2[14] The digamma—a letter probably sounded like English "w", and surviving in inscriptions—received considerable scholarly attention after Richard Bentley's discovery of its implied presence in Homer. C believed it originally had a "g" or "ng" sound: *Logic* (*CC*) 25, Hartley COLERIDGE 4 n 1.

2[15] *Ogdoa* (eighth) is "this I tie onto", in Greek and Latin.

10. Δεκα = the clasp or fingers—whence A̶t̶ Digitus, ⟨δεχομαι,⟩[16] even as our Ten is Teen (we now say, a Miss in her Teens,[17] and Twee̸nty— is tween teen) i.e. two sets of Fingers—/. For doubtless in the first language as in the Latin and Greek the Toes & Fingers were distinguished only by the adjunct of Hand or Foot—Digiti pedis, digiti manus[18]—two Tribes coming together one calling Fingers whether of Hand or Foot Fingers (from Fangen, to take hold of) the other Toes Teās, or Teen would soon desynonimize them / as two old Women, agreeing to live together now use the omnium Pot or Kettle of yore, one for their Tea, the other for Potatoes—having now two.

2[16] C is still playing with related sounds, in the Greek "ten", Latin "finger", and Greek "I take"; the connection between "ten" and "I take" was a generally accepted etymology that C would have encountered, for example, in Tooke ɪɪ 205. He uses it himself in *CN* ɪɪɪ 4436 (and see n).

2[17] The usage dates from at least the late seventeenth century; cf the title of Garrick's popular farce *Miss in Her Teens* (1747).

2[18] "The fingers of the foot, the fingers of the hand".

CHRISTIAN FRANZ PAULLINI
1643–c 1712

Christiani Francisci Paullini disquisitio curiosa an mors naturalis plerumque sit substantia verminosa? Revisa, aucta & emendata, multisque raris, selectis & curiosis Dei, naturae artisque magnalibus, mysteriis, & memorabilibus illustrata & confirmata. Frankfurt & Leipzig 1703. 8°.

Not located; marginalia pub *Green SC* (1880) 534.

DATE. 1 Oct 1803 (**1**).

1 title-page

S. T. Coleridge, I cut open this book Oct. 1, 1803, the leaves having remained uncut an exact Century, 8 years of the time in my possession. It is verily and indeed a Book of Maggots.[1]

S. T. C.   Oct. 1, 1803, Greta Hall, Keswick.

[1] A mocking allusion to the title, "a curious disquisition as to whether natural death be not for the most part a substance full of worms".

HEINRICH EBERHARD GOTTLOB PAULUS
1761–1851

Das Leben Jesu, als Grundlage einer reinen Geschichte des Urchristentums. Dargestellt durch eine allgemeinverständliche Geschichterzählung über alle Abschnitte der vier Evangelien und eine wortgetreue, durch Zwischensätze erklärte Übersetzung des nach der Zeitfolge und synoptisch-geordneten Textes derselben. 2 vols in 1. Heidelberg 1828. 8°.

British Library C 126 h 11

"S. T. C." label in both vols. II xvii–xxiv, 41–8, 57–208 are unopened still (1985), as were I 175–352 and II 209–12 when first examined by the editors. Some cryptic numerals—"27" and "28–2"—appear on I title-page and I $^{+}$3 respectively; these were probably notes for the binder, such as appear also in PLATNER.

John Taylor Coleridge recorded a conversation in 1811 in which C appears to have said that he attended lectures by Paulus when he was in Germany, but C claims such direct acquaintance nowhere else, and it seems likely that either C or John Taylor Coleridge confused Eichhorn and Paulus on that occasion (their names are often joined in C's references to the German theologians): *TT* (*CC*) I 7 n 11. C also annotated Paulus's ed of Spinoza: see SPINOZA.

DATE. Aug–Sept 1828. Dated in ms: 3 Aug 1828 (**12**), Sept 1828 (**39**). C took this vol with him on the European tour he made with WW in 1828: see **12**. Further comments on the book appear in N 38 and N 39, which C was using 1828–9.

COEDITOR. Raimonda Modiano.

1   I $^{-}$3, pencil[a]

Oriental here, oriental there![1] the Question is—Have the words of John and Paul any meaning that can be on grounds of common sense asserted

---

1[a] At the top of this page, apparently in another hand, in pencil, is written "R VI"; see **1** n 1

1[1] The main purpose of Paulus's work was to remove the miraculous element from the prophecies and accounts of Christ, offering instead a coherent naturalistic history of his career, and arguing that it is not Christ's supernatural power but his moral grandeur that makes him admirable. While sharing Paulus's mistrust of the use of miracles as "evidence" for Christianity, C disapproves of his reductive methods, including the practice of referring awkward texts to an "oriental" frame of mind (e.g. I 47, 72). It is possible that the pencilled numerals noted in textual note *a* refer to I vi, where Paulus remarks on the importance of being aware of the qualities of Jewish culture in the time of Christ and refers to "oriental" ways of thought—though he there uses the adjective *morgenländisch* and not *orientalisch*.

to be *their* meaning, and not Professor Rosenmüller's or Paulus's, or Schleiermacher['s?][b2] If the answer be, Yes!—then I venture to affirm, that no Reduction into Allegory, Personification, or other Figures of Speech and Fancy can rescue the Character of Jesus from the charge of the most inflated and [? *Ciarlatan*][3] Vanity and Egoismus—otherwise than by impeach[ing][c] John and Paul as deliberate Falsifiers of their Master's Discourses, or by branding the Writings ascribed to them with the name of spurious—. With what just indignation would not my worthy and Jewish Friend, Hyman Hurwitz,[4] or any other biblical Jew, repel the Pretensions of Professor Paulus's Christus to the credit of any addition to or improvement on the theology and ethics of the New Testament.

S. T. C.

2 I ⁻2–⁻1 (slip tipped in)

not the least interesting point for my purposes in this strange Book is the continued reference to the Evangelia Infantiæ[1] as authentic & coetaneous parts of the original Gospels, one of them written within 10 years after the Crucifixion, as the only means of rendering his Deistico-psychological Romance even plausible—thus confirming my observation made so long ago, that the only Parties whom had any interest in maintaining the genuineness of the Christopædia were Deists and Unitarians./[2]

1[b] Insertion by editor; it may be in ms, but obscured by tight binding
1[c] Insertion by editor; it may be in ms, but obscured by tight binding

1[2] Johann Georg Rosenmüller (1736–1815) was one of the most eminent and prolific of the modern school of German biblical scholars whom C described as "Neologic Divines" (*CN* III 4401 and n); Paulus refers to his *Handbuch* (Altenburg & Leipzig 1818–19) I 101. C annotated copies of at least two works by F. D. E. Schleiermacher (1768–1834), *Über den sogenannten ersten Brief des Paulos an den Timotheus* (Berlin 1807) and *A Critical Essay on the Gospel of St. Luke* (1825).
1[3] Charlatan (Italian).
1[4] Hyman Hurwitz (1770–1844), C's Highgate neighbour, master of the Hebrew Academy at Highgate and the first Professor of Hebrew at University College, London. A general note on his relationship with

C is BLANCO WHITE *Practical Evidence* 2 n 3.
2[1] "Gospels of the Infancy", i.e. the accounts of the infancy of Christ in Matt 1–2 and Luke 1–2 that C, with other recent biblical critics, believed to have been composed at a later date than other parts of the gospels: cf his notes on SCHLEIERMACHER *Critical Essay* and DONNE *Sermons* COPY B 9 n 1; also 24–26 below.
2[2] C might have included the Roman Catholics here, as he did in CHILLINGWORTH COPY B 2, one of his earliest surviving pronouncements on the subject. Cf also BLANCO WHITE *Letters* 7. "Christopædia" (perhaps C's coinage) is the "childhood (or upbringing) of Christ".

3   i [i], pencil

King that never dies and can do no[a] wrong, = Lear, Hamlet, or Othello.

The successive Impersators[1] or Incarnations of this Idea = Betterton, Garrick, Kemble, Kean, Young—each acting the same character differently, some worse, some better.[2]—The Obscuration of the Idea, the Opacity of the Shrine, the effect and Symptom of Barbarism or of the Rude State.—This and this alone is the true contra-distinction of the genuine Tory, and Whig.—In proportion as a Man confounds the Idea with the Symbol or Idolon (ειδος ⚹ ειδωλον)[3] or even loses the former in the latter, he is a Tory, *a superstitious* Royalist. In proportion as the Shrine is *transparent* for a man, he is a Whig, a religious Loyalist.[4]

4   i [v]–vii, pencil | Preface

Unverkennbar ist, wenigstens soweit die teutsche Zunge reicht . . . dass unter allen Kirchenpartheyen, in welche man, auch uns Teutschen, die allgemein gültige, wahrhaft katholische, aber geistiglebensthätige Religion Jesu getheilt hat, dennoch Alle, die mit Uneigennützigkeit Unpartheyische seyn wollen, immer mehr darin übereinstimmend werden, dass wir mit Ernst und Redlichkeit *auf das Wesentliche des Urchristentums im Leben und in der Lehre gemeinschaftlich zurückkommen* sollten.

[It is obvious, at least in the German-speaking lands . . . across all the lines of religious faction that have divided the universally valid, truly catholic, yet spiritually living and active religion of Jesus even among us Germans, that those who nevertheless strive to stand above party interests are increasingly of the view that we should return, as a community, seriously and honestly, *to the essentials of original Christianity, both in life and in doctrine.*]

On the same grounds, as we deny our Ancestors before Luther to have

3[a]   C wrote "no do" and marked the words for transposition

3[1] Not in *OED*, nor used elsewhere by C: either a slip for "Impersonators" or a nonce usage.

3[2] Eminent Shakespearean actors of several generations: Thomas Betterton (c 1635–1710), David Garrick (1717–79), John Philip Kemble (1757–1823), Edmund Kean (1787–1833), and Charles Mayne Young (1777–1856).

3[3] "Form" (in the Platonic sense) "as opposed to image". The versatile word *eidos* can also mean shape, figure, class, kind, genus, species, etc, and C generally uses it

to express a lower degree of reality, as in *CN* III 4443. His use of "Symbol" coupled with *eidos* is unusual. *Eidolon* he often renders as "idol", e.g. in LACUNZA **19**, and *SM* (*CC*) 101, where it is "the antithesis not the synonyme" of "idea".

3[4] This statement expresses C's doctrine of the symbol in unusually political terms. The contrast between Whig and Tory elsewhere in his writings, e.g. *TT* (*CC*) I 264–5, JOHNSON **1**, **43**, **52**, is more conventionally historical, but the wording of this sentence is echoed in *C&S* (*CC*) 103.

been *Roman* Catholics, we must in fairness forbear to impute the excesses of those ages to the Romanists. They belong to the *Trunk* and to neither of the diverging Branches.—Yet this must be understood with the qualification or exception of such cases as can be attributed exclusively to the Papal Usurpation. A deep interest therefore attaches to the Christian Churches, from the 8th to the 12th Century, independent of the Romish Church & Court, as the Spaniards, the British, the Albigensian/[1] under their own Bishops, & which were gradually conquered by the Pope, from the same cause as originated the primacy of Rome, viz. the necessity of a center./—*Mem.* as long as this necessity continued, i.e. as long[a] the Christian Churches were disjoined specks amid Paganism in the first Half—& till Gotho-celtic Christendom was organized in the second—the Papacy was a Good.

5   I vii, pencil

Wie können dagegen [eine Verehrung Gottes durch Geist] die durchaus unbiblischen Worte und Begriffe von *zugerechneter* Rechtschaffenheit, von *stellvertretender Genugthuung*, von Versöhnung *Gottes* durch *blutige Abbüssung* der *Sündenstrafen* für die, welche biblische Christen (nicht nur Hörer, sondern Thäter des Urchristenthums) seyn wollen, wie die Hauptsachen der Bibellehre dargestellt werden? blos weil es menschengefälliger ist, den Sündern leicht annehmbare Tröstungen und Gewissensbeschwichtigungen entgegen zu bringen, als sie nach der Bibellehre auf ein festentschlossenes Ablassen vom Sündigen durch Geistesrechtschaffenheit, als das unumgängliche Mittel zur Aussöhnung und zum Frieden mit Gott kräftig, unnachsichtlich und durch selbsteigenes Beyspiel hinzuweisen. *

[In contrast to honouring God in the spirit, how can utterly unbiblical expressions and concepts such as *imputed* righteousness, *vicarious compensation*, or appeasement *of God* through *bloody expiation* of the *punishment for sin* be presented as the main points of the lessons of the Bible to those who wish to be biblical Christians (not mere hearers, but practitioners of original Christianity)? Simply because it is more pleasing to humanity to give out agreeable comforts to sinners and soothe their consciences than to be consistent and, by setting a strong example, point them the way, according to biblical teaching, to a decisive forsaking of sin through spiritual righteousness, as the indispensable means of reconciliation and peace with God. *]

* I ask Prof. Paulus, what learned Protestant, Lutheran or Calvinist, has

4[a] Probably a slip for "as long as"

4[1] The Albigenses, a heretical sect that emerged in the south of France in the 11th century, had been eradicated by the end of the 14th.

ever stated the former as possible *Substitutes* for the latter? or questioned the indispensableness of this "festentschlossenes Ablassen vom Sündigen"?[1]

6 I x–xi

Mein grösster Wunsch ist, dass meine Ansichten über die wunderbaren Erzählungen bey weitem nicht für die Hauptsache genommen werden möchten. Ach, wie leer wäre die Gottandächtigkeit oder Religion, wenn das Wahre davon abhinge, ob man Wunder glaube oder nicht glaube. Die Allmacht oder Machtvollkommenheit Gottes glaubt doch ein jeder gewiss, der einen vollkommenen Geist zu denken vermag; *ohne dass dieser sein Glaube erst noch einiger kurzer Andeutungen und Erzählungen bedürfte, nach denen da oder dort etwas Einzelnes erfolgt ist, ohne dass wir dabey die Gesetze der Natur oder der allgemein erkennbaren Weltordnung Gottes und deren Würksamkeit bemerkt finden.

[*My greatest wish is that my views on the miracle stories should not be mistaken for the main issue.* Oh, how empty would devotion to God or religion be if its truth depended on one's believing or disbelieving in miracles. Surely, anyone who has the capacity to conceive an infinite spirit must believe in God's omnipotence or perfect power; *such belief does not first need to be supplied with brief allusions and accounts that tell of singular events observed here or there, while omitting to mention the operation of the laws of nature, the universally known, divinely appointed order of the universe.*]

*   In part, not true: for miracles may have a *subjective* propriety as *causes* ⟨*of,*⟩ if not ⟨as⟩ *grounds for*, the faith in the *personality* of God. In part, nihil ad rem:[1] for the miracles, as fulfilments of prophecy, were appropriate evidences to the Jews, the Contemporaries of Jesus, that he was indeed the Shilo,[2] the Jehovah-man, promised from the beginning.

S. T. Coleridge.[3]

7 I xi

Der Hauptpunkt ist immer schon zum voraus sicher, dass die unerklärlichsten Aenderungen in dem *Natur*lauf *keine geistige Wahrheit weder

---

5[1] "Decisive forsaking of sin": in textus.

6[1] "Nothing to the point", "irrelevant".

6[2] C alludes to the "Shiloh" of Gen 49.10, traditionally identified with the Messiah: "The sceptre shall not depart from Judah, nor a lawgiver from between his feet, until Shiloh come; and unto him shall the gathering of the people be."

6[3] C's position on miracles is usually less accommodating—as when he refers to them as "superfluous Garnish" in **8** below; cf LIGHTFOOT **2** and n 1. But he could resist modern attempts to use the "evidence" of miracles to support Christianity while accepting the value of miracles at the time of the introduction of Christianity.

umstossen noch beweisen können, da an keinem Naturerfolg zu sehen ist, *aus welcher geistigen Absicht* er so und nicht anders geschehe.

[The main point should already be clear: the most inexplicable alterations in the course of *nature* can neither invalidate nor establish *any *spiritual* truth, since in merely observing a natural event we cannot know *what spiritual design* made it happen in this way and not in some other way.]

* Argumenti causâ,[1] be it so!—but what becomes of the *Revelation*? Wherein differs Jesus from Paul, or Paul from Professor Paulus of Heidelberg? Saviour, *only* Mediator, *the* Son of God, the *only*-begotten of God—what becomes of all of these terms?—

8 I xiv–xv

* Der Wunderbeweis selbst fordert, wie er muss, immer zuerst, dass die Behauptungen gotteswürdig und nicht vernunftwidrig seyn sollen. Sind sie dies, so ist für sie kein Wunder mehr als Beweis nöthig.

[* The proof from miracles itself demands, as it must, that, above all, its claims should be worthy of God and not contrary to reason. If they be so, a miracle is no longer necessary for proof.]

* I cannot conceive—an orthodox Divine could scarcely wish—a more decisive Proof of the untenibleness of the Unitarian Scheme. If the Points here enumerated constitute all that is essential in Christianity, it is most true, that Miracles must be a most superfluous Garnish.

9 I xvi | End of Preface

[Paulus concludes his preface with a summary of his position, arguing that the teaching of Jesus is more important than the miracles, and that judgment by reason and understanding, ideas and concepts, must guard faith against superstition.] Wer durch Ahnen und Fühlen das Wahre und Gute entscheiden meint, nimmt den ersten Anfang für den Endpunct, für das Höchste. Die Begeisterung der Empfindung ist das Höchste, aber sie selbst setzt auch, nach Ephes. 4, 23. die Thätigkeit der ganzen Denkkraft (des Nus) voraus. Und deswegen ist diese des ganzen Menschen mächtig gewordene Begeisterung, dieses auf das Heilige gerichtete Pneuma, überall das höchste Wort des *Urchristentums*. In dieser Begeisterung für wahre Rechtschaffenheit besteht die Verehrung Gottes, der vollkomme-

---

7[1] "For the sake of argument".

nen Geistigkeit. Joh. 4, 23. 24. Und wie Jesu Worte dieses der Samari-
tischen Frau aussprachen, so sage es uns—jeder Zug aus seinem Leben.

[He who thinks to determine the true and the good through surmise and feeling mistakes the first beginning for the end, for the highest. The spiritualisation of the sensibility is the highest, but this itself presupposes, according to Eph. 4.23, the activity of
the reasoning power (the *nous*). And it is on this account that this inspiration of the
spirit, taking control of the whole man, this Pneuma directed towards the holy, is the
highest Word of *early Christianity*. It is in this inspiration to true righteousness that
the worship of God, of perfect spirituality, consists. John 4.23, 24. And just as Jesus's
words declared this to the Samaritan woman so let every draught from his life say the
same to us.]

N.B. I wish it to be understood, that my radical difference is with the
Scheme of our English Unitarians, the Priestlëian Psilanthropists.[1] As to
Pr. Paulus, I differ perhaps only as having more nearly completed the Circle than he seems to me to have done. We both set off by receding from
the point, m— $\bigcirc$[m] [2]

10   I 2, pencil | Introduction § 1

Am allerwenigsten aber will man diesen so *welthistorisch gewordenen
Gekreuzigten* als den betrachten oder zeigen, der Er geschichtlich un-
läugbar war und bleibt, das Musterbild eines Menschengeistes, der *nur
durch lebensthätige Wahrheiten gotteswürdiger Geistesrechtschaffenheit und durch Selbstausübung derselben das innere und äussere
Besserwerden der Menschen zu begründen unternahm* . . . die Kraft der
das Wollen aufregenden Ueberzeugungen, worauf allein Er vertraute, hat
die Welt, und gerade den bildungsfähigeren Theil der Welt, überwun-
den!!

[But the last thing that is looked for is a consideration or portrayal of the *crucified one*,
this *figure of world history*, as historically He undeniably was and still is: an exemplary human spirit who *set out to base the inner and outer improvement of mankind
solely on the vitally active truths of godly spiritual righteousness and on the putting
of these into practice* . . . the strength of the conviction that animated His will, and on
which alone He trusted, has overcome the world, even the culturally more advanced
part of the world!!]

How could Paulus contrive to forget that *not* HIS Christianity, nor aught
that resembled it, is that which has conquered the World!—

[1] The followers of Joseph Priestley
who regarded Christ as "mere man" ("psi-
lanthropy" and "psilanthropist" being C's
coinages). C's personal involvement with
the Unitarians and subsequent public attacks upon them are summarised in LESS-
ING *Sämmtliche Schriften* **26** n 1.

[2] I.e. C had begun by thinking as Paulus
did but has gone beyond him, coming round
again to a belief in the major miracles and
in the Christian mysteries.

11 ɪ 16, completed in pencil | § 4

Ein Mann von dieser erhabenen Gemüthsbeschaffenheit [Abraham, der bereit war, sein Liebstes aufzuopfern] war es demnach, der solche menschenartige Machtgötter, wie er sie durch seine Voreltern geerbt hatte, nicht für die seinige erkennen konnte. Weil er selbst seinem kräftigem Willen nach viel besser, wie sie, war, wurde es ihm gewiss, dass ein Höherer seyn müsste, der an ihm Wohlgefallen haben, ihn seines Segens würdig achten könne.

[Thus it was a man of exalted sensibility [Abraham, who was willing to offer up his beloved son,] who refused to acknowledge the anthropomorphic gods of power which he had inherited from his ancestors. Because he was himself much better than they with respect to the strength of his will, he became convinced of the existence of a higher being, one which bore him goodwill and regarded him worthy of blessing.]

But how romantic and anomalous is all this hypothetical Story compared with the narrative in Genesis! Paulus distorts the facts, and swells the marvellous into the incredible by confining to the *"effects* what in the original is shared by the assigned *Causes.*

12 ɪ ⁺3, referring to ɪ 23 | § 5

Jehova, heisst es, rief dem Mose zu, vom Berge. Der gottbegeisterte Mann erkannte das, was das Wohl der Menschen machen würde, mit Zuverlässigkeit als den wahren Willen, als die Stimme seiner Gottheit. Das Alterthum hat dies nach seiner Weise wie eine Begeisterungsrede oder, wie wir zu sagen pflegen, als poëtisch 2 M. 19, 3–5, aufbewahrt . . .

[Jehovah, it says, called to Moses from the mountain. Divinely inspired, the man confidently recognised as the true intent and voice of his God what would be of benefit to mankind. The ancient world, after its manner, has preserved this as an inspired statement or, as we are accustomed to say, as poetry Exod 19.3–5 . . .]

p 23—Readily should I admit (what in fact for 30 years past I have acted on, on my own suggestion) the necessity of reducing the poesy of the old-hebrew Documents to their matter of fact import. But in the detailed account of the Delivery of the Law from Mount Sinai, the preparations, the series of Incidents and Appearances, the repeated and positive declarations of the Writer respecting their uniqueness and superhuman character are such, as leave no pretext for the resolution of the Statements into figurative language & poetic drapery (*Begeisterungsrede*)[1]—and permit no alternative but *literal* matter-of-fact Truth, or intentional and deliber-

---

11[a] Remainder of note in pencil

12[1] From textus, "inspired statement".

ate Fiction meant to be received as truth.—S. T. C. 3 August 1828.—
Antwerp, Le Grand Laboureur—Saturday.[2]

13   I [+]3, referring to I 24

Die Gerichte selbst waren also von den Priestern unabhängig und eine
ächt bürgerliche Anstalt, um immer Gleiche durch Ihresgleichen in Ordnung zu halten und ausser Streit zu setzen. Nur für schwere Fälle war
Mose Oberrichter geblieben. [2 Mose 18] (v. 26). Für den *Krieg* hinter-
liess Mose einen obersten Heerführer.

[The courts themselves were thus independent of the priests and represented a genuinely civil institution; they served to maintain order among equals through their peers
and keep them from conflict. Only for serious cases did Moses remain supreme judge.
Exodus 18.26. In the event of *war* Moses called for a supreme army commander.]

p. 24. But surely it must, in this statement, be admitted to have been a
strange and gross Oversight on the part of the Hebrew Legislator, that no
positive Command and Arrangement has been introduced into his Constitutional Code for the election of a First Magistrate Temporal & Mili-
tary/ Provision indeed is made for a King, as a possible future Event—[1]

14   I 35, pencil

Denn dieser, auf Erden ein Davidssohn geworden, bleibt nun in der höchsten Seeligkeit bey Gott *als der immerwährende und unveränderliche
Messias Gottes* aufgestellt. Dies ist Er, weil er Regent ist durch eine
Lehre, deren innerste Heilsgrundsätze immer wahr sind, immer eben
dieselben bleiben.

[For he who became a son of David on earth is now raised up with God in highest bliss
as the everlasting and unchanging Messiah of God. This status is his because he rules
through a doctrine whose innermost principles of salvation are always true, always remain the same.]

Paulus dreaming!

15   I 38, pencil | § 9

[In making the point that all "Messiahs" (the "anointed" rulers of Israel)
were called "Sons of God":] Diesem Messias wagt dann der Dichter V.

12[2] C was coming to the end of a six-
week holiday (21 Jun–7 Aug) with WW and
Dora Wordsworth. On the day before, he
had seen an exhibition of pictures and annotated the catalogue: see NOTICE, in *CM*
(*CC*) III.

13[1] C alludes perhaps to Deut 17.14–15,
"When thou art come unto the land which
the Lord thy God giveth thee, and shalt possess it . . . one from among thy brethren
shalt thou set king over thee".

7. [Ps 45.6] zu sagen: "Dein Thron, o *Elohim* (o Hochverehrter) ist eine lange Zeitendauer; denn deines Reiches Scepter ist ein gerader Königsstab."

[In verse 7 [Ps 45.6], the poet dares to address the Messiah as follows: "Thy throne, O Elohim (O highly reverenced one) is of long duration, for the sceptre of thy kingdom is a sceptre of equity."]

Paulus's translations of Hebrew Terms seem to me arbitrary, and too evidently subservient to his argument. Ex. gr. I should render Elohim, the Strengths.[1]

16   I 42, pencil | § 10

[Paulus surveys the qualities predicted of the Messiah.] Noch eine Hauptstelle dieser Art bei Jesaiah lesen wir im elften Kapitel. Aus Davids Nachkommenschaft müsse denn doch entstehen das Heil der Nation, durch vorzügliche Eigenschaften dieses oder jenes dorther regierenden Königs!

[Another important passage of this kind is found in the eleventh chapter of Isaiah. The nation's salvation is to come from among the descendants of David, through the virtues of this or that reigning king!]

Had this been true and applicable to Christ, why no reference to his Davidical origin in the genuine writings of the Apostolic Age?

17   I 55, pencil | § 12

Nur das historisch begründete Zurückgehen in die althebräische Geschichte und die ruhige Beobachtung, inwiefern allmählig der Davidische Messiasbegriff zu einer allgemeineren Idee erhöht worden ist, kann uns gewiss machen, wie die jüdischen Zeitgenossen Jesu ihn verstehen konnten und mussten, wenn er ihnen zuerst von Johannes dem Täufer und alsdann durch sich selbst und seine Lehrgesandte, ohne eine andere Erklärung der Worte, als Messias (Joh. 1, 42) dargestellt wurde. Gleichbedeutend war es dort schon dem Täufer, ihn nach dem Amtsnamen Christus (Joh. 1, 25.26) oder (v. 34) nach dem Namen seiner Geisteswürde "den Sohn der Gottheit" zu nennen. *

15[1] In EICHHORN *Alte Testament* **21**, C similarly addresses the problem that the plural *Elohim* is used as a name of God. He wrote to Hyman Hurwitz (**1** n 4 above) about it, and in Jan 1821 announced a solution, that "Jehovah Elohim is undoubtedly, 'The self-exist[ent] *Strengths*'—Elohim being a plural derived from [the] Hebrew word for the Trunk of an Oak . . ." (*CL* v 134).

[Only historically-based research into ancient Hebrew tradition and an appreciation of the degree to which the Davidic concept of the Messiah was gradually elevated to a more universal idea can give us certainty about the manner in which the Jewish contemporaries of Jesus could and must have understood him; for he was presented to them, without further explanation, as the Messiah (John 1.42) [AV John 1.41], first by John the Baptist and later by Jesus himself and his disciples. For the Baptist there was already no difference between calling him by the name of his office, Christ (John 1.25, 26) or by that of his spiritual authority, "the Son of God" (verse 34).*]

* All this sounds to me a *Dream* of Paulus's. And yet this Phrase does not occur thrice in the whole Old Testament, and is applied to no one of the Davidic Kings, not even to the best!!![1]

18   I [+]2 (slip tipped in, verso of **48**), referring to I 56

Und was war feierlicher, als da der Hohepriester (Mt. 26, 63) in der über Leben und Tod entscheidenden Synedriumssitzung Jesu zurief: ich beschwöre dich bei der lebendigen Gottheit, dass du uns sagest, *ob du bist der Christus, der Sohn der Gottheit.* Nur in dem durch die althebräische Geschichte bis auf ihn herabgekommenen Sinn konnte der jüdische Hohepriester diese Frage machen. Jesus aber bejaht die gerichtliche Untersuchungsfrage, ohne eine andere Erklärung. Nur nimmt er zugleich auf die letzte in Daniels Namen ausgesprochene Beschreibung des Messiasgeistes, als eines Himmlischen, Rücksicht. Wie dieser dort als Geist vor die Gottheit tritt in der Gestalt eines Menschgebornen, aber kommend in Himmelswolken, in einer geistigen Erhabenheit, so erwiederte Jesus dem Fragenden: Ich bin das, was du sagst (ich bin es jetzt in dieser irrdischen Erniedrigung). Aber Ihr werdet auch in dem, was von jetzt an kommt (Ap'arti) zu sehen haben, dass Ich, dieser Menschensohn, eben der Geist bin, der in den Wolken des Himmels kommt und zur Rechten auf dem Ehrenplatz bei der Gottheit als der Regent sitzt, dem sie dort ein unvergängliches Regieren (das Reich der Wahrheit Joh. 18, 36.37. die fortdauernde Lehrregentenschaft durch innere Kraft und äussere Macht) für immer bestimmt hat.

[And nothing was more solemn than when the high priest in the Sanhedrin session that decided over life and death called on Jesus (Matt 26.63): I adjure thee by the living God, that thou tell us *whether thou be the Christ, the Son of God.* The Jewish high priest was able to frame such a question only by drawing on what had come down to him from ancient Hebrew history. But Jesus answered this legal interrogation affirmatively without offering further explanation. At the same time, however, he alluded

---

17[1] The phrase "Son of God" appears only once in OT (AV), in Dan 3.25, where it is used as a simile ("like the Son of God") to describe the fourth figure observed in the fiery furnace with Shadrach, Meshach, and Abednego.

to the last description of the Messiah's spirit, given under Daniel's name, that of one in heaven. Just as in that passage a spirit appears before God in the form of a man, coming in the clouds of heaven, in spiritual majesty, so Jesus answered his interrogator: I am that which thou hast said (now in this earthly abasement). But hereafter (*ap'arti*) ye shall see that I, this Son of Man, am the very Spirit who shall come in the clouds of heaven and sit as the reigning monarch on the right hand of God in the place of honour, on whom He has appointed forever an imperishable kingdom (the kingdom of truth—John 18.36, 37—the eternal kingdom of instruction through inner strength and outward power).]

p 56 Paulus unites what according to St John were two distinct Questions/ and without any authority asserts it to have been asked in the Jewish Synedrium which by the bye had not at this time jurisdiction in *capital* questions.—[1]

19   I 77–9 | "Evangelische Geschichts-Erzählung" § 2

[Following Paulus's point that Mary had an even greater conviction that she would be the mother of the Messiah than Elizabeth had had in regard to *her* son, John the Baptist:] Hierauf folgen noch manche recht merkwürdige Andeutungen, wie die verschiedenen Personen dieses messianisch-frommen Kreises ihre Erwartungen und Ansprüche wegen des kommenden Gottgesalbten in sich gestaltet und ausgedrückt haben. Alles *psychologisch*—wie verwandte Seelenstimmungen auf einander zu würken pflegen, *zusammenhängend*!!*

[After this come several really noteworthy hints of the manner in which the different members of this pious Messianic circle began to give shape and utterance to their hopes and expectations concerning the coming Anointed of God. Everything here is *psychologically interdependent*—in the way that related psychic states normally tend to reinforce one another.*]

* Heaven forgive me, if I speak rashly; but I am tempted to say that if these Seele-verwandten Träumer und Träumerinnen had been *physisch* as well as psychologisch *Zusammenhangend*[1] from the same Gallows, no wise ones would have been *in suspense*—according to Professor Paulus's Representation, I mean! Delusion justified and explained by Delusions— Dreams dotingly mistaken or knowingly passed off for real occurrences and the Destiny of the World grounded on Fancies and Prejudices that

18[1] Paulus paraphrases question and answer in the interrogation of Jesus by the high priest Caiaphas, as recounted in Matt 26.63–4, and then adds a paraphrase of John 18.36, part of the interrogation by Pilate (the encounter with Caiaphas being told in different words in John 18.19–23). The high court or Sanhedrin is not mentioned in either narrative.

19[1] If these "psychically-related dreamers and dreameresses" had been "*physically*" as well as "psychologically *hanging together*"—C paraphrasing and punning on textus.

would disgrace an Old Clothesman/[2] and on this foundation we are required by Professor Paulus of Heidelberg to rest our Consolation in this Life, and our Hopes in the Life to come—& Pr. Paulus is a philosophico-psychological Theologian.—Yea, and verily, O dear & learned Germany! Sound Common Sense is not among thy Attributes!   S. T. Coleridge

20   I 77, pencil | Following **19** textus

Gewiss sehr denkwürdig ist's, eben dadurch zu erfahren, mit welch beschränkten Messiasbegriffen gerade das Kind,* das dieselbe alle in der Folge durch eine so herrliche Vergeistigung übertraf, von seinen ersten irdischen Augenblicken an bey den Seinigen aufgenommen und genährt worden sey.* Wären die Evangelien Erzeugnisse späterer Zeit, könnten sie nach andern Spuren von der Geschichte selbst wenigstens etwa um ein Jahrhundert entfernt seyn, so könnte man leicht zweifeln, ob nicht dieses Früheste Alles nur eine Einkleidung, nur eine Art von *mythischer Sagengeschichte* sey . . .

[It is certainly worth considering how limited the understanding of the Messiah was which the child * absorbed from his family and was nurtured on, right from the beginning of his earthly existence—an understanding which he later surpassed in a magnificent spiritualisation.* If the gospels were products of a later time, if other indications could place them at least, say, a century after the events themselves, then it could easily be doubted whether this earliest indication were not all merely metaphorical drapery, a kind of *mythical legend* . . .]

* And is it not strange, that Paulus should never have asked himself, on what *evidence* he received as *historic* facts, Incidents so palpably incapable of all historic verification!

21   I 85, pencil | § 5

[Paulus argues that the narrative in Luke 1–2 gives the impression of being a family history rather than a late invention like the legends in the later, apocryphal gospels.] Würde ein Erfinder die messianischen Hoffnungen der verschiedenen Personen in eine so angemessene Abstufung und Uebereinstimmung mit dem, was jedem das natürlichste war, gebracht haben? Maria sieht in ihrem Sohn den Mächtigen, welcher die Usurpatoren des davidischen Throns vertreibt, und ihre lang herabgesunkene Königsfamilie in Güter und Ehren einsetzt Vs. 50–55. Spricht sie nicht ganz *wie das Mitglied eines solchen verdrängten, im Stillen stolz harrenden Geschlechts*!! voll von uralten, grossen Ansprüchen?

19[2] I.e. a dealer in old or second-hand clothes.

[Would a story-teller have been able to differentiate the Messianic hopes of the various persons so carefully and to have them correspond to what was most natural in each? Mary sees in her son the mighty one who will drive out the usurpers of David's throne and return the royal family, now long in decline, to riches and honour (verses 50–5). Does her utterance not resound with the grand, ancient claims *of a member of a noble house who has quietly and proudly endured its misfortunes*?!]

How many Questions, how many "Woulds" might be urged on the opposite side? And stronger than all, the absence of any allusion to this Relationship in all the rest of the N.T.—

22 i 92, pencil | § 8

[Commenting on Matt 1.1–18, Paulus stresses the fact that Mary was evidently convinced that she had not sinned, and that Joseph's strong inclination to believe her was confirmed by his dream.]

A *lame* account this, Friend Paulus! Either Mary was bonâ fide impregnated without the co-agency of a Man—and if so, why not take all the rest ⟨too⟩ as bonâ fide superhuman? Or there had been & was a Human Father of her Child: and then—why *then*, thro' what fanciful improbable and impure Suppositions must Paulus flounder, to get out of the way of the plain obvious inference, that M. had sworn the Child falsely to the H. G.—

23 i 95, pencil | § 10

[In discussing the appearance of the angels to the shepherds, Paulus cites Shaw's *Travels* in order to indicate that this "appearance" could be explained as an exaggeration of a natural phenomenon seen in Judea in the spring as lights that change and flicker over the landscape like lanterns or streaks of exploding gunpowder.]

That in a country in which the luminous Vapors described by Shaw,[1] Shepherds in the habit of watching their flocks by night—that Shepherds of all men in the World should mistake Jack a Lanthorns for great and small Angels, and pale flames for Loud Music & Halleluias!—

24 i 96, pencil

Wenn in einem solchen Ort gerade Alle Davids-Abkömmlinge, auch die sonsthin zerstreuten, in diesen Tagen zusammen gekommen seyn

---

23[1] Shaw is cited by Paulus in textus: i.e. Thomas Shaw (1694–1751) *Travels, or Observations Relating to Several Parts of Barbary and the Levant* (2 vols Oxford 1738).

mussten; wenn unter solchen erst nur ein Gerede, dass eine begeisterte junge Frau hier sey, welche die zuversichtliche Andeutung, den Messias zu gebähren, habe, von Einem zum Andern ging; wenn nun wirklich von Ihr ein Knabe gebohren ward, so gestaltet, wie ohne Zweifel Jesus eine vielsagende Gestalt gehabt hat; wenn dann noch die laute Freude und Verwunderung der Hirten, ihre Gewissheit, dass die Engel Gottes an dem neugebohrnen Kinde den frohsten Antheil nähmen, hinzukam; so war es gewiss das Wenigste, was noch gesagt werden konnte, dass, wie Lukas es ausdrückt, alle Hörenden sich wunderten über das, was von den Hirten zu ihnen geredet ward.

[When it so happened that at this time all of David's descendants, including those who had been scattered, were required to gather together in such a place; when among them a rumour began to spread that an excited young woman was present who claimed to have given birth to the Messiah; when she did in fact give birth to a boy who displayed the promising appearance which Jesus undoubtedly had; and added to this, the loud rejoicing and amazement of the shepherds, their certainty that the angels of God shared in the joy over the newborn child; surely the very least that could be said was, as Luke puts it, that all they who heard wondered at what they were told by the shepherds.]

When a few hours old!!

25   I 105–7, pencil | § 15

[In commenting on the fact that Luke 2.22–39 omits the story of the flight into Egypt, given in Matt 2.12–23:] Von der Zeit der priesterlichen Reinsprechung im Tempel zu Jerusalem spricht Lukas so, dass die Flucht nach Ägypten ihr nicht vorangegangen seyn kann. Jenes Darbringen im Tempel musste nach 40 Tagen geschehen. Für die späterhin aus Ägypten zurückkommende wäre sie nicht mehr nöthig gewesen. . . . Lukas also, der die Geschichte der Magier und die ägyptische Flucht, wenn er wahrscheinlich das Mathäusevangelium in Palästina schon gelesen hatte,* doch als Etwas, das weiter keine Folgen gehabt hatte, für seinen Theophilus nicht wiederholen wollte, macht, wie oft Geschichtschreiber zu thun pflegen, ohne die Auslassung anzumerken, eine Verbindung zweier nicht ganz unmittelbarer Erfolge, nämlich der Darstellung im Tempel und der Rückkehr nach Nazaret.

[According to Luke's account of the rite of purification in the temple at Jerusalem, it is not possible that the flight into Egypt had already occurred. This presentation in the temple had to take place after 40 days. If they returned from Egypt later, it would no longer have been necessary. . . . Thus Luke, who had probably already read Matthew's gospel in Palestine* but did not wish to review for his Theophilus the stories of the Magi and the flight into Egypt, events that he felt had no further consequences, links up two not immediately sequential events—namely, the Dedication at the Temple and the return to Nazareth—without indicating the omission, a frequent practice among historians.]

If Paulus's hypothesis of Oral Gospels be received, this previous acquaintance with a Gospel written by an Eye-witness and Apostle, a thing on all other accounts exceedingly improbable, would be in direct contradiction to Luke's own assurances.[1] And as to Paulus's way of reconciling the absurd Magi Tradition with the narrative in the Ev. Inf. prefixed to Luke's Gospel,[2] I would fain know what criterion of historic Truth or Falsehood would be left to us—for on the same privilege of inserting supposed spaces of Time ad libitum and against the plain sense of the Historian's Words, and at other times imaginary events, there would be no difficulty in harmonizing Sir John Falstaff's narrative of the Robbery on Gads-hill into a very consistent account.[3] But Paulus's motive is evident. The Incidents of this symbolic Christopædia, which in the 3rd Gospel still retain its poetic character, with the contents of some similar Poem or Hymn adopted as grave prosaic matter of fact by the far later compiler of the first Gospel duly blooded and purged by Paulus's psychological Process, &c would help him to account for our Lord's Self-persuasion &c[4] without the necessity of ~~other~~ any superhuman ministry, ~~but that~~ or of supposing Christ other than an hereditary Enthusiast, the Dupe of his Mother's, and two or three other *dreaming* Dotards' and Gossips', Enthusiasm. ~~S. T. C.~~ But all this is sadly foolish and mawkishly dishonest, on the part of the Heidelberg Professor of exegetic and hermeneutic Theology!   S. T. C.

26   I 126, pencil | § 18–19

[In dealing with the apparently discrepant genealogies of Christ (Matt 1.1–17 and Luke 3.23–38), Paulus points out that this linkage with the line of David was neither needed nor provided until Jesus began his Messianic ministry at the age of thirty, that Matthew and Luke trace the lin-

---

25[1] Luke 1.1–4 introduces the narrative as based on the testimony of "eye-witnesses" but not on a written gospel.

25[2] The "Ev. Inf." is the "Gospel of the Infancy" (cf **2** n 1 above). In the evolving Christian traditions of the first few centuries, the unnamed and unnumbered "wise men" of Matt 2 became three kings—Caspar, Melchior, and Balthasar. Paulus describes the kings' encounter with Herod at I 106–13.

25[3] In *1 Henry IV* II iv Falstaff lies about having been attacked by a large body of men at Gadshill, and claims to have killed several—the number rises from two to eleven in successive versions of the story—before being overwhelmed and robbed.

25[4] In the incident of "the Dedication at the Temple" referred to in the textus, when Simeon recognised Jesus as the Messiah and "Joseph and his mother marvelled at those things which were spoken of him" (Luke 2.33).

eage back along two, out of several possible, different routes, that errors of tradition had crept into their statements, and that the linkage was made not according to natural descent but according to that of traditional legitimisation.]

All this might pass, as *possible*—or even if mistakes had crept into both genealogies—what would it matter? if only the existence ⟨at so early a period as 10–20 ỹ post Chr.⟩ of the first two Chapters of our Greek Matthew, and those of Luke, had been made evident.[1] But no answer does Paulus give to the Objection from the utter silence of the rest of the New Testament—not even an allusion. See Eichhorn.[2]

27   I 130, pencil | § 20

[Paulus is commenting on the opening statement in the ministry of Jesus, as given in Matt 4.17, "Repent: for the kingdom of heaven is at hand", which is identical with the preaching of John the Baptist, as given in Matt 3.2.] Um diese Zeit also trieb eine innere Stimme Gottes, weil der lang erwartete Zeitpunkt, öffentlich wirksam zu werden, eintrat, den Vorarbeiter Jesu, des Messias, zum Antritt seiner lebensthätigen (praktischen) Unternehmung, die ganz einfach auf den *Hauptgedanken* zurückkam: "Wenn ein Reich, wie es im Himmel gedacht wird, ein Zustand, in welchem man den heiligen Willen Gottes als Gesetz befolgt, also eine Regierung des göttlichen Unterregenten oder Messias, für euch näher gekommen seyn soll, so müsset ihr in eine andere Gesinnung oder Willensrichtung übertreten, als bisher eure gewöhnliche ist." Eben diese Foderung und keine andere Art von Lehr-Gläubigkeit wird in der Folge auch als das Hauptwort Jesu von Matthäus angegeben, 4, 17. Er und Johannes haben nur *ein* Thema.

[When the long-awaited moment to begin public ministry had arrived, an inner voice of God impelled the forerunner of Jesus the Messiah to begin his active career; his message was a return to the *central point*: "If the kingdom ordained by heaven is to come, a state in which God's holy will is followed as law, then you must adopt a different frame of mind or set of priorities from those you have had in the past." It is precisely this demand, and not some other kind of religious doctrine that Matthew will

26[1] Paulus agreed with the tradition that Matt was compiled within ten years of Christ's death (I 66) and Luke no later than AD 60 (I 78).

26[2] In the periodical *Allgemeine Bibliothek der biblischen Litteratur* of which he was the editor from 1787 to 1800 (C annotated 2 vols of it), as well as in his *Einleitung in das Neue Testament* (3 vols Leipzig 1804–14) of which C annotated two copies, J. G. Eichhorn argued that most of the first two chapters of Matt and Luke were composed long after the apostolic age and interpolated in their respective gospels: e.g. *Neue Testament* I 430 ff, 630. C eventually accepted this position: cf **2** n 1 above. Eichhorn makes the point about the silence of the rest of the NT in *Neue Testament* I 163.

subsequently describe as Jesus's main concern (Matt 4.17). He and John have but *one* theme.]

The single word, *"Now"*, or the words, "is coming", "is at hand"—suffice to sweep away this finely spun Cobweb of Proffessor[a] Paulus's. A moral axiom, occurring 50 times or twice 50 in the Old Testament, and familiar to every educated Jew—and that's all!!

28 ɪ 131, pencil

Nur wo der Allwissende eine redliche, würksame Entschlossenheit, das Gute zu wollen, im Gemüth weisst, da darf der Mensch ruhig seyn darüber, dass seine sonst begangene Sünden das Wohlwollen der Gottheit gegen ihn nicht hindern. Aber redlicher, fester Ernst vor dem Ewigen, als Herzenskenner, muss allerdings diese Gesinnungsänderung erst geworden seyn! Und desswegen foderte auch Johannes eine äussere *sinnbildliche Bekenntniss und Erklärung*, wie sie ein Erwachsener doch nicht leicht, wenn er nicht sehr gerührt und überzeugt ist, sich gefallen lässt.

[Only where the All-knowing finds an honest, effectual determination to desire what is good, can a man be assured that his previous sins will not keep him from the favour of God. But first this change of attitude must lead to a sincere and firm commitment in the eyes of the Eternal who knows all hearts! And for this reason John, too, required an outward *symbolic confession and declaration*, something that might not be easy for an adult if he were not strongly moved and convinced.]

Who told Paulus this?

29 ɪ 132–3, pencil

Mk. fasst vielmehr Alles darin zusammen, dass Jesus als *Messias* den grossen Würdenamen *"ein Sohn der Gottheit"* trug, nach Lk. 1, 35.*

[Mark, rather, expresses all of this when he says that Jesus as *Messiah* bore the majestic title *"a Son of God"*, as in Luke 1.35.*]

* I am almost provoked and call this a Lie! Not *a* Son of God; but *the* Son, the *only*-begotten Son, of God, was the name & peculiar Attribute of our Lord: who commanded his Disciples, Call no *man* Master: yet said, Ye call me Master, and rightly I *am* your master./[1]

27[a] A slip for "Professor" caused, probably, by anticipation of the long "s" in "ss" following

29[1] Matt 23.9–10, and John 13.13: "And call no man your father upon the earth: for one is your Father, which is in heaven. Neither be ye called masters: for one is your Master, even Christ" and "Ye call me Master and Lord: and ye say well; for so I am." On the phrase "Son of God" see also **17** and n 1 above; for "only begotten Son" see e.g. John 1.18.

30   I 137–9, pencil | § 22

Der von Beiden wegen der Geburtsverhältnisse Vornehmere soll der
zweite, der geringere aber, der Davidische Nachkomme, ungeachtet
dieses Geschlechts in Maria und Joseph in den dürftigen Bürgerstand her-
abgesunken war, der erste, und so sehr der Erste seyn, dass kein Israëlite
mehr, als Er, seyn konnte. Denn der Messiasgeist wurde, besonders nach
Daniel,* als der höchste gedacht, so dass, wenn er nicht möglich gewesen wäre, Gott die Welt nicht geschaffen haben würde.

[Of these two, the one from the more distinguished family was to take second place;
first place was to go to the humbler one, the descendant of David, despite the fact that
in Mary and Joseph this family had sunk into a state of poverty; and He was to take
first place to such a degree that it could not have been any Israelite but He. For the
Messianic spirit, especially in Daniel,* was conceived as being so great that, had its
existence not been possible, God would not have created the world.]

* And yet in one passage only do I find reference to Daniel, and this too
only in the first Gospel,[1] the Compiler of which has in so many instances
inserted his own exposition of the words or incidents by quotation of parallel or appropriate text from the Old Testament as to make it by no means
improbable that our Lord had simply said—When ye shall see the abomination (i.e. Heathen Idols) placed in the Temple. But be it that our Lord
did refer to the Book of Daniel, he refers to the text for its historic content not as a prophecy.

31   I 137, pencil

[In commenting on the fact that nothing is given in the gospels concerning events in the lives of Jesus and John the Baptist before the baptism of
Jesus:] Darüber hängt ein undurchdringlicher Schleier; oder es muss
vielmehr darin Nichts von der Art vorgekommen und bekannt geworden
seyn, was als ein bedeutendes äusseres Ereigniss den Ueberlieferern und
Sammlern denkwürdig und der Aufzeichnung werth geschienen hätte.
Denn warum würden sie dergleichen sonst übergangen haben?

[An impenetrable veil hangs over this matter; or rather, among the events which were
known to have taken place, there must have been nothing on this score that redactors
and compilers regarded as a significant event worth recording. For why else would
they have passed over such things?]

Paulus wilfully forgets, that this is one of the many & weighty Objections
brought by Eichhorn, Schleiermacher, &c *against* the apostolic date of

---

30[1] Matt 24.15 refers to "the abomination of desolation, spoken of by Daniel the
prophet"; and cf Mark 13.14. Paulus, however, is evidently referring to Dan 7.13–14,
a passage C comments on in **37** below.

the Chapters—and the proofs, that the original Gospels all began with the Baptism of John.[1]

32 I 138, pencil

Nur über die Behandlung einiger andern Krankheiten fehlen uns genauere Anzeigen der Umstände, insofern hie und da auf gebrauchte Mittel hingedeutet ist. Ob die Kenntniss dieser Mittel und die Vorbereitung, sie auszuüben, in die vorhergegangenen 30 Jahre gefallen sey, kann man nur fragen, ohne eine traditionelle Antwort zu finden. Aber auf Kunsterfahrungen, welche mit Wissenschaft der Ursachen verbunden gewesen wären, weisen auch sie nicht hin.

[No detailed account of the circumstances surrounding the treatment of several other illnesses is given, though there are hints here and there of the use of remedies. Whether the knowledge of these remedies and of how to apply them was acquired during the preceding 30 years is a question to which there is no traditional answer. There is nothing which would indicate training in the art [of medicine] and scientific knowledge of causes.]

Why this is absolute Delirium!!!!

33 I 139, pencil

Von der Geburt an war er [Jesu] zum Messias bestimmt zu seyn versichert worden. Und jetzt nähert er sich dennoch dem, der auf den "kommenden" Messias hin tauft oder einweiht, erst mit der Bitte, *auch Ihn* zu taufen. *Selbst von seinem Freunde Johannes will er noch nicht entschieden als Messias behandelt werden; so hoch ihn dieser achtete.

[From his birth on, Jesus had been assured that he was called to be the Messiah. And now he comes to the one who has been baptising or consecrating in preparation for the "coming" Messiah and asks that *He too* be baptised. *He does not want to be treated unequivocally as the Messiah even by his friend John, highly as John revered him.]

* Is *this* an honest way of writing history? In what chapter is John spoken of, as a Friend or even as an Acquaintance of our Lord's?

34 I 143, pencil | § 23

Und dieses Abweisen des Unrichtigen zeigt ihn uns um so erhabener, wenn dabey zugleich vorauszusetzen ist, dass er sogar in einem traumar-

---

31[1] This is the position adopted by Eichhorn (**26** n 1 above); by Schleiermacher in *A Critical Essay on the Gospel of St. Luke* (1825), which C annotated in 1826; and by Herbert Marsh, a section of whose *Authenticity of the New Testament* (1820) C mentions as an authority for this line of argument in a letter of May 1820 (*CL* v 46 and n 1). By "Baptism of John", here and elsewhere, C means the baptism of Jesus *by* John (as in Matt 21.25, Luke 7.29).

tigen Zustand (denn Visionen können wir uebrigens uns doch kaum anders, als wie einen erhöhten Traumzustand vorstellen) diese mit alttestamentlichen Gründen unterstützte Entschlossenheit gehabt habe.

[And this rejection of evil shows him in an even more sublime light, when we consider that such determination, grounded in the Old Testament, was even maintained in a dreamlike state (for visions, it must be said, can only be imagined as being like a heightened dream state).]

There must be an original incurable Coarseness and Vulgarity in Paulus's mind—not to mention the psychological ignorance implied in this converted[a] the beautiful Parable of the Temptation into a Dream![1] not one single character of which it possesses. In no one instance does "the Spirit"—"in the Spirit" "led by the Spirit" relate to a State of Sleep;—but on the contrary to the free exertion of the very faculties which Sleep suspends—viz. the contemplative and prospective. But putting this aside, the meanness and meagreness of Paulus's Interpretations are marvellous. He is a perfect *Flatting*-machine![2] But above all, the absurdity of treating with all the scrupulous respect due to the most authentic modern History Works that require or permit such interpretations!

35 I 150, pencil | § 24

So sehr wahrscheinlich es aber nach allen diesen Umständen ist, dass die geschichtlichen Stücke dieses Evangeliums von Johannes selbst herkommen, so unterscheidet sich doch der Verfasser, welcher sie als ein Ganzes aufzeichnete, von ihm als dem "Zeugen" bestimmt und ausdrücklich.* Nach der letzten Erzählung nämlich von dem, was Jesus über Petrus und Johannes gesprochen habe und was damals zu einer unrichtigen Deutung, wie wenn Johannes gar nicht sterben, sondern die baldige Wiederkunft des Messias auf die Erde erleben musste, Anlass gegeben hatte, wird (21, 24.) mit den Worten geschlossen: Dieser ist *der* Lehrschüler, welcher von diesen Dingen *zeugt*.

[As probable as it may appear from all these circumstances, that the historical parts of this gospel derive from John himself, the redactor who set them down to form a whole nevertheless explicitly distinguishes himself from John, the "witness".* Thus after the

34[a] A slip for "converting"

34[1] The textus is a comment on the Temptation of Christ in the wilderness after his baptism.

34[2] A flatting-machine or flatting-mill was a machine like a wringer that squeezed ingots of silver or gold into ribbon or wire. (Cowper used it as an analogue for the poet in his poem "The Flatting Mill", composed in 1781 and published in *Poems* ed John Johnson [3 vols 1815].) C refers similarly to Eichhorn's reductive arguments as "the art of *flatt'ning* with a vengeance!" in EICHHORN *Neue Testament* COPY A 20.

final account of what Jesus says concerning Peter and John, which at the time was misinterpreted to mean that John should not die but instead live to see the imminent return of the Messiah on earth, the gospel closes (21.24) with these words: "This is *the* disciple who *testifies* of these things."]

* I expected this. But how much simpler and more probable is the received opinion among the Learned, that the last Chapter, or at least the latter Half of it, was a Postscript or Note added by John's Successor at Ephesus.[1]

36 I 151–3, pencil

Er [Johannes] schreibt an Personen, die er durch ein "Ihr" als ihm Bekannte anredet (20, 31. wie 19, 35). Und seine erklärte Absicht ist, damit sie treu überzeugt wären, von zweierlei Hauptpunkten:* Vorerst dass Jesus der Messias, der Sohn der Gottheit, sey; und dann, dass derjenige wahrhaft lebe, welcher jener Ueberzeugung treu und folgsam leben wolle.

[He [John] is writing to persons whom he addresses as "you" as though they are known to him (20.31 and 19.35). And his express intent is to convince them of two main points:* first, that Jesus is the Messiah, the Son of God; and second, that they will truly live only if they strive to live in faith and obedience to that conviction.]

* To say the least, this is a very imperfect statement of the Evangelist's Object/ which was evidently the establishment of the twofold Position, that Jesus was bonâ fide a Man, and yet not a Spirit distinct from the Allfather, yet in closest union with him ⟨who had⟩ become Flesh and an incarnate Person—in other words, that an eternal Being, having life *in* himself, tho' not *of* himself, became a true Man, and that this *Man* Jesus was—Truly and essentially divine/ against those who held him in degree only different from John the Baptist—truly and in all essentials *human*—against the Docetæ[1] who supposed his Body a mere Phænomen Illusion.

S. T. C.

37 I 155–8, pencil

Vom Messiasgeist dachte der palästinische Jude, dass Gott eine Menschenwelt, die so verkehrt werden könnte, gar nicht hätte werden lassen,

35[1] Biblical scholars debated then—and still debate now—the question as to whether the epilogue to the Gospel of John, John 21, was written by the evangelist or not. In this matter C and Eichhorn were on opposite sides: EICHHORN *Neue Testament* COPY A **39**, COPY B **7**.

36[1] Paulus himself points out (I 352–4) that the Evangelist affirms the reality of Christ's human body, as opposed to the Docetae, who believed that all matter was evil. Cf FLEURY **98** and n 3.

wenn in derselben nicht auch das Einwirken jenes verbessernden Geistes möglich gewesen und vorausgesehen worden wäre. Der Palästiner drückte diese Gedanken, wenn er kurz seyn wollte, so aus: *Diese Menschenwelt ist *wegen* des Messias (unter der Voraussetzung, dass der menschenwerdende Messias Alles wieder zu Gott zurückführen könne) geschaffen worden, wie diese Ansicht auch der Hauptstelle bei Paulus (I Kor. 15, 22–28) zum Grunde liegt.

[Regarding the Messianic spirit, the Palestinian Jew thought that God would never have permitted the existence of a human world that could become so corrupt, had not the influence of that improving spirit been possible and foreseeable. The Palestinian sometimes expressed this thought in an abbreviated form as follows: *this human world was created *because of* the Messiah (assuming that, in becoming man, the Messiah could lead all back to God); this view also underlies the central passage in Paul's writings (1 Cor 15.22–8).]

* Where is the Proof of this to be found? Even if the passage in Daniel[1] authorized the interpretation, which I deny, it would only prove the writer to have been infected by Greek Notions. Would that proof could be given that the idea expressed in lines 6, 7,[2] was genuine Jewish, and anterior to the Birth of Christ! It would decide the dispute at once in favor of the orthodox doctrine. But the fact is that *if* (as I am inclined to believe) the idea and expectation of a Jehova-Man, were entertained by the most ancient Hebrew Church, they had been long superseded/ or overlayed, by the narrow Superstition of a Messiah—a Jewish Napoleon.[3] But Paulus gives no dates! Every Rabbinical Flight is quoted by him, as a doctrine of the Jewish Church before Christ!

38   I 155, pencil

Auch Koloss. 1, 15. spricht Paulus nach der Palästinischen Ansicht, dass der Messiasgeist der Erstgeborne der Schöpfung, *in welchem* all diese Erdenwelt geschaffen sey; indem dieses "in ihm" ausdrückt, dass sein Daseyn und Würken das übrige möglich gemacht habe, welches "ohne ihn" nicht geworden wäre.

37[1] Probably Dan 7.13–14 (as in **43** below), which describe a vision of "one like the Son of man" brought before the Almighty and given "an everlasting dominion, which shall not pass away".

37[2] The first sentence of the textus.

37[3] Paulus devotes a long introductory section of his work (I 1–64) to explaining the evolution of the concept of the Messiah, including both kingly and soldierly ideals. C took up the Jewish notion of the Messiah as a conqueror again in marginalia to IRVING *Sermons*, written two or three months later than these, in Nov–Dec 1828; there he refers to "the ruinous & fleshly fancies entertained by the Jews … of a ⟨Messiah King, a⟩ Warrior Monarch & Conqueror" (**20**).

[Also in Col 1.15 Paul expresses the Palestinian view that the Messianic spirit is the firstborn of creation, *in whom* the whole world is created; here "in him" means that his being and deeds made everything possible that "without him" would not have come into being.]

false!—the words are "by" & not "in" him.[1]

39 I 161, pencil

In diesen einen Centralpunkt, in den Zweck, zu beweisen, dass Jesus der wahre, das beseeligende Geistesleben erregende Erleuchter der Menschheit und dadurch der Anordner des Gottesreiches gewesen sey, laufen alle die folgenden geschichtlichen Angaben zusammen. Bey jeder derselben ist der Schluss zu denken: Der, welcher so anerkannt wurde, so dachte, redete, handelte, endlich selbst durch die Beharrlichkeit in seiner Hinrichtung die Welt überwand, durch seine Wiederbelebung aber die Niedergeschlagenen zur höchsten Ermuthigung, zur unwiderstehlichen Verbreitung seiner lehrenden Lebensgeschichte und geistvollen Grundsätze erhob, dieser war durch die That das, was irgend von dem geistigen Messias oder Unterregenten der Gottheit erwartet werden konnte.

[All the historical statements that follow converge on this one central point, on the purpose of proving that Jesus had become the true light of mankind, the kindler of soul-giving spiritual life and by this means establisher of the kingdom of God. In each one of these the conclusion is to be understood: He who was so acknowledged, so thought, spoke, behaved, and finally conquered the world by his steadfastness under crucifixion, yet by his resurrection raised the oppressed to the greatest heights of courage and inspiration, to the irresistible spreading of the history of his life as a teacher and his spiritual principles, this man was indeed everything that could be expected from the spiritual Messiah, the vice-regent of God.]

What I said 20 years ago, I say now—Sept. 1828. This Philosophy is true or false/ if true, why reject the faith *in* Christ grounded on it? If false, there can be no faith at all. Jesus must have been an enthusiast, and his Disciples Dupes.[1]   S. T. C.

40 I 164, pencil | § 25

[In regard to John the Baptist's phrase, "Behold the Lamb of God, which taketh away the sin of the world", which Paulus believes has been misinterpreted to mean that Jesus was a sin offering for the world—a misin-

---

38[1] Coloss 1.15–16, "the firstborn of every creature: For by him were all things created . . . all things were created by him, and for him". The Greek prepositional phrases are ἐν αὐτῷ (lit "in him"), δι' αὐτοῦ ("through him"), and εἰς αὐτὸν ("for him").

39[1] Similar claims of the persistence and consistency of his own views over twenty years or longer are made in **12** and **46**.

terpretation based in turn, from the Church Fathers, on an erroneous view of the efficacy of sacrificial animals in the Mosaic Code:] Nur wer über einen *Irrthum* im Handeln oder wegen einer *Uebereilung* Reue hatte, mochte dies durch den Verlust eines Opferthiers als Schuld oder als Uebereilung bekennen und es sich desto mehr von seinem Gewissen wegschaffen. Wegen vorsätzlicher Sünden oder gar für Verbrechen gab es nach Mose keinen Gedanken an Sünd- oder Sühnopfer, und das christliche Kirchentum wurde unter das Mosaische Judenthum herabgesetzt, so oft man das Christentum als ein Mittel darstellte, eben so und noch leichter als durch die Hekatomben des Heydentums entsündigt und versöhnt zu werden.

[Only those who were repentant for some *oversight* in trade or for some *rashness* were allowed to confess it as guilt or rashness by slaying a sacrificial animal, and thereby to clear their consciences. For Moses, however, there was never any question of allowing a sin offering or expiatory offering for deliberate sin, let alone for crime; and every time Christianity was represented as a means of procuring reconciliation and release from sin, just as easy and even easier than through the hecatombs of heathenism, this lowered the Christian church beneath the level of Mosaic Judaism.]

Agreeing with Paulus in rejecting the doctrine of atonement in its vulgar sense,[1] I cannot but smile at this new discovery of a contra-distinction between Sin and Oversight in the Mosaic Code!!

41　ɪ 165, pencil

Zu seinen Lehrschülern gewendet, unter denen ohne Zweifel der Apostel Johannes selbst damals war, fuhr der Täufer fort, was er sonst unbestimmter vorausgesagt hatte, jetzt auf die bestimmte Person Jesu zu deuten.

[Turning to his disciples, who at that time no doubt included the Apostle John himself, John the Baptist went on to apply to the specific person of Jesus what his prophecy had earlier left unspecified.]

I have sought in vain for proof of this "ohne Zweifel"[1] Assertion.

42　ɪ 165–6, pencil

[Paulus paraphrases and expounds the speech of John the Baptist in John 1.32–4:] Auch ich, sagte Er noch einmal vor den Ohren des nachmaligen Apostels,—auch Ich würde ihn nicht so (durch jenen symbolischen Anblick) erkannt haben. Aber die Gottheit, welche mich angetrieben hat,

---

40[1] C's major statement about atonement appears in *AR* (*CC*) 320–34; see also *SM* (*CC*) 55–6, Irving *Sermons* **31** and n 1.

41[1] "Without doubt", from textus.

meine Wassertaufe zu beginnen, gab mir (in jenem Augenblick, als wir die Taube sahen) im Herzen das (innere) Wort: Ein solcher, auf den Du die Begeisterungskraft (bildlich und zugleich in der Würklichkeit) als bey ihm beharrend herabgekommen, erblickt hast, ist der nun nicht in Wasser allein, vielmehr in heilige Begeisterung Eintauchende. "Und gesehen hab' ich es und bezeugt will ich es haben, dass dieser ist 'der Sohn der Gottheit', der von uns für die Nation erwartete Gotteskönig." (1, 50 [34].)

[And I too, he said yet again in the hearing of the future Apostle,—I too would not have recognised him so (in that symbolic manifestation). But the God who urged me to begin baptising with water put into my heart (at the moment we saw the dove) this (inner) word: he on whom you see the quickening power descend as if to remain with him (metaphorically as well as in reality) is now the baptiser, not only in water but, much more, in the holy Spirit. "And I have seen, and will have it on record that this is 'the Son of God', the divine king whom we have awaited for the nation" (1.50 [34]).]

The cool quiet composed way in which Prof. Paulus gives his own fanciful interpretations of, and inferences from, the texts, as acknowleged History, is exceedingly humorous. Ex. gr. The Pigeon or Dove.—[1]

43 I 172/3, slip of paper tipped in, referring to I 169 | § 26

Jesus liebt öfters sich den Menschensohn zu nennen, wahrscheinlich mit Rücksicht auf jene Stelle von Daniel (7, 13.).

[Jesus was fond of calling himself the Son of Man, probably with reference to that passage in Dan 7.13.]

P. 169 This reference to Daniel (c 7, v 13)[a] is absolutely dishonest—to Daniel which Paulus himself acknowleges for a political Forgery of the age of Antiochus Epiphanes[1]—and to a text, palpably and confessedly imitated (or rather borrowed) from Ezekiel I.26—and which proves the words to be, like *a* Son of man, i.e. in a human form.—[b2]

44 I 170–1, pencil | § 27

[In regard to the first miracle of Jesus, the turning of water into wine at Cana (John 2.1–12), Paulus states that the circumstances are shadowy

43[a] MS gives "c" and "v" as superscript letters directly above the numerals

43[b] This note was evidently written upside-down at the end of a used leaf of paper, then torn off. Traces of the end of the earlier text can be deciphered as reading "inflicted on thyself.   S. T. Coleridge"

42[1] *Taube*, in textus, can mean dove or pigeon, doves being in the pigeon family. C chooses to use the prosaic "pigeon" rather than the AV "dove" to convey the humorously flattening effect of Paulus's interpre-

tations: cf **44** and **45** below.
  43[1] Paulus I 49.
  43[2] The phrase in Dan (q **37** n 1 above) is "like the Son of man" (AV); in Ezek 1.26 "the likeness as the appearance of a man".

around this whole matter of wine and water, and the way is thus left open to an interpretation of it as a miracle of transformation, but that the significance of this first public act of Jesus lay then, and lies now, not in the irrelevant question of whether or not six pots somehow filled with wine proved his Messiahship, but in the fact that it showed in his character a deep concern for the well-being of his fellow men:] Recht rührend bemerkt das Evangelium: das Erste, wodurch Jesus als Messias ein Zeichen seines Charakters gab, war dieses! Ein Zeichen theilnehmender Menschenliebe, ein Zeichen freundlicher Vorsicht, welche schon, bis seine Stunde käme, fürgesorgt hatte. Und so, fährt das Evangelium fort, machte Er, nämlich durch viele andere Zeichen seiner vortrefflichen Eigenschaften, seine Vorzüglichkeit so sehr bekannt, dass seine Lehrschüler immer inniger für ihn überzeugungstreu wurden.

[The Gospel very touchingly remarks that this was the first of the signs that Jesus as the Messiah gave concerning his character! A sign of sympathetic love for man, a sign of kindly care, providing for others even until his own hour came. And thus, the Gospel continues, by many other signs of his excellent qualities he made his superiority so evident that his disciples grew ever more deeply committed to their belief in him.]

It is scarcely too strong language, to exclaim—Disgusting! I cannot laugh at the absurdity of or the pain inflicted by its shameless dishonesty. "And this is the Beginning of the Miracles, &c!["][1] Precious Beginning, if we must take Prof. Paulus for our interpreter!

45   ɪ 173, pencil | § 28(a)

[In regard to Jesus's scourging of the money-changers in the Temple (John 2.13–22), Paulus states that many of the bystanders would ask what this was a sign of, for the Oriental is accustomed to look for a significance beyond the act itself:] Auch hier denken sie richtig, nicht um das Wegschaffen dieses Gelärms allein sey es zu thun. Wozu soll Deine That uns noch weiter einen bedeutsamen Wink geben? fragen sie. Und nur auf diesen Sinn ihrer Frage bezieht sich auch Jesu Antwort: "Löset Ihr diesen Tempel—die jetzige in mancher Rücksicht verkehrte Tempeleinrichtung auf, !! so werde Ich euch in drei Tagen (in ganz kurzer Zeit) ihn weit besser darstellen!"

[Here, too, they were right in supposing that more was at issue than the mere removal of this noise and commotion. What do your actions signify, they asked. And Jesus's reply is directed only to this sense of their question: "Destroy this temple—the present institution that has in many respects become so corrupt !!—and in three days (in a very short time) I will set up a far better one for you."]

<hr/>

44[1] John 2.11: "This beginning of miracles did Jesus in Cana of Galilee, and mani- fested forth his glory; and his disciples believed on him."

* It is, I own, too bad to laugh at; but certainly, Pr. Paulus ought to take
out a Patent for his *Flatting-mill!*[1]

46   I 352–3 pencil | § 107

[In regard to the miracle of the feeding of the five thousand (Matt
14.13–22, Mark 6.30–45, Luke 9.10–17, and John 6.5–14), Paulus points
out that, despite the minute descriptions of detail, it is stated only that
Jesus blessed the food and broke it, that he and his disciples had five
loaves and two fishes, apparently for themselves. He argues that in all
probability the others, rich and poor, had brought their own dinners from
their camels.] Nach den vier Texten lesen wir nichts anderes. Denn unser
Deutsches "Einsegnen" (eulogein) erklärt Johannes durch das *Dank-
sagen* (eucharistesas). Kein Wort folgt von einem Vermehren. Aber ausdrücklich wird gesagt: Er habe die Brode zerbrochen und sie nun durch
seine Jünger hinlegen lassen; eben so habe Er die zwey Fische in Theile
getheilt für Alle.

[Nothing else is indicated by the four texts. For John glosses our German "blessing"
(*eulogein*) with "giving of thanks" (*eucharistesas*). There is no mention of any multi-
plication. Rather, it is explicitly stated: "He broke the bread and had his disciples set
it out, and in the same manner he divided the fish in parts for all."]

The same interpretation has occurred to me 5 and 20 years ago, as what
an Infidel might suppose to have been the *origin* and *occasion* of the *Report* of Jesus having multiplied the Loaves and Fishes, but that *this* and
no more was intended to be understood by the Writers or Compilers of
the Gospels, above all, by the Author of the Gosp. according to [St] John—
no! such an absurdity never could spring up in my Head!—   S. T. C.

47   I 432, pencil | End of volume

The undeniable verbal coincidences of the 1st and 3rd G.[1] would form a
strong presumption against the Apóstolíchrony ($\cup - \cup/- \cup \cup$)[a] of the Ev.
Inf.[2]—on either Hypothesis/ that Luke knew the first Gospel, or that the
Matthew had seen Luke's. Even granting what I hold extravagant, that
the two Ev. Inf. can be conjured into compatibility—still the primâ facie
differences and seeming Contradictions are too many, too important, too
prosilient, not to have been noticed & explained by the Compiler.

47[a] The metrical marks were placed in ms below the vowels of "Apostolichrony"

45[1] See **34** and n 2.
47[1] Gospels.
47[2] The "apostle-time-ness"—C's coinage—of the *Evangelia infantiae*—for
which see **2** n 1 and **26** n 1 above.

48   I +1 (slip tipped in, the recto of **18**), pencil

Quite affecting to think, what a blessed change might have taken place, had the first Leaders of the French Revolution been Catholics of the School with the Authors of the Della Riforma d'Italia, and of the Disordini & della Corte da Roma instead of Infidels/[1]

49   II vi–vii, pencil

[In commenting on the gospels as historical documents for a reconstruction of the life of Christ, Paulus assumes that Matthew wrote the gospel attributed to him:] Der jüdische Zöllner, Matthäus, und der im jüdischen Lande der nahen Vorzeit nachgegangene Lukas behielten nur meist das jüdisch fasslichere, einzelne . . .

[The Jewish publican Matthew, and Luke, who followed up the events that had recently occurred in Judaea, tended to retain only that which was more intelligible to the Jewish mind, the particular . . .]

That there existed in early times a Syro-chaldaic Gospel, or memorabilia of Jesus, used by the Churches in Palestine: that this Gospel was compiled or revised ⟨by,⟩ or in some way received the Sanction of, Matthew; and that this was the Original or Groundwork of which our first Gospel was a free translation, with explanatory comments interwoven—I find no motive for denying[1]—tho' as to any sound & convincing evidence from the Fathers and Ecclesiastic Historians, the attribution of the Gospels to the Apostles might very rationally be doubted, were there an adequate motive for the denial.—But that the Greek Gospel in its present form was written by Matthew and within 14 years after the death of Christ, I reject on what to me appears the clearest internal evidence.

48[1] "Of the reform of Italy" and of the "Disorders and of the Court of Rome": i.e. C wishes that the rationalist leaders of the Revolution had been reformers of their own Roman Catholic Church rather than revolutionaries subversive of religion in general. This note, which may have some connection with **4** above, alludes to two books by writers who appeared to be pious Catholics but who opposed the claims of the papacy to temporal power: C. A. Pilati di Tassulo *Di una riforma d'Italia* (3rd ed 3 vols 1786, referred to in *CN* IV 5468 and in *C&S—CC*—80, 122) and Girolamo Vincenzo Spanzotti *Disordini morali e politici della Corte di Roma* (2 vols Turin 1801, q N 40 ff 19–21).

49[1] C alludes to the Hebrew or Aramaic version of Matt, posited by some biblical scholars to account for the textual relationship of the first three books of the NT (the "Synoptic Problem").

JOHN PEARSON
1613–1686

An Exposition of the Creed. By John, Lord Bishop of Chester. 12th ed rev. London 1741. F°.

William Andrews Clark Memorial Library, University of California

Inscribed on p ⁻5 "Johann: Mapletoft E: Coll: Au: Nas: Oxon. 1750"; bookplates of Pull Court Library, C. K. Ogden, and William Andrews Clark, Jr, on p ⁻6 (p-d). A small cross in ink on p 19, pencilled marks pp 38, 250, and pencilled crosses pp 235, 245 do not appear to have been made by C.

The existence of an extensive set of notes on Pearson, probably in a lost notebook, is testified to by C's reference of Dec 1829 to "the Mss Mem. Book of Notes on Pearson on the Creed" (N42.54) and by a letter written by John Sterling in 1833, in which he mentions his having been permitted to copy C's notes on Pearson: Anne K. Tuell *John Sterling: A Representative Victorian* (New York 1949) 249, 251.

DATE. Probably before 1820, possibly (since the work docs not appear to have been among C's books at his death) before 1816 when C moved into the Gillmans' house. C refers familiarly to this work on several occasions, notably in late annotations on DONNE *Sermons* COPY B **125** and LUTHER *Colloquia* **23** (see n 1).

---

1   p 381, pencil | Article 11 "The Resurrection of the Body"

But as it is necessary to a resurrection that the flesh should rise, neither will the life of the Soul alone continuing, amount to the reviviscence of the whole Man, so it is also necessary that the same Flesh should be raised again; for if either the same Body should be joined to another Soul, or the same Soul united to another Body, it would not be the resurrection of the same Man.

Personal Identity is all that is necessary. And this may be had without ~~ou~~ the Resurrection of our Individual Bodies—St Paul says that there is a natural Body, & there is a spiritual Body. And that the spiritual Body is that which is raised.[1]—As to our individual Bodies, framed as they now

---

[1] 1 Cor 15.44: "It is sown a natural body; it is raised a spiritual body. There is a natural body, and there is a spiritual body."

are, nothing can be more inconvenient for the purpose of Life eternal—
They are now [? either] ⟨for [? knowing]⟩ for the Purpose of eating &
drinking & sleeping: or for Reproduction of the Species—all which Purposes are done away in the Life to come

SAMUEL PEPYS
1633–1703

Memoirs of Samuel Pepys, Esq. F.R.S. Secretary to the Admiralty in the reigns of Charles II. and James II. Comprising his diary from 1659 to 1669, deciphered by the Rev. John Smith, A.B. of St. John's College, Cambridge, from the original short-hand MS. in the Pepysian Library, and a selection from his private correspondence. Edited by Richard, Lord Braybrooke. 2 vols. London 1825. 4°.

Victoria College Library (Coleridge Collection)

The name "Samuel Prince" appears on the title-page of each volume. (Prince published a version of these notes in *N&Q* VI—1852—213–16.) There are pencilled notations and page numbers referring to C's notes, in an unidentified hand, on I 189, 442, and [+]4. C's notes, with the exception of **2A**, were overtraced in ink, perhaps after the MS TRANSCRIPTS had been made, since the person who did the overtracing introduced such errors as "hypertropkiid" for "hypertrophied", which is correct in the transcripts and in *NTP*. In the text presented here, substantive errors made in overtracing have been recorded in the textual notes, but the neglect of a comma or full stop in the overtracing has not.

   This first publication of Pepys's diary included about a quarter of the material available.

MS TRANSCRIPTS. (*a*) VCL BT 37: SC transcript. (*b*) VCL LT 64: a transcript prepared apparently for *NTP*.

DATE. Possibly as early as May 1826 (*CN* IV 5363 and n); some notes or all after Jun 1831 (**5** n 1); and possibly as late as 1834 (**11** n 4).

1   I 84, pencil, overtraced | Diary 7 Nov 1660

Went by water to my Lord, where I dined with him, . . . he, in discourse of the great opinion of the virtue—gratitude, (which he did account the greatest thing in the world to him, and had, therefore, in his mind been often troubled in the late times how to answer his gratitude to the King, who raised his father,) did say it was that did bring him to his obedience to the King; and did also bless himself with his good fortune, in comparison to what it was when I was with him in the Sound, when he durst not own his correspondence with the King; which is a thing that I never did hear of to this day before; and I do from this raise an opinion of him, to be one of the most secret men in the world, which I was not so convinced of before.

Exquisite specimen of dry grave *Irony*

2   I 189, pencil, overtraced | 26 Dec 1662

26th. To the Wardrobe. Hither come Mr. Battersby; and we falling into discourse of a new book of drollery in use, called Hudebras, I would needs go find it out, and met with it at the Temple: cost me 2 *s*. 6 *d*. But when I come to read it, it is so silly an abuse of the Presbyter Knight going to the warrs, that I am ashamed of it; and by and by meeting at Mr. Townsend's at dinner, I sold it to him for 18 *d*.

P. 167. Pepys pronounces the Midsummer Night's Dream, the most insipid ridiculous Play, he had ever seen.[1]

2A   I 368, pencil | 14 Sept 1665

To the Duke of Albemarle, where I find a letter of the 12th from Solebay, from my Lord Sandwich, of the fleet's meeting with about eighteen more of the Dutch fleet, and his taking of most of them; and the messenger says, they had taken three after the letter was wrote and sealed; which being twenty-one, and the fourteen took the other day, is <u>forty</u>-five sail; some of which are good, and others rich ships.

thirty

3   II i 10, pencil, overtraced | 3 Feb 1666/7

Among other discourse, we talked much of Nostradamus his prophecy of these times, and the burning of the City of London, some of whose verses are put into Booker's Almanack this year: and Sir G. Carteret did tell a story, how at his death he did make the town swear that he should never be dug up, or his tomb opened, after he was buried; but they did after sixty years do it, and upon his breast they found a plate of brasse, saying what a wicked and unfaithful people the people of that place were, who after so many vows should disturb and open him such a day and year and hour; which, <u>if</u>[a] true, is very strange.

3[a] Underlining not overtraced

2[1] Pepys's words 29 Sept 1662, I 167 in this ed. To this entry someone has added a note in pencil referring to related margina-lia by C: "167 p 197. 265 See his remarks on Othello 444 [442]".

If!! but still more strange would be the *truth* of the story. Yet only suppose the *precise date* an addition of the reporter's: and nothing more natural. Mem. the good old story of a jealous Husband's sending his confidential servant to his wife, forbidding her to see a certain gentleman during his absence, & to bring back her solemn oath & promise that she would not, & how the shrewd fellow instead of this took her oath, not to ride on Neptune's Back, their huge Newfoundland Yard-dog./

4 II i 13, pencil, overtraced | 10 Feb 1666/7

We had much talk of all our old acquaintance of the College, concerning their various fortunes; wherein, to my joy, I met not with any that have sped better than myself.* Mrs. Turner do tell me very odde stories how Mrs. Williams do receive the applications of people, and hath presents, and she is the hand that receives all, while my Lord do the business.

* Most valuable on many, various, and most important accounts, as I hold this Diary to be, I ~~regard~~[a] deem it ~~as~~[b] invaluable, as a faithful Portrait of enlightened (i.e. calculating) Self-love and Self-interest in its perihelion ⟨to Morality,⟩ or ⟨its⟩ nearest possible neighbourhood ⟨to,⟩ or ~~its~~[c] least possible distance,/[d] from, Honour & Honesty!—And yet what a cold and torpid Saturn, with what a sinister & leaden Shine, spotty as the Moon, does it appear, compared with the principles & actions of the Regicide, Colonel Hutchinson, or those of the Puritan, Richard Baxter, (in the autobiography edited by Sylvester) both the Contemporaries of Pepys![1]

S. T. C.

5 II i 46, pencil, overtraced | 26 Apr 1667

And Mr. Evelyn tells me of several of the menial servants of the Court lacking bread, that have not received a farthing wages since the King's coming in. He tells me the King of France hath his mistresses, but laughs at the foolery of our King, that makes his bastards princes, and loses his revenue upon them, and makes his mistresses his masters.

4[a] Deletion not overtraced   **4**[b] Deletion not overtraced
4[c] Deletion not overtraced   **4**[d] Deletion not overtraced

4[1] The reference is to two other works of 17th-century biography or autobiography. Both C and the Wordsworths were admirers of the *Memoirs* of Colonel John Hutchinson (1615–64), written by his widow and first pub 1806; for C's annotated copy see HUTCHINSON. C also annotated two copies of Richard Baxter's autobiographical *Reliquiae*: see BAXTER.

Mem. Earl of Munster. This, with Wit and Condescension, was all that was wanting to a perfect parallelism in the character of George IVth with that of Charles II. And this he left to be supplied by his worthy Brother & Successor![1]

6 II i 55, pencil, overtraced | 16 May 1667

It is remarkable that this afternoon Mr. Moore come to me, and there among other things did tell me how Mr. Moyer the merchant, having procured an order from the King and Duke of York and Council, with the consent of my Lord Chancellor [Clarendon], and by assistance of Lord Arlington, for the releasing out of prison his brother Samuel Moyer, who was a great man in the late times in Haberdashers'-hall, and was engaged under hand and seal to give the man that obtained it so much in behalf of my Lord Chancellor; but it seems my Lady Duchesse of Albemarle had before undertaken it for so much money, but hath not done it.

And this is one of the three Idols of our Church—for Clarendon ever follows Charles the Martyr, & the Martyr Laud![1]—Alas!—What a strange thing the Conscience seems to be—when such actions & deliberate falsehoods as have been on strong grounds imputed to Lord Clarendon—among others, the suborning of assassination—could be made compatible in his own mind with professions of religion & habitual religious meditations & exercises!   *S. T. C.*

7 II i 62–3, pencil, overtraced | 3 Jun 1667

. . . and we had a good dinner of plain meat, and good company at our table: among others my good Mr. Evelyn, with whom after dinner I stepped aside and talked upon the present posture of our affairs; which is, that the Dutch are known to be abroad with eighty sail of ships of war, and twenty fire-ships, and the French come into the Channell with twenty

---

5[1] I.e. George IV left the wit and condescension to be supplied by his brother, William IV, who succeeded him in 1830. In Jun 1831, William IV raised his illegitimate son, George Augustus Frederick Fitzclarence, to the peerage as the first Earl of Munster. C's bitterness has a personal source, his pension having been withdrawn on William's accession: as he said in 1834, he had not "a shilling of my own in the world since King William the Fourth took my poor gold chain of a hundred links . . . to emblazon d'or the black bar across the Royal arms of the Fitzclarences" (*CL* VI 982).

6[1] Laud and Clarendon were not literally named in the special service for Charles I, "our martyred Sovereign", in BCP; C means that as heads of church and state under Charles they share his reputation. C, of course, disapproved of all three: in MACDIARMID 11 and elsewhere, he charges Clarendon with having suborned assassins, encouraged the king's "prelatical superstition", being his "accomplice" in deceitful treaties, and abandoning the religious rights of the British people "to the fury of the Bishops after the Restoration".

sail of men-of-war, and five fire-ships, while we have not a ship at sea to do them any hurt with, but are calling in all we can, while our Embassadors are treating at Bredah . . . and all this through the negligence of our Prince, who had power, if he would, to master all these with the money and men that he hath had the command of, and may now have, if he would mind his business.

There were good grounds for the belief, that more & yet worse causes than sensuality and sensual sloth, were working in the King's mind & heart—viz. the readiness to have the French King *his* Master & the Disposer of his kingdom's power, as the means of becoming himself the uncontrolled Master of its Wealth. He would fain be a Despot, even at the cost of being Another's Underling. Charles IInd was willing, nay anxious, to reduce his Crown and Kingdom under the domination of the Grand Monarque, provided he himself might have the power to shear & poll his Subjects without leave, and unchecked by the interference of, a Parliament. I look on him, as one of the moral Monsters of History.

S. T. C.

8   II i 108, pencil, overtraced | 4–8 Aug 1677

R^a To initiate a young Student into the mystery of appreciating the value of modern History, or the books that have hitherto passed for such.— First, let him carefully peruse this Diary; and then, while it is fresh in his mind, take up & read Hume's History of England, Reign of Charles the 2nd. Even of Hume's Reign of Elizabeth, generally rated as the best & fullest of the work, I dare assert, that to supply the Omissions alone would form an Appendix ⟨occupying⟩ twice the space ~~of occupied~~^{b} allotted by him to the whole Reign—and the necessary rectifications of his Statements half as much. What with omissions, and what with perversions, of the most important incidents, added to the false portraiture of the Characters,^{c} the work from the Reign of Henry VIIth is a mischevous Romance.[1] But alike as Historian and as Philosopher, Hume has, meo saltem judicio,[2] been extravagantly overrated.—Mercy on the Age, & the People, for whom Lock is profound, and Hume subtle.[3]   *S. T. C.*

8^a Deletion not overtraced   **8**^{b} Deletion not overtraced
8^c Only "Character" is overtraced

8[1] In 1802 C used a similar phrase to describe Hume's popular *History of England*: *EOT* (*CC*) I 388.

8[2] "In my opinion, at least".

8[3] C consistently pitted himself against these two giants of philosophy whose work seemed to him ultimately atheistical: cf *BL* ch 12 (*CC*) I 291–2.

9   II i 110–11, pencil, overtraced | 12 Aug 1667

To my bookseller's, and did buy Scott's Discourse of Witches; and do hear Mr. Cowly mightily lamented (his death) by Dr. Ward, the Bishop of Winchester, and Dr. Bates, who were standing there, as the best poet of our nation, and as good a man.

!!—Yet Cowley *was* a Poet, which with all my unfeigned admiration of his vigorous sense, his agile logical wit, and ⟨his⟩ high excellencies of diction and metre, is more than (in the *strict* use of the term, Poet) I can conscientiously say of DRYDEN.[1] Only if Pope was a *Poet*, as Lord Byron swears—then Dryden, I admit, was a very *great* Poet.[2] W. Wordsworth calls Lord Byron the Mocking Bird of our parnassian Ornithology[3]—but the Mocking bird, they say, has a very sweet song of his own native[a] Notes proper to himself. Now I cannot say, I have ~~been~~[b] ever heard any such in his Lordship's Volumes of Warbles; & spite of Sir W. Scott I dare predict, that in less than a century, the Baronet's & the Baron's *Poems* will lie on the same Shelf of Oblivion—Scott will be ~~known~~[c] read and remembered as a Novelist and the Founder of a new race of Novels—& Byron not remembered at all except as a wicked Lord who from morbid & restless vanity pretended to be ten times more wicked than he was.[4]

S. T. C.

9[a] Overtraced as "in true"   **9**[b] Deletion not overtraced
9[c] Deletion not overtraced

9[1] Applying, that is, such high standards as those expressed in *BL* ch 14 (*CC*) II 15–17, Cowley retains a place—though not in the highest ranks (*BL*—*CC*—I 84)—among genuine poets, while Dryden does not. This remark is characteristic of C's general estimate of Dryden, whom he admired as the best representative of a faulty school.

9[2] C's contribution to a classic dispute; cf Johnson's "If Pope be not a poet, where is poetry to be found?" in *Lives* ed G. Birkbeck Hill (Oxford 1905) III 251. Byron's championing of Pope is prominent in his poetry, e.g. *English Bards and Scotch Reviewers* lines 93–112, 187–8, or "Thou shalt believe in Milton, Dryden, Pope; / Thou shalt not set up Wordsworth, Coleridge, Southey" in *Don Juan* I ccv and also in his prose, notably the 1821 *Letter on the Rev. W. L. Bowles's Strictures on Pope*. For C's disparagement of Pope in comparison with Dryden, cf *TT* (*CC*) I 315–16.

9[3] WW's remark has not been traced in his published works, and may have been made simply in conversation. In his journal for Jul 1822, William Ellery Channing records such a remark: WW spoke "of Ld Byron, whom he thinks destitute of all true love of nature, & owing his success in delineating it, which is very rare, to his mocking-bird or imitative propensities": quoted from John Beer "William Ellery Channing Visits the Lake Poets" *RES* ns XLII (1991) 224.

9[4] C never thought highly of Scott's poetry, but he was an avid reader of his novels and annotated several of them: see SCOTT, and cf the judicious criticism of *CL* V 32–5. Scott warmly reviewed Cantos 3 and 4 of Byron's *Childe Harold* in the *Quarterly Review*, and praised his "mighty genius" in a tribute written on the occasion of his death for the *Edinburgh Weekly Journal*, reprinted the same year in Cosmo Gordon *The Life and Genius of Lord Byron* (Paris 1824) 3–10.

10   II i 125, pencil, overtraced | 9 Sept 1667

To the Bear-garden, where now the yard was full of people, and those most of them seamen, striving by force to get in. I got into the common pit; and there, with my cloak about my face, I stood and saw the prize fought, till one of them, a shoemaker, was so cut in both his wrists that he could not fight any longer, and then they broke off: his enemy was a butcher. The sport very good,*a* and various humours to be seen among the rabble that is there.

! Certainly, Pepys was blest with the queerest & most omnivorous Taste, that ever fell to the lot of one man!

11   II i 151, pencil, overtraced | 1 Nov 1667

To the King's playhouse, and there saw a silly play and an old one, "The Taming of a Shrew."

This is, I think, the fifth of Shakespear's Plays, which Pepys found silly, stupid trash & among them Othello![1]—Macbeth indeed he commends— for the *shews* &—music but not to be compared with the 'Five Hours Adventures'!![2]—This and the want of *Wit* in the Hudibras,[3] is very amusing—nay, it is seriously instructive. Thousands of shrewd, and intelligent men, in whom and in S. Pepys, The *Understanding* is *hypertrophied**a to the necrosis or marasmus[4] of the Reason & Imagination, while far-sighted (yet oh! how short sighted) Self-interest fills the place of Conscience, would say the same, if they dared.

   * A new-invented verb by the Doctors; meaning over-grown or over-nourished.*b*

10*a* Underlining not overtraced   **11***a* Overtraced as "hypertropkiid"
      11*b* Now very faint, "nourished" was not overtraced

11[1] For Pepys's adverse comment on *Othello*, see **11** n 2; he also wrote harshly of *The Merry Wives of Windsor* (15 Aug 1667), *A Midsummer Night's Dream* (29 Sept 1662), *Romeo and Juliet* (1 Mar 1662) and *Twelfth Night* (6 Jan 1663).

11[2] Pepys records enjoying *Macbeth*, in Davenant's spectacular musical adaptation, nine times, four times in 1667 alone. He never explicitly compares the play with Samuel Tuke's *Adventures of Five Hours*, which he saw twice in Jan 1663 and described (5 Jan 1662/3—I 193) as "the best, for the variety and the most excellent continuance of the plot to the very end, that ever I saw, or think ever shall". C has perhaps confused Pepys's remarks about *Macbeth* and *Othello*, for on 20 Aug 1666 (I 442) Pepys wrote, "To Deptford by water, reading Othello, Moore of Venice, which I ever heretofore esteemed a mighty good play, but having so lately read The Adventures of five Houres, it seems a mean thing."

11[3] Pepys said of *Hudibras* (10 Dec 1663) that it was "the book now in greatest fashion for drollery, though I cannot, I confess, see enough where the wit lies"; cf **2** textus.

11[4] Slow death or wasting away. The first recorded use of "hypertrophy" in *OED* is 1834, of "hypertrophied" 1835.

12   II i 254–5, pencil, overtraced | 3 Aug 1668

To church, and heard a good sermon of Mr. Gifford's at our church, upon "Seek ye first the kingdom of Heaven and its righteousness, and all things shall be added to you." A very excellent and persuasive, good and moral sermon. He shewed, like a wise man, *that righteousness is a surer moral way of being rich, than sin and villany.

* Highly characteristic. Pepys's only ground of morality was Prudence—a shrewd Understanding in the service of Self-love,—his Conscience. He was a *Pollard* Man—without the *Top* (i.e. the Reason, as the source of *Ideas*,^{a} or immediate yet not sensuous truths, having their evidence in themselves; and^b the Imagination, or idealizing Power, by symbols mediating between the Reason & the Understanding) but on this account more broadly and luxuriantly branching out from the upper Trunk. For the sobriety and stedfastness of a worldly Self-interest substitute inventive Fancy, Will-wantonness (stat pro ratione voluntas),[1] and a humorous sense of the emptiness & dream-likeness of human pursuits—and Pepys could have been the *Panurge* of the incomparable Rabelais.[2]— Mem. It is incomprehensible to me, that this great and general Philosopher should have been a Frenchman, except on my hypothesis of a continued dilution of the Gothic Blood from the reign of Henry IVth, Des Cartes, Malbranche, Pascal and Moliere being the ultimi Gothorum the last in whom the Gothic predominated over the Celtic.[3]   *S. T. C.*

13   II i 260, pencil, overtraced | 4 Sept 1668

To the fair to see the play "Bartholomew fair," with puppets. And it is an excellent play; the more I see it, the more I love the wit of it; only the business of abusing the Puritans begins to grow stale and of no use, they being the people that at last will be found the wisest.

Pepys was always a Commonwealth's man in his heart—N.b. Not a Democrat; but even more, than the W^a Constitutional Whigs, the very An-

12^a Underlining not overtraced   12^b Overtracing reads "or"
13^a Deletion not overtraced

12[1] "Let will take the place of reason": Juvenal *Satires* 6.223.

12[2] The same line of thought is recorded in *TT* (*CC*) I 165–6, where Pantagruel and his crafty companion Panurge also appear: "Rabelais is a most wonderful writer. Panurge is a pollarded man; the man with every quality except the Reason. Gargantua is the Reason; Panurge the Understanding." SCHELLING *Denkmal* 16 n 1 below gives references for significant formulations of this fundamental distinction.

12[3] C's distaste for the French is well documented: see, e.g. DESMOULINS 1 n 1, DUBOIS 4 n 1.

tipode of the modern Jacobins, or *Tail-up, Head-down* Politicians. A Voluptuary, and without a spark of bigotry in his nature, he could not be a Puritan; but of his free choice he would have preferred Presbyterianism to Prelacy, and a mixed Aristocracy of Wealth and Talent to a Monarchy or even a mixed Government—such at least as the latter was in his time— But many of the more enlightened Jacobites were Republicans who despaired of a Republic. Si non Brutus, Cæsar.[1]   *S. T. C.*

14   II i 319, pencil, overtraced | 20 Mar 1669

Sir W. Coventry did tell me it as the wisest thing that ever was said to the King by any statesman of his time, and it was by my Lord Treasurer that is dead, whom, I find, he takes for a very great statesman,—that when the King did shew himself forward for passing the Act of Indemnity, he did advise the King that he would hold his hand in doing it till he had got his power restored that had been diminished by the late times, and his revenue settled in such a manner as he might depend on himself without resting upon Parliaments, and then pass it. But my Lord Chancellor, who thought he could have the command of Parliaments for ever, *because for the King's sake they were awhile willing to grant all the King desired, did press for it being done; and so it was, and the King from that time able to do nothing with the Parliament almost.

* Can a more impressive proof be desired of the truth and wisdom of the E. of Carnarvon's recent remark in the House of Lords—that before the reign of Anne the Constitution had but a sort of uterine life, and[a] or but *partially*[b] appeared as in the birth[c]-throes—/ and that it is unworthy of a ⟨British⟩ Statesman to quote[d] any precedent anterior to the Revolution in 1688![1] Here, an honest, high-principled and patriotic Senator criminates

---

14[a] Deletion not overtraced   **14**[b] Underlining not overtraced
14[c] Overtraced as "book"; hyphen not overtraced   **14**[d] Overtraced as "requite"

13[1] "If not Brutus, Caesar", i.e. if it is not possible to keep the republic which Brutus (Marcus Junius Brutus, c 85–42 BC) unsuccessfully defended, then a monarchy under Caesar will have to do instead.

14[1] Henry George Herbert, 2nd Earl of Carnarvon (1772–1833) was an advocate of piecemeal parliamentary reform and a vocal opponent of the Reform Bill, as was his son Henry John George Herbert (1800–49), who was MP for Wotton Basset when the Bill was passing through Parliament. The remark that C cites has not been traced in

Hansard, though there are some remotely similar passages: Carnarvon's speech of 6 Oct 1831 in the House of Lords alludes to the Revolution of 1688 as a turning-point in British history (until then, "there was a constant struggle between prerogative and privilege. Since that period the collision had ceased, and the people had enjoyed real practical liberty"); and his speech of 13 Apr 1832 applies the image of new birth to young constitutions, arguing that all the "constitution-mongering" of recent years in Europe had produced only one or two "new-

Lord Clarendon for having prevented Charles the IInd from making the Crown independent of the Parliament!—& this when he knew & groaned under the infamous vices & folly of the KING! Sick and weary of the factious and persecuting temper of the H. of Commons, many true Lovers of their Country & its freedom would gladly have dispensed with Parliaments, & have secured for the King a Revenue, which wisely & economically managed might have sufficed for all ordinary demands— Could they have discovered any other way of subjecting the Judges to a periodical rigorous account for their administration of the *Law*.—In the *Laws* and the Rights established by Law these men placed the proper liberty of the Subject.—Before the Revolution, a Parliament at the commencement of a Reign, and of a War, under an economic & decorous Court[e] would have satisfied the People generally.—

15   II i 342, pencil, overtraced | 10 May 1669

Thence walked a little with Creed, who tells me he hears how fine my horses and coach are, and advises me to avoid being noted for it;* which I was vexed to hear taken notice of, being what I feared: and Povy told me of my gold-lace sleeves in the Park yesterday, which vexed me also, so as to resolve never to appear in Court with them, but presently to have them taken off, as it is fit I should.

* This struggle between the prudence of an Atticus, and the *Sir Piercy Shafton* Taylor-blood[1] working as an instinct in his veins, with extreme sensitiveness to the *Opinions* of men as the combining Medium, is very amusing.

16   II i 348, pencil, overtraced | 31 May 1669

And thus ends all that I doubt I shall ever be able to do with my own eyes in the keeping of my Journall, I being not able to do it any longer, having done now so long as to undo my eyes almost every time that I take a pen in hand; and therefore, whatever comes of it, I must forbear: and therefore resolve from this time forward to have it kept by my people in

---

14[e] Overtraced as "law†"

---

born, ricketty bantlings, already perishing in their cradles of infantine decrepitude".

15[1] As a contrasting figure to Cicero's loyal friend Atticus (109–32 BC), C chooses a foppish, mannered knight, Sir Piercie Shafton, from Walter Scott's novel *The* *Monastery* (1820). Sir Piercie's grandfather had been a tailor, "old Overstitch" of Holderness. C's annotated set of Scott includes notes on *The Monastery*, which incidentally in ch 11 (I 329) pays tribute to C as "the most imaginative of our modern bards".

long-hand, and must be contented to set down no more than is fit for them and all the world to know . . . . And so I betake myself to that course, which is almost as much as to see myself go into my grave: for which, and all the discomforts that will accompany my being blind, the good God prepare me!

Truly may it be said, that this was a greater & more grievous loss to the Mind's eye of his Posterity, than to the bodily Organs of Pepys himself. It makes me restless & discontented to think, what a Diary equal in minuteness & truth of portraiture to the preceding from 1669 to 1689 or 90 would have been for the true causes, process, and Character of the Revolution

17   II ii 65, pencil, overtraced | Correspondence: Will Howe to Pepys, 2 May 1683

It is a common position among these factious sectaries, that there is noe medium betweene a true Churchman of England and a Roman Catholic; soe that those that are for strict monarchy and arbitrary government[a] must needs be Roman Catholicks, or well wishers to them, which is brand enough to prevent elections of such men, and is alsoe a colour for theire other disobediences to theire Prince and his lawfull succession.

!!—It is only too probable, that James's Bigotry alone baffled his Despotism; and that he might have succeeded in suppressing the liberties of the Country, if he would—for a time at least—~~have~~[b] have kept aloof from its Religion. It should be remembered in excuse for the Supporters of James II, that, the practicability of conducting the affairs of the State with and by a Parliament, had not yet been demonstrated—nay, seemed incompatible with the theoretic division of the Legislative from the Executive— and indeed only by blending the two *in fact*, & preserving the division in words & appearances, was this effected.—And even now the practicability of governing the Empire with and by a perfectly free & freely elected Parliament, remains to be demonstrated.

18   II ii 71, pencil, overtraced | John Evelyn to Pepys, 10 Aug 1683

Were it not possible to discover whither any of thos *Citrine*-trees are yet to be found, that of old grew about the foote of *Mount Atlas*, not far from *Tingis*; and were here-to-fore in *delicijs* [favoured] for their politure and natural maculations, to that degree, as to be sold for their weight in gold?

17[a] Underlining not overtraced   **17**[b] Deletion not overtraced

* That lady of masculine intellect with all the woman's sense of Beauty (Mrs *Emerson*—was that the *name*?—but long a botanical correspondent & contributor to Nicholson's Phil. Magazine—O! Mrs *Ibbetson*) believed herself to have discovered the principle of this precious Citrine wood and the means of producing it[1]—And I see no reason for doubting it—though ⟨of⟩ her phytological anatomy, by help of the Solar Microscope I am sceptical. The Engravings instantly call up in my mind the suspicion of some kaleidoscope delusion—from the singular *Symmetry* of all the forms[2]— But she was an excellent & very remarkable Woman—and her contributions in the Phil. Magazine worth studying even for the Style.

19   II ii 73, pencil, overtraced | John Evelyn to Pepys, 8 Jun 1684

Sir, With your excellent book [Thomas Burnet's *Sacred Theory of the Earth*], I return you likewise my most humble thanks for your inducement of me to read it over again, finding in it, as you told me, several things omitted in the Latin (which I had formerly read with great delight), still new, still surprising, and the whole hypothesis so ingenious and so rational, that I both admire and believe[a] it at once.

!—Strange!—Burnet's Book is a grand Miltonic Romance[1]—but the contrast between the Tartarian Fury and Turbulence of the Burnetian and

19[a] Underlining not overtraced

18[1] Between 1809 and 1822 Agnes Ibbetson, née Thomson (1757–1823), published over 50 botanical articles in two journals that merged as the *Philosophical Magazine and Journal* after 1813: Alexander Tilloch's *Philosophical Magazine* and William Nicholson's *Journal of Natural Philosophy, Chemistry, and the Arts*. C alludes specifically to her paper "On the Flower-buds of Trees passing through the Wood, as noticed by Cicero and Pliny" *Philosophical Magazine and Journal* LIX (1822) 3–8. Here she develops her (erroneous) theory that buds originate in the tree-roots and force their way upwards and outwards: this phenomenon, she argues, accounts for the "curled figured wood" that Pliny and Cicero admired in citron wood, and that one can procure from other trees by cutting them down at the right moment.

18[2] C would have seen engravings illustrating Agnes Ibbetson's articles e.g. in the 1810 volume of Nicholson's *Journal* that he

annotated: NICHOLSON. See Plate 2. The solar microscope, invented in 1739 and available by this time in various sizes, used sunlight and lenses as in a *camera obscura*; by having the light pass through the specimen, it projected an enlarged image onto a wall or screen. C likens the effect to the effect of the more recently-invented (1817) and popular toy, the kaleidoscope. He expresses the same admiration of Mrs Ibbetson's work and the same reservations about the "optical and imaginative delusion, which depreciates all phænomena obtained by Glasses of high powers and the Solar microscope" in STEFFENS *Geognostisch-Geologische Aufsätze* (Hamburg 1810) 250. About 1821–2 he planned to present her with a set of his works: *CN* IV 4842.

19[1] Thomas Burnet (1635–1715) enlarged his influential *Telluris theoria sacra* (pt 1 1681, pt 2 1689) when he published an English version (pt 1 1684, pt 2 1690). C owned the 1689 Latin version (now at

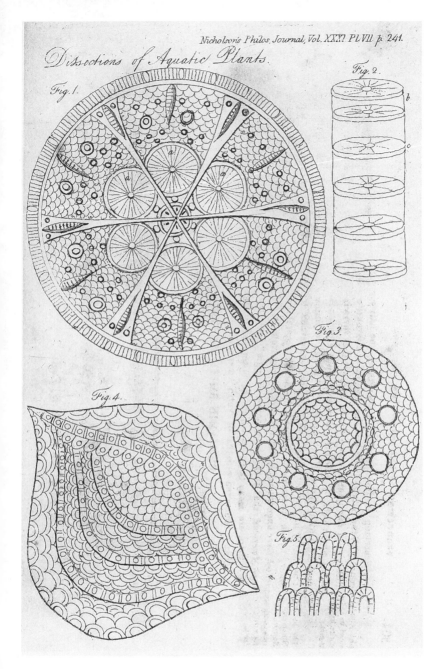

2. Agnes Ibbetson "Dissections of Aquatic Plants" Nicholson's *Journal* XXXI
(1810) plate 7. See PEPYS **18**.
The Houghton Library, Harvard University; reproduced by kind permission

the almost supernatural tranquillity of the Mosaic, Deluge is little less than comic.

20   II ii 197, pencil, overtraced | Henry, 2nd Earl of Clarendon to Pepys, 27 May 1701

After dinner, as we were standing and talking together in the room, says my Lord Newborough to the other Scotch gentleman, (who was looking very steadfastly upon my wife,) "What is the matter, that thou hast had thine eyes fixed upon my Lady Cornbury ever since she came into the room? Is she not a fine woman? Why doest thou not speak?"—"She's a handsome Lady indeed," (said the gentleman,) "but I see her in blood." Whereupon my Lord Newborough laughed at him; and all the company going out of the room, we parted: and I believe none of us thought more of the matter; I am sure I did not. My wife was at that time perfectly well in health, and looked as well as ever she did in her life. In the beginning of the next month she fell ill of the small pox . . . . Upon the ninth day after the small pox appeared, in the morning, she bled at the nose, which quickly stop't; but in the afternoon the blood burst out again with great violence at her nose and mouth, and about eleven of the clock that night she dyed, almost weltering in her blood.

It would have been necessary to cross-examine this Scotch Deuteroptis,[1] whether he had not seen the duplicate or spectrum of *other*[a] persons in blood: It might have been the result of an inflammatory[b] condition of his own brains or a slight pressure on the region of the optic Nerves.—I have repeatedly seen the phantasm of the page, I was reading, all spotted with blood—or with the letters all blood./

20[a] Underlining not overtraced   **20**[b] Overtracing reads "inflamatory"

VCL), and as early as 1795–6 thought of publishing a dual-language ed: *CN* I 61 and n. In *BL* ch 14 (*CC*) II 14, he cites Burnet's work as proof that a poem need not be written in verse.

20[1] "Second-seer", or one gifted with second sight; the word appears to be C's coinage, and is not in *OED*. Interest in the phenomenon of second sight, esp associated with the Hebrides, was stimulated by Samuel Johnson's careful suspension of disbelief: *A Journey to the Western Islands of Scotland* (1785) 178. C alludes to it as a nervous disease in Lessing *Leben* 24 (see n 1) and declares his own incredulity in Scott copy a **36**.

ROBERT PERCIVAL

1765–1826

An Account of the Island of Ceylon, containing its history, geography, natural history, with the manners and customs of its various inhabitants; to which is added, the journal of an embassy to the court of Candy. London 1803. 4°.

Victoria College Library (Coleridge Collection)

Thomas Poole's copy: half-title contains his signature, "Thoˢ Poole | 1805 | p _____ [? bow]" and (in pencil) the initials of a later owner, "G E J | 1898". C has corrected a typo p 236. There is a pencilled correction in neither C's hand nor Poole's on p 36, and there are a few pencilled booksellers' notes on p ⁺3.

DATE. Jun–Sept 1807, while C was staying with Poole.

1   p 152

Their common drink is water, or the juice of the *palmyra*; although some of them make no scruple to drink arrack when they can procure it. All day long they chew the betel or penang, and smoke *bang*. From this last herb a species of opium is prepared, which they chew in great quantities, as Europeans use strong drinks, to exhilarate their spirits. Too much of it, however, entirely deadens their senses, and reduces them to a state of complete stupefaction. I have frequently seen these people, after having chewed too large a portion of this noxious drug, lying speechless on the ground with their eyes fixed in a ghastly stare. Yet, such is the effect of habit, that they get completely infatuated with fondness for this drug, and absolutely cannot do without it.

The Bang is the powder from the dried Leaves of the Cannabis Indica, or Indian Hemp/ It is commonly blended with opium; & in Turkey and Barbary with Saffron & Spices. It is either chewed in large Pills, or smoked in the Powder. I have both smoked & taken the powder/ so did my ever-honoured ever-lamented Benefactor, T. Wedgewood: the effects in both were the same, merely narcotic, with a painful weight from the flatulence or stifled gas, occasioned by the morbid action on the coats of the Stomach. In others however it had produced, as we were informed by Sir

84

J. Banks, almost frantic exhilaration.[1] We took it in the powder, and as much as would lie on a Shilling. Probably, if we had combined it with opium and some of the most powerful essential Oils, to stimulate & heat the stomach, it might have acted more pleasantly. On the coast of Barbary the charitable Mahometans give it to poor Criminals, previous to the amputation of their Limbs; and it inspires a complete insensibility to suffering, and in these circumstances does not commonly disturb the understanding. Tippoo Saib gave to each of his Horse soldiers a pipe immediately before the engagement—likewise to those sent to storm forts.[2]

S. T. Coleridge.

2 p 157

Before entering upon any desperate enterprise, it is customary with the Malays to take opium, or, as they term it, to *bang* themselves. This plant, the bang, which is used among the natives of India as an instrument of intoxication, is found over all that continent as well as in Ceylon. It is a small shrub, with a leaf in shape and texture resembling that of the tobacco, but not larger than the leaf of the sage. From this plant a species of opium is extracted, and being made into balls, is taken internally, and operates in the same manner as a dram of spirits among the European nations. The leaf of the bang is also dried and smoked like tobacco, with a still stronger intoxicating effect than the opium.

See p. 152.—The account there given I received from Sir J. Banks thro' Mr Purkis with a Bottle of the Powder—which I after gave to Mr Ridout, a truly respectable medical practitioner, in Paternoster Row.[1] Sir J. B. had made the most exact inquiries—whether he or Mr Percival wereas misinformed, or whether the Bang of Ceylon is different from that of Turkey & the Barbary Coast, I have no means to conjecture.   S. T. C.

1[1] C and Tom Wedgwood experimented with bhang in Feb 1803 (in the period also sp "bangue") which, like hashish, is prepared from the dried leaves of Indian hemp. C obtained the bhang from Sir Joseph Banks, President of the Royal Society, through Samuel Purkis (a friend he had made through Thomas Poole who was, like Poole, a tanner), along with an account of the drug that supplied most of the facts mentioned in this note (*CL* II 919–20, 933–4).

1[2] The anecdote about Tippoo Sahib (1751–99), Sultan of Mysore, is not in Banks's letter, and C's source is not known.

2[1] J. G. Ridout was the uncle of Thomas Ward, Poole's amanuensis. C saw him occasionally in London 1802–4, and Ridout helped C to arrange his life insurance before the Malta journey (*CL* II 787, 941, 1098).

3 p 204

The priests of the inferior deities . . . are easily distinguishable by the smaller degree of respect which is paid them. They are continually met in their wandering excursions over the island, and, like all these of the same class in India, are a set of lazy, impudent vagabonds, who, without any exertion or industry, are enabled to live well by the extortions which they practise on the people. Even those who supply their demands are conscious of their vices; but superstitious fears have taken too deep a hold on the minds of the votaries to permit them to withdraw themselves from the yoke.

I have met with many affecting instances of this in Sicily & Calabria/ the peasants, especially the women, painted their priests as the vilest wretches, liars, libidinous, gluttonous/ yet still—"they alone, you know, can get us out of purgatory"/ concludes all. In cases of unmerited & boughten absolution they believe their own souls cleansed, but that the Priest, unless absolved afterwards, will be damned.[1]   S. T. C.

4 p 288

The buffalo is of a dirty grey or mouse colour; the hairs, or rather bristles, are thinly scattered over his thick coarse skin. The flesh and milk, though sometimes used, are very rank and disagreeable. These animals are very dirtily inclined, and are constantly to be seen like hogs wallowing up to the neck in mud and water.

It is no doubt the link between the Hog and Bull.

5 p 292

I was present at an experiment tried at Colombo to ascertain the reality of this circumstance [that the Indian ichneumon "on seeing a snake ever so large, will instantly dart on it and seize it by the throat, provided he finds himself in an open place where he has an opportunity of running to a certain herb, which he knows instinctively to be an antidote against the poison of the bite"]. The ichneumon, procured for the purpose, was first shewn the snake in a close room. On being let down to the ground, he did

---

3[1] C was in Sicily Aug–Nov 1804 and again Sept–Dec 1805; he passed through Calabria on his way to Naples Dec 1805. His letters and notebooks for the Mediterranean period frequently express his distaste for a Roman Catholic society, e.g. in Syracuse, C observes, "I found no one native with whom I could talk of any thing but the weather & the opera/ ignorant beyond belief—the churches take up the third part of the whole city, & the Priests are numerous as an Egyptian Plague" (*CN* II 2261).

not discover any inclination whatever to attack his enemy, but ran prying about the room to discover if there was any hole or aperture by which he might get out. On finding none, he returned hastily to his master, and placing himself in his bosom, could not by any means be induced to quit it, or face the snake. On being carried out of the house, however, and laid down near his antagonist in an open place, he instantly flew at the snake and soon destroyed it. He then suddenly disappeared for a few minutes, and again returned as soon as he had found the herb and eat of it. This useful instinct impels the animal to have recourse to the herb on all occasions, where it is engaged with a snake, whether poisonous or not.

A tale very loosely told. What was the Herb? Does it grow everywhere, yet remain invisible, tho' within "a few minutes" space of a House in Columbo? "*Suddenly disappeared*" a phrase for a Ghost.

6   p 297

Among a great variety of smaller birds, we particularly distinguish the honey-bird. It is so called from a particular instinct by which it discovers the honey concealed in trees. As if designed for the service of the human species, this bird continues to flutter about and make a great noise till it has attracted the notice of some person, and induced him to follow the course it points out to him. It then flutters before him, till it has led him to the tree where the bees have lodged their treasure. The man then carries off the honey, leaving a little for the use of the bird, which silently and contentedly watches till it is permitted to enjoy its reward. As soon as it has eaten up its portion, it renews its noise, and goes in quest of another tree, followed by the man, who finds a guide here provided for him by nature.

A story, the gross exaggerations in which, if not its falsehood, have been more than once pointed out by intelligent Travellers.[1]

7   p 307

But the most mischievous species of these vermin is the white ant, which is equally destructive in the fields and the dwelling-houses. They build

6[1] The moroc, honey-guide, or honey-guide cuckoo, was one of the wonders of travel narrative usually reported uncritically esp in accounts of Africa, e.g. James Bruce *Travels to Discover the Source of the Nile* (2nd ed 8 vols Edinburgh 1805) VII 275–8; Andrew Sparrman *A Voyage to the Cape of Good Hope* (2 vols 1785) II 186–94. DW in Jan 1807 mentions C's recommendation of Bruce: *WL* (*M* 2) pt 1 129. What sceptical travellers C has in mind is not known, and in fact the original account of the bird has remained substantially unchallenged to this day.

their nests of a very fine clay, which they throw up in large mounds, and carefully prepare for the purpose. It is made into such an excellent cement, that as soon as it is dried up by the rays of the sun, it becomes so hard that it requires great exertion even with a pick-axe to level the heaps.

Improperly so called/ it is the same with the Termites of the Sierra Leone & other parts of tropical Africa, and perhaps the most wonderful in its instincts of the whole living Creation. See Phil. Trans—[1]

8   p 308, continuing **7** textus

These ant-hills are often from six to eight feet high, and have large openings both at the top and around the sides to serve for entrances and communications.

In Africa they have been found from 10 to 14 feet high: and Buffaloes seen on the tops, browzing on the Bushes.[1]

9   p 313

The *mango* is of an oblong cylindrical form, in shape and size resembling an egg. Its taste and flavour are peculiar, and it is reckoned one of the most delicious fruits in India. One remarkable circumstance is, that no one mango resembles another plucked from the same tree in taste or flavour.

not even *resemble*?

10   p 313

The mango-tree grows to a vast size, and extends its large and beautiful branches like our oak; but the timber is not applied to any useful purpose.

is it or is it not applicable? Throughout this work I have noticed with pain the apparent unthinkingness of the Writer.

11   p 315

The *plaintain* is a small tree with wood of a soft nature. The leaves are very broad, long and green. As soon as this tree has borne fruit, the trunk

7[1] During the same summer's visit to Poole in which C annotated this copy of Percival, he appears also to have annotated Poole's set of the abridged *Phil Trans* 1665–1800 in which he would have found the article to which he alludes here and which supplied the information given in **8**:

Henry Smeathman "Of the Termites in Africa and other Hot Climates" *The Philosophical Transactions ... Abridged* (18 vols 1803–9) xv 60–85. See ROYAL SOCIETY below.

8[1] See **7** n 1.

dies, and a new one springs up through it from the root. The fruit grows at the top of the tree in bunches, resembling in shape our hog's puddings, from six to twelve inches long, and from ten to twenty in a bunch. It is covered with a coat of a lemon colour, which is easily peeled off; the inside when ripe is of a white or yellowish colour.

This is properly the Banana[1]

12   p 359

The water [of "the hot-wells of Cannia"] . . . contains no acid nor alkali in a disengaged state; for upon mixing a delicate vegetable colour with it, no change to a green or red colour was perceptible.

a color? was it blue for the acid?

11[1] The plantain and banana are closely related to one another and in practical usage are virtually undifferentiated: *OED*. C's assurance seems to be unfounded.

THOMAS PERCY

1729–1811

Reliques of Ancient English Poetry. Consisting of old heroic ballads, songs, and other pieces of our earlier poets, together with some few of later date. 4th ed. 3 vols. London 1794. 8°.

Harvard University (Houghton Library)

Wordsworth's copy, inscribed by him on the half-title of Vol I: "Bought at Hamburgh ~~1797~~ 1798 by William Wordsworth"; and on the half-title of Vol III: "Bought at Hamburgh by William and Dorothy Wordsworth 1798—". The inscription on the half-title of Vol II—"William Wordsworth Bought at Hamburg 1798"—appears to be in another hand. The signature "W. Wordsworth" on the title of Vol I is in the hand of Wordsworth's son. Inscribed on the half-title of Vol III, below the Wordsworth inscription: "See foot-note on page 131—'S. T. C.' (Samuel Taylor Coleridge) H. B. W. 1905."

DATE. 5 Sept 1800.

1   III 131 | *Sir John Grehme and Barbara Allen* lines 9–12

> O hooly, hooly raise she up,
>   To the plaice wher he was lyan;
> And whan she drew the curtain by,
>   Young man, I think ye're dyan.*

[Footnote:]   *An ingenious friend thinks the rhymes* Dyand *and* Lyand *ought to be transposed; as the taunt* Young man, I think ye're lyand, *would be very characteristical.*

Damn the "ingenious Friend!"—he must have been a Scotchman or a Lawyer—.[1]   S. T. C.   Sept. 5. 1800.

---

[1] C's scorn for the Scots is evident also in PARNELL 1 above (and see analogues in MACDIARMID 2 and n 1); of lawyers, he observes in LAW MAGAZINE 3 that they "are sorry moralists, and . . . in whimsical wise contemptuously jealous of literary men".

GOMETIUS PEREIRA

b 1500

Antoniana margarita, opus nempe physicis, medicis, ac theologis non minus utile, quam necessarium, per Gometium Pereiram, medicum Methinae Duelli, quae Hispanorum lingua Medina de el Campo appellatur, nunc primum in lucem aeditum. [Medina del Campo] 1554. F°.

Not located; marginalia from MS TRANSCRIPT

RS's copy, evidently wanting the title-page. Described in *Southey SC* as "with a long and very curious MS. Note of two pages, closely written, by S. T. Coleridge, at Keswick, in 1812." This work is associated with the collaboration of RS and C in the 1812 *Omniana*: see esp **5** n 1.

MS TRANSCRIPT. VCL LT 63, transcribed by SH. The transcriber's cancelled errors have not been reproduced.

DATE. Feb 1812 (**2**).

1 "Written in the blank Leaf at the beginning of the Book", referring to **2**

The first half of the following note is an answer to the humorous *Bold-Thinkers*, the weakly and nervous *Fort-Esprits*, who dare not affirm animals insentient, and yet abjure Instinct—*a* raising Brutes to Men for the humane purpose of degrading Men to Brutes. To Dr Darwin let it be addressed;[1] but to Señor Anthony Purl the latter half is, I conceit, a sufficient though general Reply.[2]—I hope to shake a Fist with him at Heaven's Gate. What! tho he be in the wrong? 'Tis in the right way & I love him the better therefore.[3]

1*a* TRANSCRIPT has full stop instead of dash

1[1] C addresses Erasmus Darwin chiefly as the author of *Zoonomia; or, the Laws of Organic Life* (2 vols 1794–6), to which C alludes in *BL* ch 10 (*CC*) I 171. Of his own meeting with Darwin in 1796, C had written enthusiastically but with characteristic reservations on religious grounds: "Derby is full of curiosities, the cotton, the silk mills, Wright, the painter, and Dr. Darwin, the everything, except the Christian!" (*CL* I 177).

1[2] "Señor Anthony Purl"—the last word probably a mistranscription of "Pearl" (as it appears in **2** and **5** below)—stands for the book itself, the title of which, *Anthony's Pearl*, C playfully takes as a name.

1[3] "I love him the better there*fore*" appears as an allusion in *CL* IV 868 (var) and in LUTHER *Colloquia* 7—but the source remains untraced. C uses it again at the beginning of **6** below.

91

2 Front flyleaf, referring to col 12 | "Improbatur opinio aliquorum, qui negant affirmare bruta, & sentire ea testantur"

Quod si praedictis convictus, confitearis bruta noscere inimicorum & amicorum existentiam, & negaveris eadem in suis mentibus habere aliquas propositiones attestantes inimicos & amicos esse, qui sunt, dicam, te in re nobiscum convenire, verum quod tu nesciens confiteris eadem, quae ego sciens assevero. Quid enim est dicere, agnus cognoscit lupum existentem, quam agnum in mente propria habere hanc, Hic qui adest, lupus est? Nos enim conscii sumus cum sensibus cogniscimus amicos, qui adsunt, mentibus formare propositiones, quae testantur, amici sunt, qui adsunt. Quin aliud in nobis non esse sensibus cognoscere amicos praesentes, quam mente formare relatas propositiones.

[But if, convinced by the arguments I have given, you were to admit that animals recognise the existence of enemies and friends, and were to deny that they have in their minds some sort of propositions which attest that they are enemies and friends who are such, then I should say that you agreed with me in substance, in that you unconsciously admit what I knowingly assert. For what other meaning has the statement that the lamb recognises the existence of the wolf than that the lamb has this statement in its own mind, "This which is here is a wolf"? We are consciously aware that when we with our senses recognise friends who are present we form propositions in our minds which attest that they are friends who are present. In fact, that in us the recognition through our senses of the presence of friends is nothing other than the formation in our minds of connected propositions.]

P. 12.[1]

Surely, that yet unexplained Mode of causation (which is acting on the memory, Imagination, and the instruments of Motion both external & internal as well as the Sensations we all know as a *fact*: & which later Psychologists have called the Law of Association) is abundantly sufficient, even without Instinct, to explain a Lamb's flight from a Wolf, without supposing the mental discourse, the est Lupus—or more accurately in English—This is a Wolf—ergo!/ Now this is to all intents and purposes a brace of enthymemes[a] true syllogisms in the understanding. 1. All Wolves are Lamb-eaters—but this a Wolf—ergo, This wolf is a Lamb-eater. 2. All Lambs meeting a Wolf must run off in order not to be eaten—But I am a Lamb—ergo, I must run off. Besides the argument would prove too much—for it would evince, that not only impressions are accompanied with correspondent self-conscious propositions in all living Beings, but that these *propositions*, must have pre-existed, and that if a tame and if a wild Ducks Egg, both hatched under a farmyard Hen, the

---

2[a] A short space—perhaps for an undeciphered word—follows in TRANSCRIPT

2[1] The text is actually numbered by columns, not by pages.

first was born with this "sermone mentali"[b]:[2] "—I am a tame Duck, ergo, I must content myself with this puddle—& the other, I am a wild Duck— ergo, I must fly off.["] To retort that in *man* all conscious perceptions involve universal propositions, what is it but to affirm what no one denies— that the rational, the understanding, and the sensitive powers are not three separate[c] Hypostases, but three undivided tho' distinct *faculties* of the same *person*. But tho' unseparated[d] in the personality of Man, must they therefore be inseparable?[e] Because a Watch & a Leaf are both organized,[f] must the Watch therefore grow? Because a Pea-blossom & a Butterfly are both living things, must they needs be both loco-motive & sentient? Even so, I cannot see why a Dog & a Man may not both in different degrees possess Organization, Life, Sensation, Instinct, and even a categorical understanding, i.e. innate or immanent Forms, under some one or all of which all *Impressions* mould themselves, & are co-adunated into a true and distinct *Perception*, and yet the Man alone be gifted with proper *Self-consciousness* and consequently Reason—i.e. the Power of *Ideas* & of *universal necessary* Truths.—I have explained my sentiments more at large in two Notes in the FRIEND,[3] and I am convinced, whatever this *Oyster, to whom his Namesake St Anthony probably cast one of his Pearls, may have thought that Des Cartes' assertion did not extend beyond my own. See his letter to D.[r] Henry More on this subject, annexed to a minor edition of More's enchiridion.[5]   S. T. Coleridge.

* Let not this idle joke mislead to a supposition, that I think meanly of this Writer. On the contrary, his acuteness as a Logician, his Originality & "holy Insurrection[g] of a gallant Intellect"[4] against *mere* Authority,

---

2[b] TRANSCRIPT reads "scomone mentals", underlined in pencil
2[c] TRANSCRIPT: seperate   2[d] TRANSCRIPT: unseperated
2[e] TRANSCRIPT: inseperable   2[f] TRANSCRIPT: orgundized
2[g] TRANSCRIPT: Insurrection

2[2] "Mental discourse".

2[3] C refers to two long notes on reason in the original 1809–10 *Friend*: *Friend* (*CC*) II 104*, 294–7.

2[4] Not traced.

2[5] Presenting a passage from Pereira's work in *Omniana* § 234 (**5** n 1 below), RS mentions the theory that Pereira was the source of Descartes' view "that animals are non-sentient". More's *Enchiridion ethicum* contains a letter *about* Descartes; his *Enchiridion metaphysicum* discusses Descartes but contains no letters; no edition of either work has been traced that includes a letter to More from Descartes. C may have had in mind a letter by Descartes that summarises

his arguments in favour of the view that animals are without reason, published among the letters in Henry More's *Collection of Several Philosophical Writings* (1662) pt 4 70. The letter is dated 9 Feb 1649 in this ed, but 5 Feb 1649 in modern eds, e.g. Descartes *Oeuvres* ed Charles Adam and Paul Tannery (2nd ed 11 vols Paris 1964–74) v 267–79. There is a later reference to this letter in SCHELLING *Einleitung* **22**. C's annotations in four other works by More appear in *CM* (*CC*) III, and a version of this statement about the letter was published in the 1809 *Friend* (*CC*) II 76 (and n 3).

as a man, and as a man of genius, and his graceful Perspicuity as a Writer, have even my admiration & when I consider the Age and the Nation in which he wrote, that admiration is blended with wonder.

S. T. Coleridge.   Feb. 1812.   Keswick.

3   col 15 | "Textus Aristot. explicatur"

Qui enim solvunt hanc rationem, dicendo, quod bruta quodam naturali instinctu prosequuntur matres, odióque habent à natura creatos inimicos, ideóque agnus hoc instinctu fugit à lupo nunquam ante viso, & non à cane sat simili, amátque matré & non aliam ovem, verbis tantùm satisfecisse existimo, re ipsa nequaquam. Nam aut hunc naturalem instinctum appellant facultatem aliquam, ac proprietatem, quae agno & matri insita est, ut ferro & magneti trahenti idem, & ferro & altero magneti abigenti, aut quid aliud.

[For those who solve this problem by saying that it is by some natural instinct that animals follow their mothers and hate their natural enemies and, thus, that it is by this instinct that the lamb flees the wolf it has never before seen, and not the dog which looks like a wolf, and loves its mother and not some other sheep—these men I consider have given a solution in words only, in fact not at all. For either they call this natural instinct a faculty and property which is in the lamb and its mother such as is in iron and the magnet which attracts it, and in iron and another magnet which repels it, or they call it something else.]

But instinct, tho' the term convey no positive, yet may & does give a negative or limitative knowledge, even as gravitation when opposed to spontaneous motion? On similar arguments as these against Instinct, we might ground Atheism, for it would follow that the word "Spirit" was no Word (λογος)[1] but merely articulated air or figured Ink.—

4   col 16

Si quid aliud, cum instinctum naturalem dicunt, intelligunt, id explicent: nam medium nullum inter proprietatem, qua trahitur, aut fugatur quid piam, & vim sentiendi & extimandi, qua prosequitur utile, & fugatur inutile, percipi potest.

[If they understand something else by natural instinct let them explain it; for we can see no mean between a property, by which a thing is attracted or repelled, and a power of feeling and thinking, by which the profitable is pursued and the unprofitable avoided.]

What? no tertium[1] between the flowing of a River & a Man's swimming across it? Does not the Blood circulate, & the Vessels absorb & secrete

---

3[1] Greek *logos*—word, also "Word".   **4**[1] "Third thing".

by a Law diverse from either? The Author had duped himself by the word *Medium*, which is a term of Comprehension and Science, whereas the question here is of *Facts* not whether we can conceive a *medium*, but whether we do not know a tertium vel quartum.[a2]   S. T. C.

5   Front flyleaf, referring to col 22 | "Bruta si sentirent universa naturae benignitas aboleretur"

Ac ultra hanc immanitatem, quae tantò atrocior, quantò frequentior habetur; crudelitatis apicem obtineret taurorum agitatorum tormentum, sudibus, ensibus, lapidibúsque caesis ipsis: nec in alium humanum usum, quam ut iis flagitiis humanus visus delectetur, quibus bestia vindictam mugitu supplex poscere videtur. Atque non tantùm hominis pravus affectus culpandus offertur, dum haec ita percipi à tauris, ut nutus eorum indicant, creduntur, sed omnis benignitas naturae aboletur & culpatur, quae genuerit viventia illa, ac quam plurima alia, ut vitam adeò aerumnis & miseriis plenam agant.

[But worse than this inhumanity, as atrocious as it is common, the prize for cruelty would be won by the baiting of bulls with stakes, swords and even with hewn stones, and this for no other human profit but to delight men's eyes by these sufferings, for which the poor beast seems to implore vengeance with its bellowing. And not only is man's evil disposition to be blamed, if these sufferings are believed to be felt by the bulls in the way that their movement suggests, but all the goodness of nature is annulled and arraigned since it created those living beings and so many more to live lives so full of pain and wretchedness.]

Page. 22.—Notice this dearest Southey![1] as a curious specimen of the Argumentum ad hominem[2] from a Spanish Metaphysician to his Spanish Readers! If you do not admit the cogency of these & the following arguments it is impossible for you without the most flagrant, as well as demonstrable, Inhumanity, or rather Anti-*christian* Atrocity, to continue to enjoy your BULL-FIGHTS!—O nobly-meaning *Pearl* of all the Antonios from the Hero of St. Athanasius's blessed biography to the Hero of the sinner Godwin's damned Tragedy![3] and did it never occur to thee, that

4[2]   "Third or fourth thing".

5[1]   RS followed C's suggestion and quoted this passage in *Omniana* § 234, "The Souls of Brutes", pub 1812.

5[2]   "Argument against the man": the fallacy produced by addressing personal failings of an opponent rather than the weakness of his reasoning.

5[3]   Pereira is a "Pearl" from his own title

(as in **1** n 2). The other Anthonys are St Antony of Egypt (c 251–356), whose biography, the *Vita Antonii*, is attributed to St Athanasius (c 296–373); and Antonio, the hero of Godwin's tragedy *Antonio, or the Soldier's Return*, which failed (was "damned") at its one performance in Dec 1800.

thou wert too honest, a too plain-hearted Man of Genius, to be, or ever to become, a Pope?—therefore not infallible? But & IF deceived in this Point, O how wilt thou stand the prosecution of Bull versus thy Bull in the Court of Conscience?[4] Then too, when all the sucking Pigs, whipt to death, shall squeal anew against thee, and the crimped Cods *answer* thy sermon, O Anthony![5] and the Lobsters, that had died thro' every line of every degree from 40 of Fahrenheit to 212, shall claw thee? When all the Vivæ Sectiones[6] of all the Hospitals of Medical Universities of Christendom shall arm themselves with their tormentors Lancets & Bellowses to *cut* thee up, & bleed thee up? Whither wilt thou flee?—See yonder is a Horse! And the rider will take thee up behind him!—Alas! Alas! the horse was bought at Smithfield for Dogs meat, having been lamed, excoriated & wind-broken in dragging chaise after chaise of Voters to a contested York Election, to give their Votes to M[r] Wilberforce:[7]* & the man had been a Negro, proved by Lord Kaim,[9] & by his Overseer, & by his colour, to be only "a †Live Neger" of course a *Sub-human*, who had been burnt alive for having killed the Overseer who had kicked his pregnant

* And half devoured by his Companions in the house-less, straw-less Repository at Hammersmith, before they were bought up by the King's Huntsman!—(This is a *fact*)[8]

† From the Charles-Town Advertiser, since the pretended Whole Abolition of the Slave Trade by the American Congress,—"Just arrived & to be sold at public Vendue a Cargo of *Live Negroes* &c."[10]

5[4] C perpetrates a favourite pun (the same as in RHENFERD **5** below), implying that if so honest a person as Pereira were (improbably) to become Pope and were to promulgate a Bull declaring (as he does throughout this work) that animals have no feelings, then the persecuted bull of the textus would have a solid case against Pereira's Bull, which is also an Irish Bull based on false reasoning (cf **6** below at n 5).

5[5] Another Anthony, St Antony of Padua (1195–1231), a preacher of such legendary fascination that fish were said to have leapt out of the water to hear him. The pig is associated with St Anthony of Egypt (cf n 2, and *OED* "tantony").

5[6] The animals used for vivisection.

5[7] In spite of the high reputation he enjoyed after the passing of the bill for the abolition of the slave trade in Britain early in 1807, William Wilberforce almost lost his Yorkshire seat in the general election of that year: in the end, he won by 11,806 votes

to his rivals' 11,177 and 10,989; and his expenses amounted to £28,600, but theirs to £200,000 (*DNB*).

5[8] C is perhaps alluding to an incident made famous by Lord Erskine in a speech in which he introduced to the House of Lords his Bill (which failed) for Preventing Cruelty to Animals. He told of old horses kept starving until the right moment on the market, so that they were driven to eat one another's manes: House of Lords *Parliamentary Debates* 15 May 1809 (cols 553–71).

5[9] Henry Home, Lord Kames (1696–1782), pub *Sketches of the History of Man* (1774), in which he argued that the different races reveal different levels of development, whites showing more progress than other races.

5[10] An act against the importation of slaves into the United States was passed in 1807, but as C says, it did not effectively put an end to the trade. The periodical cited has

wife in the belly, because she had fainted in the gang and it was "all damned laziness, and sham Abraham!"[11]—Nay, noble heart, thou has yet a shield! Were man as alive to the exclusive grandeur of his Nature, as thou wert sincerely tho' strangely labouring to make him, he would shudder for his own sake at representing such horrors to himself even on Idols of Wood or mock-animals of Straw!

6 col 27 | "Rationes speculativae, quibus probatur bruta non sentire"

[Pereira argues that animals do not have feelings:] Quod in idem rediret ceu affirmare, bruta, & homines, eiusdem esse speciei. Quod non tantùm manifestè absurdum, verum et impium est, ergo antecedens ex quo sequitur.

[This would amount to the same thing as saying that animals and men are of the same kind; which is not only manifestly absurd but also truly impious and so therefore is the antecedent reasoning from which it is concluded.]

"I like it the better therefore,"[1] says the Darwinian to himself—[a] "& here I stop."—Aye! at the *Result*—[b] but the grounds of deductions if admitted, would raise the brutes so very high, that Man himself would suffer no debasement if he were arranged as the Monarch species of the *genus*. Now this would not answer the purposes of the Modern Gallo-Gallinaccan[2] *Psilo*sophists.[3] *Raise* Brutes a *little, pull down* Man *altogether,* as far at least as he is *man* per *differentiam,*[4] and to the very point beyond which (not common sense merely but) all human Language would whistle a *Lillibullero Lie in your face for a contradiction in terms—but still remember the 5th of November. Never be forgot our grand End & Plot[5]—[c]that both the one & the other, the Brutes & the Man, are to be made *Beasts*.

6[a] TRANSCRIPT has full stop instead of dash
6[b] TRANSCRIPT has full stop instead of dash
6[c] TRANSCRIPT has full stop instead of dash

not been traced; C quotes extensively the advertisements for runaway slaves from a similarly ephemeral work, "the Kingston Mercantile Advertiser", in *Omniana* § 160, "Hint for a new species of History".

5[11] Proverbial, originally nautical slang for feigning illness: *The Oxford Dictionary of English Proverbs* ed F. P. Wilson (3rd ed rev Oxford 1970).

6[1] See **1** n 3 above. The Darwinian following is an Erasmus Darwinian, as in **1** n 1.

6[2] "French-cocky"—C punning on the connection between "Gallic" and *gallina*,

"a hen": cf a similar piece of word-play, *Cristogalli*, in LUTHER *Colloquia* **59**, which C translates as "French Christians, or Coxcombs".

6[3] "Shallow thinkers": C's coinage, as in JUNG **8**.

6[4] "Distinctively".

6[5] C's language echoes the jingle still recited by children in commemoration of Guy Fawkes' unsuccessful plot to blow up the Houses of Parliament on 5 Nov 1605: "Remember, remember, the Fifth of November, / The gunpowder treason and plot."

* id est: Lie, Lie, a Bull & a Blunder:[6]—ero a corruption of error—or rather a true genesis, an etymon de fonte psychologico[7]—a *wilful* blunder, an error of my whole Being, the being a wretch, quia *ero*, because *I will be*—it is a true *heresy* κρεατος ψυχικου αιρεσις[d], the *choice* of the fleshly heart.[8] Forbid it, Justice! Let Love & Goodness forbid, that the Author of this Volume should be otherwise placed contiguous to such Ouran-Outangs than as the Law of "*Extremes* meet" enforces[9]—otherwise than an East & West on a Globe.—Antonio[10] erred only from a too ardent zeal to preserve unneighboured[e] the dignities of Man.

S. T. C.

7   col 40 | "Colores qualitatem occultam habere probatur"

Coloribus consimilis occulta proprietas à natura collata est. Album enim, ac eximiè lucidum, videndi facultatem disgregat, ac raram efficit, ceu nigrum congregat, adeò immodicè, ut nonnunquam dolorem inducat. Qui motus partium organi, quo cernimus, tanta admiratione digni sunt, prout illi, qui relati fuêre, ferri, ac festucae. Qui colorum effectus in calorem & frigus reduci non poterunt, nive eximiè frig[i]da disgregante, & pipere calido nigredine congregante.

[Colours have been given a similar occult property by nature. For a white and excessively bright object dissipates and rarefies the faculty of sight, just as a black object concentrates it, so violently as sometimes actually to cause pain. These movements of the parts of the organ of vision are as worthy of remark as those which I adduced earlier, of iron and straw. It will not be possible to attribute these effects of colours to heat and cold, since very cold snow causes diffusion and hot pepper by its blackness causes contraction.]

I see no occult quality here—the white, as = all the rays, tends to contract the pupil, if it be excess of Light; the Black for the opposite cause to contract[a] it. That the Eye should have this power of adapting itself to circumstances, that indeed is so far an occult quality, as it depends on *Life*.

6[d] TRANSCRIPT reads κεατος ψυχικου διρεσις   6[e] Underlined in pencil
7[a] Probably in error for "dilate"

6[6] The refrain that gives its title to the anti-Irish song *Lillibullero*, popular from about 1688 and given increased currency by Sterne in *Tristram Shandy* (where it is Uncle Toby's habit, when perplexed, to whistle it). The word is generally thought to be meaningless, but C jokingly etymologises it.
6[7] "From a psychological source".

6[8] The transcriber had difficulty with the Greek, and it may still be not quite what C wrote. C's translation emphasises the two meanings of the Greek *hairesis*, "heresy" and "choice".
6[9] A favourite paradox: cf BLANCO WHITE *Practical Evidence* 9 n 2.
6[10] I.e. Antonio Pereira.

AULUS PERSIUS FLACCUS
34–62

Auli Persi Flacci Satirarum liber. Isaacus Casaubonus recensuit, & commentario libro illustravit. Tertia editio, auctior & emendatior ex ipsius auctoris codice: curâ & operâ Merici Casauboni Is. F. accessit & graecorum, ubi opus est, interpretatio. 2 pts in one vol. London 1647. 8°.

Victoria College Library (Coleridge Collection)

Note about this vol by EHC with additions by Alwyn Coleridge loose in vol. Inscribed on p ⁻1: "Wm. Young", with the letter "n" below the name and "C" and "X" below "n" but obscured by C's note **1** written over them. Holograph signature "S. T. Coleridge" at the head of the title-page. Also in ink on the title-page in an unidentified hand: "[? Bountry/Bounting] | Mʳ Powles | Powles | Powles | Harden". A reference "pag. 487", written in ink on ii 23, is not in C's hand; nor are the correction of a typo i 9, the pencilled numbers in the margins of i 1–5, and pencilled crosses and question-marks ii 4, 6, 8, 9, 12, 14, 15, 198, 200, 201, 207, 208, 248.

DATE. 1807? HNC in *LR* dates the note 1807 without giving evidence. The hand is rather large and sprawling, as in many of the volumes annotated early in C's annotating career.

---

1 pp ⁻2–⁻1, and the last word on title-page; the leaf torn at the edges

616 pages in this Volume, of which 22 are text; and 594 Commentary and introductory matter. Yet when I recollect, that I have the whole works of Cicero, [of]ᵃ Livy, and Quintilian, with many others, the whole works of each in a single Volume, either thick Quarto with thin paper & small yet distinct print, or thick Octavo or duodecimo of the same character & that they cost me in the proportion of a Shilling to a Guinea for the same quantity of worse matter in modern Books, or Editions, I a poor man yet one whom "βιβλίων κτήσεως ἐκ παιδαρίου δεινὸς εκτέτηκε πόθος"[1] feel

---

1ᵃ Word obscured by patch on paper, as is the case with other letters given in square brackets in this note

1¹ C quotes Julian the Apostate, Roman emperor, in a letter to Ecdicius, prefect of Egypt. Tr Wilmer Cave Wright (LCL 1913–23) III 73: "I, from childhood, have been penetrated by a passionate longing to acquire books". C might have found this sentence in his SCAPULA, under ἐντήκω, or in a copy of Julian's works, perhaps one of the ones ordered in 1796 (*CL* I 262), which may in turn have been the edition that

the liveliest Gratitude for the Age, which produced such Editions, and for the Education, which by enabling me to understand and taste the Greek and Latin Writers, has ~~likewise~~ thus put it in my power to collect on my own Shelves ⟨for my actual use⟩ almost all the best Books in spite of my so small Income. Somewhat too I am indebted to the ostentation of expense among the Rich, which [has o]ccasioned these cheap editions [to be]come so disproportionately cheap.

stayed in C's family and contains marginal   *omnia* (Paris 1583), now at VCL.
notes by DC—Julian *Opera quae extant*

PETRARCH

1304–1374

Copy A

Il Petrarca di nuova ristampato, & diligentemente corretto. Con argomenti di Pietro Petracci, &c. Venice 1651. 24°.

Harvard University (Houghton Library)

Inscribed on p ⁻2: "To Leigh Hunt from A M D—the most valuable gift she can bestow Bodryddan Sept 2—1835"; and below this in pencil in another hand: "A. M. D.—Anna Maria Dashwood, whom Hunt visited at Bodrydden in 1835." On p ⁺3, a word in pencil not in C's hand, and a librarian's note in pencil (same hand as identification of A. M. D.).

DATE. 21 Mar 1819.

1   p ⁻3, the interpolated note on p ⁻4

21 March 1819   Highgate
E dono viri reverendi, *H. F. Carey. Nunquam mihi e memoria excidet, *quomodo* vir optimus et amicissimus hoc mihi volumen dedit. Fuerat e parvulâ, selectâ tamen, bibliothecâ filiæ ejus dilectissimæ, eheu! nusquam nunquam non desideratæ, de quâ vix loquitur audet, nec nisi voce suppressâ, festinanti et formidolosa loquitur. "Illi (inquit) placuerit, credo, hunc suum Petrarcham *te* possidere, te quem poetam ea ετ' ενι ζωοις εναριθμιος plurimum admirabatur et amabat["].[1]

S. T. Coleridge.

* cujus ingenio istam veram metempsychosin debemus, quâ Dante apud nos et Anglus et Poeta redivivus fit.

[1] Taking in C's footnote, the inscription may be translated as follows: Given by the Reverend H. F. Cary [footnote:] to whose genius we owe that true metempsychosis by which Dante was restored to life among us, as an Englishman and a poet [footnote ends]. I shall never forget *in what manner* this most excellent man, my close friend, gave me this volume. It was from the small, yet select, library of his most beloved daughter, alas! everywhere and always lamented, of whom he scarcely dares to speak and of whom he does speak only in a low, hurried and trembling voice. "It would have pleased her, I believe," he said, "that *you* should own her Petrarch, you, the poet she most admired and loved 'while still numbered among the living'." Jane Sophia Cary had died in Apr 1815 aged 16. Her father, whom C met first in Sept 1817, had taught her French, Italian, and Spanish. In 1818 Cary had moved to Kentish Town to be close to C at Highgate. The Greek phrase is adapted from Theocritus Idyll 7.86. Possibly the intended meaning was ". . . you, the living poet she most admired . . ." in which case, however, -ος should have been changed to -ον or -ων.

Copy B

Le Rime di Francesco Petrarca. 2 vols. London 1778. 12°.

British Library   C 132 c 15

Inscribed "Edith Coleridge" on I ¯3; "H. N. Coleridge. *1829.*" and "Edith Coleridge *1852*" on I [i]; and "H. N. Coleridge. 1829." on II [1]. Passages on I 23 and 29 are marked in pencil with a double line that is not characteristic of C; I 182 "Sonetto CI" ("S' amor non è"), I 274 "Sonetto CLXXVIII" ("In nobil sangue vita"), I 290 "Sonetto CXCIV" ("I' mi vivea"), I 307 "L'aura, che 'l verde Lauro", and II 2 "Canzone I" ("Che debb' io far?") are marked with pencilled crosses that might be C's but might as easily have been made by the unknown person, probably *a* Coleridge, who wrote the date, "Feb. 14. 1889", in pencil at the end of the first volume, I 332.

TEXTUS TRANSLATION. *Petrarch's Lyric Poems* tr and ed Robert M. Durling (Cambridge MA 1976). Italic is used to indicate passages circled by C in the original.

DATE. About 1810–12? HNC dated the marginalia before 1812 and noted that the book was in his possession in 1836 (*LR* I 84n). It seems likely that C gave it to Mrs C to use in SC's Italian lessons, which she began about 1810; by 1812, he could say she read Italian "fluently": *CL* III 375.

1   I ⁺4 (p-d)

Gòod or pléasing Sonnets &c.
p. ì.—7̀. 1́1. 1́2. 1́3. 2́0.[1]

2   I ⁺4 (p-d)

2́4 to 3́0 = a poem imitated by our old Herbert, ridiculous in the Thoughts simple & sweet in diction.—[1]

1[1] C's notes **1**, **2** and **4** employ the code of the grave accent for "good" and the acute for "pleasing". According to the conventional numbering of Petrarch's poems, these are # 1 ("Voi, ch'ascoltate"), # 7 ("La gola, e 'l sonno"), # 11 ("Lassare il velo"), # 12 ("Se la mia vita"), # 13 ("Quando fra l'altre"), and # 20 ("Vergognando talor . . .").

2[1] *Canzone 1* (# 23), "Nel dolce tempo della prima etade . . .". What poem by Herbert C is referring to—if he means a particular poem and not a composite—is obscure: possibly *Love Unknown*, q *BL* ch 19 (*CC*) II 96–7. Several notebook entries from the summer of 1809 show that C was reading Herbert then: *CN* III 3532, 3533, 3580.

3 I $^+$4 (p-d)

35 to 39—*dignified.*[1]

4 I $^+$4 (p-d)

45. 48. 49. 50. 51.[1]

5 I $^+$3

98 & 99 the first half of this (IX) Canzone is exquisite; & 9 lines in Can. VIII.—p. 95. "O poggi" to "cura", are expressed with vigour & chastity.[1]

6 I 99, pencil, overtraced | *Canzone 9* [# 72] ("Gentil mia Donna, i' veggio")

> Da quel di innanzi a me medesmo piacqui,
> Empiendo d' un pensier' alto, e soave
> Quel core, ond' hanno i begli occhi la chiave.*

[(. . . but from then on I have been pleasing even to myself), filling with one high sweet thought that heart *of which her lovely eyes have the key.**]

O the Devil or the Pope take these eternal ~~ciphers~~ Keys that so for ever ~~on the~~ turn the Bolts on the finest passages of true passion—

7 II 6, pencil, overtraced | *Canzone 2* [# 270] ("Amor, se vuo' ch' io torni")

> Riponi entro 'l bel viso il vivo lume,
> Ch' era mia scorta, e la soave fiamma,
> Ch' ancor, lasso! m' infiamma
> Essendo spenta: or che fea dunque ardendo?

[Put back in her lovely eyes the living light that was my guide *and the gentle flame that still, alas! inflames me though it is extinguished—oh, what did it do when still burning?*]

Deleri possint utinam! et quæcunque ⟨alia⟩ hunc in modum includuntur nota pennicillari *e la soave fiamma.*[1]

3[1] # 28, "O aspettata in ciel".

4[1] These are # 32 ("Quanto più m'avvicino"), # 35 ("Solo, e pensoso"), # 36 ("S'io credessi per morte"), and the first half of # 37 ("Si è debile il filo").

5[1] *Canzone 8* is # 71, "Perché la vita . . .". The lines cited (37–45) read (tr) "O hills, O valleys, O rivers, O woods, O fields, O witnesses of my heavy life, how many times have you heard me call Death! Ah, dolorous fate! staying destroys me and fleeing does not help me. But if a greater fear did not rein me in, a short and speedy way would bring to an end this bitter and hard suffering; and the fault is hers who does not care."

7[1] "Would that they could be deleted! and whatever else in this mode that is enclosed in a pencil-mark, [starting from] 'and the gentle flame'."

7A II 8, pencil, overtraced

> Movi la lingua, ov' erano a tutt'ore
> Disposti gli hami, ov' io sui preso, e l'esca,
> Ch' i' bramo sempre . . .

[Move that tongue *where were ever set the hooks that caught me and the bait that I ever desire* . . .]

7B II 8–9, pencil, overtraced

> L'arme tue furon gli occhi, onde l' accese
> Saette uscivan d'invisibil foco,
> E ragion temean poco;
> Che contra 'l Ciel non val difesa umana . . .

[Your weapons were those eyes *from which came forth arrows lit with invisible fire, and they feared reason but little, for no human defense avails against Heaven* . . .]

8 II 9, pencil, overtraced

> * Poser' in dubbio, a cui
> Devesse il pregio di più laude darsi.

[. . .* which often left one in doubt which to praise more.]

rather flatly worded.

9 II +3 (p-d)

11. 13.[1]

10 II +3 (p-d)

117.   2; but not equal I think to p. 6. tho' more faultless.[1] Omitting half a dozen Conceits & Petrarchisms of Hooks, Baits, Flames, and F Torches this Canzone 2 from p. 6 to p. 10. is a bold & impassioned Lyric, & leaves no doubt of Petrarch's having possessed a true poetic genius.

9[1] C notes # 272 ("La vita fugge") and # 274 ("Datemi pace").

10[1] "117" is a page reference, noting (presumably with approval) the sonnet # 351 ("Dolci durezze"); the second page number, "2", refers to *Canzone 1* ("Che debb'io") in II 2–5, which is marked with two pencilled crosses at the beginning, and which C prefers to *Canzone 2* in II 6–10— itself the subject of **7–8** above.

JOHN PETVIN

b c 1690

Letters concerning Mind. To which is added, a sketch of universal arithmetic; comprehending the differential calculus, and the doctrine of flux-
ions. London 1750. 8°.

Henry E. Huntington Library

CL's copy. In Aug 1841 HCR amused himself at the Athenaeum "by copying
some marginalia of Coleridge in *Letters Concerning Mind,* by Petvin, a book I
found at Miss Lamb's on Wednesday and brought away": *CRB* ii 598, and see MS
TRANSCRIPT below. The book was included in the Lamb Sale in New York in
1848, and was bought by G. T. Strong, whose initials are on the title-page; it was
later presented to the Huntington by a Mrs Farrand. See R. F. Brinkley *HLQ* viii
(1945) 277–8.

MS TRANSCRIPT. Dr Williams's Library, HCR Bundle 1.v.3.

DATE. Oct 1820 (**1**).

1   pp ⁻3 (p-d) to title-page, footnote in pencil

~~Tho'~~ At the time, in which these Letters were written, the Haut Ton
philosophique[1] ⟨was ascendant⟩, ~~that~~ according to which Plato, Aristotle
and the rest of the unfortunate Ante-Nati,[2] who wrote before "John Locke
had thrown the *first* ray of Light on the nature of the human mind and the
true source of all ⟨our⟩ Ideas",[3] ~~was ascending;~~ were mere Dreamers or
word-splitters. Yet still there were many of a better mould, who retaining their love and veneration of the ancients were anxious to combine it
with the new Orthodoxy by explaining ~~Plato~~ Aristotle and even Plato
down into John Locke. Such was that excellent man, and genuine *Classic* Scholar, the Poet Gray.[4] Others there were, and Petvin appears to have
been one of the number, who, if they did not *love* the Ancients more than
the former class, *understood* them better; and yet ~~either~~ want~~ed~~ing either
will or courage to oppose the reigning Dynasty. These men ~~combined~~ at-

---

[1] "Philosophical high style".
[2] Those "born before" Locke.
[3] C is not quoting but paraphrasing
Petvin, whose respect for Locke is apparent
even when he ventures to correct him, as in

17 below.
[4] C is recalling his reading of "Some
Account of the Dialogues . . . of Plato" in
Mathias's ed of Gray's *Works*: see GRAY,
esp **5** and n 1.

105

tempted to reconcile the old with the new Authority by a double operation—now, like the former class, lowering down Pl. and Arist. to John Locke, & now pully-ing John Locke up to Plato and Aristotle. The result was, now a confusion in their own thoughts & an inconsistency in their several positions; now & more frequently, an expression of the Truth in lax, & inaccurate, & inappropriate Terms. But the general Effect, a nearly universal Neglect of Metaphysics altogether, & the substitution of a shallow semi-mechanical Psychology under the pretended *Law* (but in fact no more than a vague generalization) of ASSOCIATION:[a] in which a mode of causation is made the ground & cause ~~of~~ and explanation of Causation itself.[5]

But the whole scheme of Locke is an Hĕtĕrozētēsis[6]—by which the Sun, Rain, Air, Soil &c are made to *constitute* the germs (as of Wheat, Oat, or Rye) ⟨of⟩ the *growth* & *manifestation* of which they are the efficient *Conditions.*—Instead of the words, "give, convey" and the like, write wherever they occur, "excite, awaken, bring into consciousness" or words equivalent—& little will remain in Locke's Essay to be complained of, but its dullness & superficiality, its putting up of Straw-men to knock them down again—in short, the making a fuss about nothing, & gravely confuting Nonsense, which no man ever *had*[b] asserted & which indeed no man ever *could* believe—ex. gr. (as Des Cartes says to the Jesuit, Voetius, who had assailed him in the true Locke [? ~~book~~] Style, tho' before Locke's Essay), that a men saw before they saw, heard before they heard, & the like 2 + 2 = 5, cross-readings!—[7]

S. T. Coleridge

1[a] C's pencilled footnote on the facing page (⁻3) may once have had a corresponding footnote indicator here, but no trace remains
1[b] Underlined in pencil

1[5] The chief of several similar diatribes upon the popular psychology of association as a mechanical model of the mind produced by a profoundly materialistic age appears in *BL* chs 5–8 (*CC*) I 89–139.
1[6] The fallacy of "looking for something else", i.e. using an argument that proves something other than what is claimed to be proved. Echoing Maass, C makes the same charge about Locke's work in *BL* ch 9 (*CC*) I 142 and n 3.
1[7] C makes a remark rather similar to this one in *Logic* (*CC*) 184* about Voetius, but no exact source has been located. Gisbertus Voetius (1589–1676), rector of the University of Utrecht, was a consistent opponent of Descartes, and C may be paraphrasing or generalising upon either Descartes' published response to charges of atheism in the *Epistola . . . ad D. Gisbertum Voetium* (Amsterdam 1643) or his letter to his own follower Regius (Henry de Roy), which includes detailed instructions as to how to answer the attacks of Voetius: *Epistolae* (3 vols Amsterdam 1682) I 292–303. Both works contain passages expressing the point C attributes to Descartes, though neither uses exactly C's wording. Neither is included in C's copy of Descartes *Opera philosophica*: see DESCARTES.

OXFORD, Oct. 14. 1820.—Saturday Afternoon. (Left Highgate, Friday—
& London, by the three o'clock Shrewsbury Stage—arrived in Oxford,
Friday Night, 11)—God grant me a safe return on Monday.—Sunday
morning 1/2 past 11. am to have my interview with Dr Coplestone.[8]

* ^{c}substitute—under the pretended Law of Association, which, however, is in fact no *Law* at all, but a mere vague general or *common* Term
for causal connection as far as the same is seen in living & thinking, as
distinguished from inanimate things, thus making one particular mode of
causal connection the ground &c—

2   p 35, pencil | Letter 4

What is it in general, *to find out Truth*; and *How do we come by it?* To
find out Truth is, *to find out general Ideas*. And how are these got into the
Mind? By means of *Sense*; Two Ways. The one easily, and as it were of
a sudden; the other with more Difficulty, and Expence of Time. [He illustrates the first in our knowledge of a triangle, the second in the empirical procedure of generalising from observing Callias drinking or Callias
sweating to the connection between drinking and sweating.]

So *very* near to the Truth was this writer that nothing but the Locke-
dynasty could have prevented him from seeing, that the difference here
is *diversity*—not a difference in *degree* but in *kind*. The proof is, that the
Latter (the kind of empirical deduction instanced in Callias) remains as
unlike the former after the fullest Acquaintance with the several facts, as
at the first enunciation, while the Former (τα νουμενα)[1] never *wax*, nor
wane, but are either known wholly or not at all—and at all times are accompanied by the Sense of Universality & Necessity.

It was the fashion, even among Men far above Lockianism, in this age
to accomodate Locke to all that they admired in the Ancient Philosophers;
as it was the fashion of a lower order of minds, but yet reverencers of the
Ancients, to explain all into Mr Locke. So Gray.—[2]

3   p 41, pencil | Letter 6

The Things that have been, and shall be, have respect, as we said before,
to Present, Past, and Future. These, likewise, that *now* are, have moreover

1^c Footnote in pencil

1[8] C was in Oxford to see Edward
Coplestone (1776–1849), then provost of
Oriel, in a last attempt to prevent the with-
drawal of HC's fellowship on grounds of
"sottishness". Coplestone's letter to C after
the interview is pub *CL* v 73–4.

2[1] Noumena, objects of intellect, as opposed (by Kant) to phenomena.

2[2] Cf 1 n 4.

*Place; that, for Instance, which is here; that which is to the East; that which is to the West.

Pray, did Petvin's Love to his Wife stand N. E. or South West of his Esteem for his Friend?[1] But here P. was misled by Aristotle who has erroneously placed the ubi among the categories of the pure Understanding.[2]

3A   p 42, marked with a pencilled stroke in the margin

[By what kind of "mind" was the universe created?] 'Tis nothing like the Human Mind; we have no notion of it, only this, It does not understand Things by *Images*, and *abstract Ideas*, but by *being everywhere present to Things*.

4   pp 54–6, completed in pencil | Letter 7

Plato, in his Tenth Book of Laws, speaks of this Way of Representation by a Circle, and circular Motion, as only an Image . . . . And *Timaeus* himself, just after he has done with the Division of the Soul, reminds us, *that 'tis Mind only sees God, as the Eyes see the visible and sensible World.*

  Perhaps 'tis a mistaken Notion of this Passage of *Timaeus*, or others like it of the antients, that has made the Moderns go about to prove immediately a Deity by his Idea.

By the Moderns the Author can have meant Des Cartes only, tho' the same notion occurs in Anselm, & the Ante-scholastic Theologians.[1] I am far from think*[a]* it a mistaken attempt: nor has Kant's distinction of Existence, as the position of Attributes, from Attributes, convinced me[2]— *[b]*The argument is briefly this: The ⟨absolute⟩ equidistance of the radii from the center of a Circle is a necessary Truth of Reason because it is

---

4*[a]* For "thinking"   4*[b]* Note switches to pencil at this point

3[1] C makes the same mocking remark in his attack on associationism in *BL* ch 8 (*CC*) I 130.

3[2] Aristotle includes "where", or place, among the ten categories e.g. in *Categories* 4 (1^b26), *Topics* 1.9 (103^b23). In *BL* ch 5 (*CC*) I 102, C follows Maass in observing that Aristotle himself excluded place from his discussion of the mind: ". . . in his treatise 'De Anima,' he excludes place and motion from all the operations of thought . . . as attributes utterly and absurdly heterogeneous."

4[1] This is the "ontological proof of God" propounded by Anselm (c 1033–1109) and reformulated by Descartes, as noted in *BL* ch 10 (*CC*) I 200 n 4. C's formulation of the argument later in this note is more extended than the *Biographia* version.

4[2] In the comparable passage in *BL*, C quotes the Kantian text from *Der einzig mögliche Beweisgrund zu einer Demonstration des Daseyns Gottes* (1763)—C himself perhaps following Jacobi: *BL* ch 10 (*CC*) I 201 and n 2.

contained in the ~~Idea~~ Theorem, or necessary Contemplamen, of ~~our~~ Circle, which is one with ~~the~~ our Reason itself.—Even so is the *Existence* of God a necessary Truth of the Reason, for it is contained in the necessary idea of God, which is one with Reason itself. The only difference is that in the Circle the Reason creates a correspondent to the Truth by an act of the pure Imagination—in the other, it does & may not, *imagine* at all—tho' the Imagination is so prone to do of its own accord that almost all the World are more or less *Idolators.*

5   p 62, pencil | Letter 8

For, in short, properly speaking, 'tis by Induction we get all our Knowlege, of what Kind soever; and even what I now say is only to be understood by Induction. [Petvin gives an inductive proof *"that every Angle in a Semicircle is a Right one".*]

I will not say, that a man might not be led originally to the Conclusion in this manner, but it either presumes a mathem: Intuition of a Circle which has no adequate Correspondent in the physical World: or it is purely empirical & contingent. It is painful to see the influence of Locke on so clear a mind as that of this Writer. How otherwise could we explain such a gross confusion of probability with absolute certainty, of contingency with necessity as is betrayed in the next instance!—[1]

6   p 63, pencil

After this manner you will see the Reason which *Aristotle* gives, why *a Boy* may understand *Mathematics,* but not *Morality.* That Passage of *Aristotle* to me is extremely beautiful, in his manner of Writing, as well as of the highest Importance.

This of itself should have led the Writer to the opposite Inference—viz. that Math. not requiring ⟨outward⟩ Experience may be learnt by a Boy; but not Ethics (prudential or applied Morality) which do.

7   p 64, pencil

And if we do not make the Induction the Way he leads us, we must do it some other way with more Difficulty, or else never pretend to know the Principles of Reason or Knowlege.

5[1] In pp 62–3, Petvin concludes from the fact that the last few times *he* has drunk tea "to such a Degree" he injured his nerves, that drinking tea to such a degree *generally* injures the nerves.

Then there *is* another way: & what becomes of Petvin's Mr Locke? Petvin is discoursing on the *nature* of Truth; namely, of metaphysical Truth, or that which transcends the evidences of the Senses. And in an instant he passes off into the way of exciting the mind's attention to metaphysical Truth per alterum,[1] i.e. by physical Induction.

7A   pp 66–7, marked with a pencilled brace in the margin | Letter 9

And if we lay aside this *relative* View of Nature, and consider her as she is *in herself*, not as ACTING, but as SPECULATING, I mean, as having SENSE and INTELLIGENCE; in this View, she likewise appears to *harmonize and correspond with herself*; from whatever Point of the UNIVERSE she directs her Eye, having there the same *full* and *easy* Prospect of the *Universe*, which she has any-where else, together with the same INTELLECTUAL OBJECTS there in her Mind, some of them copied in what she sees, some not, and only within herself.

8   pp 68–9, pencil

How *intimate* is this UNION of NATURE! Not of many Things, one here, and another there; but of ONE THING every-where the SAME. How different *this Union* from that of other Things! IMMUTABLE, ETERNAL, SIMPLE, PURE, UNMIXT! *How wide*, and *extensive*! COMPREHENDING ALL THINGS; and, though COMMENSURATE to the *Understanding*, yet exceeding the Bounds of Imagination, or any thing which has something beyond it!

Bravo! dear Honest Man! and what if in thy Aristotelian Exaltation, thou didst forget for a moment that thou wert the *Reverend* John Petvin—didst forget that thou wert either spouting Spinosism, & Physiolatry, or Nonsense.[1]—The very term, Nature, as the futurition of those than[a] never *are*, but always *becoming*,[2] should have hinted a less *pagan* doctrine.

8[a] A slip for "that"

7[1] "By another way".

8[1] The first use of "physiolatry", nature-worship, recorded in the *OED* is from 1860. C reiterates his usual position on Spinoza, that his error was that by "making Substance a Synonime of God [he] confounds or identifies God and the sensible World" (KANT *Metaphysische Anfangsgründe* **29**).

8[2] A point of considerable importance to C, who published in *AR* (*CC*) 251 the observation that "nature", the Latin *natura*, was identical with the future participle of *nascor*, "I am born", hence "Natura, that which is *about to be* born, that which is always *becoming*". The first note referring (apparently) to this etymology appears in 1803 (*CN* I 1728).

9   p 71, pencil | Letter 11

Outward Things proceed in one immutable Order, and so do *inward Things* too. Mr. *Locke* says, we do not think always. But he allows, that we think always when we are awake.

Who told Mr L. this? Thought & recollectible Thought, are very different positions: & it is the latter only that L. had any right to negative.

10   p 72, pencil

Dr. *Clarke* says, MORALITY *consists in a Power of doing otherwise than you do at the time of doing.* I think the contrary. *We have no Power to do otherwise than we do at the time of doing.*

At the least, this remark is most worthy of being considered. None but a *Thinker* could have made it.

11   p 73, pencil

PHILOSOPHY is nothing but the LOVE OF TRUTH . . .

O no! no! This were Philo*logy*—Philo*sophy* is the Love of Truth in the speculative, + Goodness in the practical, = Wisdom.[1]

12   p 73, pencil | **11** textus continued

. . . and he that does not know how to pursue TRUTH in the Way of INDUCTION, as well as in the Ways of SYNTHESIS and ANALYSIS; in short, he that is not Master of all those Ways of proceeding, is *no Philosopher.* *

* Nor Philologist either.

13   p 73, pencil | **12** textus continued

He that is so, *is a complete one.* *

* God forbid! for then the first shrewd Knave, I met with, might be a Philosopher.

11[1] The conjunction of philosopher (lover of wisdom) and philologer (lover of discussion) was made by Plato in *Republic* 582E, the contrast between philosophy and philology (as discussion of the writings of others) by Seneca in *Moral Epistles* 108.24. C's own frequently made distinction is between philology as love of *logos* in the sense of word, discourse, learning, etc, and philosophy as the love of wisdom (*sophia*). Cf *P Lects* Lects 13, 14 (1949) 390, 397; *CN* IV 5080 and n, 5132; and TENNEMANN **53** below.

14 p 73, pencil | **11–13** textus

Truth + Good = Wisdom. Love of Truth + Love of the Good = Philosophy. Philosophy is the Wisdom of Love, as well as the Love of Wisdom.[1]

15 p 77, pencil | Letter 12

This will explain, I suppose, the μονοειδὲς [uniform, of one kind] of *Plato* in his *Symposium*, and the πολὺ πεγαλος τοῦ καλοῦ [great sea of beauty]. By which, I have a Fancy, he hints, that we are here and there, and everywhere, in the Universal Mind, as Fishes in the Sea.

What in the name of Plato can Mr Petvin have meant by this *Fishery*!— A Fish is not here, there, & everywhere, but one here & one there.

16 pp 85–6, pencil concluded in ink | Letter 14

As to the Subject of HAPPINESS, it never was once a Question with me, Whether GOD *was happy*. But it has been a very serious one, Whether he was *good*, and what Reason I had to rejoice in his Being. But in this latter Question I have been long quite satisfied. I had never any Notion of proceeding *a priori.*

In a work like this from a mind so amiable I can not read these words without feeling, how much was done by Kant, in strictly ~~defining~~ appropriating the term "a priori."[1] Had this been fully elucidated, Locke would never have had the suffrage of men, like Petvin. ^a^But in ~~wh~~ this there is an inconsistency in the statement, that surprizes one in so clear-headed a man, as Petvin must have been. The very word "happy" as applied to the Being above Fate & Chance, that is strangely lax and slovenly.[2] But we will suppose the proper word—viz. blest or blissful—this at least implies mind, self-comprehension—not merely an infinita cogitatio sine centro,[3]

16^a^ The remainder of the note is in ink

14[1] See **11** n 1.

16[1] E.g. in the 2nd ed of the *Critique of Pure Reason* (B xvii–xviii). C formulates the concept thus in *BL* ch 12 (*CC*) I 293*: "By knowledge, *a priori*, we do not mean, that we can know any thing previously to experience, which would be a contradiction in terms; but that having once known it by occasion of experience . . . we then know, that it must have pre-existed, or the experience itself would have been impossible. By experience only I know, that I have eyes; but then my reason convinces me, that I must have had eyes in order to the experience."

16[2] In a notebook entry of 1809 (*CN* III 3558) C remarked upon the etymological connection between "hap" or chance and "happy", and desynonymises happiness from blessedness, joy, etc.

16[3] "Infinite thought without a centre".

but a Self as the Copula or proper *Oneness* of all Positives. But a blessed self-possessing mind, omnipotent, and omniscient, is by necessary synthesis of the Terms, knowledge, reality and causality an all-wise agent— and wherein does wisdom consist, what is the meaning of the term, but the union of the best means & the best end/ i.e. Goodness?—In short, Good absolutely, & God are Synonymes—A God not good were a Circle not round. "Why callest thou me *good*? There is none good but the Father."[4]

17   p 88, pencil | Letter 15

But to return to the consideration of Νοῦς [Mind] and ἐπιστήμη [knowledge] above, after the Manner of *Aristotle*. And here it is plain, that *every self-evident Principle* must be a *general Idea*, because 'tis a *Medium* by which *general Conclusions* are drawn. I should hardly have made so obvious a Remark, but that, as obvious as it is, it seems to have escaped Mr. *Locke*, or not to have been considered by him in a right manner.

At length, Petvin dares *use* his own eyes. But what an instance of the effect of a *great Reputation* on an honest & even superior mind! For with this ground-falsity the *whole* of L's system as far[a] it is System, sinks & is overturned.

18   p 90, pencil

And the 47th of *Euclid* is as much a *general Idea*, as the Definition of a Triangle.

most true.[1]

19   p 90, pencil

. . . and, could Man go no further in Numbering than *One*, or the singular Number, *Plato* says, in his *Epinomis*, he would be ἀφρονέστατον ζῷον.

A most unthinking animal.[1]

17[a] For "as far as"

16[4] Matt 19.17 var.

18[1] Petvin's illustration is the famous proposition that the square on the hypotenuse of a right-angled triangle is equal to the sum of the squares on the other two sides (*Elements* 1.47).

19[1] C translates the Greek phrase, slightly tendentiously giving "animal" for "creature" or "living being".

20   p 100, pencil | Letter 17

These ARE's [the ὄντα, or things that are] are the Objects of Knowlege, and for this Reason *immutable* and *invariable*; because, were all Things *variable* and *mutable*, and were there not something of a *contrary Nature*, KNOWLEGE COULD NOT BE.

These ARE's then, depend not upon the WILL of GOD; but they depend upon HIS BEING.

This is sound—*excellent*!

21   p 101, pencil, overtraced by C | Continuing **20** textus

Every succeeding Step of Demonstration depends upon every preceding one; and they all depend upon the TO ΔIA TI ΠPΩTON [The First Cause], the SOURCE OF MIND, the ALL-TRUE and PERFECT. And if the ARE's before-mentioned are not temporary Things, but *eternal* and *immutable*; if neither any, nor all of them, can have any Being, without the FIRST; then, I suppose, we may conclude this FIRST οὐσία [being] *necessarily* IS. But this Way of Proof is not *demonstrative* . . .

This depends on the sense given to the term *demonstrative*.

22   pp 101–2, begun in pencil, overtraced by C | Continuing **21** textus

. . . and as for the *Idea of* GOD, perhaps the most perfect one may be exhibited from the Consideration of the *Harmony, Union*, and *Correspondence* of *Nature*, considered as ANIMATE and INTELLIGENT; but this, surely, will never be admitted by any honest Lover of Truth, till he sees it perfectly answer to the best Knowlege he can get of the Things within and without him, of the ὄντα [things that are] and γενέσεις [becomings].

How can he *help* it? *a*But the whole may be made conspicuous by considering the old argument so exquisitely put & worded by Bishop Berkley in his "Minute Philosopher":—in which the comparison of the World with Homer's Iliad or Euclid's Elements is shewn to be no simile but in strict analogy—the only difference being *visual*, & tactual Language in the one & *words* in the other.[1]—Still this supposes a prior possession of

22ᵃ Note continues in ink

22[1] In the fourth dialogue in *Alciphron: or the Minute Philosopher*, an argument is made for the existence of God as analogous to the existence of wise, reasoning human beings, namely that their existence is manifest in their communication by "the arbitrary use of sensible signs . . . having no resemblance or necessary connexion with the things they stand for and suggest"—Homer and Euclid (C's examples) through words the Truths awakened/ for what would Homer be to a man who could not read? or to an animal?—Just what the starry Heavens are to a Child or a Savage—viz. the one a multitude of strait & curved strokes, the other a multitude of glittering Points with blue inter spaces.—Even so, the *Idea* of Space is presumed in every act of filling or making Limits therein, as Squares, Circles, &c—tho' this act of limiting, this perception of limits, be the *means* of bringing the pre-existing Idea *b* ⟨or subjectum *limitabile*⟩[2] into our *Consciousness*. In short, the Sophism is grounded on the identification of consciousness (or rather, the Consciousness of *having been* conscious) with the Truths of which we become conscious—of the Milestones with the Mile or given quantum of Road.—

23   pp 105–6 | Letter 18

When we are given to understand by *Pythagoras*, in his mysterious Way, that KNOWLEGE is the *Harmony* of Ideas, we take no Notice of it, except as it affords us Diversion.—But when we are told by a *Locke*, that KNOWLEGE is the *Agreement* and *Disagreement of Ideas*, and have it immediately explained to us, without the least Mystery, wherein this Agreement and Disagreement consists, by enumerating the Sorts of it; we are serious, and give up our Attention and Assent, in a manner, together, admiring the Clearness of the Writer . . .

The Deuce! Where lies the difference, excepting that Pythagoras expresses himself more accurately by confining the definition to Locke's first term. For how can "*disagreement* of *Ideas*" be knowlege? A Knowlege *of* the disagreement of certain Terms as ["]A is always all white: & A is always black" is or gives the knowlege that such terms are not exponents of Ideas—but that Knowlege is itself an Agreement or Harmony. This on the supposition, that Pythagoras did use the term, "Ideas," whereas more probably he would have said "Numbers"[1]—2nd that the Ideas of the (later) Pythagoreans & the Platonists were the same as Locke's Ideas—the identity of which is scarcely more affirmable that*a* the Sameness of a Syllogism & an Apple-dumpling.[2]

22*b* C has written the following Latin phrase at the end of the note, and marked it for insertion here
23*a* For "than"

and figures, God through the created world (*B Works* III 149).
22[2] "Subject susceptible of limitation".
23[1] Nevertheless C had accepted the numbers of Pythagoras as equivalent to the idea of Plato, in *P Lects* Lect 3 (1949) 115.
23[2] See C's long note on the degeneration of the term "idea": *BL* ch 5 (*CC*) I 96–8*.

24　p 106 | **23** textus continued

For this Character [clearness], I think, is universally given to Mr. *Locke*, considering, as they say, the abstract* Nature of his Subject.

Abstract! Aye, with a vengeance! For this is what we complain of in Locke, that he has reduced the whole Intelligile[a1] to an Aggregate of Sensory Abstractions! And that an empty warmthless lifeless Idealism is an inevitable deduction from his Principles! But this was the character of the Times. *Locke* was to be cried up, at the very moment that Positions the most subversive of Locke's premises, were admitted as truths—

.

24[a]　Presumably for (Latin) "Intelligibile" or "Intelligible"

24[1]　The "intelligible", as opposed to the "sensible" world.

PINDAR

c 522–c 440 BC

ΠΙΝΔΑΡΟΥ ΠΕΡΙΟΔΟΣ hoc est Pindari lyricorum principis, plus quam sexcentis in locis emaculati, ut jam legi & intelligi possit, Ὀλυμπιονῖκαι. Πυθιονῖκαι. Νεμιονῖκαι. Ἰσθμιονῖκαι. Illustrati versione nova fideli. Rationis metricae indicatione certa. Dispositione textus genuina. Commentario sufficiente. Cum fragmentis aliquot diligenter collectis. Indice locuplete, victorum, autorum, rerum & verborum. Discursu duplici; uno de dithyrambis: altero de insula Atlantica ultra Columnas Herculis, quae America hodiè dicitur. Opera Erasmi Schmidii Delitiani, graec: & mathemat: professoris publ. 4 pts in one vol. [Wittemberg] 1616. 4º.

Wisbech Museum and Literary Institute

Inscribed in pencil on the flyleaf ⁻2: "This copy belonged to the poet Coleridge, & has notes in his own handwriting. Given me by his Son Derwent. C. H. Townsend." The signature "Chauncey Hare Townsend" is written in full on the title-page, again without the "h" which he customarily inserted from 1828 onwards: this suggests that the book was in Townshend's possession before 1828. The vol contains both Greek and Latin versions; the textus is given in Greek or in both languages, according to the point C is making. Line numbering begins afresh with each stanza in this ed; we give first its numbers and then a modern line numeration following Sir John Sandys *The Odes of Pindar with an English Translation* (2nd ed rev LCL 1937).

The English translations given in the textus are as far as seems feasible a plain rendering of Schmied's Latin translation, though without any attempt to match word for word or line by line.

Notes or symbols have been made in pencil, apparently by Townshend, in the Genealogical Table (which also has one word in ink), the Chronological Table, and on i 22, 23, 57, 61, 113, 187, 216, 298, iv 155 (Catalogus Victorum). Lines of Greek text are marked with a short pencil line in the margin on i 164, 186, 192, 216, 232, 234. A cross in ink on i 57 beside *Olympian* 1.1 may be C's: he recalled the Greek phrase from it, Ἄριστον μὲν ὕδωρ ("Water is best"), in a notebook entry of Oct 1807: *CN* II 3174.

DATE. Oct 1806, at which date there is a notebook quotation from this work (*CN* II 2887) and a sequence of Pindar entries from the *Olympian Odes* (*CN* II 2881, 2882, 2911, 2912).

COEDITOR. Lorna Arnold.

1   i 134–5, referring to *Olympian* 4 Strophe 1.1–6, Antistrophe 1.13–15, Epode
1.9–12 | Lines 1–3, 17–18, 26–8

Ἐλατὴρ ὑπέρτατε βροντᾶς
ἀκαμαντόποδος
Ζεῦ. Τεαὶ γὰρ ὧραι
ὑπὸ ποικιλοφόρμιγγος ἀοιδᾶς
ἑλισσόμεναί μ᾽ ἔπεμψαν,
ὑψηλοτάτων μάρτυρ᾽ ἀέθλων . . .

**Οὐ ψεύδεϊ τέγξω
λόγον. Διάπειρά τοι
βροτῶν ἔλεγχος . . .

Φύονται δὲ καὶ νέοις
ἐν ἀνδράσι πολιαὶ
θαμά, καὶ παρὰ τὸν ἁλικίας
ἐοικότα χρόνον.

[Brandisher of tireless-footed thunderbolt, most high Zeus, your Hours, revolving to
the lyre's harmonious song, have sent me as witness to the most exalted contests. . . .
**I shall not dye my word in falsehood. Trial is indeed the test of mortals. . . . But grey
hairs grow often even on young men's heads before the fitting time of life.]

⟨* There *seems* an anticlimax in the conclusion of this Ode, in relation
to its commencement; but⟩[1]

* ~~It~~ it is not improbable, that as these Odes were *bought* of the Poets
by the successful Combatants, ~~the~~ occasionally at least part of the subjects to be introduced were stipulated for. On this supposition, which is
indeed more than a mere supposition, the Poet's *management* must compel our *admiration*, where his *choice* would excite our *wonder*, & sometimes not without a mixture of the Ludicrous.   S. T. Coleridge.

2   i 141 | *Olympian* 5

An Ode of truly admirable construction. How little was to be said, how
much is said, and how well!   S. T. C.

1[1] The second asterisk in C's annotation
(on p 135) is level with the line of the Greek
(on p 134) which he has marked with two
asterisks, and it seems that he wrote what
precedes this second asterisk as an afterthought, though after no great lapse of time
since there is no obvious change in hand or
ink. Schmied remarks (i 137) that Pindar is
at this point referring to the improbability

already controverted by the event, that a
man already grey-headed should win such a
contest. In *CN* II 2886 C commented on the
dying away of Pindar's odes into a languid
interest, and in *CN* II 2911 copied out the
last four lines of this ode (included in textus). For the conclusion of *Olympian* 5 cf **4**
below, and on the beginnings and endings
of the odes see also **8** below.

3   i 143 | Antistrophe 1.8–9 | Line 12

καὶ σεμνοὺς ὀχετούς, Ἵπ-
αρις οἷσιν ἄρδει στρατὸν . . .

& *venerandos canales, Hip-*
paris quibus aquas-suppeditat populo . . .

[. . . and the venerable channels with which [the river] Hipparis supplies water to the
people . . .]

gives vivifying waters to an Host,[1]

4   i 145 | Epode 1.13–17 | Lines 23–5

Ὑγί-
εντα δ᾽ εἴ τις ὄλβον
ἄρδει, ἐξαρκέων κτεάτεσσι, καὶ
εὐλογίαν προστιθείς· μὴ ματεύ-
ση Θεὸς γενέσθαι.

Sobri-
am autem siquis felicitatem
auget, abundans possessionibus, &
laudem adjungens; ne quae-
rat Deus fieri.

[But if anyone increases his wealth in a healthy way, having enough of possessions
and adding to these good report, let him not seek to become a god.]

* or who on his Wealth, as on a healthy growing Plants, sheds increase-
giving dews,[1]

5   i 149 | Note on Epode 1.13–14 (in **4** textus)

ὑγίεντα ὄλβον] vel *divitias Sanas*, id est, sano & justo animo partas &
usurpatas: vel *sanam felicitatem*, id est, sanitatem.

[ὑγίεντα ὄλβον: either *healthy riches*, i.e. acquired and used in a healthy and just
spirit, or *healthy prosperity*, i.e. health.]

Oh! FLAT.

3[1] Commenting on the last two words of
textus, C evidently wishes to bring out what
he feels is the full significance of ἄρδει (on
which see also **4** below).

4[1] C is translating only as far as ἄρδει

(*auget*, "increases", lit "waters", as in **3**
above) but he expands into paraphrase, perhaps in part inspired by what follows in
textus.

6 i 161 | *Olympian* 6 Epode 4.10–13 | Lines 82–3

Δόξαν ἔχω τιν᾽ ἐπὶ
γλώσσᾳ ἀκόνας λιγυρᾶς,
ἅ μ᾽ ἐθέλοντα προσέλκει
καλλιρόοισι πνοαῖς.

Opinionam habeo quandam in
lingua cotis acutae,
quae me volentem attrahit
pulchrifluos ad flatus.

[I have a feeling of a shrill whetstone upon my tongue, that draws me, willingly, towards its fair-flowing breathings.]

* forse, ακοᾱς: vide Pyth: Θ (IX) Stroph. δ. 1.2. ακοα σοφοις[1]

7 i 163 | Last line of **6** textus

pulchrifluis suis flatibus.[1]

8 i 187 | *Olympian* 7 Antistrophe 3.1–8 | Lines 45–9

Ἐπὶ μὰν βαίνει τι καὶ
λάθας ἀτέκμαρτα νέφος,
καὶ παρέλκει πραγμάτων ὀρ-
θὰν ὁδόν γ᾽ ἔξω φρενῶν.
Καί τοι γὰρ αἰθούσας ἔχοντες
σπέρμ᾽ ἀνέβαν φλογὸς οὔ:
τεῦξαν δ᾽ ἀπύροις ἱεροῖς
ἄλσος ἐν ἀκροπόλει.

[A cloud as it were of forgetfulness often arises unexpectedly, and draws the right way of doing things from the mind. For indeed they went up not having the seed of blazing flame and made the sacred place on the citadel with fireless sacrifices.]

It is difficult to reconcile the first 7 lines of this Strophe, as well as many other passages of Pindar, with the dignity, and characteristic *import*ful-

6[1] "Perhaps ἀκοᾱς; see *Pythian* 9 Strophe 4 line 2 ἀκοὰ σοφοῖς [a sound for wise men to hear]". C would have these lines mean, apparently, "I seem to have a shrilling sound upon my tongue, that draws me willingly onward with its fair-flowing breathings". Most editors accept the metaphor of the whetstone (ἀκόνας) as not excessively far-fetched for Pindar (though interpretations still differ), and they prefer

the reading προσέρπει ("creeps upon") in line 83. C's "with" is quite as compatible with the grammar as Schmied's *ad* ("towards").

7[1] "With its fair-flowing breathings": see **6**. C singled out a picturesque passage from this poem in *CN* II 2882, where his references make it likely that he is using Schmied's ed.

ness, of his writings in general. And indeed the conclusion of this & some other odes, by their memorandum-like & to us almost *gossiping* manner seem to *contrast* oddly with the beauty & majesty of the Introduction.[1] Vide p. 135.[2] That remark & temporary Allusions may help to explain it.

S. T. Coleridge

8[1] This ode ends with the remark that the wind changes from one moment to the next. It begins dazzlingly with a wedding feast, where a wealthy father pledges his son-in-law from a golden bowl, making him envied for his harmonious marriage; with him is compared the poet himself, pledging his patron with the nectar of his songs.

8[2] I.e. **1** above, "it is not improbable" etc.

ERNST PLATNER

1744–1818

Ernst Platners Philosophische Aphorismen nebst einigen Anleitungen zur philosophischen Geschichte. 2 vols. Leipzig 1793, 1800. 8°.

British Library C 126 c 5

Autograph signature "S. T. Coleridge" on the title-page of Vol I, and the "S. T. C." labels now (1985) loose in Vol I but on the title-page verso of Vol II. A large "22" is written in pencil at the top of I ⁻3 and in the margin of the title-page of Vol I. C appears to have annotated Vol I after binding, but Vol II before: his notes fit the cut margins of the former, but in the latter the pages were folded up to preserve the notes when the volume was cropped in binding. The two vols are uniformly bound.

DATE. The last sentence of **25** indicates that these notes belong to more than one reading, but most if not all appear to have been made c 1814–15. Several are early formulations of ideas expressed in *BL* (**1**, **2**, **3**, **6**, **16** and nn) and must have been written before Sept 1815; HD, who was knighted Apr 1812, is referred to as "Sir H. Davy" in **9**. For the possibility of annotation before 1809, however, see **25** n 6 and *CN* IV 5094n, which points out that C made reference to this ed in a note of 1801, *CN* I 905.

COEDITORS. Lore Metzger, Raimonda Modiano.

---

1   I ⁻3–⁻1, ⁺1, pencil, rubbed and partly illegible

1 The last & fundamental know[lege] must be some thing, which being thought of must *be*, which *being* must think: in short, the perfect co-incidence of Reality & Conception[.][1] This condition is realized in the two terms Sum, and Cogito—Sum implies sum cogitans, Cogito involves cogit*ans*—i.e. cogit[?ans] ens.[2]

---

[1] This note is indebted to Schelling's *System des transcendentalen Idealismus*, where Schelling argues that the task of transcendental philosophy is to establish an absolute principle of knowledge which is completely certain. For his view that such a principle involves the coincidence of being and knowledge and resides in the "I AM" or self-consciousness, see esp *System* pt 1, "Vom Princip des transcendentalen Idealis-

mus". The philosophical position adopted in this note corresponds closely to that of the "theses"—derived largely from Schelling—in *BL* ch 12 (*CC*) I 264–84, esp 272–84.

[2] "'I am', and 'I think'—'I am' implies 'I am, thinking', 'I think' involves 'thinking'—i.e. 'a thinking being'". This analysis is echoed in *BL* ch 12 (*CC*) I 276–8* and n 2.

2 If any thing be known, some thing must be known certainly—& be present as the source & soul of all other certainty. ⟨3⟩ Whatever is essential to any thing, abides in that thing thro' all its modifications.

4 There can be one thing thus absolutely certain. For if there were more, I have or will have a ground for affirming their equally independent Certainty, but this I cannot do but by comparing them. Therefore my certainty of them is derived from my comparing them/ therefore, dependent on that comparison—therefore not necessary or independent.

But [. . . . . ? comparans] is a modification of Sum = Cogito = sum cogitans.[3]

5. But tho' the [? forming/foregoing] I cannot, of course, have any *sense* of its *certainty*, yet that Certainty may involve or derive from itself another certainty of a something prior to that Thing, of which we are absolutely certain. [? No doubt, from that] instance, that I [? receive/record] the primor Certainty; that I must have had [. . . . .] I am or a posteriori knowlege of a prior Thing.—Thus if I say, Sum, & ask again how I *know* that, or how is that *certain*, I can only answer, Sum quia sum;[4] but if conscious of its independently Certainty, I am asked or ask myself, How is this *possible*, I answer:—Whatever is real, must be possible and yet in this sense instance is not possible, unless there be one primary "I AM" who *is*, *because* he is, as well as *knows* himself to be because he is. Scio quód sum, quia sum; an sum vero, quia Deus est.[5] I can only*[a]* sum nunc temporis, et certe scio me esse quia sum; but the great "I am" *est* ab eterno ad eternum, quia est.[6]—As far as in accord to the Laws of the human Mind we speak of God in metaphors of Time, Deus solus est fuit, quia [. . .] est [? erat], fuit et [? erit].*[b]*[7]

The primary Certainty or Knowlege absolute is, when considered for itself alone, thetic or positive; in relation to the certainties rising out of it, hypothetical or suppositive.—

From § 3, deduce the translated universal Substance—and under what

---

1*[a]* A slip for "I can only say"?

1*[b]* Note continues, "Turn to blank Leaf at the end of the Volume", and the following text, on +1, is prefaced by "(continued from the blank Leaf at the beginning of the Volume—"

1[3] "'I am' = 'I think' = 'I am, thinking'."

1[4] "I am because I am", as in *BL* ch 12 (*CC*) I 274 and n 1.

1[5] "I know that I am, because I am; but I am, because God is." A similar formulation in *BL* ch 12 (*CC*) I 274 suggests that this idea might be put "more philosophically" as (tr) "because I exist in God".

1[6] I.e. I can only say "I am at this point in time, and know myself with certainty to be because I am"; but the great I AM "*is* from everlasting to everlasting because He is".

1[7] "God alone has been because [. . .] he is [? was], has been and [? will be]".

conditions we universalize the Idea—& how it degenerates into an idolum.[8]

2　ɪ xii–xiii, pencil | Preface

Wollte der scharfsinnige Verfasser der Kritik mit einem Beyspiele der kritischen Mässigung vorangehen: so durfte er hier, dünkt mich, nicht mehr sagen, als so viel: "Liegt auch unsern Vorstellungen von Raum und Zeit etwas in der Aussenwelt zum Grunde: so werden doch auf jede Weise zu diesen Vorstellungen Anlagen vorausgesetzt. Diese Anlagen sind allein hinreichend, jene Vorstellungen zu erklären: und im übrigen ist die Frage, ob ihnen etwas in der wirklichen Welt entspricht, eine blosse Spekulazion; über die sich mit apodiktischer Gewissheit, zwar nichts verneinen, aber auch eben so wenig etwas behaupten lässt."

Nicht weniger Dogmatiker ist Kant in der Darstellung seiner kritischen Resultate.

[If the perspicacious author of the *Critique* had wanted to set an example of critical restraint, it seems to me that he should here have said no more than the following: "Whether or not our representations of space and time are grounded in something in the external world, in any case they presuppose corresponding capacities. These capacities alone suffice to account for those representations; to go further and ask whether anything in the real world corresponds to them is pure speculation; here, to be sure, nothing can be ruled out with apodictic certainty, but neither can anything be confirmed." Kant is no less dogmatic in the presentation of his critical results.]

⟨See blank Leaf at the end of this Vol.⟩[a1]

Does K. affirm more than that what we call Space and Time are not Things but relations necessarily arising out of our mode of *seeing* Things? Is there any dogmatism in asserting that the tune from an Eolian Harp is neither in the Harp nor in the Breeze but the result from both for ⟨and in⟩ the perceptive power of the Hearer?[2] It seems to me a mere determining the ⟨only⟩ Intelligible sense of certain words.—Besides, Kant is far from denying possible *correspondents* to T. and Sp. see his Essay De Mundi

---

2[a]　The direction was written at the end of the paragraph of textus, presumably after the note itself had filled the margin

1[8]　An idol (Greek *eidolon*), an object of the senses and consequently, as C says in *SM* (*CC*) 101, "the antithesis not the synonyme" of an idea. See also Paulus **3** n 3.

2[1]　I.e. **3** below.

2[2]　A variant of this formulation appears in *BL* ch 7 (*CC*) ɪ 117, only to be dismissed as unsound: ". . . this caput mortuum of the Hartleian process has been rejected by his followers, and the consciousness considered as a *result*, as a *tune*, the common product of the breeze and the harp: tho' this again is the mere remotion of one absurdity to make way for another, equally preposterous." This history of the eolian or aeolian harp itself is outlined in Kant *C d r V* **4** n 2.

Sens. et Intell.[3] But correspondents to A and B are not A and B. Die Frage, statt eine blosse Speculazion zu seyn, ist gar keine Frage—ist ein blosses Nichts.[4]

3 I $^+$1–$^+$2, footnote on I 656 (facing), referring to I xii, pencil | **2** textus

P. XII *preface.*

What would Platner wish that Kant should say? Kant's Ding in sich* is evidently an x y z in his philosophy, defined by exclusion of a, b, c &c—so far, however, is clear that Mind or Subject-Object is meant in distinction from Product, or mere Object—and that by subsuming this idea under the form of the Finite, we have Dinge in sich—^{a}i.e. self-subsisting Minds. Now has Kant hinted that the Intuitions of Time and Space do not exist, where finite Minds are there to exercise them? In any other sense, it seems to amount to this—X is X as contradistinguished from Y, by being inward; and Y = Y as χ^2 X by being outward—but whether X may not be Y, and Y = X, whether ⟨the word⟩ inward is not of the same meaning as the word outward, it would be dogmatism to decide!!—In other words, Scepticism is the right of thinking, or rather of talking, just as you like—so that nothing which the Sceptic says in this moment, is to limit his free will or preclude him from asserting the contrary in the moment following.[3]—And this was the Genius of Platner and the Eclectic School—then the Fashion in Germany, and still the f. in England

* a postulate that imposes a conclusion, that he did not begin from the beginning but involved all anterior to reflection in the inward i.e. Ding in sich[1]

3^a The note continues on the following page, with C's direction "(turn over)" intervening

2^3 C may have in mind specifically the passage from Kant's Inaugural Dissertation, *De mundi sensibilis atque intelligibilis forma et principiis* (Königsberg 1770) § 1—*VS* II 439–40—that he quoted extensively and translated in *BL* ch 12 (*CC*) I 288–9, and quoted again in *Logic* (*CC*) 244. For C's admiration for this work see KANT *VS* COPY A **3** n 1.

2^4 "The question, rather than being pure speculation, is no question at all—it is a mere nothing." C takes up phrases from textus.

3^1 Properly *Ding an sich*, "thing in itself", mentioned again in **4** below. Of this central Kantian concept C speaks more critically in *BL* ch 9 (*CC*) I 155: "In spite therefore of his [Kant's] own declarations, I could never believe, it was possible for him to have meant no more by his *Noumenon*, or THING IN ITSELF, than his mere words express . . .".

3^2 "In opposition to"—as in SHAKESPEARE COPY D **2** below—or, as in **4** below, "contradistinguished from".

3^3 Platner discusses and advocates the tradition of scepticism in §§ 705–18 (pp 353–74), and C addresses his argument directly in **12** and **13** below. Platner defines scepticism as a mode of thinking that resists

4   I [1] (half-title), evidently referring to I xii–xiii, pencil | **2** textus

It was clearly Kant's Notion of Time and Space, that they were the mode (Handlungsweise)[1] in which a finite mind attempts successively to realize for itself, or comprehend that Sum in parte,[2] its own *ideas* of Eternity and Omnipresence. These are the only Dinge in sich, as ✗[3] from the finite Minds that are to contemplate them. Thus there are, first, the finite Minds, second, the permanent and self-subsisting Objects of the finite Mind; and thirdly, the Relations and as it were, Perspectives, arising out of the limits, and yet realities, of the former—the + − in its apprehension of the absolute + −[4] and the two first are what K. means by Dinge in sich.

5   I 47, pencil | § 50

Aber es kann ja Herr *Herzen*, der sehr gut weiss, was die von dem Gesichte getrennten Vorstellungen des Gefühls sind, nicht unbekannt seyn, dass Erhöhung und Vertiefung, ohne Einfluss jenes Sinnes, für sich selbst gar nicht zu den Gegenständen des Gefühls gehören *. . .

[But surely Mr Herzen, who knows very well what the representations of the sense of touch are as distinct from the sense of vision, cannot be ignorant of the fact that without the influence of vision, elevation and depression as such cannot become objects of touch *. . .]

* I doubt this—Berkley's Essay on Vision and the Inferences drawn from it by Plʳ & others require sifting.[1]

6   I 200–1 | § 420

[Note:] *Plato* . . . redet von seinem ewigen *Weltideal* in dem göttlichen Geiste, und von den *Ideen* desselben, welche sich in die Geschlechter . . .

---

all systems claiming universal validity by rejecting dogmatism and holding generally to the view that "all human representations have the appearance of being nothing but relations: consequently, one cannot be sure of their objective reality" (pp 361–2, tr).

4[1] "Mode of procedure", as in JACOBI *Ueber die Lehre* **4** n 4 and **15** (at n 4).

4[2] That "I Am in part". There may be echoes of Paul's "now I know in part" (1 Cor 13.12) here.

4[3] "Contradistinguished from".

4[4] The formulation is obscure. Perhaps C means the finite polarity (positive and negative) in its apprehension of the absolute polarity.

5[1] Platner cites (p 199n) Berkeley's *Principles of Human Understanding* but does not mention the *Essay towards a New Theory of Vision* (1709) by name. C identifies Berkeley's work as an influence on Platner, thinking perhaps of §§ 49–65 of the *Essay*, in which Berkeley accounts for the perception of magnitude of objects and concludes: "As we see distance, so we see magnitude. And we see both in the same way that we see shame or anger in the looks of a man. Those passions are themselves invisible, they are nevertheless let in by the eye along with colours and alterations of countenance, which are the immediate objects of vision . . ." (*B Works* I 195).

wie Stempel abgedrückt hätten, sodann auch die erschaffenen Geister er-
füllten, und in der menschlichen Seele die angebohrne Wissenschaft der
Wahrheit, Vollkommenheit, Tugend und Schönheit ausmachten: in
solchen Ausdrücken, als ob er wirkliche, für sich bestehende Wesen
damit meine, ja dieselben, soviel die materielle Welt anlangt, für die
thätigen und wirkenden Kräfte der endlichen Natur ansehe.

[Plato . . . speaks of his eternal *ideal world* in the divine mind and of its *ideas*, which,
having been imprinted like seals . . . on the species, were then also infused into the
created minds and constituted the innate knowledge of truth, perfection, virtue and
beauty in the human soul: and he speaks in a way that suggests that he meant real self-
subsistent beings, and that he even regarded them as far as the material world is concerned as the active and effective forces of finite nature.]

P. owns, that Substance is attributed to the Soul by mere translation from
matter—if so, what can the Spirit be but action? And is Action (ex. gr.
the actus sine potentiâ[1] = i.e. God) ~~more~~ less widersinnig,[2] than Intelligence—i.e. a species of spiritual action. Doubtless Plato believe[a] the actual being of Ideas—how could *he* do otherwise, who held Substance to
be only an abstraction from matter, and matter to be το μὴ ον?[3] Pl. is an
excellent Logician, a good Psychologist, a learned & meritorious Historian of spec. Philos. but he is not a metaphysical Self-Thinker.—

7   I 243, pencil | § 515

Ein Urtheil, sofern es wörtlich ausgedrückt ist, heisst ein Satz; und weil
alle Urtheile in wörtlicher Einkleidung gedacht und vorgetragen werden:
so werden sie . . . zugleich betrachtet als Sätze.

[A judgment that is expressed verbally is called a proposition; and because all judgments are conceived and presented in verbal clothing, they are . . . also regarded as
propositions.]

Now I should say, Ein Sätz[a] in seinen constitutiven Theilen vorgetragen,
heisst ein *Ur*theil, oder *ur*theilen heisst.[1]

8   I 261, pencil | § 546

[Note:] . . . Diesem nach kann ich schliessen: einige Dreyecke sind rund.
Denn *Figur* ist ein Merkmal von dem Subjekte Dreyeck: dem Begriffe

6[a] For "believed"   7[a] A slip for "Satz"

6[1] The "act without potentiality", a variant of the common Scholastic definition of
God invoked by C e.g. in *BL* ch 9 (*CC*) I 143
and n 2.

6[2] "Absurd".

6[3] "Non-being".

7[1] C adapts textus: "A sentence presented in its constitutive parts means a
judgment, or to judge." Playing on the etymology of *urtheilen* from *ur* ("original")
and *teilen* ("divide"), he indicates that judgment proceeds by division into primal
elements.

Figur kommt zu . . . *Rund*: also kommt Rund dem Subjekte Dreyeck zu.

[From this I can infer that some triangles are round. For *figure* is a feature of the subject "triangle": *round* . . . belongs to the concept "figure": therefore round belongs to the subject "triangle".]

Nay!—for Triangular is a (contingent) Predicate of Figure; and co-ordinate Predicates can not belong to each other.

9 I 358, pencil | § 705

[Note:] . . . er [Heraclitus] sagt ausdrücklich, dass in der Materie allzeit zweyerley widersprechende Zustände zugleich statt haben . . .

[. . . he [Heraclitus] says explicitly that in matter there are always two sorts of contradictory states at the same time . . .]

I regard as the most profound and fruitful Truth of all handed down to us from the Greek Philosophers, this assertion of Heraclitus, w̄ch Platner has grossly misconceived. Is it not possibly a true, and certainly a consistent, Idea, that all combination mental & physical subsists in a balance of opposing Energies?[1] To have seen this & acted on it, forms the permanent merit of Sir H. Davy, as a Chemist.[2]   *S. T. C.*

10 I 363–4, pencil | § 709

Die sinnlichen Vorstellungen werden, selbst von den strengsten Dogmatikern, angesehen nur als das Resultat der Verhältnisse unbekannter Objekte mit unerklärbaren Organen, und dieser wiederum mit einem durchaus unbegreiflichen Vorstellungsvermögen. Sonach sind sie nur Schein.*

[Sensory representations are regarded by even the strictest dogmatists as merely the result of the relations of unknown objects to inexplicable organs and of these, in turn, to a completely incomprehensible power of representation. They are therefore mere semblances.*]

* What means Schein in this place? *Nur* Schein too?[1] Surely, all here ad-

9[1] C similarly traces the "universal Law of Polarity or essential Dualism" to Heraclitus in *Friend (CC)* I 94*. Platner had represented Heraclitus as one of the philosophers who deny the reliability of the senses.

9[2] C's early admiration of HD led to public tributes such as that in the "Essays on Method" in *Friend (CC)* I 471, where he names him among eminent scientists in whose work poetry is "substantiated and realized in nature". In SCHELLING *Darlegung* 21 below, C says that in his electrochemical experiments HD "adopted my suggestion that all Composition consisted in the Balance of opposing Energies".

10[1] "Semblance" and "*mere* semblance", from textus: see n 2.

vanced may be allowed & yet the Result be mehr als Schein—Erscheinung nehmlich.[2]

11   I 364–5, pencil

Gäbe es ein reales Kriterium, so müssten aller Menschen Urtheile ihm anpassend seyn; * und der Einfluss der körperlichen Anlagen und Zustände, so wie der äussern Verhältnisse . . . in die menschliche Denkart, würde wegfallen.

[If a real criterion existed, the judgments of all men would have to accord with it; * and the influence on the human mind of bodily predispositions and states, as well as of external circumstances . . . would cease.]

* Who would affirm, that there can be no certain rule for calculating Eclipses, because the reason is not equally developed in all countries, and in all men of all countries?—

12   I 366–7, pencil

Diese theoretische und praktische Befolgung des subjektiven Scheines ist aber keineswegs das Werk eines von uns entdeckten Interesse . . . sie ist die unabänderliche Wirkung der Vorstellungen auf unsere uns unbekannte Natur. Mithin ist es nicht etwa eine Mässigung des Skeptizismus, wenn wir die Wirklichkeit der materiellen Welt und die Wahrheit aller unserm Erkenntnissvermögen angemessenen Denk- und Schlussarten annehmen; sondern es ist bloss das Eingeständniss von der Wirklichkeit unserer Vorstellungen, und von der weder abzuändernden, noch zu verleugnenden Herrschaft, welche sie über unser ganzes Denken und Leben ausüben.

[This compliance with the subjective appearance, both in theory and in practice, is by no means the work of an interest that we have discovered . . . it is the unalterable effect of the representations on our nature, a nature that remains unknown to us. It can therefore hardly be called a moderation of scepticism to assume the reality of the material world and the truth of all the modes of thought and inference proper to our cognitive faculty; it is instead merely the admission of the reality of our representations, and of their unalterable and undeniable rule over all our thought and life.]

* The word "unser"[1] so often repeated by Platner is a self-confessed Confutation of Scepticism, as he has stated it. What greater claims on All-

10[2] "More than semblance—namely appearance". C draws attention to the fact that *Schein* is contained in *Erscheinung*, so that the latter ("appearance") is more than the former ("illusion" or "semblance"). He comments on Kant's sharp distinction between the two in KANT *C d r V* 5 (and n 8).
12[1] "Our": in textus.

gemeingültigkeit[2] does the dogmatist make, than those contained in
§ 12?[3]

13   I 368–9, pencil | § 710

[Note:] . . . Dass *Kant* über den Skeptizismus etwas gewonnen habe, will
mir durchaus nicht einleuchten; indem seine Philosophie doch nicht über
die Subjektifität des Erkenntnisses hinauskommt, welche die Skeptiker
so wenig als die Wirklichkeit der Vorstellungen leugnen.

[It is not clear to me that Kant has triumphed over scepticism since his philosophy
does not go beyond the subjectivity of knowledge, which the sceptics do not deny any
more than the reality of the representations.]

Then the Sceptics have battled about *nothing*. That Thoughts are but
Thoughts, Perceptions only Perceptions, &c, who ever denied? and if the
Sceptics admit that certain Judgements are by the very constitution of the
Human Mind in all men, who pass them unconsciously combined with
an irresistible Sense of their necessary Truth, what & with whom are they
disputing?

14   I 370, pencil | § 711

[Note:] Wie es *Cartes* versteht, wenn er (Resp. 6.) sagt: das Widersprechende könne doch wohl vielleicht in dem göttlichen Verstande
gedenkbar seyn: das ist mir ein Räthsel/[a]

[What Descartes means when he says (Reply VI) that contradiction could perhaps be
conceivable in the divine mind, is a mystery to me./]

, das Platner niemals zu erklären bestimmt war.[1]

15   I 382–3, tipped in | § 732

[Note:] . . . Aber das will mir nicht einleuchten, wie der reine Begriff
Existenz nicht abgeleitet seyn sollte von dem Begriffe Kraft und weiter
zurück von dem Begriffe Ursache; d.h. wie er etwas anders seyn sollte
als der Begriff *Wirken*. Nach *Kants* selbsteigenen Grundsätzen . . . heisst
Existieren nichts anders als in der Erfahrung wahrnehmbar seyn: ist aber
etwas wahrnehmbar, das nicht wirke?

14[a] C changed Platner's full stop into a comma in order to incorporate his own comment

12[2] "Universal validity". The term is
used by Platner a few lines further on, p 366,
where he says that the sceptic "through his
doubts makes no claim upon universal

validity".
   12[3] Textus.
   14[1] C adds "that Platner was destined
never to explain".

[But it is not clear to me why the pure concept of existence should not be deduced from the concept of force and, prior to that, from the concept of cause; i.e. how it could be anything else but the concept of *effect*. According to Kant's own principles . . . existence means nothing other than being perceivable in experience: but is anything perceivable which does not produce an effect?]

Phil. Aphor. p. 383.

Platner confounds the simple Notion, Existence, with the occasional cause of our attention thereto—the *subject* of a conscious reflection with the exciting Means. First of all, it is sufficient to assert that the Notion of Existence is not the same with the Conception of Power—which (as far as Existence is something more or other than Being) is presupposed in order to the possibility of Existence. Secondly: neither is Existence the same with the conception of Force, i.e. Power in actu:[1] for Force presupposes both Existence & Power & the synthesis of both.[2] Lastly, Platner confounds the indivisibility of the corresponding realities with the identity of the Notions & Conceptions, *as* Notions and Conceptions. The relative Sharpness of the edge of a steel blade is indivisibly one with its relative Hardness—but Platner would not say that Sharpness and hardness are not two distinct *conceptions*. *S. T. C.*

16   I 400, pencil | § 753

[Note:] . . . Stärker sind die Einwendungen des Herrn Pr. *Kant* gegen die Beweise der Spiritualisten, da wo er auf den Grund des Begriffes Substanz dringt. Meines Bedünkens kommt nicht so viel darauf an, als dieser scharfsinnige Philosoph denkt, ob dem Selbstgefühl *Ich* eine Anschauung, vornehmlich von Beharrlichkeit und Identität, zum Grunde liegt, oder nicht. . . . Das ist keine Anschauung, sagt Herr *Kant* . . . das ist weiter nicht als die Einheit des Bewusstseyn.

[Professor Kant's objections against the evidence of the spiritualists are stronger when he probes the ground of the concept of substance. In my opinion it matters less than this perspicacious philosopher thinks, whether or not the self-consciousness *I* is grounded on an intuition, particularly of permanence and identity. . . . This is no intuition, says Mr Kant . . . this is nothing more than the unity of consciousness.]

In Kant's constant Sense of Anschauen, i.e. sine medio intueri sensualiter,[1] the Self = das Ich, is certainly not eine Anschauung[2]—but that there is possible a kind of direct Knowing, a Finding which may by fair

---

15[1] "In act".

15[2] In KLUGE 9 C distinguishes three sometimes synonymous terms: "Force is distinct from Power, Power still more so from Strength".

16[1] C goes from German to Latin: "To intuit, i.e. to apprehend through the senses without a medium".

16[2] "An intuition": in textus.

analogy be called eine geistige Ansch^{ng3} I agree with Fichte and Schelling in holding.[4]   *S. T. C.*

17 I 409, pencil | § 756

[Note:] . . . ich kenne keinen dogmatischen Idealismus als den Berkleyischen; von welchem Herr *Kant* ganz mit Unrecht, sagt, dass er den Unterschied *zwischen Traum und Wirklichkeit als unerweislich ansehe . . .

[. . . I know of no dogmatic idealism other than the Berkleian, of which Mr Kant has quite unjustly said that it regards the difference * between dream and reality as indemonstrable . . .]

* If K. meant a difference *in toto genere*,[1] he is in the right. But—

18   I 516–17, pencil | § 887

Aussernatürliche Wirkungen in der Welt seyen möglich auf die eine, oder auf die andere Weise . . . so setzt derselben Wirklichkeit, wenn die Welt regiert wird von einem unendlichen Geiste, allzeit voraus höchstwichtige Endzwecke, welche nicht anders, als durch dieses Mittel, erreicht werden können.

[Suppose that supernatural effects in the world are possible in one way or another . . . then, if the world is governed by an infinite spirit, their existence always presupposes highly important ultimate purposes which cannot be realised except by this means.]

The best view of miracles is, I think, the length, successive dependency, and convergence of a Series to some one End and that an End equally commensurate with^a Idea of God as that of the Series in the natural World.—This is Butler's view.[1]

18^a The next word should be "the", but C has omitted it in moving from one page to the next

16[3] "A spiritual intuition".

16[4] Cf C's comment on Kant's use of the term "intuition" in *BL* ch 12 (*CC*) I 289* (cited also in **2** n 3 above): ". . . here and elsewhere Kant uses the terms intuition, and the verb active (Intueri, *germanice* Anschauen) . . . exclusively for that which can be represented in space and time. He therefore consistently and rightly denies the possibility of intellectual intuitions. But as I see no adequate reason for this exclusive sense of the term, I have reverted to its wider signification . . . [i.e.] all truths known to us without a medium." The note to that passage cites support for this usage in (inter

alia) J. G. Fichte *Grundlage der gesammten Wissenschaftslehre* (Jena & Leipzig 1794) 191–3 and F. W. J. von Schelling *System des transcendentalen Idealismus* (Tübingen 1800) 51.

17[1] "*In the whole kind*", i.e. a complete difference in kind.

18[1] Joseph Butler (1692–1752), bp of Durham, considers miracles in his widely known *Analogy of Religion* (1st ed 1736) 161–8, saying, for example, that "a Miracle, in its very Notion, is relative to a Course of Nature; and implies somewhat different from it . . ." (164); and "Miracles must not be compared, to common natural Events . . .

19   I 552 | § 923

[Note:] Das Weltall, so schliesst *Xenophanes* . . . muss . . . dem Ursprung und der Dauer nach ewig seyn; aber auch . . . unendlich . . . und aus eben diesem Grunde: weil nämlich Bewegung veränderte Ortverhältnisse mehrerer Dinge voraussetzt, leerer Raum aber nicht existiert, *als ein Ganzes betrachtet,* unbeweglich seyn.

[The universe, so Xenophanes concludes . . . must . . . be eternal in respect to its origin and duration; but also . . . infinite . . . and for precisely this reason: namely because motion presupposes change in the spatial relations of different things but empty space does not exist; [the universe] *considered as a whole* [must] be immovable.]

* I cannot construe this sentence. Is there a Line dropt out?—No! I now see, that it relates to the "muss"[1] 9 lines before. But it is an awkward sentence.

20   I 598, pencil | § 982

[Note includes a quotation from Johann Georg Heinrich Feder *Institutiones logicae et metaphysicae* (Göttingen 1797):] Neque enim odium vitiorum, personae odium in sapiente fit, neque sui causa alteri malum inferre, perfectissimae naturae conveniens duci potest. Quae itaque a sanctitate summi numinis oriri possunt poenae, vel naturales esse eaeque privativae, vel iis, quae ipsa sapientissima bonitate necessariae fiunt, contentae esse videntur.

[For neither does hatred of the sins become hatred of the person, in the wise nature, nor can it be considered appropriate to the most perfect nature that for its own sake it should inflict evil on another. The punishments which can originate from the holiness of the supreme divinity therefore seem either to be natural and privative or to be included in those which become necessary because of the very existence of the most wise goodness.]

I know of no Problem so strangely refracted in the stating as this—even the far-famed Hatred of the Sin and not of the Sinner is a mere figure of Speech.

What is *Sin* but a generalization of Sinners, thought of collectively?[1]

---

but to the extraordinary Phenomena of Nature. And then the Comparison will be between, the Presumption against Miracles; and the Presumption, against such uncommon Appearances, suppose, as Comets, and against there being any such Powers in Nature as Magnetism and Electricity . . ." (167). C offered to assist Estlin in editing and annotating Butler's *Analogy* in 1798 (*CL* I 385–6). For his own annotations see BUTLER in *CM (CC)* I.

19[1] "Must" at beginning of textus.

20[1] For other comments on sin see RELLY **1**, **2**, and for a summary of C's position on the subject, see *CCD* 109–12.

21 ɪ 609, pencil | § 1008

Die Lebendigen haben für den Schmerz kein Gedächtniss; für das
Vergnügen aber Einbildungskraft, die es sogar erhöhet.

[The living have no memory for pain; but for pleasure they have imagination, which
may even heighten it.]

A Sophism. We can not reproduce the very *sensation* in either case; but
the Tortures of the Inquisition have thrown a gloom, yea, an irremovable
Horror, over the whole Being of the Sufferer during the remainder of his
Life.

22 ɪɪ [2] (verso of half-title), pencil | Moralphilosophie § 1

Wenn des Elends viel ist auf der Erde, so beruhet der Grund davon, nach
Abzug des . . . Uebels der Naturwelt, ganz allein in den moralischen
Handlungen der Menschen. Dieses ist auch denn noch wahr, wenn man
schon zugesteht, dass der Mensch nie Böses thut, um Uebels zu wirken.*

[If much misery exists on earth, one can find the reason for it, after discounting . . . the
evil of the natural world, only in men's moral actions. This is still true even if one admits that man never does anything wicked in order to bring about evil.*]

* What ў puniness of intellect does not imply "Thut er je Böses, ohne
Böses thun." Das "um—zu *wirken*," eine nichtige Frage.[1]

23 ɪɪ 50 | § 93

Der von dem Gesetze der praktischen Vernunft abhängigen Foderung,
Moralität anzunehmen als den Endzweck der Welt, ist nicht weniger entgegen das moralische Uebel, als das physische den Gründen der theoretischen Vernunft für den Endzweck der Glückseligkeit.

[The demand, which is dependent on the law of practical reason, to accept morality as
the final cause of the world, is no less contrary to moral evil than the physical is to the
grounds of theoretical reason as the final cause of happiness.]

Strange that Platner should not have seen that moral good would cease to
be *moral* good if it were the blank gift or necessary effect of any thing or
person—whereas Happiness[a] is Happiness, however we come by it.—

23[a] Written in large letters

22[1] C rephrases textus: "'. . . he ever   to *effect* [evil]' a vain question."
does evil without doing evil.' The 'in order

24   II ⁻1,ᵃ referring to II 50 | **23** textus

P. 50. It is a question withᵇ how far Plattner's Theory: that the Happiness of the World is the ultimate end of the Supreme Reason is tenible with the belief of a *creation* of the World.—Pl. affords one of a thousand confirmations of the two Genera of Men, Stagyrite & Platonic—.[1] Clear, orderly, distinct, satisfying in all CONCEPTIONS—the moment he treats of an IDEA,[2] all is mist, & blind groping, and a series of failures & tentative quæ pro quibus!—[3]

25   II 68–9 | §§ 124–36

Die Empfindung hat eben so viel Recht auszusprechen, was absolut Gut (66), als die Vernunft, was absolute Vollkommenheit ist (70, 75). Jene spricht Glückseligkeit ist das absolute Gut, weil sie allgemein begehrt; diese spricht Moralität, ist die absolute Vollkommenheit, weil sie nothwendig geachtet wird. . . . Mit dem Satze: Glückseligkeit ist das absolute und mithin allgemeine objectife Gut (67): wird nur gesagt, dass sie der Endzweck der Welt, nicht aber, dass Genuss der Glückseligkeit die höchste Bestimmung eines vernunftigen Geschöpfes sey . . . . Eine Vollkommenheit kann zwar ein Gut seyn, in der Beziehung, in welcher das Mittel ein Zweck seyn kann (43, 72): aber sie ist allemal ein relatifes Gut, nie das Absolute . . . . Nennt man also die Tugend ein Gut: so ist sie ein relatifes. Das Absolute ist die Glückseligkeit. . . . Ein grosses Mittel eines grossen Zwecks, welches noch überdem . . . einen verdienstlichen Werth hat in sich selbst . . . wird kräftiger empfohlen unter dem Titel eines Zwecks: weil der Mensch, getäuscht durch einen falschen Schein der Sprache, den Namen des Mittels weniger zu ehren pflegt.

[Sensation has just as much right to declare what is absolute good as reason has to declare what is absolute perfection (70, 75). The former says happiness is the absolute good, because it is universally desired; the latter says morality is the absolute perfection, because it is necessarily observed. . . . With the sentence "Happiness is the absolute and therefore universal objective good" (67) one merely says that it is the final aim of the world, and not that the enjoyment of happiness is the highest purpose of a rational creature . . . . Perfection can be a good to the extent that the means can be an

---

24ᵃ This note was written inside the original paper cover, which was carefully folded in to preserve the note when the volume was bound. It is written on the lower half of the page, below **28**
24ᵇ For "with me"

24[1] For C's formulation of the two classes into which all thinkers can be divided, namely Platonists and Aristotelians, see HOOKER **22** and *TT* (*CC*) I 172–3 and n.
24[2] The distinction between idea and conception—the latter merely a product of sense and understanding—came to be crucial to C: cf *C&S* (*CC*) 12–13 and n 1.
24[3] "Exchanges"—pluralizing *quid pro quo*.

end (43, 72): but it is at all times a relative good, not the absolute . . . . If then one calls virtue a good, it is accordingly relative. The absolute [good] is happiness. . . . An important means of an important purpose, which moreover . . . has a meritorious value in itself . . . is more forcefully recommended under the title of end: because man, deceived by the false appearance of language, tends less to honour the name of means.]

Surely much of this might have been spared by a definition of Happiness. Giebts Empfindung in Gott? im Geiste?[1] If not, how can that which belongs only to the Peritura, the τα μη οντα,[2] of the world of sense be the Ultimate end of the divine and human Reason? But if the word Happiness be capable of another & higher derivation, (& so the ancients used it) must it not be identical with Perfection—Vollkommenheit?—And so the Dispute becomes a Logomachy. Surely, the Happiness [of a pur]e[a] Spirit is either a contradiction [in][b] terms, or it must mean the same as actus purus arbitrii rationalis—.[3] I approve altogether of the phraseology of the Ancients; and think it a bad Symptom that the moderns call Pleasure in the aggregate Happiness. Kant appears to me to have demonstrated his Point[4]—& had he adopted the Ancient Terms few noble minds would have been startled at his opinions. In justification however of Kant, I must admit, there is something in the combination of Gluck[c] & Seligkeit revolting[5]—and that it carries with it the Smell of the Dregs in its Etymon more than Happiness.—. N.B. When I wrote the above, I had not considered the etymon of Happiness—i.e. Hap.—[6]

26   II 71 | § 145

So ist also die Tugend allerdings Zweck sich selbst; und sie hat, subjektif, keinen andern Zweck, als sich selbst oder die moralische Vollkom-

25[a] The edge of the page has been torn off here   25[b] Edge of page torn
                    25[c] For "Glück"

25[1] "Is there sensation in God? in the mind?"

25[2] "That which will perish, the things that are not".

25[3] "The pure act of rational choice".

25[4] In the *Critique of Practical Reason*, Kant argues that happiness is a secondary element of the *summum bonum*, the primary one being morality. Happiness, like morality, he says, "must postulate the *existence of God*, as the necessary condition of the possibility of the *summum bonum*" (bk 2 ch 2 sec 5, tr T. K. Abbott).

25[5] *Glückseligkeit* (in textus), a compound of *Glück* (good fortune) and *Seligkeit* (blessedness).

25[6] C has a long note of Jul–Sept 1809 (*CN* III 3558 and n) taking up Kant's ideas about happiness in the *Critique of Practical Reason* and *Metaphysic of Morals*; in that note, he traces "happiness" to "hap" or chance and draws distinctions among terms that are often treated as synonyms—happiness, blessedness, gladness, pleasure, joy. For further discussion of this point see *AR* (*CC*) 50 n 8. The earlier part of the note here may actually have been written before C made his notebook entry (therefore before the summer of 1809), or simply at a time when C was not thinking of the etymological point.

menheit. Aber weil kein subjektifer Zweck der absolut höchste seyn kann
(48): so ist ihr absolute höchster Zweck der * Endzweck der Welt . . .

[Thus virtue is indeed its own end and has subjectively no other purpose than itself or
moral perfection. But since no subjective end can be the absolutely highest (48), its
absolutely ultimate end is the * ultimate purpose of the world . . .]

* Endzweck der *Welt*—Ultimate *End* (final cause) of *the World*—what
World?—what is the World? Does the word include or exclude pure In-
telligences, *Spirits*? If the former, who is to determine the comparative
number of sensuous, intelligent, and mixed, Beings?

27 II 117 | § 220

[Note:] Der rechtschaffene Mann . . . der sich freywillig und nur um seine
Pflicht zu erfüllen, zur Armuth und zu einem äusserlich ganz freuden-
losen Leben entschloss, fühlt sich doch gewiss glückseliger . . . als, in
dem Besitz aller irdischen Güter, der Ungerechte, der sein Gewissen ver-
letzt hatte, und sich nun lebenslang wie einen schlechten, nichtswürdigen
Menschen verachten muss.

[The honest man . . . who decided on poverty and to all appearances a completely joy-
less life voluntarily and only in order to do his duty surely feels happier . . . than the
dishonest man who, in possession of all worldly goods, has violated his conscience
and must now despise himself all his life as a wicked, worthless human being.]

Is there then no stupor, no suspended animation of the pure Conscience
possible? Some of the worst men, I know, have the highest opinion of
themselves, and instead of "sich lebenslang wie schlechte, nichtswürdige
menschen zu verachten,"[1] enjoy a state of vivid Self-complacency that
might tempt the envy of many a good man struggling with his Frailty, suffering for Virtue, and yet still humbled by consciousness of manifold Infirmities.

28 II ⁻1, referring to pp 443–56 | Angewandte Moralphilosophie oder Karakteristik

[On pp 443–56 Platner states that men are not all moral in the same degree, then goes on to divide virtue into higher and lower types and establish a correspondence between these types and "mannered" and "unmannered" classes in society:] Einleitung. Ueber den Unterschied des
Karakters der höhern, und der niedern Tugend; an sich selbst und in Hinsicht auf die zwey Stände der bürgerlichen Gesellschaft. . . . Auf diesen
Zweck der bürgerlichen Verfassung beziehen sich, in kultifierten Staaten,

---

27[1] "Despising themselves all their lives   textus.
as   wicked,   worthless   men"—adapting

die mannichfaltigen Klassen der beschäftigten Mitglieder der Gesellschaft. Einige sorgen für Gesundheit, Erkenntniss, Religion, Tugend,
Geschmack, Sicherheit, Freyheit und Recht. Andere arbeiten für die
Nothwendigkeiten, Bequemlichkeiten und für die Lust des menschlichen
und bürgerlichen Lebens. Jene machen überhaupt den gesitteten, diese
machen den ungesitteten Stand aus.

[Introduction. On the difference of the characteristics of lower and higher virtue; considered in itself and with reference to two classes of civil society . . . . In cultivated
states, the various classes of the employed members of society apply themselves to
this objective of the civil constitution. Some attend to health, knowledge, religion,
virtue, taste, security, freedom and law. Others work for the necessities, comforts and
for the pleasure of human and civic life. The former constitute the mannered class of
the whole, the latter the unmannered class.]

P. 443 and following pages.

Platner's Division of Mankind into Mannered and unmannered, the
former comprehending the Nobility, Gentry, and liberal Professions—the
latter all the rest of Mankind; and the assignment of different *sorts* of
Virtue to each Division—is really from the coolness, with which it is
done, a positively *Comic* specimen of Aristocratic Prejudice—

PLATO

c 427–347 BC

The Cratylus, Phacdo, Parmenides and Timaeus of Plato. Translated from the Greek by Thomas Taylor. With notes on the Cratylus, and an explanatory introduction to each dialogue. London 1793. 8°.

Wordsworth Library, Grasmere

Inscribed by WW on title-page: "Wm Wordsworth". Unopened (1987) pp 49–128. On p $^+$4 (p-d), a few figures: "[? 120] 1818". Passages marked with a pencil line in the margin pp 178–80, 181, 182–3, 185, 186, 187, 195, 197, 198, 200, 205, 208, 226, 227–8, 237–8: all these occur in the *Phaedo*, and do not appear to have been marked by C. One sentence is marked in ink (not by C) p 229. Copy of a letter by H. E. Cookson from *TLS* 25 Nov 1926 attached to p $^−$2. Letter to Ernest de Selincourt 31 Jul 1939 from Cookson, donating the book to the Wordsworth Trust, loose in vol.

CONTENTS. [iii]–xi Preface; [xv]–xxiii Introduction; 1–134 *Cratylus*; [135]–243 *Phaedo*; [245]–365 *Parmenides*; [367]–554 *Timaeus*.

DATE. May–Jul 1810, or earlier. C did most of his reading of Thomas Taylor's translations of Plato and the Platonists very early in his (C's) career, c 1794–1800, but a group of notebook entries of May–Jul 1810 (*CN* III 3802, 3824, 3901, 3934, 3935 and nn) show a spurt of interest in Platonism and Taylor that tends to support the later date.

1   p 454, pencil | *Timaeus* 27C–29D

§I. TIM[AEUS]. Indeed, Socrates, since those who participate but the least degree of wisdom, in the beginning of every undertaking, whether small or great, call upon divinity, it is necessary that we (unless we are in every respect unwise) who are about to speak concerning the universe, whether it is generated or without generation, invoking the gods and goddesses, should pray that what we assert may be agreeable to their divinities, and that in the ensuing discourse we may be consistent with ourselves. And such is my prayer to the gods, with reference to myself; but as to what respects the present company, it is necessary to pray that you may easily understand, and that I may be able to explain my meaning about the proposed subjects of disputation. In the first place, therefore, as it appears to me it is necessary to define what that is which is always *real being*, but

139

is without generation; and what that is *which is generated indeed*, or *consists in a state of becoming to be*, but which never *really* is. The former of these indeed is apprehended by *intelligence* in conjunction with *reason*, since it always subsists according to *fame*. But the latter is perceived by *opinion* in conjunction with *irrational sense*; since it subsists in a state of generation and corruption, and never truly is. But whatever is generated is necessarily generated from a certain cause. . . .

§2. I denominate therefore this universe *heaven*, or the *world*, or by any other appellation in which it may particularly rejoice. . . . To discover therefore the *artificer* and *father* of the universe is indeed difficult; and when found it is impossible to reveal him through the ministry of discourse to all men.

§3. Again, this is to be considered concerning him, I mean according to what paradigm extending himself, he fabricated the world. Whether towards an exemplar, subsisting according to that which is always the same, and similarly affected, or towards that which is generated. But indeed if this world is beautiful and its artificer good, it is evident that he looked towards an eternal exemplar in its fabrication. But if the world be far from beautiful, which it is not lawful to assert, he necessarily beheld a generated instead of an eternal exemplar. But it is perfectly evident that he regarded an eternal paradigm. For the world is the most beautiful of generated natures, and its artificer the best of causes. . . . But to describe its origin according to nature is the greatest of all undertakings. . . . But that when we speak concerning the image of that which is immutable, we should employ only probable arguments, which have the same analogy to the former as a resemblance to its exemplar. And indeed as essence is to generation, so is truth to faith. You must not wonder, therefore, O Socrates, since many things are asserted by many concerning the gods and the generation of the universe, if I should not be able to produce the most approved and accurate reasons on so difficult a subject . . .

This seems to be a most beautiful mode of Prayer.—1st to give the mind certain definite objects of Thought by utterance of words; & then leaving the mind in silence to attach to those Thoughts, undisturbed by an ⟨exertion⟩ of the will in the motion of the organs, or by impressions on the bodily senses, a *feeling* of Devotion & Dependence.

2   p 455, pencil | 1 textus

I can not believe, but there must be *sense* at least under all the Passages, however nonsensical in appearance, of a work written by one and the same mind, and in the same æra of its powers, that could write so excellent a passage, as the whole of § I, and 2, and 3.—

3 p 457, pencil | 29D–E

TIM. Let us declare then on what account the composing artificer constituted generation and the universe. The artificer indeed was good: but in that which is good <u>envy</u> never subsists about any thing which has being.

envy, φθονος, better rendered by ~~intention~~ arbitrary *withholding*.[1]

4 pp 457–8, pencil | 30A

For as the divinity was willing that all things should be good, and that as much as possible nothing should be evil; [a]hence, receiving every thing visible, and which was not in a state of rest, but moving with confusion and disorder, he reduced it from this wild inordination into order, considering that such a conduct was by far the best. For it[b] neither ever was lawful, nor is, for the best of causes, to produce any other than the most beautiful of effects.

requires a Comment. I seem to anticipate that I could expound it into a meaning, that did not imply the co-eternity of ⟨actual⟩ Chaotic Matter with the Deity. Thus: God's *Idea* of the visible Universe included the opinions it would occasion in men, as ⟨a vi: universe⟩[c] self-subsistent; yet so that they would attribute its order & beauty to an interfusion of an alien & intellectual Arbitrement. But as this visible world, quoad visible,[1] subsists in *Opinion*, the idea of the opinion ~~of~~ would be the idea & ⟨would⟩ constitute the *order* in the divine mind, of this production of the Opinion—He himself for ever abiding the sole absolutely *actual* Being. I would however, I had the Commentary of Proclus on this Dialogue.[2]

S. T. C.—

4[a-b] Marked with a brace in the margin   4[c] Insertion possibly in another hand

3[1] Plato's argument is that God, being free of *phthonos* ("envy" or "jealousy"), would wish all his creatures to be as like himself as possible. "Meanness" in the distribution of his gifts would be a reasonable translation, but it is noteworthy that in Jun 1810, referring specifically to this passage, C himself used the word "jealous": *CN* III 3901. On Taylor as a translator see PROCLUS **3** below).

4[1] "Insofar as it is visible".

4[2] A memorandum of Jan 1808 (*CN* III 3276) shows C determined "to hunt for Pro-

clus"; the editor's note indicates the state of his knowledge of Proclus about that time, and points out that in the summer of 1810 he specifically recommended his *Commentary on the Timaeus of Plato* (*CN* III 3934 and n), which was at that time available in print only in an edition of 1534. It is not clear whether in this note C is still hoping to acquire the *Commentary*, or regretting that he does not have his own copy to hand, but he is not known to have used it or quoted from it.

5   p 457, pencil | 30в; continues **4** textus

In consequence of a reasoning process, therefore, he found that among
the things naturally visible, there was nothing the whole of which if void
of intelligence could ever become more beautiful than the whole of that
which is endued with intellect: and at the same time he discovered, that
it was impossible for intellect to accede to any being, without the inter-
vention of soul.

(I doubt)

6   p 458, pencil | 30d

For the divinity being willing to assimilate this universe in the most exquisite degree, to that which is the most beautiful and every way perfect
of intelligible objects, he composed it one visible animal, containing
within itself all such animals as are allied to its nature.

admirable.

PLOTINUS

205–270

Plotini Platonicorum facile coryphaei operum philosophicorum omnium libri LIV. in sex enneades distributi. Ex antiquiss. codicum fide nunc primùm Graecè editi, cum Latina Marsilii Ficini interpretatione & commentatione. Basle 1580. F°.

Collection of N. F. D. Coleridge

Inscribed "S. T. C." on title-page; bookplate of DC ⁻5 (p-d); inscribed by C on ⁻2 "S. T. Coleridge | 14. Dec. 1805. | Naples. | d. D.—". A number of newspaper clippings, some of them dated 1832, are loose in the vol.

MS TRANSCRIPTS. (*a*) by EHC, in the volume; (*b*) VCL LT 50 (k), in an unidentified hand. A copy owned by C but not annotated by him is in the British Library: C 126 1 8.

DATE. Possibly as early as Dec 1805 when it was acquired, but the hand looks later; possibly as late as 1832 when the newspaper clippings were tucked in. A plausible intermediate date is about 1814–15, when quotations from the Greek text appear in C's "Essays on . . . Genial Criticism" (*SW & F—CC*—379) and in *BL* chs 6, 12 (*CC*) ɪ 114–15, 240*.

1   p ⁻2

It is one of Kant's greatest errors, that he speaks so slightingly of Psychology/ and the weakest parts of his System are attributable to his want of the habits & facts of Psychology[1]—which with all its imperfections & uncertainty is next to necessary in order to prevent Metaphysics from passing into Theosophy and Theurgy—i.e. Dreaming & Conjuring. How can we otherwise explain the woful fact of the contemptible Spirit-raising, and wizardry of Plotinus, Porphyry, and Proclus?[2]

2   sig [α 5ʳ] | Proemium (by Ficino)

Divinitùs profectò videtur effectum, ut dum Plato quasi renasceretur, natus Picus heros sub Saturno suo Aquarium possidente, sub quo & ego

---

[1] C makes a similar remark in KANT *Grundlegung* 1: ". . . Kant, & all his School, are miserable Reasoners, in Psychology & particular Morals".

[2] This observation is given more expansive treatment in **4, 5,** and **6** below.

143

similiter anno prius trigesimo natus fueram: ac perveniens Florentiam, quo die Plato noster est editus, antiquum illud de Plotino herois Cosmi mihi prorsus occultum, sed sibi coelitus inspiratum, idem et mihi mirabiliter inspiravit.

[It seems truly to have been brought about by divine agency that the late Pico, born (while Plato was being born anew, as it were) with his star Saturn occupying Aquarius (under which star I too had been born thirty years earlier), and arriving in Florence on the day my Plato was published, marvellously inspired me with that old project of the late Cosimo concerning Plotinus, which was then totally unknown to me but communicated to him by the inspiration of heaven.]

Singular! that this same Picus so astrologically fraternized wrote a work in 7 books against Astrology—a work of great merit.[1]

3   sig [α 6^r] | Exhortatio (by Ficino)

Mementote praeterea, vos haud quaquam vel <u>sensu</u> comite, vel humana <u>ratione</u> duce, sed <u>mente</u> quadam sublimiore excelsam Plotini mentem penetraturos.

[But remember that it is certainly not with <u>sense</u> as your teacher, or with human <u>reason</u> as your guide, but by a sort of exaltation of the <u>mind</u> that you will enter into the supreme mind of Plotinus.]

[1]_____ = the understanding confining itself to facts and images given by the Senses.

_____ = the understanding extending itself by abstractions, general terms, and analogical deductions

= the mind bearing witness to new Truths by acts of direct self-intuition/ without images or general terms.

4   sig β 4^r | Plotini vita (by Porphyry)

[Shoulder-note:] *Plotinus magorum maleficia superavit: daemonem suum divinum vidit: paucis indiciis mirabiliter divinabat.*

2[1] Pico della Mirandola (1463–94) *Disputationes adversus astrologiam divinatricem*, in twelve books, the first and only completed part of a projected sevenfold attack upon enemies of the Church. C probably knew of it through Christoph Meiners's biographical and bibliographical study of Pico, from which C took some notes in 1798–9 (*CN* I 374n): "Ueber das Leben und die Schriften des Grafen Johannes Picus von Mirandula" *Lebensbeschreibungen berühmter Männer aus den Zeiten der*

Wiederherstellung der Wissenschaften (Zürich 1795–7) II 3–110, esp 90–105. Ficino was, as he says, thirty years older (1433–99). Ficino's translation of Plotinus into Latin, which Pico inspired, was first printed 1492; the Greek was not printed until 1580, as the title-page announces.

3[1] The underlined words in the textus—in the nominative *sensus, ratio, mens*—are understood to fill the three gaps before the equals signs in this note.

[*Plotinus rose above the wickedness of the magicians: he saw his own divine genius: he saw the truth marvellously from a few clues.*]

One among the many lamentable effects of Despotism with civil Wars, is this monstrous conjunction of philosophy with magic—Gloom from perpetual insecurity, and hopeless alienation from the duties and honorable aims of public Life will always generate Superstition/ Hence Logic, Geometry, Rhetoric, and moral Philosophy have been the offspring of Republics—but Theosophy and its half-brother Witchcraft, or Diabolosophy,[1] of Empires that have been military Democracies under a succession of Dictators.[2]—In the present instance it is impossible to say, how much of this infamous Imposture was a *scheme* of the Pagans to counteract Christianity and invalidate the evidence of Miracles by reducing it into an αδιαφορον τι,[3] to be found on each side. The lofty speech of Plotinus, 14th line overleaf, appears a blasphemous imitation of Christ.[4]

5   sig β 4[v]

Quum igitur ex diviniorum ordinc Dæmonum familiarem sibi Plotinus haberet, merito & ipse semper divinum suae mentis oculum ad illum sublimius erigebat. Quam etiam ob causam de suo cuiusque familiari Dæmone librum deinde composuit: ubi sanè conatur causas de familiarium numinum differentia diligenter afferre.

[Thus Plotinus had for indwelling spirit a Being of the more divine degree, and he kept his own divine spirit unceasingly intent upon that inner presence. It was this preoccupation that led him to write his treatise upon *Our Tutelary Spirit*, an essay in the explanation of the differences among spirit-guides. (Tr Stephen MacKenna)]

Quere.
    Whether Witchcraft in Christendom did not originate in concealed Paganism, after the establishment of Christianity by penal Laws? Idolatry divorced from the [? right/light] Fancy and from local and national associations, and practised under the influence of Terror and in Secrecy would very soon pass into Witchcraft: and would often be mistaken for it. An

---

4[1] "Devil-wisdom", not in *OED*.
    4[2] C's interest in accounts of witchcraft, possession, etc. is well documented—e.g. in MORE *Theological Works* 1 n 8; *Friend* (*CC*) II 117, 118*; *Lects 1808–1819* (*CC*) II 196–211.
    4[3] "Something indifferent". The adjective is common in theological usage, applied to beliefs or rites not essential for salvation: cf BAXTER *Reliquiae* COPY A 31

and n 2.
    4[4] C alludes to the response of Plotinus when he was invited to join in the observation of holy days: "It is for those Beings to come to me, not for me to go to them" (tr Stephen MacKenna). No close NT parallel has been found; remoter ones might include John 14.23, "If a man love me . . . we [I and my Father] will come unto him, and make our abode with him."

accurate examination of the oldest Writers and judicial records of Wizards, Witches, &c might perhaps detect various remnants of ancient Sacrifices & sacrificial rites and libations.

6 sig β 4ᵛ

Plotinus, ꝑ this Plato under a huge Despotism, O Shame! a vulgar Conjurer, Cunning Man, White-witch, and Caster of Nativities!![1] Verily, who can wonder at the Victory of Christianity over Paganism, when the Heroes of the Latter were so sunk in anility!

6[1] In these pages, Porphyry tells of Plotinus's involvement in conjuring (an Egyptian priest summons up Plotinus's own presiding spirit) and mentions that Plotinus foretold the future of the children entrusted to his household.

POETAE MINORES GRAECI

Poetae Minores Graeci. Hesiodus, Theocritus, Moschus, Bion *Smyrn.*, Simmias *Rhod.*, Musaeus, Theognis, Phocylides, Pythagoras, Solon, Tyrtaeus, Simonides, Rhiânus, Naumachius, Panyasis, Orpheus, Mimnermus, Linus, Callimachus, Evenus *Par.*, Eratosthenes, Menecrates, Posidippus, Metrodorus fragmenta quaedam. Philemonis, Alexidis, Amphidis, Anaxandridae, Antiphanis, Apollodori, Diphili, Menandri, Diodori *Sinop.*, Eubuli, Hipparchi, Nicostrati, Pherecratis, Philippi, Philippidae, Sotadae, Cratêtis, Eriphi, Posidippi, Timoclis, Clearchi. Et aliorum incertorum autorum. . . . Accedunt etiam observationes Radulphi Wintertoni in Hesiodum. London 1712. 8°.

Private collection

Bookplate of DC.

DATE. Early, perhaps even earlier than the c 1807 note in PERSIUS which also expresses gratitude to the editor—though for quantity of apparatus rather than for quantity of text.

1 p ¯3 (p-d)

Honour & praise to Ralph Winterton/[1] Oh that we had more such instead of your ponderous Note-makers. There should be a [? twin] collection of the Greek Lyrical Poets as a companion to this.

1[1] The editor of the collection.

SIR JOHN PRINGLE
1707–1782

Observations on the Diseases of the Army. 5th ed rev. London 1765. 4°.

Not located; marginalia printed from MS TRANSCRIPT.

MS TRANSCRIPT. VCL LT 69 (by Mary Coleridge?).

DATE. 8 May 1821 (1).

1 p 7 | Pt 1 ch 1

In proportion to the coolness of the season, to the height and dryness of the grounds, this fever [gall-sickness] is milder, remits or intermits more freely, and recedes farther from the nature of a continued putrid, or an ardent fever. But to judge from its worst state, we must refer most of the symptoms to a septic origin; since these fevers are attended with intense heat and drought, foulness of the tongue, bitterness in the mouth, desire of acids, a *nausea*, aversion to animal food, offensive vomitings, great oppression about the stomach; sometimes with livid spots, and the like indications of corrupted humours. And as, with such symptoms, the disease still puts on an intermitting or remitting form, it should seem as if even the more benign intermittents of the season were owing, in a lesser degree, to the same cause.

8th May 1821.

Sir J. Pringle's septic hypothesis is well worthy of attention, and is capable of great enlargement by distinction of species, though I should prefer the wider and generic name of Virus to the unnecessarily narrow one of septic or putrid Principle.[1] There seem to me three distinct kinds, as the origin of the three genera of Fevers.[2]

1[1] In this book, a classic in the history of medicine, Pringle revived and redefined the term "septic" and the phrase "septic principle". The "septic principle" is that which causes rotting or putrefaction. Pringle's experiments led him to identify chalk, ground shells, and table salt as the most common "septics" (xxxv) for the way in which they accelerate the process of decomposition in meats and other substances. C suggests "virus" as a wider term for any noxious matter introduced into the body or generated by the body itself in response to the introduction of foreign matter.

1[2] The classification of fevers varied considerably in the medical literature of the period. Pringle himself categorises the fevers to which members of the army were subject according to the seasons (summer, winter) and places (camp, garrison) in

1. The Hydroseptic or vegeti-aqueous,[3] originating agues, &c., from the mild Intermittents of Essex, to the Fever of the Pontine Marshes,[4] in which the violence of the poison prevents the reaction, or rather counter-action of the Arterial system. 2. The aero-septic, or chemico-atmospheric. Typhus and Plague. 3. Zooseptic[5]—Small Pox, and those Fevers which do not regularly recur to the same Patient. The *second*, or aero-septic, may or may not derive its materials from animal corruption, which is then rendered poisonous by chemical combination; but the third, or *Zoo*septic, is a Poison elaborated by the Life itself in the living Body, that is both its parent and its birthplace. Hence its greater affinity with the living Principle, and the fact, that it can be as it were familiarized and domesticated with the living Principle, as in the majority of inoculated variolous cases, with so little disturbance of the Organs, and the Organic Functions.—To these may be added, perhaps, the disputed Synocha,[6] or pure inflammatory Fever from undue excitement of the Arteriality or the Irritable system,[7] from excessive exercise of the muscles and respiratory Organs, as in harvesting, running races, and so forth; though it is to be expected, that if not removed by depletion, abstraction of Heat, et similibus,[8] it will soon affect the other systems, and only in the earlier stages therefore exist and appear as pure inflammatory Fever.

Thus then we should have four kinds of Fever, which may likewise be named in reference to the systems attacked, or the primary seats and objects of the disease. 1. The Synocha or the Fever of Irritability. 2. The remittent and intermittent, from injury and disturbance of the Skin and reproductive system, and the reactions set up by Nature to counterpoise this, and restore the balance of the Powers. 3. The *Nervous*, &c. Typhus, and Typhoid Fevers. 4. Affection of the Life or vital Principle, as the

---

which they occurred. Gall-sickness he describes as a bilious or autumnal or intermitting fever, different from inflammatory fever and from hospital or pestilential fever (73).

1[3] "Water-septic" or "plant-and-watery".

1[4] Swamps and bogs were such notorious breeding-grounds for illness that physicians discussed marsh fever as a distinct disease arising, it was believed, from "marsh miasma": cf William Cullen *First Lines of the Practice of Physic* (4 vols Edinburgh 1796) I 126–8. The Pontine Marshes of Rome were a well-known malarial area (though Pringle does not mention them specifically in his account of marsh fever). In the spring of 1832, when

the physicians of London were struggling with a cholera epidemic, C discussed the range of contagious diseases in terms very similar to those used here: cf *CL* VI 888 and *TT (CC)* I 282–3, esp n 3.

1[5] "Life-septic": C goes on to explain.

1[6] The ancient name for a continued, unremitting fever. Pringle, who makes a point of avoiding medical jargon as much as possible (x), does not appear to use the term.

1[7] C came to identify the "surface" power of electricity in nature and of irritability in living creatures with the bloodstream, perhaps because of the visibility of veins near the surface of the body: cf e.g. *TL* in *SW & F (CC)* 557.

1[8] "And by like things".

Root, Unity, or Band of the three Constituent Powers, and yet subsisting for itself, as a distinct and *inwarder* Power, and under certain conditions and circumstances capable of being affected singly, while neither the Systems nor the Organs, in which they are severally predominant, are affected, either structurally or functionally; or so slightly at least, as to bear no proportion to the Affection or Change which the Life or Vital Principle is undergoing.   S. T. C.

THOMAS PRINGLE

1789–1834

African Sketches. London 1834. 8°. Proofs of pp 3–18, containing *The Bechuana Boy, Afar in the Desert, Song of the Wild Bushman*, and the first five pages of *The Coranna*.

South African Library, Cape Town

Pringle himself has made some corrections to pp 15, [16], 17, 18. The presentation copy of the published vol is in VCL. For another gift to C from Pringle see ANALYSIS.

DATE. Early 1834: the work was pub May 1834 (*EC*).

1   p [3]*ᵃ*

I am, I fear, becoming fastidious, I daresay, there may be several "'neaths' in my own poems[1]—worse barbarisms, I am sure, there are!—But purity of Style, and even *severe* propriety of Words, appear to me more and more, the especial Duty of a Poet—who whatever political party he may favor, ought in this respect to be at once a *Radical* and a *Conservative*. For this reason I suggest the following alterations—   S. T. C.[2]

2   pp [3]–4 | *The Bechuana Boy* lines 1–16

I sat at noontide in my tent,
   And <u>looked across</u> the Desert dun,
   <u>That</u> 'neath the cloudless firmament
   Lay gleaming in the sun,

1*ᵃ* Unnumbered by printer; someone (not C) has put a number "2" in by hand

1[1] C suggests changing "'neath" to "beneath" in **2** below.

1[2] Pringle, a Scot, had emigrated to South Africa in 1820 but returned in 1826, settling eventually in Highgate. C warmly praised his poem *Afar in the Desert* when Pringle introduced himself in 1828 (*CL* VI 732), and subsequent letters reflect their shared interests in literature and in the abolition movement (Pringle became Secretary of the Anti-Slavery Society in 1827).

Pringle intervened on C's behalf in the effort to get funds from the government to make up for his lost annuity (*CL* VI 867), and published several of C's poems in *Friendship's Offering* in 1834. In the revised (published) version of these opening stanzas, Pringle changed lines 3, 8, 9, 10, and 12 as C directed, and used a semicolon for C's colon in line 7; his revised line 11 reads, "Caressing with a gentle hand".

When from the bosom of the waste
A swarthy Stripling came in haste,
With foot unshod and naked limb,/:
And a tame Springbok following him.   (ʼd)

He came with open aspect bland,
   And modestly before me stood,
Caressing with a kindly hand
      That Fawn of gentle brood;
Then, meekly gazing in my face,
Said in the language of his race,
With smiling look yet pensive tone,
"Stranger—I'm in the world alone!"

? With open ⟨fearless?⟩ Aspect, frank yet bland
  And with a modest mien he stood,
Caressing gently with his hand
    The Beast of gentle brood:

3   p 4 | Lines 17–32

/\"Poor boy!" I said, "thy kindred's home,
   Beyond far Stormberg's ridges blue,
Why has thou left so young, to roam
    This desolate Karroo?"
The smile forsook him while I spoke;
And when again he silence broke,
It was with many a stifled sigh
He told his hapless history.

"I have no <u>kindred!" said</u> the boy: ⟨Home! replied⟩
   "The Bergenaars—by night they came,
And raised their murder-shout of joy,
    While o'er our huts the flame
Rushed like a torrent; and their yell
Pealed louder as our warriors fell
In helpless heaps beneath their shot:
—One living man they left us not!

? /\ Poor Boy! (I said) I've seen thy Home,
  Be~~yond~~hind yon Stromberg's ridges blue:
Why hast thou left it, Boy! to roam
    This desolate Karroo?

a"His face grew sadder while I spoke:
The Smile forsook it; and he broke
Short Silence with a sob-like sigh,
And—[1]

3*a* The first part of the note is at the foot of the page, but the remainder, from this point, in the left-hand margin

3[1] Pringle's revised version of lines 17–18 reads "'Poor boy!' I said, 'thy native home / Lies far beyond the Stormberg blue: . . .'". In the remainder of the passage he has followed all C's suggestions.

PROCLUS

412–485

The Philosophical and Mathematical Commentaries of Proclus, on the First Book of Euclid's Elements. To which are added, a history of the restoration of Platonic theology, by the latter Platonists: and a translation from the Greek of Proclus's Theological Elements. [By Thomas Taylor.] 2 vols. London 1792. 4º.

British Library C 126 l 9

Initials "S. T. C" on the title-page of Vol II. Inscribed on I ‾6 by John Duke Coleridge: "C | Coleridge | Heath's Court | 1892 | This book belonged to S. T C— ". "S. T. C." label on the title-page of each volume. A typographical error has been corrected on I iv, possibly by C.

DATE. Between 1808 and 1810, probably 1810. Although he had some acquaintance with his works in 1803 (*CN* I 1727, 1728 and App. B), it was in Jan 1808 that C made a determined memo to "hunt for Proclus" (*CN* III 3276); in Jan 1810 he comments on the inadequacy of Taylor's translation (*CL* III 279); between May and Jul 1810 occasional references to Proclus may or may not be associated with this translation (*CN* III 3802, 3934).

---

1   I cxxvii | Thomas Taylor "A Dissertation on the Platonic Doctrine of Ideas, &c." Sec 4 § 6

But after science, and its study, it will be necessary to lay aside compositions, divisions, and multiform discourses, and from thence to ascend to intellectual life, to its simple vision, and intimate perception. For science is not the summit of knowledge, but beyond it is intellect; not that intellect only which is separated from soul, but the illustration infused from thence into the soul, which Aristotle affirms to be the intellect by which we acknowledge the principles of science; and Timaeus says, that this exists in no place but the soul.

It is unfortunate that the English Platonic Philosophers should have been misled by the Latins constantly to translate the word, Νοῦς, by *Intellect*— which yet is clearly synonnimous by right of its Etymon with Understanding[1]—Now in our Language we have no means of emxpressing the

---

[1] The Latin verb *intellegere*, meaning to perceive, apprehend, understand, shares the root of "intellect", and most English translators and commentators have found it

154

superior & ⟨the⟩ inferior faculty of knowing, each contradistinguished, except by the words, *Reason*, and Understanding—Νοῦς therefore in English ought to be translated "pure Reason"—.[2] The great question between the Masters of the new and of the newest Philosophy, the *Kant*eans and the *Fich*teans or *Schelling*ites as to the existence of intuitive *Intellect*, (i.e. ⟨intuitive⟩ *Reason*) or intellectual Intuition, might perhaps be softened by the adoption of some such phrase, as Possession, συναφη,[3] or inhabitation, or immanence—or lastly knowlege by immanence.—or better than all perhaps, by the words "immediate Perception", or "impassive & *actual* Perception."—At least, the Question would then be reduced to a question of the Fact—& not be obnoxious to any dispute or misunderstanding from an equivoque—the one taking it the word "intuition" in the literal, the other in an analogical Sense.[4]

2 i cxxviii

When you have ascended thither, and are placed among incorporeal beings, you will behold above the fluctuating empire of bodies, the sublime animal order, self-moving, spontaneously energizing in itself, and from itself possessing its own essence, yet multiplied, and anticipating in itself a certain apparition or image of the essence divisible about the unstable order of bodies.

vital—eine wirkende, lebendige *Ordnung—ordo ordinans*.[1]

3 I 44 | Proclus *Commentaries* bk 1 ch 1 "On the Middle Nature of the Mathematical Essence"

It is necessary that the mathematical essence should neither be separated from the first nor last genera of things, nor from that which obtains a sim-

convenient or necessary to use the Latin-derived family of words (intellect, intelligible, intellectual, etc) as technical terms corresponding to the neoplatonic *nous, noeton, noeron*, etc. QUARTERLY REVIEW 27 n 1 raises a related issue.

1[2] One of C's extended attempts to distinguish reason from understanding appeared in the 1809–10 *Friend* (*CC*) II 294–7, where a further qualification produces "the pure Reason" (295). C continued to use "pure reason" as his own rendering of *nous*: cf *Logic* (*CC*) 33, 34.

1[3] Greek *synaphe*, "conjunction" or "grasp". For other uses of this and related terms see *CN* II 2167 and n, III 4351, 4381;

BÖHME **24** n 9.

1[4] This area of disagreement about the concept of intuition between Kant and the German Idealists who followed him is outlined in PLATNER **16** n 4 above.

2[1] "An active, living *order*—an *ordering order*". C uses the latter phrase also in *BL* ch 9 (*CC*) I 160. The words are Fichte's, defending himself against a charge of atheism in "Aus einem Privatschreiben im Januar 1800" *Philosophisches Journal* IX (1800) 364–6. C adopted the Latin phrase also in a letter of 1806 (*CL* II 1189), in *BL* ch 9 (*CC*) I 160—in a passage concerned with Fichte—and elsewhere.

plicity of essence; but that it should obtain a middle situation between substances destitute of parts, simple, incomposite and indivisible, and such as are subject to partition, and are terminated in manifold compositions and various divisions.

I regret, that I have not the Original.[1] This enunciation appears (as far as I can *guess* from Taylor's strange English)[2] to approach more nearly to the great discovery of the mediation between the Intellect and the Sense by the "Intuitus puri", or "Formæ Universales Repræsentationis",[3] i.e. Space & Time, (in which subsists the possibility of the demonstrable Certainty of Geometry) than any passage that has occurred to my reading before the De Mund. Int. et Sens. of Immanuel Kant.[4] But the Translator instead of noticing this as the true solution of that Difficulty which drove Plato to his fiction of intelligible Aspections, Ideas, κατα Πλατ.[5]—with his characteristic χρηστοτητι (bonhommie)[6] brings Plato's fiction to explain the Text.[7]—I by no means suppose Proclus to have *mastered* the truth contained in this passage; yet it is educible from the words.—

S. T. C.

4 ɪ ⁻2, referring to ɪ 54–9 | Ch 6 "Concerning the Essence of Mathematical Genera and Species"

Let a prepared* Scholar attentively perused Chapter VI, Book I.. [a]⟨Con-

* *prepared*—i.e. 1. by common logic 2. by the elements of Geometry and universal Arithmetic. 3. by psychology empiric—4. by philosophical Grammar—5. by Dialectic, or transcendental Logic[1]—that which de-

4[a] C has indicated this insertion by putting a dagger † after "Chapter" and repeating the symbol, with this title, above the other footnotes after his signature

3[1] In **6** below, C says that he has never yet come across a Greek version of this text, and his remark is not contradicted by his comments on Taylor's ineptitude as a translator (n 2 below), since he had had opportunities of comparing other translations by Taylor with the originals. JHG presented him with a Greek Proclus in Nov 1820—an event noted in *CN* ɪᴠ 4744.

3[2] Cf C's view of Taylor, "difficult Greek is transmuted into incomprehensible English", in a letter of Jan 1810 to Lady Beaumont (*CL* ɪɪɪ 279). *CN* ɪɪɪ 3276n suggests that C already had access to the Greek text of *In Platonis theologiam . . . libri sex* (Hamburg 1618), part of which is tr by Taylor as *Elements of Theology* in Vol 2 of this Proclus.

3[3] "Pure intuition" or "universal forms of representation".

3[4] I.e. Kant's "Inaugural Dissertation", *De mundi sensibilis atque intelligibilis forma et principiis* (Königsberg 1770), which C may have read as early as 1800 (*CN* ɪ 887 and n), and which he wrote about with consistent enthusiasm: cf Kant *VS* copy ᴀ **3** and n 1. In the Latin here C uses Kant's own terminology to summarise and paraphrase secs 2 and 3 of the work.

3[5] "According to Plato".

3[6] I.e. with good nature (the French is *bonhomie* but the English used both this and C's spelling: *OED*).

3[7] I.e. in a footnote, 44-6, including his tr of the end of *Republic* bk 6, 509ᴅ–511ᴇ.

4[1] In *CN* ɪɪɪ 3934, the note of Jun–Jul

cerning the essence of Mathematical Genera and Species.⟩ i.e. from p. 54 to p. 59—and if possible, in the original Greek:[2] and the result in his mind will inform him, whether nature has intended him for metaphysical Research.—If I have any conception of Sublimity as arising from a majestic Vision of tranquil Truth, it will be found in this Chapter.

S. T. Coleridge.

---

termines on the legitimacy of the major or premise of every Syllogism by ~~that~~ such discrimination of the faculties, ~~which~~ as gives to each its due, & precludes false predicates, (ex. gr. accidents of time† and space of νοουμενα, the ideas of the pure Reason) & (6.) lastly, by a subdued and loving habit of Soul.

† Thus: *"whatever is anywhere, is"* is a universal position, & legitimate; but *"whatever is, is somewhere"* is false, for PLACE can be predicated necessarily, only of *phœnomena*, and the *passive* knowledge of the Soul: what is true of a part, is assumed as true of the whole.

5   I 57

If then, mathematical species do not subsist by material abstraction, nor by a collection of those common properties inherent in individuals; nor are at all, in their origin, posterior to sensibles, nor derived in any manner from them: it is necessary that the soul should either deduce them from herself, or from intellect; or lastly, from herself and intellect united.

It seems clear, that the Critical Philosophy, as contained in the works of Immanuel Kantius, is a junction of the Stoic *Moral* with the Platonic *Dialectic*: which ~~he~~ Kant has unfairly confounded with the *Sophistic* (Logik der *Schein*)[1] but which is in truth the same with his own transcendental Logic:[2] even as the Mathesis of Plato, so finely determined in this chap-

---

1810 that specifically recommends "Proclus's Platonic Theology & Elements of Theology" as part of a course of reading for clergymen, C begins by advising "the study of the true transcendental Logic—i.e.—the Logic which by strict investigation of the human faculties . . . [identifies] to what they are collectively & to what exclusively applicable". He is thinking of course of Kant's *Critique of Pure Reason*, which he later says would have been more appropriately entitled *Transcendental Logic: Logic* (*CC*) 205–6.

4[2] C himself would have *liked* to have

had the Greek text, but at this time did not, as he observes in **3** and **6**.

5[1] C is quoting Kant *C d r V* B 85–6 (tr Norman Kemp Smith): "However various were the significations in which the ancients used 'dialectic' as the title for a science or art, we can safely conclude from their actual employment of it that with them it was never anything else than the *logic of illusion*."

5[2] See **4** n 1.

5[3] "Pure intuition", as in **3** above; cf Kant's phrase at the beginning of the "Transcendental Aesthetic" in *C d r V* B 34–5 (tr

ter by Proclus, is Kant's transcendental *Æsthetic* (intuitus puri).[3] The Wissenschaftslehre of Fichte and Schelling is pura puta the Alexandrine Philosophy[4]—Fichte being to Kant, & Schelling to Fichte, as Plotinus to Plato, and ⟨as⟩ Proclus to Plotinus.—

> Kant = Plato + Zeno
> Fichte = Plotinus
> Schelling = Proclus.[5]

6　ɪ 60 | Ch 7 "What the Employments and Powers are of the Mathematical Science"

Nor is its [i.e. of the mathematical science] energy immoveable, like that of intelligence, nor is it affected with local motion and alteration, like sense, but it revolves with a vital energy, and runs through the ornament of incorporeal reasons . . .

κοσμον?[1] the *universe* of abstract reasons?—but the whole version is such that it is mere *game of Guess* to read it. I have unfortunately never met with the Original.

7　ɪ 60 | Taylor's footnote (ɪ 59–60) to ɪ 59

Every thing without generation, is incorruptible, and every thing incorruptible, is without generation . . . if it possesses a capacity of being destroyed . . . it is endued with a capacity of being destroyed and ceasing to be, in every instant of infinite time, in which it necessarily is. . . . If then the soul is essentially immortal, with respect to the past and future circulations of time; and if she is replete with forms or ideas of every kind . . . she must, from her circulating nature, have been for ever conversant in alternately possessing and losing the knowledge of these.

What a cheerless creed is this, in which the Soul ~~is~~ measures her Exis-

---

Kemp Smith): "I term all representations *pure* (in the transcendental sense) in which there is nothing that belongs to sensation. The pure form of sensible intuitions in general . . . must be found in the mind *a priori*. This pure form of sensibility may also itself be called *pure intuition*. . . . The science of all principles of *a priori* sensibility I call *transcendental aesthetic*."

5[4] I.e. the "philosophy" of Fichte and Schelling is the Alexandrine (or neoplatonic) philosophy "pure and simple". There may be an echo here of the title of one of the earliest works by Fichte that C read, *Ueber*

den Begriff der Wissenschaftslehre: *CM* (*CC*) ɪɪ 594.

5[5] It is impossible to be sure to what extent C means to make a correlation of ideas as opposed to a rough correspondence of sequence between Plato and the Platonists and Kant and the Kantians, but the combination of Plato and Zeno repeats the point made at the beginning of the note about "the Stoic *Moral*" and "the Platonic *Dialectic*".

6[1] C guesses (correctly) that the word that Taylor translates as "ornament" is the Greek *kosmon* ("order", "universe").

tence only by diminutions of Loss—and the more rapid these diminutions, the more rapid is her approximation to the State of total Loss: so that her Progression is truly at the same time a tremendous retrogression! Thank Heaven! the System may be demonstrated impossible: for according to the perfection of her reminiscences must be the difficulty & improbability of her Oblivion—and every step in advance is likewise an obstacle to retrogression—so that she would become retrograde just at that point, in which all the impulses to progression are the strongest, & the obstacles to retrogression the most & most numerous.—Besides, amid all these fine flights concerning the Soul, the Intellect, and the One, what becomes of poor "*I*"—of the *Self* of each person? Whence comes, whither goes, the personality?

8   I 69, slightly cropped | Ch 10 "A Solution of another Objection of certain Platonists, against the Utility of the Mathematical Sciences"

But, perhaps, some of our own family will here rise up against us, and, proposing Plato as a witness, will endeavour to provoke ruder understandings into a contemptuous disregard of the mathematical disciplines.

Plato is speaking of the mere mathematici[an] who rests in his science instead of using it as a means of elevating himself to a capacity of a yet higher, whic[h] attained will flow back upon & illumine the knowlege acquire[d] anteriorly, impregni[ng] it with a new and more glorious Life.[1] And he judges mos[t] wisely: for the mere Mathematician degrades his intelle[c]tual faculties into a machine, and tho' he strengthens t[he] power of attention, he injures that of *discrimination*, an[d] dwarfs the *growth* of the Soul*/*.— ~~and~~ He abstracts from the *matter* of Bodies only to become *rigid*, and (as it were) to stiffen in *its forms*—and ever remains *dead*.

                                                                    S. T. C.

9   I 76 | Ch 13 "Another Division of the Mathematical Science, according to Geminus"

[Footnote:] . . . that great reformer of philosophy, *as he is called*, Lord Bacon, commending pursuits which come home to men's businesses and bosoms. Indeed, if what is lowest in the true order of things, and best administers to the vilest part of human nature, is to have the preference, their opinion is right, and Lord Bacon is a *philosopher*!

8[1] C and Proclus are thinking of the discussion of the mathematical sciences in *Republic* 7.521–6, where they are described as a form of study able "to draw the soul away from the world of becoming to the world of being" (521D), although they can also be limited to mere "huckstering" (525D).

Southey very happily called Thomas Taylor a *Pagan Methodist!*[1] He is indeed a thorough blind Bigot, ignorant of all with which he is intoxicated—rather, with the *slang* of which he is bewitched. Every Platonist must revere Lord Bacon, as the great Restorer of the genuine Platonic Logic—viz—Progress by Induction.[2] The modern Chemists *talk* of Bacon; but with the exception of Humphrey Davy, I know of none who have not as grossly offended against his Laws of Investigation in this one extreme, as the Schoolmen did in the other.[3] The Schoolmen wished to find all things *in* their brains; the Priestleys to find every thing *without* brains.—[4]

10 i 78

[Footnote:] By this [sciography] is to be understood the art now called Perspective: from whence it is evident that this art was not unknown to the ancients, though it is questioned by the moderns.

It is strange, that it should: for Vitruvius in his 7th Book not only names its Inventor, but in the most expressive words describes the objects of Perspective, and mentions the manner in which it was borrowed from Scenic Representation, ⟨and applied⟩ to Architecture—[1]

9[1] Apparently in conversation: in the late 1790s both C and RS habitually referred to Taylor, with whom they were acquainted, as "Taylor the Pagan": *S Letters* (Curry) i 188; cf *CL* i 260.

9[2] C was to publish an essay in the 1818 *Friend* extolling Bacon as "the British Plato": *Friend* (*CC*) i 488.

9[3] For a decade or so, C praised HD as a *philosophical* chemist, but he was disappointed by what seemed to him to be Davy's defection to French principles, esp after Davy was knighted in 1812. Böhme **9** and **17** illustrate the two phases: "Humphrey Davy in his Laboratory is probably doing more for the Science of Mind, than all the Metaphysicians have done from Aristotle to Hartley, inclusive", and "Alas! Since I wrote the preceding note, H. Davy is become Sir Humphry Davy, and an *Atomist!*"

9[4] C usually refers to Joseph Priestley (1733–1804) as a leader of the Unitarian movement, but here introduces him as a prominent chemist and philosophical materialist.

10[1] C also alludes to Vitruvius *On Architecture* bk 7 in lectures on drama in 1808 and 1811: *Lects 1808–1819* (*CC*) i 46 and n 8, 347 and n 4.

BRYAN WALLER PROCTER
("BARRY CORNWALL")
1787–1874

Dramatic Scenes and Other Poems. London 1819. 12°.

Victoria and Albert Museum: Forster Collection

Inscribed on the title-page "J. F. [i.e. John Forster] from his old friend B. C.", above the signature "B. W. Procter". On p $^{+}1$, apparently in Procter's hand: "The following is in the handwriting of Samuel Taylor Coleridge". Corrections by Procter on pp 115, 140, 142, 153, 157.

In *LR* II 377n, this work is described as "Mr. Lamb's copy of the 'Dramatic Scenes'", but the marginalia were pub in the *New-York Mirror* 11 Apr 1835 as from a copy in Procter's own hands. (CL died 27 Dec 1834.) The *New-York Mirror* text includes a report of Procter's explanation: "the book was given me some years ago by a friend at whose house Coleridge had been staying, for the sake of the criticisms that great man did me the honour to write at the end" (324). C was not "staying" with CL but they paid visits back and forth. Given these facts and the tone of the marginalia, it seems likely that Procter asked his friend CL to solicit C's opinion, that CL gave C this copy and then gave it back annotated to Procter, and that HNC, receiving it for use in *LR*, either misunderstood about the ownership of the vol or chose to emphasise its association with CL. Procter himself presented a copy of his *Marcian Colonna* (1820) to C: it is now at VCL.

DATE. 30 Jul 1819 (1).

---

1   pp $^{+}1$–$^{+}3$, pencil

Barry Cornwall is a Poet, me saltem judice:[1] and in that sense of the term in which I apply it to C. LMB and WW.[2] There are poems of great merit, the Authors of which I should yet not feel impelled so to designate.—

The faults of these Poems are no less things of Hope than the Beauties—Both are just what they ought to be: i.e. NOW.

If B. C. be faithful to his Genius, it in due time will warn him that as Poetry is the *identity* of all other Knowleges, so a Poet cannot be a *great* Poet but ~~in~~ as being likewise & inclusively[a] an Historian and Naturalist

---

[a] The words following the deletion up to this point are all inserted above the line

[1] "In my opinion, at least".

[2] Charles Lamb and William Words-   worth. CL's *Works* had appeared in 2 vols in 1818.

161

in the Light as well as the Life of Philosophy.[3] All other men's ~~Knowleges~~ Worlds (κοσμοι) are *his* Chaos.[4]

Hints *obiter* are—Not to permit Delicacy & Exquisiteness to seduce into effeminacy.

Not to permit Beauties by repetition to become Mannerism/

To be jealous of *fragmentary* Composition—as Epicurism of Genius, ⟨and Apple Pie made all of Quinces.⟩

Item, that Dramatic Poetry must be Poetry *hid* in Thought and Passion, not T. or P. ⟨disguised⟩ in the dress of Poetry.[5]

Lastly, to be economic and withholding in similies, figures, &c.—They will all find their place sooner or later, each as the Luminary of a sphere of its own. There can be no *Galaxy* in Poetry; ~~but~~cause it is Language, ergo, successive, ergo, every the smallest Star must be seen singly.

There are not five Metrists in the Kingdom, whose works are known to me, to whom I could have held myself allowed to have spoken so plainly. But B. C. is a Man of Genius, and it depends on himself (Competence protecting him from gnawing or distracting Cares) to become a rightful *Poet*—i.e. a great Man.

O! for such a man worldly Prudence is transfigured into the highest spiritual Duty. How generous is Self-interest in *him*, whose true Self is = all that is good and hopeful in all ages, as far as the Language of Spencer, Shakspeare and Milton shall become the Mother Tongue!

A map of the road to Paradise drawn in Purgatory on the Confines of Hell by S. T. C.[6]—July 30, 1819.—

P.S. The pause after the second Syllable in Pentameter Iambic Blank Verse is frequent in the Poems of M[r] Southey and of his Imitators. But

---

[3] C echoes remarks made in *BL* chs 14 and 22 (*CC*) II 15–16 and 156, where he asserts that "The poet, described in *ideal* perfection, brings the whole soul of man into activity" and proclaims that WW is capable of producing "the FIRST GENUINE PHILOSOPHIC POEM".

[4] That is, the point from which creation begins—C using the conventional opposition of chaos and *kosmos*.

[5] Procter's *Dramatic Scenes* was influenced by CL's *Specimens of English Dramatic Poets who Lived about the Time of Shakespeare* (1808); C's opinion that WW was not suited to the dramatic form for which he had, however, an "undue predilec-tion" is expressed in *BL* ch 22 (*CC*) II 135.

[6] C represents himself as having almost given up hope of achieving what Barry Procter may yet achieve. The immediate context for his remark, given the association of this volume with CL, may be CL's dedication of the 1818 *Works* to him: ". . . you will find your old associate, in his second volume, dwindled into prose and *criticism. . . .* is it that, as years come upon us, (except with some more health-happy spirits,) Life itself loses much of its Poetry for us? . . . You yourself write no Christabels, nor Ancient Mariners, now": *L Works* (1903) V 1.

should it be imitated? Milton uses it, when the weight of the first Iambic, Trochee[b], or Spondee, of the second Line, requires a *pause* of preparation at the last foot of the preceding.

1[b] Having come to the foot of the page, C makes a footnote symbol and finishes the note in the space above "P.S."

QUARTERLY JOURNAL

The Quarterly Journal of Foreign Medicine and Surgery; and of the sciences connected with them. Vol I (2 pts). London Nov 1818–Aug 1819. 8°.

Not located; marginalia printed from MS TRANSCRIPT.

MS TRANSCRIPT. VCL BT 37, SC transcript.

DATE. Possibly as early as the dates of publication 1818–19, but more probably in the late 1820s, when grammar and colour-theory appear prominently in C's writings (**3** n 1, and see also **3** n 4).

---

1   p 89 | Geoffroi St Hilaire on the Operculum of Fishes

Nature constantly employs the same materials, and only displays her ingenuity in varying their forms. As if, in fact, she had been confined to certain primary data, we see her always bringing forward the same elements, in the same number, under the same circumstances, and with the same connexions. If one organ is found of an extraordinary size, the neighbouring parts are less developed; yet each of them is not the less preserved, although in a degree so minute, as frequently to render them almost useless. They become so many rudiments, which bear witness in some measure to the permanence of the general plan.

i.e. In the simplest living organism, ex. gr. the Polyp, all the powers of life are potentially contained in the lowest; but as productive power cannot be without product, we must presume even in the minimum of energy a correspondent minimum of Product—and a production bearing the character of *potentiality*, answering to the potential state of the productivity—viz. of no or obscure use to the animal, yet prophetic of an important function in some higher genus or species—or again historic of a by-gone use. *S. T. C.*

2   p 319 | A Comparative View of the Foreign and British Institutions for the Deaf and Dumb

From the number of mutes who are attached as guards and messengers to the courts and seraglios of some Eastern potentates, we may learn the general fact, that in these countries there are probably as many as in Europe; and from Mr Marianer's account of the Tonga Islands, as well as from travels and the histories of other uncivilized nations, we may infer, that it is not in civilized life only that such imperfections in the organs of hearing occur.

But how many of these Mutes are mutilated? Assuredly the Mutes of the Asiatic Courts are not all deaf: and of those who are not, it is fair to presume that a large proportion have been made mutes by extirpation of the Tongue. *S. T. C.*

3   p 331

[The author describes a class in a French school for the deaf and dumb.] The children . . . began by the alphabet both written and manual. They next proceeded to classified arrangements of substantives. To these they joined classified adjectives and next connected them by what is called absurdly the substantive verb . . . having no correspondence with anything in nature, serving merely to connect words in writing . . . . From adjectives to the class of substantives called abstract, the step is easy. The adverbs and prepositions, united with the substantives and adjectives already learned, are taught together, because it is obvious that, "with ease" and "easily" mean the same. The conjunctions follow, and are the most difficult, and though it is attempted here, as at Paris, to derive aid from grammatical philosophy, in teaching the conjunction, and indeed every other part of speech; yet, we are satisfied, that when the pupils have learned a great variety of prepositions and phrases, the difficulty of learning the conjunctions is in a great measure done away, and that it is practice alone which can surmount what remains of difficulty.

Prothesis—identity of Act and Being, or a Being essentially Act, an Act essentially Being: Noun = Verb + Verb = Noun. Verb Substantive, I AM.[1]

Thesis	Mesothesis	Antithesis
Noun	Infinitive Mood	Verb

Synthesis
Participle

The modification of the noun by the verb is the ADNOUN or Adjective: the modification of the Verb by the Noun is the *Adverb*.

Every language must have five parts of speech: no language can have more than seven. Conjunctions and Prepositions are one or the other of the preceding, but most commonly the Verb in the imperative mood—as *But*[2] i.e. divide, δε corrupt imper. from Δαω divido, δη (= then) from δεω, connecto;—or the participle.[3] The visual image, as expressing a *concrete*, is, by the frequent recurrence, made to express a *relation*, either of Time or Space—in the same way, in which Foot, Cubit, &c lose their visual image by abstraction of length. When such a word governs a whole sentence, we call it a conjunction; when only part of a sentence, a preposition: ex. gr. we encountered many obstacles; but we all went on

3[1] The prothesis is the first term in the pentad of grammar; the other terms follow. Similar expositions of "philosophical" or "universal" grammar appear in *CN* IV 4644 (Mar 1820); in the *Logic* of c 1822 (*Logic—CC*—lxv–lxvii, 16–17); in LACUNZA 45 (a note of 1827), and *TT* (*CC*) I 69–70; and esp in the letter of 16 Sept 1829 to Hyman Hurwitz (*CL* VI 818).

3[2] C may be indebted in his example to Tooke, who analysed the English conjunctions as originally the imperative forms of certain verbs, e.g. I (1798) 135, where the two meanings of "but" are traced to two Anglo-Saxon verbs, the second of which (cf the 2 in angle brackets at n 4 below) according to Tooke means "to Be-out" or to except. Tooke's main discussion of "but" appears in I 190–215. The article on which C is commenting at this point includes a footnote recommending "Horne Tooke's Observations on the conjunctions, and their derivation from verbs, &c."

3[3] C here treats the Greek particle δέ (*de*) as meaning "but" rather than "and" (it may mean either) and links it with the hypothetical verb δάω ("I divide", imperative δάε or δᾶ) and with δή ("then" or "indeed") as from δέω ("I bind", imperative δέε or δεῖ). C uses the same example in PASINI 2.

⟨2⟩[a] but (i.e. except) James.[4] An Interjection or Exclamation is no part of *Speech*, i.e. it does not express a thought, but a *sensation*, and is common to men and brutes.

This is the Logical Pentad; Prothesis, Thesis, Antithesis, Mesothesis (or the *Indifference* of Thesis and Antithesis, i.e. that which is both in either, but in different Relations; while the Prothesis is both as one in one and the same relation) and lastly the Synthesis. The modification of Thesis by Antithesis, and *vice versa*, constituting Adnoun & Adverb, convert the Pentad to an Heptad—analogous to the law of colours.[5]

The Interpenetration of Light and Shade in the highest unity, or the Identity of Light and Shadow is RED, Color κατ᾽ εξοχην,[b6] in positive energy. It is the Zenith, to which BLACK is the harmonious opposite, or Nadir—Color in negative energy.

Prothesis
Red

Thesis	Mesothesis	Antithesis
Yellow	Green indecomponible	Blue

Synthesis
Green—compon and decomponible.

But from the Prothesis, Red, to the Thesis an oblique line may be drawn, the bisecting point of which constitutes the Mesothesis of Red and Yellow, i.e. Orange, and in like manner a line from the Prothesis to the Antithesis, the bisecting point of which is the Mesothesis or Indifference of Red and Blue i.e. Violet or Indigo. And this is the Heptad of colours

The Infinitive mood is the Mesothesis or Indifference of Noun and Verb.

For not *to dip* the Hero in the Lake
Could save the son of Thetis from *to die*.
Spenser[7]

3[a] IN TRANSCRIPT, "2" is written directly above "but"   3[b] TRANSCRIPT: εξοκην

3[4] C's example suggests that he may have written this note with James Gillman, Jr, in mind—perhaps as the next reader. Several of C's instructional letters to this young man (b 1808) survive from the late 1820s, e.g. *CL* VI 628, 633, 700. The figure over "but" links "but" in this sense with Horne Tooke's "Be-out": see n 2 above.

3[5] The analogy between heptads in grammar and in colour-theory appears also in the 1829 letter cited in **3 n 1** above. Note that C himself has given "Adjective" as a synonym for "Adnoun" a few lines back.

3[6] "Pre-eminently": C uses the same phrase with reference to red in *TT* (*CC*) I 289.

3[7] *The Ruines of Time* lines 428–9 (var). C invoked this illustration—which he had

Now here "to dip" is a Verb relative to "the Hero", as its objective or accusative case; but it is a *noun* and the Nominative, relatively to the Verb "could save." In the Greek and Italian languages this form is of perpetual occurrence—from to die, απο τοῦ θανεῖν, Could hinder him from to destroy brave Hector. Here "to destroy" is the Noun governed by the preposition (i.e. abbreviated Verb), from; and a Verb governing the Noun and Adnoun, brave Hector.

Thesis $\quad\quad$ $\overset{8}{\nparallel}$ $\quad\quad$ Antithesis

Alkali $\quad\quad\quad\quad\quad\quad\quad\quad\quad\quad$ Acid

Now hydrosulphurate is the *Mesothesis* i.e. an Acid relatively to an Alkali, an Alkali relatively to an Acid. Music (and Verse as its Articulate Analogon) is the Mesothesis of Order and Passion, or of Law and Life— of controlling, predetermining Will of Reason, and of Spontaneity, or lawless Will—*Will* of the Flesh, φρονημα σαρκος,[9] Will surging up toward and against Reason as blind Life. Painting is the Mesothesis of Thing and Thought. A coloured wax Peach is one *thing* passed off for another thing—a practical lie, and not a work appertaining to the fine Fine Arts—a delusion, not an Imitation. Every Imitation, as contradistinguished from a Copy,[10] is a Mesothesis, but which, according to the variable propiority[11] to the Thesis, or the Antithesis, may be called the *librating* Mesothesis. Thus, Real and Ideal are the two poles, the Thesis and Antithesis. The Sophoclean Drama, or the Samson Agonistes, is the Mesothesis in its propiority or comparative proximity to the Ideal—the tragedies of Heywood, Ford &c. (ex. gr. The Woman killed by kindness) is the Mesothesis in comparative proximity to the Real, while the Othello, Lear &c is the *Mesothesis* as truly as possible ἐν μεσῳ, tho' with a *clinamen* to the Ideal.[12] The Tragic dance of the Horatii and Curiatii, to the Music of Cimarosa, such as I saw and heard at Leghorn,[13] was the

---

from James Harris *Hermes: or a Philosophical Inquiry Concerning Universal Grammar* (1751)—repeatedly: *Logic (CC)* 17 n 3 lists several instances, and cf LACUNZA **45** (where the lines are given in Latin) and IRVING *Sermons* **2** (in English and Greek).

3[8] "As opposed to": cf C's presentation of this and other symbols in JOANNES **4**, SHAKESPEARE COPY A **117**.

3[9] *Phronema sarkos*, from Rom 8.7, "the carnal mind" (AV) or "mind of the flesh" in C's own version: *AR (CC)* 239. Several instances of C's use are identified in LEIGHTON COPY B **15** n 1.

3[10] The distinction between imitation and copy was a favourite: cf *BL* ch 18 (*CC*) II 72 and n 4. In the same chapter (II 84) C offers a marble peach as an illustration.

3[11] "Nearerness" or as C says later "comparative proximity": not in *OED*.

3[12] I.e. "in the middle" though with a slight inclination towards the ideal.

3[13] This appears to be the only reference to this experience in C's writings, though he evidently enjoyed it. C was in Leghorn briefly about the middle of Jun 1806, and sailed from there to England on the 23rd. What he saw must have been a performance of the serious opera *Gli Orazi ed i Curazi*

most perfect specimen of imitation, i.e. of a Mesothesis of Likeness and Difference, under the Maximum of the latter that I can even conceive. The proportions may vary manifoldly, but not lawlessly, and the proof of the legality is found in the *unity* resulting. Oil and Alcohol are both and equally *Units*, tho' their common components, Carbon and Hydrogen, are in almost reverse proportions, the one Hydrogen with predominance of Carbon, the other Carbon with predominance of Hydrogen: and the Atmospheric air as true a Unit as the nitrous oxyde, tho' the one gas be as 4 Nitrogen to 1 Oxygen, and the other as 2 1/3 N. to 21/2 Ox./ Hence the possible varieties in the fine arts, yet none *arbitrary*. The Arbitrary at once betrays itself, as a genus hybridum, a *patch* work—like our modern inflated *prose* tragedies, Verse and Prose, Singing and Dialoguing Comic Operas, &c &c Chinese Mermaids, by stitching on the bust of monkeys to the tails of Seals.[14]   S. T. C.

(1796), with a libretto by Antonio Simone Sografi (1760–1825) and music by Domenico Cimarosa (1749–1801). In *Friend* (*CC*) I 129–30, he describes listening to Cimarosa (there he suggests a symphony) as a sort of oscillation between opposite qualities such as originality and familiarity.

3[14] In his account of the mermaid racket, Altick prints a contemporary etching of an especially celebrated specimen exhibited in London in 1822, and observes that not China but Japan "was the world headquarters of the mermaid industry" (302).

QUARTERLY REVIEW

The Quarterly Review. Vol X, containing Numbers xix (Oct 1813) and xx (Jan 1814). 8°.

Not located; marginalia printed from MS TRANSCRIPTS.

MS TRANSCRIPTS. (*a*) University of Texas (Humanities Research Center): transcript by SC of notes **1–26**, and fair copy in another hand of notes **23–25, 27–30**. (*b*) VCL LT 46, 47: transcript by SC of **27–30**. The transcript by SC, being closer to the original, is used here, i.e. (*a*) for notes **1–26**, (*b*) for **27–30**, except that SC's practice of adding the initial(s) of the author to each passage copied has not been followed.

CONTENTS. The following are reviewed (titles abridged): 1–30 *Reports and Papers on the Impolicy of Employing Indian-built Ships in the Trade of the East-India Company* (1809), *The First Report of the Commissioners of His Majesty's Woods, Forests, and Land Revenues* (1812); 31–41 Elizabeth Montagu *Letters* vols III–IV (1813); 41–57 [D. Ryder] *Substance of the Speech of the Earl of Harrowby [18 Jun 1812]* (1812); 57–90 J. B. A. Suard ed *Correspondance littéraire, philosophique, et critique . . . par le Baron de Grimm, et par Diderot* pt 3, 5 vols (Paris 1813); 90–139 David Bogue and James Bennett *History of Dissenters [1688–1808]* 4 vols (1808–12), Walter Wilson *The History and Antiquity of Dissenting Churches* 4 vols (1808–14), Daniel Neal *History of the Puritans* abridged by Edward Parsons 2 vols (1812); 139–57 Robert Bland et al *Collections from the Greek Anthology* (1813); 157–75 W. T. Comber *An Inquiry into the State of National Subsistence* (1808); 175–203 J. C. Hobhouse *A Journey through Albania [1809–10]* (1813); 203–11 [O. Felix et al, ed] *The Speech of Doctor D. Antonio Joseph Ruiz de Padron, Deputy to the Cortes [18 Jan 1813] . . . Bread and Bulls: An Apological Oration . . . By Don Gaspar Jovellanos* (1813); 211–21 *A Letter on the Conduct and Situation of Denmark [30 May 1813]* (1813); 222–50 John Chetwode Eustace *A Tour through Italy* vols I–II (1813); 250–92 J. C. Adelung et al *Mithradates, oder allgemeine Sprachenkunde* vols I–III (Berlin 1806–12); [293–300 consist of a list of new publications and the table of contents to Number xx]; 301–22 Maria Edgeworth *Patronage* 4 vols (1814); 323–31 Thomas Duer Broughton *Letters Written in a Mahratta Camp [1809]* (1813); 331–54 Byron *The Giaour* 11th ed (1814), *The Bride of Abydos* 7th ed (1814); 355–409 A. L. G. de Staël-Holstein *De l'Allemagne* 3 vols (1813); 409–27 Charles Butler *Some Account of . . . Bossuet* (1812), *The Life of Fenelon* (1810); 427–42 J. W. von Goethe *Zur Farbenlehre* 2 vols (Tübingen 1810); 442–63 ΕΡΜΗΣ ὁ ΛΟΓΙΟΣ Η ΦΙΛΟΛΟΓΙΚΑΙ ΑΓΓΕΛΙΑΙ [*The Learned Hermes, or*

Philological News (in modern Greek) Bucharest n.d.]; 463–7 [James Kirke Pauld-
ing] *The Lay of the Scottish Fiddle* (1814); 467–81 *Resolutions of a General
Meeting of the Committee of Ship-Owners for the Port of London, held the 9th
April, 1812* (1812), *Various Returns of Thames and Indian-built Shipping* (1813);
481–94 *Dépêches et lettres interceptées. Copies of the original letters and dis-
patches [sent] to the Emperor Napoleon, at Dresden* (1814); 494–539 [Charles
Jared Ingersoll] *Inchiquin the Jesuit's Letters* (New York 1810); [540–60 "New
Publications" and index to the volume].

DATE. Dec 1814 (**22**).

1   p 92 | [RS] review of books by Bogue and Bennett, Wilson, and Neal

Messrs. Bogue and Bennett, when they speak of the death of Priestley,
are not less bigotted. . . . They say of him, "when he bids his family good
night, and speaks of death as *a good long sleep*, we almost fancy ourselves transported to Paris at the era of the infidel and revolutionary fury;
for alas! Priestley speaks only of sleeping in the grave, and not, like Paul,
of sleeping in Jesus!" Whatever Priestley might have been, this is a
wicked misrepresentation of him: these writers know . . . that his belief
in the resurrection was as sincere as their own, founded upon the same
premises, and producing the same consolations.

Which said Priestley denied the existence of a soul, and whose fable of
Resurrection is neither more nor less than a system of creating B. in such
a manner as to force him to believe a Lie, viz. that he was A. in order to
torment him with a shew of justice![1] Lie supporting Lie! Injustice barri-
caded by Injustice! A strange *Positive* of Right resulting from two Negatives!—and these (*horresco referens*)[2] attributed to the Holy One! Why
will not our Laureate keep within his sphere, i.e. narration, not analysis
of opinions?

1[1] In *Disquisitions relating to Matter
and Spirit* (1777) and its sequel, *A Free Discussion of the Doctrines of Materialism,
and Philosophical Necessity* (1778), Joseph
Priestley, rejecting the dualism of body and
soul as scientifically and philosophically
untenable, argued in favour of materialism,
rehabilitating matter, however, by redefin-
ing it as active power rather than inert object, "a substance possessed of the property
of *extension*, and of *powers of attraction or
repulsion*" (*Disquisitions* xxxviii). His doctrine of the materiality and homogeneity of
body and mind led him to the conclusion
that the individual was extinguished in
death, and that the resurrection referred to
in the Bible was a general resurrection: ". . .
whenever the system is dissolved, it continues in a state of dissolution, till it shall
please that Almighty Being who called it
into existence to restore it to life again"
(*Disquisitions* 49). In C's view, if Priestley
were right, God must have created man as
material and subject to necessity but then
have led him through Scripture to believe
himself possessed of an immortal soul and
of free will "in order to torment him with a
shew of justice!" A letter of Apr 1814 to his
Socinian acquaintance Estlin clarifies this
argument: *CL* III 465–7.
     1[2] "I shudder as I say it": Virgil *Aeneid*
2.204.

2   p 92 | **1** textus continued

Bigotry makes as dismal an effect upon the understanding as upon the heart.

Makes for produces, a Gallo-barbarism not less anti-logical than anti-Anglican.[1]

3   p 94

Even Milton has joined in this ill-deserved reproach. "I persuade myself," says he, "if our zeal to true religion, and the brotherly usage of our truest friends were as notorious to the world as our *Prelatical schism*, and captivity to *Rochet apophthegms*, we had ere this seen our old conquerors, and afterwards liegemen, the Normans, together with the Britains, our proper colony, and all the Gascoins . . . come with cap and knee, desiring the shadow of the English sceptre to defend them from the hot persecutions and taxes of the French. But when they come hither and see a tympany of Spaniolized bishops swaggering in the foretop of the state, and meddling to turn and dandle the royal ball with unskilful and pedantic palms, no marvel though they think it as unsafe to commit religion and liberty to their arbitrating as to a synagogue of Jesuits." But against the opinion of those who think that we ought to have departed as widely as possible from all the forms and institutions of the Romish church . . . there is the weighty testimony of Sully. . . . [who] remarked that if the French Protestants had retained the same advantage of order and decency, there would at that time have been many thousands more Protestants in France.

I will yield to no man in attachment to the Church of England, yet I dare justify this passage of Milton's as equally wise & accurate as it is forcible. Had the Church adopted Usher's plan of moderate Episcopacy by anticipation, all the Protestant Churches of Europe might have gathered under her wings.[1] There is nothing in the assertion of Sully[2] at all irreconcilable with this.

2[1] C was given to making fastidious remarks about RS's use of the language: cf DANIEL **16** and n 2. In SOUTHEY *Joan* **5**, he began to develop a special abbreviation, "*S.E.* means *Southey's English*, i.e. no English at all." "Anti-Anglican" means "anti-English" and has nothing to do with the C of E.

3[1] James Ussher (1581–1656), abp of Armagh, was one of the episcopalian members of the Westminster Assembly appointed in 1643 to reform the English Church; he pub *The Original of Bishops* in 1644. C alludes to his moderate position approvingly in MACDIARMID **13** and in a note to Jeremy TAYLOR *Polemicall Discourses* (1674) i 1 (**13**).

3[2] In textus.

By the bye, what stronger proof can we desire than the known fact that Laud's and Hammond's tenet concerning the *jus divinum*[3] of Bishops &c. is obsolete, at least, *inter inusitatissimæ*[a]—*dogma omnimodo insolens*?[4]—So that the[b] Church is lumbered with the huge machinery without the power—a steam-engine without the steam.

4   p 95

In the latter years of her reign, when the Pope made use of religion to excite rebellion and conspiracies against her, Elizabeth offered concessions to the Puritans, which, had they been accepted, would have driven many of these men out of the church: but it was then seen that concessions which would have materially diminished the number of converts from popery, would have done little towards reclaiming those who had imbibed the temper as well as the doctrines of the Genevan school. For when Walsingham offered, in the Queen's name, that if they would conform in other points, the three shocking ceremonies, as they accounted them, of kneeling at the communion, wearing the surplice, and the cross in baptism, should be abolished, they replied in the language of Moses, *Ne ungulam esse relinquendam,*—they would not leave even a hoof behind.

A powerful mind states first all that can be wisely said on the one side of a question—then the same on the other—and lastly effects the process of comparison, and subtracts the result. Now there are certain people, who catch up and carry off the first and the second part, either as that which they happened to hear, or as that which best suited their predilections, and publish it in their own names as the whole. Hence arises a sort of perplexity in the mind of a philosophic reader, how being no better it should be so good.

5   p 95, footnote

A Puritan rampant, who calls himself J. S. Gent., who was evidently a man of learning, and might have been a man of genius if the disease of the times had not made him stark mad, gives, both in prose and verse, the

3[a] The word should be "inusitatissima": possibly an error of transcription
3[b] SC wrote "the" twice, at the end of one line and beginning of the next

3[3] The "divine right"—C alluding to Laud's famous formulation but extending it from kings to bishops, as Laud and other uncompromising prelatists of his party implicitly did. C includes in this group Henry Hammond (1605–60), another member of the Westminster Assembly. For other comments on this controversy, see HERBERT **19** and n 1, MACDIARMID **13** (on the "No Bishop, no King" maxim).

3[4] "Among the most infrequent[ly held (tenets)]—an entirely unfamiliar dogma".

feelings of his party respecting this appellation. "Puritan," he says, "the invention of hell, the language of profaneness, the blasphemy of God, the evomition of a heart desperately wicked, a glorious defamation, an undermining of, an open thrust at, the very heart, life, and power of religion; an evident preferring of pharisaical forms and Laodicean neutrality; a *match-devillian* device to kindle fire in church and state; a sly practice of the old serpent's old maxim, 'divide and reign;' &c.["]

In his crazy rhymes, he says—

> A Puritan? what's that? an hypocrite.
> Nay hold there man, for so thou dost but fit
> The noose for thine own neck.—I tell thee, man,
> Thou art an atheist, or a Puritan,
> Thou art a devil or a Puritan.—&c. &c.
>
> *Soliloquies Theologicall* 1641.

The *quotation* at least is neither crazy prose nor crazy rhymes, but sound theology in spirited diction. Are not the Epistles of Peter and John equally decisive? In short, the most important division, I had almost said, the only important one, inasmuch as all others of importance are implied in this or deducible from it, is—whether the essence of Christianity be to make us *better* men only, or to make us *other* men—"*create* in us a *new* heart."[1]

6 p 96

By whatever name the puritans might have been denominated, their history would have been the same; their rise was one of the inevitable consequences of a religious revolution, and the civil war was as inevitable an effect of their progress.

This is an unthinking way of thinking. It is easy to talk of past events as having been inevitable, because we are forced by the forms of the Understanding* to review them by the logical functions of Cause and Effect.

* The "*ipse Intellectus*" (*per intellectionem, sibi ipsi revelatus)*[1] of Leibnitz in his admirable reply to the Lockian assertion of the old Peripatetic "*Nihil in Intellectu quod non prius in sensu*":[2] an adage which my

---

5[1] A variant of Ps 51.10, "Create in me a clean heart". For variants on the distinction between other and better, see NICOLAI 7, *BL* ch 7 (*CC*) I 123, *CL* III 463.

6[1] "Mind itself (itself revealed to itself by intellection)".

6[2] The Aristotelian maxim anticipates the premises of Locke, i.e. "There is nothing in the mind that was not previously in the senses". C quotes this saying in BAXTER *Reliquiae* COPY B **112** (where he also gives a variant of the joke about Boyer that follows here, and where the footnote glosses the Leibnizian addendum "except the understanding itself") and in *BL* ch 9 (*CC*) I 141.

The writer did not consider that in the very same way we are obliged to reflect on our own past actions, and that the very same principle, if admitted other than as logical, would do away free-agency. Endless are the errors and not a few of them most pernicious, from not distinguishing *Principia Logica* from the *Principia Entitiva*.[3]

old Master at Christ's Hospital, Bowyer, used to quote when we were under the rod. You must make a lad *feel* before he will *understand*. All true knowledge is derived *a posteriori*—& therefore properly entitled too we say, Such a man has been well *bottomed*. Fundamental. Hence,[a]

7   pp 96–7

It is easy to talk of toleration, and say that the church should have tolerated these schismatics; they would not tolerate the church.—... "We intended not," says Baxter, "to dig down the banks, or to pull up the hedge and lay all waste and common, when we desired the prelates' tyranny might cease. We must either tolerate all men to do what they will which they will make a matter of conscience or religion ... or else you must tolerate no error or fault in religion, and then you must advise what measure of penalty you will inflict. My judgment I have always freely made known; I abhor unlimited liberty, or toleration of all."

Southey did not advert to Baxter's use of the word "Religion", which meant with him the *Regula Fidei*, or Apostles' Creed; and this too limited to an open opposition to the words of the Creed.[1] Whoever could conscientiously use[a] the words was not to be further questioned.

This is a most unfair quotation from Baxter, who was the nearest to absolute toleration of all Theologians. He proposed that all persons admitted as Church members should be ready to declare, that they desired what was prayed for in the Lord's Prayer, believed what was declared in the Apostles' Creed, and held themselves bound to obey what was enjoined by the Ten Commandments, and that all beyond should be free to each.[2]

6[a] Transcript breaks off here
7[a] SC wrote "use" twice, at the end of one line and beginning of the next

6[3] I.e. "logical principles" from "principles of being".
7[1] "*Regula fidei*"—"rule of faith"—is a term traditionally applied to the Apostles' Creed. C uses it in connection with Baxter in BAXTER *Reliquiae* COPY B **100**.
7[2] C's own notes on Baxter's writings

take notice of complicated and even contradictory attitudes in Baxter (e.g. BAXTER *Reliquiae* COPY A **37**, COPY B **92**), but C's general impression was of a "mild and kindhearted old man" (COPY A **37**), "the mild and really tolerant Baxter" (COPY B **59**).

8   pp 97–8

[RS records evidence of the opposition to toleration in religion during the Commonwealth period.] All this is moderate to the language of Edwards in his Gangraena, where he exhorts ministers to "pray to God and call upon him night and day to give a miscarrying womb to the sectaries, that they may never bring forth the misshapen bastard monster of a toleration.["] Toleration, says he, "will make the kingdom a chaos, a Babel, another Amsterdam, a Sodom, an Egypt, a Babylon. Toleration is the grand work of the devil, his masterpiece and chief engine to uphold his tottering kingdom: it is the most compendious, ready, sure way to destroy all religion, lay all waste, and bring in all evil: it is a most transcendant, catholique and fundamental evil. As original sin is the fundamental sin, having the seed and spawn of all sins in it, so toleration hath all errors in it, and all evils." This was the temper of the puritans; but to say that toleration would have contented men who laid claim to supremacy, and accounted intolerance in their own hands a christian duty of the first magnitude, is as absurd as it would be to attempt to reason a madman into sanity.

The answer to all the foregoing page is that the reviewer should have made himself precisely acquainted in the then sense of the word "Toleration", and in this sense he himself seems to fight against it.

9   p 98

Messrs. Bogue and Bennett fail not to notice, with due indignation, "the most infamous tragedy acted in the treatment of Burton, Prynne, and Bastwick," and to describe the bloody manner in which the shocking sentence was executed; but they pass over the bloodier and deeper tragedy of Laud, by simply saying that he was "brought to the block," and repeating the old and oft confuted calumny, that, under his primacy, "it was every day becoming more difficult and less important to distinguish between the church of England and that of Rome;" . . . . is it possible that they, being christians themselves . . . can disbelieve the last solemn declaration of Laud himself? "I was born and baptized," said he, "in the bosom of the church of England established by law; in that profession I have ever since lived, and in that I come now to die. . . . I do therefore here, in the presence of God and his holy angels, take it upon my death, that I never endeavoured the subversion of law or religion . . ."

And what is there in Laud's last confession (to attribute, by the by, to such confessions the weight, Southey does is what Wordsworth would not do)

what is there in it, that is incompatible with Bogue's & Bennett's affirmation? Laud was not a believer in those articles of *faith* in which the Romanists differed from the Reformers—nay, he was one of the very ablest of the antagonists of those articles, Transubstantiation, Purgatory,   [a]
But who ever suspected this? It was the pomp, pride, vanity, and temporal tyranny of the Roman Church that Laud was suspected of being attached to, and these, not mistakes in faith, are the poison-bag on which the Papal fang rests. What follows is so childish that I mourn for it.[1] If this were evidence what villainous conduct might not find a *martyr* of its rectitude?

10   p 99

Will this convince those persons who still asperse the intentions of Laud? will they believe him, that in the bosom of the Church of England he lived and died?

But what did Laud mean by "the Church of England?"

11   p 99

In Mr. Parsons's new and condensed edition of Neal's History of the Puritans, Laud's dying declaration that he had never endeavoured the subversion of the laws of the realm, nor any change of the Protestant religion into popish superstition, is printed in large capital letters, obviously for the purpose of shewing that Mr. Neal considered it a falsehood.

Who told Southey that?

12   p 99, continuing **11** textus

This author, whose coarse, bold, self-satisfied countenance at the beginning of this book may teach any one who can read the most legible characters of nature, what kind of feeling he is to expect in it, says that the archbishop declared himself upon the scaffold a Protestant according to the church of England, but "with more charity to the church of Rome than to the foreign Protestants."

Which? Neal? or Parsons? Not having the book I cannot say what was intended;[1] but this is most certain that Laud did think more charitably

---

9[a] Space left in ms, presumably for a word indecipherable in the original

9[1] I.e. **10** and **11** textus.   the ambiguity in RS's prose.
12[1] The portrait is of Neal; C objects to

of the Church of Rome, while he was in power, than of the foreign non-episcopal congregations, whom he did not allow to be Churches.

13   pp 101–2

We are not the apologists of Laud: in some things he was erroneous, in some imprudent, in others culpable. . . . The bloody sentences of the Star Chamber brought down upon him a more tragic catastrophe than he attempted to avert by them; a milder primate could not have saved the church from her enemies, but he would not have perished by their hands. And in return, it cannot be doubted that when the clergy regained their ascendancy, the severity with which they treated the Dissenters was in no slight degree exasperated by the remembrance of his execution.

God knows my heart, how bitterly I abhor *all* Intolerance—how deeply I pity the actors, when there is reason to suppose them deluded. But is it not clear that this theatrical scene of Laud's death, who was the victim of almost national indignation, is not to be compared with "bloody sentences" in the coolness of secure power? As well might you palliate the horrible atrocities of the Inquisition, every one of which might be justified on the same grounds that Southey has here defended Laud, by detailing the vengeance taken on some one Inquisitor.

14   p 102

That which has happened may happen again; the passions of men remain the same; progressive as we are, we have often to go through the same lessons as the ages before us; and therefore it especially behoves the historian to inculcate charity, and take part with the oppressed, whoever may have been the oppressors. Of all beasts, the many-headed one is the most ferocious; and it is fearful to think how soon and how surely the taste of blood creates the appetite for it!

When men after long habits of blind obedience in religion, began to search the Scriptures and to frame articles of belief for themselves, it was impossible that they should not differ; and as they were all agreed that any error upon these points was damnable, they all became in some measure intolerant; and the dominant party persecuted both in duty and in self-defence. Here it was that both parties erred, but thus it was that both felt, and thus in justice both ought to be represented. To write history in the true spirit of general goodwill no suppression is needed, no falsification, no affectation of candour; it is but to represent men in their actions as they have appeared to themselves, and, God be praised, there are few characters so unredeemed, that we should then regard their sufferings without compassion, or their errors without excuse.

I know well how imprudent and unworthy these my opinions are! The Dissenters will give me no thanks, because I prefer and extol the *present* Church of England; and the partizans of the Church will calumniate me, because I condemn particular members, and regret particular æras, of the former Church of England. Would that Southey had written the whole of his[a] review in the spirit of this beautiful page!

14A   p 103

The fanatic who, in this country, would drive the nervous part of his hearers mad by railing at the sins of his neighbours, was taught by the wise policy of the Romish church to expend his fervour upon his own; he was furnished with knotted scourges, hair shirts, and drawers composed of wire and bristles; if this did not content him, he might add a nutmeg-grater waistcoat, and then he had put on the whole papistical armour of righteousness.!!

15   p 104

A little more thought, with the help of a little more charity, might have shewn these writers that all the virtues are not on one side, and all the vices on the other. Hooker and Travers divided the opinions of their contemporaries for the palm of ability and learning; for that of piety and humility and all christian virtues, none on earth is worthy to judge between them. Among the puritan sufferers there is not a fairer name than that of Udal; even among churchmen in his own times many, says Fuller, conceived the proceedings against him "*rigorous* in the *greatest*, (which, at best, is *cruel* in the *least* degree,) considering the worth of his person, and the weakness of the proof against him." And when he died in prison, "for an higher judge had formerly past another sentence on Udal's death, that his soul and body should not by shameful violence be forced asunder, but that they should take a fair farewell each of other; right glad were his friends that his death prevented his death; and the wisest of his foes were well contented therewith, esteeming it better that his candle should *go* than be *put out*." This man's son, inheriting his father's piety and fearless spirit, but not his opinions, held the living of St. Augustine in London during the civil wars, and was as active against the Puritans as his father had been in their behalf. At a time when he was "aged, of very weak and

---

14[a]   SC wrote "his (? this)", recording her own emendation

infirm body, his strength exhausted with continual labour in preaching the word of God, visiting the sick, and in execution of other ministerial functions," he was not merely ejected from his living, but compelled to hide himself lest he should be committed to close prison; while his house was plundered, and his wife, a bed-ridden cripple, forcibly taken out and left in the streets. Here were father and son, both of known and exemplary virtue and unimpeachable sincerity, the one the martyr the other the victim of puritanism.

Who that is not blind does not see the colouring in this relation? There is a riot and an obnoxious character hides himself, and his wife is turned into the street—the whole = the sufferings of two or three hours; while the father is murdered in cold blood!—the Father's fate minutely detailed and capable of strict law court evidence, the other little more than hearsay. So "plundered". Of what?—and a bedridden cripple left in the streets? By whom? and who the witnesses? and from what author is the quotation? Possibly, from that lying bigot, Walker, who pronounced the victories of Marlborough parts of a hellish plot against the Church![1]— Charity, Charity, Southey! is an excellent impulse in the   [a] but Truth, dispassionate balancing of evidence, is the end and worth of an historian.

16   pp 104–5

Three Protestants suffered under the Six Articles, and three Papists for denying the king's supremacy, at the same time and place . . . . Insomuch that a certain stranger being there present, and seeing three on one side and three on the other side to suffer, said . . . *"Deus bone! quomodo hic vivunt gentes! hic suspenduntur Papistae, illic comburuntur Antipapistae.* [Good God! What a way people live here! On the one hand Papists are hanged, on the other Antipapists are burned.]"

Here again one of the bloody tyrannies of Henry the VIIIth is adduced as a fact of joint persecution by two parties. The Papists were burnt by the

15[a] Space left in ms, presumably for an illegible word: "Christian"?

15[1] John Walker *An Attempt towards Recovering an Account of the Numbers and Sufferings of the Clergy of the Church of England, Heads of Colleges, Fellows, Scholars, &c. who were Sequester'd, Harrass'd, &c. in the late Times of the Great Rebellion* . . . (1714): C alludes to this work in BM Egerton MS 2801 f 243[r] (*SW & F— CC*—1061). Walker tells the story of Udal in pt ii 178–9; in the preface to his work he describes a continuing conspiracy against the Church in England, and says of the conspirators in the reign of Anne that "they soon got themselves possess'd of all the Profitable and Important Posts in the Kingdom, and Resumed their Attempts of compleating the Ruine of it, under the same unfortunate Circumstances of an Expensive and Bloody War, and with the same Methods of Plunder and Rapine" (viii).

tyrant for treason; the Protestants by the same tyrant, as a doctrinal Romanist, for heresy.

17 p 105

. . . unquestionably error has had its martyrs as well as truth, but we may well acknowledge that the faith of him who gives his body to be burnt will atone for all the errors of his frail and fallible understanding.

Errors *of* the understanding will never condemn us, but errors *in* the understanding *from* the heart.—Faith is not in the Christian sense mere heat of conviction, or why not canonize Ravaillac?[1]

18 p 106

George Fox was as confused in his writings as Cromwell in his speeches. Yet there is one passage in his journal which describes the state of his mind in one part of its progress more beautifully than the ablest psychologist could have done. "One morning," says he, "as I was sitting by the fire, a great cloud came over me, and a temptation beset me, and I sate still. And it was said, all things come by nature; and the Elements and Stars came over me, so that I was in a manner quite clouded with it; but in as much as I sate still and said nothing, the people of the house perceived nothing. And as I sate still under it and let it alone, a living hope arose in me, and a true voice arose in me which cried, there is a living God who made all things. And immediately the cloud and temptation vanished away, and life rose over it all, and my heart was glad, and I praised the living God."

This passage I myself pointed out to Southey: who did not, it is clear, understand it.[1] For what has it to do here? And the "Psychologist" is one of my words, only used in the very opposite sense that this passage required.[2]

17[1] François Ravaillac (1578–1610), alarmed by rumours that Henri IV was about to make war on the pope, killed the king in 1610. His name appears often in debates about regicide and tyrannicide, e.g. in C's own *Friend* (*CC*) I 320–1, *EOT* (*CC*) II 209.

18[1] George Fox *Journal* ed William Penn (1694) 16. C refers to this ed in a letter of Dec 1808 that is full of admiration and gratitude towards the Quakers: *CL* III 156. Fox himself was one of C's "Revolutionary Minds" (JOHNSON 2 n 2) and one whom he defended against the pride of readers like RS (*BL* ch 9—*CC*—I 149–50). The anecdote told by Fox belongs to the year 1648: *Journal* 16.

18[2] The *OED* shows that "psychologist" was already in the language in the early eighteenth century, when Nathan Bailey included it in his dictionary; but C did make a deliberate attempt to introduce a related group of terms—"psychology", "psychologist", "psychological"—into more precise

19   pp 106–7

[One of Fox's converts, James Naylor, a poor fanatic, who marched into Bristol "with a set of crazy people before him, singing, Holy, holy, holy, Hosannah in the Highest," was savagely punished by Cromwell at the insistence of certain "public preachers", "Caryl, Manton, Nye, Griffith, and Reynolds".] He recovered both from his madness and his sufferings, and his after-life was a reproach to those who, in the hardness of their hearts and the blindness of their understandings, had treated insanity like guilt.

No sooner are Puritan Divines concerned than Southey can find "hardness of heart," and "blindness of understanding": while the Prelatic party, sweet Lambs! had only some *errors* common to their age! And this is modern impartiality! He does not tell us, which yet is most true, that at any former period poor Naylor would have been burnt alive, and no hint that so saint-like a man as Reynolds might have been conscience-scared from the dread of not resenting blasphemy against the Saviour: for Naylor declared himself God in the flesh.

20   p 108

Cromwell indeed was frequently favoured with their admonitions, and the old Quakers were firmly persuaded that the overthrow of his family was a judgment upon him for not interfering more authoritatively to stop the proceedings against them.

There is much truth in this opinion. Cromwell's dynasty fell a sacrifice to indecision and cross-catching.[1]

21   pp 117–18

[Quoted from the *Nonconformists' Memorial*:] ". . . Being on a journey he [Flavel] set himself to improve the time by meditation, when his mind grew intent, till at length he had such ravishing tastes of heavenly joys, and such full assurance of his interest therein, that he utterly lost the sight and sense of this world and all its concerns, so that for hours he knew not where he was. At last perceiving himself faint through a great loss of

---

usage. He used "psychologist" in 1810 in a marginal note to one of RS's books, James SEDGWICK *Hints to the Public and Legislature* (1808–10) ii 40; "psychological" appears in a lecture on Shakespeare in 1811 (*Lects 1808–1819—CC*—i 253 and n). C himself defined "psychology" as the philosophy of mind in *Method* 32; his objection to

RS here is perhaps that RS's psychologist *describes* but is not said to *analyse* the mind.

  20[1] This word is not in *OED* or other dictionaries, nor in dictionaries of slang. The context suggests that it means working at cross-purposes, but it could also be a transcriber's misreading.

blood from his nose, he alighted from his horse and sat down at a spring, where he washed and refreshed himself, earnestly desiring if it were the will of God, that he might then leave the world. His spirit recovering he finished his journey in the same delightful frame. . . ."

This is one of those facts, common in Romish biography, and not unfrequent in that of our own enthusiasts, which clearly belong to nosology. . . . it is remarkable that Calamy, and his modern editor, should relate the case without suspecting its real nature . . .

But does any nosologist record an instance of exalted pleasurable tranquillity during the stupor of an apoplectic fit? If any, this of Flavel's must have been *apoplexia sanguinea*, the symptoms of which, as accurately detailed by Dr W. Sainsbury Junr in his "Doctrinal Thesis," p. 7 & 8, are scarcely compatible with symptoms of voluptuous tranquillity.[1] I rather incline to conjecture, that the hæmorrhage from intense thought acted as opium is often known to do on persons new to its influence, when it produces no disorder in its first action on the stomach. The loss of blood would be sedative, and the action of the reproductive secretories would balance the sedative effect in the nature of a stimulant. Now all pleasure rests on the equatorial point of satisfaction, indifference at one, and rapture at the other pole,—i.e., is a balance. I doubt not that by this law, applied to the lungs, we must account for the effects of the nitrous oxygen of Davy.[2]

22 p 139, at the end of the review

Southey writes nothing that is not replete with point and amusing facts; but this review is less happily put together than almost any of his longer articles; for, with all his defects and deficiencies, he is the very king of reviewers, quotque sunt et fuêre.[1]

S. T. Coleridge Dec[br] 1814 Corsham.[2]

21[1] William Sainsbury *Disputatio medica inauguralis de apoplexia sanguinea* . . . (Edinburgh 1809) 7–8 lists among the symptoms of the disease headache, vertigo, nausea and vomiting, seeing black spots before the eyes, temporary deafness, insomnia, grinding of the teeth during sleep, difficult breathing, convulsive muscular movements, and many other symptoms none of which, as C says, would normally be thought of as compatible with pleasure.
21[2] When HD conducted experiments with nitrous oxide ("laughing gas") at the Pneumatic Institution of Bristol in 1799, RS and C were among his volunteers. HD published C's account of the effects he felt from the gas in *Researches, Chemical and Philosophical; chiefly concerning Nitrous Oxide* (1800) 516–18, and it is included in *SW & F (CC)* 103–4.
22[1] I.e. of all, past or present—"as many as are or have been".
22[2] C was on a visit to the family of Paul Cobb Methuen (1752–1816) at Corsham House near Bath. He amusingly describes his introduction there in a letter of Oct 1814: *CL* iii 535–6.

23   p 197 | Review of J. C. Hobhouse *Journey through Albania*

It is asserted then, and we believe with truth, both by Mr. Hobhouse, and by Dr. Pouqueville in the best part of his book, his account of the Morea, that the modern Greeks themselves have little idea of the benefits to be derived from their emancipation, beyond the establishment of their own corrupted form of Christianity; that the exaltation of their Church, and the bringing back the days of the good King Constantine, for they look no higher for their progenitors, is the only object of their prayers.

"S'ils parlent," says the Doctor, "de la liberté, ils s'exaltent, de manière à faire croire qu'ils sont prêts à tout entreprendre, même à tout sacrifier pour l'obtenir, mais au fond cette indignation qu'ils manifestent contre leurs oppresseurs, provient moins de leur amour pour l'affranchissement, que de l'envie de voir dominer leur culte.—Les Grecs modernes, je ne balance pas de la dire, ne verraient dans une révolution que le triomphe de leur religion, sans s'embarrasser beaucoup de plus ou moins de liberté publique." ["If they talk of freedom, they puff themselves up so that you'd think they were ready to undertake anything, and sacrifice every-thing to obtain it, but fundamentally this indignation that they express against their oppressors arises less from their love of emancipation than from their desire to see their own sect rule. I have no hesitation in saying that in a revolution, modern Greeks would see only the triumph of their religion, and would not be much concerned about the liberty of the people."]

A true French feeling. But a philosopher would wish no better stuff to work on and with.

24   p 197

Undoubtedly it is not easy, for those who never felt or enjoyed it, to es-timate the value of liberty, or even to conceive the benefits which it brings in its train; much less can such a people comprehend the connexion of those benefits with that liberty. Our ancestors, when they made a stand against the tyranny of the Popedom, little reflected perhaps on the ulte-rior advantages to be derived from the Reformation; and if none but those who looked farther than to the rescue of their Church (though we would not be thought to undervalue that blessing) had been admitted to the ben-efit of the change, we fancy that the number, even among the best in-formed, would have been but small. As we therefore, perhaps uncon-sciously, have arrived at our present unlooked-for prosperity both external and domestic, we are not unwilling that others also should be cheated into happiness.

These observations tantalize one. They seem truths that some noble mind had taught the Reviewer, which the word "cheated" proves he did not understand *anschaulich*,[1] as the Germans say.

25 p 199

What is most to be desired for the language in its present state, for its defect in enunciation is probably irremediable, is to fix in some degree its orthography and phraseology. The former is comparatively easy, but the latter is most difficult; not from any want of fit expressions, but of limitation to the introduction of new ones.

Me judice,[1] a weak remark. Let but a weekly newspaper be published, and set the priest attacking the heretics, and in half a century the Romaic would be Greek. The pronunciation would keep pace with the *a*desire and necessity*b* of distinctness. How many words accurately distinguished by the Educated and Reflecting are confounded in pronunciation by our clowns in England! Pail and pale, field and fill'd, καὶ ἄλλα χίλια.[2]

26 p 250 | Review of J. C. Eustace *A Tour through Italy*

[The reviewer quotes Eustace p 650:] In fact, many of my readers may be inclined, with a late eloquent writer, (Châteaubriand,) to discover something sublime in the establishment of a common father in the very centre of Christendom, within the precincts of the Eternal City, once the seat of empire, now the metropolis of christianity; to annex to that venerable name sovereignty and princely power, and to entrust him with the high commission of advising and rebuking monarchs; of repressing the ardour and intemperance of rival nations; of raising the pacific crosier between the swords of warring sovereigns, and checking alike the fury of the barbarian, and the vengeance of the despot.

This was Leibnitz' plan;[1] but to steal from their neighbours, especially from the Germans, is the privilege of the French literati, and their half brothers, the Scotch. The Scotch (they call themselves Scotsmen, as if conscious of the qualities involved in the *tch*, as proved in all words so terminating[2]—botch, blotch, crotch, scratch, scritch, stitch, letch, fetch

25*a–b* SC originally wrote "necessity and desire", then indicated with a curved line that the terms should be reversed

24[1] "Intuitively".
25[1] "In my opinion".
25[2] "And thousands of others".
26[1] Leibniz, who had been dead for half a century before Chateaubriand was born, had been involved in plans to reunite the Christian church. C alludes to his ideas also in *C&S* (*CC*) 131–2.
26[2] C habitually spoke scornfully of the Scots: cf PARNELL **1** above, MACDIARMID **2** and n 1.

(and carry, as spaniels,) ditch, pitch (*vid.* Shak: Henry IV.)[3] quitch (grass, a creeping weed that intertangling can scarce be cleared out of a place, it has been once suffered to take root in. &c &c.[)]

27 p 253 | Review of Adelung

If the resemblance or identity of a single word in two languages, supposed to be exempt from the effects of all later intercourse, were to be esteemed a sufficient proof of their having been derived from a common stock, it would follow that more than half the languages of the universe would exhibit traces of such a connexion, in whatever order we might pursue the comparison. Thus we find in a very great number, and perhaps in a majority of known languages, that the sound of the vowel A, with a labial consonant, is employed for the name of Father: and if this be supposed to be something like an onomatopoeia, or an application of the first sounds which an infant naturally utters, the same reason cannot possibly be assigned for the still more general occurrence of the combination NM in the term Name, which is by no means likely to have originated from any natural association of this kind. But neither these points of resemblance, nor any other that can be assigned, are universal, for besides the numberless varieties referable more or less immediately to Abba, Father, we have at least twenty different and independent terms for the same relation in the old world; Tia, Issa, Plar, Hair, Rama, Diam . . .

Why not epithets substantiated into the sense of the omitted word: as, she is "my Dear", for ["]Wife". Name is, I doubt not, a compound: therefore not a case in point—ὅ μενει ἐν ᾧ νῷ νουμένοῖν.[1]

28 p 254

Without dwelling on the unnecessary hypothesis and the tedious details with which some parts of Professor Adelung's work are filled, and without animadverting very severely on the occasional display of an inflated

---

26[3] *1 Henry IV* II iv 410–13: "There is a thing, Harry, which thou hast often heard of, and it is known to many in our land by the name of pitch. This pitch (as ancient writers do report) doth defile . . .".

27[1] "What *remains* in mind [is] noumenon" or, losing the pun, "What *dwells* in pure reason [is] noumenon". For *nous* as pure reason, rather than mind or intellect, see PROCLUS **1**. C often repeated the suggestion that the English *name* and the Latin equivalent *nomen* are cognate with and

overlap in meaning with *numen* (divine power) and ν[ο]ούμενον, the present participle passive of νοέω ("I think" or "I know"). For the theological and philosophical importance of this etymological connection see, e.g., BROWNE *Works* **42**, *CN* IV 4770 f 46, *CL* VI 896, *AR* (*CC*) 230–1, and James SEDGWICK **53**. Here, perhaps uniquely, C constructs *noumenon* from *nous* and *meno* ("I remain"), presumably implying that the latter is involved in all such participles, middle and passive.

insipidity of style, which too often <u>assumes</u>, in the writings of the modern Germans, <u>the place</u> of a dignified simplicity, we shall attempt to profit, as far as our limits will permit, by the solid accumulation of knowledge, which usually characterizes the productions of that laborious and accurate nation, among whom our author is well known to have stood in the first rank as a grammarian, a lexicographer, and an etymologist.

I should like to learn under what class of style this phrase "*inflated insipidity*"!! is to be arranged—Query—under co-action of incompatibles?—and an inflated insipidity *assumes* a *place*!!

29   pp 429–32 | Review of Goethe *Zur Farbenlehre*

The second volume of the work is occupied principally by a historical abstract of the discoveries and opinions of all philosophers, ancient and modern, respecting light and colours; in which the author has exhibited some industry, but little talent, and less judgment. He does not fail to triumph over the "detestable Newtonian doctrines," on occasion of the discoveries of Dollond; and although he is disposed to admit, that an accident may have given rise to the experimental error of Newton, he still very truly infers from the circumstance, that "a great philosopher may have a phenomenon completely within his view, and yet suffer it to escape his observation." . . . [The reviewer quotes a long passage from Goethe's account of his personal involvement in these investigations, including another reference to Newton:] "I have indeed to acknowledge, with gratitude, the kindness and confidence of the Duke of Weimar, Duke Ernest and Prince Augustus of Gotha, and the Prince Primate, who was at that time at Erfurt; as well as of many celebrated anatomists, chemists, scholars, and moralists; but not of a single natural philosopher. I corresponded long with Lichtenberg: for a time he answered my letters; but when I became more urgent, and expressed more violently my abhorrence of the nauseous doctrine of the Newtonian white, he abruptly dropped the subject, and notwithstanding our intimacy, he had not even the friendship to mention my essays in the last edition of his Erxleben."

I suspect that the word here translated "nauseous" is *widrige*, i.e. contrary to our natural feelings. I have a similar suspicion concerning the word "detestable": even were it *hässliche* in the original, yet the Latin *informis*, deforming, would be the truer version.[1] The insolence, with which this

---

29[1]   The word Goethe used was *ekelhafte* ("nauseous, disgusting, loathsome"), and not *widrige* ("contrary, obnoxious") or *hässliche* ("hateful"). The reviewer's ear- lier "detestable" does not appear in the section about Dolland, and may be a paraphrase rather than a quotation.

coxcomb Review-monger scribbles concerning a Goethe,[a] is very amusing. Fifty such scribes, heaped Pelion on Ossa in Lilliput, would not reach Goethe's[b] ancle.

30   p 433

Much as we have been entertained by the singularity of this statement, we cannot think it necessary to make any serious remarks on it, and shall now take our leave of Mr. von Goethe's work, as far as his own discoveries and opinions are concerned: but we cannot omit to give some account of two short contributions of his friends, which appear to us to be far the most valuable part of the compilation.

Who that has even a common acquaintance with Goethe[a] would take this statement as other than the slander of a vulgar Kenocranioni*?

   * or Cenocranion. Empty-skull to wit.

29[a] TRANSCRIPT Göethe   **29**[b] TRANSCRIPT Göethe's
30[a] TRANSCRIPT Göethe

FRANÇOIS RABELAIS

c 1490–1553/4

The Works of Francis Rabelais. Translated from the French, and illustrated with explanatory notes, by M. Le Du Chat, and others. 4 vols. London 1784. 12°.

Private collection

Bookplates on the front p-d of each vol of James Gillman; Robert, Marquis of Crewe; and Monckton Milnes.

Four annotations, probably in the elder James Gillman's hand, are in Vol I, as follows. A passage on I 158–9, marked with an ink line in the margin, on "Pillicock, her Fiddle-Diddle, her Staff of Love . . . my pretty Rogue", with the note on I 159: "For these *37* names there are only *13* in Rabelais." On I 168 the words "Arse-wisps, Bum-fodders, Tail-napkins, Bung-hole-cleansers and Wipe-breeches" are underlined, with the comment: "all this stuffed in by the translator, as if Rabelais had not known how much filth was enough." On I 216–17 the passage "blockish Grutnols, Doddipol Joltheads . . . turgy Gut" is underlined, with the comment: "inserted by translator". On the back flyleaf, I ⁺2, the note: "Speaking of the Genius of Swift, S. T. C. observed. It was Anima Rabelæsii habitans in sicco = the Soul of Rabelais dwelling in a Dry Land": cf *TT* (*CC*) I 167 n 6.

DATE. Possibly 1825 (*LR* I 138: "about the year 1825") to 1829 (**12**: 15 Sept 1829). C had lectured on Rabelais in 1818: *Lects 1808–1819* (*CC*) II 179–80.

1 I ⁻2

One cannot well help regretting, that no friend of Rabelais (surely, friends he must have had) has left an authentic account of him—/ His buffoonery was not merely Brutus's rough stick that contained a rod of gold.[1] It was necessary as an Amulet against the Monks & Bigots. Beyond doubt, he was among the deepest as well as boldest Thinkers of his Age. Never

---

[1] Lucius Junius Brutus, whom C mentions also in *Lects 1808–1819* (*CC*) II 179, survived under the Tarquins by pretending to be a harmless fool. Dionysius of Halicarnassus *Roman Antiquities* 4.69 tells how the sons of Tarquinius laughed at Brutus when he dedicated only a wooden staff to Apollo at Delphi, not knowing that he had cunningly hollowed out the staff and inserted a rod of gold. Brutus alone interpreted the answer of the oracle correctly: when it told them that he who first kissed his mother would be the next king, Brutus kissed the earth of Italy as soon as they landed there.

was a more plausible, & seldom, I am persuaded, a less appropriate, Line than the 1000 times quoted

Rabelais laughing in his easy chair

of Mr Pope.[2] The *caricature* of his Filth & Zanyism proves how fully he both knew & felt the danger, in which he stood.   S. T. C.

2 I $^-2^a$

We have "Reading made easy"—Why not Rabelais made decent—alias Pantagruel in Small clothes/ mem. *modern with flaps.*[1]   S. T. C.—

3 I $^-1$

I could write a treatise in praise of the morality and moral Elevation of Rabelais' Works, which would make the Church stare, and the Conventicle groan—and yet should be the truth, & nothing but the truth.

S. T. Coleridge/

3A I xx, marked in the margin with a pencil line | The Life of Dr. Francis Rabelais

. . . he is said not to have been able to refrain his satyrical Temper, even while he was reading Public Service; and instead of *Qui moechantur cum illâ* [Rev 2.22 AV, "that commit adultery with her"], as the Vulgate has it, to have said aloud, *Qui monachantur cum illâ* ["that commit monkery with her"—*monachor* meaning "to be a monk"].

3B I xlvi | The Preface

. . . what the Word *Utopia*, from οὐ and τόπος, signifies, *viz. What is not found*, or, *a Place not to be found*.!!!!![1]

1[2] Lines 1–4 of *Inscriptio*—verses addressed to Swift in a letter of Jan 1729: "And thou! whose sense, whose humour, and whose rage, / At once can teach, delight, and lash the age, / Whether thou choose Cervantes' serious air, / Or laugh and shake in Rab'lais' easy chair . . .": Pope *Poems* ed John Butt (1963) 497.

2[1] Smallclothes are knee-breeches. C specifies the kind with buttoned flaps front and back. A century earlier, the whole garment had to be let down: cf Swift *A Tale of*

a Tub ed A. C. Guthkelch and D. Nichol Smith (Oxford 1973) 78: "Is not Religion a *Cloak*, Honesty a *Pair of Shoes*, worn out in the Dirt, Self-love a *Surtout*, Vanity a *Shift*, and Conscience a *Pair of Breeches*, which, tho' a Cover for Lewdness as well as Nastiness, is easily slipt down for the Service of both."

3B[1] The etymology, from "no" and "place", is correct, but C preferred to derive the "U" from εὐ- ("well-"): cf FLÖGEL **15** and n 1.

4 ɪ lii

By the *Anticyrian Hellebore* (17), with which he purged *Gargantua*'s
Brain, may be meant powerful Arguments drawn from Reason and the
Scripture, opposed to the Authority of the *Popish* Church . . . [Footnote:]
(17) Ἀντίκυρία potestas, apud Suidam [Anticyrean power, in Suidas (a
Greek lexicon)].

!!!! *tribus Anticyris*[1]

5 ɪ 270–1, pencil | Bk 1 ch 41

. . . at their Pleasure, was he [the Monk] armed *Cap-a-pe*, and mounted
(8) upon one of the best Horses in the Kingdom, with [a] good slashing
Sabre by his Side . . . [Footnote:] (8) . . . M. *Du Chat* will have it that *Rabelais* here means a *Neapolitan Horse*, and that he speaks after the Way
of the *Italians*, who by the bare Word *Kingdom*, commonly understand,
and would have others also understand the Kingdom of *Naples* . . .

Possibly, Rabelais means that tho Luther would have fought the good
fight of the Reformation by himself & with the weapons of the Spirit; yet
he *was* supported by some of the ablest and most warlike Princes of the
Age/—[1]

6 ɪ 286–7, pencil | Bk 1 ch 46

[The Monk, Friar John, had not asked for ransom money to be paid for
his prisoner, Touchefaucet.] Then *Grangousier* commanded, that, in
Presence of *Touchefaucet*, should be delivered to the *Monk* for taking
him, the Sum of threescore and two thousand *Saluts*, which was done,
whilst they made a Collation to the said *Touchefaucet* . . . . After this,
Touchefaucet, got to his Horse, and *Gargantua* for his Safety allowed him
the Guard of thirty Men-at-Arms, and sixscore Archers . . . . As soon as
he was gone, the *Monk* restored unto *Grangousier* the threescore and two
thousand *Saluts*, which he had received, saying, Sir, it is not as yet the
Time for you to give such Gifts.

4[1] Two towns in Greece, both named
Anticyra, were in ancient times famous for
producing the plant hellebore, believed to
be a cure for melancholy and madness. C
quotes a phrase from Horace *Ars poetica*
300—"[not to be cured even] by three An-
ticyras".
5[1] As C's notes, starting with **1** above,
indicate, C interpreted the work of Rabelais
as intermittent religious allegory. As he said
in *TT* (*CC*) ɪɪ 109, "Some of the commentators talk about his book being all political;
there are contemporary politics in it, of
course, but the real scope is much higher
and more philosophical."

Of the difference between mannerly, and moral—yea, and between meanness of mouth and delicacy of mind. What true delicacy was it not in Friar John to receive the 62000 Crowns & to wait for Touchfaucet's departure before he returned them.

7 ɪɪ ⁻3

Rabelais & Luther born in the same year—1483 Cervantes two years after Shakespear. C. 1561. S. 1563.[1]

8 ɪɪ 139–40, pencil, overtraced in ink | Bk 2 ch 21 "How *Panurge* was in Love with a Lady of *Paris*"

The hidden sense in this uncleanly Mythos is the Gallican Church,—the folly in not gaining over to herself the men of Talents & Learning (the πανουργοι)[1] and the consequent contempt, which mere Erasmians & Rabelasians excited against her.

9 ɪɪ 154–5 | Bk 2 ch 24

And I, said *Carpalim*, will get in there [the enemy camp], if the Birds can enter; for I am so nimble of Body, and light withal, that I shall have leaped over their Trenches and ran clean through all their Camp, before that they perceive me: neither do I fear Shot, nor Arrow, nor Horse, how swift soever, were he the *Pegasus of Persee* (*Perseus*) or *Pacolet* [the "wonderful Horse, used . . . by the Hero of the Romance of *Valentine and Orson*" (footnote)]; being assured that I shall be able to make a safe and sound Escape before them all without any Hurt. I will undertake to walk upon the Ears of Corn, or Grass in the Meadows, without making either of them do so much as bow under me; for I am of the Race of *Camilla* the *Amazone*.

Even in this wild grotesque, besides the humorous Parody of the Old Romances, there is a serious Moral—that by Invention, Experience, Vigor, and rapidity of Movement, a kingdom may supersede the necessity of calling forth its main Strength, and reserve it for extreme emergencies—

7[1] Either C or his sources are mistaken about every birth-date except Luther's: Rabelais was born c 1490, Cervantes in 1547, Shakespeare in 1564. The biography of Rabelais in this ed gives 1483 as his birth-date.

8[1] *Panourgoi*, or "Panurges", by deriva-tion "people who do everything", from a Greek adjective meaning "crafty" (as applied by Aristotle to the fox) or "roguish", "knavish". C comments further on the significance of the name in **13**, **17**, and **18** below.

10   II 157–8 | Bk 2 ch 26 "How *Pantagruel* and his Company were weary in eating salt Meats; and How *Carpalim* went a hunting to have some Venison"

It was a triumphant and incomparable Spectacle to see how they ravened and devoured. Then said *Pantagruel*, Would to God every one of you had two Pair of *Sacring* Bells hanging at your Chin, and that I had at mine the great Clocks of *Rennes*, of *Poitiers*, of *Tours*, and of *Cambray*, to see what a Peal they would ring with the Wagging of our Chaps.

Ch. 26 The advantage of Light Horse Cavalry in Foraging is here humorously allegorized in Carpalim—But was there ever anything richer or more joyous than the 3 last lines of p. 158, and the three first lines of p. 159.[1] It is the Glorification, the Apotheosis, of genial Gourmandize! Elysian Gluttony! One's Imagination lives 40 days on this single meal & remains fat at the close.

11   II 164–5 | Bk 2 ch 27

. . . with the Fart, that he [Pantagruel] let, the Earth trembled nine Leagues about; wherewith, and with the corrupted Air, he begot above three and fifty thousand little Men, ill-favour'd Dwarfs; and with one Fisg (Fizzle) that he let, he made as many little Women, crouching down, as you shall see in divers Places; which never grow but like Cows Tails, downwards, or like the *Limosin* Radishes, round. How now, said *Panurge*, are your *Farts* so fertile? By G— here be brave *farted* Men and *fisgued* Women; let them be married together, they will beget fine Hornets and Dorflies.

Tho' it would be frigid to attempt an interpretation of each & every wild flash of Rabelais's phantasmagoria, yet one may conjecture that Rabelais here means the swarm of petty Scribblers and small poets, which the National Exultation in the celebration of a Victory is apt to engender. Vive la grande Nation! pedit Panurge[1]—and the Grand Nation, "whose celestial Breath is sulphurous to smell" (Cymbeline)[2] vivat, repetit, et repedit—/[3]

12   II 254–5 | Bk 3 ch 8

Behold how Nature, having a fervent Desire after its Production of Plants, Trees, Shrubs, Herbs, Sponges, and Plant-animals, to eternize, and con-

—

10[1] Textus.

11[1] C passes from French to Latin: "'Long live the great Nation!' farted Panurge".

11[2] Shakespeare *Cymbeline* v iv 114–15 (var).

11[3] The Nation "repeats, and refarts 'Vivat'".

tinue them unto all Succession of Ages . . . unruinable, and in an ever-lasting Being, hath most curiously armed and fenced their Buds, Sprouts, Shoots, and Seeds, where in the above-mentioned Perpetuity consisteth, by strengthening, covering, guarding, and fortifying them with an admirable Industry, with Husks, Cases, Scarfs, and Swads, Hulls, Cods, Stones, Films, Cartels, Shells, Ears, Rinds, Barks, Skins, Ridges, and Prickles, which serve them instead of strong, fair, and *natural Codpieces:* As is manifestly apparent in Pease, Beans, Fasels, Pomegranates, Peaches, Cottons, Gourds, Pumpeons, Melons, Corn, Lemons, Almonds, Walnuts, Filberts, and Chesnuts . . .

It is impossible to read Rabelais without an admiration mixed with wonder at the depth & extent of his Learning, ~~and~~ his multifarious Knowlege—and original Observation, beyond what Books could in that age have supplied him with!   S. T. C.   15 Septr 1829.

13   II 258–61 | Bk 3 ch 9 "How *Panurge* asketh Counsel of *Pantagruel* whether he
should marry, yea, or no"

In Ch. 9. Pantagruel stands for the *Reason* as contra-distinguished from the understanding & choice[1]—i.e. Panurge—and the humour consists in the latter asking advice of the former on a subject, in which the Reason can only give the necessary Conclusion, the Syllogistic Ergo, from the Premise provided by the Understanding itself—which puts each case so as of necessity to pre-determine the verdict thereon. It is (independent of the Allegory) an exquisite satire on the spirit, in which people commonly ask advice.

14   II 311–12 | Bk 3 ch 18 "How *Pantagruel* and *Panurge* did diversly expound the
Verses of the *Sybil* of *Panzoust*"

Verily, verily, quoth *Panurge*, brave are the Allegations which you bring me, and Testimonies of two-footed Calves. These Men were Fools, as they were Poets; and Dotards, as they were Philosophers; full of folly, as they were of Philosophy.

The whole Chapter is concomparable;[1] but the concluding §ph,[2] transcendent. Panurge exerts all his marvellous ingenuity in wrenching the Text of the Oracle out of its clear & obvious meaning—to make it answer

[13][1] An idea extended in **15** and **18** below. Cf C's use of the distinction in PEPYS **12** (and n 2).

[14][1] Not in *OED*; C may mean "incomparable".
[14][2] I.e. textus.

his own wishes & previous Determination—/ and when he comes to one stiff passage that will not yield, takes shelter in his effrontery: & cries out: and so such & such Commentators take *this* to be ⟨the⟩ Sense of the passage? A pack of numbsculls, bats, moles, Asses. Ha! Ha!—They are not worth confuting.

14A   II 317 | Bk 3 ch 19

I truly, Madam, would have done the like with all my Heart and Soul, quoth Sister *Fatbum*, but thɥat fearing I should remain in Sin . . . I did confess myself . . .

15   II 317

* You will not, quoth *Pantagruel*, with all your Jesting, make me laugh; I know that all Monks, Friars, and Nuns, had rather violate and infringe the highest of the Commandments of God, than break the least of their provincial Statutes.

* This reply of Pantagruel is quite in character. The accidents of the Tale make you laugh; but the tale exemplifies a general truth, that makes me (= the Reason) serious.

16   II 327, marked with a line in the margin | Bk 3 ch 22

Panurge, at his issuing forth of [an "old poet"] *Raminagrobis*'s Chamber, said, as if he had been horribly affrighted, By the Virtue of God, I believe that he is an *Heretic*; the Devil take me, if I do not; he doth so villainously rail at the *Mendicant* Friars, and *Jacobins*: who are the two Hemispheres of the Christian World; by whose gyronomonic Circumbilivaginations, as by two celivagous Filopendulums, all the autonomatic Metagrobolism of the *Romish* Church, when tottering and emblustricated with the Gibble-gabble Gibbrish of this odious Error and Heresy, is homocentrically poised. But what Harm in the Devil's Name, have these poor devils the *Capucins* and *Minims* done unto him? Are not these beggarly Devils sufficiently wretched already? Who can imagine that these poor Snakes, the very Extracts of *Ichthyophagy*, are not thoroughly enough besmoaked and besmeared with Misery, Distress, and Calamity? Dost thou think, Friar *John*, by thy Faith, that he is in the State of Salvation? He goeth, before God, as surely damned to thirty thousand Baskets full of Devils, as a Pruning-bill to the lopping of a Vine-branch.

Admirable! whether considered as exquisite Humour, as keen Satire or as profound Allegory. O Rabelais! Thou *wert* a Man!—

17 II +1

All Rabelais Personages are phantasmagoric Allegories, but Panurge above all.—It is throughout the πανουργαια,[1] the Wisdom, no, Cunning, of the Human Animal/—the Understanding, as the faculty of means to purposes without ultimate Ends, in the most comprehensive sense, including Art, sensuous Fancy, & all the passions of the Understanding made evident.

18 III 10–11, pencil | Bk 3 ch 29 "How *Pantagruel* convocated together a *Theologian*, *Physician*, *Lawyer*, and *Philosopher*, for extricating *Panurge* out of the Perplexity wherein he was"

Admirable even in the unexpected Detail does Rabelais preserve the distinct characters of Pantagr. as the Nous, and Panurge as the animus infra mentem.[1] The former contemplates Classes in reference to the ultimate end of each class; the latter contemplates the class in its accidents, Defects and exceptions—

19 III 40 | Bk 3 ch 34

Welcome (6) in good Faith, my dear Master, welcome; it did me good to hear you talk, the Lord be praised for all.
[Footnote:] (6) . . . It is not said, by *Rabelais*, who it is that speaks here. *However it must be *Panurge*; and his calling *Carpalim Monsieur Maitre* induces M. *du Chat* still the more to think *Carpalim* was a Student of Law, that being the Compellation by which such are distinguished.

* It is not Carpalim with whom Panurge had been during the whole tale but Ponocrates, who is here addressed.[1]

19A IV 156, marked with a pencil line in the margin | Bk 5 ch 11

. . . if you still live but six Olympiads, and the Age of two Dogs more, you'll see these *Furr'd Law-cats* Lords of all *Europe*, and in peaceful Possession of all the Estates and Dominions belonging to it; unless by divine Providence, what's got over the Devil's Back, is spent under his Belly; or the Goods which they unjustly get, perish with their prodigal Heirs: Take this from an honest Beggar.

Among 'em reigns the *Sixth Essence*; by the Means of which they gripe all, devour all, conskite all, burn all, draw all, hang all, quarter all, behead

17[1] Normally πανουργία: cf **8** n 1.
18[1] "Soul/spirit below the mind".
19[1] The text is obscure, as the footnote

indicates. The speech appears, however, to be addressed to Epistemon by Panurge.

all, murder all, imprison all, waste all, and ruin all, without the least Notice of Right or Wrong: For among *them* Vice is call'd Virtue; Wickedness Piety; Treason Loyalty; Robbery Justice. *Plunder* is their Motto, and when acted by them, is approved by all Men, except the Hereticks; *and all this they do because they dare*; their Authority is Sovereign and Irrefragable.

19B   IV 157, marked with a pencil line in the margin

... false Zealots of the Cowl, Heretical Bigots, false Prophets and broachers of Sects, to the villainy of griping Usurers, Clippers, and Coiners; nor to the Ignorance, Impudence, and Imprudence of Physicians, Surgeons, and Apothecaries, nor to the Lewdness of Adulteresses and Destroyers of By-blows; but charge 'em all wholly and solely to the inexpressible, incredible, and inestimable Wickedness and Ruin, which is continually hatch'd, brew'd, and practis'd in the Den or Shop of those *Furr'd Law-cats.*

19C   IV 159, marked with a pencil line in the margin

... some large, stately Mangers were fix'd in the Reverse. Over the chief Seat was the Picture of an Old Woman [Injustice] holding the Case or Scabbard of a Sickle in her Right-hand, a Pair of Scales in her Left, with Spectacles on her Nose: The Cups or Scales of the Balance were a Pair of Velvet-pouches; the one full of *Bullion*, which over-pois'd t'other, empty and long, hoisted higher than the Middle of the Beam ...

19D   IV 161–2, marked with a pencil line in the margin | Bk 5 ch 12

Our Laws are like Cobwcbs; your silly little Flies are stopt, caught, and destroy'd therein, but your stronger ones break them, and force and carry them which Way they please. Likewise don't think we are so mad as to set up our Nets to snap up your great Robbers and Tyrants: No, they are somewhat too hard for us, there's no meddling with them; for they would make no more of us, than we make of the little ones ...

19E   IV 168–9, marked with a pencil line in the margin | Bk 5 ch 15

What made *Hercules* such a famous Fellow, d'ye think? Nothing, but that while he travell'd, he still made it his Business to rid the World of Tyrannies, Errors, Dangers, and Drudgeries; he still put to Death all Robbers, all Monsters, all venomous Serpents, and hurtful Creatures. Why then do we not follow his Example, doing as he did in the Countries through which we pass? He destroy'd the *Stymphalides*, the *Lernaean Hydra*, *Cacus*, *Antheus*, the *Centaurs*, and what not; I am no *Clericus* [clerk (in the sense of man of learning)]; those that are such tell me so.

In imitation of that noble By-blow, let's destroy and root out these wicked Furr'd Law-cats, that are a Kind of ravenous Devils; thus we shall remove all Manner of Tyranny out of the Land.

SIR WALTER RALEGH

c 1552–1618

The History of the World. [Anonymously published. 5 pts in 1 vol, paginated in two groups, bks 1–2 containing 555 pp, and bks 3–5 669 pp.] London 1628. F°.

The engraved title-page bears the date 1614, as did all eds up to 1634; the colophon at the end of bk 5, however, is correctly dated 1628. The usual printed title-page is lacking in this copy.

Victoria College Library (Coleridge Collection)

Thomas Poole's copy, with his signature on p ⁻2, along with the price he paid, "11, 6". On p ⁻1, possibly in Poole's hand, "The first edition printed by Walter Burre". (This page also contains a bookseller's pencilled note, "The colophon is dated 1628".) On p ⁻5, the signature "C. Mansfield Ingleby 1855"; further bibliographical and biographical notes by Ingleby pp ⁻5–⁻6. Ingleby published C's notes from this vol in *N&Q* 1st ser XII (1855) 5–6. Later owners have pasted in newspaper or magazine clippings referring to Ralegh, Poole, or Coleridge at pp ⁻3–⁻4, ⁻5, ⁻8 (p-d). One column about marginalia and three clippings about Ralegh are loose in the vol, as is a note quoting Ralegh, addressed to Mrs Mathewson, Helen's Bay, Co Down, posted from Belfast 8 Jul 1916. Passages are marked in pencil with vertical strokes or thick crosses on sigg A[1]ᵛ, A3ʳ, B[1]ᵛ, B3ʳ, B[4]ʳ, B[5]ʳ, C[1]ʳ, and C2ʳ, and there is a tiny "x" in ink on sig A3ᵛ; but since these marks are not typical of C, and his notes in the vol are in ink, the marked passages have not been recorded.

DATE. 1807? Note **4** is dated 1807, coinciding with a series of notebook entries containing extracts from the *History* (*CN* II 3079–91, 3096–7), and although the ed used is stated to have been a different one (1677: *CN* II 3087n), all the passages including the verses in 3087 appear also in this copy and it seems reasonable to suppose that the extracts and annotations were made at the same time and using the same copy.

---

1   sig A[5]ᵛ | Preface

It is true that hereof we do not yet finde the effect. But had the Duke of Parma in the yeare 1588. *ioyned the army which he commanded, with that of Spaine, and landed it on the south coast; & had his Maiesty at the same time declared himselfe against us in the north: it is easie to divine*

199

what had become of the liberty of England, certainely we would then
without murmur have brought this union a farre greater praise than it
hath since cost us.

Forsan, bought——at a far greater price.[1]

2   sig B3ᵛ

[Quoting Eccles:] The living (*saith hee*) know that they shall die, but the
dead know nothing at all: for who can shew unto man, what shall be after
him under the Sun?

? But of the Dead?

3   sig B[6]ᵛ

Hee [philosophising man] *will disable Gods power to make a world, with-*
out matter to make it of. He will rather give the mothes of the Aire for a
cause, cast the worke on necessity or chance; bestow the honour thereof
on Nature; make two powers, the one to be the Author of the Matter, *the*
other of the Forme; *and lastly, for want of a worke-man, have it Eternall:*
which latter opinion Aristotle *to make himselfe the Author of a new Doc-*
trine, brought into the World: and his Sectatours have maintained it . . .

I do not think that Aristotle made the world eternal, from the difficulty of
aliquid a nihilo *materiale*;[1] but from the idea of God as an eternal *Act—*
actus purissimus,[2] and eternity = simultaneous Possession of total
Being—for strictly God neither was or will be, but always *is*. We may
without absurdity or contradiction combine the faith of Aristotle & the
Church, saying—God from all eternity creates the world by & through
the Λογος.[3]

4   i 65 | Bk 1 ch 5 § 5 "Of the long lives of the Patriarchs . . ."

The third Obiection is, that the great difference of yeeres betweene those
of the first Age, whereof some of them had well neere seene a thousand
yeares, makes it disputable, whether the account of times were of the

1[1] C suggests "perhaps, bought . . .".
This is indeed the reading of the 1st ed
(1614).
3[1] "Something [created] from no *mat-*
ter".
3[2] "*Absolutely pure act*"—part of a

scholastic definition of God frequently invoked by C, e.g. BAXTER *Catholick Theol-*
ogy 1 and n 2.
3[3] The Logos, i.e. the Son or Word (John
1), the second person in the Trinity.

same measure as in after-Ages, seeing, that soone after the Floud, men lived not a third part of that time, and in succeeding Ages and to this day, not the tenth.

They that have hereon resolved that those years were but Lunary yeeres, (to wit) of a Moneth or thereabouts, or Egyptian yeares, are easily confuted.

It is said, that the first ycars were 3 moons: that the Ideal of each Animals life (of the warm-blooded) is 8 times its full growth: that man is at his *full* at 25, which by 8 = 200—and that, taking 3 as the first perfection of number by Unity (that is, 3 is *tri-une*), & 3 moons as the first year, this would agree with the age of Methusalem, the only man who ever reached the Ideal.[1] A negro in Peru who was still living eight years back, was then 186 as known by public registers of sales.—[2]   1807.

5   i 132 | Ch 8 § 11 (2) "Of the time about which the name of Egypt beganne to be knowne"

These Riddles are also rife among the *Athenians* and *Arcadians*, who dare affirme, that they are more ancient than *Iupiter* and the *Moone*; whereof *Ovid*:

> Ante Iovem *genitum terras habuisse feruntur*
> *Arcades:* & Luna *gens prior illa fuit.*
> The Arcadians the earth inhabited
> Ere yet the *Moone* did shine, or *Iove* was bred.

This may be *equally true*, whether the Moon were a Comet stopped by the attraction of the earth, and compelled, tho' not without some staggering, to assimilate its orbit; or whether the inward fire-matter of the

[1] Gen 5.27: "And all the days of Methuselah were nine hundred sixty and nine years: and he died." Rival theories of longevity coexisted in the late 18th century; the source of C's has not been traced, but it may have been based on that of Buffon, who suggested that an animal might expect to achieve an age six or seven times its period of growth. (Buffon, however, considered that period in humankind as lasting 14 years.) Combining this calculation with the hypothesis of a three-month year, Methuselah still reaches an exceptional 242.

[2] No direct source has been found for this assertion. The connection between longevity and Peru appears, however, to have been established, and to have been prominently displayed in 1807 (a putative date for the marginalia): the Jan 1807 issue of *Ed Rev*, reviewing a Peruvian periodical entitled *Mercurio Peruano*, cites figures to support the remarkable longevity of the Peruvians (*Ed Rev* IX—1807—441); longevity in general is the topic of James Sinclair's *Code of Health and Longevity* (4 vols Edinburgh 1807) and James Easton's *Human Longevity* (Salisbury 1799), though neither of them mentions Peru specifically.

Earth turning an ocean suddenly into Steam projected a continent from that hollow which is now filled up by the Pacific & South Sea/ which is about the size of the moon.[1]

5[1] C alludes to these rival theories about the formation of the moon also in SCHU-BERT *Ansichten* **21** below. Other contemporary references indicate that they were general knowledge. The comet theory is mentioned, for example, by Laplace, in the context of the claims of the Arcadians (as in textus), in *The System of the World* tr J. Pond (2 vols 1809) II 95: "Other philosophers, struck with the singular opinion of the Arcadians who thought themselves more ancient than the Moon, have imagined that this satellite may formerly have been a comet which passing near the Earth may have been forced by its attraction to accompany it." The "fire-matter" theory is raised by Erasmus Darwin in both *The Economy of Vegetation* (1791; pt i of *The Botanic Garden*) canto 2 lines 73–93 and *The Temple of Nature* (1803) Additional Note 3—which reads, in part, "If the moon be supposed to have been thus thrown out of the great cavity which now contains the South Sea . . .".

THOMAS RANDOLPH
1605–1635

Poems. With the Muses Looking-Glasse. Amyntas. Jealous Lovers. Arystippus. . . . 4th ed rev. 5 pts in one vol. London 1652. 8°. Each of the titles listed has its separate title-page and pagination.

New York Public Library (Berg Collection)

Inscribed on title-page "S. T. Coleridge—given me by Robert Southey". Bookplates on p ⁻3, of "Sea Serjeants Meeting" and William Harris Arnold; bookseller's pencilled description p ⁻2. Throughout the *Poems*, *The Muses Looking-Glasse*, and *The Jealous Lovers*, misprints and unusual spellings are underlined with a discreet pen-stroke, perhaps by RS; on *Poems* p 100, two of these are reinforced with pencilled corrections not in C's hand.

DATE. May 1810, when there is a notebook entry about this work (*CN* III 3828), or earlier—these are comparatively scanty notes, such as are associated with C's earliest annotations: *CM* (*CC*) I lxxxi.

1   i 95 [*for* 93], pencil, with a pencilled line in the right-hand margin | *Poems*: "A Pastorall Courtship" lines 1–64

> Behold these woods, and mark my *Sweet*
> How all these boughes together meet!
> The *Cedar* his fair arms displayes,
> And mixes branches with the *Bayes*.
> The lofty *Pine* dains to descend,
> And sturdy *Oaks* do gently bend.
> One with another subt'ly weaves
> Into one loom their various leaves;
> As all ambitious were to be
> Mine and my *Phyllis* canopie!
>   Let's enter, and discourse our Loves;
> These are, my dear, no tell-tale groves!
> There dwell no Pyes, nor Parrots there,
> To prate again the words they heare.
> Nor babling Echo, that will tell
> The neighbouring hills one syllable.
>   Being enter'd lets together lye,
> Twin'd like the Zodiaks *Gemini*!

How soon the flowers do sweeter smell?
And all with emulation swell
To be thy pillow? These for thee
Were meant a bed, and thou for me,
And I may with as just esteem
Presse thee, as thou mayst lie on them.
And why so coy? What dost thou fear?
There lurks no speckled Serpent here.
No Venemous snake makes this his rode,
No Canker, nor the loathsome Toad.
And yon poor spider on the tree,
Thy spinster will, no poysoner be,
There is no Frog to leap and fright
Thee from my arms and break delight;
Nor Snail that o're thy coat shall trace,
And leave behind a slimy lace.
2   This is the hallowed shrine of Love,/!
1   No wasp nor hornet haunts this grove,/:[1]
    Nor Pismire to make pimples rise
Upon thy smooth and ivory thighes.
No danger in these shades doth lye,
Nothing that wears a sting: but I:
And in it doth no venome dwell,
Although perchance it make thee swell.
        Being set, let's sport a while my Fair,
I will tie Love-knots in thy hair.
See *Zephyrus* through the leaves doth stray,
And has free liberty to play:
And braids thy locks: And shall I find
Lesse favour then a saucy winde?
Now let me sit, and fix my eyes,
On thee that art my Paradise.
Thou art my all; the spring remains
In the fair violets of thy vains:
And that it is a summers day,
Ripe Cherries in thy lips display.
And when for Autumn I would seek,
'Tis in the Apples of thy cheek.

---

[1] I.e. C would reverse the lines and alter the punctuation accordingly: "No wasp nor hornet haunts this grove: / This is the hallowed shrine of Love!"

But that which onely moves my smart,
Is to see winter in thy heart.
Strange, when at once in one appear
All the four seasons of the year!
I'le clasp that neck where should be set
A rich and Orient Carkanet;
But swains are poor, admit of then
More naturall chains, the arms of men.

The first 64 lines make a pleasing poem, with the omission of six.

1A   p 95, pencil | Lines 65–81, continuing textus **1**

Come let me touch those breasts, that swell
Like two fair mountains, and may well
Be stil'd the Alpes, but that I fear
The snow has less of whitenesse there.
But stay (my Love) a fault I spie,
Why are these two fair fountains dry?
Which if they run, no Muse would please
To tast of any spring but these.
And *Ganymed* employ'd should be
To fetch his *love Nectar* from thee.
Thou shalt be Nurse fair *Venus* swears,
To the next *Cupid* that she bears.
Were it not then discreetly done
To ope one spring to let two run?
Fy, fy, this Belly, Beauty's mint,
Blushes to see no coyn stampt in't.
Employ it then, for though it be . . .

2   i 99, pencil | "Upon a very deformed Gentlewoman, but of a voyce incomparable sweet"

a very spirited Copy of Verses

1A[1] C's emphatic crossing-through ends here, at the foot of the page. There is also a faint pencil-line, however, through two-thirds of the next page (lines 82–104), and another, firmer line from line 125 to the end of the poem.

PAUL DE RAPIN-THOYRAS
1661–1725

Lost Book

The History of England. Written in French by Mr. Rapin de Thoyras. Translated into English, with additional notes, by N. Tindal . . . . 3rd ed. 5 vols. London 1743–7. F°.

Not located; marginalia not recorded. *Gillman SC* 504.

AUGUST WILHELM REHBERG

1757–1836

Ueber das Verhältniss der Metaphysik zu der Religion. Berlin 1787. 8°.

British Library C 134 b 13

Inscribed by C on p ⁻1 (inside of original paper wrapper): "Sara Hutchinson S. T. Coleridge", the names joined with a brace. In pencil, the numbers "27-1", which also appear in ink at the top of p ⁺2.

The vol was presented to the BM by Bernard Flexner, who in presenting the book states in a letter of 9 Nov 1934 (once tipped into the book but removed in rebinding on 30 Aug 1954): "Some years ago, in this City [New York], I picked out of a box of books on sale, a volume entitled 'Ueber das Verhaltnisz der Metaphysik der Religion' by August Wilhelm Rehberg, Berlin 1787." Because he identified the marginalia as C's, he presented the book to the BM. The BM rebinding of 1954 preserves the original paper wrappers and incorporates a typescript of C's notes in the front flyleaves.

DATE. Aug 1804; **3** is dated 29 Aug 1804.

COEDITORS. Lore Metzger, Raimonda Modiano.

---

1 p ⁻1 (the book inverted), pencil

Ulrich
Hemsterhuis[1]

---

2 p 10, pencil

Die Bemühungen mehrerer vortrefflicher Männer der neuesten Zeiten, sind dahin gerichtet, das Wesentliche der christlichen Religion, von den

---

1[1] Johann August Heinrich Ulrich (1746–1813) was professor of philosophy at Jena and author of *Institutiones logicae et metaphysicae*, a work cited by Rehberg on pp 52, 95, 116. Franciscus Hemsterhuis (1720–90) was a Dutch scholar of philosophy and aesthetics who had a great influence on Herder, Hölderlin, Jacobi, and other German writers. Rehberg cites his *Lettre sur l'homme et ses rapports* (1772) on pp 74 and 76 and his *Aristée; ou de la divinité* (1779) on p 102. There is no evidence suggesting that C ever read the works of Ulrich or Hemsterhuis. C refers to Hemsterhuis in *The Friend* (*CC*) I 155, but his familiarity with the Dutch philosopher was most likely limited to an indirect source, Jacobi's letter to Hemsterhuis in *Ueber die Lehre des Spinoza* pp 100–57, as also in *Logic* (*CC*) 230n. (C annotated this letter: JACOBI *Ueber die Lehre* **9, 10**.)

Untersuchungen der gelehrten Theologie unabhängig zu machen, und dadurch dem He~~rr~~ere von Zweifeln in der Quelle zuvorzukommen . . .

[In recent times the efforts of several excellent men have been directed towards showing that what is essential in the Christian religion is independent of the investigations of scholarly theology; they thus hope to forestall the host of doubts at their source . . .]

dem Heere = the Host of Doubts.[1] "Dem Strome"[2] would have been the better metaphor.

3 p +2, pencil, referring to pp 46–50

Es entsteht ferner noch immer mehr Schwierigkeiten, wenn man weiter fragt, wie aus der Verschiedenheit in der Zusammensetzung der Monaden, die specifisch unterschiednen sinnlichen Vorstellungen entstehen? das ist . . . warum von zween Körpern, die sich nur darum von einander unterscheiden, dass die Theile des einen, sich in einer andern Lage gegen einander befinden, als die Theile des andern, der eine roth und der andre blau erscheint? Diese letzte Frage hat noch keiner aus der Schule, die sonst alle Erscheinungen in der menschlichen Seele, aus dem mehr oder minder erklärt . . . beantworten können. . . . Zweitens deutet das Selbstgefühl an, unsre Seele bestehe aus mehr als blosser Erkenntniss und Empfindung, indem aus diesen beyden Begriffen noch nicht erklärt werden kann, warum mit grösserer Erkenntniss, mit dem Gefühle eines vollkommnen Zustandes, die Empfindung des Vergnügens, und mit der Vorstellung von der Abnahme dieser Vollkommenheit, die Empfindung der Schmerzens verbunden seyn müsse. . . . Die Leibnizianer entgehn dieser Schwierigkeit dadurch, dass sie alle Empfindung in Erkenntniss von Vollkommenheit auflösen, und (wiewohl immer vergeblich) aus dem Wesen eines Geistes zu beweisen suchen . . .

[Even more difficulties arise when one asks a further question: how do the individually differentiated sensible representations originate from differences in the composition of the monads? that is . . . given two bodies which differ only in this, that the parts of the one are arranged in a different relation to each other from the parts of the other, why does one appear as red and the other as blue? No one from the school which otherwise explains all appearances in the human soul in terms of more or less . . . has yet been able to answer this last question. . . . Second, self-consciousness indicates that our soul consists of more than mere knowledge and sensation; for no one has yet been able to explain by means of these two concepts why a sense of pleasure should be associated with greater knowledge, with the consciousness of a perfect state, and why a sense of pain should be associated with the idea of the loss of this perfection. . . . The

[2][1] This correction and the other two noted by C on pp 55 and 119 (**3A** and **7A** below) appear in the errata annexed to the front of the book, which lists 25 misprints.
[2][2] I.e. "stream" would be better than "host".

followers of Leibniz evade this difficulty by resolving all sensation into the knowledge of perfection and by trying (although always in vain) to use as proof the essence of mind . . .]

S. T. Coleridge August 29th, Syracuse ⟨1804⟩ read this masterly Work/
p. 47 & 50 admirable indeed/ & yet I have the courage (the impudence?) to *hope*, that I shall give the *wie* and *warum*[1] of color; & of pain & pleasure aus dem mehr und minder[2] of the ⟨monadic⟩ τo ζην —[3]

3A   p 55, pencil

[Footnote:] ~~Er~~ So sagt er [Spinoza] im 73sten Briefe, dem letzten vor seinem Tod unter den vorhandnen.

[So he says in his 73rd letter, the last extant before his death.]

4   p 56, pencil

Wolf stellt den Begriffen und Beweisen des Spinoza nur seine eignen entgegen . . . . Denn er bemerkt zwar sehr gut, dass die Attribute das Wesen der Substanz nicht völlig erschöpfen, und wenn man ihm die Instanz machte, dass er selbst die Vorstellung als das Wesen der Monaden angiebt, so würde er sich durch den Unterschied der Vorstellung von der Vorstellungskraft retten, in welcher letztern eigentlich das Wesen jener bestehen soll.

[Wolf opposes Spinoza's concepts and proofs only by substituting his own . . . . For he does indeed observe that the attributes do not fully exhaust the essence of the substance; and if one were to accuse him of declaring representation to be the essence of the monads, he would save himself by distinguishing representation from the mental power of representation, in which latter the essence of the monads is strictly speaking supposed to consist.]

In the same way might Spinoza justify himself by distinguishing Ausdehnung from Ausdehnungskraft.[1]

3[1] The "how and why", as at beginning of textus. C's interest in optics generally and in colour specifically appears in late notes such as QUARTERLY JOURNAL 3 above, but also in relatively early notes, e.g. a notebook entry of 1807 based on the Young-Helmholtz theory: *CN* II 3116. The Newtonian theory of colours, which C later took pains to attack, was the basis of David Hartley's observations about colour in *Observations on Man* (1791) I 41–2, 192–7.

3[2] From textus: "in terms of more or less".

3[3] Literally "the to live", i.e. life, or living.

4[1] "Extension" from "power of extension". The concept appears in Spinoza's exposition of Descartes and, more controversially, in *Ethics*, e.g. pt 2 prop 2 (tr) "*Extension is an attribute of God*, or *God is an extended thing*."

5 p +2, referring to p 62

Sollten diese Attribute, oder irgend ein Begriff, das Wesen der Substanz an sich ausdrücken, so müsste aus demselben nicht nur die Möglichkeit, sondern auch die Wirklichkeit der Verschiedenheit ihrer Accidenzen erhellen. Diese Forderung, deren Gültigkeit . . . Spinoza in Ansehung der Körperwelt wohl einsahe . . . enthält einen Widerspruch. Denn wie kann Ein allgemeiner Begriff die Nothwendigkeit mannichfaltiger Beschaffenheiten desselben enthalten? Wie kann der Grund der Verschiedenheit in dem liegen, was der Verschiedenheit gemein ist?

Es werden daher die Metaphysiker allemal genöthigt, bey dieser Erklärung noch etwas ausser dem Begriffe der Substanz zu Hülfe zu nehmen, und das ist denn der Wille des Schöpfers.

[If these attributes, or some concept, were to express the essence of the substance in itself, then the same would have to reveal not only the possibility, but also the reality of the diversity of its accidents. This requirement, the validity of which . . . Spinoza could understand in the case of the material world . . . contains a contradiction. For how can *One* general concept contain the necessity of its having manifold features? How can the ground of diversity lie in that which is common to diversity?

Thus, to give an explanation here, the metaphysician has always needed to draw on something beyond the concept of substance, and that is the will of the creator.]

p. 62 ADMIRABLE ADMIRABLE.

6 pp 75–6, pencil

In den sinnlichen Vorstellungen aber liegt noch nicht die Nothwendigkeit ihrer Verbindung mit einander in einer sinnlichen Erscheinung, welche doch Nothwendigkeit enthält. . . . Wenn wir zum Exempel ein grünes Blatt sehen, so ist es uns unmöglich . . . die Vorstellung von der grünen Farbe, von der Figur und den übrigen Eigenschaften dieses Begriffes vom grünen Blatte zu trennen. . . . Dass die Träume und Einbildungen hierin der sinnlichen Erscheinung gleich sind, das kann keinen Einwurf abgeben; denn eben dieses beweiset nur, dass die Träume und Einbildungen noch etwas mehreres enthalten, als Vorstellung, etwas Substantielles an sich . . .

[The sensible representations alone contain no necessity for their connection with one another in a sensible appearance, something that does contain necessity. . . . If, for example, we see a green leaf, it is impossible for us . . . to separate the representation of the green colour from the shape and other properties of the concept of the green leaf. . . . It is impossible to deny that in this respect dreams and fantasies are similar to the sensible appearance; for this proves only that dreams and fantasies include something more than representation, something substantial in itself . . .]

Why should not a Vorstellung, a Thought, be as necessary as a Substance? Is there any Thought, to which this does not apply? What is it to me whether I *have*, or whether I *imagine*, the green Leaf before me!—In either case I can *substitute* but not *alter*.

7   p 93, pencil

Erstlich wird behauptet, dieser Begriff [der Ursache] müsse nicht bloss auf die wechselnde Erscheinung eingeschränkt werden, indem wir zu jeder Erscheinung eine Ursache ausser unsrer Vorstellung suchen. Der Schlüssel zu dieser und vielen daraus abgeleiteten Schwierigkeiten, liegt in dem nicht genug beachteten Unterschiede der Ursache und der Kraft .... Ursache ist die vorhergehende Erscheinung; Kraft hingegen der Grund der Veränderung ...

[First it has been maintained that this concept [of cause] should not be limited to the changing appearance only, since for every appearance we seek a cause outside our representations. The key to this difficulty, and to many derived from it, lies in the insufficiently noticed difference between cause and force .... Cause is the anterior appearance; force, on the other hand, the ground of the alteration ...]

Is there not a Confusion here of *Cause* with *Occasion*? Tho' it might be well, if Use permitted it, to consider *Causes* as the *Continuum vehiculare*[1] of Power.—

7A   p 119

[Footnote:] Wer von diesen Ideen der Gottheit mehr zu wissen verlangt, wird interessante Vermuthungen und schöne Träume darüber im *Parmenides* des Plato finden, welcher die UnVollkommenheit in der Ausführung, der Materie zuschreibt.

[He who wants to know more about these ideas of the divine, will find interesting conjectures and pleasant dreams in the *Parmenides* of Plato, who ascribes to matter the imperfection of their realisation.]

8   p 121, pencil

Die einfache Verbindung des Vergnügens oder Schmerzes mit einer Wahrnehmung der Sinne, ist blosse Begierde oder Abscheu. Ganz sinnliche Wesen werden durch solche einfache Verknüpfungen jeden Augenblick regiert. So die Thiere, wenigstens mehrenteils. [Footnote:] In dies-

---

[1] What realises and keeps power going, the "continuum that transmits power".

em Verstande können die Thiere Maschinen heissen. Hingegen ist die gänzliche Empfindungslosigkeit derselben eine grundlose und in der practischen Sittenlehre schädliche Hypothese.

[The simple connection of pleasure or pain with a sense perception is mere desire or repulsion. Wholly sensual beings are ruled by such simple connections every moment. Animals [are ruled] thus, at least for the most part. [Footnote:] In this sense animals may be called machines. On the other hand, the hypothesis that animals are completely unable to experience physical sensations is groundless and, in practical moral philosophy, pernicious.]

In the first sense only did Des Cartes deem the Brutes Machines.[1]

9 pp 142–3, pencil

Es ist daher die gewöhnliche Vorstellung, dass aller Streit unter den Menschen aufhören würde, wenn sie alle vollkommen moralisch handelten, ganz falsch. Sie würden mit einander streiten, aber ohne einander zu hassen, denn die Vernunft eines jeden würde billigen, was der andre, durch einen andern Gesichtspunkt und andre Empfindungen bewogen, gegen ihn thäte.

[Therefore the common idea that all discord among men would cease if they all acted morally is utterly false. They would quarrel with each other but without hating each other, for each one's reason would approve what the other did against him, being affected by a different viewpoint and different feelings.]

I believe, that Experience rather shows its truth[a] all immoral feelings removed, Man is more inclined to believe the superiority than the inferiority of ~~others~~ others, because he knows his own ~~per~~ Imperfections more *intuitively* & vividly than theirs; whereas the kindness of his nature prompts to take their virtues as more perfect than his own/ rather, as his own magnified & defecated by Imagination.

9[a] ms thus, but the sense indicates a pause or stop here

8[1] Descartes speaks of animals as machines in *Discourse on Method* pt 5 where, as C rightly points out, he does not argue that animals lack sensibility, but that they lack reason "and that it is the nature which acts in them according to the disposition of their organs, just as a clock, which is composed of wheels and weights[,] and is able to tell the hours . . ." (*D Works* I 117). The issue of Descartes' "animal machines" comes up also in PEREIRA 2 above (and n 5), where other texts are cited.

Untersuchungen über die Französische Revolution nebst kritischen Nachrichten von den merkwürdigsten Schriften welche darüber in Frankreich erschienen sind. 2 vols. Hanover & Osnabrück 1793. 8°.

Victoria College Library (Coleridge Collection)

Autograph signature "S. T. Coleridge" on the title-page of Vol I. Description by EHC, marked "Green Bequest", in pocket attached to I +3 (p-d). The book was cropped for binding after C's one note was written, but the leaf was folded in to preserve the note.

DATE. After 1798, perhaps c 1804 like the preceding work.

COEDITORS. Lore Metzger, Raimonda Modiano.

1 I 48

[Rehberg asserts that "reason, which determines the natural rights of man, is silent on the subject of social relations, and with respect to these refers us to human deliberation and arbitrary choice" (p 45). He then discusses the question of the political inequality that may be caused by property laws such as those based on primogeniture.] Aber so lange bis jemand auftreten, und aus dem Naturrechte beweisen wird, dass das Eigenthumsrecht an ein Feld demjenigen der es bebauet hat, Zustehe, und dass die Kinder dieses Eigenthümers, an das Feld das nehmliche Recht haben, welches alle andere Menschen respectiren müssen, ohne dass darüber ein positives Gesetz gemacht worden: so lange werde ich immer ohne Gefahr behaupten dürfen, dass freywillige und willkührliche Bestimmungen des Eigenthums, rechtmässig sind. Wenn das Gesetz der Natur . . . darüber nichts mit evidenter unwidersprechlicher Gewissheit bestimmt, so muss das willkührlich erdachte Gesetz des Menschen zu Hülfe kommen, und die Bestimmungen angeben, die für rechtmässig gelten sollen.

[But until someone comes and demonstrates that according to natural law the right of ownership of a field belongs to the one who tills it, and that the children of this owner have the same right to the field, a right which all others must respect without there being a positive law to that effect: until then I will always be able safely to maintain that deliberate and arbitrary determinations of property are legitimate. If natural law . . . here determines nothing with evident and incontrovertible certainty, then arbitrarily conceived human law must come to its aid and determine what is to be considered legitimate.]

But surely there must be some guide. Does not the Writer fall into the fault of making Vernunft & Verstand two separate Persons?[1] Can Man ever cease to be amenable to the moral Law?—If Primogeniture be for the advantage of a State, doubtless his arguments hold.[2] For it is not a case of positive Duty, in which we are forbidden to rest our conduct on calculations. But where this does not take place, assuredly, the next law of morals does, that of promoting the happiness of the greatest number.—

[1] "Reason" and "understanding"—the crucial Kantian distinction adopted and extended by C throughout his career: cf PEPYS 12 and n 2, and esp SCHELLING *Denkmal* 16 n 1. In this passage, Rehberg uses *Vernunft* consistently, although *Verstand* appears elsewhere, e.g. p 49.

[2] C comments on the "mournful alienation of brotherly Love occasioned by Primogeniture in noble families" in SHAKESPEARE COPY D 75.

JOHANN ALBERT HEINRICH REIMARUS
1729–1814

Ueber die Gründe der menschlichen Erkentniss und der natürlichen Religion. Hamburg 1787. 8°.
Bound as second with RICHTER *Das Kampaner Thal*, and with an unidentified (unannotated) pamphlet on slavery written after 1803.

Princeton University Library

Autograph signature "S. T. Coleridge" on p ⁻2 of the composite volume; bookplate of M. Taylor Pyne on ⁻5 (p-d). Numerals pencilled on pp ⁺2, ⁺3, partly obliterated, may be C's—as is the pencilled diagram on p ⁺3 (**24** below). For a note on the flyleaf of the vol that may refer to this work see RICHTER *Kampaner Thal* **1** and n 1.

DATE. Probably between the spring of 1811 and the summer of 1815. Although C was familiar with some writings of Reimarus as early as Dec 1803 (see *CN* I 1720, 1724), these marginalia seem to be of the same date as the marginalia in RICHTER *Das Kampaner Thal*. C alludes to Reimarus, probably meaning this work, in *BL* ch 6 (*CC*) I 106 (and n 2) and in FICHTE *Bestimmung* **10** (and n 1).

COEDITORS. Lore Metzger, Raimonda Modiano.

1   pp 3–5 | §§ 2–3

"Das Element aller menschlichen Erkentniss (sagt er [Jacobi]) sey *Offenbarung*, und *Glaube* an dieselbe." Als man nun hierüber weitern Aufschluss verlangte, erklärt es der Verfasser der Resultate, dass unter dieser Offenbarung die *sinnliche Evidenz* oder *anschauende Erkentniss* verstanden werde . . . . "Durch den Glauben (an diese Offenbarung) wissen wir, dass wir einen Körper haben"—Wissen wir? Ich denke—durch den Glauben glauben wir nur, oder *meinen* zu wissen. . . . Kann also die sinnliche Erkentniss irgend eine Probe der Gewisheit seyn? . . . Eben so ist es mit den Dingen, welche wir uns als *ausser uns* befindlich vorstellen. Wir können glauben Flammen zu sehen, Töne zu hören, ohne dass etwas von aussen unsere Sinne rührt. Was entscheidet dann in allen diesen Fällen die Täuschung? Doch nicht eine unmittelbare Ueberzeugung: nein—nichts als . . . der Gebrauch der Vernunft.

["The principle of all human knowledge (he [Jacobi] says) is *revelation* and *belief* in the same." Since further explanation of this matter was asked for, the author of the *Re-*

215

sults has now explained that by revelation is understood *sensory evidence* or *intuitive knowledge* . . . . "Through belief (in this revelation) we know that we have a body"— Do we know? It seems to me through belief we only believe or *think* we know. . . . Can sensory knowledge, then, be any kind of test of certainty? . . . The same goes for the things which we imagine as existing *outside ourselves*. We can believe we see flames and hear sounds without there being anything from the outside affecting our senses. How then do we decide that these are all cases of delusion? Certainly not by immediate conviction: no—solely by . . . the use of reason.]

Reimarus did not understand Jacobi who, I suspect, did not thoroughly understand himself. Not the impressions and sensations which are the *Stuff* of the phænomenal world, not was *scheint* ausser uns zu seyn,[1] but the existence of a supporting reality corresponding to it, as a sense does to its proper word—this we know by an ipse dixit of our Conscience, which Jacobi borrowing the language of the first Quakers entitles a revelation.[2] He would have conveyed his meaning more clearly, had he said that Conscience or the moral Postulate, is the Antecedent of human Consciousness, and its necessary Condition. But there is an ambiguity in the German, Glaube, which does not necesssarily accompany the word, *Faith*—& this misled Jacobi, and made him confuse ~~the~~ two perfectly distinct conceptions—i.e. Faith and Belief:[3] And Reimarus, who understood him to speak wholly of the latter, and who had no reason to understand him otherwise, has manifestly the whip hand of him in the argument. To know by Belief, is = to believe that we know—or rather it is nonsense.

2   pp 15–17 | § 9

Doch ich will das Entstehen unserer Begriffe, wie sie, nach und nach aus der Vergleichung entspringen, nicht weiter erörtern. Ich wolte hier nur von dem sinnlichen oder anschauenden Erkentnisse reden, und, da die Resultate sagen—"ohne Erfahrung sey die Erkenntniss des Daseyns unmöglich"—zu bedenken geben, dass ohne Vernunftgebrauch keine Erfahrung empfunden oder geoffenbaret werde . . .

[But here I will end the discussion of the origin of our concepts, how they originate little by little from comparison. I wished only to speak of sensory or intuitive knowledge; and—since the *Results* say that "without experience knowledge of existence is impossible"—to suggest that no experience can be felt or revealed without the use of reason . . .]

1[1] "What *appears* to be outside us": C echoes textus.

1[2] C does not appear to have associated this usage with the Quakers elsewhere; for the idea itself, see also his assertion in HOOKER 26 that "reason in man must have [been] first actuated by a direct Revelation from God".

1[3] C insisted on this distinction elsewhere, e.g. HEINROTH 11, LUTHER *Colloquia* 80.

Not only is there, ὡς ἐμοίγε δοκεῖ,[1] a confusion of Image and Conception throughout this reasoning; but an inadvertency to the Quantum of Thought blended with and as it were interpolating the mere visual impressions in the total Picture or Presentation, der Vorstellung, oder dem Ganzen, was wir uns vorstellen.[2] In omnem actum Perceptionis influit Imaginatio—says Wolff, and truly![3] But it is equally true, that in omnem actum Imaginationis influit Conceptio sive Intellectus.[4] As a Philosophy of Reflection, the Kantéan rightly reduces the total Sum of what is received from without to Sensation and errs only in describing it as a Chaos. All Form is, I concede, in and from the mind[a]; but this is modified and particularized in correspondence to the plus, and minus, nay, to the distinction in kind, of the impact or resistance from without.

3   pp 18–20 | § 9 note 13

Er [unser Begriff vom Raume] ist auch allerdings, wie Herr Kant lehrt, blosse *Form* unserer Anschauung: nur sehe ich nicht, wie es eine Vorstellung *a priori* zu nennen sey, die in Gemüthe selbst läge, und vor aller Empfindung hergehen müsse. . . . Die Vorstellung des Raums betrift doch auch nur das Verhältniss zweier Sinne, des Gesichts und Gefühls . . . die Verhältnisse aber, welche wir Geschmack, Geruch und Gehör nennen, geben keinen Begrif von Ausdehnung oder vom Raume.

[Our concept of space is also, to be sure, merely a *form* of our intuition, as Mr Kant has taught; only I fail to see how it can be termed an *a priori* representation that inheres in the mind itself and that must precede all sensation. . . . The representation of space refers only to the relation between two senses, those of sight and touch . . . the relations however that we call taste, smell, and hearing, do not yield any concept of extension or space.]

Clearly as Kant has explained the sense, in which he uses the phrase "a priori" as determining ~~the~~ a fontem sive natale solum, minime vero *tempus*, et *occasiones*, idearum—the ubi oriuntur, not the quando;[1] yet still

2[a] The word "mind" is written in large (but not capital) letters

2[1] "As it seems to me, at least".

2[2] In "the representation, or the whole that we represent to ourselves". For the "confusion of Image and Conception" see also *BL* ch 12 (*CC*) I 288 and n 1; the related distinction of conceptions from ideas arises in RELLY 2 n 2 below.

2[3] "The imagination enters into every act of perception": this observation, originating in Christian Wolff *Psychologia rationalis*, was quoted by Ernst Platner in

Philosophische Aphorismen (2 vols Leipzig 1793) I 76, and copied from Platner by C in a notebook entry of 1801, *CN* I 905. For other instances of C's use of it, see KLUGE 7 n 5.

2[4] "The conceptual faculty or intellect enters into every act of imagination."

3[1] A "source or birthplace, but not in the least the *time* and *occasions* of ideas—the 'where they arise', not the 'when'": C uses similar phrasing in *Logic* (*CC*) 184*. Kant

the unhappy *Temporality* of the term acts by force of association as an ignis fatuus—& has prevented this sensible writer from comprehending Kant's meaning.—I on the whole should prefer the phrase "ab intra"[2] to "a priori"—both are metaphors—the latter from Time—the former from Space—but that from Space leads to fewer delusions: because Space is so compleatly heterogeneous with thought & forms of Thinking—while Time is not indeed *homo-* but yet homoio geneous.[3]

4   p [+]3,[a] referring to pp 34–5 | § 19

So dünkt mich, können wir wohl verstehen, wie man bald künstliche Demonstration nach dem gesunden Menschenverstande *orientiren*, bald aber desselben Urtheile durch genauere Zergliederung *berichtigen* muss. Sogar die Rechenkunst erfodert zuweilen ein solches Orientiren. Ich will nur ein Beyspiel geben—Vier Arbeiter brauchen sechs Tage: wie viel brauchen acht Arbeiter? Der Schüler sezt nach der Kunst 4 : 6 = 8: und findet 12. Wenn er sich aber nach dem gemeinen Menschenverstande orientiret, so siehet er im Ganzen voraus, dass die Anzahl der Tage kleiner seyn, und das Verhältniss umgekehrt, wie 8 zu 4, berechnet werden müsse.

[Thus, I think, we can easily see that sometimes we have to *orient* scientific proofs according to sound common sense, and at other times *correct* these judgments through more precise analysis. Such an orientation is occasionally required even in arithmetic. I will give only one example—Four workmen need six days: how many do eight workmen need? The pupil proceeds according to the rule 4 : 6 = 8: and concludes 12. If, however, he orients himself by common sense, he will generally foresee that the number of days ought to be smaller and the inverse proportion ought to be calculated, as 8 is to 4.]

35. orientiren[1] 4 Laborers need 6 days—how many will 8 need?—
            The Arithmetician by Rote, or   }
            Schoolboy states the sum   } 4 : 6 = 8
and finds 12 as the answer—. The prevention of this blunder by analysis

---

4[a] Written over **24**

---

defines *a priori* in the Introduction to *C d r V* (B 2), and C gives a definition of his own in *BL* ch 12 (*CC*) I 293*, q above PETVIN **16** n 1.

3[2] "From within".

3[3] C coins a word, on the model of the theological term *homoiousios* ("of like substance"). Time is not "of the same kind" but "of a similar kind".

4[1] From textus, "to orient oneself". C may have recalled at this point Kant's essay "Was heisst: Sich im Denken orientieren?" ("What does it mean, to orient oneself in thought?"): Kant *VS* III 61–88. Kant, however, does not use etymological analysis as C does.

of the Proposition into its terms, & steady consideration of each term in its own meaning is, *s'orientir*—to *east* oneself—²

5   pp 54–6

[On pp 51–6 Reimarus lists various tenets of Kant's philosophy such as the position that one can merely know the representations arising from the relationship between objects and our sensibility, but never things-in-themselves; that all concepts that are not referred to intuition are empty; that what we call the "real" consists only in appearances or in our representations; and that even the thinking "I" belongs to the order of appearances and the search for necessary firm grounds of knowledge is delusive. He then comments:] Denn, was bliebe uns noch übrig, wenn wir uns selbst sowohl als die Sinnenwelt nur für blosse Erscheinung halten, und ausser aller Erscheinungen auf nichts weiter schliessen solten; wenn keine würkliche Gegenstände den Erscheinungen zum Grunde lägen, und wenn die vermeinte Nothwendigkeit der Ursachen nur in einer Regel bestünde, nach welcher die Folge dieser grundlosen Erscheinungen . . . sich richtete. So lohnte es aber auch nicht der Mühe, dass eine Erscheinung mit der andern disputirte, da jede derselben weniger als Gespenst, nur ein augenblickliches vorübergehendes Nichtetwas wäre, und eine solche Feen-Welt noch leerer als Träume geachtet werden müsste, indem wir diesen doch einen würklichen Grund zuschreiben können.

[What would we have left if we regarded both ourselves and the sensory world as mere appearances and could infer nothing else beyond these appearances; and if the appearances were not grounded in any real objects, and if the supposed necessity of causation consisted only in a rule according to which the succession of these groundless appearances . . . was ordered? In that case it would be futile to have one appearance dispute with another, since every appearance would be less than an apparition, only a momentary, transitory nonentity, and such a fairy land would have to be regarded as even emptier than dreams, since one can still ascribe to the latter a real ground.]

All these §ˢ convey the notion of a sensible, clear-headed, truth-loving Man, who seeks for Reality & Certainty as goods exceedingly precious. But yet all seem to me grounded on a mistaken idea of the subject & the purpose of Kant's Critik der R. V.: as if it were an investigation of the human Being, whereas, in fact, it is a Critik or Ordeal of the scientific Faculty alone, or the pure (i.e.) formal Reason—and the purpose that of preventing Scepticism by proofs that from other faculties of our Being,

---

4² If C intends the French verb, it should be *s'orienter*. He draws attention (correctly) to the etymology of the verb.

ex. gr. from our sensuous nature, or *receptivity*; & from the peremptory Postulates of our moral Being, (i.e. the practical Reason) must we acquire the facts, which are to elevate the *Wenn—so*,[1] into So it *is*, & *being* so, therefore—&c. Kant's Substratum of Intellect is Morality: & in this he manifests himself as a true Philosopher (a lover of Wisdom) as contradistinguished from the Philologist, or amateur of coherent ratiocination.   *S. T. C.*[2]

6 p 56 | § 24 note 64

[Reimarus attacks statements made by Kant.] Nach S. 205. 217. besagter Prüfung "sind beides, wir selbst und die Sinnenwelt, blosse Erscheinung im Raume." So heisst es auch (das. S. 211.) "Der Satz: es ist eine Sinnenwelt, oder wenigstens Ich selbst—ist falsch, denn er nimt das *ist* objective, so dass Sinnenwelt und meine Person, oder Ich, als Dinge *an sich* angesehen werden . . ."

[According to pp 205, 217 of the previously-mentioned *Examination*, "both we ourselves and the world of the senses are mere appearances in space." And again (ibid p 211), "The proposition that there is a world of sense, or at least I myself—is false, for it takes 'is' in an objective sense so that the world of the senses and my person, or I, are regarded as things *in themselves* . . ."]

This is a mistake. Not that which thinks and wills is a mere Phænomenon, but its Thought of itself, as an *Object* ⚹ Subject as φαινεται αει υπο τοις φαινομενοις.[1]

⚹ ⚹ means in contradistinction to.

7 p 62 | § 26

Ist denn das Bewustseyn keine Erfahrung? Ist es nicht vielmehr die einzige ursprüngliche Erfahrung? und wie kann irgend ein Wesen von dem Daseyn oder der Würklichkeit irgend eines Wesens, oder Subjects, eine nähere oder völligere Kentniss erhalten als durch Selbstbewustseyn? . . . Also lässt sich doch nicht sagen, dass wir unser Ich oder Selbst nur *als* Erscheinung kennen . . . denn, wo schwebte dann der innere Sinn, der nicht im Ich wäre, sondern sich das Ich nur als ein Fremder vorstellte? So hätten wir dann doch an uns selbst schon das Daseyn eines von Erschein-

---

5[1] The "*if—then*".

5[2] On the difference between philosopher and philologist see Petvin **11** n 1 above. Cf other complaints about the misinterpretation of Kant in e.g. Jacobi *Werke* **4–6**, Lessing *Leben* **2**, and the Richter

work bound with this, Richter *Kampaner Thal* **2** below.

6[1] "It always appears [*phainetai*, whence 'phenomenon'] as dependent upon phenomena", or "it is always manifested by the phenomena".

ungen unterschiedenen *würklichen Wesens* (intelligibelen Subjects) entdeckt. . . . Nur ein selbständiges Wesen, d.i. welches seine Kraft aus sich
selbst schöpft, kann den Grund und die innere Beschaffenheit der Kraft
einsehen.

[Is consciousness therefore not experience? Is it not rather the only original experience? And how can any being attain a closer or fuller knowledge of the existence or
reality of any other being or subject except through self-consciousness? . . . Therefore
it cannot be said therefore that we know our "I" or self only *as* appearance . . . for
where then would the inner sense float if it were not in the "I" but, instead, represented
the "I" to itself as something alien? In that case surely we would already have discovered in ourselves the existence of a *real being* (intelligible subject) distinguished
from appearance. . . . Only a self-subsistent being—i.e. one that derives its own power
from within itself—can understand the ground and inner structure of the power.]

This good and sensible man, a worthy Son of a worthy Father,[1] seems by
mere force of sound sense & a good heart to have arrived at the same Conclusions, which Schelling has come to by phil! Genius.[2]

8   pp 67–8 | § 27

Dies ist das eigentliche *Gesetz der Gesellung* (Association) und des *Rück-
rufs der Ideen*, oder der Erinnerung . . . . Weder die Verwandschaft, noch
das Gegentheil der Empfindungen, führt uns an und für sich von der einen
Vorstellung auf die andere, sondern wenn dies geschiehet, so ist es nur
deswegen, weil . . . diese Vorstellungen ehemals verbunden worden sind.

[This is the true *law of association* and of *recollection of ideas*, or of memory . . . .
Neither affinity in sensations nor the opposite leads us in and of itself from one representation to another; if this happens it is only because . . . these representations were
once connected with each other.]

This is true of all mere passive associations—or rather would be true, if
any such existed. But to *recollect* is an *act* of the will and reason/ and we
more often exert it by means of Likeness, Contrast, & Cause & Effect,
and Arrangement, than by the accident of Contemporaneity. Hartley who
rejected all Will as a separate power, consistently admitted Time as the

---

7[1] J. A. H. Reimarus was the son of Her-
mann Samuel Reimarus (1694–1768), author of the controversial *Fragmente eines
Ungenannten* published by Lessing (see
LESSING *Schriften* **19** n 1). He was also the
author of a work on animal instinct that interested C: see *CN* II 2319n.
    7[2] The view that our knowledge of
reality has no other source but self-
consciousness is basic to Schelling's phi-

losophy. For the position, comparable to
that of Reimarus, that the self does not belong to the world of external objects but becomes an object in itself see e.g. *System des
transcendentalen Idealismus* (Tübingen
1800) 48–50 (*SW* III 367–9), *Abhandlungen
zur Erläuterung des Idealismus der Wissenschaftslehre—Philosophische Schriften*
(Landshut 1809) 222–5 (*SW* I 365–7).

only Law of Association.[1] But it remains a question whether Time itself is not a confused Sense of Likeness & Difference, *empirical* Time I mean.

9   p 69

. . . ist es nicht ein Urtheil das sich auf Vergleichung entgegen gesetzter Vorausetzung stützet—diese Erscheinungen einer Ursache *ausser uns* zuzuschreiben?

[To attribute these appearances to a cause *external to ourselves*—is this not a judgment based on comparison of opposing presuppositions?]

It is even more than an Urtheil; it is ein Vorurtheil.[1] Yet still it is *capable* of an *ideal* explication. The very notion "ausser uns"[2] suggests a doubt to the mind, that has convinced itself that *outness* is a mere sensation—as is proved in fevers, & by a 100 other instances.[3]

10   p 70 | § 28

Hiezu komt noch sowohl das *Beharrliche* in den Vorstellungen, aus welchem wir auf die ihnen zum Grunde liegenden *Substanzen* schliessen . . . . Wie man jenes Beharrliche, welches auf die Substanz oder das Ding selbst deutet . . . bloss in unserer Vorstellungsart, oder in den Erscheinungen an und für sich selbst finden kann, sehe ich doch nicht ein. Die Erscheinungen selbst sind ja augenblicklich verschwindend und wieder anhebend. Von den Farben des Regenbogens bleibt nichts übrig wenn sich die Wolke verzieht, oder wenn ich die Stelle verändere aus welcher ich ihn betrachtete. Man könnte also nur sagen, dass *ähnliche* Erscheinungen wiederkehren: aber wo wäre das Beharrliche, da es doch immer neue sind, die nur wechseln?

[There is in addition the *permanent* contained in those representations from which we infer underlying *substances* . . . . How this permanent, which signifies the substance or the thing itself . . . is supposed to be located in and for itself merely in our mode of representation or in the appearances is something I fail to see. The appearances themselves disappear and reappear every moment. Nothing remains of the colours of the rainbow when the cloud moves away or when I change the position from which I observed it. The most that could be said is that *similar* appearances recur: but where would there be anything permanent, since there are always new appearances that merely change?]

8[1] C's sustained critique of Hartleian associationism, including the objection to the principle of contemporaneity, appears in *BL* chs 5–7 (*CC*) I 89–128.

9[1] "Judgment . . . prejudice [lit prejudgment]".

9[2] From textus, "external to ourselves".

9[3] "Outness" is a term gratefully adopted from Berkeley: cf *CN* III 3325 and n. For examples of C's use of the term elsewhere, see MATTHIAE **5**, SCHELLING *Philosophische Schriften* **22**, *Friend* (*CC*) I 140, *SM* (*CC*) 18 n 2.

The Rain-bow is no happy instance for Reimarus—The common people supposed it a thing—why should not we too be common people a little more advanced.—

R. seems to forget, that the co-existence of things perceived successively will give the feeling, we call Substance. The fire circle formed by a point of fire whirled round is an instance.[1] Were it perpetual, we should imagine a Substratum.

11 p 72

Wir finden heute wieder was wir gestern gesehen und gefühlt hatten . . . . Nicht so bey den Träumen oder andern innern Vorstellungen der Einbildungskraft: da verändert sich und entspringt eins nach dem andern ohne Verhältniss von Ort, Zeit, Kraft, oder äussern Ursache.

[Today we find again what we saw and touched yesterday . . . . Not so in the case of dreams or other inner representations of the imagination, where one thing after another changes and arises without relation to place, time, force, or external cause.]

This is all sound sense; but yet it *proves* no more than that Sleep is—a different state from Waking. Besides, R. confounds our remembrance of our Dreams with the Dreams themselves.

12 p 72 | § 28 note 80

Die Träume geben doch auch Vorstellungen im Raume und in der Zeit— also Würklichkeiten.

[But dreams, too, produce representations in space and time—hence realities.]

R. here confounds Würklich und reäle—actual & real.

13 pp 89–90 | § 32

Dass aber ein Gegenstand ausser den Grenzen der Erfahrung liegt, sezt ihn doch nicht ausser den Grenzen der Schlussfolgen.

[But the fact that an object lies beyond the limits of experience hardly means that it is beyond the limits of inference.]

But Reimarus takes the Term, Experience, in a narrower sense, than Kant in his Crit. d. r. V./ ausser den Grenzen der Anschauung,[1] i.e. the Forms

---

10[1] C uses this illustration elsewhere: see esp *Logic* (*CC*) 75 and n 2.

13[1] C adapts textus in this phrase, "beyond the limits of intuition" in a reworking, in the spirit of the original, of Kant's own repeated assertion that there can be no knowledge "beyond the limits of experience" (e.g. *C d r V* B xx). There is further commentary on C's sense of the significance of *Anschauung*, "intuition", in JACOBI *Ueber die Lehre* 4 n 4 and *BL* ch 12 (*CC*) I 289n.

of Space and Time, is Kant's meaning/: and yet it remains true, that the actual Existence of the Thing, as of a perfect Circle, &c, can be only ascertained by Experience, i.e. a perception of its existence. Whatever is real, must be possible; but it is ⟨not⟩ so clear, tho' asserted by Spinoza & Schelling, that whatever is possible, is likewise real: other than as an Idea.[2]

14   pp 132–3 | § 48

In dem *Willen* Gottes müssen wir uns also nur keine solche Handlung vorstellen, wo, nach menschlicher Weise, erst verschiedene Gründe abgewogen, dann gewählt und ein Entschluss gefasst würde: keinen äussern Endzweck, der dem Willen vorausgienge.

[Only we must not conceive of God's *will* as an action where, according to the human way, first different reasons would be weighed, then a choice made and a decision arrived at: no external final cause would precede the will.]

But still the Answer of the Sceptic is: "You bid me remove the limitations when I apply the ideas of Will, and Intelligence to the Infinite—But in these limitations the very *essence* of those qualities consists—It is, as if you called God a ~~Circle~~ Square, without the 4 Sides & Angles—or "a circle, whose center is every where and circumference no where"[1] i.e. as a center has no meaning but in reference to a circumference, a Circle without center or circumference/ i.e. a Circle that is no Circle.["]

The Rejoinder to this must be a Denial that the Essence of Intelligence is, like that of a geometrical Figure, in its Limits. But then why not admit Spinoza to have adopted ⱥ less objectionable Terms in the Words, Love and Wisdom?[2]

15   pp 134–5 | § 49 notes 141–2

So lässt auch *Jacobi* . . . den *Spinoza* sagen: "Gott, welcher nur aus dem Grunde handelt, und handeln kann, aus dem er ist, und der nur durch sich

---

13[2] C may have in mind Schelling's observation that Spinoza opposed the separation of external things and our ideas: ". . . he perceived that the ideal and the real (thought and thing) are intimately united in our nature". Schelling goes on—in a work annotated by C—to suggest that Spinoza should have explained this unity of the ideal and real by means of the self: *Ideen zu einer Philosophie der Natur* (2nd ed Landshut 1803) 56–7 (*SW* II 35–7).

14[1] This paradoxical scholastic description of God is invoked elsewhere by C, e.g. *AR* (*CC*) 233*. In *Logic* (*CC*) 115, needing an example of an absurd question, he says one might as well "ask what a circle is, exclusive of its circumference, or a square, exclusive of its sides and angles".

14[2] In *Ethics* pt 1 prop 17 Spinoza denies that intellect and will properly pertain to God's nature, and in pt 5 props 33–7 he writes of God as manifesting an intellectual love which is at once self-love and love of man.

selbst ist, besizt demnach die absolute Freiheit.["] Z.B. Ein Rad, das durch äussern Trieb bewegt wird, liegt unter mechanischer Nothwendigkeit: die Magnetnadel bewegt sich (dem Anscheine nach) aus innerer Kraft. Geschähe dieses mit Bewustseyn, dass sie diese Stellung nähme, weil sie sich dort am besten befände; so müsten wir ihr Freiheit zuschreiben. Ein Mensch, der gestossen, gezogen, oder durch andere Macht bestimmt wird, ist gezwungen: er handelt frey, wo er wissentlich seine Handlungen selbst bestimmt.

[Thus Jacobi, too, has . . . Spinoza say: "God, who only acts, and can only act, because of what he is, and who is by means of himself alone, thereby possesses absolute freedom.["] For example, a wheel that is set in motion through external impetus is subject to mechanical necessity: the magnetic needle moves (apparently) as a result of inner force. If it were to take this position consciously because it felt best there, then we would have to attribute freedom to it. A man who is pushed, dragged, or pressured by another power, is bound: he acts freely when he knowingly determines his actions himself.]

But the consciousness of a thing does not constitute the Thing. Who calls a Plant free?[1] If then our freedom arises only from adding to the vis interna[2] a consciousness of it, either the Plant is free or we are not. This is the evil of seeking analogies for things essentially sui generis—such as moral Freedom must of necessity be, if it exist at all. If R. had said, what Magnetism is in the first & lowest Power that Freedom is [in][a] the highest & atoning Power—I should not have objected.

16 pp 145–7 | § 52 and note 152

Herr *Jacobi* will sogar seine [Spinozas] Folgerungen unter den philosophischen für die bündigsten erklären, welches doch andere Untersucher nicht finden. [Footnote 152:] Und gewiss Herr *Kant* nicht, auf den er sich sonst zu berufen scheint: der aber ausdrücklich dagegen spricht, (Berl. Monatschr. 1786. S. 323. Not.) und der nothwendig folgert, dass die Grundursache von allem nicht zur Reihe der abhängigen Dinge, auch nicht als oberstes Glied gehören könne, sondern ausser der Welt gesezt werden müsse. (*Crit.*)

[Mr Jacobi even wishes to declare [Spinoza's] deductions as among the philosophically most valid, a view which others, however, do not share. [Footnote 152:] And certainly not Mr Kant, whose authority he seems to invoke elsewhere; for the latter explicitly opposes such a view (*Berlinische Monatsschrift* 1786 p 323n) and necessarily

15[a] Word concealed in binding

15[1] C argues the same point in his own   15[2] "Inner power".
comment on JACOBI *Ueber die Lehre* 1.

concludes that the first cause of everything could not possibly belong to the series of dependent things, not even as its highest member, but must be postulated as existing outside the world. (*Critique*.)]

Aye! but was für einer Welt?[1] The World of Phænomena. It is clear, that Reimarus did not understand Spinoza: & even Jacobi wrote under a *Warp*—the fear of appearing a Convert to Spinozism. And after all what meaning can we attach to a Grund-kraft *ausser* der Welt?[2] We may *distinguish* the Kraft die Thätigkeit or Kraftaüsserung and the Würkung[3] but not *separate* them. And after all, I miss the LIVING God, the *Personal* Ruler, as much in Reimarus, as in Spinoza: nay, far more. See p. 139.[4] How can I, but with self-delusion, *pray* to a Being, before whom no Individual, "als ein besonderer Gegenstand, vorschwebt"?[5] In short, I am more and more convinced, that without personality there can be no God for Religion: & that the Xtn[a] Trinity is the only possible Medium between a mere Ordo ordinans,[6] and Idolatry, which may co-exist with Monotheism no less than with Polytheism.   S. T. C.

And as to the quotation from Müller, was it first beym Verfall der Kirche, or not rather in St John's Gospel, that this Mystic is taught to Christians?[7] And no less plainly, tho' less frequently, in St Paul?[8] With

---

16[a] C's abbreviation for "Christian"

16[1] But "what kind of world"?

16[2] "Fundamental power *outside* the world"—adapting textus.

16[3] I.e. the "power, the activity or manifestation of power, and the effect".

16[4] C refers to a passage in which Reimarus employs the German phrase following. Tr: "If we recognise that everything is dependent on the singular power of an omniscient creator, and adapted for the welfare of every possible sentient being, we must certainly not assume that each is present to him as a particular object, or that he orders every object by virtue of a specific external cause or uncertain arbitrary power."

16[5] From the passage q n 4, "is present as a particular object".

16[6] "Ordering order", a phrase used also in PROCLUS 2 above.

16[7] C is referring to the following passage from Müller's *Geschichte der Schweizer* (*History of the Swiss*) q by Reimarus pp 146–7. Tr: "In the heyday of

antiquity—he says—a certain mysticism arose in the warmest Orient, which was carelessly adopted by pious men at the beginning of Christianity, maintained by zealous teachers at the decline of the Church, and retained in various forms to this day by many good people. All is in God, God is all, all is from Him, all takes place in Him. In us there is a light, but matter oppresses us with chains. Perfection consists in breaking through these chains. The break from them consists in contemplation through which we become immersed in God and thus also become God, and Alpha and Omega, God, Christ, Heaven and we ourselves would be one, from one, for one, in one. The more incomprehensible, the more divine . . . ." C objects specifically to the phrase "at the decline of the Church".

16[8] Meaning perhaps the line he often cites (e.g. *CL* IV 768), "In whom [God] we move and live and *have* our being", Acts 17.28 var.

exception of the Perruption, (Durchbruch)[9] the very words are in the N. Test.

17   p 148 | § 53

Spinoza urtheilt also: das selbstständige Wesen müsse, als vollkommen, alle mögliche Realität in sich begreifen. Realitäten achtete er, nach dem *des Cartes*, die körperliche* Ausdehnung und das Denken: also muste es unendlich ausgedehnt seyn, und unendliche Gedanken besitzen.

[Spinoza reasons thus: since it is perfect, the autonomous substance must comprise within itself all possible reality. Following Descartes, he considers corporeal* extension and thought as realities: thus this substance must be infinitely extended and must possess infinite thoughts.]

* No! SPIN. directly guards against it/ Cogitatio et Extensio in Spinoza's sense, are the Same as Being and Existence.[1]

18   pp 148–9 | § 53 note 155

Ich halte mich theils an dem, was Herr *Jacobi* selbst in seiner Schrift über die Lehre des *Spinoza* erklärt, theils an des Herrn de *Jariges* Abhandlung über das System des Spinoza. . . . *De Jariges* hat sich nämlich ebenfalls die Mühe genommen, die Schriften des Spinoza durchzustudiren, aber so wenig als *Mendelsohn* . . . etwas Zusammenbestehendes herausbringen können.

[I follow partly Mr Jacobi's own explanation in his book on the doctrines of Spinoza and partly Mr de Jariges' commentary on Spinoza's system. . . . De Jariges has likewise taken the trouble to study the writings of Spinoza attentively, but he managed as little as Mendelssohn . . . to bring out something consistent.]

Spinoza's works were, previously to the late re-publication of them by Prof.̣ Paulus, far more uncommon in Germany, than in England.[1] On this ground I explain what would otherwise appear strange & unjustifiable— that Reimarus "hält sich theils &c &c—"[2] instead of consulting the original "Ethice" itself.—It is evident to me, however, that neither Reimarus

16[9] "Breaking through", in the passage cited, tr, in n 7.

17[1] E.g. Spinoza *Ethics* pt 1 props 14, 21, which assert that extension and thought (*extensio* and *cogitatio*) are both infinite attributes of God; and pt 1 def 4, "By attribute I understand what the intellect perceives of a substance, as constituting its essence."

18[1] Heinrich Eberhard Gottlob Paulus (1761–1851), author of the annotated *Leben*

Jesu above, edited Spinoza *Opera quae supersunt omnia* (2 vols Jena 1802–3). C annotated HCR's copy, which he kept from Nov 1812 to Nov 1813: SPINOZA. The only other collected ed available earlier was the Dutch ed of *Opera posthuma* identified in n 4 below; C must mean that it was easier to find in England than in Germany.

18[2] From beginning of textus, "partly follows".

nor his Father nor Mendelsohn understood Spinoza[3]—& I after my last
Perusal of the Opera Posthuma[4] begin to doubt, whether Jacobi's Statement is a just one.

19   pp 150–1 | § 53

Nun protestirt zwar Spinoza einerseits, dass dies [Gott, oder Substanz]
keine Abstraktion, kein blos abgezogner Begrif sey, weil er den Inbe-
grif aller würklichen Individuen verstehe, und andererseits, dass es kein
Aggregat, keine Zusammensetzung sey, weil er ein untheilbares Ganze
annehme. Dies sind aber doch Vorstellungen, die sich einander wider-
sprechen, und es ist *protestatio facto contraria*, eine Entschuldigung, die
durch seine eigenen Worte widerlegt wird.

[Now Spinoza protests on the one hand that this [God, or Substance] is not an abstraction, a merely generic concept, because he meant the sum total of all real individuals; on the other hand, he says it is not an aggregate, not a conglomerate, because
he supposes an indivisible whole. But these are concepts that contradict each other and
constitute a "declaration contrary to fact", a defence that his own words refute.]

In other words, R. does not understand Sp: ergo, Sp. is not to be understood! My mind I regard neither as an Abstraction, or generic Term, nor
yet as an Aggregate of all ~~my~~ the Thoughts inexistent in my mind—and
yet cannot allow this to be protestatio facto contraria.[1]   S. T. C.

What follows is curious[2]—R. puts *his* notion of an individual Body
in the place of Spinoza's, as Spinoza's, & then makes him contradict himself. Spinoza says no more than this: What I have affirmed of God is
equally true of each Individual—It is neither an Abstraction, ~~or~~ nor an

---

18[3] For Reimarus's father see **7** n 1
above. C's notes on Moses MENDELSSOHN
complain occasionally of his misrepresentation of Spinoza, e.g. *Morgenstunden* **13**.

18[4] C was familiar not only with the
Paulus ed referred to in n 1 above, but also
with Spinoza *Opera posthuma* (Amsterdam
1677), from which he took a motto for the
1809–10 *Friend*: *Friend* (*CC*) I 165.

19[1] From textus, "declaration contrary
to fact".

19[2] Following upon the textus are these
sentences (tr): "He says quite clearly, 'Just
as every body or individual is made of individual components of a different nature and
manner, so likewise the whole of nature is a

single individual whose parts—that is all
bodies—change in infinitely diverse ways,
without causing the least change in the
whole individual.' Here, then, are obviously
diverse, that is multiple, things which in
themselves always remain multiple and
only with respect to their connection and interaction or the purpose which they serve
can be comprised in a concept or called *a*
thing. *Spinoza* had in mind not an empty
universal concept, but all that is real . . . but
that which several things have in common
with one another constitutes only . . . a deduced concept, and not a being that contains
these individual things or is one with them."

Aggregate.[3] The whole Confutation is of the same kind/ R. and Sp. hold two contrary Faiths—R. takes his for granted, and thence deduces the falsehood of Spinoza's. But *Reim's* very axioms were in Spinoza's view the Errors & Prejudices, which he wrote to overthrow. It is if[a] A should say $9 + 11 + 9 + 11 = 42$. No, says B. they are $= 40$. Nay, rejoins A. $9 + 11$ being $= 21$, twice that must be $= 42$.—

20   p 152

* Das allgemeine ist doch nur in jedem besondern Dinge wiederholt, oder in der Mehrheit wirklich, und nur in der Einbildung eins und dasselbe. Alle Menschen haben es mit einander gemein, dass sie einen Kopf haben: es sind und bleiben aber immer mehrere Köpfe, und nicht Abänderungen eines unbestimmten Kopfes.

[* The universal after all is only repeated in each particular thing or becomes real in a plurality; only in the imagination is it one and the same. All human beings share the characteristic of having a head: however, these are and will always remain several heads, and not modifications of one indeterminate head.]

* Now this is exactly the point, to which Spinoza drives: that das Eins allein is in der Würklichkeit, das Mehrere in der Einbildung allein.—Die Köpfe sind Erscheinungen:[1] and do not belong to the point in Question.[2]

21   p 153 | § 54

Ich übergehe, dass Spinoza Ausdehnung, welche doch nur eine Vorstellung unsers Gesichts und Gefühls ist, als etwas Wesentliches angiebt. . . . Aber das muss ich doch anmerken, dass, da Spinoza das Eingebildete in der Ausdehnung für Würklichkeit nimt, er hingegen das Würkliche, welches dieser Erscheinung zum Grunde liegt, nämlich die Mehrheit, Verschiedenheit, verschwinden und zu Eins werden lässt.—Wir wenden uns also zu dem *Denken*, welches doch eine Realität . . . ist, die wir in uns selbst unmittelbar wahrnehmen. So, wie nun das Bewustseyn in jedem

---

19[a] A slip for "as if"

19[3] Cf *Ethics* pt 1 prop 25 coroll: "Particular things are nothing but affections of God's attributes, *or* modes by which God's attributes are expressed in a certain and determinate way." Spinoza also expresses the view that substance is not an aggregate of component parts, but one and indivisible, e.g. *Ethics* pt 1 props 12–15.

20[1] "The one alone exists in reality, the many only in the imagination.—Heads are appearances . . . ."

20[2] C may have been thinking of *Ethics* pt 1 prop 15 scholium, defending the concept of corporeal substance as "infinite, unique, and indivisible".

Subjecte absolute Einheit darstellt, weder theilbar ist, noch sich theilen lässt, so kann doch auch die Verschiedenheit des Bewustseyns nichts anders als Verschiedenheit der Subjecte anzeigen . . .

[I pass over the fact that Spinoza declares extension, which is only a representation of our sight and touch, to be something essential. . . . But I cannot help observing that while Spinoza accepts extended imagined things as real, he at the same time makes the reality that lies behind this appearance—that is, plurality and diversity—vanish and merge into one.—Let us now turn our attention to *thought*, which is a reality . . . that we perceive directly in ourselves. Just as consciousness makes up an absolute unity in every subject and is neither divisible nor can be divided, so too the diversity of consciousness must always present itself as a diversity of subjects . . .]

Reimarus could not have understood the first Book of Kant's Crit. der r. V.—[1]

22   p 154 | § 54 note 170

Eine deutliche Vorstellung konte es auch nicht seyn, dass Spinoza sich selbst nur für eine Abänderung oder Beschaffenheit des Alleinwesens hielte, und sich dabei doch die Mühe gab, uns andere eben so nothwendige Abänderungen dieses Alleinwesens die Moral zu lehren, oder überhaupt mit uns zu disputiren.

[It could hardly have been a distinct idea when Spinoza considered himself a mere modification or attribute of the one substance and yet took pains to moralise or even to dispute with us—who are equally necessary modifications of this one substance.]

a note worthier of the Sophist Bayle,[1] than the honest Searcher, Reimarus.—

23   p 161 | § 56

Wie viel Menschliches und Ungereimtes ist nicht ehedem der Gottheit zugeschrieben worden? . . . Dass dieses indessen nicht bloss Einbildungen des dummsten Volkes gewesen, liesse sich aus vielen Abhandlungen gelehrter Schriftsteller und Volkslehrer beweisen. *

[How much that is human and irrational has not been attributed to the deity in times past? . . . That this, however, did not just amount to the fantasies of the ignorant could be proved by many treatises of learned authors and popular teachers. *]

21[1] I.e. the *Transcendental Aesthetic*, an inquiry into the *a priori* intuitions of space and time.

22[1] Pierre Bayle (1647–1706), whom C describes in BM Egerton MS 2801 f 2ᵛ (*SW & F—CC*—613) as "the Founder and Father of Modern Scepticism and religious Indifference", used the "Spinoza" entry in his famous *Dictionnaire historique et critique* (1697; 1st English ed 1710) as the occasion for an attack upon Spinoza.

S[t] Augustin, Luther, Melanchthon, &c—and yet what one conception or proof of Deity has Reimarus adduced, which is not to be found in the writings of these men?—

24   p $^{+}$3, turned sideways, pencil[a1]

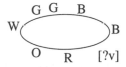

24[a] Written on the same leaf as **4**, which partly obscures the diagram

24[1] The purpose of the diagram is obscure: it looks like a seating plan.

KARL LEONHARD REINHOLD
1758–1823

Lost Book

Versuch einer neueren Theorie des menschlichen Vorstellungsvermö-
gens. Prague & Jena 1789. 8°.

Not located; marginalia not recorded. *Green SC* (1880) 660, "MS Notes by S. T.
Coleridge, but cut into in binding".

JAMES RELLY

c 1722–1778

The Believer's Treasury; or, the union, consanguinity, and affinity, of Christ and His Church, illustrated in the light of scripture. . . . Rev ed. To which is added, an essay on the apostolic manner of preaching the gospel. London 1824. 8°.

British Library C 126 h 2(8), bound in "Pamphlets—Divinity"

Autograph inscription on the title-page: "S. T. Coleridge Sent to me by some unknown Donor—I hope, friend—". Unopened pp 27–30, 89–92.

DATE. Summer 1825, perhaps Jun. In a notebook entry of Sept 1825, C records the gift of this work "soon after the publication of the Aids to Reflection" (*CN* IV 5243, a note that elaborates upon C's disagreement with Relly). *AR* (1825) appeared in May.

1   p 59

Objec. But doth not the doctrine of union, which supposes Christ to suffer under the character of the sinner, contradict the apostle, who saith, Christ also hath once suffered for sin, the just for the unjust.
Answ. To intimate that Jesus was a sinner in thought, word, or deed, is what I never intended, but would abhor the thought as highly blasphemous; nay, the prince of this world, when he came, having nothing in him, was therefore constrained to appear in visible form and tempt him by his outward senses.

ingenious as it here stands and capable of a true and noble Meaning—viz. that the Evil Principle having no set[a] in the Will of Jesus could only present itself to the Fancy—i.e. could appear only in ~~th~~ its proper nature, as the *Posse*—its *esse*[1] being in all cases ~~derived~~ acquired ~~by~~ from the correspondent Act in the Will of the Individual, to & for whom therefore γινεται. Το Πονηρον ~~ȷ~~ εστι ⟨, υπαρχει,⟩ εν αυτω, και αυτος γινεται πονηρος.[2]

1[a] Possibly a slip for "seat"

1[1] The "potentiality" and its "existence".
1[2] To and for whom therefore "it comes into being. The Evil *is* ⟨, it exists,⟩ in him,   and he himself becomes evil". Implicit in C's usage is the distinction that he makes elsewhere (e.g. *CN* IV 5078 f 34) between

233

2   pp 60–2

And this accounting of him [Jesus] a sinner, in the eye of justice, as it was equitable; so was it not from any personal guile, for he knew no sin; but from his union unto the sinful people, which rendered the punishment of their sin upon him, an act of divine and strict justice.

Whoo!—Here is a substantiated Metaphor with a vengeance![1] Strange Nonsense! If the ⟨sinful⟩ blood and nervous Spirits circulated thro' the Head how could it the Head be sinless? If they did not, how could it be that Body's Head?—But if the former were *subposed* (for *conceived* or *imagined* it could not be)[2] in the same instant & by virtue of the supposition, the punishment of the a sinfulness, which was not existing was, = must be an act of "divine and strict justice"[3] that was is likewise = 0—; and if for negative Sin we supposed positive merit, then this pure "divine and strict justice" must be = pejor humanâ et omni jure soluta Injuriastitia, dissolutissima Tyrannis et Διαβολη.[4] For if the shooting *accusation* of guilt against the Guiltless is strictly διαβαλλειν,[5] to shoot both ⟨the⟩ imputation and the punishment must a fortiori be αυτοτατος ο διαβολος— —.[6] In short, the misery of all these reasonings consists in a trick of the idoloplastic[7] Fancy, which gives to Guilt a sort of ⟨guiltless⟩ materia or stuff, abstractable from the *form*—just as in a wooden ma-

---

the neuter *to poneron* "the evil [thing]" or abstract "evil" or "the Evil Principle" (as here) and the masculine *ho poneros*, which sometimes in NT is a synonym for the Devil himself though not so translated, e.g. Matt 13.19. Ambiguity arises when the phrase is used in the genitive, because the forms for the masculine and neuter are the same: cf Howie **8** and n 13, Luther *Colloquia* **103**. (Both C and Relly are commenting on the temptation of Christ in the wilderness: Matt 4.1–11 etc).

2¹ Metaphors, according to C in Luther *Colloquia* **68**, are "sorry Logic"; in Southey *Wesley* **18** "tricksy companions". C had recently published an extended analysis of metaphorical language, in *AR* (*CC*), 205–6, 318–32.

2² By using "subposed" (not in *OED*) for "supposed", C draws attention to the etymologically reduced meaning of the word as something "placed under" something else; cf the discussion of "hypothesis", "supposition", and "suffiction" in *BL*

ch 5 (*CC*) I 101–2 and 102 n 1. To "conceive" is to "take this with that" (*C&S*— *CC*—13 n 2), and to "imagine" is to have a visual image—which in this case would be an impossibility. Conceptions are discussed in distinction from ideas e.g. in Hooker **3**, Luther *Colloquia* **41**, *C&S* (*CC*) 12–13.

2³ In textus.

2⁴ This justice must amount to "Injustice worse than human and unrestrained by any law, a most unbridled Tyranny and Devilry".

2⁵ In view of its component parts the Greek verb *diaballein* may mean "to cast/throw over" (hence "to shoot at") and hence also "to accuse", "to be an adversary", and "to slander/traduce". Cognate with it is *diabolos*, i.e. "accuser", "slanderer", "devil".

2⁶ "The devil himself". C comments elsewhere on the derivation of *diabolos* and "diabolical" from "slanderer": see *EOT* (*CC*) II 454 and n 3, Fielding *Tom Jones* **2**.

2⁷ "Idol-making": not in *OED*.

hogany Table there is ⱥ the Conception, Mahogany, that is quite independent of the image, Table—or as the ~~Sea~~ Conception, Salt Water, remains unaffected by the superinduced or assumed accident of the Wave.

But Guilt has its essence & substance in the FORM—~~in~~ Its only *Substance* or *Stⱦuff* is BEING—which again is a mere *Ens* logicum,[8] the moment it ceases to be contemplated as *Ens veré ens*,[9] and falling therefore under the Axiom—Omne Ens *Quoad Ens Bonum.[10]

S. T. Coleridge

* Some 19 or 20 years ago I amused myself ~~with~~ by puzzling a Priest at Noto in Sicily[11] with the following ⟨Enthymeme or⟩ Syllogism, by transposition of Terms and Conversion of the affirmative into its[a] equivalent negative form.—"Omne ens est bonum. Imo, quoth the Priest.—Diabolus est omnino non bonum. Pro certissimo, quoth he.—Ergo, Diabolus est ⟨omnino⟩ Non-ens.[12] Now, Signor: you must either contradict Aristotle, which you know is pæne Hæresis,[13] or you must agree with an English Proverb That the Devil may be painted too black/ For I take for granted, that you will not allow him to be Non-entity.—Ah! replied the Priest with a deep sigh/ What advantages you English possess!—Such loads of Money—such Ships of War—and no one can withstand you in the use of the Pistol—and what *Philosophers* you ⟨all⟩ are!! Now *here* we are ⟨all⟩ forced to be Christians—our Bishop would play the Devil with me, if I said the Devil was a Non-entity [? ~~led~~], or if I did not say, that he was altogether a Good for nothing Fellow.["]

3 p 61, written at the end of **2**

And where the Scriptures speak of our being in him . . . it appears that we were in him, and with him, through all, but not active; we were altogether in a passive state, whilst the toil and torment was wholly his. Yet through all, he was greatly conscious of his including the people in himself, his life and death, being that of the whole body; for if one member suffers,

2^a Reading not certain: could be "to", in error

[8] "Logical *Entity*".

[9] An "*entity that truly is*".

[10] "Everything that is, insofar as it is, is good." The "Axiom" has not been traced in precisely this wording, but cf e.g. Joannes Scotus Erigena *De divisione naturae* (Oxford 1681) 3.2, with the same meaning, "Omnia siquidem quae sunt, in tantum sunt, in quantum bona sunt." C annotated this work, though not this passage: JOANNES.

[11] C travelled in Sicily in Oct 1805, and a notebook entry of that period mentions Noto as part of a possible itinerary: *CN* II 2709.

[12] "All being is good. Yes indeed, quoth the Priest.—The Devil is definitely *not* a good thing. That is most certain, quoth he.—Ergo, the Devil is altogether a Nonentity."

[13] "Almost Heresy".

all the members suffer with it. Thus though <u>we</u> were not with him, as helping or assisting him, according to the prophet, yet were we always in him, and with him, according to the doctrine of union so abundantly taught in the Scriptures.

P.S. It would have been amusing to have asked Relly, what he meant by "*We*".

4   p 81 | Essay on Apostolic Preaching

The scripture saith, to him that worketh not, but believeth on him that justifieth the ungodly, his faith is counted for righteousness . . . [Rom 4.5]

Some years ago as I was travelling on foot thro' a part of Somersetshire I saw a sturdy Lad trenching the ground on a Plot of Land divided from the road by a Sweet-briar ⟨Hedge⟩, with so much life & spirit—that I stopt, & asked him—Whose Labourer are you? Who are you working for? He answered rather resentfully—I am no Laborer. I ~~can~~ do not work at all. It is my own Father's Garden.—This is the Sense in which St Paul uses the word.

JOHN REYNOLDS

fl 1620–1640

The Triumphes of Gods Revenge agaynst the Cryinge, & Execrable Sinne, of (Willfull, & Premeditated) Murther expressed in thirtye severall, tragicall Historyes (Digested into Six Bookes) wch contayne great variety of mournefull, & memorable Accydents Amorous, Morall, & Divine. The whole Worke nowe compleatlye finished. 3rd ed. London 1657. F°.

[Text from engraved title pasted to p ‾1, the printed title-page being missing from this copy.]

Harvard University (Houghton Library)

CL's copy, with corrections in his hand to the running headlines on pp 121, 325, 347, 467. An illegible signature is heavily cancelled at the head of p ‾2 and a correction to the text deleted p 2; on p 213 the signature "Thom May" is written; on p 438 a stray "m" in the margin; and on pp ‾2, 243, 255, 398 a few arithmetical calculations. The initials "G. T. S", for George T. Strong, appear on sig A; bookplates of "E. R. McC." and A. Edward Newton on pp ‾3 and ‾5 (p-d) respectively. Extract from bookseller's catalogue loose in vol.

DATE. Uncertain; perhaps in the early years of C's residence in Highgate, i.e. after Apr 1816. **7** n 3 suggests 1812 at the very earliest.

1   p ‾5 (p-d), concluded on p ‾2 (recto of p ‾1 to which is pasted the engraved title-page)

It is exceedingly entertaining to observed, how absolutely & integrally J. Renynold's heart & soul are swallowed up in the notion "Murder", & in all other crimes only as far as they lead to Murder. The most execrable Wretch about to be murdered, becomes "poor innocent man"—"worthy harmless Gentleman", &c[1]—and the most heroic Character, as that of chaste Perina, "execrable bloody Lady", as soon as she forms the thought of punishing the horrible crimes to herself and her poisoned Lord & Husband, & his Mother, on the old Monster who had perpetrated them.[2]—

[1] As in **5–7** below.

[2] C is not quoting but paraphrasing Reynolds's account of Perina, who avenges the murder of her husband and mother-in-law by her father-in-law, has her right hand cut off, is sentenced to imprisonment for life, and dies of grief, a "graceless and bloody" woman according to Reynolds (119).

237

And then his never for a moment, not for half a sentence, relaxing or elanguescing,[3] from the height & high top gallant of Sensibility & impassioned Moralizing upon all & every act, however often repeated, from p. 1. to p. 486—so flatly delicious, so deliciously flat!—I LIKE JOHN REYNOLDS. *S. T. C.*

P.S. Almost every tale in this Folio is maimed, as a Tale, thro' its being catastrophied by Torture—& yet, so totus in illis[4] is J. R., that it seems never once to have suggested itself to his mind, tho' he was an Englishman, that the same horrible agonies which overpowered the guilty, spite of all their Interests & strongest predeterminations, would equally overpower the Innocent, nay, more so for the Innocent & Guilty would be the same in preferring Death to such Tortures (or else the Guilty would not have confessed) and the former would have hopes in another world which the latter could not have.—But no such notion occurred to honest Murthero-maniacal[5] John Reynolds—& then the Judges—they are such glorious Abstracts, one & all, of omnisciency, incorruptibility, & firmness. They are not Judges; but Justice & Judgement.—But the Beauties of this Work are endless. There is something half-celestial in that infantine Combination of intense feeling with the vulgarest Truisms, the merest mouldy Scraps, of generalizing Morality. "It is an excellent felicity to grow from Vertue to Vertue, & a fatall misery to run from Vice to Vice. Love & Charity are always the true marks of a Christian, & Malice & Revenge &c &c"[6]—but the nicest feeling is that concerning Duels, which verbally he always condemns as Loss both of Body & Soul/ of course, as leading to the same Hell as Murder—but yet this is all matter of course. In the Author's *feelings* as shewn in the event of his Stories, the⟨se⟩ Duels are always innocent or virtuous.[7] O what a beautiful Concordia Discordantium[8] is an unthinking good-hearted Man's Soul!—

---

[3] Growing feeble, relaxing: not in *OED*, but based on the Latin *elanguescere*.

[4] "Wholly absorbed in these things": Horace *Satires* 1.9.2.

[5] I.e. obsessed with murder: C's playful epithet adopts Reynolds's obsolete spelling.

[6] The quotation is from p 12, where the sentence ends, "those of an Infidell, or rather of a Devill".

[7] Duels are indeed common motifs in Reynolds's stories; they are often graphically represented in the engravings that tell the story without words (cf Plate 3). The first story annotated by C, "Pisani and Christeneta" (12–22), contains a duel, and Reynolds there remarks parenthetically that in duels honour "is bought and sold at so dear a price, as the perill and losse both of body and soul" (17).

[8] "Harmony of Discordant Things". Cf Horace's *concordia discors* "harmony in discord" (*Epistles* 1.12.19) and the *Concordia discordantium canonum* "Concord of Discordant Canons" of the 12th-century monk Gratian. C uses a variant to describe Augustine and Jeremy Taylor in Jeremy TAYLOR *Polemicall Discourses* **110**.

Gods revenge againſt the Crying and Execrable Sinne of Murther.

HISTORY III.

Mortaign, under promiſe of Marriage, gets Ioſſelina with Child, and after, converting his love into hatred, cauſeth his Lackey La Verdure, and La Palma, to murther both her and her young Son; the jealouſie of Iſabella to her Husband La Palma is the cauſe of the diſcovery hereof: they are all three taken and executed for the ſame.

IT is a juſt reward for the vanity of our thoughts, and a true recompence for the errours of our youth, that we buy pleaſure with repentance, and the ſweetneſſe of ſin with the bitterneſſe of affliction: but if we violate the Laws of Chriſtianity, and abandon our ſelves to luſt and fornicati-on, then we ſhall ſee with ſhame, that men will not pitty us, and find with grief, that God will pu-niſh us. In is an excellent vertue in Maidens, not to liſten to the lewd temptations of men; and in men not to hearken to the ſugred charms of the Devil; for commonly that folly gives the one ſhame, and this madneſſe brings the other deſtruction: but if we firſt forget our ſelves, and then our God, by adding and heaping ſin upon ſin, as firſt, to perpetrate Fornication, and after Murther, then aſ-ſuredly our eſtate is ſo miſerably wretched, and ſo wretchedly miſerable, as we have no hope left for better fortunes, nor place for worſe. And becauſe Example is both pleaſing to our memory, and profitable to our judgement, this mournfull enſuing Hiſtory ſhall make good, and confirm it to us: therefore let us ſhut the door of our thoughts againſt the power of ſin, and that of our hearts a-gainſt the malice of Hell, and we ſhall not only make our fortunes immoveable in this World, but our felicity eternall in that to come.

In the South-eaſt part of *France*, within a dayes journey of the famous City of *Lyons*, at the foot of the Mountain of *Tarara*, upon the border and boſome of that ſweet River *Lignon*, ſo famouſed by the Minion of Honour, and the Darling of the Muſes, the Marqueſſe of *Vrſe*, in his beautifull and Divine *Aſtrea*, neer *Dareny* (a certain ſmall Village) there dwelt a poor Countrey Farmer named

3. John Reynolds *The Triumphes of Gods Revenge agaynst the Crying,
& Execrable Sinne, of . . . Murther* (1657). See REYNOLDS 1
The Houghton Library, Harvard University; reproduced by kind permission

2   p 18 | Bk 1 "Pisani and Christeneta"

[Letter from Gasparino to Pisano:] *You have given the first breach to our friendship: for sith you have treacherously bereaved me of my Mistris, you must now both in honour and justice, either take my life, or yeeld me yours in requitall. If you consider your own ingratitude, you cannot tax, much lesse condemn this my resolution: the Place, the West end of the Park; the hour, four or five after Dinner; the manner, on foot, with Seconds; the Weapon, if you please, two single Rapiers, whereof bring you one, and I the other, and I will be content to take the refusal, to give you the choyce. If your courage answer your infidelity, you will not refuse to meet me.*

Reminds one of Shakespere, who in his affected *brevities epistolary*[1] probably had his eye on similar Stories. The style was not imaginary. This Letter might have occurred in Shakespere, & no one have found the least Dissonance with his manner.

3   p 22

The chief pain, I feel, in reading these stories is that of a true Theorist.[1] I cannot but perceive, what apparent strength they lend to the Lockians & Materialists, who hold Conscience to be nothing more than the Prejudice of Education—to the same being the most atrocious action will make no pang in the Conscience, if it be but according to the custom of the Age—& the most innocent the cruellest pangs of Remorse, if against the Custom.[2] This *may* be sufficiently answered; but then the answer requires powers of reflection extraordinary, & the statement seems to be of undeniable facts, which every man understands at once.

4   p 23 | "Mortaign and Iosselina"

Notice thro' all these tales, & in the writings of Sir P. Sidney & many others, that the natural antipathy (as has been since supposed) of English to

---

2[1] An allusion to *2 Henry IV* ii ii, where Bardolph delivers a letter from Falstaff. The letter contains the line, "I will imitate the honourable Romans in brevity", to which Poins retorts, "He sure means brevity in breath, short-winded."

3[1] C appears to be using "Theorist" here in the same positive sense as appears in *LS* (*CC*) 14: "Yet it would not be difficult . . . to demonstrate that the most important changes in the commercial relations of the world had their origin in the closets or lonely walks of uninterested theorists . . .". Cf his definition of "theory" in PARK *Dogmas* 2.

3[2] Locke *Essay concerning Human Understanding* bk 1 ch 3 §§ 7–10, part of Locke's argument against innate ideas. C on the contrary maintained that conscience was antecedent to consciousness: cf IRVING *Sermons* 9, REIMARUS 1.

French Men, had not commenced.[1] E contra,[2] our Writers in general speak of the French with a manifest predilection, and of all the nations we find the feeling of the great Commonwealth of Christendom predominant. A King is a King, sacred tho' an enemy—a Nobleman always a Nobleman/ the ranks common to all as yet outweighed the differences, by which country was distinguished from Country. With them the Emphasis was layed on the last word, as with us on the first, in the phrase—French Nobleman.

5   p 64 | Bk 2 "Sypontus and Victorina"

But as it is the nature of Adultery to be accompanied and waited on by other sins, so *Victorina* is not only content to love *Sypontus*, but she makes a farther progression in impiety, and will needs hate her Husband *Souranza*; who poor honest Gentleman, sick with the Gout, and a Cough of the Lungs, is now distastfull, and which is worse, odious to her . . .

damn'd old Scoundrel.

6   p 65

. . . *Sypontus*, not to fail of his promise to *Victorina*, in the execution of his bloody and damnable attempt, takes his *Gondola*, and hovers in the direct passage betwixt *Lucifizina* and *Venice*, for *Souranza* his arrivall, who, poor harmlesse Gentleman, loved his young wife so tenderly and dearly, as he thought this short time long that he had wandred from her . . .

filthy old Dotard!

7   p 459 | Bk 6 "Sanctifiore and Ursina"

She very secretly provides her self of a Friers compleat weed, as a sad russet Gown and coule . . . and in one of the pockets of this Frock, she puts a small begging box . . . as also a new breviary . . . but in the other pocket thereof she puts a couple of small short Pistols which she had secretly purloined out of her Father *Placedo*'s Armory, and had charged each of them with a brace of Bullets, fast rammed down, with priming

---

4[1] For a set of references to C's own acknowledged prejudice against the French, see DESMOULINS **1** n 1. The supposedly natural antipathy of the two nations is a commonplace: cf "the wars of whist were comparable to the long, steady, deep-rooted, rational antipathies of the great French and English nations" in CL's essay "Mrs. Battle's Opinion on Whist" *L Works* (1903) II 34.

4[2] "On the contrary".

powder in the pans, and all these fatall trinckets, she . . . packs and tyes up close in the Gown, expecting the time and hour to work this her cruell and lamentable feat on <u>innocent</u> *Sanctifiore*, who little thinks or dreams what a bloody Banquet his old love, and now his new enemy *Ursina* is preparing for him.

there is something very amusing in this Writer's sudden change of Feeling as soon as a Villain, a Monster, or even a Murderer himself, is about to be murdered.[1] And the levis macula[2] on the conscience when these murders are effected by Duels, how ever unfair & savage, is curious, as a proof how much of what Superstition *calls* Conscience, is mere Love of Reputation, Character, Admission into accustomed Society, &c. Hence the utility of penal Laws, Death not so much as deterring from the crime when tempted to it, but as by prior blind horror precluding the temptation & the very thought. O Mr Clarkson & Co little think how much of the *guilt* of Murder &c in men's Consciences originate in the Gallows & the Newgate Calendar.[3]

7[1] Sanctifiore had jilted Ursina, leaving her pregnant.

7[2] "Slight spot", "light stain".

7[3] The *Newgate Calendar*, which C mentions enjoying as a boy (James SEDG-WICK **63**), told the life stories of notorious criminals. (It first appeared in 5 vols about 1773, and was followed by numerous imitators.) Here C expresses a reservation about the movement for prison reform that was active esp from 1814 (when the state of Newgate was deplored by a parliamentary inquiry) to 1823–4, when prison reform acts were passed through parliament. The Quaker minister Elizabeth Fry (1780–1845) was a prominent reformer in this period; C himself had praised her predecessor John Howard (?1726–90) in *Reflections on Having Left a Place of Retirement* lines 49–50: *PW* (EHC) I 107. C's acquaintance Thomas Clarkson was an Honorary Member of the Society for Diffusing Information on the Subject of Capital Punishment and Prison Discipline (founded in 1812); the Society's tract *On the Effects of Capital Punishment, as Applied to Forgery and Theft* (1818) contains his attack on the death penalty (specifically, for forgery) as unchristian. C points out that worldly considerations such as loss of reputation may themselves be deterrents when moral and religious—genuinely spiritual—inhibitions are lacking.

JACOB RHENFERD

1654–1712

Opera philologica, dissertationibus exquisitissimi argumenti constantia. Accedunt orationes duae, altera de fundamentis et principiis philologiae sacrae, altera de antiquitate baptismi ante inedita. Praemittitur oratio Cl. Andalae in obitum Rhenferdii habita. Elenchus dissertationum post praefationem exhibetur. Utrecht 1722. 4°.

British Library C 126 g 8

Inscribed by C on p ⁻6 below the price-mark £1.15.0: "S. T. Coleridge, Jany 1818." Note in an unidentified hand on p 205. Unidentified pencil marks and underlinings on pp 44, 45, 48, 64, 82, 83, 84, 90, 92, 93, 101, 102, 106, 108, 117, 122, 167, 169, 176, 187, 190, 193, 212, 226, 297, 481, 482, 483, 919, 926, 927, 946, 947, 951, 952, 953, 955. Note by EHC bound in at pp ⁻8/⁻7: "For Rhenferd vid. Table Talk *Bohn* pp. 54. 60. 273. These notes are unpublished". Note **22** has been recorded as in its original position, although recent rebinding has moved it from the back to the front of the book.

CONTENTS. Praefatio; Oratio funebris . . . dicta . . . a Ruardo Andala; 1–33 Dissertatio de stylo Apocalypseos cabbalistico; 34–51 De phrasi graeca N. T. ὁ Αἰὼν ὁ Μέλλων . . . non denotare DIES MESSIAE; 52–75 Testimonia recentiorum Rabinnorum de seculo futuro & diebus Messiae; 76–124 De fictis Judaeorum haeresibus; 125–64 De fictis Judaeorum & judaizantium haeresibus; 165–93 De Sethianis; 194–224 De redemtione Marcosiorum & Heracleonitarum; 225–53 De antiquitate literarum Judaicarum; 254–479 De decem otiosis synagogae; 480–583 Investigatio praefectorum & ministrorum synagogae; 584–613 De Arabarcha vel Etnarcha Judaeorum; 614–38 De ratione observandi genuinam vocabulorum Hebraicorum significationem; 639–85 Periculum Palmyrenum; 686–711 De statuis & aris; 712–31 Ad loca Hebraea Novi Testamenti; 732–69 Periculum Phoenicium; 770–5 Conjectura de tecto sabbathi; 776–81 Periculum criticum in loca depravata Eusebii Caesariensis, & Hieronymi; 782–92 Exercitatio philologica II ad loca deperdita Eusebii & Hieronymi; 793–800 Exercitatio philologica III ad loca vexata Eusebii & Hieronymi; 801–8 Exercitatio philologica IV ad loca depravata & vexata Eusebii, & Hieronymi; 809–15 Notae criticae & observationes in Eusebii & Hieronymi Onomasticum locorum sacrorum; 816–21 Exercitatio Eusebio-Hieronymiana de angulo Arabiae; 822–7 Epistola ad amicum de origine . . . vocis ATTA; 828–86 Rudimenta grammaticae harmonicae linguarum orientalium; 887–916 Vindiciae sententiae de seculo futuro; 917–41 Oratio de fundamentis et principiis philologiae sacrae; 942–57 De antiquitate baptismi; Index locorum scripturae; Index rerum et verborum.

DATE. Jul 1827, and perhaps earlier, since C acquired the book in 1818. Dated in ms: 6 Jul 1827 (**2**), Jul 1827 (**14, 22**). Further evidence of C's reading this work in Jul 1827 appears in N 33 (dated 5 Jul 1827) and N 34 (dated 31 Jul 1827), *T T* (*CC*) I 80, and OXLEE **2**.

COEDITOR. Lorna Arnold.

1   p ⁻6

Liber rarissimus—qui per multos annos erat mihi in votis. Spes meas minime fefellit: est enim opus egregium, et spiritum *Semiticum* alte spirat.   S. T. C.

   N.b. utor verbo isto, "Semiticum," quia "Linguæ Orientales" nimis latum—nempe ut quod Hindostanicum, Tartaricum, Sinensem, &c &c includit. Linguæ Semitarum (descendants of Shem) vocantur Hebraica, Syro-chaldaica, Arabica, Phoenicia, et si quae aliæ.—¹

2   p ⁻4, pencil

This truly excellent and enlightened Theologian constantly reminds me of Erasmus—or rather of our Jortin.¹ Jortin & Rhenferd were the spiritual Heirs of Erasmus— ~~but~~ ᵃ⟨or more truly still, I might have said that J. Rhenferd is an *Amphoteros*² of his ⟨Senior yet⟩ Contemporary Selden,³ and of his by more than a century Junior Dʳ Jortin—⟨J. Rhenferd had⟩ the wit and humor & classical taste of the latter, ~~and~~ with the vast Learning and robust ~~good Sense~~ Intellect of the former—& the *good sense* common to both.   6 July, 1827.—⟩ᵇ

   2ᵃ⁻ᵇ The long insertion is marked with two carets and written on the lower half of the page.

1¹ "A very rare book—which I had wanted for many years. It has fallen little short of my hopes; for it is an excellent work and breathes deeply of the *Semitic* spirit. S. T. C.   N.B. I use the word 'Semitic' because 'Oriental languages' is too wide a term, in that it includes Hindustani, Tartar, Chinese, etc, etc. Hebrew, Syro-Chaldaic, Arabic, Phoenician, and any others there may be, are called languages of the Semites (descendants of Shem)."
   2¹ John Jortin (1698–1770), to whom C likens Rhenferd also in *T T* (*CC*) I 80 (q in n 3 below) and in OXLEE **2**, was in fact the author of a *Life of Erasmus* (1758–60). C writes approvingly of his wit but disparagingly of his biography, in *Friend* (*CC*) I 61,

134*.
   2² Not in *OED*; C transliterates the Greek word meaning "both" or "either" from which is derived the adjective "amphoteric"—"partaking of the qualities of both"—which he used in a scientific context in a note of 1823 (*CN* IV 4942) and in a theological one c 1825 (IRVING *Missionaries* **9**).
   2³ John Selden (1584–1654), whose *Table-Talk* C had annotated many years before: see SELDEN. Cf his remark to HNC 8 Jul 1827 (*T T*—*CC*—I 80): "Rhenferd possessed the immense learning and robust sense of Selden with the acuteness and wit of Jortin."

Jacob Rhenferd, Sixth Child of Jacob Rhenferd, Minister of the Gospel at Mulheim on the Rhine—who had eleven children, 4 of whom survived the Father—born 15 August, 1654 at Mulheim[4]

3 sigg **3^r–[4^r]

[David Mill, the editor, devotes the last nine of the eleven pages of his preface to Rhenferd's controversy with Herman Wits on the meaning of the Hebrew phrase translated as *Seculum Futurum*, or "Age to Come". Mill adduces passages against Rhenferd's view that Jewish authors clearly distinguish it from *Dies Messiae*, "the Days of the Messiah".]

It appears to me that Rhenferd's ⟨principal⟩ error lay in expecting & asserting a greater consistency in the Rabbinical Comments & Tractates, than either the difference of the ages in which they were written, or the number & unequal attainment of the Writers, or lastly the fantastic and *minutial* Genius of the whole Tribe, rendered probable or possible. It would be a curious & not unprofitable subject to present the parallelisms in the ⟨theological⟩ divisions of the Jewish and the Christian Church from the 2nd Century. So in the instance of the Millennarian Dogma/ For them a time it counted a majority in both Churches among its Adherents—/ But in the Christian Church as the expectation of the ⟨speedy⟩ personal Return of Christ grew fainter & fainter, and the multitude of Gentile Christians quite overlayed that of the Jewish Christians, the Asserters of a Kingdom of Christ on Earth before the general Resurrection dwindled gradually into a small & insignificant Minority; while in the Jewish Church the major number of their Rabbis & Doctors adhered to it. And tho' there appears to have been a greater confusion in the use of the terms, Dies Messiae et Sec. Futurum, than Rhenferd was willing to admit,[1] the both terms being used by different Rabbis of both either Epochs, yet in the distinction itself I fully believed that Rhenferd has advanced the truth, of as to the Rabbis of highest Authority—and the majority of the Learned Jews.

P.S. What ever may be thought of the Question itself, it is of great interest & importance in the interpretation of the New Testament, and of

2[4] This information is given in the funeral oration printed in this vol, sigg ***3^v–[4^v].

3[1] The phrase given in Latin as "Seculum Futurum" is implied in NT at Matt 12.32 (AV tr "the world to come"); "Dies Messiae", with *dies* "day" in the singular, in

Phil 1.6, 10 and 2 Thess 2.2—the Greek in these reading τοῦ Χριστοῦ (the anointed, the Messiah; AV has "Christ" here as a proper name). Equivalent expressions such as "the day of the Lord" are frequent, with "day" always in the singular; for its lasting a thousand years see 2 Pet 3.8–10.

yet greater in the controversy with the Jews as to the marks of the messiah in Jesus![2]

4   pp ⁻6–⁻5, referring to p 2

II. Cabbala enim . . . *acceptionem* notat, sive oralem aut viva voce traditam, auribusque perceptam doctrinam, seu illam institutionem quam Graeci κατήχησιν appellant; à qua etiam vix differre deprehendas, nisi quod praeter communia, usuque recepta & vulgo intellecta vocabula, etiam literas quasdam, & voces nove usurpatas, & res quoque externas adhibeat, divinorumque mysteriorum, de quibus agit, signa & symbola constituat.

III. Hujusmodi olim Cabbalam ab ipso Deo in primitivae Ecclesiae institutione usurpatam; Patribus familias, Ecclesiaeque Doctoribus, ut usurparent, praescriptam; ab iisdem inde à primo rerum principio observatam; ad tempora usque Christi continuatam; circa ea vero κακοζηλιά & fastu Doctorum, qui populum indignum judicabant, cui . . . *fidem sanctis semel traditam* revelarent, obscuratam & foede contaminatam; & tandem, ne intercideret tam insignis scientia, ad instar Talmudis in literas relatam esse; id praesentis non fert ratio instituti ut probemus.

[II. For "Cabbala" denotes . . . a *receiving*, or a teaching handed on orally, or by word of mouth, and heard with the ears, or the custom that the Greeks call *catechesis*, from which you would scarcely find any difference except that besides ordinary words, generally used and commonly understood, the Cabbala introduces also certain letters, and words used in new ways, as well as external objects, and sets them up as signs and symbols of the divine mysteries with which it deals.

III. That this kind of Cabbala was used long ago by God himself in instituting the primitive Church, its use being prescribed to heads of families and Doctors of the Church; that by them it was observed from the first beginning and continued to the time of Christ; that about then it was obscured and badly corrupted by the mistaken zeal and arrogance of the Doctors, who thought the people unworthy to have revealed to them the faith . . . "which was once delivered unto the saints"; and that, at last, lest such a noble learning should be lost, it was committed to writing, like the Talmud— it is not relevant to our present purpose to demonstrate.]

P. 2. De Stylo Apoc. Cabbal.—
It is greatly to be regretted that Rhenferd had not applied his rabbinical lucubrations in determining the probable Date of the Cabbalistic Tracts

3[2] That is, the controversy as to whether the "marks", characteristics, or signs of the Messiah found in OT prophecies and in some apocryphal ones were fulfilled in Jesus, in particular whether they referred to the reign on earth of a king who would lay low the enemies of Israel or to the reign in heaven of the saviour of mankind. For a set of cross-references to C's reflections on the theory that there was a collection of the prophecies, actually entitled "Marks of the Messiah", see SCHLEIERMACHER *Luke* **1** n 1.

still extant, the oldest & most important of them I mean/ as likewise that he had not given the learned Public his Authorities for assigning so high an antiquity to the Cabbala itself. I should myself refer its Origin to the Maccabaic Period—tho' probably its verbal drapery & letter-fancying[a] was posterior to the Masora./[1]

5   p ⁻5, referring to pp 34–75

De seculo futuro.[1] In the same manner, as the present Romanists who quasi per taurum æneum (= a brazen-faced Irish *Bull*) sese Catholicos *boant* et reboant,[2] apply the phrase, "the future Life," indiscriminately to their purgatory and to their Heaven and Hell: so the Jews their seculum futurum to the state of immortality (such at least as had elevated their minds to this conception) and to their fancied Messianic Monarchy or Millennium. The controversy therefore was like that of the gold and sil-

---

4[a] The word is smudged and *might* be "latter-fancying"

4[1] The dating of the Cabbala depends on what one means by "Cabbala". Rhenferd accepts it as part of the rabbinical tradition going back to Adam or Abraham or Moses, but also as including what C refers to as the "most important" of the "Tracts still extant", the *Jezira* (or *Yetsira*) and *Sohar* (or *Zohar*), attributed to rabbis of the 2nd century AD. C himself assigned various dates to it, usually within the first two centuries BC. In marginalia to TENNEMANN (**64, 138**) and in the 1819 *P Lects* Lect 10 (1949) 299 he argues in favour of an early date "Before Christ" (TENNEMANN **64**): cf BREREWOOD **1** n 4. In EICHHORN *Apocrypha* **18** he suggests a date more than a century before the birth of Christ. Here, however, he assigns the origin of the Cabbala to the slightly earlier time of the revolts led by the Maccabees (beginning 168 BC) but the final touches ("verbal drapery") to the Middle Ages. The Masora or Masoreth, a body of traditional information about the text of the OT, is generally thought to have been complete about the 10th century; the connection between it and the Cabbala is made in Rees under both headings, and both entries describe the minute attention given to the very letters of the text.

5[1] "Concerning the age to come"—alluding to the fourth and fifth items in CON-TENTS, for which the running heads are "Dissert. I de seculo futuro" and "Dissert. II de seculo futuro". C elsewhere proposes that "Seculum Futurum" properly refers to a 3rd Epoch following the "Dies Messiæ" or 2nd Epoch: LACUNZA **59** and n 2. Cf **3** above.

5[2] Romanists who "as though through the Brazen bull . . . *bellow* and bellow again that they are Catholics". Phalaris, tyrant of Acragas in Sicily c 570–554 BC, was said to have dealt with his enemies by roasting them in a brazen bull; their cries represented the bellowing of the bull. C makes a complicated joke by linking the "brazen" bull with the self-contradictory utterance known as an "Irish bull" (cf *BL* ch 4—*CC*—I 72* and n 2), implying that it was outrageous that the Irish of his own period who were demanding reform called themselves Catholics; from C's point of view "Roman" and "Catholic" are contradictory terms (cf *CN* III 3872). Milton said the same thing, calling the phrase "Roman Catholic" "one of the Pope's bulls": *Of True Religion* (1673), q by Samuel Johnson "Milton" *Lives of the English Poets* ed G. Birkbeck Hill (3 vols Oxford 1905) I 148. (C himself annotated an ed of Milton containing this work: MILTON *Complete Collection.*)

ver shield—the phrase meant either—and which of the two must be determined by the context.[3]   *S. T. C.*

6 p 59 | § 15

[Moses Maimonides] . . . quid de promissionibus & comminationibus corporalibus, quae in Lege toties occurrunt, de annonae vilitate & caritate, pace & bello, regno & servitute, possessione terra & exilio, sentiendum sit, exponit; quae omnia cum *Hujus* tantum *Seculi* sint, neque praemii neque poenae loco aestimanda tradit, sed solummodo consideranda tanquam media, quae studium Legis, & virtutis exercitium, unica *Futuri Seculi* obtinendi media, vel promoveant vel impediant. Et hanc adeo piis ait causam fuisse desiderandi *Tempora Messiae*, quibus procul negotiis & soluti omnibus curis & aerumnis hujus vitae, soli Deo cognoscendo & colendo operam dare possent, & vitam aeternam mereri . . .

[[Moses Maimonides] . . . expounds what one ought to think about the material promises and threats that so often occur in the Law, the cheapness and dearness of grain, peace and war, kingship and slavery, possession of land and exile, all of which, since they are only of *This Age*, he lays down as to be reckoned neither as rewards nor as punishments but to be considered only as means to the promotion or hindering of the study of the Law and the practice of virtue, which are the only means of attaining the *Age to Come*. And this, he says, is why the pious should long for the *Times of the Messiah*, when, removed from business and free from all the cares and troubles of this life, they may apply themselves solely to knowing and worshipping God and deserving eternal life . . .]]

This doctrine of the more judicious Rabbis, tho' imperfect and below the dignity of the Event in sundry Particulars, is yet in the main, ὡς ἐμοίγε δοκεῖ,[1] confirmed by the New Testament, and gives a meaning and purpose to the resurrection of the Body, which Sherlock and other Christian Theologians have wrested their wits to discover without success.[2]

5[3] The shield that is gold on one side and silver on the other is a traditional figure; cf C's use of it in *Logic* (*CC*) 123 and n 4.

6[1] "As it seems to me (at least)".

6[2] C has in mind the interpretation of Rev 20.4–6 as meaning that at the Second Coming the departed souls of the dead will be restored to bodily life and live and reign "with Christ a thousand years". As to the "imperfect" particulars in Maimonides' account (in textus), C's marginalia in theological and millenarian books emphasise the importance of correct definitions of "body" (e.g. IRVING *Sermons* **29**; LACUNZA **36**;

LUTHER *Colloquia* **40**) and endorse the Pauline view that it is not the "natural" but the "spiritual" body that is to be raised: PEARSON **1**, DE WETTE **4**. Passages in which Sherlock might be said really to have "wrested" his wits over the issue of the resurrection of the body include *A Practical Discourse concerning Death* (3rd ed 1690) 35–68 and *A Practical Discourse concerning a Future Judgment* (1692) 346–8. Sherlock stresses what C himself felt, that body and soul are both essential to the whole man and his individual personality.

7   p 109

[The Nazarenes must have had a Hebrew gospel written by one of the Apostles, probably the Gospel of Matthew in Hebrew.] Nam si Deus infinitam suas gratiam & sapientiam eo olim comprobatam dedit, quod V. Testamentum mature in linguam Graecam curavit transferri; quod item N. Foederis libros Graece scribi voluit, ut gentiles haberent, quo de Deo & voluntate ejus ad salutem erudirentur: qui nobis vero simile fiat, Christum & Apostolos ejus primam Ecclesiam ex Hebraeis, Hebraea tantum lingua utentibus, collectam adeo negligere voluisse, ut peregrino idiomate apud illos uti voluerint? *Graeca autem lingua Judaeis in solo patrio barbara erat, neque Apostoli ante Sp. Sancti effusionem, caeterique de vulgo Judaei, qui quidem Hierosolymam reliquaque Judaeae loca incolebant, magis Graece callebant quam Latine. Unde neque Christus, neque Apostoli ejus, in Judaea ad populares suos aliter, quam Hebraice, locuti leguntur.

[For if God once showed his infinite grace and wisdom by providing in good time for the OT to be translated into Greek and by willing that the books of the NT should be written in Greek, in order that the Gentiles might have the means of being instructed about God and his will for their salvation, how is it to be made probable to us that Christ and his Apostles so wished to neglect the first Church, recruited from Hebrews, who used only the Hebrew language, that they deliberately used a foreign language with them? *For the Greek was a foreign language to the Jews in their native land; and the Apostles before the outpouring of the Holy Spirit, and the rest of the Jews of low rank, who lived in Jerusalem and the rest of Judaea knew no more Greek than Latin. Hence neither Christ nor his Apostles are said to have spoken any language but Hebrew to their fellow-countrymen in Judaea.]

*   O the power of a received Fancy on the soundest Judgements. Here is a stupendous Miracle asserted of at least 500 men—& yet not one single instance on record![1]—in Palestine ⟨itself⟩ the number of Natives who spoke & understood the Greek *only* was greater than that of those who understood the Hebrew—i.e. Aramaic only.[2]

7[1] The "stupendous Miracle" is the "gift of tongues" which, according to the traditional interpretation of Acts 2, enabled the Apostles to speak all the languages of those present, including Greek, when they met in Jerusalem on the day of Pentecost. On 23 Feb 1828 C recorded his growing conviction that Acts 2.6–11, giving the countries of origin of those present, was a later addition: N37 f4ᵛ–5. See also **10** below, as well as FIELD **4**. Here he argues that there is "not one single instance on record" of any change in the linguistic abilities of any person present. C has apparently taken the number "at least 500" from 1 Cor 15.6, assuming that all who had seen Jesus after the resurrection would be present at the meeting in Jerusalem.

7[2] Cf *CN* IV 5324 and n. Judaea had been under Roman rule since 68 BC, but Greek was still the lingua franca of the Eastern provinces of the Empire, and Aramaic rather than Hebrew was the local vernacular. (It was often by earlier scholars, like Rhenferd here, not distinguished from Hebrew, and was often, as by C elsewhere, called Syro-Chaldaic.)

8   p 114 | § 80

Epiphanius Haeres. XXIX. §. 7. *Hoc igitur uno tam à Judaeis, quam à Christianis differunt: ab illis quidem, quod in Christum credant; à Christianis vero; quod Judaicis adhuc ritibus implicentur, velut Circumcisione, Sabbatho, aliisque caerimoniis. Et Haer. XVIII. § 1. de Nazaraeis. Pentateuchum ipsum repudiat. Nec Mosen quidem abjicit, neque oblatam huic à Deo legem esse diffitetur, sed aliam fuisse dicit, quam quae vulgo circumfertur. Ex quo factum est, ut Judaeorum reliquas caerimonias observent, utpote Judaei: à sacrificiis abhorreant; neque animata re ulla vescantur. Itaque carnes in cibum adhibere, vel sacrificare nefas esse ducebant. *Conficta enim haec esse volumina: neque eorum quicquam à majoribus profectum.*

[Epiphanius *Heresies* 29 § 7. "They [the Nazarenes] are, then, as different from the Jews as they are from the Christians in this one respect: from the Jews, in that they believe in Christ; from the Christians in that they still engage in Jewish practices, such as Circumcision, the Sabbath, and other observances." And *Heresies* 18 § 1 on the Nazarenes. "[This sect] repudiates the Pentateuch itself. It does not reject Moses, nor deny that the law was given to him by God, but it says that it was different from the law that is commonly circulated. From this it comes about that they observe other Jewish ceremonies, just as the Jews do, but abhor sacrifices and eat no living thing. So they considered it unlawful to eat or to sacrifice meat. *For these volumes were forgeries and none of them came from the fathers."]

*   a capital specimen of the malignant credulity of the Fathers respecting those, whom they considered as Heretics.[1]

9   p 114 | § 82

Sed, age, videamus, quam haec justa & gravis causa fuerit. Erant Nazaraei illi omnes, erant Cerinthus ille & Ebion, si tamen uterque fuerint, genere Judaei, semen Abraham, cui circumcisio à Deo mandata erat, & data signum foederis & sigillum justitiae fidei; neque vero ipsi tantum, sed & semini ejus . . . *in generationes eorum* . . . *in foedus aeternum,* quamdiu posteri Abrahami superstites erant futuri, adeo ut Deus piaculum pronunciaret, singulari judicio vindicandum, si quis circumcidi nollet. Gen. XVII. Rom. IV. 11.

[But come, let us see how justified and how serious this charge was. They were all Nazarenes; the notorious Cerinthus and Ebion, if indeed either existed, were Jews, the seed of Abraham, to whom circumcision was commanded by God and given as a sign

8[1]   C was especially impressed by Rhenferd's success in explaining away the Fathers' reports of early heresies among the Jewish Christians in his four dissertations on the subject, all of which C annotated. Cf his appreciative comment in *T T (CC)* I 460, and the parallel passages gathered in nn 22, 23 there.

of his covenant and a seal of the righteousness of the faith, and not indeed to him alone, but to his seed also ". . . in their generations . . . for an everlasting covenant" for as long as the descendants of Abraham were to survive, so much so that God prescribed a propitiatory sacrifice, to be enforced by a singular judgment, if anyone should refuse to be circumcised. Gen 17. Rom 4.11.]

Because the Palestine Christians retained Circumcision, not as Christians but as descendants of Abraham—therefore they retained the cerimonial[a] Law—But because they did not retain the Ceremonial Law, regarding Sacrifices as superseded by the Substance—therefore they rejected the Pentateuch, as a recent Forgery!!!—[1]

10   pp 115–16

At, inquies, Circumcisio jam pridem abrogata erat, & cum reliquis Veteris T. caeremoniis sepulta. Sic vulgo ajunt, atque uno omnes ore praedicant. Sed si quis hujus novae legis tabulas desideret, si vocem praeconis funus illud indicentis requirat; ubi inveniat, quis ostendat? De Paulo Apostolo jam olim fama . . . illud vulgavit, et ab ipsis aliquamdiu Nazaraeis creditum fuit, illum hujus legis funerisque praeconem fuisse; sed falsissima illa erat, & mox prudenti Jacobi consilio & promto Pauli obsequio publice est refutata. Ut mirum sit, potuisse vanum rumorem tam altas in Christianorum gentilium animis radices agere, ut per tot secula in hunc usque diem nequiverint evelli.* [Rhenferd then quotes Acts 21.20-5.]

["But," you will say, "circumcision had long ceased to be required and had been buried with the other observances of the OT." Such is the common and unanimous account. But if one looks for the tablets of this new law, or listens for the voice of the crier announcing this burial, where will he find anyone to show it to us? Rumour . . . had already long ago reported it of the Apostle Paul, and it had long been believed by the Nazarenes that he was the announcer of this law and burial; but the report was utterly false and was early refuted in public by the prudent advice of James and by Paul's prompt compliance. So that it is extraordinary that an empty rumour was able to strike roots so deep in the minds of gentile Christians that they have been ineradicable for so many centuries up to the present day.*]

* This excellent remark of this learned and (a far rarer gift) sensible Critic would furnish me with an answer to himself, should he object to me the antiquity & universality of the tradition respecting the ⟨polyglot⟩ miracle—thro' the mistaking Luke's "other," i.e. profane, Languages for "diverse."[1] Item, de Mariâ nunquam non Virgine—vel ut rem omnem

9[a] For "ceremonial" (correct below)

9[1] C reinforces Rhenferd's objections to Epiphanius' reasoning as reported in **8** textus.

10[1] Acts 2.4: "And they were all filled with the Holy Ghost, and began to speak with other tongues, as the Spirit gave them

fatear, de toto isto Evangelio Infantiæ, duplici quidem & miro modo bilingui.[2]

11   pp 118–21

[Rhenferd continues (pp 115–19) to defend the Nazarenes against Epiphanius (see **8** textus), citing NT texts (Acts 21.20–5, Rom 3.2, Gal 5.2–4, 6.15, 1 Cor 7.17, 19) to prove that the Jewish law applied to Jewish but not to gentile Christians, and that the Nazarenes were right to retain circumcision in particular because it was not given by Moses but was from the fathers (John 7.22) or Abraham (Gen 17.10).]

Rhenferd has omitted to notice one essential point—viz. that these declarations were made & these commands enjoined by the Apostles before the destruction of the Temple, and while the Jewish *State* still subsisted, in both its constituent parts; the Hierarchy and the People, as the *Subjects,*/ or Citizens of ~~the~~ a Republic. When the Heaven (= the ~~Parlia~~ Government ⟨as the *Head*⟩) and the Earth (= the Governed, as the *Body* of *this* Corpus Politicum[1]) were removed, the Law ceased of course with the Subjects & Object[2]—as a Tune when both Player & Instrument are no more. Till that time Christ demanded of his disciples being members of the Jewish State the most scrupulous Observance of the Law—declaring the contrary conduct ~~or~~ and doctrine, not indeed a damning Heresy but an instance of rash & premature Zeal, which would ~~determine prove the~~ place the Individual in the lowest rank of Christians—i.e. mark him at once as a man very imperfectly enlightened as to the true object & character of the Gospel Dispensation.—If the Palestine Christians after the destruction of the Jewish *State* under Hadrian[3] not only retained Cir-

utterance." For C's consistent interpretation of this verse, see also *TT(CC)*ı62; FLEURY 6; HERBERT 24; OMNIANA **11** and nn.

10[2] "The same goes for the perpetual Virginity of Mary—or, to tell all, the whole notorious Gospel of the Infancy, bilingual in a remarkable and double way." C usually argued that the "Gospel of the Infancy" in Matt was woven into it at a comparatively late date, and that the longer account in Luke 1–2 was an interpolation: cf PAULUS **2** and SCHLEIERMACHER *Luke* **9** and n 2. These accounts could be called "bilingual" as having been translated from Hebrew into Greek, as well as for containing inconsistencies—"bilingual" in the sense of "two-tongued".

11[1] "Body politic".

11[2] Alluding to Matt 5.17–18: "Think not that I am come to destroy the law, or the prophets: I am not come to destroy, but to fulfil. For verily I say unto you, Till heaven and earth pass, one jot or one tittle shall in no wise pass from the law, till all be fulfilled." Cf *CL* v 2, where C defends this interpretation at greater length; also *CN* III 4402.

11[3] The more usual date given for the end of the Jewish state is AD 70, when Titus sacked Jerusalem and destroyed the Temple, but in AD 135 Hadrian expelled the Jews from Jerusalem and founded a Roman colony there.

cumcision as Descendants of Abraham, which in my opinion they were bound to do; but both this and other parts of the ceremonial Law, as the Law of *Moses*—they assuredly were in an error, and S[t] Paul's argument applied to them. Gal. V. 2.—[4]

12   p 121

[Rhenferd has quoted Jerome on Isa 66, where Jerome implies that there were some who thought that Jewish Christians could offer animal sacrifices without harm to themselves.] In quo quid sit, quod haereseos magnopere accusari possit, lubens equidem fateor me non videre, cum ipse Apostolus sacrificia procul dubio obtulerit, quae completo Naziraeatus voto debebat, Act. xviii. 18. & myriades illae Judaeorum, quorum Jacobus meminit, iis non abstinuerint . . . . Quod cum absque ullo Christianismi & salutis Pauli detrimento factum sit, quid mirum; si illi quoque Hebraei, quorum Hieronymus mentionem facit, nullam admodum difficultatem ea in re viderint.

[What there is in this seriously to justify an accusation of heresy I freely admit that I for my part cannot see, when the Apostle himself doubtless offered the sacrifices that a Nazarite owed on completing his vow (Acts 18.18) and those thousands of Jews that James mentioned did not abstain from them . . . . As this was done without any detriment to the Christianity and salvation of Paul, why should we be surprised if those Jews whom Jerome mentioned found no difficulty whatever on this point?]

Another reason might probably influence the Palestine Christians—the prophecies of Ezekiel respecting the new Temple, ~~of~~ which, many believed, would be literally fulfilled at the Return of our Lord in Glory.—[1]

13   p 123

[Rhenferd translates from Epiphanius, interspersing his own comments:] Haeres. xxix. . . . Porro *(enim more omnium Christianorum)[a]* non solum Novo sed & Veteri Testamento Judaeorum *(Christi, inquam, & Apostolorum)* instar utuntur. * Neque enim apud illos Legis libri, Prophetae, aut Hagiographa prohibentur *(quasi sc. ad veri naturam Christianismi pertineat, Veteris Test. libros prohibere)* . . .

[Epiphanius *Heresies* 29. ". . . Further *(i.e. like all Christians)*, they use not only the

---

13[a] Square brackets in the original have been converted to parentheses throughout this passage in order to avoid confusion with editorial matter

11[4] "Behold, I Paul say unto you, that if ye be circumcised, Christ shall profit you nothing." Rhenferd (116) quotes Gal 5.2–4 and points out that Paul is addressing Gentiles there.

12[1] Ezek 41.

New, but also the Old Testament, like the Jews (*like Christ, I say, and the Apostles*).*
For among them the books of the Law, the Prophets, and the Hagiographa are not prohibited (*as though, forsooth, it pertained to the true nature of Christianity to prohibit
the books of the Old Testament*) . . ."]

* This, however, is a noticeable passage. Taken in combination with the
Letter of Melito, a Bishop, to his Brother, likewise a Bishop, and sundry
other passages in the Fathers of the 3 first Centuries, it shews, how little
known, and how little valued, the Jewish Canon (= O.T.) was by the Gentile Christians:[1] a fact of no mean importance in accounting for many of
their wild notions & strange interpretations of the N.T.—of the Apocalypse, especially.

14 pp 132–3

[The Gentile Christians heard those who lived in Judaea called Ebionim,
meaning "poor men" . . .] Sed cum non adeo ipsi ingenio destituti essent,
quin facile perspicerent, quo nomine Christus suos beatos praedicat, eo
se Ebionaeis illudere ac male dicere non posse; detorserunt non nihil
phrasin, & πτωχοὺς τῇ διανοίᾳ vocaverunt, id est *mentis inopes*, vel
potius, Hebraismi emphasi quodammodo retenta, *humiliter atque abjecte
sentientes*, de Jesu Christo scilicet, quem (sic Patres aliunde nova calumniae ansa arrepta fingunt) more caeterorum hominum ex Josepho &
Maria natum, & ψιλὸν ἄνθρωπον, *merum hominem*, nequaquam Deum
esse crediderint.

[But as they were not themselves so destitute of intelligence as not to see that they
could not use the name by which Christ describes his blessed ones to mock and abuse
them, they slightly altered the phrase and made it "poor in mind" or rather, keeping
the emphasis of the Hebrew, "thinking poorly and abjectly", of Jesus Christ, that is.
They are supposed to have believed (thus, yet again, the Fathers grasp a new handle
to fashion calumny wherever they can) that he was born in the same way as other people, of Joseph and Mary and [*psilon anthropon*] *mere man*, not God at all.]

* I cannot help suspecting, that credulous as the malignity of the Fathers
was,[1] there must have been some—not ground; but—*pretext* for this
charge of Psilanthropism[2] against the Palestine Christians. A false
Charge, assuredly; but what if they had asserted the Evangelia Infantiæ
to have been no ~~pe~~part of the Apostolic κηρυγματα?[3] The Fathers would

---

13[1] Melito, bp of Sardis (115–85), does
imply uncertainty about the OT canon—but
not a low estimate of it—in a letter to Onesi-
mus that C could have found quoted in full
(from Eusebius *Historia ecclesiastica* 4.26)
in Eichhorn *Alte Testament* I 120.

14[1] Cf **8** above.
14[2] "The assertion of the mere humanity
of Christ". Cf textus. This word may be C's
coinage: see *OED*, *LS* (*CC*) 176–7 and n 4,
CHANNING 1.
14[3] I.e. what if they had asserted the "In-

at once infer a disbelief of our Lord's Divinity: tho' in fact there is not the slightest connection between the two Opinions.—

S. T. C.   1827   July.

15   p 137, pencil | § 22

[On the phrase "poor in spirit" (Matt 5.3) as not applying to the Ebionites, whose Hebrew name means "poor men":] At cum illa *animi humilitas, humilis* cujusque *de se ipso sensus* exprimendus est, Hebraei nunquam voce אביון utuntur, nedum illam cum substantivis לב vel רוח construunt, sed voce ענו *anav* sive absolute posita, sive cum memoratis substantivis constructa, unde ענוה *humilitas, mansuetudo,* & Rabbinis Syrisque עגון *anvaan,* & ענוגות *anvnuth, humanus, mansuetus* . . .

[But when that *humility of mind,* someone's *humble opinion of himself* is to be expressed, the Hebrews never use the word *evyon* [poor, needy] nor combine it with the nouns *lev* [mind] or *ruach* [spirit], but rather use the word *anav* [humble] either absolutely or combined with the above-mentioned nouns, whence *anavah humility, gentleness,* and the rabbinical and Syrian words *anvaan* and *anvnuth, humane, gentle.*]

Q.ᶻ Hinc Germanum "*Anmuth?*" Haud putem.—[1]

16   p 139, pencil | § 28

Hic [Barnabas] cum esset vir bonus & Spiritu Sancto & fide plenus, postquam aliquandiu Pauli fidus comes & collega in opere domini fuisset, tandem jurgio aliquo oborto Paulum reliquit, & *cum Marco in Cyprium navigavit.* Act. xv, 39.

[After he [Barnabas], being a good man and full of the Holy Spirit and of faith, had for a long time been Paul's loyal companion and colleague in the work of the Lord, at length some contention arose, and he left Paul and "sailed unto Cyprus with Mark." Acts 15.39.]

This *jurgium*[1] adds to the probability, that the Epist. of Barnabas is authentic:[2] and I doubt not, the strong-minded Apostle alluded if not to the

---

fancy Gospels" (**10** n 2 above) to have been no part of the Apostolic "pronouncements"—which latter C generally, as in **17** below, considers essential doctrines as opposed to *doxa* or "opinion of Divines". Cf HERDER *Von der Auferstehung* **16** n 3, EICHHORN *NT* COPY A **1**, LACUNZA **47**, and **17** below.

15[1] "Hence the German *Anmuth*? I shouldn't think so." *Anmuth* (now *Anmut*),

meaning "grace" or "charm", was one of the "untranslatable" words C said he envied the Germans: SCHELLING *Darlegung* **20**. Here he toys with the idea that it might have descended from the Hebrew *anvnuth*.

16[1] "Contention": in textus.

16[2] This note is closely related to remarks in *TT* (*CC*) I 460 and to C's reading of the General Epistle of Barnabas (now believed to be not by the apostle Barnabas but

Epistle yet to the Foible & known Fondness of the holy and zealous but not very judicious, Saint in his caution against the innutritive inflating tendency of the γνωσις—[3]

17   pp 159–62

[Quoting Irenaeus *Adversus Haereses* 3.24 on the Ebionites:] *Non ergo vera est quorundam interpretatio, qui ita audent interpretari scripturam; Ecce, adolescentula in ventre habebit & pariet filium: quemadmodum & Theodotion Ephesius est interpretatus, & Aquila Ponticus, utrique Judaei proselyti; quos sectati Ebionaei ex Joseph generatum eum dicunt, tantam dispositionem Dei solventes &c.* Ex eo, quod dicti interpretes vocem עלמה apud Jesaiam non per παρθένος sed per νεᾶνις verterunt, calumniae illos seu malitiosae interpretationis arguit; quorum versionem cum Ebionaei, qui Graece Biblia legebant, adoptassent, ceu textui originali Hebraeo convenientiorem, hinc eos negatae nativitatis Christi ex Virgine reos agit: *Quos sectati Ebionaei ex Joseph generatum eum dicunt.* Tanti constitit Ebionitis veterem & receptam in Ecclesia versionem, quam τῶν Ο΄. appellabant, relinquere, ac novas Aquilae & Theodotionis recipere ac lectitare: ut cum hi in versionibus suis aliquid innovarent, id illi orthodoxiae suae periculo & aperta haereseos accusatione luere debuerint.

["Therefore the interpretation of certain persons who dare so to interpret scripture is incorrect: 'Behold a young woman shall be with child and shall bring forth a son': this is how Theodotion of Ephesus interpreted it, and Aquila of Pontus, both Jewish converts. Following these, the Ebionites say that he was begotten by Joseph, undoing God's great dispensation, etc." From the fact that the above-mentioned translators rendered the word *almah* in Isaiah not by "virgin" but by "young woman" he accuses them of calumny or of malicious mistranslation, and since the Ebionites, who read the Bible in Greek, adopted their version, as closer to the Hebrew text, he charges them with denying that Christ was born of the Virgin: "Following these, the Ebionites say that he was begotten by Joseph." The price to the Ebionites of this departure from the old translation accepted in the Church, the so-called Septuagint, and their adoption and reading of the new ones by Theodotion and Aquila was that when these made any innovations in their translations, the orthodoxy of the Ebionites was questioned and they had to face a public accusation of heresy.]

by an Alexandrian Christian of rather later date) in *The Apocryphal New Testament* ed William Hone (1820) in Apr 1826: *CN* iv 5351–5, Bible *NT Apocrypha*.

    16[3] 1 Cor 8.1–2 (the "strong-minded Apostle" being Paul): ". . . Knowledge [*gnosis*] puffeth up, but charity edifieth.

And if any man think that he knoweth any thing, he knoweth nothing yet as he ought to know." Cf comments on *gnosis* in Donne *Sermons* copy b 39, Eichhorn *Neue Testament* copy b 5, Irving *Sermons* 5 at n 3.

The easiest way of reconciling this apparent contradiction would be found in the hypothesis, that tho' the Ebionites or Converts from Judaism, generally, received the Tradition of their Church respecting the miraculous Conception, yet the more learned among them regarded it as a credible δοξα, worthy of all reverence, but denied that it was an Apostolic κηρυγμα.[1] For the probability of this conclusion of theirs, many grounds might be advanced, without contravening the truth of the Tradition. We all know the reason assigned for the omission of that most momentous miracle, the raising of Lazarus, by the three earlier Evangelists[2]—Much more might ⟨it⟩ be a duty of Apostolic Prudence, or even of Mary herself, not to tempt the ribbald Blasphemies of their unbelieving Countrymen by the assertion of a Miracle insusceptible of Proof—& where the ⟨public⟩ attestation of the only Witness, the Mother of our Lord, could scarcely be reconciled with the σεμνῳ & και πρεποντι[3]—with the great maxim of the First Preachers of the New Covenant—παντα κατα το πρεπον εστω.—[4]

18   pp 170–1

Cum itaque Eberus talis tantusque esset, ut ab illo omnes qui in avita & vera religione casti manebant, *Ebraei* dicerentur, id primum Semo laudi datur, quod hujus Eberi pater sit, quod tam praeclara indole nepotem genuerit; quemadmodum e contrario Chamo hoc stigma inuritur, quod improbum illum Canaanem genuerit, Gen. IX. 18. . . . *Hic* [Cham] *est pater Canaanis*, cui ob insignem impietatem atque flagitium adversus avum commissum ipse Noachus praeter caeteros omnes Chami posteros maledixerat, Ibid vs. 25. seq.*

17[1] See **14** n 3.

17[2] John 11.33–44. Cf the general note on John 11 in *The New Testament . . . with a Commentary* ed Adam Clarke (3 vols 1817) I: "It is surprising that the other Evangelists have omitted so remarkable an account as this is, in which some of the finest traits in our Lord's character are exhibited. The conjecture of *Grotius* has a good deal of weight. He thinks that the other three Evangelists wrote their histories during the life of Lazarus; and that they did not mention him for fear of exciting the malice of the Jews against him. And indeed we find from chap. xii. 10. that they sought to put Lazarus to death also, that our Lord might not have one monument of his power and glory remaining in the land. Probably both Lazarus and his sister were dead before St. John wrote." Cf DONNE *Sermons* COPY B **92**.

17[3] "Reverence and decorum". There are injunctions to be σεμνός in Phil 4.8, 1 Tim 3.4, 8, 11, and Tit 2.7 (AV "honest" or "grave"); and various forms of the verb πρέπει—though not this participle—in 1 Cor 11.13, 1 Tim 2.10, Tit 2.1 (AV "becomes" or "is comely").

17[4] "Let all things be in accordance with decency". Cf 1 Cor 14.40, "Let all things be done decently and in order"—where, however, the Greek is quite different from C's.

[So while Eber was of such character and greatness that after him all who remained faithful to the old ancestral religion were called *Hebrews*, the praise was given to Shem first, for being the forefather of this Eber, for producing a descendant of such outstanding character; just as, on the other hand, Ham was branded with the shame of being the father of the wicked Canaan, Gen 9.18. . . . "he [Ham] is the father of Canaan" whom, for the gross impiety and crime committed against his grandfather, Noah himself cursed above all the descendants of Ham. Gen 9.25 ff.*]

* May not this suggest the probable solution of the difficulty respecting the Language of the Canaanites—viz. that the Descendents of Chamus or Ham by Canaan, Ham's Son, should speak a dialect of the Semitic Tongue, instead of Coptic or some Sister-dialect of the Hammonic? But if we suppose the Tribes destroyed, or driven out of Palestine by Joshua to have been the Offspring of misalliances or mixt marriages the i.e. descendants of Shem but likewise of Ham by forbidden intermarriage, & that they or their posterity had apostatized from the Sethite and Semitic Faith, and become Canaanites in Religion—all is clear.[1]

19   pp 187–9

Sic ex eodem fonte est eorundem *Archonticorum*, qui & ipsi *Sethiani* fuerunt, ἡ ἀκατονόμαστος δύναμις *innominata*, vel *quae nullo nomine comprehendi potest Virtus*, Haer. xl. cap. 7. כוה הנסתר Cabbalistis, *Pater* nostris, opposite ad *Filium*, qui est כוה הנגלה Virtus illa manifesta & manifestans omnia. Hinc illa Gnosticorum *Achamoth*; ipsa Cabbalistarum הכמה, *Sapientia*: Hinc item alia multa, quae hic non est dicendi locus.

[So these same *Archontici*, who also were Sethians, have from the same source "the unnamed power", or the Virtue which can be comprehended in no name. [Epiphanius] *Heresies* 40 ch 7. [It is] *koach hanistar* [hidden power] to the Cabbalists, the *Father* to Christians, as opposed to the *Son*, who is *koach hanigleh* [revealed power], the Power manifest and manifesting all things. Hence the Achamoth of the Gnostics, the *chokmah Wisdom* of the Cabbalists: hence much more too, for which this is not the place.]

If the Cabbalists have thus stated the Supreme Mystery, the Scheme is deficient—by the confusion of the Prothesis with the Thesis, and thus giv-

18[1] For C's theory based on the tradition of the origin of nations and of languages in the migrations of the sons of Noah and their descendants cf his notes for a lecture of 30 Jan 1818 in *Lects 1808–1819* (*CC*) ii 70–2; *CN* iv 4548 (Jun 1819); and BLUMENBACH **4**. All these refer to the "mixt marriages" with the polytheistic Canaanites, which were to be avoided, or were specifically forbidden (Gen 24.3, 28.1; Exod 34.11–16; Deut 7.1–3) but nevertheless took place (e.g. Judges 3.5–7). That the languages of the Hebrews and the Canaanites were identical is implied by Isa 19.18 and by the absence of any sign of difficulties in communication. It was assumed by most earlier commentators that their differences amounted to no more than dialectal variations on Hebrew, the original language of mankind, at least since Babel.

ing the 3 (Trias) without preposing the Tetractys, which provides for the unity of the Trias. The order is ·∴·, i.e. 4 = 3 = 1.[1] 1. The absolutely immanifestable Identity. 2. The I AM, or Ipseity self-manifest ⟨implicitè⟩[2] and manifested in suo Altero et per Alterum[3] = The Father. 3. The Alterity, the Supreme Being, or substantial Reason—The WORD = The Son—3.[a] The Community, energic Love, the Divine Life = Holy Ghost.—And these are *one* and God, by the ακατομ́νομαστον δυναμιν του υπερουσιου προπρωτου.[4] S. T. C.—

20 pp 204–8, part in pencil

[Rhenferd emends and interprets the two baptismal formulas (in corrupted Syriac) of the Marcosians and the Heracleonites, given by Irenaeus and by Epiphanius; in the teaching about redemption and the formulas in which it is expressed, he finds parallels between Jews, Christians, and these so-called heretics.]

Assuredly, it must to a candid mind appear a strong Presumption in favor of a Scheme of Faith, that its principal articles are found in so many forms, in so many different countries and ages—that a succession of Individuals, in many instances without knowlege of each other, should arrive at the same truths, yet expressed in the greatest variety of terms and symbols, according to the presence or absence of a learned education, to the different climates, different *positive* Religions &c ⟨of the individual Writers—⟩[a]—a decisive proof, that they did not learn them by rote, in a line of succession from a common source, but must have found them in themselves. [b]In fact, no man *could* learn them from a Book who had not previously discovered the clue in himself: for in this system the first Idea contains the whole, and generates the Second. The second generates the third, and by reflected Ray, lumine retrorso,[1] manifests the first—and so on thro' the whole descent and expansion. In my own instance, I solemnly bear witness and declare that every Idea, Law, or Principle, in which I coincide with the Cabbala, or the School of Plotinus, or the Christian Gnos-

19[a] "3" in error for "4", which has been added above the line in pencil, probably not by C
20[a] Insertion in pencil
20[b] Note continued in pencil

19[1] The adaptation of the Pythagorean tetractys to the Trinity is a typically Coleridgean manoeuvre: cf GREW **1**, IRVING *Sermons* **2**, **3**, and esp C's remark in LACUNZA **1** that "divine truths are ever a *tetractys*, or a triad equal to a *tetractys*: 4 = 1 or 3 = 4 = 1".
19[2] "Implicitly".
19[3] "In its Other and by the Other".
19[4] "By the unnameable power of the being above, which is before the first".
20[1] "By the light directed backward".

tics, or the Mystics of the middle Ages from Hugo de Sancto Victore to Tauler, or the Protestant Masters of the interior way, as Behmen, Zinzendorf &c,[2] I *recognized* in them, as truths already known by me in my own meditation. Indeed, the language of the greater number of the Mystics, from causes explained in my "Biog. Literaria",[3] is so inadequate and arbitrary, & the Writers themselves ⟨are⟩ so imperfectly Masters of the Ideas; (possessed by fragments of the Truth rather than possessing ~~the~~ even these) that it would have been impossible to have decyphered the true import of their Strivings, without the hounding Scent of Sympathy and without the Key of a previous and superior Insight.

S. T. Coleridge

21   pp 214–17, pencil

[Quoting James 5.14–15:] *Si quis inter vos aegrotet, arcessat Seniores Ecclesiae; & orent pro illo, ungentes illum oleo in nomine Domini. Et preces cum fide conjunctae servabunt aegrum, & Dominus illum suscitabit. Et si peccata commiserit, venia illi dabitur.*

[[AV:] *"Is any sick among you? let him call for the elders of the church; and let them pray over him, anointing him with oil in the name of the Lord: And the prayer of faith shall save the sick, and the Lord shall raise him up; and if he have committed sins, they shall be forgiven him."]

* The most profitable use, we can make of this (for protestant and spiritually minded Christians) somewhat repulsive passage, is: that we should learn from it the necessity of supplying those *qualifying* conditions, which, the Apostle might safely take for granted, ~~as~~ would be understood by ~~by the first Readers~~ those, to whom this Letter was more immediately addressed—either limiting the otherwise too general proposition (as —"if it be ~~for~~ the true interest of the Patient & for the advancement of the

20[2] C's sense of the importance of a mystical tradition is well documented in the marginalia, and explanatory annotation for most of the names given here will be found in earlier entries. For the Cabbala see e.g. **4** above, OXLEE **13**; for Plotinus and the Neoplatonists LUTHER *Colloquia* **62** n 2, PLOTINUS, PROCLUS; for the Christian Gnostics CHILLINGWORTH COPY B **1** n 2, FLEURY **32–34**, **35–39** and nn; for Hugh of St Victor the headnote to HUGH (but see also *TT—CC—*I 298 and n 10); for Böhme the headnote to the long BÖHME entry; for Zinzendorf LAVINGTON **2** and nn. The one

exception is Johann Tauler (c 1300–61), the German mystic whom C enquired about in 1817 (*CL* IV 742) and whose "very rare Works . . . were with difficulty procured for me in Germany last year" according to a letter of Jan 1822 (*CL* V 205).

20[3] In his tribute to the mystics who "contributed to keep alive the *heart* in the head", *BL* ch 9 (*CC*) I 152, C points out that unlearned writers "made their words immediate echoes of their feelings" and were consequently misunderstood as claiming direct revelation (150).

Church spiritually") or by choosing purposely expressions capable of, nay, actually conveying to spiritually minded Readers a double sense— the removal of spiritual Sickness, the Saving him from the Death truly such, as the contrary of true Life.—The ~~taking refuge in the notion~~ flying off to the excuse, that it was written during the age of miracles may *serve a turn/* if there be no Catholic within hearing to demand a *scriptural* authority for the Assertions, that Miracles were confined to the Life-time of the Apostles. *I* should have another question to ask—By what facts or credible documents we are to support the assumptions, that *Miracles*— such as *we* should consider ~~as such~~ Miraculous—i.e. Miracles objectively, as distinguished from assumed "answers to our Prayers", from "Remarkable *providences*", from *special Gifts* & Graces, &c &c, were things of frequent occurrence at any period after the Day of Pentecost, or before the Baptism of our Lord.—[1]

22 p +1[a], pencil

It is, I humbly trust, from ~~the~~ a deep sense ⟨(derived from History & my own observation)⟩ of the mischievous direct & indirect effects of all error in mens'[b] religious Creeds, unmixed with vanity or busy-body restlessness, that I am influenced in so anxiously desiring that the questions respecting the true nature of the Authority of the Canonical Scriptures, collectively, with the true import of the Inspiration vouchsafed to the writers;—the Grounds of Authenticity of the several Books; and the validity of the received notions concerning the immediate effects of the Descent of the Spirit and ⟨concerning⟩ the character of the Jewish & Gentile Christians during the apostolic Age & the age of the next generation—/ should be submitted to a cautious but free inquisition.[1]—Especially solicitous am I to determine the right apprehension of our blessed Saviour in his two-fold character, as the Son of God and the Son of Man.—

S. T. Coleridge

Grove, Highgate   July 1827

22[a] The original position of the note, which was removed to ⁻2 in rebinding in 1970
22[b] For "men's"

21[1] In response to Hume's scepticism on the one hand and Paley's materialism on the other, C carefully formulated his position on the supererogatory status of miracles about 1807 and revised it very little in many later statements on the subject. His views are summarised in *CCD* 38–42; cf HERDER *Briefe* 11, LIGHTFOOT 2 and n 1, LESSING *Sämmtliche Schriften* **8**, **9**; *CN* III 4452, IV 5228.

22[1] C attempted such an "inquisition", at least on the questions of authority and inspiration, in *CIS*, composed c 1820–4 and pub posthumously in 1840. (It is now included in *SW & F—CC* —1111–71.)

JOHANN PAUL FRIEDRICH RICHTER
"JEAN PAUL"
1763–1825

Jean Pauls Geist oder Chrestomathie der vorzüglichsten, kräftigsten und gelungensten Stellen aus seinen sämmtlichen Schriften; mit einer Einleitung und einzelnen Bemerkungen begleitet. 2 vols. Weimar & Leipzig 1801. 8°. Vol I lacks title-page.

Dr Williams's Library

Inscribed on the title-page of Vol II, slightly cropped: "H. C. Robins[on]". A slip of paper pasted to II ⁻5 (p-d) inscribed by HCR: "The Mss notes in this Vol: are by Coleridge", and below, in pencil in another hand (perhaps E. W. Field): "Handwriting of H Crabb Robinson". Bookplate of Edwin Wilkins Field, HCR's literary executor, in each vol: cf RICHTER *Museum*.

In Vol I many passages are marked in pencil and ink, and in Vol II also many passages are marked and cross-references written: these are presumably by HCR. A few words are written in pencil, not by C, on I 377, 378, 414, 424.

DATE. Between Mar and Jul 1811? C borrowed these vols from HCR on more than one occasion. *CL* III 305–6 and 462 request the loan of *some* work by Jean Paul, probably this one, in Mar 1811 and Nov 1813 respectively. *CRB* I 150 records an urgent request for *Jean Pauls Geist* in Oct 1814. But the clearest evidence is two series of entries in N 18 dated (by ed) May–Jul 1811: *CN* III 4087–8, 4090, 4092, 4094 and nn.

COEDITORS. Lore Metzger, Raimonda Modiano.

---

1   I 27–8, pencil, cropped | § 3

Da die geistigen Thätigkeiten keine körperlichen sind, sondern ihnen blos entweder *nach-* oder *vorgehen*, und da jede geistige so gut im Geiste, wie im Körper Spuren lassen muss; sind denn, wenn der Schlagfluss oder Alter die körperlichen weglöscht, darum auch die geistigen *verloren*?

[Since mental activities are not physical ones, but only either *follow* or *precede* them, and since every mental activity must leave traces in the mind as well as in the body; if then apoplexy or age blot out the physical traces, are the mental ones *lost* too?]

All these poetico-philosophical Arguments strike & shatter themselves into froth against that stubborn rock, the Fact of *Consciousness* or rather its depend[ence] on the body. Th[at] this sho[uld] be the last, the only

261

Strong[hold] of Materialism—& to be successfully stormed by pure *Idealism* alone. Alas!—& yet again, alas! But M. & I. are irreconcilable with an [? honest/earnest] Faith, and the latter Common Sense, (i.e. Dualism = Soul + Body = Person) is (if possible) yet more irreconcilable with Science—[1]

2   I 199, cropped | § 129

* Gute Menschen können sich leichter in schlimme hineindenken, als diese in jene.

[* Good people can more easily understand wicked people than the latter can the former.]

There are no *good* men—but the bett[er] men have the germs of the Evil mostre often than the wicked have those of the Good, consc[?ience] developed.

3   II 12, pencil, overtraced, cropped | § 373 footnote

Es ist leider eine nur zu wahre Bemerkung, dass blos das ausgezeichnet Vortreffliche, oder das entschieden Schlechte seinen Platz in der Weltgeschichte findet. Die Menge von guten Menschen, die im Stillen ihre Rolle spielten . . . werden . . . vernachlässigt, vergessen und von jenem überglänzt.

[It is unfortunately only too true an observation that only what is supremely excellent or decidedly bad finds a place in world history. The multitude of good people, who quietly played their part . . . are . . . thereby neglected, forgotten, and eclipsed.]

a most piteous pitiful and pitiable remark that leider![1] alias alas! Mr Mawkish looks into a Register of extraordinary Events for ordinary ones and did not [. . . . .][2]

4   II 27, cropped | § 393

Nicht die Vernunft (d.h. das Gewissen) macht uns gut.

[Reason (i.e. conscience) does not make us good.]

1[1] C's commentary on these pages continues in *CN* III 4087–8, where C asserts that "The Materialist is the Idealist of the intelligible World" (4087).

3[1] "Unfortunately": in textus.
3[2] "Mr Mawkish" appears to be C's invention.

The Reaso[n] is not the Conscience the latter is a *sensation* sui generis, the spiritual feeling ~~of~~ that results from the perceived Consonance or inconsonance of an Act or Purpose with the Universal Will or Reason.[1]

5   II 58, cropped | § 441

Ein Flockengewimmel von Aethergestalten stand schwebend über einer weiten Insel, um welche ein rundes Geländer von grossen Blumen aufgeblättert spielte;—mitten über den Himmel der Insel flogen Abendsonnen hinter Abendsonnen . . .

[A flock of ethereal forms hovered above a large island, about which fluttered a round hedge of large flowers;—midway across the sky above the island, setting suns rushed after setting suns . . .]

A fair specimen [of] unimaginable Images. I could describe the births [&] vanishings of those bright [m]aniform [o]cular Spectra, which people a new world of Space when my nervous system is feverous,[1] [? as] a strange intermundium[2] between the ideal space in the Soul, & the outward space—even these I could translate into more intelligible words

---

4[1] There is a very similar definition in *LS* (*CC*) 66–7.

5[1] Erasmus Darwin coined the phrase "ocular spectrum" to denote an image left on the retina after a person had been gazing at a bright object, in *Phil Trans RS* LXXVI (1786) 313, and popularised it in "Interlude III" of *The Loves of the Plants* (Lichfield 1789) 128–9. C was interested in this phe-nomenon, recording some experiences of his own (e.g. *CL* II 961; *CN* I 1681, 1765) and incorporating it eventually in his ghost-theory: *TT* (*CC*) I 54 n 7.

5[2] "Space between worlds", a word C adopted from Latin and for which his use in *Omniana* (1812) is the earliest cited in *OED*. Cf *Omniana* § 175 in *SW & F* (*CC*) 337 and *BL* ch 2 (*CC*) I 32 and n 2.

Das Kampaner Thal oder über die Unsterblichkeit der Seele; nebst einer Erklärung der Holzschnitte unter den 10 Geboten des Katechismus. 2 pts. Erfurt 1787. 8°.

Bound as first with REIMARUS *Ueber die Gründe der menschlichen Erkentniss*, and with an unidentified, unannotated pamphlet on slavery written after 1803 (the title-page is missing; the opening words are, "Bei den mehrsten Nationen, welche vor der Römer Herrschaft in der Geschichte . . ." and it ends, at p 86, ". . . der Partheien gänzlich aufzuheben").

Princeton University Library (Grenville Kane Collection)

DATE. Between the spring of 1811 and the summer of 1815. The notebooks show that C was reading Richter eagerly during 1810–11, but notes of 1811 that might appear to be derived from *Das Kampaner Thal* have been traced with some certainty to RICHTER *Geist* (see headnote above); therefore it seems that his reading of *Das Kampaner Thal* and REIMARUS came later. The allusion to REIMARUS in *BL* ch 6 (*CC*) I 106 suggests the summer of 1815 (when *BL* was being composed) as the latest possible date for the reading of that work, and presumably of the Richter bound in the same vol.

COEDITORS. Lore Metzger, Raimonda Modiano.

TEXTUS TRANSLATION. Juliette Gowa tr *The Campaner Thal: or, Discourses on the Immortality of the Soul* (2nd ed 1857), slightly revised. Gowa did not translate the second work in the vol (where **12** appears).

1　p $^-$1, pencil

Transfer to [? p] Mem. B. Science + y as superseding KNF and its state and accompaniments—[1]

2　i 61, pencil, marked with a pencilled line in the margin | Station 503 [The work begins at 501.]

---

[1] This puzzling note is on a flyleaf and might therefore belong with REIMARUS rather than with the Richter title. It seems to be a memorandum addressed to C himself to copy a note from this vol to a memorandum book (one of the notebooks) kept for scientific topics; this memorandum book together with "Y" (there is a reference to "two pocketbooks, L and Y" in *P Lects*—1949—151n, but *CN* III—Notes—xxxiii is unable to identify Y, which may be lost; or "y" may be one of the loose sheets to which C sometimes gave such headings) would supersede KNF. KNF remains a mystery.

Der Hauskaplan replizierte: "Ueberhaupt wil Kant damit die Unsterblichkeit nicht demonstrieren: er sagt selber, sie sei uns darum so ungewis gelassen, damit der reine Wille nur durch sich und durch keine eigennüzigen Aussichten in die Ewigkeit bestimmet werde."

"Sonderbar, sagte Karlson! Da wir nun aber diese Endabsicht heraushaben, so wäre sie ja eben dadurch verfehlt. . . . Es ist ein eigener Zirkel, *aus der Unbeweislichkeit eines Sazes seine Wahrheit zu vermuthen. Entweder die Unsterblichkeit ist darzuthun—und dan ist die eine Hälfte Ihres Sazes nicht richtig—oder sie ist es nicht: dan ist der ganze falsch. Noch dazu: wenn der Glaube an sie die Tugend eigennüzig macht:[a] so thuts ja das Erleben derselben in der zweiten Welt noch mehr."

[The chaplain replied: "Kant does not at all intend to demonstrate immortality by this argument. He says even, that it has been left so uncertain in order that a free will shall be influenced only by itself and by no selfish prospects of immortality."

"Strange," said Karlson! "But as we have now discovered this intention, its object appears to be defeated. . . . It is a strange circular argument *to presuppose the truth of a proposition from its indemonstrability. Either immortality can be proved, then one half of your argument is right, or it cannot: then the whole of it is wrong. Besides, if belief in immortality makes virtue selfish, the experience of it in the next world would make it more so."]

Whenever I meet with positions stated universally or exclusively, I suspect a Sophism. Thus, l. 5 after "Wille" insert "nicht", ⟨and for "keine" before, read "allein" after, eigen. Aussichten:⟩[b1] and *then* the doctrine, said to be Kant's, will approximate to the Truth, and pluck out beforehand the sting, of Karlson's Objections.

3 i 60, pencil | **2** textus

* Why so? What Kant asserts, is this only: the Truth of a Dogma, for the belief of which other sufficient grounds exist, may be confirmed by its *indemonstrability* in the strict sense of Demonstration.[a1] Is not this the Case with all rational Hopes & Fears? With all ultimate Truths?

2[a] C has marked the textus from * to this point with a line in the margin
2[b] C has written this afterthought in the margin, with a symbol indicating where it is to go
3[a] The note continues at the top of the page with the direction, "*From the bottom of the page*"

2[1] If these alterations were made, the textus tr would read, ". . . in order that a free will shall not be influenced by itself and by selfish prospects of immortality alone". **3[1]** C's interpretation of Kant's argument may be based chiefly on Richter's account, but it also reflects his reading of Kant's discussion of proofs of the immortality of the soul—specifically, his refutation of Mendelssohn's argument—in *C d r V* B 423–6.

4   i 61, pencil | **2** textus

In short, the whole argument proceeds on an absurd application of the Totum simul[1] i.e. the Eternal to a Being assumed to be finitely progressive.

5   i 75 | Station 505

Es ist mir selber kaum glaublich; aber die *melodische* Fortschreitung zu sublimierten Wesen hinauf wurde bisher doch warlich nur—*angenommen*; ich glaube an eine *harmonische*, an ein ewiges Steigen, aber an keine erschafne Kulminazion.

[It seems scarcely credible to me. But truly the *melodious* progression to sublime beings has hitherto been merely taken for granted. I believe in a *harmonious* one, in an eternal ascension, but in no created culmination.]

There neither are nor can be more or other *Kinds* of living Existence than God, Man, and Beast: and even of these the third is rather assumed than conceived. So thought St Augustine/[1] and so far I agree with Jean Paul,— but the ewige Steigen I as little believe as die *erschafne* Kulmination.[2] What then? Re-ascension *aus* dem Erschafnen.—[3]   *S. T. C.*

6   i 86–7, pencil | Station 506

Dan fragte Karlson, warum man denn bei dieser immerwährenden Erfahrung, dass jede körperliche Einbiegung eine geistige Narbe grabe, und bei diesem unaufhörlichen Parallelismus des Körpers und der Seele, blos nach dem lezten Ris und Bruch dieser alles wiedergeben wolle, was man mit jenem scheitern sah.

[Karlson then asked why, with the continual experience that every bodily twisting leaves a spiritual scar, and with this unceasing parallelism of body and soul, it is only after the final cracking and breaking of the latter that we want to recount everything we have seen fail in the former.]

This is *not* fairly stated. There is nothing absurd or even anomalous in supposing a successive Development involved in one and the same plastic Power. There are biennial & triennial Plants, that yet each Autumn rot to the invisible Root—i.e. a root that would be invisible to the Plants tho' not to superior Beings. But this Argument, like all others adduced by Ma-

4[1] "The whole simultaneously".

5[1] C attributes the same position to Augustine elsewhere, e.g. Noble **4**, Oxlee **10**, *C&S* (*CC*) 169—where the editor's note indicates relevant passages in Augustine but is unable to identify a direct source.

5[2] "Eternal ascension" and "*created* culmination"—in textus.

5[3] Reascension "*out of* the Created".

terialists, involves the conclusion in the unproved Premise. It takes the Product (das Körpergen)[1] as identical with the Producent. While the Caterpillar remains co-organic with the Fly, the Fly must suffer with and from the Caterpillar—even where the Caterp. suffers from the growth of the Fly.[2]

7 i 90–2, pencil

Aber der Resonanzboden des Körpers ist weder die geistige Tonleiter noch ihre Harmonie; die Betrübnis *hat keine Aehnlichkeit mit der Thräne, die Beschämung hat keine mit dem in die Wangen gesperten Blute . . .

[But the sounding board of the body is neither the soul's scale, nor its harmony. Grief *has no resemblance to a tear, shame none to the blood that rushes to the cheeks . . .]

* Neither less nor greater resemblance (the materialist might reply) than the Wind with the Wave, or than any antecedent with a different phænomenon that is its ordinary Consequent—ex. gr. Mackerel with Goose-berry Sauce. That A = B, i.e. Non-A, is a Mystery common to all Systems.[a] Were it possible, the Spiritualist should prove the contrary—viz. that B = A: ergo, that B is not Non-A, in *essence*. In other words, there may be a more intimate analogy between Grief &c and Tears &c, than is at present conjectured—Δακρυ τι υδατοειδες. ὑδωρ τι δακρυοεν.[1]

8 i 93, pencil

Unterscheidet denn der Geist eines *kindischen* Greises sich in nichts von dem Geiste eines *Kindes*? Büsset Sokrates Seele, in Borgia's Körper wie in ein Schlambad eingescheidet, *ihre moralischen Kräfte ein und tauschet sie auf einmal ihre tugendhaften Fertigkeiten gegen lasterhafte aus?

[Is there no difference between the soul of a *childish* old man, and that of a *child*? Does the soul of Socrates imprisoned in Borgia's body as in a mud bath, lose *its moral powers, and does it suddenly change its virtuous qualities for vicious ones?]

7[a] The note continues on p 91 with the direction "(turn over)"

6[1] C uses a diminutive (now only dialect): "little body".

6[2] C uses "Fly" here (conventionally) in the sense of butterfly: the butterfly emerges at the cost of the caterpillar. This was a fertile image for C, especially when he drew upon the traditional symbolic identification of the butterfly and the soul (*psyche*), as in his poem *Psyche—PW* (EHC) I 412—or in such a remark as the following, from *CL* II 1032: ". . . my miserable carcase—the Caterpillar Skin which, I believe, the Butterfly Elect is wriggling off, tho' with no small Labor and Agony."

7[1] "A tear is somewhat waterlike and water somewhat tearlike."

* Alas! the Negative ~~of~~ to this Question is the Object *sought for* in this argument, not a *part* of it. Who would not gladly answer, No! and who, that has known the dreams and the passions and impulses that agitate the Soul in ~~Cases~~ the Dreams of aggravated Indigestion, but must feel a momentary hesitation in returning that Answer?[1]

9 i 95, pencil | End of Station 506

One thing robs Jean Paul's reasoning of its value—that a *Karlson* is a non-*descript*. For who ever admitted the distinct and diverse existence of a Soul in the Body and yet asserted the mortality of the former?—Admit a Soul as the proper subject of all the powers spiritual, and therefore a self-subsistent Conscious Individual: and Karlson's arguments are mere Difficulties versus Impossibilities.[1]

10   i 117 | Station 507

". . . Denn der ewige Hunger im Menschen, die Unersätlichkeit seines Herzens wil ja nicht *reichlichere*, sondern *andere* Kost, nur Speise stat Weide: bezöge sich unser Darben nur auf den Grad, nicht auf die Art, so müste uns wenigstens die Phantasie einen *Sättigungsgrad* vormalen können; aber sie kan uns mit der gemalten Aufthürmung aller Güter nicht beglücken, wenn es andere als Wahrheit, Tugend und Schönheit sind."

[". . . For the eternal hunger in man, the insatiability of his heart, wants not a *richer*, but only a *different* food; fruit, not grass. If our wants referred but to the degree, not to the quality, then the imagination, at least, might paint a *degree of satiety*. But imagination cannot make us happy by showing us innumerable heaps of treasures, if they be other than those of truth, virtue, and beauty."]

But remove these Dirt-clods, the Suns, Planets &c that make up the Material Universe, and what provender shall we have for Truth?—remove the Passions & Appetites: & what is Virtue/ And these lost, where is Beauty?—

11   i 118–19

"Aber die schönere Seele?" sagte Nadine. Ich antwortete: "diese Unförmlichkeit zwischen unserem Wunsche und unserem Verhältnis, zwischen

---

[8][1] C often attributed his own disturbed sleep to a disturbed stomach, e.g. *CN* II 2078; *CN* III 3692; *CL* II 976, 991.

[9][1] C's note sums up his reaction to the dialogue as a whole, and particularly to the position adopted by one of the speakers, Karlson, with counter-arguments by the Chaplain, the narrator, and others.

dem Herzen und der Erde bleibt ein *Räthsel*, wenn wir dauern, und wäre eine *Blasphemie*, wenn wir schwinden."

["But the more beautiful soul?" asked Nadine. I answered: "This discrepancy between our wishes and our circumstances, between the heart and the earth, will remain an *enigma*, if we are immortal, and would be a *blasphemy* if we perish."]

Whatever *is*, must *be* a mystery: and must *appear* a Miracle if we reflect on it as having *become*. For ~~all that is~~ the ⟨sole⟩ Bond of Beings, is their *Relations*: and these *are* not, but exist only in the focus of the Percipient. And how Being*s*? The *one* needs no Bond: & how can that verily *be*, which is other than *One*? There is an eternal History implied in *Being*, by force of its *Existence*. ~~and~~ It is History that ties the Gordian Knot, & it is History alone that must cut it. The Philosophy, that *begins*, is History: the History, that begins in A WILL, is the only true Philosophy.

12   ii 37 | *Erklärung der Holzschnitte unter den zehn Geboten des Katechismus* § 1

Aber das sag' ich nicht gern in den Wind, dass Fet ein Zeichen und Siz des körperlichen Wohlbehagens ist: da nun nach Bellarmin zeitliche Glükseligkeit unter die Merkmale der wahren Kirche gehört, so darf den Dienern derselben dieses Merkmal am wenigsten fehlen . . .

[But I'm not wasting my breath when I say that fat is the sign and seat of bodily comfort; since according to Bellarmin, temporal happiness is one of the distinguishing characteristics of the true church, its servants ought least of all to be without it.]

As far as my Experience of the Lutheran Clergy in N. Germany extended, this is a most ungrounded Charge. Lax Faith even to an infra-socinian mere Philochristianism[1] may be justly laid to the Charge of too many; but in general they are men of Learning & exemplary Lives. But the Undervaluing of Protestantism is one of the worst Diseases of the later German Philosophers & Poets.

12[1] "Philochristianism", love of the Christian, appears to be C's nonce-word; "infra-socinian", below the Socinian, i.e. going further than even the Socinians do when they deny the divinity of Christ and consider him merely an extraordinarily gifted human being.

Museum von Jean Paul. Stuttgart & Tübingen 1814. 8°.

Dr Williams's Library

Inscribed on p ⁻2: "Carl Aders December 1817"; and in HCR's hand on p ⁻3 (p-d), "N.B.: The M:S: notes in this Vol: are by *Coleridge*, either written in ink by him, or in pencil: and written over by me H. C. Robinson", followed by a list of the pages on which C's notes are written. Pencil autograph signature of HCR's executor E. W. Field on p ⁻3, and librarian's notation "Donation from Miss Field 1916." The headnote to DE WETTE gives an account of Aders's importance to C as a source of German books.

DATE. Perhaps 1818, shortly after Aders acquired the book and during the period of C's intense interest in animal magnetism; perhaps later.

COEDITORS. Lore Metzger, Raimonda Modiano.

1   p ⁻2, pencil, overtraced

I am sorry to say, that I look upon this book as an affair between Jean Paul and his booksellers with which the Public have no other concern but that of keeping their money in their Pocket./   S. T. C.

P.S. From this censure (whether of Jean Paul or of those whose neglect in patronizing so admitted a Genius may have compelled him to these Catch-pennies I know not) I except p 195[1]—& a few other patches of Sunshine. But it applies in its full force to the wretched Compilation from Wienholt, Wolfart, Gmelin,[2] &c and to the Learning [. . . . .]

2   p ⁻1, referring to p 7 | Pt 1 § 2

Die Lichtmaterie, welche an einem trüben Tage durch die Luftschichten, durch die Wolkenschichten, und zuletzt durch ein Stückchen Glas hin-

[1] On p 195 Richter contends that all suffering, including physical pain, is spiritual and originates in mental representations (*Vorstellungen*). As these representations are replaced by others, pain disappears. The remedy against painful thoughts is the realisation that whatever affects a person is already a past event. Another comment on this passage appears in **12**.

[2] On pp 4–5 Richter lists works by Wienholt, Wolfart, Gmelin, and Kluge to which he refers frequently in his subsequent discussion of animal magnetism. These works include E. Gmelin *Über den thierischen Magnetismus* (Tübingen 1787), A. Wienholt *Heilkraft des thierischen Magnetismus* (3 vols Lemgo 1802), K. C. Wolfart *Darstellung einer lebensmagnetischen Kur* (1812), C. A. F. Kluge *Versuch einer Darstellung des animalischen Magnetismus* (2nd ed Berlin 1815). C annotated Kluge's work and Wolfart's *Erläuterung zum Mesmerismus*: see MESMER.

durch uns alle Gegenstände zeigt, vermag diess nicht mechanisch durch Poren zu thun, weil z.B. in einem Linsen grossen Glas . . . welches alle einzelne Punkte des weiten halben Gesichtkreises durchgehen oder schauen lässt, in jedem denklichen Punkte Poren, also gar nichts, da sein müsste . . .

[The luminous matter, which on an overcast day must pass through layers of air, through layers of clouds, and finally through a small piece of glass to show us all objects, cannot do so mechanically through pores; for in that case a lens-sized piece of glass . . . that allowed a view of all the points contained in fully half of one's field of vision would have to have pores at every conceivable point, i.e. would be nothing . . .]

P. 7.—This objection (viz. that the Glass must be *all pore*, or it could not shew us the whole Landscape) is not *coercive* to my mind. I am indeed strongly disposed by analogical reasoning and my pre-established aversion to the atomic physics, to adopt a successive action, instead of a continuous prolongation, of Light; but I cannot but think that it would be possible even for man to make a porous substance which would transmit outward Objects [? ~~or~~] sufficiently near to Glass to leave no doubt as to what motion might do.—[1]

3   pp 38–9, pencil, overtraced | § 5

Und ist denn das helle Einschauen einer Hellseherin in das verwickelte körperliche Geflecht und Gebäu kein jetziges Anschauen, sondern nur eine Notiz von frühern Anschauungen, wenn gleichwol . . . *der Hellseherin sowol frühere anatomische Anschauungen als Kenntnisse von allen den Nervengewinden und Farben mangelten, die sie doch in der Krise richtig zu bezeichnen weiss?[a]

[And is a clairvoyant's clear insight into the intricate plexus and structure of the body not a present perception but merely a record of previous perceptions? for the fact remains that . . . *even though she had access neither to previous anatomical observations nor to knowledge of all the nerve clusters and colours, she was nevertheless able to designate them correctly in the crisis.]

*   The grand prudential Error of the Magnetists consists in the eager haste with which they have published their own Beliefs and Interpretations of unusual Phænomena without weighing the proportion of the Appearances

3[a] C's note indicator here is a long line in the margin stretching from "der Hellseherin" to the end of the textus

2[1] It is, as C says, consistent with his rejection of material atomism that he dismissed Newton's corpuscular theory of light (and with it the doctrine of pores, for which see IRVING *Sermons* 51 and n 16). On the other hand, he does not explicitly endorse the available alternative, the wave-theory of Christiaan Huygens.

to the positions deduced from them. This is particularly striking in the ~~eas~~ instances of supposed anatomical Beholdings, and of Prescience. The facts are meagre compared with the assertions.[1]

4   pp 46–8, pencil, overtraced

Ich erinnre nur flüchtig noch an die Kraft menschlicher Berührung, welche sich am Gelde zeigt, das der Hund seinem Herrn aus dem Wasser holt, *ferner an dem Auswittern von dessen Fussspuren unter tausend andern auf meilenlangen Wegen . . .

[I draw attention only in passing to the power of human touch, which is demonstrated by the dog's retrieving money from the water for his master, and *furthermore by his scenting out his master's footprints among a thousand others along mile-long paths . . .]

Jean Paul has not hit the true Puzzle viz. not the Seeing nor yet the Not-Seeing: but the co-existence of both ~~in~~ as to the same Object, in the same person. The paper, on which the Somnambulist was writing (in the case recorded by the Archbishop of Bourdeaux in the French Encyclop:) was changed and the writer made an erasure, and put the correction with a caret /\ exactly over the erasure without perceiving the Blank.[1] This would seem to *prove* that not the Sight, but the memory as its substitute, was the Agent—yet a stool being placed in his way, where no stool ever had been or could have been before, he avoided it exactly as one that saw it.—

5   pp +1–+2, referring to pp 46–7

In all the publications of the Magnetists hitherto (& this work of Jean Paul's is merely a careless compilation from them with a little Gossip thereon) there is a strange confusion arising from the metaphysical and physical mode of contemplating the same subject at the same time. In the former *the Will* is every where represented as the Source—and yet in the very next sentence perhaps, we have "recht viele anfassende Verstärk-menschen"[1] recommended: as if Will were capable of arithmetical addi-

3[1] Similar complaints about the proponents of animal magnetism—their claims about clairvoyance in particular—appear in e.g. KLUGE **7**, **8** and LOEWE **4**.

4[1] C refers to the *Encyclopédie, ou dictionnaire raisonné des arts et des métiers* xv (Neuchâtel 1765) 340–1, where the article "Somnambule, & somnambulisme" records a case reported by the Archbishop of Bordeaux: a young clergyman was found at night composing and reading sermons with his eyes shut.

5[1] A quotation from p 47, referring to the magnetisers' use of assistants to boost the power of the mesmeric "battery": tr "a great many supporters for reinforcement".

tion, or the truth of a Geometrical Demonstration were increased by the increasing number of the Demonstrators! Where indeed the effect is produced not by the Will, which is so far a mere *accident*, as when I turn something over by means of a Lever which might as well have been overturned by the Wind or by a Flood—then I can understand the value of numbers—but not, when the Will itself is the immediate agent.

Thus again, p. 46,[2] the instances from the Dog & Coin, and the deserted Birds Eggs are as little to the purpose, i.e. in proof of any wonder-working powers of Touch (Berührung) as a bottle of Ether placed under or near a piece of Meat, & after some time taken away. Our quantum of Smell enables us to know that the meat has been exposed to some specific effluvia—and so does the Dog's without regard to the Coin piece of Money, and the Bird's with regard to her Eggs.—

The remark in 47[3] is equally applicable to Opium, in short to all Drugs which increase the Sensibility while they diminish the muscular irritability. Nothing can be more celestial or intellectual—alas! because the goings on in the body, that stimulate to the sensual, are laid asleep. What mystery in this? When the contrary appears in *Old age*, does it not become an Object of Disgust? The two points, which ought to be insisted on by Magnetists at present, as the foundation of future researches, are: I. that Man can act on the bodies of other men, immediately, at least without Visible or known Media—2. that the persons acted on acquire the sense of Presentation without the Eye or Ear.[4]

6   pp 48–9

Auch die Beobachtungen Wienholts, dass stumpfe, dumme Seelen* des Magnetismus nicht empfänglich sind, hilft hier bestätigen.

[Wienholt's observations that dull, stupid souls* are not susceptible to magnetism also serve here as confirmation.]

* And yet Trees and Water are! But the strange *dreamy* way in which single instances are generalized here, is enough to give a sensible mind a distaste and suspicion. Never did Animal Magnetism find a more wretched Advocate. J. Paul is no *reasoner*.

5[2] I.e. **4** above, with the additional evidence that birds will abandon eggs that have been touched by human beings.

5[3] On p 47 Richter says that the increase in spiritual and moral sensibility experienced by the subjects of animal magnetism cannot be attributed to ordinary physical causes.

5[4] In his statements about animal magnetism, C quite consistently maintains that the champions of animal magnetism would do better if they worked more empirically, building up physical evidence rather than speculating about the causes of the phenomena recorded: cf *CL* IV 886–7, *CN* IV 4908.

7   p ⁻1, referring to p 50 | § 6

* Dazu kommt noch das Eisen im Menschenblute selber . . . welches . . .
von ihm nicht erst aufgenommen, sondern selber erschaffen wird; denn
blos eingenommenes Eisen geht unvermindert wieder ab, und sogar in
den Nährmitteln kommt es nur selten und zufällig in uns . . .

[* Add to this the fact that there is iron in human blood itself . . . which . . . not originally absorbed by it, is instead itself produced; for iron that is merely ingested is entirely discharged, and even by way of food it enters us only rarely and accidentally
. . .]

P. 50. I am ⟨as⟩ strongly inclined to believe with Schelling, Steffens, and
others, that the Iron in the Blood is a Product of the Life, as Jean Paul can
be.[1] But the arguments here adduced by him in this page are either mere
assertions, or proofs of *possibility*. The Iron may have pre-existed in our
food or even in the air; but it *may* likewise have been produced as well as
the Phosphate of Lime, &c. But there it will be answered, that the Lime,
Soda, &c *may* likewise have been taken up into the body/ and at all events
are *known* to be compounds/ and [? ever/even]

8   pp 54–5, pencil, overtraced | § 8

Schon in der ganz gemeinen Erfahrung thut der Wille sein Vermögen,
ohne Muskeln zu bewegen, kund, dass wir ein auf den beiden ungeregten
Zeigfingern hängendes Eisen,? z.B. einen Schlüssel durch blosses
Wollen in Drehung oder in Ruhe bringen können.

[The will reveals its power without moving muscles even in everyday experience, such
as when through pure volition we can make a piece of iron suspended from the two
motionless index fingers,? as for example a key, turn or come to a standstill.]

? *I* cannot: and is it not more probable that the muscular motion should
be unnoticed from its being less or other than what the Eye has learnt[a]
and used itself to see—than that it should not exist?

8[a]   Word not overtraced

7[1] Schelling, Steffens and other *Natur-
philosophen* would welcome the presence
of iron in the blood, iron that was somehow
generated by the living body itself and not
introduced from outside it, as a confirmation of certain important hypotheses of their
system, e.g. that there is no essential difference between organic and inorganic matter,
all naturally-occurring phenomena being
derived ultimately from a single source.
Schelling contributed a short notice on iron
in the blood anonymously, as editor of the
journal, to *Zeitschrift für spekulative Physik*
I ii (1800) 148–9: *SW* IV 544. (C read and
annotated this journal.) C himself speculates about iron in the blood in BÖHME **23**.

9 pp 72–3, pencil, overtraced | § 13

... Scheinertrunkne vernahmen (nach Unzer)* im Wasser das ferne Glockengetön in einem seelig-wogenden Sein, gleichsam liegend an der halb-offenes Todes- und Paradieses-Pforte und einsaugend einen Rausch von Erdenduft.

[... seemingly drowned persons (according to Unzer)* heard in the water the distant tinkling of bells, swaying in a blissful state of being, as though they were lying at the half-open gate of death and paradise, and breathing in an intoxicating fragrance of the earth.]

I can attest from *my own experience* that this is the Case with outward insensibility in consequence of Frost. For I was recovered from such a state, with a distinct recollection of my feelings during the earlier part—what they were, if any, during the *interval*, I cannot say.

S. T. Coleridge—

10 p 83 | § 14

Wenn uns der irdische Magnetismus das <u>erhebende</u>* Schauspiel von Seelen-Vereinen blos durch ätherische Körper-Vereine gibt . . . so dürfen wir wol furchtsam-kühn ahnen . . . dass künftig jenes unbegreiflich ätherische Medium . . . dass vielleicht als Eine Aetherhülle, als Ein Welt-*Körper* oder Welt-Leib eine aus tausend Seelen zusammengeflossne Welt-*Seele* umschliessen und tragen könne.

[If terrestrial magnetism offers us the <u>elevating</u>* spectacle of the union of souls simply through the union of bodies in an ether . . . we may surely surmise with trembling boldness . . . that in the future that incomprehensible ethereal medium . . . may perhaps as a single ethereal envelope, as a single world *body* or world carcass, enclose and carry a world *soul* of a thousand commingled souls.]

* Erhebende? elevating? Can a more degrading, depressing, immoral Idea be formed, that[a] of Spiritual affections and perfections by a mere coercion, of the *bodies* intermingling? ätherische![1] nonsense! body is body, thick or thin.[2]

10[a] A slip for "than", or omitting "than" before it

10[1] "Ethereal"—in textus.

10[2] Here C uses "body"—an immensely complex term for him, as IRVING *Sermons* 29 and n 12 indicate—in the limited sense of his definition in a letter of 1818, "Body, phaenom. ponderabile et fixum [something that is stable and can be weighed]" (*CL* IV 807). This note expresses his typical complaint about *Naturphilosophie*, that it confused spiritual powers with physical products: cf GOLDFUSS **2** n 2.

11   p 163, pencil, overtraced | Pt 3 Postscript

Dieser furchtsame Versuch, wiewol er mehr die Liebe* als die Kraft der Untersuchung offenbart, sei als Herzens-Nachfeier des *achten Februars* dem erhabnen Verfasser der *"Betrachtungen über das Universum"* zugeeignet.

[Although it reveals more a love for* than strength in research, this timid assay shall be dedicated to the distinguished author of the *Observations on the Universe* as a heartfelt late celebration of the *eighth of February*.]

* If for Liebe[1] we⟨re⟩ substituted Schreibsucht = the itch of Scribbling, verily, Amen! O Jean Paul! Jean Paul! This (= die Kraft der Untersuchung)[2] is not *thy* Forte: a more confused Tangle of common place Thoughts I have seldom read!— —

12   pp 195–6, pencil, overtraced | Pt 7 § 4

Nun ist aber die Trauer über eine Vergangenheit . . . ob sie eine Stunde oder ein Menschenalter alt ist, weiter nichts als ein Wehklagen über das Dasein eines Winters, Todes, oder Jahrhunderts.

[But grief over something in the past . . . be it an hour or a lifetime ago, is nothing but a lament over the existence of a winter, a death, or a century.]

There is a something Whimsical in this Sophism, that almost atones for its absurdity. The Blunder consisting in confounding the reflecting on a Pain, which must therefore be Past, with the Sensation, Pain, which is as necessarily present! When this latter does not exist, the former is most often accompanied with pleasure as ex. gr. even*a* a *moment's* compleat Ease in severe pain.

13   pp 198–9, pencil, overtraced | § 5

Eigentlich haben wir unbewusst die Reue und Qual nur über den *noch fortlebenden* Wurmstock des Unmoralischen in uns, ob wir gleich auch diesen mit Einem Tritte tapfern Entschlusses zerknirschen könnten.*

[Unawares, we actually experience remorse and pain only for the *still perpetuated* wormwood of immorality in us, although we could easily crush it with one step of bold resolution.*]

* Alas! here lies the unfortunate Equivoque, which makes us equally incapable of denying, and of fully assenting to the position—viz. in the

12*a* Word not overtraced

11[1] "Love"—marked in textus.   11[2] "Strength in research"—in textus.

word *könnten!*[1] Who dares deny that in ~~every~~ach immoral act he *could* have abstained? Who dares assert, that he *can* be throughout life perfect even as his heavenly Father is perfect?[2] in all and every act?—

14 p 201, pencil, overtraced | § 6

Eine vierte Täuschung ist, unser (schon vorhin gerügtes) Zusammenrechnen.* Alles ist zu ertragen, was nur Einen Augenblick dauert.

[A fourth error (already criticised previously) is our way of adding things up.* Anything that lasts only one moment is bearable.]

* This is a repetition of a former Sophism. Reflection is always fragmentary and on the Past; but Suffering is continuous & present—

15 p 203, pencil, overtraced

* Indess halte man nur den Entschluss stets in jedem Unglück, sich heil und heiter zu machen, recht eisenfest: so wird der Geist seine kurze Bewölkung bald wieder licht durchbrechen . . .

[* But if, in every misfortune, we just hold fast to the unshakable resolution to make ourselves hale and hearty, the spirit will soon break through the clouds again . . .]

* Not the least doubt of it: and thank you, kind Sir! for the information!—Only contrive to feel no pain: and no pain will be felt.

16 pp 212–13, pencil, overtraced | Pt 8 § 2

Es ist eine leben-verwirrende Gewohnheit, dass der Mensch sich das fremde Hassen viel lebhafter und öfter in das Herz hineinmalt als das fremde Lieben,* daher er das eine stärker erwiedert als das andere; so werden auch die Engel meistens nur klein und halb als Köpfchen mit Flügelchen vorgemalt . . .

[One habit that much perplexes life is that man pictures others' hatred in his heart more vividly and frequently than others' love,* and for that reason he returns the one more strongly than the other; similarly, angels are usually depicted as small, with only half their bodies showing, little heads with little wings . . .]

* How constantly J. P. Richter reminds his Reader, that his Simile was made first and then a Something looked about for to be assimilated thereto. Hence his positions are such as are perfectly intelligible of themselves—and the whole puzzle if any lies in "the illustration"—

13[1] "Could"—at end of textus.   13[2] Alluding to Matt 5.48.

17   pp 214–17, pencil, overtraced

Der erste Gedanke eines Menschen, der etwas nicht findet, ist der, man hab' es ihm gestohlen;? und so häufig auch das blosse Verlieren und Verlegen gegen das seltene Bestehlen vorkommt, so glaubt er doch das nächstemal wieder an einen Dieb.

[A person's first thought when he cannot find something is that it has been stolen from him;? and no matter how much more frequent losing and misplacing are than the occasional theft, nevertheless he will believe in a thief again the next time.]

? This is, I am sure, a mere *subjective* peculiarity. *I*[a] never think of any thing ⟨having⟩ been stolen that I had mislaid; but always that the *Women* had swept it or put it away in their rage of neatness. The cause is obvious in[b] the act of mislaying or overlaying presents no *image*[c] round which one's pet and vexation may climb up and support itself. And yet the image must be uncertain, and wavering—for a distinct individualized[d] Image rather puts a sudden stop to the Pet—for all Passions can neither do without Images or *with* clear and definite ones. The Reason alone is self-sufficing—The Passions are all Parasite Plants, the strangling Joy; Tempers the Tree, Mosses affections the Grape-vines &[e] Woodbines

18   p 226, pencil | § 5 note f

* Ein hochgesinnter Fürst mit grauen Haaren, zu dessen Füssen seine Länder blühen, gleicht den hohen Bergen mit Schnee bedeckt, unter welchen die Auen und Thäler, die von ihren Gipfeln gewässert werden, umher liegen voll Blumen und Ernten.

[* A high-minded, grey-haired prince, whose lands are flourishing at his feet, resembles high snow-capped mountains, beneath which lie meadows and valleys that receive water from the peaks and are full of flowers and crops.]

* Observe, Jean Paul first *turns* the Prince into a Mountain, by the words, zu dessen Füssen Länder blühen—and then *likens* him to one.[1]

17[a] The italicised "*I*" was underlined twice in ms
17[b] Thus overtraced, but the original may have been a dash
17[c] The word "image" is repeated as the note runs over to the next page
17[d] Word not overtraced   17[e] Ampersand not overtraced

18[1] "Whose lands are flourishing at his feet"—in textus. Cf C's objection to Jean Paul's similes in **16**. This direction—"Observe"—may be addressed to Aders, who owned the book.

Palingenesien von Jean Paul. 2 vols. Leipzig & Gera 1798. 8°. [The BM copy, Gera 1798, has a second title-page in both vols: *Jean Paul's Fata und Werke vor und in Nürnberg.*]

Not located; marginalia from *NLS* II 276–7.

Apparently HCR's copy: the notes were "communicated by Mr. H. C. Robinson" to the editor of *NLS*. (There is also an unannotated copy of Vol I that belonged to HCR in Dr Williams's Library, however: see *CN* III 3684n.)

DATE. About Feb 1810 or after Oct 1810. It seems most probable that C annotated these vols at the same time as he made a series of notes based on his reading of them, but the dating of the notes is itself uncertain: *CN* III 3684n.

COEDITORS. Lore Metzger, Raimonda Modiano.

1   Front flyleaf

—S ist zu merken, dass die Sprache in diesem Buch nicht sey wie in gewöhnlich Bette, darin der Gedankenstrom ordentlich und ehrbar hinströmt, sondern wie ein Verwüstung in Damm und Deichen.[1]

2   I xxxi | Preface

[Footnote:] Zwei Revoluzionen, die gallische, welche der Idee oder dem Staate die Individuen, und im Nothfal diesen selber opfert, und die kantisch-moralische, welche den Affekt der Menschenliebe liegen lässet, weil er so wenig wie Verdienste geboten werden kan, diese ziehen und stellen uns verlassene Menschen immer weiter und einsamer aus einander, jeden nur auf ein frostiges unbewohntes Eiland; ja die gallische, die nur Gefühle gegen Gefühle bewafnet und aufhezt, thut es weniger als die kritische, die sie entwafnen und entbehren lehrt, und die weder die Liebe als Quelle der Tugend noch diese als Quelle von jener gelten lassen kan.

[Two revolutions—the Gallic, which sacrifices the individual to the idea or to the state, and if need be sacrifices the state itself; and the Kantian moral revolution, which disregards the emotion of human love because it cannot be commanded any more than

[1] "It should be noted that the language in this book is not like an ordinary channel in which the stream of thought flows on properly and honourably, but rather like a wilderness of dam and dike." The German is inaccurate—but it might have been mistranscribed.

merit can—these draw us and place us poor forsaken men ever farther apart, each alone on a cold deserted island; indeed the Gallic revolution, which only arms and incites feelings against feelings, does so less than the Critical, which teaches us to disarm and renounce feelings; it admits neither love as the source of virtue nor virtue as the source of love.]

But surely Kant's aim was not to give a full *Sittenlehre*,[1] or system of practical material morality, but the *a priori* form—*Ethice formalis:*[2] which was then a most necessary work, and the only mode of quelling at once both Necessitarians and Merit-mongers, and the idol common to both, Eudæmonism.[3] If his followers have stood still in lazy adoration, instead of following up the road thus opened out to them, it is their fault not Kant's.   S. T. C.

[1] "Doctrine of morals" or "ethical theory".

[2] "Formal ethics". C's objection is justified: in his preface to *Grundlegung zur Metaphysik der Sitten* (which C annotated in 1803) Kant points out that he is strictly concerned with the metaphysics of morals, that is, with the purely rational part of ethics dealing with the establishment of *a priori* moral laws, and not with its empirical part which belongs to practical anthropology. "The present treatise," Kant writes, "is, however, nothing more than the investigation and establishment of *the supreme principle of morality*, and this alone constitutes a study complete in itself, and one which ought to be kept apart from every other moral investigation" (tr T. K. Abbott).

[3] "Eudaemonism", "that system of ethics which finds the foundation of moral obligation in the tendency of actions to produce happiness" (*OED*)—from the Greek *eudaimonia* "happiness"—is *described* by Kant in *Grundlegung zur Metaphysik der Sitten* but Kant does not appear to have used the word itself. The *OED* attributes the earliest use that it records of this and related terms to C, De Q (writing on Kant), and Bentham, though it had been familiar for centuries before in its Greek and Latin forms.

HEINRICH RIMIUS

fl 1750–1759

Lost Book

A Candid Narrative of the Rise and Progress of the Herrnhuters, commonly call'd Moravians, or, Unitas Fratrum; with a short account of their doctrines, drawn from their own writings. To which are added, observations on their politics in general, and particularly on their conduct whilst in the country of Büdingen in the circle of the upper-Rhine in Germany. London 1753. 8°. [Bound with] A Solemn Call on Count Zinzendorf, the author, and advocate of the sect of Herrnhuters, commonly call'd Moravians, to answer all and every charge brought against them in the Candid Narrative &c; with some further observations on the spirit of that sect. London 1754. 8°.

Not located; marginalia not recorded. *Southey SC* (1844) 2445, "S. T. Coleridge's copy, with many MS. notes in the margins, and three pages entirely filled with his autograph Notes".

JOSEPH RITSON
1752–1803

Ancient Songs, from the time of King Henry the Third, to the Revolution. London 1790. 8°.

Inscribed on p ‾1 (p-d): "W. Wordsworth." Bookplate on p ‾1 indicates that the book was given to the Wordsworth Trust by Dorothy Dickson in Sept 1967. Someone has altered the date on the title-page to "MDCCXCII."

In this reprinting of Ritson's text, the "t" and "u" have been normalised, but the multivalent thorn (þ) and yogh (ʒ) have been retained.

DATE. Between 1803 and 1810, perhaps Apr 1803 when SH was on a visit to Dove Cottage but more probably during the period of the *Friend*, 1809–10. These notes were written for women in the Wordsworth and Hutchinson families: DW and SH are referred to in **14** and **5**.

TEXTUS TRANSLATION. For all but **16**, the translations are based on *The Oxford Book of Medieval English Verse* ed Celia and Kenneth Sisam (Oxford 1970).

1   p 24 | "In praise of the author's mistress, whose name was Alysoun"

It would make the delightful metrical romances quite mother-tongue to my fair friends, if they would but sit down doggedly to *construe* these old Songs. What is omitted, or left as not understood in the Glossary,[1] I have either explained from the Gothic, Theotiscan, & Low German (as Sisters of the Saxon)[2] or at worst *guessed at*.

2   p 24

> Jch libbe in louelongínge
> For semlokest of alle þýnge,
> He maÿ me blisse brínge,
> Jcham in hire bandoun.   <u>I am</u>

---

[1] At the back of the book, pp 315–29.
[2] C means to draw on his philological studies at Göttingen in 1799. Cf *CL* I 494: "The learned Orientalist, Tychson, has given me instruction in the Gothic, [and] Theotiscan Languages, which I can now read pretty well; & hope in the cou[rse of a] year to be thoroughly acquainted with all the Languages of the north, both [GERMAN] & Celtic."

[I live in love-longing / For the fairest of all creatures, / She can bring me bliss, / I am in her power.]

3   p 25

I trust, that the etymological inform*ations* in these marginal illustr*ations* will atone, as intellect*ual*, for the marginal Obscur*ations*, with which they deform the page, visually: n.b. a sentence worthy of *W. T.* of Norwich, ʄ or Mr A. Aiḳin, for affect*ution* & pedantry.[1]   S. T. C.

4   p 25

*   On hen híre her ís fayr ẏnoh,
          Híre browe broune, híre eȝe blake;

[*   In hue her hair is fair enough, / Her eyebrows brown, her eye black.]

   1 2   3
*   on hen hire her—no part explained in the Glossary, and the 3rd referred to as uncertain.[1] The meaning however is either *"and then"*—or else it is half erratum, half contraction, either for *on hered*, i.e. *on her head*, or else—~~an~~ "on heaven", i.e. By heaven!—her *Hair* is fair enough![2]

5   p 25 | **4** textus continued

        Wiþ lossum^a chere <u>he</u> on me loh . . .

[With lovable looks <u>she</u> smiled on me . . .]

—This "he" for "she", & 500 similar Instances explain the 's in our genitive Case, as "Sara*'s* Hair heaves with my Heart*'s* Heaving"[1]—& shew

       5^a In more modern eds "lofsum"

3[1] C refers disparagingly to two active reviewers. William Taylor of Norwich (1765–1836), RS's friend and a contributor to his *Annual Anthology* (see ANNUAL ANTHOLOGY **1** and n 7), was a tireless contributor to periodicals. C makes fun of his pretentious language in a letter of 1805, *CL* II 1161, and it was satirised by others as well: see *DNB*. Arthur Aikin (1773–1854), who eventually made his name as a scientist, was a nephew of Anna Laetitia Barbauld and from 1803 to 1808 editor of the *Annual Review and History of Literature*, from which C indignantly copied part of a review in Jan 1804 (*CN* II 1848 and n). C's

sneers against Aikin are recorded in *CL* I 392–3 and in *De Q Works* I 127n.
   4[1] Of these four words only "her" appears in the Glossary, and that is given a page reference but no translation. Modern editions read "On hew", "in hue", where C's text has the mysterious "On hen".
   4[2] For SH's hair see **5**.
   5[1] Cf SC's much-quoted description of SH: "She had fine, long, light brown hair, I think her only beauty, except a fair skin, for her features were plain and contracted, her figure dumpy, and devoid of grace and dignity" (*SC Memoir* I 19–20).

that the 's is really = *his*, spite of Lowth's & Took's imagined Confutation:[2] for He, & his meant alike He, She, it, His, hers, its,[b] even as *hir* meant he, him &c.[3]

6   p 25

> Leuedi al for þíne sake
> Longinge ís ẏlent me on.

[Lady, all for your sake / Longing is come upon me.]

ex referred to in Gloss: as unknown; but it is from the German, *anlehnen* i.e. is fastened on me, is become my *Tenureant*—a metaphor from feudal Tenures—& thence our common word "to *lean* on a person & to *hold* of him["] The latter is still extant in Law Books.[1]

7   p 26

> Jcham for wowing al for wake,
>   Wery so water in wore;
> Lest eny reue me mẏ make,
>   Ychalbe ẏȝẏrned ȝore.
> Betere ís þolien whẏle sore
> Þen mournen euermore,
>   Geynest vndergore,
>   Harkne to mẏ roun.

5[b] Ms reads "her's, it's" according to C's usual spelling of the possessive, normalised throughout this ed

5[2] The dispute over the English possessive form is referred to in the "Grammar" prefixed to Johnson's *Dictionary* (1755; 4th ed Dublin 1775) I sig n[1ᵛ]: "These genitives are always written with a mark of elision, *master's*, *scholar's*, according to an opinion long received, that the *'s* is a contraction of *his*, as the *soldier's valour*, for *the soldier* his *valour*: but this cannot be the true original, because *'s* is put to female nouns, *Woman's beauty* ... and collective nouns, as *Women's passions* ... in all these cases it is apparent that *his* cannot be understood." Horne Tooke does not appear to discuss the matter in *The Diversions of Purley*, but Robert Lowth makes the same point as Johnson in *A Short Introduction to English Grammar* (Philadelphia 1775) 17–18 and 18 n 2.

5[3] C is correct about the possibility of a confusion or telescoping of genders in the nominative case in Middle English, but not about the other cases.

6[1] *OED* gives the German *lehnen* "to lean" (whence also *anlehnen* "to lean on") as a corresponding verb but not as the etymological source of the ME *lenen*. "To hold of", in the sense of possessing property from or through the office of someone (*OED* quotes *Othello* I iii 118, i.e. "The trust, the office, I do hold of you") was still in use, and not only in legal contexts, in C's day. The use of "lean on" in the sense C appears to mean—to invest with or entail upon—is not recorded by *OED*; C may be illustrating colloquial usage, or confusing "lean" with "lien".

[Through wooing I am worn out by lack of sleep, / Weary as the waters in a troubled pool, / Lest anyone rob me of my mate, / Whom I have so long desired. / It is better to suffer pain for a time / Than to mourn forever, / Most gracious woman under clothing [i.e. alive] / Hearken to my song.]

"Better to suffer a *sore* i.e. grief awhile than mourn for ever."[1] The foregoing & remaining part of the Stanza is referred ⟨to⟩ as unintelligible in the Glossary.[2] The last line but one I can only *guess* to be—"by suffering (by being an *Undergoer*)[3] thou gainst["], as in the Latin Ad⟨a⟩ge— Patiens es tibi lucro:[4] the former most obscure lines I take to mean / I am wasted by wakefulness, or ⟨weakness⟩ thro' wooing, or love-longing, as restless (weary) as water, at a wear[5] (from whence it is perpetually falling) lest ⟨(or if)⟩ any one bereave me of my Mate, I shall be sorely indignant. yzurned, from the German Zürnen.[6] Mem. Did Ritson not understand German or Saxon? It seems, as if he did not: or if he did, that he must have been rather dull than otherwise.[7]   S. T. C.

8   p 26 | "A Love Song, whose author describes his beautiful, but unrelenting mistress"

> Menskful maiden of mẏht,
> Feír ant fre to fonde.

[A gracious maiden of virtue, / Fair and excellent to see.]

Mense. North Country still.[1]

compleatly, to the very bottom: referred to as unintelligible in the Glossary.[2]

7[1] Textus lines 5–6.

7[2] C is right: the several hard words in lines 1–4, 7–8 are listed in the Glossary with page references but no translation, the omission indicating that they were unintelligible to the editor.

7[3] C's speculation is based on the common semantic origin of these English synonyms, "suffer" being derived from the Latin *sub* "under" and *ferre* "to carry" or "to bear". The word should, however, have been printed as two words, "under gore" i.e. "under clothing" and hence "alive".

7[4] C's own translation is given in quotation marks above.

7[5] "Wear" was indeed an early alterna-tive spelling for "weir", obsolete long before C's time.

7[6] "To be angry".

7[7] This is a more tentative version of C's judgment of Ritson's dullness than appears in RITSON *Select Collection* 1 and in *CN* III 3437 (1808–9).

8[1] *OED* confirms that "mense", a variant of the obsolete "mensk", was still in use in Scotland and the north of England during the nineteenth century, with the meaning "propriety, decorum; neatness, tidiness".

8[2] The Glossary includes *fonde* but only to give a cross-reference to this passage; there is no translation or explanation.

9   p 27

> Wiþ lossom*a* eye, grete ant gode,
> Wiþ browen blȳsfol vnderhode,
> He þᵗ reste hī on þe rode
> Þᵗ leflych lȳf honoure.

[With lovable eye, great and good, / With blissful eyebrows under a hood, / May He who hung upon the cross / Honour that beautiful lady.]

omitted in the Glossary. *blissful*? or *flashing*? from *blitz*, i.e. Flash of Lightning?[1]

10   p 28

> Heo is paruenke of prouesse,
> Heo is solsecle of suetnesse

[She is the periwinkle of perfection, / She is the sunflower of sweetness.]

the pink or *periwinkle*
sun-flower, quod *solem sequi fertur*.[1]

11   p 28

þ is *th*: ꞇ is t. ȝ, either y, or g, or gh, or z.[1]

12   p 29

> For hire loue ẏ carke ant care,
> For hire loue ẏ droupne ant dare,
> For hire loue mẏ blisse is bare,
> Ant al ich waxe won.

[For love of her I fret and grieve, / For love of her I droop and despair, / For love of her my bliss is gone, / And I grow all pale.]

a beautiful Stanza.

9*a* In more modern eds "lofsom"

9[1] The idea of a connection with "blitzen" appears to be unfounded.

10[1] The flower-names are both translated in the Glossary. *Solsecle* is commonly traced to the Latin *solsequium*, of which C's phrase "which *is made to follow the sun*" is a variant.

11[1] C is simply explaining the typographical equivalents of the Middle English letters. As the headnote indicates, "t" is normalised in this edition.

13   p 30 | "A Song on his Mistress, whom he admires as the fairest maid bituene Lyncolne & Lyndeseye, Norhampton and Lounde (i.e. London)"

> When þe nyhtegale singes þe wodes waxen grene,
> Lef & g<u>a</u>s & blosme sp͡nges ín aueryl ẏwene . . .   <u>grass</u>
> Jch haue siked moni syk lēmon for þín <u>ore</u>

[When the nightingale sings, the woods grow green, / Leaf and <u>grass</u> and blossom spring in April, I ween . . . / I have sighed many a sigh, sweetheart, for your <u>mercy</u>]

ehre—grace, favor, to be honored by thee.[1]

14   p 31, referring to the poem as a whole

The above well worthy of translation, and capable of retaining its tender, sweet, and natural beauties in a translation almost literal. Dear Theodore![1] do, try it

15   pp 35–7 | "A Song upon the Man in the Moon"

[Ritson's note, after quoting Num 15.32–6:] . . . *But with due reverence to omnipotent authority, such a decision* [to stone a person for gathering sticks on the Sabbath] *from any other quarter must have been deemed rigid justice; considering that the fact had never happened before, was prohibited by no express law, and, for anything that appears, an act of the utmost necessity. Whoever, therefor, altered the sentence to a perpetual pillory-like imprisonment in the moon, seems to have proceeded upon the more just and rational principles,—on the supposition, that is, of its being criminal for a poor wretch to pick a few thorns in church-time to keep his family from starving.*

Surely, sincere and earnest Believers have the honestest & fairest reason to complain of this ambush-fighting against Revelation. Is a Collection of old Songs the proper place to smuggle in an Infidelity, which the writers of the Songs would have been burnt alive rather than have subscribed to: & *cui ~~bonono~~*?[1] Well, *can* any mind be made better, who is seduced to abandon the faith of its childhood by mere *sneers* & *scoffing*. Reason ⟨of⟩, and *then*, for or against what you like—I will defend the *arguer* whatever I may deem of his *arguments*; because victorious Reason always puts something in the place of what it removes. Sneers leave a

---

13[1] Modern scholarship in this case confirms C's linguistic speculation about the link between the OE *ar*, the ME *ore*, and German *Ehre*, "honour".

14[1] I.e. DW, "Dorothy" becoming "Theodore" by metathesis.

15[1] "To whose advantage?"

vacuum, which as nature acts (old philosophers thought) *horrore vacui*,[2]
the Devil's Winds soon rush in & fill up.   S. T. C.

16   p 44 | "Ayen me will I take mi leue"

> Now B'nes, Buírd, bold and blyþe,
> To blessen ow her nou am I boūde,
> I þoke ȝou alle a þousend siþe,
> And preí god saue ȝou hol and soūde;
> Where eṹ ȝe go, on gras or grounde,
> He ow gouerne, w*touten greue,
> For frēdschipe þᵗ I here haue foūde,
> Aȝeyn mí wille I take mí leue.

[Now gentlemen and ladies, bold and blithe, / I am here now bound to bless you, / I
thank you all a thousand times, / And pray God save you whole and sound. / Where'er
you go, on grass or ground, / May he govern you without grieving. / Because of the
friendship I have found here, / Against my will I take my leave.]

One of the oldest, & for many sorts of Subjects, one of the most pleasing
metres. See, p. 35.—[1]

15[2] "In abhorrence of a vacuum", from
the proverbial "Nature abhors a vacuum".

16[1] Since C does not actually scan the
lines, it is hard to be sure how he would
have analysed them metrically. His page
reference is to p xxxv, part of the preliminary "Dissertation on the Songs, Music, and
Vocal and Instrumental Performance of the
Ancient English", where Ritson declares
that "it is perhaps impossible to produce
even the bare name of a song or dance-tune
in use before the year 1500".

A Select Collection of English Songs. 3 vols. London 1783. 8°.

Wordsworth Library, Grasmere

Each vol is inscribed, I ⁻2, II ⁻1, III ⁻1: "To William Wordsworth with the best love of A B Skepper". On p ⁻3 (p-d) of each vol is a bookplate indicating that the work was donated to the Wordsworth Trust by Dorothy Dickson in Sept 1967. A correction has been made in ink in the "Directions to the Binder" on the page preceding I [i].

DATE. Probably between Sept 1808 and Mar 1810, a long period of domestication with the Wordsworths and the production of the *Friend*; but for the possibility of a date after 1815, see **7** n 1.

1 I x | A Historical Essay on the Origin and Progress of National Song

[Quoting the Bishop of London's tr of Callistratus:]

> In myrtle leaves I'll wear my sword,
> As did Harmodius and his friend so true,
> What time the tyrant king they slew,
> And freedom to her seat restor'd.

> Thou, lov'd Harmodius, art not dead;
> Thou to the Happy Isles art fled;
> Where Peleus' son, as poets tell,
> And matchless Diomedes dwell.

[Two more quatrains follow.]

O the *Crush* of Dullness! the substantial *Flatness* of this Version![1] It reminds me of Southey's remark on two Versions of Milton, that M. had been *overset* ("overgeset") into Dutch, and traduced (traduit) in French.[2]

S. T. C.

1A I xiv

Horace is the only Latin lyric with whose works we are acquainted. Most of his odes are real songs, which he is supposed to have sung!! either at

---

[1] Cf C's similar comment in RITSON *Ancient Songs* **7** (and n 7), though Ritson himself is not the target here.

[2] RS's multilingual joke appears to have been a private, not a published one.

Overgeset is one of a number of Dutch equivalents for "translated" (lit "over-set") and the French is *traduire* (of the same root as "traduce"). C makes the same pun in FLÖGEL **3**.

table with his friends, to his mistresses, or in societies where men of pleasure used to assemble.

2   I xvi–xvii

Italy, however, though the residence of the muses, and nursery of the fine arts, does not boast of the number and excellence of these smaller lyrics [composed by "Lorenzo de' Medici . . . the Pulcis, Politian, Giambullari, and other first rate poets of the fifteenth century"].

Chiabrera, Redi, &c &c.[1] Never was a false Remark—it[a] not merely different from, but opposite to, the Fact—No language has more lyrics, or greater variety of metres. The Italians fail only in blank Iambics, because of the necessary trochaic ending ($- \cup$) of almost all their Lines. They cannot stop *firm* on *one* foot. Chiabrera has performed *wonders* in blanks; but he could not work impossibilities. But this excepted, there is no verse, the Italians have not given specimens of—there is a greater variety of metres in Chiabrera alone, than in our whole Language.

3   I xvii

The ancient language of France was Latin, established by the long residence of the Roman armies, and corrupted by Tudesque, the jargon of the Franks, and other Gothic barbarians, who settled among or had commerce with the old inhabitants.

Why *Jargon*?[1] was it not an homogeneous language? & probably the *parent* of the Greek & Latin?/[2] Is not the German, at present, the richest & most energetic Language of the World, Greek excepted.[3]

2[a]   For "it is"

2[1] As App A to *CN* II explains, C had read little if any literature in Italian before he went to Malta in 1804. He owned a copy of the first 3 vols of Gabriello Chiabrera's *Opere* (Venice 1782); the first evidence of his reading of Chiabrera seems to be 1808: *CN* III 3318. The poetry of Chiabrera figures prominently in the *Friend*, notably in an extract included in the issue for 7 Sept 1809 (*Friend—CC*—II 55) and in Wordsworth's translations of several epitaphs (*Friend—CC*—II 248–9, 269–70, 334–5). There is also a quotation in a letter of Dec 1809: *CL* III 264. C does not appear to refer elsewhere to the physician-poet Francesco Redi (1626–97), whose best known poetical

work is *Bacco in Toscana* (1685).

3[1] In the sense not of a specialised language but of "unintelligible talk; gabble; gibberish" as in the definition in Johnson's *Dictionary*.

3[2] "Tudesque" is the same as "THEO-TISCAN, or the transitional state of the Teutonic language from the Gothic to the Old German of the Swabian period": *BL* ch 10 (*CC*) I 209; cf RITSON *Ancient Songs* 1 and n 2. The desire to trace all languages to one common ancestor was strong among philologists in the period; C mentions Lessing's attempt to trace Greek and German to a single source in LESSING *Leben* 13.

3[3] In a notebook entry of Jul–Sept 1809,

4   I xix

Whether these celebrated compositions [of Peter Abelard] were in Latin or French, we are no where certified. *We may, therefore, conjecture them to have been in both.

* From what part of the "Organon"[1] is this Logic deduced? It is *original*, I suspect.

5   I xxii

Chaucers Cuckow and Nightingale, Flower and Leaf (so beautifully *modernised by Mr. Dryden), and some other of his poems, are quite in the Provençal mode, and, not improbably, from Provençal compositions.

* Read—*"damnably infernalized"*[1]

6   I xxxv

. . . Edward I. who was so irritated at the continual insurrections and disturbances fomented by their songs, that he caused most of them [the bards] to be hanged by martial law: an event which has been immortalized by the sublime genius of the English Pindar.

!! poor *Pindar*. for what crime of his was his sacred name to be blended with that of the Ferruminator of Verses in "The Bard"?[1]

7   I lix

And of the following song by Ben Jonson, Anacreon, had Anacreon written in English, need not have been ashamed.

Drink to me only with thine eyes . . .

Was Ritson ignorant that this is a *mere Translation* of a Greek Epigramma, or more probably, *Scolion*?[1]

C even more daringly commented "On the superiority of the German Language to all others": *CN* III 3557.

4[1] Aristotle's treatises on logic.

5[1] It is not that C believes Chaucer should not be modernised, but that he dislikes Dryden's versions. It may be significant that Wordsworth had been modernising some of Chaucer's tales, including "The Cuckoo and the Nightingale": *WPW* IV 217–28. C's views about Chaucer's language remained fairly stable: cf *TT* (*CC*) I 466–7. His attitude towards Dryden was more ambivalent, but a letter to Godwin in 1801 protests "Of Dryden I am & always have been a passionate admirer": *CL* II 743.

6[1] C's main public attack on Thomas Gray appears in *BL* chs 1, 2 (*CC*) I 20, 40–1*; for a more balanced view see GRAY headnote. A "Ferruminator" is one who fastens things together with cement or, as we would say, cobbles them together. The *OED* does not include the word, but gives examples from C for "ferruminate" and "ferrumination".

7[1] In *Monthly Magazine* XXXIX (Mar

8 I 10–11 | "I lik'd, but never lov'd, before"

It is sufficient proof to me, that these Writers were not in love, or at least did not truly express what they felt if they were, thall[a] all is attributed to the Beauty &c as a *cause*: whereas in true Love—or rather, for which we want a word = ποθος,[1] "*the being in Love*", the beauty is felt & as one of the *Effects*, & is created by the Passion, & valued by it as its own creation, as a language, it has discovered externally, which expresses that something, it *believes* itself to have an intuition of in the peculiar Essence of the Soul, in the person beloved.

9 I 11 | "By Mr. Addison"

> My love was fickle once and changing
> Nor e'er would settle in my heart;
> From beauty still to beauty ranging,
> <u>In every face I found a dart.</u>

an instance of the corruption of Language. In savage times "a dart" might thus have been caused to be the word for "attraction, pleasingness of feature, &c"; but when a Language had been formed, such phrases, equally void of Logic, Grammar, & Imagination, are intolerable.

9A I 16 | "Fain would you ease my troubled heart"

> Your counsels may my thanks engage,
> But not my love controul;
> * Alas! such juleps ne'er asswage
> This fever of the soul.

8[a] For "that"

1815) 123–4, John F. M. Dovaston responded to Ritson's praise of Jonson here by proving that Jonson had "*most closely* translated" lines "from the Greek love-letters of Philostratus" and passed them off as his own. Although this article appears to be the first *published* account of Jonson's use of this source, Dovaston indicates that it was not his own discovery, "as I find it among other papers I transcribed some years ago at Oxford". Since C does not identify the Greek original at all precisely, it seems most likely that Dovaston was not the direct source of his own information, but that the fact that there was a Greek source was fairly common knowledge in academic circles.

8[1] I.e. longing or yearning. Personal and sexual associations of this word, often used in connection with SH, are glossed in BÖHME **52** n 2.

10   I 17 | "Why, Delia, ever when I gaze"

> Absence may bring relief, I cried,
> And strait the dreadful hope I tried;
> Alas! in vain was ev'ry care;
> Still in my heart I bore my fair;
> Ah! whither, whither shall I rove,
> To shun despair, or fly from love?

very beautiful & natural thoughts, tho' languidly exprest.

ROBERT ROBINSON
1735–1790

Miscellaneous Works of Robert Robinson, Late Pastor of the Baptist Church and Congregation of Protestant Dissenters, at Cambridge . . . to which are prefixed brief memoirs of his life and writings. 4 vols. Harlow 1807. 8°.

This work was edited by C's friend Benjamin Flower, whose name is given as the printer on the title-page of each vol, and whose initials appear at the end of the Preface in Vol I.

Henry E. Huntington Library

Josiah Wade's copy, with "J Wade" in pencil on I title-page and notes by him I lxxxviii, lxxxix, cix, cxxv, 225; he was probably also responsible for a pencil line in the margin of II 13. Typed librarian's description pasted in at I ⁻3; extract from bookseller's catalogue loose in I. On I ⁻3, II ⁻2, III ⁻2, IV ⁻2, in pencil, "Rev. W. Bird—Morton—1854". Someone—apparently Bird—has written notes in pencil on I ⁻4 (p-d): "Mʳ Wade's Copy the Friend of Coleridge with MS Notes by him published 1856. Sold at the Sale of Mʳ Wade's library abᵗ '42 bought by Mʳ Pickering—after whose death it came into my hands—in '54—W. B.—Kerslake the Bristol Bibliographer, of whom I had it thinks the notes were written early—or so—See Cottle's Reminiscences of S. T. C.—" On the same page, in pencil, in another hand, "Autog of Robinson". A list of pages annotated by C, in pencil, on III ⁻3 (p-d) and IV ⁻3 (p-d).

MS TRANSCRIPTS. (a) VCL BT 37: EHC transcript, incomplete; (b) University of Texas (Humanities Research Center): transcript possibly by Edward Irving, incomplete.

CONTENTS. I [v]–vii Preface; [ix]–clvi Memoirs of the Life and Writings of the Author [by George Dyer]; [1]–63 Memoirs of the Reformation in France; [65]–86 Remarks on Deism; [87]–134 Reflections on Christian Liberty, Civil Establishments of Religion, and Toleration; [135]–44 Remarks on Christian Morality; [145]–59 Remarks on Saurin's Sermons; [161]–219 Remarks on the Life of the Rev. John Claude; [221]–92 A Brief Dissertation on the Ministration of the Divine Word; by Public Preaching. [Note: in this copy, I 225–40 are by error bound in between 208 and 209.] II [1]–139 Arcana: or the Principles of the late Petitioners to Parliament for Relief in the Matter of Subscription. In Eight Letters to a Friend; [141]–86 The History and the Mystery of Good Friday; [187]–256 A Plan of Lectures on the Principles of Nonconformity, for the Instruction of Catechumens; [257]–362 A Political Catechism. III [1]–136 A Plea for the Divinity of Our Lord Jesus Christ; [137]–93 The General Doctrine of Toleration Applied to the Particular Case of Free Communion; [195]–360 Sermons [1–6]. IV [1]–153 Sermons [7–13]; [155]–77 A Discussion of the Question [of marrying the sister of a deceased wife]; [179]–87 Memorial Addressed to the Congregation of Protestant Dissenters, in Cambridge; [189]–203 The Circular Letter of the Eastern Association; [205]–15 An Essay on Liberality of Sentiment; [217]–345 Letters; 346–8 [Two Hymns].

DATE. Between Oct 1813 and Sept 1814, when C stayed with Wade in Bristol; an earlier and less likely occasion is May–Jun 1807.

A   III 7, marked with a pencil line in the margin

At present I affirm, because I believe, that JESUS CHRIST IS TRULY AND PROPERLY GOD.

B   III 14, marked with a pencil line in the margin

The word was GOD. GOD *was manifest in the flesh. His name is Emanuel,* GOD *with us. John turned many to* THE LORD THEIR GOD. *The Jews crucified the* LORD OF GLORY. GOD *purchased the church with his blood.* GOD *laid down his life for us. Jesus Christ is* LORD OF ALL. *Christ is* OVER ALL GOD BLESSED FOREVER. *We shall all stand, before the judgment-seat of* CHRIST; *so every one of us shall give an account of himself to* GOD. These are a few of many propositions, which the new testament writers lay down relative to Jesus Christ.

C   III 23–5, marked with a pencil line in the margin

Is CREATION a work of God? *By Jesus Christ were all things* CREATED, *that are in heaven, or that are in earth, visible and invisible, whether they be thrones or dominions, or principalities, or powers, all things were created by him, and for him.*

   Is PRESERVATION a work of God? *Jesus Christ* UPHOLDS *all things by the word of his power. By him all things* CONSIST.

   Is THE MISSION OF THE PROPHETS a work of God? *Jesus Christ is* THE LORD GOD OF THE HOLY PROPHETS; *and it was* THE SPIRIT OF CHRIST, *which testified to them beforehand the sufferings of Christ, and the glory that should follow.*

   Is the SALVATION of sinners a work of God? *Christ is the* SAVIOUR *of the world; the* AUTHOR OF ETERNAL SALVATION *to all them that obey him.*

Is THE FORGIVENESS OF SINS a work of God? *The son of man hath power* TO FORGIVE SINS.

The same might be said of the *illumination* of the mind; the *sanctification* of the heart; the *resurrection* of the dead; the *judging* of the world; the *glorification* of the righteous; the *eternal punishment* of the wicked; all which works in one part of scripture are ascribed to GOD, and all which in another part of scripture are ascribed to JESUS CHRIST.

Consider now into what contradictions these writers must fall if Jesus Christ be not God. They contradict one another, they contradict themselves. They degrade writings, which, they pretend, are inspired, below the lowest scribbling of the meanest authors. *In the beginning*, said Moses, GOD *created the heavens and the earth.* It is a mistake, says the Apostle John, *In the beginning* THE WORD THAT WAS MADE FLESH, *made all things, and without him was not any thing made, that was made.*

Elihu asks, WHO *hath disposed the whole world?* Jehovah asks *out of the whirlwind,* WHO *laid the measures thereof?* WHO *stretched the line upon it?* WHO *laid the corner stone thereof?* All the old Testament writers reply, THE LORD OF HOSTS *founded the heavens, the earth, the world, and the fulness thereof.* No such thing, says the Apostle John, THE WORD, *that was made flesh, and dwelt among us, made the world.*

Hezekiah looks up to heaven, and says, O LORD GOD *of Israel, thou art* THE GOD, *even* THOU ALONE, *of all the kingdoms of the earth, thou hast made heaven and earth.* Paul lifts up his eyes to Jesus, and says, THY THRONE, O GOD! *is for ever and ever.* THOU LORD *in the beginning hast laid the foundation of the earth, and the heavens are the work of* THY *hands.* This is Paul's language to his countrymen: but, behold! when the same Paul arrives at Athens, he contradicts himself, and tells the Athenians, that GOD *made the world and all things therein;* HE *is Lord of heaven and earth;* HE *giveth to all life, and breath, and all things.* If Jesus Christ and the Father be ONE God, all these seeming inconsistencies vanish; if not, it ill becomes such writers to say, *as God is true, our word towards you was not yea and nay.*

---

1   III 27, pencil | A Plea for the Divinity of our Lord Jesus Christ

Was Stephen then guilty of idolatry? "No," adds Mr. Lindsey, "the blessed martyr *saw* Jesus *with his eyes,* and called him the son of man; but this can be no precedent for directing prayer to him *unseen,* or addressing him as God." I have a profound respect for this conscientious apologist; but I cannot help astonishment at this reasoning. According to this reasoning, idolatry does not consist in worshipping a creature; but in worshipping an *unseen* creature.

See page, 69.—[1]

2   III 42–3, pencil

Let us take a single passage of the old testament, and let us see what the application of it to Jesus Christ proves. John the Baptist sends two of his disciples to Jesus Christ to ask him, Whether he were the expected Messiah? The messengers find him in a crowd of diseased people. To one, who had been blind, he gives sight. To another, who had been deaf, he gives hearing. He cleanseth lepers, and makes the lame walk. Having healed the infirmities of their bodies, he addresseth himself to the disorders of their minds, and speaks with an authority unknown to the scribes. By the gracefulness of his deportment, he obtains the attention of his hearers. By the truth of his doctrine, he obtains the assent of their minds. By cloathing his ideas with images, the archetypes of which had produced pleasure and pain in his hearers, he obtains an authority over their hearts, and excites, as he pleases, the hopes, the fears, the joys, the sorrows, of his audience. Having opened these grand springs of human action, he gives plain and profitable rules of conduct for the producing and promoting of social happiness.

I scarcely miss any *"desiderand"* in this fine treatise, but an occasional reply to, or rather Anticipation of, natural and unavoidable Objections, not from the Socinians but from the sincere Searchers after Truth.[1] A case is very imperfectly stated by giving the arguments on *one* side/ Audi alteram partem!/[2] Now I confess, that all the arguments *ostensibly* in favor of Socinianism would if *proved & real*, be *to me* proofs of Deism, or rejection of Revelation—therefore, those not grounded on verbal criticism, & trifles of that sort, but on plain common sense ought to be met or anticipated. Such is the present Instance/ John had baptized Christ, his own Cousin/ of whom such miracles must have been told him both by his Aunt, Mary, & his Mother Elizabeth—at the Baptism he recognized him

---

1[1] I.e. **3** below. Acts 7.55–6 describes Stephen as looking into heaven, where he "saw the glory of God, and Jesus standing on the right hand of God, And said, Behold, I see the heavens opened, and the Son of man standing on the right hand of God."

2[1] The Socinians (in C's day, specifically the Unitarians) are taken care of because the entire treatise addresses their denial of the divinity of Christ.

2[2] "Hear the other side!"—proverbial.

as Messiah—& his recognition was confirmed by a Voice from Heaven—
yet *now* he sends to enquire as of one unknown—[3]　　　S. T. C.—

3　iii 69–72, pencil

We will illustrate this remark by two passages from the worthy and reverend Mr. Lindsey. These are his words.

"Rev. v. 13. *Blessing and honour, &c. be unto him, that sitteth on the
throne, and to the Lamb for ever and ever. The blessing and honour is
tendered to the object* PRESENT *and* VISIBLE." But we have observed in
St. Stephen's case, that idolatry doth not consist in worshipping an *invisible* object. The *visibility* and the *invisibility* of the object have nothing to
do with the nature of the act. Is a papist less an idolater when he worships
the host exposed to *view* than when he worships the same host inclosed
in a pix?

In this §, as likewise in p. 27, 28, R. has fallen into an unintentional
Sophism: first, in making "Worship" a specific, whereas it is a general,
term to be specified by its Object. "The people fell on their faces, and
worshipped God, and the King" (David.) *Chronicles*.[1]—secondly,
(herein perhaps misled by Lindsay's lax phraseology) in confining the
words "seen & unseen" to the sight, whereas the word *was* meant to imply
the knowlege of actual, yet contingent, Presence, however obtained.[2]
Surely, a blind man (see p. 27)[3] may discover that Such a one is in the
Room, as certainly as one with eyes. Exprest philosophically Lindsay's
argument would run thus: Worship is either of God or of a Creature; but
the former is distinguished from the latter by always implying the acknowlegement of *necessary* Presence (i.e. omnipresence)/ while in the

2[3] The story of the baptism of Christ is
told in Matt 3.13–17; John's later sending
disciples to enquire about him, in Matt
11.2–6, Luke 7.19–23.

3[1] C means "the King, David". He is
paraphrasing—perhaps with a recollection
also of Rev 11.16—1 Chron 29.20: "And
David said to all the congregation, Now
bless the LORD your God. And all the congregation blessed the LORD God of their fathers, and bowed down their heads, and
worshipped the LORD, and the king." This
whole note is closely connected with a ms
note of 1830 or later which reproduces this
quotation and goes on to discuss prayer in
similar terms: *SW & F (CC)* 1484.

3[2] Robinson at this point is responding

to arguments made in the *Apology* of the
Unitarian Theophilus Lindsey which explains Lindsey's reasons for leaving the C
of E. The second sentence in quotation
marks in the textus is not from the Bible; it
is Lindsey's gloss on the verse from Rev. C
objects that the verb "to see" in the Bible (cf
"unseen" in **1** textus, and "visible" here) is
not limited to physical vision. "Unseen" itself does not occur in AV, but "not seen" is
fairly common, esp in Paul, e.g. Col 2.18, 1
John 4.20, Heb 11.1. Article 1 of the Thirty-
Nine Articles refers to God as "the Maker,
and Preserver of all things both visible and
invisible".

3[3] I.e. **1** above.

latter an accidental Presence (ergo, Absence elsewhere) only is attributed. The people worshipped, i.e. *adored religiously*, the omnipresent Jehovah, & they likewise worshipped, i.e. *honored & did homage to*, King David who *happened* then to be present. Now the *essence* of Idolatry consists in destroying the essence of all Religion, viz—the sense of necessary Presence by attributing it to a creature, or vice versâ, by attributing accidental & creaturely Presence to the Creator. I agree therefore with Lindsay, that the *divine* worship of Christ cannot be *certainly* deduced from THIS Text,[4] which *may be* explained as Χριστο δουλεια not Χστολατρεία[a5] tho' the words "for ever & ever" would incline me to the Latter/ but that Christ was visually present to St Stephen at the moment of his Death is a mere Presumption of the Unitarians.[6] Besides, are we not commanded to pray to God thro' Jesus Christ, our *Lord & Mediator*?[7] Now it is impossible for me to pray to A *through* B. without implying that B. hears my prayer either first, or at the same time as A. Whatever Presence is attributed to A, is equally applied to B.—In the present instance this is Omnipresence/ Therefore, the Unitarian, who obeys the Scripture, adores Christ as God.[b]

4   III 75, pencil

The Lord Jesus encouraged his followers to believe, that the spirit of truth should abide with them for ever: yet it appears by the event, Jesus Christ did not include in the promise that first great truth of christianity, on which all the rest are founded, the doctrine of his *person*; the Turks are in possession of this Truth, the generality of christians have lost it.

Though there is, doubtless, a certain degree of weight in this argument, yet, I think, Robinson rests too much upon it, & repeats it too often—for it is a fact not less certain than melancholy, that an immense majority of Christians (ex. gr. all the Russias, all the Christians of Asia, & of Africa, and of S. America, the larger & more populous Portion of Poland & of Germany, nine tenths of France, & all Spain, Portugal, Italy, Sicily, &c &c) have been given up to the most despicable & idolatrous Supersti-

3[a] For Χριστολατρεία
3[b] The initials "S T C" have been added in pencil in another hand

3[4] I.e. from Rev 5.13, the first sentence in quotation marks in textus.
3[5] C gives in Greek the distinction that he elsewhere makes in English, between "Christoduly" and "Christolatry" (for which latter term the *OED* cites his as the earliest

recorded use), i.e. "Christ-veneration" and "Christ-worship". Cf FIELD **18** and n 1.
3[6] Of the Rev Mr Lindsey, for example, cf in **1** textus.
3[7] E.g. in John 16.23–4, 26–7; 1 Tim 2.5.

tions, when Christ comes, shall he find Faith on the Earth? I say unto you, Nay!

5   iii 84–5, pencil

Happy for christians, had they rested here [in "revelation"] without *philosophical explications*! Were this a proper place, (but I am not writing on the doctrine of the Trinity,) I believe, it would be very easy to prove, that the primitive christians received this simple testimony, just as revelation gave it; and that when, about 200 years after Christ, they began to practise the art of explaining what they did not understand, they produced a novel notion called a Trinity, and with it disputes, creeds, subscriptions, proscriptions, persecutions, wars, and other calamitous consequences, which have disgraced christianity, and divided christians from that day to this.

A SCRIPTURE TRINITY undoubtedly there is: but our present concern is with our Lord's divinity . . .

Is not this strange? If not writing on the Trinity, how could he justify this harsh gratis dictum[1] ("*a novel notion called* a *Trinity*["]) to plain unlearned People?—If there be "*undoubtedly a Scripture Trinity*" there must be a Scripture Tri-unity: & what other there can be than that of the Nicene Creed, or wherein this differs from Scripture, I am at a loss even to imagine. *All* Scripture from Genesis to the Apocalypse declares, there is but one God. In the N. Testament three distinct agents are spoken of = the Father, the Son, & the Paraclete or Holy Ghost. (My *Father* and *I* will come; & *we* will dwell with you—Sins against the Father & against the Son may be expiated; but not against the Holy Ghost[2]—&c &c)—To each of these the Name, names, & incommunicable Attributes of the Supreme Being are given. Ergo, there are Three, & these Three are One.—This is the Scripture Trinity: & what other is contained in the *Nicene* Creed?—Of the unauthorized Creed of the ⟨fierce⟩ Individual, whom from ignorance of his real name we may call Pseudo-Athanasius, I agree with many learned and orthodox Fathers of the English Church in wishing *that we were well rid.*[3]   S. T. C.

[1] "Gratuitous expression of opinion".

[2] None of these clauses is an exact quotation, but C is recalling John 14.23 ("If a man love me, he will keep my words: and my Father will love him, and we will come unto him, and make our abode with him"—a verse similarly misremembered in connection with another work by Robinson in *CN* iv 4750) and Matt 12.31 ("All manner of sin and blasphemy shall be forgiven unto men: but the blasphemy against the Holy Ghost shall not be forgiven unto men").

[3] For C on the "pseudo-Athanasian Creed" (the attribution to Athanasius having been disproved in 1642), see BÖHME **33** and n 1, LUTHER **78** and n 2, *TT* (*CC*) i 78

6   III 87, pencil

They know not the *nature*, but they do know the *use* of objects. A man may be a good mariner, who can neither account for the saltness of the sea, nor for the action of the air.

Q. Does not the christian faith discard reason?

A. God forbid! Reason asks and obtains evidence that God speaks, and faith believes what he says. Is it irrational to believe him, who *cannot lye?* A believer admits the *evidence of things* NOT SEEN. . . . *All* the patriarchs *died in the belief* of a proposition, of which they had but obscure and imperfect ideas.

Here is the Gap in the Evidence: & unless this be filled up, all the rest can but perplex the mind. Reason *cannot* obtain evidence that it is God who hath spoken, unless what is spoken is compatible with the co-existence (or if I dared coin such a phrase, with the *sub*-existence[1] at least) of Reason.—As the ground-work therefore of all positive Proof, the negative Condition must be premonstrated, that the Doctrine does not contradict, tho' it may & must transcend, the Reason: that it is incomprehensible but not absurd.   S. T. C.

7   III 89–90, pencil

God requires me to believe the deity of Jesus Christ. Deity is an invisible object. I never saw, nor ever conceived an object analogous to it. I cannot reason about it; I believe it.

This is strange! We cannot believe without knowing what it is we believe/ and this we cannot know but by distinguishing it from all other notions, at least by *negatives*—& what is this but reasoning? A cannot be at once 1 and 3, *reasons* the Socinian. Not in the same sense, *reasons* the Trinitarian; but A, which in one sense is 3, in another sense may be 1.—Both alike *reason*, or they could not believe. Were I to work a miracle & then say to an illiterate Englishman, "Εἰς οιωνος αριστος αμυνεσθαι περι πατρης,[1] is a divine Truth."/! the man might have good reason to believe

and n 4. The immediate source for C's assertion about the "Fathers of the English Church" here may well have been the article "Creed" in Rees. It cites Chillingworth, Taylor, Tomline, and Horsley as opponents of the "damnatory clauses" of the Creed, and quotes Tillotson as follows: "'The account given of Athanasius's Creed,' says the excellent archbishop Tillotson, in a let-

ter written from Lambeth, Oct 23, 1694, to a right reverend prelate, 'seems to me nowise satisfactory; I wish we were well rid of it.'" The letter itself was published in Tillotson *Works* ed Thomas Birch (3 vols 1752) I xcv.

6[1] "Under-existence", not in *OED*.

7[1] "The one best omen is, to fight for the fatherland": *Iliad* 12.243.

my *veracity*, & that *I something* (*what*, *I* knew, tho' *he* did not) was true, but *that* Truth he could not believe. I dwell the more on this, because I am convinced by experience, that this mode of arguing is & has been the main occasion of Socinianism in liberal minds. It is one thing to *apprehend*, & another to *comprehend*—Reason apprehends the existence of the Supreme Being, tho' that Being alone can comprehend it.

7A   iii 96

[Robinson is quoting Lindsey's *Apology*.] *The principal argument for Christ's divinity is to be fetched from* religious worship and *prayer being addressed to him.*

8   iii 98, pencil

For example. There are many passages in the new testament, which express the inferiority of Jesus Christ to the Father. *My Father is* GREATER *than I. All power is* GIVEN *unto me. Of that day knoweth no man, no not the angels,* NEITHER THE SON; *but the Father.* If I embrace the doctrine of Christ's mere humanity, I meet with no difficulty in two of these texts, and but a few in the middle one.

I believe, that the sense of this Text (wc̄h in its ordinary interpretation seems equally hostile to the Socinian & the Trinitarian, & therefore naturally the *pet* text of the Arians)[1] is—"no not the Angels—neither the Son in his character as contra-distinguished from the Father, but as one with the Father, or as in the Father.["][2] Were the sense what the Arians[a] the words should be αλλα ⟨μονος⟩ ο πατηρ—but the Father alone. This is confirmed by the corresponding text in St Mark.—[3]

9   iii 120–1, pencil

There is (if I may express my meaning so) a REAL and a RELATIVE infinity. Real infinity belongs to God alone. Relative infinity may belong to one creature in regard to another. I possess an infinity of ideas in regard

8[a] A word is omitted: "say" or "claim"?

8[1] The Arian heresy, which considers the Son as "of *like* substance" with the Father, but created by him, may be considered as falling between Trinitarian insistence on the "one substance" of the Trinity and the Socinian denial of the divinity of Christ.
8[2] C's interpretation of Mark 13.32, q in textus.

8[3] C appears to have confused the two versions of this text: it is Mark 13.32 (q in textus) that reads "not the angels which are in heaven, neither the Son, but the Father", and Matt 24.36 "not the angels of heaven, but my Father only", the Greek reading (in the latter case) εἰ μὴ ὁ πατὴρ μόνος more or less as C recalls it.

to my canary-bird; and an angel possesseth an infinity of wisdom in regard to me: but all infinity, relative or real, is consistent with the nature of the being in question.

The real distinction is infinite *impropriè*, i.e. *præter*, numerum; & infinite *propriè*, i.e. contra numerum, quicquid numerum excludit.[1]—The one (as the material Universe for instance) is the excess of number & measure—the other (pure Spirit) is the Opposite, the contradiction, to number & measure. The immortality of the first created Angel may, or will hereafter, include the excess of Time—God's Eternity the Absence of Time./

10 iii 124, pencil

Had I been born a Canadian savage, I should certainly have thought, that the GREAT SPIRIT CREATED the world. Had I been born a Greenlander, I should have said, "My kajak did not make itself. More skill is displayed in the structure of the meanest bird, than in that of the best kajak, and more still in that of man than in the composition of either. Certainly there must be some Being, who MADE all these things, a Being that always was, and can never cease to be."

Had Robinson been a ~~Canadian Savage~~ Greenlander, he would have thought thus: My kajak was *made*—the bird *grew*—& never have reasoned from one to the other.

11 iii 130, pencil

It became fashionable in time for men of science to speak and think as Plato spoke and thought; and Philo the Jew, and after him many christian divines, took up the *Platonic* logos, and thus brought the *Memra* of the old Targumists, and the *logos* of St. John, into obscurity and disgrace, although it does not appear that St. John knew any thing about Plato's ideas of it.

I suspect, that Robinson had not studied Plato or Philo very profoundly. Horsley did not hesitate to pronounce the agreement of the Platonic with the Christian Trinity.[1]

9[1] C proposes as alternatives to Robinson's "relative" and "real" infinity the "*improperly*" infinite, "*i.e. beyond* number" as opposed to the "*properly*" infinite, "*i.e.* against number, that which excludes number".

11[1] C is recalling his reading of Letter 13 in Samuel Horsley *Letters from the Archdeacon of Saint Albans in Reply to Dr. Priestley* (1784) from Feb 1805 (*CN* ii 2447, 2448 and nn).

12   IV 17–18 | Sermon 7 "The Sufficiency of the Holy Scriptures"

As I may avoid fire without feeling its effects, so I may avoid the truths of christianity; but I cannot admit them without admitting at the same time the effects, which the belief of these truths never fails to produce. On these principles the apostle . . . connects salvation with faith alone, because faith is not alone, but is inseparably connected with repentance, and love, and zeal, and good works, and every other christian excellence: and on these principles we praise the understandings of those, who give sailors bibles *only*, because the gift implies several just and honourable principles; principles, I mean, which do honour to the understandings and hearts of those, who admit them.

First: this donation implies, that in the opinion of the donors, the bible is a *plain*, easy book; either that all the truths of revelation are simple, plain, and clear, or that such truths as are essential to salvation are so. This is a very just notion of revelation . . .

!! What if I were to ~~say~~ call Newton's "Principia" a *plain*, easy Book, because certain detached passages were axiomatic, & because the results were evident to common-sense?—What? The Pentateuch? the Solomon's Song? The Prophets in general, & Eze¢kiel in particular? What? the Ecclesiastes? The praise of Jael? of Ehud? of David?—What? Sᵗ John's Gospel, & his Revelations? the *apparent* Discordances of the Evangelists in the most important narration, that of the Resurrection? What? Sᵗ Paul's Epistles, declared by a contemporary Apostle, dark & hard?[1]—are these parts of a plain & easy Book?

The Writer of the preceding Note reverences the Bible, he trusts, ⟨as much,⟩ & believes its contents with a far stricter Consistency with Protestant Orthodoxy (in the common received meaning of the word, Orthodoxy) than the amiable Author of this Discourse as appears by his own Letters—but never, never, can he believe that the many & various Writings of so many, various, and distant ages, as brought together form "the Book"; that this Book, or Collectaneum, the interpretation of which *has* occupied, & will occupy all the highest powers of the noblest & best Intellects even to the Consummation of all things; can be called in toto, or even on the average, "a plain & easy Book![")]—That what is necessary for each man's Salvation, (in *his* particular state, he making the best use of the means in his Power, & walking humbly ~~in~~ with his God) is sufficiently plain for that *his* purpose, the Writer of the note cheerfully ac-

12[1]   2 Pet 3.16.

knowleges, & with thanks to the Author of all Inspiration & of all good
Gifts!   S. T. Coleridge

13 IV 18

The nature and perfections of God, the superintendance of providence,
the folly, the guilt, the misery of sin, the purity and perfection of the law,
the depravity of human nature, the imperfection of unassisted knowledge
and obedience, the nature and offices of Christ, the place and use of scripture, the influence of the holy spirit, the nature and necessity of faith and
obedience, the promise of eternal life to the righteous, the threatening of
endless punishments to the wicked, the resurrection of the dead, and the
final judgment, how clear and explicit are the oracles of God on all these
important subjects!

And yet on every *one* of these Points have long & obstinate Controver-
sics ~~have~~ been carried on by Learned, & by Unlearned. And yet scarce
any can be mentioned, which some one Sect does not interpret in a sense
different from, or opposite to, that of another.

14 IV 18

Some pretended mysteries are not scripture propositions at all, but mere
creatures of the schools. Others called mysteries are contained in scripture, but are not mysteries; the Lord's supper never was accounted a mystery till transubstantiation made it so.

Whoo!

15 IV 19

Secondly: the donation of a bible only, implies, that each reader hath *a
right of private judgment*. This is another just notion, truly scriptural, and
entirely protestant. To give a man a book to read, and to deny him the
right of judging of its meaning, seems the summit of absurdity.

Doubtless!—but may there not be folly in giving a Child (and an ignorant man is a Child in Knowlege) a Book, he cannot understand, without
any assistances to enable him so to do? To an ignorant Man I would not
give Newton at all: for not only he can not understand it, but he may do
very well without it. To the same man I *would* give the Bible, tho' a very
large part would be worse than unintelligible, for it would be misintelli-
gible—yet as it does concern him, I would give it, only with "all the

means & appliances to boot",[1] that would preclude a dangerous misinterpretation.   *S. T. C.*

16 iv 109–10, pencil | Sermon 11 "On Sacramental Tests"

This [parental] dominion, which hath been exercised for many ages, continues to be so. When children first begin to think, christianity is not proposed to their examination, but they are informed they are christians already disposed of by a contract made for them by proxies, whom they are taught to call godfathers, and godmothers . . .

Who dare presume himself secure against prejudice, when the Historian of Baptism[1] could so merge in himself the rational *common-sense* R. Robinson, as to call from his Pen such *Rosseau* Trash, as is contained in this §!![2]—What? do not the Baptists teach their Children to pray to and thro' Christ, long before they can understand Christianity? Do they defer teaching them to read & write, till the age of Discretion has enabled them to have such a conviction of its advantages, as inspires the spontaneous wish, produces a request to be taught? In the English Church does not Confirmation supply the same means as Baptism with the Baptists? When the Baptist says, "I attribute no saving importance to Baptism, no loss of divine favor to infant Baptism; but I think myself obliged to obey Christ scrupulously, & believing that he did not command infant baptism, but on the contrary baptism under conditions incompatible with Infancy (Faith and Repentance) therefore I cannot with innocence, because I cannot in faith, baptize an infant at all, or an adult otherwise than by immersion"/ I honor the man, & incline to his Doctrine as the more scriptural.[3] But to declaim ⟨about⟩ ~~over against~~ *offering* Xtnty to a Child's *Choice* &

15[1] Shakespeare *2 Henry IV* iii i 29 var.

16[1] Robinson published a *History of Baptism* in 1790; C alludes to it with respectful disagreement in a statement of his own position about baptism (he was convinced that the practice of infant baptism did not arise until after the apostolic period, and that no ceremony was essential to salvation) in Nov 1820, though it is evident that he knew Robinson's work before that date: *CN* iv 4750. The notebook entry is associated with Lancelot Wade, son of the owner of these vols.

16[2] Though he favoured certain kinds of reform in education, C never followed the radical theories associated with Rousseau's notorious *Émile* (1762), in bk 4 of which,

for example, Rousseau declares, "If I had to depict the most heart-breaking stupidity, I would paint a pedant teaching children the catechism; if I wanted to drive a child crazy I would set him to explain what he learned in his catechism. . . . there are mysteries which the heart of man can neither conceive nor believe, and I see no use in teaching them to children, unless you want to make liars of them" (tr Barbara Foxley). A letter of 1818 tells a story designed to contrast the Christian education of C's own children with the Rousseauistic projects of John Thelwall: *CL* iv 879–80.

16[3] Cf C's arguments against infant baptism in *CN* iv 4750, *AR* (*CC*) 359–81.

Judgement, and to treat the inculcation of it on his docile & believing Spirit as a truth & a duty, as being an instance of Superstition & tyrannidos patriæ[4]—o this should have been in the Emilias of the sickly Genevan, not in ~~the~~ a sober Sermon of ROBERT ROBINSON!—

S. T. C.

17   IV 110, pencil

When Constantine entered into the christian church he brought along with him all his imperial titles, and his absolute dominion. Like a true politician he joined himself to the most numerous and the most powerful party of christians, [a]and they, being at the same time the least enlightened, and the most depraved of all other parties of christians,[b] taught him to exercise his pagan authority over all his subjects both pagan and christian.

This assertion should have been accompanied with proofs.

18   IV 118, pencil

They [Protestant dissenters from "the reformation to the revolution" (117)] rejected canonical obedience to an ordinary upon oath. In brief, they refused to conform; and for non-conformity they suffered fines and bonds, exile and death. I own, it is not in my power to censure this numerous host of christians. Would I, a freeborn native of this enlightened country, exchange my christian liberty for a state of such servility? I would not.

But these very Non-conformists were, 9 out 10,[a] equally eager & pitiless in imposing their *Covenant Oath* & the Articles of Westminster—and as soon as they possessed the power in N. America, began hanging & imprisoning & burning with more than episcopal Glee.[1]—In short, Intoler-

---

17[a-b] Marginal line contains this passage   **18**[a] For "9 out of 10"

16[4] "Of paternal tyranny".

18[1] C reminds Robinson that the Nonconformists of the Civil War period and later were not always the *victims* of intolerance. The Solemn League and Covenant (1643) between the English Parliament and the Scottish Presbyterians aimed to impose Presbyterianism on the English Church; it greatly influenced the Westminster Assembly (itself dominated by Presbyterians), which began meeting in 1643 to revise the 39 Articles but eventually produced a completely new formula, the Westminster Confession, which was approved by Parliament in 1648 and became "the definitive statement of Presbyterian doctrine in the English-speaking world" (*ODCC*). The cruelty of the Nonconformists in North America is represented, e.g. in Cotton Mather *Magnalia Christi Americana: or, the Ecclesiastical History of New-England, from its First Planting in the Year 1620. unto the Year of Our Lord 1698* (1702), which C annotated (MATHER).

ance was the Vice of the age, not of particular Sects: tho' Toleration was the peculiar Virtue & Glory of the Quakers & Independents—[2]

19   IV 122, pencil

Some complain of a profanation of a sacred institute. Whether we, sinful men, have any religion, or not, surely there are some, who have given unsuspected proofs of piety; and they say, we always think of the Supreme Being with the most profound reverence: we consider the worship of him, with the deepest veneration, as the most serious and important business of life: we adore the father of mankind for all his works, and chiefly for sending his son to enlighten our minds, and to regulate our actions; and when we behold the holy institutes of a kingdom not of this world, now imposed upon the wicked, and now refused to the good, diverted from the original end of their appointment, and prostituted to secular purposes, we blush and tremble at the sight.

I don't know exactly, *how* it is; but *so* it is, that the same Phrases which in the N. Testam! I read with awe & delight, yet introduced as they are in this §, and a thousand others of like kind in other writings, shock me with the grossness of the *Anthropomorphism*. In the N.T. God assumes the Human Nature (νούμενον)—in paragraphs, like these, the Author seems to turn God into ⟨(φαινόμενον)⟩[1] man.   *S. T. C.*

20   IV 123–4, pencil

But it is not this sort of men, it is not atheists, deists, and profligates, upon whom the test law is intended to spend its force, but another, a class of virtuous characters exposed to scorn for imaginary offences called schism and heresy. Yet what have states to do with heresy? They create the crime, and then punish it; but could statesmen be persuaded to let religion alone, there would remain no such crime to be punished. Among the brave and virtuous Goths, there was no such word in all their primitive codes of law; and * opinions the most preposterous do no injury to

18[2] Cf C's remark in Jeremy TAYLOR *Polemicall Discourses* **23**: "the recent *cruelties* of the Star-chamber under Laud (I do not say the *intolerance*: for that, which was common to both parties, must be construed as an error in both rather than a crime in either)". For C on the Quakers, see MORE

Theological Works **17** and nn 1, 2.

19[1] C invokes the Kantian distinction between "noumenon" and "phenomenon", that which is apprehended by the intellect alone as opposed to that which is apprehended by the senses.

the state, as daily experience proves. Where men's lives are inoffensive, their speculations ought to be free.

* No! neither do the *Nits* in a ~~man's~~ child's Head bite him; but Nits become Lice/ Adders before Birth have no phangs—but we kill the y[a]

20[a] Word—and note—left unfinished

HUGH JAMES ROSE

1795–1832

Prolusio in Curia Cantabrigiensi recitata, Nonis Jul. MDCCCXVIII. In comitiis maximis, &c. [Half-title:] Quaest. Inter Graecos et Romanos Historiae Scriptores comparatione facta, cujusnam stylus imitatione maxime dignus esse videtur? Cambridge 1818. 8°.

British Library C 126 h 3(7), bound in "Pamphlets—Miscellaneous"

Inscribed on the front of the original grey-brown paper wrapper: "S. T. Coleridge Esq. with the Authors most kind & respectful Comp[ts]". Rose made corrections to the text on pp 8, 13, 16, 20, 32.

DATE. The latter half of 1818, the lecture being dated (in the title) 9 Jul. Rose had been in correspondence with C and had visited him in Highgate since writing to express his enthusiasm for the *Friend* in 1816: *CL* IV 669.

---

1   p 24

Quod mihi quidem verissime dictum esse videtur: omnibus, enim, quaecunque Xenophon scripserit, quamvis legentium animos summa orationis comitate atque elegantia teneant atque delectent, deesse sentio pondus illud auctoritatis sine quo nemo potest esse omni laude cumulatus Historicus. *Id, enim, in animo tenendum, quod initio posuimus, non satis esse ut delectet Historia, accedat, autem, oportet ut legentes doceat.

[And this still seems to me a very true remark: I feel that everything Xenophon wrote, although it seizes and delights the readers' minds with its outstanding affability and elegance of style, lacks that weight of authority without which no man can receive the highest praise as historian. *For what we stated at the beginning should be borne in mind: that it is not enough that history delight the reader; beyond that, it should teach.]

This is most appropriate—it hits the very center of the White.[1] Throughout Xenophon I feel the want of a *commanding point*, of a *staple*, both as an Historian and as a moralist. For in my strictest sense of the term, I should hesitate to admit Xenophon as a *Philosopher*.[2]

---

[1] A metaphor from archery, the white being the centre of the target.

[2] I.e. as a true lover of wisdom: see PETVIN **11** n 1. C's *Friend*, revised in 1818, nevertheless quotes Bacon's account of Xenophon as a celebrated example of the philosopher (disciple of Socrates) who was also an effective man of action: *Friend* (*CC*) I 119–20.

2   p 36, at the end of the treatise

In ⟨the perusal of⟩ this very sensible Treatise, which bears no other mark of a young man's composition but the life and spirit with which it is conceived, some points suggested themselves to me which I could have wished to have had added, none which I wished ~~to~~ removed. I am alike satisfied with the Author's conclusion, and with the grounds advanced in support of it.[1]   S. T. Coleridge

2[1] In response to the question assigned, namely, "When Greek and Roman historians are compared, whose style appears most worthy of imitation?", Rose weighs the virtues of Herodotus, Thucydides, Xenophon, Sallust, Caesar, Livy, and Tacitus, and concludes that Thucydides is most to be recommended.

ROYAL SOCIETY

Lost Book

The Philosophical Transactions of the Royal Society of London, from their commencement, in 1665, to the year 1800; abridged, with notes and biographic illustrations, by Charles Hutton, George Shaw, Richard Pearson. 18 vols. London 1809. 4°.

Not located; marginalia not recorded. Sotheby Sale Catalogue 18 Dec 1908 gives the following information (the dating being mistaken): "This interesting copy was formerly in the library of Thos. Poole of Nether-Stowey. . . . Several of the volumes contain profuse pencil notes in the margins in the handwriting of Coleridge dating from 1796 onwards until his leaving the village." C's last visit to Poole was in 1807. Since the work was issued in monthly parts between c Jun 1803 and 1809, Poole's copy, if this was his, could not have been complete by 1807, but it is possible that C annotated the parts that had appeared by then.

DATE. Most probably Jun–Sept 1807, when C stayed with Poole. George Whalley discusses the dating problems for this work in *CM* (*CC*) I lxxvii and points out that "If these notes were in fact written from 1796 to 1798, they precede by about five years all other evidence of copious annotation".

FERDINAND FRIEDRICH RUNGE

1795–1872

Neueste phytochemische Entdeckungen zur Begründung einer wissenschaftlichen Phytochemie. Erste Lieferung. [General title-page preceding:] Anleitung zu einer bessern Zerlegungweise der Vegetabilien durch Theorie und Versuche erläutert von Ferdinand Runge, Doctoren der Heilkunde. 2 pts in 1 vol. Berlin 1820, 1821. 8°.

In this copy Pt ii pp xiii–[xxiv] are bound in error after Pt ii p 16.

British Library C 126 g 5

"S. T. C." label on verso of fly-title to Pt i.

MS TRANSCRIPT. VCL BT 22.

DATE. After 1827 (**1** n 3), in conjunction with C's continuing study of German philosophy of science with JHG (**19, 20**).

COEDITOR. Raimonda Modiano.

---

1   pp ⁻2–⁻1, pencil, badly rubbed

Light : Sound :: Harmony : A Melody, a Series translated into Simultaneity.[1]

A State is the pattern (εἶδος)[2] of a kaleidophone[3]—/ the visualized Product of its "λογοι"[4] (discords resolved & neutralized) acting as one— the visual Incarnation of its numberless Series of Sounds—every free [? Member] or Citizen being a [? Genus]

1[1] "Light is to sound as harmony is to a melody", sound and melody representing series and light and harmony simultaneity. Speculation about a common source for light and sound appears regularly in C's work, notably in the "sound-like power in light" of the 1817 version of *The Eolian Harp* line 28 (*PW*—EHC—I 101); cf *CL* IV 750–1; also KANT *VS* COPY B **2**, where C asserts that varying vibrations in the ether may produce sound or light or heat. In *The Loves of the Plants* (Lichfield 1789) 128–30, Erasmus Darwin gives an extended account of Newton's "discovery" of the coincidence of the colours in a prism and the notes in the gamut, and describes some experiments in "luminous music".

1[2] *Eidos*, "pattern", as C says here; cf PAULUS **3** and n 3.

1[3] The kaleidophone or "phonic Kaleidoscope" was invented in 1827 to exhibit sound-waves.

1[4] *Logoi*, "words" or "language".

a – b – c

. . .

. . .

. . .

. . .

and the State the Spiritual Kaleidophone that simultenizes these all into a one *Eidos*—Eidos : Idea :: Species : Genus.[5] But [? the law] abstracted the Idea antecedent and evolutive/ S. T. C. The Genus expresses the mode, in which we acquire the Consciousness of the Idea. The Idea is the living Substance of every objective Genus—the vis substans unific[?a]. Ἐν καὶ Ὄν = ἕν[6]

2   p $^{-}$1 (recto of general title-page)

1 Q.y Ductility = Coherismus + & ⚹[1] Dilativity, under the predominance of the former?[2]
2 Connection of Malleability with Ductility, and of Fusibility with both—what?—
3 But is not coherismus itself the duplication of Length by difference of directions? | and ——— ?[3] the ~~identity~~ μεσοθετον[4] of | and ——— —and again of the punctual and the lineal? ········· Bring these points into contact, and we have the horizontal line———

3   i 4–6, pencil, offset | Ch 1 § 11–13

Was sich aus dem Anorganischen entwickelt, muss dieses selbst in sich aufnehmen, in sich enthalten.—Daher ist das Lebendige nicht ohne Todte, die Pflanze nicht ohne das Mineral und somit auch Pflanzen-chemie nicht ohne Mineralchemie. Hieraus ergiebt sich der Zusammenhang beider, so wie auch das Wesentliche ihres gegenseitigen polaren Verhältnisses. . . . Diesemnach steht die Phytochemie nicht der Mineral-

1[5] *"Eidos* ['form' or as C says above 'pattern'] is to idea as species is to genus". C's views on the *idea* of the state are developed in *C&S* chs 1–2 (*CC*) 11–31. "Simultenize" is not in *OED*.

1[6] The "substantial [i.e. underlying] unifying force. One plus Being = one".

2[1] "In addition to and opposed to"—two of C's standard symbols.

2[2] This entry attempts to work out the relationship of ductility to other forces in the dynamic scheme or compass of nature (as in e.g. GOLDFUSS 2, OERSTED 1 and n 1, OKEN *Lehrbuch der Naturgeschichte* 1 and

n 9, *CN* III 4226). It is noteworthy that C does not appear to use the term "Coherismus" elsewhere for coherence or cohesion: this usage may be an echo from a German text or a late attempt to find an alternative to "coherence" and "cohesion", which he had tried to distinguish from one another in 1818 or 1819: *CN* III 4433.

2[3] I.e. the north–south magnetic line of being and the east–west electrical line of becoming.

2[4] *Mesotheton*, that which is placed in the middle, the mid-point.

chemie gegenüber, wie ein Pol dem andern ... sondern wie zwei Pole gegen einen Pol, *so dass die Phytochemie eigentlich noch einmal so viel ist als die Mineralchemie.* . . . . Das Mineral ist ein *Einfaches* im Verhältniss zur Pflanze, die Pflanze aber ein *Doppeltes* im Vergleich mit dem Mineral, nehmlich Mineral mit *Leben* begabt oder philosophisch ausgedrückt: die Pflanze ist das *lebendig gewordene Mineral.* Auf gleiche Weise verhält sichs mit der Phytochemie ... die der Definition der Pflanze entsprechend, eine *lebendig gewordene Mineralchemie genannt werden kann.*

[Whatever evolves from the inorganic must absorb the inorganic within itself and contain it.—Thus, that which lives is not without that which is dead, nor is the plant without the mineral; accordingly, the chemistry of plants is not without the chemistry of minerals. From this arises the connection between them, as well as the essence of their mutual polar relationship. . . . Thus phytochemistry does not stand in relation to the chemistry of minerals as one pole to the other ... but as two poles in relation to one, *so that in fact phytochemistry [contains] as much again as the chemistry of minerals.* . . . The mineral is *simple* in relation to the plant; the plant, however, is *double* as compared with the mineral, that is, [it is] mineral endowed with *life* or, expressed philosophically, the plant is *mineral come to life.* It is the same with phytochemistry ... which, corresponding to the definition of the plant, can be called a *chemistry of minerals come to life.*]

The polar relation is in my judgement most unfairly brought in here.—[1]

Mineral = Metalleity $\cancel{*}$ Light[2] is synthesis—but not to Light as tho from Antithesis of the Metalleity [? i.e.] το Αλλον as $\cancel{*}$ of the Μεταλλον[3] for this synthesis of direct opposites (ex. gr. Carbon & Nitrogen or Cyanogen[)],[4] are never permanent/ but to Light corporized or rather corporealizing *in statu mobili*[5]—but in the negative pole/ = Oxygen, Chlorine,[6] &c and with Sulphur in the Amphoteric[7] of mobile &

3[1] C believes Runge misrepresents the polar logic of *Naturphilosophie,* and he sets out to correct him, using the dynamic scheme of the Compass of Nature as in 2.

3[2] The magnetic north–south line, representing metalleity, has carbon as the negative pole (N) and nitrogen as the positive (S); the electrical east–west line, representing light, has oxygen as the negative pole (E) and hydrogen as the positive (W). The symbol means "opposed to". The relationship between metalleity and light is considered in similar terms in OKEN *Lehrbuch der Naturgeschichte* 5.

3[3] The *allon* (other) as opposed to the *metallon* (that which seeks the other): C refers to these also in FULLER *Holy State* 7 (at n 8) and OKEN *Lehrbuch der Naturgeschichte* 5.

3[4] Cyanogen, a gas isolated and named by Gay-Lussac in 1815, is a compound of carbon and nitrogen—a synthesis, therefore, of directly opposite N and S poles in C's scheme.

3[5] "In a mobile state".

3[6] Chlorine, identified as an element by HD in 1810 (cf OKEN *Lehrbuch der Naturgeschichte* 1 and n 6), had a place between oxygen and hydrogen, but closer to oxygen, in the system of relations represented by the Compass of Nature (OKEN *Lehrbuch der Naturgeschichte* 2, *CN* III 4420).

3[7] C here uses "amphoteric" ("partaking of the nature of both") to represent a midpoint or "indifference" as in IRVING *Missionaries* 9; see also 8 below.

fixed—But the Plant is corporealized Light in the synthesis of the [. . .] state fixed = the Carbon, the base or negative Matter or visible form, and mobile in both Poles: but with the Positive Hydrogen predominantly appropriated—

This awakening ab intra[8] into functional power—Light individualized, and as such nascent Life, the mesothesis or indifference of Light & Life. Hence the exquisite sensibility of Plants to Light ab extra.[9]

4   i 10–11, pencil | §§ 27–8

Die Qualität eines Stoffs ist nur durch die Wechselwirkung mit einem andern Stoff (Körper oder Potenz), mit dem man ihn in Conflict bringt, zu ergründen. Alles, was hiezu dient, wird in der Chemie Reagens gennant. . . . *Es giebt so viele Reagentien, als es Stoffe und Potenzen in der Natur giebt*! Man kann nach einer allgemeinen Ansicht der Körperwelt drei Stufen in derselben unterscheiden:

*1. die cosmische oder physicalische,
   2. die anorganische oder mineralchemische,
   3. die organische oder dynamische Stufe.

[The quality of a substance can be ascertained only through its interaction with a different substance (body or power) with which it is brought into conflict. In chemistry, anything that serves this function is called a "reagent". . . . *There are as many reagents as there are substances and powers in nature*! Taking a general view of the corporeal world, one can distinguish three stages: *1. the cosmic or physical, 2. the inorganic or mineral-chemical, 3. the organic or dynamic stage.]

* O—my hopes begin to flag. Nothing can come of such divisions. Far better, Universal—a. particularized. b specialized c. individualized d. coexisting—e. relative f. opposed./ But even these find their best use as forms, and determinants of position, as exponents of Dynamics not of Stuffs.[1]

5   i 15–16, pencil | § 40

Man legt noch immer der Chemie zur Last, dass sie die ursprünglichen Verhältnisse zernichte und neue schaffe, diess können jedoch nur Unkundige thun, * denn wer z.B. von der Phytochemie verlangt, dass sie das primäre oder natürliche Seyn des Pflanzenstoffs *nicht zerstören* soll, der hat ihr Wesen nicht begriffen.

3[8] "From within".
3[9] "From without".
4[1] This note reiterates one of C's fundamental objections to the writings of the German *Naturphilosophen*, whose work in general he admired, namely their tendency to confuse the ideal symbols of dynamic powers with actual physical substances. Cf Oken *Lehrbuch der Naturgeschichte* 1 and n 13.

[Chemistry is still blamed for destroying the original conditions and creating new ones. This, however, is the attitude of the ignorant;* in fact, those who, for example, require of phytochemistry that it *not destroy* the primary or natural character of the vegetable substance, have misunderstood its essence.]

* The charge is here falsely stated. No one blames the chemist for destroying the life of the Plant, or of the Atmospheric Air in dissolving the specificating potentiating nexus; but drawing the same consequences as if he had done so, and thus making the ⟨qualities of the⟩ carcase the adequate exponent of those of the living Body. It is his Logic, we blame.[1]

6   i 24–5 | §§ 50–1

So wird es im Blatt z.b. wieder Stoffe höherer und niederer Dignität geben, Stoffe, die der Wurzel, dem Stengel, dem Blatt, und endlich der Blume *dem Werthe nach* entsprechen. . . . Was die Wurzel nicht erreicht, geschieht im Stengel, was dieser nicht vollbringt, erhält vielleicht erst im Blatt Vollendung, und Stoffmetamorphosen, die der individuellen Thätigkeit des Blattes noch nicht gelingen, treten erst in der Blüte und ihren Theilen in höchster Vollendung auf. So ist z.B. der narkotische Stoff der *Datura Stramonium* in der Wurzel noch sehr unvollendet und von geringer Wirksamkeit, im Blatt schon vielmehr und häufiger entwickelt, und in der Frucht von grösster Intensität.—

In unserer Kartoffel (*Solanum tuberosum*) macht die Entwicklung des wirksamen, giftigen Stoffs denselben Cyclus. In der Knolle hat sich die Masse (das Nährende) auf Kosten der Kraft (der dynamischen Wirkung) gesteigert, das Giftige sich in Nahrung verwandelt. . . . Auf einem andern Wege gelangt man zu dem nähmlichen Resultate. Steht die Blume höher als das Laub, dieses höher als der Stengel, und ist der Stengel von vollendeterer Ausbildung als die Wurzel, so folgt nothwendig, dass Wurzel, Stengel, Laub u.s.w. als in sich geschlossene, durchaus von einander verschiedene Ganze auch bestimmte eigenthümliche Bestandtheile haben müssen, die sich von einander so unterscheiden wie die angeführten Pflanzenorgane und Systeme selbst unter sich differiren.

[Thus the leaf, for example, will also contain substances of higher and lower dignity which correspond *in value* to the root, the stem, the leaf, and finally, the flower. . . . Whatever is not attained by the root, takes place in the stem; what the stem does not complete, is perhaps only accomplished in the leaf; and the metamorphoses of substances that the individual activity of the leaf cannot perform reach the highest perfection only in the blossom and its parts. Thus the narcotic substance of the *Datura*

5[1] Cf IRVING *Sermons* **29** at n 18 (annotated 1828–9), where C similarly explains the difference between a living body and a carcase as "the extinction or withdrawing of the operative *Form*".

stramonium, for example, remains quite undeveloped and with little potency in the root; in the leaf it is already much more abundant and developed; and in the fruit it reaches its greatest intensity.

The development of the potent poisonous substance in our potato (*Solanum tuberosum*) undergoes the same cycle. In the tuber the mass (the nutritive element) increases at the expense of the force (the dynamic effect) and the poisonous element turns into nutrition. . . . The same result can be reached by a different route. If the flower is higher than the leaves and the leaves higher than the stem, and if the stem is more fully developed than the root, it necessarily follows that root, stem, leaves, etc, being self-contained, radically different units, must also have specific individual components that differ from one another just as much as the above-mentioned plant organs and systems themselves.]

Is not this a little fanciful? In reference to what criterion does Runge determine the comparative height and dignity! Why, is a poison—i.e. a poison for *man*—in the *fruit* of the Potatoe a product marking superior dignity, and the nutritive farina of inferior? And on what principle does the Author identify the Mass & the Nutritive (*v. p. 23. last line but two*)[1]— But let his point of reference & the order of his ascending Scale be this, that, or any other—Runge, if I am not greatly mistaken, will find his Rule crushed to Death by the crowd of Exceptions. Ex. gr.: Surely, the fruit must rank higher than the mere Capsule—and yet the fruit (the seeds) of the Poppy contain a bland nutritive Oil, the Capsule or Shell a deadly poison.[2]—On what pretence would the insignificant flower & seed of the Carrot, Turnip, &c be ranked higher than the Roots? (except indeed ⟨the seeds⟩ on universal Grounds, viz. the power of self-reproduction—but these are not what Runge means!) Or the blossoms of the Cabbage & Cauliflower?—Mem. The Elm.[3]

7   i 24, 25, referring to p 25 | § 53

Wir haben (§. 27, 28, 29.) den drey Hauptformen der Körperwelt entsprechend, ein dreyfaches Qualitätsverhältniss der Stoffe unterschieden, nehmlich ein physicalisches, ein chemisches und ein dynamisches als Resultate der Wechselwirkung zwischen dem Pflanzenstoff und den cosmischen, anorganischen und organischen Potenzen. (§. 30.) Sie geschieht hier 1) nach der Wechselwirkung mit den dem solaren Pol angehörigen Reagentien (§. 29.): *Licht, Wärme, Schwere*; 2) nach der

[6]¹ Second sentence of second paragraph in textus.

[6]² The seeds of *Papaver somniferum* are pressed to produce a bland, edible oil; the capsules or seed-cases produce opium.

[6]³ C chooses the elm probably as an example of a plant whose infertile seeds were not considered to be of much use compared with other parts, the trees being propagated in Britain normally by cuttings and suckers. The bark was used medicinally as a diuretic and in treating skin disorders.

Wechselwirkung der entsprechende tellurischen: *Wasser, Luft, Erde* und *Voltaismus*.

[We have distinguished three relationships of quality among the substances (§ 27, 28, 29) corresponding to the three main forms of the corporeal world; these relationships, the physical, the chemical, and the dynamic, result from the interaction between the vegetable substance and the cosmic, inorganic, and organic powers (§ 30). This interaction occurs 1) as an interaction with the reagents belonging to the solar pole (§ 29), *light, heat, gravity*; 2) as an interaction of the corresponding terrestrial reagents *water, air, earth*, and *voltaism*.]

Psha! solar Pol Parrot!/[a1]

P. 25. § 53. One great defect of the existing or second Generation of *Natur-philosoph* Physiologists is, ὡς μοι δοκει,[2] their disposition to cheat and satisfy themselves with arbitrary or at best fancy-aided Antitheta—ex. gr. Solarisch, and Tellurisch.[3] How can Water and Air be *opposed* to Light and Warmth, which are contained in their constitution? See my Note, p. 10.[4]

8   i 34 | § 74

Der Chemismus ist im Allgemeinen ausgesprochen ein Thätigkeits-process von Stoffen, vermittelt durch das *Wasser*: wo *kein Wasser* ist, *stellt keine chemische Action sich ein.* Der Electrismus ist ganz dasselbe, aber statt Wasser durch *Luft* vermittelt: wo *keine Luft* ist, kann kein electrisches Phänomen statt haben. Jedes hat demnach sein eignes Element, folglich auch seine eigene Sphäre, und man kann sagen: Chemismus unterscheide sich von Electrismus, wie Wasser sich von Luft unterscheidet.

[Generally speaking, chemism is an active process in substances and is mediated by *water*: where there is *no water, no chemical activity occurs.* The same is true of electrical activity, except that it is mediated by *air* instead of water: where there is *no air,* no electrical phenomenon can take place. Accordingly, each has its own element and thus its own sphere, and chemism may be said to differ from electrical activity as water differs from air.]

Q.y Does not Potassium in perfectly dry Oxygen Gas burn to ⟨pure⟩ Potash = oxide of Potassium: tho' common Potash, we know, is a hydrate?[1]—

7[a] This remark is in the margin, the remainder of the note at the top of p 24

7[1] C scoffs at Runge's "solaren Pol" (solar pole), the pun on "Poll Parrot" perhaps including the insinuation that Runge is echoing the terminology of the earlier and superior generation of *Naturphilosophen* that included Schelling and Steffens.
7[2] "As it seems to me".

7[3] "Solar" and "terrestrial", in textus.
7[4] 4 above.
8[1] C's objection is sound: these chemical reactions do not necessarily involve water. A contemporary source of information about potassium (which had been discovered by HD in 1807), W. T. Brande *A*

If so, here is Chemismus without Water: for surely the combination of Metals with Bases, Anti-bases, & Amphoterics[2] must ~~be a~~ come under the name of Chemistry.

9   i 35–6 | § 79

Hiernach zerfallen die Pflanzenstoffe in 3 grosse Abtheilungen:
1. *in Gift,*
2. *in Nahrung,*
3. *in Arzney.*

[Vegetable substances accordingly fall into three major divisions: 1. *poison*, 2. *nutrition*, 3. *medicine*.]

§. 79. the nullity of these divisions will be easily seen by reflecting that all three being that, which they are called, only ⟨relatively, and⟩ by an indefinitely variable relation, each is the other—and ⟨one and⟩ the same Pflanzenstoff[1] all three, Poison to one animal, food for a second, medicine for a third.—As definition of *Words*, not of *Substances*, that which is digestible but not assimilable, is POISON, weak or strong according to the power of *re-action* which the digested but not naturalized Alien retains. That which is both digestible and assimilable is Food.—*Medicine* has no business here—it being defin~~ed~~able by its finality or Aim alone— tho' doubtless the greater ~~part~~ number of Medicines are Poisons administered in conquerable doses for the purpose of overcoming and expelling a more dangerous disease by the production of a less dangerous one of an opposite character. Many Drugs may indeed be characterized as Assimilable substances, that in the process of assimilation exert their alien powers, as re-agents—of course, difficultly or imperfectly assimilable: & such Medicines might indeed form an intermediate class between food & medicine. 1. Digestible without assimilation = Poison. 2. Assimilable with reaction = Doctor's Stuff. Assimilable. = Food.[2]

     P.S. Almost all Food contains an unfoodful portion; but where this is

---

Manual of Chemistry (1819), a book with which C was familiar, notes (185): "When potassium is thrown into water it instantly takes fire; hydrogen gas is evolved, and *oxide of potassium*, or *potassa*, is found dissolved in the water." For a further reference to HD's work on potassium see SCHUBERT *Ansichten* **35**.

   8[2] I.e. with alkalis, acids, and intermediate substances (cf C's use of "amphoteric"

in **3** at n 7). The only example given in *OED* for "amphoteric" in a chemical sense, as a neutral substance neither acid nor alkaline, dates from 1849.

   9[1] "Vegetable substance", from textus.

   9[2] C repeats and develops this three-way distinction, suggested by Runge here and in **10** textus, in SOUTHEY *Wesley* **28** and in *TT* (*CC*) I 374–5.

separable and eliminable by the vital powers and organs provided for that purpose, it may be taken as = 0.

10   i 36 | §§ 80–2

Gift heisst derjenige Stoff, der den lebenden Organismus im Wechselkampf *besiegt, ihn tödtet* (§. 78.); besitzt demnach eine so *ausgezeichnete dynamische Qualität*, dass die lebende Kraft sie nicht überwältigt. *Nahrung* bildet zum Giftstoff einen Gegensatz. Ihr Hauptcharakter besteht in einem Ueberwiegen des Materialen und im gleichmässigen Zurücktreten des Dynamischen. . . . Der Nahrungstoff hat also eine so *geringe dynamische Qualität*, dass die Wirksamkeit des Organismus sie sogleich zernichtet und ihn sich assimilirt. *Der Arzneystoff* hält das Mittel zwischen beyden Extremen, er wird weder aufgelöst und assimilirt vom Organismus, noch reibt er diesen auf, wie es der Giftstoff thut.

[*Poison* is defined as any substance which, in struggling with a living organism, *overcomes* and *kills it* (§ 78); it possesses such a *superior dynamic quality* that the vital force cannot overpower it. *Nutrition* represents the opposite of poison. Its main characteristic is a preponderance of the material quality with correspondingly less of the dynamic. . . . The nutritional substance thus has such a *low dynamic quality* that the functioning of the organism immediately destroys and assimilates it. *Medicine* holds the middle ground between the two extremes: it is neither dissolved and assimilated by the organism, nor destructive of it, as is poison.]

Q! Are theire ingestible but not digestible Substances, capable of exerting a hostile *dynamic* (i.e. not merely mechanic) action on the living body, preventing or counteracting their elimination?—If there are, it would be easy so to word the preceding definition as to include them.—

11   i 60–1 | Ch 2 § 133

Organisches und *Dynamisches* ist zweyerley, und unterscheidet sich wie *Lebloses* und *Lebendiges*. Das erwürgte Thier oder der einzelne Thier- und Pflanzenstoff ist noch organisch, aber nicht mehr dynamisch zu nennen, weil das, was man mit "*Leben*" bezeichnet, nicht mehr daran zu bemerken ist. Dennoch gehören beyde Zustände ausschliesslich dem *organischen Reiche* an, daher die von uns sogenannten "*organischen Reagentien*" in zwey Hauptabtheilungen sich spalten, nehmlich in *organische* und *dynamische*.

[The *organic* and the *dynamic* are two kinds of thing, and differ from each other in the same way as something *lifeless* does from something *living*. A strangled animal or an animal or vegetable substance taken singly is still called organic, but no longer dynamic, since we can no longer observe anything in it that we would designate "life".

Yet both states belong exclusively to the *organic realm*; consequently, what we have called *"organic reagents"* fall into two main divisions, namely *organic* and *dynamic*.]

§. 133. Surely this is a most unphilosophic Distinction. A slaughtered Ox is not an organic body, but a body disorganizing./ Independent of Organization, every compound of matter so far resists a change of form, as to require a *time* for the transition, longer or shorter according to the activity and relative intensity of the Agents, mechanical, chemical or vital, acting thereon, and its own torpor or susceptibility thereof. This indispensable transit-time is the cause and ⟨co-⟩condition of a *Carcase*.[1]—Besides, how grossly illogical to oppose disparate times—ex. gr. Ens perstans, and Ens per transitum.[2] It is, however, expedient, nay, necessary to introduce a mid term—viz. Animant or animated—*Dis*animated. Inanimate. Organized, disorganized, inorganic. In our Language "dead" expresses this middle term—Living, lifeless, dead.—In vegetable Life, the Humus or Vegetable Mould is dead or devitalized matter.

12   i 76, pencil | § 165

Es ist . . . der Begriff Reagens auf die Sinne als Funktionen übertragen, nicht richtig, sondern zu weit ausgedehnt. . . . die fungirenden Sinne nur Reagentien secundärer Art sind; sie benachrichtigen das Subject von Stoffqualitäten, die *nicht durch Wechselwirkung des Eines mit dem Stoff entstehen, sondern ausserdem vorhanden sind.*

[It is incorrect to apply the concept "reagent" to the functions of the senses; that would extend it too far. . . . the functioning senses are only reagents of a secondary order; they inform the subject of material qualities which *do not arise from the interaction between the senses and matter but exist independently of them.*]

Many words with much superfluous effort to confute an error into which no man ever had fallen, and no man is likely ever to fall. Any school-grammar would have spared RUNGE this trouble under the Rules for the Verbs of Sense as Verbs active determinant but not transitive—i.e. they determine an object, but not act on it.[1]

11[1] On "carcase" cf **5** above. C's most extended speculation about the nature of life and degrees of vitality in the universe is *TL*, most of it composed in 1816.

11[2] E.g. "a persisting entity" and "a transitory entity".

12[1] Cf Runge's definition of "reagent" in **4** textus. In his reference to a "school-grammar", C may be thinking of the distinction made in the Port Royal *Grammaire générale et raisonnée* [by Claude Lancelot and Antoine Arnauld] (Paris 1660) 116. In the English translation, *A General and Rational Grammar* (1753) 115, it reads: "Those verbs may properly be called active, which signify action, to which is opposed passion, as *to beat, to be beaten; to love, to be beloved*: whether these actions be determined to a subject, which is called a real action; as *to beat, to break, to kill*, &c. or only determined to an object, which is called intentional action, as *to love, to know, to see.*"

13   i 83, pencil | § 176

* Die Iris als das Lichtathmungsorgan des Auges ist in steter oscilla-torischer Bewegung, Diastole und Systole begriffen, was sich bey einem schnellen Wechsel von Finsterniss und Licht sehr deutlich zeigt.

[* The iris as the eye's respiratory organ of light is in continuous oscillatory motion, diastole alternating with systole; this can be clearly observed when there is a sudden change between darkness and light.]

* There *may* be some analogy between the oscillating motion of the Iris, and the process of Breathing; but wherein it consists, and what therefore the meaning of Lichtathmung[1] is, I cannot even conjecture.   *S. T. C.*

14   i 103, pencil | Ch 5

Ueber kein Objekt der Phytochemie ist so viel gefaselt als über dieses, und es wäre wirklich für das Geschichtliche der Narkotica wichtig, wenn man alles das sammelte und zusammenstellte, was Schriftsteller (Chemiker und Nichtchemiker) über das Chemische der Narkotica, über den "Narkotischen Stoff" gesagt und—geträumt haben.

[There has been more foolish talk about this part of phytochemistry than any other, and it would be really valuable for the history of narcotics if one collected and com-piled what writers (chemists and non-chemists) have said—and dreamt—about the chemistry of narcotics and the "narcotic substance".]

I hazard the anticipation that the principle of the Narcotic will be found

neither in $\begin{array}{c} N \\ | \\ S \end{array}$ nor in W——E, but in the pentad or centrality, differenced

from all four yet opposite to neither.   S. T. C.[a1]   As Sinn to Leben,[2] so Bitter to Narcotic./ The several Narcotic Stoffs[3] differ by the modifica-

---

14[a] C adds a caret at the end of his marginal note, and continues at the bottom of the page

13[1] "Light-breathing" as in "light-breathing organ" or "respiratory organ of light" in textus and tr.

14[1] C invokes again the scheme of the Compass of Nature, as in 2 and 3 above. Runge goes on, after the textus, to say that the chemists of his day were aware that their analyses of narcotics were still imperfect; C guesses that whatever narcotics have essen-tially in common will be found at the deep-est and most central point of the imagined sphere, a point that in an earlier version of the Compass he refers to as the "Internal Center" where, at one level of existence, "Gold, or Cube of Gravity" is to be found: *SW & F (CC)* i frontispiece. Cf "Centrific Power" in **15**.

14[2] As "sense" to "life".

14[3] "Stuffs" or (as in textus tr) "sub-stances".

tion of the Narcotic by one or other of the four Poles, & by the quantity of the modification/ Ex. gr. Opium, = Narc. + Hydr[?ogen]⁴

15 i 116–17, pencil

Mit dieser Analyse und dem durch dieselbe dargestellten wahren Verhältnisse des narkotischen Stoffs als einem basischen oder alkalischen wären nun . . . alle jene schiefen Ansichten und ungegründeten Meynungen, die man über einen durch alle narkotische Pflanzen verbreiteten narkotischen Stoff hegt, widerlegt und berichtigt. Es ist weder die organische Combination der Bestandtheile, noch die Blausäure, noch das Morphium, was in der Bilse als eine so mächtige dynamische Potenz auftritt, sondern ein ganz eigenthümlicher Stoff, der sich durch seine *Pupillenerweiternde Eigenschaft* von allen in chemischer Hinsicht noch so ähnlichen Stoffen unterscheidet. Der Name *"narkotischer Stoff"* ist demnach aus dem Register der Pflanzenbestandtheile völlig zu streichen . . .

[In establishing the true relationship of the narcotic substance as basic or alkaline, this analysis should now . . . refute and correct all those false views and unfounded opinions that supposed a single narcotic substance to be diffused throughout all narcotic plants. Neither the organic combination of components, nor hydrocyanic acid, nor morphine can account for the strong dynamic potency of henbane; but it is due, rather, to a special substance which differs chemically from all similar substances through its *iris-dilating property.* The name *"narcotic substance"* should therefore be completely struck off the register of vegetable components . . .]

Runge's Aim is good and wise; but he has neither a distinct view of it, nor of the path to it. In order to both, the Logos, Law, or informing Exemplar, must be distinguished from the Nature, even as the dynamic Nature = Natura naturans¹—as well as the *dynamic* from the *Material.*— The *Stoffe,*² Carbon, Azote, Metal, Oxygen, Hydrogen, and the unembodiable 5ᵗʰ, or Centrific Power,³ must be reduced to their dynamic genesis and import.—Their relative proportion to each other will then no longer appear so insignificant or generalized as R. sees them—tho' still they will be no more than necessary conditions of qualities, the full solution of which can be given only by the specific susceptibilities & re-active forces of the several Objects, on or together with which the

14⁴ C guesses that opium—his example also in **6** above—will be found to consist of a modification of the narcotic principle by the forces associated with the positive, western pole in the electrical axis or line of becoming.

15¹ The Spinozistic distinction between nature as informing spirit or law (*natura naturans* "nature naturing") and nature as an ensemble of external objects (*natura naturata* "nature natured") appears frequently in C's work, e.g. *CN* III 4397 f 50ᵛ and n, *AR* (*CC*) 251–2*.

15² "Stuffs" or "substances" as in textus.

15³ Cf **14** and n 1; extended accounts of the evolution of powers in creation occur in *TL* and in *CN*, e.g. *CN* III 4418, 4420.

specific Quality is brought to act. What does the *Mind* gain by naming the Narcotic base of the Hensbane an iris-~~contrae~~dilating Stuff? This simply [? depicts/rejects] the *fact*, not solves or renders it intelligible.

16   i $^+$1, pencil, faded

I do not know by what perverse Spirit I have been pushed and shoved on to read thro' this much ado about nothing Book. But this I know that it has been an unqualified Waste of time.   S. T. C.

17   ii 29, pencil | Ch 1 § 29

Die Wissenschaft von der Einwirkung des *bewussten Willens* des Menschen auf die Pflanze würde also hier ihre wahre Stelle finden. . . . Ein Hauptkapitel dieser Wissenschaft ist noch die Einwirkung der Pflanze auf den Menschen, einmal mehr realiter (stoffig), ein andermal mehr idealiter (geistig). Das Erstere giebt jeder zu, die ernährenden, vergiftenden und arzneyenden Pflanzen im Gedanken habend, das letztere möchte jeder bezweifeln, auf den magnetischen Baum als eine Charlatanerie hindeutend. Es ist hier der Ort nicht, über diese Sache ins Einzelne zu gehen, jedoch ersuchen wir die Zweifler, sich vor allen Dingen die Frage zu beanworten: * *ob es möglich sey, dass zwey Dinge sich neben einander befinden, ohne nicht auch zugleich in einander zu seyn, d.h. ohne auf einander einzuwirken?*—

[The science of the effects of the *conscious will* of man on plants would thus find its proper place here. . . . A principal theme of this science is the effect of plants on man, considered first under the aspect of reality (materially), and then under the aspect of ideality (spiritually). All will acknowledge the first aspect, having in mind the nutritive, poisonous, and medicinal plants; but everyone casts doubt on the second, pointing to the magnetic tree as charlatanry. This is not the place to enter into detailed discussion of this matter, but those who doubt should first answer the question: * *whether it is possible for two things to be beside each other without being simultaneously in each other, that is, without acting upon each other?*]

* This is exquisitely characteristic of the German Mind: "You think the pretence of infusing or awakening an operative Life in a Tree mere Humbug?[1]—Now tell me—ob *es möglich sey &c!!*—["]² i.e. abstract meta-

---

17[1] As the textus indicates, Runge has raised the example of the "magnetized" tree of mesmerism, that is, a tree to which the mesmerist had communicated mesmeric power and which could in turn work cures on patients who were attached to it by ropes. The phenomenon is described by Robert Darnton in *Mesmerism and the End of the Enlightenment in France* (Cambridge MA 1968) 8 and in many of the books and journals that C read on the subject of animal magnetism, e.g. KLUGE **1** and n 9. A comprehensive note about C's interest in mesmerism or animal magnetism is given in *TT* (*CC*) I 96–7 n 6.

17² "Whether *it is possible*"—in textus.

physique!*a3* The absurdity too of the argument—for if it proved any thing, it must apply to every tree magnetized or not—yea, to every chair, table &c/

18   ii 38 | § 39

Kiesers Eintheilung der Pflanzenwissenschaft, die derselbe *Phytonomie* nennt, ist eine mit unsern Hauptabtheilungen identische, nemlich
1. *Phytonomie* = unserer *Phyto-Morphologie*;
2. *Phytophysiologie* = unserer *Phyto-Biologie*;
3. *Phytochemie* = unserer *Phyto-Stöchiologie* . . .

[Kieser's division of botany, which he calls *Phytonomy*, is identical with our main divisions, namely: 1. *Phytonomy* = our *Phyto-morphology*; 2. *Phytophysiology* = our *Phyto-biology*; 3. *Phytochemistry* = our *Phyto-stoichiology* . . .]

The minting of Greek Compounds with German Endings seems to engage the better half of the Author's exertions.—But surely, every desirable distinction is obtained by dividing Botany into—1. the Physiography of Plants: 2. The Physiology of Plants: and 3. The Physiogenie[1] of Plants—What need of this barbarous prefix of *Phyto*?[2]

Phyto-physiography/. The reader takes up the ~~Work~~ Book as a botanical Work.

19   ii 44 | Ch 2 § 2

* Der Charakter der Ellipse ist *Bipolarität*. Sie ist doppelter Kreis, zwey Centra (*focus*) in sich habend, deren gegenseitiges Verhältniss das Wesen und die Form der Ellipse giebt.

[* The ellipse is characterised by *bipolarity*. It is a double circle with two centres (*foci*) whose mutual relationship determines the essence and form of the ellipse.]

* Within the Ellipse? Take the Ellipse described by the Planet Uranus.[1] The Sun being in one of the Foci, where is the other? The Law of

17*a*   C adds a caret at this point and finishes the note at the top of the same page

17[3]   "Metaphysics". Why C should have used the French word at this point is mysterious; perhaps, given his usual attitude towards French thought, it conveys more contempt than English would.

18[1]   C adopts a German term since "physiogeny" was not yet current in English. He seems to have been a pioneer in the use of "physiography", of which the *OED* gives a published use in 1828 and then cites

C (from marginalia to Henry MORE *Theological Works* **1**, in *LR* III 158) and JHG—for whom see **19**.

18[2]   The Greek prefix *phyto* "of a plant" was not extensively adopted into English botanical vocabulary until the second half of the nineteenth century (*OED*), but C himself used it in English words as well as Greek, e.g. BÖHME **17**, *CN* IV 5168, 5254.

19[1]   Discovered by Herschel in 1781; re-

Bi-centrality we (J. H G + S. T. C.) had evolved some ten years ago—
but bi-polarity in the sense here intended is senseless.[2]

20   ii 46 | § 5

Wenn Stoff und Thätigkeit nur in der Einigung real werden, und diese als
Form erscheint (§. 4.), so kann nichts anderes real werden als die Form.
Da nun aber diese Einigung zweyer Pole auf eine dreyfach verschiedene
Weise möglich ist, nemlich einmal mit vorwaltender Thätigkeit, ein andermal mit vorwaltendem Stoff und drittens mit relativem Gleichgewicht
beyder, so wird die Form auch hienach eine dreyfach unterscheidbare
seyn. Der dritte Fall stellt nemlich die Form am reinsten dar, diese heisst
daher "*Form*" im engern Sinne, im erstern hingegen wird sie durch das
prädominirende Thätigkeitseyn getrübt und heisst dann *Leben*, und
endlich im zweyten Fall, wo sie unter der Herrschaft des Materiellen der
sinnlichen Wahrnehmung als Form sich fast entzieht, giebt sie den *Stoff*
als Erscheinendes.

[If matter and activity become real only through unification, and if this appears as form
(§ 4), then nothing but form can become real. Now this unification of two poles is possible in three different ways: activity may predominate, or matter may predominate
or, thirdly, there may be a relative equilibrium of both. Similarly, form can also be distinguished in three ways. The third case represents form at its purest and is therefore
called *form* in the stricter sense; in the first, however, form is clouded by the predominance of activity and is thus called *life*. Finally, in the second case, where form is
dominated by matter to such a degree that it is almost unavailable to sensory perception, it yields *matter* as that which comes to appearance.]

Mercy on us! What a word![a]

As we have repeatedly set forth in the Chloro-esteesian Method,[1] it is
expedient, as soon as the evolution of Matter has reached to the Organic,

---

20[a] The remainder of the note appears at the top of the page

---

ferred to by C (as "Georgium Sidus", the
name originally proposed by Herschel) in
SW & F (*CC*) 678.

19[2] C elsewhere formulates a positive
natural law of bicentrality thus: "that every
Whole, whether without parts . . . or composed of parts . . . must be conceived as a
possible center in itself, and at the same
time as having a Center out of itself, and
common to it with all other parts of the same
System": *CN* IV 5464, Nov 1826. In a
metaphoric and pejorative sense, having
two centres means being pulled out of an
ideal shape, as in BÖHME **6**. "Bipolarity" or
"polarity", however, has a different meaning, referring to the coexistence of opposite
and dynamic polar forces that C describes
throughout his work as operative at all levels of existence. The dating of "some ten
years ago" refers to C's studies of Schelling
and *Naturphilosophie* with JHG in 1818
and later, the fragmentary records remaining mostly in *CN* and the *Opus maximum*.

20[1] The system worked out by C and
JHG (*chloros* is the Greek word for
"green"). C uses other playful compounds

to exchange the terms Materia or Hyle and Dynamis for Product and Productivity.[2]   S. T. C.

---

elsewhere, e.g. "Ja—aitchgee and Ess Teesi" in SCHUBERT *Allgemeine* 2.

20[2] I.e. "Matter" (Latin and Greek) and "Power" (Greek) should be replaced by the terms "Product" and "Productivity" adopted from *Naturphilosophie* and specifically from Schelling (who uses them, how-ever, to refer to inorganic as well as to organic nature, as C's annotated copy of *Einleitung zu seinem Entwurf eines Systems der Naturphilosophie*—Jena & Leipzig 1799—i 3 and passim indicates). *LS* (*CC*) 29 n 1 notes a deliberate change from "*educts*" to "*Produce*" in an annotated copy of *LS*.

GIROLAMO RUSCELLI

d 1566

Del modo di comporre in versi nella lingua italiana, trattato di Girolamo Ruscelli, nel quale và compreso un pieno, & ordinatissimo rimario, con la dichiaratione, con le regole, & co'l giudicio per saper convenevolmente usare, ò schifar le voci nell' esser loro, così nelle prose, come ne i versi. Venice 1594. 8°.

British Library C 132 c 14

This work is not paginated but foliated. A transcript of **1** and a note by EHC dated 10 Feb 1918 are bound in at the end of the volume.

DATE. Possibly Malta about Aug 1804, when C's interest in Italian versification revived: *CN* II Appendix A 399.

1   f 110ᵛ, left-hand column of a list of verbs, C's translations written above each word

A. active.   N. Verbs neuter
Strale = Freccia = Saetta = dardo[1]
Tacca = the notch in the ~~Bow~~ Arrow, nella quale entra la corda dell'
arco.[2]
[? mistra . . .][3]

Abbacinare	To blind
Abbagliare	To dazzle
Abbruciare	To burn
Abituare	To accustom
Accarnare	To cut thro' the Skin
Accattare	To borrow
Accertare	To certify
Accoccare	To fit the arrow to the Bow
Accomunare	To *communify*[4]
Accoppiare	Couple
Accortare	To shorten
Accupare	To hollow?[5]
Acquistare	To acquire
Additare	To point out
Addoppiare	To double
Adeguare	To equalize + appraise
Adimare	To sink A.[6]
Adombrare	Oershadow
Adorezare	To be in Shade
Affamare	To starve A & N.
Afferrare	To hold by force.*
Affigurare	To conceive†
Affollare	Crowd
Affumicare	To smoak—black
Aggiornare	To fix a day
Aggrappare	Grapple
Agiare	⟨To *loiter*⟩ To make oneself at *ease*.
Aguagliare	To compare &c
Aguzzare	To sharpen
Aizzare	To set on.

* To grapple?—[7]
† To body forth—affigurarsi = immaginarsi[8]

2   p ⁻2, referring to *Accomunare* in **1**

In using a quaint self-coined word such as communify, I mean that the Italian has many senses implied in this word, tho' not expressed by any one English word that at least occurred to my memory—Thus accommunare = metter commune,[1] in medium conferre, communicare, participem facere, impertire, participare: and accomunarsi = socium se præbere[2] = our word "to club" answers to many of these senses.

3   f 224ᵛ

upo/ cupo, deep.[1]

1[1] Alternative terms for "arrow", probably connected with *accoccare* below.

  1[2] "Which the string of the bow goes into".

  1[3] The conjectured reading does not make sense in connection with the vocabulary of archery above: *mistrà* is "aniseed". But it may be the beginning of another word ("mistranslation"?) or not intended to have any connection with the foregoing.

  1[4] This translation, C's own, which he discusses in **2**, suggests that for at least some of these verbs he was departing from his dictionary.

  1[5] Related to **3** below. C's guess is based on etymology: one of the meanings of *cupo* is "deep". But this is a variant of *accupire* "to grow sad" or "become gloomy".

  1[6] I.e. an active verb.

  1[7] "Grapple" is one of the possible meanings of the verb.

  1[8] *–arsi* is a suffix with reflexive force, so these words mean "to figure to oneself" and "to image to oneself".

  2[1] C probably intends the Italian *mettere* rather than the French *mettre*; in either case the phrase would mean something like "to put into common use".

  2[2] "Bring into the midst, make one with, make a participant, confide, participate; . . . offer oneself as a companion to".

  3[1] C has inserted this entry between two groups of words ending in *–iunto* and *–ura* respectively; *–upo* is an ending, not a word. Cupo may mean "deep" but also "gloomy", "dejected", etc.

SAMMLUNG . . . GEDICHTE

Sammlung vorzüglich schöner Gedichte, welche in Absicht auf Geschmack und Sitten bey Unterweisung der Jugend mit grossen Nutzen gebraucht werden können, und aus denen berühmtesten und neuesten Dichtern mit Fleiss zusammen getragen worden. 2 vols in 1. Leipzig & Halberstadt 1759. 8°.

Victoria College Library (Coleridge Collection)

Autograph signature "S. T. Coleridge—" on the title-page of Vol I only, suggesting that this copy was already bound in one vol when C acquired it. There is a German inscription in an unknown hand on I $^{-}$1. EHC description in pocket on p $^{+}$4 (p-d), indicating "Green Bequest".

DATE. About 1799, in Germany? An early date is indicated both by the restraint of the marginalia (cf BÜRGER) and by the use of symbols (cf ANDERSON COPY C).

1 I $^{-}$2

Tho' it is an hopeless Business, yet I have resolved to look thro' this Volume: and mark what seems readable. If any after reader in consulting the pages, pointed out to him, co-incide with my Taste, he may perhaps thank me for saving his time & eye-sight as to the rest—if not, he may rather read thro' the volume for himself/.

$\mathbf{\mathcal{F}}$ = good $\mathbf{X}$ = not amiss
66 Der junge Gelehrte. $\mathbf{\mathcal{F}}^{1}$
68 Der rohe Diamant $\mathbf{X}^{2}$

1[1] The poem appears on p 66, among a group of narrative poems ("Fabeln und Erzählungen"); it is not marked in any way.

1[2] *Der Diamant und der Bergcrystall* appears pp 68–9, in the same section as the preceding; it is likewise not marked. C's version of the title is recollected from the first line, which introduces the two main figures of the fable, the rock crystal and the rough diamond.

GEORGE SAMOUELLE
fl 1819

Lost Book

The Entomologist's Useful Compendium; or an introduction to the knowledge of British insects, comprising the best means of obtaining and preserving them, and a description of the apparatus generally used; together with the genera of Linné, and the modern method of arranging the classes crustacea, myriapoda, spiders, mites, and insects, from their affinities and structure, according to the views of Dr. Leach. Also an explanation of the terms used in entomology; a calendar of the times of appearance and usual situations of near 3,000 species of British insects; with instructions for collecting and fitting up objects for the microscope. Illustrated with twelve plates. London 1819. 8°.

Not located; marginalia not recorded. *Gillman SC* 452: "with MS. Note by S. T. Coleridge".

DANIEL SANDFORD
1766–1830

The Remains of the Late Right Reverend Daniel Sandford, D.D. Oxon. Bishop of Edinburgh in the Scottish Episcopal Church; including extracts from his diary and correspondence, and a selection from his unpublished sermons. With a memoir, by the Rev. John Sandford, Vicar of Chillingham. 2 vols. Edinburgh 1830. 8°.

Not located; marginalia pub from TRANSCRIPT. In L. E. G. Watson *Coleridge at Highgate* (1925) 153 the book is described as the last C annotated. C mentioned this work to HNC on 5 Jul 1834 (*TT—CC*—I 496–7) and in fact the notes may be addressed to him (**4**).

TRANSCRIPT. BM Add MS 63785 ff 5ᵛ–8ᵛ. The transcription, made about 1840, is included along with other Coleridge entries in a notebook that belonged to Frances Sarah Bunyon (1816–93), who in 1846 married John William Colenso (1814–83), later bp of Natal. The discovery and contents of the notebook are described by Hilton Kelliher in "A Stray Notebook of Miscellaneous Writings by Coleridge" *British Library Journal* XIV (1988) 136–53. In publishing the marginalia here, we have silently converted the transcriber's consistent "yᵉ" and "wh" to C's consistent "the" and "which", and expanded the textus.

DATE. Jun–Jul 1834.

1   I 77 | Memoir ch 11

In the society of his daughters he was always happy and always delightful; and there never was a more beautiful picture than that exhibited in his intercourse with them. His manner towards women was uniformly that of deference and courtesy,—towards his daughters it united tenderness with respect.ᵃ The closeness of affinity, which is sometimes considered a plea for indifference, was with him only an argument for more exact and delicate attention.

I have never met with this remark in any other book—it is most beautiful, & of the deepest & dearest moral interest. The Father recognises in his Daughters the Representations & as it were the renewed Types of their

---

1ᵃ Here the transcriber began C's note, but crossed it out after the first sentence to expand the textus

dear Mother; & repeats towards *them*, delicately modified by the difference of the relation [b]the tender reverence, the inward gentle awe, inseparable from all true love, that is at once pure & deep[c]; & which even in the stirring gay & summer tide, the blossoming May and the sapful "leafy June"[1] of our *natural* life, can & will preserve the purer, permanent & spiritual Element, undebased by the earthly accessaries which it elevates, refines, cloathes ⟨& fills⟩ with its own Light, & finally almost transubstantiates into its own Essence. From the Father the same Tone and Feeling, again modified by the different relation, will pass to the Brother, & thus the parental Home be a *rehearsal* of the finest duties, of the *continuous* affections of the conjugal state. For Reverence of Womanhood is the *Ground* of all *manly* virtues, & a main *condition* of all *female* excellence.[2]   STC.

2   I 83

[a]Prayer is the natural expression of want to Him who alone can relieve it, and its fervency is proportioned to the sense of need. The Bishop knew the value of prayer. As a confession of sin, an acknowledgment of blessing, an application for pardon and strength, a medium of communion with God, prayer was peculiarly grateful to his humble and pious spirit. He lived in prayer. How frequent were his addresses is known only to him who reads the heart. "Do you know what it is," he once said to a beloved child, "to be unable to leave off praying?—oh! I feel sometimes as if I could pray for ever." His voice was repeatedly heard breathing forth petitions, and its solemnity and sweetness will never be forgotten. A few months before his death, when on a visit to one of his children, the low murmur of prayer was heard proceeding from his chamber during the whole of a sleepless night. Such was his habit in the acutest suffering.[b] Pain was familiar to him,—prayer was its anodyne.

Grace forbid! that I should ever *think* of myself & of Bᴾ S. in the same

1[b-c] Lightly underlined in pencil in TRANSCRIPT
2[a-b] Transcriber notes of textus "The whole of this was marked"

1[1] An allusion to *AM* line 370 (PW—EHC—I 201), "In the leafy month of June".

1[2] C's many pronouncements upon love insist upon its special status as a spiritual force or element, e.g. DE WETTE **22** (and n 1), KANT *Metaphysik* **2**, **3**. The 1811 lecture on *Romeo and Juliet* is a locus classicus; C there remarks, for example (cancellations omitted), "One certain criterion in forming an opinion of man was the reverence in wᶜʰ he held woman. Plato had said that by this we rose from sensuality to affection, from affection to love, & from love to pure intellectual delight & by which we became worthy to conceive that infinite in ourselves without which it were impossible for man to have believed in a God": *Lects 1808–1819* (*CC*) I 315.

thought. But I owe it to my fellow men to declare that I *know* & can solemnly *attest*, the truth & efficiency of what is here written.[1]

STC.

3 I 96

His theology he drew from the scriptures; but from the Augustan age of the English church he had caught the diction, as well as the spirit, in which its masters wrote.

What age does the writer mean? It was once the fashion to call the age of Queen Anne & George 1st our *Augustan* age[1] But if Mr S means the age from Elizth to the Restoration, or from Hooker to Jeremy Taylor & Stillingfleet,[2] I fully agree with him in his *meaning*, tho' I do not think the age of Augustus the *golden* age of Roman Literature, but the century preceding.[3]

STC.

4

Pray, read at least the 1st 100 Pages of this volume & mark the book down for a 2nd reading—[1]
As far as I have read—for alas! thro weakness of the body & over-activity of the suggestive mind I now crawl thro' a book like a fly thro a milk splash on a Tea-tray![2] I who 20 years ago, used to read a volume, stereo-

2[1] Towards the end of his life, C came to believe he had gained new insight into the nature and efficacy of prayer. He announced (but did not publish) an essay on prayer to follow *AR*: *AR* (*CC*) 381n, *CL* VI 545. Cf *CL* VI 577, a letter of Apr 1826: "But in one point I have attained to a conviction which till of late I never had in any available form or degree—namely, the confidence in the efficacy of Prayer. I know by experience, that it is Light, Strength, and Comfort.—"

3[1] Anne reigned 1702–14, George I 1714–27. This period in English literature was soon identified with the reign of Augustus in Rome (27–14 BC) or, more broadly, the period from the death of Julius Caesar (44 BC) to the death of Ovid (AD 17), when Virgil, Ovid, and Horace were active. The label "Augustan" was commonplace in C's day and has persisted to our own in spite of scholarly attempts to dislodge it.

3[2] The great age of the Church of England is earlier than Queen Anne, spanning half the sixteenth century and most or all of the seventeenth: the reign of Elizabeth began 1558 and the Restoration took place in 1660; Hooker was born 1554 and Stillingfleet died 1699.

3[3] C may be referring to the "Ciceronian age", variously dated from c 80 BC to c 44 BC (Cicero died in 43 BC), in which the great prose writers were Cicero, Caesar, and Sallust, and the major poets Lucretius and Catullus; or, less conventionally, to the whole century preceding the reign of Augustus (27 –14 BC) and so including the dramatists Plautus and Terence. For a similar list of preferences taught at C's school see *BL* ch 1 (*CC*) I 8–9.

4[1] This injunction was addressed to HNC (cf n 5 below), who noted C's enthusiasm for this book and in a letter of Aug 1834 recommended it, in words that suggest that he had read it himself: *TT* (*CC*) I 496–7 and n 13.

4[2] C had used the same image in a letter of 13 Mar 1832: *CL* VI 889.

type-wise by whole pages at a glance:[3] as if my eyes & brain had been a claude Lorrain Mirror, or a Camera Obscura or D[r] Woolaston's Camera Lucida or M[r] Burton's new patent Paneidolon,[4] specimens of the produce of which you have seen in Sir F Head's "Bubbles from the Brunnen[a]"[5]

STC.

5   I 353 | Letter of 5 Oct 1819

... "Paley's Horae Paulinae," the most invaluable work Paley ever produced.

True & the mere English Reader may well be thankful for it.[1] But it is likewise true, that for those acquainted with the German theologians of the 20 or 30 years before the publication of Paley's works, the Horae Paul[ae] contains nothing that could be new to him.[2]   STC.

4[a] TRANSCRIPT has a closing parenthesis here

4[3] The stereotype method, perfected in 1800, printed the whole forme of text at once from a single plate.

4[4] These were all devices used by artists to reduce a scene to a scale suitable for viewing at a glance or for copying: the Claude Lorraine Glass was a slightly convex, darkened hand-mirror, the camera obscura an ancestor of the pin-hole camera (cf *BL* ch 22—*CC*—II 128 "the whole picture flash'd at once upon the eye, as . . . in a camera obscura"), the camera lucida a device patented by William Hyde Wollaston in 1807 that used a prism to produce a reduced image onto paper for tracing. The paneidolon—the name is based on the Greek for "an image of everything"—was a device similar to the camera lucida but one that involved a box that accommodated the artist's head; it was invented and patented in 1832 not by "M[r] Burton" but by Caroline Eliza Ann Burges, the cousin of Francis Bond Head, for whom see the following note.

4[5] Francis Bond Head's *Bubbles from the Brunnens of Nassau* (1834) was pub anonymously as "by an old man". C read and annotated the work in Mar 1834, addressing a note of 16 Mar to HNC and wondering who the author might be (HEAD 1). By 16 Apr 1834, when he referred to the work in *TT* (*CC*) I 473, he knew the answer. Head describes the "Paneidolon" pp 324–5 and includes as illustrations engravings of drawings made with its help (as H. Kelliher points out in the article cited in the headnote to this entry, 149–50).

5[1] C's early enthusiasm for the works of William Paley (1743–1805) began to wear off about 1796, and Paley is a frequent target of attack as a Grotian in C's own writings on religion: cf LUTHER *Colloquia* 4 and n 1. Nevertheless, he consistently spoke well of the *Horae Paulinae* (1790), written, as C says, "to exhibit the Harmony & unconscious Coincidences of the Epistles of Paul with Luke's Acts of the Apostles": BLANCO WHITE *Practical Evidence* 1, where n 1 gives a comprehensive account of C's opinion of Paley.

5[2] I.e. German scholars who studied the historical construction of the text of the NT, notably Johann David Michaelis (1717–91), Johann Salomo Semler (1725–91), and Gotthold Ephraim Lessing (1729–81).

JACOPO SANNAZARO
1458–1530

Jacobi Sannazarii, patricii neapolitani, Opera omnia, accedit vita authoris per Paulum Jovium. Frankfurt 1709. 8°.

Henry E. Huntington Library

Printed extract from bookseller's catalogue loose in vol; bookplate of Henry W. Poor on p ⁻7 (p-d). A deletion in ink on p 125 does not appear to be C's. This book was bound or rebound after C's notes were made, and the pages concerned were folded in to avoid cropping.

DATE. Probably between Jul 1804 and Jun 1806, when C was in Malta, Sicily, and Italy; a note of Aug 1805 (*CN* II 2633) refers to someone apparently unable to translate the title-page of one of Sannazaro's works, possibly from this copy.

1 p ⁻2, evidently referring to p 5 | *De partu Virginis* bk 1 lines 71–2

This Book more infamous for typographical Blunders than any work, I remember to have read, excepting Anderson's British Poets.[1]

polo   altoque
Digna *paulo* regnare, *alioque* effulgere divum—
—as
Concilio, *et nostris* æternum habitare penates.[2]

This is a fair Specimen.—

2 p 85, pencil | *Ad Petrum de Roccha-Forti Maximum Regis Galliarum Cancellarium*

Hæc elegia si puritatem et suavitatem s̶p̶ et linguæ et carminis consideres; nec non orationem modestè figuratam, cum summa cum summâ[a] per-

---

2[a] Here C continued the note in the foot-margin, using a footnote indicator and repeating the words "cum summa"

[1]1 For the typographical errors in that work, see ANDERSON headnote.

[1]2 C's corrected version translates: "Worthy to reign in heaven, to shine in the high concourse of divinities, and ever to dwell in our household shrines." C has corrected "for a little while" to "in heaven", and "another" to "high". His change of *nostris* to *nostras* (f) where *nostros* (m) is required is puzzling; he may have been confused about the gender of *penates*, or have considered that household shrines were occupied predominantly by female saints.

spicuitate, videtur ~~proximos~~ proximas Tibull⟨i⟩~~osa~~nas æmulari posse. [. . . . .]*b* [? Hæc] vero sensu et ingenio facile superat, sapientiâ ⟨quadam virili⟩ validior; prudentiæ politicæ sententias lyrâ Alcæo dignâ et sustinens et [? commemorans].[1]

3 p 85, pencil | Lines 17–22, circled in pencil by C

> Deprimor audaccis inter derisa ministros:
> Nec fas ingenuum tollere ad astra caput.
> Quodque diu partum est virtute, & fortibus armis
> Imperium, foedè servit avaritiae.
> Nec mirum, vestro tantùm cum distet ab orbe,
> Terraque censura sit procul illa tua.

[[Astraea, the goddess of justice, speaks of the state of Naples:] I am mocked and trampled upon in the press of insolent underlings, and may not raise my innocent head to the stars. The realm long since won by virtue and by courage in war now basely serves avarice. No wonder, when it is so far from your world, and that land is so far from your seat of judgment.]

Inclusa omittas; non quod mala, sed quod non optima.[1]

4 p 86, pencil | Lines 37–8

> * Delentur nullos hominum benefacta per annos,
>   Quaque licet faciunt nos ratione <u>Deos</u>.   <u>suos</u>?

[* The good deeds of mankind are not obliterated by any lapse of years, and so far as is lawful they make us into <u>Gods</u>. <u>theirs</u>?]

* Beneficence is immortal; & as far as we dare use such an expression, it makes Gods of us.—Potuisset scribi—

> Dius Amor hominum diademate [? pulchrior/pulchrius] [. . .]
> Illustrat reges et facit esse deos[1]

2*b* C has deleted a line, leaving it illegible

2[1] "This elegy, if you consider the sweetness and purity both of language and versification—the modest ornamentation of style combined with the utmost clarity— seems very nearly able to vie with the elegies of Tibullus. Indeed in feeling and spirit it easily surpasses them, being stronger in a sort of manly good sense sustaining and recording the maxims of political wisdom with a lyric quality worthy of Alcaeus."

3[1] "Omit the lines encircled; not because they are bad, but because they are not excellent."

4[1] "He could have written—Divine love of humankind, fairer than any crown [or— if *pulchrius*—more beautifully than by a crown], ennobles kings and makes them into gods." The word needed to complete the first line may have been *omni* or *ullo* ("fairer than *every* or *any* crown") or perhaps *ornans* ("adorning more beautifully than with a crown").

5   p 86, pencil | Lines 39–40, following **4** textus

> At si quis serae spernit praeconia famae,
> ~~Quercubus Alpinis~~ adnumerare potes.

[But if anyone scorns the proclamation of his glory, thought late, you may count him among the mountain oaks.]

Iam nunc oblitis[1]

5[1] C's substitution would read "*among those now forgotten*".

FRIEDRICH CARL VON SAVIGNY

1779–1861

Of the Vocation of our Age for Legislation and Jurisprudence, translated
... by Abraham Hayward. London [1831]. 8°.

Not located; marginalia pub from MS TRANSCRIPT.

C may have owned more than one copy of this work, or else his note may have
been removed from the vol before it went to the binder, for the BM holds a presentation copy to C from the translator, not annotated by C but inscribed p ⁻2
"S. T. Coleridge Esq: (presented as an humble token of profound respect by the
Translator) *see p. 48. ante*"—the page reference being to a footnote in which Hayward, the translator, quotes from *C&S* and comments on the resemblance between
Savigny's and C's "cast of mind". This copy (BM C 126 g 12) has an "S. T. C."
label on the title-page verso, and the monogram of John Duke Coleridge on p ⁻6.

MS TRANSCRIPT. University of Texas (Humanities Research Center): transcription by SC.

DATE. 1831 or later.

1   "Blank leaf before the title page"

The purely evil nature of the ambition, which agitates, like a *lust*, The
French Nation, is betrayed and evinced by the merely *physical* character
of their pretexts: Ex. gr. That the *Rhine* is the natural boundary of
France—that the interspace between the Rhine and the Pyrenees cannot
endure a divided sovereignty.[1] Languages, manners, religion, historical
recollections, even *race*, may be diverse. What of all these compared with
a *River*?—though the said River never, for a short week, stopped the
march of a superior force! But alas! incapable of the sense of duty the
French seek a substitute for it by generalizing their Self-lust in a demand
for *Rights*. God and the Devil cannot be more strikingly contrasted than
in this different ordination of the two Antithetæ, Persons ⨉ Things, Duties ⨉ Rights.[2] According to the will of God it is, *Persons* and Things in

---

[1] This example is not derived from
Savigny. The idea of the Rhine as a "natural
boundary" appears to have been commonplace: see for example the casual reference
in NICOLAI **12A**.

[2] For the "sacred principle ... which is
the *ground-work* of all law and justice, that
a person can never become a thing, nor be
treated as such without wrong" (*Friend*—
CC—I 190); see also *C&S* (*CC*) 15–16. C's

order to Persons, Duties and thence Rights as derived from the obligation to perform Duties. According to the Devil the Cotton-factors & the West Indian Planters and the Revolutionists[3] it is, Persons as Things and in order to Things—*Rights* i.e. Desires, and *other Men's duty*[a] to submit to them.

1[a] SC originally wrote "Duty"

---

symbol ⚹ means "opposed to". The distinction between rights and duties (and at the same time, the reciprocity between them) is maintained by C e.g. in *Lects 1795* (*CC*) 43, *Watchman* (*CC*) 122*, NICOLAI **12**. He was not alone in holding this position: cf William Godwin *Political Justice* bk 2 chs 2, 4.

1[3] The "Cotton-factors" are the factory-owners who resisted the shortening of working hours for children, an issue C addressed in a series of pamphlets in 1818 (*SW & F—CC*—714-51); the "West Indian Planters" similarly opposed the movement to abolish the slave trade; the "Revolutionists" are both the Jacobins of the French Revolution (whose *Declaration of the Rights of Man and of Citizens*, however, dealt with duties as well as with rights) and their supporters in other countries, such as Thomas Paine, author of the inflammatory *Rights of Man* (pt 1 1791).

JOANNES SCAPULA

fl 1580

Joan. Scapulae Lexicon Graeco-Latinum, e probatis auctoribus locuple-
tatum, cum indicibus, et Graeco & Latino, auctis, & correctis. Additum
auctarium dialectorum, in tabulas compendiosè redactarum. Accedunt
lexicon etymologicum, cum thematibus investigatu difficilioribus &
anomalis. Et Joan. Mersii glossarium contractum, hactenus desideratum.
Rev ed. 2 pts in one vol. Lyons 1663, 1662. F°.

University of Kentucky

With autograph inscription on a front flyleaf: "S. T. Coleridge | Bought at Naples
for six Dollars—". C appears to have signed his name in the book, with the note
of price below, when he bought it in Naples in Nov 1805, but to have written his
note (1) at a later date. Comments on C's note in another hand (WW's, according to *W Library*) are recorded in the footnotes.

DATE. 8 Feb 1808 (1).

1 p⁻1

N.B. Twenty years ago, this Edition in as good condition might have
been purchased for ~~12 11 Sh~~ 20 Shillings: inferior Editions from 7 to 14
so great has been the advance on the price of Books in general, but especially on good editions of valuable Works in classical Literature—; and
so remarkably has the Scapula risen in estimation; that the Catalogue
Price of this Edition in a copy equally neat is at present ~~ten~~ from 8 to 10
Guineas. The Stephani Thesaurus (the Greek) apud H. Steph. 1572 sells
for twenty guineas.[1]   Feb. 8ᵗʰ, 1808.

N.B. This is the best Edition; the second or *next best* is the Elzevir,
printed TEN[2] years before. It is a thinner Folio than this Edition—[3]

---

[1][1] Early in 1808 C made a note "To
spend half an hour in Cuthell's Shop, examining Stephens's Thesaurus in order to
form an accurate idea of its utilities above
Scapula". Cf his notes from a catalogue issued by Cuthell and Martin of Holborn, *CN*
III 3276 and n.

[1][2] Corrected in another hand: "eleven".
But the 1652 Elzevir ed—unpriced but described as "the best" in the catalogue mentioned in the preceding n—is ten years older
than Pt ii of this ed.

[1][3] A comment follows in another hand:

"In Longman's Catalogue the Elzevir Edition L. Bat. 1652 is called 'Editio Optima[']
its price bound in Russia is £12—" We have
been unable to locate a Longman's catalogue for 1808, or any Longman's catalogue before 1813 that includes this
Scapula. Longman, Hurst, Rees, Orme, and
Brown *Bibliotheca Curiosa: Pt* II *A Catalogue of Rare, Curious, and Valuable
Books* (7 Jun 1813) lists as # 481 "Scapulae Lexicon, *fine* Copy, best Edition, hand-
somely bound in russia Elzevir 1652".

343

FRIEDRICH WILHELM
JOSEPH VON SCHELLING
1775–1854

Darlegung des wahren Verhältnisses der Naturphilosophie zu der verbesserten Fichte'schen Lehre. Eine Erläuterungsschrift der ersten von F. W. J. Schelling. Tübingen 1806. 8°.

British Library C 126 f 7(2), bound as second with JAHRBÜCHER DER MEDICIN (Tübingen 1805–6), edited by Schelling

This copy lacks a title-page; the notes that were made in pencil are badly rubbed, and some notes have been cropped in rebinding. Two notes written on the back fly-leaves, referring to JAHRBÜCHER, show that the two works were already bound together when C used them; in rebinding since C's time, however, parts of some notes have been obscured. Someone, possibly C, has corrected a typographical error in pencil on p 87, changing *wir* to *wie*.

This *"small pamphlet against Fichte"* was one of the three vols of Schelling that C had been able to procure by 1815 (*BL* ch 9—*CC*—I 164 and n 3; on which see SCHELLING *Ideen* headnote), and he included a free translation of two paragraphs from it in *BL* ch 9 (*CC*) I 147–9, with a general acknowledgment. C's annotations on several works by Fichte are included in *CM* (*CC*) II.

We do not know when C began to read Schelling, but we can trace the climax and the decline of his enthusiasm for Schelling's works in the period from 1815 to the end of 1818. In *BL*, C refers familiarly to several works that he had apparently read by Aug or Sept 1815. The editors of *BL* (*CC*) document an indebtedness to the first volume—the only one published—of Schelling's *Philosophische Schriften*, which included *Vom Ich als Princip der Philosophie, Über das Verhältniss der bildenden Künste zu der Natur, Ueber das Wesen der menschlichen Freyheit*, and *Philosophische Briefe über Dogmatismus und Kritizismus*, as well as less unequivocal debts to the *System des transcendentalen Idealismus, Abhandlungen zur Erläuterung des Idealismus der Wissenschaftslehre, Ideen zu einer Philosophie der Natur, Darlegung des wahren Verhältnisses der Naturphilosophie zur verbesserten Fichte'schen Lehre, Philosophie und Religion*, and *Ueber die Möglichkeit einer Form der Philosophische Schriften*: *BL* (*CC*) I cxxi. A year later, in Aug 1816, C wrote to a bookseller who supplied him with German books agreeing to purchase *Denkmal der Schrift von den göttlichen Dingen* and requesting *all* the books by Schelling that he did not already possess (*CL* IV 665). An important letter of Sept 1817 outlines a philosophical system so closely resembling Schelling's that C draws attention to the resemblance and, while claiming to have worked it out for himself before reading Schelling, welcomes Schelling as a "fellow-laborer" in the field (*CL* IV 775). Similarly, a letter of 23 May 1818 recommends Schelling as a philosopher of religion (*CL* IV 863). About the same time, however, doubts began to come to the surface. Although C had recommended Schelling as a philosopher of nature to JHG in Dec 1817 (while disparaging his theology—*CL* IV 792), he found increasing reason to question the soundness of the system after he and Green began a regular study of *Naturphilosophie* (*CL* IV 873–6). By 24 Nov 1818, C was describing Schelling and his "Sect" as fundamentally pantheistic (*CL* IV 883), and this was the position he maintained throughout the 1820s.

Besides the works represented in the following pages, C annotated two periodical publications of which Schelling was an editor: JAHRBÜCHER and ZEITSCHRIFT.

DATE. 1815 or later; JAHRBÜCHER, bound together with this work, was most likely annotated Aug 1816–Sept 1818.

SPECIAL ABBREVIATION. *SW*: F. W. J. Schelling *Sämmtliche Werke* ed K. F. A. Schelling (14 vols Stuttgart 1856–61). In a departure from normal *CM* practice, the generic reference following the vertical rule in each headline (in some cases, following the *second* vertical rule) consists of a reference to this standard ed, to which subsequent major eds also refer. Where the German text varies from the text of *SW*, it is because *CM* reproduces the text that C actually used.

COEDITOR. Raimonda Modiano.

1   p 7 | *SW* VII 25

Ein Hauptsatz der Fichte'schen Lehre . . . war bekanntlich die: dass der Begriff des Seyns ein bloss negativer sey, indem er nur die absolute Verneinung von Thätigkeit ausdrücke; desgleichen dass er von Gott und göttlichen Dingen völlig verbannt werden müsse. Nun tritt Hr. Fichte herzhaft hin und spricht: Alles Seyn ist lebendig, und es giebt kein andres Seyn als das Leben. Das Absolute, oder Gott ist selbst das Leben. Gott ist alles Seyn, und ausser ihm kein Seyn . . .

[As is well known . . . it was one of the chief principles of Fichte's teaching that the concept of being is merely a negative one, in that it expresses only the absolute negation of action; likewise, it must be utterly excluded from God and divine things. Now Mr Fichte steps forward resolutely and says that all being is alive and that there is no other being but life. The absolute, or God, is itself life. God is all being and apart from him there is no being . . .]

1*a* This word is also written above in pencil

I have ever thought that all this Dispute resolves[a] itself into the mystery of Perception: & that the Question is, can you do this away without substituting an equal or greater mystery?[1]

2 p 7, pencil, overtraced by C, cropped | **1** textus continued | *SW* vii 25

Sonst lehrte er: In Ansehung des Absoluten oder An-sich besteht ein ewiger Widerspruch, denn es soll etwas für das Ich, und folglich in ihm, und doch zugleich nicht im Ich, sondern ausser ihm seyn; sonst wäre es kein An-sich. *Diess ist der nie zu durchbrechende Zirkel, dessen Entdeckung das Verdienst der Wissenschaftslehre ist, und in welchem alle endlichen Naturen unrettbar befangen und ewig eingeschlossen sind.

[Moreover he professes that with regard to the absolute or the In-itself there is a permanent contradiction, in that it must be something for the I, and consequently must be in the I, and yet at the same time it is not inside but outside the I; for otherwise it could not be the In-itself. *This is the circle which can never be broken through, the discovery of which is the merit of the theory of knowledge. Within it all finite beings are irretrievably caught and permanently enclosed.]

But is it [? not] the same, differing [only] as the Sch[. . .][1] and the Rh[etori]cal, to s[ay] that alle[s] Seyn is [a] Derivative [of] dem *Thun*[2] and in [the] popular [? belief] that all [? this] Being i[s] *Life*? F[or] it is evid[ent] that by S[eyn] or "the to [be"] Fichte meant Substance, *Thing* = Ding in S[ich.][3] So again in the next Charge of Inconsist[ency] I seem to perceive the same meaning under different Conditions—that what [in] the former Fichte using Kantéan Phrase calls Faith (Glauben) in the latter—die Liebe.[4]

3 p 8, pencil | *SW* vii 25–6

Hr. Fichte hatte seine ganze Philosophie zu Stande gebracht und vielfach dargestellt, ohne dass er nöthig gefunden, von Gott oder göttlichen

---

1[1] C makes a similar observation in **8** below. A note written earlier than this one, SCHELLING *System* **1**, expounds C's views about "the mystery of Perception" and the controversy it entails; FICHTE *Bestimmung* **5** also touches on it.

2[1] Perhaps "Scholastic", to go with "Rhetorical".

2[2] That "all being" is a derivative of (derived from) "action": cf textus **1**.

2[3] The Kantian *Ding an sich*, the "thing in itself", which is unknowable.

2[4] "Love", in **3** textus. The "next Charge of Inconsistency" is presented in **3**, which outlines arguments made in Fichte's *Einige*

Vorlesungen über das Wesen des Gelehrten (Jena & Leipzig 1794; Schelling quotes from the expanded version, *Ueber das Wesen des Gelehrten und seine Erscheinungen im Gebiet der Freiheit in Vorlesungen gehalten 1805*—Berlin 1806). Kant uses *Glaube* in religious contexts, e.g. in C *d r V* B xxx (tr Norman Kemp Smith): "I have therefore found it necessary to deny *knowledge*, in order to make room for *faith* [*Glaube*]." C complains on several occasions that German has only one word, *Glaube*, to signify both "faith" and "belief": LUTHER **56**, SCHELLING *Philosophie* **1**, STEFFENS *Caricaturen* **6**.

Dingen die geringste Erwähnung zu thun; bis er im Jahr 1798 die *Resultate* seines Philosophirens über diesen Gegenstand mittheilte . . . . Nunmehr aber soll alles Philosophiren beginnen von der göttlichen Idee und die Liebe . . . . Sonst . . . wusste der Philosoph zu gut, dass nur eine verirrte Philosophie, in der Verlegenheit etwas zu erklären dessen Daseyn sie nicht läugnen kann, von der Sinnenwelt auf einen Gott schliesst . . . . Denn "dass ein Gott *ist*, leuchtet dem, *nur ein wenig* ernsthaften Nachdenken über die Sinnenwelt ohne Schwicrigkeit ein["]; man muss (*muss*) *zuletzt doch* damit *enden*, demjenigen Daseyn, das immer nur in einem andern Daseyn gegründet ist, ein Daseyn zu Grunde zu legen, welches (Daseyn?) den Grund seines Daseyns in sich selbst habe . . .

[Mr Fichte brought his entire philosophy to completion and presented it in various ways without finding it necessary to make the least mention of God or divine things; he finally communicated the *results* of his philosophy on this matter in 1798 . . . . But all philosophy should begin with the divine idea and love . . . . However . . . the philosopher knew all too well that only a confused philosophy, caught in the embarrassment of having to explain something whose existence it cannot deny, infers the existence of a God on the basis of the sensible world . . . . For the fact "that a God *exists* is easily evident with *only a little* serious reflection on the sensible world["]; in the *final analysis* one must (*must*) *conclude* by grounding that being, which always has its ground in another being, in a being whose (being?) has the ground of its being in itself . . .]

*a*But is not this captious? Fichte spoke of the modern cosmological in contrast with the old ontological argument.[1]

4   p 9, first sentence in pencil and overtraced | **3** textus continued | *SW* vii 26

Nicht dass Hr. Fichte diese oder jene Sätze aufstellt, sondern dass Er überhaupt in dieser Region angetroffen wird, ist das Verwundersame. Wir hatten ihm nachgewiesen, dass er das eigentliche Princip der Sünde, die Ichheit,* zum Princip der Philosophie gemacht (Philosophie u. Religion S. 42. u.f.); nun erklärt er eben dieses Zeitalter für das Zeitalter der vollendeten Sündhaftigkeit. Es war gezeigt worden, dass die ganze Fichte'sche Philosophie ein in Reflexionsaberglauben verhärteter und in

---

3*a* This note in ink is preceded by a few words in pencil, so rubbed as to be completely illegible

3[1] Schelling himself gives a reference for the work from which he is quoting, Fichte's *Ueber das Wesen des Gelehrten* (see previous note). The "modern cosmological" argument infers the existence of God from the evidence of the sensory world, asserting that the universe must have been brought into being by some self-sufficient primary cause. The "old ontological argument" is the *a priori* argument, associated with Anselm, "that the existence of the idea of God necessarily involves the objective existence of God" (*ODCC*).

formeller Wissenschaft erstarrter Verstand sey. . . . Jetzt spricht er von
Liebe und vom Apostel Johannes, und die in Gott sich selbst vernicht-
ende Reflexion ist das Höchste.

[The curious thing is not that Mr Fichte sets up certain principles rather than others,
but that he is to be found working in this field at all. We had proved that he had made
the actual principle of sin, the Ego, * into a principle of philosophy (*Philosophy and
Religion* p 42 ff); now he declares this particular age to be the age of utter sinfulness.
The entire Fichtean philosophy had been shown to be a way of thinking hardened in
superstitious reliance on reflection and frozen in formal science. . . . Now he talks
about love and the apostle John, and says that the greatest thing is reflection which
annihilates itself in God.]

* But not in Schelling's sense. The ichheit[1] of Fichte was = the universal Will, not the individualizing Self. Besides, Fichte had to oppose Spinozism,[2] which he fought as Kant did Hume, by extending his Doctrine.[3]
He shewed that [? all] Science, i.e. distinct Knowlege, began and ended
in the acts of Self-knowlege/ And that all our *clear* tho' not distinct, Possessions were Faith. We *live* by Faith, said the philosophic Apostle.[4] O
that Schelling & Fichte had both considered, how *strong* an objection,
tho' invalid, against their Philosophy, is given by the unphilosophic Passions of the Teachers.

5   p 9 | *SW* vii 26

Jeder Glaube an ein Göttliches, der mehr enthielt als den Begriff der
moralischen Weltordnung, war ihm ein Gräuel, eines vernünftigen

4[1] "Ego", from textus.

4[2] For Fichte's view of and opposition to
Spinoza's system, particularly with regard
to Spinoza's representation of the absolute
"I" or pure consciousness, see e.g. *Grundlage der gesammten Wissenschaftslehre*
(Leipzig 1794, the edition C annotated) i
16–17. Here Fichte concludes that any system which bypasses the "I AM" necessarily
ends up in Spinozism, there being only two
consistent philosophies, the critical philosophy which acknowledges the boundaries
of the "I AM" and the Spinozistic philosophy which omits these boundaries. In a note
to "Philosophische Untersuchungen über
das Wesen der menschlichen Freyheit",
Philosophische Schriften (Landshut 1809)
416–17 (these pages not annotated; *SW* vii
348n–9n), Schelling mentions a review of
Fichte's writings by Friedrich Schlegel in
which Schlegel advises Fichte to "devote
himself to Spinoza in his polemical undertakings". Schelling finds this advice strange

given that (tr) "Mr Fichte is doubtless of the
opinion that he already refuted Spinozism
(qua Spinozism) in his *Wissenschaftslehre*,
in which his opinion is altogether correct."

4[3] At several points in the *Critique of
Pure Reason*, Kant praises Hume for having
pursued an issue further and with more success than other philosophers, although still
not far enough: *C d r V* B 19–20, 127,
773–4, and esp 788–97, which concludes,
"While, therefore, the sceptical procedure
cannot of itself yield any *satisfying* answer
to the questions of reason, none the less it
prepares the way by arousing reason to cir-
cumspection, and by indicating the radical
measures which are adequate to secure it
in its legitimate possessions" (tr Norman
Kemp Smith).

4[4] Not exactly, though C uses the same
phrase in *SM* (*CC*) 18 and *Friend* (*CC*) i
97. Paul's words, in Rom 1.17, Gal 3.11,
and Heb 10.38, are "The just shall live by
faith".

Wesens höchst unwürdig, höchst verdächtig. . . . . Ebenso war alle Treff-
lichkeit, Schönheit und Seligkeit menschlicher Natur völlig erschöpft in
der Pflichtmässigkeit und Sittlichkeit, ja diese war das einzige Reale der
Welt und des Menschen.

[Any belief in a divine being that went beyond the idea of a moral cosmic order was
to him an abomination, utterly unworthy of a rational being, highly suspect. . . . In the
same way all the excellence, beauty, and blessedness of human nature were for him
completely expressed in dutifulness and morality, and this was the sole reality of the
world and of man.]

So think I!—but in this O! what is not, that should *be*!

6   p 11 | *SW* vii 27

Indess das alles hat nun Herr Fichte einmal an sich gebracht, (sein eigner
Ausdruck): die göttliche Idee, die unmittelbare Erkenntniss des Absoluten, das selige Leben und die Liebe selber, und wir wenigstens sind
nicht gemeynt, ihm dieses Erwerbthum zu verkümmern. Vielmehr wir
freuen uns innig und aufrichtig, dass es ihm so gut geworden, diess alles
so weit zu erkennen; wir freuen uns, dass er die Hoffnung der Blöden zu
Schanden gemacht hat, da die meynten, er werde die Erkenntniss des
Göttlichen ferner, wie sie, läugnen, er werde statt des heitern und seligen
Gottes das finstre Götzenbild der Subjektivität und einer schnöden Moral
wieder auf den Thron heben; wir freuen uns jeder lebendigeren Idee,
jedes einzelnen Lautes ächter Wissenschaft bey ihm, und betrachten sie
als ein indirektes, äusseres Zeugniss der Wahrheit.

[Mr Fichte, however, has taken up these points himself. His own terms here are the
divine idea, immediate knowledge of the absolute, blessed life, and love itself. We certainly have no intention of detracting from his achievement. Instead we rejoice heartily
and sincerely that he has succeeded in gaining such insights. We rejoice that he has
overturned the hopes of fools who supposed that he would, like them, continue to deny
knowledge of the divine, and that he would set the sinister graven image of subjectivity and a rank morality on the throne in place of the serene and blessed God. We rejoice over every vital idea, every utterance of true knowledge that comes from him,
for we regard these as an indirect and external witness to truth.]

What is the meaning of all this? Can any thing be right and lovely, and
not included in the Ich soll?[1]

7   p 15, pencil | *SW* vii 30

Er giebt zu, dass Gott die Realität, die reine Wirklichkeit selbst ist: suche
er nun die Welt, oder die Sphäre, in der Gott die Wirklichkeit ist! Es wird

---

6[1] "I ought", the imperative of con-   between religion and morality.
science. C rejects Schelling's distinction

ihm wohl weder jetzt noch künftig eine andre Welt aufgehen, in der Gott noch ganz besonders die Wirklichkeit wäre, ausser eben der gegenwärtigen und so genannten wirklichen Welt . . .

[He admits that God is reality, pure actuality itself: let him now look for the world or sphere in which God is the actuality! He will surely not find any other world, either now or in the future, in which God is actual in a fuller sense than in the present and so-called real world . . .]

What means "Wirklichkeit"[1] here? The old Philosophy distinguished the Actual from the Real;[2] but in the later Germans I have never been able to translate their Realität Wirklichkeit[3] systematically

8   p 15, pencil, cropped | *SW* VII 30

Denkt er nur wirklich Gott, so denkt er ihn als das allein-Reale, das wesentlich selbst das *Seyn* ist. Gott kann daher nicht in der Gedanken-welt seyn, ohne eben darum das allein-Positive einer wirklichen oder Naturwelt zu seyn; und es ist in Ansehung seiner überhaupt kein Gegensatz einer idealen und realen Welt . . . . Wer das läugnet, mag wohl von einer Natur träumen, die nicht-ist, oder von einer Wirklichkeit, die nicht Wirklichkeit ist. Wie kommt er aber dazu, zu träumen, da er doch wachen sollte? . . . Ist also Philosophie Wissenschaft des Göttlichen als des allein-Positiven, so ist sie Wissenschaft des Göttlichen als des allein-Wirklichen in der wirklichen oder Natur-Welt, d.h. sie ist wesentlich Naturphilosophie.

Wäre sie nicht Naturphilosophie, so würde sie behaupten, dass Gott allein in der Gedankenwelt, also nicht das Positive der wirklichen oder Naturwelt sey, d.h. sie würde die Idee Gottes selbst aufheben.

[If he really thinks of God, he thinks of him as the sole reality, that is essence itself, *Being*. God cannot be in the world of ideas, therefore, without being the only positive of a real or natural world; and in this respect there is absolutely no opposition between the ideal and the real world . . . . Whoever denies this, however, may well dream of a nature that does not exist, or of a reality that is not reality. But how is it that he is dreaming, since he should be awake? . . . If philosophy is the science of the divine as the solely positive, then it is the science of the divine as the solely real in the real or natural world, i.e. it is essentially the philosophy of nature [*Naturphilosophie*].

If it were not *Naturphilosophie*, it would maintain that God exists only in the world

---

7[1] "Actuality", in textus.

7[2] I.e. Platonism and its descendants, which contrast an ideal realm with the realm of actual existence. Cf C's letter to James Gillman, Jr, written in a copy of *C&S*, on "the double Sense of the term, *Real, Real-*

ity": *C&S* (*CC*) 234.

7[3] To translate their "reality actuality". C would like to be able to translate *each* of them, *Realität* and *Wirklichkeit*, systematically as "reality" and "actuality", as he does in SCHELLING *Philosophische Schriften* 3.

of ideas and therefore is not the positive of the real or natural world, i.e. it would eliminate the idea of God itself.]

All that I read, refers me to the desideratum of a Critique on *Perception.* Idealism & Materialism both are ground[ed] on the assertion, that Perception is but the [? affection in modification].[1]

9   pp 21–2 | *SW* vii 34

Die Erkenntnis, die er von Gott hat, d.h. von dem, was allein das *Seyn* ist, ist eine Erkenntnis durch das blosse *Denken*, d.h. durch das allem Seyn, aller Wirklichkeit Entgegengesetzte. "Das Ewige kann allein durch den Gedanken ergriffen werden." . . . Das göttliche Leben ist im *wirklichen, unmittelbaren* Bewusstseyn unwiederbringlich *ausgetilgt* und kann nur in dem sich darüber erhebenden *Denken* wiederhergestellt werden.

[The knowledge which he has of God, i.e. of that which alone is *being*, is a knowledge acquired merely through *thinking*, i.e. through that which is opposite to all being and all reality. "The eternal can only be grasped by thought." . . . The divine life has been irretrievably *obliterated* in *actual, immediate* consciousness and can only be restored in *thought*, which rises above it.]

But still I ask, what did F. mean by "den Gedanken", and by "Ερgriffen?"[a1] Does it differ from what both He and Schelling entitle intellectual Intuition?[2] If Fichte ⟨do indeed⟩ assert, that all our knowlege of God is *mediate*, and that be the sense of "der Gedanke", then indeed there is an essential difference between them. But the words quoted do not quite convince me of this. I cannot but suspect, that by wirklichen, unmittelbaren Bewusssein,[b3] F. meant that which men ordinarily so call—& which Schelling calls ein absehen.[4] When two opinions are verbally in direct and *total* contrariety, I always begin to suspect, that they ⟨arguers⟩

9[a]   C uses a Greek *rho* for "r"   **9**[b]   A slip for "Bewusstsein"

8[1] See **1** and n 1, as well as C's complaint about a "gratuitous Assumption", in FICHTE *Bestimmung* 5, that what we call perception is "a mere consciousness of self-modification".

9[1] Schelling gives a page reference for the quotation from Fichte's *Anweisung zum seeligen Leben* (Berlin 1806); C is simply questioning terms from the quotation in the textus, "thought" and "grasped".

9[2] In German, *intellektuelle Anschauung*. With regard to this important concept,

C adopted the term in the "wider significATIon" associated with Fichte and Schelling, in opposition to Kant, and so defined "intellectual intuitions" as "all truths known to us without a medium": *BL* (*CC*) i 289* and n 1; cf PLATNER **16** n 4.

9[3] From textus: "actual, immediate consciousness".

9[4] "A seeing", i.e. an act of perception. Schelling uses the verb *absehen* and its derivatives in contrast to *anschauen*, for example *absehenden* in **16** textus below.

mean the same: as here—that what the one calls Denken, reine Denken, the other calls reine or intellektuelle Anschau⟨u⟩ng:[5] and vice versâ.

10   p 25 | *SW* vii 36

Ist doch die Natur noch der einzige Damm gegen die Willkühr des Denkens und die Freiheit der Abstraktion! Darein hatte nun Hr. Fichte von jeher wissenschaftlich eingestimmt, da auch ihm die Natur nie anders, denn als eine Schranke der freien Thätigkeit erschien, die uns überall im Wege ist; aber in der Bestimmung des Menschen ist dieser Hochmuth und wahnsinnige Dünkel der Erhabenheit über die Natur vollends heilig gesprochen.

[For nature is the only bulwark against arbitrariness of thought and freedom of abstraction! With this Mr Fichte's works have always been in agreement, since nature never appeared to him otherwise than as a barrier to free action, everywhere in our way; but in *Die Bestimmung des Menschen* this pride and insane arrogance of superiority over nature is pronounced holy without any reservation.]

I must confess that the §, alluded to here, always struck me as the maddest Bellow of Bull-frog Hyperstoicism, I ever met with under the name of Philosophy.[1]

11   p 33, pencil, rubbed, cropped | *SW* vii 42

Der Verstand ist eben auch die Vernunft und nichts anderes; nur die Vernunft in ihrer Nichttotalität, und er ist eben so nothwendig und ewig bey der Vernunft, als das Zeitliche überhaupt bey dem Ewigen ist und es begleitet. Der Verstand hat kein Leben für sich, sondern allein durch die Vernunft, nicht als ein unbiegsames, sondern als ein nachgiebiges Werkzeug derselben.

[The understanding is nothing other than reason, but not reason in its totality; for just as the temporal is in the eternal and necessarily accompanies it, so the understanding is necessary to reason and ever with it. The understanding has no life of its own, except through reason, of which it is not an inflexible but a pliant tool.]

What can [this] mean? I[f] Vern. & Ver[st.] be the sam[e] [? but/not] dif-

9[5] "Thought, pure thought" and "pure or intellectual intuition". For Schelling, intellectual intuition is always unmediated. When he defines it in *System des transcendentalen Idealismus* (Tübingen 1800—the ed annotated by C) 50–2 (*SW* iii 369–70), he cites Fichte for support.

10[1] C annotated *Die Bestimmung des Menschen* but did not on that occasion record such a reaction. He uses a similar phrase, "the hyper-tragic histrionic Stoicism borrowed from late Theories of the Greek Drama" in notes on K. W. F. Solger's *Erwin* (2 vols Berlin 1815): *SW & F* (*CC*) 597.

ferent, how can the former be the latter's Instrument?[1] The Schoolmen expressed this by the Intuitive and the Discursi[ve] Faculty./[2]

12 p 34, pencil, rubbed, cropped | *SW* VII 42

Alle Irrthümer des Verstandes entspringen aus einem Urtheil über die Dinge in der Nichttotalität gesehen. Zeige sie ihm in der Totalität und auch er wird begreifen, und seinen Irrthum erkennen.

[All errors of the understanding arise from a judgment about things not seen in their totality. Show them to the understanding in their totality and it too will understand and recognise its error.]

This is among the difficult parts of Schelling. Can the Reason (Vernunft) exist in different degrees in [t]he same [P]erson in [the] same [A]ct? Or ⟨now⟩ must [w]e conceive [it] as a Whole acting [a]s a Whole [? without] [the] Past act [? being] the same [. . . . .]

13 p 35 | *SW* VII 43

Du sagst z.B., die Ursache, durch welche irgend ein Körper in elektrischem Zustand ist, sey ein andrer Körper, mit dem er in Berührung getreten. Diess erklärt nichts. Denn durch welche Ursache hat nun wieder die Berührung des andern Körpers Elektricität erweckt? Der Körper ist Bedingung, Veranlassung der Erweckung, aber nicht ihre Ursache, und in's Unendliche kannst du die Reihe dieser Bedingungen verläugnenngern[a], ohne je zur wahren Ursache zu gelangen.

[You say, for example, that the cause of one body's being electrically charged is another body with which it has come into contact. This explains nothing. For through what cause has the contact with the other body produced electricity? The body is a condition or occasion of the charge, but not its cause, and you can extend the series of these conditions into infinity without ever attaining to the true cause.]

So said Spinoza, so Berkley[1]—but what does this mean more or other

13[a] C corrects a typographical error

11[1] "Vernunft & Verstand", "reason and understanding", in textus; but C has the relationship inverted.

11[2] On this point C liked to quote Milton *Paradise Lost* v 486–8, ". . . whence the soul / REASON receives. And reason is her *being*, / Discursive or intuitive": *BL* ch 13 (*CC*) I 295. See also *SM* (*CC*) 69.

13[1] C may have in mind Spinoza *Ethics* pt 1 prop 28 (tr Curley): "*Every singular thing*, or *any thing which is finite and has a* determinate existence, can neither exist nor be determined to produce an effect unless it is determined to exist and produce an effect by another cause, which also is finite and has a determinate existence; and again, this cause also can neither exist nor be determined to produce an effect unless it is determined to exist and produce an effect by another, which also is finite and has a determinate existence, and so on, to infinity." See also props 24–7, esp 25, for the view

than the Schoolman's occasional caus[e]² and who ever supposed that a *thing* any but God & Spirit, could be a cause in any other sense, than as— the Phænom[enon] A would not be if B. had not been?

14   p 36, cropped | *SW* VII 43

Jede wahre Ursache ist also unmittelbar erste Ursache und da diess von allem Wirkenden gilt, so ist im Grunde *nichts* Ursache, weil nichts Wirkung, alles gleich absolut, ist, und das Gesetz vernichtet sich selbst.

[Every true cause is therefore an immediate first cause and since this is the case for everything that produces an effect, *nothing* basically is a cause because nothing is an effect; everything is equally absolute, and the law destroys itself.]

The more I think, the less can I see any essential difference between Schelling & Kant. Who ever mean by Cause any more than such [a] cor-res[p]ondence [b]etween two Phænomena, that [A] + B = C. Sch. seems to talk as [i]f by Cause [w]ere meant *Creation.*

15   p 45 | *SW* VII 49

Jene einfache Zeit ist nicht mehr, wo die Kantische Scholastik, zwar mit bleiernem Zepter aber doch sanft einwiegend, die Köpfe beherrschte und das Andenken alles Lebendigen in der Wissenschaft verdrängte.

[Those simple times are now gone when Kantian scholasticism reigned over all minds with a leaden sceptre, yet also softly lulled the mind and displaced from memory all that was vital in science.]

Would either Fichte or Schelling have existed as Writers, but for the Kantean Scholastic?[1]

16   pp 67–8 | *SW* VII 63–4

Zuvörderst diese Ansicht lehrt: dass wir recht eigentlich die Dinge an sich anschauen, ja dass diese das einzig Anschaubare sind, keineswegs aber

---

that God is the ultimate cause of the existence and essence of things. For Berkeley's view that causality does not reside in natural phenomena such as figure, weight, motion or other sensible qualities but must be found in "the will of a spirit", see *A Treatise Concerning the Principles of Human Knowledge* esp §§ 64–6, 102–8: *B Works* II 68–70, 85–9.

13[2] Various degrees of what was later called occasionalism have been identified in the Schoolmen. A work with which C

was familiar, J. J. Brucker *Historia critica philosophiae* (6 vols Leipzig 1766–7) III 184–5, declares that in claiming that God was the sole active cause of all things, the Arabs had already anticipated the followers of Descartes in inventing a system of occasional causes.

15[1] C defends Kant against his detractors in a similar way in SOLGER **6**: "What since Kant is not in Kant as a Germ at least?"

das was nicht an-sich ist, als welches bloss gedacht oder imaginirt wird. Eben aus diesem Grunde läugnet sie alle Erkenntniss *a priori*, schlechthin und durchaus; denn was von Kant und Fichte so benannt worden, näm- lich die angebliche Erkenntniss durch Verstandsbegriffe ist ihr keine nothwendige, sondern eine bloss angenommene und wieder abzulegende Denk- und Betrachtungsweise, die nicht einmal im Subjekt einen ab- soluten Grund hat, und lediglich das Produkt eines von dem Wahren ab- sehenden d.h. nicht-anschauenden Denkens ist. Die Vernunfterkenntniss ist aber auch kein Erkenntniss *a priori*; denn für diese existirt nichts, zu dem sie sich als das *Prius* verhalten könnte. Das *Posterius* müsste die Wirklichkeit seyn . . .

[First of all, this view teaches that we really intuit things in themselves and that these are all that we can intuit; we never intuit that which is not in-itself, i.e. what is merely thought or imagined. For that very reason this view denies all *a priori* knowledge, sim- ply and absolutely; for that which was called so by Kant and Fichte, that is, alleged knowledge by means of concepts of the understanding, is in this view not a necessary but merely an assumed point of view which can be laid aside again. It does not even have an absolute basis in the subject, but is simply the product of a thinking that does not take in the true, that is, of a non-intuiting thinking. But neither is the knowledge that originates in the reason an *a priori* knowledge, since nothing exists for it to which it could stand *prior*. The *posterior* must be reality . . .]

I vehemently suspect a play on words here [—]*a* that which the one calls Seeing, Sensuality the other calls Thinking, Fancying—yet both mean the same.[1] Does Schelling pretend [to]*b* have no consciousness of Quantity, Quality, Relation, Mode?

Besides, K. has repeatedly explained that a priori has no relation to Time; but = a mente ipsâ.[2]

17   p 105 | *SW* vii 87

Nicht zu vergessen, dass selbst da, wo, wie er sagt, das göttliche Seyn "ungetrübt durch irgend eine in der Selbständigkeit des Ich liegende und eben darum beschränkende Form hervortritt" doch die unzerstörbare Form der unendlichen Mannichfaltigkeit (mit dieser auch der unend- lichen Zeit) ausdrücklich ausgenommen wird; in *diese bleibt* das gött- liche Seyn auch dann noch gebrochen, denn sie ist eine im wirklichen Be- wusstseyn nie aufzulösende oder zu endende Form.

16*a* Edge of page worn away   **16***b* Edge of page worn away

16[1] Verbal misunderstanding is a re- peated theme in these notes: cf **9** above.
16[2] "From the mind itself". C is correct in insisting that Kant's *a priori* has nothing to do with priority in time. He makes this point also in NICOLAI **17** and in *BL* ch 12 (*CC*) i 293*.

Gleich vorn im seligen Leben, (S. 6), findet sich folgendes: "Nicht im Seyn an und für sich liegt der Tod, sondern im tödtenden Blicke des todten Beschauers." So, sprach ich zu mir selbst, begreife ich nun, wie die Naturphilosophie das Todte (das sie gar nicht kennt) vergöttern kann. Hr. Fichte schiesst in den Grundzügen gar ergrimmte Blicke nach ihr: diese mögen wohl die obige Wirkung, die Eigenschaft des Basiliskenblicks gehabt, und das lebendige Seyn in ihr in ein todtes verkehrt haben.

[It should not be forgotten that even when, as he [Fichte] says, divine being "emerges unclouded by any form which, due to the independence of the ego, would be limiting," the ineradicable form of the infinite manifold (including infinite time) is still made an explicit exception; even then, divine being *remains* broken in *this form* which, belonging to actual consciousness, can never be dissolved or brought to an end.

Right at the beginning of the *Blessed Life* (p 6) is a passage that reads, "Death is found not in being in and for itself, but in the killing glance of the dead observer." At last, I said to myself, now I understand how *Naturphilosophie* is able to idolise what is dead (without even recognising it). In *The Foundations* Mr Fichte casts angry glances in the direction of *Naturphilosophie*, and these glances have no doubt had the effect already indicated: like the gaze of the basilisk, they have turned its living being into something dead.]

Forced Wit and out of place. Surely, Fichte is entitled to ask, Have *you* acquired the power of not seeming to see what you call spots, shadows, nothings? If you answer—"I know them to be only such," F. would reply—So do I! but I write not for my possible future, but for the imperfect Present. The "ineradicable" he might so explain—i.e. durante Peccato.[1]

18　　pp 110–12 | *SW* vii 90n–1n

[Footnote:] Er [Fichte] führt an: . . . b) *Dass ich dieses vom Bewusstseyn unabhängige Reale erst in der Intelligenz durchbrechen lasse zum Bewusstseyn.*—Hierauf liegt die Antwort schon im Vorhergehenden. Wenn das von allem subjektiven Bewusstseyn unabhängige, mit ihm gar nicht in Gegensatz zu bringende, mit Einem Wort durchaus absolute und von sich selbst seyende Seyn—oder Gott—wesentlich ein Selbstbejahen ist: so kann wohl mit tieferem Grunde, als Hr. Fichte einzusehn vermag, behauptet werden, dass diese göttliche Selbstbejahung in der Intelligenz zu der Form der Selbstbejahung durchbreche, die sich als persönliches Bewusstseyn durch das: Ich bin, ausspricht, und die Hr. Fichte sonst als das Höchste im ganzen Universum betrachtet hat.

[He [Fichte] states . . . b) *that I let that which is real and independent of consciousness break through to consciousness only in the intelligence.*—The answer to this is

17[1] "As long as the Sin continues". "Ineradicable" is from textus.

already contained in the preceding. If the being that is independent of all subjective consciousness and cannot be brought into opposition with it, in a word the completely absolute being existing out of itself—or God—if this being is essentially a self-affirmation, then one can assert, with deeper reason than Mr Fichte can appreciate, that this divine self-affirmation breaks through in the intelligence to that form of self-affirmation which is expressed as personal consciousness in the "I am", which Mr Fichte has otherwise regarded as the highest thing in the whole universe.]

This convinces me, that Schelling's System does not essentially differ from the Spirit of Kant: i.e. from Kant as Schelling himself interpreted him in his "Ich", his Letters, &c[1]—tho' even then I felt his Difference from the Wissenschaftlehre,[a2] of which he then believed himself the Ali,[3] tho' he was in truth what certain Writers have falsely represented St *Paul* to have been, i.e. the *Founder* of a new & truly universal Religion in the guise of a *Commentator*.—How much more amiable, were Schelling's then reverential Expressions concerning *Kant*; and the sharp contrast, he then religiously preserved, of Kant with the Kantian Textualists![4] I cannot endure these *Slights* on Kant; but for whom Schelling himself would not have been Schelling! and from Fichte they are quite abominable.[5]

19   pp 118–19, cropped | *SW* vii 95–6

Wir haben behauptet, und behaupten als eine bewiesene Sache, dass die Welt als ungebrochen und farblos nicht nur zu denken, sondern in der That zu schauen ist und wirklich geschaut wird; so wie wir auch in der Farbe nicht eigentlich die Finsterniss, sondern eben das Licht sehen und nur mittelst desselben sein Gegentheil bemerken . . .

[We have asserted, and assert as a proven point, that the world is not only to be thought of as unbroken and colourless, but in fact is to be seen as such and really is seen that

18^a A slip for "Wissenschaftslehre"

18[1]   C refers to *Vom Ich als Prinzip der Philosophie* and *Philosophische Briefe über Dogmatismus und Kriticismus*, the first two titles contained in Vol I—the only vol published—of Schelling's *Philosophische Schriften* (Landshut 1809), which C annotated and to which he refers ("his collected Tracts") in *BL* ch 9 (*CC*) I 164.
18[2]   C appears to mean Fichte's "theory of knowledge" in its entirety, and not merely a particular work with the word in its title (though he annotated one of them, the *Grundlage* of 1794). In *BL* ch 9 (*CC*) I 157–60 he outlines what seemed to him to

be the strengths and weaknesses of what he there called "Fichte's Wissenschaftslehre, or *Lore* of Ultimate Science".
18[3]   I.e. the faithful disciple and spokesman. Ali ben Abu Talib (c 600–61) was adopted and educated by Mahomet, married his daughter Fatima, and eventually succeeded him as the fourth of the caliphs. C applies the name to John Elliotson in *SW & F* (*CC*) 904.
18[4]   E.g. in *Philosophische Schriften* x–xi, 28, 69 (*SW* I 154–5, 181, 210).
18[5]   Cf **15** and n 1 above.

way, just as we do not truly see the darkness in the colour, but see the light, and only notice its opposite by means of it . . .]

Still does [a]ll this [a]ppear to [m]e a mere [P]lay on [the] word, ["S]eeing." [G]ranted, [fo]r instance, [th]at in the [g]reen Fields & Woods the colourless Light is the sole positive, yet surely [t]hat Light so modified is distinguished, [a]s green. Do I not feel the Frost, tho' [the] sole positive be Heat? Is there no sense [of] the Plus and Minus?—But bemerken for sehen[1]—& the whole difference is a[t] an end, ως εμοιγε δοκει.[2]   S. T. Coleri[dge]

20   p 121 | *SW* vii 97

Hr. Fichte hat sich nun auch eine solche todte und unendlich gebrochne Welt *erdacht*; wollte er behaupten dass sie für ihn *wirklich* ist, so müsste er behaupten, dass er sehen kann und sieht, was nicht ist und nicht seyn kann, d.h. er müsste behaupten auch der *Sinn* sey in ihm zum Wahn, also zum *Wahn*-Sinn geworden.

[Mr Fichte too has now *made up* just such a dead and infinitely broken world; if he were to assert that it is *real* for him, then he would have to assert that he can see and does see that which is not and cannot be, i.e. he would have to assert that *sense* too had become a delusion in him, and hence had become *non*-sense.]

This "WAHN-*Sinn*"[1] is among the many untranslatable Words, which (in the innocent sense of "envy") I envy the Germans. I mean to make a catalogue of them. Anmuth[2] is another.

21   pp 125–6 | *SW* vii 100

So, um uns wenigstens durch Ein Beyspiel deutlich zu machen, hat die Physik über den Hergang im chemischen Process erst seitdem Wissenschaft erlangt, als sie erkannt hat, dass das in der chemischen Erscheinung eigentlich *Seyende* nicht die Materie als solche, das Verbundene als das Verbundene ist, sondern das lebendige Band, oder die Kopula der beyden Elektricitäten.*

[Thus, in order to make it clear by at least one example, physics was able to give a scientific account of the course of events in a chemical process only when it recognised that what really *exists* in a chemical phenomenon is not matter as such, the composition as compounded, but the living bond or the copula of the two electricities.*]

* Well, if so it were: and so I hoped, it would have been when Sir H. Davy adopted my suggestion that all Composition consisted in the Bal-

---

19[1] I.e. substitute "to notice" for "to see".

19[2] "As it seems to me, at least".

20[1] "Delusion" or "madness" ("*non*-sense" in textus tr).

20[2] "Charm" or "grace".

ance of opposing Energies.[1] But alas! this still doubtful Copula of the neg. and pos. Electricities is a mere plausible Datum[2] for Hope as ~~if~~ the union of two or more in a third/ but has not thrown a ray of Light on Iron as Iron, Gold as Gold—Hitherto, it has merely de-elemented x to introduce y, as inexplicable as x.—

21[1] C's relationship with HD is outlined in ANNUAL ANTHOLOGY **16A** n 1, and the history of his attentive following of HD's success as a scientist is given in Levere 20–35. In PLATNER **9**, C declares that HD's strength consists in his having grasped the idea that "all combination mental & physical subsists in a balance of opposing Energies". Similar remarks appear elsewhere in C's writings, but he does not elsewhere claim to have been the source of the idea.

21[2] A something "given"; a premise or presupposition.

Denkmal der Schrift von den göttlichen Dingen &c. des Herrn Friedrich Heinrich Jacobi und der ihm in derselben gemachten Beschuldigung eines absichtlich täuschenden, Lüge redenden Atheismus. Tübingen 1812. 8°.

British Library C 126 f 8(1), bound first with SCHELLING *Philosophie und Religion* and *Ueber die Gottheiten von Samothrace*.

"S. T. C." label on verso of title-page. The pencil notes are badly rubbed, and many of them have been cropped in rebinding. A few notes (both pencil and ink) that are contained within the present margins may have been written after the cropping took place.

DATE. Late 1816 to early 1817 (C had the *Denkmal* in his hands by Aug 1816—*CL* IV 663—and **10** is dated 27 Feb 1817); and later undated additions.

COEDITOR. Raimonda Modiano.

1   p $^-$2

In addition to the harsh quarrelsome and vindictive Spirit that displays itself in this Denkmal, there is a Jesuitical dishonesty in various parts that makes me dread almost to think of Schelling. I remember no man of any thing like his Genius & intellectual Vigor so serpentine & unamiable. To give one instance—his exaltation of the Understanding over the Reason. What Understanding? That of which Jacobi had spoken?[1] No such thing! But an understanding *enlightened*[2]—in other words, the whole Man spiritually regenerated. There is doubtless much true and acute observation on the indefinite&ness, the golden mists, of Jacobi's Scheme—but it is so steeped in Gall, as to repel one from it—And then the Fancy is unlithesome & wooden-jointed in the wilful open-eyed *Dream*—and the Wit, the Would-be-Smile, sardonic throughout. *Dry* Humor with a vengeance!—

[1] Schelling's work was written in response to the attack on *Naturphilosophie* in Jacobi *Von den göttlichen Dingen und ihrer Offenbarung* (Leipzig 1811). Jacobi defined the understanding (*Verstand*) in opposition to the reason (*Vernunft*), understanding belonging to the realm of temporality and materiality (Jacobi 34–5, 177–82); Schelling asserted on the contrary that the understanding was a gift of God (138) and that the elevation of reason over understanding was a major error (140). Though it is arguably confusing or even misleading to persist in translating these terms as "understanding" and "reason", we have opted for consistency in this case.

[2] C is quoting Schelling's own phrase from p 144: cf **18** textus below.

2   pp 2–3, pencil | *SW* VIII 23–4

[Quoting Jacobi:] "Als vor zwölf Jahren die leibliche Tochter der kritischen Philosophie, die Wissenschaftslehre, behauptete, die moralische
Weltordnung allein sey Gott: da erregte diese Behauptung doch! *noch
einiges Aufsehen*" . . . . Aber . . . "kurz darauf die *zweyte* Tochter der kritischen Philosophie . . . die von der ersten noch stehen gelassene Unter-
scheidung zwischen Natur- und Moralphilosophie, Nothwendigkeit und
Freyheit vollends, d.h. auch *namentlich* aufhob." . . . "Es erregte nämlich
diese auch namentliche Aufhebung *schon gar kein Staunen mehr*".
S. 117. 118.

Es ist schwer zu sagen, was nach der Meynung dieser pragmatischen
Erzählung dem Urheber der zweyten Lehre nach Kant hätte geschehen
müssen, um das *Staunen* über seine Unternehmung mit dem *Aufsehen*,
das die Fichte'sche veranlasste, in einiges Verhältniss zu setzen. Zum
wenigsten musste er doch von Amt und Stelle verjagt werden. Es
geschah—leider, nicht. Der Erzähler bezeugt, dass er an dieser Gleich-
gültigkeit keinen Theil hat. Er wäscht seine Hände—in Unschuld.

["Twelve years ago the very daughter of critical philosophy, the theory of knowledge,
stated that the moral cosmic order is God alone, a statement which *caused quite a sensation*" . . . . But . . . "shortly afterwards the *second* daughter of critical philosophy
[appeared] . . . and utterly, i.e. *explicitly*, cancelled the distinction which the first had
left in place, the distinction between natural and moral philosophy, necessity and freedom." . . . "This explicit cancellation, then, *no longer caused any astonishment*."
P. 117. 118.

It is difficult to say what, according to the opinion of this pragmatic account, should
have been done to the author of the second theory after Kant, in order that the *astonishment* regarding his undertaking might be made comparable to the *sensation* caused
by Fichte's theory. At the least he should have been driven from his office and position. This, unfortunately, did not happen. The writer testifies that he had no part in this
carelessness. He washes his hands of it.]

In what a *moody* state of passion Schelling began and ended this Denkmal, is clear from the special Pleading Tricks in the 2nd and 3rd page: in
which the sensation excited in the philosophic world is maliciously transmuted into civil persecution.

3   p 6, pencil | *SW* VIII 25

[Quoting from his own *Darstellung meines Systems der Philosophie*
(114):] "Wir verstehen unter *Natur* die absolute Identität, so fern sie nicht
als *seyend, sondern als Grund ihres eignen Seyns* betrachtet wird." Hier
wird die *seyende* absolute Identität von der nicht-*seyenden, die nur
Grund* (in meiner Sprache so viel als Grundlage) ihrer Existenz ist, unter-

schieden, und die letzte *allein* als Natur erklärt. Ich behaupte also, die *Natur* sey die (noch) nicht *seyende* (bloss objektive) abs. Identität. . . . Da ferner das Seyende allgemein *über* dem Seyn muss, was nur Grund (Grundlage) seiner Existenz ist, so ist offenbar, dass . . . die *seyende* abs. Identität, (Gott im eminenten Verstand, Gott als *Subjekt*), über der Natur, als der nicht-*seyenden*—bloss *objektiven*—abs. Identität gesetzt wird.

["By *nature* we understand an absolute identity, insofar as it is regarded not as *existing, but as the ground of its own existence.*" Here, the *existing* absolute identity is distinguished from the non-*existing one, which is only the ground* (in my language the same as "basis") of its existence, and the latter *alone* is defined as nature. I therefore assert that *nature* is the not (yet) *existing* (merely objective) absolute identity. . . . Furthermore, since the existing must generally be *above* being, which is only the ground (basis) of its existence, it is obvious that . . . the *existing* absolute identity (God understood *eminently*, God as *subject*) is posited *above* nature, as the non-*existing*— merely *objective*—absolute identity.]

What but words are won by this distinction? The World, as the aggregate of Particulars and Individuals, is *it* or is it not distinguished from Nature der nicht-seyende?[1] If not, the position is nonsense. If it be, then the World according to Schelling is God—and ["]über ihr sey nichts."[2]

4   p 63, pencil | *SW* VIII 54

* Der Erste, dem auf dem Wege reiner Vernunftforschung als die alles versöhnende Lösung des grossen Räthsels der Gedanke in die Seele sprang, dass ein persönliches Wesen Urheber und Lenker der Welt seyn möge, war davon unstreitig wie von einem Wunder gerührt, und in das höchste Erstaunen versetzt. Es war nicht nur ein kühner, es war schlechthin der kühnste aller Gedanken. Wie durch diesen erst alles menschlich wurde, so hatte der erste Finder (wenn es je einen solchen gab) von jenem persönlichen Wesen sicher eine ganz menschliche Vorstellung.

[* It must undoubtedly have been a moment of great astonishment and an experience, as it were, of the miraculous, when, in the course of purely rational investigations, the idea was first conceived that would solve the great riddle, the idea that a personal being might be the originator and ruler of the world. It was not only a daring idea; it was absolutely the most daring of all ideas. In the same way as it made everything human, so the first finder of it (if ever there was such a person) certainly had an entirely human concept of that personal being.]

* Bring together all the words *underlined*: and does not this first § become a romance founded on contradictions?

[1] Nature "the non-existing", from textus.

[2] A phrase from Jacobi 118, quoted by Schelling (4): "above it there is nothing".

5   p 66 | *SW* viii 55–6

Zu sehr ist in unserer Zeit der wissenschaftliche Geist angeregt, als dass sich eine solche, den Menschen entadelnde Lehre mit der offenen Freyheit, wie noch vor Kurzem, ankündigen dürfte. Selbst Herr Jacobi, dessen Jubel über das vermeynte schmähliche Ende der Wissenschaft durch Fichte keine Gränze kannte, fühlt, dass es zum Beweis einer solchen Meynung noch etwas mehr als seiner blossen Versicherung bedarf. . . . Hr. Jacobi versichert uns, Kant habe die Unmöglichkeit, zu einer wissenschaftlichen Einsicht von Gott und göttlichen Dingen zu gelangen, *unwiderleglich* dargethan (S. 115.). Was soll uns diese Versicherung? Sie heisst entweder soviel: die Vordersätze, die Schlüsse, durch welche Kant zu jener Folge gelangte, sey'n unwiderleglich . . . . Oder, sie besagt nur soviel: das Kantische Resultat sey unwiderleglich, wenn auch nicht die Kantischen Gründe. In diesem Fall ist sie nichts als eine Wiederholung der eignen Versicherung unter anderer Form, oder ein Versuch durch den grossen Namen Kants sich selber zu ermuthigen.

[The scientific spirit is too much stimulated nowadays for the kind of teaching that debases human beings to be promulgated with the same openness as it was a little while ago. Even Mr Jacobi, whose exultation about the supposed ignominious end of science at the hands of Fichte knew no bounds, feels that something more than simple assertions are needed as a proof of such an opinion. . . . Mr Jacobi assures us that Kant has demonstrated *irrefutably* the impossibility of achieving a scientific insight into God and divine things (p 115). What does this assurance mean? Either it means that the premises and inferences by which Kant arrived at his conclusion are irrefutable . . . . Or it merely means that the Kantian result is irrefutable, even if the Kantian grounds are not. In this case it is no more than a repetition of his [Jacobi's] own assertion in a different form, or an attempt to cheer himself by invoking the great name of Kant.]

Schelling uses the word "*scientific*" *wissenschaftlich*, in a different sense from Kant, and on this artifice grounds his pretended superiority over him.[1]

5[1] For Kant the term "science" (*Wissenschaft*) or "scientific" (*wissenschaftlich*) pertains exclusively to a system of knowledge derived from *a priori* concepts whose certainty is absolute as opposed to empirical knowledge based on sense experience. In his *Critique of Pure Reason* Kant argues that metaphysics can become a science and defeat dogmatism only by first undertaking a rigorous critique of reason which leads to the recognition that reason cannot provide theoretical (i.e. scientific) knowledge of God or of related transcendental ideas. The term *Wissenschaft* for Kant also implies a system that is a self-subsistent and complete unity based on a principle that must answer "all the questions to which it itself gives birth" (tr Kemp Smith 10). As early as 1794 Schelling began to explore the meaning of the term *Wissenschaft*, most notably in his essay "Ueber die Möglichkeit einer Form der Philosophie". Like Kant, Schelling claims that philosophy can aspire to the status of science only if it develops a system of

6   p 69, pencil, cropped | *SW* viii 57

[Quoting Jacobi:] "Allemal und nothwendig ist *ja* der Beweisgrund *über* dem, was durch ihn bewiesen werden soll; er *begreift* es *unter* sich, aus ihm fliessen Wahrheit und Gewissheit auf das zu Beweisende erst herab, es trägt seine Realität von ihm zum Lehn." . . . *Diesem Axiom gemäss wird künftig die Zahl 3 für höher als die Zahl 9 angesehen werden; denn die Zahl 9 bedarf der Zahl 3 zu ihrem Erweis, sie trägt ihre Realität von dieser zum Lehn; 3 ist also mehr wie 9 und alle aus ihr folgenden Potenzen.

["The ground of proof is indeed always and necessarily *above* that which is to be proved; it *includes* the latter *beneath* itself; only from it do truth and certainty flow to that which is to be proved; the latter holds its reality in fee from it." . . . *In accordance with this axiom, the number 3 will in future be regarded as higher than the number 9; for the 9 requires the number 3 for its proof, it holds its reality in fee from it. Therefore 3 is more than 9 and all powers arising out of it.]

Schelli[ng] seems h[ere] to conf[use] the mo[de] or for[m] [of] Demons[tration] with the [Proof], die Bewei[s-]weise [mit] dem [Be]weisgr[und.]
   * This seems to me a mere Sophism: a[nd] Schelling himself on any other occasion would have repelled it. the Idea of On[e] and then that ⟨of⟩ III as the ⟨first⟩ manifestation[—]the One not as barren abstraction but as a [. . . . .]

7   p 80, pencil, badly rubbed, cropped | *SW* viii 63

[Quoting Jacobi, who outlines an argument in favour of the idea that perfection may arise out of imperfection:] "Denn so sehen wir täglich, dass aus einem Unwissenden durch Bildung und Entwicklung ein Wissender werde; der Mann sich aus sich selber als Jüngling, der Jüngling aus sich selber als Knaben, und dieser wieder aus sich selber als Kind, welches doch lauter unvollkommnere Zustände sind, emporarbeite."

["For we see daily how an ignorant person becomes knowledgeable by means of education and development; the man works his way up from his youth, the youth from his boyhood, and the boy from his childhood—which are, after all, in each case less perfect conditions."]

[A]ye! but—[fi]rst a [B]aby [G]od? A [B]oy God? [A] Youth, [a] Man?

---

logically connected propositions and becomes a self-subsistent unity. But unlike Kant, for whom reason alone can guarantee the systematic unity that science calls for, Schelling, like Fichte, attributes this function to the absolute ego. Furthermore, while for Kant the absolute is unavailable to rational cognition, for Schelling it is fully available to intellectual intuition.

[W]hy not [an] old man?—then [a ? deity] [a]nd still a God [. . .] [? would . . . ever effect.]¹

8   pp 80–1, pencil, badly rubbed, cropped | *SW* VIII 63–4

[Quoting Jacobi:] "*Nothwendig* muss nämlich das Allervollkommenste— dasjenige, welches die Vollkommenheit aller Dinge in sich hat—*vor allen Dingen* seyn; die Frage ist aber, ob es *als* das Allervollkommenste zuerst war, welches schwer zu glauben ist . . ."

["For the most perfect one—that which has in itself the perfection of all things—must *necessarily* exist *before all things*; the question is, however, whether it existed first *as* the most perfect, which is hard to believe . . ."]

* But what can Zu erst¹ mean, applied to an eternal Being? I am really giddy in [? attempting] [. . . . .]

9   p 81, pencil, badly rubbed, cropped | *SW* VIII 64

[Quoting Jacobi:] "Wie, wenn jemand . . . der sagt, dass Newton der voll- kommenste Geometer ist, damit nicht behauptet haben will, dass er es schon als Kind gewesen, und doch auch nicht läugnet, dass *der Newton, welcher* das Kind war, eben der *Newton* ist, *welcher* der vollkommenste Geometer ist."

["Just as when someone . . . who says that Newton is the most perfect geometrician does not mean to assert by this that he was so even as a child; nor does he deny that *the Newton who* was the child is the same *Newton who* is the most perfect geometri- cian."]

But [what] is thi[s?] a sel[f-]*caus*[ing] Being[?] Newt[on] did n[ot] make him[self]. I should have understood it at on[ce]: to wit, that the man was applyin[g] the phantom Beginning, & the Relative, Priority, to the [? su- perior] Reality in Whom, not for whose [. . . . .]

10   pp 82–3, pencil, cropped | *SW* VIII 64

[Quoting Jacobi:] "Wie wenn man z.B. sagte, des eigentlichen Wesens Art bestehe in Liebe und Güte, * so könne die von dem Wesen unzer- trennliche, ja von ihm gewissermassen vorausgesetzte *Natur* des Wesens nicht auch in Güte und Weisheit bestehen, weil sonst kein Unterschied wäre; in ihr müsse also ein Mangel, wenigstens selbstbewusster Güte und Weisheit, oder sie müsse blosse Stärke seyn."

7¹ Jacobi's analogy is intended to sup- port the idea of growth or development even in God; cf **8** and **9** below.

8¹ "First"—in textus.

["As if one said, for example, that the quality of actual being consisted in love and goodness* and that therefore the *nature* of being, which is inseparable from being, and is even to a certain extent presupposed by it, could not also consist in goodness and wisdom, because otherwise there would be no distinction; in it [the nature] there had therefore to be a lack, at least of self-conscious goodness and wisdom, or it [the nature] had to be mere strength."]

Might not the same be said with equal reason of Love and Wisdom that Love must at least be negative Folly—Wisdom a defect of Love? [It] is not my *Nature* that is darksome a[nd] chaotic but my confused perceptions [of] my Nature. Schelling makes separati[on] in God—and not distinction only.[1] If [it] be abs[urd] to cal[l] God Wisd[om,] streng[th,] or we[. . .] surely [it] is equ[ally] so to c[all] his Stre[ngth] unwi[se] *or bli[nd] also*? warum Weder dieses noch jenes sonde[rn] gleich und gleich *ewig*—oder *bild*lich—anthropomorphisch zu sprechen, gleichzeitig.[2]

S. T. Coleridge

27 Feby 1817.	Third [? perusal]

11	p 85, pencil, cropped | **10** textus

After all, I am, after a *fifth* re-perusal, inclined to think that the Bug-bear is only in the Hi[. . .] nay, to suspect that Schelling ha[s] [. . . . .]

12	p 123, pencil, cropped | *SW* viii 87–8

Denn obwohl ein philosophischer Staat nie, auch entschiedne Gottesläugner verfolgen wird, (weil aller Glaubenszwang unvernünftig) so könnten doch nach meiner Ueberzeugung Menschen, welche mit dem Namen Gott nur *Spiel* und *Betrug* trieben, unmöglich öffentlicher Aemter fähig gehalten werden . . .

[For although a philosophical state will never persecute even decided atheists (because all compulsion of belief is unreasonable) yet, according to my convictions, people who do nothing but *play* with the name of God and use it *fraudulently* could not possibly be held capable of holding public positions . . .]

10[1] The concept of distinction without separation or division was important to C, as e.g. in *Friend* (*CC*) I 177*. JHG contributed a pamphlet to debate about reform in the medical profession with a relevant title: *Distinction without Separation: A Letter on the Present State of the Profession* (1831). Cf, on the general issue, C's view that Schelling and the *Naturphilosophen* introduce polarity in the absolute: *CL* IV 874 (which includes a comment on *Denkmal*), *CN* III 4449, and OKEN *Lehrbuch der Naturphilosophie* 3.

10[2] "Then why Neither this nor that but both and both *eternal*—or, speaking *figura*tively and anthropomorphically, simultaneous". C's "Weder . . . noch" may be echoing the phrasing of a passage from Jacobi quoted in a footnote (82): "Von sich selbst übt die Natur weder Weisheit noch Güte aus, sondern überall nur Gewalt" ("Nature in itself exhibits neither wisdom nor goodness, but everywhere power").

But who is to *prove* that the man mit dem Namen Gott nur SPIEL und BE-TRUG trieben?[1] And is it from *Schelling* that we are to hear of an *Oath* and other appeals to ~~the~~ Invisibles grounded o[n] [. . . . .][2]

13 pp 124–5, pencil, cropped | *SW* VIII 88

Hier hat die öffentliche Meynung ein *Recht*, die offenste unumwundendste Erklärung zu fodern, damit nicht entweder ein Unwürdiger das Vertrauen, welches ihm der Charakter eines wissenschaftlichen Mannes erwirbt, missbrauche, oder der Andre, welcher das Mittel einer so frevelhaften Verläumdung angewendet, durch die öffentliche Impunität ein einladendes Beyspiel zu ähnlichem Frevel für andre werde, und auf solche Art öffentliche Skandale, anstatt verhindert und gemindert, vielmehr befördert und vermehrt werden.

[Here, public opinion has the *right* to demand the most open, frank explanation in order that it should not happen either that an unworthy man should misuse the trust gained through a reputation for learning, or that another, who has used the means of so outrageous a defamation, should become an example to others, inviting them to similar outrage because of public impunity, and in this way public scandals, instead of being prevented and lessened, should rather be furthered and increased.]

[? W]here [? sho]uld this [? sto]p? Not [to] mention [the] silly [. . . .]ction involved: f[o]r if [. . .] Oath & the Voice of conscience are [pr]esumably inefficient in such a man, [. . .] what can the *Fodern*,[1] the Demand, effect? How can "the openest most unravelled Explanation"[2] be relied on? [. . . . .] developed of the anti-creation philosophy, and the assertion (attributed to Plato)[3] of a not good, and often intractable Infinite prior actu et tempore[4] the Finite Measure and Ordonnan[ce . . .][5]

12[1] *"Play* with the name of God and use it *fraudulently"*—from textus.

12[2] I.e. grounded on the name of God. Schelling goes on, on p 124, to justify his position on the grounds that an unbeliever could not be expected to consider an oath sacred.

13[1] "Demand", in textus .

13[2] C's translation of "die offenste unumwundenste Erklärung", from textus.

13[3] The attribution of an "anti-creation philosophy" to Plato (an attribution made by Schelling pp 96–7 and echoed by C in BÖHME 31 at n 7) may be supported by such passages as *Timaeus* 29B–30A and 53A–B in the "probable account" put into the mouth of a Pythagorean that the Creator (a subordinate deity) gave order to preexistent

unformed matter.

13[4] Prior "in act and in time". Plato, however, clearly states (*Timaeus* 37E–38D) that time began only with the heavens. C took the same view: cf BÖHME 165 and ETERNAL PUNISHMENT 18 and n 2 for "the timeless" and "time without time".

13[5] Although the gaps in the ms make C's position uncertain, it appears that he is criticising Schelling's "Explanation" of Jacobi. Schelling quotes from Jacobi's summary of Plato (tr), "Do not call God infinite Being, says Plato, for existence is opposed to the infinite . . .". The original passage in Jacobi continues (tr), "Call Him—the one who *gives* measure, in whom measure originally is; say '*He is himself measure*'": JACOBI *Werke* III 211–12 (not a passage an-

14   p 131, pencil, slightly cropped | *SW* VIII 92

[Schelling replies to Jacobi by listing the principles of true theism; though in quotation marks, the words are Schelling's own.] "Der erste Artikel dieses Glaubens war von Anbeginn bis jetzt, dass Gott diese gegenwärtige Welt freywillig erschaffen, dass sie also nicht von Ewigkeit her existire,—sondern ihrer Natur nach anfänglich und endlich*—somit überhaupt die Zeit dieser Welt eine *bestimmte* Zeit sey."

["The first article of this belief has always been that God voluntarily created this present world, that it therefore has not existed from eternity, but has, according to its nature, a beginning and an end*—and that therefore time in this world is a *delimited* time."]

* The direct contrary is asserted in Vol. I. Jahrbücher der Medicine first Treatise.[1]

15   p 135, pencil, cropped | *SW* VIII 94

[Quoting Jacobi:] ". . . Sie wollen andern Theismus lehren, und wissen sich in den wesentlichen Elementen desselben nicht zu finden . . . . Sie beschuldigen fälschlich eine Ihnen persönlich verhasste Lehre, sie habe nebst der Idee von Gott und Freyheit auch die der Unsterblichkeit aufgeben müssen* . . . für sie sey ausser der Natur nichts . . . aber mit deutlichen Worten läugnen Sie den Gedanken der Geisterwelt, diesen liebsten zugleich und liebevollsten Glauben der Menschheit, mit welchem der Begriff einer persönlichen Fortdauer ebenfalls dahin ist . . ."

[". . . You want to teach others theism and do not know how to accommodate yourself to its basic elements . . . . You falsely impugn a doctrine which is repugnant to you personally, saying that it has had to give up the idea of immortality as well as that of God and freedom* . . . and that it believes in nothing but nature . . . but you distinctly deny the idea of a spirit world, that most beloved and most lovely of mankind's beliefs, together with which the concept of a personal continuation likewise stands or falls . . ."]

* If Schelling alter his faith year[ly] as Serpents cast their skins; or if he

---

notated by C). C recurred several times to the statement that God is not infinite, but measure: cf HEGEL **10**, *CN* IV 5087, *C&S* 168 and n 6.

14[1] C refers to Schelling's own article—which C annotated—"Aphorismen zur Einleitung in die Naturphilosophie" in *Jahr-*

bücher der Medicin als Wissenschaft I (1806) 1–74 (*SW* VII 140–97). There Schelling asserts the divinity and eternity of the whole of nature, and the unity of the real and the ideal. C refers specifically to this article again in **16**, **17**, **19**, and **20** below.

publish under his own authority as Editor tracts positively denying a future stat[e] [. . . . .][1]

16   p 143, pencil, cropped | *SW* viii 98

* In allen Sprachen, allen Reden der Menschen, wird der Verstand über die Vernunft gesetzt. Niemandem vor der Kantischen Sprachverwirrung war eingefallen, daran zu zweifeln. Vernunft ist das *allgemeinmenschliche*, unpersönliche . . . . Vernunft schreiben wir allen Menschen zu; wie vielen aber *Verstand*?

[* In all languages, in the speech of all mankind, the understanding is placed above the reason. Before Kant's muddling of the language no one had dreamt of doubting this. Reason is that which is *universally* human, impersonal . . . . We ascribe reason to everybody, but *understanding* to how many?]

* What can be a more childish Log[o]machy than this? If the Understandi[ng] be confined to Relations in Time an[d] Space, and its only implements be gener[al] terms and [? notions] (Schell[ing's] own de[fin]ition),[1] then assure[dly] the Rea[son] must have [? its] first [. . .] in the things above Space [&] Time.

17   pp 142–3, pencil, cropped | **16** textus

Kant, Fichte, Jacobi—all alike, Schelling will quarrel with his own words in the mouth of another. No man dare have any merit [. . . . .][a] Who could believe this written by the same man who a few years before wrote the 31, 32, 33 to 48 Aphor. Zur Einleitung in d. N. P., Jahrbuch d. M. [. . . . .][b1]

17[a] A line is lost by cropping at the foot of 142
17[b] A line is lost by cropping at the foot of 143

15[1] C alludes presumably to *Jahrbücher der Medicin als Wissenschaft*, edited by Schelling with A. F. Marcus: cf **14** and Jahrbücher.
16[1] For Schelling's "definition" see **17** and n 1 below; also **19**. C's position on the crucial distinction between reason and understanding is outlined in Leighton copy c **12** and nn 5, 6; see also *Friend* (*CC*) i 154–61, *BL* ch 10 (*CC*) i 173–4 and nn, *AR* (*CC*) 214–36.
17[1] In Aphorisms 31–48 in the *Jahrbücher* article referred to in **14**, Schelling defines the functions of reason and understanding, considering the former—reason—as the superior faculty, in contrast to his position in *Denkmal*. He asserts that understanding knows only "empty unity" without infinity, "clarity without depth", whereas reason contains within it sense, understanding and imagination, and unifies oneness and infinity, clarity and depth (Aphorisms 33–5). Reason is also the faculty that affirms God and that reproduces in the individual human being God's eternal act of self-knowledge and self-affirmation (Aphorisms 42–8).

18   p 144, pencil | *SW* viii 99

* Erleuchteter Verstand ist Geist, und *Geist* ist das Persönliche, das allein Thätige des Menschen, was allein auch geistliche Dinge versteht.†

[* Enlightened understanding is spirit, and *spirit* is that which is personal; it alone is the active principle in human beings and it alone understands spiritual matters.†]

* Woher die Erleuchtung? Von der Vernunft?[1]

19   p 145, pencil, cropped | **18** textus

† Allgemeinbegriffe bildend vergle[icht] der VERSTAND die Dinge und hebt d[ie] Gottlichkeit aller und eines jeden insbesondere auf, indem er es nur W[. . . . .][1]

20   pp 164–5, pencil, cropped | *SW* viii 109–10

[Schelling imagines a "stranger" in dialogue with Jacobi:] "Sie sagen in Ihrem [Jacobis] Buch, die Wissenschaft müsse in Ansehung der Lehre von Gott, Freyheit und Unsterblichkeit *neutral* bleiben.—Neutral? In Ansehung der allergeistlichsten Wahrheiten! . . . Meynen Sie, dass vor Gott eine Theilung des Menschen gelte—in Kopf und Herz, Verstand und Vernunft?"

["You say in your [i.e. Jacobi's] book that learning must remain *neutral* with regard to the doctrines of God, freedom, and immortality." "Neutral? With regard to the most spiritual truths! . . . Do you think that before God a division of the human being into head and heart, understanding and reason, is valid?"]

[The] injustice of this Attack provokes me. The [?fir]st incautious passage quoted from Jacobi, p. 18 [is] hypothetical—*in diesem* Sinn.[1] I would [?ch]arge to Schelling [? as] the Leader of a *Sect* tho' not as [the]

18[1] "Whence the enlightenment? from reason?"

19[1] C is quoting a passage from Aphorism 33 of the article cited in **14** n 1. The sentence ends, "indem er es nur im Widerschein andrer, nicht an sich selbst begreift", and the full sentence may be translated as follows: "In forming general concepts the UNDERSTANDING compares things; it suspends the divinity of them all, and of each one in particular, by grasping each one only in the reflection of the others and not in itself."

20[1] "In this sense". C alludes to *Denk-*

mal 17–18 (*SW* viii 30), where Schelling quotes (and then responds to) the following passage from Jacobi: "Der Naturalismus in diesem Sinn muss nie reden wollen—auch (!) von Gott und von göttlichen Dingen, nicht von Freyheit, von sittlich Gutem und Bösem, von eigentlicher Moralität; denn nach seiner (wessen?) *innersten Ueberzeugung sind* diese Dinge *nicht*, und von diesen Dingen reden sagt er, was er in Wahrheit nicht meynt. Wer aber solches thut, der redet *Lüge*." ("Naturalism in this sense must never want to say anything—also (!) about God and divine things, nor about freedom,

Author,[2] the [f]acts [sta]ted [by] him, [and] all [?fou]nding [prin]ciples, [. . .] objected [? to by] Him—[. . .]is Schell. The [. . .] and [. . .]?—[. . .] epithet, [?*Hei*]*lige* [?mig]ht [. . .]isably [ha]ve [?mis]led [Jac]obi into the comment of the "allein [wa]hre Gott["].[3]—Either Schelling means [? by] his Verstand the same as in his [A]phorisms (33-48) Jahrb. d. M. vol. I,[4] [. . .] Verstand with the philosoph[y]. If the latter, Jacobi is not speaking [of] it; but of the wilfully insulated Und[er]standing—and had he not the same right and the same Temptation of Schel[?ling] If the former, what he says follows Schelling's own repeated definitions of [. . . . .]

21   p 168 | *SW* viii 112

[The dialogue continues, the words of the stranger appearing in quotation marks and the other words being attributed to Jacobi.] Gott bewahre uns vor einem Himmel im blossen Verstande. "Gott bewahre uns aber eben so sehr vor einem Himmel ohne allen Verstand.—Irren Sie sich nicht! Der Verstand könnte wohl einmal die Rede umkehren und sagen: 'du schiltst mich unvermögend; du *willst*, dass ich es sey. Dein Neutral-bleiben-wollen mit dem Kopf ist am Ende nichts anders als deine leidige Herzensträgheit. Du vermagst nicht das geringste zu erkennen, da dein Herz nicht dabei ist.['"]

[God preserve us from a heaven in the mere understanding. "God preserve us likewise from a heaven without any understanding. Do not be mistaken: the understanding could very well reverse the account and say: 'you are in no position to blame me: you *want* me to exist. Your willingness to remain neutral in your head is in the end nothing more than your accursed slowness of heart. You are not able to recognize anything at all, since your heart is not involved.'"]

What may not an ingenious man make out against another, if he will put his own definitions on the other's words?

---

nor about moral good and evil, nor about morality proper; for according to its (whose?) *inmost conviction*, these things *don't exist*, and so when it speaks of these things it says what it does not really mean to say. But whoever does that utters *lies*.")

20[2] Cf *CL* iv 883 (Nov 1818): "Schelling is the Head and Founder of a philosophic Sect, entitled Natur-philosophen, or Philosophers of Nature." C goes on to say, however, that Schelling's achievement consisted in the "revival" of "the Law of Polarity", i.e. as he indicates

here, that Schelling was not the "Author" of it.

20[3] The epithet *heilige* ("holy") and the phrase *allein wahre Gott* (the "sole true God") are taken from a passage from Jacobi quoted at length by Schelling (*Denkmal* 13). Jacobi affirms (tr) that "nature or absolute productivity is *the holy, eternally creative primary force of the world, which begets all things out of itself and skilfully brings them forth; it is the sole true God, the living one*".

20[4] See **16** and **17** above.

22   pp 192–3 | *SW* viii 125n

[Footnote, referring to the work of Johann Georg Hamann (1730–88):]
... Auch dass Vernunft von Vernehmen herkommt, ist ja eine Hamann'sche Tradition.

[. . . Furthermore, that *Vernunft* comes from the word *Vernehmen* is a Hamann tradition.]

Wahr evidently the same word with Verum; and Nunft the same as Zunft.
Vernunft = Veragium, Veritatum Consociatio.[1] So Wahrnehmen, vernehmen.?[2] The *tas* or *itas* of the Latin—what? τις, τι?[3]

23   p [216, errata], pencil (first two words in ink) rubbed and cropped

Spite of all the superior Airs of [th]e Natur-philosophen, I confess [that] in the perusal of Kant I [b]reathe the free air of Good Sense [a]nd logical Understanding, with [th]e Light of Reason shining in it [an]d thro' it[1]— While in the Physics [of] Schelling I am amused with happy [con]jectures ~~and~~ but in his theology [be]wildered by Positions which in their [? *be*]*st* sense are transcendent (*überfliegend*)[2] [but] in their literal sense scandalous [. . .] in the controversy with Jacobi—and [. . . . .]

22[1] *Vernunft*, in philosophical terminology translated as "reason", is indeed cognate with *vernehmen* "to become aware of" or "to take notice of a fact". *Ver-* in these words is not, however, cognate with *wahr* "true" (Latin *verum*) but with *wahr* (a suffix with various meanings) as in *gewahr* "aware". *Nehmen* means "take" or "grasp" and *Zunft* "association". C paraphrases his coined word *Veragium* as "association of truths".

22[2] So "to perceive, to grasp". Modern scholarship traces these two verbs to differ-

ent roots.

22[3] C suggests that the Latin suffix that makes a noun or adjective into an abstract noun, as *veritas* ("truth") was derived from or equivalent to the Greek pronoun *tis*, *ti* ("which" or "what").

23[1] Among other expressions of C's preference for the reasoning of Kant over that of the *Naturphilosophen*, see HEINROTH 6, 25.

23[2] *"Flying over"*. The word is not usually used as an equivalent for "transcendent".

Einleitung zu seinem Entwurf eines Systems der Naturphilosophie. Oder: Ueber den Begriff der spekulativen Physik und die innere Organisation eines Systems dieser Wissenschaft. [[*With*]] Erster Entwurf cines Systems der Naturphilosophie. Zum Behuf seiner Vorlesungen von F. W. J. Schelling. 2 pts in 1 vol. Jena & Leipzig 1799. 8°.

Dr Williams's Library

HCR's copy, with his signature on p ⁻3 (p-d); inscribed on the title-page in pencil, "Field", referring to E. W. Field, HCR's executor.

DATE. Sept–Oct 1818. These notes almost certainly belong to the period of C's careful rereading of the work in conjunction with his studies with JHG. A letter of Sept 1818 and a notebook entry of Oct 1818 refer to specific passages in the same book: *CL* IV 873–6, *CN* III 4449.

COEDITOR. Raimonda Modiano.

1   i 3 and pp ⁻2–⁻1, referring to i 3, pencil, PS in ink | *SW* III 271–3

["Die Regelmässigkeit in allen Bewegungen der Natur":]—dies alles wird daraus erklärt, dass es eine bewusstlose, aber der bewussten ursprünglich verwandte Productivität ist, deren blossen Reflex wir in der Natur sehen, und die auf dem Standpunkt der natürlichen Ansicht als ein und derselbe blinde Trieb erscheinen muss, der von der Crystallisation an bis herauf zum Gipfel organischer Bildung, (wo er auf der einen Seite durch den Kunsttrieb wieder zur blossen Crystallisation zurückkehrt), nur auf verschiednen Stufen wirksam ist.

Nach dieser Ansicht, da die Natur nur der sichtbare Organismus unsres Verstandes ist, *kann* die Natur nichts andres als das Regel- und Zweckmässige produciren, und die Natur ist *gezwungen*, es zu produciren. Aber *kann* die Natur nichts als das Regelmässige produciren, und producirt sie es mit Nothwendigkeit, so folgt, dass sich auch in der als selbstständig und reell gedachten Natur und dem Verhältniss ihrer Kräfte wiederum der Ursprung solcher regel- und zweckmässigen Producte als nothwendig muss nachweisen lassen, *dass also das Ideelle auch hinwiederum aus dem Reellen entspringen und aus ihm erklärt werden muss.*

Wenn es nun Aufgabe der Transcendentalphilosophie ist, das Reelle dem Ideellen unterzuordnen, so ist es dagegen Aufgabe der Naturphilosophie, das Ideelle aus dem Reellen zu erklären; beyde Wissenschaften sind also Eine, nur durch die entgegengesetzten Richtungen ihrer Aufgaben sich unterschiedende Wissenschaft; da ferner beyde Richtungen nicht nur gleich möglich, sondern gleich nothwendig sind, so kommt auch beyden im System des Wissens gleiche Nothwendigkeit zu.

[["The regularity of all movements in nature":]—all this is explained by the fact that there is an unconscious productivity—though one that is originally related to conscious productivity—of which we see the mere reflex in nature. From the point of view of nature it must appear as one and the same blind urge which manifests its efficacy at different levels, from crystallisation up to the peak of organic formation (where on the one side it returns to mere crystallisation through artistic impulse).

According to this view, since nature is only the visible organism of our understanding, it *can* produce nothing but what is regular and purposeful, and nature is *forced* to produce this. But if nature *can* produce nothing but what is regular, and if she produces it of necessity, then it follows that even in nature, thought of as independent and real, and in the relationship of its powers, one must be able to prove the origin of such regular and purposeful products as necessary. It follows, therefore, *that the ideal must in its turn arise from the real and be explained from it.*

If it is the task of transcendental philosophy to subordinate the real to the ideal, then it is the task of natural philosophy on the other hand to explain the ideal from the real. Both sciences are therefore one science and are distinguished only by the opposing orientations of their tasks. Furthermore, since both orientations are not only equally possible but equally necessary, each possesses the same degree of necessity in the system of knowledge.]]

See the remarks written on the blank Leaf, before the Title-page.[a]

P. 3. The *method* of teaching the prima principia[1] of his System is not, ὡς ἐμοίγε δοκει,[2] so *happy* as might have been wished. An unconscious activity that acts intelligently without intelligence, an intelligence that is the product of a Sans-intelligence, are positions calculated rather to startle or confuse the mind by their own difficulty, than to prepare it for the reception of other Truths[3]—the more so, that Schelling has given no preparatory remarks on the nature of Consciousness itself, and has left the Student to guess, whether the term is used in the sense of primary Consciousness, or of secondary, i.e. the consciousness of having been conscious, the secondary reflective, or recollective Consciousness.[4]

S. T. C.

1[a] This sentence alone is written on p 3

1[1] "First principles".

1[2] "As it seems to me, at least".

1[3] C alludes to the two preceding paragraphs, the opening of Schelling's text, which define two kinds of intelligence, the "unconscious" intelligence that is at work in the order of the natural world, and the "conscious" intelligence that functions in the ideal world—both of which have, according to Schelling, a single "root". Cf SCHELLING *System* 5.

1[4] C recorded a similar objection in SCHELLING *System* 4 two or three years earlier. The relationship between primary and secondary consciousness here corresponds to the distinction between primary and secondary imagination in *BL* ch 13 (*CC*) I 304.

[b]P.S. See the second § of p. 3.[5] Will not the Student ask, is this Organismus separate from the Understanding, as an Eye-glass or Pair of Spectacles from the Eye?[6] Or is it only a term for the Understanding acting in certain directions? If the former, nothing is solved. On the contrary, the Gegensatz (Antithesis) is fixed/ How the Understanding can be acted upon by the Organ/ why it should need it—needing it, how could it have organized it—i.e. acted without it, & therefore *not* needed it &c.—If the latter, how can the Consciousness Activity be an unconscious One?— N.b. I am speaking exclusively of Schelling's *Method*.

So again, if the Nature be only the organic System; or the sum of the Organs, of the our Understanding, there must need (thinks the Student) another Needature to be the stimulant, the fuel, and the Object of these organs. Can the Glass *be* the Landscape, seen by means of it?—All these objections (or Schelling might say) imply an ignorance of our Science. Doubtless. But that *is* the ground of the Objections—that the Student of the first Chapter is must be supposed to be ignorant, and reads in order to remove his ignorance—. It is not the doctrine itself that I am here blaming but the *method*—but the selection of the Metaphors, the explanation of the ideas from Organs &c, instead of Organization from the Ideas./ In the following § too, the transcen. and Natur-Wissenschaften[7] must appear to the student more likely to supersede each other than to form one Science—like a Candle placed horizontally and lit at both ends.[8] At least, a Plot to be found out in the last Scene of the 5th Act, but so shallow that it is seen thro' in the first of the first Act. For it will appear to the Learner, in his first perplexity, a mere Trick—viz. that one and the same Thing is called I, or Intelligence, or our Intellect (Verstand) at one end, and Nature at the other/ If he begin at A,

$$\text{A}\ \underline{\text{a b c d e f e d c b a}}\ \text{B}$$

B. is the Effect: if at B. B. becomes the Cause/ if coinstantaneous, so aa.bb &c/ and it is mere ABC = CBA—not by any real change of the order but by arbitrarily turning the same round link upside down, or looking at it thro' a doubling Glass.[9]

1[b] From here the note is in ink

1[5] The second paragraph of the textus, beginning "Nach dieser Ansicht" ("According to this view").

1[6] The analogy of the pair of spectacles occurs also in SCHELLING *System* **18**, where, however, a different point is made.

1[7] The "transcendental and natural sciences", adapting textus.

1[8] C uses the same image of a candle lit at both ends in the letter of 30 Sept 1818 in which he offers JHG a critique of this book: *CL* IV 874.

1[9] C may be referring simply to the mirror-image, but the preposition in that case would normally be "in" and not "thro'". The use of "thro'" rather suggests a lens that produces a double image.

2   p ⁻3 (p-d), referring to i 6 | *SW* iii 274

Unsere Wissenschaft ist dem bisherigen Zufolge ganz und durchein rea-
listisch, sie ist also nichts anders als Physik, sie ist nur *speculative* Physik;
der Tendenz nach ganz dasselbe, was die Systeme der alten Physiker und
was in neuern Zeiten das System des Wiederherstellers der Epicurischen
Philosophie, *le Sage's* mechanische Physik ist, durch welche nach
langem wissenschaftlichem Schlaf der speculative Geist in der Physik
zuerst wieder geweckt worden ist.

[Following from the above, our science is entirely and wholly realistic; it is therefore
nothing but physics; it is only *speculative* physics, just the same in its tendency as the
systems of the old physicists and, in more modern times, the system of that restorer of
Epicurean philosophy, the mechanical physics of Le Sage. It was through the latter
that the speculative spirit in physics was first reawakened, after having long been dor-
mant in science.]

P. 6. Think of Immanuel Kants Works written before his 23ʳᵈ year, that
on the Living Forces, asserted by Leibnitz, the Bernouilli, &c, and controverted by the French & English Geometricians;[1] and the Himmel's
System, of which La Place's Celeste Mechanique is but a exposition in
detail[2]—think of his Metaphysics of ~~Natural Philosophy~~ Physical Science;[3] his Critique of the Judgement;[4] his Essay on the introduction of
~~the~~ Negative Forces in Speculative Philosophy[5]—that on the *Races* of

2[1] The only one of the works listed in
this note that was published before Kant
was 23 was *Gedanken von der wahren
Schätzung der lebendigen Kräfte*, pub 1747,
which C annotated about 1816: KANT VS
COPY B 1. It proposes an analysis of and an
independent solution to a dispute between
Leibnizian and Cartesian physicists—the
two Bernouillis, Jacques (1654–1705) and
Jean (1667–1748) having been identified by
Kant as members of the Leibnizian group
that "asserted" living forces. In *AR* (*CC*)
399–400*, C summarises Kant's position,
including his objection that "Leibnitz, with
the Bernouillis, erred in the attempt to
demonstrate geometrically a problem not
susceptible of geometrical construction".

2[2] *Allgemeine Naturgeschichte und
Theorie des Himmels*, pub 1755: C's annotations are KANT VS COPY B 2–4 and COPY
c 2–6. C habitually makes the connection
with the (in England) better known *Traité
de mécanique céleste* of Laplace, calling
Kant's work the "germ and original idea" in

Logic (*CC*) 195 and the work of Laplace an
"unprincipled Plagiarism" in a letter of Jan
1818 (*CL* IV 808). Levere (143) argues that
these views represent "a fair indication that
[C] had never read Laplace".

2[3] *Metaphysische Anfangsgründe der
Naturwissenschaft*, of which C annotated a
copy of the 2nd ed (Riga 1787). This is one
of a small group of texts by Kant that C sin-
gles out in *BL* ch 9 (*CC*) I 153 as having
"[taken] possession of me as with a giant's
hand".

2[4] Another from the group described
in the previous note: C annotated a copy of
the 3rd ed, *Critik der Urtheilskraft* (Berlin
1799).

2[5] *Versuch den Begriff der negativen
Grössen in die Weltweisheit einzuführen*,
pub 1763 and reprinted in Kant *VS* I 611–76
(not annotated). C summarises a part of the
argument of this work in his account of the
evolution of the concept of the imagination
in *BL* ch 13 (*CC*) I 297–9.

Man[6]—and then appreciate the base envy and Jealousy that could impel Schelling to this compliment to the French Man, *Le Sage!*—[7]

3   i 10-11, pencil | *SW* iii 277

Angenommen z.B. was angenommen werden muss, *dass der Inbegriff der Erscheinungen nicht eine blosse Welt, sondern nothwendig eine Natur, d.h. dass dieses Ganze nicht blos Produkt, sondern zuglcich produktiv sey, so folgt, dass es in diesem Ganzen niemals zur absoluten Identität kommen kann . . .

[Assuming, for example, what must be assumed, *that the essence of phenomena is not a mere world, but necessarily a nature, i.e. that this whole is not simply a product, but at the same time productive; then it follows that an absolute identity can never emerge from the whole . . .]

* Warum "angenommen ⟨werden⟩ *muss*"? Warum "*nothwendig*"?[1] That the position is susceptible of proof, I do not doubt; but I see likewise that it requires that proof. That, surely, cannot be self-evident, the contrary of which has been believed by such minds as Des Cartes, Newton, &c.[2]

4   i 11, pencil | *SW* iii 277

Diese absolute Voraussetzung muss ihre Nothwendigkeit in sich selbst tragen, aber sie muss noch überdies auf empirische Probe gebracht worden, denn *woferne nicht aus dieser Voraussetzung alle Naturerscheinungen sich ableiten lassen, *wenn im ganzen Zusammenhange der Natur eine einzige Erscheinung ist, die nicht nach jenem Princip nothwendig ist, oder ihm gar widerspricht, so ist die Voraussetzung eben dadurch schon als falsch erklärt*, und hört von diesem Augenblick an auf, als Princip zu gelten.

[This absolute presupposition must bear its necessity in itself, but beyond this it must be subject to empirical proof. For *if all natural phenomena cannot be derived from this presupposition, if in the whole nexus of nature there is a single phenomenon that is not necessary according to that principle, or that even contradicts it, then the pre-

2[6] *Von den verschiedenen Racen der Menschen*, pub 1775 and reprinted in *VS* ii 607–32 (not annotated).

2[7] C is outraged at the omission of the name of Kant from an account of the recent reintroduction of theory in physics; and his outrage is exacerbated by the compliment to a *French* (actually Swiss) scientist, Georges Louis Le Sage (1724–1803). (For C's general hostility to the French, see

Desmoulins 1 n 1.) Le Sage is paired with John Dalton as a proponent of atomism in a letter of Jul 1817: *CL* iv 760.

3[1] "Why '*must* ⟨be⟩ assumed'? Why '*necessarily*'?" C echoes textus.

3[2] These are general references to systems in which the world of phenomena is in fact assumed to be "simply product", inert and not itself generative.

supposition is by that fact alone declared false and ceases, from that moment, to be valued as a principle.]

* That the Voraussetzung auf empirische Probe gebracht worden ⟨muss⟩[1] is clear; but the compatibility of this "must" with the preceding tragen ihre Nothwendigkeit in sich selbst,[2] is by no means clear.

5 i 12–13, pencil, slightly rubbed | *SW* iii 278–9

Es würde dieser Anmerkung nicht bedürfen, wenn nicht die noch immer herrschende Verwirrung an sich deutlicher Begriffe einige Erklärung hierüber nothwendig machte.

Der Satz: die Naturwissenschaft müsse alle ihre Sätze *a priori* ableiten können, ist zum Theil so verstanden worden: Die Naturwissenschaft müsse der Erfahrung ganz und gar entbehren und ohne alle Vermittelung der Erfahrung ihre Sätze aus sich selbst herausspinnen können, welcher Satz so ungereimt ist, dass selbst Einwürfe dagegen Mitleid verdienen.— *Wir wissen nicht nur dies oder jenes, sondern wir wissen ursprünglich überhaupt nichts als durch Erfahrung, und mittelst der Erfahrung* . . . . Zu Sätzen *a priori* werden diese Sätze nur dadurch, dass man sich ihrer als nothwendiger bewusst wird . . . so dass jeder Satz, der für mich blos historisch ist, ein Erfahrungssatz, derselbe aber, sobald ich unmittelbar oder mittelbar die Einsicht in seine innere Nothwendigkeit erlange, ein Satz *a priori* wird. Nun muss es aber überhaupt möglich seyn, jedes ursprüngliche Naturphänomen als ein schlechtin nothwendiges zu erkennen . . . . Die Einsicht in diese innere Nothwendigkeit aller Naturerscheinungen wird freylich noch vollkommner, sobald man bedenkt, dass es kein wahres System gibt, das nicht zugleich ein organisches Ganzes wäre. . . . *Nicht also* WIR KENNEN *die Natur, sondern die Natur* IST *a priori*, d.h. alles Einzelne in ihr ist zum Voraus bestimmt durch das Ganze oder durch die Idee einer Natur überhaupt.

[This note would not be needed if the still prevailing confusion about concepts that are in themselves clear did not make some explanation necessary.

The statement that "natural science must be able to derive all its propositions *a priori*" has in part been understood to mean that natural science must do without experience altogether and, without any mediation by experience, be able to spin forth its propositions out of itself. Such a notion is so absurd that even objections to it deserve sympathy.—*It is not that we know only this or that through experience; originally we*

4[1] That the "presupposition ⟨must⟩ be subject to empirical proof": from textus. C gives "Anticipation" as a translation of "Voraussetzung" in **5** below.

4[2] The preceding "bear its necessity in itself": textus. C pursues his objection to Schelling's notion of empirical proof in relationship to *a priori* principles in **5** below.

know nothing at all except through experience and by means of experience . . . . These propositions become *a priori* only when we become conscious of their necessity . . . so that every proposition that is merely historical for me—i.e. an empirical proposition—becomes an *a priori* proposition as soon as I arrive, whether directly or indirectly, at an insight into its internal necessity. Now, on principle it should be possible to understand every original natural phenomenon as utterly necessary . . . . Our insight into this internal necessity of all natural phenomena becomes, of course, still more complete, as soon as we reflect that there can be no true system that is not also an organic whole. . . . *It is not, therefore, that* WE KNOW *Nature, but that Nature* IS, *a priori*, that is, everything individual in it is predetermined by the whole or by the idea of Nature as such.]

In truth, this is too frequent with Schelling to support rash assertions by contemptuous language. If his position, that a principle, strictly a priori, nay absolute, and yet relative to Physics, could involve its own necessity, were true, we should have a right to infer that "Die Natur-Wissenschaft müsse der Erfahrung (der äusseren, naturlich) ganz und gar entbehren können":[1] and Schelling's *Italics* are but an evasive equivocation on the *word*, Experience.[2]—But his Position is false—The Anticipation acquires necessity by becoming an *Idea*; but it becomes an Idea in the moment of its coincidence with a Law of Nature—& vice versâ, a constant Phænomenon becomes a Law in the moment of its coincidence with an Idea.[3]

---

6   i 20, pencil | *SW* iii 283

Die Physik als Empirie ist nichts als Sammlung von Thatsachen, von Erzählungen des beobachten, des unter natürlichen oder veranstalteten Umständen geschehenen. . . . Der Gegensatz zwischen Empirie und Wissenschaft beruht nun eben darauf, dass jene ihr Object im *Seyn* als etwas fertiges und zu Stande gebrachtes; die Wissenschaft dagegen das Object im *Werden* und als ein erst zu Stande zu bringendes betrachtet.

[Physics as empirical knowledge is nothing but a collection of facts, of accounts of observations, of what has happened under natural or artificial circumstances. . . . The distinction between empirical knowledge and science is based precisely on the fact that the former regards its object in *being* as something finished and completed; science, however, looks at the object as it is *becoming* and as something which has yet to be completed.]

5[1] "Natural science must be able to do without experience (external [experience], naturally) altogether": based on textus.

5[2] C refers to the first italicised passage in the textus. He reiterates and elaborates upon his objections to this passage in *CL* iv

875, a letter which appears to have been based in part on this note; and cf *CN* iii 4449.

5[3] The last sentence is echoed almost word for word in *CL* iv 876.

This appears to me arbitrary and contrary to the received meaning of Empirie = experimental Knowlege.[1]

7 i 22, pencil | *SW* iii 284

Insofern wir das Ganze der Objecte nicht blos als Product, sondern nothwendig zugleich als productiv setzen, erhebt es sich für uns zur *Natur* . . .

[Insofar as we posit the totality of objects not only as product but at the same time as necessarily productive, it is elevated to [the status of] *nature* for us . . .]

I find in Schelling a frequent confusion of what is necessary for his system and what is necessary in itself.

8 i 23–4, pencil | *SW* iii 285

Nur von der Natur als Object kann man sagen, dass sie *ist*, *nicht von der Natur als Subject, denn diese ist das Seyn oder die Productivität selbst.

[One can say of nature as object only that it *is*, *not of nature as subject, for the latter is being or productivity itself.]

* The question here is—Did Sch. understand himself? And if he did, is it more than a truism masked in a paradox? By "is" I mean a "thing", aliquid definitum:[1] what therefore is exclusively definient,[2] is not aliquid definitum. Certainly. But what authorized you to attach this sense to the word "is"? If all Stones are men, and all men think: all stones think.

9 i 24, pencil | *SW* iii 285

* Die ursprünglich unendliche Reihe (das Ideal aller unendlichen Reihen) ist die, worin unsre intellectuelle Unendlichkeit sich evolvirt, die *Zeit*.

[* The original infinite series (the ideal of all infinite series) is the one in which our intellectual infinity evolves, *time*.]

* A strange combination, *ursprünglich* and *unsre*![1]

6[1] C's point here appears to be essentially an objection to the distinction between *Empirie* and *Wissenschaft* when *Wissenschaft* is thought of as "knowledge" broadly. If *Empirie* is itself a kind of knowledge or way of knowing, the distinction collapses.

8[1] "Something defined" or determined.

8[2] "Defining" (not in *OED*), i.e. the determining power.

9[1] "*Original*" and "*our*", from textus. C's objection here seems to be related to his objection to a failure to distinguish between the universal and the merely individual or collective in ESCHENMAYER 3 (and n 1) and 8—notes made about the same time as these.

10   i 31–2, pencil

This therefore is at last purely hypothetical. An *absolute* voraussetzung[1] is little less than a contradiction in terms, if the voraus[2] be more than a superfluous word.—"In assuming a nature (says Sch.) I assume this."[3] Be it so! But what compelled you to assume a nature? *My* System.—Grant it me: and I will solve the problem of the World. It *was* granted: and the Grantèe got tired of the attempt—and has not (I grieve to say) had the honesty to recant a promise which he has found himself unable to perform.—

11   i 36–7, pencil, partly rubbed | *SW* iii 292–3

Wäre die unendliche Evolution der Natur *vollendet*, (was unmöglich ist), so würde sie zerfallen in ursprüngliche und einfache *Actionen*; oder wenn es erlaubt ist, so sich auszudrücken, in einfache Productivitäten. . . . Zu beweisen ist also hier nicht mehr, als behauptet wird, nämlich dass solche ursprüngliche Productivitäten *gedacht* werden müssen als Erklärungsgründe aller Qualität.

[If the infinite evolution of nature were *completed* (which is impossible), then it would break up into original and simple *actions*, or, if one may express it thus, into simple productivities. . . . Thus nothing more is to be proven here than is asserted, namely that such original productivities must be *thought of* as the basis for the explanation of all quality.]

Let me dare assert the superiority of my own view, which contemplates the same idea as Multëity, but first clearly deduces it:[1] but then I would

---

10[1] "Presupposition" or (C's tr) "Anticipation": C is reverting to **4** textus. Cf his summary in *CN* iii 4449: "In my letter to Mr Green I detect two fundamental errors of Schelling—I. The establishment of Polarity in the Absolute—and 2. the confusion of Ideas, with Theorems on oncce side, and ⟨with⟩ Anticipations on the other, so as to make one and the same at once self-evident and yet dependent on empirical Proof.— But these and all his other errors . . . are referable to . . . the making *Nature* absolute."

10[2] The "before", i.e. the "pre" in "presupposition". An absolute admits nothing prior to itself.

10[3] C alludes to **3** textus.

11[1] *CN* iii 4449 discusses the same passage, in which, he says, Schelling "attempts

to represent as aboriginal the same idea as I have deduced under the name Multeity". The concept of multeity—indeed the term itself—was important to C: his use and defence of the term are outlined in *BL* ch 12 (*CC*) i 287 n 3, ATHENAEUM **31** n 3, and the concept is variously explained by C himself in aesthetic, scientific, and theological contexts. DONNE *Sermons* COPY B **123** alludes, for example, to "Hades, the Multëity, the Many [without number and below number]". Especially relevant here are his attempts to work out an alternative to Schelling's *Naturphilosophie*, e.g. *CN* iii 4449 with its account of the *Logosophia*; *Op Max* Vol i ff 15^r, 64–5 (on 15^r he says, "These powers, in their most comprehensive forms, we have recognized & already explained as multeity & unity"); and STEF-

not say, dass solche einfache Actionen *gedacht* werden müssen.[2] They
must perhaps be so *imaged*, for unity is essential to the Imagination, but
at the same moment the Imagination must make it many—or it would not
be extension, therefore not imaginable. But *thought* so it cannot be. This
again is an instance of the errors into which Schelling is led by making
Nature absolute.[3] Noticeable that Aristotle as soon as ✳ to Plato he did
the same, but [. . . . .][4]

12   i 44–5, pencil | *SW* III 298

Wo die Natur in Gestaltlosigkeit sich verliert, erschöpft sich die Productivität in ihr. . . . Umgekehrt, wo die Gestalt überwindet, wo also die Productivität *begränzt* wird, tritt die Productivität hervor;* sie erscheint
nicht etwa als (darstellbares) Product, sondern *als* Productivität, obgleich ins Product übergehende, wie in den Erscheinungen der Wärme.

[Where nature gives itself over to formlessness, its productivity becomes exhausted. . . . On the other hand, where form conquers, that is, where productivity is
limited, productivity becomes prominent;* it does not appear, for example, as product
(that can be represented) but *as* productivity, although merging into the product, as in
the phenomena of heat.]

*   *Wo* die Natur—*wo* die Gestalt[1]—but unless this *Wo* be *causatively* predetermined, little more, methinks, is done but new-naming known facts.

13   i 59, pencil | *SW* III 307

So wie diese drei Stufen im *Individuum* unterscheidbar sind, so müssen
sie *in der ganzen organischen Natur* unterscheidbar seyn, und die Stufenfolge der Organisationen ist nichts anders als eine Stufenfolge der *Productivität selbst.*—(. . . Die eigentliche Naturgeschichte, die nicht die

FENS *Beyträge* **17**, where C again represents his system as opposite to that of
Schelling: "Now I take the reverse, and explain all out of the Multeity involved in
each, and presupposed as the condition of
its existence."

11[2] "That such simple actions must be
thought"—bringing together two phrases
from textus.

11[3] See the quotation in **10** n 1 above.

11[4] The symbol means "contrary" to
Plato (cf JOANNES **4**): i.e. Aristotle contrary
to Plato made nature absolute. C's most sustained account of the differences between

the philosophies of Plato and Aristotle appears in *P Lects* Lect 5 (1949) 185–9, where
he carries the contrast suggested here a little further, saying that although Aristotle
declared that "the objects of the senses"
were "the true realities of nature", he formulated the doctrine of entelechy in an attempt to avoid the "utter destitution of all
religion and all morality" into which such
doctrine might have led him. In TENNE-
MANN **13**, C remarks that Schelling was to
Kant as Aristotle to Plato.

12[1] "*Where* nature . . . *where* form":
from textus.

Producte, sondern die *Natur selbst* zum Object hat, verfolgt die *Eine* der Freiheit sich gleichsam wehrende Productivität durch alle Wendungen und Krümmungen hindurch bis zu dem Punkt, wo sie im Product zu ersterben endlich gezwungen ist.)*

[Just as these three stages are distinguishable in the *individual*, so they must be distinguishable *in the whole organic nature*. The sequence of stages in the organisations is nothing but a sequence of stages in *productivity itself*. (. . . The true history of nature, which does not have the *products* but *nature itself* as object, pursues the *one* productivity, even as it seems to offer resistance, freely through all turns and windings, up to the point where it is finally forced to expire in the product.)*]

* The old scheme of Emanation, against which Schelling in other places declares so vehemently.[1] But this of course must follow from taking either the οδος ανω or the οδος κατω alone.[2]

14   ii 30–2 | *Erster Entwurf eines Systems der Naturphilosophie* | *SW* III 35

Das Absolutflüssige aber kann sein Daseyn nicht anders als durch Decomposition offenbaren. . . . *Aber das Absolutflüssige ist seiner Natur nach das decomponibelste*, denn es ist in ihm das vollkommenste Gleichgewicht der Actionen, das sonach durch die leiseste Veränderung gestört wird.—Es leuchtet ferner von selbst ein, dass das Absolutflüssige nur *decomponibel*, aber nicht *componibel* ist.

[*The absolutely fluid cannot, however, demonstrate its existence in any other way than through decomposition.* . . . *But the absolutely fluid is by its nature that which is most easily decomposed.* For it represents a most perfect equilibrium of actions and is accordingly disturbed by the slightest alteration. Furthermore it is self-evident that the absolutely fluid can only be *decomposed*, but not *composed*.]

It seems to me that Componible and Decomponible are not Antitheta of a common Root, as here used. At least, it sounds odd, to call an alterableness of Temperature Decomponibility, by which, as in the Earths for instance, we mean the reduction of a Compound to its several Compo-

---

13[1] For C's view that the Neoplatonic doctrine of emanation erred by making the creator continuous with the creation, see Luther *Colloquia* 62 and n 2; and cf Schubert *Ansichten* 32 below, where Schubert's system is called "the old Emanation Scheme in a new chemical Dress". Schelling wrote against emanation e.g. in *Philosophische Untersuchungen über das Wesen der menschlichen Freyheit*, pub in *Philosophische Schriften* (Landshut 1809,

annotated by C) I 413–14, 425–6, 451n, 504–5 (*SW* VII 346–7, 355, 373n, 411–12).

13[2] The "way up" or the "way down", Heraclitean concepts glossed by C in further notes to the *Einleitung* in *CN* III 4449 f 28; there, C contrasts Schelling's error in following only *one* "method" or "way" with his own four-phase one. C also used the latter phrase as a motto: *Friend* (*CC*) I 424 and n 1.

nents. It is in this sense, that the Metals are called indecomponible.[1] Now componible ought to mean a something (a Salt for instance) which we can give origin to by bringing two or more bodies together. But here it is made to signify the capability of being united to other bodies—i.e. Apponible or προσσυνθετον,[2] *dynamically*, as distinguished from mere mechanical *juxta*-position.[3]

S. T. C.

15   ii 82–4 | *SW* iii 81–2

α) Das Princip des Lebens zeigt sich, *wo* es sich äussert, als eine Thätigkeit, die jeder Anhäufung des Stoffs von aussen, jedem Andrang äussrer Kraft sich widersetzt; aber diese Thätigkeit *äussert* sich nicht, ohne durch äussern Andrang erregt zu *seyn*, die negative Bedingung des Lebens also ist *Erregung durch äussre Einflüsse.* . . . Die äussre Natur also wird gegen das Leben ankämpfen; die meisten äussern Einflüsse, die man für lebensfördernd hält, sind eigentlich destructiv für das Leben, z.B. der Einfluss der Luft, der eigentlich ein Verzehrungsprocess—ein beständiger Versuch ist, die lebende Materie chemischen Kräften zu unterwerfen. β) Allein eben dieses Ankämpfen der äussern Natur erhält das Leben, weil es immer aufs neue die organische Thätigkeit aufregt, den ermattenden Streit wieder anfacht; *so* wird jeder äussre Einfluss auf das Lebende, welcher es chemischen Kräften zu unterwerfen droht zum *Irritament* d.h. er bringt gerade die entgegengesetzte Wirkung von der, welche er seiner Natur nach hervorbringen sollte, wirklich hervor.

[α) *Wherever* it is manifest, the principle of life appears as an activity that opposes every accumulation of matter from without and every pressure from an external force; but this activity does not become *manifest* without *having been* excited by external pressure; the negative condition of life is therefore *excitation through external influences.* . . . Thus external nature strives against life; most of the external influences that are thought to promote life are actually destructive to life, e.g. the influence of the air, which is actually a corrosive process, a constant attempt to subjugate living matter to chemical forces. β) But it is this very strife of external nature that sustains life, because it continually stimulates organic activity and fans the languishing discord back into flame; *in this way* every external influence on the living thing becomes an agent of *ir-*

14[1] C was personally responsible for bringing these terms over from the vocabulary of chemistry into more general use: the *OED* gives his use in the *Friend* as the first example for "indecomponible", and a phrase of HC's—much later—for "decomponible".

14[2] "Apponible", which could mean as C indicates something "capable of being put

to" another thing, is not in *OED*; the Greek compound *pros-syntheton* (non-existent in this form in classical Greek and probably C's coinage) would mean "something put together with" something else.

14[3] For "mere mechanical *juxta*-position" as opposed to constructive synthesis cf *SW & F* (*CC*) 289—"The Imagination is the synthetic Power".

ritability by threatening to subjugate it to chemical forces, etc—that is, it in fact produces exactly the opposite effect to the one it should by nature produce.]

There is a relique of Brunonianism[1] in §phs α and β—reducing the vis vitæ (Lebenskraft)[2] to mere excitability—which Sch. would perhaps have avoided, had he been acquainted with the proofs that Oxygen acts in ~~the~~ or rather *on* the Lungs by Decarbonization exclusively.[3] I should rather say that + Life, ως πῦρ ασωματον,[4] acts destructively on the stuff or matter of the Organs supplied by external Nature, than vice versâ. The Opposite Factor of Life, = − Life, and therefore the negative Condition of the continu~~ing~~ance of the Organismus, and its self-reproduction, is Carbon, the ⟨only⟩ *excess* of which it is the business of Oxygen to prevent.[5] As Man employed the Dog as his ally in warring against the wild Beasts, the Dog's Congeners, so + Life seems to employ Oxygen in its conflicts with the other Stuffs—externum versus externa.[6]

16   p ‾3 (p-d), referring to ii 93 | *SW* iii 91

Aber Innres und Aeussres scheidet sich nur im Act der Entgegensetzung, es muss also zwischen dem Individuellen und seiner äussern Natur eine wechselseitige Entgegensetzung seyn, d.h. wenn jenes in Bezug auf diese *organisch* ist, muss diese in Bezug auf jenes *anorgisch* seyn.

[But inner and outer are distinguished only in the act of opposition. There must therefore be a mutual opposition between the individual and its outer nature, i.e. if the former is *organic* with regard to the latter, the latter must be *inorganic* with regard to the former.]

p. 93.—This assertion may too easily lead a young Thinker into the error of confounding positive Depth, or absolute *In*-ness with relative Inwardness,—the proper with the merely metaphorical use of the phrases, within, from within &c—In like manner, the relative organic & inorganic with the actually so—A's Head or Fist impinging on B's Nose or Forehead is *relatively* [in]organic[a]—but the ? here is of the positive—!

16[a] Letters torn off edge of page

15[1] I.e. of the system of John Brown (1735–88), which taught that "excitability" is the quality that distinguishes all living matter from dead matter: cf MESMER **13** and n.

15[2] "Life-force" (Latin and German).

15[3] This remark shows C to be up to date in the current scientific literature about respiration: cf GOLDFUSS **5** and n 1, C's note reading (in part), "the Continental Physiologists seem ignorant of Allen & Pepys's Experiments proving that in Breathing the Blood ~~is~~ decarbonates itself by an exudation of Carbon on the surfaces of the Airvessels".

15[4] "Bodiless, like fire".

15[5] See n 3.

15[6] "An external thing against [other] external things".

17　ii 102–3 | *SW* iii 98

Dieser grosse Gedanke liegt wirklich in *le Sage's* System. Zwar sagt er an einer Stelle: "Die allgemeine Gravitation könne die Erscheinungen der Verwandschaften nicht vollkommen erklären, man müsse daher die wahren chemischen Verwandschaften, die nicht von Gesetzen noch von der Ursache der allgemeinen Schwere abhängig sind, von den uneigentlich sogennanten Verwandschaften, die nur besondre Fälle des allgemeinen Phänomens der Anziehung seyen . . . wohl unterschieden". Allein—nur, dass die Ursache der Schwere nicht *unmittelbar* Ursache der chemischen Affinitäten seye, folgt daraus. Denn *diese* sucht *le Sage* in einem secundären Fluidum, dem Aether und seinen Agitationen, die ihm doch durch das schwermachende Princip eingedrückt werden.

[This grand conception is actually found in the system of Le Sage. True, he says in one place: "General gravitation cannot fully explain the phenomena of affinity; therefore one must clearly distinguish true chemical affinities, which are dependent neither on laws nor on the cause of general gravitation, from the improperly called affinities which are only particular instances of the general phenomenon of attraction". But from this it can only be inferred that the cause of gravity is not *directly* the cause of chemical affinities. For Le Sage supposes the *latter* to reside in a secondary fluid, in the ether and in the agitations that are, however, imposed on it by the principle of gravity.]

I cannot imagine the ground of Schelling's partiality to this monstrous Scheme, or rather Knot of arbitrary suppositions. The spirit of detracting from Kant, from whose juvenile Himmels-system Le Sage borrowed the only tenable parts of his Cosmoplasm?[1] See the blank leaf, p. 2 at the end of the Volume.[2]

18　p ⁺2, referring to ii 103 | **17** textus

P. 103.—No wonder! How could it appear otherwise. Le Sage enumerates the phænomena, and then christens the abstract notion of the ultimate inexplicable cause by ~~an~~ the picture-name of an ultimate inexplicable Fluid—and this too in the clumsiest possible way, and in utter incompatibility with the requisites and desiderata of a Cause—i.e. the reduction of multitude to unity. But here the causes are as numerous as the single effects, and the pretended ultimate Cause (a Fluid) a mere *aggregate*—of course therefore, itself an *effect*—But any thing to *set up* against his immortal Countryman, who yet may be truly said to have *set up him* (Schelling)[1]

17[1] See **2** and nn 1, 2, 7 above.
17[2] I.e. **18** following.
18[1] For C's exasperation at what he con-

sidered to be Schelling's disloyalty to his master Kant, cf **2** n 7 and **11** n 4 above.

19   ii 137–9 | *SW* iii 129

Dieses Princip muss Mittelglied aller chemischen Verwandtschaften seyn. Alle andern Materien müssen sich nur dadurch chemisch verwandt seyn, dass sie gemeinschaftlich nach Verbindung mit diesem *Einen* streben.—Dieses Princip ist, wie aus der Erfahrung erhellt, das, was wir *Sauerstoff* nennen.

[This principle must be the intermediate link in all chemical bonds. All the other substances form chemical bonds with each other only because they all strive for combination with this *one* substance. This principle, as is made clear by experience, is what we call *oxygen*.]

Here again Schelling had been seduced by the then existing state of Chemical Theory to confine a Principle to a one Product, in which a high *Grade* of this Principle is embodied, or specificated.[1] Chlorine and Iodine are as primary Products & then Functionaries of the Contractive Power, as Oxygen: and doubtless, we shall make similar Discoveries in the opposite Sphere of the Dilative Power and dethrone or split Hydrogen in the same manner.[2] Either some new Indecomponible of dilative force will be discovered, or some supposed Compound will be found to be equally simple as Hydrogen itself, falsely assumed as its main Factor or Constituent.

20   ii 146–9

[Schelling in these pages develops a position stated p 139 (*SW* iii 131):]
Der Sauerstoff hat bei allen chemischen Processen der Erde die *positive* Rolle. Nun ist aber der Sauerstoff ein der Erde fremdes Princip, ein Erzeugniss der Sonne.

[Oxygen plays the *positive* part in all chemical processes of the earth. However, oxygen is a principle alien to the earth, a product of the sun.]

This is, or perhaps was, a Hobby Horse of Schelling's—this solar Origin of Oxygen.[1] But why more than Hydrogen, I could never guess, or more than Nitrogen. That Air in order to be both Air and Atmosphere must have the Contractive and the Volatile or Dispersive in determined proportions, as its factors, I understand—and that the substances exercising contrac-

---

19[1] C considered this to be a common and fatal error among the *Naturphilosophen*: cf GOLDFUSS 2, where C begins his catalogue of their "great mistakes" with this, "that they confound the Ideal Polar Powers with the Bodies entitled to represent them".

19[2] The scheme of the Compass of Na-

ture in which iodine and chlorine, situated in the south–east quadrant, are associated with oxygen at the eastern pole, is glossed by C himself in *CN* iii 4420; the recent discovery of chlorine and iodine confirmed his faith in his system: cf OKEN *Lehrbuch der Naturgeschichte* 1 and nn 6, 9, 13, 14.

20[1] E.g. ii 137–54 of this text.

tive Functions are representatives of Light, and ⟨positive⟩ Conditions of the phænomenon. But the representatives of Dilation, as Hydrogen, are no less the negative Conditions.[2] But Schelling's Logic is so exquisite! Oxygen is of Solar Birth. Nay, it is extricated from a 1000 bodies on and in the Earth. Yes! and that proves that those bodies have all been in the Sun, & thence exploded![3]

21   p [+]1, referring to ii 184 | *SW* III 169–70

Was ist denn nun nach dem bisherigen eigentlich *Sensibilität*? Alle Nebenvorstellungen, die diesem Wort anhängen, müssen nun ausgeschlossen werden, und darunter nichts als der *dynamische Thätigkeitsquell* gedacht werden, den wir in den Organismus so nothwendig, als in die allgemeine Natur überhaupt setzen müssen. Aber es geht auch aus unsrer Ableitung der Irritabilität hervor, dass *Sensibilität* wirklich sich in die Irritabilität als ihr Objekt *verliert*, dass es sonach unmöglich ist, zu sagen, was jene *an sich* seye, da sie selbst nichts Erscheinendes ist. Denn nur das Positive wird erkannt, auf das Negative wird nur geschlossen. Aber Sensibilität ist nicht selbst Thätigkeit, sondern *Thätigkeitsquell*, d.h. *Sensibilität* nur *Bedingung* aller *Irritabilität*. Aber Sensibilität ist *an sich* nicht, ist nur in ihrem Objekt, (der Irritabilität) erkennbar . . . . Wie übrigens Sensibilität in Irritabilität übergehe, ist eben dadurch erklärt, dass sie nichts anders, als die organische Duplicität selbst ist. Der äussre Reiz hat keine andre Function als diese Duplicität wiederherzustellen.

[What, then, is *sensibility* according to the above? We must now exclude all the connotations attached to this word and think of nothing but the *dynamic source of activity* that has to be posited in the organism just as necessarily as in nature at large. But something else that follows from our derivation of irritability is that *sensibility* really becomes *absorbed* into irritability as its object. Thus, it is impossible to say what it is *in itself*, since it doesn't itself appear. For only the positive can be known; the negative has to be inferred. But sensibility is not activity itself, rather it is the *source of activity*, i.e. *sensibility* is only the *condition* of all *irritability*. *In itself* sensibility is not knowable, but only in its object (irritability) . . . . Moreover, how sensibility passes into irritability can be explained from the fact that it is nothing but organic duplicity itself. External excitation has no other function than to restore this duplicity.]

184. This and the pages preceding strikingly exemplify the inconveniency of using one word for two Relations—Sensibility for the Prothe-

20[2] For C oxygen represents merely one of the four poles of the natural world as the manifestation and symbol of the force of contraction. It therefore does not occupy a more privileged position than hydrogen (dilation), carbon (attraction), or nitrogen (repulsion).

20[3] Schelling's general hypothesis—that the cosmos has evolved from an original mass of matter (the sun)—precedes the argument about oxygen specifically, in ii 113–37.

sis or (Antecedent Ground and Condition) of the Vital Powers, and for the third and highest Power. Why not thus?

$$\text{Excitability} = \text{Life}_{(0}$$
$$\text{Productivity} = \text{Life}_{(1}$$
$$\text{Instinctivity} = \text{Life} = \text{Life}_{(2}$$
$$\text{Incitivity} = \text{Life}_{(3}{}^{a1}$$

The Excitant from without awakes the center, which re-acting becomes Incitive & being itself not phænomenal ($\alpha\varphi\alpha\nu\varepsilon\varsigma\ \tau\grave{\iota}$)[2] appears either in product, when it incites the first power or in act (instinctive Motion) when it incites the second power.—⟨But the first power is the re-agency of the third on the (relatively) inorganic & therefore organizable Excitant.⟩

Q.y The nerves excitable ab extra[3]—i.e. alive to the relatively lifeless or subject~~ly~~ive to the relatively Objective—but inexcitable ab intra, ~~no~~ or rather a centro[4]—i.e. lifeless to^b the vital activity, and ~~indifferent~~ alien—therefore ~~as~~ the *conductors* of the *power*, which begins to be a *force*, i.e. a power in *act* or an *efficient* power at the moment of its arriving at the irritable System—i.e. first manifests itself in the instinctivity?—In other words, the Nerves act on the Brain; but the Brain does not act on the Nerves—but *thro'* them?—[5]

22   ii 209 | *SW* iii 188

Der Haupteinwurf, auf den sich alle andre reduciren, die wir erwarten müssen, ist der, dass wir die Thiere zu blossen Cartesischen* Maschinen herabsetzen . . .

[The chief objection we can expect, and the one to which all others reduce, is that we degrade animals to mere Cartesian* machines . . .]

* I have for more than 20 years wanted to know, on what part of Des Cartes' Writings this charge is founded. Certain it is, that in his Letter to Dr H. More Des Cartes himself repels the charge with contemptuous Indignation.[1]

21^a Written "Life$^{(0}$ . . . Life$^{(1}$" etc, and printed as "Life$_{(0}$" etc to avoid confusion with footnote indicators

21^b In ms, "to to", at the end of one line and beginning of the next

21[1] "Incitivity" is not in *OED*, and the first example for "incitive" as an adjective (below) is dated 1888.

21[2] "Something unseen" or "not appearing".

21[3] "From without".

21[4] "'From within', or rather 'from the centre'".

21[5] The most systematic exposition of C's approach to physiology (specifically, to the relationship of productivity, irritability, and sensibility) appears in *TL*.

22[1] This is an overstatement: in the letter to More Descartes admits the possibility of counter-arguments but basically reaffirms his own position that animals are de-

23 ii 244 | *SW* iii 212–13

Dieser dritte Körper ist im thierischen Lebensprocess das Blut,* das
allein unmittelbar den Sauerstoff berührt, und im Lebensprocess nur als
sein Repräsentant auftritt.

[In the vital process of animals, this third body is the blood;* it alone is in direct contact with oxygen and appears in the vital process only as its representative.]

* To how many false Conclusions has Priestley's and Lavoisier's Theory of the actual oxydation of the Blood in the act of Breathing given
birth![1]

24 ii 268–9 | *SW* iii 232

Auf der höchsten Stufe hat die Sensibilität das entschiedne Uebergewicht, aber hier geschehen auch die Irritabilitätsäusserungen* mit
grössrer Leichtigkeit zwar, aber geringerer Energie, als auf der Stufe, wo
mit allmählich sinkender Sensibilität, jenes Uebergewicht der nach
aussen gehenden Kräfte in den sthenischen Naturen des Löwen z.B. und
seiner Mitkönige unter den Thieren hervortritt.

[At the highest level, sensibility has a definite preponderance; here the manifestations
of irritability* occur more easily, it is true, but with less energy than at the level where,
with sensibility gradually decreasing, that preponderance of power directed outwards
appears in the sthenic natures of the lion, for example, and other kings among the
animals.]

* A co-efficient Something is wanting here: viz. an activity *within* the
retro-itive Power, an Irritability *within* the Sensibility. And this is often
in Man so strong as to nullify the excitement to the proper extro-itive tendency, by which the Sensi- transforms itself into Irrita bility. In other
words, there is a mental activity which Sch. vainly explains into a *degree*
of that, which the Lion has in common with Man, in kind.[1]

---

void of reason (and hence of soul). For an
earlier reference to this letter, see Pereira
2 and n 5.

23[1] Invoking again the corrective
though still imperfect work of Allen and
Pepys referred to in **15** n 3; C identifies it
specifically as a response to Priestley and

Lavoisier in *CN* iv 4854.

24[1] C himself attempted to supply the
perceived deficiency systematically in *TL*,
and in a more piecemeal way in such later
works as the analysis of instinct in *AR* (*CC*)
243–50.

Ideen zu einer Philosophie der Natur. Als Einleitung in das Studium dieser Wissenschaft. Erster Theil. 2nd ed rev. Vol I [all published]. Landshut 1803. 8°.

British Library C 43 b 9

On p 22, as in SCHELLING *Philosophische Schriften* and *System*, someone has noted a passage parallel to *BL*.

DATE. Perhaps before 1815, but possibly much later. C made a *critical* study of Schelling's writings on *Naturphilosophie* in 1818, in connection with *Op Max* and his studies with JHG: these notes are in the spirit of that period, and of C's later attitude towards Schelling. The editors of *BL*, starting with SC in 1847, have found traces of *Ideen* in *BL*, esp in ch 8, where a case can be made for C's having taken "about fifty words from two different places in the Introduction to *Ideen zu einer Philosophie der Natur*" (*BL—CC*—I cxx); but these turn out all to be passages in which the ideas are ones that appear also in other works by Schelling or his contemporaries, and they are not conclusive evidence of C's acquaintance with *Ideen* by the date of composition of *BL*. This is not one of the group of Schelling's works that C himself claimed to have been acquainted with by that date: *BL* ch 9 (*CC*) I 164.

COEDITOR. Raimonda Modiano.

TEXTUS TRANSLATION. Errol E. Harris and Peter Heath *Ideas for a Philosophy of Nature as Introduction to the Study of this Science* (Cambridge 1988).

1   p 60 | *SW* II 53

§ Gehen wir endlich zurück auf den ersten Ursprung des dualistischen Glaubens, dass eine vom Körper verschiedene Seele wenigstens in mir wohne, was ist denn wohl jenes in *mir*, was selbst wieder urtheilt, dass ich aus Körper und Seele bestehe, und was ist dieses *Ich*, das aus Körper und Seele bestehen soll? Hier ist offenbar etwas noch höheres, das, frey und vom Körper unabhängig, dem Körper eine Seele giebt, Körper und Seele zusammendenkt und selbst in diese Vereinigung nicht eingeht— wie es scheint, ein höheres Princip, in welchem selbst Körper und Seele wieder identisch sind.

[§ If in the end we go back to the original source of the dualistic belief, that a soul distinct from the body dwells at least in me, then what is it in *me* which itself in turn judges that I consist of body and soul, and what is this *I* which is supposed to consist of body and soul? Here, clearly, there is something still higher, which, freely and independently of the body, gives the body a soul, conceives body and soul together, and does not itself enter into this union—a higher principle, as it seems, in which body and soul are themselves again identical.]

§. Sophistical. The preceding §ph is excellent.[1]

2   p 195 | *SW* II 145–6

Noch merkwürdiger in dieser Rücksicht sind die von Herrn *van Marum* angestellten Versuche zum Erweise, dass in dem elektrischen Fluidum Wärmestoff zugegeben ist. . . . Diese Versuche verstatten also anzunehmen, dass der Wärmestoff, welcher sich im elektrischen Fluidum befindet, daselbst mit einer andern Substanz verbunden ist, welche ihn hindert, bey einigen elektrischen Erscheinungen frey zu wirken . . . . Können also Auktoritäten gelten, so sieht man, dass die vorgetragene Erklärung, die Hypothesen sowohl als die Versuche bedeutender Naturforscher für sich hat, und es ist kein Zweifel, dass Experimente in der Absicht, sie zu *prüfen*, angestellt, sie bald eben so sehr bestätigen würden, als sie bereits durch die oben angeführten Versuche des Herrn van *Marum* (vorzüglich die Verkalkung der Metalle in mephitischen Luftarten, vermittelst des elektrischen Funkens,) * *bestätigt* ist.

[Still more remarkable in this connection are the experiments performed by van Marum to show that caloric is present in the electric fluid. . . . These experiments therefore permit us to assume that the caloric which occurs in the electric fluid is even there combined with another substance which prevents it, in some electrical phenomena, from acting freely . . . . So if authorities can be credited, it is clear that the proposed explanation has on its side the hypotheses as well as the experiments of distinguished scientists, and there is no doubt that experiments set up with a view to *testing* it would soon confirm it just as much as it has already been *confirmed* by the abovementioned experiments of van Marum (especially the calcination of metals in mephitic types of air by means of the electric spark). *]

This did indeed seem decisive—till Davy proved that the Electricity *conveyed* the Oxygen.[1]

1[1] In the preceding paragraph (57–60; *SW* II 251–3), Schelling attacks the philosophy of the dualism of body and soul and explains how one attains consciousness of oneself, of things outside the self, and of other independent agents.

2[1] Van Marum was thought to have proved that electricity was a compound fluid in which caloric is combined with another still unknown substance, but HD's experiments at the Royal Institution had led him to conclude that electricity was not a compound of caloric with anything, but a power which might be identical with chemical affinity, and which through a series of combinations and recombinations transported the components of water invisibly through the electrolyte to the electrodes, where they were then released.

3   p 202, completed in pencil, cropped | *SW* II 151

Wir führen in dieser Beziehung nur die Beschränkung der Electricität auf die Oberfläche der Körper, *und, was noch mehr ist, ihre Bestimmbarkeit z.b. in Ansehung der quantitativen Vertheilung zwischen verschiednen Körpern durch die Gleichheit und Aehnlichkeit der Oberflächen an . . .

[We cite in this connection only the confinement of electricity to the surface of bodies, * and what is more, its determinability, for instance, in regard to the quantitative distribution between different bodies through the uniformity and similarity of the surfaces . . .]

* How does this agree with p. 183? *a*["die] Zers⟨t⟩örung, die sie im *Innern* der Körper [anr]ichtet"—ihre gewaltsame Wirkung auf animal[ischen Körper . . .][1]

4   pp 302–3, pencil | *SW* II 215–16

Der *blosse* Begriff ist ein Wort ohne Bedeutung, ein Schall für das Ohr, ohne Sinn für den Geist. Alle Realität, die ihm zukommen kann, leiht ihm doch nur die *Anschauung*, die ihm vorangieng. Und deswegen kann und soll im menschlichen Geist, Begriff und Anschauung, Gedanke und Bild nie getrennt seyn.

[The *mere* concept is a word without significance, a sound to the ear, without meaning for the mind. All the reality that can accrue to it is lent to it solely by the *intuition* that preceded it. And hence, in the human mind, concept and intuition, thought and image, can and should never be separated.]

l. 10.[1] Here, as in too many places, Schelling equivocates: for if he confines the term, Intuitus, to the Kantean sense,[2] in the first place; and if in the second place he does not take the presence of an non-appropriate Intuitus for *the* Intuitus; the assertion is not tenible. Thus, I have a clear con-

3[a]   The quotation, to the end of the note, is written in pencil

3[1] "The destruction that it causes in the interior of bodies—its violent effect on the animal body": C is quoting from pp 182–3 (*SW* II 137), a passage that contradicts assertions in textus about external, superficial effects.

4[1] The line beginning with *Sinn* and ending with *zukommen*: but C means the sentence that starts on that line, "Alle Realität" etc.

4[2] The term is "intuition", in German *Anschauung*, one of the crucial and contro-

versial terms in Kantian philosophy. C remarks in several places that the followers of Kant used the term to mean an intellectual or spiritual event rather than (as in Kant) a sensory one: cf **6** below, SCHELLING *System* **17**, and PLATNER **16** n 4 above; also *BL* ch 12 (*CC*) I 289 and n. Indeed, although Kant repeatedly and explicitly denied the possibility of non-sensory intuition, Fichte and Schelling gave it a central role in their philosophical systems.

ception of the Sun as 1/2 a million times larger than all the Planets taken together, ~~the~~ without *the* intuition. Even in a microscope that magnifies 300 times, the Angeschaute[3] or Image is that, by contradicting which I deduce the Notion of the Animalcule's true size. Even so throughout the whole important realm of Truths known only by an insight into the absurdity of the contrary position.   S. T. C.

5   p 305 | *SW* II 217n

[Footnote:] Dieses Bild ist uralt—(derselbe Philosoph, der es brauchte, sagte das treffliche Wort: λογου αρχη [ου][a] λογος, αλλα τι κρειττον.)

[This image is an ancient one—(the same philosopher who employed it uttered the telling words: "The foundation of arguments is not an argument, but something superior."]

"My Father is greater than I."[1]

6   pp 312–13, pencil | *SW* II 222

Daraus ist klar, warum Anschauung nicht—wie viele vorgebliche Philosophen sich einbildeten—die unterste—sondern die *erste Stufe* des Erkennens, *das Höchste* im menschlichen Geiste, dasjenige ist, was eigentlich seine Geistigkeit ausmacht.

[From this it is clear why intuition is not—as many pretended philosophers have imagined—the lowest level of knowledge, but the *primary one*, the *highest* in the human mind, that which truly constitutes its mental nature.]

Here again Schelling forgets, that *relatively that* can⟨not⟩ be the *Highest* in Man which is common to Man and Brute.[1] Not the *primary* Anschauung, but the intellectual* Anschauung is the Highest—suprema quia ultima.[3] And such in fact is Schelling's own opinion.

    * Anschauung des Angeschauten, und Ansch. der Ansch. des Angesch.[2]

       5[a] By a typographical error, the negative is omitted in this ed

4[3] The "thing intuited".

5[1] John 14.28. C's note indicates that he interpreted the Greek in a Christian way, seeing it probably as a variant of John 1.1 Ἐν ἀρχῇ ἦν ὁ λόγος, "In the beginning was the Word . . .". Neither Schelling nor his translators gives a reference for the quotation.

6[1] See **4** n 2 for the different meanings of the term "intuition" in Kant and Schelling.

6[2] "Intuition of the thing intuited, and intuition of the intuition of the thing intuited". C invokes the ascending order of levels of knowing culminating in self-reflexive human consciousness, as it was outlined by *Naturphilosophie* and by C himself in *TL*.

6[3] "Highest because last of all": C uses a similar formulation in FABER **2** (and see n 1).

7   p 366, pencil | End of ii ch 6 | *SW* ii 256

I but imperfectly understand this Chapter on Cohesion, and do not see at last *what comes* of it, but a classing of facts [? as] in reference to the abstract terms, Universal and Specific.[1]

Q? Has not Schelling forgot that there are other Fluids besides Water, ex. gr. Ether and Sulphuric Acid?[2]

8   pp 402–3, pencil | *SW* ii 280

Die Natur hat sehr deutlich die beyden Extreme bezeichnet, zwischen welchen Lichtentwickelungen überhaupt möglich sind. Die minderelastischen Luftarten (die mephitischen nicht entzündbaren) taugen dazu eben so wenig, als die am meisten elastischen (die mephitischen entzündbaren). In der Mitte zwischen beyden liegt die Quelle des Lichts, die Lebensluft.

[Nature has marked very clearly the two extremes between which light-production is possible at all. The less elastic kinds of air (the mephitic non-inflammable) are of as little use for the purpose as the most elastic (the mephitic inflammable). Midway between the two lies the source of light, vital air.]

Here and throughout the whole of Schelling's speculations on Light, and of the Natúr-philosophen generally, there is an inadequacy, that often borders on confusion—the cause being the want of a clear previous insight into the distinction between Elasticity and Dilation, and likewise between + and − Elasticity or Elastic and Spring—[? predicable].[1] The mephitic inflammable Gases are near the Maximum of − Elast. and in the act of kindling pass into the opposite pole, i.e. become + or positively Elastic = Light.[2] Nature, (and the Earth, in like Manner, as Halley long

---

7[1] In this chapter "Of Contingent Determinations of Matter", Schelling defines cohesion as "the cause whereby matter is confined to a specific limit". He then goes on to make a series of distinctions—between original and derived cohesion; dynamical, mechanical, chemical, and organic cohesion; absolute and relative cohesion; and finally, in a supplementary passage added in the 1803 ed, general (C's "Universal") and special ("Specific") cohesion.

7[2] Water is Schelling's only example of a fluid in the supplementary passage, and although he elsewhere refers to ether, it is not in the sense of a particular chemical compound, as C apparently intends here, but in the generalized sense of the hypothetical universal ether.

8[1] For C's repeated objections to the *Naturphilosophen*, see GOLDFUSS 2 and nn 1, 2. In KANT *Metaphysische Anfangsgründe* 8, C clarifies his notion of positive and negative elasticity (which Kant identified with the force of expansion): "By Elastic I have always understood a tendency to re-expand combined with a *compressibility*—a passio motûs followed by a re-action on itself, or a *suspensible* expansive force without destruction."

8[2] In C's model of the "compass of nature" (for which see the analysis and references gathered in GOLDFUSS 1 n 3, and 2)

ago asserted) has four Poles and one Center—correspondent to the five Powers, Attraction, Repulsion, Contraction, Dilation, Gravitation.[3]

9   p 402, pencil | *SW* II 281

Das Phänomen des Schattens, oder der völligen Dunkelheit, sobald der erleuchtete Körper dem Licht entzogen wird, beweiset, dass das Licht, indem es den Körper berührt, seine Natur völlig ändert. Denn warum leuchtet der Körper, dem Licht entzogen, nicht fort, wenn mit dem letztern keine Veränderung vorgegangen ist?

[The phenomenon of shadow, or of total darkness, as soon as the illuminated body is removed from the light, proves that light, in touching the body, entirely changes its nature. For why does the body not continue to shine when removed from the light, if no change occurred when the removal took place?]

How should it reflect the Light when the L. is not there to be *reflected*!

10   p 403, pencil | *SW* II 281

Mehrere berühmte Chemiker (Richter, Gren, u.a.) lassen das Licht aus Brennstoff und Wärmestoff bestehen.

[A number of well-known chemists (Richter, Gren, et al) take light to consist of matter of fire and heat.]

Zundstoff? the incendent or comburent ⊁ the inflammable or combustible?[1]

11   p 406, pencil | *SW* II 283

Hier ist es also ganz anders, als beym Licht. Denn wir kennen bis jetzt nur Eine Materie (die Lebensluft und einige, die sich ihr annähern), als solche, welche zu dem Grad von Elasticität, der von dem Phänomenen des Lichts begleitet ist, übergehen können. Darum haben wir das Recht, von einer Lichtmaterie zu sprechen. Allein *erwärmt* werden kann unmit-

---

carbon and nitrogen appear at the north and south poles respectively. Carbon monoxide is mephitic and combustible ("inflammable"), and nitrogen dioxide is mephitic and non-combustible: these may be the gases C has in mind.

8[3] The astronomer Edmund Halley (1656–1742) proposed an explanation of the variation of the magnetic needle based on the hypothesis of four magnetic poles: *Phil Trans RS* XIII (1683) 208–21 and XVI (1692) 563–78.

10[1] *Zündstoff*, "matter that enkindles". C's symbol means "as opposed to". "Incendent", "that which enkindles", is not in *OED*, but it is an easy formation from the Latin; it is introduced as an alternative to "comburent", a term especially associated with Lavoisier and one that C himself uses elsewere, e.g. in SCHELLING *Philosophische Schriften* 43.

telbar in sich selbst (durch Reibung) *jede* Materie, und das nicht durch den *Beytritt* eines unbekannten Fluidums allein, sondern durch gleichzeitige Veränderung, die im Körper selbst vorgeht.

[So here the situation is very different from that of light. For till now we know of only one matter as such (vital air, and some others that approximate to it), which can take on the degree of elasticity that is accompanied by the phenomenon of light. We are therefore entitled to speak of a light-substance. But *every* matter can be *heated* directly in itself (through friction), and this not by the *advent* of an unknown fluid alone, but by a simultaneous change that takes place in the body itself.]

Well! but jede Materie in einem gewissen Grad von Erwärmung übergeht ins Licht? Auch versterbt das Licht in Wärme.[1]

[a]The Atmosphere at the height of 90 miles is by calculation a thousand times rarer than the most perfect artificial Vacuum: and yet Meteors of brilliant Light have been seen at a yet greater height.

11[a] The first paragraph is written beside the textus, the second in the head-margin

11[1] I.e. "every matter at a certain temperature passes into light? Light also dies into heat".

Philosophie und Religion. Tübingen 1804. 8°.

British Library C 126 f 8(2), bound with *Denkmal* and *Ueber die Gottheiten von Samothrace*.

DATE. Perhaps 1817, like *Denkmal*, and in a period of intensive reading of Schelling.

COEDITOR. Raimonda Modiano.

1 p +2, referring to p 5 | *SW* vi 18

Was er [Eschenmayer] aber ausser der Unmöglichkeit, gewisse Fragen durch Philosophie befriedigend zu beantworten, zur Begründung seines Glaubens Positives anführt,—kann allerdings nicht beweisend seyn, da der Glaube, könnte er bewiesen werden, aufhörte Glaube zu seyn, aber es ist im Widerspruch mit dem von ihm selbst Zugegebenen.

[Aside from the impossibility of answering certain questions satisfactorily by means of philosophy, what he [Eschenmayer] adduces as positive support for his belief cannot in fact prove anything, since belief would cease to be belief if it could be proved. In any event, his evidence is contradicted by what he himself has admitted.]

Philos. und Religion. p. 5. Here we have strikingly exemplified the ill effects of a ambiguous (i.e. double meaning) word even on highest minds. The whole Dispute between Schelling and Eschenmayer arises out of this—that what Esch.͏ asserts of FAITH (the fëalty of the partial faculti[es,][a] even of Reason itself as mainly speculative to the *focal* Energy—i.e. Reason + Will × Understanding = Spirit) Schelling understands of *Belief*, i.e. the Substitution of the Will + Imaginati[on] + Sensibility for the Reason.[1]

2 p 7, cropped | *SW* vi 19–20

[Schelling discusses Eschenmayer's argument concerning the dichotomy between rational cognition and religious intuition.] Jeder . . . ist von Natur getrieben, ein Absolutes zu suchen, aber indem er es für die Reflexion fixiren will, verschwindet es ihm. . . . Nur in Augenblicken dieses

---

1[a] Here and in the following lines, a few letters have been obscured by tight binding

1[1] C elaborates on the distinction be-   BLANCO WHITE *Letters* 1, REIMARUS 1.
tween faith and belief elsewhere, e.g.

Streits, wo die subjective Thätigkeit sich mit jenem Objectiven in eine unerwartete Harmonie setzt . . . tritt es vor die Seele. Aber kaum ist jene Harmonie gestiftet, so kann die Reflexion eintreten, und die Erscheinung flieht. Religion . . . ist demnach ein blosses Erscheinen Gottes in der Seele, sofern diese auch noch in der Sphäre der Reflexion und der Entzweyung ist: dagegen ist Philosophie nothwendig eine höhere und gleichsam ruhigere Vollendung des Geistes: denn sie ist immer in jenem Absoluten, ohne Gefahr, dass es ihr entflieht, weil sie sich selbst in ein Gebiet über der Reflexion geflüchtet hat.

[Everyone . . . is driven by nature to seek an absolute, but as soon as one attempts to grasp it for the purpose of reflection, it disappears. . . . Only in certain moments of this conflict, where the subjective activity unexpectedly falls into harmony with the objective . . . does the absolute appear before the soul. But that harmony is hardly established before reflection steps in and the phenomenon vanishes. Religion . . . is therefore the mere appearance of God in the soul insofar as the soul is still in the sphere of reflection and division. Philosophy, on the contrary, is necessarily a higher and, as it were, more peaceful fulfilment of the spirit: for it ever resides in the absolute. There is no danger that the absolute might flee from it because philosophy itself has taken refuge in a realm that is beyond reflection.]

Whatever St Paul (the Apostle to a[?nd] thro' the *Understanding*) may have done, yet Christ and John use the word, ["]*Faith*" not as Eschenma[yer] &c. but as a *total Energy* of the moral and intellectual Being, destr[oying] all Antithesis—as [. . . . .][1]

3   pp $^+$1–$^+$2, referring to pp 21–2 | *SW* vi 29–30

So gewiss nämlich jenes schlechthin einfache Wesen der intellectuellen Anschauung, für das uns kein anderer Ausdruck zu Gebot steht, als der der Absolutheit, Absolutheit ist: so gewiss kann ihm kein Seyn zukommen, als das durch seinen Begriff, (denn, wäre diess nicht, so müsste es durch etwas anders ausser sich bestimmt seyn, was unmöglich ist): es ist also überhaupt nicht *real*, sondern an sich nur *ideal*. Aber gleich ewig mit dem schlechthin-Idealen ist die *ewige Form*; nicht das schlechthin-Ideale steht unter dieser Form, denn es ist *selbst* ausser aller Form so gewiss es absolut ist: sondern diese Form steht unter ihm, da es ihr, zwar nicht der

---

2[1] This assertion is consistent with C's position in other discussions of the relationship between faith and will or faith and reason (cf *CCD* 35–7). In KANT *Religion* 2, "Gospel *Faith*" is described as a "*total Energy*" of Will . . . one act of the whole Being"; in *Friend* (*CC*) I 315, "faith is a *total* act of the soul". Although C often, as here, insisted that the words of Paul were addressed to the understanding and were therefore to be interpreted metaphorically, whereas those of Christ were to be read literally and symbolically (*AR*—*CC*—205, 318–34), he quotes Paul in support of the view that faith is "a *total* energy of the Soul" in LEIGHTON COPY C **12** (at n 12).

Zeit, doch dem Begriff nach, vorangeht. Diese Form ist, dass das schlechthin-Ideale, *unmittelbar* als solches, *ohne also aus seiner Idealität herauszugehen*, auch als ein *Reales* sei.

[For just as certainly as that purely simple essence of intellectual intuition is absoluteness, for which indeed no other expression is available to us but that of absoluteness, so with equal certainty it can have no existence except by means of its concept. (For were this not so, it would have to be determined by something outside itself, which is impossible.) It is therefore not *real* at all, but in itself only *ideal*. But *eternal form* is coeternal with the purely ideal. The purely ideal is not subordinate to this form because, insofar as it is absolute, it exists *itself* outside all form. Rather, the form is subordinate to it since the purely ideal precedes the form, if not chronologically then conceptually. This form is such that the purely ideal is also, *immediately* as such, something *real without abandoning its ideality*.]

Philosophie und Religion. p. 21, 22—

If I do not deceive myself, the truth, which Sch. here *toils* in and after, like the Moon in the Scud and Cloudage of a breezy November Night, is far more intelligibly and adequately presented in my Scheme or Tetraxy—[1]

1. Absolute Prothesis

WILL, absolutely and essentially causative of Reality.—
Therefore

2. Absolute Thesis

of its own Reality. MENS—PATER.[2]—But the Absolute Will Self-realized is still absolutely causative of Reality.—It has all reality in itself; but it must likewise have all reality in another—that is, all eternal Relations are included in all reality—and here there can be difference but of *relation/* but this must be a *real* relation—an

3. Absolute Antithesis—

but the absolute of MENS is IDEA absolutè adequata—Deus Filius[3]— But where Alterity exists without Difference of Attribute, the Father ~~loveth~~ beholdeth ⟨himself in⟩ the only-begotten Son & the Son acknowlegeth the Father in himself, an *Act* of Absolute Unity is given—proceeding from the Father ~~toward~~ into the Son from the Son into the Father—περιχφορησις, processio inter-circularis.[4]

4. ~~Sy~~ Absolute Synthesis. Love. Deus Spiritus.[5]—

---

[3][1] Or tetractys ("tetraxy" is not in *OED*). There are many versions of this Pythagorean formulation in C's notebooks, letters, and marginalia: cf GREW **1** (where the notes indicate other versions), IRVING *Sermons* **2**.

[3][2] "MIND—FATHER".

[3][3] The absolute of "MIND" is "the absolutely adequate Idea—God the Son".

[3][4] "Perichoresis, inter-circular procession". C alludes to the doctrine of perichoresis or circumincession also in BÖHME **103** (and see n 1), FIELD **23**, LACUNZA **58**.

[3][5] "God the Spirit".

From the beginning I avoid the false opposition of Real & Ideal which embarrasses Schelling.—Idea with me is contra-distinguished only from Conception, Notion, Construction, impression, Sensation—[6]

3[6] This is a fair statement of C's steady position. For his distinction between ideas and conceptions, see e.g. *C&S* (*CC*) 12–13, HOOKER **23**.

F. W. J. Schelling's Philosophische Schrifte[n]. Vol I [all published].
Landshut 1809. 8°.

British Library C 126 g 7

"S. T. C." label recorded by George Whalley on verso of title-page is no longer
there (1989), the corner of the page having been replaced with new paper. Inscribed by C in pencil p [iii], "To Burkitt, ⟨£⟩3,, ⟨S⟩6,, ⟨D⟩6. Nov. 30 [? 1812]".
EHC's transcript of **3** is tipped in at pp ⁻3–⁻2. Many notes have been heavily
cropped in binding, but some annotation occurred after cropping (**50**); the pencil
notes are badly rubbed and offset. Some pencil notes have been overtraced in ink,
apparently by JHG: although it must often have preserved C's notes, the overtracing sometimes makes nonsense of them by misreading, obscuring, or obliter-
ating words. In another, later hand, passages on pp 112–13 are marked as parallel to passages in *BL*.

CONTENTS. [v]–xii Vorrede; i–xxiv, [1]–114 *Vom Ich als Prinzip der Philosophie*; [115]–200 *Philosophische Briefe über Dogmatismus und Kriticismus*;
[201]–340 *Abhandlungen zur Erläuterung des Idealismus der Wissenschaftslehre*; [341]–96 *Ueber das Verhältniss der bildenden Künste zu der Natur*;
[397]–511 *Philosophische Untersuchungen über das Wesen der menschlichen
Freyheit und die damit zusammenhängende Gegenstände*.

MS TRANSCRIPT. VCL S MS 19: hand of SC, incomplete. For the transcript of **3**,
see headnote.

DATE. 1812–15 and later, including at least a partial re-reading about Mar 1818
(*CN* III 4397). C himself refers to his "repeated perusal" of this collection, and
some passages were annotated more than once, e.g. **17**. C probably owned this
copy before 13 Aug 1812, when HCR recorded C's statement that "Schelling . . .
appears greatest in his last work on *Freiheit*" (*CRB* I 107–8), referring to the fifth
and last work in this collection. According to his own statement in *BL* ch 9 (*CC*)
I 164, this was one of only three volumes of Schelling's works that C had acquired
by Sept 1815 when *BL* was written. For his use in *BL* of material from the third
item in this collection, see *BL* ch 12 (*CC*) I 260, 278–80; for the use of material
from the fourth in 1818 in what became the essay "On Poesy and Art" see *Lects
1808–1819* (*CC*) II 214–25, *CN* III 4397.

COEDITOR. Raimonda Modiano.

1   p ⁻3, pencil, overtraced in another hand

I believe in my Depth of Being, that the three greatest Works since the introduct[ion]ᵃ of Christianity are—*Bacon's* Novum Organon, & his other Works as far as they are Commentaries on it—*Spinoza's* Ethice, with his Letters &c as far as they are Comments on his Ethics—and *Kant's* Critique of the pure Reason, & *his* other works as Commentaries & ~~Aids~~ Applications of the same.¹

2   p ⁻3, pencil

Iajá—em-em—cebéeᵃ¹

3   p ⁻2, pencil, conclusion in ink

¹Το ασκ εμεμσῆ, ᵃ[ει θε μεανς καν βε ρασδ]ᵇ ὑεθερ
Θαι ὀυδ σπενδ α [? ενιαυτον]ᶜ συν εμοι εν
Γερμανιᾳ ἡ Σουιτσερλαντ.
Δηρ Φρενζ, Jajá, Εμ-Εμ—Σιβῆ!
Λυφ, ασ ηυρ λυφτ βει, Εϛ-Τι-Σῆ.

1ᵃ The overtracing appears to have been done after the vol was bound; in binding, some letters were obscured

2ᵃ Binder's mark "3", in ink and in pencil, beside and above this line

3ᵃ⁻ᵇ The pencil is almost illegible, and EHC's transcription has been used to piece out these words

3ᶜ EHC's transcription

1¹ C's major tribute to Bacon appears in the essays on method in *Friend (CC)* I 482–95; he calls him "the British Plato" (I 488). MORE *Theological Works* 1 represents him as a British Kant, the *Novum Organum* having led the way in the "Critique of the human intellect" that came to fruition in Kant. As late as 1825, C was actively associated with the *Novum Organum*, having "engaged to translate [it] with comments &c." (*CL* v 493). C annotated HCR's copy of Spinoza *Opera* (2 vols Jena 1802–3) between Nov 1812 and Nov 1813, and Kant *C d r V* perhaps as early as 1800: see KANT *C d r V* and SPINOZA. Both Kant and Spinoza are warmly praised in *BL* ch 9 *(CC)* I 152–4.

2¹ Like many of his contemporaries, C wrote "I" and "J" interchangeably for J. He is spelling out the initials "J.J.—M.-M.—C.B."—"John James—Mary Morgan—

Charlotte Brent". The Morgans and Mary Morgan's sister Charlotte Brent were C's hosts off and on from Nov 1810 to Apr 1816, when he moved into the Gillman house in Highgate.

3¹ The note consists mostly of English words transliterated into Greek, but a few words are Greek or transliterated German. (The German will be noted separately below.) Tr: "To ask M. M. C. [Mary Morgan and Charlotte], if the means can be raised, whether they would spend a [? year] with me in Germany or Switzerland.
Dear Friends, J. J., M. M.—C. B.!
Love, as you're loved by, S. T. C.
  Sein = Being
  Dasein = Existence
  Wirklichkeit = Actuality
  Realität = Reality
Dear Friends, J. J.—, M. M., C. B.!
Love, as you're loved by, S. T. C."

²Σεῖν = βεινγ
Δασεῖν = εξιστενς
Φιρκλιχειτ = Actuality
Ρεαλιτατ = Reality
^{d}Δηρ Φρενδς, Ια-ια—, Ḛεμ-Εμ, Σι Βῆ!
Λυφ, ας ηυ'ρ λυφδ βει, Ες Τι Σῆ.

4   p [1], pencil | *Vom Ich als Prinzip* § 1 | *SW* 1 162

Wer etwas wissen will, will zugleich, dass sein Wissen Realität habe. Ein
Wissen ohne Realität ist kein Wissen. Was folgt daraus?

[He who wants to know something, at the time wants his knowledge to have reality.
Knowledge without reality is no knowledge. What follows from this?]

Ja, was?[1]

5   p [1], pencil | Continuing **4** textus

Entweder muss unser Wissen schlechthin ohne Realität—ein ewiger
Kreislauf, ein beständiges wechselseitiges Verfliessen aller einzelnen
Sätze in einander, ein Chaos seyn, in dem kein Element sich scheidet,
oder—

Es muss einen letzten Punkt der Realität geben, an dem alles hängt,
von dem aller Bestand und alle Form unsers Wissens ausgeht, der die El-
emente scheidet und jedem den Kreis seiner fortgehenden Wirkung im
Universum des Wissens beschreibt.

[Either our knowledge must be absolutely devoid of reality—an eternal cycle, a constant mutual flowing of all individual propositions into one another, a chaos in which
no element is differentiated, or—
There must be an ultimate point of reality on which everything depends, from which
all permanence and every form of our knowledge takes its origin, and which separates
the elements and prescribes to each one the sphere of its continual efficacy in the universe of knowledge.]

But is this a logical, or an actual, necessity?—

6   pp [1]–xxiv, pencil, cropped, badly rubbed and offset | **4, 5** textus

There are two ways of *Studying* (i.e. not merely eye-reading) an Author
1st that of Learning with childish docility, knowlege or *hints* to know-

---

3^d The remainder of the note is in ink

3² The next four lines transliterate (ap-   4¹ "Yes, what?"
proximately) and translate German terms.

lege no[t] acquired before—the 2nd that of examining, whether this knowlege i[s] conveyed aptly & scientifically. That refers to the matter, the second to the ~~matter~~ manner/. In this latter sense, [I] objec[t] to the use o[f] the wor[d] "Wiss[en"] in, an[d]^a *as* in the *same* § of t[he] work.[1] [? Taken as "Wahrnehmen"] or "to perceive": it is [a] fruitless Truism: & in any other sense as "*to know*" it can not but be obscure to the Student. [. . . . .] In the second §[2] the same cloud hovers [be]tween thc Sun & the Student. A *real* [? definition], an exemplified Explication [? of] Wissen should have preceded. As it [. . .] here, I have no *logical* compulsion [. . . . .]

P.S.^{b} May it not [b]e said too, that the Author either *assumes* [. . .] of *Things* (which is not his [com]petence) or else confounding or identifying [th]is with modes [of] thinking [c]omprehending cause & effect. [. . .] the latter [for] the former [. . .]s, *supposes* [th]at he should [. . .] instruct.

7 pp 2–3, pencil, rubbed and cropped | *SW* i 162–3

Giebt es überhaupt ein Wissen, so muss es ein Wissen geben, zu dem ich nicht wieder durch ein anders Wissen gelange, und durch welches allein alles andre Wissen Wissen ist. Wir brauchen nicht eine besondre Art von Wissen vorauszusetzen, um zu diesem Satze zu gelangen. Wenn wir nur überhaupt etwas wissen, so müssen wir auch Eines wenigstens wissen, zu dem wir nicht wieder durch ein andres Wissen gelangen, und das selbst den Realgrund alles unsers Wissens enthält.

[If I know anything at all, I must have some knowledge which I don't attain through other knowledge but by which alone all other knowledge becomes known. We need not assume a special kind of knowledge in order to arrive at this proposition. If we know anything at all, we must know at least one thing which is not in turn the result of other knowledge and which itself contains the real ground of all our knowledge.]

I write, (*dramatically*) not my own present Convictions; but assume the character of a young Searcher after [T]ruth. [N]ow [(w]ould not a [? man] say) [? to] SEE [an]y thing [im]plies [Se]eing [üb]erhaupt[1]—[Er]go, [th]ere [mu]st be [som]e one [Si]ght, or [sor]t of [se]eing, [wh]ich [i]s the [s]ource [of] all other Sights &c—Strange notion [(]he might say to him-

6^a In the cropping of the margin a few letters or a short word may have been lost here
6^b At the head of p xxiv, beginning: "P.S. (continued from the bottom)"

6[1] *Wissen* is both the verb "know" and the noun "knowledge"—in 4 textus. C's objection is to Schelling's use of it here at all, as well as to the sense he gives it, without definition.
6[2] The first paragraph of 5.
7[1] "Generally"—translated "at all" in the phrase "anything at all" in textus.

self). Is not Seeing a Power common to all its appropriate [. . . . .] &c—
whether seen first, second, or thir[d] does it not depend on accidents? So
in Science/ the Sciential[2] Faculty of seeing [. . . . .]

8   p 5, pencil | § 2 | *SW* I 164–5

Allein ein Objekt realisirt sich niemals selbst; um zur Existenz eines Objekts zu gelangen, muss ich über den Begriff des Objekts hinausgehen;
seine Existenz ist kein Theil seiner Realität: ich kann seine Realität
denken, ohne es zugleich als existirend zu setzen.

[However, an object never realises itself; in order to reach the existence of an object
I must go beyond the concept of the object; its existence is no part of its reality: I can
think its reality, without at the same time positing it as existing.]

Ich kann seine Reälitabilität denken, nicht aber seine Reälität,[a] ohne &c[1]

9   p 9, cropped | § 3 | *SW* I 168

Ich bin, weil Ich bin! das ergreift jeden plötzlich.

[I am, because I am; that comes upon everyone as a sudden [revelation].]

jeden?[1] [I] doubt i[t.] Many w[ould] say, I a[m] becaus[e] God ma[de]
me.[2]

10   p 81, cropped | § 16 | *SW* I 219

* So kann A = B ein thetischer, obwohl kein identischer Satz seyn, wenn
nemlich durch das *blosse* Setzen von A, B, aber nicht umgekehrt durch
das blosse Setzen von B, A gesetzt ist.

[* Thus A = B can be a thetic statement but not a statement of identity when B is
posited by *merely* positing A but A on the other hand is not posited by merely positing B.]

* applied to the Logos as gese⟨t⟩zt in the το ον.[1]—N.B. gesetzt = posi-
tum, how can we render it i[n English?]

8[a] A slip for "Realität"

7[2] I.e. knowing, having to do with
knowledge.

8[1] C adapts the last sentence of the textus, coining the word "Realitabilität": "I can
think its realisability, but not its reality,
without etc".

9[1] Upon "everyone"? C questions textus.

9[2] Cf *BL* ch 12 (*CC*) I 274: "If a man be

asked how he *knows* that he is? he can only
answer, sum quia sum [I am because I am].
But if . . . he be again asked, how he, the individual person, came to be, . . . he might
reply, sum quia deus est [I am because God
is], or still more philosophically, sum quia
in deo sum [I am because I exist in God]."

10[1] "The Word as posited in what is".
The Platonic expression τὸ ὄν (*to on*) may

11 *a*p 91, pencil, cropped | **10** textus | *SW* I 225

Is it, yet *comprehends* it.

Quere—At once to *be* the ~~heart~~ ignorant human *Heart* (& it [a] dreadful Abyss!) & yet to *comprehend* it = Man + God = Θεανθρωπος.[1]—The mystery of the Incarnation truly μυστηρι[ov.][2] We close the Lips *naturally*, when we intensely meditate inward.*b*

12 pp 118/19, tipped in, referring to p 119 | *Philosophische Briefe*: Letter 1 | *SW* I 284–5

[C is referring to the first two pages of this letter, in particular to the following passages:] Ich verstehe Sie, theurer Freund! Es dünkt Ihnen grösser, gegen eine absolute Macht zu kämpfen und kämpfend unterzugehen, als sich zum Voraus gegen alle Gefahr durch einen moralischen Gott zu sichern. Allerdings ist dieser Kampf gegen das Unermessliche nicht nur das Erhabenste, was der Mensch zu denken vermag, sondern meinem Sinne nach selbst das Princip aller Erhabenheit. . . . Der consequente Dogmatismus geht nicht auf Kampf, sondern auf Unterwerfung, nicht auf gewaltsamen, sondern auf freywilligen Untergang . . . . Aber dafür hat jene Unterwerfung eine *reinästhetische* Seite. Die stille Hingabe ans Unermessliche, die Ruhe im Arme der Welt, ist es, was die Kunst auf dem andern Extreme jenem Kampfe entgegenstellt . . . . Ist das Schauspiel des Kampfs dazu bestimmt, den Menschen im höchsten Moment seiner Selbstmacht darzustellen, so findet ihn umgekehrt die stille Anschauung jener Ruhe im höchsten Momente des Lebens. . . . Be-

11*a* C continues to reflect on **10** textus, writing his note in the next available large space
11*b* A cropped line at the foot of the page appears to include a repetition of the diagram of two circles

mean here the sphere of true existence, the physical world being μὴ ὄv (*me on*) "notbeing". For the Logos itself as the Ὁ ῎Ωv (*Ho On*) or "I AM" of Exod 3.14 see BIBLE COPY B **119** and nn 1, 2.

11[1] C uses the Greek *Theanthropos*, "God-man", normally in conjunction with the Logos incarnate, Christ: cf "The Potential (= Λογος θεανθρωπος)" in T. FULLER *Holy State* **7** and the projected section of "5 Treatises on the Logos" described in a letter of 25 Sept 1816, "Commentary in de-tail on the Gospel of St John—or Λόγος θεάνθρωπος" (*CL* IV 687).

11[2] Truly "a mystery", that is, inexpressible. As C more than once pointed out, the word is connected with μύειν (*muein*), to close the lips (or the eyes): *CN* IV 4832 f 59*v*, 4931 f 98*v* and nn. C provides a further gloss in LEIGHTON COPY C **12** (at n 18): "They are *therefore* Mysteries, *because* they are wholly and solely *Reason* itself. They are not indeed to be *understood*—for their *Sub*stans is in themselves."

trachten wir also die Idee eines moralischen Gottes von dieser Seite (der ästhetischen), so ist unser Urtheil bald gefällt. . . . Denn der Gedanke, mich der Welt entgegenzustellen, hat nichts grosses mehr für mich, wenn ich ein höheres Wesen zwischen sie und mich stelle, wenn ein Hüter der Welt nöthig ist, um sie in ihren Schranken zu halten.

[I understand you, dear friend! You think it greater to struggle against absolute might and go down in the struggle than to secure yourself beforehand against all danger by means of a moral God. This struggle against the Immeasurable is indeed not only the most sublime object that man is able to think of, but in my opinion it is itself the principle of all sublimity. . . . Consistent dogmatism concerns itself not with struggle, but with submission, not with forcible but with voluntary destruction . . . . But that is why this submission has a *purely aesthetic* side to it. Quiet surrender to the Immeasurable, rest in the arms of the world—this is what art sets in opposition to that struggle at the other extreme . . . . If the scene of struggle represents man at the highest moment of his own power, the quiet view of that rest shows him at the highest moment of life. . . . Thus, if we consider the idea of a moral God from this side (the aesthetic), we soon reach a judgment. . . . For the thought of setting myself in opposition to the world no longer has anything great in it for me if I put a higher being between the world and myself, and if a guardian of the world is needed in order to keep it within its bounds.]

Schelling (Phil. Schrift. p. 119)

I have made repeated efforts, and all in vain, to understand this first Letter on Criticism and Dogmatism—Substitute the World (*die Welt*) for a moral God, what do I gain, in der *reinästhetischen* Seite,[1] more than in any other point of view?—How can I combat ~~a~~ or fight up against that which I ~~am~~ myself am? Is not the very Impulse to contend or to resign one of the Links in the very chain of necessary Causes, which I am supposed to struggle against? If we are told that *God* is in us both to will and to do,[2] i.e. is the sole actual Agent, how much* more must this apply to the World or Fate, or whatever other phantom we substitute. Der Gedanke, mich der Welt entgegensetzen, not only hat nichts grosses für mich,[3] but seems mere pot-valiant Nonsense, without the idea of a moral Power extrinsic to and above the World as much inconceivable by a sane mind, as that a single Drop of the Falls of Niagara should fight up against the whole of the Cataract, of which itself is a minim.—

How much more sublime, and in other points of view, how infinitely more beautiful, even in respect of Taste, or aisthetic Judgement, is the Scriptural representation of the *World* as in enmity with *God* & of the continued Warfare, which calls forth every energy both of act and of en-

12[1] "On the *purely aesthetic* side"— from textus.

12[2] Phil 2.13: "For it is God which worketh in you both to will and to do of his good pleasure."

12[3] "The thought of setting myself in opposition to the world not only has nothing great in it for me"—a slight variant of the phrasing in textus.

durance, from the necessary vividness of Worldly Impressions and the sensuous Dimness of Faith, in the first Struggles! Were the Impulses and Impresses from the Faith in God equally vivid, as the sensuous Stimuli, then indeed all Combat must cease—& we should have Halleluiahs for Tragedies & Statues. Cruel Loss!!

* I say, how much more: because admitting a supersensual Being this may possibly be, & we therefore from other reasons do not doubt, that it is really compatible with Free Will; but with a *World*-God this were a blank Absurdity.

13   pp 122/3, tipped in | *SW* I 287

Aber die theoretische Vernunft wird, ob sie gleich jene Welt [der absoluten Causalität] nicht finden konnte, doch nun, da sie einmal entdeckt ist, auch das Recht haben, sich in Besitz davon zu setzen. Die theoretische Vernunft soll für sich selbst zum absoluten Objekt nicht hindurchdringen; nun aber, da ihr es einmal entdeckt habt, wie wollt ihr sie abhalten, an der Entdeckung auch Theil zu nehmen? Also müsste nun wohl die theoretische Vernunft eine ganz andre Vernunft, sie müsste durch Hülfe der praktischen erweitert werden, um neben ihrem alten Gebiete noch ein neues zuzulassen.

[But now that that world [of absolute causality] has been discovered, theoretical reason will also have the right to take possession of it, even though it could not discover that world. Theoretical reason is not for itself supposed to penetrate to the absolute object; but now that you have discovered it, how could you prevent theoretical reason from taking part in this discovery too? Thus theoretical reason would now have to become an entirely different reason; it would have to be enlarged with the help of practical reason in order to admit a new sphere in addition to its old one.]

Schelling's Phil. Schrift./ p. 122.

I cannot see the force of any of these arguments. By theoretic Reason as opposed to practical, Kant never meant two *Persons* or *Beings*; but only that what we could not *prove* ~~in~~ by one train of Argument, we might by another—in proportion to the ~~necessity~~ purposes of the Knowlege—.[1] I cannot theoretically *demonstrate* the existence of God, as a moral Creator & Governor; but I can theoretically adduce a multitude of Inducements so strong as to be all but absolute Demonstrations; and I can ~~so~~ demonstrate, that not a word of Sense ever was or ever can be brought against it. In this stage of the argument my Conscience, with its categor-

---

13[1] C offers an exposition of Kant's distinction between theoretical reason and practical reason as Kant himself applied it to theological issues, e.g. in the "Critique of all Theology based upon Speculative Principles of Reason" in *C d r V* B 659–70.

ical Command, comes in & proves it to be my Duty to *choose to* believe in a God—there being no obstacle to my power so to choose.[2] With what consistency then can Schelling contend that the same mind having on these grounds fixed its belief in a God, can then make its former speculative infirmities as applied to the Idea of God, a pretext for turning back to disbelieve it?—

14   pp 122/3, tipped in, referring to pp 123–4 | *SW* I 288

Am kürzesten wäre es, zu sagen, jenes Wesen sey selbst Urheber des Moralgesetzes. Allein diess ist dem Geiste und Buchstaben eurer Philosophie zuwider.—Oder soll das Moralgesetz unabhängig von allem Willen vorhanden seyn? so sind wir im Gebiete des Fatalismus: denn ein Gesetz, das aus keinem unabhängig von ihm vorhandenen Daseyn erklärbar ist, das über die höchste Macht, wie über die kleinste gebietet, hat keine Sanktion, als die der Nothwendigkeit.

[To put it in the briefest terms, that Being is itself the originator of the moral law. But precisely this is contrary to the spirit and letter of your philosophy. Or is the moral law to be independent of all will here, so that we are in the realm of fatalism? For a law that cannot be explained in terms of a being existing independently of it and reigning over the highest power as well as the smallest has no sanction but that of necessity.]

p. 123. 124—Just as well might Schelling have asked, concerning the Wisdom or any other attribute of God—and if we answered, they were essential—i.e. God himself, then object, that this was Fatalism. The proper answer is that God is the originator of the Moral Law; but not per arbitrium (Willkühr)[1] but because he is essentially wise and holy and good—rather, Wisdom, Holiness, and Love.—[2]

15   pp 142–3, pencil | Letter 5 | *SW* I 301

Ist es doch kein so seltner Fall im menschlichen Leben, dass man die Aussicht auf einen künftigen Besitz /\ für den Besitz selbst nimmt!*

[Is it not often the case in human life that one takes the prospect of a future possession /\ for the possession itself?*]

* Is there not some omission of the Press here? viz—"für den Besitz"

13[2] For a similar statement by C and other sources in Kant, see Nicolai **4** and n 1.

14[1] Not "by arbitrary choice". C elsewhere—as in the 1812 *Omniana* quoted in *BL* ch 12 (*CC*) I 293—makes a clear distinction between "will" and "choice" in human beings. *AR* (*CC*) 333–4 distinguishes between "the absolute Will . . . and the Election and purpose of God in the personal Idea".

14[2] For a further note on this section of the work, see *Annex*.

after "Besitz"?—that we take the *Look out* on a future Possession for the Possession itself—.[1]

16   p 153, cropped | Letter 6 | *SW* I 309n

Aber noch unerträglicher wird dem denkenden Kopf das Gerede von *Beweisen* des Daseyns Gottes. . . . Man dachte sich Gottes Seyn nicht als das *absolute* Seyn, sondern als ein *Daseyn*, das nicht *durch sich selbst*, sondern nur insofern absolut ist, als man über ihm kein höheres weiss. Diess ist der empirische Begriff, den jeder der Abstraction unfähige Mensch von Gott sich bildet. Um so mehr blieb man bey diesem Begriff stehen, als man sich *fürchtete*, mit der reinen Idee des absoluten Seyns auf einen Spinozischen Gott zu gerathen.

[But even more intolerable for the thinking mind is the talk of *proofs* of God's existence. . . . God's existence was not thought of as *absolute* existence, but rather as a *being* that is absolute, not *in itself*, but only insofar as nothing greater above it was conceivable. This is the empirical concept of God formed by those incapable of abstraction. People retained this concept all the more as they *feared* that the pure idea of absolute existence would lead to a Spinozistic God.]

But h[?ow can we] know that a[?nything is,] except [so] far as [it] *works* [on] or in [us;] and [what] is th[at] but existence? Answer. The mean[s] by which we arrive at the consciousness [of] an Idea, are not the Idea.

17   pp 175–6, cropped | Letter 8 | *SW* I 324–5

Wo *absolute Freyheit* ist, ist *absolute Seligkeit*, und umgekehrt. Aber mit *absoluter* Freyheit ist auch kein Selbstbewusstseyn mehr denkbar. Eine Thätigkeit, für die es kein *Objekt*, keinen Widerstand mehr giebt, kehrt niemals in sich selbst zurück. Nur durch Rückkehr zu sich selbst entsteht *Bewusstseyn*. Nur *beschränkte* Realität ist *Wirklichkeit* für uns.

Wo aller Widerstand aufhört, ist unendliche Ausdehnung. Aber die Intension unsers Bewusstseyns steht im umgekehrten Verhältniss mit der Extension unsers Seyns. Der höchste Moment des Seyns ist für uns Uebergang zum Nichtseyn, Moment der *Vernichtung*. . . . Wir erwachen aus der intellektualen Anschauung, wie aus dem Zustande des Todtes. Wir erwachen durch *Reflexion* . . . . Der Mensch aber soll weder lebloses noch bloss lebendiges Wesen seyn. Seine Thätigkeit geht nothwendig auf Objekte, aber sie geht eben so nothwendig in sich selbst zurück. Durch *jenes* unterscheidet er sich vom leblosen, durch *dieses* vom bloss lebendigen (thierischen) Wesen.—

15[1]   C's emendation is correct.

[Where there is *absolute freedom*, there is *absolute bliss*, and vice versa. But with *absolute* freedom, self-consciousness is no longer conceivable. An activity for which there is no *object*, no more resistance, never returns into itself. *Consciousness* arises only through the return upon the self. Only *limited* reality is *actuality* for us.

Where all resistance ends there is infinite extension. But the intensity of our consciousness stands in inverse relation to the extension of our being. The highest moment of being for us is the transition to not-being, the moment of *extinction*. . . . We awaken from intellectual intuition as from the state of death. We awaken through *reflection*. . . . Man, however, should be neither an inanimate being nor a merely animate one. His activity is necessarily directed toward objects, but it is just as necessarily directed back into itself. By means of the *former* he is distinguished from inanimate being, by means of the *latter* from merely animate (animal) being.]

It is clear to me, that both Schelling an[d] Fichte impose upon themselves the *Schem*[*e*] of an expanding Surface and call i[t] *Freedom*[.][1] *I* should [say], where absolute Freedo[m] is, the[re] must absolu[te] Power [be;] therefo[re] the free[dom &] power [are] Introit[ive.][2] Strang[e] that F[.] and Sch. both h[old] that t[he] very Obj[ect] whic[h] is t[he] conditio[n of] Self-con[sc.] is no[thing] but the Self its self by an act of *free* self-limitation!—

The above I wrote a year ago; but the more I reflect, the more [am] I convinced of the gross materialism, [which lies under the whole system.][a3] All this arises from the Duplicity of human Nature—or perhaps, [Tri]plicity. ["Ho]mo [an]imal [tri]plex":[4] [th]e facts [sta]ted are [m]ere [sen]sations, [the] corpus [mo]rtuum [of] vol[a]tilized [me]mory.[5]

18   p 177, cropped | *SW* I 326

Vielleicht erinnerte ich Sie an Lessings Bekenntniss, dass er mit der Idee eines unendlichen Wesens eine Vorstellung von unendlicher *Langeweile* verbinde, bey der ihm angst und wehe werde—oder auch an jenen (blas-

17[a]   SC's version in *BL* (1847) I 311 is here used in the reconstruction of a cropped line

17[1] The notion that the self or self-consciousness unites two contrary motions, the one infinite, free, and ideal, and the other self-limiting, determined, and real, is central to both Fichte's and Schelling's philosophies: see e.g. Fichte *Grundriss des Eigenthümlichen der Wissenschaftslehre* (Jena & Leipzig 1795) 53–6, Schelling *System des transcendentalen Idealismus* (Tübingen 1800) 83–99. C annotated both these works at an early date.

17[2] A rare term meaning literally "of an ingoing nature". For references to C's use of

this and related words see BÖHME **143** n 1.

17[3] This line of thought led C eventually to the conclusion that Schelling's system was fundamentally pantheistic: *CL* IV 883.

17[4] "Man is a threefold animal". Cf **29** below; also AURELIUS **27**, *CN* III 3901.

17[5] The "dead body" of a volatilised memory: a variant (as in BÖHME **71** and n 2) of the more normal alchemical and chemical image of the "caput mortuum" or "dead head" or residue, as in *BL* ch 7 (*CC*) I 117 and n 4.

phemischen) Ausruf: Ich möchte um alles in der Welt willen nicht selig werden!

[Perhaps I reminded you of Lessing's admission that he connected the idea of an infinite being with the concept of endless *boredom*, which frightened him unutterably— or of that (blasphemous) exclamation: I would not be saved for anything in the world!]

Surely this i[s] childi[sh—] a confus[ion] of Space with Intensity, of Time with Eternity. I cannot think that by the word "adequate" Spinoza meant "commens[u]rate"; but simply "*immediate*".[1]

19   p 219, pencil, overtraced, cropped | *Abhandlungen* § 2 | *SW* I 363

Schon einigemal habe ich die Frage gehört, wie es doch möglich sey, dass ein so ungereimtes System, als das der *sogenannten* kritischen Philosophen in eines Menschen *Kopf—nicht etwa nur kommen, sondern darin gar—Stand fassen konnte?

[I have already heard several times the question as to how it is possible that a system as preposterous as that of the *so-called* critical philosophers could not only get into a man's *head, but also take a firm hold there.]

* I cannot see the mystery. The man persuaded of the ~~Nature~~ Being of Self, seines Ichs[1] as a Thing in it[self,] and that the bodily symbols of it were phænomena (Erscheinung[en)] by which it manifested its bein[g] to *itself* ⟨&⟩ others, easily [how]ever un[reason]ably conce[ives] all other phæn[omena] as m[ani]festa[tions] of other[s as] consci[ous] or un[conscious] yet *actually* sep[arate] Powe[rs] or Ichs or Monads.

20   p 221, pencil, overtraced, cropped | *SW* I 364

Man liess also die Dinge zugleich mit ihren Bestimmungen aus dem *schöpferischen* Vermögen einer Gottheit hervorgehen; * allein man begreift wohl, wie ein Wesen von schöpferischem Vermögen äussre Dinge sich *selbst*, nicht aber wie es dieselbe andern Wesen darzustellen vermag, oder mit andern Worten: wenn wir auch den Ursprung einer Welt *ausser uns* begreifen, so begreifen wir doch nicht, wie die Vorstellung dieser Welt *in uns* gekommen sey.

18[1] C harks back to a footnote by Schelling p 164 (part of his discussion of the philosophy of Spinoza). Tr: "According to Spinoza, all adequate, that is unmediated experiences are intuitions of divine attributes, and the thesis upon which his ethics depends (insofar as it *is* a system of ethics) is the proposition that 'The human mind has an adequate idea of the eternal and infinite essence of God.' *Ethics* pt 2 prop 47."

19[1] "Of his 'I'".

[Therefore things, and their determinations as well, were thought to have arisen through the *creative* power of a deity;* although we may indeed understand how a being with creative power is able to represent external things to *itself*, we cannot understand how it can represent these things to other beings; or, in other words, even if we can conceive of the origin of a world *outside ourselves*, yet we cannot grasp how the representation of this world has got *into us*.]

I cannot comprehend how it can be more difficult to assume a po[wer] of Perception than of Sensation, i.e. Self-perception. God who create[d] [. . . . . ? percipient][1]

21   pp 224–5, pencil, part of first sentence overtraced, cropped | *SW* i 367

Was nun Objekt ist (ursprünglich), ist als solches nothwendig auch ein *Endliches*. Weil also der Geist nicht ursprünglich Objekt ist, kann er nicht ursprünglich seiner Natur nach endlich seyn.—Also unendlich? Aber er ist nur insofern *Geist*, als er *für sich selbst Objekt*, d.h. insofern er *endlich* wird.

[Now what is an object (originally) is as such necessarily *finite* also. Since the spirit is not originally an object it cannot originally be finite according to its nature. Is it therefore infinite? But it is *spirit* only insofar as it is *its own object*, i.e. insofar as it becomes *finite*.]

[a]That the Spirit is, in the modified sense here [no]ted, infinite, may be proved by other[b] reasons; [? &] this is, surely, a strange Twist of Logic!— If [al]l Finites were necessarily Objects, then [in]deed the Spirit, as far as it is no Object, [might be infinite. But that it *is*][c] therefore infinite, by no means follows. The Finite may be the common Predicate of both, the one essentially, the other by will of the Creator.

22   p 229, pencil, partially overtraced | *SW* i 369–70

Der Gegenstand der Anschauung also ist nichts anders, als der Geist *selbst* in seiner Thätigkeit und seinem Leiden. Der Geist aber, indem er sich selbst anschaut, kann sich nicht zugleich von sich selbst unterscheiden. Daher in der Anschauung die absolute Identität des Gegenstandes und der Vorstellung; (daher, wie sich bald zeigen wird, der Glaube, dass in der Anschauung allein Realität sey; denn jetzt noch unterscheidet der Geist nicht, was real und was nicht real ist).

[The object of intuition is thus nothing but the spirit *itself* in its activity and passivity. But the spirit, insofar as it intuits itself, cannot at the same time differentiate itself from

---

21[a–b] Overtraced   **21**[c] SC's reconstruction, in *BL* (1847) i 312

20[1] C has an extended discussion of the   in Schelling *System* **1**.
relation between sensation and perception

itself. Hence the absolute identity of object and representation in intuition; (hence, as will soon be shown, the belief that reality exists in intuition alone; for the spirit does not as yet distinguish what is real and what is not real).]

Spite of Schelling's contempt of Psychology, the fact of outness is more clearly[a] stated in psychology, as dependent on *vividness*.[1] In a fever yet retaining our understand[ing] we see objects a[s] outward[,] yet wel[l] know, t[hey] are no[t] real.

23   p 233, pencil mostly illegible | *SW* I 373–4

Wir, die wir wissen, dass ursprünglich Form und Materie Eins sind . . . kennen nur die einzige Alternative: Entweder muss uns beydes, Materie und Form, *von aussen gegeben*, oder beydes, Materie und Form, muss erst *aus uns* werden und entspringen.

Nehmen wir das erstere an, so ist Materie etwas, das *an sich*, und ursprünglich wirklich ist. . . . Gesetzt aber, sie wäre Etwas *an sich*; obgleich es widersinnig ist, dies nur zu sagen . . . so könnten wir nicht einmal wissen, was sie *an sich* ist. Wir müssten, um das zu wissen, die Materie selbst seyn. . . . So lang wir also Materie *voraussetzen*, d.h. annehmen, sie sey Etwas, das unsrer Erkenntniss *vorangeht*, verstehen wir nicht einmal, was wir reden. . . . *Ursprünglich* also verstehen wir nur *uns selbst* . . . so bleibt für uns, die wir *uns selbst* verstehen wollen, nichts anders übrig, als die Behauptung, dass nicht der Geist aus der Materie, sondern *die Materie aus dem Geist geboren werde*;—ein Satz, von welchem der Uebergang zur praktischen Philosophie . . . sehr leicht gemacht werden kann.

[We who know that form and matter are originally one . . . know of only one alternative: either both matter and form must be *given* to us *from the outside*, or both matter and form must first evolve and originate *from us*.

If we assume the former, then matter is something that exists *in itself* and is originally real. . . . If, however, we posit that matter were something *in itself*, notwithstanding the fact that it is absurd to say this . . . then we can never know what it is *in itself*. In order to know this, we would have to be matter itself. . . . As long as we take matter for granted, i.e. we assume that it is something that *precedes* our knowledge, we shall never understand what we are talking about. . . . *Originally*, then, we understand only *ourselves* . . . hence we who want to understand *ourselves* have no choice but to assert that it is not the spirit which is born out of matter, but is *matter which is born out of the spirit*—a proposition by means of which the transition to practical philosophy . . . can be made quite easily.]

<hr />

22[a] Overtraced to this point

22[1] A note of May 1808 linking the need for vivid symbols and the property of "outness" acknowledges Berkeley as the source of the term: *CN* III 3325. Another Coleridgean variant is "outerance": BÖHME **100** and n 2.

A very profound Remark; [? that] to many [. . . . .]—which far more than
Jacobi often remind[s] me of Plato's *Mode* [? of] convey[ing a] hidde[n]
Truth [in a] Mode which [the] first of [. . . . .]

24   p 237, pencil, rubbed and cropped | § 3 | *SW* I 377

Erstens, die ganze Hypothese [unsere Anschauung ist lediglich passiv]
(denn mehr ist es nicht) würde schon deswegen nichts erklären, weil sie
höchstens einen Eindruck auf unsre Receptivität begreiflich macht, nicht
aber, dass wir einen wirklichen *Gegenstand* anschauen. Läugnen aber
wird niemand, dass wir den äussern Gegenstand nicht bloss *empfinden*,
sondern dass wir eine *Anschauung* von ihm haben. Nach dieser Hypothese würde es ewig nur beim Eindruck bleiben; denn wenn man sagt, der
Eindruck werde erst auf den äussern Gegenstand (als seine Ursache) be-
zogen, und dadurch entstehe die Vorstellung des Letztern, so bedenkt
man nicht, dass wir uns im Zustande der Anschauung keiner solchen
Handlung . . . bewusst sind, auch, dass die Gewissheit von der Gegenwart
eines *Gegenstandes* (der doch etwas vom Eindruck verschiednes seyn
muss) nicht auf einem so unsichern Schlusse beruhen kann. . . . Nun ist
aber *zweytens* gewiss, dass die Ursache niemals *zugleich* ist mit ihrer
Wirkung. Zwischen beyden verfliesst eine Zeit. Es muss also, wenn jene
Annahme richtig ist, eine Zeit geben, in welcher das Ding an sich auf uns
wirkt, und eine andre, in der wir uns dieser Wirkung *bewusst* werden.

[First, the whole hypothesis [that our intuition is merely passive] (for it is no more than
an hypothesis) would explain nothing if for no other reason than that it, at the most,
makes understandable an impression on our receptivity, but not that we are intuiting
a real *object*. But no one will deny that we not only *sense* the external object but also
have an intuition of it. According to this hypothesis, we would always stop short at the
impression; for when it is said that the impression is first of all referred to the external object (as its cause) and that the idea of the external object arises in this way, it is
forgotten that we are not conscious of any such action when we intuit an object, and
that certainty of the presence of an *object* (which must be something different from
the impression) cannot rest on such an uncertain inference. . . . *Secondly*, it is certain
that the cause is never *simultaneous* with the effect. Between the two time passes.
Thus, if that assumption is correct, then there must be a time in which the thing in itself *acts* on us, and another time in which we become *conscious* of this effect.]

This is, ~~surely~~ methinks, all very weak. The Realist may surely affirm that
an Impre[ss]ion of [a] given force [is] what [we] call a[n] Object as
Sch[elling] affir[ms,] ⟨tha[t]⟩ the me[re] self-[exc]itati[on] of its o[wn]
self-di[rected] opera[tions] are wha[t] we m[ean] by O[bjects,] and [?
that] assert[ed] in the § is indee[?d so.] I alw[ays] though[t,] one of the
difficulties attending the notion [? of] cause was its co-instantaneity with

effect. The Heat & the Fire, for instance. [In] all things, the effect is the *presence* of some [? other force as] its cause.*a*

25   p 340 (end of work), referring to p 239 | *SW* I 378

Zwischen der Ursache und ihrer Wirkung endlich findet nicht nur Continuität der Zeit, sondern auch Continuität dem Raume nach statt. Beydes aber kann zwischen dem Gegenstande und der Vorstellung nicht gedacht werden. Denn, was ist wohl das gemeinschaftliche Medium, in welchem, so wie Körper und Körper im Raume, der Geist und das Objekt zusammentreffen?

[Between the cause and its effect there is, finally, not only continuity of time but also continuity as regards space. However, neither can be thought of between the object and the representation. For what then is the common medium in which, as body meets body in space, the spirit meets the object?]

P. 239 Kant⟨, justifying the logical possibility of attraction, as a cause acting at a distance,⟩ has shewn the sophistry of this Assertion in his Verm. Schrift:[1]—and Schelling himself adopts and confirms the Argument of Kant in his Syst. d. t. Id.—[2]

26   pp 355–6, pencil, cropped | *Ueber das Verhältniss* . . . | *SW* VII 301–2

Kaum zweifelhaft kann es nun seyn, was von dem so durchgängig gefoderten und so genannten Idealisiren der Natur in der Kunst zu halten sey. Diese Foderung scheint aus einer Denkart zu entspringen, nach welcher nicht die Wahrheit, Schönheit, Güte, sondern das Gegentheil von dem allem das Wirkliche ist. Wäre das Wirkliche der Wahrheit und Schönheit in der That entgegengesetzt: so müsste es der Künstler nicht erheben oder idealisiren, er müsste es aufheben und vernichten, um etwas Wahres und Schönes zu erschaffen. Wie sollte aber irgend etwas ausser

---

[24]*a* SC reads "some other thing than the cause": *BL* (1847) I 313

[25][1] The sophistry that Kant exposed appears to have to do with the analogy of continuity in space. C may be thinking of parts of Kant's *Allgemeine Naturgeschichte und Theorie des Himmels*, which he annotated in *VS*, e.g. *VS* I 359n–60n; but the concept is discussed more than once by Kant and a more apposite text, which is actually cited by Schelling, is *Metaphysische Anfangsgründe der Naturwissenschaft*, where Kant devotes several pages to the phenomenon of attraction as a form of action at a distance.

In a passage in the 2nd ed (Riga 1787) that C annotated, for example, he asserts (tr): "this attraction is a penetrative force and acts *directly* at a distance . . . through every space as an empty space" (69).

[25][2] In *System des transcendentalen Idealismus* 169–76 (*SW* III 440–4), Schelling cites Kant's *Metaphysische Anfangsgründe* as the source of his own view of attraction as operating "immediately, or at a distance" (174, tr; *SW* III 443).

dem Wahren wirklich seyn können, und was ist Schönheit, wenn sie nicht das volle mangellose Seyn ist? Welche höhere Absicht könnte demnach auch die Kunst haben, als das in der Natur in der That Seyende darzustellen? . . . Die Kunst stellt in der bloss oberflächlichen Belebung ihrer Werke in der That nur das Nichtseyende, als Nichtseyend dar.

[There is now no doubt about what is to be thought of the so-called idealising of nature in art that is so universally called for. This demand seems to arise out of a manner of thinking that views not truth, beauty, goodness, but their opposites as the real. If the real were in fact the opposite of truth and beauty, the artist would have, not to elevate or idealise it, but to transcend it and destroy it in order to create something true and beautiful. But how could anything but the true be real? And what is beauty if not absolute faultless being? Accordingly, what higher intention could art have than to present what in fact exists in nature? . . . In the merely superficial animation of its works, art, then, actually presents the non-existent as not existing.]

It seems to me unworthy of a great Philosopher (& such Schelling is) to give the right sense of words, & then to speak contemptuously of [. . . . .]ᵃ notions arising out of this wrong sense. Thus: those who contended *for* the Ideal in opposition to the actual (*Wirkliches*) meant by the latter what Schelling would call the *unreal*, "das nicht-seyendes".ᵇ

27   pp 358–9, pencil, cropped | *SW* VII 304

Von ihren ersten Werken an ist die Natur durchaus charakteristisch; die Kraft des Feuers, den Blitz des Lichtes verschliesst sie in harten Stein,* die holde Seele des Klangs in strenges Metall . . .

[Right from its very first works, nature is entirely characteristic: it locks up the power of fire, the spark of light in hard stone,* the beautiful soul of sound in austere metal . . .]

* If this be a mere poetic illustration, like those of the Phœnix, the Centaur, &c, it is somewhat out of its place; but if it be intended as fact of exemplification, the [. . . . .]ᵃ either new or obsolete. We understand the fire & flash from Flint & Iron to proceed from ignition by vehement Friction on the same principle as two pieces of Soft-wood [. . . . .]ᵇ

28   p 364, pencil, cropped | *SW* VII 308–9

Die Plastik im genaueren Sinne des Worts verschmähet ihrem Gegenstand den Raum äusserlich zu geben; er trägt ihn in sich. Aber eben dieses verbietet ihr grössere Ausbreitung, ja sie ist genöthigt, die Schönheit

---

26ᵃ Line cropped at foot of 355   26ᵇ A slip for "das Nichtseyende", in textus
      27ᵃ Line cropped   27ᵇ Line cropped

des Weltalls fast auf einem Punkte zu zeigen. . . . Dagegen kann die Mahlerey im Umfang schon mehr mit der Welt sich messen und in epischer Ausbreitung dichten. . . . Hier zählt der Einzelne kaum für selbst; das Ganze tritt an seine Stelle, und was für sich nicht schön wäre, wird es durch die Harmonie des Ganzen. Würde in einem ausgebreiteten Werk der Mahlerey, welche ihre Gestalten durch den beygegebnen Raum, durch Licht, durch Schatten, durch Widerschein verbindet, das höchste Mass der Schönheit überall angewendet: so entstünde hieraus die Naturwidrigste Eintönigkeit, da, wie Winckelmann sagt, der höchste Begriff der Schönheit überall nur Einer und derselbe ist und wenig Abweichungen verstattet.

[The plastic arts in a more exact sense of the term disdain to give to their object space externally; space carries the subject within itself. But this is just what prohibits them from achieving greater expansion; the plastic arts are thus compelled to show the beauty of the universe in a single point. . . . On the other hand, painting can begin to compare itself with the world in scope and can compose on an epic scale. . . . Here the individual part hardly counts in itself; the whole takes its place and what would not be beautiful in itself becomes so through the harmony of the whole. If a large-scale work of painting applied the highest degree of beauty equally in all its parts, combining its figures through the adjoining space, through light, through shadows, and through reflection, the result would be a most unnatural monotony; as Winckelmann says, the highest concept of beauty is everywhere one and the same and allows for little variation.]

This is the fault common to [both] Lessing [a]nd Winckelmann, that in their Theory they [m]anifestly, tho' unconsciously, confined their [I]ntuitions to Statuary. What an endless [re]petition [and] how [fe]w Forms [w]ould Painting [?conve]y, were [it] imprisoned [wi]thin the [C]ordon [o]f [L]essing's [L]aocoon![1]

29   pp 368–71, pencil, cropped | *SW* vii 311–12

Der Geist der Natur ist nur scheinbar der Seele entgegengesetzt; an sich aber das Werkzeug ihrer Offenbarung: er wirkt zwar den Gegensatz der Dinge, aber nur damit das einige Wesen, als die höchste Milde und Versöhnung aller Kräfte, hervorgehen könne. Alle andern Geschöpfe sind von dem blossen Naturgeist getrieben, und behaupten durch ihn ihre In-

---

28[1] J. J. Winckelmann's *Gedancken über die Nachahmung der griechischen Wercke in der Mahlerey und Bildhauer-Kunst* (Friedrichstadt 1755) provided a point of departure for G. E. Lessing's famous essay *Laokoon: oder über die Grenzen der Mahlerey und Poesie* (Berlin 1766), which is included in the set of Lessing's *Sämmtliche Schriften* (30 pts Berlin 1784–98) annotated by C. Lessing discusses painting as well as sculpture, but since the Laocoön group is central to his argument, he necessarily gives more attention to sculpture than to painting.

dividualität; im Menschen allein als im Mittelpunkt geht die Seele auf, ohne welche die Welt wie die Natur ohne die Sonne wäre.

Die Seele ist also im Menschen nicht das Prinzip der Individualität, sondern das, wodurch er sich über alle Selbstheit erhebt, wodurch er der Aufopferung seiner selbst, uneigennütziger Liebe, und, <u>was das Höchste ist</u>, der Betrachtung und Erkenntniss des Wesens der Dinge, eben damit der Kunst, fähig wird.

[The spirit of nature is only seemingly opposed to the soul; in itself, it is the means of the latter's manifestation. Although it produces the opposition of things, it does so only so that the one being, as the greatest benevolence and the reconciliation of all powers, may come forth. All other creatures are driven by the mere spirit of nature and maintain their individuality through it; only in man, as at the midpoint, does the soul arise, without which the world would be like nature without the sun.

Therefore the soul in man is not the principle of individuality but that by means of which man rises above all selfhood, that through which he becomes capable of the sacrifice of the self, of selfless love and—<u>this is the highest of all</u>—of contemplation and knowledge of the essence of things and thereby also of art.]

[It] had [been] better, [methi]nks, to have adopted St Paul's terms, & to [ha]ve named this the Spirit, while [So]ul might be left to designate the [? first] individualizing Principle, and the Σαρξ, [the] Flesh or Nature,[1] or the Body for whatever Man possesses in common with other Animals & even with the (so called) *In*animates—thus Animus, Anima: Spirituality, Animity, Animality.[2] Here we modify the previous [. . . . .] the first [. . .] the third. I *cannot* approve the choice of the Proper Name, Naturephilosophie,[3] because it is 1. a useless Paradox, 2. chosen to make the dif-

---

29[1] Paul uses different Greek terms to designate "soul" and "spirit" and another term again, of course, for "body"—a point made by C elsewhere, e.g. IRVING *Sermons* 27, where the main texts are 1 Cor 15.40, 45. For further attention to this tripartite distinction, see AURELIUS **18, 27, 37** and nn.

29[2] C now attempts to assemble three cognate terms with the Latin root *anim-*, the basic meaning being "breath". Although the meanings of these terms overlap and are confused, the standard Latin dictionary, Robert Ainsworth's *Thesaurus linguae latinae compendarius* (1736; numerous revised eds) under "anima" would have told C that (tr) "*anima* properly signifies the part by which we live and have vigor, *animus* that by which we reason, have wisdom, and are immortal; but they are often confounded". So C probably intends *animus* as spiritual-

ity and *anima* as soul in the Pauline sense. But he finds himself without a word for the fleshly part, the sensual, purely animal part. He begins again, with abstract nouns, coining *Animity* to represent the quality of the *anima*, Schelling's *Naturgeist* or "spirit of nature".

29[3] "Nature-philosophy". The term continued to be in current use as roughly equivalent to English "natural philosophy", "natural science", or "physiology", when Schelling appropriated it for his own system. As C explained to C. A. Tulk in a letter of 24 Nov 1818, "Schelling is the Head and Founder of a philosophic Sect, entitled Natur-philosophen, or Philosophers of Nature. . . . as a *System*, it is . . . reduced at last to a mere Pantheism" (*CL* IV 883). C sometimes used "physiology" in the wider sense to avoid the paradox of describing the study

ference [. . . . .] and his old Master (Fichte's) systems greater than it is[4]—
& 3. because the phrase has been long & universally appropriated to the
knowlege, which does not include the *Peculia*[?*rs*][5] of Man/ i.e. to Phys-
iolog[y.] The Identity of the one with the other is to appear as the *Result*
of the System; but for its Title, i.e. its Proper (*appropriated*) name, Qui
bene distinguit, bene docet.[6]

30   p 369, pencil, cropped | **29** textus (last paragraph)

Strange morality, to place contempla[tion] & Painting above the most
heroic & pure Virtues in Action. This eulogy of the Soul is taken from
the Alexandria[n] School, especially Proclus, but by him applie[d] to the
το Εν.[1]

31   p 403, cropped | *Philosophische Untersuchungen* | *SW* vii 339

Die meisten, wenn sie aufrichtig wären, würden gestehen, dass, wie ihre
Vorstellungen beschaffen sind, die individuelle Freyheit ihnen fast mit
allen Eigenschaften eines höchsten Wesens im Widerspruch scheine, z.B.
der Allmacht.

[Most people, if they were honest, would admit that, according to the way their ideas
are constituted, individual freedom seems to them to be in contradiction with almost
all characteristics of a highest being, e.g. omnipotence.]

But is no[t] this still [a] carrying [of] the *physic*[*al*] Dynamic[s] into the
moral? [? Even] admitting the incongruous Predicate Time, in the Deity,
I cannot see an[y] absolute incompossibility of Foresight with Freedom.

---

of nature as philosophy. For Schelling's use
of the word in both senses, as well as for C's
use of "physiologist", see **36** below.

29[4] Although Kant and Fichte were formative influences in his thought, Schelling
aimed with *Naturphilosophie* to establish
an objective idealism that would supersede
the subjectivism of Fichte's *Wissenschaftslehre* ("theory of knowledge") and counter
Kant's objections to dogmatic philosophy.

29[5] *Peculia* (Latin) "special properties";
or the archaic English equivalent.

29[6] "He who distinguishes well, teaches
well". C uses this scholastic maxim also in
CN iii 4058 f 73, *Logic* (*CC*) 253, *SW & F*
(*CC*) 107.

30[1] To "the One". Plotinus, who is usually considered to be the first as well as the

greatest of the Neoplatonics (or Eclectics or
Alexandrians or Alexandrines as they were
then, in England, more commonly called)
maintained that the active virtues were only
the first steps in the ascent of the soul
through contemplation of its own divine nature to union with Beauty, the Good, and the
One; the work of art is beautiful insofar as
the soul of the artist has a vision of Beauty
itself. See e.g. *Ennead* 1.6.9, 5.8.1 (passages to which C alludes in *CN* iv 5280 f
10ᵛ), and 6.9.11. For a comparable passage
in Proclus see Proclus **1** and **2** textus.
Proclus **5** links Schelling—or aspects of
Schelling's thought—specifically with Proclus, as do *P Lects* Lect 13 (1949) 390, *CL*
iv 873–4.

32   p 413 | *SW* vii 346

Es ist nicht ungereimt, sagt Leibnitz, dass der, welcher Gott ist, zugleich gezeugt werde, oder umgekehrt, so wenig es ein Widerspruch ist, dass der, welcher der *Sohn eines Menschen ist, selbst Mensch sey. Im Gegentheil, wäre das Abhängige oder Folgende nicht selbständig, so wäre diess vielmehr widersprechend. . . . Das Nämliche gilt vom Begriffenseyn in einem Andern. Das einzelne Glied, wie das Auge, ist nur im Ganzen eines Organismus möglich; nichtsdestoweniger hat es ein Leben für sich, ja eine Art von Freyheit, die es offenbar durch die Krankheit beweisst, deren es fähig ist.

[Leibniz says that it is not nonsense that he who is God is at the same time begotten, or vice versa, just as it is not a contradiction that he who is the *son of a man is himself a man. On the contrary, if the dependent or consequent were not independent, this itself would be contradictory. . . . For this is a case of being comprehended in another. The individual member, such as the eye, is possible only in the totality of an organism. Nevertheless it has a life of its own, even a kind of freedom, which it clearly displays in the illness of which it is capable.]

* I do not see the propriety of the Instance: unless "God" is here assumed as an *Ens genericum*,[1] even as "Man"—and if this be a mere nominalism, it proves nothing—and as a realism, it is a petitio principii sub Lite.[2] Just so, that of the Eye: but this is a far better Illustration.

33   p 421, cropped | *SW* vii 351–2

Es wird aber immer merkwürdig bleiben, dass Kant, nachdem er zuerst Dinge an sich von Erscheinungen nur negativ, durch die Unabhängigkeit von der Zeit, unterschieden, nachher in den metaphysischen Erörterungen seiner Kritik der praktischen Vernunft Unabhängigkeit von der Zeit und Freyheit wirklich als correlate Begriffe behandelt hatte, nicht zu dem Gedanken fortging, diesen einzig möglichen positiven Begriff des An-sich auch auf die Dinge überzutragen, wodurch er sich unmittelbar zu einem höhern Standpunkt der Betrachtung und über die Negativität erhoben hätte, die der Charakter seiner theoretischen Philosophie ist.

[It will always remain a curious fact that after Kant had distinguished things in themselves from phenomena only negatively with reference to independence of time, and had afterwards treated independence of time and freedom as really correlated concepts in the metaphysical expositions in his *Critique of Practical Reason*, he did not proceed to the thought of transferring this, the only possible positive concept of the in-

32[1] "Generic Being".
32[2] "Begging the question in dispute", the logical fallacy of taking for granted something that is still under discussion or unresolved. C gives an account of "the two great schools of the Schoolmen, the Nominalists and the Realists" in *P Lects* Lects 9, 10 (1949) 278–80, 290–2 (the quotation being from 278).

itself, to things as well. That way he would have attained directly a higher level of reflection and gone beyond the negativity which is characteristic of his theoretical philosophy.]

But would not this have been opposite to Kant's aim? His object was a καθαρτικον τῆς ψυχης.[1] In order to effect this thoroughly, within this he by an act of choice, confined himself—[. . .]wise & good!

34   p 422 | *SW* vii 352

Denn ob es einzelne Dinge sind, die in einer absoluten Substanz, oder eben so viele einzelne Willen, die in einem Urwillen begriffen sind, ist für den Pantheismus, als solchen, ganz einerlei.

[For pantheism, as such, it is irrelevant whether single things are comprehended in an absolute substance or many individual wills are comprehended in a primal will.]

The ? is, do not these single Wills so included in the one "Urwille"[1] become "Things"?

35   p 424, slightly cropped | *SW* vii 354

Es könnte jemand versuchen, jenem Dilemma durch die Antwort zu entgehen: das Positive, was von Gott herkommt, sey die Freyheit, die an sich gegen Böses und Gutes indifferent sey. Allein wenn er nur diese Indifferenz nicht bloss negativ denkt, sondern als ein lebendiges positives Vermögen zum Guten und zum Bösen, so ist nicht einzusehen, wie aus Gott, der als lautere Güte betrachtet wird, ein Vermögen zum Bösen folgen könne.

[Someone might try to escape that dilemma by answering that the positive, which comes from God, is freedom, which in itself is indifferent to good and evil. However, if he thinks of this indifference not only as something negative but as a living, positive capacity for good and evil, it is not evident how a capacity for evil could derive from God who is regarded as pure goodness.]

But God will not do impossibilities [a]nd how can a Vermögen[1] for moral Good exist, (in a *Creature*) which does not *imply* a Vermögen zum Bösen?[2]

36   p 428, pencil, cropped | *SW* vii 357

Wir haben es bereits erklärt: nur aus den Grundsätzen einer wahren Naturphilosophie lässt sich diejenige Ansicht entwickeln, welche der hier stattfindenden Aufgabe vollkommen Genüge thut. Wir läugnen darum

---

33[1] "Cleansing of the soul".
34[1] "Primal will"—in textus.

35[1] "Capacity"—in textus.
35[2] "Capacity for evil"—in textus.

nicht, dass diese richtige Ansicht nicht schon längst in einzelnen Geistern vorhanden gewesen sey. Aber eben diese waren es auch, die ohne Furcht von den von jeher gegen alle reelle Philosophie gebräuchlichen Schmähworten Materialismus, Pantheismus, u.s.w. den lebendigen Grund der Natur aufsuchten, und im Gegensatz der Dogmatiker und abstrakten Idealisten, welche sie als Mystiker ausstiessen, Naturphilosophen (in beyderlei Verstande) waren.

[We have already explained that a view fully adequate to the problem which concerns us here can only be developed on the basis of the fundamental principles of a genuine philosophy of nature. We do not however deny that this correct view has for a long time already been present in individual minds. It was indeed these very individuals who sought out the vital ground of nature, without fear of those terms of reproach—materialism, pantheism, etc—that have always been used against all genuine philosophy. They were nature-philosophers (in both senses of the word) in contrast to the dogmatists and abstract idealists who dismissed them as mystics.]

[Be]hmen, [B]runo [na]y, tho' [in] meteor [fl]ashes [on]ly, even the writings of Paracelsus.—[1]

37　　p 438 | *SW* VII 364

Indem nun die Seele lebendige Identität beyder Prinzipien ist, ist sie Geist; und Geist ist in Gott. Wäre nun im Geist des Menschen die Identität beyder Prinzipien eben so unauflöslich als in Gott, so wäre kein Unterschied, * d.h. Gott als Geist würde nicht offenbar. Diejenige Einheit, die in Gott unzertrennlich ist, muss also im Menschen zertrennlich seyn,—und dieses ist die Möglichkeit des Guten und des Bösen.

[Now insofar as the soul is the vital identity of both principles, it is spirit; and spirit is in God. If the identity of both principles were as indissoluble in the spirit of man as in God, there would be no distinction, * i.e. God as spirit would not be revealed. That unity which is indivisible in God must therefore be divisible in man—and this is the possibility of good and evil.]

* But the Problem was—How to prove this Distinction (Unterchied)[a] and here it is *assum⟨ed⟩* as a ground of Proof.—

37[a]　A slip for "Unterschied"

36[1] C suggests Böhme, Bruno, and Paracelsus as representatives of the sort of "individual minds" described by Schelling as precursors of the "nature-philosophers" of his own school. Böhme and Bruno he associates elsewhere with Schelling (e.g. *CL* IV 775, 883), but Paracelsus is a more unusual choice, though in a note that was probably written about the time when C was most immersed in Schelling, C prophesies that Paracelsus will eventually be recognized "either as a Repository of the Arcana . . . of the Samothracian . . . Mysteries, or as the greatest Physiologist since the Christian Æra": LESSING *Sämmtliche Schriften* **47**. For a later statement see Thomas FULLER *Holy State* **7** and nn. On Böhme see also **38** n 2 below.

38   pp 438–9 | **37** textus

* How exactly does this seem to resemble Schelling's Objection to
Fichte—"It must be so.["] Why?—"Because else my Theory would be
false."[1] Well! and what if it were?—In truth, from p. 429. I find little but
Behmen—which a Reader must have previously understood in order to
understand.[2] And in the names of Candor and Common Sense wherein
does this Zertrennlichkeit differ from the rejected Vermögen zum Bösen
involved in dem freyem[a] Vermögen zum Guten?[3]

39   pp 438–9, leaf tipped in, referring to p 438 | Continuing **37** textus | *SW* VII 364

Wir sagen ausdrücklich: die Möglichkeit des Bösen, und suchen vorerst
auch nur die Zertrennlichkeit der Prinzipien begreiflich zu machen. Die
Wirklichkeit des Bösen ist Gegenstand einer ganz andern Untersuchung.
Das aus dem Grunde der Natur emporgehobne Prinzip, wodurch der
Mensch von Gott geschieden ist, ist die Selbstheit in ihm, die aber durch
ihre Einheit mit dem idealen Prinzip *Geist* wird.

[We stress that it is the possibility of evil [that is at issue here], and for the time being
we are only trying to explain the divisibility of principles. The reality of evil is the object of an entirely different investigation. The principle, derived from the ground of
nature through which man is separated from God, is the selfhood in him—which, however, becomes *spirit* through its unity with the ideal principle.]

Schelling, p. 438.—
    We will grant, for a while, that the Principle evolved or lifted up from
this mysterious *Ground* of Existence, which *is* and yet does not exist, is
separate (geschieden) from God: yet how is it separate from the Ground
itself? How is it individualized? Already the material phænomen of Part-
ibility seems to have stolen in.—And at last I cannot see what advantage

38[a] A slip for "freyen"

38[1] In *Darlegung* Schelling objects to
Fichte's tendency to offer purely hypothetical assertions as indubitable facts and his
expectation that readers will take his words
for granted. See e.g. *SW* VII 16 where
Schelling accuses Fichte of an authoritarian
and egotistical mode of reasoning while appearing to deny this very fact. C alludes
to a later passage in *Darlegung* where
Schelling objects to Fichte's notion that
knowledge, viewed as absolute self-posit-
ing and self-affirmation, is an accomplished
fact (*Thatsache*) of our consciousness and
that generally we cannot know anything but

"such accomplished facts of our consciousness." He wonders how Fichte arrived at
this notion and criticises Fichte for presenting such hypothetical conjectures as "purely
factual" as if "it would not have occurred to
anyone to doubt" them (*SW* VII 67).
    38[2] For C's association of Schelling
with Böhme see **36** and n 1 above, **42** and n
1 below, as well as BÖHME **52** and n 15.
    38[3] C combines phrases from **39** and **35**
textus: "Wherein does this divisibility differ
from the rejected capacity for evil involved
in the free capacity for good?"

in reason this Representation, this form of Symbol, has over the old more reverential Distinction of the Divine Will relatively to the End from the same Will relatively to the Means: the latter of which we term his Wisdom, and to the former appropriate the name of the Divine Will κατ' εμφασιν.[1]

40   pp 438–9, leaf tipped in

Schelling has more than once spoken of the necessity of a thorough "Study of Logic["]—he has admitted that a Logical Work suited to the present state & necessities of scientific Discipline does not exist.[1] Would that he had prefixed to this work a Canon of his own Logic: and *if he could*, have taught us, wherein his forms of Thinking differ from thate transrealization of not Ideas alone but more often of Abstractions and arbitrary general Terms, in Proclus.—[2]

41   pp 440–1, apparently referring to pp 438–9,[a] pencil, partly overtraced | *SW* vii
          364

Der Geist ist über dem Licht; wie er sich in der Natur über der Einheit des Lichts und des dunkeln Prinzips erhebt. Dadurch, dass sie Geist ist, ist also die Selbstheit frey von beyden Prinzipien. Nun ist aber diese oder der Eigenwille nur dadurch Geist, und demnach frey oder über der Natur, dass er wirklich in den Urwillen (das Licht) umgewandelt ist, so dass er zwar (als Eigenwille) im Grunde noch bleibt, (weil immer ein Grund seyn muss)—so wie im durchsichtigen Körper die zur Identität mit dem Licht erhobne Materie desshalb nicht aufhört, Materie (finstres Prinzip) zu seyn—aber bloss als Träger und gleichsam Behälter des höhern Prinzips des Lichts.

[The spirit is above the light, just as in nature it rises above the unity of light and the dark principle. By being spirit, selfhood is therefore free from both principles. But this selfhood or self-will is spirit—and accordingly free or above nature—only because it

41[a]   The foot-margins of pp 438–9 had already been filled with **38**

39[1] "Emphatically".

40[1] E.g. in this work, tr: "Such misunderstandings, if they are not intentional, imply a degree of dialectical immaturity that Greek philosophy transcended almost in its first beginnings, and make the recommendation of a thorough course in logic an urgent duty" (407; *SW* vii 342).

40[2] In WHITAKER **7**, when Whitaker describes Philo as "subtilizing being into power", C makes a similar remark: "Who

that had ever rested but in the porch of the Alexandrine Philosophy, would not rather say—of substantiating Powers and Attributes into Beings? What is the whole System, from Philo to Plotinus, and thence to Proclus inclusively, but one fanciful Process of hypostasizing logical Conceptions and generic Terms? In Proclus it is Logolatry run mad." On the connection between Proclus and Schelling see also **30** and n 1 above.

has really changed into the primal will (light) in such a manner that it is indeed fundamentally preserved (as self-will)—for there must always be a ground—but merely as the vehicle and, as it were, container of the higher principle of light—just as the matter in a transparent body does not cease to be matter (the dark principle) when it is raised to an identity with the light.]

It is difficult to conjecture what advantage Schelling proposed to himself in this allegorizing [b](αλλον αγορευειν)[c1] & yet so imperfectly whatever he might dream as to the hidden identity of Light [. . . . .] and of Darkness with the natural [? dawning/yearning][d]: yet no man can avoid distinguishing Day-light from [? dark].[e] In short, Light here means *some*⟨thing.⟩ Why not substitute that meaning?   S. T. C.

---

42   p 442, cropped | *SW* vii 366

Diesen allein richtigen Begriff des Bösen, nach welchem es auf einer positiven Verkehrtheit oder Umkehrung der Prinzipien beruht, hat in neueren Zeiten besonders Franz Baader wieder hervorgehoben und durch tiefsinnige physische Analogien, namentlich die der Krankheit, erläutert.

[This sole true concept of evil, according to which evil is based on a positive perversity or inversion of principles, has in recent times been re-emphasised by Franz Baader and elucidated by profound physical analogies, in particular those of illness.]

How can I explain the strange Silence [r]especting Jacob Böemen?[1] The Identity of his [&] Schelling's System was exulted in by the TIEKS [? in/at] Rome in 1805, to *me*:[2] & these were [Sch]elling's [in]timate [fr]iends—[an]d the [co-]incidence [of] the express[io]ns, illustrations, [e]ven in the [m]ystical [ob]scurities, [is] too glaring [to] be solved [as] a mere [in]dependent [co]-incidence [in] Thought and [in]tuition.

[Pr]obably, pru[d]ential motives [re]strain Schelling [for] a while: for [I w]ill not think, [th]at Pride or [a] dishonest lurking Desire to appear not only [*an*] original, but *the* Original, can have influenced [a] man of Genius, like Schelling.   S. T. Coleridge.

41[b-c] Not overtraced   **41**[d] Overtraced as "yearning"
41[e] SC reads "the mere sense of day-light": *BL* (1847) i 303

41[1] "To say something else". For this derivation of "allegory" cf *CN* iii 4183 and n, *Lects 1808–1819* (*CC*) ii 99.

42[1] C comments on the resemblance between the works of Schelling and Böhme in **36** and **38** above.

42[2] This is one of very few records of C's early acquaintance with Ludwig Tieck, whom he did not meet again until Jun 1817:

CL iv 738–9, 742–3, 744–6. According to Roger Paulin *Ludwig Tieck: A Literary Biography* (Oxford 1985) 172, they met in the Humboldt house in Rome, Tieck's brother Friedrich being the beneficiary of a travelling scholarship arranged by Humboldt. C arrived in Rome just after Christmas 1805; he must mean 1806 when he refers to the Tiecks.

43   p 443, pencil, overtraced, slightly cropped | *SW* vii 367n

[Footnote, quoting from *Jahrbücher der Medicin* iii 203:] "Einen lehr-
reichen Aufschluss giebt hier das gemeine Feuer (als wilde, verzehrende,
peinliche Glut) im Gegensatze der sogenannten organischen wohlthuen-
den Lebensglut, indem *hier* Feuer und Wasser in Einem (wachsenden)
Grunde zusammen, oder in Conjunction eingehen, während sie *dort* in
Zwietracht auseinander treten . . ."

["An instructive example is here provided by common fire (as a wild, consuming, dis-
tressing blaze) in contrast to the so-called organic and benign glowing fire of life. In
the *latter* fire and water form a common (growing) ground or conjunction, whereas in
the *former* they divide in disunity . . ."]

Water is the great Nurse & Mediatrix of all growth. Now Water is an in-
stru[ment] of union, a marriage, of the Comburent and the Combustible
principles = Oxygen & Hydrogen.[1] Fire on^a the cont[rary] is the fierce
Combat of the two. This is better as well as more accurate than Feur und
Waser^b in einem *Grunde*.[2]

44   pp 444–5, pencil, partly overtraced | *SW* vii 368–9

Denn schon die einfache Ueberlegung, dass es der Mensch, die vollkommenste aller sichtbaren Kreaturen ist, der des Bösen allein fähig ist,
zeigt, dass der Grund desselben keineswegs in Mangel oder Beraubung
liegen könne. Der Teufel nach der christlichen Ansicht war nicht die
limitirteste Kreatur, sonder vielmehr die illimitirteste. Unvollkommenheit im allgemeinen metaphysischen Sinn ist nicht der gewöhnliche
Charakter des Bösen, da es sich oft mit einer Vortrefflichkeit der einzelnen Kräfte vereinigt zeigt, die viel seltner das Gute begleitet.

[For even the simple reflection that it is only man, the most perfect of all visible creatures, who is capable of evil, shows that the cause of evil cannot lie in want or depri-
vation. In the Christian view the devil was not the most limited creature but rather the
most unlimited. The normal character of evil is not imperfection in the general metaphysical sense, since it often appears combined with an excellence of individual powers which accompanies the good much more rarely.]

Thus [. . .] world [. . . .] not [. . . ? general] as moral evil, but as the limitation of a given Quantum of Perfection, or Powers, all below as well as

---

43^a Overtraced as "in"   **43**^{b} A slip for "Feuer und Wasser"

43[1] "Comburent" and "combustible"
were adopted by Lavoisier to describe that
which causes combustion (esp oxygen) and
that which undergoes combustion; C uses

them elsewhere in the context of *Naturphilosophie*, e.g. OERSTED **5**.
    43[2] "Fire and water in one *ground*"—in
textus.

above being exactly as such in the scale of Being; must [. . .] a Man of Horns?[1] I do not mean to deny the truth of Schelling's position, but the force of some of his reasons in support of it. It seems evil [? for] that Evil is excluded by Substitute [. . . . .]

45 p 445, pencil, overtraced | Continuing **44** textus | *SW* VII 369

Der Grund des Bösen muss also nicht nur in etwas Positiven überhaupt, sondern eher in dem höchsten Positiven liegen, das die Natur enthält, wie es nach unsrer Ansicht allerdings der Fall ist, da er in dem offenbar gewordnen Centrum oder Urwillen des ersten Grundes liegt.

[The cause of evil must reside not just in something positive in general but rather in the highest positive contained in nature. In our view this is indeed the case, for it resides in the now apparent centre or primal will of the primal ground.]

* But what is the Cause or Condition of this?

46 p 445, pencil, partly overtraced, cropped | **44** textus

The modern (English) Unitarians contemplate the Deity as mere Mercy, or rather Good-nature, without reference to his Justice & Holiness; and ~~in~~ to this Idol, Deifica[tion] of a hum[an] Passion[,] is their whole system confined. The Calvinis[ts] do the same with [the] Omnipo[tence] of God with as little referen[ce] to his Wisdom and Love.[1]

47 pp 449–50, pencil, overtraced | *SW* VII 371

Denn die Schwäche oder Nichtwirksamkeit des verständigen Prinzips kann zwar ein Grund des Mangels guter und tugendhafter Handlungen seyn, nicht aber ein Grund positiv-böser und tugendwidriger.

[For weakness or ineffectiveness of the principle of understanding can, it is true, be a reason for the lack of good and virtuous actions, but not a reason for positively wicked or unvirtuous actions.]

Why not? if the Inertia be voluntary. Suppose *Heat* to be a moral agent, and voluntarily to withdraw itself. Would not the splitting of the Vessel

---

44[1] I.e. as in traditional representations of the Devil.

46[1] Having spent a few critical years as a Unitarian in his youth, C made many analyses of its errors in his maturity, notably *LS* (*CC*) 93–100, 181–4*, *AR* (*CC*) 208–13*, *CN* III 3581. His observations about Calvinism are more scattered: IRVING *Sermons* **10** describes the emphasis on God's "Sovereignty" as contradictory to "Holiness" as the "radical error of Calvinism"; and "modern" Calvinism is the subject of many notes, e.g. A. FULLER **4**, LUTHER *Colloquia* **33**, *C&S* (*CC*) 135 and n, *AR* (*CC*) 157–60.

by the frozen water be a positive act? I find a confusion in Schelling of the visible with the conceivable.[1] As well might I say, that when I tossed a child into the air, & wilfully did not catch it again, that[a] this being a mere negation of motion was no moral act.

48   pp 452–3, leaf tipped in | *SW* vii 373–4

Denn jedes Wesen kann nur in seinem Gegentheil offenbar werden, Liebe nur in Hass, Einheit in Streit. Wäre keine Zertrennung der Principien, so könnte die Einheit ihre Allmacht nicht erweisen . . . . Der Mensch ist auf jenen Gipfel gestellt, wo er die Selbstbewegungsquelle zum Guten und Bösen gleicherweise in sich hat: das Band der Principien in ihm ist kein nothwendiges, sondern ein freyes.

[For every being reveals itself only through its opposite—love through hatred, unity through conflict. If there were no separation of principles, unity could not manifest its omnipotence . . . . Man is placed on that summit where he possesses within himself the source of the self-impulsion toward good and evil in equal measure: the bond of the principles within him is not a necessary but a free one.]

Schelling puzzles me for ever by his Man *made up* of two separate Principles—and yet *he* (as a tertium aliquid[)],[1] *whose* not *who* these principles are, has the free power of separating them—

49   p 456, cropped | *SW* vii 376

Aber es sind in der Natur zufällige Bestimmungen, die nur aus einer gleich in der ersten Schöpfung geschehenen Erregung des irrationalen oder finstern Prinzips der Kreatur—nur aus aktivirter Selbstheit erklärlich sind. Woher in der Natur . . . Erscheinungen, die auch ohne Rücksicht auf ihre Gefährlichkeit für den Menschen dennoch einen allgemeinen natürlichen Abscheu erregen. [Footnote:] So ist die nahe Verbindung, in welche die Imagination aller Völker, besonders alle Fabeln und Religionen des Morgenlandes, die Schlange mit dem Bösen setzen, gewiss nicht umsonst.

[But in nature there are accidental conditions that can be explained only as the result of an excitation of the irrational or dark principle of the creature that occurred at the original creation—only as the result of activated selfhood. Whence in nature . . . [the

47[a]   C's comma and "that" overtraced as semi-colon and dash

47[1] A perennial complaint of C's against materialism and the materialist frame of mind: cf *BL* ch 12 (*CC*) i 288, where he attacks "the creed of our modern philosophers" that "nothing is deemed a clear conception, but what is representable by a distinct image. Thus the *conceivable* is reduced within the bounds of the *picturable*."
    48[1] A "third something"—as in *BL* ch 13 (*CC*) i 300 and n 2.

existence of] phenomena which, even regardless of their danger for man, nonetheless excite a general, natural repugnance. [Footnote:] Thus the close connection between the snake and evil, found in the imagination of all peoples, and in particular in all the fables and religions of the East, doubtless does not exist without good reason.]

But some have [s]upposed [i]t the Ape. [T]he Ape is the [v]ery opposite of the Serpent. The Eel—the Trout—the Salmon—these excite no "Abscheu"[1]—nor the common Earth-worm.—   S. T. C.

—I doubt the truth of my own remark. The Eel & Earth-worm [. . . . .]

50   p 458

The Book-binder has docked my former notes; but I understand enough to find that my first impressions were the same as my present are: after repeated perusal, and too strong a pre-possession. It is a mere Day-dream = somnium philosophans![1]

51   p 458, cropped | *SW* vii 378

Wie aber die ungetheilte Macht des anfänglichen Grundes erst im Menschen als Inneres (Basis oder Centrum) eines Einzelnen erkannt wird: so bleibt auch in der Geschichte das Böse anfangs noch im Grunde verborgen . . . . Auf dieselbe Art nämlich, wie der anfängliche Grund der Natur vielleicht lange zuvor allein wirkte, und mit den göttlichen in ihm enthaltnen Kräften eine Schöpfung für sich versuchte, die aber immer wieder, (weil das Band der Liebe fehlte), zuletzt in das Chaos zurücksank, (wohin vielleicht die vor der jetzigen Schöpfung untergegangenen und nicht wiedergekommenen Reihen von Geschlechtern deuten), bis das Wort der Liebe erging, und mit ihm die dauernde Schöpfung ihren Anfang nahm; so hat sich auch in der Geschichte der Geist der Liebe nicht alsbald geoffenbaret . . .

[But just as the undivided might of the inchoate ground is first recognised in man as the inside (basis or centre) of an individual, so too in history evil at first remains hidden in the ground . . . . In the same way, that is, as the primal ground of nature may have operated alone long before and, through the divine forces contained within it, may have attempted a creation on its own which, however, in the end always sank back into chaos because the bond of love was lacking. (Possible evidence for this is the series of species that were destroyed before the present creation and never returned.) At last the word of love went forth and with it the permanent creation had its beginning; likewise in history the spirit of love did not reveal itself straight away . . .]

[I h]ave often [dr]eamt of [th]is, as [a] Theory of [Hy]datids, [Ta]pe-

49[1] "Repugnance"—in textus.   **50**[1] "A philosophising dream".

worms [an]d other [ex]crescences [of] Life.[1] Supp⟨ose⟩ [a] brief [me]tathesis of [? the] Bildungstrieb = nisus formativus,[2] from its [ap]propriate Organs in Male or Female, to the [St]omach, or Liver. Uxores steriles, vel saltem [α]παιδες, præsertim quæ ob defectum Mariti [. . . . .][3]

52   p 459, cropped | *SW* VII 378–9

. . . so hat sich auch in der Geschichte der Geist der Liebe nicht alsbald geoffenbaret; sondern weil Gott den Wille des Grundes als den Willen zu seiner Offenbarung empfand, und nach seiner Fürsehung erkannte, dass ein von ihm (als Geist) unabhängiger Grund zu seiner Existenz seyn müsse, liess er den Grund in seiner Independenz wirken, oder, anders zu reden, Er selbst bewegte sich nur nach seiner Natur und nicht nach seinem Herzen oder der Liebe. Weil nun der Grund auch in sich das ganze göttliche Wesen, nur nicht als Einheit, enthielt, so konnten es nur einzelne göttliche Wesen seyn, die in diesem Für-sich-wirken des Grundes walteten. Diese uralte Zeit fängt daher mit dem goldenen Weltalter an, von welchem dem jetzigen Menschengeschlecht nur in der Sage die schwache Erinnerung geblieben, einer Zeit seliger Unentschiedenheit, wo weder Gutes noch Böses war . . .

[. . . likewise in history the spirit of love did not reveal itself straight away; but because God perceived the will of the ground to be the will to its revelation, and in his providence recognised that there must be a ground independent of him (as spirit) for its existence, he allowed this ground to act in its independence, or to put it differently, he himself moved only according to his nature and not according to his heart or love. Since the ground contained in itself the whole divine being, only not as a unity, there could only be individual divine beings which reigned in this acting-for-itself of the ground. This primordial time therefore begins with the golden age, of which mankind today has only a faint memory preserved in legend, a time of blessed indecision, where there was neither good nor evil . . .]

Why not have quoted all this from Böemen, as an extract raisonnè?[1] B[ut]

51[1] By "hydatid" here C means the larva of a tapeworm. The example would be a common one—and C uses intestinal parasites as metaphors elsewhere, e.g. *CL* II 1001, BIBLE COPY B **118**—but it is worth noting that all C's family were troubled occasionally by worms, C having his own theories about such infestations, e.g. *CL* II 909.

51[2] *Nisus formativus* with the German equivalent *Bildungstrieb*, "formative impulse", was a phrase coined by Blumenbach, whose lectures C attended at Göttin-

gen (*BL* ch 10—*CC*—I 207), to denote the vital power that acts on matter and "imparts to it a *form* regular and definite": J. F. Blumenbach *Institutions of Physiology* tr John Elliotson (2nd ed 1817) 335.

51[3] "Infertile or at least childless wives, particularly those who [are sterile] from a defect in the husband".

52[1] C does not mean that this passage is to be found verbatim in Böhme, only (as he has said before, e.g. **38** and n 2, **42** above) that Schelling's philosophy in many ways

does the Hypothesis ([or] hypo-p[oiesis] rather)[2] explain [the] problem [of] Evil?—A Nature, [the] Groun[d,] the *Sub-s[?tans]*[3] of God [it is] which y[et] is not "e[r] selbst" [—] not God himself but out of whic[h] God [? himself] exists, & which y[et] is bego[t] by the se[lf-]existent[,] & yet is evil, morally evil—& yet the cause & parent, yea the very essence o[f] Freedom, without which, ⟨as antecedent,⟩ das Böse[4] cann[ot] be— what is all this?—Here is neithe[r] [. . . . .]

---

53   p 461, cropped | *SW* vii 380

Denn nur Persönliches kann Persönliches heilen, und Gott* muss Mensch werden, damit der Mensch wieder zu Gott komme.

[For only the personal can heal the personal, and God* must become man so that man will come to God again.]

* What[ever] this me[ans] Water [is] not [to be] mixed [with] Wine, unles[s] Wine [has] been [pre]vious[ly] mixed [with] Water.

---

54   p 462, cropped | *SW* vii 381

Erst nach Erkenntniss des allgemeinen Bösen ist es möglich, Gutes und Böses auch im Menschen zu begreifen. Wenn nämlich bereits in der ersten Schöpfung das Böse mit erregt und durch das Für-sich-wirken des Grundes endlich zum allgemeinen Prinzip entwickelt worden, so scheint ein natürlicher Hang des Menschen zum Bösen schon dadurch erklärbar, weil die einmal durch Erweckung des Eigenwillens in der Kreatur einge- tretne Unordnung der Kräfte ihm schon in der Geburt sich mittheilt. Allein es wirkt der Grund auch im einzelnen Menschen unablässig fort, und erregt die Eigenheit und den besondern Willen, eben damit im Gegensatz mit ihm der Wille der Liebe aufgehen könne. Gottes Wille ist, alles zu universalisiren, zur Einheit mit dem Licht zu erheben . . . der Wille des Grundes aber, alles zu partikularisiren oder kreatürlich zu machen. . . . Darum reagirt er nothwendig gegen die Freyheit als das

---

resembles Böhme's: for Böhme's discus- sion of similar topics and C's responses see BÖHME **110**, **165**. An extract *raisonné* would be one in which a position was fully developed or "reasoned out".

52[2] A favourite distinction, elucidated in a note of 1809 (*CN* iii 3587): "Hypothe- sis: the placing of one known fact under oth- ers as their *ground* or foundation. Not the fact itself but only its position . . . is imag-

ined. Where both the position and the fact are imagined, it is Hypopoeesis not Hy- pothesis, subfiction not supposition."

52[3] "Standing-under"—again, an ety- mology to which C recurs, e.g. in BLANCO WHITE **13** (at n 8), or in *AR* (*CC*) 17*. In *AR* (*CC*) 394, he observes that "*Subject* and *Substance* are words of kindred roots, nay, little less than equivalent terms".

52[4] "Evil"—in textus.

Ueberkreatürliche und erweckt in ihr die Lust zum Kreatürlichen . . . .
Schon an sich scheint die Verbindung des allgemeinen Willens mit einem
besondern Willen im Menschen ein Widerspruch, dessen Vereinigung
schwer, wenn nicht unmöglich ist.

[Only after recognising universal evil is it possible to comprehend good and evil in
man too. For if evil was already aroused in the first creation and was finally developed
into a general principle by the self-centred operation of the ground, then man's natural inclination to evil seems at once explicable, because the disorder of forces that
entered creatures on account of the awakening of self-will is already transmitted to
man at birth. But the ground operates incessantly in individual man too, and rouses
egotism and a particularised will so that the will of love might arise in opposition to
it. It is God's will to universalise everything, to lift everything to unity with light . . .
but the will of the ground is to particularise everything or to make it creature-like. . . .
Thus it necessarily reacts against freedom, freedom being something above the creaturely, and awakens in it the desire for the creaturely . . . . The combination of the universal will with a particular will in man seems in itself to be a contradiction; their union
seems difficult, if not impossible.]

But where, after all, is the *Evil*, as contra-distinguished from Calamity,
& Imperfection? How does this solve the diversity, [the] *essential*
[diffe]rence, [betw]een [re]gret & [rem]orse?[1] [Ho]w does [it] concur
[ev]en with [th]e Idea [of] Freedom? [I] own, [I] am [dis]appointed: [and]
that [I r]eject [this] system [& rea]lise, that [I r]emain [in] the same State,
with the same harrying [?dim]ly & partially light-shotten Mists before
[my] eyes, as when I red*a* the same things [f]or the first time in Jacob
Behmen!—[2]

55   p 463, cropped | *SW* VII 381–2

Daher die allgemeine Nothwendigkeit der Sünde und des Todes, als des
wirklichen Absterbens der Eigenheit, durch welches aller menschlicher
Wille als ein Feuer hindurchgehen muss, um geläutert zu werden. Dieser
allgemeinen Nothwendigkeit ohnerachtet bleibt das Böse immer die
eigne Wahl des Menschen; das Böse, als solches, kann der Grund nicht
machen und jede Kreatur fällt durch ihre eigne Schuld.

[Hence the universal necessity of sin and death as the real mortification of individuality, through which all human will must go, as through a fire, in order to be purified.
Despite this universal necessity, evil always remains man's own choice; the ground
cannot make evil as such and each creature falls through its own fault.]

54*a* A slip for "read"

54[1] C uses the example of the difference   18, NICOLAI 4, James SEDGWICK 57.
in kind between regret and remorse as evi-   54[2] See 52 n 1.
dence of original sin elsewhere, e.g. JUNG

But i[s] Death [to] the Wick[ed] as to t[he] Better[?][a] Shall we say that th[e] Redeem[ed] die *to* [the] *Flesh* [and] therefo[re] *from* [it?] but [then] ⟨the⟩ Repro[bates] die *in* the Flesh and therefore *with* it?— *S. T. C.*

56 p +2, referring to p 465 | *SW* vii 383

Die Hauptsache ist, dass dieser Begriff eine gänzliche Zufälligkeit der einzelnen Handlungen einführt und in diesem Betracht sehr richtig mit der zufälligen Abweichung der Atomen verglichen worden ist, die Epikurus in der Physik in gleicher Absicht ersann, nämlich dem *Fatum* zu entgehen. Zufall aber ist unmöglich . . . und wenn Freyheit nichts anders, als mit der gänzlichen Zufälligkeit der Handlungen, zu retten ist, so ist sie überhaupt nicht zu retten. Es setzt sich diesem System des Gleichgewichts der Willkühr . . . der Determinismus (oder nach Kant Prädeterminismus), entgegen, indem er die empirische Nothwendigkeit aller Handlungen aus dem Grunde behauptet, weil jede derselben durch Vorstellungen oder andre Ursachen bestimmt sey, die in einer vergangenen Zeit liegen, und die bei der Handlung selbst nicht mehr in unsrer Gewalt stehen. . . . Beyden [Systemen] gleich unbekannt ist jene höhere Nothwendigkeit, die gleichweit entfernt ist von Zufall, als Zwang oder äusserem Bestimmtwerden, die vielmehr eine innere, aus dem Wesen des Handelnden selbst quellende, Nothwendigkeit ist. . . . Ueberhaupt erst der Idealismus hat die Lehre von der Freyheit in dasjenige Gebiet erhoben, wo sie allein verständlich ist.

[The main point is that according to this concept individual actions are completely accidental, and in this respect it has been compared quite rightly to the accidental swerving of atoms which Epicurus invented in physics for the same purpose, namely to escape *fate*. Accident, however, is impossible . . . and if freedom is to be saved in no other way except by making actions completely accidental, then it cannot be saved at all. Determinism (or, as Kant calls it, predeterminism) stands opposed [to this system of the equilibrium of choice] . . . in that it asserts the empirical necessity of all actions on the ground that each of them was determined by past representations or other causes that are no longer in our control at the time of the action. . . . Both [systems] alike are ignorant of that higher necessity which is equally far removed from accident and from compulsion or external determination, and which is, rather, an inner necessity that springs from the being of the agent itself. . . . It was indeed Idealism that first raised the doctrine of freedom into that realm in which it can alone be understood.]

P. 465. I still feel myself dissatisfied with the argument against Freedom derived from the influence of Motives, Vorstellungen,[1] &c—for are these *things?* and not rather mere general Terms, signifying the Mind deter-

55[a] SC reads "better mortal": *BL* (1847) i 305

56[1] "Representations"—in textus.

mining itself? For what is a motive but a determining Thought? And what is a Thought but the mind acting on itself in ~~a given~~ some one direction?—all that we want is to prove the *possibility* of Free Will, or what is really the same, a Will. Now this Kant had unanswerably proved by shewing the distinction between Phænomena and Noumena, by demonstrating that Time and Space were Laws of the former only (ἁι Συνθεσεῖς ἁι πρῶται τῆς αισθησέως· Ὁ χρονος μεν, η πρωτη, καθ' ολον συνθεσις τῆς αἰσθησεως τῆς ἔσω, ο δε χωρος, τῆς ἔξω)[2] and irrelative to the latter, to which Class the Will must belong.[3] In all cases of Sense the Reality proves the possibility; but in this instance (which ~~might~~ must be unique if it be at all) the proof of the Possibility only is wanting to effect the establishment of the Reality. Therefore, I cannot but object to p. 468—sie fällt ausser aller Zeit, und *daher* mit der *ersten* Schöpfung zusammen.[4] This has at least the appearance of a contradiction.

57   pp 467–8, cropped | *SW* vii 384

Das intelligible Wesen kann daher, so gewiss es schlechthin frey und absolut handelt, so gewiss nur seiner eignen innern Natur gemäss handeln, oder die Handlung kann aus seinem Innern nur nach dem Gesetz der Identität und mit absoluter Nothwendigkeit folgen, welche allein auch die absolute Freyheit ist: denn frey ist, was nur den Gesetzen seines eignen Wesens gemäss handelt, und von nichts anderem weder in noch ausser ihm bestimmt ist.

[In acting perfectly freely and absolutely, an intelligible being can, to be sure, act only in accordance with its own inner nature. Or the action can proceed out of its inner nature only according to the law of identity and with absolute necessity, which alone is absolute freedom as well; for that alone is free which acts according to the laws of its own being and which is determined by nothing else external or internal to itself.]

And is not this a confirmation of the old Remark—that he, who would *understand* Freedom instead of knowi[ng] it by an act of Freedom (the myste[ry] in the mystery[)] must either flee to Deter[mi]nism a prio[ri] or ab extra[1] or to Fatali[sm] or the Necessi[ty] ex esse[ntia] propri[a].[2] In eithe[r] case ho[w] can w[e] explai[n] Remor[se] and Self-accusation

---

56[2] These are "the first synthetic acts of perception. Time is the first general synthesis of the inner perception, while place is that of the outer [perception]". C alludes specifically to the transcendental aesthetic in *C d r V*, esp secs 1–2 (B 37–53).

56[3] See, for example, Kant's "Explana-

tion of the Cosmological Idea of Freedom . . ." in *C d r V* B 570–86.

56[4] "It occurs outside all time, and *therefore* coincides with the *first* creation": from **58** textus below.

57[1] "From without".

57[2] "From its own nature".

other than as Delusions[,] the necessity of which does not preve[nt] the necessity of knowing them to be Delusions—& consequently, renews that civil war between the Reason and the unconquerable Feeling, which it is the whole Duty & Promise of Philosophy to reconcile?[3]

58   p 468 | *SW* vii 385

Der Mensch ist in der ursprünglichen Schöpfung, wie gezeigt, ein un entschiedenes Wesen . . . nur er selbst kann sich entscheiden. Aber diese Entscheidung kann nicht in die Zeit fallen; sie fällt ausser aller Zeit und daher mit der *ersten Schöpfung . . . zusammen.

[Man in the original creation is, as has been shown, an undecided being . . . only he himself is capable of decision. But this decision cannot take place in time; it takes place outside all time and therefore . . . coincides with *first creation.]

* But this makes it time.[1]

59   p 469 | *SW* vii 386

Eben so verhält es sich mit dem Guten, dass er nämlich nicht zufällig oder willkührlich gut, und dennoch so wenig gezwungen ist, dass vielmehr kein Zwang, ja selbst die Pforten der Hölle nicht im Stande wären, seine Gesinnung zu überwältigen. In dem Bewusstseyn, sofern es blosses Selbsterfassen und nur idealisch ist, kann jene freye That, die zur Noth-wendigkeit wird, freylich nicht vorkommen, da sie ihm, wie dem Wesen, vorangeht, es erst *macht*; aber sie ist darum doch keine That, von der dem Menschen überall kein Bewusstseyn geblieben . . .

[The same applies to the good: it is not good by chance or arbitrarily, and yet it is so little forced that, on the contrary, no compulsion, not even the gates of hell, would be able to prevail against it. That free action which becomes necessity cannot, it is true, occur in consciousness insofar as the latter is mere self-comprehension and only ideal, because it precedes self-comprehension as well as being and in fact *produces* self-comprehension; it is nevertheless for that very reason not an act of which man has re-mained completely unconscious . . .]

Far better to have proved the *possibility* and to have left the mode un-touched—The Reality is sufficiently proved by the Fact.

57[3] Cf Schelling 507 (*SW* vii 413) tr: "These considerations lead us back to our point of departure. A system which contra-dicts the most sacred sentiments and feel-ings and moral consciousness can, at least in these characteristics, never be called a system of reason but only of unreason. On the other hand, a system in which reason ac-tually realises itself would have to unite all the demands of the spirit as well as of the heart, of the most conscientious feeling as well as of the strictest understanding."

58[1] The last sentence of textus is quoted at the end of **56** above.

60   p 470 | *SW* VII 386–7

Wie oft geschieht es, dass ein Mensch von Kindheit an, zu einer Zeit, da wir ihm, empirisch betrachtet, kaum Freyheit und Ueberlegung zutrauen können, einen Hang zum Bösen zeigt, von dem vorauszusehen ist, dass er keiner Zucht und Lehre weichen werde, und der in der Folge wirklich die argen Früchte zur Reife bringt, die wir im Keime vorausgesehen hatten . . .

[How often does it happen that a person from childhood—at a time when, regarding the matter empirically, we can hardly believe him capable of freedom and reflection—displays a tendency to evil from which we can foretell that he will not yield to any discipline or teaching, and which in the end actually produces the bad fruits that we had foreseen from the seed . . .]

D^r· Bell would deny this lustily, & charge the result on blunders in the Education.[1]

61   pp 470–1, pencil, rubbed, partly overtraced, cropped | *SW* VII 387

. . . so hat der Mensch, der hier entschieden und bestimmt erscheint, in der ersten Schöpfung sich in bestimmter Gestalt ergriffen, und wird, als solcher, der er von Ewigkeit ist, geboren . . . . Von jeher war die angenommne Zufälligkeit der menschlichen Handlungen im Verhältniss zu der im göttlichen Verstande zuvor entworfnen Einheit des Weltganzen, der grösste Anstoss in der Lehre der Freyheit. Daher denn, indem weder die Präscienz Gottes noch die eigentliche Fürsehung aufgegeben werden konnte, die Annahme der Prädestination. Die Urheber derselben empfanden, dass die Handlungen des Menschen von Ewigkeit bestimmt seyn müssten; aber sie suchten diese Bestimmung nicht in der ewigen, mit der Schöpfung gleichzeitigen, Handlung, die das Wesen des Menschen selbst ausmacht, sondern in einem absoluten, d.h. völlig grundlosen Rathschluss Gottes, durch welchen der eine zur Verdammniss, der andre zur Seligkeit vorbestimmt worden, und hoben damit die Wurzel der Freyheit auf.

[. . . therefore man, who here appears as decided and determined, took on a determinate form in the first creation and was born as that which he is from eternity . . . . The

---

60[1] Andrew Bell (1753–1832) developed an inexpensive method for teaching children by using senior children as monitors. He became involved in controversy with Joseph Lancaster (1779–1838), the proponent of a similar, rival system. C, who was acquainted with Bell, joined the fray in his support, lecturing on his system in 1808 (*Lects 1808–1819*—*CC*—I 96–109) and writing in the 1809 *Friend* (*Friend*—*CC*—II 69–70) to praise him as one whose system inculcated virtue as well as knowledge.

greatest obstacle to the doctrine of freedom has always been the relation of the assumed accidental character of human actions to the unity of the universe as previously planned in divine reason. Thus there came the assumption of predestination, since neither God's prescience nor actual providence could be relinquished. The authors of the doctrine of predestination felt that human conduct must have been determined from eternity. Yet they did not seek this determination in the eternal act contemporaneous with creation, which constitutes the being of man himself, but in an absolute (i.e. wholly unfathomable) decree of God through which one individual was predetermined for damnation and another for blessedness; and thus they destroyed the root of freedom.]

I have long believed this; but surely, it is no explanation beyond the simple idea of free will itself, which still in the first instance [co]mes [b]ack [to] the [. . .] *absolute*, or *Indiff*[e]*rence* which if Schelling [f]rom [. . .]ingly [. . .] [fo]rce [. . . . .] himself & Fichte or rather Kant—and again (p. 471) does not ["]völlig grundlosen Rathschluss",[1] [with] difficulty remain the same?

62   pp 472–3, pencil, overtraced | *SW* vii 388

Nur jenes durch eigne That, aber von der Geburt, zugezogne Böse kann daher das radikale Böse heissen, und bemerkenswerth ist, wie Kant, der sich zu einer transcendentalen alles menschliche Seyn bestimmenden That in der Theorie nicht erhoben hatte, durch blosse treue Beobachtung der Phänomene des sittlichen Urtheils in späteren Untersuchungen auf die Anerkennung eines, wie er sich ausdrückt, subjektiven, aller in die Sinne fallenden That vorangehenden Grundes der menschlichen Handlungen, der doch selbst wiederum ein Aktus der Freyheit seyn müsse, geleitet wurde . . .

[Only that kind of evil that results from one's own deed, but originates in birth, can therefore be called radical evil. It is worth noting that Kant, whose theory did not introduce a transcendental deed to determine all human existence, was led in his later works, merely by faithfully observing the phenomena of moral judgment, to the acknowledgment of (as he put it) a subjective ground of human actions preceding all deeds occurring to the senses, a ground that had itself, in its turn, to be an act of freedom . . .]

But why this asserted superiority over Kant? Where is the Proof? Where the probability? that by *mere faithful observation* he could arrive (he alone of all other philosophers) to this awful Conclusion? Lastly what has Schelling added to Kant's notion?

61[1] The "wholly unfathomable decree"—in textus.

63   pp 478–9, pencil, partly overtraced, cropped | *SW* vii 392

Es sey uns erlaubt, diess, der ursprünglichen Wortbedeutung nach, durch Religiosität auszudrücken. Wir verstehen darunter nicht, was ein krankhaftes Zeitalter so nennt, müssiges Brüten, andächtelndes Ahnden, oder Fühlen-wollen des Göttlichen. Denn Gott ist in uns die klare Erkenntniss oder das geistige Licht selber, in welchem erst alles andre klar wird, weit entfernt, dass es selbst unklar seyn sollte; und in wem diese Erkenntniss ist, den lässt sie wahrlich nicht müssig seyn oder feyern. Sie ist, wo sie ist, etwas viel Substantielleres, als unsre Empfindungsphilosophen meynen. Wir verstehen Religiosität in der ursprünglichen, praktischen Bedeutung des Worts. Sie ist Gewissenhaftigkeit, oder dass man handle, wie man weiss, und nicht dem Licht der Erkenntniss in seinem Thun widerspreche. Einen Menschen, dem diess nicht auf eine menschliche, physische oder psychologische, sondern auf eine göttliche Weise unmöglich ist, nennt man religiös, gewissenhaft im höchsten Sinne des Worts. Derjenige ist nicht gewissenhaft, der sich im vorkommenden Fall noch erst das Pflichtgebot vorhalten muss, um sich durch Achtung für dasselbe zum Rechttun zu entscheiden.

[This can perhaps best be expressed by the term religiosity, taken in its original sense. We do not thereby mean what a morbid generation designates by this term: indolent brooding, pious presentiments, or pretended sensations of the divine. For God is the clear knowledge or the spiritual light itself in us. Only in it does anything else become clear; that this light itself should be unclear is hardly possible. And when this knowledge is present in someone, it truly does not allow him to be indolent or festive. Wherever it is found, it is something much more substantial than our philosophers of sensibility suppose. We understand religiosity in the original, practical meaning of the word. It is conscientiousness, acting as one ought and not contradicting the light of knowledge by one's deeds. Someone for whom such contradiction is impossible, not in a human, physical, or psychological manner, but in a divine manner, is religious or conscientious in the highest sense of the word. A man is not conscientious who must in a given situation first remind himself of the command of duty and can decide what action is right only by observing the command.]

[B]ut how unfair this is, to attribute to Kant a slow motive-seeking process [? at/in] separate [in]tervals [of] *time* [me]rely [bec]ause [a] man [ca]n [*u*]*tter* [an]y thought in [the] forms [of] time & space [b]ut if [Sch]elling [had] tried [? the] same Law!—Most true, most reverently true is it, that a Being imperfect does feel an *awe* of [. . . . .] it as in the presence of a holier Self—alter et idem,[1] where the tr[ue] I, distinguishable thro' imperfection [. . . . .]

<hr />

63[1]   "Other and the same"—a phrase C attributed to Philo and generally used in a   Trinitarian context, as in BÖHME **178** (at n 1), and below, **69** at n 6.

64   p 493, pencil, partly overtraced, cropped | *SW* VII 403

[There is only one answer to the question why there is not perfection from the beginning:] . . . weil Gott ein Leben ist, nicht bloss ein Seyn. Alles Leben aber hat ein Schicksal, und ist dem Leiden und Werden unterthan. Auch diesem also hat sich Gott freywillig unterworfen, schon da er zuerst, um persönlich zu werden, die Licht- und die finstre Welt schied.

[. . . because God is a life, not merely a being. All life, however, has a destiny, and is subject to suffering and change. God has submitted himself voluntarily to this also, even when he, at the beginning, separated the light and the dark world in order to become personal.]

These are hard Sayings. Is not the Father *from all Eternity*[1] the [? Seiend][2] one?—and frey-willig sich unterwor[fen] um persönlich zu werden![3] Do not [. . . . .] the end

65   pp 495–6, pencil, overtraced | *SW* VII 405

Sein Zustand [des Bösen] ist daher ein Zustand des Nichtseyns, ein Zustand des beständigen Verzehrtwerdens der Aktivität, oder dessen, was in ihm aktiv zu seyn strebt. Es bedarf darum auch zur Realisirung der Idee einer endlichen allseitigen Vollkommenheit keineswegs einer Wiederherstellung des Bösen zum Guten, (der Wiederbringung aller Dinge) . . .

[Its [evil's] state is therefore one of non-existence, a state of constant consuming of activity or of that which strives to be active in it. That is why it is not at all necessary that evil be restored to good (the return of all things) for the realisation of the idea of an ultimate universal perfection . . .]

Then will not the Darkness become again Light? What was before its union with Light, & of course the Object of the same process repeated?—Surely, this has too much the appearance of subjecting the supersensual to the Intuitions.

66   p 496, pencil, overtraced, cropped | *SW* VII 405

Das Ende der Offenbarung ist daher die Ausstossung des Bösen vom Guten, die Erklärung desselben als gänzlicher Unrealität. Dagegen wird das aus dem Grunde erhobene Gute zur ewigen Einheit mit dem ursprünglichen Guten verbunden . . .

64[1] This is not an uncommon phrase, but C's underlining it suggests that he had a particular source in mind, perhaps Milton *Paradise Lost* VIII 406.

64[2] The "existing" or "being" one; the one who simply *is*. Schelling regularly uses this term—on the same page as textus, for example.

64[3] "Voluntarily submitted himself in order to become personal"—in textus.

[The end of revelation is therefore the expulsion of evil from the good and the declaration that it is complete unreality. On the other hand, the good which is taken up from the ground will be bound in eternal unity with the original good . . .]

[It] really looks [. . . ? peculiar] in a thing merely to take it out. And still [the] Question returns, Why not this in [the] first place? What can the [?pro]cess have [exp]ected?

67   p 502

It seems to me, that this whole Work presupposes Des Cartes's "quod clare concepimus, verum est.["][1]

67A   p 506, final sentence marked with a pencil line in the margin | *SW* vii 412

Wir im Gegentheil sind der Meynung, dass eben von den höchsten Begriffen eine klare Vernunfteinsicht möglich seyn muss, indem sie nur dadurch uns wirklich eigen, in uns selbst aufgenommen und ewig gegründet werden können. Ja, wir gehen noch weiter, und halten mit Lessing selbst die Ausbildung geoffenbarter Wahrheiten in Vernunftwahrheiten für schlechterdings nothwendig, wenn dem menschlichen Geschlecht damit geholfen werden soll.

[We, on the contrary, are of the opinion that a clear, rational understanding must be possible even of the most exalted concepts, since only thus can they become truly ours, enter into us and be eternally grounded. Indeed we go still further and with Lessing regard even the development of the truths of revelation into truths of reason as absolutely necessary if the human race is to be helped by them.]

68   p +1, pencil, badly rubbed, partly overtraced[a]

[. . . . .]iction in fact to the [. . . . .] Idea, [. . . . .] discovery which [. . . . .] Wissenschaftslehre,[1] & of Schelling's Erweiterung und Vervollkommung derselben[2]—[. . . . .] not THINGS (= Sachen), but Acts! LIVING Powers[3]

68[a]   Only the overtraced words are now legible

67[1] "That which we have clearly conceived, is true": Descartes *De methodo* pt 4 var. (C may be quoting from memory.) He annotated a copy of the philosophical works of Descartes containing this essay: DESCARTES.

68[1] Presumably a reference to Fichte's *Wissenschaftslehre* or "theory of knowledge": the word appears in the titles of several of Fichte's works (some of which were annotated by C) and is used by extension for his whole philosophy. In *BL* ch 9 (*CC*) i 157 C translates the word as "*Lore* of Ultimate Science".

68[2] His "enlargement and improvement of the same". Cf "the Wissenschaftslehre of Fichte and Schelling" in PROCLUS **5**.

68[3] The subject of the final clause must have been words, for C affirmed repeatedly that words are not things but acts or thoughts or living powers: cf *CL* vi 630, *AR* (*CC*) 10.

69   pp [+2]–[+7],[a] slightly cropped

There are ~~so~~ indeed many just and excellent Observations in Schelling['s] Phil. Unt. üb. das Wes. der Mensch. Fr.[1] and yet ~~so many~~ even more *over*meaning or unmeaning Quid pro Quos— ~~so many~~ ex. gratiâ, *Thing*-phrases, (such as Licht, Finsterniss, Feuer,[2] center, circumference, Ground, &c &c) which seem to involve the dilemma, that either they are mere similies, when that, which they are meant to illustrate, has never been stated; or that they are *degrees* of a *Kind*, which Kind has not been defined. Hence ṃ Schelling seems to be *looking objectively* at one thing, and imagining himself *thinking* of another. And after all this mysticism, what is the result? Still the old Questions return, & I find none but the old answers.—This Ground to God's existence either lessens, or does not lessen, his Power—in the first, it is in effect a co-existent God, evil because the ground of all evil—in the second, it leaves us, as before. With that *"before" my* understanding is perfectly satisfied—and, vehemently as Schelling condemns that Theory of Freedom, which makes it consist in the paramouncy of the Reason over the Will, wherein does his own solution differ from this—except in expressing with uncouth mysticism the very same notion?—For what can be meant by the individuality, or Ichheit, becoming excentric—& usurping the circumference[3]—if not this?—He himself plainly says that moral Evil arises not from Privation much less Negation, but from the same Constituents leaving their proper

---

69[a] The note begins on [+6], continues to [+7], returns to [+4] and [+5], and ends on [+2]

69[1] The title of the last work in the volume—*Philosophische Untersuchungen über das Wesen der menschlichen Freyheit und die damit zusammenhängende Gegenstände*.

69[2] "Light, darkness, fire"—as in **41** and **43** textus above.

69[3] Schelling describes the dual movement of selfhood away from or towards the universal will as respectively a movement from the centre of a circle to the periphery and the opposite movement, from the periphery to the centre. C may have had in mind a particular passage, pp 439–40 (*SW* VII 364–5), tr: "But because selfhood possesses spirit . . . it can separate itself from light. Self-will may seek to be, as a particular will, that which it is only in its identity with the universal will. It may seek to be at the periphery that which it is only insofar as it remains at the centre, or as creature. . . . Will which deserts its supernatural status in order to make itself, as universal will, both particular and creaturely strives to reverse the relation of the principles, to exalt the ground above the cause and to use the spirit which it received only for the centre, outside the centre and against the creature, an action that leads to disorganisation within itself and outside itself. Man's will may be regarded as a nexus of living forces; as long as it abides in its unity with the universal will these forces remain in their divine measure and balance. But hardly does self-will move away from the centre which is its station, than the nexus of forces is also dissolved; in its place a merely particular will rules which can no longer unite the forces among themselves as before . . .".

ordination—i.e. C. B. A. instead of A. B. C.[4]—But wherein does this differ from the assertion, that the Freedom of Man consists in all the selfishness of his nature being subordinated to, and used as the instrument and materia of his Reason—i.e. of his sense of the universal will?

In short, nothing seems gained—. To Creation (werden)[5] he himself admits that we must resort—he himself admits it, in even a far higher sense, in the Logos—or the alter Deus et idem[6]—Other creations were still possible, from the will of God, and not from his essence—and yet partaking of his *Goodness*—A mere machine could be made happy, but not deserving of Happiness—but if God created a Being with a power of *choosing* Good, that Being must have been created with a power of choosing Evil—or there is no meaning in the word, Choice. And thus we come again to the necessity arising out of Finiteness, with Leibnitz & Plato for it is evident, that by Matter Plato & Plotinus meant Finiteness,[7] or how else could they call it the το μη ov[8]—without any qualities, & yet capable of all? The whole Question of the origin of Evil resolves itself into one—Is the Holy Will good in & of itself or only relative, i.e. as a means, to Pleasure, Joy, Happiness, &c?—If the latter be the truth, no solution can be given of the origin of Evil compatible with the attributes of God—but (as in the problem of the Squaring of a Circle) we can demonstrate, that it is *impossible* to be solved.[9] If the former, be true, as I more than believe, the Solution is easy and almost self-evident. Man cannot be a moral Being without having had the Choice of Good & Evil—he can-

69[4] The passage quoted in n 3, among others, suggests this position.

69[5] "Becoming", as opposed to being: in a passage that C may have had in mind, p 431 (*SW* VII 358–9), Schelling observes (tr), "First, the concept of immanence must be completely set aside, insofar as it is understood to express a dead conceptual inclusion of things in God.... But the process of their becoming [*Werden*] cannot be in God (viewed absolutely), since they are altogether—or more accurately, infinitely—distinct from him."

69[6] The "God that is other and the same"—the second Person of the Trinity, as in BÖHME **178** (at n 1) and in **63** above. Schelling discusses the concept of God as one with yet different from "God himself" p 431 (*SW* VII 359).

69[7] At pp 441–8 (*SW* VII 364–73), Schelling establishes a context for his own

views about the origin of evil by outlining the arguments of certain other philosophers, specifically Plato, Leibniz, and Baader (of the last of whom he writes approvingly). According to him, Plato considered matter as inherently evil, while Leibniz replaced the matter of the ancients with "the realm of eternal verities" as "the ideal cause of evil and good" (443 tr; *SW* VII 367).

69[8] "That which is not"—"the το μη ov, whose essence is negation", as C says in EICHHORN *Apocrypha* **12**. Cf ARGENS **18** nn 1–3 where Plato's created matter is defined as existing by limitations, that is, in so far as it negates the one and good.

69[9] On this perennial mathematical puzzle, see e.g. Spinoza *Ethics* pt 1 prop 11 dem (tr Curley): "the very nature of a square circle indicates the reason why it does not exist, viz. because it involves a contradiction".

not *chuse* Good without having been able to choose Evil. God, as infinite & self-existing, is the alone One, in whom Freedom & Necessity can be one and the same, from the Beginning—in all finite Being, it must have been arrived at by a primary act, as in Angels, or a succession of acts as in man.   *S. T. Coleridge*

P.S. Schelling unfairly represents Kant's System & that other of other as the mere subjection of the appetiteses[b] to the Reason/ Kant makes the *enjoyment* of Freedom, not Freedom itself, consis[t] in the subjection of the particular to the universal Will, in order to their Identification[10]—and does not Schelling use Freedom often where he means no more than others mean by *Life*—i.e. the power of *originating* motion?

Annex

An additional fragment of a note written, like **12, 13, 14**, and **39**, on a separate piece of paper, its whereabouts now unknown, is described in a Sotheby sale catalogue 7–8 Dec 1959, Lot 391. It appears to refer to p 126 of this work, i.e. to Letter 2 (126–9; *SW* I 290–2), probably and particularly to the first paragraph, printed as textus. The note is described in the catalogue as consisting of 2 pp, the text incomplete at the foot of the second page, and the "second paragraph . . . initialled 'S. T. C.'". The catalogue prints as an extract the text presented here as C's note.

Der Kriticismus, mein Freund, hat nur schwache Waffen gegen den Dogmatismus, wenn er sein ganzes System nur auf die Beschaffenheit unsers *Erkenntnissvermögens*, nicht auf unser ursprüngliches Wesen selbst gründet. Ich will mich nicht auf den mächtigen Reiz berufen, der dem Dogmatismus insofern wenigstens eigenthümlich ist, als er nicht von Abstraktionen oder von todten Grundsätzen, sondern (in seiner Vollendung wenigstens) von einem *Daseyn* ausgeht, das aller unsrer Worte und todten Grundsätze spottet. Ich will nur fragen, ob der Kriticismus seinen Zweck—die Menschheit frey zu machen—wirklich erreicht hätte, wenn sein ganzes System einzig und allein auf unser Erkenntnissvermögen, als etwas von unserm ursprünglichen Wesen verschiedenes, gegründet wäre?

[The critical philosophy, my friend, brings feeble weapons against dogmatism if it bases its whole system solely on the constitution of our *cognitive faculty* and not on our original essence itself. I will not speak of the powerful attraction that inheres in dogmatism, at least insofar as it proceeds not from abstractions or dead principles but (at least in its most perfect form) from a *being* that mocks all our words and dead principles. I only wish to ask whether the critical philosophy would have attained its purpose—to set humanity free—if its whole system were based solely on our cognitive faculty as something distinct from our original essence?]

69[b] A slip for "appetites"

69[10] See **56** and nn above.

... 126 This attack on Kant like most of Schelling's is really *slanderous*. The very phrase Vernunft-glauben, Faith of Reason, gives the sufficient answer.[1] Kant's Position is this: that in the great truths of Religion the Moral being of Man supplies those premises which in the science of Nature are given by the Sense, and Experience; but that as in the latter the conclusions cannot go beyond the Data, so neither ought they in the former. That is: the conclusions are limited by the *moral* interest, in which the Ratiocination had its origin . . .

ANNEX[1] Kant is not explicitly named by Schelling, but his system is the implied target. C defends him by reference to one of Kant's own terms, *Vernunft-Glauben* (*C d r* *V* B 857), i.e. "rational belief" or—as C himself translates it in *CL* IV 863, "a *belief* consistent with reason".

System des transcendentalen Idealismus. Tübingen 1800. 8°.

British Library C 43 b 10

Three passages on pp 112–13 have been marked in an unidentified hand as parallel to specific passages in *BL*. Some of C's notes have been seriously cropped in rebinding.

TRANSCRIPT. VCL S MS 19 (by SC).

DATE. Two readings at least, one about 1813–15, before the composition of *BL*; one after 1818 and possibly later than 1825 (**1** n 4). According to his own statement in *BL* ch 9 (*CC*) I 164, this was one of only three vols by Schelling in C's possession before the composition of *BL*; its role in that work is discussed esp in the notes to *BL* chs 8, 12 (*CC*) I 132–6, 252–60, and in *CN* III 4265n. C returned to this work and to his notes in it in Nov 1825: *CN* IV 5276, 5280–3, 5286, 5288.

TEXTUS TRANSLATION. *System of Transcendental Idealism*. Tr Peter Heath. Charlottesville 1978.

COEDITOR. Raimonda Modiano.

1   pp ⁻1, ⁻3

*a*Berkley's Scheme is merely an evolution of the positions—All perception is reducible to Sensation; and all Sensation is exclusively *subjective* (He, who feels, feels himself)—Ergo, all Perception is ~~subje~~ merely subjective/ [? so] "Perceptum = percipi": or "Dum percipitur, est."[1] The principium *cognoscendi* is raised into the principium *essendi*.[2] Now I*b* should commence my reply to Berkley by denying both positions—or (which is tantamount) the second—~~Error~~ Sensation, I would say, is never merely subjective; but ought to be classed as a minimum, or lower degree of Perception.[3] Sensation, I assert, is not exclusively subjective; but of all

1*a* This note begins below the end of **4** (on p ⁻1), and must have been written after it
1*b* Here C has written "(see Cover)", and at the end of p ⁻3 (which he has marked "*Cover*") has continued the note with "from next leaf, p. 2."

1[1] "What is perceived = the being perceived" or "While it is being perceived, it exists".
1[2] The "principle of *knowing*" is raised into the "principle of *being*".
1[3] C referred specifically to this note when he took up the critique of subjective idealism again in Nov 1825 (*CN* IV 5276):

"As rationally might I ~~ackn~~ assert a Tree to be a Bud, as Bp. Berkley ~~that~~ Perception ~~is Sens~~ to be Sensation—which is itself but the minimum, lowest grade, or first manifestation of Perception. In the covers & blank Leaves of my Copy of Schelling's System des Transcendentalen Idealismus I have proved this succinctly yet clearly". An

the *known* Syntheses of Subject + Object it is the *least* Objective; but for that reason still objective. Or (to express my Position in a somewhat more popular form) Sensation is Perception within the narrowest sphere.—But this admitted, Berkleianism falls at once.—

Now the Facts of Zöology are all in favor of *my* position, and the whole Class of Protozoa so many instances of the Truth.[4] Nay, as Extremes meet,[5] Sensation in its first manifestation is eminently *Objective.* The Light, & Warmth, and surrounding Fluid are the Brain & Nerves of the Polyp: even as the true Objective (the Corporeal World as it *is*) exists only *subjectively*—i.e. in the *Mind* of the Philosopher, while the true Subjective (i.e. the Appearances resulting from the position and mechanism of the Percipient) exists for our ⟨common⟩ Consciousness[6] ~~only~~ as independent & pure *Object.*

2   pp 4–6, pencil, cropped, marked with two pencilled crosses in the margin | *SW* III 341

Die vollendete Theorie der Natur würde diejenige seyn, kraft welcher die ganze Natur sich in eine Intelligenz auflöste.—[a]Die todten und bewusstlosen Producte der Natur sind nur misslungene Versuche der Natur, sich selbst zu reflectiren, die sogenannte todte Natur aber überhaupt eine unreife Intelligenz, daher in ihren Phänomenen noch bewusstlos schon der intelligente Charakter durchblickt.

[The completed theory of nature would be that whereby the whole of nature was resolved into an intelligence.—The dead and unconscious products of nature are merely abortive attempts that she makes to reflect herself; inanimate nature so-called is actually as such an immature intelligence, so that in her phenomena the still unwitting character of intelligence is already peeping through.]

2[a]   From here to the end the textus is marked with an ink line in the margin

important early note on the relationship between sensation and perception is *CN* III 3605 (1809). The argument against Berkeley is pursued—perhaps on the basis of this and other notes in this vol—in *BL* ch 8 (*CC*) I 137.

1[4] The designation "protozoa" for the simplest single-celled animals is attributed to Goldfuss in 1818 (*OED*)—a fact that helps to date this note. The 2nd ed of *AR* (1831) 85 elucidates this remark: "The lowest class of Animals or Protozoa, the Polypi for instance, have neither brain nor nerves.

Their motive powers are all from without. The Sun, Light, the Warmth, the Air are their Nerves and Brain" (*AR*—*CC*—97–8).

1[5] A favourite proverb; cf BLANCO WHITE **9** n 2.

1[6] Presumably Schelling's (tr) "merely empirical consciousness" (*SW* III 366), or what C in *BL* ch 12 (*CC*) I 236 calls "the spontaneous consciousness natural to all reflecting beings" (in the same passage he translates "spontaneous consciousness" into Latin as *conscientia communis*).

True or *false*, this assertion [w]as too early. Nothing precedent [? has ex-plained, much less proved . . . . .] it *true*.   S. T. C.

P.S.—with exception [. . . . .] the finite is the Wisdom of the infinite, Intelligence.

3   pp +3–+4, referring to pp 15–16, afterthought on p +2 | *SW* iii 347–8

C. Aber mit diesen beyden Problemen sehen wir uns in einen Wider-spruch verwickelt.—Nach B wird gefordert eine Herrschaft des Ge-dankens (des Ideellen) über die Sinnenwelt; wie ist aber eine solche denkbar, wenn (nach A) die Vorstellung in ihrem Ursprung schon nur die Sklavin des Objektiven ist?—Umgekehrt, ist die wirkliche Welt etwas von uns ganz Unabhängiges, wonach (als ihrem Urbild) unsere Vorstel-lung sich richten muss (nach A), so ist unbegreiflich, wie hinwiederum die wirkliche Welt sich nach Vorstellungen in uns richten könne (nach B).—Mit einem Wort, über der theoretischen Gewissheit geht uns die practische, über der practischen die theoretische verloren; es ist un-möglich, dass zugleich in unserem Erkenntniss Wahrheit, und in unserem Wollen Realität sey.

Dieser Widerspruch muss aufgelöst werden, wenn es überhaupt eine Philosophie giebt—und die Auflösung dieses Problems, oder die Beant-wortung der Frage: *wie können die Vorstellungen zugleich als sich richt-end nach den Gegenständen, und die Gegenstände als sich richtend nach den Vorstellungen gedacht werden?* ist nicht die *erste*, aber die *höchste* Aufgabe der Transcendental-Philosophie.

[C. But with these two problems we find ourselves involved in a contradiction.—*B* calls for a dominance of thought (the ideal) over the world of sense; but how is this conceivable if (by *A*) the presentation is in origin already the mere slave of the objec-tive?—Conversely, if the real world is a thing wholly independent of us, to which (as *A* tells us) our presentation must conform (as to its archetype), it is inconceivable how the real world, on the contrary, could (as *B* says) conform itself to presentations in us.—In a word, for certainty in theory we lose it in practice, and for the certainty in practice we lose it in theory; it is impossible both that our knowledge should contain truth and our volition reality.

If there is to be any philosophy at all, this contradiction must be resolved—and the solution of this problem, or answer to the question: *how can we think both of presen-tations as conforming to objects, and objects as conforming to presentations?* is, not the first, but the *highest* task of transcendental philosophy.]

P. 15, 16.

C.[1]—Ye Gods! annihilate both Space and Time—and then this §ph.

3[1] The capital letter identifies the paragraph in textus.

may become cogent Logic. But as it is, one might ⟨with equal plausibility⟩ from the fact of one man's lying on his back deduce the incompossibility of another Man's standing on his feet; or from the incompossibility of both positions in the same Man at the same time infer the impossibility of the two positions successively.—

Besides, the antitheta are not adequate Opposites, much less Contraries.[2] A Wheel ~~is~~ presented to me generates without apparent materials the image of ~~a~~ the Wheel in my mind. Now if the preconception of a Wheel in the Artist's mind generated in like manner a corporeal wheel in outward Space—or even in a mass of timber—then indeed (tho even so I can see no contradiction in the two hypotheses) a problem would arise, of which the equality or sameness of kind ~~of~~ in the two Generators ~~would~~ might be the most natural Solution—. Yet even here there is a Flaw in the Antithesis: for to make it perfectly correspondent, the Mass of Wood ought to generate the Image, Wheel/—Where is the inconsistency between the reality (i.e. actual realizing power) of the Will in respect of the relative *position* of Objects and the reality of Objects themselves independent of the *Position*? Is the Marble of a *Statue* less really Marble, than the Marble in the Quarry?—What after all does the problem amount ~~more~~ to more than the Fact, that the Will is a vis motrix,[3] and the Mind a *directive* power at one moment & in relation to the Will, and a Re- or Percipient in relation to objects moving, or at rest? Schelling seems at once to deny and yet suppose the Objectivity—on no other ground than that he commences by giving objectivity to Abstractions—A *acting* he calls Will: the same A acted on he calls *Truth* and then, because acting, and being acted on, are Antitheses or *opposite States*, he first turns them into *contrary things*, and then transfers this contrariety to the Subject A/— ~~Doubtless~~ That A acts on B, and is itself acted on by C, is a fact, to the *How*? respecting which I may have no other answer than Nescio/[4] but that my ignorance as to the How makes any contradiction in the Fact, I can by no means admit—any more than that a Mail Coach moving 10 miles an hour on the Road contradicts the fact of the same standing in a Coach House the night following. [a]⟨The whole difficulty lies in the co-existence of Agere et Pati[5] as Predicates of the same Subject⟩

[a] This sentence is written on p +2 below a line at the end of **19**

[2] The distinction between "opposite" and "contrary" is a tool that C often employs in logical analysis: cf e.g. BÖHME **158** and n 2, GOLDFUSS **2** n 8. C departs from the philosophical relationship of these terms in Aristotle's *Categories* (11^b16–12^a25), where "contrary" is merely a sub-category of "opposite".

[3] "Motive power".

[4] "I do not know".

[5] "To act" and "to be acted upon", or simply "active and passive" as C says in *Logic* (*CC*) 268. Cf **4** following.

4   pp $^-$2–$^-$1, referring to pp 15–16 | **3** textus

P. 15, 16. §ph. C.—

The remarks on the blank leaves at the end of the Volume are, I still think, valid: so far that all Schelling's "Contradictions" are reducible to the one difficulty of comprehending the co-existence of the Attributes, Agere et Pati,[1] in the same subject—and that the difficulty is diminished rather than increased by the facts of human *Art*, in which the Pati and the Agere take place in different relations and at different moments.—Likewise—that Schelling's position of Opposites, viz. Nature and Intelligence as the same with ~~Subject~~ Object and Subject already supposes Plurality, and this being supposed, the whole Hypothesis becomes *arbitrary/* for the conception of Plurality once admitted, Object and Subject become mere relative terms: & no reason can be assigned why each existent should not be both Object and Subject. But if he begins at the beginning, then the objection applies—viz. that Schelling arbitrarily substantiates attributes. For in the very act of opposing A to B, he supposes an X common to both viz. Being, οὐσία; but this given, there is no necessary reason, why Objectivity and Subjectivity should not both be predicable of both—so namely that the Subject B is an Object to the Subject A; and the Subject A an Object to the Subject B: as in the instance of a Lover & his Mistress gazing at each other.—Finally, it is a suspicious Logic when no answer can be given to the question *"What do you mean? Give me an instance."*—The fact is: that every instance, Schelling could have brought, would imply an Object as the Base of the Subject—and his bewusste Thätigkeit ohne Bewüsstein[a2] I do not understand. At least, if he mean the Will, it is a strange way of expressing himself—and at all events, he should have previously explained the distinction between primary consciousness, ceasing in the co-incidence of O. and S.; and the secondary—or Consciousness of having been conscious—which is *memory*. It would be well to shew, how much better Schelling's meaning might have been given in simple common-life words.[3]

4[a]   A slip for "Bewusstsein"

4[1] "Active and passive", as at the end of **3**.

4[2] "Conscious activity without consciousness": C appears to be collapsing the distinction Schelling makes in **5** textus between a kind of activity that may exist either with *or* without consciousness. He makes the same objection in SCHELLING *Einleitung* **1**. In **8** textus below, which it seems C had not read when he wrote this note, Schelling himself combines the categories of conscious and unconscious activity.

4[3] This whole note, but esp the reference to primary and secondary consciousness, has a direct bearing upon *BL* chs 12 and 13 (*CC*) I 232–306, as does the *Einleitung* note cited in n 2.

5 pp 16–17, pencil, cropped | *SW* III 348

Wie zugleich die objective Welt nach Vorstellungen in uns, und Vorstellungen in uns nach der objectiven Welt sich bequemen, ist nicht zu begreifen, wenn nicht zwischen den beyden Welten, der ideellen und der reellen, eine *vorherbestimmte Harmonie* existirt. Diese vorherbestimmte Harmonie aber ist selbst nicht denkbar, wenn nicht die Thätigkeit, durch welche die objective Welt producirt ist, ursprünglich identisch ist mit der, welche im Wollen sich äussert, und umgekehrt.

Nun ist es allerdings eine *productive* Thätigkeit, welche im Wollen sich äussert; alles freye Handeln ist productiv, nur *mit Bewusstseyn* productiv. Setzt man nun, da beyde Thätigkeiten doch nur im Princip Eine seyn sollen, dass dieselbe Thätigkeit, welche im freyen Handeln *mit Bewusstseyn* productiv ist, im Produciren der Welt *ohne Bewusstseyn* productiv sey, so ist jene vorausbestimmte Harmonie wirklich, und der Widerspruch gelöst.

[How both the objective world accommodates to presentations in us, and presentations in us to the objective world, is unintelligible unless between the two worlds, the ideal and the real, there exists a *predetermined harmony*. But this latter is itself unthinkable unless the activity, whereby the objective world is produced, is at bottom identical with that which expresses itself in volition, and *vice versa*.

Now it is certainly a *productive* activity that finds expression in willing; all free action is productive, albeit *consciously* productive. If we now suppose, since the two activities have only to be one in principle, that the same activity which is *consciously* productive in free action, is productive *without consciousness* in bringing about the world, then our predetermined harmony is real, and the contradiction resolved.]

But is this *fair* Logic? If indeed whatever I *imagined, appeared*, even as whatever appears, as real, I am [u]nder a necessity [o]f [*i*]*magining*—[th]en [i]ndeed the [. . . . .] would be [j]ust. Think of a Table as an empty [. . .] but no Table has these in[. . .] As to the modifications of matter pro[. . .] by the mind, it would be to the purpose if the mind acted upon matter immedi[ately,] but al[l] that *w*[*e*] perceive is tha[t] phænome[non] acts u[pon] phæn[omenon,] the w[ill] on t[he] [? Soul,] the Wa[. . .] the H[. . .] on th[e] [. . . . .] &c. In short, the effect of matter [upon] mind = perception, is ⟨immediate &⟩ constant [. . .] Mind = Will on matter [. . . . .]

6 Title-page, referring to p 17, cropped | **5** textus par 2

[? This argument] grounds itself on the assertion, "es ist allerdings eine PRODUCTIVE Thätigkeit, welche im *Wollen* sich aüssert*ᵃ*",[1] in the very

---

6ᵃ A slip for "äussert"

6[1] From **5** textus: "it is certainly a *pro-* *ductive* activity that finds expression in willing".

same sense of the word "productive["] in which Nature "im produciren der Welt *productive* sey":[2] only that the former is "*mit*", the latter "ohne Bewusstein[b] *productiv*."[3] Now this is merely *asserted*. I deny it: & for the reasons above stated.   S. T. [C.]
⟨i.e. at this moment. A book, I value, I reason & quarrel wit[h] as with myself when I am reasoni[ng.]⟩[c]

P.S. Add to this one scruple which always attacks my mind when I read Schelling or Fichte—Does Perception imply a greater mystery, or less justify a Postulate, than the Act of Self-consciousness—i.e. Self-perce[?ption] Let Perception be [? demanded] as an Act specified of the mind, & how many of the grounds of Idealism become $0 = 0!$—*

⟨* No! I am wrong. For grant this mysteri[ous] [P]erception; yet ask yourself *what* you per[ceive] and a contradiction arises. The Percepti[on . . . . .]⟩

7   p 17 | 5 textus par 2

A + B produce a Child = D; A and B remaining undiminished.

8   p 17 | *SW* iii 348–9

Setzt man, dies alles verhalte sich wirklich so, so wird jene ursprüngliche Identität der im Produciren der Welt geschäftigen Thätigkeit, mit der, welche im Wollen sich äussert, in den Producten der ersten sich darstellen, und diese Producte werden erscheinen müssen als Producte einer zugleich *bewussten und bewusstlosen* Thätigkeit.

[Supposing that all this is really the case, then this fundamental identity, of the activity concerned in producing the world with that which finds expression in willing, will display itself in the former's products, and these will have to appear as products of an activity at once *conscious and unconscious*.]

What analogy is there between this, & my shaping a Log into a Stool?

9   pp +1–+2, referring to p 40 | *SW* iii 363

Wie wir in Ansehung solcher Sätze, in welchen ein ganz fremdartiges Objectives mit einem Subjectivem zusammentrifft—(und dies geschieht in jedem synthetischen Urtheil A = B; das Prädicat, der Begriff,

---

6[b] A slip for "Bewusstsein", as in 4 also
6[c] This sentence written in a different pen and squeezed in below C's initials

6[2] From 5 textus: "is *productive* in bringing about the world".
6[3] The former is "productive *with* con-

sciousness", the latter "without": from 5 textus.

repräsentirt hier immer das Subjective, das Subject das Objective,) zur Gewissheit gelangen können, ist nicht zu begreifen . . .

[In every synthetic judgment, A = B, a wholly alien objective coincides with a subjective; the predicate, the concept, always stands here for the subjective, and the subject term for the objective; and how we can attain to certainty in regard to such propositions is unintelligible . . .]

P. 40, two last lines.[1]

It seems to me, that the Logician *proceeds from* the Principles of Identity, Alterity, and Multëity or Plurality, as already known;[2]—that the Logical *I* attributes its own Subjectivity to whatever really *is*, & takes for granted that a not-he really is—& that it is a *Subject*/ And this he proceeds to make objective for himself by the predicate.—N.B. It does not follow, that the Logical I attributes its *Egöity* as well as its *subjectivity* to the *not*-itself as far as it *is*/ [? ~~your n~~]

In other words, the Logical *I* seems to me to represent the INDIVIDUAL I, which must indeed be this or that or some other, not without determining which it is—individuality, or singularity, in *genere*,[3] as when we say—every man is *an* individual.[4]

In the position, Greeks are handsome, Schelling says—The *Subject* "Greeks" represents the Object, the Predicate "handsome" the Subjective.[5] Now I would say, ~~th~~ "Greeks" as a Subject assumed by apposition with my Self as ~~far as~~ a Subject—. Now this Subject I render objective for myself by the predicate./ By becoming objective it does not cease to be a Subject—

It follows of course that I look on Logic as essentially empirical in its pre-conditions & Postulates—& *posterior* to Metaphysics, unless you would name these the Higher Logic.[6]

9[1] The remark in parentheses—or strictly speaking, that part of it that begins with "synthetischen" and ends with "Subjective, das".

9[2] C discusses these terms in his own *Logic* (*CC*) e.g. 46, 91. In this section of the *System*, Schelling distinguishes between propositions of identity which are subjective and presuppose a purely logical subject that is completely abstracted from any real subject, and synthetic propositions which presuppose an object alien to and distinct from the subject.

9[3] In *"kind"*.

9[4] These terms are not from Schelling's text, nor does Schelling identify the logical I with the individual I.

9[5] The example is C's.

9[6] In his own *Logic* (*CC*) 36 and 70, in a discussion consistent with the statement here, C variously considers logic as a *branch* of metaphysics and as distinct from metaphysics; in both cases he makes it clear that logic belongs to the faculty of the understanding, as opposed to the pure reason. "Higher Logic" here seems to correspond to the "pure common logic" of *Logic* (*CC*) 139–40. C's interpretation of "metaphysics" as meaning "beyond nature" or "transcendental" (*Logic*—*CC*—36) is based on a widely-held but false etymology: cf MILLER 4 n 8.

10   p ⁻2ᵃ, referring to pp 54, 59–62 | *SW* iii 371–2, 375–6

Ist das Princip der Philosophie ein Postulat, so wird das Object dieses Postulats die ursprünglichste Construction für den *innern Sinn*, d.h. das *Ich* . . . . Durch diese ursprüngliche Construction, und in dieser Construction kommt nun allerdings etwas bestimmtes zu Stande. . . . Aber das Product ist *ausser* der Construction schlechterdings nichts, es *ist* überhaupt nur, indem es construirt wird, und abstrahirt von der Construction so wenig, als die Linie des Geometers.—Auch diese Linie ist nichts existirendes, denn die Linie an der Tafel ist ja nicht die Linie selbst, und wird als Linie nur erkannt, dadurch, dass sie an die ursprüngliche Anschauung der Linie selbst gehalten wird.

Was das Ich sey? ist ebendeswegen so wenig demonstrabel, als was die Linie sey; man kann nur die *Handlung* beschreiben, wodurch es entsteht . . . . Das reine Selbstbewusstseyn ist ein Act, der ausserhalb aller Zeit liegt, und alle Zeit erst construirt . . . . Dieser Begriff muss wohl höher seyn, als der des Dings, da die Dinge selbst nur als Modificationen einer auf verschiedene Weise eingeschränkten Thätigkeit zu begreifen sind.— Das Seyn der Dinge besteht wohl nicht in einer blossen Ruhe, oder Unthätigkeit. Denn selbst alle Raumerfüllung ist nur ein Grad von Thätigkeit, und jedes Ding nur ein bestimmter Grad von Thätigkeit, mit welchem der Raum erfüllt wird.—

Da dem Ich auch keines von den Prädicaten zukommt, die den Dingen zukommen, so erklärt sich daraus das Paradoxon, dass man vom Ich nicht sagen kann, dass es *ist*. Man kann nähmlich vom Ich nur deswegen nicht sagen, dass es ist, weil es das *Seyn-selbst* ist. Der ewige in keiner Zeit begriffene Act des Selbstbewusstseyns, den wir *Ich* nennen, ist das, was allen Dingen das Daseyn giebt, was also selbst keines andern Seyns bedarf, von dem es getragen wird, sondern sich selbst tragend und unterstützend, objectiv, als das *ewige Werden*, subjectiv als das *unendliche Produciren* erscheint.

[If the principle of philosophy is a postulate, the object of this postulate will be the most primary construction for *inner sense, i.e.*, for the *self* . . . . Now in and through this original construction, something determinate does indeed come about . . . . But the product is in no sense *external* to the construction, it *exists* at all only in being constructed, and has no more existence in abstraction from the construction than does the geometer's line.—And this line also is nothing existent, for the line on the blackboard is by no means the line itself, and is only recognized as linear by relating it to the original intuition of the line itself.

What the self *is*, is for that reason no more demonstrable than what the line is; one

10ᵃ The writing crowded in a small hand into the head of the page and between the opening lines of **4**

can only describe the *action* whereby it comes about. . . . Pure self-consciousness is an act lying outside time, and by which all time is first constituted . . . . This concept must certainly be higher than that of a thing, since things themselves are to be understood merely as modifications of an activity limited in various ways.—The being of things assuredly does not consist in mere rest or inactivity. For even all occupancy of space is merely a degree of activity, and every thing merely a specific degree of activity with which space is filled.

Since the self actually possesses none of the predicates that attach to things, we have an explanation of the paradox that one cannot say of the self that it *exists*. For one cannot say of the self that it exists, precisely because it is *being-itself*. The eternal, timeless act of self-consciousness which we call *self*, is that which gives all things existence, and so itself needs no other being to support it; bearing and supporting itself, rather, it appears objectively as *eternal becoming*, and subjectively as a *producing without limit*.]

P. 54—and then p. 59–62 the *Spinosism* of Schelling's System first betrays itself: tho' the very comparison des reinen Ichs zum geometrischen Raume[1] ought by its inadequacy & only partial fitness to have rescued him.[2] Im Raume[3] the *materia*[4] & the limiting power are diverse./.

11   p 59, pencil | *SW* III 374

Kant findet es in seiner Anthropologie merkwürdig, dass dem Kind, sobald es anfange, von sich selbst durch *Ich* zu sprechen, eine neue Welt aufzugehen scheine. Es ist diess in der That sehr natürlich; es ist die intellectuelle Welt, die sich ihm öffnet; denn was zu sich selbst *Ich* sagen kann, erhebt sich ebendadurch über die objektive Welt, und tritt aus fremder Anschauung in seine eigene.

[Kant, in his *Anthropology*, finds it remarkable that as soon as a child begins to speak of itself by the word "I", a new world appears to open up for it. In fact this is very natural; it is the intellectual world that opens to the child, for whoever can say "I" to himself uplifts himself, by that very act, above the objective world, and steps out of the intuition of others into his own.]

I dare not absolutely deny this but suspect it to be a *verbal* D[?istinction][1]

10[1] The comparison "of the pure I to geometrical space": C is summarising the textus, not quoting from it.

10[2] C probably sensed that Schelling's characterisation of self-consciousness as a timeless act and as "being-itself" brought it close to the ontological status usually attributed to divinity; hence Schelling's comparison of the pure act of self-consciousness with geometric space appears Spinozistic or pantheistic. By Nov 1818 C was describing Schelling and his "Sect" as fundamentally pantheistic (*CL* IV 883), and this was the position that he held, vis à vis Schelling, for the rest of his life.

10[3] "In space".

10[4] "*Matter*".

11[1] Schelling alludes to sec 1 "Vom Bewusstsein seiner selbst" in Kant *Anthropologie in pragmatischer Hinsicht* (Königsberg 1798) 4, a passage that C annotated disapprovingly in copies of both the 1st (1798) and 2nd (1800) eds: KANT *Anthropologie* COPY A 1, COPY B 1.

12   p 78 | *SW* III 386

Da nun die ideelle ursprünglich nur als die *anschauende* (subjective) von jener gesetzt ist, um durch sie die Begräntztheit des Ichs *als* Ich zu erklären, so muss *angeschaut*—und *begräntzt* werden für die zweyte, objective Thätigkeit Eins und dasselbe seyn. Dies ist zu erklären aus dem Grundcharakter des Ich. Die zweyte Thätigkeit, wenn sie Thätigkeit eines *Ich* seyn soll, muss zugleich *begräntzt* werden, und *angeschaut* werden als begräntzt, denn *eben in dieser Identität des Angeschautwerdens* und *Seyns* liegt die Natur des *Ich.* . . .

 Beyde Thätigkeiten, ideelle und reelle, *setzen sich wechselseitig voraus.* Die reelle ursprünglich in's Unendliche strebende . . . ist nichts ohne ideelle. . . . Aus dieser wechselseitigen Voraussetzung beyder Thätigkeiten zum Behuf des Selbstbewusstseyns wird der ganze Mechanismus des Ich abzuleiten seyn.

[Now since the ideal activity is originally posited merely as the *intuitant* (subjective) of the other, so as to explain thereby the limitation of the self *as* self, to be *intuited* and *limited* must, for the latter, objective, activity, be one and the same. This must find its explanation in the basic character of the self. The latter activity, if it is to be activity of a *self*, must simultaneously be *limited* and *intuited* as limited, for *in this very identity of being intuited* and *of being* lies the nature of the *self.* . . .
 Both activities, the real and the ideal, *mutually presuppose each other.* The real, originally striving into infinity . . . is nothing without the ideal . . . . From this reciprocal presupposition of the two activities, for the sake of self-consciousness, the entire mechanism of the self will have to be derived.]

The "To Be" whose act of Being is the self-affirming, that it *is*, is a Spirit or Intelligence.

13   pp 86–7, cropped | *SW* III 391

Weder durch die begräntzende, noch durch die begräntzte Thätigkeit für sich kommt es also zum Selbstbewusstseyn. Es ist sonach eine dritte aus beyden zusammengesetzte Thätigkeit, durch welche das Ich des Selbstbewusstseyns entsteht.

 5) Diese dritte zwischen der begräntzten und der begräntzenden schwebende Thätigkeit, durch welche das Ich erst entsteht, ist, weil Produciren und Seyn vom Ich Eins ist, nichts anders als das *Ich des Selbstbewusstseyns selbst.*

[Thus neither through the limiting nor the limited activities, by themselves, do we arrive at self-consciousness. There is, accordingly, a third activity, compounded of these two, whereby the self of self-consciousness is engendered.
 5. It is this third activity, oscillating between the limited and the limiting, whereby

the self is first engendered; and, since the producing and the being of the self are one, it is nothing other than the *self of self-consciousness itself.*]

When I sink into myself, I have ever possessed intuitions like these; but when I read Fichte or Schelling, & of course judge by my discursive Intellect, then I am puzzled. For in order to account for the first limit or [o]bject, [S]elf-Consci[o]usness is [p]re-assumed—[as] the [c]ause—& [ye]t again [f]ind it a new [bi]rth, & [its] product a [co]mpound [ac]tivity [res]ulting from the presence of the Bound [or] Obstacle.[1] It is true, the Author warns us, [th]at these predicabilia[2] of Time, fore & after, [a]re but metaphors of necessity,[3] but then[a] an unnecessary verbal Confusion! At leas[t] it seems exposed to Schelling's own objection [to] Hypotheses, that they are made *for* the Fact, [or] rather f[or] the Sys[tem.][4] In short, [I do] not clear[ly] see the use of this Ru[le] of *Fac[t.]* I can[not] conce[ive] Distin[ction] in ex[tent] of Spa[ce] as ea[sily] as i[n the] succes[sion] of Tim[e.] It *is* create[d:] Self-c[onscious] it *is* [? not.]

Mil[ton's] Line may perhaps be applied to, if not justified [by,] the System of the Wissentschaftslehre[b]—And at each *Bound* high overleaps [. . . . .][c5]

14   p 103, cropped | *SW* III 401

(Bliebe das Ich bey jener ersten Construction stehen, oder könnte jenes Gemeinschaftliche wirklich fortdauern, so wäre das Ich leblose Natur, ohne Empfindung und ohne Anschauung. Dass die Natur von der todten Materie herauf bis zur Sensibilität sich bildet, ist in der Naturwissenschaft, (für welche das Ich nur die von vorn sich schaffende Natur ist)

13[a] A line may have been cropped here (but no trace remains) or a word omitted as C moves on to the top of p 87
13[b] A slip for "Wissenschaftslehre"
13[c] A line cropped

13[1] C is troubled by a circularity in Schelling's argument: the original unity of self-consciousness must be assumed in order to have the opposition between subject and object, between limited and unlimited activity, yet this opposition is in turn resolved through the mediating activity of self-consciousness, which therefore appears at once as a primary activity prior to division and as a third-phase synthetic activity reconciling opposition.
13[2] "Things to be predicated", "predicables".
13[3] Schelling often insists (e.g. pp 2,

112) on the actual simultaneity of the phases of self-consciousness that may be distinguished from one another by logic and for purposes of analysis. They should not be conceived of as succeeding one another in time, but as presupposing one another in every instance.
13[4] See SCHELLING *Philosophische Schriften* **38** n 1 above.
13[5] Milton *Paradise Lost* IV 181: Satan "At one slight bound high overleap'd all bound", a line C liked to apply to audacious methods of argument (though not elsewhere to Fichte), e.g. in *BL* ch 7 (*CC*) I 118.

eben nur dadurch zu erklären, dass auch in ihr das Product des ersten
Aufhebens der beyden Entgegengesetzten nicht fortdauern kann.)

[[If the self halted at this first construction, or if the common product were really able
to endure, the self would be inanimate nature, without sensation or intuition. That nature rears itself up from dead matter to sensibility is explicable in natural science (for
which the self is merely nature creating itself anew) only by the very fact that even
there the product of the first cancellation of the two opposites is unable to endure.]]

But h[ʊw] can "d[as] Ich"[1] then [be] essential if still the sa[me] "I am",
can y[et] lose i[ts] essent[ial] Powe[r?] If fro[m the] very B[?irth] of
Bei[ng] [? no] Comm[on] or Sy[?stematic] Link conn[?ects] how [? can]
that be & be "Ich", the essence of whi[ch] is that it *does* last? The answer
must b[e:] we here involve Time inappropriately.

15   p 115, pencil | *SW* iii 408

Er behauptet nur, das Ich empfinde niemals das Ding selbst, (denn ein
solches existirt in diesem Moment noch nicht), oder auch etwas von dem
Ding in das Ich Übergehendes, sondern unmittelbar nur sich selbst, seine
eigene aufgehobene Thätigkeit.*

[It [idealism] claims only that the self never senses the thing itself (for nothing of the
kind yet exists at this stage), nor even anything passing from the thing into the self;
what it senses immediately is only itself, its own suspended activity.*]

* Still I complain that the "itself", "its own", "seine eigene",[1] &c are anticipations of an *I*, not yet existing.

16   p 486 (last page of text), referring to p 118 | *SW* iii 410

Dass ich überhaupt begräntzt bin, folgt unmittelbar aus der unendlichen
Tendenz des Ichs, sich Object zu werden; die Begräntztheit überhaupt ist
also erklärbar, aber die Begräntztheit überhaupt lässt die bestimmte
völlig frey, und doch entstehen beyde durch einen und denselben Act.
Beydes zusammengenommen, dass die bestimmte Begräntztheit nicht
bestimmt seyn kann durch die Begräntztheit überhaupt, und dass sie doch
mit dieser *zugleich* und durch Einen Act entsteht, macht, *dass sie das Un-
begreifliche und Unerklärbare der Philosophie ist.*

[That I am limited as such follows directly from the self's unending tendency to become an object to itself; limitation as such is therefore explicable, but it leaves the de-
terminacy entirely free, even though both arise through one and the same act. Both
taken together, that the determinate limitation cannot be determined through limitation as such, and yet that it arises along with the latter, *simultaneously* and through one
act, means *that it is one thing that philosophy can neither conceive nor explain.*]

14[1] "The I" or "self": in textus.   15[1] From textus: "its own".

But why if (p. 118) there are many Ichheiten,[1] should *not* N? 1 I act on n? 2 I? If I act on itself, it is acted on—therefore actible-on by an I. But to assert, that it can only be acted on by this, & no other incomprehensibly-determined-in-its-comprehensible-determinateness-I, is—to *assert!* and no more. In short, the Attributes of the Absolute Synthesis, the I Am in that I am are falsely transferred to the I AM in that God is.—[2]

Aye (replies Schelling) this would be secundum Principium Essendi; but I speak only secundum Principium Sciendi—.[3] True (I rejoin)—but you assert that the two principles are *one* p. 118, l. 17, 18.—What is this but to admit that the I itself even in its absolute Synthesis supposes an already perfected Intelligence, as the ground of the possibility of its existing as it does exist? And what is Schelling's "Begränztheit überhaupt" but the algemeinerte[a] abstraction from the bestimmten Begranztheiten[b4]—a mere ens logicum,[5] like Motion, Form, Color &c—?

17   p 121 | *SW* III 411

Das Ich empfindet, indem es sich selbst als ursprünglich begräntzt anschaut. Dieses Anschauen ist eine Thätigkeit, aber das Ich kann nicht zugleich anschauen, und sich anschauen, als anschauend.*

[The self has sensation, in that it intuits itself as originally limited. This intuition is an activity, but the self cannot at once both intuit, and intuit itself as intuiting.*]

I more and more see the arbitrariness and inconveniences of using the same term, Anschauen,[1] for the productive and the contemplative Acts of the Intelligential Will, which Schelling calls das Ich.[2] If * were true, the I could never become ~~self~~ conscious: for the same impossibility for the same reason would recur in the second act—& so in fact it is. We can no more pass without a saltus from mere Sensation to Perception, than from Marble to Sensations.[3]

Whether it is better to assume Sensation as a minimum of Perception,

16[a] A slip for "allgemeinste"?

16[1] Many "selves".
16[2] On the importance of the "I AM" in C's thinking see PLATNER 1 and nn, *TT* (*CC*) I 77 and n 3; *BL* ch 12 (*CC*) I 272–5 and nn; *Friend* (*CC*) I 515 and n 3.
16[3] "According to the Principle of Being" and "according to the Principle of Knowing".
16[4] From textus: what is Schelling's "limitation as such" but the "most general" abstraction from the "determinate limita-

16[b] A slip for "Begränztheiten"

tions"?
16[5] "Logical entity" having no other than mental existence.
17[1] "Intuit", a crucial term in German Idealism but one that was used and interpreted differently by different writers: cf PLATNER 16 and n 4, *BL* ch 12 (*CC*) I 289* and n.
17[2] "The I".
17[3] C makes a similar argument in 1, 3, 4 above and uses a similar illustration in 3.

N. B. The following Remarks 492 apply merely to the
Logical Form, not to the substance of Schelling's
Philosophy.

Schelling finds the necessity of splitting not
alone Philosophy but the Philosopher as well of
Rehama p. they personal at two several Gates—
The system may be represented by a straight
Road from B & B. ———— C ———— Bβ

Bα ———— II ————
A

with a Gate at A, the massive Door
of which is barred on both the sides: so
that when he arrives at A from B & A—
must return back & go round by C to Bβ
in order to reach the same point from
that direction—

And I appear to myself to obviate
this inconvenience by d° simply reversing
the assumption that Perception is a
Species of which Sensation is the Genus.
or that Perception is only a more finely
organized Sensation—with me, Perception
is the essentia prima, and Sensation
= perceptio unius, while Perception as
so called is = perceptio plurium
simultaneorum. Single Intuition/Perception
is Sensation, Comparative/complex
Intuition is Perception.—The consequences
of this Index are wider & ampler—

The whole difficulty lies in the co-existence
of Agere et Pati as Predicates of the
same Subject

4. Note on the endpapers of F. W. J. von Schelling *System des
transcendentalen Idealismus* (Tübingen 1800). See SCHELLING *System* **19**
The British Library; reproduced by kind permission

or to take them as originally diverse, and to contend that in all Sensation a minor grade of Perception is comprised deserves consideration.[4]

18   p 260, cropped | *SW* III 494

Wenn nun also die Intelligenz die Evolution des Universums, so weit es in ihre Anschauung fällt, in einer Organisation anschaut, so wird sie dieselbe als identisch mit sich selbst anschauen.

[So now if the intelligence intuits the evolution of the universe, so far as this falls within its intuition, in terms of an organisation, it will intuit this latter as identical with its own self.]

Whether from acquired Habit or no, I [do] not, & seem to myself never to have [re]garded my Body as identical with [my]self—my Brain no more than my [n]ails or [ha]ir—or [mo]re than [a p]air of [sp]ectacles.

S. T. C.

19   p [+]2

[a]⟨N.B. The following Remarks apply merely to the logical form, not to the Substance, of Schelling's Philosophy.—⟩

Schelling finds the necessity of splitting not alone Philosophy but the Philosopher—a sort of *Kehama* twy-personal at two several gates—[1]

This system may be represented by a strait Road from B to B

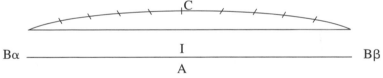

with a Gate at A, the Massive Door of which is barred on both sides: so that when he arrives at A from Bα he must return back, & go round by C to Bβ in order to reach the same point from that direction—.[2]

Now I appear to myself to obviate this inconvenience by simply reversing the Assumption that Perception is a Species of which Sensation is the Genus, or that Perception is only a more finely organized Sensa-

19[a] Insertion written in a cramped hand at the top of p [+]2 evidently after C had written the following note

17[4] Cf C's argument in **1** above (and n 3).

19[1] In RS *Curse of Kehama* (1810) canto 24 Kehama storms the eight gates of Hell ("Paladon") by multiplying himself and appearing on all sides at once.

19[2] This diagram, like **13** above, ex-presses C's sense of the circularity of Schelling's philosophical system: see Plate 4. In SCHELLING *Einleitung* **1**, a note that coincides with this one at several points, C describes the system as "a Candle placed horizontally and lit at both ends".

tion—. With me, Perceptio[n] is the essentia prima,[3] and Sensation = perceptio unius:[4] ⟨while⟩ Perception so called ⟨is⟩ = perceptio plurium simultanea.[5] Or ⟨thus⟩: Single ~~Perception~~ Intuition is Sensation, Comparative & complex Intuition is Perception.—The consequences of this [? Practice] are wide & endless.[6]

19[3] "Prime essence".
19[4] "Perception of a single thing".
19[5] "Simultaneous perception of many things".

19[6] The issue of the relationship between sensation and perception is raised also in **1, 6, 17** above.

Ueber die Gottheiten von Samothrace, vorgelesen in der öffentlichen Sitzung der Baier'schen Akademie der Wissenschaften am Namenstage des Königes den 12. Oct. 1815. Beylage zu den Weltaltern. Stuttgart & Tübingen 1815. 8°.

British Library C 126 f 8(3), bound as third with *Denkmal* and *Philosophie und Religion*.

DATE. First half of 1817? Ordering German books from Thomas Boosey in Jun 1817, C requested "Schelling's 'Welt-altern', if it be published" (*CL* IV 738). The *Weltalter* was not completed and was published posthumously in a fragmentary form, but it seems likely that C knew about it from his reading of *Ueber die Gottheiten von Samothrace*, which is described on the title-page as a supplement (*Beylage*) to the *Weltalter*, and therefore that his request to the bookseller is evidence of the date of his reading of this work. There is also a brief notebook entry, made some time between Jan 25 and Mar 1817, that could have been derived from this text: *CN* III 4335. C may have drawn upon *Ueber die Gottheiten von Samothrace* later, in his literary lectures of Jan–Mar 1818: FABER headnote, *Lects 1808–1819* (*CC*) II 56 and nn 27–9; but see the doubts expressed in *Lects 1808–1819* (*CC*) II 188–9. It was certainly central to the philosophical lecture of 8 Mar 1819: *P Lects* Lect 11 (1949) esp 321–3. Allusions to it appear also in the "Prometheus" essay of 1825 (*SW & F* 1254-5 and n 1) and in BÖHME **140, 174**. Schelling in turn paid C a compliment on his understanding of the *Gottheiten* as revealed in the "Prometheus" essay, in *Einleitung in die Philosophie der Mythologie* (*SW* XI 196n).

COEDITOR. Raimonda Modiano.

1   p 62, pencil | *SW* VIII 383

[Schelling wishes to establish the separate identities of three deities whose nearly synonymous names may be translated as Love, Desire, and Yearning.] In Megara sah man von der Hand desselben Skopas drey Werke, Eros, Himeros und Pothos, von denen gesagt wird: ἔιδη διάφορά ἐστι κατὰ τάυτα τοῖς ὀνόμασι καὶ τὰ ἔργα σφίσιν, eine Brachyologie, die nur so aufzulösen ist: "Es sind Gestalten verschieden (gebildet) nach den einem jeden zukommenden Werken, die sich ihren Namen gleich und auch so (verschieden) wie diese verhalten."

[In Megara three works by the same Skopas could be seen, Eros, Himeros and Pothos, of which is said: "Of different kinds, in accordance with their names, are their functions also," a brachyology which can only be resolved as follows: "They are figures differently (represented) according to the functions appropriate to each, which are behaving like their names and also as (differently) as these."]

I do not remember any such instance of Brachiology,[1] nor do I see how words without any grammatical connection can be so called—[2]

---

[1] Normally "brachylogy", with "brachyology" and (less commonly) "brachilogy" as alternative spellings: "condensed expression" (*OED*).

[2] The Greek is from Pausanias *Description of Greece* 1.43.6. The translation in textus of the dubious Greek is, at least, consistent with "grammatical connections". Modern editors have preferred to read εἰ δὴ . . . "if indeed their functions are as different as their names" tr W. H. S. Jones (LCL 5 vols 1918–35). Schelling's German version is apparently aiming at paraphrase rather than exact translation of the obscurities of the Greek. Beginning on the same lines a fairly literal though still obscure translation might run: "They are figures different in the same ways with reference to their names as are their functions with reference to [the gods] themselves."

AUGUST WILHELM SCHLEGEL
1767–1845

Gedichte von August Wilhelm Schlegel. Tübingen 1800. 8°.

British Library C 126 g 11

"S. T. C." label on title-page verso; John Duke Coleridge's monogram on p ⁻6.

DATE. Between 1803 and 1810, perhaps c 1805. Probably early, given the light annotation, the large loose hand, and the use of a list of page references as in COWLEY 2 (1801). If the reference in 1 to "the almost fiendish Tyranny of an evil Habit" is an allusion to C's experience of opium addiction, it is not likely to have been written before 1803; cf other internal evidence in 3 nn 1, 3.

COEDITOR. Hans Eichner.

1   p ⁻3, inside front of original grey wrapper

God prevents us from having any vivid pre-experience of the conse-quences of our actions, in order to preserve us in some measure *free-agents*—Else, if the Youth could have given to him not merely the know-lege, (for that *can* be given) but the feelings accompanying the actual Experience, of Unchastity, Intemperance, &c: & above all the almost fiendish Tyranny of an evil Habit;[1] it would be so impossible for him to err, as to render this Life not that for which it was manifestly intended (doubtless for the wisest & most beneficent ends) *a Life of Probation.*

S. T. Coleridge

2   p ⁻2

$$\Phi\upsilon\lambda.\gamma.\ 3.[1]$$
$$\sim\zeta.\ 6.[2]$$
$$\sim v.\ 13.[3]$$

[1] Cf "the horrible Tyranny of *Habit*" in LEIGHTON COPY A **7** (Apr 1814)—but oblique references to opium-taking as one of C's "infirm Habits" go back at least to 1803: *CN* I 1421.

[2] The Greek "Φυλ." stands for φύλλον, "a leaf" i.e. a page; the first four letters cor-respond to the Arabic numbers after them, and so identify the page on which a note-worthy poem is to be found. On p 3 is the first poem in the collection, *Sonett* ("Ob-schon der Jünger ungehirnte Rotte").

[2] Pp 6–8 *Kleomenes an Chariton.*

[3] P 13 *Das Lieblichste: Sonett.*

∼π. 16.[4]

∼φ. 30.[5]

∼ψη. 57. ∼μαρκτ ιν βυργερς αλμαναχ.[6]

∼Aβ. 72.[7]

∼Cγ. 103. καλοκαγάθων αριστοκαλλιστον.[8] If there be a Speck-let in this Diamond, it is, perhaps, the rather too *Lucianic* phrase "die ewigen *Zeccher*"[9] = the eternal Tipplers. A favorable Critic would call it *Homeric*.[10]

3   pp 190–1, cropped | *Shakespeare's Sonette und übrigen Jugendgedichte*

Nothing yet (plausible) has been advanced in explanation of Shake-spear's Sonnets. That they have been strangely jumbled & misplaced, I doubt not; but remove all the light & less worthy ones, & confine the attention to the connected suite, (forming a sort of poetic conjunction disjunctive, a divine Holomery,[1] all making one Whole, and yet each component Stanza a Whole of itself) still a [? conviction] that they were addressed ~~as~~ to a Woman, but yet as Swift's Stella,[2] under the disguise of a man, to escape suspicion.—What if to blind the jealous Parents or Guardian they were nominally addressed to the Brother of the Beloved (he the Friend & Confidant of the Poet[)]—& to heighten the disguise

[2][4] Pp 16–18 *Abendlied: für die Entfernte.*

[2][5] Pp 30–1 *An Einen Kunstrichter.*

[2][6] Pp 57–71 *Pygmalion.* C's note continues, the Greek characters a transliteration of "markt in Burgers almanach", but in this reference there is some confusion: *Pygmalion* had previously been published not in the *Musenalmanach* of Göttingen of which G. A. Bürger was for a time the editor, but in Schiller's *Musen-Almanach für das Jahr 1797* (Tübingen, n.d.) 126–41. Some other poems from this collection had appeared in Bürger's periodical. C annotated a copy of Bürger's poems (BÜRGER), but the whereabouts of his marked copy of the *Musen-Almanach* is not known.

[2][7] Pp 72–86 *Prometheus.*

[2][8] Pp 103–7 *Lebensmelodieen.* C's comment, in Greek, is "best and most beautiful of the beautiful and good".

[2][9] From *Lebensmelodieen* (105), actually *die ewigen Zecher*, accurately translated by C.

[2][10] Lucian is to Homer as a satirist is to a writer of serious epic poetry: either one might use such a hyperbolic phrase.

[3][1] "Holomery" (not in *OED*), is a compound from Greek meaning "whole-part" so perhaps "whole [composed] of parts". There are such things as "disjunctive conjunctions" in the jargon of grammarians (Johnson's *Dictionary*, under "disjunctive", quotes Isaac Watts to this effect), but C applied the phrase to the witty epigrams of Samuel Butler in *CN* II 2112 (May–Jun 1804) and of Pope in *BL* ch 1 (*CC*) I 19.

[3][2] Cf a letter of 1796, to John Thelwall (*CL* I 260): "My Wife is well & desires to be remembered to you & your Stella, & little ones. N.B. Stella (among the Romans) was a Man's name. All the *Classics* are against you; but our Swift, I suppose, is authority for this unsexing." The final reference is to Swift's *Journal to Stella*, addressed to Esther Johnson, which was composed 1710–13.

some really so, & to him exclusively applicable—while the others were read & understood by her/?—/[3]

[3] C's remarks reflect the fact that the identity of the addressee of the sonnets was a notorious puzzle in his day, one that he himself wrote about as early as 1803 (AN-DERSON COPY A 1) and discussed as late as 1833: *TT* (*CC*) I 377–8, and esp n 15. In the *Table Talk* entry the one sonnet explicitly addressed to a man is described as "a pur-posed blind", and C's position generally was that although Shakespeare expressed very powerfully the love of men for one an-other, such a love could not be sexual and the sonnets must therefore have been writ-ten to a woman.

Lost Book

Ueber dramatische Kunst und Litteratur. Vorlesungen von August Wilhelm Schlegel. 3 pts in 2 vols. Heidelberg 1809, 1811. 8°.

Not located; marginalia not recorded. There may have been two annotated copies of this work: in *Green SC* (1880) 701 it is described as containing "a loose MS. note by S. T. Coleridge, upon the Eichhornian Hypothesis, placed inside cover"; the copy in *DC SC* (1888) 919 is said to have "autograph notes of S. T. Coleridge". For C's celebrated use of this work, see the index to *Lects 1808–1819 (CC)*.

FRIEDRICH DANIEL
ERNST SCHLEIERMACHER
1768–1834

A Critical Essay on the Gospel of St. Luke. With an introduction by the translator [Connop Thirlwall], containing an account of the controversy respecting the origin of the three first Gospels since Bishop Marsh's Dissertation. London 1825. 8°.

British Library C 126 h 9

Bookplate of DC on p ⁻5 (p-d). Inscribed by John Duke Coleridge on p ⁻2: "C | Coleridge | Heath's Court | 1891—" "S. T. C." label on title-page verso. Pencil note on p ⁻3, perhaps by DC, attesting to the handwriting as C's. Some passages of textus marked in pencil for TRANSCRIPTS; also a pencilled biblical reference p 246. This copy C described as having been "sent to me by my Publisher (Mr Taylor) in a very handsome letter announcing *his own conversion* by the Aids to Reflection": *CL* VI 543 (19 Jan 1826). At the same time he borrowed from the Aderses their copy of Schleiermacher's sermons; he comments on them in *CL* VI 545–6, 555, and in *CN* IV 5318.

MS TRANSCRIPTS. (*a*) VCL LT 59 (**1–5**), LT 60 (**6–13**); (*b*) University of Texas (Humanities Research Center); fragmentary transcript in an unknown hand.

DATE. 20 Jan 1826 (**7**), and a little later. There is a corresponding sequence of notes in *CN* IV 5318–23 (Jan–Feb 1826), going back and forth between Eichhorn and Schleiermacher.

1   pp lxxxvii–lxxxviii | Introduction by the Translator

[Thirlwall discusses the hypothesis of Eichhorn, modified by Gratz, that the first three gospels were derived from an earlier lost narrative text, the *Urevangelium*.] He [Gratz] imagines it to have been used by the apostles . . . [for] their converts, for whom it was to supply not only the absence of their instructors, but also the historical facts which they omitted in their public discourses.

The supposition that the first propagators of Christianity provided themselves with copies of a written document for such a purpose appears to me to be not only unwarranted, but directly contradicted by every memorial we have remaining of the earliest transactions in Christian history. . . . For as the preachers must be supposed to have impressed their

469

hearers with every fact essential to the reception of Christianity, we should be obliged actually to believe what Gratz suggests . . . that the apostles were willing to gratify the propensity to the marvellous already excited by their preaching in their hearers, by leaving with them some more miraculous stories concerning Jesus.

This almost always candid and judicious Critic seems to have overlooked the strongest and most probable Particular of Eichhorn's Hypothesis:— viz, that the Proto-evangelium had for its object to prove the Messiahship of Jesus by the perfect coincidence of his Life and Actions with the Marks of the Messiah, which Herod sent for from the Priests.[1]

2   pp cxi–cxii

St. Luke, in the introductory verses prefixed to his Gospel, evidently describes the motives which induced him to undertake his work, and the means by which he was enabled to accomplish it. Such being the object of his introduction, it seems nearly certain that if his Gospel had been founded either on a document such as that imagined by Eichhorn, or on the works of St. Matthew and St. Mark, he would have made some allusion to these sources; and accordingly the advocates of each hypothesis have drawn arguments in favour of it from this passage in St. Luke. Still all that can be collected from it with certainty is, that at the time when St. Luke wrote there were several accounts relating to the transactions which form the subject of his Gospel, that these accounts were inaccurate or imperfect, and that he believed himself able to give information which might be more safely relied on.* To deduce any thing more than this from his language requires a rather subtle and elaborate argument.

* This fact at least we learn, that there were (not *several*; but) *many* απομνημονευματα,[1] Memorabilia, or Gospels by *many* Writers; & these

1[1] C was well read in the controversy among Continental, especially German, theologians about the composition of the gospels—the "Synoptic problem" as it came later to be called—and in *CN* IV 5323 (Jan–Feb 1826) he describes the then unpublished *Confessions of an Inquiring Spirit* as having been written in order to prepare students of theology in his own country for engagement in that controversy. C uses "Proto-evangelium" unconventionally, here and elsewhere, as a synonym for Eichhorn's *Urevangelium* or "original gospel". He annotated several works by Eichhorn and tended on the whole to seek a compromise between Eichhorn's hypothesis and Schleiermacher's "Counter-theory" (*CN* IV 5323) that the separate gospels were made up out of fragmentary written records of oral teaching. For "the Marks of the Messiah", for which C supposes Herod may have sent (Matt 2.4), see BAXTER *Reliquiae* COPY B 2, EICHHORN *NT* COPY A 12 and n 3, LESSING *Sämmtliche Schriften* 21, RHENFERD 3 n 2 above, and *CN* IV 5075 and n.

2[1] "Memoranda" or "memorials" or as C says in *CN* IV 5323 "Recollections"—a

Writers were not Apostles or Eye-witnesses, but persons who had ~~collected the~~ put in writing the substance of ~~their~~ discourses, & narrations which they at first or second hand had heard from the Preachers—Now how will this apply to Matthew?—This we *find*; & but from this we may fairly deduce the probability, that some one of these many Memoirs or *Ana* of Jesus was the *first*, and that the *first* was ~~made~~ undertaken on the ~~best~~ Authority, or at least not without the sanction of the Apostles. And what more does Eichhorn's Theory require?—

3   pp cxvi–cxxv

One of the most interesting and valuable contributions to this inquiry is the Essay by Dr. Gieseler, to which Schleiermacher alludes in his preface, *On the Origin and Early History of the Written Gospels*. It first appeared in a periodical work, and was afterwards published separately with considerable enlargements and additions. Gieseler conceives the only common source of our three first Gospels to have been oral tradition.

If I am right (and I am persuaded, that I am) in my premise, that the first Discourses of the Apostles, whether held in the ordinary Synagogues or to Assemblages of Jews & Jewish Converts consisted mainly in the Collation of Passages from the Old Testament which the Jewish Church had before the Birth of Christ agreed to interpret of the Messiah, with the gradual addition of other passages, in which the Apostles themselves discovered a̸ this prophetic Bearing ~~on Christ~~ —the collation of these with the Acts and incidents of the Life of Christ, each with each, yet so that all converged and found a focal fulfilment in Jesus, Schleiermacher's theory of a multitude of detached unconnected Narratives must appear alike improbable and unnecessary. Indeed, the very notion of Jewish or other Converts so shortly after the Death of Christ undertaking, each on his own impulse and each taking a different road, set pedestrian tours thro' Palestine for the purpose of collecting Anecdotes of Christ, strikes me as so grossly arbitrary and improbable that I scarcely know which most to wonder at, (i.e. in a writer of Schl$^{r's}$ Learning and Genius) the strangeness of the hypothesis itself, or the slightness of the Grounds, on which it is ~~tr~~ rested.—the occasional presence, to with, and the *conjectured* Omission, of *apparent* introductory Sentences to the various *supposed* separate Collections! Could no other account be given of ~~those~~ these sentences of this kind,

---

phrase from Justin Martyr taken up by the German commentators: cf *CN* iv 5172n, 5323 and n; EICHHORN *NT* COPY A 5; and

Jeremy TAYLOR *Polemicall Discourses* **29**. It appears also in this work, e.g. p lxiv.

that actually do exist in Luke's Gospel, [? ψ] it would ⟨be⟩ enough to reply—that such is the character of inartificial Narration. See the Essay on Method, Friend, Vol. III.[1] But in the way, in which I believe the Ǥ Materials of the three ~~firs~~ Gospels to have originated, it could not have been otherwise. On this supposition too, we can at once understand the tendency to *increase*, and the insertion or addition of ~~nar~~ Traditions grounded on Mystic Hymns, or suggested by other verses of the Prophets, or by Legends of other extraordinary Men. (*Speusippus's* Story of the miraculous Conception of his Uncle Plato, preserved by Origen, and Elijah's Fast of Forty Days, are cases in point.—[)][2] Hence would arise the necessity of revision, and Selection: and those would of course be ~~selected~~ preferred, which the Writers declared to have heard from an Apostle or Apostolic Man—. The one was *according* to Matthew; another according to Mark, the Companion of St Peter & supposed to have been himself one of the Seventy. This "according" appears to me the same with the καθως in the Preface or Dedication of Luke.[3] On this theory there can be no reason to doubt that the third Gospel is *authentic*, in the proper sense of the word—i.e. revised by Luke—and of these *Revisions*, I doubt not, the first in time.[4]—But here it behoves us to remember, that the Revisors of our Matthew and Mark may, on the strongest grounds of internal evidence, be referred to a later date than Luke—they were not im-

---

3[1] At the beginning of the "Essays on Method" in the 1818 *Friend*, C says that the conversation of an educated man is distinguished by "the unpremeditated and evidently habitual *arrangement* of his words, grounded on the habit of foreseeing, in each integral part, or (more plainly) in every sentence, the whole that he then intends to communicate": *Friend* (*CC*) I 449. The "ignorant" man, on the other hand, depends on memory exclusively and always tells the same story in the same order.

3[2] I.e. it would be consistent with the hypothesis of the *Urevangelium* that supplementary materials should have been added to the basic story of Christ so as to produce different versions in the oral tradition and hence different written accounts. As examples of legends that could have been adapted in this way, C goes to both Greek and Jewish sources: the story of the miraculous conception of Plato, attributed to his nephew Speusippus, was scornfully rejected by Origen—who does not, however, actually name Speusippus—in *Contra Cel-*

sum I 37 (C alludes to it in a note of 1825 on the same subject, *CN* IV 5240 ff 28^v–29); and Elijah's fast of forty days, analogous to the forty days that Christ spent in the wilderness, is described in 1 Kings 19.4–8.

3[3] Cf Luke 1.1–2: "Forasmuch as many have taken in hand to set forth in order a declaration of those things which are most surely believed among us, even as [*kathos*] they delivered them unto us, which from the beginning were eyewitnesses, and ministers of the word". C refers to his hypothesis that *kata* ("according to") in the titles of the Gospels is the same as this *kathos* in Luke in EICHHORN *NT* COPY A 1; and indeed they are etymologically related.

3[4] Cf C's assertion, at the end of this note, of "the priority and known authenticity of Luke" (as compared with the revisions of the gospels of Matthew and Mark). The eminent critic Nathaniel Lardner had already maintained this view in *The Credibility of the Gospel History: Works* (11 vols 1788) VI 41–2.

probably revised by the Bishops of Jerusalem, or some other of the earliest Jewish Churches (το κατα Μαρκον perhaps, by a Bishop of Alexandria[)][5]—and then we ought to take our Ignatius (if *any* parts be genuine), Justin Martyr, and above all Tertullian in hand, in order to form a correction notion, of what sort of men these Bishops were—fervent, pious, and holy Men but neither Critics nor Philosophers, nor accustomed too to value the *question* of Fact by its bearings on Doctrine.[6] The analogy of Faith was the Test, on which the primitive Church relied—& compared with which Documents, Autographs, & the et cetera of Historical Research stood in small honor.—Lastly, to this View, ὡς εμοίγε δοκεῖ,[7] [? throu] is capable of suggesting the motives that impelled the Evangelist John to compose a Gospel κατα πνευμα;[8] not ⟨so much⟩ to correct Matthew, Mark, and Luke, as to counteract the carnalizing passion for biographical anecdotes of Jesus—And what if the acquaintance with a number of these απομνημονευματα,[9] and a perception of the undue importance attached to them, had given an additional emphasis to S[t] Paul's resolve not to know Christ himself *after the Flesh*.[10] We cannot, however, be too thankful to Providence, that the Revisions of Matthew and Mark are such as they are—with so much of inestimable Worth, and with so little dross. And both this, and the Confinement of the Choice to these, may fairly be attributed to the priority and known authenticity of Luke.

---

4   pp cxxvii–cxxx

[Thirlwall continues to summarise Gieseler's arguments.] In the meanwhile the apostles at Jerusalem, previous to their separation and departure* for the purpose of propagating Christianity in foreign lands, exercised themselves in rendering the original cyclus [from Aramaic] into Greek, the language in which it was probable that they would have the most frequent occasion to deliver it, and with which their acquaintance was so imperfect that they must have stood in need of mutual assistance.

3[5] I.e. "The [Gospel] according to Mark" by a bp of Alexandria. Eusebius (*Hist. Eccl.* 2.16, 2.24) reports that Mark established the Church in Alexandria, and that the first bishop was Annianus.

3[6] The works of these early Christian writers, that is, reveal a great deal about qualities of mind as well as about the conditions and personnel of the early Church. St Justin Martyr (c 100–c 165) and Tertullian (c 160–c 220) were not themselves bishops. On the authenticity of the letters of St Ignatius, bp of Antioch (c 35–c 107) see

FLEURY 26 and n 3.

3[7] "As it seems to me, at least".

3[8] "According to the spirit" as opposed to the first three gospels "according to the flesh" (the latter phrase coming from 2 Cor 5.16, cited below at n 10): cf e.g. BLANCO WHITE *Letters* 1 and n 2.

3[9] "Memoranda", as in 2 above.

3[10] 2 Cor 5.16: "Wherefore henceforth know we no man after the flesh: yea, though we have known Christ after the flesh, yet now henceforth know we him no more."

They were by this means enabled to deliver even in Greek one and the same Gospel with scarcely greater variations than are presented by different copies of the same manuscript.

* On what authority that deserves the name of historical are these Apostolical missionary Travels founded? And how are they to be reconciled with S[t] Paul's peculiar Title, and Privilege, the Apostle of the Gentiles?[1] If such was the understood Office, Duty, and Intention of the Apostles, of each and all, must it ⟨not⟩ appear strange, that not even an incidental allusion to any one of the Twelve, as thus employed, should have escaped from S[t] Luke in the Acts of the Apostles? The last 12 verses of Mark the Translator gives up, and with good reason, as spurious.[2] And the longer I examine the text, Go into all the world, or Go unto all nations,[3] the firmer is my conviction, that the Aramaic words used by our Lord himself signified no more than the rescinding of his former Command which had confined the preaching of the 70 to the children of Israel.[4] Henceforward they were to offer the Gospel to men of all Nations, indifferently. I do not by this mean to refuse all credit to the tradition, that Mark was at Alexandria, and John at Ephesus: & we learn from Peter's Letter, that he was at Babylon (for I see no reason, why Babylon should mean Rome.)[5] In all these Cities there were Jewish Communities & Synagogues: & nothing can be more probable, than that numerous Converts were made during the annual Conflux of Jews from all parts of the Roman Empire to Jerusalem—and these on their return to their homes would naturally be solicitous to receive a visit from their Spiritual Fathers, for the ordering of their Churches & the confirmation of their Faith. But this admission goes but a small way toward the vindication of the historic claims of Cave's Lives of the Apostles.[6]   *S. T. C.*

4[1] Rom 11.13.

4[2] C refers to Thirlwall's Introduction lxxxviii, where he summarises the arguments of Peter Alois Gratz (1769–1849) regarding Mark 16.9–20 and concedes that there is "very strong external and internal evidence" that these verses constitute "an apocryphal addition made by a later hand". This was and is a common opinion: cf C's allusion to it in BIBLE COPY B **101** and n 1.

4[3] Mark 16.15 (one of the disputed verses): "And he said unto them, Go ye into all the world, and preach the gospel to every creature." And Matt 28.19: "Go ye therefore, and teach all nations . . .".

4[4] Luke 10.1: "After these things the Lord appointed other seventy also, and sent them two and two before his face into every city and place, whither he himself would come."

4[5] The traditions C mentions having to do with John and Luke are recorded e.g. by William Cave (whom C is about to refer to) *Antiquitates Apostolicae: or, The Lives, Acts and Martyrdoms of the Holy Apostles of Our Saviour. To which are added the Lives of the Two Evangelists, SS. Mark and Luke* (1675) 116, 162. As to Peter, the first Epistle is sent as from Babylon (1 Pet 5.13), though "Babylon" is usually interpreted as meaning Rome. C's doubts about the *general* equation of Babylon and Rome appear also in LACUNZA **69, 70**.

4[6] See the preceding note.

5 pp cxxxii–cxxxv

. . . I cannot conceive that our Gospels represent in a literal sense the public preaching of the apostles. In their private intercourse with one another and their most confidential scholars, the scenes they had witnessed and the speeches they had heard, as they undoubtedly formed their most delightful recollections, might also be frequently the theme of conversation. . . . And that to these communications we are indebted for some passages of our Gospels is not improbable; though when we consider how fully the time of the apostles was occupied . . . we shall not be disposed to expect many such instances, and still less to assign this as the origin of a collection embracing the whole public life of Jesus.*

* This confutation of Gieseler[1] is sensibly and pleasingly written—but it consists almost entirely of ὡς ἐμοὶ δοκεῖ[2] declarations of the writer's *Opinion. He* imagines that the Apostles' Discourses were chiefly polemical or docential,[3] and seldom narrative. I with equal right imagine, that the narrative part of their Preaching would follow the first and simplest articles of faith. Nay, I cannot imagine or conceive, that any number of Converts could have met together, without desiring to hear from the Companions of their Lord something like a connected Relation of Events and Actions, ⟨of⟩ which some had seen one or two only, some had seen at a distance, and others not at all. But in fact I do not see, how the Apostles could prove that Jesus was the Christ promised and predicted by the Prophets without first quoting the prophetic passage, and then relating the event or miracle that had fulfilled it. Suppose this done (and done it must have been) successively to each of the preadmitted "Marks of the Messiah"[4]—& suppose only that some one "ready Writer"[5] among the Auditors had *taken notes*—and we have the Proto-evangelium, for which Eichhorn contends.[6] Now that the Jews were in the habit of using tablets, on which they took down the aphorisms or pointed SENTIMENTS of their Rabbis, may be shewn from the Talmud, even if the very existence of such Books, as "Proverbs" and "Ecclesiasticus" did not supersede all other proof.[7] It is to this custom, common both to the Jews and the Ro-

5[1] A large section of Thirlwall's introduction (cxvi–cxliii, including 3–5 textus) is taken up with a summary of a work by Johann Karl Ludwig Gieseler, the *Historisch-kritischer Versuch über die Entstehung und die frühesten Schicksale der schriftlichen Evangelien* (Leipzig 1818)—which title Thirlwall renders simply as *On the Origin and Early History of the Written Gospels.* As Thirlwall says, "Gieseler conceives the only common source of our first three Gospels to have been oral tradition."

5[2] "As it seems to me".
5[3] "Docential"—not in *OED*—means "instructional".
5[4] Referred to also in 1 above.
5[5] Ps 45.1.
5[6] See 1 and n 1.
5[7] From the aphoristic form common in the wisdom literature of the Talmud, OT,

mans, that we may probably attribute the coincidence of the Gospels in the Speeches of our Lord.—Finally, this is not merely hypothetical. S! Peter's Harangue (Acts of the Ap. C. II.) is an instance:—first, a Prophecy quoted—then a miracle appealed to as the fulfilment.[8]

6   p 34 | On Luke 2.1–20

It is in the highest degree improbable that the account of this vision [the announcement to the shepherds] found its way at that time even so far as Jerusalem, and that when Christ made his public appearance and attracted notice, this as well as the following incident [the visit of the shepherds to the manger] had been circulated. Had this been the case,* the massacre of the infants at Bethlehem could not have taken place, nor even, if there be any who will not admit it as a fact, have been invented . . .

* Perche? non?[1] Does Schl. mean that *if* Herod had heard the story of the Shepherds, he would have believed it & turned Christian by anticipation? This I cannot suppose of a Schleiermacher; and yet what else he can have meant, I do not see.

7   pp 35–7 | Continuing 6 textus

. . . in that case too it would be almost astonishing that we find in our Gospels no hint, that the reputation of Jesus among the multitude and the report of his being the Messiah were founded in part on such accrediting presages. We must therefore suppose that this story was only drawn forth from the dust of oblivion by the recollections of individuals after the fame of Jesus was already established, and therefore probably did not obtain farther publicity till after his death. *But that it is neither an empty bubble, nor a fabrication designed to exalt the dignity of Jesus by such presages, we have an assurance, in the opportunity which the Christians of that district had to inquire of Mary, who must have known of it, or of the disciples with whom she spent most of her life, upon the subject.

Schleiermacher is too good a man for me to suspect, that he was laughing in his Sleeve when he wrote this §ph. Yet how he could be in earnest, puzzles me. What do we know of "the Christians of that district?" Or on what grounds can we build "an assurance"[1] that this Poem or Legend ever

---

and OT Apocrypha, C infers "the habit of using tablets". Cf *CN* IV 4603 (Oct 1819), again a note on Luke, in which C comments on the characteristic practice of the period, namely "to *take notes* &c" upon the speeches of the rabbis.

5[8] Acts 2.14–36, where Peter explains the gift of tongues at the Pentecost by reference to the prophecy of Joel (Joel 2.28–32).

6[1] "Why? not?"

7[1] Both phrases are quoted from the textus.

fell in their way? Or that it had been even written during the Life of Mary? What do we know of Christ's Mother ~~on~~ from *historical* sources? Are not the (falsely called) Traditions glaringly mythological? It would indeed be easy (and 30 years ago I amused myself with *imaginings* of this sort) to conjecture, that Mary, like all other Mothers of famous & extraordinary men, might have been fond of recollecting sundry ⟨*Remarkables,*⟩ presages &c before & after the Birth of the Child[2]—the strange Dreams & Visions, she had had, "whether in the body or out of the body"[3] she could not tell—& that these *recollections* (not seldom the mental *Echoes* of the Events, in which they had been fulfilled) might have travelled from hand to hand, with the usual improvements./ But surely facts, of which Paul probably was, and certainly wished to be, ignorant,[4] have but little claim to rank as articles of Faith at the present day.   20 Jan.ʸ 1826.—

8   pp 40–1 | On Luke 2.22–40

And to this incident too [the presentation of the child Jesus in the Temple] the same remark is applicable as to the former, that it was certainly forgotten during the interval between the infancy of Jesus and his public appearance, and was only brought forward again at a later period. It could not but excite attention at the moment, and that in no slight degree, as we must suppose Simeon, should we even disclaim all further acquaintance with him, to have been a well known and respected man. *But the prospect of that which an infant was to be and perform in his riper years was too distant, especially in such unquiet times, when one shock followed another, to engage continued attention.

Werthester Schleiermacher, mache den Schleier ab, und lasse dich sehen![1] What! a solemn agnition & prophetic annunciation in the Temple by a venerated Priest during the performance of a solemn and public Act—⟨an agnition⟩ of what? Of a Maccabeus, or of a Prophet?—No! Of the Messiah, at the very time that the whole East, nay, "the prophetic Soul of the whole World,"[2] were unquietly and anxiously expecting his advent, speedily *forgotten*! and no eye follow the proclaimed Saviour of Israel into his retirement!—And even after he had entered on his public Mission, no reference made by him or by his Apostles—to this fact!— Credat quid credere possit.[3]

7[2] C recorded the same speculation in a note of Dec 1823: *CN* iv 5075.
7[3] 2 Cor 12.2 var.
7[4] In reflecting on Paul's wilful ignorance, C is perhaps alluding to 2 Cor 5.16, as in **3** and n 10 above.
8[1] "Most worthy Schleiermacher, put the veil aside and let yourself see!" C puns on the name *Schleier-macher* i.e. veil-maker.
8[2] Shakespeare Sonnet 107 lines 1–2 var.
8[3] "Let him believe [it] who is capable of believing [it]."

9   pp 44–7 | On Luke 2.41–52

Since however this superior purity prevails in the main throughout the whole narrative, and reminds us more than any thing that has hitherto appeared of the introduction, one might conjecture, that the compiler and arranger of the whole [Luke 1 and 2] was also the first who committed to writing this last piece [the account of Jesus with the learned doctors in the Temple], after an oral narrative derived directly or indirectly from Mary, and annexed it to the earlier accounts of Jesus's infancy which he found already collected, so that we should here meet with his own hand again for the first time since the introductory passage. *This however is a conjecture which does not admit of being more firmly established.

* I ask but one question of Schl.ʳ· In the whole World of historical Literature, comprizing Biographies, Memorials, Memorabilia, &c does there exist a parallel or similar instance? What! take a *Poem*, which Sch. himself regards as at best a fiction grounded on facts, Wahrheit und Dichtung[1] (tho' after the poetic machinery, ɪs the fictions, are detached, it is not easy to discover what the *facts* are)—Leave this poem as he found it, then procure from Mary information on events or incidents subs immediately subsequent to the assumed date of the fiction—and cooly add the to this known fiction a matter-of-fact Narrative, without any inquiry of Mary what truth (if any) was the ground or occasion of the ⟨preceding⟩ fiction, & without pointing out the difference between the two narratives by a single word! What reliance could place[a] on a Compiler, so deficient in common honesty or common sense or both? Must it not affect the credibility of the whole Gospel, as far as Luke is concerned? And is it not incomparably safer, as well as simpler, to consider the whole from the Dedication to the 3ʳᵈ Chapter as an accidental Prefix to the best authenticated Copy of Luke's Gospel, which the Church was in possession of?—*This* may be removed without knife or ligature—while the Evang. Infantiæ in Matthew can be detached only by excision.[2]

9[a] For "could we place" or "could one place", the pronoun accidentally omitted at the turning of the page

9[1] "Truth and poetry"—but also an oblique allusion to the title of Goethe's autobiography, *Dichtung und Wahrheit* (pts 1–3 pub 1811–14).

9[2] "Evangelium Infantiae", "Gospel of the Infancy", is a phrase applied by C and others—e.g. Thirlwall in the introduction to this translation (lxxxix), EICHHORN in *Neue Testament* I 500—to accounts of the infancy of Jesus, whether apocryphal or

canonical. Most of C's notes about Luke have to do with the argument that the first two chapters consist of a separate "infancy gospel" tacked on to the beginning of the text: cf e.g. DONNE *Sermons* COPY B 9, IRVING *Sermons* 2, PAULUS 2 and n 1, RHENFERD 10 and n 2. In BLANCO WHITE *Letters* 7 C refers, as here, to the relative ease with which these chapters may be separated from Luke, compared with Matt: "the Evan-

10   pp 51–5 | On Luke 1 and 2

Can it at all lessen the credibility of the two evangelists [Matthew and Luke], that each admitted into his history some passages not purely historical?* Certainly not with a candid judge, who reflects, in the first place, that all this serves still only as a prelude to the proper subject of the history, which was the public life of Jesus . . .

* I cannot repress ~~my~~ the indignation which the perusal of this and the two preceding pages has excited. Better, a thousand times better, reject the three Gospels altogether as the spurious patchwork of the II.nd Century— ~~It an~~ The worst, that could happen *then*, would be, the want of any certain & authentic History of "Christ according to the Flesh.["]^1 We should have the Faith & Religion of Christians without knowing the particular incidents which accompanied the ~~first~~ Revelation—further than the Creed and unvarying Tradition had preserved for us—a great Loss indeed, but not a mortal ~~wound~~ injury. But these Imaginations of Schleiermacher poison the very sources of the Christian Religion while he represents the Eye-witnesses, the chosen Apostles & Preachers of the Faith, the only competent Recorders of the Actions and Doctrines of Christ, as men capable of blending Facts & Fictions, without leaving any clue to the Labyrinth. I dare affirm, that it is impossible/. One or the other of three cases must be supposed. Either all is fiction; or all is fact; or the former is not apostolic. Even in reading the Par. Reg. of Milton, and most oppressively in reading the Messiah of Klopstock, tho' both are avowed Poems, the juxta-position and immediate neighborhood of what we know to be fictitious with facts, incidents and discourses which we had received as truths with a ~~more~~ deeper and more passionate Faith, than mere History, even the most authentic, can inspire, shocks our moral sense as well as offends our Taste & Judgement—and by the violence of the contrast gives to poetic fiction the character & quality of a Lie. The more than historic faith in the one prevents us from yielding even a poetic faith to the other.^{2} How impossible then must it appear, that ⱥ the chosen Companions of our Lord, ~~an~~ Eye-witness⟨es⟩ of his wonderful Acts, many of

---

gelia Infantiæ, prefixed to the Gospel of Luke and concorporated with the canonical Revision of Matthew's".

10^1 2 Cor 5.16, q above **3** n 10.

10^2 This passage echoes C's famous formulation about the "willing suspension of disbelief for the moment, which constitutes poetic faith" in *BL* ch 14 (*CC*) II 6; but more specifically, it echoes remarks about Klopstock's epic *Messias* in a letter of Jun 1817

(*CL* IV 743): "In Klopstock's Messiah, for instance, the *truths*, the glorified Facts, being connected with more than historic Belief in the minds of men, the *fictions* come upon one like *Lies*.—" This criticism of *Paradise Regained* is unusual for C, who usually discusses the poem respectfully though describing it as inferior in kind to *Paradise Lost*, e.g. HAYLEY **1**.

which were worked for *their* sake, and in order that they might deliver them to all Nations, could for a moment endure to *hear*, much less themselves to *relate*, to *record*, known falsehoods, ⟨or truths⟩ magnified & fantastically refracted into falsehoods, in close connection with and under the ~~distinct foresight~~ immediate impression of actions and events, that *lived* on their very eyes, and filled their souls with Love, Joy, Reverence, affectionate Grief and Devoted Loyalty even to Death!

11   pp 66–7 | On Luke 4.16–30

Thus then did it happen that Luke, when he sought for accounts of the commencement of Jesus's ministry, met with these three sections, the abstract of the memoirs of John, the account of the baptism of Christ, and the history of the temptation, in a somewhat different form indeed from Matthew, but yet in the same order.

If however he found these three sections already connected, as I suppose . . . Luke loses the praise of the chronological determination contained in III.1 ["Now in the fifteenth year of the reign of Tiberius Caesar"]. . . . For this determination of time was to be sure very meritorious and seasonable in a memoir of John; but is it also very praiseworthy in a biography of Christ to state more exactly when John made his first public appearance, than when Christ began to teach, or when he was born? And is it much to be commended that Luke distributed his dates unconnectedly and injudiciously in three different places?

Schleiermacher wearies me out with his ipse dicos,[1] and unsupported Assertions, the self-evidence or even decisive probability of which is far from apparent to *my* mind.—If ~~the~~ Luke, the Evangelist, be St Paul's Luke,[2] we might expect that he would not trouble himself with any hearsays concerning Jesus previous to his public Mission, as the Christ. But this public Mission began with the Baptism by John, and (inasmuch as an introductory Chapter is component part of a Book) with the Baptism *of* John. In precisely determining by all the several dates intelligible to several Readers ⟨the time⟩ of John's Baptism, he best determined the date of the proper Epiphany of Christ, and therefore deserves the praise, he has received.[3]

---

[1] Anglicised plural of "I myself say [it]", a variant on *ipse dixit*; i.e. dogmatic statements.

[2] Paul refers to Luke "the beloved physician" (Col 4.14) as his companion on his missionary journey to Rome (2 Tim 4.11) and Acts records his presence on other journeys.

[3] In Irving *Sermons* 36, C describes himself as one "for whom the Gospel commences with and from the Baptism of John"—the final phrase, though ambigu-

12   pp 220–1 | On Luke 15.1–17.10

Should however any one object, that the result of this whole view of the subject is that Christ favoured the law more than the subsequent proceedings of his disciples would induce us to suppose, I should be inclined to say, in the first place, that where Christ appears as the defender of the publicans it was very seasonable to lay greater stress on this head, and in the next place, that Christ certainly intended to make the law in its utmost rigour (as is proved by his whole way of treating it in his speeches against the Pharisees and also by other expressions not connected with them) the foundation of his church, so far as a considerable portion of the Jewish nation was to form its first stock, and in this very spirit the Christians of Palestine afterwards acted.

* Here is another rash and hasty assertion: as if such an *intention* was compatible with the distinct foreknowlege of the utter cessation of the Jewish Government and State so soon to be accomplished! Or as if Christ had not known that the Law had done its work—& was *dead*—i.e. utterly unfit to the minds & conditions of men henceforward. As long as the Heaven (the Jewish Hierarchy) and the Earth (the Jewish People, as the subjects of a State) remained, so long not a jot was to be disobeyed—i.e. Christianity no pretext for Sedition.[1] Can aught be more offensive to the *taste* no less than the moral sense, to suppose that the privilege & superior dignity of the Jewish People, had they received the Redeemer of the World, was to have consisted in this—that they alone were to be confined to the slaughter-house of a sacrificial Institution!

ous, one that probably simply echoes AV and means baptism "*by* John" (as in PAULUS **31** and n 1). In a note of May 1825 C again remarks that "the original Gospels" "all began with the Baptism of John": *CN* iv 5228 f 89ᵛ. Here he may, however, have had in mind the extra-scriptural tradition, based on Matt 3.14–15, that after baptising Christ, John was baptised by him in turn (cf Nathaniel Lardner *Works*—11 vols 1788— v 292); or he may have inferred, from Luke 3.2 ("the word of God came unto John the son of Zacharias in the wilderness"), that John himself had already experienced some form of baptism. He challenges the authority of the infancy narratives by considering the spiritual mission of Christ as not having

properly begun until he was an adult, at the time of his baptism, when "a voice came from heaven, which said, Thou art my beloved Son; in thee I am well pleased" (Luke 3.22). The Feast of the Epiphany, originally and in the Eastern Church still associated with the Baptism of Christ, came to be identified with his birth and the revelation to the Magi, in the Western Church after the 4th century.

12[1] Matt 5.17–18: "Think not that I am come to destroy the law, or the prophets . . . . For verily I say unto you, Till heaven and earth pass, one jot or one tittle shall in no wise pass from the law, till all be fulfilled."

13   pp 246–7 | On Luke 18.15–34

In the prediction, XVIII.31–4 [Christ's prediction of his trial and crucifixion], Luke alone has the addition, verse 34, which does indeed at first sight appear to accord but ill with the openness and precision of Christ's discourse ["And they understood none of these things . . ."], and has been used by many to throw suspicion on that very precision, as if it were to be laid only to the account of the disciples and did not lie in the words of Jesus. But how has it escaped reflexion, that all the expressions in this verse, as Jesus at all events spoke in a language intelligible to his disciples and they were able to understand his meaning, can be only relative, and are meant to describe the imperfect degree in which they understood him, in comparison with the manner in which, after his resurrection, they came to perceive the necessity of his sufferings and the reference of prophetical passages to him?

* This again is one of those arbitrary Assertions, of which I complain in this Essay. Words cannot be more express, than those in Luke 18.34.— or less capable of bearing a qualified & merely comparative sense. Thrice in three different forms of expression, each stronger than the other, does the Evangelist affirm the incapability of the Disciples to comprehend the true meaning of Christ's Declarations. "⟨1⟩[a] And they understood none of these things: ⟨2⟩ and the saying was hid from them; ⟨3⟩ neither knew they the things that were spoken["][1]—(or as we should say in English, & which is the true force of εγινωσκον in this sentence,[2] *they had not even a conception of any such things.*)—And now take Schleiermacher's paraphrase—And they understood him sufficiently well; and the meaning of his words was clear enough to them; but yet not with that fullness of insight into the necessity of the events, ~~or~~ nor in that connection with the whole scheme of the Christian Faith, which they afterward attained.!! If this be allowable, every Reader is his own Evangelist.—

14   p 266 | On Luke 20, 21

Christ repels this attempt [that by the chief priests and scribes to get him to make seditious statements against the Roman government—Luke 20.19–23] in a way that involves no contradiction with his invitations to a union in a βασιλεία τοῦ θεοῦ [Kingdom of God], which should be quite

---

13[a]   The figures printed here as ⟨1⟩, ⟨2⟩, and ⟨3⟩ were originally written by C above the line; they have been brought down to avoid confusion with editorial notes

13[1] Luke 18.34 var.
13[2] C's rendering of the Greek is correct, but Schleiermacher's point is also

valid, i.e. that the words made sense to the disciples although they did not understand their full meaning.

independent of civil circumstances. To this answer the question XX.41–44 is evidently the second part. I too, Christ says as it were, will propose to you ensnaring questions, which you cannot answer without either being inconsistent with your theory or saying something for which I might instigate the Romans against you. For as they applied the psalm to the Messiah they could not answer otherwise than that *David might call the Messiah his Lord, because he was to be a far more powerful king than he was himself, and this certainly implied above all that he could not be a subject of the Romans, and, like the house of Herod, even a servant.

* This is little less than impudent. The King of England might call the Emperor of China Monarch, ⟨or Sovereign;⟩ but would he call him *my* Monarch, *my* Sovereign? The stress is on the word, *his* Lord.

15 pp 266–7 | Continuing from **14** textus

And who knows whether in discourses directed against Christ, which no doubt they did not neglect in the Synagogues and porches of the Temple, they had not availed themselves of this construction, in order to prove that Jesus of Nazareth could not be the Messiah. In this close connexion with the preceding occurrence this proceeding of Christ is perfectly intelligible and perfectly worthy of him, but loses both characters, according to my impression, if it be separated, and Christ made to act, in the spirit of this question, on the offensive.

* Worthy of a Special pleader; but of Christ?—The Aff. or Neg. to this question depends on an *If. If* Jesus were no more than the Socinians believe him to have been—I answer: perfectly so! Quite in character! To play with double meanings, of which the least obvious was always the one really meant, appears to have been his habit./ But when I answered thus, I should at the same instaneet turn my back on both.—Besides, how would this have offended the Romans? Were they silly enough to be angry with the Priests of a country for sharing with the rest of their countrymen in a popular Belief common to all parts of the *Roman* East? If they had declared, the Messiah is come—or we may expect during the next month—or had pointed out an existing person, as the Messiah—then indeed a prudent Government would have reason to look about/. But no such danger was involved in the answer, Sch. supposes.

16 pp 292–3 | On Luke 22.1–23.49

A closer inspection will I think satisfy us, that this piece was originally written as an account of the institution of the Lord's Supper [rather than as a description of the entire evening]. To this necessarily appertained

Christ's expressions, that he knew this to be his last meal; so likewise that no one knew beforehand of such an institution being designed, but that Christ only gave commission to prepare the Passover. These points are only touched upon; all others are entirely omitted. The disproportionate minuteness at the beginning admits of two explanations. On the one hand every unpractised writer and narrator is apt to deliver himself more explicitly at the beginning than he chooses or is able afterwards to continue. In the next place the framer of this narrative, who had the transaction indirectly, or in the most favourable case directly from an apostle, seems to have found in the manner in which Jesus gave the commission something marvellous, or at least very striking and remarkable, which certainly does not in fact belong to it; and he was thereby induced to relate this part more circumstantially than the rest. This point of view being fixed, there is very much which, according to my impression, speaks very plainly in favour of the genuineness and originality of our narrative.

* If the Apostles generally had ⟨not⟩ found in this transaction and command "something marvellous",[1] how could this have become the universal faith of all the Churches from the very beginning; or St Paul have adopted the mysterious language, which he has done?[2] But if the Apostles generally did so understand their great Master, where did Schl. obtain *his* more correct information?

16[1] In textus.   in 1 Cor 10.16–21, 11.23–9.
16[2] In writing about the Lord's Supper

Ueber den sogenannten ersten Brief des Paulos an den Timotheos. Ein kritisches Sendschreiben an C. H. Gass, &c. Berlin 1807. 8°.

British Library C 43 a 16(1), bound as first (*after* C's note-making) with three other Schleiermacher books, all unmarked: *Ueber die neue Liturgie für die Hof- und Garnison-Gemeinde zu Potsdam und für die Garnisonkirche in Berlin* (Berlin 1816), *Gelegentliche Gedanken über Universitäten in deutschem Sinn* (Berlin 1808), and *Ueber die für die protestantische Kirche des preussischen Staats einzurichtende Synodalverfassung* (Berlin 1817).

DATE. Probably early in 1826, as indicated by notebook references of Jan and Apr 1826: *CN* IV 5312, 5347 and nn.

1   p 193, cropped

[In a discussion whether the phrase ἑνὸς ἀνδρὸς γυνή ("Wife of one man") in 1 Tim 5.9 implies a prohibition against polygamy, polyandry, adultery, or bigamy:] Vielmehr wird gewiss jeder der unsern Brief unbefangen für sich liest, und an keine Aufgabe denkt, ihn mit sonst etwas als nur mit sich selbst in Harmonie zu bringen,* hier gewiss ein Verbot der zweiten Ehe finden, und zwar nicht ein allgemeines sondern nur für die welche nach kirchlichen Aemtern streben. Dies ist nun offenbar nicht Paulinisch, sondern steht in der Mitte zwischen der Paulinischen Praxis und der späteren . . .

[Rather, anyone who reads this letter for himself without prejudice and without thought for any problem other than bringing it into harmony with itself* will find here a prohibition against second marriage, not indeed a general one but solely for those who aspire to Church offices. This is obviously not Pauline, but stands midway between Pauline practice and that of later times . . .]

* Tho' convinced with Schl. of the spurious[ness] of I. Timothy, or rather with Eichhorn holding nei[ther] of the 3 Pastoral Epistles for Paulline;[1] yet I [do] not see why the ενος ανδρος γυνη may n[ot] mean the Wife of a man who has no other wi[fe.][2]

[1] As late as 1824 C was still referring to the Pastoral Epistles 1 and 2 Tim, and Tit, as authentically Pauline (e.g. *CN* IV 5169), but early in 1826 he came to accept the arguments of Eichhorn and Schleiermacher against Paul's authorship and there are numerous later assertions to this effect: see esp *CN* IV 5312, 5347 and nn; BIBLE COPY B **116** and n 1; EICHHORN *NT* COPY B **32** and n 1; *TT* (*CC*) I 388 and n 6. J. G. Eichhorn's argument appears in *Einleitung in das Neue Testament* (3 vols Leipzig 1804, 1810–11, 1812–14) III 315–410.

[2] 1 Tim 5 deals, among other things,

with the role of what came to be known as the deaconess, and 5.9 exhorts, "Let not a widow be taken into the number under threescore years old, having been the wife of one man". C is elsewhere more concerned about 5.11–12, which he interprets as "The imposing a Vow on the Deaconesses not to marry again—& making the breach of it a crime": *CN* IV 5312; cf ETERNAL PUNISHMENT **16**). No standard commentary appears to endorse C's suggestion that the phrase might mean the *only* wife. Cf the note on this passage in *The New Testament ... with a Commentary* ed Adam Clarke (3 vols 1817) III, where "having been the wife of one man" is thus explained: "Having lived in conjugal fidelity with her husband; or, having had but one husband at a time; or, according to others, having never been but once married."

GOTTHILF HEINRICH VON SCHUBERT
1780–1860

Allgemeine Naturgeschichte oder Andeutungen zur Geschichte und Physiognomik der Natur. Erlangen 1826. 8°.

British Library C 44 d 36

Autograph signature of JHG on p ‾4 (recto of original brown paper wrapper). On p ‾2 an account of the provenance of the book, dated Jun 1908, with a list of the pages on which C has written notes.

MS TRANSCRIPT. VCL LT 61.

DATE. About May 1827 (**25** n 3), and later: a note of c May 1830 (N 45 f 2) refers to this work. C evidently had the book on loan from JHG, and some of the notes (**2**) appear to have been written with him in mind.

COEDITOR. Raimonda Modiano.

---

1   p ‾3, pencil

The great defect, meo saltem judicio,[1] of Schubart's System or Scheme of Thought is the sort of contrasted divinity which he assigns to Light, and quasi proprio quodam jure,[2] to the Solar Light or Atmosphere![3] But throughout Schubart too much confounds the powers, and the eternal Laws, that are the *conditions* of the actualization of the Powers.[4]

---

2   p 193, pencil, cropped | § 19

Es wird in unserm jetzigen Meere, durch die Wirkung des Gefrierens, ein Theil des Meereswassers fast ganz entsalzen und in Süsswasser umgewandelt. *Vielleicht dass auch andre Naturkräfte und ihre Wechselwirkung in dem alten, weniger an Salz als an Kalk reichem Meere, stellenweise, bald hier bald dort eine Entkalkung des Wassers und

---

[1] "In my judgment at least".

[2] "In its own right, as it were".

[3] C is probably referring especially to ch 3 (on the sun and the planets) secs 9–11 (pp 70–91), where Schubert celebrates the power of the sun, calling it (tr) "the queen of day" and describing the atmosphere of the sun in semi-mystical language as "ani-

mate and animating".

[4] C's considered and repeated objection to *Naturphilosophie* as a whole: cf GOLDFUSS **2** and nn 1, 2, this work of Goldfuss being in fact a contribution to Schubert's *Handbuch der Naturgeschichte* (4 vols Nürnberg 1813–23).

kristallinische Süsswassergebilde der Tiefe, die nicht blos Sandstein sondern vollkommener Granit wurden, hervorrief.

[In our present-day sea, part of the sea-water is almost entirely desalinated and changed into fresh water by freezing. *Perhaps other natural forces and their interaction in the ancient sea, which was less salty than calcic, also led in places, now here, now there, to a decalcification of the water and to crystalline fresh-water formations in the depths; and these forms turned not merely into sandstone but into perfect granite.]

* Yes! this is easily said. What ⟨products⟩ might not [be] supposed, if we suppose the productive causes. But what is the connection? Why Süsswasser, rat[her] than the *Urluft* or Urfeuer?[1]—Ja—aitchgee and Ess Teesi[2] determine the dynamic Factors of the teeming Mother-waters, and the characteristic Stagger of their Equilibriu[m] as compared with the barren water-Masses of the present Epoch—& then construct [? the new].

3　p 285, pencil, cropped | § 30

Am häufigsten aber unter allen scheint damals der noch jetzt vor allen Säugethieren des Landes langlebende, ruhig überlegende, einer ausdauernden treuen Erinnerung fähige, keusche Elephant gewesen zu seyn: ein Thier, in welchem sich jene Eigenschaften am meisten fixirt und vergestaltet haben, welche noch jetzt, auch bei unsrem Geschlecht, die im kräftigsten Wachsthum stehende, nach innen geistig sehr empfängliche, nach aussen unbeholfnere, vom Geschlechtstrieb noch unbewegte Kindheit auszeichnen.*

[Commonest of all in those days seems to have been the chaste elephant, of all mammals still the longest-living, most calmly reflective, and most capable of tenacious and faithful memory: in this animal those traits have become established and most fully formed which still, even in our race, characterize childhood, a period of strongest growth in which the child is inwardly very impressionable, outwardly awkward, and as yet unmoved by the sexual instinct.*]

* Poor Chiny at the Exeter Exchange would have told Schubart a different tale.[1] Like all other large Herding Beast[s] the Male Elephants are sexuall[y] tranquil for the far larger portion of the Year, and tempest-

2[1] "Why fresh water, rather than the *original air* or the original fire?"

2[2] "J. H. G. and S. T. C."—Joseph Henry Green and S. T. Coleridge, fellow-critics of *Naturphilosophie*.

3[1] The permanent menagerie at the Exeter Exchange is described in colourful detail in Altick 307–16. Altick describes the elephant Chunee as "the prime attraction" from 1812 onwards. Well known for his un-

governability "at certain seasons", Chunee had to be destroyed on 1 Mar 1826: 152 shots were fired into his body, but it was a harpoon that finally dispatched him. Altick reproduces a contemporary print of the scene and describes the press coverage in terms that would support C's "poor Chiny": "The obedient Chunee murdered by his friends" seems to have been the refrain (312).

driven, maddene[d] during the remainder. Their Chastity stands on the same footing with their accredited modesty. Compare Sir W. Jones's Statement.[2]

4   p 327, pencil, cropped | § 32

Diese Sprache entstehet bei dem Menschen, wie schon das Beispiel verwilderter Individuen zeiget,* nicht so unwillkührlich und von innen, als der schreiende Ton eines gemarterten oder sich ergötzenden Thieres, sondern sie ist etwas Gegebenes, Mitgetheiltes, allenthalben Erlerntes.

[As the example of individuals raised in the wild demonstrates,* language does not arise in man as involuntarily and as much from within as the cry of a tortured or delighted animal, but is something given, communicated, and everywhere acquired.]

* These facts of solitary Individuals prove nothing for or against the possible growth of Language ou[t] of the Living Mind. Suppose from 12 to 20 male and femal[e] Infants to be reared *humanly* with human comfo[rt] and Kindness by a dumb Nurse in some Elysian Isle of the Pacific. Would or would not they gradually organize the exclamations of Joy, surprize, fear &c in⟨to⟩ articulate sounds? I incline to think, that this would be the result.[1]   S. T. C.

5   p 329, pencil

Die 3 Füsse des Pferds Kalzi—Trimurti der Inder—Tao der Chinesen, = Dreieins,—Har, Jafhnar und Tredie der Edda, so wie die die Erde schaffenden Drei: Odin, Vile und Ve, oder Odin, Thor und Freya, und der dreiköpfige Swandewit, dessen Bild zu Arcona auf Rügen verehrt war; Artugon, Schugotengon und Tangara der Tartaren (nach Oberst Grant); die Münze am Flusse Kemptschik gefunden (nach Parson und Strahlenberg); das Götzenbild Tangatanga (Eins in Drei) in Cuquisako, nach Acosta's Gesch. von Westindien; Sonne als Apomti (Vatersonne) Churunti (Sohn Sonne) Intiaquacqui (Brudersonne) verehrt; auch Cuquilla, Gott der Luft in drei Bildern; die Trias des Amelias nach Proclus; des Orpheus βουλη, φως, ζωη u.f. in Stolbergs Kirchengeschichte I. v. 440 u.f.

3[2] Jones's statement is not about elephants, but about modesty. His essay "On the Loris, or Slowpaced Lemur" *Works* (6 vols 1799) i 544–8 describes a pet lemur that was inclined to have nocturnal fits: "a *Pandit*, who saw my *Lemur* by day light, remarked that he was *Lajjàlu* or *modest* (a word which the *Hindus* apply to all *Sensitive Plants*), yet he only seemed bashful, while in fact he was dim sighted and drowsy" (547).

4[1] A fundamental postulate in C's lifelong exploration of the origin and nature of language is the idea that properly speaking, language is an attribute of "the Human Species alone" (BLUMENBACH 2). His *Logic*, which has much to say on the subject, asserts that "language originates in reflection" and that words are to be regarded "as living growths, offlets, and organs of the human soul": *Logic* (*CC*) 234, 126.

[The three feet of the horse Kalzi—Trimurti of the Indians—Tao of the Chinese, = Triune,—Har, Jafhnar and Tredie of the Edda, like the Three Creators of the Earth: Odin, Vile and Ve, or Odin, Thor and Freya, and the three-headed Swandewit, whose image was venerated at Arcona in Rügen; Artugon, Schugotengon and Tangara of the Tartars (according to Colonel Grant); the coin found near the river Kemptschik (according to Parson and Strahlenberg); the idol Tangatanga (one in three) in Cuquisako, according to Acosta's *Geschichte von Westindien*; the sun venerated as Apomti (father sun) Churunti (son sun) Intiaquacqui (brother sun); also Cuquilla, god of the air in three images; the triad of Amelias according to Proclus; the Will, Light, Life of Orpheus and so on in Stolberg's *Kirchengeschichte* I. v. 440 ff.]

I fear, that too much significance is assigned to these Triads.

6   p 347, pencil | § 36

Allerdings könnte dann die Geschichte der vulkanischen Erscheinungen, so wie der Erdbeben, im Kleinen uns noch eben jene Kräfte kennen lehren, welche zu der Hervorbringung der grossen Fluth, und der sie begleitenden Katastrophe in Bewegung gesetzt worden; jene Erscheinungen lehren uns einen Quell der unterirdischen Wärme kennen, welcher unter gewissen Umständen schon allein im Stande gewesen, dem Pole . . . ein mildes Clima zu gewähren . . . . Nicht minder wird aus jenen Erscheinungen mit Recht auf das Daseyn grosser unterirdischer Wassermengen geschlossen, welche nur den 286ten Theil der Erdmasse auszumachen brauchen, um weit grösser als die ganze obere Wassermasse und hinreichend zu seyn, die ganze Oberfläche des Planeten bis zur Spitze der höchsten Gebirge zu bedecken. Es hat überdies schon die frühere Physik auf die Wirkung von Gasarten und vulkanisch entwickelten Dämpfen aufmerksam gemacht, welche in die unteren Wasserbehältnisse hineintretend, den flüssigen Inhalt derselben für einige Zeit auf die Oberfläche herausdrängen konnten. Wohl könnte dann bei der grossen Katastrophe die vereinigte Kraft des Feuers und des Wassers thätig gewesen, und vielleicht seit derselben durch irgen eine tiefergreifende Ursache jene Wärmeleitung unterbrochen seyn . . . . Wenigstens könnte es, nach v. Humboldts oben erwähnten Wahrnehmungen über das geognostische Vorkommen der vulkanischen Gebilde auf der westlichen Halbkugel der Erde scheinen: dass seit der grossen Veränderung, die jetzige vulkanische Gewalt des Feuers nur ein sehr schwacher, kleiner Rest von jener sey, welche das gebährende und zerstörende Element der Tiefe vormals auf und unter der Erdrinde ausgeübt.

[The history of volcanic phenomena and of earthquakes could certainly teach us, on a small scale, about precisely those forces that were unleashed to bring about the great flood and its accompanying catastrophe. Those phenomena inform us about a source of subterranean heat which by itself could, under certain conditions, bring a mild climate to the pole . . . . Furthermore, one can rightly deduce from these phenomena the existence of large quantities of subterranean water, which need only make up the 286th part of the mass of the earth in order to be much larger than the whole surface mass of water and sufficient to cover the whole face of the planet up to the tip of the highest mountains. Besides, earlier physics has already drawn attention to the action of gases and volcanically developed fumes, which, penetrating into the lower water depositories, can at times force their fluid content to the surface. It may well be that during the great catastrophe the combined forces of fire and water were active, and perhaps since then, owing to some more far-reaching cause, the transmission of heat was interrupted . . . . However, in light of Humboldt's above-mentioned observations regarding the geological occurrence of volcanic formations in the Western hemisphere, it is possible that since the great change, the present volcanic power of fire is only a very much weaker and smaller remnant of that power which once functioned as the parturient and destructive element of the depths both above and below the earth's crust.]

When a Boy, I used to fancy that in the ante-diluvian Ages when men ~~were~~ had Millennial longevity, the Earth-rind on which they lived, might have been like a Pewter warming-plate—viz. with ⟨a⟩ boiling subterraneous Ocean under it. But it seems odd that Schubart should not have hit on the enormous Evaporation that must have followed the Deluge—& which of itself would have sufficed to erect the two Girdles of Ice at given distance from the Equator—

7   p 455, pencil | § 49

Das Leben, sagt *Cuvier*, gleichet dem Wirbel eines Stromes, der mehr oder minder reissend, mehr oder minder zusammengesetzt, nach derselben Richtung hinströmt, indem er immer Theilchen derselben Art in sich aufnimmt und wieder ausstösst, *so dass die Form der lebendigen Körper beständiger ist, als die Materie aus der sie bestehen.*

Den Satz: Leiblichkeit ist das Ende der Werke Gottes, hat Oettinger in seinem Wörterbuch, (unter dem Art. Leib u.f.) trefflich beleuchtet.

[Life, Cuvier says, resembles the eddying of a river that with more or less violence, more or less composure, always flows in the same direction, continually taking up or thrusting out parts of the same kind, *so that the form of living bodies is more constant than the matter of which they consist.*

The proposition "corporeity is the end of God's works", has been excellently illustrated by Oettinger in his dictionary (in the article on "Body" and following).]

Oracular!—But whether it be as deep as it is dark, is not so clear. The mystery lies in the Indistinction (Chaos, Hades)[1] and the Multeity of

7[1] C's concept of chaos or "Hades" or the state of original darkness and indistinction is developed more fully in an important note of Aug 1818, *CN* iii 4418 f 13; cf BÖHME **146** n 1, IRVING *Sermons* **12** and n 4.

Wills or Spirits, one neither[a] with God nor with each other, nor with themselves. Assume this, and that they are being and to be redeemed from this state of darkness; and the Corporeity is easily explained.[2]   S. T. C.

8   pp 626–9, pencil, cropped | § 56

Schon die Geschichte der Wärme lehret uns, dass, vermöge einer beständigen Entgegensetzung der wirksamen Naturkräfte, stettig, so viel auf der einen Seite gebunden und fest wird,* so viel auf der andren flüssig und frei werde, und dem beständigen Gebundenwerden des Flüssigen, im Innern der Pflanze, stehet ein Freiwerden des gebundenen Elements ausser derselben (z.B. als Sauerstoffgas) entgegen, während im Thiere das Freiwerden nach innen, einem beständigen Binden- und Festmachen nach aussen . . . entgegengesetzt ist.

[Even the history of heat teaches us that, thanks to a constant opposition of dynamic natural forces, there is a perpetual balance between what becomes fixed and solid* and what becomes fluid and free, and that the constant binding of fluids inside a plant is opposed by the release of the fixed element (e.g. oxygen gas) outside it, whereas in an animal the inward release [of the fixed element] is set off by a constant outward binding and solidifying.]

* I fear, that there is more of fancy than of fact in this neat antithesis. The Plant under certain states & circumstances exhales pure Oxygen, at other times Oxygen + Carbon as Carbonic acid Gas[1]—the respiring animal the latter only with all or the larger portion of the Hydrogen inhaled i.e. *supposing* either one or the other to be *corpuscularly* absorbed. Now all this seems to me Mystery out [of] place. A Philosopher knows, that the A1[1] is Mystery; and on this ground he proceeds to precipitate the myster[y] from each particular portion—*not* by plunging specific products into universals, but by evolving the former from the latter. Ex. gr.—He [w]ill ⟨not⟩ explain Electricity & Warmth into [? *mimic*] Light—before he has secured an insight into Light itself. Least of all, will he confound what it is his special function to distinguish & *determinate*—ex. gr. Warmth and Electricity.—For the philosophic Naturalist is a minister of the *Logos*— i.e. of the *distinctive* Intelligence, *by* whom ar[e] all things, even as all things and the Log[os] itself are *from* the Father./[2]

7[a] C originally wrote "neither one" and marked the words for transposition

7[2] Here C conforms to his own definition of "body" (and hence of "corporeity") as meaning not matter filling space, but "the visible Organismus of living Creatures": IRVING *Sermons* 29 (and see n 12).

8[1] I.e. carbon dioxide.
8[2] Cf John 1.3: "All things were made by him; and without him was not any thing made that was made."

9 pp 641–3, pencil, cropped | § 61

In den *Zoophyten*, als den äussersten Enden des eigentlichen, selbst-
ständigeren Thierreiches, erscheint *die Pflanze* von der übermächtig
gewordnen thierischen Natur verschlungen,* in diese aufgenommen . . .
dennoch aber, mitten in der umfangenden, noch deutlich vorhanden.

[In *zoophytes*—on the utmost fringe of the true, independent animal kingdom—*the
plant* appears engulfed in the overpowering animal nature,* taken up in it . . . and yet,
though encompassed, still clearly present.]

* DEAR Schubart! but what, *what*, WHAT, I say, do these visualities,
these pictures of both by altitudes, *mean*? the verschlungen und die umfangenden[1] &c &c The true Problem is: so to state the inferiority of the
Vegetable antecedence & Creation as to preserve & imply its counterpo-
sition to the Animals—i.e. so to place V. = Veg., I. Insect; and A =
anim[al] that they may be at once

10 pp 702–3, pencil | § 66

Es giebt im vollkommneren Thiere ausser dem Knochen viele Aus-
sonderungen von feinerer Natur, und das auf einer niederern Stufe der
Lebensthätigkeit Ausgeschiedene und Sterbende, wird das Lebens-
element einer höheren Stufe: die Lymphe zum Blute, das Blut zum
Nervenaether.

Denn hierin eben liegt die Wichtigkeit und Bedeutung jenes beständigen Sterbens und Ausgeschiedenwerdens, dass aus dem Austretenden ein
lebensfähiges Element, ja der Anlass zu einem neuen, höheren Leben selber wird. . . . Und wie das Volk der Bienen, Tausende von Einzelnen
zusammengenommen ein gemeinsames Kunstwerk hinstellen; so gehet
von dem unzählbaren Gesammtheer der Lebendigen, unsichtbar, oder im
gröberen Abbild sichtbar, ein gemeinsames Vermittelndes aus, welches
die Lebensstrahlen von oben in sich empfängt und auffasset . . . diese
wiederum austheilend nach allen Richtungen: gleich der verwittlenden

9[1] The "engulfed and the encompassed": in textus.

Atmosphäre, durch welche das Herabblicken der Sonne zur Erde, für diese erst zum erhellenden und wärmenden Lichtstrahl wird.

[In the more developed animals there are, aside from bones, secretions of a finer nature; and what is discharged and moribund at a lower level of vital activity becomes the element of life at a higher stage: lymph becomes blood, blood becomes nerve-ether.

The importance and significance of this perpetual dying-off and discharge lie precisely in the fact that from the outflow an element capable of life arises, indeed the start of a new and higher kind of life. . . . And just as a colony of bees—thousands of individuals—together produces a common work of art, so a common intermediary, which receives and comprehends the rays of life from above, emanates invisibly or, in a cruder form, visibly from the innumerable host of living creatures . . . and these rays in turn spread out in all directions: just as it is only through the mediation of the atmosphere that the sun's looking down upon the earth ever becomes a bright, warming beam for it.]

Schubart, throughout, cheats himself with fanciful Progressions, and double, triple, quadruple Refineries, ~~and~~ Distillations, and Filtrations *per ascensum.*[1] His nerve-ether—is there any sound reason for supposing it different in kind from the Galvanic?[2] Yes or no, it can be but an exciting force, and the mystery is in the *Subject* = in [? senses] & nerves, so marvellously excited: Not the Horsewhip but the man, it makes skip & yell.

As from thousands of Bees = one Bee there is secreted the one Honeycomb: *so* from the thousand sorts of Animals = one animal (ideale Animal collectivum)[3] there is secreted invisible—what? what? why, a common mediating somewhat, that takes into itself Life-rays, like an atmosphere!!! was ever such a [. . .]*[a]* such an abortive [? as—so!—]

11   p 704, pencil

Gewiss ist aber, dass im Thierreich öfters das, was von einer höheren Lebenskraft ergriffen zum harmlos Wirksamen wird, auf einer niederen Stufe, wo es noch ein bloss Sterbendes, Ausgestossenes ist, als gewalt-

---

10*[a]* Here there is a gap in ms where a word has been omitted, or possibly erased

10[1] "Upward".

10[2] C's scepticism about the materialist assumptions involved in the idea of a "nerve-ether" (he refers to it scornfully in *BL* ch 6—*CC*—I 106 as "Hartley's hypothetical vibrations in his hypothetical oscillating ether of the nerves"; and cf MESMER 6 n 1) seems to have given way gradually to a revised, comprehensive concept of "ether" as a name for one of the primary "essences", manifest in different forms

under different circumstances: see KANT *VS* COPY B 2, OKEN *Lehrbuch der Naturgeschichte* 5. In *TL* and related scientific speculation, C considers magnetism, galvanism (or sometimes electricity), and chemical combining power as increasingly sophisticated manifestations of the same active principle in nature: see e.g. *SW & F* (*CC*) 507–8, 532–3 and nn.

10[3] "Ideal composite animal".

sam nach aussen wirkende Kraft, ja selbst als zerstörendes Gift erscheint, und auf diese Weise wird eben jene Kraft, die anderwärts von dem Nerven auf andre Organe ausströmend, bewegend und lebenerregend wirkt, auf einer niederern Stufe als elektrisch schlagende erscheinen, ja wir werden anderwärts sehen, dass jene Wechselwirkung des thierischen Lebens, welche in der Schlange noch das Gift bewirket, auf einer höheren Lebenstufe—im Vogel—zur Ausbildung und Bewegung der Organe der Stimme und des Gesanges wiedergeboren und umbewandelt wird.

[But in the animal kingdom it is certain that what has a harmless effect under the control of a higher vital force often appears as a violent outward force—even as destructive poison—at a lower level where it is merely moribund, discharged matter. And in this way that very force which elsewhere produces through the nerves a radiating, animating, and vitalising effect upon the other organs works like an electric shock at a lower level. Indeed we shall see elsewhere that the same interaction of animal life which produces the poison in snakes is reborn and transformed at a higher level of life—in birds—in the formation and exercise of vocal organs and song.]

Indeed! O for the proof!

12   pp 748–9, pencil | § 70

So ist namentlich ein sehr grosser Theil des Reiches der Insekten darauf angewiesen, dass er der Vermehrung des andern in seinen Geschlechtern und Arten Einhalt thue, und Millionen von Insekten haben keine andre Bestimmung, als dass sie andre Millionen von Insekten vernichten und auffressen, und die Verminderung, welche jene Thierklasse aus ihrer eignen Mitte erfährt, ist ungemein viel bedeutender als jede sonstige, die ihr von andern Seiten her, durch Vögel, Amphibien und andre Thierklassen kommt. . . . Wenn irgendwo in der Natur, so ist es hier im sinnig webenden und zusammenwirkenden Reiche der Insekten, wo der fragende Verstand das nahe Wehen eines durch Alle wirkenden und lebenden höheren Geistes bemerken kann.

[In particular, a very large part of the insect realm lives by checking the increase of others of its own species and kinds, and millions of insects have no other purpose than to annihilate and devour other millions of insects. The reduction which this class of animals undergoes by its own doing is far more significant than the reduction to which it is subjected in other ways by birds, amphibia, and other classes of animals. . . . If anywhere in nature, it is in the remarkably intertwined and cooperative realm of the insects that the inquiring mind can discern the stir of an all-pervasive and living higher spirit.]

Now I on the contrary see no where the godless Self-will in all its forms, to have, to hold, to get another for a Self by the destruction of the other; so manifestly declared—as likewise in no class the great compulsion of

evil workings into good effects by the eternal Word—than in this Insect
Realm.[1]   S. T. C.

But throughout Schubart confounds the Law, which determines the
total Result, with the ground and incipient principle of the instrumental
Agency.

13   pp 755–7, pencil | § 71

* Eben bei solchen zusammengesetzteren Wirkungen des Instinktes
drängt sich uns ein andrer Vergleich auf, dessen wir hier im Vorbeigehen
erwähnen wollen. Wenn die mütterliche Mauerbiene, in ihr eigenes
Innres schauend, wohl bemerket, von welchem Geschlecht das Ei seyn
werde . . . und schon jetzt die Einrichtung zu einer grösseren Zelle trifft,
wann das Ei, welches sie gebähren soll, ein weibliches, zu einer
kleineren, wann es ein männliches ist . . . wenn überhaupt der Instinkt,
sowohl in der Sorge für die künftige Brut, als auch für die Selbererhalt-
ung . . . prophetisch in die Ferne siehet: so erinnert dies an ein ähnliches
Vermögen, welches wir bei den Hellsehenden bemerken. Auch diese sind
eines magischen Hineinsehens in das Innere des eigenen oder fremden
Leibes fähig; wissen und schauen was fern von ihnen jedoch in einiger
Beziehung auf sie geschieht . . .

[* These more complicated workings of the instinct suggest a further comparison,
which we should mention in passing. When the mother bee, looking inside itself and
discovering what sex its egg will be . . . proceeds immediately to build a bigger cell
when the egg to which it will give birth is female, and a smaller cell when it is male
. . . when instinct in general, in caring both for the future brood and for self-preserva-
tion, looks prophetically into the distance—then one is reminded by all of this of a
similar power, which can be observed in clairvoyants. They too are capable of seeing
magically inside their own body or the body of a stranger; they know and perceive
what is far from them and yet affects them in a certain respect . . .]

* I can not find in this second series of facts any such essential difference from the former as to require a solution of a different kind. If indeed
the Clair-voyance of the Magnetic Patient were a known, universally admitted fact; if the recorded Cases were not liable to sundry, not groundless objections—then indeed an Analogy might be suspected, and Light
might be thrown from the magnetic to the instinct powers. But it only increases the perplexity, to explain the obscure by the vague and uncertain.[1]

12[1] C's most extensive reflections on
the insect realm appear in *TL* (*SW & F*—
CC—541–5); cf Goldfuss **10** and n 1, *TT*
(*CC*) I 111–12 and nn. But all these passages are celebratory or, at worst, neutral in
judgment.

13[1] In 1817 C was converted from a conventional scepticism to a position of cautious support for the claims of animal magnetism (mesmerism). He did a great deal of

4. Unser Baquet.

Nach diesen vorläufigen Bemerkungen, durch welche, als auf geschichtliche Thatsachen sich stützend, ich mich von der bisher angenommenen mesmerschen Theorie der Wirkung des Baquets völlig frei gemacht, und einen allgemeineren Standpunct der Betrachtung zu erlangen versucht habe, komme ich nun zu der speciellen Angabe der Construction meines Baquets, wie es mir in den nachfolgenden Krankheitsgeschichten gedient hat, womit ich unsern Lesern einen doppelten Gefallen zu erzeigen glaube, indem ich sie zugleich mit der in Mesmers Schriften sehr complicirt und selbst undeutlich angegebenen Einrichtung desselben bekannt mache.

Was die Dimensionen und Form desselben betrifft, so bemerke ich hier für manche meiner Leser, daß erstere (so viel mir jetzt zu schließen erlaubt, da alle genaueren Angaben noch fehlen) nur durch die beabsichtigte Intensität der Wirkung bestimmt wird, letztere mir aber ganz gleichgültig scheint.

Mein Baquet besteht aus einem viereckigen Kasten (S. die Zeichnung a) in Form eines kleinen Altars mit einem etwas breiteren Fußgestell von 2 Fuß 8 Zoll (rheinisch) Höhe, und von 1 Fuß 5 Zoll Breite, aus starkem Eichen- oder Buchenholz zusammengefügt, und nach Belieben angestrichen oder polirt, und mit einem 1½ Zoll breiten aus einem Stücke bestehenden hölzernen Deckel (b), versehen, der vermittelst einer ½zölligen Leiste auf den Kasten gepaßt, und wenn der Kasten gefüllt ist, durch

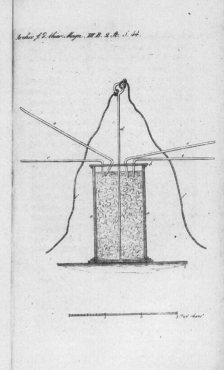

Archiv f. d. thier. Magn. III B. 2 St. S. 44.

5. Dietrich Georg Kieser "Unser Baquet" *Archiv für den thierischen Magnetismus* III (1818) ii 44–5. See SCHUBERT *Allgemeine Naturgeschichte* **14**

14 p 759, pencil

Er [der Magnetiseur] kann auch überdies jene Kräfte, welche den magnetischen Schlaf und alle seine begleitenden Erscheinungen hervorrufen, auch auf ein ganz lebloses Ding, z.B. eine Flasche, eine Baguette u.f. übertragen, und die an der Baguette Sitzenden empfangen dasselbe vermittlende, belebende Einwirken, welches ihnen sonst durch die unmittelbare Berührung des Magnetiseurs wird.

[Moreover, he [the magnetist (or mesmerist)] can transfer the powers that produce the magnetic sleep and its accompanying symptoms to a completely lifeless object, for example to a bottle or a baguette, and those seated at the baguette receive by means of it the same animating influence as is otherwise obtained through direct contact with the magnetist.]

I had understood that Keiser himself had found the same effects on his patient from a Baguette not magnetized, and merely in the outward Shape resembling the former.[1] Such experiments must be tried & repeated, *fairly* tried, before we are permitted to assume the power of the Baguette as a *fact*.

15 pp 766–7, pencil

* Durch Verwirrung des Instinkts legt die Aasfliege ihre Eier in die wie Aas riechende *Stapelia*; die Stubenfliege die ihrigen zuweilen statt in Mist, in Schnupftabak, wenn sie im Herbst eine offene Schnupftabakdose im Zimmer stehen findet.

[* By a bewilderment of its instinct, the carrion-fly lays its eggs in the *Stapelia*, which smells like carrion; in autumn the common fly sometimes lays its eggs in snuff instead of dung if it finds an open snuffbox in the room.]

* I would not say, bewilderment, but limitation, and inadequate Sub-

---

reading in the field and took a special interest in attested cases of "inside-seers" or "clairvoyants". For a comprehensive account of C's engagement with the subject see *TT* (*CC*) I 96n–7n; relevant marginalia include Böhme **26** and n 3, Jahrbücher *passim*, Jung, Kluge, Loewe, Mesmer, Richter *Museum*, Southey *Wesley passim*.

14[1] C perpetuates an error of Schubert's here. The mesmerist sometimes used a *baguette*, i.e. a wand or baton, but more typically a *baquet*, i.e. a tub, supposedly full of mesmeric fluid, with rods coming out of the top to which several seated patients could be attached at a time. Schubert has mistaken the one for the other, giving the name *baguette* to the tub. C recalls, however, an article by Dietrich Georg Kieser in *Archiv für den thierischen Magnetismus* III (1818) ii 1–180, which includes the case history of a patient cured of epilepsy by means of an *unmagnetised* baquet. See Plate 5. C read this journal and refers to it elsewhere, e.g. Kluge **7**, **28**. C's spelling of Kieser's name, as of others, was erratic.

tlety—which perceives the likeness without the difference probably because the instinctive judgement is in this instance determined by a single Sense.—Einfachkeit = *Simplicity* of Instinct and of Comparison, solves these accidents best.[1] It is a melody, not a harmony of recognitions. The dog can associate.[2]

16   p 906, pencil | § 73

Die Gliederung des Insektenleibes ist eine Wirkung jenes (magnetischen) Gegensatzes, der am organischen Leibe als oben und unten, als vorn und hinten, oder als jener zwischen Haupt und Gliedern erkannt wird. Dieser ist allerdings der ursprüngliche und erste, welcher dem Chaos der noch tropfenartig unentschiedenen, niederen Formen entsteiget.

[The articulation of the insect's body is the result of the (magnetic) opposition that is manifested in an organic body as upper and lower part, as front and back, or as the opposition between head and limbs. This is indeed the original and first opposition, which rises out of the chaos of the inferior forms that are still droplike and indeterminate.]

With the best possible dispositions I am unable to discover the appropriateness of this metaphor or hypothesis of the magnetic or N ⚹ S. Polarity,[1] as explanatory of the distinction into Head and Trunk—whether I think of the Magnet, or of the inner strivings of the Spirit.

17   p 997, pencil, cropped | § 79

Im sogenannten thierischen Magnetismus . . . wird durch die Manipulation des Magnetiseurs die waltende Kraft des oberen Systems: des Gehirns und seiner Sinnen auch auf die andren und unteren Systeme des Leibes übergetragen; diese werden zu einem Sehen, zu einem Hören, zu einem Fernbemerken fähig, wobei kein Auge, kein Ohr und kein Sinnesorgan des Hauptes nöthig ist: die unteren Systeme des Leibes werden ihrerseits dem oberen . . . gleichbedeutend und gleichkräftig gemacht. Der Zustand der Ruhe und des Schlafes deutet es an, dass das Untere gegen das Obere indifferent, für seine bewegende Einwirkung unerregbar geworden.

15[1] C invariably identified the insect realm with the vital power of irritability, and with instinct (or "instinctivity" as he calls it in **19** below), as the texts cited in **12** n 1 demonstrate.

15[2] C's favourite example of the higher mental powers found in the animal kingdom is the form of understanding exhibited by the dog at a crossroads, when it eliminates three paths by using its sense of smell, then chooses the fourth by a process of deduction: *Friend* (*CC*) I 160–1. In *AR* (*CC*) 248–50, he gives the dog as his example of the "dawning of a *moral* nature".

16[1] North "as opposed to" South.

[In so-called animal magnetism . . . the governing force of the higher system—that of the brain and its senses—is transferred to the other, lower systems of the body by the magnetist's manipulations; these lower systems become capable of sight, hearing, and remote perception without needing eyes, ears, or the senses located in the head. For their part, the lower systems of the body become equal to the higher ones . . . in power and significance. The state of rest and sleep shows that the lower systems have become indifferent to the higher ones and unresponsive to their influence.]

To an English Reader who knows the only not universal opinion of professional men and men of science in his own country, it is very amusing—this easy coo[l] matter-of-course 2 + 2 = 4 Reference to the FACTS (i.e. for English Naturalists the pupil-dilating, grinenkindling Narrations) of the Animal Magnetists.[1] It is as if a Physiologist had proved the probability of the flying Lizard (by the analogous *fact* of Witches riding thro' the [? Air] in the [? night].

18   p 997, pencil, cropped | Continuing **17** textus

Wenn auf diese Weise der untre Leib zur Natur des höheren Systemes erhoben und veredelt worden ist, wird allerdings dieses des beständigen, mühevollen Geschäftes jene zu bewegen und an den Ausgängen der oberen Sinnen für sie und ihre Bedürfnisse zu wachen und zu überhoben . . . um seinerseits in eine neue, empfangende und aufnehmende Wechselwirkung mit dem allgemeinen und höheren Gegensatz und Grund alles einzelnen Lebens zu treten; eine Wechselwirkung, aus deren fruchtbarem Momente die neue, höhere Stufe des Selbstbewusstseyns und Empfindens geboren wird.

[If the lower body is thus raised to the nature of the higher system and ennobled, the higher system too is released from the constant and burdensome task of setting the lower one in motion and of watching and caring for it and its needs at the outlets of the higher senses . . . so that the higher system in turn enters into a new, receptive, and assimilative interaction with the universal and higher antithesis and ground of all individual life—an interaction that in its productive moment gives birth to the new and higher stage of self-consciousness and sensation.]

A most [? pernicious] Naturalism[.] But the facts are the first principles i[n] Schubart's System. Out of these noth[ing] else could come.

S. T . [C.]

19   pp 1040–3, pencil | § 81

Allerdings mag eine von unten nach oben, etwa vom Infusionsthier oder Polypen bis hinan zum Menschen aufwärts steigende Stufenleiter der

17[1]   For C's position on animal magnetism see **13** and n 1 above.

Entwicklung, eben so schwer in der uns umgebenden Sichtbarkeit nachzuweisen seyn, als etwa die Quadratur des Zirkels. Es ist der kühne, immer ein oft verkanntes Höheres begehrende und erstrebende Menschengeist, welcher . . . die Gestalt seines *nur vorwärts* strebenden Traumes und Wunsches in die Natur überträgt.

Wollte man dennoch eine solche Stufenleiter . . . auf äusserliche Aehnlichkeiten und scheinbare Uebergänge begründen; so würde sich am leichtesten eine aus den Strahlenthieren zu den Mollusken . . . und von hier zu den Fischen und Reptilien und so weiter zu den Säugthieren gehende, wenigstens scheinbar aufzeigen lassen. Die Ordnungen der Gliederthiere vorscheinen hierbei als eine Episode, als ein eben so wie das drei und drei und das sechsgliedrige System der Krystalle für sich bestehendes Ganzes . . .

[In our visible world, it may indeed be as difficult to demonstrate an ascending scale of development, from low animal forms upward, from the infusoria or the polyp up to man, as to square the circle. It is the dauntless human spirit, always desiring and striving for something higher—though this latter often remains unrecognised—which . . . transfers to nature the form of its own dreams and wishes: *always* striving *onwards*.

If, however, one wanted to establish such a scale . . . based on external similarities and apparent transitions, it would be easiest and least specious to show it by proceeding from the radiates to the molluscs . . . and thence to fishes and reptiles, and beyond to mammals. The orders of articulata appear in this scheme as an episode, as a whole existing for itself just like the three-and-three and the six-membered system of the crystals.]

If the ascent modified by collateral expansion, the first being the *Air*, the second the *Variation*,[1] can be exhibited in *any* scheme of Classification, it must be one which takes its first principles in the three Forms of Organic Life, Productivity, Irritabil- or Instinctivity, and Sensivity—In such a scheme the Insects would form no episode but represent the paramouncy of Life$_{(2}$[a] = Instinctivity/ the Productivity energetic the more or less subordinate, as Life$_{(3}$ = Sensivity latent or mere⟨ly⟩ instrumental.[2] The Fish are the true transitional Creatures, in whom the Nervous *System* is *being* made but not or very dimly anordinated[3] so as scarcely, in most instances at least, to be called sub- co- or super-ordinated. In the Birds

19[a] The raised figures of the ms have been converted to subscripts, to avoid confusion with editorial matter

19[1] As in music: cf the musical analogy of melody and harmony in **15**.

19[2] One of the earliest and certainly the fullest exposition of the evolution and interrelationship of "the three Forms of Organic Life"—usually given the names productivity, irritability, and sensibility— appears in *TL*, composed in 1816: *SW & F* (*CC*) 534–51. Cf *C&S* (*CC*) 179–82, HEINROTH **14** and n 3, JAHRBÜCHER **15** and n 1. HEINROTH **38** and n 2 provides precedents for "Life$_{(2}$" and "Life$_{(3}$".

19[3] I.e. put together: not in *OED*.

Sensivity energetic but subordinate to the mammalia varying from co- to super-ordination—In Man it being the material Basis of a higher Principle, and both in *its* right and in its own establishes its undisputed Primacy.—

20   p 1041, pencil, cropped

Vergleichen wir die Amphibien mit den höheren Thierformen der Säugthiere und Vögel, so erinnern uns einige Geschlechter jener Klasse, namentlich die der Füsse und Flossen beraubten, wurmartig kriechenden Schlangen, in ihren giftigen, zerstörenden Eigenschaften an jene Misgestalten, welche auch im Reiche des Geistigen, das in seinem Laufe gehemmte und gehinderte Streben und Sehnen anzunehmen pflegt. Denn es entzündet sich die vorhin ruhig in ihrem Strombette gebliebene Neigung, ihres Gegenstandes beraubt, oder in seinem Besitzen gehindert, zur giftigen Eifersucht oder zum zerstörende Neide, ein, der natürlichen Mittel sich zu äussern beraubter Unmuth zur giftigen Heimtücke.

[When we compare the amphibia with the higher forms of animal life in mammals and birds, the poisonous, destructive characteristics of some species of that class—the snakes which, deprived of feet and fins, crawl like worms—remind us of the monstrous forms that also arise in the spiritual realm when strivings and yearnings are curbed and obstructed in their course. Deprived of its object or prevented from possessing it, the inclination which until then had quietly remained within certain bounds now flames up into poisonous jealousy or destructive envy; deprived of its natural means of manifestation, the ill-humour turns to poisonous malice.]

If *all* Amphibia were Snake[s] and if *all* Snakes had poison-fangs *then* indeed.

21   p 1041, pencil, cropped

News from the Moon. "The Celebra[ted] Jac. Behmen has made h[is] escape from our Luna[tic] Hospital. If any ⟨Soul⟩ &c/ [. . .] reward.["][1]

21[1] This note, repeated with variations below (**24**), is not obviously prompted by any passage in Schubert, unless **20** textus and what follows led C to imagine Böhme's soul inhabiting Schubert's body. It puns conventionally on the connection between the moon (Latin *luna*) and lunacy (periodic madness attributed to or associated with the phases of the moon), and is perhaps making use of the satiric tradition of using the moon as a fantasy location to stand for one's own society, as in Cyrano de Bergerac's *Histoire comique des états et empires de la lune* (pub 1656) or William Blake's *An Island in the Moon* (composed c 1784). Böhme was widely regarded by C's contemporaries as a lunatic, but C defended and praised him, saying, for example, in a note of 1810 (*CN* III 3975), "Aye, poor B! there came more Light and ~~reliable~~ precious Light thro' the cranny of thy Madness than ever passed thro' all the doors & windows of these Psilosophists' sober Sense, & acute penetration".

22   p 1043, pencil

* Der grössere Theil der Amphibien ist stumpfsinnig, träge . . .

[* The greater part of the amphibia are dull-witted and sluggish . . .]

* What then is the probable Origin of the Choice of the Serpent as the Emblem or Symbol of Understanding, Invention, Subtlety?—Its motion?—Not impossible.[1]

23   p 1043, pencil, cropped

Die Verdauung geschieht sehr langsam, und was dieser, so wie der Kraft der meist nur zum Beissen eingerichteten, nicht käuenden Zähne abgeht; das ersetzt bei einigen Arten ein die Verwesung und leichenhafte Auflösung der ergriffenen Thierkörper beförderndes Ferment: das *Gift*.

[Digestion takes place very slowly; and where this process together with the force of the teeth (usually reserved for biting and not for masticating) fails to function, it is replaced in some species by a ferment that promotes putrefaction and carrion-like decomposition of the ingested animal body: *poison*.]

* But in how small a proportion? The final cau[se] being gen[eral] the provi[?sion/dence] ought to [be] so. Where[as] few if an[y] Lizards—(the Gecko) & only the 7th of Snake[s] are poisoners.[1]

24   p 1296, pencil, cropped | End of index

News from the Moon
    The celebrated Jacob Behmen has made his escape from the Lunatic Hospital in [. . .]shire. Ten Moon-[? notes/dollars] reward to any Soul, that shall secure & [. . .] him. N.B. [. . . . .][a1]

24[a] Two lines illegible from rubbing and cropping

22[1] C—and others, e.g. SCHELLING *Philosophische Schriften* **49** textus—noted the emergence and persistence of this image of the serpent in a number of mythologies, though especially in the Judaeo-Christian account of the Fall, in *AR* (*CC*) 258*; in *C&S* (*CC*) 24*, he refers to the serpent as "the most mobile of creatures".
23[1] Whether it was the source of his information or not, Blumenbach's *Handbuch der Naturgeschichte* (6th ed Göttingen 1799) 235, 237n confirms these statements (though Blumenbach was mistaken about the gecko). This is the ed C himself refers to in *CL* I 590 (the footnote in *CL* is in error), but the page numbers are the same for editions of 1802 and 1817. C once thought of translating this work: *CN* I 1738n, *CL* I 590.
24[1] See **21** n 1 above.

25 p⁺1

Next to that, to which there is no Near, the γυιλτ¹ and the avenging Dæmon of my Life, I must place the neglect of Mathematics under the strongest motives, and the most favorable helps and opportunities for acquiring them. Not a week passes in which I do not regret this [? er] Oversight of my Youth with a sort of remorse that turns it to a Sin.²—This day I read the account of Faraday's Microphone³—& instantly recognized a fond and earnest dream-project of my own, of 30 years' standing—with sundry other imaginations respecting what might be effected in the only embryo Science of Acoustics.⁴ The Walls of Jericho were to fall before my Wartrumpets.⁵ But where were the *Hands*, where the Tools, of my Reason? I had not the *Organ* of all Sciences that respects Space and Quantity. My Dreams were akin to Reason: but I could not awake out of my prophetic Sleep, to effectuate their objectivization—for I was ignorant of the Mathematics!—   S. T. C.

25¹ "Guilt" (not a Greek word but Greek letters): C alludes covertly to his addiction to opium.

25² A repeated theme: see also BÖHME **66** and n 4.

25³ The reference is to a contribution by Charles Wheatstone (1802–75) to the issue of the Royal Institution's *Quarterly Journal of Science, Literature, and Art*—as it was then called—for Jul–Oct 1827, which seems to have been published about the end of Sept 1827, since it advertises lectures by Brande and Faraday that were to begin Oct 9. (C would have associated the article with Faraday because of Faraday's deep involvement with the Institution and its journal.) The article, entitled "Experiments on Audition" (pp 67–72), describes the invention of "an instrument, which, from its rendering audible the weakest sounds, may

with propriety be named a Microphone" (69). The instrument consists of flat metal disks to cover the ears, joined by metal rods; it looks like a modern headset rather than like the modern microphone, which according to the *OED*—which records this instance of the early use of the word—was not invented until 1878.

25⁴ Cf a note of Jul 1810 (*CN* III 3959): "Jericho/Cathedral Organ—Pipe—What a new Power may not Acoustics give!—perhaps, greater than that of steam & gunpowder!"

25⁵ An allusion to Joshua 6.20: "So the people shouted when the priests blew with the trumpets: and it came to pass, when the people heard the sound of the trumpet, and the people shouted with a great shout, that the wall fell down flat . . .".

Ansichten von der Nachtseite der Naturwissenschaft. Dresden 1808. 8°.

British Library C 43 b 13

In this copy, pp 159–60 are bound between pp 144 and 145 by transposition from sig K8 to J8, and pp 319–20 are bound between pp 304 and 305 by transposition from sig U8 to T8. This copy may have belonged to or at least have been shared with JHG, who studied *Naturphilosophie* with C: **13** is addressed to a "you", and many of the notes seem to have been written with a sympathetic reader in mind.

DATE. Probably 1818–21 and earlier. Dated in ms: 4 Aug 1818 (**1** 2nd PS) as a reperusal, 18 Feb 1819 (**46**), Mar 1821 (**49**). Cf the reference to "Schubert's Nachtseite, 156 p.—for the Lectures" in *CN* III 4457 (c 1 Nov 1818)—the passage cited not having been annotated. There is a passing reference to Schubert's geological speculations in *CN* IV 4551 f 74ᵛ (Jun 1819), and *CN* IV 4973 (? 1823) contains an interesting allusion to the title of this work.

COEDITOR. Raimonda Modiano.

1   p ii (title-page verso) and iii, pencil, rubbed

To select, out of a vast wilderness of mythology, traditions &c. the few facts that may be drawn or forced into coincidence with a pre-conceived Belief; to reason from these as if they were ~~all~~ the whole or at least the fair representatives of the Whole, without noticing the mass of incompatible nonsense unquestionably of the same date; and [? ~~after~~] then salient conclusions that might well have scared the modesty of the Rhodian Leaper[1]—these, with a fine sandy Mist over all, contain the sum and character der neuesten Logik der mythosophischen Teutschen Physiosophen![2]*

O ihr verbrüderte Geister, Tiefsinn und Gemeinsinn! ihr sind

*   Besser vielleicht, Oneirosophen.[3]

[1] Aesop tells the story of a braggart who boasted about the great leap he made at Rhodes; a sceptical listener challenged him to imagine himself at Rhodes and do it again (*Fables* # 33, in some eds # 51): cf *CN* III 4415 and n. In this context C is drawing attention to the huge gulf in the reasoning between the evidence and the conclusions.

[2] "Of the newest logic of the mytho-sophical German physiosophs"—"mythosophisch" and "Physiosoph" being apparently terms of C's own invention to describe the combination of mysticism and nature-study in certain post-Kantian thinkers.

[3] "Better perhaps, oneirosophs"—again a nonce-word based on *Philosoph* "philosopher" and meaning "one who seeks wisdom in dreams".

vorübergeflogen und statt Immanuel Kant haben wir Cant*ᵃ* †im Manuale!⁵

P.S. Disappointment, perhaps, has rendered me too severe; but really, even when in a milder and therefore wiser mood I seek for the Truths, of which the Dreams in this book are the dim Shadows, the Caricature is *so* gross! Thus, the instances of an apparent Arithmetical Instinct, as in the Amer[ican] Boy,⁶ might be quoted in favor of Schubart,⁷ &c. but—

Second Post-script, 4 August, 1818. I am glad, I have reperused this work. For tho' I have not found any reason to annul any of my former particular Objections, yet I find more merit to counterbalance them, than from the glaringness of the Faults I had been able to see and appreciate in the first perusal. S. T. C.

† *Punicé*, statt *bey den Handbüchern.*⁴

2   p 14, pencil

. . . und neben Keplers erhabenen Ansichten, hat sich noch zu derselben Zeit, in Frankreich, eine mechanische und handwerksmässige Ansicht einer todten Natur gebildet, in welcher sich wie Würmer, welche ein moderndes Gebein benagen nur noch die mechanischen Kräfte bewegen.

[. . . and alongside Kepler's lofty views there arose about the same time in France a mechanical and artisan-like view of a dead nature in which merely mechanical forces are in motion, like worms gnawing at a mouldering bone.]

a most unhappy Simile.

3   p 20, pencil

So, um wieder mit der erhabensten Naturwissenschaft zu beginnen, lassen es in der Astronomie das Gesetz der Schwere, und zum Theil selbst

1*ᵃ* This word is written in large widely-spaced letters though not in capitals

1⁴ "*Punningly*, in place of *in the textbooks*".

1⁵ "O you brother-spirits, Deepthinking and Commonsense! you have flown off above our heads and instead of Immanuel Kant we have cant in manual!"

1⁶ Zerah Colburn (1804–39) was exhibited in London in 1812 as a mathematical prodigy. A contemporary report describes him as "a child, *under eight years of age*, who, without any *previous* knowledge of the common rules of arithmetic, or even of the *use and power* of the Arabic numerals

. . . possesses (as if by intuition) the singular faculty of solving a great variety of arithmetical questions *by the mere operation of the mind*, and without the usual assistance of any visible symbol or contrivance": *Philosophical Magazine* XL (1812) 120.

1⁷ C generally spells the name this way (cf SHUBERT *Allgemeine Naturgeschichte* 1), and his spelling is repeated in the lettering on the spine of the vol. Schubert discusses instinct pp 27–8, but the "American Boy" is C's own example.

die Keplerischen Gesetze . . . noch unentschieden, ob das System der
Weltkörper ein nach nothwendigen Gesetz verbundenes Ganze bildet, wo
ein Glied das andre voraussetzt, oder ob blos die Anziehung der Materie,
die durch höheren Zufall einzeln entstandenen Massen, mechanisch
zusammenhält. . . . Nimmt man aber selbst nur das schöne von Bode
aufgestellte Verhältniss der Entfernungen, von welchem es neuerdings
erweisbar ist, dass selbst die Differenzen an die man sich bisher
gestossen, aus einem nothwendigen Gesetz entstehn; nimmt man einige
andre, neuerlich zur Sprache gekommene Verhältnisse der Grössen, Son-
nenfernen, Eccentricitäten und Tageslängen der einzelnen Planeten
hinzu; so zeigt sich auf einmal das Planetensystem als ein organisch verbundenes Ganze, wo jedes Einzelne in der innigsten und nothwendigsten
Beziehung auf die übrigen Glieder, und auf das Ganze steht.

[Thus—to return to the most sublime of the natural sciences—in astronomy the law
of gravitation and in part even Kepler's laws . . . leave it undecided whether the system of heavenly bodies, according to a necessary law, forms a connected whole in
which each member presupposes the other, or whether the attraction of matter, by mechanical means, merely holds together individual masses that have arisen by accident. . . . Even if one considers only the wonderful relation (established by Bode) of
distances, a relation in which even the previously encountered deviations can now be
proved to have arisen from a necessary law, and if one considers some other recently
discussed relations of the sizes, aphelia, eccentricities, and lengths of the day of individual planets—then the planetary system reveals itself at once to be an organically
connected whole in which each individual part is inherently and necessarily related to
the other parts and to the whole.]

This *tantalizes* Curiosity. The ? is: are these Astron. Relations the necessary results of the Law of Gravitation, or not. If they are, what point is
gained? It would, methinks, tend rather to confirm the mechanic Philosopher in his view of the Creation. The point is—to prove Grav. itself a
product of once anterior and still co-existing Laws.[1]

4   p 26

Wenn Religion, ein Erzeugniss der Furcht, aus rohem Anfange entstanden, wie kommt es denn, dass die Religionen, je älter sie sind, desto
reinere und erhabnere Ansichten enthalten? wie man z.B. von der Religion der Indier seit einiger Zeit zugestehen müssen, sie sey bisher fast
durchaus verkannt worden, und erst bey den vielseitigeren Ansichten der
letzten Jahrzehende eröffne sich das Innre ihres tiefen, weisen Sinnes.

[If religion, a product of fear, arose from crude beginnings, then how is it that the older
religions are, the purer and sublimer the views they hold? For some time this has had

----

3[1] For C's view "that Gravitation is not   see BÖHME **79**; cf KANT *Metaphysische*
merely Attraction but a synthetic Power"   *Anfangsgründe* **14** and n 5.

to be conceded, for example, of the religion of the Indians, though before that it had been almost completely misunderstood. Only to the less one-sided views of recent decades did the heart of its deep, wise meaning reveal itself.

Doubtful, to say the least.

5   p 26 | Continuing **4** textus

Wenn die Sprache durch Mittheilung der von verschiednen Individuen verschieden aufgefassten Naturlaute (thierischer Stimmen z.B.) entstanden, als die Menschen von der äussren Noth zur Gesellschaft gezwungen worden, und sich von den unvollkommensten Anfängen allmählig entwickelt hat, wie kommt es, dass, wie sich beweisen lässt, die vollkommnere Sprache—die metrische, früher gewesen als die Prosa? Denn nicht etwa Griechenland allein erwähnt des ersten Gebrauchs der ungebunden Rede als einer neuen Erfindung, sondern es ist die Mythologie, diese älteste historische Urkunde der alten Welt, von den Ufern des Ganges bis zu der Küste des Eismeers, in Versen enthalten, und auch die ältesten astronomischen Beobachtungen und Naturtheorien der asiatischen Völker, sind in Gedichten bewahrt.

[If language arose from the communication of natural sounds (e.g. animal voices), differently apprehended by different individuals, at the time when external necessity forced human beings to form societies, and if it has gradually developed from such imperfect beginnings, how is it that the more perfect language, the metrical one, was older than prose, as it can be proved to be? For it is not only in Greece that the first use of prose was regarded as a new invention; rather, mythology itself, the oldest historical document of the ancient world, from the banks of the Ganges to the shores of the Arctic, is contained in verse; and the oldest astronomical observations and theories of nature of the Asiatic peoples are also preserved in poems.]

And this easily explained by the antagonism of high Excitement.[1]

N.B. I do not object to the opinion itself, but to the arguments by which Schubart has supported it.

6   p 26 | Continuing **5** textus

Wenn Mangel und Dürftigkeit dem Menschen die Wissenschaften gelehrt, warum hat sich die alte Welt gerade mit solchen Untersuchungen am meisten und angelegentlichsten beschäftigt, welche, wie zum Theil meine heutige Vorlesung zeigen wird, mit der Nothdurft des Lebens in gar keinem unmittelbaren Zusammenhang stunden?

5[1] C's ideas about the relationship between metrical language and "the antagonism of high Excitement" are elucidated in *BL* ch 18 (*CC*) ɪɪ 64–5, 71–2, where he traces "the *origin* of metre" to "the balance in the mind effected by that spontaneous effort which strives to hold in check the workings of passion" (64).

[If want and need taught men the sciences, why did the ancient world concern itself mostly and most intensively with precisely those investigations which, as my present lecture will partly show, had no direct connection with the necessities of life?]

This now is sound and strong—O si sic omnia![1]

7   p 40, pencil

Das Kopernicanische System ist nach Bailly bey den Indiern ur- sprünglich einheimisch, obgleich ein Theil der Brahminen die Erde für unbeweglich hält.

[According to Bailly, the Copernican system originally belonged to native tradition in India, although some Brahmins think the earth immoveable.]

But how is this probable, on the supposition that the Copern: was the elder system? What could have persuaded a learned class to have exchanged so simple a scheme for the crude notion of the senses?

8   p 43, pencil

Gewisse Kenntnisse, welche nicht minder mehreren Völkern gemein- schaftlich waren, sind von Etlichen als ein Beweis angesehen, dass man sich in der ältesten Zeit der Telescope bediente. So die Annahme von Gebürgen im Monde und die Kenntniss der eigentlichen Beschaffenheit der Milchstrasse, die man als aus lauter kleinen Sternen zusammen- gesetzt betrachtete.

[Some items of knowledge, likewise common to several peoples, have been consid- ered by some as a proof that in ancient times the telescope was in use. Thus, for ex- ample, the assumption that there are mountains on the moon and the knowledge of the peculiar nature of the Milky Way, which was believed to consist of nothing but small stars.]

What more obvious conjectures can be imagined than either of these? Even Children would fall on it.

9   pp 60–1, pencil

Es wurde von der ganzen älteren Zeit der Rede ein unmittelbarer Ur- sprung aus dem höheren Einfluss gegeben, und fürwahr die Meynung; es habe die gesellschaftliche Noth dieselbe, aus einzeln aufgefassten und gestammelten Naturlauten erfunden, konnte nur in neuerer Zeit erdichtet werden. Hierin glich die Sprache der Vorwelt dem Dichten, dass, wie es

---

[6][1] "O if only [he had said it] all like this!" A common tag based on Juvenal   *Satires* 10.123–4, where the phrase is used of the ineffectiveness of Cicero's bad verse.

scheint, alle Rede metrisch, in Versen ausgesprochen war, und die älteste Sprache die wir kennen, die Sanscrit, ist nicht etwa die unvollkommenste, wie nach der gemeinen Ansicht zu vermuthen wäre, sondern gerade die vollkommenste, reichste, und doch einfältigste, die wohlklingendste und rythmischste. [Footnote:] M. s. Jones Werke.

[Throughout ancient times speech was thought to originate directly from the higher influence, and indeed the opinion that the needs of society invented it from single nat ural sounds which were apprehended and stammered out could only be fabricated in more recent times. The language of the primitive world resembled poetry in that all speech was apparently spoken metrically in verse; and the oldest language we know, Sanscrit, is not the most imperfect, as is commonly assumed, but is precisely the most perfect, the richest and yet the simplest, the most euphonious and rhythmical. [Footnote:] See Jones's *Works*.]

* As the Nose to Mephitis, so is the Ear placable to Cacophony: especially when either are co-existent with pleasurable associations. It does not therefore seem wonderful, that Sir W. Jones should have found the Sanscrit the most perfect, richest and yet simplest, and above all most suavi-sonorous and rhythmical; but that an Scholar who had not attached a⟨n⟩y glory to the knowlege of Sanscrit, but who had barely heard it read, should think it such,—this *does* seem strange![1] But what is of more importance, the variety of the Moods and Tenses, &c. in conjunction with the polysyllabic *honorificabilitudinitabatibus* length of the words is a proof of its Barbarism.[2] The Greek was happily fixed at the mid point, or rather suspended for many centuries, but at length even this completed the process of simplification, even as the Latin did.[3]　　　S. T. C.

10　p 62, pencil

Wie der Mond und die Sonne noch jetzt einen sichtbaren und merklichen Einfluss auf die Veränderungen des Luftkreisses haben, wie nach Einigen noch jetzt verschiedene Stellungen und wechselseitige Beziehungen der entfernteren Planeten auf einander durch verschiedene neue Bewegungen in der Atmosphäre ausgezeichnet sind; so müsse dieser Einfluss

9[1] The second scholar is Schubert. C is simply echoing the textus reference to the Orientalist Sir William Jones—with whose works, however, he had some direct acquaintance. A typical statement appears in "The Third Anniversary Discourse" *Works* (6 vols 1799) I 26: "The *Sanscrit* language [is] . . . more perfect than the *Greek*, more copious than the *Latin*, and more exquisitely refined than either".

9[2] C's example of an exceptionally long word is an old favourite cited by Dante and Shakespeare (*Love's Labour's Lost* v i 41) among others: see *OED* s.v. "honorificabilitudinity".

9[3] The elegant brevity of Greek was a commonplace: cf one of C's contributions to RS's 1812 *Omniana* (# 205, based on *CN* I 1613; in *SW & F—CC*—341–2), where he gives "an instance of compression and brevity in narration, unattainable in any language but the Greek".

früher, bey einem, wie sich beweisen liesse, viel empfänglicherem Zustand des Luftkreisses, viel merklicher gewesen seyn. Man fände noch jetzt in der Bildungsgeschichte des Planeten Spuren der heftigsten Bewegungen in der flüssigen Atmosphäre, einige Planeten unsres Systems, deren Beschaffenheit dem Urzustande des Unsrigen noch nahe scheint, gäben noch jetzt fast täglich ein Beyspiel von solchen heftigen Bewegungen in ihrer Atmosphäre . . .

[Just as the moon and the sun still exercise a visible and noticeable influence on atmospheric changes, and just as, according to some, the different positions and mutual relations of the more distant planets continue to be marked by various new movements in the atmosphere, so must this influence have been much more noticeable in earlier times, as could be demonstrated, because of a much more susceptible state of the atmosphere. In the history of the formation of the planet one can still find traces of the most violent movements in the fluid atmosphere, and some of the planets of our system that closely resemble the original condition of our own still offer almost daily examples of such violent movements in their atmosphere.]

Welche *einigen*? und *wie* lässt sich die frühere grössere Empfänglichkeit des Luftkreisses beweisen?[1] The heftige Bewegung of Stones from a vulcano proves no grössere Emp![2] but only the vehemence of the moving forces.

11   p 63, pencil

Wenn es wahrscheinlich sey, dass jene äussern Einflüsse, welche Veränderungen in der Atmosphäre zu bewirken pflegen, in jenem Zustand der Erde, welcher dem jetzigen des Jupiter näher stund, Bewegungen der Luft erzeugten, die an Geschwindigkeit dem Schalle wenigstens gleich kamen, so sey die Frage nicht ungereimt: ob nicht das, was jetzt als Sturm mit einem rohen und anorganischen Laut erscheint, damals als wirklicher Ton vernommen sey, ob nicht die alten Sagen von der Harmonie der Weltkörper, von den Tönen des Universums, wirklich einige Wahrheit enthielten? Hieraus würde dann begreiflich, warum Astronomie unter den Wissenschaften, Musik unter den Künsten das Aelteste sey. Den Rythmus der Bewegungen der Welten, wie er sich in der Atmosphäre abspiegelt, habe der Mensch zuerst nachgesprochen, und hierdurch eingeweiht in das harmonische Gesetz des Ganzen, habe sein Gemüth den Zusammenhang der Naturereignisse, und die Beziehung der einzel-

---

10[1] C challenges assertions made in textus: "[According to] which *ones*? and *how* can the greater susceptibility of atmospheric conditions in earlier times be demonstrated?"

10[2] The "violent movement" of stones from a volcano proves no "more susceptible state": German phrases from textus.

nen Dinge auf das Ganze erkannt. Auf diese Weise sey die älteste Naturweisheit und die Sprache selber, durch unmittelbare Offenbarung der
Natur an den Menschen entstanden.!!

[If it were probable that, at a time when the earth's condition was closer to the current
condition of Jupiter, those external influences which customarily bring about changes
in the atmosphere produced air movements whose velocity reached that of sound, then
it is not unreasonable to ask whether a storm which now has a rough and inorganic
sound was not heard as real tone then. Might not the old legends of the harmony of
the planets and the tones of the universe contain some truth? Thus it would be understandable why astronomy is the oldest of the sciences and music the oldest of the arts.
Man would at first have imitated the rhythm of the movements of the worlds as it is
reflected in the atmosphere, and having been initiated thus into the harmonic law of
the whole, his mind would have recognised the coherence of natural phenomena and
the relationship between individual things and the whole. Thus the oldest natural wisdom and language itself would have come into existence by man's receiving direct
revelation of the natural world.!!]

Are there traditions older than Pythagoras? In *him* was it not a most intelligible *metaphor*? Do we not even now speak of the Harmony of the
Universe?[1]

12   p 63, pencil | Continuing **11** textus

Es lassen sich freylich zur Bestätigung dieser Meynung keine direkten
Beweise führen.*

[To be sure, there are no direct proofs to substantiate this opinion.*]

* In this one point I perfectly agree.

13   p 63, pencil

[Schubert's footnote:] Das musicalische System der Chinesen fängt nach
Roussier eben da an, wo das der Griechen aufhöret.

[The musical system of the Chinese, according to Roussier, begins at the point where
the Greek system leaves off.]

!!! Did you ever happen to hear Chinese Music? Of all damnable Noises
it is the most ridiculously damnable!

11[1] C consistently represents the philosophy of universal harmony and the doctrine
of numbers of Pythagoras (6th century
BC)—the man "to whom the name [of
philosopher] seems due first of all", as he
says in a general lecture upon the Pythagorean system in *P Lects* Lect 2 (1949) 97—
as symbols, like Plato's Ideas, of the inner
life: cf *BL* ch 6 (*CC*) I 107; *Logic* (*CC*) 243
and n 1; *CN* III 4436; and, on the tetractys
specifically, BÖHME **6** and n 10.

14   p 67, pencil

Sey es aber, dass der Geist des ersten Menschen, wie der der Kinder,
empfänglicher und abhängiger von der Gewalt der Natur, ein Instrument
geworden, auf welchem der Geist derselben seine ewigen Harmonien
ausgesprochen, oder sey es dass die Natur noch in der Kraft der eben vollendeten Schöpfung, einer tieferen Einwirkung auf ihr letztes Werk fähig
war und dass so die Gewalt der noch jugendlichen Mutter über das neu-
gebohrne, noch zarte Kind grösser, der Zusammenhang zwischen beyden
inniger war: so musste entweder der selbstständiger und vollendeter
werdende Mensch sich jener Obergewalt mehr entziehen, oder der
Mensch wurde allmählig, während die Gewalt jenes höheren Einflusses
der (veraltenden) Natur abnahm, auf seine eigne Kraft zurückgewiesen,
und zur Selbstständigkeit genöthigt.

[Whether it be that the mind of primitive man, like that of children, being more receptive to and dependent on the power of nature, became an instrument on which the
mind of nature expressed its eternal harmonies; or that nature, still full of the power
of the just completed creation, was capable of exerting a greater influence on its last
work and that, as the control of a young mother over her new-born and still delicate
child is greater, so the connection between the two was more intimate: still, growing
more independent and perfect, man either had to free himself from that higher control,
or was gradually forced to rely on his own strength and to develop his independence
as the control of the higher influence of (ageing) nature diminished.]

I like this now. For it is poetry, tho' it is not philosophy: whereas the former is as dull as it is illogical.

15   p 68, pencil | **14** textus

It is to be regretted that Schubart has not thought fit to explain what he
means by Nature/ then perhaps we might guess what *die veraltende*
Natur[1] could be.

16   pp 85, 87, pencil

Die Mysterien bilden einen schönen Uebergang der alten Welt zur neuen.
In ihnen, oder mit ihnen zugleich, bewahrten die egyptischen Priester die
noch übriggebliebenen Trümmer der alten Naturweisheit. Diese wurden
nicht auf jene Weise mitgetheilt, wie wir zu unsrer Zeit die Wissenschaft
mittheilen, sie wurden allem Anschein nach im gewöhlichen Sinne weder
gelehrt noch gelernt; sondern ein Abbild der alten Naturoffenbarungen,
musste das Verstehen aus der Seele des Schülers selber, als Begeisterung
kommen.

15[1] "Ageing Nature": in **14** textus.

Aus diesem Grunde scheinen jene vielfältigen Vorbereitungen und Läuterungen gekommen, deren Strenge Viele von der Einweihung der egyptischen Priester zurückgeschreckt, ja nicht selten den Schülern das Leben geraubt hat.

[The mysteries represent a fine transition from the ancient to the modern world. In them, or through them as well, the Egyptian priests preserved the fragmentary remains of the ancient natural wisdom. These were not communicated in the same manner as we communicate knowledge now; they were apparently neither taught nor learned in any ordinary sense; as they were an image of the ancient nature revelations, the understanding of them had instead to come like enthusiasm from the disciple's soul.

Hence those varied preparations and purifications the severity of which frightened many away from initiation into Egyptian priesthood; it was such that it frequently entailed even the death of the disciples.]

That moral and religious Doctrines, true or false, may be conveyed to minds, already acquainted with the rudiments, during the excitement of enthusiastic feelings, and that the mind may thus be rendered more susceptible of the same, I can well believe;—but that the scientific truth of Astronomy or that the true system of Astronomy, should either excite, or the communication thereof be facilitated by, a state of turbulent sensation, I find it right difficult to comprehend. The Greeks are said to have borrowed the planetary names of the Metals from Egypt:[1] from which and from the Mosaic Account of the 5th days Work (Gen 1)[2] I conjecture, that the Moon was believed the largest of the celestial Bodies after the Sun.

17   pp 94–5, pencil, concluded in ink

[Schubert argues that the ancient oracles were the result of illness, and cites Justin, Tertullian, Athanasius, Cyprian, and Eusebius in support of his view. He points out that the phenomena recorded of oracles bear a strong resemblance to the phenomena associated with "somnambulism", the trance experienced by some patients under mesmerism.] Es beruhen bey diesen hierauf einige Heilarten, welche das Volk anzuwenden pflegt, bey jenen ist es bekannt genug, wie die Nähe einer Person von einem festen und entschiedenen Unglauben, die besten Somnambülen ... in einen solchen unangenehmen geistigen Zustand setzt, wie die Annähe-

[1] The earliest alchemical works known in C's day were by Alexandrian Greeks, and it was debated whether Egypt or Babylon was the birthplace of alchemy. For a list connecting various metals with the sun, moon, and planets see BOERHAAVE **3**, where, however, the compilers naturally give the modern Latin names of the planets, and where they attribute the symbols for them to the Persians.

[2] Fourth, rather than fifth. Gen 1.16, 19: "And God made two great lights; the greater light to rule the day, and the lesser light to rule the night: he made the stars also. . . . And the evening and the morning were the fourth day."

rung eines gesunden und starken Menschen, der mit ihnen in keinem Rapport steht, sie körperlich beängstigt.

[On these depend a number of cures that the common people employ, knowing well that the proximity of a person of firmly settled disbelief puts the best somnambulists . . . into an unpleasant frame of mind similar to the physical alarm they experience at the approach of a healthy, strong man with whom they have no rapport.]

Alas! Where is the *Proof* of all this? Have not Justin, Athanasius, &c asserted *as* boldly the most ridiculous Anilities? Ex. gratiâ: Does not Tertullian challenge for every true Christian the power of restoring the Dead to Life? the power of making any one of the Heathen Gods flee from his Temple, audibly yelling forth his proper Name in Hell, Beelzebub, Moloch, or Asmodeus?[1] And does Schubart believe *this*?[a]—And then the supposed Fact of the disentrancing influence of einem festen und entschiednen Unglauben[2] on the best Magnetic Somnambules but ill applies to the credulous Primit. Christians, who did fully believe the spiritual nature of these Catalepsies. Assuming the exorcism of Christians as a fact, and the Analogy to Anim. Magnet[m] as just, it must rather be attributed to a more intense Faith with an opposite Will.

18   p 96, pencil

So müssen wir, schon was die äussere Form anbetrifft, in den Orakeln die Wirkungen einer krankhaften menschlichen Natur erkennen. Wenigstens sind sie dieses in den spätern Zeiten durchaus gewesen, wenn auch noch einige Spuren eines edleren Ursprungs und einer früheren Verwandschaft mit der besseren Vorwelt in ihnen gefunden werden, wohin vielleicht die Anfangs unwillkührliche, aus der Natur der Sache selber hervorgehende metrische Form der Orakel, und die Einrichtung einiger der ältesten Orakel deutet, obgleich auch die metrische Form später blos willkührlich, als eine einmal hergebrachte Gewohnheit beybehalten scheint.

  Aber auch diese Aussprüche der Orakel selber bestätigen jene Ansicht, indem in ihnen die Zukunft trübe, und in einem zweydeutigen Lichte, gleich den Phantasien im Traume erscheint.

17[a] Note concluded in ink

17[1] This rhetorical question is based ultimately on Tertullian *Apologeticus* 23, which describes the early Christians' powers in exorcism; but C's immediate source was probably Edward Gibbon *The Decline and Fall of the Roman Empire* ch 15. This famous chapter considers five causes of the spread of Christianity, including the "miraculous powers of the primitive church".

Gibbon describes the public ceremony of exorcism, citing the Tertullian text in a footnote; more significantly, he goes on in the same paragraph to point out that about the end of the second century, according to Irenaeus, the resurrection of the dead was a fairly common event in Christian churches.

17[2] Of "a firmly settled disbelief": in textus.

[So we must conclude that the oracles, even as regards their external form, are the results of a diseased human nature. At least in later times they were so, even if they still bore traces of a nobler origin and an earlier relation to a better, former world. This one might see in the metrical form of oracles, which originally arose spontaneously out of the thing itself—also in the organisation of some of the oldest oracles. It appears, however, that even the metrical form later became something purely arbitrary and was retained out of mere custom.

But also the utterances of the oracles themselves substantiate this view, since in them the future appears vaguely and ambiguously, like fancies in a dream.]

In short, all, we *know*, of the Oracles, proves them impostures: but we may, if we like, *guess*, that in times, of which we know nothing, it might be otherwise.

19   p 107, pencil

In dieser Hinsicht sey vorzüglich der sonderbare Nebelfleck im Orion . . . bedeutend. . . . Seine unregelmässige Gestalt ist veränderlich, und oft in wenig Tagen sieht man ihn nach einigen Seiten sich ungeheuer ausdehnen, nach andern sich zusammenziehen. Die Stellen, innerhalb welchen solche plötzliche Veränderungen vorgehen, übertreffen öfters an Umfang unser ganzes Planetensystem bey weitem, und nicht selten sieht man solche ungeheure Strecken mit einem ungewöhnlichen Lichte aufflammen, andre dagegen verlöschen, wie dieses besonders die merkwürdigen Schröterschen Beobachtungen eines zur Seite gleichsam herauswachsenden Zweiges jener Nebelsubstanz im Jahr 1797, und der nach 6 Tagen wieder verschwindenden Lichtmasse, die . . . einen Durchmesser von 418 Millionen Meilen hatte, und noch mehr jene im Durchmesser wenigstens 29000 Millionen Meilen betragende Contraktion des ganzen Lichtnebels, nach einer Seite hin, im Jahr 1800, gezeigt haben.

[In this respect the strange nebula in Orion is especially . . . significant. . . . Its irregular shape is changeable, and often within a few days one can see it expanding enormously in some directions and contracting in others. The spaces encompassed by such sudden changes often greatly surpass in size our entire planetary system and it is not unusual to see enormous stretches flare up with exceptional brightness while others are extinguished. Such occurrences were demonstrated by Schröter's remarkable observations in the year 1797 when a branch was seen growing, as it were, out of the side of the nebula; its luminous mass, which disappeared again after 6 days, . . . had a diameter of 418 million miles; and even more, in the year 1800 the contraction of the entire luminous nebula on one side had a diameter of at least 29000 million miles.]

Contradicts the statement in a following § of the non-attractive Power of Comets, as luminous masses.[1] And the irregularity too! 29000 Millions

19[1]   C is probably thinking of the passage printed as **22** textus below.

of German miles, each = 5 of our miles! How could not[a] dilations & contractions take place without the least disturbance of gravitation?

20   p 109

Es ist jener Lichtnebel im Orion . . . nicht der einzige in seiner Art, und wir finden in einer der letzten Herschelschen Abhandlung über den Bau des Himmels, mehrere ähnliche Erscheinungen aufgeführt. Es gehören hieher unter andern jene milchweissen Nebelmassen, von runder Gestalt, welche in ihrer Mitte einen kleinen hellen Stern enthalten, indem sich eben aus der Sichtbarkeit des Sterns in ihrer Mitte beweisen lässet, dass sie nicht aus sehr entfernten, nicht mehr erkennbaren Sternen bestehen. Auch diese Weltsysteme, die noch fast ganz im . . . flüssigen Zustand scheinen, indem nur erst in der Mitte die Ausbildung zu Sonnen ihren Anfang genommen, übertreffen nach einer beyläufigen Schätzung im Durchmesser die Entfernung des Sirius von uns mehrere hundertmale.

[The Orion nebula is not the only one of its kind. Herschel, in one of his latest treatises on the structure of the sky, cites similar phenomena. To these belong, among others, those milk-white nebulous masses of round shape which have a small bright star in their centre; and the fact that this central star is visible proves that they do not consist of very distant, indistinguishable stars. These cosmic systems, which still appear to be in an almost entirely liquid state, and in the middle of which the formation of suns has only just begun, exceed in diameter (by a rough estimate) the distance of the planet Sirius from us by many hundreds of times.]

Why may not this central Star be a double or treble Star somewhat nearer than the Galaxy? or even the central Body by its immensely greater magnitude alone—distinguishable as a single Star?

21   pp 126–7

Es ist nämlich der Weltkörper, welchen wir bewohnen . . . aus flüssigem Zustand . . . entstanden. Die Wassermenge war . . . in den ersten Zeiten der Erdbildung verhältnissmässig ungemein häufig . . . . Die grössere Wassermenge, der flüssigere Zustand, bezeichnen uns mithin den Zustand der frühen Jugend der planetarischen Natur, während der mehr Wasserleere, trocknere Zustand, ein höheres Alter dieser Welten andeutet.

   In dem Zustand des hohen Alters finden wir demnach den Mond, von dem ich anderwärts erwähnt habe, dass er fast gänzlich ohne Wasser, fast ganz in dem letzten starren und trocknen Zustand sey . . .

19[a]   C's "not" seems to be superfluous

[The planet which we inhabit . . . originated from a fluid state. In the early period of the formation of the earth the quantity of water was in comparison exceedingly abundant. . . . Thus a greater quantity of water and a more fluid state indicate to us a youthful state of the planetary nature, whereas a drier condition and less water indicate a greater age of these planets.

Accordingly, we find the moon in a state of advanced age, since, as I mentioned elsewhere, it is almost entirely without water, almost wholly in the final condition of rigidity and dryness . . .]

a less improbable Inference would be, that our Moon was a detachment from the Earth, a sort of After-birth projected during or towards the close of the Orgasm of Solidification, either in the revulsionary Re-action of the expansile Force, or as the consequence and accompaniment of the intension of the contractive energy in the Lunar Mass itself?[1] Q.y Trapp? or Porphyry? Mem. The remarkable Cup or Saucer Forms of porphyritic masses super-posed on the Ridge of other Formations.[2]

22 p 137

So wurde die Bahn des merkwürdigen Kometen von 1770, von verschiedenen Astronomen, vorzüglich aber von den berühmten und geschickten Herrn Messier und Lexel sehr sorgfältig beobachtet und . . . berechnet. . . . Aus allen Beobachtungen erhielt man einstimmig das Resultat: dass dieser Komet 5½ Jahr zu seiner Umlaufszeit brauchte. Und doch ist dieser so genau und von so treflichen Astronomen berechnete Komet weder vorher noch nachher erschienen . . . . Zwar haben Einige dieses unverhoffte Aussenbleiben jenes Kometen aus der Störung oder der Anziehung, welche Jupiter . . . auf ihn ausgeübt habe, hergeleitet . . . . Auch gehörte dieser Komet immer nicht zu den kleinsten . . . und wir haben, so oft auch Kometen in der nächsten Nachbarschaft der uns näheren Weltkörper vorübergiengen, noch nie Spuren einer solchen auffallenden Störung oder Unterbrechung des gewöhnlichen Laufs, sowohl bey den Kometen als bey den Planeten in deren Nähe sie kamen, bemerkt. . . . doch werden schon die Besseren unter ihnen [Astronomen], die Moglichkeit eines solchen zerstörenden Zufalls nicht zugeben mögen.

21[1] See the note on this theory about the formation of the moon also in RALEGH **5** and n 1 above.

21[2] Schubert in this work (197) refers to porphyry as a relatively young sort of rock, and in *Allgemeine Naturgeschichte* 190–1 he outlines the main periods of geological evolution, identifying porphyry as relatively recent and trapp as even more so. The general issue in these discussions, carried on with growing intensity since the late seventeenth century, is the theory of the formation of the earth: C like most of his contemporaries believed that the earth began in a fluid state and took shape gradually by a process of drying out, perhaps cooling, and compacting.

[Thus, several astronomers, especially the celebrated and skilled Messier and Lexel, have carefully observed . . . and calculated the path of the remarkable comet of 1770 . . . . The unanimous result obtained from all observations was that this comet needed five years and a half to complete its revolution. And yet this very comet, whose path was so precisely calculated by such excellent astronomers, never appeared either previously or afterwards. . . . Some astronomers have attributed the comet's unexpected failure to return to the disturbance or attraction that Jupiter . . . exerted on it. . . . This comet is, however, by no means one of the smallest ones . . . and comets have often come into close proximity to planets near us; and yet no noticeable disturbance or disruption of their usual course was ever observed either in comets or in the planets they approached. . . . thus none of the best among them [astronomers] would admit the possibility of such a destructive coincidence.]

Later Astronomers, however, have established the fact, I understand, that the Attraction of Jupiter does exert an influence on the Comets, short'ning or prolonging their times of Return.[1]

23 p 140, pencil

"Es muss nämlich, wenn man die Umlaufszeit aus Beobachtungen unmittelbar bestimmen will, die elliptische Theorie zu Grunde gelegt werden. Wie unsicher aber diese Rechnungen seyn müssen, erkennt man schon dadurch, dass man ohne merklichen Fehler, den beobachteten Theil der Bahn als parabolisch betrachten, mithin die Umlaufszeit unendlich annehmen kann. . . ." So erscheint nach diesen Worten eines geistreichen Astronomen, selber die Bahn der Kometen als etwas Unbestimmtes, noch Formloses-Flüssiges . . .

["In order to determine the period of the orbit [of a comet] through direct observation it is necessary to suppose the elliptical theory. But it is clear how uncertain such calculations are, since without noticing one's error one can regard the observed part of the comet's path as parabolic and thus assume that its period is infinite. . . ." According to these words of a witty astronomer, even a comet's path appears as something indefinite, still shapeless—fluid . . .]

Is not this a deduction a diverso?[1] from the Observations of the Path to the Path itself?

22[1] Edmund Halley (1656–1742) had proposed that the orbits of comets were affected by the influence of Jupiter, among other things; his predictions based on this assumption were generally accepted as having been accurate with regard to the 1682 comet that reappeared in 1759. The matter continued to be debated, however, as textus indicates. What C refers to as the current state of the debate in England—in favour of Halley's hypothesis—is confirmed by Rees (s.v. "Comet") and by the 1817 *Encyclopaedia Britannica* (s.v. "Astronomy" § 326), the latter offering recent evidence that "comets may have their motion disturbed by the planets, especially by the two largest, Jupiter and Saturn".

23[1] "From a different thing".

24 p 143, pencil

Man hat ferner schon behauptet, dass die leuchtende Atmosphäre die den
Kern der Kometen . . . umgiebt, nichts anders als der Aether sey . . . .
Müsste nicht auch eine bestimmte Quantität Flüssigkeit, sey es dass das
Quantum von aussen (gleichsam durch das Gefäss, wie bey dem Blutum-
lauf) oder durch die herbeyführende Kraft bestimmt sey, wenn sie sich
zu einer Kugel geformt durch den ewigen Aether bewegte, auch auf
einem Theile ihrer Bahn, wo gleichsam wenig oder nichts von ihr con-
sumirt würde, von einer bestimmten Grösse erscheinen?

[Further, it has been asserted that the glowing atmosphere that surrounds the core of
the comet is nothing but ether. . . . Would it not also have to be true that when a certain quantity of fluid—whether the quantity be defined from without (by means of a
container, as in the circulation of the blood) or through the causal force—takes on
spherical form and moves through the eternal ether, this quantity would appear to have
a definite size in that part of its orbit where, as it were, little or nothing of it was con-
sumed?]

But here the Fluidum is made distinct from the Ether.

25 p 144, pencil

Könnte nicht selbst, man erlaube mir das Bild, die Grösse der Kometen
ohngefähr eben so mit der Bahn (von der wir nur den Ort des Kometens
und die Neigung meinen) im Verhältniss stehen, wie die Grösse der
Blutwelle die sich durch diese oder jene Region des Körpers bewegt,
davon abhängt, dass sich in dieser Region grössere oder kleinere Gefässe
befinden?

Selbst das Periodische der Wiederkehr der Kometen (der periodische
Umlauf) hienge damit zusammen, und vielleicht liesse sich diese selbst
noch auf eine andre Weise als aus der elliptischen oder parabolischen
Berechnung der Bahn finden, ja vielleicht dass selbst das was neulich ein
Arzt in einer erdichteten Witterungsprophezeihung über die periodische
Wiederkunft der Kometen, ohngefähr wie die der Nordlichter im Scherze
gesagt hat, im Ernste wahr wäre.

[Is it not possible that the size of the comets, if I may use this image, is proportionate
to their orbits (by which we mean only the position and inclination of the comet), just
as the size of the blood-current which flows through this or that part of the body depends on the larger or smaller size of the vessels?

Even the periodicity of the return of the comets (the periodic revolution) would be
connected with this, and perhaps it would be possible to measure the period by other
means than by way of elliptic or parabolic computation of the orbit; in fact, it may well
be that the doctor who recently composed a humorous weather forecast was near the

truth when he said that the periodic return of the comets resembled that of the northern lights.]

Alas! but this does not "hang together" with the preceding §: which seems to require a continuous action.[1] Perhaps if Pulsation were better understood, some analogy might be supported—at present, it seems obscurum per obscurius.[2] Yet I myself have often had wild notions, yea shapings of worlds, while gazing at the Waves and counting their intervals—or in hanging over a torrent stream as from Greta Bridge—[3]

26   p 146, pencil

Die Bahnen der Kometen sind im Verhältniss zu den Bahnen der Planeten eben so wenig bestimmt, als die Richtungen der nach allen Dimensionen auslaufenden, und an der Gränze des Körpers auf einmal (erst als Arterie dann als Vene) und ohne alle Vorbereitung in die gerade entgegengesetzte Richtung umkehrenden Blutgefässe . . . . Noch unausgebildete Weltkörper, oder vielmehr Weltenmasse, sind die Kometen allerdings, wie Einige behauptet haben, nur werden sie so für sich auch nie zur festen Existenz der übrigen Weltkörper gelangen. Neuen Lebensstoff *diesen* zuführend, von *jenen* den alten wieder zurücknehmend, treibt dieses seltsame Geschlecht sein dunkles Spiel mitten in dem ewigen Aether.

Merkwürdig ist noch das Verhältniss der Zahl der rückläufigen und vorwärtsgehenden, was ohngefähr ist wie das der Venen und Arterien nämlich sich gleich . . .

[The orbits of the comets, in relation to the orbits of planets, are just as indefinite as the course of blood-vessels, which run out in all directions to the end of the body where, suddenly (first as arteries, then as veins) and without any preparation, they reverse their course and go in exactly the opposite direction. . . . The comets, as some have held, are planets that remain unformed, or rather planetary masses, yet as such they will never attain the solid existence of the other planets. Giving new vital matter to *some* bodies and taking the old from *others*, this curious genus plays its mysterious part in the midst of the eternal ether.

It is remarkable that the relative proportion of those in progression and in retrogression, as with veins and arteries, remains the same . . .]

25[1] The "preceding §" is **24** textus. In "hang together", C adopts a literal translation of the verb *zusammenhangen*, used in textus and here translated as "be connected with".

25[2] I.e. to explain "what is obscure by reference to what is more obscure": C uses the phrase also in HARTLEY **6**.

25[3] The River Greta ran close by C's house in Keswick, a fact he mentions particularly in *CL* i 610, 614, 619. For some observations on "hanging over" the bridge by moonlight, see *CN* i 1616, 1624.

Stuff? What Stoff,[1] and how connected with *Comets* in particular? To assertions so vague it is impossible to say, Yes or No.—To the Pro- and Retro-grade Comets—the arterial blood *is* the venous—carbon, and the transit in the Heart.[2] But the retrograde Comet remains retrograde thro' its whole path. But perhaps I am confused by the double meaning of the term, retrograde. Would not planetary and anti-planetary motion be better than direct and retrograde? Tho' as they cut thro' the orbits of the Planets in all directions ⋈ as well ♃ , even this seems not general enough.

27 p 147, pencil

Die Knoten haben sich auch noch in einem Stück den elektrischen Meteoren ähnlich gezeigt, das ich hier nicht ganz übergehen darf, besonders da ein Beobachter wie Schröter neuerdings wieder darauf aufmerksam gemacht hat. Es haben nämlich nach dem übereinstimmenden Zeugniss mehrerer der besten Beobachter die Schweife mehrerer grosser Kometen eine eigenthümliche "fluctuirende und vibrirende" Bewegung gezeigt, als ob sie in solchen Momenten neue Strahlen schössen, so dass jetzt der Schweif sich verkürzte und zurückgezog, dann in einem Augenblick durch einen neuen Strahlenschuss wieder verlängerte und ausbreitete.

[The nodes are similar to the electric meteors in one respect which should not go unmentioned here, particularly as an observer like Schröter has recently called attention to this again. The majority of the best observers agree that the tails of several large comets have shown a peculiar "fluctuating and vibrating" movement; it is as if at such moments they were shooting out new rays, so that at one point the tail shortened and contracted, and then in an instant it lengthened and expanded again by shooting out new rays.]

But what has the electro-pulsatory motion in the Tails to do with their Nodes? It must be a press-error for Kometen.[1]

27A p 153, marked with a pencil line in the margin

Ausser diesem möge uns der Innhalt der heutigen Vorlesung ein nicht nach mechanischen Kräften sich hier und dahin untereinander bewegendes, sondern lebendig zusammenwirkendes Weltganze, und—in dem

26[1] *Lebensstoff*—literally "life-stuff"— in textus, tr "vital matter".

26[2] C's point appears to be that it is the *same blood* that circulates in veins and arteries, although the arterial blood carries oxygen, and the venous blood carbon dioxide.

27[1] *Knoten* ("nodes") is not an error: Schubert has been describing comets observed in 1790, some of which moved forward and some backward, some of which had their nodes on the northern and some on the southern side of the ecliptic.

Reich der Kometen, ein solches gemeinschaftliches, um Alle geschlung-
enes Band anerkennen lassen.

[With this exception, the content of today's lecture allows us to envision the cosmos
not as a set of movements connecting this to that according to mechanical forces, but
as a living, co-operative whole, and—in the realm of the comets—as a common, all-
encompassing bond.]

28   p 154, pencil

Bekanntlich war am Anfange der neuen Zeit jenes Vorurtheil fast allgemein herrschend, dass die Sonne und alle Weltkörper unsers Systems, ja
selbst die ungeheuer fernen Fixsterne, sich täglich, und in einer grösseren
Periode jährlich um unsre kleine Erde, die in der Mitte still stünde, bewegten. So weit hatte der schlimme Geist des Egoismus den Menschen
von der einfältigen, klaren Wahrheit, die ihm von Anfang an gar nicht unbekannt war, abgeführt.

[At the beginning of modern times, as is well known, the prejudice prevailed almost
everywhere that the sun and all the heavenly bodies in our system, including the re-
motest fixed stars, moved daily and, during a longer period, yearly round our small
earth, which stood motionless in the middle. Thus far had the evil spirit of self-love
carried man away from the clear, simple truth known to him from the very beginning.]

I cannot see that the Self-love of Men was much concerned in the slow
admission of the Copernican system—easily solved first by the contradiction of the Cop. System to the *words* of Scripture, and secondly, by
the excessive difference between the real and the apparent magnitudes of
the heavenly Bodies—so that even at this day a common mind thinks, you
are speaking of one thing while he means another. "1000 times big^a than
the whole world! what? you can't mean that star there, surely?"

29   p 162, pencil

So hat, kann man sagen, Kepler das Gesetz der Schwere nicht blos ge-
ahndet, sondern wörtlich und klar ausgesprochen . . . . Die Wahrheit des
Gesetzes . . . war ihm demohnerachtet so einleuchtend, dass ihm nach
seinem eignen Ausdruck dieser Streit des wahren Gesetzes gegen eine
früher gebildete Ansicht, wirklich *quälend* war, und dass er ihn deshalb
auf alle Weise auszuweichen gesucht. . . . Er hielt sich, indem er das, was
er mit tiefen und wahrhaften Schlüssen über das Gesetz der Schwere gefunden verwarf, nach seiner Ueberzeugung mehr an das, was ihm die
Natur unmittelbar zu lehren schien, und es würde wohl jeder ächte Natur-

---

28^a A slip for "bigger"

forscher, wo in einem ähnlichen Fall zwischen den auch noch so wohl zusammenhängenden Schlüssen des Verstandes, und dem unmittelbaren Zeugniss der Natur gewählt werden muss, auf dieselbe Weise handeln.

[So it can be said that Kepler did not merely surmise the law of gravity, but enunciated it literally and clearly . . . . For him the truth of this law . . . was nevertheless so compelling that, as he puts it, the conflict between this true law and a view he had formed earlier was really *agonising*, and he therefore tried to avoid the conflict in every way . . . . In repudiating what he had discovered by profound and truthful inferences concerning the law of gravity, he formed his convictions more on what nature seemed to teach him directly; and every genuine natural scientist faced with a similar choice between the conclusions inferred by the understanding, however coherent, and the immediate evidence given by nature would do likewise.]

How? But this whole §ph is very obscurely expressed

30   p 177, pencil, partially overtraced in pencil

Wenn die Materie, je näher sie ihrem Ursprung, jenem Zustand der reinen Lebensempfänglichkeit der sie bey ihrem Entstehen auszeichnet, stehet, einer um so vollkommneren und höheren Lebenswirkung fähig, wenn sie auf dieser frühern Stufe ihres Daseyns einer viel innigeren Gemeinschaft mit dem höheren Einfluss theilhaftig ist; so finden wir sie dagegen in jenem Zustand, worinnen wir den grössten Theil der uns umgebenden Natur erblicken, dem Anschein nach aller selbstständigen Thätigkeit nach aussen beraubt, und gleichsam gefühllos für alle höheren Einflüsse.

[The nearer matter is to its origin, to that state of sheer receptivity to life so characteristic of matter at the moment of its inception, the more perfect and the greater its influence on life; at this early stage of its existence matter participates in a closer communion with the higher influence. By contrast, where matter is found in that state in which we see most of surrounding nature, it is apparently deprived of all independent outward activity and, so to speak, apathetic to all higher influence.]

So unlike the elder German Philosophers! *They* (even to a fault) were anxious to employ no terms not previously defined and explained. Now here is *Matter*, *Fluid*, &c &c/ and no clue to the Writer's meaning—only a mess of Hylozoism[a1]—The cause of this, as if[b] almost every other, mistake of the Natur-philosophen is to be found in their Pantheism.[2] The

---

30[a] Overtracing ends here, and note is continued at top of page, with the direction "see above"
30[b] A slip for "of"

30[1] Hylozoism contends that matter is endowed with life: cf C's use of the term, and comments on his use, in Dubois **2** and n 2, Jacobi *Werke* **10** and n 3. In *CL* IV 874 (30 Sept 1818), he comments scathingly on Schelling's "Hylozoic Atheism".
30[2] The pantheistic tendency of *Naturphilosophie* is a recurrent theme: cf

nearer the origin, the more evident the God. Yet *why*, if all be at all times God? Now I believe, the near⟨er⟩ the Chaos, the farther from God.[3]

S. T. C.

31   p 178, pencil

Wenn man diesen Zustand der anorganischen Welt mit jenem ursprüng-lichen vollkommneren vergleicht, erscheint derselbe als ein tiefes Herab-sinken von einer höheren und früheren Stufe; und schon jene chemischen Gegensätze, wenn sie vorher flüssig, und mit den ersten Spuren einer höheren selbstständigen Thätigkeit, jetzt in der gegenseitigen Vermisch-ung sich zu einem festen Körper gestalten, verlieren alle ihre frühere Thätigkeit nach aussen.

[This state of the inorganic world, when compared with its originally more perfect state, appears as a deep descent from a higher and earlier stage; and if those chemical oppositions had earlier been a fluid, possessing the first traces of a higher independent activity, they now intermingle and form a solid body, losing all their previous outward activity.]

How strange must it not appear, if a work of God were to deteriorate from the first moment of its Construction! What should we say of a human Work that did so?

32   pp 178–9, pencil | **31** textus continued

Es ist, wie anderwärts gezeigt worden, jeder lebendigen Natur, so wie auf der einen Seite der höhere Einfluss, so auf der andern ein untergeordnetes Material, eine Basis nöthig, an welcher sie das innre Leben schaffend (nach dem Vorbild des höheren Einflusses) übt und vollendet. Zu dieser Basis verhalten sich jene schon untergeordneten Naturen wie höherer Einfluss; und wenn sich nun so die Natur bis ins Unendliche aus sich sel-ber entfaltet, und das Bild des höheren Einflusses sich immer mehr in endlichen Formen darstellt, trübt und "verfinstert" sich zuletzt die Klarheit des ursprünglichen Zustandes, in dem der Materie.

[As has been demonstrated elsewhere, all living nature—the higher influence on one hand as well as the subordinate material on the other—needs a basis on which to prac-tise and attain perfection in creating the inner life (after the model of the higher influ-ence). Both the subordinate natures and the higher influence relate to this basis; and

---

SCHELLING *System* **10** and n 2 above; also "pantheistic or rather atheistic Absolute" in OKEN *Lehrbuch der Naturphilosophie* **2**.

30[3] As C wrote in LACUNZA **2**, "the whole march of nature and history, from the

first impregnation of Chaos by the Spirit, converges toward this kingdom [of God and his Word] as the final cause of the world. Life begins in detachment from Nature, and ends in union with God."

since nature unfolds itself endlessly and the image of the higher influence is presented increasingly in finite forms, the clarity of nature's original state is finally dimmed and "obscured" in that of matter.]

The old Emanation Scheme in a new chemical Dress.[1] But after all this Senescence or Languescence of Nature in her Descent is a mere assertion.—The Poppy presents itself in a thousand Seeds, each of which evolves into an undegenerate Poppy. So the Oak and the Eagle: so the Tyger of India, the Whale of the frozen North.

33   p 180, pencil

Wenn uns auch die jetzige irdische Natur in einem grossen Theil ihres Umfanges nur einen starren und unwirksamen Zustand der Körper zeigt, so ist ihr doch dieser Zustand nicht immer eigenthümlich gewesen, und es finden sich von allen Seiten Spuren eines viel bildsameren, und an den Einflüssen des höheren Ganzen theilnehmenderen Zustandes: jenes der allgemeinen Auflösung und Flüssigkeit. . . . Es sieht der Mensch auf den Gipfeln der Gebirge, welche jetzt mehr als 13000 Fuss über der Meeresfläche erhöht sind, die Ueberreste von Thieren und Pflanzenartigen Wesen, welche den Grund des ehemaligen Meeres bewohnt haben.

[Even if the present terrestrial nature shows us to a great extent merely the fixed and inactive state of the body, this state was not always characteristic of it: one finds traces everywhere of a much more plastic state, one participating in the influences of the higher whole, a state of general dissolution and fluidity. . . . On top of mountains that are now 13000 feet above sea level one finds the remains of animals and plant-like beings which lived at what was once the bottom of the sea.]

!! And are these shells of Worms, Snails, and Zoophytes the proofs "eines viel bildsameren und an den Einflüssen des höheren ganzen theilnehmenden Zustandes"?[1]

34   p 188, pencil

So sieht das Auge in jenen Gebirgsmassen, in denen sich der Bildungstrieb der Erde zuerst ausgesprochen, den Boden und die zu Stein erstarrten Wogen eines ungeheuren Meeres. . . . Einst haben sie auch, lebendige Theile der Erde, mitten im dem fröhlichen Kreise der Wechselwirkung und des allgemeinen Lebens gestanden, als sie, noch nicht zu diesen einzelnen Massen erstarret, Theile der von dem Geist des allgemeinen Lebens bewegten Fluth waren.

32[1] On the "old Emanation Scheme" see SCHELLING *Einleitung* 13 and n 1.

33[1] From textus: "a much more plastic state, one participating in the influences of the higher whole".

[In those mountainous masses in which the formative instinct of the earth first expressed itself, one can see the bottom and petrified waves of an immense sea. . . . These masses, when they were part of the tide moved by the spirit of universal life and had not yet petrified into individual masses, were once living parts of the earth and stood in the midst of the happy circle of interaction and universal life.]

On what (but *poetic*) grounds can Schubart appropriate an intenser participation "of the Spirit of universal Life" to the Drops of a Surge or a Sea, than to the particles of a Stone or a Mountain? Both are moved and both statically:—[a] neither moves.

35   pp 200–1, pencil

Ueberhaupt muss, wie ich anderwärts gezeigt habe, der Uebergang aus dem Steinreich in das der Pflanzen und Thiere, in jeder Hinsicht in den Metallen gesucht werden.

[The transition from the realm of stones to that of plants and animals must, as I have shown elsewhere, always be sought in the metals.]

How does this square with the late chemical discovery of the metallic Bases of the Earths?[1] If for instance Lime and its Congeners are Metal + Oxigen, how are we to conceive the transition from the Inorganic to the Organic by the simple resilience of ~~the~~ each Component to its single and original State?[2] This rather seem[a] a retrograde movement than a means of progress. Suppose a moment in the history of the Earth, in which Potassium existed prior to its combination with Oxygen—i.e. prior to its appearance as Potash.—Wherein, I ask, ~~does~~ can the Potassium procured from Potash be supposed to differ in quality or tendency from the Potassium in the first case?[3]   N.B. I am far from asking this question in the

34[a] After the dash, an ampersand has been inserted in ink, apparently not by C
35[a] A slip for "seems"

35[1] C alludes to work by HD, notably "Electro-Chemical Researches, on the Decomposition of the Earths; with Observations on the Metals Obtained from alkaline Earths, and on the Amalgam Procured from Ammonia", a paper presented before the Royal Society 30 Jun 1808: *Phil Trans RS* xcviii pt 2 (1809) 333–70. HD observes that the "results of the experiments on potash and soda . . . afforded me the strongest hopes of being able to effect the decomposition both of the alkaline and common earths; and the phenomena obtained in the first imperfect trials made upon those bodies countenanced the ideas that had obtained from the earliest periods of chemistry, of their being metallic in their nature" (333).

35[2] HD published reports of his experiments in the decomposition of lime and barytes: *Phil Trans RS* xcviii pt 2 (1809).

35[3] See HD "On the Properties and Nature of the Basis of Potash" in a paper read 19 Nov 1807, "The Bakerian Lecture, on some new Phenomena of chemical Changes produced by Electricity" (*Phil Trans RS* xcviii pt 1—1809—44) and "Of Potassium" *Elements of Chemical Philosophy* (1812) 321–31.

belief that it is unanswerable. I intend it as an *objection*, which I wish to have solved, not as a confutation of Schubart's conjecture. S. T. C. At present, however, I prefer the scheme, according which[b] the reduction of the metals is a consequence rather than an antecedent of the transition.

36   p 205, pencil

Es wird nämlich auch schon in den kosmischen Momenten der anorganischen Natur, jenes momentane Leben des Einzelnen durch die Vermittlung eines höheren Ganzen erhalten.

Im Magnetismus sind es die beyden physicalischen Erdpole, oder die beyden erregbarsten Punkte des Planeten, durch deren Vermittlung der Magnet, dessen herrschender Pol sich stets nach dem nächsten von jenen Punkten hinwendet, den höheren Lebenseinfluss empfängt, und auch in der Elektricität ist es der Erdkörper, aus dessen mittelbarer oder unmittelbarer Gemeinschaft die Körper den Schimmer des ersten selbstständigen Lebens empfangen.

[That momentary individual life is already contained, through the mediation of a higher whole, in the cosmic moments of inorganic nature.

In magnetism it is through the mediation of the two physical poles of the earth, or the two most excitable points of the planet, that the magnet, whose dominant pole always turns towards the nearer of these points, receives the higher influence of life; and in electricity too it is through mediate or immediate communion with the earth that bodies receive a first glimmer of independent life.]

Alas! that the Author had but told us, what he means by *Life*![1] The Foci of Glasses; the concentric Circles of on a Pond, are beautiful WORDS for its phænomena, could we but first learn what *it* is. If I say, I *know* it—yet how can I then apply *that* "it" to a magnet?

37   p 228, pencil, rubbed

Es muss auch nach dem Südpol hin vor Zeiten das Land von üppiger Vegetation und einer reichen Thierwelt geschmückt gewesen seyn. Zwar hat man auf dem Feuerland und den angränzenden Gegenden nach Versteinerungen noch nicht nachsuchen können, da selbst in den langen Sommertagen dieses traurige Land, das die schaffende Natur zu verlassen anfängt, von öfteren Schnee erstarrt, man hat aber fast auf jeder Seereise in dieses Clima, die schwarzen und kahlen Klippen jener Wildniss von

---

35[b]   For "according to which"

36[1]   In *TL* (composed 1816), C surveys a number of unsatisfactory definitions of "life" and then offers his own (*SW & F—*   *CC*—I 510): "*the principle of individuation*, or the power which unites a given *all* into a *whole* that is presupposed by all its parts".

häufigen vulkanischen Feuer rauchen sehen, und das zerspaltene jähe Aussehen der Felsen spricht von einer langen Arbeit der Vulkane. Dieses Eyland scheint mithin an Brennmaterialen, und an Fülle der Vorräthe, die aus einer früheren Vegetation erhalten sind, Island nichts nachzugeben.

[In past times the land towards the South Pole must have been adorned with luxurious vegetation and abundant animal life. So far it has not been possible to examine the petrification on Tierra del Fuego and its neighbouring regions; for even in the long summer days this sad land, which the active [forces of] nature begin to forsake, is frequently snowbound. And yet on almost every voyage into this climate seafarers have noticed the abundant smoke of burning volcanoes rising from the black and bare cliffs of the wilderness, and the broken steep appearance of the rock attests to the long activity of volcanoes. This island seems to be equal to Iceland in the abundance of fuel and resources obtained from earlier vegetation.]

Does this follow? Is it proved, that all Vulcanoes are fuelled by Co[al]?

38   pp 232–3

Wir sehen in vorzüglich feuchten oder heissen Jahren gewisse Gegenden voller Kräuter, von denen in andern Jahren keine Spur da war.

[Especially in humid or hot years we find some certain regions full of vegetation of which there was not a trace in other years.]

This is a Longing Desire to make a Mystery out of a plain matter. Schubart does not dare to say downright, that the germs and seeds of these plants did not pre-exist in the Soil, either left there since the last Season favorable to their vegetating or wafted thither: for there are too many facts/ in proof of the contrary, some of the lowest Fungi alone presenting any difficulty. But he would forget this and have the Reader forget it: it is so pleasant to both parties to wander and wonder awhile in gleamy dreamy Twilight.

39   p 235, pencil

Das Leben zeigt sich so zuerst als kosmische Erscheinung, bey welcher sich das Einzelne selbstständig und unmittelbar von demselben Geist des Lebens ergriffen zeigt, welcher die ganze Natur bewegt. Das Einstimmen in die Harmonie der allgemeinen Wechselwirkung der Weltkräfte, ist das Leben.

[Life at first presents itself as a cosmic phenomenon in which the individual is independently and immediately animated by the same spirit of life that moves all of nature. Life means joining in with the harmony of the universal interaction of world forces.]

Surely not. For then all things would live—which may be true, but ⟨not⟩ in Schub's present sense of the word, Life. Microcosm, or a Part representative of the whole, would be a better definition; but far from adequate.[1] Individual Centrality of different Parts? A chrystal is centrality of like parts. The Polypus &c therefore lowest Life.

40   p 237, pencil

Es pflegen alle ausgepressten Pflanzensäfte, denen die Möglichkeit einer Gährung nicht ganz genommen ist, zu jener Zeit, wenn die Pflanzen von denen sie herkommen, blühen, eine neue Gährung zu erleiden, und viele können nur bis zu dieser Zeit aufbewahrt werden.

[All juices squeezed out of plants and not entirely deprived of the possibility of fermentation tend to undergo a new fermentation at the time when the plants from which they are extracted come into bloom, and many can be kept only until that time.]

Gospel? Or Apocrypha?

41   pp 384–5, pencil, referring to p 237 | **40** textus

~~P. 273~~ P. 237. §. 2.—This fact I have often met with in Books—I wish, I could meet with some individual verification of it. At the reblossoming of *the* Vine from whose Grapes a Cask of Wine had been expressed, the Wine will ferment anew if it have not passed beyond the last Fermentation. And this is asserted of all expressed Plant-juices.—

On mentioning this fact a young Lady assured me on her own repeated Experience that a spot or stain from Fruit on a Gown may be washed out while that sort of Fruit continues in season; but becomes indelible if delayed beyond that time.[1]

42   p 237, pencil

Eben in der Zeit, wenn die Blüthen, von denen sie sich zu nähren pflegen, sich eröffnen, sieht man auch die verschiedenen Arten der Insekten aus ihren Gräbern hervorgehen. Die schöne Sympathie der Nachtigall und der Rose, ist von den Persern in unzähligen Liedern besungen, wie in dem blühenden Hayn der kleine Sänger von der Liebe zur schönen Blume ergriffen, die ferne Kluft, welche die Natur zwischen der Blüthe und dem Thiere befestiget, beklagt.

39[1] See **36** n 1.   1818: *CN* III 4417.
41[1] C recorded this conversation 3 Aug

[One also sees various kinds of insects emerging from their graves just at the time when the blossoms on which they are accustomed to feeding open. The lovely sympathy of the nightingale and the rose was the subject of countless Persian songs in which the little singer in the blossoming grove, seized by love for the beautiful flower, laments the great chasm established by nature between flowers and animals.]

! Why with the *Rose* of all other Flowers[a] On my own account, answers the *Poet*. But the Naturalist—?

43   p 261, pencil

Ein scharfer Geruch sehr entfernter riechbarer Gegenstände, ist bey verschiedenen Insekten bemerkt worden, ohne dass die Organe desselben entdeckt wären. So zieht die Bienen der Geruch der blühenden Linden in einer bedeutenden Entfernung an, und jene ausländischen Insekten, die sich seitdem bey uns eingefunden haben, seitdem die Pflanzen, auf denen sie sich gewöhnlich aufhalten, bey uns ausgesäet wurden, könnte nur dieser Sinn aus jenen grossen Fernen hergeführt haben, wenn man ihre selbstständige Erzeugung aus den Pflanzen nicht zugeben will.

[It has been observed that various insects have an acute sense of smell for very distant odoriferous objects, although their olfactory organs themselves have not been discovered. Thus bees are attracted to the smell of flowering linden trees from a considerable distance, and those insects that have established themselves in our country ever since the plants on which they live began to be sown here could only have been brought from such distances by the sense of smell—for one could hardly suppose them to have been engendered independently out of the plants.]

Why may not the Eggs of the Insect have been imported in or with the seeds?

44   pp 268–9, pencil

Das Leben des ganzen Thierreichs scheint sich durch ein stetes Vorwärtsstreben nach dem des Menschen hinzudrängen, und nach diesem gleichsam zu sehnen.

[By continually striving onwards, the whole animal kingdom seems to strain towards human life, to long for it, as it were.]

To the *Animal*, Man, doubtless the *animal* World presses onward as in a dense Crowd, each part of which seems to move, and yet the whole is stationary—or rather compare it to the column of blue Smoke from a Cottage Chimney on a calm day. But to Man, as Man, to that which constitutes his *kind*, I find no Approximation. The Elephant and Ape seem as

---

42[a] Last word crowded in at edge of page

distant as the Ant and the Bee—.[1] Even as the Light the nearest the Focus is as warmthless as that which is the most remote. But man we will make in our own Image: and the Mighty One, the Covenanter, breathed into man a living soul[2]—In what sense Animals may be said TO BE, is a Problem, the solution of which will remain hopeless, as long as we can conceive no medium between the οντως ον and το οντως μη ον—[3]

45 p 271, pencil

Die bekannten Versuche einiger Chemiker, welche Pflanzensaamen in destillirtem Wasser und im verschlossenen, der Sonne ausgesetzten Gefässen keimen und aufwachsen liessen, lehrten: dass die so erhaltenen Pflanzen alle jene Erden und sonstigen Bestandtheile enthielten, welche in der Asche der freywachsenden gefunden werden. Das Wasser wäre mithin in diesen Versuchen durch die Vegetation in Stoffe von fester Natur übergegangen, von denen es vorhin keine Spur zeigte.

[The well-known experiments of certain chemists who let plant seeds sprout and grow in closed vessels of distilled water which were exposed to the sun have shown that plants produced in this way contained all the soils and component elements that were found in the ashes of plants that grew in the open. In these experiments, then, water was changed by means of vegetation into solid materials of which there had been no trace before.]

Ellis positively denies this, and Davy's experiment with the vetches appears to contradict it.[1]

44[1] Elsewhere C firmly rejects the idea of the evolution of humankind from primates—"the Ouran outang Hypothesis" (*CL* VI 723)—and insists that man is different in *kind* from other animals, see e.g. *SW & F* (*CC*) 1406, 1409; *AR* (*CC*) 348–50; *CN* IV 4984.

44[2] Gen 2.7: "And the Lord God formed man of the dust of the ground, and breathed into his nostrils the breath of life; and man became a living soul."

44[3] Between "the truly existing" and "the truly non-existing": traditional Platonic terms; cf *CL* II 1197 "the absolutely inanimate is called by the Platonists, τὰ μὴ ὄντα".

45[1] Chemists and botanists of the period were attempting to understand the processes involved in what later came to be called photosynthesis. C alludes here as elsewhere to Daniel Ellis *An Inquiry into the Changes Induced in Atmospheric Air, by the Germination of Seeds, the Vegetation of Plants, and the Respiration of Animals* (Edinburgh 1807), and possibly also to his *Farther Inquiries* (Edinburgh 1811)—the latter work one that frequently cites HD's earlier papers. It is not quite clear what part of Schubert's statement Ellis should be thought of as "positively" denying, but C may be referring to *Farther Inquiries* pp 197–8, where Ellis suggests that the alkali "which so much abounds in the ashes of the green parts of vegetables" was probably derived from the fluids absorbed by growing plants—i.e. that there *would* have been traces of it in the water. In a chart in *Elements of Agricultural Chemistry* (1813) 103, HD provides a chemical analysis of the ashes of several plants and shows that vetches "raised in distilled water" did *not* contain the same elements as vetches grown in soil.

46   p 284, pencil

Durch ein nicht minder verlohren gegangenes Geschlecht, jenes Riesen-
thier, das Cuvier Megatherium nennt, und das in seinem Bau von allen
jetzt vorhandenen Thiergattungen ungemein weit abweicht, sieht man . . .
ein Weiterschreiten der Reihe. Dieses Thiergeschlecht . . . bey der Grösse
seines Körpers, welche die natürliche Beschwerde noch vermehren
musste, ist es von der Natur auf einen engen Raum, auf das Thal oder den
Sumpf, in welchen es gebohren worden, beschränkt gewesen.

[One can see the progress of this series of animals in a no less extinct species, that
giant beast which Cuvier calls Megatherium and whose bodily frame differs widely
from all existing types of animals. This species . . . whose physical size can only have
multiplied its natural difficulties, was confined by nature within a small area, the val-
ley or morass in which it was born.]

If we may trust the American Travellers, this Beast the Skeleton of which
is preserved at Madrid, has been recently seen alive on the banks of the
Missouri.[1]   Feb. 18, 1819.

47   p 290, pencil

Dieses sinnreiche Thier [der Delphin], dessen beständige Liebe zu dem
Menschen und zur Musik, schon von den Alten gepriesen war, gesellt
sich wirklich in Meere immer zu den Schiffen, und das vom festen Lande
verbannte Geschlecht scheint sich . . . der Nähe des Menschen vor allen
andern Thieren zu freuen.

[This intelligent animal [the dolphin], whose constant love towards man and towards
music was already praised by the ancients, always joins the ships in the sea; and ex-

---

[46][1] In the early days of the discovery
and classification of fossil remains, C was
not alone in confusing the mammoth and
the megatherium. (For a note that treats
them as interchangeable examples, see
ANDERSON COPY B **16** and n 2.) American
travellers had indeed reported sightings.
From "the banks of the Mississippi" there is
a report of a living mammoth in the Feb
1819 issue of the *Philosophical Magazine*
LIII (1819) 156; and Thomas Ashe, whose
Travels in America (3 vols 1808) C had
read, had exhibited American specimens of
mammoth and other bones in Liverpool in
1806, publishing a catalogue that included
an account of such an animal (he does not
refer to the megatherium specifically) as
"still existing" somewhere to the west and
north of the Missouri: *Memoirs of Mammoth, and Various Other . . . Bones* (Liverpool 1806) 11. The megatherium, described
and named by Cuvier in 1797 on the basis
of an illustrated article about a fossil discovered near Buenos Aires and shipped to
Madrid in 1789, is almost exclusively associated with South America. In 1804, Cuvier
published an important, expanded account
of the animal in an article, "Sur le mégath-
erium: autre animal de la famille des pa-
resseux, mais de la taille du rhinocéros, dont
un squelette fossile presque complet est
conservé au cabinet royalle d'histoire naturelle de Madrid" *Annales du Muséum national d'histoire naturelle* v (1804) 376–87.
See Plate 6.

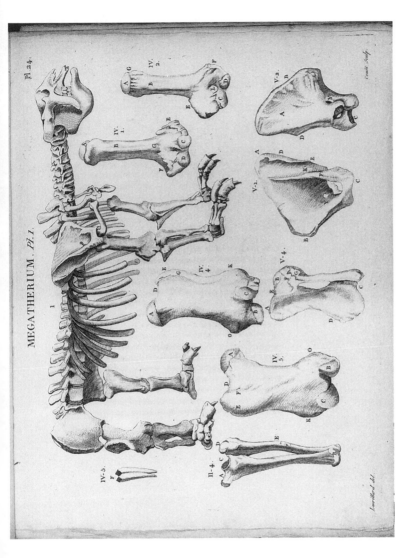

6. Georges Cuvier "Megatherium" plate 1, from *Annales du Muséum d'histoire naturelle* v (1804). See SCHUBERT *Ansichten* **46**

iled from the firm land, this species appears . . . to rejoice in the close presence of man above all other animals.]

Has not Schubart confounded the Dolphin with the Porpoise, which latter is the Dolphin of the Ancients? It is the former only that follows Ships; but I never saw or heard ⟨of⟩ any instance of philanthropy in the latter.[1]

48 p 291

Jener Uebergang der Elephantenartigen Thiere, durch das Flusspferd und die Lamatine in die Geschlechter der Cetaceen . . . lassen uns die Cetaceen als eine merkwürdigere Abtheilung der Säugethiere betrachten, als sie gewöhnlich scheinen. Vielleicht dass auch hier, wie in andern Thierklassen, die Natur, ehe sie ihr höchstes Werk beginnt, einer Wiedergeburt aus dem Element, aus welchem im Anfang Alles ward, bedarf.

[The transition of the elephant-like animals, from the hippopotamus and the manatee to the species of cetaceans . . . sets off the cetaceans as a more remarkable division of mammals than they usually appear to be. Perhaps in this case also, as with other classes of animals, nature, before beginning its highest work, needs a rebirth out of the element from which everything originated.]

I can not help doubting whether Schubart ever fairly asked himself, what he meant by these words—that perhaps Nature was obliged to go back to the Water, and make River-horse, Lamantines, Dolphins and Grampuses in Rivers and the Sea before she could make *men* on dry land!! and why? Ὕδωρ μεν πρωτον!![1]

49 p 296

Die grössten Thiere der zweyten Reihe sind der Eisbär und der grosse bengalische Tieger, während sich die körperliche Grösse in der ersten Reihe, nachdem schon früher die Geschlechter der Stiere und des Rosses,

47[1] C is right in observing that dolphins and porpoises are often confounded with one another, but in this case the confusion seems to be his rather than Schubert's. Naturalists of their day, e.g. Blumenbach *Handbuch der Naturgeschichte* (Göttingen 1799) 127, recognised three kinds of "dolphin"—*delphinus phocaena* "porpoise", *delphinus delphis* "dolphin", and *delphinus orca* "grampus". *Delphinus delphis*, the common dolphin of the Mediterranean and Atlantic, tends to travel in herds and to follow ships; it is also the one associated with legendary kindness towards man, as notably in the case of the lyric poet and musician Arion, rescued and carried away by a dolphin from the sailors who planned to rob him: Herodotus 1.23.

48[1] "Water [was] first". The allusion is to Thales, traditionally the founder of Greek philosophy, with his theory that water was the first material principle. The exact collocation of words is probably C's own. C outlines the philosophy of Thales in *P Lects* Lect 2 (1949) 95–6.

das Kameel und die Giraffen ... aufgetreten, noch bis zu dem Ele-
phanten, ja bis zu dem grössten bekannten Thier der Erde, (wenn wir den
fabelhaften Kraken ausnehmen) zum Wallfisch erhebt.

[The largest animals of the second series are the polar bear and the great Bengali tiger,
while physical size in the first series (after the earlier appearance of the bull and horse
species, the camel and the giraffe ...) reaches that of the elephant, and even that of
the largest known animal on earth (if we exclude the legendary Kraken), the whale.]

Relata refero:[1] March, 1821. Lieutenant Matthews while off the Cape of
G. H. on his return from the East Indies in Capt[n] Cochrane's Ship$ saw
& the whole Ship's Crew saw with him, a Kraken with a vengeance![2] So
he assured me on his word and honor: and authorized me to use his name,
and to make enquiries of Capt[n] Cochrane. The vessel was going six knots
an hour; & by his watch which he held in his hand the whole time they
were ten minutes and a half in passing the enormous Lubber from Head
to Tail, running close alongside it: and discharged a cannonade into it, at
the moment of parting. Matthews (who is now the Lithographer at the Admiralty)[3] saw the Blood spout up, & Kraken surlily sunk down!—

50   p 297, pencil

Ein viermal so kleines Raubthier bezwingt und tödtet öfters ein Pflanzen-
fressendes, das gegen ihm ein Riese scheint. Dagegen sind die von Vege-

49[1] "I report what has been said".

49[2] The kraken, a fabulous sea-monster
believed to be the largest living creature,
was said to be something like a jellyfish in
shape: it rose to the surface of the ocean,
producing the appearance of a cluster of
islands; put out tentacles to gather in food;
and when satisfied—or disturbed—sank
slowly out of sight. See Walter SCOTT
COPY C **3** n 1 for further references.

The Navy List for 1821 includes three
Captain Cochranes and three lieutenants
named Matthews or Mathews, but the only
record of a Matthews and a Cochrane working together dates from 1816–17, when
Henry Bathurst H. Matthews (commissioned 13 Jun 1815, d 1827) served under
Nathaniel Day Cochrane (commissioned
26 Mar 1806) aboard HMS *Orontes* in St
Helena. Since C mentions the East Indies
and the Cape of Good Hope, however, it
seems unlikely that it was on the St Helena
voyage that Matthews saw the kraken. The

Orontes had previously been stationed at
the Cape of Good Hope, and most probably
Matthews's story refers to a period ante-
dating his lieutenancy: cf John Marshall
Royal Naval Biography Supplement pt 1
(1827) 123.

49[3] The Navy Lists do not record any
Lieutenant Matthews or Mathews employed at the Admiralty in or about 1821,
though he might have been there in some
minor office. What C can mean by "Lithographer" is also a puzzle: although the Admiralty had created the very important office of Hydrographer in 1795 there was no
corresponding Lithographer, and the word
in the sense of one who deals with
stones, or geology, or landforms was already obsolete. Charts in C's day were usually engraved, although some experiments
in lithography for maps and charts had been
carried out in England since 1808, notably
by the army: Michael Twyman *Lithography
1800–1850* (1970) 32–3.

tabilien lebenden Thiere im Durchschnitt sinnvoller, gelehriger und klüger.

[A carnivore can often subdue and kill a herbivore four times its size, though the latter looks like a giant beside it. However, the herbivores are in general more intelligent, more clever, and more sensible.]

But what an exception in the DOG!![1]

51   p 298

Erst das Thier wird vom Boden frey und selbstständig beweglich, während die Pflanze gleichsam nur noch ein Theil des Bodens ist, in welchem sie wurzelt. Es geht also auch in der organischen Welt jener passivere Zustand, wo das Einzelne nur noch in unmittelbarer Vereinigung mit seinem Ganzen besteht, *jenem* voraus, wo das Einzelne ein Ganzes in sich, und unabhängig wird. Endlich haben wir im Thierreich, und zwar vorzüglich in der Klasse der Säugethiere . . . eine Reihe vorausgehen sehen, wo die Geschlechter durch ihre grössere Körpermasse und Schwerfälligkeit . . . durch die Unfähigkeit zum eigentlichen Gehen, statt dessen nur ein mühsames Kriechen möglich war, von dem Boden abhängiger, der allgemeinen Schwere mehr unterworfen waren . . .

[Only the animal is free of the ground and moves independently, whereas the plant, as it were, remains a part of the ground in which it is rooted. Similarly, in the organic world the more passive condition, in which the individual subsists only in immediate union with the whole, precedes that condition in which the individual becomes whole in itself and independent. In the animal kingdom, and especially in the class of mammals . . . we have finally seen the emergence of an order whose members were more dependent on the ground and subject to universal gravity on account of their greater corpulence and heaviness . . . and their inability to walk properly, instead being only able to crawl with difficulty . . .]

Schubart must have forgotten the Stag, Deer, Antelope, Mountain Goat, Horse, Zebra, and the horned Horse-like Beasts of South Africa.

52   p 312

Wenn nämlich die in der Cohärenz und Schwere unbewegt ruhenden Körper, eine stärkere Kraft als die ihrer Schwere ist, gegen einander bewegt,* wenn auf diese Weise gleichsam eine höhere geistigere Welt in die gröbere des jetzigen Daseyns eingreift, wird als Electricität, die wech-

---

50[1] The dog was often C's example of almost human sympathy and intelligence: cf *Friend* (*CC*) I 160–1, *AR* (*CC*) 248–9.

selseitige Anziehung, das Streben nach Vereinigung erregt, und selbst
das, was auf den höchsten Stufen des chemischen Processes, als wirkliches innres Wesen der Körper hervortritt, das Licht, wird im elektrischen Process schon als Funke gesehen.

[When bodies resting motionless in coherence and gravity are driven against one another by a force more powerful than that of their gravity,* and when in this way a
higher, more spiritual world intervenes, as it were, in the coarser world now existing,
a mutual attraction or striving for unification is provoked as electricity; and even that
which emerges at the highest stages of the chemical process as the real, inner essence
of bodies, namely light, is already seen in the electrical process as a spark.]

* I do not understand the Author's meaning here. *Wenn* (= when or if)
a power stronger than that of Gravity takes place in bodies, *then* that
stronger power shews itself.—Who can doubt it? But what has this to do
with the argument: unless it be proved, that the power originate in the
bodies, not in friction &c ab extra?[1] But I feel that I do not understand
the passage.

53   pp 334–5, pencil

Der Somnambulismus kündigt sich sogleich als eine mit dem gewöhnlichen Daseyn nicht unmittelbar zusammenhängende Erscheinung an.
Denn obgleich die Somnambülen mit der grössten Lebendigkeit und
Klarheit auf alle ihnen vorgelegte Fragen antworten, und in jeder Hinsicht witziger sinn- und geistreicher erscheinen als jemals im Wachen, so
dass selbst Naturen von sehr mittelmässigem Umfang, in diesem Zustand, <u>fast über die Gränzen</u> der gewöhlichen menschlichen Kräfte <u>hin-
austreten,</u> bleibt doch von diesem allen bey dem Erwachen noch weniger
zurück, als von dunklen Träumen.

[Somnambulism presents itself from the start as a phenomenon that is not directly connected with ordinary life. For although the somnambulists have the quickest and clearest answers to all the questions they are asked, and in all respects show greater intelligence and wit than when awake—so much so that even average people in a state of
somnambulism <u>almost surpass the bounds</u> of ordinary human ability—they retain on
waking even less than what remains after shadowy dreams.]

Where are the Proofs of this? I have carefully examined the greater number of the answers and discourses taken down from the mouths of the
most celebrated somnambulistic Clair-voyantes: and have found nothing
to justify this assertion, tho' proofs enough of the weak judgement of the
Amanuenses.[1]

52[1] "From outside".
53[1] C's extensive reading in the literature of mesmerism and clairvoyance is documented in SCHUBERT *Allgemeine Naturgeschichte* **13** n 1.

54 pp 351–2, pencil, slightly cropped

Die Geschichte jenes römischen Mönches, der dieses Vorgefühl auf dem Krankenlager hatte, und dessen Vorhersagung bey allen genau eintraf, ist bekannt. Merkwürdig ist auch in dieser Hinsicht die Pest zu Basel (am Ende des 16ten Jahrunderts) wo die Ansteckung mit einer Art von Bewusstseyn geschahe, und wo fast jeder Sterbende, selbst in den bewusstlosen Phantasien der letzten Augenblicke, den Nahmen dessen anrief, der zunächst nach ihm sterben musste.

[The story of that Roman monk whose premonitions and prophecies from the sickbed all came true is well known. In this connection it is also worth remarking on the plague at Basel (at the end of the 16th century) when contagion took place with a kind of consciousness; almost every victim about to die, even in the last moments of delirium, called out the name of the person whose death was immediately to follow his own.]

Jenes?[1]—one would really suppose, that some notorious part of classical history was alluded to!—and as to the obvious solution of these stories by the doctrine of chance Coincidence, and the extinction of the negative in the memory, Schubart does not even hint at. I am far from any contemptuous rejection of these stories; but I cannot receive them on such evidence. Ex. gr. the Plague at Basle: firstly, the State of philosophy—& then the great probability, that any name mentioned would be that of a Person attacked—& lastly, was the prophecy *always* fulfilled?

55 pp 358–9, pencil

[Schubert writes that clairvoyance reminds him of the awakening of phosphorescent substances in ignitable bodies which, when burning, become capable of much greater interaction with the outside world.] Das Sehen selber ist, wie wir anderwarts sahen, mit Recht ein Selberleuchten des Auges genannt worden, welches mithin blos durch die Eigenschaft des Leuchtens mit der Aussenwelt in jene Beziehung tritt, die wir Anschauen nennen.

[The act of seeing itself, as we saw elsewhere, has been rightly called a self-lighting of the eye, for it is only through its property of lighting that it enters into the kind of relation with the external world that we call intuition.]

Indeed?? Then it must needs follow, that the Day time is the time of *outward* Darkness: for all phosphorescent bodies are bright in proportion to the darkness. Besides, what gross sensuality is the whole System! What

---

54[1] "That?"—from the first line of the textus.

endless confusion of Terms![1] The *faculty* of seeing has no more connection with the flame than with the tallow of a Candle.

56 p 360, pencil

So bezeichnet das Erwachen des brennbaren Wesens, wie im Anorganischen das Erscheinen des Lichts, überall den Moment, wo die irdischen Dinge sich über die Natur des Planeten erheben, wo sie von diesem frey werden, und in eine höhere Ordnung der Dinge eintreten. Auch für das menschliche Daseyn scheint sich zuletzt die Befreyung von dem Planeten auf eine ähnliche Weise nach Aussen Kund zu geben, und vielleicht ist die Geschichte unsrer letzten Verwandlung, schon mit dem Erscheinen des Phosphors geendigt.

[The awakening of the inflammable, like the appearance of light in the inorganic world, always marks the moment when earthly things rise above the nature of the planet, when they become free from the latter and attain to a higher order of being. In human existence, too, a liberation from the planet seems at last to be manifesting itself in a similar externalized way, and perhaps the history of our latest transformation ended with the appearance of phosphorus.]

Ergo, a ~~good~~ bright fire is the apotheosis of Coal: and Mary, our Firemaker,[1] a maker of black Angels, and other beatified Super-planetaries!—While I laugh, I grieve in anger—not that trash should be published in Germany, more than in London—but that such *mawkish* Trash should have a *name*, be quoted as original Genius, &c—& by such men as Tiek![2]—O I begin to be sick of all the Post-Kantean Philosophers.

S. T. C.

57 p 364, pencil

Auch die Vorahndungen müssen aus denselben oder ähnlichen Ursachen hergeleitet werden. Wir werden diese dunkle Erscheinung der Seelenlehre leichter verstehen, wenn wir sie mit verwandten Phänomenen der untergeordneten Körperwelt zusammenstellen.

[Presentiments must also be deduced from the same or similar causes. We shall understand this obscure phenomenon of psychology better if we compare it with related phenomena of the subordinate physical world.]

55[1] Cf earlier objections to Schubert's "confusion of Terms": **15, 29, 30, 36**; also **60** below.

56[1] Presumably a maid at the Gillmans'.

56[2] Ludwig Tieck, whom C had met in Rome in 1806 (SCHELLING *Philosophische Schriften* **42** n 2), had passed through London in Jun 1817 and renewed their acquaintance. He may also have been instrumental in bringing C and JHG together (*CL* IV 738, 739–40), and the reference to him here is a reminder that some of these notes are perhaps addressed to JHG.

But first prove the separate existence of these Vorahndungen[1]—i.e. that they differ from other fancies, of fear and hope, in any thing but the accident of the event.

58   p 365, pencil

Unter den Vögeln soll es aus ähnlichen Gründen vorzüglich der Kukuk seyn, an welchem eine solche Vorempfindung der noch künftigen Witterungsveränderungen wahrgenommen wird, und es ist bekannt, dass dieses Thier, vermöge einer minder vollkommnen Organisation, selten, oder wie Einige behaupten, niemals, die eignen Jungen auszubrüten vermag.

[For similar reasons, it is supposed that among the birds the cuckoo, above all, can sense approaching changes in the weather; and it is well known that owing to a less perfect structure, this animal is rarely able, or, as some have claimed, is never able to hatch out its own young.]

a fable?

59   p 376, pencil

Endlich wird in dem Licht des Verbrennungsprocesses, welcher erst durch die Gegenwart der Atmosphäre möglich wurde,* in dem positiven Gegensatz jenes höhere Ganze, die Sonne selber dargestellt.

[That higher whole, the sun itself, is at last presented in this positive opposition, i.e. in the light from the combustive process which was only made possible by the presence of the atmosphere.*]

* not *as* atmosphere: ex. gr. the Oxymuriate of Potash, that burns under water.[1] Rather is the process of Combustion the cause or condition of an Atmosphere.

60   pp 376–7, pencil

* Es ist dieselbe, die hier als Schwere, dort als Licht, hier als Leben, dort als Bewusstseyn und Begeisterung erscheint.

[* It is the same whether it appears here as gravity, there as light, here as life, there as consciousness and animation.]

57[1] "Presentiments"—in textus.

59[1] C must mean potassium oxymuriate, now known as potassium chlorate. (In 1786 Berthollet had shown that it could be prepared by the action of oxymuriatic acid gas—i.e. chlorine—on caustic potash.)

William Brande's *Manual of Chemistry* (1819), a work C used, says of it that "When sulphuric acid is poured upon mixtures of this salt and combustibles . . . under water by means of a long funnel, inflammation also ensues" (188).

* O that it were as easy to understand this as to say it! *"There* as Light, *here* as Life"[1]—what is this but an *equivoque*, or two opposite senses under one word? Lux facta ⚹ Lux lucifica.[2] If the latter be assumed as an invisible living agent, what mean the "there" and "here"? Might we not say, on the same ground,—it is the same Life which appears here as sitting, there as writing, and at another moment as thinking and composing?

61   p 377, pencil

Bald nach dieser Zeit wurden die Spuren einer vollkommneren organischen Welt gefunden, minder <u>vollkommne</u>* Wesen hatten schon in früheren Perioden gelebt, und waren unter ihren Gebirgen begraben.

[Soon after this time there were found traces of a more perfect organic world; less <u>perfect</u>* beings had already been alive in earlier periods and were buried under their mountains.]

compare with * below.[1]

62   p 377, pencil

Jene glückseeligere und <u>kräftigere</u> Vergangenheit,* von welcher dieser Nachlass der Vorwelt zu uns spricht . . .

[That more blissful and <u>more powerful</u> past,* which the legacy of the former world tells us about . . .]

* Is not this a contradiction to * above?

60[1] Schubert's subject is the hypothetical power that is the cause of life in general.
60[2] "Light made"—the actual phenomenon of light—as opposed to "light-making light". This often-invoked distinction is glossed in Böhme **80** n 1.
61[1] I.e. with **62**.

Die Symbolik des Traumes. 2nd ed rev. Bamberg 1821. 8°.

British Library C 43 b 17

Two notes in C's hand, headed "Schubert's Symbolik des Traume", are written on the first three pages of four leaves of writing paper sewn in at pp 184/5. There are no true marginalia in this vol.

DATE. After 1821, the year of publication.

COEDITOR. Raimonda Modiano.

1   pp [1–3] Insert (at pp 184/5), referring to p 4 | Ch 1

Ohne dass wir deshalb in Versuchung kommen könnten, dem Traume vor dem Wachen, dem Närrischseyn vor der Besonnenheit, der Trunkenheit vor der Nüchternheit irgend einen Vorzug einzuräumen, ja indem wir uns sogar daran erinnern, dass der Mensch jenes innere Organ, was dem Geiste die Traumbilder reflectirt, mit dem Thiere gemeinschaftlich besitze, dürfen wir uns doch nicht läugnen: dass jene Abbreviaturen und Hieroglyphensprache, der Natur der Seele in mancher Hinsicht angeeigneter erscheine, als unsere gewöhnliche Wortsprache. Jene ist zum Theil ausdrucksvoller, schnell und viel umfassender, der Ausgedehntheit in die Zeit viel minder unterworfen, als diese. Die letztere müssen wir erst erlernen, dagegen ist uns jene angebohren, und die Seele versucht diese ihr eigenthümliche Sprache zu reden, sobald sie im Schlafe oder Delirio aus der gewöhnlichen (wachen) Unterwürfigkeit unter ihren Geist und aus der Verkettung mit ihrem gröberen Körper, etwas los und frei geworden, obgleich es ihr damit ohngefähr nur eben so gelingt, als es einem nachherigen guten Fussgänger gelungen, wenn er als Fötus im Mutterleibe, die künftigen Bewegungen versuchte. Denn, beiläufig: wir würden es, falls wir es auch vermöchten, jene *disjecta membra* eines ursprünglichen und künftigen Lebens, schon jetzt an Licht und Luft hervorzuziehen, doch vor der Hand in der Geistersprache kaum zum Lallen bringen, oder höchstens zu einem Grade von Bauchrednerei.

[Without being tempted to prefer dreaming to waking, folly to presence of mind, drunkenness to sobriety, and remembering that man shares with the animals the inner organ which reflects dream images to the mind, we cannot deny that such a language of abbreviations and hieroglyphics seems in some respects more appropriate to the nature of our soul than our usual word-language. The dream-language is in part more expressive, rapid, and comprehensive and takes much less time than ordinary word-language. We have to learn the latter, whereas the former is innate; the soul tries to speak this language, which is peculiarly its own, as soon as sleep or delirium begins to free it from its usual (waking) submission to the mind and from its connection with the gross body. Of course, it succeeds in doing so only in the way that a foetus destined to become a good walker might practise the future movements while still in the womb. For, incidentally, even if we succeeded in bringing to light and air these *disjecta membra* [scattered remains] of an original and future life, we would only get as far as stammering in the language of spirits, or at most reach a certain degree of ventriloquy.]

Schubart's Symbolik des Traume.

p. 4. aus der Verkettung mit der gröberen Körper etwas los?[1]—*I*[a] should have inferred the Contrary.

The astounding rapidity and complexity of the successions in ⟨the⟩ Somnial State—Q[y]—how far may it depend on the suspension of the *Personal* Volition;[2] on the potential or negative state of the connexive *Life* of the Muscles (Life$_{(2}$[b], "Vis ~~Vitæ~~ Zöoelectrica muscularis["])—;[3] and above all, as the most proper definition of Sleep, the − Subjectivity of the Mind = the rational Will in the I AM, the Animus Objectivus,[4] ~~I ha~~ inner Sense as Sensuous Fancy, with the Adaptivity or ~~Automatic~~ instinctive Understanding being +: or the Positive Pole? I walk from Grosvenor Square to Mile End—& now from the ~~successive~~ onward rolling broad Stream of multifarious Objects, which *scious*ly[5] if not with reflective consciousness I have apprehended, let me abstract or subtract all the acts and efforts of the Mind to connect or unite all these successive groups of Forms, Sounds, &c with my own Identity, with the I AM,

---

1[a] The word "I", italicised here, was underlined twice in ms

1[b] C's superscript has been printed as a subscript to avoid confusion with editorial matter

1[1] "Free from its connection with the gross body?"—adapted from textus. C's lifelong interest in the experience of dreaming and nightmare is manifest in many thoughtful observations, and he often notes a direct connection between the content of the dream and the state of the body, e.g. *CN* II 2073, 2543, III 4046, 4409 and n; JUNG **15**, **34**, **44**; *Lects 1808–1819* (*CC*) I 130–1 and n 19.

1[2] This idea is a refrain and a source of alarm in many of C's remarks about dreams, e.g. TENNEMANN **43**, where he declares that "the Suspension of the Free-will is a main Constituent of Sleep" and where he describes dreams in general as "a shifting Current in the shoreless Chaos of the Fancy in which the streamy *Continuum* of passive Association is broken into *zig-zag* by Sensations, from within or from without—ex. gr. distension from wind in the Stomach, or a knot in the bed-cloathes".

1[3] "The zooelectric muscular power". For similar formulations see SCHUBERT *Allgemeine Naturgeschichte* **19** and n 2.

1[4] The "objective mind": for the distinction between *animus* and *anima* see SCHELLING *Philosophische Schriften* **29** and nn.

1[5] *OED* gives "scious" ("having knowledge"), its only example being from C himself, but not "sciously".

of *translating* them, as it were, and construing them, as so many various *pro*nouns representing the infinitely modifiable *Me* (the universal Accusati[ve]^c or Objective Case)—in short, all the acts of the Reason in the Understanding, "of ^{d}the *Discourse of Reason*"/^{6} to give the⟨m⟩ af firm objectivity, to judge and affirm their *objective* Being;—causation ab extra;^{7} and again, of distinguishing this per antithesin^8 from causation ab intra;^{9} and this again as *contingency* from free Will, &c &c how prodigiously should I diminish the *sense* of Time? Every one of these Acts are so many suspensions of, drags put to, the wheels of the ⟨Chariot of⟩ Associative— ~~Vehicle~~ chrystallizations, as of Frost, in the rapid Current— —

Now in Sleep all *relative* Objectivity is swallowed up in this its *own monopoly*.—Hence all contingency—& no contingency &c &c.—

2   p [3] Insert, referring to p 6

Dieser [unsre Seele im Traume] gelingt es deshalb, sobald sie ihre Traumbildersprache redet, Combinationen in derselben zu machen, auf die wir im Wachen freilich nicht kämen; sie knüpft das Morgen geschickt ans Gestern, das Schicksal ganzer künftiger Jahre an die Vergangenheit an, und die Rechnung trifft ein, der Erfolg zeigt, dass sie uns das, was künftig ist, oft ganz richtig vorhersagt. Eine Art zu rechnen und zu combiniren, die ich und du nicht verstehen; eine höhere Art von Algebra, noch kürzer und bequemer als die unsrige, die aber nur der versteckte Poet in unserm Innern zu handhaben weiss. [Schubert then recounts a number of prophetic dreams which were instrumental in preventing an otherwise certain loss of lives.]

[As soon as it speaks the language of vision, our soul [in a state of dreaming] thus succeeds in making connections which, to be sure, we do not come upon when we are awake; it skilfully links the tomorrow with the yesterday, the fate of future years with the past, and the record confirms, the results show that it often predicts the future quite accurately. This type of reckoning and combining neither you nor I understand; it is a higher type of algebra, even more concise and convenient than ours, but which only the poet hidden within us knows how to handle.]

p. 6.—Schubart's prophetic and artistic Dreams form a *distinct* Kind— and ought not to have been confounded with those of proper Sleep—.

1^c Letters lost in binding   1^d C repeats opening quotation marks before "the"

1^6 Shakespeare *Hamlet* I ii 150—a favourite phrase used e.g. in FIELD **10**, JOHNSON **16**, *SM* (*CC*) 69, *Friend* (*CC*) I 156.

1^7 "From without".
1^8 "By antithesis".
1^9 "From within".

They are far more akin to Madness.—In all these cases, the Brain is not diffusedly, or in balance as a whole Organ, *Asleep*.—The *outward* Senses themselves are rather to be deemed in a state of *Torpor*, than of genuine *Sleep*.[1]

2[1] A state C describes in connection both with (but also distinguished from) dreams and with the "clairvoyant" phase of mesmerism, but especially memorably in the Preface to *Kubla Khan*—"The Author continued for about three hours in a profound sleep, at least of the external senses": *PW* (EHC) I 296.

JOHN SCOTT

1638–1694/5

The Christian Life, from its beginning to its consummation in glory. With proper and useful indexes. 9th ed. London 1729. F°.

Cornell University, Wordsworth Collection

DATE. Perhaps 1807–8, when C was staying with the Wordsworths; perhaps even earlier. The provenance of the vol is Wordsworthian (Coffman S87); the hand looks "early", being large and sprawling. An internal reference to the bp of London (**4** n 5) indicates a date before May 1808.

1   pp ⁻1–⁻2, pencil

Passages excellent or otherwise remarkable.
   P. 7¹
      7 & 8²
      8 (6 last lines) & 9.—³
      39— 4̶3̶ to—45.⁴
      45–57 inclusive.⁵

2   p 28, pencil

So that being left utterly destitute of all her dear Delights and Satisfactions, which are such as she [the Soul] knows she can never enjoy but in *Conjunction* with the *Body*, all her Appetite and Longing must necessarily be an outragious Desire of being *Embodied* again, that so she may be capable of repeating her old *sensual* Pleasures, and acting over the *brutish* Scene anew.

And this, as some think, is the Reason why such *gross* and *sensual* Souls have appeared so often, after their Separation, in the *Church-yards*,

---

1¹ ANNEX **4**.
1² ANNEX **5**.
1³ ANNEX **6**.
1⁴ C did not mark this long passage in the text, a rhapsody upon the desirability of loving and imitating God, with this conclusion (45): "So that if we carry with us into Eternity a Frame and Disposition of Nature like God's we shall always so *imitate* as still to *love* him, so *love* as still to *contemplate* him, so *contemplate* as still to *adore* him, so *adore* as still to *imitate*, and *love* and *contemplate* him a-new; and in this blessed Circle we shall move round for ever, with unspeakable Vigor and Alacrity."
1⁵ In these pages C marked two passages, pp 50 and 56–7 (ANNEX **14, 2A**). See **6** for a continuation of this note.

or *Charnel-Houses*, where their Bodies were laid; because they cannot please themselves without them . . .

See Milton's Comus, l. 453–475.[1]

2A   pp 56–7

. . . if in the *cool* and *standing* Temper of our Souls, we are hearty Well-wishers to all Men, and hearty Lovers of all that do in any measure *love* and *resemble* God, we are in a natural Tendency to Heaven, that perfect Element of Love . . . [a]yet do they ["those heavenly People" who are "all of them most *flagrant* Lovers of God"] all *stick fast* to one another, being *clung* inseparably together, by those attractive Virtues, which they have all derived from him: And in this State of perfect *Friendship* they converse together with unspeakable Pleasure, and all their Conversation is a perpetual Intercourse of *wise* and *holy* Endearments: And now what a blessed Society must this be, wherein perfect *Love* and *Friendship* reigns, and hath an All-commanding Empire; where every Heart *mingles* with every one; and all like precious Dusts of Gold, are melted together into one solid Ingot; where infinite Myriads of blessed Spirits, by interchangeably *clasping* and *twining* with one another, are so inseparably *united* and *grown together*, that they are all but one *compounded* Soul; and when, from the highest Angel to the lowest Saint, they are all so *tied* together by the Heart-strings, that every one is every one's dear Friend, what inexpressible *Content* and *Complacency* must they needs take in one another! When I shall pass all Heaven over, thro' Ten Thousand Millions of blessed Beings, and meet none but such as I most dearly *love*, and am

---

2A[a]   C's marginal line begins here

2[1] From a speech of the Elder Brother:

So dear to Heav'n is Saintly chastity,
That when a soul is found sincerely so,
A thousand liveried Angels lacky her,
Driving far off each thing of sin and guilt,
And in cleer dream, and solemn vision
Tell her of things that no gross ear can
    hear,
Till oft convers with heav'nly habitants
Begin to cast a beam on th'outward shape,
The unpolluted temple of the mind,
And turns it by degrees to the souls
    essence,
Till all be made immortal: but when lust
By unchaste looks, loose gestures, and
    foul talk,

But most by leud and lavish act of sin,
Lets in defilement to the inward parts,
The soul grows clotted by contagion,
Imbodies, and imbrutes, till she quite loose
The divine property of her first being.
Such are those thick and gloomy shadows
    damp
Oft seen in Charnell vaults, and
    Sepulchers
Lingering, and sitting by a new made
    grave,
As loath to leave the body that it lov'd,
And link't it self by carnal sensualty
To a degenerate and degraded state.

as dearly *beloved* by. O what unspeakable Rejoycing and Congratulations will there be between us! Especially when I shall find no Defect either of Goodness or Happiness in *them*, nor they in *me*, to damp our mutual Joy and Delight in each other; but every one shall be what every one wishes him, a *perfect* and a *blessed* Friend: For perfect Lovers have all their *Joys* and *Griefs* in common between them; but the Heavenly Lovers having no *Griefs* among them, do only communicate their *Joys* to one another: For where they love so perfectly as they do in Heaven, there can be no such Thing as a *private* or *particular* Happiness, but every one must have a share in every one's . . .

3   p ⁻1, referring to pp 79–80, marked with a double line in the margin

And certainly next to exacting the Punishment due to our Sins at our own *hands*, the most dreadful Severity he could have expressed, was to resolve not to remit it upon any other Consideration than*ᵃ* that of his own Son's undergoing it in *our stead*; by which he hath given us the greatest reason that Heaven and Earth could afford, to tremble at his Justice, even whilst we are inclosed in the Arms of his Mercy.*ᵇ* . . . *ᶜ*And as a thorow Persuasion of the Necessity of *Christ's Sacrifice* to the Forgiveness of our Sins, will fill us with awful Apprehensions of the Divine Severity, and set before us a most dismal Prospect of the vast demerit of our Sins, both which are necessary to engage us to a thorow Reformation; so a thorow Conviction of the Necessity of his *Intercession* to render our *Duties*, our *Prayers*, and Persons acceptable to God, will effectually *humble* and *abase* us in our own Eyes, which, as I shall shew you by and by, is highly conducive to a good *Beginning* of this our *Christian Warfare*. For next to *banishing* us from his Presence *for ever*, the most effectual Course God could take to *abase* us, was to exclude us from all *immediate* Intercourse with him, and not to admit of any more Addresses or Supplications from us, but only thro' the Hands of a *Mediator*; which is a plain Demonstration how infinitely *pure* he is, and how *base* and *vile* our Sins have render'd us; insomuch that he will not suffer a sinful Creature to come near him, otherwise than by a *Proxy*; that he will not accept of a *Service* from a guilty Hand, nor listen to a *Prayer* from *ᵈ*a sinful Mouth, till 'tis first *hallowed* and *presented* to him by a *pure* and *holy* Mediator.

79. the 2ⁿᵈ passage marked ‖ is manifestly *heretical*; and indeed the whole work smells rank of anthropomorphitism. Christ is equally the me-

3*ᵃ* Marginal lines begin at this point   3*ᵇ* The following paragraph is not marked
   3*ᶜ* Marginal line resumes   3*ᵈ* Remainder of textus over page, unmarked

diati~~on~~or of unfallen as of fallen Spirits; as necessary to the Father as to the Angels, to the Angels as to Man/ He is no contingency, but an eternal filiation of Intellect and of Being!—

4   pp ⁻1–⁻2, pencil, referring to p 80

And in the Virtue of this [Christ's] *Sacrifice*, as well as his own Personal *Interest* with His Father, He now interceeds in our behalf; and pleading our Cause, as He doth, with the price of our Souls in his Hand, even in his precious Blood by which He redeemed them, we may be sure that with that powerful *Oratory* He cannot fail of succeeding in our behalf. For having *purchased* for us, by his Blood, all those Favours which He *interceeds* for, He is invested with the Right and Power of bestowing them upon us. So that now, for our greater Security, all those Favours, which God hath *promised* us, are actually *deposited* in the Hands of our *Mediator:* And though His bare Promise is in itself as great an Assurance as can be given us: yet it is to be considered that guilty Minds are naturally *anxious* and full of unreasonable *Jealousies*, and consequently whilst they looked upon God as their *adverse* Party, and a Party infinitely *offended* by them, would have been very prone to *suspect* the worst, had they had nothing but his bare Word to depend on.

80. If possible, still more idolatrous, & degrading of the εν και το παν.[1] Indeed, the whole Book must be read with a perpetual guard against the *gross* eudaimonism[2] of its principles, passio voluptuaria[3] substituted for pure and holy *action*—one law of endless change of *enjoyment, fruition,* &c. all of which differ in degree not in kind/ for pleasure is pleasure & we never ask *what* it is, but how much and of how long continuance/ Alas! how has the Christian Religion declined from the Religion of Christ— This work is an eloquent disguise of Epicurism. Enjoyment! enjoyment!—not differing from the embrace of a Strumpet in *kind*, only keener, i.e. a handsomer Strumpet less transient—i.e. a more faithful Strumpet/ but Virtue for its own sake; Reason as a categorical and sine origine[4] Lawgiver, & the absolutely unconditional amenability of the Will to the Reason, ~~for~~ because it is Reason, & for no other cause (nay, if any other intervene, Vice Intervenes) this is not only not mentioned; but the Bishop of London—Antichrist's Trumpeter, preparing Papacy by Methodism, blasphemously proclaims it Atheism, & the characteristic of

4[1] "The one and the all", i.e. God (in a pantheistic system).

4[2] The system of ethics that is based on a calculation of happiness: see RICHTER *Palingenesien* 2 and n 3.

4[3] "Passion of voluptuousness".

4[4] "Without a beginning".

ą Wickedness!—He acknowleges no Virtue/ he only knows the difference between Cunning & Simple (for what differs Heaven & Stock Exchange, if we seek both by the same feelings) and yet dares use the word *Virtue & Wickedness*.[5]   S. T. Coleridge.

5   p ‾2, referring to p 97

If therefore Men would be but so kind to themselves, as to apply themselves, in all their spiritual Exigences, to a *holy*, *wise*, and *well-instructed* Guide; to *uncover* their Sores, *lay open* their Cases, and *reveal* the Secrets of their Souls to him, so far as it is necessary to enable him to make proper Applications; it is not to be expressed what a *vast* Advantage they might make of him. He would be instead of a *good Genius* or *Tutelar Angel* to their Souls, to suggest many a good *Thought* to them, and feed their Meditations with many an useful *Notion*; to enable them to *extract* from the Articles of their Belief, their just and proper Inferences, and *reduce* them to practical Principles, to *rectify* their Wandring, and *extricate* them from their Doubts; to *comfort* them in their Sorrows, and *quicken* them in their Indispositions; to *warm* their Indifferences, and *moderate* their Zeal, so as that they may neither be *becalmed* by the one, nor *overborn* by the too violent Gusts of the other; and, in a word, to direct them to the proper Methods of *Mortifying* their bad Inclinations, and *conducting* their Religion so, as to render it more *easy* and *delightful* to them.

97. Had the pious Author witnessed the effects of Confession in Catholic Countries, or reflected deeply, a priori, on the necessary consequences of such a practice, when general and imposed as a religious Duty, he would surely never have written this preparation for Popery/ but it is the mis-

4[5] Scott's book was dedicated to a bp of London, Henry Compton (1676–1714); but C's reference is to the bp of London of his own time, Beilby Porteus (1731–1808), who was sympathetic to the Evangelicals, a friend of Hannah More, and author of a pamphlet on a subject that was anathema to C—*A Summary of the Evidences for the Truth and Divine Origin of the Christian Revelation* (1800). C has a bitter note about him as one "inclined to Devil-worship": *CN* II 2440 (Feb 1805). In his remarks here, C may have had in mind particularly a lecture that Porteus delivered 27 Mar 1801 on "The Mysteries of Christianity": *Works* (6 vols 1811) v 372–415. The lecture takes up questions about the origin of evil and the punishment of sinners. Of the first question, Porteus maintains that it is too great a subject for human intellect to fathom, and that indeed it would be "a strange misapplication of talents, and a waste of labour and of time" (v 376) to try, when we are plainly told in the first book of the Bible that it was the Devil who brought moral evil into the world. With regard to the second question, Porteus—invoking worldly criteria that C heartily disapproved of—is at pains to prove that sinners will be punished sooner or later, even if it is not until the Day of Judgment, and that therefore "the religious and virtuous" ought not to "repine" at the "prosperity of the wicked" (v 411).

fortune of our Church that being Episcopal and founding their office on a succession from the Apostles, always to support with one arm the monster, whom it professes to press against with its whole Body.—

5A p 119, marked with pencil lines in the margin

When the Ship hath *sprung* a Leak, 'tis a madness for the Mariners to sit still and complain of the *Pains* and *Labour* of Pumping; for in the Extremity they are in, there is no more to be said, they must *pump* or *per-ish*; and it is not to be debated, where there is so vast an *Inequality* between the Objects of their Choice, which of the *Two* they were best to fix upon; whether to *take Pains* for the present to *secure* the Ship, or to *sit still* and suffer themselves to be *swallowed up* in the Ocean. . . . But what then; were we not better labour for a *while* than perish *for ever?* Do we talk of *Labour*, when our Souls are *at Stake*, and our immortal Life is upon the Brink of an everlasting *well* or *ill* Being? In other Cases we never think much to endure a *present* Inconvenience for the Prevention of a future Mischief . . .

6 blank page following Alphabetical Table, referring to p 132 (marked with a pencil line in the margin), pencil

. . . had we been so [i.e. Subjects and Members of the Church of Rome *de jure*], we should doubtless never have *separated* ourselves from her, could we but have *separated* her *Sins* from her Communion; *[a]* could we have profest her *Creed* without *implicitly* believing all her Cheats and Impostures, or submitted ourselves to her *Guides* without apparent Danger of being *misled* by them into the Pit of Destruction, or join'd with her publick *Services* without *worshipping* of *Creatures*, or received her *Sacraments*, without practising the grossest *Superstitions* and *Idolatries*. But when she had made it necessary for us either to *sin with*, or *separate from* her, we could have no other *honest* Remedy but only to *withdraw*; and if in this our *Separation* there had been a sinful *Schism* on either side, we could have appealed to Heaven and Earth, *whose* the Guilt of it was; *theirs* that forced us upon it, or *ours* that were forced to it. But yet the Case of *our* Separation from the *Church of Rome*, is vastly different from that of the Separation of *private* Members from their own *particular* Churches. For we affirm that the *Church of Rome* is but a *particular* Church, whose *Authority* extends no farther than to its own *native* Members, and consequently hath no more Power to impose Laws of Communion upon *us*, than *we* have upon *her*; our particular Church being altogether as *distinct* and *independent* from *her*, as *she* is from *ours*. So

6[a] C's marginal line begins here

that tho the Terms of Communion she imposes upon her own Members, were all of them *lawful* and *innocent*, yet do they no more *oblige* us as we are *Christians* of the *Church of England*, than the *lawful* Commands of the *Great Mogul* do, as we are *Subjects* of the *Kingdom of England*.

Remarkable passages continued from the blank leaf at the beginning. 132. How Bellarmin would have played with this passage, as a lion astride of a [? Mammoth] [. . .] himself with his certain prey.[1] This indeed a most [? breathless/breechless], yea, [? leafed][b] Assertion!

6A   pp 671–2, marked with a pencil line in the margin

. . . sure they will and do promote it; since in so doing they contribute to their own *Joy*.

7   p 679

For if there be no such Thing as *future Rewards* and *Punishments*, it is a Folly for any man to concern himself about any Thing but his *present* Interest; and in Reason we ought to judge Things to be *good* or *evil*, only as they promote or obstruct our *temporal* Happiness and Welfare.

can there be no virtue without selfish motives?

8   p 679

. . . whensoever we could cheat or steal *securely*, it would be highly reasonable for us to do it; because thereby we might promote our own *temporal* Happiness, which would be the *only* End we should have to pursue.

base reasoning

Annex

C has marked the following passages with a pencil line in the margin, in some places with more emphatic marking (as noted).

ANNEX 1   sig A2[v]

As for the Argument *I have undertaken, I may, without breach of Modesty, say, it is a great and a noble one; it is the* Christian Life, *which, next to the* Angelical, *approaches nearest to the Life of God.*

6[b] An illegible word is cancelled before the speculative reading "leafed"

6[1] Here as elsewhere (JOHNSON **22**, LA-CUNZA **57**), C refers to the Jesuit saint Robert Bellarmine (1542–1621) as an apol-ogist for the Roman Catholic position in controversies with the Protestants.

ANNEX 2   sig [A3]ʳ

For I have proved at large, that there is something of Heaven *and* Hell *in the very Nature of each particular* Virtue *and* Vice, *and that in the Perfection of these Two opposite* Qualities *consists the main* Happiness *and* Misery *of those Two opposite* States.

ANNEX 3   pp 6–7

And now, by this time, I think it is clear enough, that the *main* and *principal Part* of the *Heaven* of a *Man*, considered as a *reasonable Creature*, consists in *Knowing* and *Choosing* of God. But besides *this*, there are other blessed *Ingredients* of Heaven; the *Principal* whereof is, the knowing and choosing *those* that are *most like* unto God; namely, the *blessed Jesus* in his *human Nature*, and the *Holy Angels* and *Saints*, who are *all* in their several Measures and Degrees, the express and lively *Images* of God. And therefore if to know and choose God be the *supreme* Felicity of Heaven, then doubtless the *next* to *that*, is, to *know* and be *acquainted* with these blessed *Images* of him, and freely to *choose* their *Company* and *Conversation*, and be entirely *united* to them in *Affection*; without which, it would be no Felicity to dwell in the *same Place* with them. For to *cohabit* with Jesus, and with Saints and Angels, and not be *acquainted with* and *united* to them in *Heart* and *Affection*, would be rather a *Burden* than a *Pleasure*. The Happiness therefore of being in their *Society*, consists in *knowing* and *choosing* them. And this is every where implied, where our being in *them* is mention'd as a Part of our Heaven. Thus, 1 *Thess.* iv. 17. to *be ever with the Lord*, is the same Thing with being *ever in Heaven:* But then, 'tis to be ever with him upon *Choice*; for so those Words imply, *Phil.* i. 23. *I desire to depart and to be with Christ*; *which is far better.* And accordingly this is mention'd by the Apostle, as a *dear Privilege* of our being Members of the *Christian Church*, whereby we are entituled to the Society of *Holy Myriads of Angels*; *of the general Assembly and Church of the First-born*; *of God the Judge of all*; *of the Spirits of Just Men made perfect, and of Jesus the Mediator of the New Covenant*, Heb. xii. 22, 23, 24. And indeed this must needs be an *inestimable Happiness*, not only to *cohabit*, but be *acquainted with*, and in Heart and Will *united* to this blessed and glorious Company.

ANNEX 4   p 7, referred to in 1: the pencil line continuing from 3, but adding a second line in the outer margin and a double line in the inner margin

For what Soul that has any *Spark* of Cordial Love to Jesus, the *best Friend* of *Souls* that ever was, any *grateful Remembrance* of what he *did* and *suffer'd* for our sakes, would not esteem it a *mighty Felicity* to be admitted into his *Presence*, and to be an *Eye-witness* of the happy Change of his past *woful* Circumstances? To see him that was so *cruelly treated*, so barbarously *vilified*, *tortured* and *butchered* for our sakes, *raised* to the highest pitch of Splendour and Dignity, to be *Head* and *Prince* of all the *Hierarchy* of Heaven, to be *worshipped* and *celebrated* thro'out all the noble *Choir* of *Arch-Angels* and *Angels*, and *Spirits of just Men made perfect?* Verily methinks had I only the Privilege to *look in* and *see* my dear and blessed Lord *surrounded* with all this *Circle* of Glories, it would be a most *heavenly Consolation* to me, tho I were sure never to *partake* of it. The very *Communion* I should have in the *Joys* of my *Master*, would be a kind of

Heaven at *Second-hand* to me, and my Soul would be wondrous Happy by *Sympathizing* with him in his *Felicity* and *Advancement*. But, Oh! when that *Blessed Person* shall not only *permit* me to *see* his Glory, but *introduce* me into it, and make me *Partaker* of it; when I shall not only *behold his beloved Face*, but be *admitted* into his *dear Conversation*, and *dwell* in his *Arms* and *Embraces* for ever; when I shall hear him record the *wondrous Adventures* of his Love, thro' how many *woful Stages* he pass'd to rescue me from *Misery*, and make me *Happy*, and in the mean time shall have a most *ravishing Feeling* of *that* Happiness; how will my Heart *spring* with *Joy*, and *burn* with *Love*, and my Mouth *o'erflow* with *Praises* and *Thanksgiving* to him!

ANNEX 5   pp 7–8, referred to in 1

For as their *Goodness* cannot but render their Conversation infinitely *free* and *benign*, so their great *Knowledge* must necessarily render it equally *profitable* and *delightful*. And then being so *Knowing* as they are, they must needs be supposed to *understand* all the *wise Arts* of *Endearment*; and being so *Good*, they must be also supposed to be continually *practising* them. And if so, what a *heavenly Conversation* must theirs be, the *Scope* whereof is the most *glorious Knowledge*, and the *Law* whereof is the most *perfect Friendship?* Who would not be willing to leave a *foolish, froward*, and *ill-natur'd* World, for the blessed Society of these *wise Friends*, and *perfect Lovers?* And what a Felicity must it be, to spend an Eternity in such a *noble* Conversation! where we shall hear the *deep Philosophy* of Heaven communicated with *mutual Freedom* in the wise and amicable Discourses of *Angels* and *glorified Spirits*; who without any *Reserve*, or *Affectation of Mystery*, without *Passion* or *Interest*, or *peevish Contention* for *Victory*, do *freely* Philosophize, and *mutually* impart the Treasures of each other's *Knowledge*. For since all *Saints* there are great *Philosophers*, and all *Philosophers* perfect *Saints*, we must needs suppose *Knowledge* and *Goodness*, *Wisdom* and *Charity*, to be equally intermingled thro'out all their Conversation; and being so, what can be imagined more delightful! When therefore we shall leave this *impertinent* and *unsociable* World; and all our *good old Friends* that are gone to Heaven before us, shall meet us as soon as we are landed upon the Shore of Eternity, and with infinite Congratulations for our safe Arrival, shall conduct us into the Company of the *Patriarchs* and *Prophets*, *Apostles* and *Martyrs*, and introduce us into an *intimate* Acquaintance with them, and with all those *brave* and *generous* Souls, who by their glorious Examples have recommended themselves to the World; when we shall be *familiar Friends* with *Angels* and *Arch-Angels*, and all the *Courtiers* of Heaven shall call us *Brethren*, and bid us *Welcome* to their *Master's Joy*, and we shall be received into their glorious Society with all the tender Endearments and Caresses of those *heavenly Lovers*; what a *mighty* Addition to our Happiness will this be!

ANNEX 6   pp 8–9, referred to in 1

Now from what hath been said concerning this great *End* of the *Christian Life*, these *Two* Things are to be inferr'd concerning the *Nature* of it.

    *a*I. That the *main* of Heaven consists not so much in any *outward* Possession,

ANNEX 6^a C's marginal line begins here

as in an *inward* State and Temper. For tho Heaven be, doubtless, a most *glorious Place*, and all its blessed *Inhabitants* do possess and hold it by an everlasting *Tenure*; yet 'tis a great Mistake to imagine that the main Happiness of Heaven consists in living for ever in a *glorious Place*, which, separated from all the rest of Heaven, would be but a *poor* and *hungry* kind of Happiness. For *Life* is no otherwise a Happiness, than as it is the Principal of all our *pleasant* and *grateful Perceptions*; and if we could live for ever without *perceiving*, it would be the same Thing to us, as if we were nothing but a Company of everlasting *Stones* and *Trees*; and what great matter would it signify to live for ever in a *glorious Place*, unless we could be for ever affected by it with a *delightful Sense* and *Perception?* which is impossible; because all *delightful Sense* (as hath already been proved) arises out of the *vigorous Exercise* of our Faculties about such Objects as are suitable to them; but what can there be in the most *glorious Place* so suitable to a *Rational Mind* and *Will*, as to keep them for ever *vigorously* employed and exercised about it? It may, indeed, for a while, employ the *Mind* in an eager Contemplation of its *new* and *surprizing Beauties*; but how soon would the Mind dis-relish it, were it to be its *only* Entertainment for Eternity? And as for the *Will*, what would a fine Place signify to it, if it were not replenish'd with such Objects as are suitable to its own *Options?* And indeed, there is nothing that can *everlastingly* gratify a rational Mind and Will, but what has in it such an *Infinity* of *Truth* as is everlastingly *Knowable*, and such an *Infinity* of *Goodness* as is everlastingly *Desirable*; or, which is the same Thing, nothing but what hath *Truth* enough in it for the one to be vigorously *contemplating* for ever; and nothing but what hath *Goodness* enough in it for the other to be as vigorously *loving, adoring*, and *imitating* for ever. And such an Infinitude of *Truth* and *Goodness* is no where to be found but in *God*. But *God*, as well as the *Place*, and *Duration* of Heaven, being an Object that is *external* to us, neither is, nor can be a Happiness to us, unless we *act upon* him, and *freely exercise* our Faculties about him; unless we *Know* him, and *Love* him, &c. [b]So that *that* which *felicitates* all, is our own *Internal Act;*[c] 'tis by *this* that we enjoy Heaven, and perceive all the Pleasures of it. 'Tis not by *being in Heaven* that Men are constituted Happy, but by *vigorously exerting* their Faculties upon the heavenly Objects: For without *this*, to be *in* Heaven or *out of it*, would be indifferent to us. The Happiness of Heaven therefore consists in a *State* of *heavenly Action*; in being so *attempered* and *connaturaliz'd* to the Objects of Heaven, as to be always *acting upon*, and *chearfully employing* our Faculties about them. For as there is no Pleasure in Acting *coldly* upon *suitable* Objects, so there is Pain and Trouble in acting *vigorously* upon *unsuitable* ones. And therefore to make *Heaven* itself a *Happiness* to us, 'tis necessary not only that we should act vigorously upon the Objects of it, but that we should *so act* from a *Suitableness* of Temper to them: That we should contemplate God, submit to his Will, adore and imitate his Perfections from a *God-like Temper* and *Disposition*. For otherwise these Acts will be *Penances* instead of *Pleasures* to us; and the more *intensely* we exert them, the more *painful* they will be. And if we were in Heaven, all that heavenly Exercise in which the Happiness of it consists, would be but a *Torment* and *Vexation* to us, unless we had a *heavenly Temper*. For as the Parts of *Matter* can never *rest*, but do move about in a perpetual *Whirlpool*, till they *hit* into a Place or *Interstice* that is of the same *Form* and *Figure*

ANNEX 6[b–c] This passage is marked with three extra lines in the margin

with them; so there is nothing can *rest* in Heaven but what is *Heavenly*. All that is otherwise *rebounds* and *flies off* of its own accord, and can never *acquiesce* there, till 'tis of the same Form, and Temper, and Disposition with it. From hence therefore it's evident, that the Happiness of a Man in *Heaven* consists not so much in the *outward* Glory of the Place, as in the *inward* State of his own Mind, which, from a *Suitableness* of Temper to the heavenly Objects, doth always *freely* employ and exercise its Faculties about them.

ANNEX 7   pp 22–3

II. Another Virtue which appertains to a Man, considered merely as a *Rational Animal*, is *Moderation*; which consists in proportioning our *concupiscible* Affections to the just worth and value of Things; so as neither to spend our Affections *too prodigally* upon Trifles, nor yet be *oversparing* or *niggardly* of them to real and substantial Goods: But to *love, desire* and *expect* Things more or less, according to the Estimate which our best and most impartial *Reason* makes of their Worth and Goodness. For he that affects Things more than in the Esteem of Reason they deserve, affects them *irrationally*, and regulates his Passion by his *wild* and *extravagant* Imagination, and not by his *Reason* and *Judgment*. And while Men do thus neglect their *Reason*, and accustom themselves to *desire*, and *love*, and *affect* without it, they necessarily disable themselves to enjoy a *Rational Happiness*. For, besides that their Rational Faculties being thus *laid by*, and *unemployed*, will naturally contract *Rust*, and grow every Day more *weak* and *restive*; besides, that their *unexercised* Reason will *melt away* in Sloth and Idleness, and all its vital Powers *freeze* for want of motion, and, like standing Water, *stagnate* and gather mire, and by degrees *corrupt* and *putrify*, till at last it will be impossible to revive them to the *vigorous Exercise* and *Motion* wherein their Pleasure and Happiness consists: Besides this, I say, by habituating ourselves to affect Things *irrationally*, *i.e.* to love the *least* Goods *most*, and the *greatest least*, we shall disable ourselves from enjoying *any* Goods, but only such as cannot make us happy. For he that loves any Good more than it is worth, can never be happy in the enjoyment of it; because he *thinks* there is more in it than he *finds*, and so is always *disappointed* in the *Fruition* of it. And the *Grief* of being disappointed of what he *expects*, does commonly countervail the *Pleasure* of what he *finds* and *enjoys*. While he is in the *pursuit* of any Good which he *inordinately* dotes upon, he is *wild* and *imaginative*; he swells with *Fantastick* Joys, and juggles himself into *Expectations*, that are as large and boundless as his *Desires:* But when once he is *seiz'd* of it, and finds how vastly the *Enjoyment* falls short of his *Expectation*, his *Pleasure* is presently lost in his *Disappointment*, and so he remains as unsatisfied as ever. And thus if he were to spend an Eternity in such *Pursuits* and *Enjoyments*, his Life would be nothing but an Everlasting Succession of *Expectations* and *Disappointments*. So that all *inordinate* Affection destroys its own *Satisfaction*, and *necessarily* renders us by so many Degrees miserable, as it exceeds the real Worth and Value of Things.

Besides which, also, it is to be considered, that all these *lesser* Goods which are the Objects of our *Extravagant Affections*, are Things which we must ere long be for ever *deprived* of: For the *lesser* Goods are those, which are only good for the *worser* part of us, that is, for our *Body* and *Animal Life*; the proper Goods whereof are the *Outward Sensitive* Enjoyments of this World; all which, when we leave this World, we must leave *for ever*, and go away into Eternity, with nothing about us, but only the good or bad *Dispositions* of our Souls. So that if our soul be *carnaliz'd* thro' our *immoderate Affection* to the Things of this World, we shall carry that *Affection* with us, but leave the Things which we thus vehemently *affect* behind us for ever. For that which is the *prevailing Temper* of Souls in this Life, will doubtless be so in the other too; so far is that of the Poet true,

> *Quae gratia currûm*
> *Armorúmque fuit vivis, quae cura nitentes*
> *Pascere equos, eadem sequitur tellure repôstos.*

[The selfsame pride in chariot and arms that was theirs in life, the selfsame care in keeping sleek steeds, attends them when hidden beneath the earth. (Virgil *Aeneid* 6.653–5 tr H. Rushton Fairclough, LCL.)] For tho the coming into the other World, will questionless *improve* those Souls which are *really good* before; yet it is not to be imagined how it should *create* those *good*, who are *habitually bad*; and if we *retain* in the *other* World that *prevailing Affection* to these sensitive Goods which we *contracted* in *this*, it must necessarily render us unspeakably *miserable* there. For every *Lust* the Soul carries into the other World, will, by being eternally separated from its *Pleasures*, convert into an *Hopeless Desire*, and upon that account grow more *furious* and *impatient*. For of all the Torments of the Mind, I know none that is comparable to that of an outragious *Desire* joined with *Despair* of Satisfaction; which is just the Case of Sensual and Worldly-minded Souls in the other Life, where they are full of *sharp* and *unrebated* Desires, and, like starving Men, that are shut up between two dead Walls, are tormented with a *fierce* but *hopeless* Hunger, which, having nothing else to feed on, preys and quarries on *themselves*; and in this desolate Condition they are forced to wander to and fro, tormented with a restless *Rage*, an hungry and unsatisfied *Desire*, craving Food, but neither *finding* nor *expecting* any; and so in unexpressible Anguish they pine away a long Eternity. And tho they might find Content and Satisfaction, could they but *divert* their Affections another way, and reconcile them to the heavenly Enjoyments; yet being irrecoverably pre-engaged to sensual *Goods*, they have no savour or relish of any thing else, but are like *Feverish Tongues* that disgust and nauseate the most grateful Liquors, by reason of their own *over-flowing Gall:* So impossible is it for Men to be happy, either here or hereafter, so long as their Affections to the lesser Goods of this World do so immoderately exceed the worth and value of them.

One Essential Part therefore of the *Christian Life*, which is the Great *Means* of our Happiness, is the Virtue of *Moderation*; the peculiar Office whereof is to bound our *Concupiscible* Affections, and proportion them to the Intrinsick Worth of those outward Goods which we *affect* and *desire:* For tho the word *Moderation*, according to our present acceptation of it, be no where to be found in the New Testament, yet the Virtue expressed by it is frequently enjoined; as particularly where we are forbid to *set our Affections upon the Things of the Earth*, Col. iii. 2. *To love the World, or the Things that are in the World*, 1 John ii. 15. Which Phrases are not to be so understood, as if we were not to love the Enjoyments of the World *at all*; for they are the Blessings of God, and such as he has proposed to us in his Promises, as the *Rewards* and *Encouragements* of our Obedience; and to be sure, he would never encourage us to obey him by the Hope of such Rewards as are *unlawful* for us to desire and love: The meaning therefore of these

Prohibitions, is, that we should so *moderate* our Affections to the World, as not to permit them to exceed the real Worth and Value of its Enjoyments. For it is not *simply* our loving it, but our loving it to *such a degree* as is inconsistent with our Love of God, that is here forbidden: For *he that loveth the World* (saith St. *John*) *the love of the Father is not in him*; *i.e.* he that loves it to such a degree, as to *prefer* the Riches, Honours and Pleasures of it, *before God*, and his *Duty* to him, hath no real Love to God, *i.e.* he loves not God *as God*, as the chiefest Good, and supreme Beauty and Perfection. And hence *Covetousness*, which is an immoderate Desire of the World, is called *Idolatry*, Col. iii. 5. because it sets the World in the place of God, and gives it that supreme Degree of Affection, which is only due to Him; and this the Apostle there calls *Inordinate Affection*, because it extravagantly exceeds the intrinsick Worth and Value of its Objects.

ANNEX 8   p 24

Now that this also mightily contributes to our acquisition of the *heavenly Happiness*, is evident, not only from what hath been already said, but also from hence, that till our Affections are thus *moderated*, we can have no Savour or Relish of the *heavenly Enjoyments*. For in this corrupt State of our Nature, we generally *understand* by our *Affections*, which, like *coloured Glass*, represent all Objects to us in their own *Hue* and *Complexion*. When therefore a Man's *Affections* are immoderately carried out towards worldly Things, they will be sure by degrees to corrupt and deprave his *Judgment*, and render him as unfit to judge of Divine and Spiritual Enjoyments, as a *Plowman* is to be a *Moderator* in the *Schools*. For when a Man's Thoughts have been employed another way, and the Delights of *Sense* have for a long while preoccupied his *Understanding*, he will judge Things to be *Good* or *Evil*, according as they *disgust* or *gratify* his lower Appetites: And this being the Standard by which he measures Things, 'tis impossible he should have any Savour of those *Spiritual Goods* in which the Happiness of Heaven consists. For tho in his Nature there is a Tendency to *Rational Pleasures*, yet this he may, and very frequently does, stifle and extinguish, by addicting himself wholly to the Delights and Gratifications of his *Sense*, which by degrees will so melt down his *Rational* Inclinations into his *Sensual*, and confound and mingle them with his *Carnal Appetites*, that his *Soul* will wholly sympathize with his *Body*, and have all *Likes* and *Dislikes* in common with it; and there is nothing will be capable of pleasing the *one*, but what does gratify the unbounded Liquorishness of the *other*.

Now to such a Soul the spiritual World must needs be a *barren Wilderness*, where no Good grows that it can live upon, none but what is nauseous and distasteful to its *coarse* and *vitiated* Palate; where there are noble Entertainments, indeed, for Minds that are *contempered* to them, that have already tasted and experienced them, but not one drop of Water to cool the Tip of a *Sensual* Tongue, or gratify the Thirst of a *Carnal Desire*. So that were we admitted to that heavenly Place where the Blessed dwell, yet unless we had acquired their heavenly *Disposition* and *Temper*, we could never participate with them in their Pleasures. For so great would be the Antipathy of our sensual Affections to them, that we should doubtless fly away from them, and rather choose to be for ever *Insensible*, than be condemned to an everlasting *Perception* of what is so *ungrateful* to our Natures. So that till we have in some measure moderated our *Concupiscible Affections*, and weaned them from their excessive Dotages upon *sensual Good*, it is impossible we should enjoy the Happiness of Heaven: For such perfect Opposites are a *Spiritual* Heaven and a *Carnal* Mind, that unless This be *Spiritualized*, or That be *Carnalized*, it is impossible they should ever meet and agree.

ANNEX 9 pp 24–7

And in this Latitude, *Fortitude* comprehends not only *Courage*, as it is opposed to *Fear*; but also *Gentleness*, as it is opposed to *Fierceness*; *Sufferance*, as it is opposed to *Impatience*; *Contentedness*, as it is opposed to *Envy*; and *Meekness*, as it is opposed to *Malice* and *Revenge:* All which are the Passions of *weak* and *pusillanimous* Minds, that are not able to withstand an Evil, nor endure the least Touch of it, without being *startled* and *disordered*; that are so softned with Baseness and Cowardice, that they cannot resist the most gentle Impressions of Injury. For as sick Persons are offended with the Light of the Sun, and the Freshness of the Air, which are highly *pleasant* and *delightful* to such as are well and in Health; even so Persons of weak and feeble Minds are easily offended, their Spirits are so tender and effeminate, that they cannot endure the least Air of Evil should blow upon them; and what would be only a *Diversion* to a couragious Soul, *troubles* and *incommodes* them. And whatsoever Courage such Persons may pretend to, it's merely a Heat and Ferment of their Blood and Spirits; a Courage, wherein *Game-Cocks* and *Mastiffs* out-vie the greatest *Heroes* of them all. But as to that which is truly Rational and Manly, which consists in a firm Composedness of Mind, in the midst of evil or dangerous Accidents, they are the most wretched Cowards in Nature. For the true *Fortitude* of the Mind consists in being hardned against Evil upon *Rational Principles*; in being so fenced and guarded with *Reason* and *Consideration*, as that no dolorous Accident from without is able to invade it, or raise any violent commotions in it: In a word, in having such a constant Power over its *irascible* Affections, as not to be over-prone, either to be timorous in Danger, or envious in Want, or impatient in Suffering, or angry at Contempt, or malicious and revengeful under Injuries and Provocations. And till we have in some Measure acquired this Virtue, we can never be happy either here or hereafter.

For whilst we are in this World, we must expect to be encompassed with continual Crouds of evil Accidents, some or other of which will be always pressing upon and justling against us: So that if our Minds are *sore* and *uneasy*, and overapt to be *affected* with the Evil, we shall be continually *pained* and *disquieted*. For whereas were our Minds but *calm* and *easy*, all the evil Accidents that befal us, would be but like a Shower of Hail upon the Tiles of a Musick-House, which with all its *Clatter* and *Noise*, disturbs not the Harmony that is *within*; our being too apt to be moved into Passion by them, *uncovers* our Mind to them, and lays it open to the Tempest. *a*And commonly the greatest Hurt which these outward Evils do us, is, the *disturbing* our Minds into violent Passions; and this they will never cease doing, till we have thorowly *fortified* our Reason against them: For if our Reason commands not our Passions, to be sure *outward Accidents* will; and while they do so, we are Tenants at will to them for all our Peace and Happiness; and according as they happen to be *Good* or *Bad*, so must we be sure still to be *Happy* and *Miserable*. And in this Condition, like a Ship without a Pilot, in the

ANNEX 9*a–b* Marked with a second line in the outer margin

midst of a Tempestuous Sea, we are the sport of every Wind and Wave, and know not, till the Event hath determin'd it, how the next Billow will dispose of us; whether it will dash us against a *Rock*, or drive us into a quiet *Harbour*.[b]

So miserable is our Condition *here*, while we are utterly destitute of this Virtue of *Fortitude:* But much more miserable will the want of it necessarily render us *hereafter*. For all those *Affections* which fall under the Inspection and Government of *Fortitude*, are, in their *Excesses*, naturally vexatious to the Mind, and do always disturb and raise Tumults in it: For so *Wrath* and *Impatience* distracts and alienates it from itself, and confounds its Thoughts, and shuffles them together into a heap of wild and disorderly Fancies; so *Malice*, *Envy*, and *Revenge*, do fill it with anxious biting Thoughts, that, like young Vipers, gnaw the Womb that bears them, and fret and gall the wretched Mind that forms and gives them Entertainment. And tho in this World we are not so sensible of the mischief which these black and rancorous Passions do us; partly, because our sense of them is *abated* with the intermixture of our bodily Pleasures; and partly, because while we operate as we do, by these unwieldly Organs of Flesh, our Reflections cannot be comparably so *quick*, nor our Passions so *violent*, nor our Perceptions so *brisk* and *exquisite* as they will doubtless be, when we are stript into naked Spirits; yet if we go away into the other World with these *Affections unmortified* in us, they will not only be far more *violent* and *outragious* than now, and we shall not only have a far quicker Sense of them than now; but this our sharp Sense of them shall be *pure* and *simple*, without any intermixture of Pleasure to soften and allay it. And if so, Good Lord! What exquisite *Devils* and *Tormenters* will they prove, when an extreme *Rage* and *Hate*, *Envy* and *Revenge* shall be all together, like so many hungry Vultures preying on our Hearts; and our Mind shall be continually *baited* and *worried*, with all the furious Thoughts which these outragious Passions can suggest to us. When with the meagre Eyes of *Envy* we shall look up towards the Regions of Happiness, and incessantly *pine* and *grieve* at the Felicities of those that inhabit them; when, thro' a Sense of our own *Follies*, and of the miserable effects of them, our *Rage* and *Impatience* shall be heightned, and boiled up into a *diabolical Fury*; and when, at the same Time, an inveterate *Malice* against all that we converse with, and a fierce desire of *Revenging* ourselves upon those who have contributed to our Ruin, shall, like a Wolf in our Breasts, be continually gnawing and feeding upon our Souls, what an insupportable *Hell* shall we be to ourselves! Doubtless, that *outward Hell* to which bad Spirits are condemned is very terrible; but I cannot imagine, but that the worst of their Hell is *within* themselves, and that their own *devilish Passions* are severer *Furies* to them than all those *Devils*, that are without them. For *Wrath* and *Envy*, *Malice* and *Revenge*, are both the Nature and the Plague of Devils; and tho, as Angels, they are the Creatures of God; yet, as Devils, they are the Creatures of these their devilish *Affections*; they were *these* that transformed them from blessed Angels into cursed Fiends; and could they but once cease to be *envious* and *malicious*, they would cease to be Devils, and turn blessed Angels again. If then these rancorous *Affections* have such a malignant Influence, as to *blacken* Angels into Devils, and make them the most miserable, who were once the most *happy* Creatures; how can we ever expect to be happy, so long as we indulge and harbour them?

Wherefore, to remove this great Impediment of our Happiness, Christianity strictly enjoins us to practise this necessary Virtue of *Fortitude*, which consists in the due Regulation of all these our *Irascible Affections*; in moderating our

Anger and *Impatience*, suppressing our *Envy*, and extinguishing all our unreasonable *Hatred* and desire of *Revenge*. For hitherto tend all those Evangelical Precepts, which require us to *put away all bitterness and wrath, all clamour and evil-speaking, and malice*, Eph. iv. 31. *to lay aside all malice, and to be Children in malice*, I Pet. ii. 1. I Cor. xiv. 20. *to be strengthened with all might unto all patience and long-suffering*, Col. i. 11. And accordingly all the Virtues which are comprehended in this of *Fortitude*, are reckoned among the Fruits of that Blessed Spirit, by which we are to be guided and directed: *Gal.* v. 22. *But the fruit of the Spirit is peace, long-suffering, gentleness, goodness, and meekness*; all which are nothing but this great Virtue of *Fortitude*, severally exerting itself upon those several *Irascible Affections*, that are in us, and guiding and regulating them according to those Laws and Directions which Right Reason severally prescribes them; and setting such Bounds and Limits to each of them, as are necessary to the Peace and Happiness of our Rational Natures; that so when outward Dangers or Evils do excite them, they may not start out into such wild Excesses as to become *Plagues* and *Diseases* to our Minds.

Now how much the Practice of this Virtue conduces to our heavenly Happiness, is evident from hence, That all the Diseases and Distemperatures which our Mind is capable of, are nothing else but the *Excesses* of its *Concupiscible* and *Irascible Affections*; nothing but its being affected with Good and Evil *beyond* those Limits and Measures which Right Reason prescribes. ᶜDid we but love outward Goods according to the Value, at which true Reason rates them, we should neither be vexed with an *impatient Desire* of them, while we *want*, nor disappointed of our *Expectation*, while we *enjoy them*.ᵈ And when our Desires towards these outward Goods are reduced to that Coolness and Moderation, as neither to be *impatient* in the *Pursuit*, nor dissatisfied in the *Enjoyment* of them, it is impossible they should give any Disturbance to our Minds. And so on the other hand, did we but take care to regulate our Resentments of outward Evils and Dangers as Right Reason advises, they would never be able to *hurt* or *discompose* our Minds: For Right Reason advises, that we should not so resent them, as to *increase* and *aggravate* them; that we should not add the Disquietude of an *anxious Fear* to the Dangers that threaten us; nor the Torment of an *outragious Anger*, to the Indignities that are offered us; nor the Smart of a *peevish Impatience* to the Sufferings that befal us; in a word, that we should not aggravate our Want thro' an *invidious pining* at another's Fulness, nor sharpen the Injuries that are offered us by a *malicious* and *revengeful* Resentment of them. ᵉAnd he that follows the Advices of *Reason*, and conducts his *Irascible Affections* by them, has a Mind that is elevated above the Reach of Injury; that sits above the Clouds in a calm and quiet Aether, and with a brave Indifferency hears the rowling Thunders grumble and burst under its feet.ᶠ And whilst outward Evils fall upon *timorous* and *peevish* and *malicious* Spirits, like Sparks of Fire upon a heap of Gunpowder, and do presently blow them up, and put them all in Combustion; when they happen to a *dis-passionate* Mind, they fall like Stones on a Bed of Down, where they sit easily and quietly, and are received with a calm and soft Compliance. ᵍWhen therefore by the continual Practice of *Moderation* and *Fortitude*, we have tamed

ANNEX 9ᶜ⁻ᵈ Marked with a second line in the inner margin
ANNEX 9ᵉ⁻ᶠ Marked with a second line in the inner margin
ANNEX 9ᵍ⁻ʰ Marked with a second line in the inner margin

and civilized our *Concupiscible* and *Irascible* Affections, and reduced them under the Government of Reason, our Minds will be free from all *Disease* and *Disturbance*, and we shall be liable to no other Evil but that of bodily Sense and Passion.[h] So that when we leave our *Bodies*, and go into the World of *Spirits*, we shall presently feel ourselves in perfect *Health* and *Ease:* For the *Health* of a Reasonable Soul consists in being *perfectly Reasonable*, in having all its Affections *perfectly* subdued to a well-inform'd Mind, and clothed in the Livery of its Reason. And while it is thus, it cannot be diseased in that *Spiritual* State, wherein it will be wholly separated from all *bodily* Sense and Passion; because it has no Affection in it that can any way disturb or ruffle its calm and gentle Thoughts. And then feeling all within it self to be *well*, and as it should be; every String tuned into a perfect Harmony; every Motion and Affection corresponding with the most perfect *draughts* and *models* of its own Reason, it must needs highly *approve* of, and be perfectly *satisfied* with itself; and while it surveys its own Motions and Actions, it must necessarily have a most delicious Gust and Relish of them, they being all such as its best and purest Reason approves of, with a *full* and *ungainsaying* Judgment. And thus the Soul being cured of all irregular Affection, and removed from *all corporeal* Passion, will live in perfect *Health* and *Vigour*, and for ever enjoy within itself a Heaven of *Content* and *Peace*.

ANNEX 10   p 28

And hence, among other Reasons, it was, that the Primitive Christians did so severely abstain from bodily Pleasures, that by this means they might gently *wean* the Soul from the Body, and teach it before-hand to live upon the Delights of separated Spirits; that so, upon its Separation, it might drop into Eternity, like ripe Fruit from the Tree, with Ease and Willingness; and that by accustoming it before to *spiritual* Pleasures and Delights, it might acquire such a savoury Sense and Relish of them, as to be able, when it came into the *spiritual* World, to live wholly upon them . . .

ANNEX 11   p 31

. . . In short, that we should so effectually represent to ourselves the little Reason we have to be proud of any Personal Accomplishment, whether it be of Body or Mind, to strut, like *Aesop*'s Crow in these borrowed Feathers, which we could neither *give* to ourselves, nor *merit* of God, but are wholly owing for to the Divine Bounty; so to inculcate upon our Minds the Folly and Ridiculousness of being proud of any *outward Goods* we possess; such as fine Clothes, great Estates, or popular Reputation, all which are so far from either *making* or *speaking* us *wiser* or *better* Men, that they are too often the Fruits and Testimonies of our *Folly* and *Knavery:* And, in fine, That we should so impartially reflect upon the many Follies and Indiscretions, Errors, and Ignorances, Irregularities of Temper, Defects of Manners, and Deviations from Right Reason, that we are guilty of, as to shame ourselves out of all those *proud* and *arrogant* Conceits, that do so *swell* and *imposthumate* our Minds.

ANNEX 12   pp 34–5

But unless we do *now* acquaint our Minds with God, by frequent *thinking* and *meditating* upon him, we shall, by degrees, grow such *Strangers* to him, that by that Time we go into the other World, we shall be so far from being *pleased* with contemplating him, that we shall look upon him as an *uncouth* Object, and out of distaste *avert* and turn our Eyes from him: For the Mind of Man must be *familiariz'd* to its Objects, before it will be able to contemplate them with *Pleasure*; and tho the Objects themselves be never so *amiable*, yet while the Mind is *unus'd* to them, its Thoughts will *start* and *fly off* from them, and, without a great deal of Violence, will never be reduced to a *fix'd* and *serious* Attention to them.

ANNEX 13   p 35

To prevent which [i.e. our pining and languishing "under an eternal Discontentedness" at loss of "one of the sweetest Pleasures that Human Nature is capable of"], the Gospel injoins us to train up our Minds to Divine *Contemplation*, and to be frequently *thinking* and *meditating* upon God; to *mind those Things that are above*, for so the Greek Word is to be rendred, *Col.* iii. 1. *To sanctify the Lord God in our Hearts*, I Pet. iii. 15. that is, by entertaining great and worthy Thoughts of him: And therefore the Gospel is set before us as a *Glass*, that therein we may *contemplate and behold the Glory of God*, 2 Cor. iii. 18. namely, that Divine Glory which is therein discovered and revealed to us; that we may set him always before our Minds, and *gather up* our Thoughts about him, and force them to *dwell* and *stay* upon him, that so they may taste and relish his heavenly Beauties, and please and satisfy themselves with the View and Contemplation of them: For tho to meditate closely upon God, may at first be *irksom* and tedious to our unexperienc'd Minds; yet when by the constant Practice of it, we have worn off that *Strangeness* towards God, which renders the Thoughts of him so *troublesome* to us, and by frequent Converses are grown better acquainted with him, we shall grow, by degrees, so *pleased* and *satisfied* with the Thoughts of him, that we shall not know how to live *without* them; and our Minds at last will be touch'd with such a lively Sense of his attractive Beauties, that we shall never be well but while we are with him; so that he will become the constant Companion of our Thoughts, and the daily Theme of our *Meditations*; and nothing in the World will be so *grateful* and *acceptable* to us, as to retire now and then from the World, and converse with God in holy *Contemplations*. And tho, by reason of our present *Circumstances* and *Necessities*; there is no Remedy but our Thoughts must be often diverted from him, and forced to attend to our secular Occasions; yet, after they have been used a while to God, we shall find they will never be so well pleased, nor so much at ease, as when they are retired from every Thing but God, and composed and settled into Divine Meditations. So that when we go away into the other World, where we shall be removed from those troublesome *Circumstances* and *Necessities*, which did here so often divert our Thoughts from God, our Minds which have been so long accustomed and habituated to him, will immediately fasten upon him, and entirely devote themselves to the Contemplation of his Nature and Glory: For our Minds being already strongly *inclined* and *biassed* towards God, by those grateful Foretastes we have had of him in the Warmths of our Meditation; when we come into the still and quiet Regions of the Blessed, where we shall immediately have a more close and intimate View of him than ever, all our Thoughts will naturally run towards him, and be so captivated with the first sight of his Glory, that we shall never be able to look off again, as long as Eternity endures; but *one* View will invite us to *another*, and what we see will so transport and ravish us, that we shall still desire to see farther and farther. And because our finite Mind will never be able fully to comprehend all that is *knowable* in his infinite Being, we shall be so delighted in every farther Knowledge of him, that we shall still desire to know farther; and that *Desire*, as fast as it springs, shall still be satisfied with a farther *Knowledge*, and so to eternal Ages, each new Satisfaction shall immediately spring a new Desire, and each new Desire immediately terminate in a new Satisfaction.

ANNEX 14   p 50

So that 'tis impossible for him to be mistaken in his Choices, because he knows as well before-hand what Things *would* be to us if they *were*, as what they *are* when they do *actually* exist. Upon the whole therefore, 'tis doubtless of inestimable advantage to us, to be in the Hands of God, and verily, next to Hell itself, I know nothing that is more formidable, than for God to let us alone, and give us up to our own Wills and Desires. And should he call to us from Heaven, and tell us, that he was resolved to cross our Desires no more, but to comply with all our Wishes, let the Event prove good or bad, we should have just reason to look upon ourselves as the most *forlorn* and *abandoned* Creatures on this side Hell, as Persons excluded from the greatest Blessing that belongs to a Creature; and if we had any hope of his re-acceptance of us, it would be infinitely our Interest to *resign* back ourselves, and all our Concerns to him, and on our bended Knees to beseech him, above all Things, not to leave us to *ourselves*, or throw us from *his* Care and Conduct.

ANNEX 15   pp 64–5

So that whatsoever wicked Temper we carry with us into Eternity, we shall be sure to meet with it in every individual Member of the Society of the Wicked; and consequently if we carry thither with us a *perverse* and *untreatable* Temper, that will not endure either to *submit* or *condescend*, we shall be sure to find the same Humour reigning thro'out all the Society of the Wicked. . . . "when all our whole Society shall consist of a Company of *stiff* and *stubborn* Spirits, that will neither *submit to*, nor *bear with* one another, but every one will have his will upon every one, so far as he is able to force and extort it; when those that are superior in Might and Power, do all rule with a *fierce* and *tyrannical* Will,[b] and will *condescend* to nothing that is beneficial for their Subjects . . . how is it possible but that they should be all of them in a most *wretched* and *miserable* Condition?

ANNEX 16   pp 88–9

IV. Consider, that when once we have *begun* it *well*, we have conquered the *main* Difficulty of this our Spiritual *Warfare*: For tho it be an easy Matter to begin *ill*, to resolve against our Sins in a *sudden* Pet, or *transient* Heat of Passion; yet it must be confessed, that to resolve *well*, and *wisely*, that is, with that firm *Belief* and thorow *Consideration* of Things, with that *Shame* and *Sorrow*, and those earnest *Cries* to Heaven for Aid and Assistance, which are necessary to the founding of a *strong* and *lasting* Resolution, is not so easy a Matter: For in all those

---

ANNEX 15[a] The intervening lines (indicated by points of ellipsis) are not marked; C's marginal line resumes here
ANNEX 15[b] Marginal line ends here

preparatory Exercises, we have a *roving* Mind, a *hard* Heart, and a *perverse* Nature to contend with; and we shall find it a very hard Matter to call in our *wandring* Thoughts, and unite them together into a *fixt* and *steady* Consideration of the Evidences of the Truth of Religion, and of the Duties and Motives and Difficulties of it. And whilst we are entertaining them with this *unwonted* Argument there are a thousand Objects with which they are better *acquainted*, that will be calling them away; so that without a great deal of Violence to ourselves, we shall never be able to keep them *together* so long, as is necessary to the forming a firm *Assent* to the *Truth*, and the passing a true and impartial *Judgment* upon the *Proposals* of Religion. And when we have fixt our Thoughts into a serious Consideration of the *Evidences* of Religion, we shall find, that our *Lusts* will object much more against them than our *Reason*; that *they* will be casting *Mists* before our Eyes and *bribing* and *byassing* our Understanding the other way; and that thereupon 'twill be more difficult than we are aware, to convince ourselves thorowly of the Truth of a Religion that is so diametrically opposite to our vicious Inclinations: But when this is done, and we proceed to consider the *Duties* of Religion, and to balance the Motives with the Difficulties of them, in order to the obtaining of ourselves a *full* and *free* Consent to them; here again we shall find ourselves at a mighty Plunge: For tho the Motives to our Duty are, at first View, infinitely *greater* and more *considerable* than the Difficulties of it; tho it be unspeakably more *intolerable* to lose the Joys of Heaven, and incur the Pains of Hell, than to endure the *sharpest* Brunts of this Spiritual Warfare; yet *these* being *present* and *sensible*, have a more immediate Access to us, and consequently are apter to move us than either of those Motives, which are both of them *future* and *invisible.* . . .
But when we have *effectually* convinced ourselves, that those Difficulties of our Duty are much less considerable than the Motives to them, we shall find it a hard Task to persuade our Wills into a *free* and *explicit* Consent to all the *Particulars* of it: For now we shall find a strong *Aversation* in our Natures to *sundry* of those Duties that call for our *Approbation*, and there will be a mighty Counter-striving between our *Reason* and *Inclinations*. Our darling Lusts, those Bosom-Orators within us, will now employ all their Rhetorick to dissuade us from parting with them; they will *clasp* about our Souls, like *departing* Lovers, and use all their *Charms* and *Allurements* to hold us fast, and reconcile themselves to us; and under these Circumstances, tho we have all the Reason in the World on our side, we shall find it will be no such easy matter effectually to dispose our Wills to *close* with so many *offensive* Duties, and *part* with so many *beloved* Sins: But when *this* is done, which, to be sure, will cost us many a violent *Struggle* and *Contention* with ourselves, there are *other* Difficulties to be mastered: For now we must *reflect* upon our past ill Life, and expose it to our own Eyes in all its natural *Horror*, *Turpitude*, and *Infamy*, and never leave reproaching ourselves with the *Foulness* and *Disingenuity*, the *Madness* and *Folly* of it, till we find our Hearts affected with *Shame* and *Sorrow* for, and *Indignation* against it. And for us that have been so long used to *cokes* and *flatter* ourselves, to *paint* and *varnish* our Deformities, and crown our Brows with *forced* and *undeserved* Applauses; for *us* to *condemn* and *upbraid* ourselves, to strip our Actions of all their *artificial* Beauty, and set ourselves before our own Eyes in all our *naked*, *undisguised* Ugliness, and not look off till we have lookt ourselves into *Shame* and *Horror*, and *Hatred* of ourselves, will be, at first especially, a very *ungrateful* Employment; and yet it may be a good while, perhaps, before our *hard* and *unmalleable* Hearts will yield to

the Impressions of *Godly Sorrow* and *Remorse:* But when this Difficulty is conquered, our Work is not yet *totally* finished: For now we must *come off* from ourselves, and all our *presumptuous* Dependences upon our own Ability and Power, and in a deep Sense of our own most wretched *Weakness* and *Impotency*, throw ourselves wholly upon God, and with *earnest* and *importunate* Out-cries, implore his gracious Aid and Assistence. And let me tell ye, to Men that have been all along inured to such glorious Conceits of themselves, such mighty Confidences in their own Abilities; that have promised themselves, from time to time, that at *such* and *such* a Time, they would repent and amend, as if, without God's Help, 'twere in *their* Power to repent when they *pleased*; for such Men as these, I say, to come out of themselves and their own *Self-confidences*, and wholly cast themselves upon a foreign Help; so sensibly to *feel*, and ingenuously to *own* their own Inability, as to fly to God, and confess themselves *lost* and *undone* without him, is a much harder Matter than we can well imagine, till we come to make the Experiment: And yet this, all *this*, must be done, before we can be well prepared to *resolve* upon the *Christian Warfare*.

This I have the longer insisted on, because I would deal *plainly* with you, and shew you the *worst* of Things: For whether you are told of it or no, you will find it, if ever you make the Experiment, that all your good *Resolutions*, without these *Preparations*, will soon unravel in the *Execution*; and that after you have resolv'd a thousand times over, you will be just where you are, and not one Step farther in Religion. But for your Encouragement, know, that when, with *these* necessary Preparations, you have *solemnized* your Resolution, you have won the *main* and *toughest* Victory in all your Spiritual Warfare; a Victory by which you have *pulled down* your Sin from its Throne, and *broken* and *disarrayed* its Power and Forces; so that now you are upon the Pursuit of a *flying* Enemy; and if you do but diligently *follow* your Blow, and *pursue* your brave Resolution thro' all Temptations to the contrary, and do not suffer your vanquished Enemy to *rally* and *reinforce* himself against ye, you will sensibly perceive his Strength decay . . .

ANNEX 17   p 91

And at first especially, while our good Resolution is yet in its *Infancy*, it will be very necessary that we should, every Day, before we go abroad into the World, spend some Portion of Time in *fore thinking* of the many Temptations that do lie in wait for us, whether in our *Business* or *Company*, or necessary *Refreshments* and *Diversions*; and *fore-arming* ourselves against them with the Motives and Arguments of our Religion; that so we may have our Weapons ready when-ever they shall assault us, and be always provided to resist them.

ANNEX 18   pp 92–3

And tho if when we were forming our Resolution, we considered the whole Matter, we could not but *foresee* great Difficulties in the Execution of it, And be very sensible what strong Inclinations from *within*, and Temptations from *without* we were to *struggle* and *contend* with; yet, alas! the Difficulties of all Undertakings are usually much less in our *Fore-sight*, than in our *Sense* and *Experience* of them: For while they are in our Fore-sight, we have only the *Notions* and *Ideas* of them to encounter, and these being not so stubborn as *the Things themselves*, are much more easily conquered by us. So that when instead of our own *easy* and *compli*-

ant Notions we come to contend with the Difficulties *themselves*, we very often find the Face of Things quite *changed*, and those Difficulties which did so easily *submit* to our *Apprehensions*, do many times make an obstinate *Resistance* to our *Endeavours*. And thus many times it is in the Matter in hand: So that when we are *fore-casting* the Difficulties of Religion in our Minds, we must always allow for the *Distance* of them, which usually *lessens* their Appearance; and conclude with ourselves, that when we are *actually* engaged with them, we *find* them much more *stiff* and *incompliant* to our *Endeavours* than they are now to our *Thoughts*; and accordingly *prepare* and *arm* ourselves against them: For when from *considering* we proceed to *encounter* them, we must expect to find, that to *discourse* and *execute*, are Things of a widely different Nature; and that those Difficulties which we so easily *vanquished* in our Thoughts and Discourses, will, when we are actually *contending* with them put us to a much harder Trial of our *Valour* and *Constancy* than we were aware of.

ANNEX 19   p 93

... and then you will need a *world* of Patience and Courage to undergo all that *Shame* and *Reproach*, *Loss* and *Pain*, *Fear* and *Suffering*, thro' which you must fight your way to Heaven if ever you come there. Since therefore this *may* happen to ye, and is not altogether *unlikely*, it concerns ye, as ye hope for Heaven, to *fore-arm* and *prepare* yourselves against it.

ANNEX 20   p 93

For when they see that he himself *practises* what he *teaches*, that is an *ocular* Demonstration to them that 'tis *practicable*. So that good Example carries in it this strong Encouragement to Goodness, that there is nothing in it but what is *possible*, and that the greatest Difficulties that attend it are such as may be *conquered* by Diligence and sincere Endeavour. And as it gives us the most *sensible* Direction and Encouragement to Virtue, so it also represents it to us to the greatest *Advantage*. And whereas Precepts and Discourses of Virtue are only the *Pictures* and *Artificial* Descriptions of it, a virtuous Example is Virtue *animated* and exposed to our view in all its *living* Charms and Attractions.

ANNEX 21   p 95

... our Saviour tells his Disciples, *John* xiii. 15. *I have given you an Example* (that is, of Humility and Charity) *that you should do as I have done to you*; and 'tis one of his great Commands that we should *learn of him who was meek and lowly of heart*, with a promise, that in so doing, *we should find rest unto our Souls*, Mat. xi. 29.

ANNEX 22   p 99

Whereas when a Man's Intention *purely* respects God, 'twill be *immoveably* fixt among all the Changes and Alterations from without. For there is no outward Change or *Capricio* of Fortune can hinder a Man from pleasing God, whose Love to us depends not upon our being *poor* or *rich*, *pleased* or *pained*, *depressed* or *advanced*, but upon our being truly *Virtuous* and *Religious*. And therefore if our

Aim be *purely* to please him, we shall be sure to continue so, which side soever Fortune smiles upon.

ANNEX 23   p 100

Wherefore to our successful Progress in Religion it is highly necessary that, so far as in us lies, we should *abstract* and *separate* our Religious Intentions from all these *worldly* Respects; and this must be done by looking frequently up to God, and actually *referring* and *dedicating* our Actions to him; by shutting our Eyes, when we are entering upon any Duty, to all worldly Considerations, and determining with ourselves, *this* I will do purely because 'tis *Godlike*, or because God hath *commanded* it; whether I shall be *commended* or *disgraced* for it, whether I shall *get* or *lose* by it, I will not now regard; it is sufficient that it is *good*, and that God hath commanded it, and therefore for this Reason *only* I will do it, without any other Respect or Consideration.

ANNEX 24   p 120

. . . if we were left to *struggle* with the Difficulty of it in our own single Strength, we might justly *despair* of Success, and so tamely *lie down* and *yield* ourselves *foil'd* and *defeated.* But, God be praised, this is not our Case; for tho when we cast our Eyes upon the many violent Inclinations to evil that are *within* us, and upon the *numberless* Temptations to evil that are *about us*; when we seriously reflect upon the *Weakness* of our Reason, and the *Strength* of our *Lust*, and the *Number* and *Nearness* and *Prevalency* of those Objects from without, that are continually *pressing upon* and *assaulting* our good Resolutions; tho, I say, when we reflect upon all this, we are ready to cry out as *Elisha's* Servant did, when he beheld the City compassed with Horses and with Chariots, *Alas Master, how shall we do?* How shall we be able to withstand all this mighty Army of Enemies? Yet if we turn our Eyes from our *own* Weakness, and our *Enemies* Strength, to those gracious Promises of *Assistance*, which the Father of Mercies hath made to us, we shall quickly be able to answer *ourselves*, as *Elisha* did *him*, *Fear not*, O my Soul, *for they that are with us are more*, and more powerful, *than they that are against us* . . .

ANNEX 25   p 121

When Men are told how many Duties are necessary to their successful *Progress* in Religion, what *Patience* and *Constancy*, what frequent *Examinations* and *Trials* of themselves, what lively *Thoughts* and *Expectations* of Heaven, &c. they are apt to conclude, that if they should engage to do *all* this, they must resolve to do nothing *else*, but even shake Hands with all their *secular* Business, and Diversions, and *cloyster* up themselves from all other Affairs; [a]which is a very great Mistake, proceeding either from their not *considering*, or not *understanding* the Nature of these Religious Exercises, the greatest Part of which are such as are to be wholly transacted in the Mind, whose Motions and Operations are much more *nimble* and *expedite* than those of the Body, and so may be very well *intermixt*

ANNEX 25[a] Line begins here

with our *secular* Employments, without any *Lett* or *Hindrance* to them: For what great Time is there required for a Man now and then to revolve a few *wise* and *useful* Thoughts in his Mind, to *consider* the Nature of an Action when it *occurs*, and *reflect* upon an Error when it's *past* and hath *escaped* him?

ANNEX 26   p 132

. . . or submitted ourselves to her *Guides* without apparent Danger of being *misled* by them into the Pit of Destruction, or join'd with her publick *Services* without *worshipping* of *Creatures*, or received her *Sacraments*, without practising the grossest *Superstitions* and *Idolatries*. But when she had made it necessary for us either to *sin with*, or *separate from* her, we could have no other *honest* Remedy but only to *withdraw*; and if in this our *Separation* there had been a sinful *Schism* on either side, we could have appealed to Heaven and Earth, *whose* the Guilt of it was; *theirs* that forced us upon it, or *ours* that were forced to it. But yet the Case of *our* Separation from the *Church of Rome*, is vastly different from that of the Separation of *private* Members from their own *particular* Churches. For we affirm that the *Church of Rome* is but a *particular* Church, whose *Authority* extends no farther than to its own *native* Members, and consequently hath no more Power to impose Laws of Communion upon *us*, than *we* have upon *her*; our particular Church being altogether as *distinct* and *independent* from *her*, as *she* is from *ours*. So that tho the Terms of Communion she imposes upon her own Members, were all of them *lawful* and *innocent*, yet do they no more *oblige* us as we are *Christians* of the *Church of England*, than the *lawful* Commands of the *Great Mogul* do, as we are *Subjects* of the *Kingdom of England*.

ANNEX 27   pp 619–20

Fifthly and Lastly, Another of the *Miseries* which affect Men's Souls is *Impotency*, or Want of *Power* to recover themselves out of their vicious Courses; for a *vicious State* doth so miserably *weaken* and *disable* Men's Faculties, so *impair* the Health and Vigour of their Minds, that it is not in their *Power* to help and recover themselves out of it. For to their Recovery it is necessary, first, that their Thoughts should be determined to a fixed and exact *Consideration* of the Evil and Danger of their Sins, and of the blessed Hopes which God hath set before them to tempt them to renounce and forsake them: And then that these *Considerations* should so prevail upon and influence their *Wills*, as to captivate them into a thorough Resolution of Amendment; both which Effects are out of the Reach of the Sinner's *Power* considered singly, and without the Concurrence of the *Divine Grace*. For his Mind is so *depressed* and *bowed* down towards these earthly and sensible Objects which have been hitherto the sole Companions of his Thoughts, that it is not *able* to raise up it self to the *Consideration* of Divine Things: And though now and then, a good Meditation may break in upon him, and seize upon his Thoughts, yet it cannot hold them a quarter of an Hour together; they are so *roving* and *slippery*, so *backward* and *averse* to any Thing that is *serious* and *divine:* So that unless the *Divine Spirit* lays hold upon them, and by his *Powerful* and *Importunate Inspirations* confines and fixes them, the *Man* will never be able to reduce them to any *fast* and *steady Consideration*. And when with the *Holy Spirit*'s Assistance he hath effected this, he hath a *perverse* and *obstinate* Will to deal with; which no Considerations will be able to determine to a fixed Resolution of Amendment, but what are set home upon his Mind, and continually *actuated* and *enlivened* with the vigorous Influence of the *Spirit of God*. So that of himself every habitual Sinner is a most *weak* and *impotent* Creature, that with all the Powers of his *Mind* and *Will*, the utmost Efforts and Strugglings of his *own Faculties*, is not able without a *supernatural* Aid to rescue himself from Sin and Misery. For how many sorrowful Instances do we every Day converse with of Men, who in their *sober Thoughts* will sadly lament their own Follies, and blush in the Morning when they remember how their Brains were set a float by their last Night's Intemperance; who yet when the *next Temptation* beckons them to their Lust again, return as greedily to it as ever; and though, when they have *repeated* their Sin, they *curse* it and *resolve* against it, yet when they are tempted, sin again, and then weep and call themselves *miserable:* but still alass! the same *Inchantment* confines them to the same *Circle?* Now in this, *Philosophy* is at a stand, nor can there any other rational Account be given of it, but only the miserable *Frailty* and *Impotence* which Men contract by *vicious Courses*. What then is to be done for these miserable Persons in this their *forlorn* and *helpless* Condition? Why, besides all the above named Instances of *Mercy*, which we are obliged even for Pity's sake to apply to them; we are also bound in *Mercy* earnestly to recommend their woful Condition to the *God* of all Grace and Compassion, to beseech *him* to commiserate their Impotence, and with the outstretched arm of *his Grace* to touch their dead Souls, and to raise them up into Newness of Life. For though in all Cases of Misery, *Prayer* is a proper Act of *Mercy*, yet there is none that doth so much need and call for our Prayers as *this:* For in all *other* Cases, either it is in the Power of the *Miserable* to help themselves, or it is in the Power of the *Merciful* to rescue and relieve them, or their Miseries are such as will quickly *end* and *expire* into eternal Ease; but as for the Misery of the *obstinate Sinner*, it is such as *God* alone can remedy, and such as if it be not remedied the sooner, will quickly determine in *endless* and *remediless* Misery. Wherefore if we have any *Bowels* of *Mercy* or *Compassion* in us, how can we sit still and see an impotent Sinner bound as it were to the Stake of Perdition, and not able to escape, though he sees the Flames of Hell rising round about him; without lifting up our Eyes to *God*, in whom alone his *Help* and *Salvation* lies, and earnestly imploring him to commiserate the perishing Wretch, and to snatch him from his approaching Ruin? Wherefore as the Law of *Mercy* obliges us in general to pray for *all* that are in *Misery*, so more especially for these *wretched Creatures*, who are already within the Suburbs of endless Misery; and unless *God* stretches forth his Arm and saves them, will be within a few moments beyond the reach of *Prayer* and *Mercy*. And thus you see what those Instances of *Mercy* are, which we are obliged to exercise towards the *Souls* of Men: And for the Enforcement of our Duty herein, I shall subjoyn some *Considerations* to excite our Christian Compassion.

I. Consider the inestimable *Worth* of those *Souls*, upon which your *Mercy* is to be employed. I confess, were the *Souls* of Men of the same Alloy with their *Bodies*, whose highest Pleasures do consist in the Gratification of a few brutish *Senses*, and are nothing else but the agreeable Touches of certain little Skins and Arteries, which are as inconsiderable as a Lutestring; and which, after they have repeated these Pleasures some Twenty or Thirty Years, do commonly expire into

Insensibility and *Rottenness*; were, I say, their *Souls* of the *same* Make and Frame, it were not so much to be admired that we are so indifferently affected towards them. But these *precious Beings* . . .

III. Another *Instrument* of *Mortification* is a hearty and well-grounded *Resolution*; and indeed without a *firm Resolution* it is in vain for us to attempt the *mortifying* of our Lusts, or any *difficult* Undertaking whatsoever. For there is a wide Distance between *Thoughts* and *Things*, and 'tis much easier to *discourse* of Things than to pass them into *Execution*; for *clear Reasonings* are accompanied with a wonderful Delight, because there we engage only with *Designs*; and fighting only with the *Idea's* of Things, they will easily suffer themselves to be conquered by us, and taken captive at our Will; but when we pass into *Practice*, that will revolt and oppose us in the *Execution*, which was so very compliant to the *Thought* and *Meditation*; then you will find that you must *wrestle* stoutly with those *Difficulties* that will make Head against you, and that these will put you to a greater Proof of your *Valour* and Constancy than ever you did imagine; so that unless you are armed with a great Strength of *Resolution*, you will be beaten off at the first Attempt, and meeting with greater *Resistance* than you expected, be forced upon a base and cowardly *Retreat*. Now to form a firm *Resolution* requires a great deal of *Prudence* and good *Conduct*; for it is of a great Avail in all Cases to *begin well*; and as a Foundation well laid doth secure the Superstructure, so a *Resolution* well form'd will render the *Execution* of what we are to do a great deal more easie and feasible. Before we do resolve therefore on *mortifying* our *Lusts*, let us be sure to make use of the former *Instrument* of *Mortification*; that is, let us acquaint our selves with all those mighty Arguments against Sin, wherewith either our *Reason* or *Religion* can furnish us; and let us consider them over and over, till they are *familiar* to our Understandings, and our *Thoughts* have extracted the *utmost Force* of them; for which End it will be necessary for us to seek Direction from our *Spiritual Guides*. Then let us seriously consider with our selves, *what* it is that we are about to do, what *Vices* we must divorce, and what *Virtues* we must espouse; and let us thoroughly inform our selves beforehand of all the foul *Ways*, and steep *Ascents*, and dangerous *Precipices* that are in the Road of our Duty; and then as you go along in your Meditations, ask your own Hearts whether there be any Passage that they *startle* at, or whether notwithstanding all, they are *seriously willing* you should go on? Remonstrate to your own Souls, that in such a Place your *Lust* will be tempting you with the *genial* Pleasures of an *adulterous Bed*, and desire them to deal *plainly* with you whether they can be deaf to those *bewitching Invitations*; tell them that before you have gone many Paces farther, the Wants of *poorer Men* than your selves will be soliciting your *Charity*, and desire to know of them whether they are willing you should *do good* and *trust God* for a Repayment; represent to them how highly you may be *provoked* at the next Step by the *injurious* Carriage of some insolent *Adversary*, and know of them whether they are willing to *contain* their savage *Passions* within the Bars of *Reason* and *Sobriety*; and so go on in your own *Thoughts* through all the Paths of your *Duty*, and never cease putting these and such like *Questions* distinctly to your own Souls, till they give an *express Consent* to every *Duty* that presses for a Resolution. And it will very much conduce to the settling of a *fixed Judgment* in you, if you do not conclude too *soon*, but *weigh* all these Things over again; if you would ask your selves the next Morning, whether you still *continue* of the same Mind, and whether your former *Consent* was not the Effect of a *present Heat*, or whether now after the Cool of the Night you do *still allow* of it; for in all probability if you *resolve* in Haste, you will repent at Leisure. And this, I doubt not, is the Bane of most of our good *Resolutions*, that generally they are the Effects of some *transitory Passion*, and not of a *sober Judgment* and *serious Deliberation*; for when Men resolve well in Heats of *Passion*, they resolve to do they know not what themselves, but swallow their Religion by the *Lump*, without considering the *Particulars* of it; and so they do by their *Duty*, as Men do with bitter *Pills*, which they can swallow *whole*, but when they come to *chew*, those prove so distasteful, that presently they spit them out again. When therefore you have calmly *considered* with your selves all the *Arguments* against your Sins, and all the *Difficulties* of forsaking them, and you have *reason'd* your Wills into an *express Consent* to part with them for ever; then betake your selves to your bended Knees, and in the most solemn Manner devote your selves unto God: *O Lord, I acknowledge, I have been a great Offender against thee, and that my past Life has been nothing else but a continued Rebellion; but now I see my Folly, and am ashamed to think what a notorious Offender I have been; wherefore here I solemnly promise in thy dreadful Presence, and in the Presence of all thy holy Angels, that where-ever I have done amiss, I will do so no more; be Witness, O thou righteous Judge of the World, that here I shake Hands with all my darling Lusts, and bid them adieu for ever; wherefore be gone ye Soul-destroying Vipers, that have twined so long about me; away, ye wretched Idols, whom I have too long adored; for in the Name of God I am fully resolved never to entertain you more.* And now having reduced our selves to a *good Resolution* of Mind, our greatest Difficulty is over; for so long as we keep our *Resolution*, we are *invincible*, and all the Powers of *Hell* will not be able to *prevail* against us. For our Wills are not to be *forced* by any Power whatsoever, and there is no *Temptation* in the World can make us *return* to our *Sin*, so long as we are heartily *resolved* against it; so that all we have now to do is to keep the Ground we have gotten, and not to suffer our *spiritual Enemies* to batter down those *good Resolutions* we have raised against them, which if we can but maintain will infallibly secure us against all their *Power* and *Malice*.

ANNEX 29   pp 672–3

Now the *holy Angels*, being the Ministers of the *divine Providence*, have great Advantages of assisting us in our *Duties*, and serving the Interests of our *Souls*; which Advantages to be sure their own *Goodness* and *Benignity* will prompt them to make the utmost Improvement of. They have many Opportunities to *present* good Objects to us, and to *remove* Temptations from us, of *disciplining* our Natures by *Prosperities* and *Afflictions*, and of *ordering* and *varying* our outward Circumstances, so as to render our *Duty* more *facile* and *easie* to us. And besides, as they are *Spirits* they have a very *near* and *familiar* Access to our *Souls*; not that they can make any *immediate Impressions* upon our Understandings, or Wills, which is a Sphere of Light to which no *created Spirit* can approach, but is under the immediate Oeconomy of the *Father of Spirits*: But yet being *Spirits*, I conceive, they may easily insinuate themselves into our *Fancies*, and mingle with the *Spirits* and *Humours* of our Bodies; and by that means suggest *good Thoughts* to us, and raise *holy Affections* in us. For that they can work upon our *Fancies* is apparent; else there could be neither *Diabolical* nor *Angelical* Dreams. And if they can so act upon our *Fancies*, as to excite new *Images* and *Representations* in them, they may by this means communicate new *Thoughts* to the *Understanding*; which naturally prints off from the *Fancy* all those Ideas, and Images which it sets and composes. And as they can work upon our *Fancies*, so they can also upon our *Spirits* and *Humours*; else they have not the Power of *curing*, or *inflicting* a Disease; and by thus working upon our *Spirits* they can in some measure *moderate* the Violence of our *Passions*, which are nothing but the *flowings* and *reflowings* of the *Spirits* to and fro from the Heart: And by working upon our *Humours* they can compose us to such a *sedate* and *serious Temper*, as is most apt to receive *religious Impressions*, and to be *influenc'd* by the Motions of the *Holy Ghost*. These Things I doubt not but the *blessed Angels* can do, and many Times do, though we *perceive* it not: And though possibly by the *Laws* of the World of *Spirits* they may be *restrained* from doing their *utmost* for us, that so we may still act with an uncontrouled *Freedom*, and be left under a Necessity of *constant* and *diligent* Endeavour, yet doubtless their *Assistance* is not wanting to us; but as the *evil Angels* are always ready to *pervert* and *seduce* us, so the *good* are no less ready to *reform* and *recover* us. And since whatsoever they do for us, they do as the *Agents* and *Ministers* of the *divine Spirit*; whatsoever we do by their Assistance, we do by the *Holy Spirit*.

IV. And *lastly*, let us consider the *internal* Motions and Operations of the *Holy Ghost* upon our *Souls*. For besides all those Assistances which the *Holy Spirit* vouchsafes to us by his *Word*, and his *Providence*, and his holy *Angels*; he does also very powerfully *aid* and *help* us by his own *immediate Motions* and *Suggestions*. For that the Ministrations of *Religion* have been always accompanied with the *internal* Operations of the *Spirit*, is evident from that *miraculous* Success that *Religion* hath found in the World: For I cannot imagine how *Christianity*, that never was beholding to *humane Force* and *Power*, but instead of that found all the Powers of the World armed *against* it, and had so many mighty *Prejudices* to combate, before ever it could be admitted to speak with Mens *Reason*; I say, I cannot imagine, how under such Circumstances it could have *thrived* and *flourished* as it did, had it not been accompanied with an *invisible Power* from *above*. For how did it *triumph* in its very *Infancy* over all the Power and Malice of the World, growing like the *Palm-tree* by Depression, and *conquering* in the midst of *Flames?* What wonderful *Alterations* did it make in the *Lives* and *Manners* of Men, transformed in an Instant the *debauched* and *dissolute* into Patterns of the strictest *Temperance* and *Sobriety*, and with its mighty Charms turning *Wolves* into *Lambs*, and *Vultures* into *Turtle-doves?* Which wondrous Effects were so very frequent, that the *Heathens* themselves took special Notice of them; which, as *St. Austin* tells us, made them to attribute its Success to the Power of *Magick*; thinking it impossible that it should do such Wonders, without the Assistance of some *powerful Spirit*. And indeed it is not to be supposed, how it could work such *strange* and *sudden Alterations* in Men, by its *external* Arguments and Motives, without a *divine Power* concurring with them and animating and enforcing them: And though now that *Christianity* hath gotten such footing in the World, and is become the Religion of *Nations*, the *divine Spirit* does not *ordinarily* work upon Men in such a *strange* and *miraculous* Way; but proceeds in more *human* Methods by joining in with our *Understandings*, and leading us forward by the Rules of *Reason* and *Sobriety*; so that whatsoever Aids it affords us, they work in the *same Way*, and after the *same Manner*, as if all were performed by the Strength of our *own Reason*; yet we have a *standing Promise* which extends to all Ages of *Christianity*, that to him who *improves* the Grace which he hath already, *more* Grace shall be given; that if we *work out our Salvation with Fear and Trembling*, God will work in us *to will and to do*; and that he will give his *holy Spirit* to every one that sincerely *asks*, and *seeks* it. For of the *Performance* of this *Promise*, there are none of us all but have had many *sensible Experiences*; for how often do we find *good Thoughts* injected into our Minds we know not *how* nor *whence?* How frequently are we *seiz'd* with *strong* and *vehement* Convictions of the Folly and Danger of our own wicked Courses, even in the *midst* of our loose *Mirth* and *Jollity*, when we are *rock'd* into a deep *Security*, when we have *endeavour'd* to *chase* good Thoughts from our Minds, or to *drown* them in *Sensuality* and *Voluptuousness?* How often have we been *haunted* with their *Importunities*, till we have been *sear'd* by them into sober *Resolutions?* And when we have complied with them, what *Joys* and *Refreshments* have we sometimes found in the Discharge of our *Duty*, to encourage us to *Perseverance* in Well-doing? All which are *plain* and *sensible* Instances of the *internal* Operations of the *holy Spirit* upon our Souls. So that when we comply with these *inward* Motions of the *Holy Ghost*, so as to forsake those Sins which they dissuade us from, we do then *mortify the Deeds of the Body by the Spirit*.

ANNEX 30 pp 673–4

And though to these *natural* Arguments God hath added sundry *supernatural* Ones in the *ª*Revelations of the *Gospel*, such as are in *themselves* sufficient to check our most *outragious Appetites*, and to baffle the *strongest Temptations*; Yet alas! our *Thoughts* are so squander'd among this great Multiplicity of *carnal* Objects that surround us, that did not the *divine Spirit* frequently suggest those *supernatural* Arguments to us, and by the powerful Influence of his *Grace* keep our Minds intent upon them, we should never recollect our selves to such a *thorough Consideration* of them, as is necessary to persuade our selves by them into a *lasting Resolution* of Amendment. So that we have very great need both of the *outward*, and *inward* Grace of God; for though we can *deliberate* what is best to *chuse*, and *chuse* what we find *best* upon Deliberation; yet we are like Men standing in *bivio*, between two contrary Roads, and are naturally indeed free to turn either to the *Right* Hand or to the *Left*; but on the *left-hand* Way there are so many *Temptations* perpetually beckoning to us, and inviting us unto that which is *Evil*, and our brutish *Passions* and *Appetites* are so ready upon all occasions to yield and comply with them; that we should certainly go that way, did not the *holy Spirit* importune us with strong Arguments to turn to the *right-hand* way of *Virtue* and *Goodness*.

ANNEX 30ª Line begins here

SIR WALTER SCOTT
1771–1832

Minstrelsy of the Scottish Border: consisting of historical and romantic ballads, collected in the southern counties of Scotland; with a few of modern date, founded upon local tradition. 2nd ed. 3 vols. Kelso & Edinburgh 1802–3. 8°.

Collection of Paul Betz

Inscribed by C on I ⁻4 (original first recto front flyleaf): "S. T. Coleridge, Pub. Sec. t. h. M. his. Commiss.ʳ | Malta, 1 August 1805.—" Below this in DC's hand: "This book was given by the above to his eldest Son Hartley Coleridge, at whose death, January 6!ʰ 18ƒ49, it came into my possession— | Derwent Coleridge | N.B. The Memorandum page xcii is in the handwriting of S. T. C." (The incorrect year of HC's death has been altered to "1849", perhaps in another hand.) On I ⁻2 the signature: "Hartley Coleridge." Booksellers' notes I ⁻7; bookplate of DC I ⁻9 (p-d). Pencilled notes by HC on I 274, 277, 282, 286; II 58, 59, 62, 337, 348.

DATE. About 1 Aug 1805 (date of acquisition note).

1   I xcii, lightly cropped | Introduction

Penances, the composition betwixt guilt and conscience, were also frequent upon the borders. Of this we have a record in many bequests to the church, and in some lasting monuments; such as the Tower of Repentance, in Dumfries-shire, and, according to vulgar tradition, the church of Linton*, in Roxburghshire. [Footnote *:] This small church is founded upon a little hill of sand, in which no stone of the size of an egg is said to have been found, although the neighbouring soil is sharp and gravelly. Tradition accounts for this, by informing us, that the foundresses were two sisters, upon whose account much blood had been spilt in that spot; and that the penance, imposed on the fair causers of the slaughter, was an order from the Pope to sift the sand of the hill, upon which their church was to be erected. This story may, perhaps, have some foundation; for, in the church-yard was discovered a single grave, containing no fewer than fifty skulls, most of which bore the marks of having been cleft by violence.

In a Copy of the first Edition of this Work, in two Volumes, under this * was written the following interesting Note by the Gentleman who had lent

574

me the Volumes, the accomplished Scholar, the gallant soldier, and truly good man, Major Walker of [th]e 20th/[1]

"If, as is not very probable, I should go home to sleep with my Fathers, our Family Burying Ground being in the center of this Church-yard, I shall repose in this green Hill. D. W. Malta—5 March 1803—"

---

[1] David Walker (d c 1840) began his career as an army officer with a commission as Ensign in the 64th Regiment of Foot in 1781, and ended it as a Major-General in the 58th, retiring in 1828 but continuing to be included in the Army List till 1840. In 1803, as C says, he was serving as Major in the 20th Regiment of Foot.

"WAVERLEY NOVELS"

C's set of the "Waverley Novels" comprises 17 novels, originally issued in 25 vols, and now bound in 13 vols in uniform binding. The novels were issued in three groups, to each of which a letter is here assigned for reference. The three sets of novels are described separately in *chronological* order of publication, and not in alphabetical order of titles.

    A *Novels and Tales*. 1823. 12 vols in 6. 9 novels.

    B *Historical Romances*. 1824. 6 vols in 3. 4 novels.

    C *Novels and Romances*. 1825. 7 vols in 4. 4 novels.

  Since individual novels do not always fall within volume-units either of the original issue or in the present bound set, a capital Roman numeral here indicates the volume-number as at present bound, and a lower-case Roman numeral in parentheses indicates the volume-number as originally issued. The series of chapter numbers begins afresh with each of the *original* vols, so that "Ch 2" may appear twice for any given novel, referring to different vols of the edition. In the following alphabetical list of novel-titles, the location of the novel in the set is shown, with the distribution of ms notes as they appear in the printed transcript.

INDEX

	Volume	MS Notes
The Abbot	B II (iv)–III (v)	B 8–19
The Antiquary	A II (iv)–III (v)	A 17A–19
The Black Dwarf	A IV (vii)	
The Bride of Lammermoor	A VI (xi), (xii)	
The Fortunes of Nigel	C I (ii)–II (iv)	C 7–9
Guy Mannering	A I (ii)–ii (iii)	A 10–16
The Heart of Midlothian	A V (ix), (x)	A 26–28, 30
Ivanhoe	B I (i), (ii)	B 1–2
Kenilworth	B III (v), (vi)	B 21
A Legend of Montrose	A VI (xii)	A 31–36
The Monastery	B I (ii)–II (iii)	B 3–4, 6–7
Old Mortality	A IV (vii), (viii)	A 23–25A
Peveril of the Peak	C II (iv)–III (vi)	C 10–14
The Pirate	C I (i), (ii)	C 2–6
Quentin Durward	C III (vi)–IV (vii)	C 15–24
Rob Roy	A III (v), (vi)	A 20–22
Waverley	A I (i), (ii)	A 1–9, B 20
General Notes		A 17, 29
		B 5, 22
		C 1

It is significant that C could tell Thomas Allsop as early as 8 Apr 1820—before any of these sets was published—that he had "read the far greater part of his [Scott's] Novels twice, & several three times, over with undiminished pleasure and interest" (*CL* v 33). He frequently praised the novels for their historical analysis, as in the letter cited, and for the comfort they brought him "in many a sleepless night when I should but for them have been comfortless" (*CL* vi 821), but he never thought very highly of Scott's poetry (e.g. *CL* iii 290–6, *TT—CC—*i 413) and he was certainly nettled both by the great success of what he considered an inferior talent and by Scott's inadequate acknowledgment of debts to C's work, notably to *Christabel* (*CL* iii 290–1 and n, 355–8 and nn, v 379–81, 437). He met Scott a few times socially, but they were never close. C's opinion of him must have been affected by his prejudice against the Scots, and the harshest remark he ever made about him was on the occasion of the catastrophic failure of Scott's publisher, when Scott's prosperity collapsed completely: C called him then "a Scotchman suffering the penalty of his Scotchery" (*CL* vi 562).

Copy A

Novels and Tales of the Author of Waverley. [Anonymous.] 12 vols (in 6). Edinburgh 1823. 18°.

British Library C 126 b 4, bound uniformly with *Historical Romances* and *Novels and Romances*, for which see COPY B, C.

Inscribed by John Duke Coleridge on I ⁻5: "This set of the Waverley Novels belonged to S. T. Coleridge. They came to me from Ernest Coleridge & as far as my wishes have weight I desire that they stay at Heath's Court | Coleridge | June—1892." A note by EHC is pasted to III (v) ⁻5: "S. T. Coleridge maintained that this portrait of Dousterswivel by his 'young American friend' Leslie was an intentional caricature of himself—vid: MS. Corr: of 1825" (i.e. *CL* v 422). For this supposed portrait, see Frontispiece. A pencilled note beside **19** (III [v] 61) reads "yes DC"—presumably agreeing with C. VI (xii) 361–8, 369–72—the better part of the glossary—are unopened. COPY B **20** appears to have been misbound, its natural place following COPY A **4**.

In COPY C **16**, C refers to these vols as "my ever circulating Copy of Scott's novels".

CONTENTS. See the General Note preceding this headnote.

DATE. After Sept 1823, the date of publication of COPY A (*EC*); but not soon after, and from 1825 on if, as seems most likely, C acquired the whole set (COPY A, B, C) at once. A reference to *Old Mortality* in a notebook entry of Oct–Nov 1823 is to another ed: *CN* IV 5038. The existence of many earlier allusions to the *Waverley* novels shows that C was by this time *re*reading most if not all of them. He must have had this set in hand by Apr 1825, however, when he complained about being identified with German quackery through the frontispiece in COPY A: *CL* v 422, quoted above.

1   I (i) 14 | *Waverley* ch 2

For it may be observed in passing, that, instead of those mail-coaches, by means of which every mechanic at his six-penny club may nightly learn from twenty contradictory channels the yesterday's news of the capital, a weekly post brought, in those days, to Waverley-Honour, a Weekly Intelligencer . . .

* This piece of Satire is post-dated. It had ceased to be applicable to London Journals, even before the publication of Waverley.

2   I (i) 139, pencil | Ch 17

The allowance of whisky, however, would have appeared prodigal to any but Highlanders, who, living entirely in the open air, and in a very moist climate, can consume great quantities of ardent spirits, without the usual baneful effects either upon the brain or the constitution.*

* It would be more correct to have said—"with less than the usual &c".

3   I (i) 140, pencil | Ch 18

. . . he would have believed his farther progress by land impossible, only that it was scarce probable but what the inhabitants of the cavern had some mode of issuing from it otherwise than by the lake.

* A Scotticism? or simply a Vulgarism?[1]

4   I (i) 196 | Ch 24

Edward observed, with some surprise, that even Fergus, notwithstanding his knowledge and education, seemed to fall in with the superstitious ideas of his countrymen; either because he deemed it impolitic to affect scepticism on a matter of general belief, or more probably because, like most men who do not think deeply or accurately on such subjects, he had in his mind a reserve of superstition which balanced the freedom of his expressions and practice upon other occasions.

In the most reflecting minds there may, nay must, exist a certain "*reserve of Superstition*["], from the consciousness of the vast disproportion of our knowlege to the terra incognita yet to be known—Between these is a region of indistinctness, sights not forms, but to which ~~you~~ we give a form/ ~~Less~~ Some few are aware, that the *form* is their own gift yet without denying a SOMEWHAT seen/ whenever the last understood *causes* may be, still aliquid *superstat*[1]—and these[a] it is, which constitutes the reason of *Superstition*, and makes it reasonable[2]

4[a] A slip for "this"?

3[1] *OED* gives examples of this usage going back to the seventeenth century without labelling it as either Scottish or vulgar; C notes its occurrence with distaste again, however, in COPY C **15**.

4[1] Literally "something *stands above*". As he often does, C is here playing on the etymological connection between *superstitio* "superstition" and other words compounded from *super* "above" and *stare* "to stand", including *superstare* "to stand above", *superstes* "one standing over" therefore "a survivor", etc. Elements of the group appear in *CN* IV 4605 f 44 and n, 4708, 5274. In JUNG **44** at n 1 "superstition" is expanded into a Latin phrase as "an assertion of things standing above yet nevertheless appearing to the senses"; here the contrast is especially between standing over and "understood". Reason stands over understanding.

4[2] C's note COPY B **20** comments further

5   I (i) 255 | Ch 30

This worthy man . . . maintained his character with the common people, although he preached the practical fruits of Christian faith, as well as its abstract tenets* . . .

* *Abstract Tenets*—i.e. whatever in the Gospel is peculiar to the Gospel!—what an Opening into the actual state of religion among the higher classes, as represented by & in Sir W. S.—! Christ's Divity,[a] the Fall of Man, Sin, Redemption—*abstract* tenets!!¹

6   I (ii) 66–8, pencil | Ch 10

But . . . no one knew better than Fergus that there must be some decent pretext for a mortal duel. *For instance, you may challenge a man for treading on your corn in a crowd, or for pushing you up to the wall, or for taking your seat in the theatre; but the modern code of honour will not permit you to found a quarrel upon your right of compelling a man to continue addresses to a female relative, which the fair lady has already refused.

* Mem. What a compleat answer to Arthur Melvyn's defence of Dueling in the former Volume!¹ "I am morally entitled to defend my Honor not less than my Life or Purse". So be it. But what *is* your Honor? And what *are* attacks on it?—Sir W. Scott here answers the question.—

7   I (ii) 84 | Ch 12

My ghastly visitant glided before me, (for I cannot say he walked,) until he reached the foot-bridge: there he stopped, and turned full round.

I doubt, whether this be natural¹

8   I (ii) 84–5

[Fergus MacIvor describes his encounter with the Bodach Glas, the Grey Spectre that forebodes death.]

<hr/>

5ᵃ For "Divinity"

<hr/>

on this passage and should really have been bound in here.

5¹ Scott satirises the villagers' preference for polemical divinity over moral instruction; C however sees the satire as evidence of an indifference to theological issues among members of the comfortable middle classes.

6¹ **15** below.

7¹ C expands upon this observation in **9** following.

Sir W. S., an orthodox Cosmolater,[1] is always half and half on these subjects. The ~~facts~~ appearances are so stated as to be readily solved on the simplest principles of Pathology: while the precise coincidence of the event so marvellously exceeds the ordinary run of Chances, as to preserve the full effect of Superstition for the *Reader*, and yet the credit of ~~an~~ Unbelief for the Writer. S. T. C.

9 I +2, referring to I (ii) 84

P. 84. These Stories of Ghosts, prophecies, dreams, presentiments, as related by Sir W. S., are calculated to produce a very ill effect—not only from the absurdly exact coincidence of the Events, but (and principally) because the Appearances themselves are not psychologically given, but in opposition to the intention of the Writer are bonâ fide præter- or rather contra- natural[1]—Ex. gr. The Ocular Spectrum "turning full round"— after the well-imagined incident of Mac Ivor's seeing the figure in all points of the Compass.[2]

10 I (ii) 218, pencil | *Guy Mannering* ch 3

"Truly," said Sampson, "I opine with Sir Isaac Newton, Knight, and umwhile master of his majesty's mint, that the (pretended) science of astrology is altogether vain, frivolous, and unsatisfactory."

This Joke stolen from [? ~~another who~~] Murphy, & by him put into the mouth of an old money-loving Citizen, is quite out of character with Dominie Sampson.[1]

11 I (ii) 221, pencil

So strongly can imagination deceive even those by whose volition it has been excited, that Mannering, while gazing upon these brilliant bodies,

---

8[1] Not in *OED*, though "cosmolatry" ("worship of the world") appears, with an illustration from Cudworth.

9[1] What C considered a crass approach to the supernatural in Scott's *Lady of the Lake* (1810) prompted him to write an "Essay on the Supernatural" which was to have been "prefixed to the poem of The Ancient Mariner": *BL* ch 13 (*CC*) I 306 and n (but a fragment of the essay remains); cf *CL* VI 1035, *SW & F* (*CC*) 401–2. This point is reiterated in COPY C 2.

9[2] C alludes to a passage following **7** textus: "'. . . to ascertain what I dreaded, I

stood still, and turned myself on the same spot successively to the four points of the compass—By Heaven, Edward, turn where I would, the figure was instantly before my eyes, at precisely the same distance!'"

10[1] The "Joke" consists presumably in the irrelevance of Newton's official position (and perhaps even of his authority) to the opinion about the futility of astrology. The line has not been traced in Murphy's plays, though C was surely thinking of the miser Old Philpot in *The Citizen* (1761); it seems to C incongruous in the mouth of the unworldly tutor Sampson.

was half inclined to believe in the influence ascribed to them by superstition over human events.

Col. Mannering is full 60 years too late to make his half-joke, half-earnest, penchant for Astrology, endurable by the imagination/[1] And there is nothing in his character to aid or account for it.

12   I (ii) 224–5, pencil | Ch 4

[In making predictions on the basis of astrological calculations, Mannering is surprised to discover that the same year is to be a "period of peril" both for the woman he is in love with, and for the newborn Harry Bartram.] . . . whether Mannering, bewildered amid the arithmetical labyrinth and technical jargon of astrology, had insensibly twice followed the same clue to guide him out of the maze;* or whether his imagination, seduced by some point of apparent resemblance, lent its aid to make the similitude between the two operations more exactly accurate than it might otherwise have been, it is impossible to guess; but the impression upon his mind, that the results exactly corresponded, was vividly and indelibly strong.

* Now this makes no difference/ It is the coincidence of the fulfillment that makes us wonder. But the whole is misconceived & mismanaged. But this is Scott's great defect. Nothing is evolved out of the character or passions of the Agent; but all is accident ab extra[1]

13   I (ii) 229–30, pencil

Mannering, after in vain attempting to make himself master of the exact words of her [the gypsy's] song, afterwards attempted the following paraphrase . . .

> Twist ye, twine ye! even so,
> Mingle shades of joy and woe,
> Hope and fear, and peace and strife,
> In the thread of human life.

> While the mystic twist is spinning,
> And the infant's life beginning,
> Dimly seen through twilight bending,
> Lo, what varied shapes attending!

11[1] *Guy Mannering* begins in the 1750s and its main action takes place about 1780. Scott himself seems to have been aware of an element of anachronism in Mannering's astrological lore: he makes it part of his education under an aged tutor, and gives him only a qualified measure of belief in it as a system.

12[1] "From outside".

Passions wild, and Follies vain,
Pleasures soon exchanged for pain;
Doubt, and Jealousy, and Fear,
In the magic dance appear.

Now they wax, and now they dwindle,
Whirling with the whirling spindle.
Twist ye, twine ye! even so,
Mingle human bliss and woe.

And this a professed *imitation* of a *Gypsy's* charm! Well does this instance the diversity of Fancy, which Sir W. S. possesses, and *imagination*, which belongs to another Grade of Intellects.[1]

14   I (ii) 233–5, pencil | Ch 5

[Epigraph]

—You have fed upon my seigniories,
Dispark'd my parks, and fell'd my forest woods,
From mine own windows torn my household coat,
Razed out my impress, leaving me no sign,
Save men's opinions and my living blood,
To shew the world I am a gentleman.
                              Richard II.

I have never seen or been able to discover any other satisfactory Solution of the Problem of the Pride of *Blood*, but that recorded in Genesis—respecting the 3 Sons of Noah.[1] Nor do I believe, that this pride is grounded on a mere *Prejudice*. The Duke of Norfolk can not be prouder of his being a Howard, than I am in the belief that I am an Iapetides—a descendant of Japhet in the North-western or Gothic Branch—& not a *Celt*, or any of the mixed Bloods, & with no infusion of the Hammonic.[2]   *S. T. C.*

13[1] Besides the philosophical distinction between fancy and imagination that is at the heart of the *Biographia*—*BL* ch 13 (*CC*) I 304–5—there are more casual contrasts, e.g. "Milton had a highly *imaginative*, Cowley a very *fanciful* mind" (*BL* ch 4—*CC*—I 84). C had written charms or spells of his own, such as the one given to Geraldine in *Christabel* lines 267–78: *PW* (EHC) I 224–5.
14[1] By "Solution of" C appears to mean "explanation of" or "genesis of". The "Problem" is, whence does it arise? The an-

swer, he maintains, is to be found in Gen 9 and 10, where Ham is the son who sees his father's nakedness, so that his race is cursed; and where the nations of the world are divided among the descendants of the three sons, Shem, Ham, and Japhet.
14[2] For other references to this myth about the origins of race and class, and for the inferiority of mixed races such as the Celts, see esp BLUMENBACH **4** but also RHENFERD **18** and n 1, *Lects 1808–1819* (*CC*) II 49–54, *CN* IV 4548.

15 I (ii) 329–31 | Ch 16

[Arthur Mervyn argues that duelling is justified by the natural right of self-defence. That right is surrendered to civil society on condition of legal protection; but the law does not protect one's honor.] If any man chuses to rob Arthur Mervyn of the contents of his purse, if he has not means of defence, or the skill and courage to use them, the assizes at Lancaster or Carlisle will do him justice by tucking up the robber:—Yet who will say I am bound to wait for this justice, and submit to being plundered in the first instance, if I have the means and spirit to protect my own property? . . . I suppose little distinction can be drawn between defence of person and goods, and defence of reputation.

This plausible Defence of Duelling *intra certos* limites[1] wants but two points to be more than *plausible*. The first is, a determination o*r*f the what are & ought[a] be regarded, as assaults on honor & reputation/ If not enumerated, yet let them at least be predefined and described. At present, it is notorious that in nine cases of ten, the offence is determined by the irascibility & pruriency ad pugnam[2] of the Person who takes the Offence— The second point is—Admit the innocence and necessity of sending or accepting a challenge on any occasion, how is a sober minded Man to be protected from your hot Candidates for duellistic fame, who may take any the most absurd pretence for *beginning* a dispute?—In short, the Law of Duelling exposes my *honor* to every Bully or Fool.[3]

16 II (iii) 214–16, pencil | Ch 22

"Some of these papers," said Bertram, looking over them, "are mine, and were in my portfolio when it was stolen from the post-chaise. They are memoranda of little value, and, I see, have been carefully selected as affording no evidence of my rank or character, which many of the other papers would have established fully. *They are mingled with ship-accounts and other papers, belonging apparently to a person of the same name."

* I do not remember, that the means by which Glossin procured the contents of the Portmanteau from the Robbers, have been explained, or even the fact itself stated. Sir W. S. seems to have confounded the Gypsey's

---

15[a] For "ought to"

15[1] "*Within certain* limits".
15[2] Itching "for a fight": from Martial *Epigrams* 3.58.11, q also *CN* II 2333, *EOT* (*CC*) II 176.

15[3] A related note on the issue is **6** above. C writes indignantly of duellists as assassins in *CN* II 1971.

Purse left at the Inn with Bertram's own portmanteau. Glossin might have procured them from Dirk Hatteraick. Sir W. has forgot to mention it.[1]

17   II (iii) [+]1 | At the end of *Guy Mannering*

Spinoza

$$K - \Theta = 0$$
$$\Theta - K = 0$$

Christian Theism

$$K - \Theta = 0$$
$$\Theta^a - K = \Theta^1$$

17A   II (iv) 70, pencil | *The Antiquary* ch 6

I had recourse to a physician, but he was also practising a more whole-~~some~~sale mode of slaughter than that which his profession had been supposed at all times to open to him.[1]

18   II (iv) 160–1, pencil | Ch 14

[Oldbuck, the antiquary, tries to find out why Lovel has decided to stay in the area, and supposes that he may have ambitions as a writer.] Lovel, who was rather closely pressed by the inquisitiveness of the old gentleman, concluded it would be best to let him remain in the error which he had gratuitously adopted.

"I have been at times foolish enough," he replied, "to nourish some thoughts of the kind."

"Ah! poor fellow! nothing can be more melancholy! unless, as young men sometimes do, you had fancied yourself in love with some trumpery specimen of womankind, which is, indeed, as Shakespeare truly says, pressing to death, whipping, and hanging, all at once."

---

[17][a] Here C has formed a capital *theta* by writing a large-scale lower-case one

[16][1] The explanation that C requires is given in the sentence preceding the textus: some of Bertram's papers "had been found by the officers in the old vault where his portmanteau was ransacked".

[17][1] Various versions of this formula appear in C's work, the closest parallel being in HILLHOUSE 1. Here, C uses K for κοσμος (*kosmos*, the world), and Θ for Θεος (*Theos*, God). To translate the code: according to Spinoza (1) the world without God is nothing (HILLHOUSE 1: "an impossible Idea"); (2) God without the world is nothing; but according to Christian theism (3) the world without God is nothing; and yet (4) God without the world is God (HILLHOUSE 1: "God, the Self-sufficing").

[17A][1] C is correct: "wholesale" is the reading of the 1st ed (1816).

This is one of the gross improbabilities which Scott's Genius enables him to skip over unnoticed. Oldbuck is every where presented as a shrewd observing man, Antiquarianism excepted. But he must have been a Dolt, an Ideot, not to have detected Lovel's passion for Isabella & consequently his motive for staying in the Neighbourhood, after the information, he has now received from Sir Arthur.[1]

19 III (v) 60–1, pencil | Ch 5

After a formal apology for the encroachment, Lord Glenallen /\ agreed to go with him, and underwent* with patience in their return home the whole history of John of the Girnell, a legend which Mr Oldbuck was never known to spare any one who crossed his threshold.

/\ went with him & this without his undergoing &c which Mr O. was never before known &c/

    * It would have been a much finer touch, had Sir W. inserted "without undergoing["], and "before" after "never known"./

20 III (vi) 196, pencil | *Rob Roy* ch 15

". . . O, Maister Frank, a' your uncle's follies, and a' your cousins' pliskies, were naething to this!—Drink clean cap-out, like Sir Hildebrand; begin the blessed morning with brandy sops, like Squire Percy;* swagger, like Squire Thorncliff; rin wud amang the lasses, like Squire John; gamble, like Richard; win souls to the Pope and the deevil, like Rashleigh; rive, rant, break the Sabbath, and do the Pope's bidding, like them a' put thegither†—But, merciful Providence! take care o' your young blude, and gang nae near Rob Roy!"

One most *characteristic* quality of Sir W. S.'s novels is the charm & yet the utterly impersonal & undramatic stuff and texture of the Dialogues. *Ex. gr.* * †.

21 III (vi) 298–9, pencil | Ch 21

I do not regard small improbabilities, numerous as they are in Sir Walter's Novels—his Genius overpowers them. But this Confusion of the Father with the Husband is so *very* gross, so utterly inconsistent with Os-

---

18[1] In the preceding chapter, Oldbuck has learnt from Sir Arthur Wardour and his daughter Isabella that Isabella had met Lovel the previous spring but had not ac- knowledged the acquaintance because of Sir Arthur's prejudice against illegitimacy (Lovel being supposed an illegitimate son).

baldistone's intimacy with Diana, as to awaken one rudely out of the Day-dream of negative Faith.[1]

22   III (vi) 321–2, pencil | Ch 23

[Frank misunderstands mysterious allusions to Sir Frederick and Diana Vernon, whom he supposes to be man and wife.] He [Sir Hildebrand] once or twice mentioned Diana, always with great affection; and once he said, while I sat by his bedside—"Nevoy, since Thorncliff and all of them are dead, I am sorry you cannot have her."

* Again—another obtrusively gross improbability that Frank with all these interviews should not have discovered that Sir Fred. V. was Diana's Father, not Husband./

23   IV (vii) 201–2 | *Old Mortality* ch 1

The peasantry continue to attach to the tombs of those victims of prelacy an honour which they do not render to more splendid mausoleums; and when they point them out to their sons, and narrate the fate of the suffer-ers, usually conclude, by exhorting them to be ready, should times call for it, to resist to the death in the cause of civil and religious liberty, like their brave forefathers.

Alas! a Liberty which in the first moment in which it asserted itself, be-came intolerance, and an exclusion of all Liberty in others! But the Scot-tish Covenanters are not chargeable with this inconsistence. It was not *Liberty*, they claimed; but Truth, which they believed themselves to as-sert. Now *Truth* can be but one. It is in its very essence *exclusive*. It is man's blindness to his own fallibility, and the lust of sway; which pervert this exclusiveness into *intolerance* & persecution.

24   IV (vii) 242, pencil | Ch 4

In their <u>excited</u> imagination the casual rencontre had the appearance of a providential interference, and they put to death the Archbishop, with cir-cumstances of great and <u>cold-blooded</u> cruelty . . .

excited imagination, & cold-blooded cruelty! Well done, Scotchman! a word for both parties!

21[1] Unless it refers to Osbaldistone's *as-sumption* that although they love one an-other, he and Diana Vernon cannot marry ("I was beloved by Diana, and was sepa-rated from her for ever") because she al-ready has a husband (he mistaking her fa-ther for her husband), this note appears to be misplaced: there is no explicit "Confusion of the Father with the Husband" in this chapter. See, however, **22** following.

25 IV (vii) 256–7 | Ch 6

". . . I should strongly doubt the origin of any inspiration which seemed to dictate a line of conduct contrary to those feelings of natural humanity,* which Heaven has assigned to us as the general law of our conduct."

* Alas! how weak̶l̶y̶ an answer to Balfour's Discourse!—not the feelings of *natural* Humanity, which by the bye is almost as inconsistent, as a round Square, but the Principles of a supernatural immutable *Reason*, that are the Criterion.

25A IV (viii), marked with a pencilled line in the margin | Ch 24

". . . But Mackay will pit him down, there's little doubt o' that; he'll gie him his fairing, I'll be caution for it."

26 V (ix) 217–18, pencil | *The Heart of Midlothian* ch 15

[Robertson begs Jeanie to perjure herself to save her innocent sister's life.] "It is not man I fear," said Jeanie, looking upward; "the God, whose name I must call on to witness the truth of what I say, he will know the falsehood."

"And he will know the motive," said the stranger, eagerly;* "he will know that you are doing this—not for lucre of gain, but to save the life of the innocent, and prevent the commission of a worse crime than that which the law seeks to avenge."

* This is admirably wrought up: and I confess with deep awe that there has been a time when this sophistry would have weighed with me in a similar instance, but God be praised! I was not exposed to the Temptation.   S. T. C.—

27 V (x) 65–6 | Ch 5

Bunyan was, indeed, a rigid Calvinist,* but then he was also a member of a Baptist congregation, so that his works had no place on David Deans's shelf of divinity.

* Calvinism never put on a less rigid form, never smoothed its brow & softened its voice more winningly than in the Pilgrim's Progress.[1]

27[1] Two annotated copies of *Pilgrim's Progress* survive: BUNYAN COPY A, B. The General Note in *CM* (*CC*) I 801 sums up C's comments on Bunyan; and see his spirited defence in James SEDGWICK below, esp **57**.

28   v (x) 252–3, pencil | Ch 19

". . . O, if the puir prodigal wad return, sae blithely as the goodman wad kill the fatted calf!—though Brockie's calf will no be fit for killing this three weeks yet."*

* This is *wit*, *head*-work, a *falsetto* imitation of Shakespear's Dame Quickly.[1] Half a dozen read-worthy sentences might be written on the difference/ Sir W. S. forgot or never had learnt, that it is the weak memory that is discursive, not the strong feeling.

[a]Sh. would have made May leave off with "the fatted Calf", & given the line following to a second character, Simple, Davy or Shallow.[2]

29   v (x) [+]1–[+]2, pencil

Perhaps, the very error of the Romish Church, for which the Heart ~~most~~ pleads most strongly and which the mere understanding finds most equitable, is of all others the error that has produced most evil—fruits most poisonous—the Doctrine of Purgatory, I mean.[1]—As if Providence warned us by a proof which all men can understand, how dangerous every addition to revealed truth is, however plausible it may appear to our narrow intellect. The Heart of man conscious of its imperfections is *naturally* too narrow to contain a full faith in the absoluteness of God's Love to us in Christ!   S. T. Coleridge

30   v (x) [+]4, pencil

There is an intensity of Wickedness, as in the character of Mother Murdockson, that is incompatible with the presence of Reason.[1] But whether

---

28[a] The note to this point covers the foot of pp 252–3; the remainder is at the top of p 253

28[1] Mrs Quickly, the Hostess of the Boar's Head Tavern in *1 Henry IV*, *2 Henry IV*, and *Henry V*: C uses her speech as an example of "the absence of Method, which characterizes the uneducated . . . occasioned by an habitual submission of the understanding to mere events and images as such, and independent of any power in the mind to classify or appropriate them" (*Friend—CC*—I 451). For "falsetto" see also COPY B 2 and n 2.

28[2] Simple is a servant of Slander in *The Merry Wives of Windsor*, Davy a servant of Justice Shallow in *2 Henry IV*. (Both are Falstaff plays, and therefore understandably linked in C's mind.)

29[1] C's remark does not appear to have been prompted by any cue in the text. For other reflections on this doctrine see BLANCO WHITE *Practical Evidence* 2, FIELD **60**, JUNG **33**; and, for a summary of C's position, *CCD* 194.

30[1] Meg Murdockson, eventually executed for her part in a robbery and murder, had killed her own daughter's illegitimate child and allowed Effie Deans to be condemned to death for infanticide although Meg herself had taken the baby away.

it be the exclusion of the Light of Reason, that has occasioned the Wickedness, or the growing Wickedness that has finally quenched the Reason—on the answer to this question it depends, whether the Culprit is to be punished for Guilt, or pitied and protected as Mad.

31   VI (xii) 81 | *A Legend of Montrose* Introduction

It was, therefore, with great pleasure, that I extracted from my military friend [Serjeant McAlpin] some curious particulars respecting that time; they are mixed with that measure of the wild and wonderful which belong to the periods and the narrator, but which I do not in the least object to the reader treating with disbelief, providing he will be so good as give implicit credit to the natural events of the story, which, like all those which I have had the honour to put under his notice, actually rest upon a basis of truth.

* This, dear Sir W., is not what we object to; but that you tell these parts in your own person, & that Serjeant McAlpin is lost in Sir W. Scott—& that is the *incongruity*.

32   VI (xii) 87–8 | Ch 1

* Leaving it to casuists to determine whether one contracting party is justified in breaking a solemn treaty, upon the suspicion that in certain future contingencies it might be infringed by the other, we shall proceed to mention two other circumstances that had at least equal influence with the Scottish rulers and nation, with any doubts which they entertained of the king's good faith.

* On this ground I should rest the Vindication of the Parliamentarians in publisheding the King's private Correspondence captured at (Naseby? or Marston Moor?)[1] In these Letters they found positive proofs of the King's hollowness and perfidy, of which indeed they had sufficient evidence before, but not such evidence as they could published with safety, or without breach of good faith towards the Furnishers and Informants.

33   VI (xii) 89

The Presbyterians,* a numerous and powerful party in the English Parliament, had hitherto taken the lead in opposition to the King . . .

32[1] The letters, captured at Naseby (14 Jun 1644), revealed secret negotiations between Charles I and foreign courts.

* A mistake. The *Anti-prelatists* indeed did; but of Presbyterians, i.e. *Anti-episcopists*, there were at that time but few. See Baxter's *Life*.[1]

S. T. C.

34 VI (xii) 89–91 | **33** textus continued

. . . while the independents and other sectaries, who afterwards, under Cromwell, assumed the power of the sword, and overset the Presbyterian model both in Scotland and England,* were as yet contented to lurk under the shelter of the wealthier and more powerful party. The prospect of bringing to a uniformity the kingdoms of England and Scotland in discipline and worship, seemed, therefore, as fair as it was desirable.

* Cromwell restrained and [? ~~eurbed~~] curbed, but did not *overset*, the Presbyterian Church, in *Scotland*. Had the Coalition of the two forms, each modifying the other, been *practicable*, it *would* have been a *most* desirable event, an irresistible arm of Strength to both Countries, and the solid foundation of their future union as *one* State. That which in an intenser form has rendered the Union with Ireland a calamitous Mockery,[1] delayed the blessings of Union more than a century for Scotland.

35 VI (xii) 128–9 | Ch 5

"Gentlemen cavaliers," he said, "I drink these healths, *primo*, both out of respect to this honourable and hospitable roof-tree, and, *secundo*, because I hold it not good to be preceese in such matters, *inter pocula* [between drinks]; but I protest, agreeable to the warrandice granted by this honourable lord, that it shall be free to me, notwithstanding my present complaisance, to take service with the Covenanters to-morrow, providing I shall be so minded."

If Sir W. S. could on any fair ground be compared with Shakespear, I should select the character of Dalgetty as best supporting the Claim.[1] Brave, enterprizing, intrepid, brisk to act, stubborn in endurance: these qualities, virtues in a Soldier, grounded on *low principles*, but yet *principles*; *low*, indeed, but clear, intelligible, and of pre-calculable influence,

33[1] C appears to be recording a general impression about the scale of Baxter's English Presbyterian party; in annotations to the work itself (two annotated copies survive), he makes one group of all "Anti-prelatic Divines, whether Episcopalians or Presbyterians" (BAXTER *Reliquiae* COPY B **78[j]**).

34[1] I.e. religious difference.

35[1] C more than once expressed indignation on hearing Scott compared to Shakespeare: LAMB **1**, *TT* (*CC*) I 497. Dugald Dalgetty is one of Scott's successful comic mixtures of courage and pedantry.

&in all Circumstances co-ercingve; & unbent by accident. I exceedingly
admire Captⁿ Dalgetty.   S. T. C.

36   VI (xii) 142–3

[Lord Menteith explains his view of Allan McAulay's "second sight".]
". . . I think that he persuades himself that the predictions, which are, in
reality, the result of judgment and reflection, are supernatural impressions
on his mind, just as fanatics conceive the workings of their own semi-
maniacal imagination to be divine inspiration—* . . ."

* I am not (tho' perhaps I ought to be) ashamed to say, that I am rather
an *Un*believer than a *Dis*believer of this semi-maniacal faculty of Sec-
ond-sight, akin to the *clair-voyance* in certain forms of Catalepsy and in
women under the excitement of the Ganglionic System induced by Animal Magnetism.[1]

36[1] For another remark about second sight see PEPYS **20** and n 1. C reported his conversion from disbelief to unbelief (i.e. suspended judgment, in the absence of firm conviction) in animal magnetism (mesmerism) in Jul 1817: *SW & F (CC)* 589–95, and cf *Friend (CC)* I 59n. His reading in the subject was extensive, and besides writing isolated remarks in books on other subjects, he annotated several works about animal magnetism—including the phenomenon of the "clairvoyants" or "inside-seers": JAHRBÜCHER, KLUGE, LOEWE, MESMER, RICHTER *Museum*. For a comprehensive note about the evolution of C's views see *TT (CC)* I 96n–7n.

Copy B

Historical Romances of the Author of Waverley. [Anonymous.] 6 vols (in 3). Edinburgh 1824. 18°.

British Library C 126 b 6, bound uniformly with *Novels and Tales* and *Novels and Romances*, COPY A and COPY C.

A doggerel poem, entitled "An Epitaph for Mr Coleridge" and signed H. A. G.—probably Henry Anthony Gillman, the Gillmans' second son—is written in an unidentified hand, in pencil, on I (ii) $^+$1.

CONTENTS. See General Note before COPY A headnote.

DATE. See COPY A headnote. COPY B **22** is dated 20 Sept 1830.

1   I (i) 111, cropped | *Ivanhoe* ch 8

This rough expostulation was addressed to no other than our acquaintance Isaac, who, richly and even magnificently dressed* in a gaberdine ornamented with lace and lined with fur, endeavoured to make place in the foremost row beneath the gallery for his daughter, the beautiful Rebecca . . . [who was] not a little terrified for the displeasure which seemed generally excited by her parent's presumption. But Isaac, though we have seen him sufficiently timid upon other occasions, knew well that upon the present he had nothing to fear.†

*—†. The reason or rather excuse assigned † is too weak to remove the improbability of this ostentation of *Wealth* i[n] I[saa]c's exposure of Rebec[ca's] b[eau]ties

2   I (ii) 233–[235] | End of *Ivanhoe*

I do not myself know how to account for it—but so the fact is, that tho' I have read and again and again turned to, sundry Chapters of Ivanhoe with an untired interest, I have never read the whole—the pain or the perplexity or whatever it was always outweighed the Curiosity.[1] Perhaps, the

---

2[1] In *Ivanhoe*, which first appeared in 1819, Scott quoted three lines from C's unpublished poem *The Knight's Tomb* and confirmed C's conviction of his authorship of the Waverley novels, not publicly acknowledged until 1827: *CL* v 24 n 2, vi 602 and n 3. A letter of 1820 refers to the novel as one of two "wretched Abortions" in the series, though C made a partial retraction of this judgment almost immediately: *CL* v 24, 33.

foreseen Hopelessness of Rebecca—the comparatively feeble interest excited by Rowena, the from the beginning foreknown Bride of Ivanhoe/ perhaps, the unmixed atrocity of the Norman Nobles, & our utter indifference to the feuds of Norman and Saxon (N.b. what a contrast to our interest in the Cavaliers & Jacobites and the Puritans, Commonwealthmen & Covenanters from Charles I to the Revolution!)—these may, or may not have been the cause—but Ivanhoe I never have been able to summon fortitude to read thro'—Doubtless, the want of any one predominant interest aggravated by the want of any one continuous thread of Events is a grievous defect in a Novel.—These form the charm of Scott's *Guy Mannering*, which I am far from admiring the most but yet read with the greatest delight—spite of the *falsetto* of Meg Merrilies,[2] and the absurdity of the tale. But it contains an amiable character, tho' a very commonplace & easily manufactured Compound, Dandy Dinmont—and in all Walter Scott's Novels I know of no other. Cuddy in *Old Mortality* is the nearest to it, and certainly much more of a *Character* than Dinmont. But Cuddy's consenting not to see and recognize his old Master at his selfish Wife's instance, is quite inconsistent with what is meant by a *good heart*. No wife could have influenced *Strap* to such an act.[3]—I have no doubt, however, that this very absence of *Heart* is one & not the least operative, ~~of m~~ among the causes of Scott's unprecedented favor with the higher Classes—[4]

3   I (ii) 311 | *The Monastery* ch 2

The savage and capricious Brown Man of the Moors, a being which seems the genuine descendant of the northern dwarfs,* was supposed to be seen there frequently, especially after the autumnal equinox, when the fogs were thick, and objects not easily distinguished. The Scottish fairies too, a whimsical, irritable and malicious tribe, who though at times capriciously benevolent were most frequently adverse to mortals . . .

*   themselves the relics of the Cabiri, Coβωλοι, Cobolts—and the Gothic Zwerg, whence our Dwarf, a corruption of Theurgi.[1] Another name of the

2[2] The gypsy Meg Merrilies foils a plot to cheat the hero, Harry Bertram, out of his estate; C uses "falsetto" metaphorically, it seems, for a strained or forced fictional character; cf COPY A **28**.

2[3] Hugh Strap is the faithful companion of the hero in Smollett's *Roderick Random*. C used a comparison of Scott's novels with *Roderick Random* and other popular successes of 18th-century fiction as evidence of a significant change in taste: *CL* V 24–5, 33.

2[4] For another remark about Scott's higher-class audience see COPY A **5**.

3[1] This note reflects C's interest in the common features of different national mythologies, and particularly his reading about the Cabiri of the Samothracian Mysteries in George Stanley Faber *A Disserta-*

Cabiric Gods is Boni Socii, the *Good Neighbors* of the Scotch Glens. Even the Fairies are the Φηρες, Peris, Persæ, all synonimes of the Cabiri, or κοβωλοι/[2]

4   I (ii) 341 | End of ch 4

[Tibb tells Elspeth Glendinning about a local spectre, the White Maiden of Avenel, whom she considers as a sort of personal saint for the Avenel family; but Elspeth says, "Our Lady and Saunt Paul are good enough saunts for me . . .".]

This mixture of the White Lady (an imitation of Baron Fouqué's Undina)[1] with a secret convert to Protestantism is exceedingly whimsical.

5   II (iii) ⁻5–⁻3, pencil

Qy One Object (and *Effect*, when it indeed *is*) of Religion to over power in the individual mind the working of the *self-comparativeness*, alike for better and for worse—alike *antidotive* to presumption and to despair.

Let A in twenty respects have gifts & qualities great compared with b.

---

tion on the *Mysteries of the Cabiri* (Oxford 1803)—see FABER passim—and esp in F. W. J. von Schelling *Ueber die Gottheiten von Samothrace* (Stuttgart & Tübingen 1815), which C also annotated—see above. (C's most extensive use of this material appears in *P Lects* esp Lect 11—1949—320–3.) The Cabiri were sometimes described as infernal or subterranean deities, and Schelling refers to their pygmy or dwarf figure (34–6); in an article published in *Blackwood's* in 1821, C remarks upon "the habit of tracing the presence of the high in the humble, the mysterious Dii Cabiri, in the form of the dwarf Miner, with hammer and spade, and week-day apron": *SW & F* (*CC*) 949. In addition to these mythological and iconographic resemblances, C here follows Schelling in proposing linguistic connections among Greek, Latin, German, and English terms: the German *Kobold* or *Kobalt* (associated by Schelling with the mischievous κόβαλοι of Aristophanes *Knights* 635) being a demon or goblin of the mines, and *Zwerg* (which Schelling derived from the latinised Greek term *theurgi* "god-workers") a dwarf.

3[2] At a dinner attended by both C and Scott on 22 Apr 1828, C spoke at length about the Samothracian Mysteries "which he considered as affording the germ of all tales about fairies past, present, and to come": *TT* (*CC*) I 557, and cf I 105 and n 28. The same point is made, with some of the same connections, many of them suggested by Schelling (*boni socii* "good fellows"; Persian peri and fairies), in *P Lects* Lect 11—1949—321, *Lects 1808–1819* (*CC*) II 56 and nn 27–9, and a *Blackwood's* article of 1822—*SW & F* (*CC*) 979*. The Φηρες (Greek *Pheres* "Beasts" or "Satyrs") are mentioned by Scott himself in "On the Fairies of Popular Mythology" *Minstrelsy of the Scottish Border* (2nd ed 3 vols Kelso & Edinburgh 1802–3) II 174.

4[1] Baron Friedrich Heinrich Karl de La Motte-Fouqué (1777–1843) *Undine* (1811, tr 1818)—a fairy story about the water-spirit Undine who gains and then loses a human soul by her involvement in human affairs. *The Monastery* features a White Lady who similarly intervenes in the lives of the characters. C compares Scott's work unfavourably to *Undine* in *TT* (*CC*) I 150.

c. d. e. f. &c A cannot redeem himself from either the *drawbacks* from these gifts & qualities, the *sets-off* against them: nor even from their own imperfection.[1] Comparatively with b. c. d, they may *appear* great; POSITIVELY and relatively to what they *ought* to be, they are *filthy Rags*—i.e. fragments. A. and Z. owe each a 1000£—A pays a 100 Shillings, Z a hundred Pence—both are insolvent.

At best, we can not redeem ourselves: at worst, God can redeem us.[2]

As a part of the *process* of discipline we may profitably for humiliation confine our comparison, first, of the apparent good with the evil in ourselves, and second, of the comparative good with the positively good. But even this must not be too long or exclusively pursued—or it would sink us into despair & faithless self-contempt. Still we must recur to the principle—No man can redeem himself—but there *is* a Redeemer, and He *all-wise*.

For a Soul in right earnest respecting its Salvation, there is but one difficult point in theology—viz. in what sense the Soul may trust in Christ's Supplement of its defeeticiency and Precipitation of its Sins.—The one practically interesting controversy, that between Pelagian and Antinomian.[3]

6   II (iii) 18–19, pencil | Ch 2

[The supernatural figure of the White Lady of Avenel appears to Halbert Glendinning, and transports him to a grotto deep in the earth.]

This Chapter might be chosen by a philosophical Critic to point out and exemplify the difference of Fancy and Imagination.[1] Here is abundance of the former with the blankest absence of the latter. Hence the "In-

---

5[1]   C's writings, and his letters in particular, frequently express a sense of the discrepancy between his capacity (and hence responsibility) and his achievement; the parable of the talents in Matt 25.14–30 was a perpetual reproach to him: *BL* ch 10 (*CC*) I 219–20, *CL* III 490.

5[2]   Other notes on the subject of redemption include *CL* V 47–8, DONNE *Sermons* COPY B **6**, HOOKER **49**, KANT *Religion* **4**; C's most extended treatment of it appears in *AR* (*CC*) 305–8, 318–34; the evolution of his views upon it is traced in *CCD* 127–47.

5[3]   Insofar as Pelagianism emphasises the active role of the individual in redemption, while Antinomianism considers redemption to be an act of grace. In BUNYAN COPY A **24** C takes a somewhat different position on the question from the one he adopts here, by affirming a middle road, a "Gospel Medium" between the Pelagians and the Antinomians, namely "It is indeed Faith alone that saves us; but such a Faith, as cannot be alone."

6[1]   See COPY A **13** and n 1. It is noteworthy that a little later in this chapter Scott quotes "the most imaginative of our modern bards"—i.e. C himself, named in the footnote.

credulus odi"[2] which it leaves on the mind—the imperious sense of the *Absurdity* of the arbitrary *fiction*.

7   II (iii) 232, referring to Ch 17

Ch. XVII. The sudden transfiguration of Mysie into a Heroine with all the tremulous delicacy & sensitive proprieties of a Damsel of Quality— & this too without the Aid which in after times a Jeanie Dean might have reccived from an austere religious Education—draws somewhat too largely on the Belief of the Reader.[1]

8   II (iv) 15–16 | *The Abbot* ch 1

She pressed her hands together, as if she was wringing them in the extremity of her desolate feeling, as one whom Heaven had written childless. A large stag-hound of the greyhound species approached at this moment, and, attracted perhaps by the gesture, licked her hands and pressed his large head against them. He obtained the desired caress in return, but still the sad impression remained.

It seems to me clear, that at this time Sir W. S. intended to *make something* of this Dog and his prophetic instinct; but I suppose, it did not *come out* as kindly and easily, as the contract with the impatient Publisher required.—

9   II (iv) 20–1

". . . the best of our feelings, when indulged to excess, may give pain to others. There is but one in which we may indulge to the utmost limit of vehemence of which our bosom is capable, secure that excess cannot exist in the greatest intensity to which it can be excited—I mean the love of our Maker."*

* This is a point of awful importance, which I cannot handle without trembling. But surely our highest possible Love of God must in some measure differ from our Love of a Child, a Sister, or a Friend, in as much

---

6[2] Horace *Ars Poetica* 188: "I disbelieve and detest".

7[1] Mysie Happer, a miller's daughter, in love with Sir Piercie Shafton, had helped him to escape when he was held under suspicion of murder. In this chapter, which is concerned with their journey on horseback together, Mysie acts with delicacy and discretion, dressing as Sir Piercie's page but avoiding intimacy. Sir Piercie, who is himself the grandson of a tailor, eventually marries her.

as the Affection does not partake of a passion—is more purely an Act of the Will confirmed by the dictate of the Reason.

10   II (iv) 21, pencil

". . . The fondness which you have lavished on the unfortunate, and, I own, most lovely child, has met something like a reproof in the bearing of your household dog.—Displease not your noble husband. Men, as well as animals, are jealous of the affections of those they love."

But, surely, H. Warden ought to have reserved the better half of his reproof for the jealous Husband.[1]

11   II (iv) 27–8 | Ch 2

[The Lady of Avenel proposes to the grandmother of Roland that he should be brought up in her own noble household.] "Received into a noble family! . . . and for what purpose, I pray you?—to be my lady's page, or my lord's jackman, to eat broken victuals and contend with other menials for the remnants of the master's meal? . . ."

How grossly unnatural is not this Speech! What mere head-work of a ~~modern~~ Sentimental Dramatist of the Kotzebue School![1] How uniformly Sir W. S. fails in his attempts at imaginative characters! They are all alike from Meg Merrilies to Norna![2]

12   II (iv) 29

[Roland's grandmother agrees to part with him for a time, on certain conditions.] ". . . *But especially swear, he shall not lack the instruction of

10[1] Henry Warden, a grave Protestant preacher and a member of the Avenel household, has been warning the Lady of Avenel against excessive display of affection towards a child (Roland) whom her dog Wolf had rescued from drowning, and whom she wants to adopt and raise as her son.

11[1] The German playwright August Friedrich Ferdinand von Kotzebue (1761–1819) had a great vogue throughout Europe about the end of the 18th century: in 1798–9, Drury Lane staged *The Stranger*, *Lovers' Vows*, and *Pizarro* (Sheridan's version of *The Spaniards in Peru*). C attacked "the pantomimic tragedies and weeping comedies of Kotzebue and his imitators" in "Satyrane's Letters": *BL* ch 22 (*CC*) II 185 and n.

11[2] C refers to a group of poor, socially outcast and more or less mentally disordered older women in Scott's fiction, his examples being the gypsy Meg Merrilies from *Guy Mannering* and Norna, the mother of the pirate, from *The Pirate*. In his notes to the latter work he makes a similar point: COPY C **6**. For C's complaint about Scott's failure of imagination see also **6** above, and COPY A **13** and n 1.

the godly man who hath placed the gospel truth high above these idolatrous shavelings, the monks and friars."

* Roland being 10 years old, this piece of desperate & useless hypocrisy
is as incredible as her vulgar mock-heroic Rudeness is disgusting.

13   ɪɪ (iv) 30

* The old woman turned short round on the officious waiting-maid. "Let
her make her obeisance to me then, and I will return it. Why should I bend
to her?—is it because her kirtle is of silk, and mine of blue lockeram?—
Go to, my lady's waiting-woman. Know that the rank of the man rates
that of the wife, and that she who marries a churl's son, were she a king's
daughter, is but a peasant's bride."

* Again, this is not the Language of a Woman of high birth, whose mind
had been unsettled by calamities; but of a mad Oyster-woman who fancied herself a Dutchess.

14   ɪɪ (iv) 42–3, pencil | Ch 3

Sir W. S. should never have meddled with the Super-natural, for he can
not blend it with the Natural.[1] Imagine the supposed experiences of Halbert in the Monastery[2]—& you feel how impossible these in themselves
justly delineated natural feelings become. The *Super-naturalist's* must be
a transitory character, never *carried on*. He must exist only in and for the
super-natural Tale.

15   ɪɪ (iv) 44

"Wolf chained up—and Wolf surly to your page!" answered Sir Halbert
Glendinning; "Wolf never was surly to any one; and the chain will either
break his spirit or render him savage—So ho, there—set Wolf free directly."

* and yet Sir W. would describe Sir Halbert as an amiable character, a
kind Husband. ~~God save me~~ But the truth probably is, that the whole of
this 'Abbot' was written, because a novel for 2 or 3000£ was engaged for.

S. T. C.

14[1] See COPY A **9** and n 1.
14[2] E.g. **6** textus above. *The Abbot* is a
sequel to *The Monastery*, and Halbert Glendinning a central character in both.

16   II (iv) 45, pencil

[Roland refuses to kiss Sir Halbert's hand.] "Nay, but do as you are commanded, child," replied the lady.—"He is dashed by your presence," she said, apologizing to her husband; "but is he not a handsome boy?"

"And so is Wolf, . . . a handsome dog; but he has this double advantage over your new favourite, that he does what he is commanded, and hears not when he is praised."

* Surely, a very cruel and unamiable Speech from the Peasant's Son to the Lady of Avenel.[1]

17   II (iv) 406–7 | Ch 26

[Roland makes love to the supposed Catherine Seyton, who is really Catherine's twin brother dressed as a woman.]

Shakespear has left us one *farce*—the Classical Model of that Genus of the drama which begins by taking some improbability for granted, & then works an comic interest out of it. But even in ~~the~~ a 'Comedy of Errors' Sh. would not have made a *Male* after close examination & excited doubt indistinguishable from a female.

The improbability of this Scene is so monstrous, & Roland's Stupidity so inconceivable, that even ~~had~~ its ~~occurred in fact~~ actual occurrence would not have justified its introduction in such a work.—

18   III (v) 16–17, pencil | Ch 1

Certainly, no Writer ever availed himself of a præternatural obtuseness in his Heroes, and an incomprehensible non-understanding or misunderstanding, of the most palpable solutions of ~~his~~ (even at first scarcely credible[)] Mistake, in the degree that Sir W. S. does, in most of his Novels.

19   III (v) 101 | Ch 6

Seyton and Douglas stood looking on the dying man, and when the scene was closed, the former was the first to speak. "As I live, Douglas, I meant not this, and am sorry; but he laid hands on me, and compelled me to defend my freedom, as I best might, with my dagger. If he were ten times thy friend and follower, I can but say that I am sorry."

*"I blame thee not, Seyton," said Douglas, "though I lament the

---

16[1] Halbert Glendinning, the son of a   to the house of Avenel.
tenant farmer, had been raised by marriage

chance—There is an over-ruling destiny above us, though not in the sense of that wretched man, who, beguiled by some foreign mystagogue, used the awful word as the ready apology for whatever he chose to do . . ."

* [D.] The Coat is black.   [Sir W.] Yea, black! I say the same: Tho' not in THY Sense, wretched Man!   [D.] What then? [Sir W.] Why, bottle-green.

    * I would fain ask *at*[1] Sir Walter's Profundity, in *what* other sense "an over-ruling DESTINY" can be asserted?

20   III (v) ⁻4, referring to COPY A I (i) 196 | *Waverley* ch 24, COPY A **4** textus

p. 196.
A *Superstition* or ~~the~~ rather the reasonable *Ground* of Superstition in the Human Mind—whatever be the last distinct *Cause* ~~in the~~ fading into the Horizon of our Knowlege, aliquid adhuc *superstat*.[1]

    An old Map of Africa compared with one of Arrowsmith's, may serve to illustrate the difference between the Superstition of the Philosopher & that of the Multitude/ Between the *lost* in distance & the Objects within the field of distinct Vision there are *Sights*, to which we ourselves *give* forms. He who is aware of this, is so far a Philosopher—as compared with him, who believes that he receives both . . .*ᵃ*[2]

21   III (v) 243 | *Kenilworth* ch 4

"Stop thy base unmannered tongue!" said the lady; "to no question that derogates from my honour, do I deign an answer."
    "You have said enough in refusing to reply," answered Tressilian; "and

---

      20ᵃ The note ends thus, with stops or points of ellipsis

    19[1] C objects to "ask at" as a Scotticism in COPY C **20**, and here uses it mockingly.
    20[1] As in COPY A **4**, to which this note is a sort of postscript, C makes an etymological point: superstition has to do with that "something [that] still *stands above*" or remains.
    20[2] Presumably, this analogy works as it were in reverse order, so that the superstition of "the Multitude" is like the old map, and the superstition of "the Philosopher" like the new one. The first fills the area of the unknown with imaginary forms; the second is aware of the hazard of the guessing process. R. V. Tooley *Collectors' Guide to*

Maps of the African Continent and Southern Africa (1969) iv makes the point: as late as the 17th century, map-makers "filled the interior with imagined mountains and rivers, fictitious kingdoms and other devices", but by the late 18th century, when Aaron Arrowsmith (1750–1833) founded his family of cartographers, "How much emptier is Arrowsmith's map, how much more accurate—and less decorative." The Arrowsmiths may have been in C's mind because they had very recently (1825) published a new map of Africa: see Oscar I. Norwich *Maps of Africa* (Johannesburg & Cape Town 1983) 188.

mark me, unhappy as thou art, I am armed with thy father's full authority to command thy obedience, and I will save thee from the slavery of sin and of sorrow, even despite of thyself, Amy."

"Menace no violence here!" exclaimed the lady . . .

Sir W. gives to his characters an occasional happy obtuseness, a felicity in *not*-under- or *mis*under-standing things plain as pike-staves, that is as convenient to himself as it seems surprizing to his Readers. Ex. gr. Tresillian's "You have said enough" &c.—

22   III (vi) ⁻2

A thought, (which something better than a thought forbad to be realized) for a Lady's ALBUM. 20 Sept^br 1830.

> If without any *Head*, & Al bum be the same,
> This Book, I opine, well merits the name.[1]   S. T. C.[a]

22[a] The note is followed by an outline of a rectangle, in pencil—perhaps the imagined album?

22[1] C must have been considerably pestered for contributions to ladies' albums but as a rule he good-naturedly produced the expected comic or sentimental epigram, as for example *PW* (EHC) II 972–3. *SW & F* (*CC*) 1506–7 is an example of a contribution in prose.

Copy C

Novels and Romances of the Author of Waverley. [Anonymous.] 7 vols (in 4). Edinburgh 1825 [1824]. 18°.

British Library C 126 b 5, bound uniformly with *Novels and Tales* and *Historical Romances*, COPY A and COPY B.

CONTENTS. See General Note before COPY A headnote.

DATE. See COPY A headnote. COPY C **6** alludes to a current periodical, the *Gentleman's Magazine* of Jun 1827.

1 ɪ ⁻3, ⁻4, ⁻2–⁻1ᵃ, pencil

Semibreve | Breve | Plusquam breve | Long | Plusquam long.[1]
In the ~~trochaic~~ Iamböid Pentameter of the Paradise Lost, I assume fifteen Breves as the total quantity of each Line—this Isochrony being the Identity or Element of Sameness, the varying quality of the Isochronous Feet constituting the difference.[2] And from the harmony or fine balance of the two opposite (N.B. *not* contrary)[3] Forces, viz. Identity and Difference results the Likeness—And again, this Likeness (quicquid *simile* est, non est *idem*)[4] reducible to a Law or Principle, & therefore anticipable & in fact,

---

[a] The note begins on pp ⁻3–⁻4 (written across the page), then continues on pp ⁻2–⁻1; ⁻3 and ⁻4 are each headed "3"

[1] "Half-short | short | more than short | long | more than long": this proposed notation appears to be C's own, a casual experiment not repeated. C was, however, fascinated by classical and English prosody and prosodic issues all his life, both as critic and as practitioner. Significant statements about poetic metre are the Preface to *Christabel* (*PW*—EHC—ɪ 215); the response to WW in *BL* chs 14, 18 (*CC*) ɪɪ 11–15, 58–88; and the lesson on prosody in *SW & F* (*CC*) ɪ 201–6. See also "metrical experiments" collected in *PW* (EHC) ɪɪ 1014–20; examples in the notebooks, esp *CN* ɪɪ 2224; observant remarks about poetic practice in e.g. BEAUMONT AND FLETCHER COPY B **10** and n 3, DONNE *Poems* **1, 2, 13**, HERBERT **13**, JONSON **45, 46**; and a comparison of his own

work with that of WW and Scott, in *CL* ɪɪɪ 111–12.

[2] On "the incomparable Excellence of Milton's Metre" see *CN* ɪɪɪ 4190 and MILTON *Poems* (annotated 1823) **4, 9, 10, 20, 24, 38**. C's "Iamböid"—meaning *resembling* iambic, or *roughly* iambic—appears to be a nonce usage and is not in *OED*; for "isochrony" the first example in *OED* is from 1953.

[3] C often made this distinction, notably in *C&S* (*CC*) 24*, where the main point is that "Opposite powers are always of the same kind, and tend to union".

[4] "Whatever is *like* is not *the same*", a maxim in logic: cf e.g. *Logic* (*CC*) 11 and n 4.

tho perhaps unconsciously expected by the Reader or Auditor, constitutes poetic Metre. Each Line is a Metre:[5] ex. gr. we should not say, that an Hexameter is a Line of six Metres, but that it is a metre of six feet. But the harmonious relation of the Metres to each other, the fine Medium [b]between Division & Continuity, Distinction without Disjunction, which a good Reader expresses by a pause without a cadence, constitutes Rhythm[c]—And it is ~~that~~is harmonious Opposition & balance of Metre and Rhythm, superadded to the former Balance of the Same in Quantity with the Different in Quality, the one belonging to the Lines, the other to the Paragraphs, that makes the peculiar charm, the *excellency*, of the Miltonic Poesy. The Greek ₽ Epic Poets left Rhythm to the Orators. The metre all but precluded Rhythm.[6] But the Ancients *sang* their poetry.[7] Now for a Nation, who like the English, have substituted *Reading*, impassioned and tuneful Reading I grant, but still *Reading*, for *Recitative*, this counter-action, this interpenetration, as it were, of Metre and Rhythm is the dictate of a sound Judgement and like all other excellencies in the Fine Arts, a Postulate of Common Sense fulfilled by Genius, the *Needful* at once contained & united in the *Beautiful*.   S. T. Coleridge

P.S.—Milton must be scanned by the Pedes Compositæ, as the Choriambus, Ionics, Pæans, Epitrites, &c[8]—taking the five notations, ◡ | ◡◡ | ◡◡◡ | — | ◡— | as the Ground.

2   I (i) vii–viii | Advertisement to *The Pirate*

The purpose of the following Narrative is to give a detailed and accurate account of certain remarkable incidents which took place in the Orkney Islands, concerning which the more imperfect traditions and mutilated records of the country only tell us the following erroneous particulars .... [A pirate named Gow, having terrorised the district and been be-

1[b] Running out of space at the end of p ⁻4, C returns to the top of ⁻3
1[c] Here C has written "(Turn over leaf,)" and continued the note on p ⁻2

1[5] In an essay on Greek metre, C defined the μέτρον (*metron*) in the singular as equivalent to "foot" and in the plural (*metra*) as the arrangement of feet to form a verse line: *SW & F* (*CC*) 861.

1[6] In the metre of epic, dactylic hexameter, the unit or *metron* was the dactylic foot, for which a spondee might be substituted; nevertheless it would seem possible to introduce rhythm as C defines it above.

1[7] Or, as C implies with "recitative" below, recited it with a musical accompaniment.

1[8] "Composite feet": the choriambus being a combination of trochee (otherwise "chorius") and Iambus – ◡ ◡ –; the ionics – – ◡ ◡ or ◡ ◡ – –; the paeons (C's "Pæans" is an error) any one of the four possible combinations of one long and three short syllables; and the epitrites any one of the four possible combinations of one short and three long syllables. The same composite feet are discussed in an 1807 lesson on English prosody: *SW & F* (*CC*) 203.

trothed to a local girl, was eventually seized with his crew, brought to
trial, and executed.] It is said, that the lady whose affections Gow had engaged, went up to London to see him before his death, and that arriving
too late, she had the courage to request a sight of his body; and then touching the hand of the corpse, she formally resumed the troth-plight which
she had bestowed. Without going through this ceremony, she could not,
according to the superstition of the country, have escaped a visit from the
ghost of her departed lover, in the event of her bestowing upon any living suitor the faith which she had plighted to the dead.

Surely, nothing more injudicious than this Advertisement can well be
conceived, as the introduction to a tale which imitates the tones of an historical Memoir!—But this is one of the distinguishing Characters of Sir
W. S.'s Novels—best explained, perhaps, as the contrary to the "*most believing mind*"[1] which Collins so happily attributes to Spenser, who

Wept as he wrote and did in tears indite.[2]

Sir W. relates Ghost-stories, Prophecies, Presentiments, all præter-super-
naturally fulfilled; but is most anxious to let his Readers know, that he
himself is far too enlightened not to be assured of the folly & falsehood
of all, that he yet relates as *truth*, & for the purpose of exciting the interest and the emotions attached to the belief of their truth—and all this, not
with the free life & most happy judgement of Ariosto, as a neutral tint or
shooting Light; but soberly, to save his own (Sir Walter's) character as
an enlightened man.—[3]

If Sir W. thought it necessar~~ily~~ by this previous assurance of the falsehood of all the ~~sup~~ pretended facts, characters & incidents to prevent the
pathos & interest of his tale from overpassing the bounds of pleasurable
excitement, I can only say that in this Novel at least it was a needless
alarm/ & that generally Sir Walter's merit does not lie in this quarter.

S. T. C.

---

3   I (i) 30, pencil | Ch 2

The kraken, that hugest of living things, was still supposed to cumber the
recesses of the Northern Ocean . . . . The sea-snake was also known,
which, arising out of the depths of ocean, stretches to the skies his enor-

2[1] C quotes his own *Frost at Midnight*
line 24: *PW* (EHC) I 241.

2[2] C is recalling a description of Spenser
in William Shenstone *The Schoolmistress*
line 167, "Sigh'd as he sung, and did in tears
indite". The idea of the "most believing
mind" occurs in Collins's tribute to Tasso in

*Popular Superstitions of the Highlands of
Scotland* lines 198–9: "Prevailing poet,
whose undoubting mind/ Believed the magic
wonders which he sung!"

2[3] Cf similar disparagement in COPY A
8, 9 (and n 1).

mous neck, covered with a mane like that of a war-horse, and with its broad glittering eyes, raised mast-head high, looks out, as it seems, for plunder or for victims.

Many prodigious stories of these marine monsters, and of many others less known, were then universally received among the Zetlanders, whose descendants have *not as yet by any means abandoned faith in them.

* No wonder! for *I* believe in the Sea-snake; R. Southey in the Kraken; and Linnéus in both.[1]   S. T. Coleridge

4   i i 224–5 | Ch 15

In this process of reasoning, it is probable that a little mortified vanity, or some indescribable shade of selfish regret, might be endeavouring to assume the disguise of disinterested generosity; but there is so much of base alloy in our best (unassisted) thoughts, that it is melancholy work to criticise too closely the motives of our most worthy actions; at least we would recommend to every one to let those of his neighbours pass current, however narrowly he may examine the purity of his own.*

* Different Men will assent to this Position in different degrees: *Some* truth the vainest heads will admit, and the purest hearts find, therein. But it is likewise true, that the blameless interpolations of the associative Memory are not seldom by misanthropes misconstrued into impulses of a corrupt Will or Motives of Self-love.

5   i (i) 280–1 | Ch 19

[Norna speaks:] ". . . Not by day-light should Norna tell a tale that might blot the sun out of heaven, and blight the hopes of the hundred boats that will leave this shore ere noon, to commence their deep-sea fishing,—ay, and of the hundred families that will await their return. The demon, whom

---

3[1] For the kraken, see SCHUBERT *Ansichten* **49** and n 2. The two mythical sea-monsters, the kraken and the sea-snake or sea-serpent, were commonly linked to one another, especially after the publication of the chapter on sea-monsters in Erich Pontoppidan's *Natural History of Norway* (tr 1755) ii 183–218. See Plate 7. Their existence was a matter of scientific controversy but it does not appear even to have been considered by Linnaeus almost a century earlier: his *Systema Naturae* (1735) does not include either of them even under "Para-

doxa", though it gives the name of sea-serpent to one of the eels, a variety however only 3–4 feet long. The same is true of a translation C used, Sir Charles Linné *A General System of Nature* tr William Turton (7 vols 1802). C is said to have discussed the kraken and mermaids and affirmed RS's belief in them (whether in mermaids alone or in both is not clear) in his famous encounter with Keats: John Keats *Letters* ed Hyder Edward Rollins (2 vols Cambridge MA 1958) ii 89.

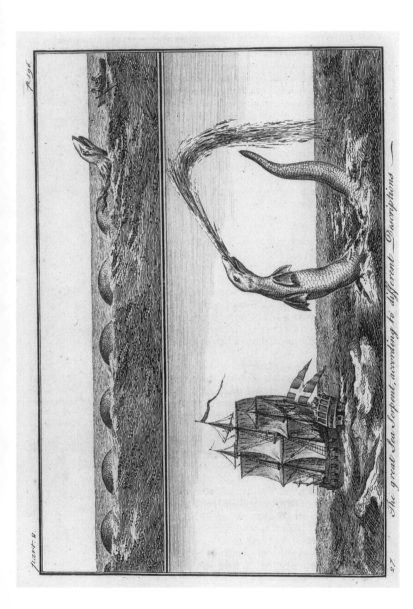

7. "The Great Sea Serpent", from Erich Pontoppidan *The Natural History of Norway* (1755). See Walter SCOTT COPY C **3**. The British Library; reproduced by kind permission

the sounds will not fail to awaken, must shake his dark wings over a ship-less and a boatless sea, as he rushes from his mountain to drink the accents of horror he loves so well to listen to."

Was it Auri sacra fames?[1] Or is it to be classed among the instances of Self-nescience? that Sir W. S. enters in competition with Mrs Ratcliff?[2] Alas! This Norna Δειμος τε φοβος τε[3] has not even the ordinary merit of Failures in the Horrible Line—to be laughable! I would call the failure pitiable, but that the Attempt was pitiful.

6   I (ii) 20–1 | Ch 2

Turning to this quarter, from which a low hollow moaning breeze then blew, Norna addressed the spirit of the winds, in tones which seemed to resemble his own,—

> "Thou, that over billows dark
> Safely send'st the fisher's bark,—
> Giving him a path and motion
> Through the wilderness of ocean;
> Thou, that when the billows brave ye,
> O'er the shelves can drive the navy,—
> Did'st thou chafe as one neglected,
> While thy brethren were respected? . . ."

Much certainly might have been expected from a "Reading Public" that had found Meg Merrilies a master-stroke of wild sublimity: but to expect, that N⟨orna⟩ would *pass*, was a bold *Spec.* verily!![1] The rhymes "brave ye, Navy" remind me of Sir Lumley Skeffington's "Desire, Maria" in his delicate Doggrel to Miss Foot, in the Gentleman's Magazine for June or July 1827.[2]

5[1] "Accursed hunger for gold": Virgil *Aeneid* 3.57 tr H. Rushton Fairclough (LCL).

5[2] Ann Radcliffe (1764–1823), author of several celebrated Gothic novels, notably *The Mysteries of Udolpho* (1794) and *The Italian* (1797). C reviewed *The Italian*: *SW & F (CC)* 79–82.

5[3] "Terror and fear": they appear personified as sons of Ares in Homer and Hesiod. This phrase occurs (var) in *Iliad* 15.119.

6[1] Cf COPY B **11**. "*Spec.*" appears to be a joking form of "expectation" or "speculation", but if the word is an allusion, its source is not traced.

6[2] *G Mag* XCVII (Jan–Jun 1827) 548 includes "The Spring and the Morning: Stanzas inscribed to Miss *Foote*. By Sir *Lumley Skeffington*, Bart." Maria Foote (c 1797–1867) was a glamorous actress, Skeffington (1771–1850) a minor playwright. C alludes to lines 7–8: "Aloud I exclaim'd, with augmented desire,/ I thought 'twas the Spring, when, in truth, 'tis MARIA!"

7   I (ii) 323 | *The Fortunes of Nigel* ch 4

"I hope it will, my lord," said the old man, with a smile; "but," to use honest John Bunyan's phrase*—'therewithall the water stood in his eyes,' "it has pleased God to try me with the loss of two children . . ."

* Is not this an Anachronism? ~~Surely~~ But the words, perhaps, are intended as the Narrator's.[1]

8   I (ii) 360–1, pencil | Ch 6

In the meanwhile, the name of the Duke of Buckingham, the omnipotent favourite both of the King and the Prince of Wales, had struck some anxiety into the party which remained in the great parlour. He was more feared than beloved, and, if not absolutely of a tyrannical disposition, was accounted haughty, violent, and vindictive.

In order not to exaggerate Buckingham's monopoly of patronage & his imperious deportment, it must be remembered that the King's Favorite was likewise what we call the Premier—& we must think of M[r] Pitt as well as the Marquis or Marchioness of Cunningham.[1]   *S. T. C.*

9   II (iv) 4–5, pencil | Ch 32

. . . the King extended his hand to be kissed, and then began to address him in a tone of grave sympathy.

"We told your lordship in our secret epistle of this morning, written with our ain hand, in testimony we have neither praetermitted nor forgotten your faithful service, that we had that to communicate to you that would require both patience and fortitude to endure, and therefore exhorted you to peruse some of the most pithy passages of Seneca, and of Boethius *de Consolatione*, that the back may be, as we say, fitted for the burthen—This we commend to you from our ain experience.

Non ignara mali miseris succurrere disco,
['Not ignorant of ill do I learn to befriend the unhappy'—Virgil *Aeneid* 1.630, tr H. Rushton Fairclough] sayeth Dido, and I might say in my own

7[1] The story of *The Fortunes of Nigel* is set during the reign (1603–25) of James I and therefore antedates the birth of John Bunyan in 1628; but as C points out, the fictitious narrator ("the Author of *Waverley*") belongs to a later era.

8[1] C elsewhere writes harshly of "the Minion, Buckingham" (MACDIARMID **8**) and of James's "*beslobbered* Minion" (HACKET *Scrinia* **6**, cf **32** and n 2). Here he attempts more impartially to account for his power: he is not only the king's close friend, like Henry Conyngham, 1st Marquis Conyngham (1766–1832), whose wife Elizabeth (Denison) (c 1766–1861), the Marchioness, was the mistress of George IV; but also prime minister, like William Pitt the Younger (1759–1806), who had long held this office (1783–1801 and again 1804–6).

person, *non ignarus*; but to change the gender would affect the prosody, whereof our southern subjects are tenacious.*. . ."

* Burlesque; not character. James I. wrote as a Pedant of Learning in a learned and pedantic Age; but he did not talk like a fool—Sir W. Scot copies Shakespear's Holofernes & call[a] him King James.[1]

10   II (iv) 121, pencil, marked with a line in the margin | *Peveril of the Peak* ch 1

The moment when a lover passes the window of his mistress—the moment when the epicure hears the dinner-bell, is that into which is crowded the whole interest of the day—the hours which precede it are spent in anticipation; the hours which follow, in reflection on what has passed; and fancy, dwelling on each brief circumstance, gives to seconds the duration of minutes, to minutes that of hours.

Worthy of Shakespear: and to men in sickness & sorrow eminently applicable.

11   II (iv) 151 | Ch 4

[A group of Puritans, led by Major Bridgenorth, approaches Martindale Castle.] "Be patient, my brother," said Solsgrace; "be patient, and let not thy soul be disquieted. We enter not this high place [breached by the Cavaliers] dishonourably, seeing we ascend by the gate which the Lord opened to the godly." The words of the pastor were like a spark to gunpowder. [They sing the hymn "Lord God, arise, and then his foes/ Shall turn themselves to flight . . ."]

Sir W. Scott is universally deemed a first rate historical Scholar: and yet this portrait puzzles me, it is so utterly unlike the character of the Bridgenorth, or so called Presbyterian Party.—It is that of the wildest portion of the Independents.[1]

12   III (vi) ⁻3–⁻1

The absence of the higher beauties & excellencies of Style, Character, and Plot has done more for Sir W. Scott's European, yea, plusquam-eu-

---

9[a] A slip for "calls"

9[1] Cf "James I. was no Fool" in HACKET *Scrinia* **32**; and the extensive note **14** to the same work. Holofernes is the pedantic schoolmaster in *Love's Labour's Lost*.

11[1] C contrasts the relatively sedate behaviour of the Presbyterians with that of more extreme Protestant sects such as the Independents—"Separatist" he calls them elsewhere (BAXTER *Reliquiae* COPY B **2** at n 5)—who argued for the autonomy of each congregation.

ropæan popularity, than ever the abundance of them ~~ever~~ effected for any former writer.[1]—His age ~~was~~ is an Age of *Anxiety*—from the Crown to the Hovel, from the Cradle to the Coffin, all is an anxious straining to maintain life, or *appearances*— ~~some~~ to *rise*, as the only condition of not falling. Interest?—A few Girls may crave purity & weep over Clarissa Harlow, & the Old Novellists![2]—For the Public at large, every man (for every man is now a Reader) has too much of it in his own needs, and embarrassments. He reads, as he smokes, takes snuff, swings on a chair, goes to a Concert, or a Pantomime, to be *amused*, and forget himself—When the desire is to be *a* musis, how can it be gratified *apud* musas?—[3]

The great felicity of Sir W. S. is, that his own ~~char~~ Intellect supplies the place of all intellect & all character in his Heroes & Heroines; & *representing* the intellect of his readers, supersedes all motive for its exertion, by never appearing *alien*, whether as above or below.   S. T. C.

13   III (vi) 75–6, pencil | Ch 5

"Christian," she [Zarah] replied, "I owe you much. Had I not felt I did so, I would, as I have been often tempted to do, have denounced thee to the fierce Countess, who would have gibbetted you on the feudal walls of Castle-Rushin, and bid your heirs seek redress from the eagles, that would long since have thatched their nest with your hair, and fed their young ospreys with your flesh."

Unworthy of Sir W. Scott as was this pilfering imitation of Goethe's *Mignon*, it was still more *unwise*.[1] For it flashes upon us the difference in kind between the Cabinet-work of Talent and the Offspring of Genius!—[2]

12[1] Cf C's letter of 30 Mar 1820 on this subject (*CL* v 24): "Walter Scott's Poems & Novels . . . supply both instance & solution of the *present* conditions & components of popularity—viz—to amuse without requiring any effort of thought, & without exciting any deep emotion." "Plusquameuropæan" i.e. "more than" European.

12[2] In the letter cited in the previous note, C likewise considers Scott's work inferior to the novels of the previous century, and cites Samuel Richardson's *Clarissa Harlowe* (1747–8) as an example.

12[3] When the desire is to be "*away from* the muses", how can it be gratified "*in the company of* the muses"? C makes the same verbal connections (this is not the accepted etymology for "amuse" or "amusement") and uses some of the same illustrations in *BL* ch 3 (*CC*) I 48*.

13[1] In *Wilhelm Meisters Lehrjahre* (pub 1795–6), the protagonist Wilhelm encounters a mysterious child, Mignon, travelling with a group of tightrope dancers; he buys her freedom and she follows him until her death. Carlyle gave C a copy of his translation in Jun 1824: *C Talker* 112.

13[2] C expounds upon the difference between talent and genius elsewhere, notably *BL* ch 2 (*CC*) I 31–2, *Friend* (*CC*) I 419; see also HERDER *Kalligone* **2** and n 3. For the analogous disparagement of Scott as a poet of mechanical fancy rather than creative imagination, see COPY A **13** and n 1.

14 III (v) pp ⁻4 and ⁻1, evidently referring to Ch 5, pencil, cropped

[In this chapter, the villain Edward Christian talks to his accomplice Zarah about past and present plots, and it is revealed that she is the supposedly dumb girl Fenella.]

A man so pre-eminent in literary & contemporary reputation, as Sir W. Scott, ought not to have transferred a character from Goëthe, at all; a Man, of such accredited frankness of temper, as Sir W. S. ought still less to have transferred it *without acknowlegement*—and lastly, so worldly-wise ~~and~~ man, a man of, among Authors, such ⟨unexampled⟩ strong shrewd Good Sense, as Sir W. S.—ought least of all to have ~~fil~~ appropriated Goethe's *Mignon* from the Wilhelm M[eis]t[ers] L[e]h[r] Jahre,[1] & thus have placed himself in rivalry with Goethe in, perhaps, the only point in which he had no possible chance of succeeding—i.e. in the Imaginative, as contra-distinguished from the Fanciful.[2] Hence ~~the~~ Goethe's Mignon, an embodied, and impassioned Ariel,[3] the most exquisite of all Goethe's Conceptions, becomes that repulsive non-descript ~~of~~ Grotesque of a mechanical Fancy-casuistry, the *incredulus odi*,[4] absurd and yet disgusting Ἑρμαφροδίτης,[5] Fenelia—Of all Scott's literary Sins this is the grossest.   S. T. Coleridge

15 III (vi) 112, pencil | Introduction to *Quentin Durward*

You seldom dine at a well-supplied table, <u>but what</u>* the intervals between the champagne, the burgundy, and the hock are filled . . . with the fall of interest and the difficulty of finding investments for cash . . .

* One of Sir Walter's favorite Vulgarisms.[1]

16 III (vi) 115–16, pencil

[The narrator explains some of the advantages of a brief spell abroad.] Whatever, in short, I spend here, is missed at home;* and the few sous

---

14[1] Mignon is identified in **13** n 1. Questions of indebtedness amounting even to plagiarism ("theft" he calls it in **23** below) were almost invariably associated with Scott in C's mind, particularly in connection with Scott's belated acknowledgment of his debt to *Christabel*: *CL* III 290–6, IV 600n, 601 and n, V 379, 437.

14[2] See COPY A **13** and n 1.

14[3] The "delicate Ariel" (I ii 442) of Shakespeare's *Tempest*.

14[4] "I disbelieve and detest", as in COPY B **6** and n 2 above.

14[5] "Hermaphrodite". The bisexual hermaphrodite or androgyne was a figure C seldom invoked without distaste, as with the dandies of *SW & F* (*CC*) 938*; it is of a piece with his usual rejection of the idea of homosexual love (as in ANDERSON COPY A **1** and n 6). He was more enthusiastic about the metaphorical androgyny of "great minds": *CN* IV 4705, *TT* (*CC*) II 191.

15[1] Noted also in COPY A **3**.

gained by the *garçon perruquier* [hairdresser], nay, the very crust I give to his little bare-bottomed, red-eyed poodle, are *autant de perdu* [so much lost] to my old friend the barber, and honest Trusty, the mastiff-dog in the yard. So that I have the happiness of knowing at every turn, that my absence is both missed and moaned by those who would care little were I in my coffin, were they sure of the custom of my executors.

* For the sake of young Readers of this, my ever circulating Copy of Scott's Novels I feel it a duty to say, that this is written in a *bad* spirit. Why *should* the Butcher, the Barber &c feel any deeper regard for a Customer, than as a Customer? Esteem and Love are due only for Esteem and Love. If my Butcher behaves civilly and serves me honestly, he has fully balanced my doings toward him, in ~~emp~~ chusing him for my Butcher, in the belief that I should be better served by him than by an other.

17   III (vi) 226, pencil | Ch 5

Sir W. Scott's Conversation scenes are always interesting because the thoughts are so—but they are utterly characterless. Neither Quentin or Ludovic speaks, but Sir W. S.[1]

18   III (vi) 325 | Ch 11

[The King speaks:] ". . . And, now I think better on it, it will be best that thou pass for a Scottish recruit, who hath come straight down from his mountains, and hath not yet acquired our most Christian language [i.e. French] . . ."

Did Quentin then talk Scotch to Maitre Pierre & the young Countess at the Inn?[1] But this is only one & among the least palpable, of the inconsistencies & improbabilities in Sir W. S's fictions.

19   IV (vii) 18, pencil | Ch 2

"I have liberty," said the Bohemian—"I crouch to no one—obey no one—respect no one.—I go where I will—live as I can—and die when my day comes."

17[1] Quentin and Ludovic are both characters from *Quentin Durward*, Ludovic Lesly ("Le Balafré") being Quentin's uncle. C expresses a similar objection to "a species of ventriloquism, where two are represented as talking, while in truth one man only speaks", in *BL* ch 22 (*CC*) II 135 and n 2.

18[1] In this scene, Louis XI suggests that Quentin should spy on inhabitants of the castle while he is on guard, by pretending that he does not speak French. C objects that at least one of the ladies involved—a young countess who had been presented as a serving-maid at the inn when Louis himself played the part of a merchant, "Maître Pierre"—is bound to recognise him.

"But you are subject to instant execution, at the pleasure of the Judge."

"Be it so," replied the Bohemian; "I can but die so much the sooner."

"And to imprisonment also," said the Scot; "and where, then, is your boasted freedom?"

*"In my thoughts," said the Bohemian, "which no chains can bind . . ."

* Characterless or anti-characteristic as Scott's dialogues too ~~fre~~ commonly are, this is *ultra*-improbable, superlatively inappropriate.

20   IV (vii) 130, pencil | Ch 9

No sooner had the Syndic and Quentin left the room, than Isabelle began to ask at Gertrude various questions concerning the roads . . .

Strange that no friend should have pointed out to Sir W. S. the frequent recurrence of this Scotticism.[1]

21   IV (vii) 225, pencil | Ch 14

"Reprieved or not, he that decoyed us into this snare shall go our fourier to the next world, to take up lodgings for us," said the King, with a grisly and ferocious smile. "Tristan, thou hast done many an act of brave justice—*finis*—I should have said *funis coronat opus*—thou must stand by me to the end."

* *funis* = a rope./ In Louis's state of mind not a very probable joke.[1]

22   IV (vii) 232, pencil | Ch 15

He found . . . the Astrologer in the corner of the public drinking-room—a <u>Stove</u>, as it is called in German and Flemish—sitting in close colloquy with a female . . .

—Exquisite GERMAN! Sir W. meant Stube.[1]

23   IV (vii) 236, pencil

"Speak'st thou of their inability to influence waters, when yet thou knowest that even the weakest, the moon herself . . . holds under her domina-

---

20[1] C uses it mockingly in COPY B **19**.

21[1] The adage is *finis coronat opus* "the end crowns the work". C corrects a typo in this edition—the King, imprisoned in a tower by the Duke of Burgundy and fully expecting to be assassinated, does pun on *funis* "a rope" and not on *funus* "a funeral procession".

22[1] Scott does mean *Stube*—a parlour or sitting-room—but the word comes from the Old High German term for a stove, so the textus is not entirely absurd.

tion ... the tides of the mighty ocean itself, which ebb and increase as her disk waxes and wanes, and watch her influence as a slave watches the nod of a Sultana?* ..."

* From the Ancient Mariner stolen and (as usual) *spoilt* in the attempt to disguise the theft.[1]

24 IV (vii) 242–3, pencil

Amidst these vulgar and ignoble countenances, nothing could shew to greater advantage, than the stately form, handsome mien, and commanding features of the Astrologer .... And, indeed, had he been distinguished by nothing else than the beauty of the graceful and flowing beard which descended over the mysterious roll which he held in his hand, one might have been pardoned regretting that so noble an appendage had been bestowed on him, who put both talents, learning, and the advantages of eloquence, and a majestic person, to the mean purposes of a cheat and an impostor.*

* Why necessarily an impostor? In a far more enlightened age even an Erasmus condemned the too great hardihood of Mirandula for his Work against Astrology.[1] Doubtless, many of these celebrated Astrologers were sincere Believers in their own Jargon.

23[1] C has in mind *AM* lines 414–17 (*PW*—EHC—I 202): "Still as a slave before his lord, / The ocean has no blast; / His great bright eye most silently / Up to the Moon is cast—". For C on Scott's plagiarism see **14** and n 1 above.

24[1] Not traced. The works of Erasmus contain very few references to Pico della Mirandola, most of them admiring. The one arguable exception occurs in the dialogue *Ciceronianus*, where Erasmus has one of his speakers comment that he was "an absolutely superhuman genius, an intellect capable of everything, but his style too was marred by his interest in languages and philosophy and even theology": tr *Collected Works of Erasmus* vol 28 ed A. H. T. Levi (Toronto 1986) 416. Both Pico and Erasmus as a rule were equally dismissive about astrology, and C refers admiringly to Pico's work against it—*Disputationes adversus astrologiam divinatricem*—in PLOTINUS **2**.

HENRY SCOUGAL
1650–1678

[Anon.] The Life of God in the Soul of Man. Or, the nature and excellency of the Christian religion; with the methods of attaining the happiness it proposes. And an account of the beginnings and advances of a spiritual life. In two letters written to persons of honour. 16th ed. London 1806. 8°.

University College London Ogden A 373

Anne Gillman's copy, with "Mrs Gillman" written in her own hand on the title-page and an additional note by C (ANNEX) transcribed by her on pp $^+$2–$^+$3. A typographical error is corrected in pencil p 110, apparently not by C. Bookseller's and librarians' marks p $^-$3 (p-d). Following C's holograph note on p $^-$2, "Samuel Taylor Coleridge" in the bookseller's hand.

DATE. After 1816, perhaps about 1820 like the comparable ms described in the ANNEX headnote and the "Essay on Faith": *SW & F (CC)* 833–44.

1 p $^-$2

This is an excellent little Book, and contains the very Ground-work on which I should wish to build up a true Philosophy, in man and in woman. Philosophy is a Greek Word meaning Love-wisdom.[1] Let but the Individual have domesticated the principles of this Work in his or her Heart: and in the Man I would raise the Love of Wisdom, in the Woman the Wisdom of Love.   S. T. C.

2 p 95, pencil

[In the preceding section Scougal considers Adam before the Fall as having had a "refulgent impression" or idea of God which at the Fall "was much darkened, so much only remaining as might serve to awaken all men, and put them in mind of a supreme and perfect Being".] This idea being so clouded, that it had no more <u>than</u> commanding authority, but was become as a twilight, then our natural propensity to love ourselves took place . . .

Q^y that

[1] A variant of C's usual etymological approach to "philosophy": cf PETVIN 11 n 1.

Annex

The following note was copied into pp $^+2$–$^+3$ by Anne Gillman—whether from a notebook or another (lost) annotated volume, or a scrap of paper, is not known. This gloss on Heb 11.1 is a shorter version of a ms now in the Liverpool University Library, pub *SW & F (CC)* 845–7.

On Faith

Few texts of Scripture have been more misinterpreted than S! Pauls definition of Faith, even the best Commentators (as M! I. Milner)[1] making the first of the verse mean the same as the latter half, an obscure way of saying what is immediately said over again. But every word in this verse has its own distinct meaning—the first referring to the Will, as the *root* of all Spiritual Being, the latter to the Reason as the eye of the Spirit—in the perfect union of which would be Faith perfected. To understand this I must use an analogy.—What is a Soldier? In and of himself, that is, *positively*, he is a *man*; but *relatively*, i.e. in consequence of his king being at war with an invading Enemy, he is a Soldier, but having conquered, and extirpated or reformed his enemies he again becomes a Man. *Substantially* therefore he is a *man*; *relatively* a Soldier. So it is with Faith. That, which in a state of warfare with & ⟨in⟩ direct opposition to the influence of the Senses is Faith, is substantially that state ⟨in⟩ which (all the world and its vanities subdued) ~~and~~ we hope to be—or that which perfected and without an opposite to contend with, is the blessedness of a Spirit, is in its militant state Faith.—Faith is the *substance* of things hoped for; and at the same time that direct Beholding of a Spiritual Truth, which now has to struggle against the over dazzling power of a world of Sense—   S. T. C.

Copy From Mr Coleridge

ANNEX[1] C, along with many of his contemporaries, commonly wrote "J" as "I". Here he is referring to Joseph Milner (1744–97), author of a well-known *History of the Church of Christ*—and specifically to his sermon on Heb 11.1, entitled "The Nature of Faith". It may be found in his *Practical Sermons* ed Isaac Milner (Cambridge 1801) 47–62, and in his *Works* ed Isaac Milner (9 vols 1819–23) VI 47–62. Milner paraphrases the Pauline text thus (47): "Here he tells us what faith is. It substantiates things hoped for, it realizes things invisible; giving such evidence of their reality to the mind, that the believer is influenced as if he saw the objects; and thus he walks by faith, as if by sight."

CHARLES SCUDAMORE
1779–1849

A Chemical and Medical Report of the Properties of the Mineral Waters of Buxton, Matlock, Tunbridge Wells, Harrogate, Bath, Cheltenham, Leamington, Malvern, and the Isle of Wight. London 1820. 8°.

British Library 7510 cc 1 (3)

Bound as third with HASLAM (in Addenda, *CM—CC—*VI) and with Charles Thomas Haden *Practical Observations on the Colchicum Autumnale, as a general remedy of great power, in the treatment of inflammatory diseases, both acute and chronic; and therefore as a substitute for bleeding, in disorders which are connected with increased action of the heart and arteries* (1820). This collection of pamphlets was bound after C's notes had been made: the annotated pages in HASLAM were folded in to protect them from cropping, but the notes in SCUDAMORE were overlooked.

Bookplate of James Gillman on p ¯3; booksellers' marks and prices in pencil on p ¯3, together with the words "Coleridge" and "With MS. Notes by Samuel Taylor Coleridge" in an unidentified hand, in pencil; and in a smaller hand, also in pencil, "Patterson". A typographical error is corrected on p 9 in ink, not in C's hand. A leaf with the signature "W. S. Jackson", now loose in the vol, was perhaps once a flyleaf.

DATE. Probably 1820–1, not long after publication.

1   p 22, pencil, cropped | Buxton

I have here, however, to add, that I have seen instances in which the sanguineous temperament has not been favourable to the use of the water, although the patient has been in the daily habit of drinking a moderate quantity of wine without suffering particular excitement.

But [?wou]ld not [. . .] Water [. . .] the [?Pa]tient in [. . . ?sup] have [. . .] indeed [? the] same [E]ffect?—[B]ut *hush*! [Co]mparisons are odious: and never more [? so] than in the Quackery of Medical Waters.

2   p 23, pencil, cropped

In the condition of stomach which gout produces, and also in the state of constitution which is associated with chronic rheumatism, the internal

617

use of the water has in many instances within my knowledge afforded decided benefit; and, therefore, although it be less sensibly active in its properties than some of the other waters of which I treat in this little volume, it deserves, I am persuaded, to be regarded as considerably medicinal and useful.

Mercy on me[!] It is not perh[aps] *so*, but yet you [? prefer] i[t] *is*—but I myself kn[ow] striking ins[tances] &c.

3   p 29, pencil, cropped

[Scudamore describes the mineral baths at Buxton.] In the instance of a plethoric habit, and more especially if there be <u>marks of congestion</u> in the vessels of the head, some loss of blood will be a necessary preliminary. If there be increased action in the general circulation, blood will be taken from the arm with more propriety; but when there is mere local fulness of the vessels, not affecting the general circulation, cupping, or the use of leeches, will deserve a preference.

!! Either Dr S. rejects the Circulati[on] of the Blood (& if so, h[e] should hav[e] said so) or he shoul[d] have told us, what he means by this local congestion[,] compatib[le] with the Circulatio[n.]

JAMES SEDGWICK
1775–1851

Hints to the Public and the Legislature, on the Nature and Effect of Evangelical Preaching. By a Barrister [James Sedgwick]. 4 pts in one vol. London 1808, 1808, 1809, 1810. 8°.

Pt i is the 4th ed, Pt ii 3rd, Pts iii and iv having no statement of edition are presumably the 1st.

Duke University Library (Dept. of Rare Books)

Bookplate of RS on p ¯1. A note by RS is written on the half-title of Pt i: "The marginal notes in this book are S. T. Coleridge's, written in pencil by him, & traced in ink by me 'that nothing be lost.' R. Southey. June 13. 1810." C annotated this work with the aim of assisting RS in the review he was to write for *QR* iv (Aug–Nov 1810) 480–514: for similar assistance given earlier, see MALTHUS headnote, though in the case of the Malthus review RS took up more of C's suggestions than he did for Sedgwick. Notes **74** and **76** address RS directly, while other notes reflect C's awareness of his special interests, e.g. in the history of Dissent. RS later wrote lives of Bunyan and Wesley: see SOUTHEY *Wesley*. Not all C's notes were written by him in pencil. Where they were, however, little remains of the pencilled original, given the overtracing and the rubbing of the notes. Substantive discrepancies between the pencilled and overtraced versions are recorded in textual notes; pencilled commas, however, are included without a textual note when the overtracer has ignored them. Sometimes only the overtracing is legible, though one wonders about its accuracy: the number of question marks where exclamation marks would be more usual is a case in point. Leaves unopened from iv 81 to end (p 159), except for iv 136–45, 152–9, which in 1986 were opened though unannotated.

On p ¯7 (p-d), a library bookplate and a clipping from a bookseller's catalogue are pasted in; on p ¯5 are pencilled notes regarding the sale and trade of the vol; on p ¯2 an advertisement for the sale of the ms of RS's *Life of Dr. Bell* is pasted in; on p ¯1 RS's bookplate and a notice of the sale of Bewick's bill of charges for the bookplate are pasted in, and some pencilled notes by an owner of the vol explain the connection between C's notes and RS's work: "See Southey's Letter to Taylor Nov 3 1810 | Taylor's Life 301 . . . Southey reviewed the book in Quarterly No 8 Vol iv 1810". A pencilled note on the half-title verso of Pt i reads "The 'Barrister' was James Sedgwick | see Gent: Mag: April 1851. p. 436." The fly-

619

title to Pt iv has a note in pencil, "See Notes p 319", although no "p 319" appears in the vol. RS has made pencil marks in the margins of i 17, 19, 34, 38, 39, 44, 63.

MS TRANSCRIPT. VCL B7 37.

DATE. Between May and mid–Jun 1810. C was back at Greta Hall with his family (and RS's) early in May; RS records retracing the notes in this vol 13 Jun 1810.

1 half-title, written above RS's ms note, pencil, overtraced

> For only that man understands indeed
> Who well remembers what he well can *do*;
> The Faith lives only where the Faith doth breed
> Obedience to the Works it binds us to.
> And as the Life of Wisdom hath exprest
> If this ye know, then do it and be blest!
>
> Lord Brook.[1]

2 half-title, pencil, overtraced

There is one Misconception running thro the whole of this Pamphlet, the rock on which & the quarry out of which, the whole Reasoning is built—therefore an Error which will not indeed destroy its efficacy as a μισητον[a][1] or Anti-philtre to inflame the scorn of the Enemies of Methodism, but which must utterly incapacitate it for the better purpose of convincing the consciences or allaying the fanaticism of the Methodists themselves.[2] this[b] is the uniform & gross Mistatement of the one great Point in Dispute, by which the Methodists are represented as holding the compatibility of an impure Life with a saving Faith whereas they only assert that the works of righteousness are the consequence not the price of Redemption. A gift included in the great gift of Salvation—therefore not of merit but of imputation thro the free Love of the Saviour[3]

2[a] Overtraced as μισητρον
2[b] Probably capitalised originally, but now too badly rubbed to be sure

1[1] Fulke Greville, Baron Brooke *A Treatise of Humane Learning* st 140 var, from *Certaine Learned and Elegant Workes* (1633). C had annotated CL's copy of this book c 1806 (see GREVILLE) and later copied several extracts, probably from RS's copy, into a notebook: *CN* III 3709–19, 3709 being the same stanza that is quoted here.

2[1] "An object of hate", but RS in overtracing has corrected the word to μίσητρον (a charm for producing hatred, or in C's phrase an "Anti-philtre").

2[2] Sedgwick's work expressed the alarm that many people felt about the spread of Methodism, and urged the government to take steps to restrict the number and activity of itinerant preachers. C regards the work as hate-mongering from an at least equally dangerous Unitarian standpoint; RS in his review describes him as a "rank libeller": *QR* IV (1810) 481.

2[3] For Sedgwick's charge and C's response cf e.g. **9** below.

3   i 49, pencil, overtraced

It is enough, it seems, that all the disorderly classes of mankind, prompted as they are by their worst passions to trample on the public welfare, should *know* that they are, what every one else is convinced they are, the pests of society, and the evil is remedied. They are not to be exhorted to honesty, sobriety, or the observance of any laws, human or divine—they must not even be entreated to do their best.—

For "know" let the B. substitute "*feel*" i.e. we know it as we know our life, and then ask himself whether the production of such a state of mind in a Sinner would or would not be of greater promise as to his reformation than the repetition of the ten commandments with paraphrases on the same.—But why not both? The B. is at least as wrong in the undervaluing of the one as the ψευδο-evangelists[1] in the exclusion of the other.

4   i 51–2, pencil, overtraced

Whatever these new Evangelists may teach to the contrary, the present state of public morals and of public happiness would assume a very different appearance if the thieves, swindlers, and highway robbers, would *do their best* towards maintaining themselves by honest labour, instead of perpetually planning new systems of fraud, and new schemes of depredation.

i.e. if these Thieves &c had a different *Will*—not a mere wish, however anxious, for this "the *Libertine*" doubtless has, as described in p. 50—but an effective *Will*.[1] Well! and who doubts this? The point in dispute is, as to the *means* of producing this reformation in the Will—which whatever the Barrister may think, Christ at least thought so difficult, as to speak of it not once or twice but uniformly, as little less than *miraculous*, as tantamount to a *re-creation*.[2] This Barrister may be resembled to an igno-

[3][1] "Pseudo"-evangelists, "false" in that in C's view they were not really preaching the Gospel. Cf "new Evangelists" in **4** textus. "Evangelical" was a relatively recent name for the party identified with the Methodists in the C of E, and C uses it seldom and self-consciously, e.g. in later notes to KANT *Religion* **3** at n 8.

[4][1] On p 50 Sedgwick maintains that "The libertine that has worn out the prime of his life in the haunts of prostitution, and who has destroyed his health, dissipated his property, and lost his character, cannot fail to *know his misery* . . .". In discussions of

repentance and conversion or "metanoia" (*AR—CC*—132 and n), C typically invokes the distinction he makes here (and in SHAKESPEARE COPY D **171**) between willing and wishing; that is, as he says in **57** below, the "essential *Heterogeneity* of Regret and Remorse". Cf *AR* (*CC*) 127–8 and n, *Lects 1808–1819* (*CC*) I 63–4.

[4][2] C is probably thinking of texts such as John 3.3 and 3.7, which include the phrase "born again", mentioned in **28** and **40** below, and discussed at some length in *AR* (*CC*) 205–6, 321–2.

rant but well-meaning Galenist, who writing against some infamous Quack who lived by puffing & vending Pills of Mercurial Sublimate for all cases of Syphilis, had no stronger argument than to extol Sarsaparilla & Lignum Vitæ, or Senna, in contempt of all mercurial preparations.[3]

5 i 56, pencil, overtraced

Not for the revenues of an Archbishop would he exhort them to a duty *unknown in Scripture*, of adding their five talents to the five they have received,—never would he direct any follower of his so to act as to have it in his power to say, when, after a long time, the Lord cometh and reckoneth with him,—"Lord, *thou hast delivered* unto me five talents, behold *I have gained* five talents more."

All this is mere calumny! and wilful mistatement of the Tenets of Wesley, who never doubted that we are bound to improve our *talents* or on the other hand, that we are equally bound, having done so, to be equally thankful to the Giver of all things for the power and the will, by which we improved the Talents, as for the original Capital which is the object of the improvement. The question is not, whether Christ will say, Well done thou good &c—but whether the *Servant* is to say it of himself.[1] Now for this Christ has delivered as positive a precept against our doing this as the promise can be that he will impute it to us, if we do not impute it to our own merit.[a2]

6 i 60, pencil, overtraced

[Sedgwick is attacking Rowland Hill's *Village Dialogues*.] The complaints of the profligacy of servants of every class, and of the depravity of the times are in every body's hearing:—and these Evangelical Tutors—the dear Mr. Lovegoods of the day, deserve the best attention of the public for thus instructing the ignorant multitude—who are always ready

5[a] Overtraced as "merits"

4[3] Doses of mercury were the established treatment for syphilis but C describes on the one hand a quack (as in **62**) who prescribes it indiscriminately, and on the other a Galenist who would use ineffectual (though harmless) herbs. Both extremes are wrong.

5[1] From the parable of the talents, Matt 25.20–1, q also in textus: "And so he that had received five talents came and brought other five talents, saying, Lord, thou deliveredst unto me five talents: behold, I have gained beside them five talents more. His lord said unto him, Well done, thou good and faithful servant: thou hast been faithful over a few things, I will make thee ruler over many things: enter thou into the joy of thy lord."

5[2] Perhaps Matt 7.21–3 and 6.1–4.

enough to neglect their moral duties,—to despise and insult those by whom they are taught.

All this is no better than infamous Slander, unless the Barrister can prove, that these depraved Servants, Thieves, &c are *Methodists*, or have been wicked in proportion as they were proselyted to Methodism. O folly! This is indeed to secure the Triumph of these Enthusiasts!

7 i 61, pencil, overtraced

It must afford him [Rowland Hill] great consolation, amidst the increasing immorality . . . that when their Village Curate exhorts them, if they have *faith* in the doctrine of a world to come, to add to it those *good works* in which the sum and substance of religion consist, he has led them to ridicule him, as *chopping a new-fashioned* logic.

That this is either false or nugatory, see proved in THE FRIEND*a* on Faith & Works.[1]

8 i 68, pencil, overtraced

Tom Paine himself never laboured harder to root all virtue out of society,—Mandeville nor Voltaire never even laboured so much;—they were content with declaring their disbelief of a future state . . .

Indeed? in what part of their Works? Can any wise man read M.'s Fable of the Bees, & not see that it is a keen Satire on the inconsistency of Christians, & so intended?[1]

9 i 71–2, pencil, overtraced

When the populace shall be once brought to a conviction that the Gospel, as they are told, has neither terms nor conditions . . . that no sins can be too great, no life too impure, *no offences too many or too aggravated, to disqualify the perpetrators of them for* *salvation . . .* it requires no very extensive foresight to predict what will be the result.

* merely insert the words "sincere repentance and amendment of Heart & Life, and therefore for" Salvation. And is not this Truth, and Gospel Truth? And is it not the meaning of the Preacher? Did any Methodist ever

7*a* Small caps omitted in overtracing

7[1] *Friend* No. 23, 8 Feb 1810 in the original issue: *Friend (CC)* II 310–20.
8[1] C adopts the same ironic interpretation of Bernard de Mandeville *The Fable of the Bees* in an annotated copy: see MANDEVILLE.

teach that Salvation may be attained without Sanctification? This B. for ever forgets that the whole point in dispute is not concerning the possibility of an immoral Christian, which the Methodist would deny as strenuously as himself, & perhaps give an austerer sense to the word immoral; but whether morality, or as the Methodists would call it, Sanctification, be the price which we pay for the purchase of our Salvation with our own money, or a part of the same free gift. God knows! I am no advocate for Methodism, but for fair Statement I am & most zealously—even for the love of Logic, putting Honesty out of sight.

10   i 73, pencil, overtraced

"In every age (says the MORAL Divine [Blair]) the practice has prevailed of substituting certain appearances of piety in the place of the great *duties* of humanity and mercy. Too many there have always been who flatter themselves with the hope of obtaining the friendship of their Creator, though they neglect to *do justice to their fellow-creatures* . . ."

Will the Barrister rest the decision of the controversy on the comparison of the Lives of the Methodists & Non-Methodists? Unless he knows that their Morality has declined, as their Piety has become more ardent, is not his quotation mere labouring—nay, absolute Pioneering for the triumphal Chariot of his Enemies?

11   i 76, pencil, overtraced

. . . it is but fair to select a specimen of Evangelical Preaching from . . . . the favourite and admired Sermons of Mr. TOPLADY.

We will preface it with the solemn and awful communication of the Evangelist John, in order to shew how exactly they accord, how clearly the doctrines of the one are deduced from the Revelation of the other, and how justly, therefore, it assumes the exclusive title of EVANGELICAL.

"And I saw the dead, small and great, stand before God; and the books were opened . . . and the dead were judged out of those things which were written on the books, *according to their* WORKS. . . ."

Let us recall to mind, at the same time, the urgent caution conveyed to us in the epistolary writings of PAUL, given as an awful warning to the whole human race—"Be not deceived, God is not mocked, for whatsoever a man *soweth, that* shall he also *reap.*"

Utinam sic omnia![1] All this is just and forcible. And surely nothing can

---

11[1] "Would that it were all like this!" Cf SCHUBERT *Ansichten* **6**.

be easier than to confute the Methodist by shewing that his very *no-doing* when he comes to explain, is not only an *act*, a *work*, but even a very severe & perseverant *energy* of the Will, & he is to be arraigned of *Nonsense* & abuse of words, rather than of Immoral Doctrines.

12   i 84–5, pencil, overtraced

The sacred volume of Holy Writ declares that—*"true religion,** and undefiled before God and the Father, IS THIS, to visit the fatherless and widow in their affliction, and to keep himself unspotted from the world."

* This is *now*[a] at least, whatever might have been the meaning of the word "Religion" in the time of the Translators, a false version.[1] St James is speaking of persons eminently zealous in those public or private *acts* of Worship, which we call "Divine Service," θρησκεια[b]. It should be rendered:[c] "True *Worship*[d], &c." The passage is a fine Burst of *Rhetoric*[e], & not a mere Truism, just as when we say, A chearful Heart is a perpetual Thanksgiving, and a state of Love & Resignation the truest utterance of the Lord's Prayer. St James opposes Xtianity to the outward Signs & ceremonial observances of the Jewish & the Pagan Religions—But these are the only sure signs, these are the most significant ceremonial observances by which your Xtianity is to be made known—to visit the fatherless, &c—True *Religion*[f] does not subsist *quoad essentiam*[2] in these acts, but in that habitual state of the whole moral Being, which manifests itself by these acts—and which acts are to the Religion of Christ that which Ablutions, Sacrifices, and Temple-going were to the Mosaic Religion—viz. its genuine θρησκεια[g]. That which was the *Religion* of Moses is the *ceremonial* or *Cult* of the Religion of Christ. Moses commanded *all good works* even those stated by St James, as the means of temporal Felicity,*[3] & to these he added a multitude of symbolical observances.† Christ[h] commands holiness out of perfect Love = Xtn Religion: and adds to this

12[a] Italics (underlining) not overtraced   **12**[b] Italics (underlining) not overtraced
      12[c] Colon not overtraced   **12**[d] Italics (underlining) not overtraced
12[e] Italics (underlining) not overtraced   **12**[f] Italics (underlining) not overtraced
      12[g] Italics (underlining) not overtraced   **12**[h] Overtraced as "Christs'"

12[1] Jas 1.27: "Pure religion and undefiled before God and the Father is this, To visit the fatherless and widows in their affliction, and to keep himself unspotted from the world." C comments in the same vein on the word (*thrēskeia*) translated "Religion" in this text in FIELD **7** ("the word *Religion* for θρησκεια in St James ought *now* to be altered to—Ceremony or Ritual") and

LUTHER *Colloquia* **3**.
      12[2] "As to its essence", "in essence".
      12[3] E.g. Deut 15.10, on giving to the poor: "Thou shalt surely give him, and thine heart shall not be grieved when thou givest unto him: because that for this thing the Lord thy God shall bless thee in all thy works, and in all that thou puttest thine hand unto."

no other ceremony or Symbol than a pure Life and active Beneficence: which (says S! James) are the true *Cult*.

   * and this was the Mosaic Religion.

   † and these formed the Mosaic *Cult* (Cultus religiosus, θρησκεια.)

13 i 86–7, pencil, overtraced

[Footnote:] There is no one whose writings are better calculated to do good [than Paley], by inculcating the essential duties of common life, and the sound truths of practical Christianity.

!!!!!!!!*ᵃ* Paley's whole System is reducible to this one Precept—Obey God, and benefit your Neighbour, because you love yourself above all.[1] Christ has himself comprized*ᵇ* his system in—Love your Neighbour as yourself, and God above all.[2] These "sound Truths of practical Xtianity" consist in a total subversion, not only of Xtianity, but of all Morality— the very words Virtue and Vice being but lazy Synonimes of "Prudence and Miscalculation"—and which ought to be expunged from our Vocabularies, together with Abraxas, and Abracadabra,[3] as *charms* ⟨ab⟩used*ᶜ* by superstitious or mystic Enthusiasts!

14 i 94, pencil, overtraced

Eventually the whole direction of the popular mind, in the affairs of religion, will be gained into the hands of a set of ignorant fanatics, of such low origin and vulgar habits as can only serve to degrade religion in the eyes of those to whom its influence is most wanted.—Will such persons venerate or respect it in the hands of a sect composed in the far greater part of bigotted, coarse, illiterate, and low-bred enthusiasts? Men who have abandoned their lawful callings, in which, by industry, they might have been useful members of society, to take upon themselves concerns the most sacred, with which nothing but their vanity and their ignorance could have excited them to meddle.

It is not the B–lch and Buffoonery of the Reverend Parasite and Joke-

---

13*ᵃ* Only three exclamation marks overtraced   13*ᵇ* Overtraced as "comprizes"
13*ᶜ* Overtraced simply as "abused"

13[1] This is the recurrent theme of C's writings against Paley's prudential morality: for a collection of cross-references including the recent *Friend* (*CC*) ii 313 see AURELIUS **38** n 1. See also *Friend* (*CC*) i 424–6.
13[2] Matt 22.37–40, Mark 12.30–1, Luke 10.27–8.

13[3] As the context indicates, these are both cabbalistic words supposed to have magic powers; each, as C says of "Abracadabra" in *Friend* (*CC*) i 440, an "idolatrous *charm*". C later came upon more specific information about "Abraxas": *CN* iv 4832 f 62 and n.

bully in the Ed. Review,[1] not the convulsed Grin of Mortification, which sprawling prostrate in the Dirt from "the Whiff and Wind" of the masterly Disquisition in the Quart: Rev. he would pass off for the broad grin of Triumph[2]—[a]no, nor even the over-valued distinction of miracles, which will prevent the Itinerant Preacher from seeing and shewing the equal applicability of this §[b] to the Apostles & the Primitive Christians.[3] We *know* that Trajan, Pliny, Tacitus, the Antonines, Celsus, Lucian, &c &c. much more the ten thousand Psilosophers & *Joke-Smiths*[4] of Rome, *did* both feel and apply all this to the Galilæan Sect—and yet—*vicisti, O Galilæe!*[5]

---

15 i 95, pencil, overtraced

. . . they throw the imputation of pride upon what they term the *self-right-eousness* of all those who strive to attain salvation by personal goodness.

14[a] Overtraced as full stop   14[b] C's symbol for "paragraph" not overtraced

14[1] Probably the renowned wit Sydney Smith (1771–1845), clergyman and co-founder of the *Edinburgh Review*. "Joke-bully" is C's own compound, not in *OED*; but see the note on "Joke-Smith" in n 4 below.

14[2] The quotation is from *Hamlet* II ii 471–4, when the First Player recites lines about the Fall of Troy: "Unequal match'd, / Pyrrhus at Priam drives, in rage strikes wide, / But with the whiff and wind of his fell sword / Th' unnerved father falls."

14[3] C's point is that in spite of altered historical circumstances—the Methodists don't work miracles and the Apostles were not subject to bad reviews—the case that Sedgwick makes against the Methodist preachers could just as well have been made against the early Christians.

14[4] "Psilosophy" and "psilosopher" are C's coinages, "psilosophy" appearing e.g. in *Friend* (*CC*) I 94*, *BL* chs 3, 10 (*CC*) I 67*, 185, JUNG **8** and nn. C himself glosses "psilosophy" as "slender . . . Wisdom, in opposition to Philosophy, the Love of Wisdom and the Wisdom of Love" (*CL* IV 922*) and "psilosopher" as "a nominal Ph[ilosopher]. without Imagination" (*CN* II 3158). For "jokesmith" ("a manufacturer of jokes") the first example in *OED* is a letter written by RS to Walter Savage Landor in 1813; it is especially appropriate for a joker named Smith, as suggested in n 1 above.

14[5] "Thou hast conquered, O Galilaean!" apocryphally reported (by Theodoret *Historia ecclesiastica* 3.20) to have been the dying words of the Roman Emperor Julian the Apostate (331–63), who had opposed the growth of Christianity. In May 1810, thinking of writing a "Defence of Christianity", C was reading accounts of the reign of Julian, and of the first centuries of Christianity, both in William Warburton *Julian* (1st ed 1750, C's ed not known) and in Edward Gibbon *Decline and Fall of the Roman Empire* (12 vols 1802): *CN* III 3805–8, 3813–16, 3818 and nn. Although neither of them repeats this story, virtually all the rest of the evidence that C cites for the low esteem in which the Christians were held *before* Julian's time may be found in ch 16 of Gibbon's work: the enquiry of Pliny the Younger (61–c 113) to the Emperor Trajan (53–117) about how to proceed legally against them; the account by Tacitus (c 55–c 120) of Nero's "cruel punishment" of them; and the contempt in which they were held by Antoninus Marcus (i.e. the emperor Marcus Aurelius Antoninus, 121–180) and by Celsus (fl c 178). Lucian (c 120–180) appears in this chapter only in a footnote, as a source of evidence about oracles, but he is mentioned in ch 2 as an effective satirist against religion "in the age of the Antonines".

They never fail to refer to the proud Pharisee, whom they term self-*righteous*, and then, having grossly misrepresented his character, they proceed to declaim on the arrogance of founding any expectation of reward from the performance of our *moral duties* . . .

* The *Evangelical[a]* has only to translate these sentences into the true statement of his opinions, in order to baffle this angry & impotent attack. Thus:[b] the self-righteousness of all who expect to claim Salvation on the plea of their own personal merit. "Pay to A.B. at sight—*value received* by me J.C."—To Mess[rs] *Stone* & Co Bankers, Heaven-Gate. It is a short step from this to the R. Catholick "Pay to A.B. *or order*."[1] Once assume *merits*, & I defy you to keep out supererogation & the old Monte di Pieta![2]

16   i 95, pencil

. . . the plain truth is, that the Pharisee was *not righteous*, but *merely arrogated to himself that character . . .

* Who told the B. this? Not the Gospel, I am sure.

17   i 97, pencil, overtraced

. . . that which is nothing more than *self-delusion*, in the Pharisee, is termed *self-righteousness*; and from thence occasion is taken to defame all those who strive to prepare themselves, during this their state of trial, for that judgment which they must undergo at that day, when they will receive either reward or punishment, according as they shall be found to have *merited the one, or *deserved* the other.

* Can the Barrister have read the N.T.? or does he know it only by quotations?

18   i 97, pencil, overtraced

All the promises which God of his infinite goodness has given to man . . . are *in fact* denied, and *in effect* frustrated, by a swarm of new Evange-

---

15[a] Italics (underlining) not overtraced   15[b] "Thus:" not overtraced

15[1] For the mercenary approach to redemption, cf C's objections to the "Debtor and Creditor" scheme in IRVING *Sermons* 11, argued at length in *AR* (*CC*) 318–34. Here C suggests that there is not much to choose between the doctrine of merit, defended by some Protestant sects, which looks upon salvation as a sort of personal contract or bargain with God, and the trans-ferable credit of certain Roman Catholic doctrines, including perhaps works of supererogation, those that are over and above normal moral duty.

15[2] The "Mount of Piety" in France and Italy was a state-run form of support for the poor, making small loans on the strength of items held in pawn: C plays with the idea of the Church as a trading centre.

lists, who are every where teaching the people that no reliance is to be placed on holiness of life as a ground of future acceptance!!—

I am weary of repeating that this is *false*. It is only denied, that *mere* actions not proceeding from Faith, are or can be *Holiness*. As surely (would the Methodist say) as the Holy Ghost proceeds from the Son, so surely does Sanctification from Redemption, and not vice versâ, much less from Self-Sanctifiedness, that Ostrich with its head in the sand, and the plucked Rump of its Merits staring on the divine Ἄτη venatrix!¹

19 i 102–4, pencil, overtraced

Since then it is plain that each must *himself* be righteous, if he be so at all, what do they mean who thus inveigh against *self*-righteousness, since Christ himself declares there is no other?

Here again, the whole dispute lies in the word "himself." In the outward and visible Sense both parties agree, but the M.¹ calls it "The Will in us," given by Grace; the Barrister calls it "our own will," or "we ourselves." But why does not the B. reserve a part of his wrath for Dʳ Priestley, according to whom a Villain has *superior* claims on the divine Justice, as an innocent Martyr to the grand *Machinery* of Providence?² for Dʳ P, who turns the whole Dictionary of Human Nature into verbs impersonal with a perpetual Subauditur of *Deus* for their common Nominative Case?³ which said Deus however is but another Automaton, *self*-worked indeed, but yet work*ed*ᵃ, not properly work*ing*ᵇ, for he admits no more freedom or will to God than to Man. The Lutheran leaves the Free Will whining with a broken back in the ditch; and Dʳ P puts the poor Animal out of its

19ᵃ Overtraced "*work*ED"   **19**ᵇ Italics not overtraced

18¹ "Ate, the huntress". The goddess Ate, in Greek mythology, personified infatuation and moral blindness, both the original guilt and the incitement to further excesses which Zeus sent as a punishment.

19¹ Methodist.

19² C attempts to turn Sedgwick's arguments against his own sect, the Unitarians, and their founder Joseph Priestley, whose materialist and necessitarian philosophy C himself espoused for a few crucial years in his youth (cf LESSING *Sämmtliche Schriften* **26** and n 1). In his statement about the "Villain", C may be extrapolating from Priestley's *Doctrine of Philosophical Necessity Illustrated; Being an Appendix to the Disquisitions Relating to Matter and Spirit* (1st

ed 1777; rev ed 1782). There Priestley makes the case for his "necessarian" philosophy, addressing the difficulties posed by the abandonment of free will and the acceptance of God's being the source of evil as well as of good in a system in which good is destined ultimately to triumph. He represents humanity as a single family, with God as the "Universal Parent" who will eventually reclaim even the worst of sinners and bring all to perfect happiness. C's early familiarity with Priestley's *Disquisitions* and its appendix is recorded in *CN* i 64n, *Lects 1795* (*CC*) 156 and n 1.

19³ I.e. with "God" understood to be the subject.

misery! But seriously, is it fair or even decent to appeal to the Legislature against the METHODISTS[c] for holding the doctrine of *Atonement*? Do we not pray *by Act of Parliament* 20 times every Sunday "*thro the only merits of Jesus Christ*?"[4] Is it not the very Nose which (of Flesh or Wax)[5] this very Legislature insists on as an indispensable Qualification for every Christian Phiz? Is not the Lack thereof a *felonious* Deformity,—yea the grimmest Feature of the Lues confirmata of Statute Heresy?[6] What says the *Joke-Smith* to this?[7] Will he not rise in wrath against the Barrister—he the CUSTOS NIGER, ⟨the Pamphagus⟩[8] of Homiletic, Liturgic, & Articular Orthodoxy? this Gargantua, whose ravenous Maw leaves not a single word, syllable, letter, no! not one i-dot unswallowed, if we are to believe his own recent Fee! Fa! Fum! since he smelt the blood of a Living ——?[d9] What says *he* to the Barrister?

20   i 105, pencil, overtraced

If the new faith be the only true one, let us embrace it; but let not those who vend these *new articles*[a] expect that we should choose them with our eyes shut.

19[c] Small caps (double underlining) overtraced as italics (single underlining)
19[d] Closing punctuation may not be in original
20[a] Underlining not overtraced

19[4] C refers to the Act of Uniformity (1662) which decreed the exclusive use of BCP in C of E services. The phrase "through Jesus Christ our Lord" and variants of it appear again and again in BCP, and "through the merits of Jesus Christ our Saviour" e.g. in the second Collect at Evening Prayer.

19[5] The "nose of wax" is proverbial for something easily altered or moulded, and *OED* records it as having been especially common in references to wresting the Scriptures; C uses the phrase in just such a context in a note of 1808–9, *CN* iii 3451.

19[6] The loss of the nose was a symptom of advanced venereal disease, "Lues confirmata" being "confirmed syphilis". C pursues the imagery suggested by the "Nose . . . of Flesh or Wax" above.

19[7] Sydney Smith of *Ed Rev*, as in **14** n 1. *Ed Rev* did not review Sedgwick's *Hints*. Sydney Smith had, however, anonymously but notoriously contributed two reviews on the subject of Methodist magazines and Methodist missions in 1808. When John Styles was provoked to respond in 1809 with *Strictures on Two Critiques in the*

Edinburgh Review, Smith reviewed that too: *Ed Rev* xiv (1809) 40–50.

19[8] "The black custodian, the all-devourer"—the former phrase just possibly implying a pun with "blackguard" (villain). "Pamphagus" sounds like, but is not, one of the gluttonous giants of Rabelais, like Panurge or Pantagruel or Gargantua (whom C proceeds to mention). The word is not unprecedented: Pliny *Natural History* 6.195 mentions an imaginary race of Pamphagi; and "pamphagous" is recorded as an English adjective with an example from 1702 (*OED*).

19[9] One of the traditional variants to the giant's line "I smell the blood of an *English* man" in the story of Jack the Giant Killer was "I smell the blood of an *earthly* man": Iona and Peter Opie *The Classic Fairy Tales* (1974) 63. Perhaps "living" was another, but in C's joke it is not a human victim at all but the lucrative position in the Church that the greedy clergyman detects. Sydney Smith held the living of Foston-le-Clay, near York, which was worth £500 p.a.: he was appointed to it in 1806, and required to be resident after 1808.

Let any man read the Homilies of the Ch of E:[1] and if he does not call this either blunt Impudence or blank Ignorance, I will plead guilty to both! *New Articles*!! Would to Heaven, some of them, at least, were! Why Wesley himself was scandalized by Luther's Commentary on the Galatians, & cried off from the Moravians, (the strictest Lutherans) on that account.[2]

21   i 115, pencil, overtraced

[Footnote:] The catalogue of Authors which this Reverend Gentleman [Mr Clayton] has pleased thus publicly to specify and recommend begins with Homer, Hesiod, the Argonautica, Aeschylus, Sophocles, Euripides, Pindar, Theognis, Herodotus, Thucydides, Xenophon, Polybius, Diodorus Siculus, &c. . . . "This catalogue,"—says he, with a gravity becoming the great occasion,—"might be considerably extended; but I study *brevity*. It is only *necessary for* ME *to add*, that the recommendation of these books is *not to be considered* as expressive of MY *approbation* of *every* particular sentiment they contain."

It would indeed be a grievous injustice if this writer's reputation should be injured by the occasional unsoundness of opinion in writers whom it is more than probable he may never have read, and for whose sentiments he ought no more to be made answerable than the compiler of LACKINGTON'S CATALOGUE, from which it is not unlikely that his own was abridged.

very good.[a1]

22   i 116, pencil, overtraced

These high-strained pretenders to godliness, who deny the power of the sinner to help himself, take good care always to attribute his *saving change* to the blessed effect of some sermon preached by some one or

21[a] Italics (underlining) not overtraced

20[1] For C's annotated copy see SERMONS below.

20[2] This is a direct allusion to the entry for Monday, 15 Jun 1741, in John Wesley's *Journal*, where he records his disappointment in this commentary ("I was utterly ashamed"), writes about its mystical and blasphemous teaching, and concludes that "the real spring of the grand error of the Moravians" is that they "follow Luther for better for worse": *Journal* (4 vols 1827) I 301. We do not know what edition of the *Journal* C had read, but an essay in the re-vised *Friend* alludes to it: *Friend* (*CC*) I 431. Wesley himself may have been led to this commentary by Bunyan, who says in his autobiography *Grace Abounding to the Chief of Sinners* par 130 that Luther's commentary on Galatians was, after the Bible, his favourite of all books.

21[1] James Lackington (1746–1815) was an enterprising London bookseller whose shop, "the Temple of the Muses", was renowned for its huge stock and low prices. His catalogue for 1810–11 contained 10,754 titles.

other of *their* Evangelical fraternity. They always hold *themselves* up to the multitude as the instruments of producing all those marvellous conversions which they relate. No instance is recorded in their Saints' Calendar of any sinner resolving, in consequence of a reflective and serious perusal of the Scriptures, to lead a new life. No instance of a daily perusal of the Bible producing a daily progress in virtuous habits.—No, the *Gospel* has no such effect—It is always the *Gospel Preacher* who works the miracle . . .

excellent and just! In this way are the Methodists to be attacked—even as the Papists were by Baxter, not from their *doctrines*, but from their *Practices*[a], & the *spirit* of their Sect.[1] There is a fine Passage in Lord Bacon concerning a Heresy of *manner* not less pernicious than Heresy of *Matter*—[2]

23   i 119, pencil, overtraced

But these Saints, who would stop their ears if you should mention with admiration the name of a Garrick or a Siddons;—who think it a sin to support such an *infamous profession* as that, through the medium of which a <u>Milton</u>[a], a Johnson, an Addison, and a Young have laboured to mend the heart . . .

Whoo!!!. See his Pref. to the Sam. Agonistes.[1]

22[a] Italics (underlining) not overtraced

22[1] C is probably referring to Richard Baxter's *Holy Commonwealth* (1659), which he had recently used for an epigraph: *Friend* (*CC*) II 197. In "An Addition to the Preface", Baxter argues against religious toleration. "Liberty in all matters of Worship and of Faith," he says, "is the open and apparent way to set up Popery in the Land." He points out that the Roman Catholic Church has large numbers of priests, backed up with money as well as with specious argument, ready to prey upon unsuspecting, uneducated people: "Consider . . . above all, what a multitude of Jesuites, Fryers, and Priests can they prepare for the work, and poure out upon us at their pleasure . . ." (sig C3).

22[2] Bacon's short essay "De haeresibus" ("Of Heresies") in *Meditationes sacrae— Works* ed D. Mallet (4 vols 1740) II 402–3—discusses two *sources* of heresy,

23[a] Italics (underlining) not overtraced

but not in the terms C uses here, and it seems more likely that he was thinking of the essay "Of Unity in Religion" *Works* (1740) III 303–5, esp 304: "Men ought to take heed of rending God's church by two kinds of controversies. The one is, when the matter of the point controverted is too small and light, not worth the heat and strife about it, kindled only by contradiction. . . . The other is, when the matter of the point controverted is great; but it is driven to an overgreat subtility and obscurity; so that it becometh a thing rather ingenious than substantial."

23[1] In the preface to *Samson Agonistes*, which he subtitled "a dramatic poem", Milton asserts that the work "never was intended" for the stage; on the other hand, in the same preface he gives several examples to vindicate the reputation of tragedy.

24   i 134, pencil, overtraced

[Footnote:] . . . in the Evangelical Magazine for the last month, is the following article:—". . . At ——, in Yorkshire, after a handsome collection [for the Missionary Society] on the preceding evening, a poor man, whose wages are about 28*s.* per week, brought the next morning, at breakfast-time, a donation of twenty guineas. Our friends hesitated to receive it, doubting whether it was consistent with his duty to his family and the world to contribute such a sum; when he answered to the following effect:—'Before I knew the grace of our Lord I was a poor drunkard: I never could save a shilling. My family were in beggary and rags; but, since it has pleased God to renew me by his grace, we have been industrious and frugal; we have not spent many idle shillings; and we have been enabled to put something into the Bank; and this I freely offer to the blessed cause of our Lord and Saviour.[']—This is the SECOND donation of this same poor man, to the SAME AMOUNT!!!"

Whatever these Evangelists may think of such conduct, they ought to be ashamed of thus basely taking the advantage of this poor ignorant enthusiast . . .

Is it possible to read this affecting Story without finding in it a compleat answer to the charge of demoralizing the lower Classes? Does the Barrister really think, that this generous & grateful Enthusiast is as likely to be unprovided & poverty-stricken in his old age, as he *was* prior to his conversion? Except indeed that at that time his old age was as improbable as his distresses were certain if he did live so long. This is singing Io Pæan![1] for the Enemy with a vengeance.—[a]

25   ii 14–16, pencil, overtraced

It behoved him [Dr Hawker in his 1808 *Letter to a Barrister*] to shew—which he has wholly omitted—in what manner a COVENANT can exist WITHOUT TERMS OR CONDITIONS.—The very supposition is absurd . . .

According to the Methodists there *is* a condition, that of Faith in the Power and Promise of Christ, and the virtue of the Cross. And were it other wise, the Objection is scarcely appropriate except at the Old Baily or the Court of King's Bench. The Barrister might have framed a second Law-syllogism, as acute as his former. The Laws of England allow of no

---

24[a] Closing punctuation overtraced as exclamation mark

24[1] "Hail, Apollo!"—a battle cry, or a shout of victory.

Covenant in transfer of goods or chattels without *value received*. But there can be no value received by God—Ergo, there can be no Covenant between God & Man—& if Jehovah should be as courteous as the H. of Commons, & acknowledge the jurisdiction of the Courts at Westminster, the Pleading might hold perhaps, & the Pentateuch be quashed after an argument before the Judges.—Besides, how childish to puff up the empty bladder of an old metaphysical Football on the modus operandi interior[1] of Justification into a shew of practical Substance! as were it no less solid than a cannon ball. Why, drive it with all the vehemence that five Toes can exert, it would not kill a louse on the Head of Methodism. Repentance, godly Sorrow, Abhorrence of Sin as Sin, & not merely dread from forecast of the consequences, these the Arminian would call "means of obtaining salvation," while the Methodist (more philosophically perhaps) names them "Signs of the work of free Grace *commencing*, and the dawning of the Sun of Redemption." And pray where is the *practical* Difference?

26   ii 18, pencil

[In a very long footnote, Sedgwick attempts to show that Hawker modelled his *Letter to a Barrister* on Burke's *Letter to a Noble Lord*; he implies that Hawker is a plagiarist.] Doctor Hawker *prays in aid* of Mr. BURKE, and his letter to the Duke of Bedford . . . is compelled to contribute a portion of its eloquence; although, stripped as it is of its connection, it makes but a very sorry figure in its new alliance.

Mr. Burke thus begins his letter to the noble Duke . . .

Contemptible

27   ii 19, pencil

[Sedgwick continues the comparison of texts, quoting Burke.] ". . . To have incurred *the displeasure* of the Duke of Orleans or the Duke of Bedford, *to fall under the censure* of Citizen Brissot, or of his friend the Earl of Lauderdale, *I ought to consider as proofs not the least satisfactory*, that I have produced some part of the effect I proposed by my endeavours."

The doctor, adopting the same strain, says . . .

Trash!

25[1] "Inner workings".

28   ii 26, pencil, overtraced

Jesus answered him thus—"Verily, I say unto you, unless a man be born of *water* and of *the spirit*, he cannot enter into the kingdom of God."— The true sense of which is obviously this—Except a man be initiated into my religion by *baptism*, (which *at that time* was always *preceded by a confession of faith*) and unless he manifest his sincere reception of it, by leading that upright and *spiritual* life which it enjoins, *he cannot enter the kingdom of Heaven*, or be a partaker of that happiness which it belongs to me to confer on those who believe in my name and keep my sayings.—

Upon my faith as a Christian[a], if Jesus Christ meant no more by being born again, than this, he had the strangest taste in metaphors of any teacher in verse or prose on record, J Bœhmen himself not excepted. The very Alchemists lag behind.[1] Pity tho' that our Barrister has not shown us how this plain & obvious business of Baptism &c squares with v. 8 of the same Chapt: "The wind bloweth where it listeth &c"[2] Now if this does not express a *visitation* of the mind by a x y z not in its own power or forethought, what are words meant for?

29   ii 30

The true meaning of being "born again," in the sense in which our Saviour uses the phrase, implies nothing more or less in plain terms, than this:—to repent; to lead for the future a religious life, instead of a life of disobedience; to believe the holy scriptures, and to pray for grace and assistance, to persevere in our obedience to the end. All this any man of common sense, might explain in a few words.

Pray then, (for we will take the B's own commentary) what does the man of common sense mean by *Grace*? If he will explain Grace in any other way, than as the circumstances ab extra[1] (which would be mere mockery

28[a]   Overtraced as "Xtian."

28[1] While C's marginalia show him struggling against an impression of absurdity in some of Böhme's assertions (e.g. BÖHME **57**, **58**, **72**, **92**, **164**), they also bear witness to the way in which "a ridiculous likeness leads to the detection of a true analogy" (**60**). The link between Böhme's language and that of the alchemists is made in BÖHME **93**. In *AR* (*CC*) esp 321–2 C was to formulate an argument about the entire absence of metaphor from the language of Jesus as recorded in the Bible.

28[2] John 3.8: "The wind bloweth where it listeth, and thou hearest the sound thereof, but canst not tell whence it cometh, and whither it goeth: so is every one that is born of the Spirit."

29[1] "From without", external.

& in direct contradiction to a score of Texts) & yet without mystery, I will undertake for D[r] Hawker & Co[2] to make the New Birth itself as plain as a pike-staff, or a Whale's Foal, or Sarah Robarts's Rabbits?[3]

30   ii 30

So that they go on in their sin waiting for a "new birth," or a miraculous and sudden conversion, which they relate to happen in the most absurd cases and situations.

"So that they go on in their Sin"! Who would not suppose it notorious, that every Meth: Meeting House was a Cage of Newgate Larks making up their minds *to die game*?[1]

31   ii 30, pencil, overtraced

The following account . . . is extracted from the Methodist Magazine for 1798, p. 273.—"The *Lord* ASTONISHED *Sarah *Roberts* with his mercy, by *setting her at liberty, while employed* in the necessary business of *washing* for her family.["]

* N.B. Not the famous Rabbit-woman—she was Roba*r*ts not -berts.[1]

32   ii 31, pencil, overtraced

A washerwoman has *all her sins blotted out*, in the twinkling of an eye, and while reeking with suds, is received in the family "of the Redeemer's kingdom!!!"

Surely this is a most abominable profanation of all that is serious!—a most monstrous burlesque of all that is sacred! Yet such, according to the evangelists of methodism, is the new birth!!!

And where pray is the absurdity of this? Has Christ declared any antipathy to Washerwomen, or the H.G. to warm Suds? Why does not the B.

29[2] Robert Hawker, D.D. (1753–1827), whose 1808 *Letter to a Barrister*, alluded to in **25** and following notes, was the first of three pamphlets written in controversy with Sedgwick.

29[3] The imagery of birth governs C's last two examples (a "Whale's Foal" being an absurdity), but no further information has been discovered about Sarah Robarts, "the famous Rabbit-Woman"—as he calls her in **31**. (Cf "the Rabbit Woman", otherwise unnamed, in OKEN *Lehrbuch der Naturgeschichte* **25**.) One woman who had

been famous for fraudulently claiming to have brought forth litters of rabbits was Mary Toft or Tofts (?1701–63).

30[1] "To die game; to suffer at the gallows without shewing any signs of fear or repentance": *A Dictionary of Buckish Slang, University Wit, and Pickpocket Eloquence* (1811). The same dictionary gives "Newgate Bird" ("A thief or sharper, frequently caged in Newgate"), but not "lark" specifically.

31[1] See **29** n 3. Sarah Robarts remains unidentified.

try his hand at *ª*abom. prof.*ᵇ*[1] in the story of the Woman with the issue of Blood who was made free by touching the Hem of a Garment without the previous knowlege*ᶜ* of the Wearer?[2] If a man were at once wicked & hard-hearted enough to repeat the same process, would not something more repulsive to decorous Ears come out than *reeking suds*? This is far, far too childish!

33   ii 32

The leading design of John the Baptist . . . was evidently this:—To pre-pare the minds of men for the reception of that pure system of moral truth which the Saviour, by divine authority, was speedily to inculcate, and of those sublime doctrines of a resurrection and a future judgment which, as powerful motives to the practice of holiness, he was soon to reveal.—

What then? Did not John the Baptist teach a pure System of moral Truth? Was John so much more ignorant than Paul before his conversion, and the whole Jewish Nation, except a few rich Free-thinkers, as to be igno-rant of the Sublime Doctrines of a Resurrection & a future Judgment? This I well know is the Strong-hold of Socinianism; but surely, one single unprejudiced perusal of the N.T., not to suppose an acquaintance with Kidder or Light-foot would blow it down, like a House of Cards![1]

34   ii 33

When the Baptist thus exhorted his hearers to amendment of life, he seems to have soared above their comprehension. The change of a CER-EMONIAL for a MORAL dispensation, was a change which they did not conceive to be an improvement at all intelligible. . . . and their *faith* in the efficacy of their own rites, and creeds, and ceremonies, and their whole train of SUBSTITUTIONS for MORAL DUTY, was so entire, and in their

---

32*ª⁻ᵇ* Not overtraced
32*ᶜ* Overtraced "knowledge", as in all occurrences here, though C characteristically omitted the "d"

32[1] From textus, "abominable profana-tion".
32[2] C repeats the point made against Sedgwick in **14**, namely that the objections he has to Methodism could be equally well applied to early Christianity. The story of the woman with an issue of blood who touched the hem of Jesus' garment and was healed is told in Matt 9.20–2, Mark 5.25–34, Luke 8.43–8.

33[1] Since the issue here is the state of Jewish doctrine before Christ, C invokes the names of two biblical scholars who spe-cialised in Jewish culture and history, John Lightfoot (1602–75) and Richard Kidder (1633–1703). C had annotated 2 vols of Lightfoot's *Works* in Sept 1809: LIGHT-FOOT.

opinion was such a *saving faith*, that they could not at all interpret any language that seemed to dispute their value, or deny their importance.

Poor strange Jews! They had, doubtless, what Darwin would call, a specific paralysis of the auditory nerves[1] to the writings of their own Prophets, which yet were read Sabbath after Sabbath in their public Synagogues! For neither John nor Christ himself ever did, or indeed could, speak in language more contemptuous of the folly of considering *rites* as substitutions for moral Duty, or in severer words denounce the Blasphemy of such an opinion. Why need I refer to Isaiah or Micah?—[2]

35   ii 34–5

Thus it was that this MORAL preacher explained and enforced the duty of repentance, and thus it was that he prepared the way for that greatest and best of teachers . . .

Well then! if all this was but a *preparation* for the Doctrines of Christ, those Doctrines themselves must surely have been something different, and more difficult!—O no! John's Preparation consisted in a compleat *Rehearsal* of the Drama didacticum,[1] which Christ and the Apostles were to exhibit to a *full* Audience!—Nay, prithee, good Barrister! do not be too rash in charging the Methodists with a monstrous Burlesque of the Gospel!

36   ii 37–8

But the logic of the new evangelists will convince him that it is a contradiction in terms even to SUPPOSE himself CAPABLE OF DOING ANY THING to help, or BRINGING ANY THING TO RECOMMEND HIMSELF TO THE DIVINE FAVOUR.

Now supposing the wisdom of these endless attacks on an old abstruse metaphysical notion, yet why in the name of common candour, does not the Barrister ~~apply~~ ring the same Tocsin against his friend, D[r] Priestley's scheme of Necessity—or his idolized Paley, who in his Nat. Theol. explains the Will as a sensation produced by the action of the Intellect on the Muscles, and the Intellect itself as a catenation of Ideas, and Ideas as

---

34[1] Erasmus Darwin classifies deafness among the diseases of irritation and notes that when it accompanies "nervous fevers", it probably arises "from a partial paralysis of the nerve of sense": *Zoonomia; or, the Laws of Organic Life* (3rd ed rev 4 vols 1801) III 239.

34[2] E.g. Isa 1.10–20, Mic 6.6–8.

35[1] "Didactic drama": the theatrical metaphor continues with "Audience" and "Burlesque" below.

configurations of the organized Brain?[1] Would not every syllable apply, yea, and more strongly, more indisputably? And would his fellow-sectaries thank him or admit the consequences? Or has any late Socinian Divine discovered, that Do as ye would be done unto, is an interpolated Text?[2]

37 ii 39–40

—"Even REPENTANCE and FAITH, (says Dr. Hawker) those most essential qualifications of the mind, for the participation and enjoyment of the blessings of the gospel, (and which all real disciples of the Lord Jesus cannot but possess) are *never* SUPPOSED as a CONDITION *which the* SINNER *performs to entitle him to mercy*, but merely as evidences that he is brought and has obtained mercy. *They* CANNOT *be the* CONDITIONS of obtaining salvation."

Ought not this single Quotation to have satisfied the Barrister, that no *practical* difference is deducible from these Doctrines? Essential qualifications, says the M.—Terms & Conditions, says the spiritual Higgler—. But if a man begins to reflect on his past Life, is he to withstand the inclination? God forbid, exclaim both!—If he feels a commencing Shame & Sorrow, is he to check the feeling? God forbid, cry both in one Breath!—But should not remembrancers be thrown in the way of Sinners, & the voice of Warning sound thro' every Street & every wilderness? Doubtless, quoth the Rationalist! We do, we do, shout the Methodists! In every corner of every Lane, in the high road, and in the waste, we send forth the voice—Come to Christ and repent & be cleansed. Aye, quoth the Rationalist—but I say, Repent and become clean, & go to Christ— Now is not Mr Rationalist as great a Bigot as the Methodist, and, me judice,[1] a worse psychologist?

36[1] For Priestley's assault on free will see **19** above. Paley, C's target in **13**, reintroduced the famous analogy of the created world as a watch and the creator as a divine watchmaker in *Natural Theology* (1802): C alludes to this figure in DONNE *Sermons* COPY B **111**. When the book came out, C wrote to RS about it: "Have you read Paley's last Book? Have you it to review?— I could make a dashing Review of it" (*CL* II 954). C's account of Paley's concept of will, etc, here is not to be found as an explicit statement in *Natural Theology*, but it is consistent with the materialist approach adopted in that work. C thought Paley a Socinian at heart; for the evolution of his opinions about him, see BLANCO WHITE *Practical Evidence* **1** n 1.

36[2] A variant of that "golden rule" of Matt 7.12, "Therefore all things whatsoever ye would that men should do to you, do ye even so to them: for this is the law and the prophets." C sarcastically suggests once more that Sedgwick and his Socinian cohorts should be prepared to be judged by the standards they apply to their opponents: cf **14, 19** above.

37[1] "In my judgment".

38 ii 40 | **37** textus continued

The former authorities on this subject, I had quoted from the gospel according to St. Luke; that gospel most positively and most solemnly declares the *repentance* of sinners to be the *condition* on which, *alone*, salvation can be obtained. But the doctors of the new divinity DENY THIS, they tell us distinctly IT CANNOT BE.—For the future, the gospel according to CALVIN, must be received as the truth.—Sinners will certainly prefer it as the more comfortable of the two, beyond all comparison.

Mercy! but only to read Calvin's account of that Repentance, without which there is no *Sign* of Election, & to call it the more *comfortable* of the two?[1] The very term, by which the German New-Birthites express it, is enough to give one Goose-flesh—*das Herzknirschen*—the very Heart crashed between the teeth of a Lock-jaw'd Agony!—[2]

39 ii 40–2

What is *faith*? Is it not a conviction produced in the mind by adequate testimony?*

* No! that is not the meaning of Faith in the Gospel! Nor indeed any where else. Were it so, the stronger the testimony, the more adequate— Yet who says, I have *Faith* in the existence of George the Second, as his present Majesty's Antecessor & Grandfather?—If Testimony, then Evidence too—and who has Faith, that the two sides of all Triangles are greater than the Third? In truth, Faith even in common language always implies some effort, something of evidence that is not universally adequate or communicable at will to others—.[1] Well! to be sure, he has behaved badly hitherto; but I have *Faith* in him.—If it were otherwise, how could it be imputed as Righteousness—Can morality exist without

38[1] John Calvin *Institutes of the Christian Religion* 3.3.4 invokes, for example, a distinction between two kinds of repentance. In a translation current in C's day— *The Institution of the Christian Religion* tr Thomas Norton (Glasgow 1762)—they are rendered as "repentance of the law" and "repentance of the gospel". In the former, exemplified by Cain and Judas among others, sinners perceive the heinousness of their sins, but have no hope of redemption. Thus "the sinner wounded with the searing iron of sin, and worn away with fear of the wrath of God, sticketh fast in that trouble and cannot wind himself out of it" (277).

38[2] The overtraced verb in the final clause is definitely "crashed", but "crushed" would make more sense and may have been what C originally wrote. The compound *Herzknirschen* has not so far been traced, but C is correct about the meaning: *knirschen* means "to crush" or "to grind"; it is used of *gnashing* teeth. By "German New-Birthites" C may mean the Moravians, as in **20**; and see LAVINGTON.

39[1] The supra-rational quality of faith is a central tenet of C's maturity: cf **41** below, SCHELLING *Philosophie und Religion* **1** and n 1 above, and *CCD* 14–52.

choice? nay, strengthen in proportion as it becomes more independent of the Will?—A very meritorious man! he has *faith* in every proposition of Euclid, which he understands!

40   ii 41

"I could as easily create a world [says Dr Hawker], as create either FAITH *or* REPENTANCE in my own heart." Surely this is a most monstrous confession.—What! is not the Christian religion a REVEALED religion, and have we not the most miraculous attestation of its truth?

Just look at the answer of Christ himself to Nicodemus—John 3.*a* 2. 3. N. professed a full belief in Christ's divine mission, why? It was attested by his miracles. What answered Christ? Well said, O good & sensible Believer!—No, not a word of this; but a reproof of the folly of such a supposition/ Verily, verily, I say unto thee, unless a man be born again, he cannot see the Kingdom of God—i.e. he cannot have Faith in me.

41   ii 42–3

How can this evangelical preacher [Dr Hawker] declaim on the necessity of seriously searching into the truth of revelation, for the purpose either of producing or confirming our belief of it, when he has already pronounced it to be just as possible to arrive at conviction as to create a world?!!!

* Did D^r H say, that it was impossible to produce an assent to the historic credibility of the facts related in the Gospel? Impossible to become a Socinian by the weighing of outward Evidences? No! but Dr H. says, and I say, that this is not, cannot be, what Christ means by Faith—which to the misfortune of the Socinians he always demands as the *condition* of a miracle, instead of looking forward to it as the natural effect of a miracle? How came it that Peter saw miracles countless—& yet was without Faith, till the Holy Ghost descended on him?[1] Besides, Miracles may or may not be adequate evidence for Socinianism; but how could miracles prove the doctrine of Redemption, or the Divinity of Christ? But this[2] is the creed of the Church of E.

40^a This number is written larger than the others to indicate that it stands for the chapter, they for verses

41[1] Matt 16.15–17, esp 17: ". . . Blessed art thou, Simon Barjona: for flesh and blood hath not revealed it unto thee, but my Father which is in heaven."

41[2] I.e. the doctrine of redemption, and the divinity of Christ.

42 ii 43 | Continuing **41** textus

What becomes all this time of the evidences of Christianity? Are the miracles to be denied, or is their force deemed inconclusive? Is all the proof, internal and external, coincident and collateral, which the gospel carries with it, to be rejected as inadequate? Is then the life, and death, and resurrection of the Saviour not authentic? Is the veracity of the apostles doubtful, or does their testimony go for nothing?

Really these ministers of the new church are a most extraordinary class of teachers!!!

It is wearisome to be under the necessity or at least the constant Temptation of attacking Socinianism in reviewing a work professedly written against Methodism? Surely, such a work ought to treat of those points of doctrine & practice, which are peculiar to Methodism. But to publish a diatribe against the substance of the Articles & Catechism of the Established Church, nay, of the whole Christian World, excepting the Socinians, & to call it Hints concerning the dangerous & abominable Absurdities of Methodism is too bad by half

43 ii 43 | Continuing **42** textus

But this Calvinistic evangelist tells us, by way of accounting for the utter impossibility of producing in himself either faith or repentance, that— "both are of divine origin, and like the light, and the rain, and the dew of heaven, which tarrieth not for man, neither waiteth for the sons of men, are from above, and come down from the Father of light, from whom alone cometh every good and perfect gift."

Is the Barrister, are the Socinian Divines, inspired, or infallible—that it is a crime for a Christian to understand the words of Christ in their plain and literal sense—when a Socinian chuses to give his paraphrase—often too, as strangely remote from the words, as the old spiritual Paraphrases on the Song of Solomon!—[1]

44 ii 46–7

According to that gospel which hath hitherto been the pillar of the Christian world, we are taught that whosoever endeavours to the best of his ability to reform his manners and amend his life, will find pardon and acceptance.

43[1] See **61** at n 1 below.

As interpreted by whom? By the Socini, or the Barrister?[1] or by Origen, Chrysostom, Jerome, the Gregories, Eusebius, Athanasius? By Thom. Aquinas, Bernard, Thomas a Kempis? By Luther, Melancthon, Zuinglius, Calvin? By the founders & martyrs of the English Church? By Cartwright and the learned Puritans? By Knox? By G. Fox?[2]—With regard to this point, that mere external evidence is inadequate to the production of a saving Faith, & in the majority of other opinions, all these agree with Wesley—So they all understood the Gospel! But it is not so!—Ergo, the Barrister is infallible./—

45 ii 47

That "when the wicked man turneth away from the wickedness which he hath committed, and doeth that which is lawful and right, he shall save his soul alive."* This gracious declaration the old moral divines of our church, have placed in the front of its liturgy.

* In the name of Patience, over and over again, who has ever denied this? The question is, by what power, his own, or by the free Grace of God thro' Christ, the wicked man is enabled to turn from his wickedness? And again & again, I ask—were not these "old moral Divines" the Authors & Compilers of the *Homilies*?[1] If the B. does not know this, he is an ignorant man: if knowing it, he has yet never examined the Homilies, he is an unjust man/ but if he have, he is a Slanderer, & a Sycophant—

46 ii 48–9

Is it not intolerable to take up three bulky pamphlets against a recent Sect, denounced as most dangerous, and which we all know to be most powerful & of rapid Increase—and to find little more than a weak, declamatory abuse of certain metaphysical dogmata concerning free will, or free

44[1] C questions the authority by which Sedgwick presents himself as an interpreter of the Bible. Is he speaking for the Socini, i.e. for the two Italian theologians, uncle and nephew, Lelio Sozini (1525–62) and Fausto Sozzini (1539–1604), who are identified with the doctrine that denies the divinity of Jesus? (As **19** and **36** above indicate, C was aware that Sedgwick was a Unitarian.) In Jeremy TAYLOR *Polemicall Discourses* **25** C describes Socinianism as "a heresy which either denies or reduces to

an absurdity the whole doctrine of Redemption". Cf **80** below.
44[2] Against the Socinian idea of redemption C arrays the whole history of the Christian church, representing by groups of individual names first the Fathers of the Church; then the Schoolmen; the Protestant Reformers; the Protestant martyrs of the time of Mary Tudor; and the Puritan and Presbyterian Dissenters.
45[1] Cf **20** and n 1 above.

will forfeited—de libero vel servo arbitrio[1]—of Grace, Predestination, &c—Dogmata, on which according to Milton God & the Logos conversed, as soon as Man was in existence—they in Heaven, and Adam in Paradise, and the Devils in Hell!![2] Dogmata common to all religions, & to all ages & sects of the Christian Religion? Concerning which the Brahman disputes with Brahman, the Mahometan with Mahometan?[a] and Priestley with Price?[3]—And all this to be laid on the Shoulders of the Methodists *collectively*: tho' it is a notorious fact, that a radical difference on this abstruse Subject is the ground of the Schism between the Whitfieldite & Wesleyan Methodists—and that the latter coincide in opinion with Erasmus, and Arminius, by which latter name they distinguish themselves—and the former with Luther, Calvin, and their great Guide, S[t] Augustine![4]—This, I say, is intolerable—yea, a crime against Sense, Candour and white Paper!

47   ii 50

"For so very peculiarly directed to the SINNER, and to HIM ONLY— (says the evangelical preacher)—is the blessed gospel of the Lord Jesus, that UNLESS YOU ARE A SINNER, YOU ARE NOT INTERESTED IN ITS SAVING TRUTHS."

Does not Christ himself say the same in the plainest, and most unmistakable words? I come not to the Healthy; but to the Sick?[1] *Can* he, who has no share in the Danger, be *interested* in the Saving? Pleased from benevolence he may be; but *interested* he cannot be. *Est*ne aliquid *inter* salvum et salutem? inter liberum et libertatem? Salvatio est pereuntis, vel saltem periclitantis; Redemptio, quasi Pons divinus, inter Servum et Libertatem—amissam, ideòque optatam!—[2]

46[a] C may originally have intended to end his note here, but it goes on, at first in a slightly larger hand

46[1] C puts his own English phrase ("concerning free will, or free will forfeited") into Latin, lit tr "concerning free or enslaved will".

46[2] *Paradise Lost* III 80–343.

46[3] The famous friendly controversy between Joseph Priestley and Richard Price was published under the title *A Free Discussion of the Doctrines of Materialism, and Philosophical Necessity*, in 1778.

46[4] The well-known division of the Methodists into two parties, the Calvinistic followers of George Whitefield (1714–70)

and the Arminian followers of John Wesley himself, is alluded to also in **52, 62**, and **80**, where C asserts that the latter greatly outnumber the former.

47[1] Matt 9.13, and var Mark 2.17, Luke 5.32: ". . . I am not come to call the righteous, but sinners to repentance."

47[2] "*Is* there something *between* the saved and salvation? between the free and freedom? Salvation concerns one who is perishing, or at least in danger; Redemption [is] like a divine Bridge between the Slave and the Freedom he has lost, and conse-

48 ii 52

It was reserved for these days of *new discovery* to announce to mankind, that unless they are SINNERS, they are excluded from the promised blessings of the gospel.

Merely read—that unless they are sick, they are precluded from the offered remedies of the Gospel: and is not this the dictate of common sense, as well as Methodism/ But, does not Methodism cry aloud, that *all* men are sick—sick to the very heart? "If we say we are without Sin, we deceive ourselves, & the Truth is not in us!"[1] This shallow-pated Barrister makes me downright *piggish*; and without the stratagem of that famed Philosopher in Pig-nature almost drives me into the Charon's Hoy of Methodist[a] by his rude and stupid tail-hawling me back from it.[2]

49 ii 53

I can assure these gentlemen, that I regard, with a reverence as pure and awful as can enter into the human mind, that *blood which was shed upon the cross . . .

* i.e. in the Barrister's Creed, that mysterious Flint, which with the subordinate Aids of Mutton, Barley, Salt, Turnips, & Potherbs, makes most wonderful fine *Flint Broth*.[1] Supposing Christ had never shed his pure & aweful *Blood* (mere Cant & Hypocrisy in this man) yet if he had worked his miracles, raised Lazarus, & *taught* the same doctrines, would not the *Result* have been the same to him?—Or if Christ had never appeared on Earth, yet did not Daniel work miracles as stupendous, which surely must give all the authority to his doctrines, that miracles can give? And did he not announce by the Holy Spirit the Resurrection to Judgment, of Glory or of Punishment!—

48[a] A slip for "Methodism"? or an error in the overtracing

---

quently longs for!" C makes a point of the etymology of "interest" similarly elsewhere, e.g. ATHENAEUM **11**, *AR (CC)* 193.

48[1] 1 John 1.8.

48[2] Charon was in Greek mythology the ferryman who transported the souls of the dead across the river Styx into the underworld. A hoy is a small boat. The stratagem appears to be affecting to forbid the very thing you want done; what "Philosopher" C has in mind is not clear, unless it is Charon himself in some untraced story. For his own

piggishness, cf *BL (CC)* I 304: "*in money concerns you have some small portion of pig-nature in your moral idiosyncracy, and . . . must occasionally be pulled backward from the boat in order to make you enter it*".

49[1] C alludes to the European folk-tale about the trickster who, pretending to make soup by cooking a stone in a pot of water, persuaded his dupes to add meat and vegetables. C makes the same analogy in his attack on Hartley in *BL* ch 6 *(CC)* I 109.

50   ii 54–5

Let them not attempt to escape it by quoting a few disconnected phrases in the epistles, but let them adhere solely and steadfastly to that GOSPEL, of which they affect to be the exclusive preachers   . . .

And whence has the Barrister learnt, that the Epistles are not equally binding on Christians, as the 4 Gospels? Surely, of St Paul's at least the authenticity is incomparably clearer/ and if he give up, as doubtless he does, the plenary Inspiration of the Gospels, the authority of the Writers of all the Epistles is greater than two at least of the 4 Evang^{ts}.[1] Secondly, the Gospel of John, and all the Epistles were purposely written to teach the Christian *Religion*; whereas the first three Gospels are as evidently intended only as memorabilia, of the History of the Xtian *Revelation*, as far as the process of Redemption was carried on in the Life, Death, & Resurrection of the divine Founder? This is the blank brazen blushless or only brass-blushing Impudence of an old Bailey Barrister, attempt to browbeat out of court the better & more authentic Half of the Witnesses against him/—If I wished to understand the Laws of England, shall I consult Hume or Blackstone—him who has written his volumes expressly as Comments on those Laws, or the Historian, who mentions them only as far as the Laws were connected with the events & characters, which he relates or describes?[2]—Nay, it is far worse than this—for Christ himself repeatedly defers the publication of his Doctrines till after his Death/ & gives the reason too, that till he had sent the Holy Ghost, his disciples were not capable of comprehending?[3] Does he not attribute to an immediate influence of especial Inspiration even Peter's acknowlegement of his Filiation to God or Messiahship?[4]—Was it from the Gospels that Paul learned to know Christ?—Was the Church sixty years without the aweful Truths taught exclusively in *John's* Gospel?

51   iii 6–7

The nostrum of the Mountebank will be preferred to the prescription of the regular Practitioner. Why is this? Because there is something in the

---

50[1] Greater than that of Mark and Luke, who were not apostles.

50[2] C makes an analogy between the narratives of the evangelists and David Hume's *History of Great Britain* (1st ed 1754–61), on the one hand, and the epistles and William Blackstone's classic *Commentaries on the Laws of England* (1765–9), on the other.

50[3] For Christ's prohibition against "the publication of his Doctrines" see e.g. Matt 16.20; Mark 7.36, 9.30; Luke 9.18–22. For the "reason" cited by C, see John 14, esp 14.26: "But the Comforter, which is the Holy Ghost, whom the Father will send in my name, he shall teach you all things, and bring all things to your remembrance, whatsoever I have said unto you."

50[4] Matt 16.15–17, q in **41** n 1 above.

authoritative arrogance of the pretender by which *ignorance is over-awed.

* This is something: and true as far as it goes. That is however but a very little way. The P̶ great Power of both spiritual and physical mountebanks rests on that irremoveable property of human Nature, in force of which *indefinite* Instincts and Sufferings find no echo, no resting place in the Definite and Comprehensible. Ignorance unnecessarily enlarges the sphere of these; but a sphere there is, *facts* of mind and Cravings of the Soul there are, in which the wisest Man seeks help from the Indefinite, because it is nearer and more like the Infinite, of which he is made the Image—for even we are infinite, even in our finiteness infinite, as the Father in his Infinity. In many caterpillars there is a large empty space in the head, the destined room for the pushing forth of the antennæ of its next state of Being.—[1]

52   iii 13–15

But the ANTI-MORALISTS aver—and it makes a prominent feature in their defence—that they are quoted unfairly;—that although they disavow, it is true, the necessity, and deny the value, of practical morality and personal holiness, and declare them to be totally irrelevant to our future salvation, yet that, by diligent attention, I might have found occasional recommendations of moral duty, which I have neglected to notice.

The same Crambe bis decies cocta[1] of one self-same ⟨charge⟩ grounded on one gross & stupid misconception and mistatement: and to which there needs no other answer than this simple fact. Let the Barrister name any one gross offence against the moral Law, for which *he* would shun a man's acquaintance/ and for that same vice the Methodist would inevitably be excluded publicly from the Society of the Faithful/ and I am inclined to think, that a fair List of the Barrister's friends & Acquaintances would prove, that the Calvinist Methodists are the austerer and more watchful Censors of the two. If this be the truth, as it notoriously is, what but the Cataract of Stupidity uncouched,[2] or the thickest Film of Bigot-slime can prevent a man from seeing that this Tenet of Justification *by Faith alone* is exclusively a matter between the Calvinist's own Heart

---

51[1] The chrysalis of the butterfly was a favourite emblem, for C, of spiritual growth, partly because of the traditional iconographical link between Psyche (the mythological, allegorised figure whose name means "soul") and the butterfly: cf RICHTER *Kampaner Thal* **6** and n 2 above.

52[1] "Twice-ten-times-cooked cabbage": a hyperbolic version of the proverbial *crambe bis cocta.*
52[2] I.e. a cataract in the eye, not a waterfall: to "couch" is to remove the cataract surgically.

& his Maker who alone knows the true source of his words and actions; but that to his neighbours & fellow-creedsmen his spotless Life & good works are demanded, not indeed as the [? the] prime efficient causes of his salvation, but as the necessary & only possible *Signs* of that Faith, which is the *means* of that Salvation, of which Christ's free Grace is the Cause, and the sanctifying Spirit the Perfecter. But I fall into the same fault, I am arraigning, by so often exposing & confuting the same Blunder, which had no claim even at its first enunciation to the compliment of a philosophic Answer. But why, in the name of common sense, all this endless Whoop and Hubbub against the *Calvinist* Methodists? I had understood, that the Arminian Methodists, or Wesleyans, are the more numerous Body by far? Has there been any union lately? And if so, have the followers of Wesley abjured the doctrines of their Founder on this Head?—[3]

53   iii 16

Impostors of every class, religious as well as political, cry down the exercise of *reason*, for they have no chance of escaping exposure but by bringing men of penetration and inquiry into disrepute. . . .

We are told, by our new spiritual Teachers, that *reason* is not to be applied in the inquiry into the truth or falsehood of their doctrines; they are spiritually discerned, and *carnal reason* has no concern with them.

Even under this aversion to *Reason*, as applied to religious grounds, a very important Truth lurks: and the mistake (a very dangerous one, I admit) lies in the confounding two very different faculties of the mind under one and the same name/ the Pure Reason, or vis scientifica;[1] and the *Discourse*, or prudential Power, the proper Objects of which are the *Phænomena* of [? un] sensuous *Experience*. The greatest Loss, which modern Psilosophy[2] has thro' wilful Scorn sustained, is the great Distinction of the Ancient Philosophers between the Νουμενα, and Φαινομενα.[3] This gives the true sense of Pliny—venerare *Deos* (i.e. their Statues, &c) et *numina* Deorum (i.e. those spiritual Influences which are represented by the Images & PERSONS of Apollo, Minerva, &c.[4]

52[3] Cf remarks in **46** above, and n 4.

53[1] "The power that gives knowledge" or "the sciential faculty".

53[2] See **14** n 4 above.

53[3] Between Noumena and Phenomena, as in ROBINSON **19** (and n 1) above. The Kantian antithesis is foreshadowed often in Plato, e.g. *Timaeus* 51D, *Parmenides*

132C–D, *Republica* 508C.

53[4] C liked to dwell on the significance of the resemblances among the words "noumenon", "name", *nomen*, and *numen*: cf QUARTERLY REVIEW **27** and n 1 above. Here he alludes to Pliny the Younger *Letters* 10.96.6–7, where Pliny tells how he had ordered to be brought into court the em-

54   iii 17

Religion has for its object the moral care and the moral cultivation of man. Its beauty is not to be sought in the regions of mystery or in the flights of abstraction. It was intended to be the regulator of life.

What ignorance? Is there a single *moral* Precept of the Gospels not to be found in the Old Testament?—Not one! A new Edition of White's Dia-Tessaron with a running Comment consisting entirely of parallel passages from the Hebrew, Greek, and Roman Writers before Christ, and those after him who, it is morally certain, drew no aids from the N.T., ~~would~~ is a grand Desideratum/ and if any thing could open the eyes of Socinians, this would do it.—[1]

55   iii 25

The masculine strength and moral firmness which once distinguished the great mass of the British people is daily fading away; METHODISM, with all its cant, with all its cunning, with all its hypocrisy, and with all its meanness, has taken place of that religion which made us what we were, and which . . . gave strength, and vigour, and dignity, to our character as men.

Well! but in God's name can Methodism be at once *the effect* and the *cause* of this Loss of masculine Strength & moral firmness—Did Whitfield & Wesley *blow* them *out* at the first puff—these grand virtues of *masculine* Strength, and *moral* Firmness? Admire, I pray you, the happy Antithesis—yet *"feminine"* would be an improvement as then the *sense* too would be antithetic. However, the sound is sufficient, and modern rhetoric possesses the virtue of Economy.

56   iii 27–8

[Sedgwick again quotes Rowland Hill's *Village Dialogues* to the effect that it would be worthwhile for all men to become tinkers if by so doing

peror's statue and images of the divine powers (*simulacra numinum*) and how all those accused of being Christians paid reverence (*venerati sunt*) to the emperor's statue and the images of the gods (*simulacra deorum*). It is fairly clear that Pliny was making no such careful distinction as C implies.

54[1] Joseph White (1745–1814), a distinguished Orientalist who was appointed Regius Professor of Hebrew at Oxford in 1804, had produced his *Diatessaron* in Greek in 1799, and a Latin version in 1802. The title is transliterated Greek signifying "through the four [gospels]": the work is a history of the life of Christ compiled from the gospels. The Latin *Diatesseron* is a small book that was used as a school textbook; C would like to see it expanded to include OT and classical analogues to the teachings of Christ.

they became preachers of the calibre of John Bunyan.] So with the Tinker; I would give him the care of kettles, but I would not give him *the
cure of souls*. So long as he attended to the management and mending of
his pots and pans, I would wish success to his industry; but when he came
to declare *himself* a "chosen vessel," and demand permission to take the
souls of the people into his holy keeping, I should think that, instead of *a
license*, it would be more humane and more prudent to give him a passport to Saint Luke's.—Depend upon it such men were never sent by
Providence to rule or to regulate mankind.

WHOO!!! Bounteous Providence, that always looks at the Baby Clothes
& the Parents' Equipage before it picks out the proper Soul for the Baby.
Ho! the Dutchess of Manchester is in labor—quick, Raphael or Uriel!
bring a Soul out of the *Numa Bin/* a young Lycurgus—or the Archbishop's Lady—Ho! a Soul from the Chrysostom or Athanasius
Locker![1]—But poor Moll Crispin is in the Throes with Twins—/ Well!
there are plenty of Cobler & Tinker Souls in the Hold—*John* Bunyan!—
Why, thou miserable Barrister, it would take an Angel an eternity a post[2]
to tinker thee into a Skull of half his Capacity!

57   iii 31–4

. . . these *anti-moral* editors [of *Pilgrim's Progress*, with notes by J. Newton, Dr Hawker, and others] assure us, in a note, that "A *truly* awakened
conscience can never find relief from the law." (*i.e.* THE MORAL LAW.)[a]
"The more he looks for peace *this way*, *his guilt*, like a heavy burden, becomes more intolerable; when he becomes *dead* to the *law*,—as to *any
dependence upon it for salvation*,—by the body of Christ, and married to
him, who was raised from the dead, then, and not till then, his heart is set
at liberty to run the way of God's Commandments." . . . But here we are
taught that the *conscience* can never find relief from *obedience to the law*
of the Gospel, and are told, directly in the teeth of it, that the more a man

---

57[a] Square brackets in original

56[1] C draws attention to the class assumptions underlying Sedgwick's statement, namely that Providence provides
members of every class with qualities
appropriate to their respective stations—
hence rulers and lawgivers as the prototypes
for the duke's son (Numa was according to
legend the second king of Rome, and Lycurgus the lawgiver was a son of the king of

Sparta), and eminent theologians for the son
of the archbishop (St John Chrysostom—c
345–407—was one of the Greek Fathers of
the Church, and Athanasius—c 296–373—
bp of Alexandria).

56[2] Meaning perhaps an eternity for
each stage, using "post" in the traveller's
sense, the distance between two post-
horses.

looks for peace *this way*, the more *intolerable* becomes the burden of *his guilt!!*

False! We are told by Bunyan, that the Conscience can never find relief for its *disobedience* to the Law in the Law itself—and this is as true of the Moral as of the Mosaic Law.[1] I am not defending Calvinism or Bunyan's Theology; but if victory, not truth, were my object, I could desire no easier task than to defend it against our doughty Barrister.—Well, but I *repent*—i.e. regret it.—Yes! and so you doubtless regret the loss of an Eye or Arm—will that make it grow again?—Think you this nonsense as applied to morality? Be it so! But yet nonsense most tremendously suited to human Nature is it, as the Barrister may find in the Arguments of the Pagan Philosophers against Christianity, who attributed a large portion of its success to its holding out an expiation, which no other Religion did.[2]—Read but that most affecting & instructive anecdote selected from the Indostan Missionary Account by the Quart. Review![3] Again let me say, I am not giving my own opinion on this very difficult point; but of one thing I am convinced, that the *I am sorry for it—that's enough* men mean nothing but *regret* when they talk of repentance, and have consciences either so pure or so callous, as not to know what a direful and strange thing *Remorse* is![4] and how absolutely a fact sui generis![5] I have often remarked, & it cannot be too often remarked (vain as this may

57[1] If C has a particular passage in mind, it is probably the episode in *Pilgrim's Progress* in which Christian, weary of his burden, is advised by Mr Worldly-Wiseman to go to the village of Morality (passing by the "hill" of Mount Sinai), where a gentleman named Legality will help him off with it. Evangelist intercepts him and corrects him, saying, "ye cannot be justified by the Works of the Law; for by the deeds of the Law no man living can be rid of his burden": John Bunyan *Grace Abounding to the Chief of Sinners; and Pilgrim's Progress* ed Roger Sharrock (1966) 157–8. C's annotated copies of *Pilgrim's Progress* belong to a much later date than the Sedgwick notes: see BUNYAN.

57[2] This assertion may be based on Gibbon, as much of **14** above is. In ch 15 of the *Decline and Fall*, Gibbon outlines reasons for the spread of Christianity, including the expiatory sacrifice of Christ. We do not know what ed of Gibbon C used before 1810, though he certainly later annotated at least one copy (GIBBON); *Southey SC*

(1844) 1099 is a 12-vol ed of 1788.

57[3] C alludes to a package review by RS of two books about India, one of them an account of Baptist missions there, in *QR* I (Feb 1809) 193–226; and specifically a story that seemed to the missionaries to show "the effect produced by offering an easier law" (215). A penitent had been sent on a pilgrimage of 500 miles in sandals that had spikes driven through them. One day as he was resting, he heard a Christian missionary preaching on the text "The blood of Christ cleanseth from all sin". "While he was preaching, the man rose up, cast off his torturing sandals, and cried aloud, this is what I want; 'And he became . . . a lively witness that the blood of Jesus Christ does indeed cleanse from all sins.'"

57[4] The difference between regret and remorse was an important concept for C. Notes for a lecture of 1808 include an exposition of it (*Lects 1808–1819—CC*—I 63–4); and cf SCHELLING *Philosophische Schriften* **54** and n 1.

57[5] "Of its own kind", i.e. unique.

sound) that this essential *Heterogeneity* of Regret and Remorse is of itself a sufficient and the best, *proof* of Free *Will*, and *Reason*: ~~on~~ the co-existence of which in man we call *Conscience*, and on this rests the whole Superstructure of human Religion—God, Immortality, Guilt, Judgment, Redemption. Whether another & different Superstructure may be raised on the same foundation, or whether the same ⟨Edifice⟩ is susceptible of important alteration, is another question—But such is the Edifice at present—and this its foundation: and the Barrister might as rationally expect to blow up Windsor Castle by breaking wind in one of its Cellars, as hope to demolish Calvinism by such arguments as his.

58 iii 36–40

"And, behold, a certain Lawyer stood up, and tempted him, saying, Master, what shall I do *to inherit eternal life?*

"He said unto him, WHAT IS WRITTEN IN THE LAW? HOW READEST THOU?

"And he answering, said, Thou shalt love the Lord thy God with all thy heart, with all thy soul, and with all *thy strength*, and with all thy mind; and thy neighbour as thyself.

"And he said unto him, *Thou hast answered* RIGHT. THIS DO, and THOU SHALT LIVE."

So would Bunyan, and so would Calvin have preached: would both of them in the name of Christ have made this assurance to the Barrister— *This do*, and thou shalt live!—But ~~if~~ what if he has not done it; but the very contrary? And what if the Querist should be a staunch Disciple of Dʳ Paley; & hold himself *morally obliged* not to hate or injure his fellow-man, not because he is compelled by Conscience to see the exceeding sinfulness of Sin, & to abhor sin as sin, even as he eschews Pain as Pain— no, not even because God has forbidden it—but ultimately because the great Legislator is able and has threatened to put him to unspeakable Torture if he disobeys, and to give him all kind of pleasure if he does not—?[1] Why, verily, in this case, I do foresee that both the Tinker and the Divine would wax warm, and rebuke the said Querist for vile Hypocrisy, and a most nefarious abuse of God's good gift, intelligible Language—What? do you call *this* loving the Lord your God with all your *heart*, with all your *soul*, &c &c—and your n. as yourself—/[2] when in truth you *love* nothing, not even your own soul; but only set a superlative *value* on whatever will gratify your selfish lust of *Enjoyment*, and en-

---

58[1] Cf **13** above, and n 1.   **58**[2] Cf **13** above, and n 2.

sure you from Hell-fire at a 1000 times the true value of the dirty property. If you have the impudence to persevere in misnaming this *Love*, supply any one instance, in which you used the word in this sense? If your
Son did not spit in your face, because he believed, you would disinherit
him if he did, & this were his main *moral obligation*, would *you* allow,
that your Son *loved* you—& with all his heart & mind, & strength, &
soul?—Shame! Shame!

Now the power of *loving* God, of willing good as good (not of desiring the *agreeable*, and of preferring a larger tho' distant delight to an infinitely smaller immediate gratification = selfish prudence) Bunyan considers supernatural, & seeks its source in the free grace of the Creator
thro' Christ, the Redeemer/[3] this the Kantéan avers to be supersensual indeed, but not supernatural, but in the original and essence of human Nature, & forming its grand & aweful characteristic. Hence he calls it die
Menschheit = the principle of Humanity[4]—but yet no less than Calvin
or the Tinker declares it a principle most mysterious, the undoubted Object of religious Awe, a perpetual witness of that God, whose Image
(Icon)[5] it is; a principle utterly *incomprehensible* by the discursive Intellect—and moreover teaches us, that the surest plan for stifling &
paralysing this divine *Birth* in the Soul (a phrase of Plato's as well as of
the Tinker's)[6] is by attempting to evoke it by, or substitute for it, the hopes
& fears, the motives & calculations, of Prudence: which is an excellent
& in truth indispensable *Servant*, but considered as Master & Primate of
the moral Diocese precludes the possibility of Virtue (in Bunyan's
phrase, HOLINESS OF SPIRIT)[7] by introducing *Legality*:[8] which is no Cant

---

58[3] Cf the episode of *Pilgrim's Progress*
cited in **57** n 1, which demonstrates—as
Bunyan necessarily does again and again—
that no merely human means will relieve
Christian of his burden and bring him to the
Celestial City. Christian's "name at the first
was *Graceless*" (176).

58[4] C was reading—and probably at the
same time annotating—Kant's *Metaphysik
der Sitten* (2 vols Königsberg 1797) in the
summer of 1809: *CN* III 3558, 3560–2;
KANT *Metaphysik*. Kant describes *Menschheit* "Humanity" as the defining characteristic of mankind, and the cultivation of humanity as the moral duty of mankind, so
that the perfection of humanity constitutes
the ideal goal of the human race: see e.g.
Metaphysik der Sitten II 15, 47.

58[5] C came later to object to the translation of εἰκων (*eikōn*, "icon") as "image" in

AV, and instead used "Idea or Icon" and
"substantial-Idea": BIBLE COPY B **131** and
n 4, LEIGHTON COPY B **11** and n 4, COPY C
7 and n 1.

58[6] The phrase itself has not been traced
in Plato or Plotinus. Plato tends to say that
only the philosopher can recover the divine
truths that all human souls saw before birth:
Meno 99E, *Phaedrus* 249B–250C.

58[7] This not very remarkable phrase
(Rom 1.4 has "spirit of holiness") has not
been traced in *Pilgrim's Progress*, though
Faithful there says that the work of grace in
the soul is manifest to others by "a life of
holiness; heart-holiness, family-holiness,
[and] . . . Conversation-holiness in the
world" (ed cit 206). It does not appear in
Bunyan's *Holy War* or *Grace Abounding*.

58[8] For Bunyan's "Legality" see **57** n 1;
Kant, in *Metaphysik der Sitten* (cited in n 4),

phrase of Methodism, but of authenticated standing in the Ethics of the profoundest Philosophers—even those, who rejected Christianity, as ⟨a⟩ *miraculous* Event, & revelation itself as far as anything *supernatural* is implied in it.—I must not mention Plato, I suppose—he was a Mystic— nor Zeno—he & his were Visionaries[9]—but Aristotle, the cold and dry Aristotle, has in a very remarkable passage in his lesser tract of Ethics asserted the same thing; and called it "a divine principle, lying deeper than those things which can be explained, or enunciated discursively."[10]

59 iii 46

Sure I am, that no father of a family, that can at all estimate the importance of keeping from the infant mind whatever might raise impure ideas or excite improper inquiries, will ever commend the PILGRIM'S PROGRESS to their perusal.

In the same spirit and for the same cogent reason, that the holy Monk Lewis prohibited the Bible to all decent families—or if they *must* have something of that kind—proposed in preference Tirant, the White![1]—O how I abhor this damnable French heart-haunting Impurity in the envelope of Modesty. Merciful Heaven! is it not a direct consequence from this System, that we all purchase our existence at the price of our Mother's purity of Mind? See what Milton has written on this subject in the passage quoted in the Friend, in the Essays on the communication of Truth.—[2]

---

repeatedly contrasts those rules of prudence that are based on experience with *a priori* intuitions of moral obligation, e.g. "Ethische Elementarlehre" pt 1 § 8, pt 2 § 32. He also makes a correspondent distinction between legality and morality: "Einleitung" § 1.

58[9] C is ironically imagining the dismissive reaction of his contemporaries to these names. For Plato's position see n 6; "Zeno" is Zeno of Citium (335–263 BC), the founder of Stoicism.

58[10] Aristotle rejected Plato's Idea of Good and even the concept of goodness as a universal in all three surviving versions of his work on ethics, that is, *Nicomachean Ethics* 1.6 (1096[a]–1097[a]), *Eudemian Ethics* 1.8 (1217[b]–1218[b]), and *Magna moralia* 1.1 (1182[b]). The words C quotes here have not been traced. Aristotle does however include references to divine inspiration of right conduct (which he equates with good fortune) and to the contemplation of God as the final

cause of virtue in *Eudemian Ethics* 7.14 (1248[a]) and 7.15 (1249[b]). It may be that C had these passages in mind in *TT* (*CC*) I 173; cf II 111.

59[1] In his review of M. G. Lewis *The Monk* in the *Critical Review* in 1797, C had already selected for special opprobrium the passage that describes a prudent mother as censoring her daughter's reading of the Bible, some parts of it containing more "indecent expressions" than "the annals of a brothel" and liable to do more harm to a young mind than "lascivious" romances such as the 15th-century *Tirant lo Blanch*: *The Monk* (1796) II 247–8; C's review is in *SW & F* (*CC*) 57–65.

59[2] C quotes Milton several times in these essays (*Friend*—*CC*—II 38–88), but the passage he has in mind is probably the one from *Areopagitica* in favour of freedom of the press: *Friend* (*CC*) II 60–1*.

60   iii 47

. . . let us ask whether the female mind is likely to be trained to purity by studying this Manual of Piety, and by expressing its devotional desires after the following example:—"MERCY, being a *young* and *breeding* woman, *longed* for something that she saw there, but was ashamed to ask. . . ."

d–mn the fellow! I could find it in my heart to suspect him of any Vice, that a Frenchman could commit![1]

61   iii 56–9

. . . wherefore he saith, 'As by one man's disobedience many were made sinners, so by the obedience of one shall many be made righteous.' [Footnote:] This text, from St. Paul, gives not the slightest countenance, when properly understood, to the unscriptural doctrine in support of which the blindfold followers of Calvin perpetually quote it. Its interpretation is simply this:—As by following the fatal example of one man's *disobedience* many were made sinners, so by that pattern of perfect *obedience* which Christ has set before us shall many be made righteous . . .

What may not be explained thus? and into what may not any thing be thus explained? Yet after all, it comes out little better than nonsense, in any other than the literal sense. For let any man of sincere mind and without any system to support look round ⟨on⟩ all his Christian Neighbours, and will he say or will they say, that the origin of their well-doing was an attempt to *imitate* what they all believe to be *inimitable*, Christ's *perfection* in virtue, his *absolute* Sinlessness?—No—but yet perhaps some particular virtues, for instance, his patriotism in weeping over Jerusalem, his active benevolence in curing the sick & preaching to the poor, his divine forgiveness in praying for his enemies—We grant all this! But then how is this *peculiar* to Christ? Is it not the effect of all illustrious examples, probably most, which we last read of, or which made the deepest impression on our feelings? Were there no good men before Christ?—as there were no bad men before Adam. Is it not a notorious fact, that those who most frequently refer to Christ's conduct for their own actions, are those who believe him an the incarnate Deity, consequently, the best possible *guide*, but in ⟨no⟩ *strict* sense, an *example*—while those, who regard

60[1] C invariably associated the French with moral, and especially sexual impurity (cf **59**). In a note written not long after this one, he comments on the use of the word "love" for the mating instinct in animals as a typically French example "of the filthiness of mock-modesty": ENCYCLOPAEDIA LONDINENSIS **1**. For his consistent hostility towards French writers, see DESMOULINS **1** and n 1.

him as a mere man,[1] the chief of the Jewish Prophets, both in the pulpit and from the press ground their moral persuasions chiefly on arguments drawn from the propriety & seemliness—or the contrary—of the action itself, or from the will of God known by the Light of Reason. To make St Paul prophesy that all Christians will owe their Holiness to their exclusive & conscious imitation of Christ's actions is to make St Paul a false Prophet—and what becomes of the boasted influence of Miracles? Even as false would it be to ascribe the vices of the Chinese, or even our own, to the influence of Adam's bad example! As well might ⟨we⟩ say of a poor scrofulous Innocent—see the effect of the bad *example* of his Father on him!—I blame no man for disbelieving, or ⟨for⟩ opposing with might and main, the dogma of original Sin; but I confess, that I neither respect the understanding nor have confidence in the sincerity of him, who declares that he has carefully read the writings of St Paul, and finds in them no consequence attributed to the Fall of Adam but that of his bad *example*, and none to the Cross of C~~ross~~hrist but the good *example* of dying a martyr to a good cause! I would undertake from the writings of the later English Socinians to collect paraphrases on the N.T. texts, that could only be paralleled by the spiritual Paraphrase on Solomon's Song in Vol. II. of "A Diction. of the Holy Bible["], by John Brown, Minister of the Gospel at Haddington/ Third Edition—Article, Song.—[2]

62   iii 64–7

Call forth the Robber from his cavern, and the midnight Murderer from his den; summon the Seducer from his couch, and beckon the Adulterer from his embrace; cite the Swindler to appear . . . assemble from every quarter all the various miscreants whose vices deprave, and whose villanies distress, mankind; and when they are thus thronged round in a circle, assure them—not that there is a God that judgeth the earth—not that punishment in the great day of retribution will await their crimes. . . . Let

<hr/>

61[1] The Socinians—in contemporary England, Unitarians like Sedgwick.

61[2] The very long entry "Song" in John Brown *A Dictionary of the Holy Bible* (3rd ed 2 vols Edinburgh 1789) consists almost entirely of an extended paraphrase of the Song of Songs by way of a defence against the "carnalists" who read it literally as a love-poem. Brown offers instead an allegorical interpretation in which, for example, the phrase "betwixt my breasts" (1.13) is rendered "amidst the two nourishing testaments of his word" and "Let him kiss me with the kisses of his mouth" (1.2) becomes "Let HIM, whose name is wonderful, inexpressible, and unmatched . . . kindly, but powerfully, apply his precious truths to my soul". HC's heavily annotated copy of this edition—probably the one his father used—is in the Humanities Research Center at the University of Texas in Austin; it is inscribed "Hartley Coleridge from his friend Mr Jackson"—i.c. William Jackson (the landlord of the Coleridges and Southeys at Greta Hall), who died Oct 1810 just after C left for London.

every sinner in the throng be told that they will stand *justified* before God; that *the righteousness* of *Christ* will be imputed to *them*; and that consequently they will be precisely in the same condition as if they had led a life of the utmost holiness . . .

Well! do so!—Nay, nay! it has been done! the effect has been tried! and Slander itself cannot deny, that the effect has been the conversion of thousands of those very Sinners, whom the Barrister's Fancy thus convokes! O shallow man! not to see that here lies the main strength of the cause, he is attacking/ that to repeat my former illustration he ~~appeals~~ draws the attention to Patients in the at worst state of Disease which perhaps alone requires & justifies the use of *the White Pill*, as a mode of exposing the frantic Quack who vends it promiscuously![1]—He fixes on the Empiric's *Cures* to prove his Murders!—not to forget what ought to conclude every paragraph in answer to the Barrister's Hints—and were it so, what does this prove against the present Methodists as Methodists? Is not the tenet of imputed Righteousness the faith of all the Scotch Clergy, who are not false to their declarations at their public assumption of the Ministry?[2] Till within the last 60 or 70 years was not the Tenet preached Sunday after Sunday in every nook of Scotland—and has the B. heard, that the morals of the Scotch Peasants & Artisans have been improved within the last 30 or 40 years, since the exceptions have become more & more common?— Was it by want of strict morals, that the Puritans were distinguished to their disadvantage from the rest of Englishmen during the reigns of Eliz. James I. Charles I. & 2.[n][d]?[3] And ~~during~~ that very period, which the B. affirms to have been distinguished by the moral vigor of the great Mass of Britons, was it not likewise the Period when this very doctrine was preached by the Established Clergy 50 times, for once that it is heard from the same pulpits in the present and preceding generation?—Never, never can the Methodists be successfully assailed, if not honestly! and never honestly or with any chance of success, except as *Methodists*—for their practices, their alarming Theocracy, their stupid, mad, and mad-driving

62[1] See **4** at n 3, where C describes a quack selling "Pills of Mercurial Sublimate".

62[2] The presbyterian Church of Scotland subscribed to the terms of the Westminster Confession of 1647 which includes the doctrine of imputed righteousness (in ch 11 "Of Justification"), but the active promulgation of this doctrine had been to some extent remitted in the later 18th century by moderates under the influence of the Scot-

tish Enlightenment.

62[3] The answer expected to this rhetorical question is "No". Cf *TT* (*CC*) I 162–5, remarks prompted by RS's life of Bunyan, esp C's championing of the Puritans as morally superior to the high-church party, and the observation (164) that "Whatever may have been the faults of the Puritans under Cromwell—to call them immoral as compared with the Cavaliers after the Restoration is really too much".

Superstitions—These are their property pro peculio:[4] their doctrines are those of the Established Church, with no other difference than that in the Church Liturgy + Articles + Homilies, Calvinism & Lutheranism are joined like the two Hands of the Union Fire Office[5]—the Methodists have unclasped them, and one is Whitfield & the other Wesley[6]

63 iii 75

". . . For the same reason that a book written in bad language should never be put into the hands of a child that speaks correctly, a book exhibiting instances of vice should never be given to a child that thinks and acts properly." [Footnote:] "Practical Education. By Maria and R. L. Edgeworth. In three volumes." Vol. ii. p. 89.

* How mortifying, that one is never lucky enough to meet with any of these Virtuosissimos, 15 or 20 years of age!! But perhaps they are such rare Jewels, ~~that~~ that they are *always* kept in Cotton! The Kilcrops![1] I would not exchange the heart, which I myself had when a boy, while reading the Life of Colonel Jack, or the Newgate Calendar, for a waggon-load of these Brilliants.[2]

64 iii 78

The following annotations hold out a very discouraging prospect to those who may feel inclined to forsake the evil of their ways, and to walk in the path of religious duty.

62[4] "As their very own", i.e. distinctively or exclusively theirs.

62[5] The Union Fire Office, in Cornhill in C's day, was one of several private fire brigades cum insurance companies operating in London, and its emblem of two joined hands was well known. (C refers to it also in *CN* III 4134.) When Drury Lane Theatre was rebuilt after a fire, James and Horace Smith published *Rejected Addresses* (1812), a collection of parodies of contemporary writers; one of the entries, "The Rebuilding. *By R.S.*", i.e. Robert Southey, reads in part as follows: "Now come the men of fire to quench the fires, / To Russel Street see Globe and Atlas run, / Hope gallops first, and second sun; / On flying heel, / See Hand in Hand / O'ertake the band, / View with what glowing wheel / He nicks / Phoenix; / While Albion scampers from Bridge-street Blackfriars . . .".

62[6] See **46** and n 4.

63[1] *OED* "killcrop": "An insatiate brat, popularly supposed to be a fairy changeling substituted for the genuine child".

63[2] In the educational debate about the proper reading-matter for children, C and his friends steadily advocated fantasies (fairy tales) and adventure stories in opposition to the "Goody Two-Shoes" school of overt moral didacticism, e.g. in Lect 12A (1808) in *Lects 1808–1819 (CC)* I 107–8 and nn 37–8, and cf "O! bring back *Jack the Giant Killer*" in PARR **1** above. Defoe's *Colonel Jack* (1722) is the fictional autobiography of a reformed thief, based on such supposedly authentic stories of the lives of criminals as were later collected in the *Newgate Calendar* (1774). For C's reading in Defoe generally see the DEFOE headnote.

"When a man turns his back on the world, and is in good earnest resolved for everlasting life, his carnal friends, and ungodly neighbours, *will pursue him with hue and cry*; but *death is at his heels*, and he cannot stop short of the City of Refuge." . . .

This representation of the state of real Christians is as mischievous as it is false.

Yet Christ's assertion on this head is positive, & universal:[1] and I believe it from my inmost soul, and am convinced that it is just as true A.D. 1810, as A.D. 33.

65   iii 82

The spirit with which all their *merciless treatment* is to be borne is next pointed out [in a note to *Pilgrim's Progress*] . . . "*Patient bearing of injuries* is true Christian fortitude, and will always be more effectual to *disarm our enemies*, and to bring others to the knowledge of the truth, than all *arguments* whatever . . ."

Is this Barrister a Christian of any sort or sect, and is he not ashamed, if not afraid, to ridicule such passages as these? If they are not true, the 4 Gospels are false.

66   iii 86–7

It is impossible to give them credit for integrity when we behold the obstinacy and the artifice with which they defend their system against the strongest argument, and against the clearest evidence.

Modest Gentleman! I wonder, he finds time to write bulky pamphlets: for surely Modesty, like his, must secure success & constant Clientage at the Bar!—Doubtless, he means his own arguments, the evidence, he himself has adduced—I say, doubtless, for what are these pamphlets but a long series of attacks on the doctrines of the strict Lutherans, and Calvinists (for the doctrines, he attacks, are common to both—) and if he knew stronger arguments, clearer evidence, he would certainly have given them!—and then what obstinate Rogues must our Bishops be, to have suffered these Hints to pass into a third Edition, & yet not have brought a Bill into Parliament for a new set of Articles, &c![1]—I have not heard, that they have even the grace to *intend* it.

64[1] On the incompatibility of Christian and worldly goals, and on the need to forsake the company of the ungodly, see e.g. Matt 10.34–9, 19.29; Mark 8.34–8; Luke 10.25–8; John 3.1–7.

66[1] I.e. to replace the Thirty-Nine Articles of the C of E.

67   iii 88–9

On this subject I will quote the just and striking observations of an excellent modern writer [Robert Fellowes, whose *Religion without Cant* is cited in a footnote]:—"In whatever village," says he, "the fanatics get a footing, drunkenness and swearing—sins which, being more exposed to the eye of the world, would be ruinous to their great pretensions to superior sanctity—will, perhaps, be found to decline; but I am convinced, from personal observation, that lying and dishonesty, that every species of fraud and falsehood—sins which are not so readily detected, but which seem more closely connected with worldly advantage—will be found invariably to increase."

In answer ⟨this⟩ let me make a very just observation, by some other man of my opinion to be hereafter quoted "from an excellent Modern Writer"[1]—and this, that from the Birth of Christ to the present Hour no Sect or Body of Men were zealous in the reformation of manners in society, without having been charged with the same vices in the same words. When I hate a man, & *see* nothing bad in him—what remains possible, but to accuse him of crimes which I cannot see—& which cannot be disproved, because they cannot be proved.—Surely, if Xtn Charity did not preclude *these* charges, the Shame of convicted Parrotry ought to prevent a man from repeating & publishing them.—The very same thoughts, almost the words, are to be found in Lucian of the early Christians[2]—of the poor Quakers, in a hundred Books—of the republicans—of the first Reformers. Why need I say this? Does not every one know, that a jovial Pot-companion can never believe a water-drinker not to be a sneaking cheating Knave that is afraid of his thoughts—that every Whoremonger swears that those who pretend to be chaste, either have their girl in a corner, or far worse—&c—&c— —

68   iii 89

The same hollowness and hypocrisy which our Saviour so fully detected and so sharply reproved in the *Godly* Pharisees of old time is manifested in their puritanic posterity. The same superstitious display of the outward and visible signs of devotion; the same *long prayers* . . . the same rigor-

---

67[1]   Textus var.

67[2]   The Greek satirist Lucian (for whom see also **14** n 5). In *De morte Peregrini* (c 165) he adopts a general tone of contempt towards the Christians; the dialogue *Philopatris*, still attributed to Lucian in C's day but now considered spurious, goes much further in its apparent ridicule of Christian doctrine; but C may simply have been relying on and echoing Gibbon, as in the earlier allusion.

ous abstinence from all appearance of recreation on the Lord's *day*; <u>and the same neglect of the weightier matters of the *moral* law, in the course of the *week*</u> . . .

This sentence thus smuggled in at the bottom of the Chest ought not to pass unnoticed: for the whole force of the former depends on it. It is a true *trick* & deserves *reprobation*.

69   iii 97

[Footnote, correcting the author of a work entitled *Lectures on Scripture Facts*:] It should have been "Lectures on *Scriptural* Facts." What should we think of the Grammarian, who, instead of *Historical*, should present us with "Lectures on *History* Facts."

But *Law* Tracts! And is not Scripture as often used thus *semi-adjectively*?

70   iii 100–1

"Do you really believe," says he [Dr Hawker], "that, because man by his apostasy hath lost his power and ability to obey, God hath lost his right to command? . . . Put the case that you were called upon, as a Barrister, to recover a debt due from one man to another, and you knew the debtor had not the ability to pay the *creditor*, would you tell your client that his debtor was under no legal or moral obligation to pay what he had no power to do? And would you tell him that the very expectation of his just right *was as foolish as it was tyrannical?*" . . . I will give my reply to these questions distinctly, and without hesitation. . . . Suppose A to have lent B a thousand pounds, as a capital to commence trade, and that, when he purchased his stock to this amount, and lodged it in his warehouse, a fire were to break out in the next dwelling, and, extending itself to *his* warehouse, were to consume the whole of his property, and reduce him to a state of utter ruin. If A, my client, were to ask my opinion as to his right to recover from B, I should tell him that this his right would exist should B ever be in a condition to repay the sum borrowed . . . but that the attempt to recover a thousand pounds from a man thus reduced, by accident, to utter ruin, and who had not a shilling left in the world, would *be as foolish as it was tyrannical.*

But this is rank Sophistry! The question is: Does a Thief (and a fraudulent Debtor is no better) acquire a claim to impunity by not possessing the power of restoring the goods. Every moral act derives its character (says a Schoolman with an unusual combination of profundity with quaintness) aut voluntate originis, aut *origine* voluntatis.[1] Now the very essence of Guilt, its dire and incommunicable character, consists in its tendency to destroy the free will—but when thus destroyed, are the *habits* of vice thenceforward innocent? Does the Law excuse the Murder because the Perpetrator was drunk? D[r] H. put his objection laxly & weakly enough; but a candid opponent would have been ashamed to have seized an hour's victory from what a move of the Pen would render impregnable.

71   iii 103–6

When, at this solemn tribunal, the sinner shall be called upon to answer for the transgression of those *moral* laws, on their obedience to which their salvation was made to depend, will it be sufficient, that, with unutterable terror and alarm, he declares himself to have been taught, when on earth, to believe that the Gospel *had neither terms nor conditions*, and that his salvation was secured by a covenant which procured him pardon and peace, *from all eternity*; a covenant, the effects of which no folly or *after-act whatever* could possibly destroy?—Who could anticipate the sentence of condemnation, and not weep in agony over the deluded victim of ignorance and imposture, who was thus taught a doctrine so fatally false?

What then? God is represented as a Tyrant when he claims the penalty of disobedience from the servant, who has wilfully incapacitated himself for yielding it—and yet just and merciful in condemning to indefinite misery "a poor *deluded victim*["] of Ignorance & Imposture? even tho' the Barrister spite of his antipathy to Methodists "would weep in agony" over him?[1] But before the Barrister draws Bills of Imagination on his tender feelings, would it not have been as well to have adduced some last dying Speech & Confession, in which the Culprit attributed his crimes—not to Sabbath-breaking & loose Company—but to Sermon-hearing on the modus operandi[2] of the divine Goodness in the work of Redemption!— How the Ebenezarites[3] would stare to find the Socinians & themselves in one flock on the Sheep-side of the Judgment-seat[4]—& their cousins, ~~the~~

70[1] "Either as being willed from its origin or as originating from the will": Alanus Magnus, better known as Alanus de (or ab) Insulis (c 1114–1203). C jotted down a number of his sayings, including this one, in Jul–Sept 1809: *CN* iii 3516 and n.

71[1] The quoted phrases are from textus, var.

71[2] "Way of working".

71[3] "Ebenezer", like Bethel, was a name sometimes given to a dissenting chapel, so "Ebenezarites" would be those who attend the chapel.

71[4] On the day of judgment, according to Matt 25.31–46, "all nations" are to be divided "as a shepherd divideth his sheep

and fellow Methodists, the Tabernaclers, all caprified[5]—Goats every man John—and why? They held, that Repentance is in the power of every man, with the *aid* of Grace—while the Goats held, that without Grace no man is able even to repent. A makes Grace the Cause, and B. makes it only a *necessary* auxiliary. And does the Socinian extricate himself a whit more clearly? Without a due concurrence of circumstances no mind can improve itself into a state susceptible of spiritual Happiness—and is not the disposition & pre-arrangement of circumstances as dependent on the divine Will as those spiritual Influences, which the Methodist holds to be meant by the word Grace? Will it[a] the Socinian find it as difficult to reconcile with Mercy & Justice the condemnation to Hell-fire of poor Wretches born & bred in the Thieves'-nests of S[t] Giles,[6] as the Methodists the condemnation of those who have been less favored by Grace? I have one other question to ask, tho' it should have been asked on occasion of a note on P. II.[7] Supposing Christ taught nothing more than a future State of Retribution & the necessity & sufficiency of good morals, how are we to explain his forbidding these truths to be taught to any but Jews—till after his Resurrection?[8] Did the Jews reject *those* Doctrines? Except *perhaps* a handful of rich men called Sadducees, they all believed them[9]—& would have died a thousand deaths rather than have renounced their faith!—Besides, what is there in doctrines common to the creed of all religions, and enforced by all the schools of Philosophy except the Epicurean, that prevented from[b] being taught to all at the same time? I perceive, that this difficulty does not press on Socinians *exclusively*; but yet it presses on them with far greater force. For they make Xtnity a mere philosophy, the same in substance with the Stoicals, only purer from errors & accompanied with clearer evidence—While others think of it, as part of a covenant made up with Abraham, the fulfilment of which was in good faith to be first offered to his Posterity. I ask this

71[a] A slip for "not"?
71[b] Perhaps a slip either of C's or of RS's in overtracing: "from" should be "their" or at a pinch "them"

from the goats", the "sheep" being set on the right hand of Christ and destined to "life eternal", the "goats" on the left, destined to "everlasting punishment".

71[5] "Made into goats": not in *OED* in this sense. "Tabernacle" was, like "Ebenezer" or "Bethel", a word that might designate any nonconformist meeting-house; but C appears to be using it in a sense closer to

its original meaning of "tent", "Tabernaclers" being thereby distinguished from other dissenters as those who met in tents, as some of the Methodists did.

71[6] A notorious slum parish in London.
71[7] Apparently C's own note **50** above.
71[8] See **50** and n 3.
71[9] The "Sadducees, which say that there is no resurrection" (Matt 22.23).

only because the B. professes to find *every* thing in the 4 Gospels so *plain & easy*!

72   iii 106

The Reformers by whom those [39] Articles were framed were educated in the Church of Rome, and opposed themselves rather to the <u>perversion</u> of its power, than the errors of its doctrine.

An outrageous Lie, or Blunder!!!

73   iii 107

Lord BACON was the first who dedicated his profound and penetrating genius to the cultivation of sound philosophy, and who taught us how best to improve those faculties which God has given to man for the perfection of his rational nature.

This very same Lord Bacon has given us his "Confessio Fidei" at great Length, with full particularity. Now I will answer for the Methodists' unhesitating Subscription to it; but would the Barrister subscribe to it?[1]

74   iii 108–9

<u>We</u> look back to that era of our history when SUPERSTITION threw her victim on the pile, and BIGOTRY tied the martyr to his stake—but we take our eyes from the retrospect, and turn them in thankful admiration to that Being who has opened the minds of many, and is daily opening the minds of more amongst us, to the reception of these most important of all truths, that there is no true faith but in practical goodness, and that the worst of errors is the error of *the life*.

Such is the conviction of the most enlightened of our Clergy;—the conviction, I trust, of the far greater part. They do not, therefore, feel it necessary to revive the exploded controversies which agitated, without purifying, the passions of the Divines of past days. They hold it more important to reform the vicious, and, after the example of their Divine Teacher, to exhort men to do justice, to love mercy, and to walk humbly

---

[1] Francis Bacon "A Confession of Faith" *Works* (1740) IV 453–7 (Spedding VII 215), which starts thus: "I believe that nothing is without beginning but God; no nature, no matter, no spirit, but one, only, and the same God. That God, as he is eternally almighty, only wise, only good in his nature; so he is eternally Father, Son, and Spirit in persons." C's point is twofold: first, that Bacon was not merely a rationalist; second, that the Methodists could subscribe to Bacon's trinitarian creed whereas the Unitarian Barrister could not.

with their God. They deem it better to inculcate the MORAL DUTIES of Christianity in the pure simplicity and clearness with which they are revealed, than to go aside in search of DOCTRINAL MYSTERIES. For as mysteries cannot be made manifest, they, of course, cannot be understood—and that which cannot be understood cannot be believed, and can, consequently, make no part of any system of FAITH; since no one, till he understands a doctrine, can tell whether it be true or false; till then, therefore, he can have no faith in it, for no one can rationally affirm that he believes that doctrine to be true which he does not know to be so; and he cannot know it to be true if he does not understand it.—In the religion of a true Christian, therefore, there can be nothing unintelligible; and if the Preachers of that religion do not make MYSTERIES, they will never find any.

Who? the Bishops? the dignified Clergy? Have they at length exploded all *doctrinal mysteries?* Was Horsley "the ~~last~~ one red Leaf, the last of its Clan",[1] that held the doctrines of the Trinity, the corruption of the human Will, and the Redemption by the Cross of C~~ross~~hrist?[2] Verily, this is the most impudent attempt to impose a naked Socinianism on the Public ~~for~~ as the general Religion of the Nation, admitted by all but a dunghill of mushroom Fanatics, that ever insulted Common Sense or common Modesty! And will "the far greater part"[3] of the established Clergy remain silent under so atrocious a Libel, as is contained in this page? Do they indeed solemnly pray to their Maker weekly, before God & Man, in the words of a Liturgy which, they know, *cannot be believed?*—For heaven's sake, my dear S.,[4] do quote this § from "Such is the &c"—& compare it with the Introduction & Petitions of the *Litany*—and with the Collects on the Advent &c.[5]

74[1] *Christabel* line 49 var: *PW* (EHC) I 217.

74[2] Samuel Horsley (1733–1806), bp of St Asaph, chosen perhaps partly because his death was a relatively recent event, but also because he had engaged in public controversy with Priestley. C appears to have been reading Priestley's *Letters* to Horsley (pub between 1784 and 1790) in Jan–Feb 1810: *CN* III 3675 and n.

74[3] From textus.

74[4] RS did in this case follow C's advice, quoting the passage in his review with the following comment: "What! the bishops? the dignified clergy? have they then exploded all doctrinal mysteries? have they ceased to hold the doctrines of the Trinity, the corruption of the human will, and redemption by the cross of Christ? Do our clergy solemnly pray to their maker, weekly before God and man, in the words of a liturgy which they know *cannot be believed?* Either this is true, or the Barrister is a libeller, a rank and convicted libeller": *QR* IV (1810) 484.

74[5] These familiar parts of BCP invoke the Trinity, confess the sinfulness of the petitioner, and pray for mercy in Christ's name—thus reiterating the doctrines identified by C at n 2.

75   iii 110 | **74** textus continued

We shall discover, upon an attentive examination of the subject, that all those laws which lay the basis of our CONSTITUTIONAL liberties are no other than the rules of religion transcribed into the JUDICIAL system, and enforced by the sanction of civil authority.

!!! Compare [? Fait] these Laws, first, with Tacitus's account of the constitutional Laws of our German Ancestors, Pagans: & then with the Pandects & Novellæ of the most Christian Justinian, aided by all his Bishops![1] Observe, the Barrister is asserting a *fact* of ⟨the⟩ historical origination of our Laws—& not what no man would deny, that as far as they are humane & just, they coincide with the precepts of the Gospel. No! they were *transcribed*.

76   iii 114–5

Where a man holds a certain system of doctrines, the State is bound to tolerate, though it may not approve, them; but when he demands *a license to teach* this system to the rest of the community, he demands that which ought not to be granted incautiously and without grave consideration. This discretionary power is delegated in trust for the common good; and to give permission to all persons, indiscriminately, to spread doctrines destructive in their tendency to the moral interests of the public, is to act in disobedience to the public safety.

All this, dear S., I leave to the lash of your Indignation. It would be oppression to do—what the Legislature could not do if it would—prevent a man's *thoughts*; but if he speaks them aloud, & asks either for instruction

---

75[1] Challenging Sedgwick's complacency, C suggests that some pre-Christian societies might have had good laws, and some Christian societies bad ones; and that our civil liberties are based in part on non-Christian traditions. Tacitus *Germania* (98), one of the most important literary sources of information about the ancient Germans, contains evidence about the election of kings and generals (7), the powers of chiefs and councils (11–12), the laws governing family life and inheritance (18–20), and land tenure (26). The Emperor Justinian I was responsible for the publication of the set of documents constituting the *Corpus juris civilis*, an authoritative statement of Roman law: it includes a Codex or collec-

tion of laws (529); the Institutes, a condensed treatise on the legal system; and the Pandects or "Digest", a collection of decisions in civil cases. The Novellae or Constitutions were unofficial collections of law made after the publication of the Codex. Gibbon—C's authority in **14** and possibly **57** above—describes the "code, pandects, novels, and institutes of Justinian" in *Decline and Fall* ch 44, describing the texts as the work of teams of lawyers and bureaucrats, with mixed and sometimes self-contradictory results; they constitute, he says, "a tesselated pavement of antique and costly, but too often of incoherent, fragments".

& confutation if he be in error, or assent and honor, if he be in the right, then it is no oppression to throw him into a dungeon! But the B. would only withhold a *Licence*? Nonsense! What if he preaches & publishes without it, will the Legislature dungeon him or not? If not, what use is either the granting or the withholding—And this too from a Socinian, who by this very book has made himself obnoxious to Imprisonment & the Pillory—and against men, whose opinions are authorized by the most solemn Acts of Parliament, & recorded in a Book, of which there must be one, by Law, in every parish, and of which there *is* one in almost every House & Hovel!!—[1]

76A   iii 139

There were some in the congregation, however, who listened to it with ears less erect. They had sit too long *under the sound* of this pulpit eloquence . . .

77   half-title to Pt iv

Pray, do not forget to quote p. 13 & 14.—In the whole Bibliotheca Theologica[1] I remember no instance of calmuny so gross, so impudent, or so infamous.[2]

78   iv 1–2

The religion of genuine Christianity is a revelation so distinct and specific in its design, and so clear and intelligible in its rules, that a man of philosophic and retired thought is apt to wonder by what means the endless systems of error and hostility which divide the world were ever introduced into it.

What means this hollow Cant—this 50 times warmed⟨-up⟩ Bubble & Squeak?[1] That such *parts* are intelligible, as the Barrister UNDER-STANDS? that such parts as it possesses *in common* with all systems of Religion & Morality, are plain & obvious?—In other words, that A B C is are so legible, that they are legible to every one that has learnt to read?—If the B. mean other or more than this, if he really mean the whole Religion & Revelation of Christ, and even as it is found in the original Records, the Gospels & Epistles, he escapes from the silliness of a Tru-

---

76[1] AV, "appointed to be read in churches" as it originally said on the title-page.

77[1] I.e. in the whole set of books on theology.

77[2] Textus of **81** below.

78[1] A variant on the classical ten-times-cooked cabbage of **52** (at n 1) above: bubble-and-squeak is a dish of reheated hashed-up meat or potatoes and cabbage.

ism by throwing himself into the arms of a broad, brazen-faced False-hood! What? is the VIth Chapter of John so distinct and specific in its de-sign, that any modest man can wonder that the best & most learned men of every age since Christ have deemed it mysterious.[2] Are the many pas-sages concerning the Devil & dæmoniacs so very easy? Has this writer himself thrown the least Light ⟨on⟩, or himself received one Ray of Light from, the meaning of the word *Faith*? or the reason of Christ's paramount ~~com~~ declarations respecting its omnific power, its absolute indispensable Necessity?[3]—If the word mean only what he supposes, a persuasion that in the present state of our knowlege the evidences for the historical truth of the miracles of the Gospel outweigh the arguments of the Sceptics, will he condescend to give ~~his~~ us such a comment on the assertion, that had we but a grain of mustard seed of it,[4] we might controul all material Na-ture, without making Christ either a madman, or the most extravagant Hy-perbolist that ever misused Language? But it is impossible to make that man blush, who can seriously call the words of Christ as recorded by S[t] John, plain, easy, common sense, ⟨out of⟩ which prejudice, artifice, & selfish Interest alone can compose any difficulty!—The Barrister has just as much right to call *his* Religion Christianity, as to call Flour & Water Plum Pudding—yet we all admit that in Plum Pudding both Flour & Water do exist!—

78A   iv 4

Against that strong fortress of error which the anti-moralists have erected, no impression can be made by a desultory shock; it becomes necessary "to set down before it, and to assail it by regular approaches."[1]

79   iv 7–8

SOCINUS can have no claim upon my veneration; I have never concerned myself with what he believed, or with what he taught. . . . The Scripture

---

78[2] Cf C's objections to literalist inter-pretations of the Bible elsewhere, e.g. ROBINSON **12** above, LUTHER *Colloquia* **21**, in both of which the Gospel of John is cited to reveal their dangerous inadequacy. John 6 includes notably the idea of Christ as the "bread of life": "Then Jesus said unto them, Verily, verily, I say unto you, Except ye eat the flesh of the Son of man, and drink his blood, ye have no life in you" (6.53).

78[3] Christ's "paramount declarations" would include the assertions about faith moving mountains in Matt 17.20 (q below

n 4) and 21.21. For C's position on faith, see also SCHELLING *Philosophie und Religion* **1, 2** and nn above.

78[4] Matt 17.20: ". . . If ye have faith as a grain of mustard seed, ye shall say unto this mountain, Remove hence to yonder place; and it shall remove; and nothing shall be im-possible unto you."

78A[1] Another erroneous or vulgar use of the same verb was noted in **76A**. The un-derlining is in ink, and may in both cases be RS's rather than C's.

is my authority, and on no other authority will I ever, knowingly, lay the foundation of my faith.

A LIE! It is not the Scripture, but such passages of Scripture as appear to him to accord with his Procrustean Bed of Reason, and to force the blankest contradictions into the same meaning, by explanations of which I defy him to furnish one single analogy as allowed by mankind with regard to any other writings but the O. and N. Testament. It is a gross, an impudent Delusion to call a Book his authority, which he receives only so far as it is an echo of his own Convictions.—I defy him to adduce one single article of his whole faith, (creed rather)[1] which he really *derives* from the Scripture! Even the arguments for the Resurrection are & must be extraneous: for the very proofs of the Facts are (as every tyro in Theology must know) the proofs of the authenticity of the Books, in which they are contained. This question I would press upon him—Supposing that we possessed the Fathers only with the Ecclesiastical & Pagan Historians, & not a page remained of the New Testament, what article of his Creed would it alter?

80   iv 10–13

If the creed of CALVINISTIC METHODISM is really more productive of conversions than the religion of CHRISTIANITY, let them openly and at once say so, and let them put their defence of it upon that ground. [Sedgwick proceeds sarcastically to propose "JOHN CALVIN as our only sound oracle, and his system of mystery as our only sure guide."]

But C.M.? Why C.M.?—Not one in an 100 of the M. are Calvinists![1] Not to mention the impudence of this Crow in his abuse of black feathers. Is it worse in a Methodist to oppose Socinianism to Christianity, i.e. the doctrines of Wesley or even Whitfield which are the same as that of all the Reformed Churches of Christendom, and differ only where the most celebrated Divines of the same Churches have differed with each other, than for the Barrister to oppose Methodism to Christianity—i.e. Socinianism, which in every *peculiar doctrine* of Christianity differs from all Divines of all Churches of all ages? For the one tenet in which the Calvinist differs from the majority of Christians, are there not ten in which the Socinian differs from all?[2]

79[1] C's qualification here evokes his customary distinction (as in REIMARUS **1** and SCHELLING *Philosophie und Religion* **1**) between faith and belief: a creed is a statement of *belief*.

80[1] Cf C's assertion about the Calvinis-

tic Methodists at the end of **52**.

80[2] C made the same point in **44**. For C's notorious opinion that Unitarianism was not Christianity, though individual Unitarians might be Christians, see *BL* ch 24 (*CC*) II 245–6 and n 3; for later discriminations be-

To what purpose then this windy declamation *about* John Calvin? How many Methodists does he think, ever saw, much less read, a work of Calvin's? If he scorns the name of Socinus as his authority, & appeals to Scripture,[3] do not the Methodists the same?—When do they refer to Calvin? In what work do they quote him?—This page is therefore mere Dust in the Eyes of the Public—& his abuse of Calvin displays only his own vulgar Ignorance both of the man & of his writings. He is too ignorant to know, that the *humane* Melanchthon, & not only he but almost every Church, Lutheran or Reformed, throughout Europe, sent Letters to Geneva, extolling the execution of Servetus, & returning their Thanks.[4] Yet it was a murder not the less—Yes! a damned Murder; but the Guilt of it not peculiar to Calvin, but ⟨common⟩ to all the Theologians of that age, N.b. *not* excepting the *Socini*, who were prepared to inflict the very same punishment on F. David for denying the adorability of Christ—.[5] If to wish, will, resolve, and attempt to realize, be morally to commit, an action, then must Socinus & Calvin hunt in the same Collar. O mercy! if every human Being were to be held up to detestation, who in *that* age would have thought it his Duty to have passed sentence de comburendo Heretico[6] on a man, who had publicly styled the Trinity "a Cerberus," and three-headed Monster of Hell, what would the History of the Reformation be but a ~~Lot~~ List of Criminals? With what face indeed can we congratulate ourselves on being born in a more enlightened age, if we so bitterly abuse *not* the practice but the agents? Do we not admit by this very

---

tween the Socinians and the Unitarians, the latter "having succeeded in disbelieving far beyond the last foot-marks of the Socini", see *LS* (*CC*) 176.

80[3] In **79** textus.

80[4] Michael Servetus (1511–53) published against the doctrine of the Trinity and denied the divinity of Christ. He was engaged in controversy with Calvin, who was responsible eventually for the arrest, interrogation, and execution of Servetus as a heretic. C alludes to Calvin's persecution of Servetus in BIBLE *NT Gospels* **2** (and see n 1); to "the Protestant Churches who applauded the act, & returned thanks to Calvin & the Senate for it" in FIELD **24**; and to the role of Melanchthon in the process in *TT* (*CC*) I 455—where n 3 suggests that Rees may have been one, at least, of C's sources of information.

80[5] "Socinus worshipped Jesus Christ, and said that God had given him the power

of being omnipresent. David, with a little more acuteness, suggested that mere audition or presence in a creature could not justify worship from men": *TT* (*CC*) I 488, where nn 1 and 2 gloss the controversy between Fausto Paulo Sozzini and Francis Dávid (1509–79), an anti-Trinitarian bishop in Transylvania who refused to worship Christ. Dávid was sent to trial and died in prison.

80[6] The English statute of 1401 *De haeretico comburendo* ("on burning a heretic"), repealed in 1533, ordered that heretics convicted in a spiritual court should be handed over to the secular courts for public execution by burning. But C may be using the phrase without specific reference, since being burnt at the stake had been for centuries the traditional punishment and was to continue so: Servetus, mentioned at n 4, was to be a victim of this sentence on the Continent.

phrase "enlightened" that we owe our exemption to our intellectual advantages, not primarily to our moral superiority? It will be time enough to boast, when to our own Tolerance we have added their zeal, learning, & indefatigable Industry.—

81   iv 14

If religion consists in listening to long prayers, and attending long sermons, in keeping up an outside appearance of devotion, and interlarding the most common discourse with phrases of gospel usage;—if this is religion, then are the disciples of Methodism pious beyond compare. But, in real humility of heart, in mildness of temper, in liberality of mind, in purity of thought, in openness and uprightness of conduct in private life, in those practical virtues which are the vital substance of Christianity,— in these are they superior? No. Public observation is against the fact, and the conclusion to which such observation leads is rarely incorrect. Simplicity and fair dealing has been usually held to mark the conduct of the QUAKERS, and they consequently stand high in the confidence of that community of which they make a part. But the character of the METHODIST has gradually unfolded itself with a very different reputation. The very name of the sect carries with it an impression of meanness and hypocrisy. <u>Scarce an individual</u> that has had any dealings <u>with those belonging</u> to it, but has good cause to remember it, from some circumstance <u>of low deception</u> or of shuffling fraud. Its very members trust each other with caution and reluctance. The more wealthy among them are drained and dried by the leeches that perpetually fasten upon them. The leaders, ignorant and bigotted,—I speak of them collectively,—present us with no counter-qualities that can conciliate respect. They have all the craft of Monks without their courtesy, and all the subtlety of the Jesuits without their learning.

Even as a single Robber ~~gets~~, I mean, he who robs one man, gets hung, while the Robber of a million is a great man, so it seems to be with Calumny—this Rascal Barrister will be extolled for this infamous Slander of thousands, for which applied to any one individual he would be in danger of the Pillory. This § should be quoted/ for were the Charge true, it is impossible that the Barrister should know it to be true.[1] He positively asserts as a truth known to him what it is impossible he should know— he is therefore a double Liar—for first, the Charge is a gross calumny, an

81[1] C also comments on this passage in   in his review, *QR* IV (1810) 483.
77 at n 2. RS did quote the marked passage

infamous falsehood—& were it otherwise, he would still be a Liar—for he could have no proof, no ground for such a charge.

82 iv 15

Illustrious as Great Britain has rendered herself in every quarter of the globe . . . yet, amidst all this progress of knowledge, amidst all this spirit of research, we find nothing,—comparatively nothing,—of advancement in that science, of all others the most important in its influence . . . . RE-LIGION,—except from the emancipating energy of a few superior minds which have dared to snap asunder the cords which bound them to the rock of error,— . . . Religion has been suffered to remain, in its principles and in its doctrines, just what it was when the craft of Catholic superstition first corrupted its simplicity.

So! So! Here it comes out at last! It is not the Methodists no, it is all & each of all Europe, Infidels & Socinians excepted! Impudent Rascal! The exquisite self-conceit of the Blunderer!

83 iv 29–30

[Footnote on the Society of United Theological Booksellers:] . . . Who are those *eminent ministers*, whose pretended patronage is held out to soothe us? If of *different denominations*, how were they thus conciliated to a society of this ominous nature, from which they must themselves of necessity be excluded by that indispensable condition of admittance, "*a union* of religious sentiment in the *great doctrines*;" which very want of union it is that creates these *different denominations?*

No, Barrister! they mean that men of *different denominations* may yet all believe in the corruption of the human Will, the Redemption by Christ, the Divinity of Christ as consubstantial with the Father, the necessity of the Holy Spirit or Grace (meaning more than the dispositions of circumstances) and the necessity of Faith in Christ superadded to a Belief of his Actions & Doctrines—and yet differ in many other points. The points enumerated are called the great points, because all Christians agree in them excepting the Arians & Socinians, who for that reason are not deemed Christians by the rest[1]—the Catholic, the Lutheran, the Calvinist, the Arminian, the Greek, with all their subdivisions do yet all accord in these articles. The Booksellers might have said, all who repeat the

83[1] See **80** and n 2.

Nicene Creed. N.B. I do not approve, or defend, nay, I abominate these "United Theol. Books—" but this Barrister Rascal is their best Friend by attacking them so as to secure to them Victory & all the advantage of ~~hav-ing been k~~ being known to have been wickedly slandered—the best shield, a faulty cause can *pro*tend against the javelin of fair opposition.

84   iv 56–8

Our Saviour never, in any single instance, reprobated the exercise of reason: on the contrary, he reprehends severely those who did not exercise it. *Carnal reason* is not a phrase to be found in *his* Gospel; he appealed to the understanding in all he said, and in all he taught. He never required *faith* in his disciples, without first furnishing sufficient *evidence* to justify it. The truth of his *divine mission* he attested by miracles. He reasoned thus:—If I have done what no *human power* could do, you must admit that my power is *from above.* You have witnessed *the miracles* which I have wrought; let this testimony lay the foundation of your faith.

Good heavens! did he not uniformly require Faith as the condition of obtaining the *evidence*, as the B. calls it—i.e. the Miracle? What a shameless perversion of the fact!—It is a Lie! He never did reason thus—in one instance only, and then upbraiding the base sensuality of the Jews, he said—If ye are so base as *not* to believe what I say from the moral evidence in your own consciences, yet pay some attention to it even for my works' sake—/[1] —And this, an argumentum ad hominem, a bitter reproach (just as if a great Chemist should say—Tho' you do not care for my science, or the important truths it presents, yet, even as an amusement superior to that of your Jugglers to whom you willingly crowd, pay some attention to me)—this is to be set up against 20 plain Texts & the whole Spirit of the whole Gospel! Besides, Christ *could* not reason so—for he knew that the Jews admitted both natural and dæmoniacal Miracles—& their faith in the latter he never *attacked*; & if words have any fixed meaning he confirmed—tho' by an argumentum ad hominem (for it is no argument in itself) he denied its applicability to his own works. If Christ had reasoned so, why did not the B. quote his words, instead of putting imaginary words in his mouth?

84[1] John 14.11: "Believe me that I am in the Father, and the Father in me: or else believe me for the very works' sake." C's campaign against dependence on the "evidence" of miracles for the defence of the Christian religion was constant throughout his maturity; for a recent example, see LIGHTFOOT **2**, a note written c Sept 1809 that explicitly links the argument from miracles with the Socinians.

85   iv 61

Religion is a system of *revealed* truth; and to affirm of any revealed truth, that we *cannot understand it*, is, in effect, either to deny that it has been revealed, or—which is the same thing—to admit that it has been revealed in vain. Just, therefore, in the proportion that we admit the existence of *mysteries* in religion which we *cannot understand*, we *so far* deny it to be a *revealed* religion.—this, the orthodox would do well to consider.

It is too worthless! I cannot go on. Merciful God! hast thou not revealed to us the Being of a Conscience, and of Reason and of Will?—And does this Barrister tell us, that he *understands* them? Miserable Railer! he does not even understand the very word, understanding.[1] Is he so ignorant as not to know the schoolboy distinction between the ὅτι ἐστι, and the διότι?[2]—But ⟨to⟩ all these silly Objections the cause of Religion must for ever remain exposed, as long as ⟨the word⟩ *"Revelation"*, is applied to any thing that can be bonâ fide *given* to the mind ab extra,[3] thro' the senses of Eye, Ear, or Touch. No! All Revelation is & must be ab intra[4]—the external Phænomena can only awake, recall, evidence—but never reveal. This is capable of strict demonstration.

85[1] C's most recent effort to explain the word "understanding" (as opposed to reason) had been in the 1809–10 *Friend*: *Friend (CC)* II 104*, 125, 294–7.

85[2] *"That* it is" and *"why* it is", i.e. the fact and the reason for it—to which Aristotle added "whether it is" and "what it is": *Posterior Analytics* 2.1 (89b24).

85[3] "From without".

85[4] "From within".

WILLIAM SEDGWICK

c 1610–c 1669

Justice upon the Aimie Remonstrance, or a rebuke of that evill spirit that leads them in their counsels and actions. With a discovery of the contrariety and enmity in thir waies, to the good spirit and minde of God. Dedicated to the General, and the Councel of War. London 1649. 4°.

Bound as eighth in "CROMWELLIAN TRACTS" II.

Not located; marginal note published from MS TRANSCRIPT (a).

C published extracts from this work in the 1818 *Friend* (*CC*) I 411–14, presenting them as "an address to his comrades" from "a common soldier" that deserved to be rescued "from oblivion, both for the honor of our forefathers, and in proof of the intense difference between the republicans of that period, and the democrats, or rather demagogues, of the present"; he prints a part of his own note as a footnote. In fact, as C indicated in 1833, he had "filtered" the text, taking sentences from here and there, reassembling and editing: *Friend* (*CC*) I 411 n 5.

MS TRANSCRIPTS. (*a*) VCL BT 37; (*b*) Humanities Research Center, University of Texas.

DATE. Summer or autumn of 1818, when C was preparing the *Friend* in 3 vols: *Friend* (*CC*) I 410.

1   "Blank page at the end of the Volume of Tracts"

8th—. Tract. 1649

Justice upon the Remonstrance of the Army, by William Sedgwick— highly interesting. I must make myself better acquainted with this W. Sedgwick who re-excites the regret, I have so often felt, that a history of Charles the first, the Republic, and Protectorate were not written with especial reference to the numberless Pamphlets, Books, &c then published or while yet there is time.—But alas! every year destroys its quota—the noble, probably unique, collection of Sir W. Lawson's Predecessor, left out of spite to the Butler, lasted the Grocers, Chandlers, and Druggists of Penrith and Kendal during a destruction of 20 years & more![1]—W. S. ap-

---

1[1] This statement is not strictly true, but C may be reporting local gossip. The will of Sir Gilfrid Lawson, bt (c 1710–94), proved with two codicils 21 Jul 1794, left his property to his son with a large bequest to his daughter. The other significant bequest was

pears an instance of an Independent sublimated into a theosophic Behmenist, greatly to the improvement of his political insight at least. Several passages on the spirit of Fear, as symptomatic of hollowness and weakness, and the contrary spirit of Co-inherence, are almost sublime. Sedwick's[a] views of immortality seem, however, to coincide with those of Spinoza, rather than with Behmen's. see p. 25. last paragraph, and the three or four following pages.[2]   S. T. Coleridge.

1[a] Almost certainly a transcriber's error: MS TRANSCRIPT (*b*) reads correctly "Sedgwick's"

---

for a sum of £100 and an annuity of £30 to be paid to his steward, Jonathan Potts. The will makes no specific reference to the library, though it may be that the trustees sold off the books in order to meet some of their obligations. C had had the use of whatever was left of the collection—in fact he called it a "magnificent Library" when he lived in Keswick in 1800–2: *CL* I 618, 619, 645, II 834.

1[2] C had been reflecting for some time on the question of immortality, and on such issues as the survival of individual personality after death: see e.g. *CN* III 4356 (Aug 1817). He had also given both Spinoza and Böhme an attentive reading and was aware of the contrast in their concepts of the status of the individual: in BÖHME **44**, for example, he comments on a passage in which Böhme asks "What dost thou bring into this World, or what dost thou take along with

thee at thy going out of it?"; and in a copy of SPINOZA *Opera* (2 vols Jena 1802–3) annotated 1812–13 he marked *Ethics* pt 2 prop 13, which has to do with the relationship between the individual entity and the universal substance. The selections from Sedgwick that C put together as a single passage in the 1818 *Friend* all come from pp 25–32. From p 25 C took reflections on death and immortality ("Death cannot hurt me. . . . I live an immortal life. What we have within, that only can we see without"); and he built up to a Spinozistic flourish on the eradication of individual entity ("we being enlarged into the largeness of God, and comprehending all things in our bosoms by the divine spirit, are at rest with all, and delight in all: for we know nothing but what is, in its essence, in our own hearts"): *Friend* (*CC*) I 411, 414.

JOHN SELDEN

1584–1654

Table-Talk: being the discourses of John Selden Esq; or his sence of various matters of weight and high consequence relating especially to religion and state. [Ed R. Milward.] London 1689. 4°. [Textus is taken from this, the 1st ed (unpaginated), it being uncertain which ed C used. The page numbers do not correspond to any ed available to us: 1716, 1755, 1777, 1786, 1789, 1797, 1798, 1818, 1819, 1821.]

Not located; marginalia (in a Westminster Library copy) preserved by H. F. Cary and published in *LR* II 361–3. The text here follows Cary's journal entries as recorded in Henry Cary *Memoir of H. F. Cary* (1847) I 323–4.

DATE. Between May 1811, when C settled in London with the Morgans and began using the Westminster Library, and 24 Feb 1814, when Cary read the book and recorded C's annotations.

1 "in the first page"

There is more weighty bullion sense in this book, than I ever found in the same number of pages of any uninspired writer.

2   p 114 | "Opinion"

Opinion and Affection extreamly differ; I may affect a Woman best, but it does not follow I must think her the Handsomest Woman in the World. I love Apples best of any Fruit, but it does not follow, I must think Apples to be the best Fruit. Opinion is something wherein I go about to give Reason why all the World should think as I think. Affection is a thing wherein I look after the pleasing of my self.

Good! This is the true difference betwixt the Beautiful and the Agreeable, which Knight and the rest of that πλῆθος ἄθεον[1] have so *beneficially* confounded—*meretricibus videlicet et Plutoni.*[2]

2[1] "Godless crowd".
2[2] "To wit, to prostitutes and to Pluto" (as a god of wealth). C is being ironical: the benefit is purely commercial, and to mercenaries. The aesthetic theories of the fashionable connoisseur Richard Payne Knight

(1750–1824) had been or were to be an easy target in C's own lectures and writing on the subject, notably the lectures of 1808 (*Lects 1808–1819—CC*—I 31–6) and the 1814 "Essays on the Principles of Genial Criticism" (*SW & F—CC*—353–86), both of

3 p 115

'Tis a foolish thing for me to be brought off from an Opinion in a thing neither of us know, but are led only by some Cobweb-stuff, as in such a case as this, *Utrum Angeli in vicem colloquantur?* ["Whether angels converse with one another"] if I forsake my side in such a case, I shew my self wonderful light, or infinitely complying, or flattering the other party. But if I be in a business of Nature, & hold an Opinion one way, and some man's Experience has found out the contrary, I may with a safe Reputation give up my side.

O what an insight into a wise man's *heart!* who has been compelled to act with the Many, as one of the Many! It explains Sir T. More's Zealous Romanism, &c., &c.[1]

4 p 117 | "Parliament"

Dissenters in Parliament may at length come to a good end, tho' first there be a great deal of do, and a great deal of noise, which mad wild folks make; just as in brewing of Wrest-Beer, there's a great deal of business in grinding the Mault, and that spoils any Mans cloaths that comes near it; then it must be mash'd, then comes a Fellow in and drinks of the Wort, and he's drunk, then they keep a huge quarter when they carry it into the Cellar, and a Twelve month after 'tis delicate fine Beer.

Excellent! O to have Selden over his glass of wine, making every accident an outlet and a vehicle of wisdom!

5 p 125 | "Poetry"

There is no reason Plays should be in Verse, either in Blank or Rhime, only the Poet has to say for himself, that he makes something like that, which some body made before him. The old Poets had no other reason but this, their Verse was sung to Musick, otherwise it had been a senseless thing to have fetter'd up themselves.

---

which endeavour to draw distinctions among aesthetic categories such as the ones Knight is said to confound. C annotated—briefly and dismissively—KNIGHT *Analytical Inquiry into the Principles* (3rd ed 1806), and alludes to it as a worldly and trivial work in *Friend* (*CC*) I 11–12.

3[1] C has another, later note on the question of More's "Zealous Romanism", in which he proposes a different solution, namely "that the Statesman and the patriot were uppermost, and that not foreseeing the rise and power of the Third Estate, he saw in the Power of the Clergy and even in the Papal Influence the sole remaining counterweights to the Royal Prerogative": G. BURNET *History* 3.

No one man can know all things. Even Selden here talks ignorantly. Verse is in itself a music, and the natural symbol of that union of Passion with Thought and Pleasure, which constitutes the *Essence* of all *Poetry*, as contradistinguished from Science, and distinguished from History, civil or natural.[1] To Pope's Essay on Man, in short to whatever is mere *metrical* good sense and wit the remark applies.[2]

6 p 126

Verse proves nothing but the quantity of Syllables, they are not meant for Logick.

True; they (i.e., verses) are not logic: but they are, or ought to be, the envoys or representatives of that vital passion which is the practical cement of logic, and without which logic must remain inert.[1]

5[1] This statement anticipates C's definition of poetry and his account of the origin of metre in *BL* chs 14, 18 (*CC*) ii 12–13, 64–5.

5[2] Pope's *Essay on Man* was a standard example of reasoning in rhyme: in *BL* ch 1 (*CC*) i 19, C describes several of Pope's most celebrated works, including this one, as "thoughts *translated* into the language of poetry."

6[1] On the logic of poetry cf *BL* ch 1 (*CC*) i 9: "I learnt from him [Boyer], that Poetry, even that of the loftiest, and, seemingly, that of the wildest odes, had a logic of its own, as severe as that of science; and more difficult, because more subtle, more complex, and dependent on more, and more fugitive causes."

DANIEL SENNERT
1572–1637
Lost Book

Danielis Sennerti Vratislaviensis, doctoris et medicinae professoris in
academia Vittebergensi, operum in quinque tomos divisorum . . . editio
novissima. . . . 5 vols. Lyons 1666. F°.

Not located; marginalia not recorded. *Wordsworth LC* 475 "Sennerti Opera: 2
Vol:"; *Green SC* (1880) 916, "With MS. notes by S. T. Coleridge, but having a
portion torn away, and autograph signature [of C] on title". C appears to have acquired this edition—"4 vol. in 2" according to *Green SC*—late in 1799: *CL* I 531.
Sennertus is quoted in a letter and notebook entries of 1800–02 (*CL* II 683–4, *CN*
I 879, 880, 1000C) and these references may coincide with the annotation of the
work.

CONTENTS. I 1–99 Epitome scientiae naturalis; 100–72 Hypomnemata physica;
173–9 Methodus discendi medicinam; 180–284 De consensu & dissensu chymi-
corum cum Galenicis; 285–306 De origine animarum in brutis. II 307–696 Institutionum medicinae, libri quinque; 697–848 De febribus, libri quatuor; 849–70
Fasciculus medicamentorum contra pestem. III 1–253 Practicae liber primus, de
capitis morbis ac symptomatibus; 254–362 Practicae liber secundus, de thoracis
morbis ac symptomatibus; 363–622 Practicae liber tertius, de ventris inferioris
morbis ac symptomatibus. IV [623]–790 Practicae liber quartus, de mulierum &
infantium affectibus praeter naturam; 791–938 Practicae liber quintus, de partium
externarum morbis & symptomatibus; 939–70 De arthritide, tractatus; 971–1095
Practicae liber sextus, de morbis occultarum qualitatum; 1096–8 Exoterica. V
1099–[1266] Epistolarum medicinalium; 1267–1366 Epitome institutionum
medicinae; 1367–1402 Epitome librorum de febris; 1403–4 Panegyricus dictus
in obitum D. Dan. Sennerti.

SERMONS OR HOMILIES

Sermons or Homilies of the United Church of England & Ireland, as they were originally appointed to be read in churches in the time of Queen Elizabeth, of famous memory. 33 pts in one vol. London 1815. 12°.

British Library C 43 a 21, [bound with] Articles, agreed upon by the Archbishops and Bishops of both provinces, and the whole clergy, in the convocation holden at London in the year 1562, for avoiding of diversities of opinions, and for the establishing of consent, touching true religion. London 1813. 12°. Both titles printed "For the Prayer-book and Homily Society".

Inscribed on the title-page: "Frn^s Green | St Lawrence".

MS TRANSCRIPT. VCL 60: ms facsimile. A visiting card of JHG is pasted to p ⁻5 (p-d), the new endpaper being cut to frame the card; an inscription is written below the printed name: "Joseph Henry Green ⟨gave this book to his Mother Fra^s Green⟩". C's note **2** is copied in JHG's hand on p ⁻4 (originally p ⁻2 now tipped to the new free endpaper ⁻2/⁻1).

DATE. Probably the mid-1820s, given the approach to the subject of prayer and the imagery of animal magnetism. JHG evidently owned this book himself and then gave the original to his mother, making a copy for himself. C had visited the Greens, senior and junior, at their farm estate "Moats" at St Lawrence in Essex in Jun 1818 and Jun 1819: *CL* IV 869–70, 943; *CN* IV 4543.

1   pp ⁺1–⁺3, evidently referring to Homily 19 | Nineteenth Homily . . . concerning Prayer

N° 19. Homily on Prayer.

Observe: we must not worship God, as if *his* Ways were as *our* ways. We must not apply to him, neither, as tho' God were the same with sensible Nature, or the sum total of the Objects of our bodily Senses. For Nature in this sense must of necessity appear to us but as a more subtle and exquisite sort of Machine—and so to think of God is a deadthly Superstition. And to speak aloud to God and by the sound and meaning of our words to suppose ourselves influencing him as we in this way influence our fellow-men, this is a *delirious* Superstition.—O in that, which ⟨comprizing both⟩ transcends both, what precious Mysteries lie hid.

Means + intreaty—/ O miraculous indeed hath been & would be such Prayer![1]

Faint dim imperfect analogy to Prayer: and yet an analogy, arbore, lacu, vitro contuso, ferri ramentis aurâ zoo-magneticâ quasi transanimatis—/Hoc modo Volitio subjectiva fit Objecta, et novis atque alienis viribus in energūmen ὡς volentem remigrat filius in Parentem. Τὸ πνεῦμα περιχωρεῖ.—Nathaniel subter Ficum.[2]—But somewhat more worthy to be glanced at analogically, will the Baquet be, if the Manipulator and Adsedent[3] do but polarize himself, make himself transmeable to the spirit of Healing by the very energy of invoking it?[4] Or what if both *?* πνεῦμα το καθολον dum invoco, πνευμα το ιδιον emisi, conjunxi, refocillavi, atque iterum atque iterum dum το θεῖον accerso, το εμαυτον αλλ' αποθεουμενον, i.e. πνευμα⟨τος μεν⟩ ̶μ̶ο̶υ̶ του ιδιογ̓υ apotheosin, revoco.[5]—In short, God is neither Man nor Nature; but of whatever excellence either partaketh, that with all other perfection God essentially *is*— and in this sense it may be said, that being neither he comprehendeth both transcendently. But as the adorable Object, so must the Prayer be, at once scheme and energy, ideal and real, final ⟋ and medial, object and efficient

2   p +3, referring to Homily 19 p 4

We read in the Book of Exodus, (Exod. xvii. 11), that Joshua, fighting against the Amalekites, did conquer and overcome them, not so much by virtue of his own strength, as by the earnest and continual prayer of

1[1] C's evolving views about prayer are summed up in *CCD* 181–5. He planned to write an essay on prayer as a supplement to *AR*: *AR* (*CC*) 381* and n 95. For other remarks about prayer in marginalia see esp BOOK OF COMMON PRAYER COPY B 1, 29; SANDFORD 2.

1[2] I.e. an analogy "when a tree, a lake, powdered glass, iron filings are transanimated as it were by a zoo-magnetic aura— / In this way subjective Volition becomes Objective, and the son returns with new powers to the Parent who efficaciously wills it. The spirit circumincedes—Nathanael under the Figtree." The point of the analogy is that a certain force exerted returns greatly augmented, or has what might seem to be disproportionately great consequences. In mesmerism or animal magnetism or "zoo-magnetism" (a term C was using in this sense about 1822, as in *CN* IV 4908), the power generated by the magnetiser was

thought to be capable of being communicated to inanimate objects and thereby to enlarge its field of action. (For C's interest in mesmerism see SCHUBERT *Allgemeine* 13 n 1.) On circumincession or perichoresis see BÖHME 103 n 1. The story of Nathanael is told in John 1.43–51 and cited by C, who identifies himself with Nathanael, in CHILLINGWORTH COPY B 3 at n 5.

1[3] The one "sitting at it": not in *OED*.

1[4] The baquet was the mesmeric tub, supposedly full of magnetised fluid that could be drawn off through rods fixed to the tub: see Plate 5.

1[5] "While I invoke the universal spirit I have sent forth my own, have conjoined it, revived it, and again and again while I summon the divine spirit I call back my own, but deified, that is, the apotheosis of my own spirit." (C habitually wrote καθολον for καθόλου: see BEAUMONT & FLETCHER COPY A 5 n 2.)

Moses, who as long as he held up his hands to God, so long did Israel prevail; but when he fainted, and let his hands down, then did Amalek and his people prevail: insomuch that Aaron and Hur, being in the mount with him, were fain to stay up his hands until the going down of the sun; otherwise had the people of God that day been utterly discomfited, and put to flight.

I believe: Lord, help my Unbelief![1] I pray: o enable me to pray!—O Word, O Spirit of the Lord, be ye unto me, as Aaron and Hur unto Moses on the Mount⟨ain!⟩ of O stay up my hands until the going down of the Sun, the day-star of my mortal Life, lest Amalek and his people, even they that are within me, prevail against me!—I would fain hold up my hands— I faint. I let my hands down—O stay up my hands—O gracious Word and O imbreathed Wisdom! O Light! O Life of God—O Light of Man! Ye stayed up my hands even when they were sinking, and in my utter Fainting ye did live in me, yea, for me and instead of me—otherwise I had been utterly discomfited!—Lo, I pray! O that I had the power of supplication! I believe! O Lord—help my unbelief.

2[1] Mark 9.24. Cf *CL* iii 499, a letter of 1814: "My main Comfort therefore consists in what the Divines call, *the Faith of Adherence*—and no spiritual Effort appears to benefit me so much, as the one, earnest, importunate, & often for hours momently [repeated], Prayer: 'I believe! Lord, help my Unbelief! Give me Faith but as a mustard Seed: & I shall remove this mountain! Faith! Faith! Faith! I believe—O give me Faith! O for my Redeemer's sake give me Faith in my Redeemer.'" C quotes this verse also in HERDER *Briefe* 14, LEIGHTON COPY A 4.

WILLIAM SHAKESPEARE

1564–1616

Four annotated copies of Shakespeare are preserved; they are here presented in chronological order of publication. COPY A is associated with J. J. Morgan and the lectures of 1808–12, and the interleaved COPY D is associated with Highgate and the two series of lectures in 1818–19. The notes in COPY B and COPY C seem to have been written between these two dates, but COPY C may have been annotated earlier than COPY B, since it has some connection with the lectures of 1813. See the DATE entries in the headnotes.

COPY A *The Works of Shakespeare* ed Lewis Theobald (8 vols 1773): BM.

COPY B *Stockdale's Edition of Shakespeare* (1784): Harvard.

COPY C *The Dramatic Works of Shakespeare* ed Joseph Rann (6 vols Oxford 1786–94): Folger.

COPY D *The Dramatic Works of William Shakespeare* ed Samuel Ayscough (2 vols 1807): BM.

This edition of the marginalia is heavily indebted to its immediate predecessor, *Lects 1808–1819 (CC)* ed R. A. Foakes, in which some of C's notes are published as lecture material, and which I have pillaged for my own footnotes. Standardised act-scene-and-line references are based on the Riverside Shakespeare, as they are also in *Lects 1808–1819 (CC)*.

With SHAKESPEARE as with SCOTT we can be sure that C was familiar with the texts long before he came to annotate them in these copies. In this case he was familiar also with a tradition of scholarship devoted to the explanation or emendation of the plays, and therefore frequent reference is made in the footnotes to *Sh* (Reed), the "first variorum" of 1803, which C is known to have used on occasion (*Lects 1808–1819—CC*—I lxvii, 383 and n 14), and to *Sh* (Arden), a convenient modern equivalent. Since some of the plays in the Arden Edition have been re-edited or are in the process of being re-edited, the following list identifies the editors of specific plays commented on by C: *All's Well* ed G. K. Hunter, *Antony and Cleopatra* ed M. R. Ridley, *As You Like It* ed Agnes Latham, *Coriolanus* ed Philip Brockbank, *Cymbeline* ed J. M. Nosworthy, *Hamlet* ed Harold Jenkins, *1 Henry IV* ed A. R. Humphreys, *2 Henry IV* ed A. R. Humphreys, *Henry V* ed John H. Walter, *King John* ed E. A. J. Honigmann, *King Lear* ed Kenneth Muir, *Love's Labour's Lost* ed Richard David, *Macbeth* ed Kenneth Muir, *Measure for Measure* ed J. W. Lever, *Merchant of Venice* ed John Russell Brown, *Merry Wives* ed H. J. Oliver, *Midsummer Night's Dream* ed Harold F. Brooks, *Othello* ed M. R.

Ridley, *Romeo and Juliet* ed Brian Gibbons, *Taming of the Shrew* ed Brian Morris, *Tempest* ed Frank Kermode, *Timon of Athens* ed H. J. Oliver, *Titus Andronicus* ed J. C. Maxwell, *Troilus and Cressida* ed Kenneth Palmer, *Twelfth Night* ed J. M. Lothian and T. W. Craik, *Winter's Tale* ed J. H. P. Pafford.

DISTRIBUTION OF MARGINALIA

	COPY A	COPY B	COPY C	COPY D
All's Well	36–40	3		10–11
Antony and Cleopatra	129–135	18	9–10	68–69
As You Like It	22–34			8–9
Coriolanus	112–115	17	6–8	59–60A
Cymbeline	136–141	20–21		73–74
Hamlet	144–153	22		127–184
1 Henry IV	72–73	8–10		56
2 Henry IV	74–77	11–12		57
Henry V	78–81			
1 Henry VI		13		
Julius Caesar	118–128			61–67
King John	64–69	7		
King Lear	82–84		11–13	75–98
Love's Labour's Lost	20–21			6
Macbeth	96–111		14–44	17–32
Measure for Measure	14–19			
Merchant of Venice			3–5	
Merry Wives	10–13A	1		4–5
Midsummer Night's Dream	4–9	2–2A		7
Othello	154–158		45–47	185–203
Richard II	70–71			33–55
Richard III		14–16A		
Romeo and Juliet	143			99–126
Taming of the Shrew	35–35A			
Tempest	2–3		1–2	3
Timon of Athens	85–93	19		
Titus Andronicus	94–95			
Troilus and Cressida	141A–142			70–72
Twelfth Night	41–52	4–6		12–15
Winter's Tale	53–63			16
General notes	1, 116, 117			1, 2

Copy A

The Works of Shakespeare. Collated with the oldest copies, and corrected; with notes, explanatory, and critical: by Mr. Theobald. Printed verbatim from the octavo edition. 8 vols. London 1773. 12°.

British Library C 45 a 21

Autograph signature "Jnº Jaˢ Morgan" on ɪ ⁻2 and ɪɪ ⁻2. See also the reference to Morgan in **86** below. The overtraced notes (e.g. **47, 52**) appear to have been overtraced by someone other than C, perhaps Morgan himself. Internal evidence suggests that the work was annotated with both Morgan and the women of the household—Mary Morgan and Charlotte Brent—in mind: some bawdy passages are censored, but **15** and **83** give a Latin explanation of an indecency, thereby enlightening Morgan while protecting the ladies. In several notes (e.g. **1**) C adopts a teacherly role. In **10**, Mary Morgan is given credit for glossing an obscure term.

A few passages from *As You Like It* that seem to have been marked for excision are collected in the ANNEX.

CONTENTS. ɪ sig A3–A4ᵛ Dedication; ix–xii Epitaph etc.; Theobald's Preface (46 pp); Shakespeare's Will (8 pp); [1]–[75] *Tempest*; [77]–148 *Midsummer Night's Dream*; [149]–216 *Two Gentlemen*; [217]–303 *Merry Wives*; [304]–95 *Measure for Measure*. ɪɪ [3]–86 *Much Ado*; [87]–170 *Merchant of Venice*; [171]–264 *Love's Labour's Lost*; [265]–346 *As You Like It*; [347]–431 *Taming of the Shrew*. ɪɪɪ [3]–[100] *All's Well*; [101]–81 *Twelfth Night*; [183]–242 *Comedy of Errors*; [243]–341 *Winter's Tale*; [343]–430 *King John*. ɪᴠ [3]–88 *Richard II*; [89]–182 *1 Henry IV*; [183]–[282] *2 Henry IV*; [283]–385 *Henry V*; [387]–478 *1 Henry VI*. ᴠ [3]–98 *2 Henry VI*; [99]–190 *3 Henry VI*; [191]–300 *Richard III*; [301]–[400] *Henry VIII*. ᴠɪ [3]–118 *King Lear*; [119]–201 *Timon of Athens*; [203]–81 *Titus Andronicus*; [283]–358 *Macbeth*; [359]–488 *Coriolanus*. ᴠɪɪ [3]–85 *Julius Caesar*; [87]–213 *Antony and Cleopatra*; [215]–339 *Cymbeline*; [341]–458 *Troilus and Cressida*. ᴠɪɪɪ [3]–99 *Romeo and Juliet*; [101]–245 *Hamlet*; [247]–370 *Othello*; Table of Editions (8 pp); Index (66 pp).

DATE. About 1810–13, when C was living with the Morgans and lecturing on Shakespeare. **82** is dated 1 Jan 1813. For an assessment of the rather remote relationship between the notes and the lectures, see *Lects 1808–1819 (CC)* ɪɪ 430.

1   ɪ ⁻4–⁻3

(= means *equal to*)
◡ = short syllable

‿ = ∪ ∪

∪ ∪   a Pyrrhic or Dibrach, as bŏdў, spĭrĭt
∪ ∪ ∪ a Tribrach, as nŏbŏdў when hastily pronounced
∪ –   an Iambic, as dĕlīght
– ∪   a Trochee as Līghtlў
– –   a Spondee, as Gōd spāke* ⟨*n.b.—The fewness of Spondees in
single words in our and indeed in the modern Languages in general makes
perhaps the greatest distinction between them & the Greek and Latin at
least metrically considered.⟩
– ∪ ∪ a Dactyl as mērrĭlў
∪ ∪ – an Anapaest as ăprŏpōs, or the first 3 syllables of cĕrĕmōnious
∪ – ∪ an Amphibrach, as dĕlīghtfŭl.
– ∪ – an Amphimacer as Ōvĕr Hĭll
– – ∪ a Bacchius, as Hēlvēllўn
∪ – – an Anti-bacchius as Thĕ Lōrd Gōd
– – – a Molossus, as Jōhn Jāmes Jōnes

These which are called Simple Feet may suffice for understanding the
metres of Shakespear, for the greater part; but Milton cannot be made har-
moniously intelligible without the composite feet, Ionics, Pæans,[1] &
Epitrites.
[a]brachus in Greek means short, and makros long: amphi on each side.
Therefore amphibrach means short on both sides with a long syllable between, and amphimacer long on both sides with a short Syllable between.
So Dibrach means twice short, and Tribrach thrice short.—The Spondee
and the Molossus might analogically have been named Dimacer, and
Trimacer. Anapæst from a Greek word signifying to strike descending,
i.e. to lay the stress on the last syllable of three.

2   I 10 | *Tempest* I ii 117–20

PROSPERO. Mark his condition, and th' event; then tell me,
    If this might be a brother.
MIRANDA.   I should sin,
    To think but nobly of my grand mother;
    Good wombs have bore bad sons.*

[Theobald's note:] How could *Miranda*, that came into this *desart island*

1[a] Note continues at top of p ⁻3

1[1] C's usual misspelling of "paeon".

an infant that had never seen any other creatures of the world, but her father and *Caliban*, with any propriety be furnish'd to make such an observation from life . . . ? But it comes very properly from *Prospero* . . .

* I cannot but believe that Theobald is quite right.[1]

3   I 21 | I ii 435–7

FERDINAND.   . . . myself am *Naples*,
        Who, with mine eyes (ne'er since at ebb) beheld
        The king my father wreck't.
MIRANDA.   Alack, for mercy!
FERDINAND. Yes, faith, and all his Lords: the duke of *Milan*,
        And his brave son, being twain.

[Theobald's note:] Here seems a slight forgetfulness in our Poet: No body was lost in this wreck . . . and yet we have no such character introduced in the fable, as the Duke of *Milan*'s son.

Must not Ferd. have believed so—in the fleet that the Tempest scattered?

4   I 83 | *Midsummer Night's Dream* I i 134–40

LYSANDER. . . . The course of true love never did run smooth;
        But, either, it was different in blood—
*HERMIA. O cross! too high to be enthrall'd to low!—
LYSANDER. Or else misgraffed, in respect of years—
*HERMIA. O spite! too old, to be engaged to young!
LYSANDER. Or else it stood upon the choice of friends—
HERMIA. O hell! to chuse love by another's eye!

** It would be a great improvement, if these 2 lines were omitted. The third "O Hell!" would then become a beauty, & most natural.

5   I 86–9 | I i 246–9

[Helena betrays Hermia to Demetrius:]
HELENA. . . . I will go tell him of fair *Hermia*'s flight:
        Then to the wood will he, to-morrow night,
        Pursue her; and for this intelligence
        If I have thanks, it is a dear expencc.

2[1] C also notes his approval of this proposed emendation in COPY C **2**.

I am convinced that Shakespear availed himself of the Title of the Play in his own mind a *Dream*, throughout;[1] but especially (& perhaps, unpleasingly) in this broad determination of ungrateful Treachery in Helena, so undisguisedly avowed to herself, and this too after the witty cool philosophizing that precedes. The act is very natural; the resolve so to act is, I fear, likewise too true a picture of the lax hold, that Principles have on the female Heart when opposed to, or even separated from, passion & inclination—for Women are less hypocrites to their own minds than Men, because they feel less abhorrence of moral evil in itself, & more for its outward Consequences, as Detection, Loss of Character, &c, their natures being almost wholly extroitive—but still, however just, the representation is not poetical—we shrink from it—& cannot harmonize it with the Ideal.

6 I 90–1 | II i 1–5

PUCK. How now, spirit, whither wander you?
FAIRY. Over hill, over dale,
  *Thorough bush, thorough briar,
  Over park, over pale,
  Thorough flood, thorough fire . . .

* What a noble pair of ~~Ass~~ Ears this worthy Theobald must have had! The ~~four five~~ 8 Amphimacers,

⟨– ˘ – | – ˘ –|⟩	Ōvĕr Hīll, ōvĕr dāle,
– ˘ – | – ˘ – |	Thōrŏ' būsh, thōrŏ' brīar,
– ˘ – | – ˘ – |	ōvĕr pārk, ōvĕr pāle,
– ˘ – | – ˘ – |	Thōrŏ' flōod, thōrŏ' fīre,

have so delightful an effect on the ear! ~~S. T. C.~~ // and then the sweet Transition to the Trochaic—Ī dŏ | wāndĕr | ēv'rў̆ | whērĕ—for where itself, as a rhyme, is almost a trochee.

7 I 95 | II i 127–33

QUEEN. . . . . Marking th' embarked traders on the flood,
  When we have laugh'd to see the sails conceive,
  And grow big-bellied with the wanton wind:
  Which she, with pretty and with swimming gate,
  <u>Follying</u> (her womb then rich with my young squire)

5[1] C was to develop a theory about Shakespeare's titles, mentioning this play among others, in lectures of 1813 and 1818: *Lects 1808–1819 (CC)* I 551 and n, 573, II 137.

Would imitate; and sail upon the land,
To fetch me trifles, and return again . . .

[Theobald accepts Warburton's emendation from the original "following":] *follying*, i.e. wantoning, in sport and gaiety; so the old writers used follity for foolishness . . .

Oh! Oh! Oh! Lord have mercy on poor Shakspere!—& on Mr. W———n's mind's Eye![1]

8   I 137, pencil, overtraced | v i 91–2

THESEUS. . . . And what poor (willing)*ᵃ* duty cannot do,(34)
     Noble respect takes it in might, not merit.

[Theobald's note (34):] What ears have these poetical Editors, to palm this line upon us as a verse of *Shakespeare*? 'Tis certain, an epithet had slipt out, and I have ventur'd to restore such a one as the sense may dispense with; and which makes the two verses flowing and perfect.

(34) To *my* ears it *would* read far more Shakespearian, thus:
     And what poor Duty cannot do, yet would,
     Noble Respect takes it, &c—
or "cannot do, tho' fain,"—[1]

9   I 146, pencil, marked with a line in the margin | v i 371–400

PUCK. Now the hungry lion roars,
     And the wolf behowls the moon:
Whilst the heavy ploughman snoars,
     All with weary task fore-done.
Now the wasted brands do glow,
     Whilst the scritch-owl, scritching loud,
Puts the wretch, that lies in woe,
     In remembrance of a shroud.
Now it is the time of night,
     That the graves, all gaping wide,

8ᵃ Square brackets in original, converted to avoid confusion with editorial matter

7[1] Warburton had pointed out that the lady could not strictly be said to "follow" the ship, "for that sailed on the water, she on land"; and he offered "follying" instead. The suggestion met almost universal outrage from later 18th-century editors: *Sh* (Reed). The phrase "mind's eye" is an allusion to *Hamlet* I ii 185.

8[1] Neither Theobald's nor C's solution to the short line here has found favour with later editors.

Every one lets forth his spright,
  In the church-way paths to glide;
And we *Fairies*, that do run
  By the triple *Hecate*'s team,
From the presence of the sun,
  Following darkness like a dream,
Now are frolic; not a mouse
Shall disturb this hallow'd house.
I am sent with broom before,
To sweep the dust behind the door.
OBERON. Through the house give glimmering light,
  By the dead and drowsy fire,
Every elf, and fairy sprite,
  Hop as light as bird from brier;
And this ditty after me
Sing, and dance it trippingly.
QUEEN. First rehearse this song by rote,
  To each word a warbling note.
Hand in hand, with fairy grace,
Will we sing, and bless this place.

Anacreon in the *Perfectness* of the Lines—Proportion, Grace, Spontane-ity![1] So far it is Greek. But then add to it, O what wealth, what wild lux-uriance, ~~the English Fancy! S. T. C.~~[a] and yet what compression & con-densation of English Fancy.

[b]There is nothing in Anacreon *more* PERFECT than these 30 lines, or *half so* rich and imaginative; a diamond speckless!!

10   I 220–1 | *Merry Wives* I i 16–23

SLENDER. . . . . they may give the dozen white luces in their coat.
SHALLOW. It is an old coat.
EVANS. The dozen white lowses do become an old coat well . . . .
SHALLOW. The luce is the fresh-fish, the salt-fish is an old coat.*

9[a] Over the cancelled words C has written "✓ ✓ ✓" twice, and resumed the note in the foot-margin with "✓ ✓ ✓"

9[b] This sentence is written in the gutter margin, the first part of the note having been written in the head and outer margin

9[1] Cf C's praise for "the perfusive and omnipresent grace" achieved in certain classical measures, including "the 'Swal-low,' the 'Grasshopper,' and all the other little loves of Anacreon" in *BL* ch 16 (*CC*) II 34 and n 2.

* an old Coat, i.e. an old Cod—Salt Fish, or Baccalao, being chiefly Cod—. This Remark Sh. owes to Mary M.[1]

Probably, ~~the Dialogue should be divided~~ thus—Shallow. The Luce is the Fresh-fish, the Salt-fish—~~Evans~~—is an old Cod.— (Shallow mistaking Evans's Pronunciation of Coat for Cod.[)][2]

11   I 224 | I i 162

PISTOL. . . . I combat challenge of this latten bilboe . . .

[Warburton's speculative note, defending "latten" as a kind of metal over the alternative reading "Latin", runs to more than a page of small type, with quotations in Greek from several learned sources.]

Monstrous Erudition!—And after all Latten is nothing but what is called Black-Tin, probably from the British Ló or Lá Black & Tin/ so Lo Dore, Lodore black water[1]

12   I 239, pencil | II i 49–53

MRS. FORD. If I would but go to hell for an eternal moment, or so, I could be knighted.
MRS. PAGE. What, thou liest! Sir *Alice Ford!* these Knights will hack, and so thou shouldst not alter the article of thy gentry.*

* I confess, I do not understand this sentence! Of course, therefore, there is no explanatory note: simply, because the Passage requires one.[1]

S. T. C.

10[1] *Bacallao* (variously spelled in English) is the Spanish word for "cod". C gives Mary Morgan credit for elucidating this culinary term.

10[2] A play on words on "cod" and "coat" (with Shallow misunderstanding Evans's pronunciation) does not seem to have occurred to Shakespearean scholarship before C—it is at any rate not included in *Sh* (Reed)—but it is now an accepted interpretation: *Sh* (Arden). C repeats his explanation of these lines in COPY B **1**, COPY D **4**.

11[1] C is not challenging the gloss, only protesting at the documentation of what he thought of as an everyday term. *OED* indicates in fact that "latten" (which was usually yellow) and "black latten" were distinct from one another. The north-country connection (the cataract of Lodore being a well-known attraction of the Lakes) is worth noting: Steevens, glossing this line (*Sh*—Reed) observed that "*Latten* is still a common word for *tin* in the North." About Lodore itself C is quite mistaken: although the etymology is disputed, no expert of his day or ours endorses his theory. The English Place-Name Society offers a compound of Old Norse and Old English meaning literally "low-door": A. M. Armstrong et al *The Place-Names of Cumberland* pt 2 (Cambridge 1950) 350.

12[1] C's predecessors (*Sh*—Reed) and successors expended much ingenuity in glosses of "these Knights will hack", but the conclusion in *Sh* (Arden) is that "No clear explanation of the word ['hack'] has ever been given".

13 I 284–5, pencil, very faint probably from erasure | IV iv 11–14

⏑ − ⏑ ⏑/ − ⏑ ⏑/ − ⏑ ⏑/ − ⏑ ⏑/ −[a]

PAGE. Be not as extreme in submission, as in offence;
  But let our plot go forward; let our wives
  Yet once again, to make us public sport,
  Appoint a meeting with this old fat fellow . . .

⏑ − ⏑ ⏑   − ⏑ ⏑/ − ⏑ ⏑

as good as [. . .] of co[. . .]tory;
4[. . .] the 5 [. . . . .] Line equipollent.

13A I 286, pencil | IV iv 52–5

MRS. PAGE.   . . . upon a sudden,
  As *Falstaff*, she, and I, are newly met,
  Let them from forth a saw-pit rush at once
    With some diffus'ed song . . .

14 I [305] | *Measure for Measure* (fly-title)

This Play, which is Shakespeare's throughout, is to me the most painful, say rather, the only painful, part of his genuine Works. The comic & tragic parts equally border on the μισητεον;[1] the one disgusting, the other horrible—and the pardon and marriage of Angelo not merely baffles the strong indignant claim of Justice (for cruelty, with Lust and damnable Baseness cannot be forgiven, because we cannot Conceive them as being *morally* repented of) but it is likewise degrading to the character of Woman.[2] Beaum. and Fletcher, who can follow Shakespear in his errors only, have presented a still ~~more~~ worse because more loathsome & contradictory instance of the same kind in his Night-Walker, in the marriage of Alathe to Algripe.[3] Of the counterbalancing Beauties of the Measure

---

13[a] The marks of scansion are written in the margin

14[1] "Hateful", as similarly in J. SEDGWICK 2; cf BEAUMONT & FLETCHER COPY A **10** n 1.

14[2] Clarified in Collier's report of the 1818 lectures: "[C] pointed especially to the artifice of Isabella, and her seeming consent to the suit of Angelo, as the circumstances which tended to lower the character of the female sex" (*Lects 1808–1819—CC*—II 245).

14[3] In *The Night-walker* (1640), incidentally not annotated in either of C's sets of BEAUMONT & FLETCHER, Maria is married against her will to old Justice Algripe, but before the marriage is consummated, he is tricked into a confession of bigamy, and so Maria is released. No character named "Alathe" appears in this play, nor in any other play by Beaumont and Fletcher.

for Measure I need say nothing: for I have already said, that it is Shakespear's throughout. S. T. Coleridge—

14A I 311 | I ii 14–20

I GENTLEMAN. .... there's not a soldier of us all, that, in the thanksgiving before meat, do relish the petition well that prays for peace.
2 GENT. *Lucio.* I never heard any soldier dislike it.
LUCIO. *2 Gent.* I believe thee: for, I think, thou never wast where grace
was said.
2 GENT. *Lucio.* No? a dozen times at least.[1]

15 I 324–5, pencil | II i 89–92, 106–7

CLOWN. Sir, she came in great with child; and longing (saving your honour's reverence) for stew'd prewns; Sir, we had but two in the house,
which at that very distant time stood, as it were, in a fruit-dish ....
Very well; you being then, if you be remembered, cracking the stones
of the foresaid prewns.

I sometimes ⟨—foolishly⟩ doubted, whether stewed Prewns ~~are~~ meant
Prunes, i.e. Plumbs—/ Stewed Prawns as other shell-fish, enjoy⟨ing,⟩
truly or falsely, famam sive infamiam Aphrodisiacam.[1] But the cracking
Stones settles the question[2]

15A I 335, pencil | II ii 151–3

ISABELLA. ... but with true prayers,
That shall be up at heav'n, and enter there,
Ere sun-rise: prayers from preserv'ed souls ...

16 I 348–9, pencil | III i 128–31

CLAUDIO. .... The weariest and most loathed worldly life,
That age, ach, penury, imprisonment
Can lay on nature, is a paradise
To what we fear of death.

[Warburton's note:] This natural fear of *Claudio*, from the antipathy we
have to death, seems very little varied from that infamous wish of *Mae-*

14A[1] This proposed redistribution of
lines does not appear to have either precedent or support from other commentators.

15[1] "The fame or infamy of being aphro-
disiac".

15[2] The lines have generally been accepted as they stand, and glossed before and
since C as referring to *stewed* prunes as
standard brothel fare.

cenas recorded in the 101st Epistle of *Seneca*. . . .

> *Vita, dum superest, bene est.*
> *Hanc mihi, vel acuta*
> *Si sedeam cruce, sustine.*
> [All is well, if my life remains.
> Save, oh, save it, I pray you,
> Though I sit on the piercing cross! (LCL)]

I cannot but think this rather an heroic resolve, than an infamous Wish. It appears to me the grandest Symptom of an immortal Spirit, even when that bedimmed & oerwhelmed Spirit recked not of its own Immortality/ The privilege to *be*, to be a Mind, a Will.

17   I 357, pencil | III ii 180–1

LUCIO. . . . the Duke, I say to thee again, would eat mutton on *Fridays.*

[Theobald refers to *Two Gentlemen*, his third note, to explain this joke. C looked it up (in I 154) and found a note on "*I, a* lost mutton, *gave your letter to her, a* lac'd mutton" (in which there is no suggestion of the reading "laes'd").]

I suspect, that "lac'd Mutton" is a corruption for læs'd Mutton (as læsa Majestas)—Flesh *kept* too long.[1]

18   I 360, pencil | III ii 263–4

DUKE. . . . Pattern in himself to know,
        Grace to stand and virtue go* . . .

* Worse metre indeed, but better English, were
   Grace to stand, Virtue to go—[1]

19   I 364, pencil, erased | IV ii 19–20

PROVOST. What hoa, *Abhorson!* where's *Abhorson*, there?
                Enter Abhorson.*

* [. . . . .][1]

17[1] "Mutton" and "laced mutton" were slang terms for prostitutes; C's suggestion that "laced" corresponds to "laesed" or "lesed" ("damaged") is improbable. The Latin means (lit) "damaged majesty", i.e. treason.

18[1] The meaning of this couplet has been much debated; C's solution is idiosyncratic.

19[1] A note of three lines has been erased here. C does not elsewhere comment on Abhorson. Perhaps the note was a speculation about the name (suggesting "whore's son" or "whoreson"), erased for decorum's sake.

20   II 259, pencil | *Love's Labour's Lost* v ii 760–5

BIRON. . . . As love is full of unbefitting strains,
   All wanton as a child, skipping and vain,
   Form'd by the eye, and therefore like the eye,
   Full of straying shapes, of habits, and of forms,*
   Varying in subjects as the eye doth rowl,/
   To every varied object in his glance . . .

* Either "stray"; or "full" thrown back to the preceding Line—"The eye,
full of straying Shapes—" I prefer the former.[1]

20A   II 260, pencil | v ii 805

PRINCESS. . . . Come challenge me; challenge ~~me,~~ by these deserts . . .

21   II 260–1, pencil | v ii 817–22

BIRON. And what to me, my love? and what to me?
ROSALINE. [a]You must be purged too, your sins are rank,
   You are attaint with fault and perjury;
   Therefore if you my favour mean to get,
   A twelve-month shall you spend, and never rest,
   But seek the weary beds of people sick.[b]

[Theobald, following Thirlby and Warburton, brackets Rosaline's lines
as being an earlier draft or later abridgment of her next speech.]

There can be no doubt respecting the last 5 lines—~~it~~ they spoil the very
page that retains them;[1] but the first line is quite in Biron's character, and
Rosamond[c] not answering, *Dumain* takes up the question for himself—
& after he & Longaville are answered, then Biron with evident propriety
says, *Studies* my Lady?[2]

22   II 269, pencil, slightly cropped | *As You Like It* I i 49–57

ORLANDO. . . . I have as much of my father in me, as you; albeit, I confess your coming before me is nearer to his reverence.

21[a–b] C has scribbled over these lines to delete them   21[c] A slip for "Rosaline"

20[1] C objects to the extra syllable in the
line: Capell and Malone had proposed to
change "straying" to "strange" (*Sh*—Rced),
but other editors see no need for emendation.
   21[1] This view has been generally
adopted. Cf *Sh* (Arden): "Rosaline's next
speech makes these lines redundant. They
are clearly an early draft, somehow left un-
cancelled by Shakespeare although he had
written new lines for Rosaline and Berowne
[Biron, in C's copy] and borrowed from the
old for Dumain and Katharine."
   21[2] At v ii 837.

OLIVER. What, boy!*

ORLANDO. Come, come, elder brother, you are too young in this.

OLIVER. Wilt thou lay hands on me, villain?

ORLANDO. I am no villain: I am the youngest son of Sir *Rowland de Boys* . . .

* There is a Beauty here. The word, *Boy*, naturally provokes and awakens in Orland[a] the sense of his manly powers—& with the retort, "elder Brother", he grasps him with firm hands, & makes him feel tha[t] he is no *Boy*.

23   II 272, pencil | I i 163–73

OLIVER. Farewell, good *Charles*. Now will I stir this gamester: I hope, I shall see an end of him; for my soul, yet I know not why, hates nothing more than <u>he</u>. Yet he's gentle; never school'd, and yet learn'd; full of noble device, of all sorts enchantingly beloved: and, indeed, so much in the heart of the world, and especially of my own people who best know him, that I am altogether misprised. But it shall not be so, long; this wrestler shall clear all; nothing remains but that I kindle the boy thither, which now I'll go about.

This has always *appeared* to me one of the most unshakespearian Speeches in all (the genuine works of) Shakespear. Yet I should be nothing surprized, & greatly pleased, to find it hereafter a fresh Beauty as has so often happened with me with the supposed Defects of the ανηρ μυριονους.[1]

24   II 277, pencil | I ii 174–8

CELIA. . . . you have seen cruel proof of this man's strength. If you saw yourself with your eyes, or knew yourself with your judgment, the fear of your adventure would counsel you to a more equal enterprise.

our?[1]

22[a] For "Orlando"

23[1] "Myriad-minded man", an epithet C began to apply to Shakespeare in Dec 1801: *CN* I 1070 and n, *Friend (CC)* I 453, *BL* ch 15 *(CC)* II 19, *Lects 1808–1819 (CC)* II 112 and n 2. He uses it again in COPY C **5**. C returns to puzzle over this speech again in COPY D **8**. A number of marked passages following this note are printed in the ANNEX.

24[1] Warburton had also found this line obscure and proposed "our eyes" and "our judgment" as C does; but subsequent scholars, starting with Johnson, defended the original reading.

25 II 281, pencil | I iii 10–11

CELIA. But is all this for your father?
ROSALIND. No, some of it is for my child's father.

[Theobald restores the original text—which had been altered by Rowe to "my father's child"—and notes:] . . . *Rosalind* would say, "no, all my distress and melancholy is not for my father; but some of it for my sweetheart, whom I hope to marry and have children by." In this sense she stiles him her *child's father.*

This is putting a very indelicate anticipation in the mouth of Rosalind, without reason: not to speak of the strangeness of the Phrase—

26 II 284, pencil | I iii 114–16

ROSALIND.   Wer't not better,
    Because that I am more than common tall,
    That I did suit me all points like a man?

somewhat*[a]* the more tall,

27 II 295, pencil | II v 54–60

JAQUES. . . . Ducdame, ducdame, ducdame;
    Here shall he see
    Gross fools as he,
    An' if he will come to me.
AMIENS. What's that ducdame?
JAQUES. 'Tis a *Greek* invocation, to call fools into a circle.

Duc ad me, i.e. Bring him to me![1]

27A II 305, pencil | III ii 125–6

CELIA. Why should this a desart be/ ?
    For it is unpeopled? no . . .

27B II 307 | III ii 174–5

ROSALIND. I was seven out of the nine days out of wonder, before you came . . .

26*[a]* The first 5 letters overtraced in ink

27[1] In C's day this was the standard explanation, proposed by Hanmer and supported by Johnson and Malone (*Sh*—Reed); it was subsequently challenged, and *Sh* (Arden) barely mentions it.

28   II 315, pencil | III iii 79–81

CLOWN. As the ox hath his <u>bow</u>,* Sir, the horse his curb, and the faulcon her bells, so man hath his desire . . .

* Bow = Yoke.[1]

29   II 320, pencil | III v 66–7

ROSALIND. He's fallen in love with your foulness,* and she'll fall in love with my anger.

* (*aside*)

30   II 323, pencil | After IV i 26

Enter Orlando.

Enter [? meeting Orlando]

31   IV 324, pencil | IV i 73–7

ROSALIND. Nay, you were better speak first, and when you were gravell'd for lack of matter, you might take occasion to kiss. Very good orators, when they are out, they will spit; and for lover's lacking, God warn us, matter, the cleanliest shift is to kiss.

hem[1]

32   I 324, pencil | IV i 94–7

ROSALIND. . . . the poor world is almost six thousand years old, and in all this time there was not any man died in his own person, *videlicet*, in a love-cause . . .

to wit[1]

33   II 328, pencil, marked with vertical lines | IV ii 10–18

SONG. What shall he have that kill'd the deer?
     His leather skin and horns to wear;

28[1] Steevens's gloss in *Sh* (Reed), fully accepted by later editors.

31[1] C may be in part meaning to draw attention to the pun—"shift" designating an undergarment as well as an expedient, and "hem" indicating the public speaker's action (like spitting), as also in **148**.

32[1] C is simply glossing "videlicet", something he would not have had to do for J. J. Morgan, but perhaps necessary for Mary Morgan and her sister.

Then sing him home:—take thou no scorn
To wear the horn, the horn, the horn:
It was a crest ere thou wast born.
Thy father's father wore it,
And thy father bore it,
The horn, the horn, the lusty horn,
Is not a thing to laugh to scorn.

I question whether there exists a parallel Instance of a phrase, that like this of Horns for Cuckoldism is universal in all Languages, yet for which no one has yet discovered even a plausible origin.[1]

34   II 346, pencil | Epilogue lines 14–23

ROSALIND. . . . and I charge you, O men, for the love you bear to women . . . that between you and the women, the play may please. If I were a woman, I would kiss as many of you as had beards that pleas'd me, complexions that lik'd me, and breaths that I defy'd not; and I am sure, as many as have good beards, or good faces, or sweet breaths, will for my kind offer, when I make cur'sy, bid me farewel.

and now for our best efforts to please.

35   II 360, pencil | *Taming of the Shrew* I i

The first & second Page read (to *my* eʒar) very unlike Shakespear.[1]

35A   II 401, pencil | IV i 124–5

PETRUCHIO. Here, Sir, here, Sir, here, Sir, here, Sir?
    You loggerheaded and unpolish'd grooms . . .[1]

36   II 7, pencil | *All's Well* I i 57–60

COUNT. If the living be not enemy to the grief, the excess makes it soon mortal.
BERTRAM. Madam, I desire your holy wishes. ⎰
LAFEU. How understand we that?   ⎱

Both, I imagine, speak together. Lafeu refers to "If the living" &c.

33[1] In *BL* ch 21 (*CC*) II 116–17, C includes an anecdote that illustrates the international viability of the symbol of "Horns for Cuckoldism".

35[1] These pages correspond to I i 1–52.

35A[1] C corrects a typographical error.

37   iii 25–9 | ii i 12–19

KING.   . . . lct higher *Italy*
   *(Those bated, that inherit but the fall
   Of the last monarchy;) see, that you come
   Not to woo honour, but to wed it; when
   The bravest questant shrinks, find what you seek,
   That same may cry you loud: I say, farewel.
2 LORD. Health at your bidding serve your Majesty!
KING. Those girls of *Italy*, take heed of them . . .

[Warburton's note:] . . . The King says, *higher* Italy;—giving it the rank of preference to *France*; but he corrects himself and says, I except those from that precedency, who only inherit the fall of the last monarchy; as all the little petty states; for instance, *Florence* to whom these voluntiers were going.

* It would be, I own, an audacious and unjustifiable Change of the Text; but yet as a mere Conjecture, I venture to suggest—"Those Bastards" for "those bated".[1] As it stands, spite of Warburton's Note I can make little or nothing of it. Why should the King except the then most illustrious States, who, as Republics, were more truly the Inheritors of Roman Grandeur? With my conjecture, the sense would be—let higher, i.e. the more Northern Part of—Italy (unless higher be a corruption for *hir'd*:[2] as the metre seems to demand a monosyllable) those Bastards, that inherit the infamy only of their Fathers/ see &c/—the following "wed & woo" are so far confirmation, as it marks Shakespear's manner of connection by unmarked influences of association from some preceding metaphor. This it is which makes his style so peculiarly vital and organic. Likewise "Those Girls of Italy" strengthens the guess.—The absurdity of Warburton's Gloss, which makes the King call Italy superior, and then except the only part, the Lords were going to, must strike every one.

38   iii 26 | ii i 52–4

PAROLLES. . . . be more expressive to them: for they wear themselves in the cap of the time; there do muster true gate, eat, speak . . .

these do[a]

38[a]   C has also written "these" over "there" in textus

37[1]   C repeats this conjectural emendation in COPY B **3**, COPY D **10**. "Bated" has always puzzled commentators. The emendation to "bastards", proposed originally by Hanmer, was rejected by Johnson and has not proved popular: *Sh* (Reed).

37[2]   C repeats this conjectural emendation in COPY D **10**. Other critics have debated the meaning of "higher Italy" without proposing to change it.

39   III 33 | II iii 1–3

LAFEU. They say, miracles are past; and we have our philosophical persons to make modern, and familiar, things supernatural and causeless. . . .

[Note discusses punctuation:] This, as it has hitherto been pointed, is directly opposite to our poet's, and his speaker's, meaning. As I have stop'd it, the sense quadrates with the context; and, surely, it is one unalterable property of philosophy, to make seeming strange and preternatural *Phaenomena* familiar, and reducible to cause and reason.

Sh. inspir'd, as it might seem, with all knowlege, here uses the word "causeless" in its strict philosophical sense, ~~as~~ cause being truly predictable only of phænomena, i.e. things natural, not of noumena or things supernatural.

40   III 57–8 | III v 48–51

HELENA.   His name, I pray you?
DIANA. The Count *Rousillon:* know you such a one?
HELENA. But by the ear, that hears most nobly of him;*
     His face I know not.

* Shall we say here, that Shakespear has unnecessarily made his loveliest Character utter a Lie? or shall we dare think, that where to deceive was necessary, he thought a pretended verbal verity a double crime equally with the other a Lie to the Hearer, & at the same time an attempt to lie to one's own Conscience.—   *S. T. C.*

41   III 104–5, pencil, overtraced | *Twelfth Night* I i 14–15

DUKE. . . . (1) so full of shapes in fancy,
     That it alone is high fantastical.

[Warburton's note (1):] . . . I am persuaded, the alteration of *is* into *in* has giv'n us the Poet's genuine meaning; that *love* is most *fantastical*, in being so variable in its *fancies*.

(1) Fancy may very well be interpreted "exclusive Affection", or "passionate Preference"/ thus, Bird-Fanciers, Gentlemen of the Fancy—i.e. Amateurs of Boxing &c W's alteration is needless: which the Play of assimilation, the meaning one sense chiefly, and yet keeping both senses in view, is perfectly Shakespearian.[1]

41[1] Other editors concur with C's view   "is" to "in".
that there is no need to change the reading

41A   III 117 | I v 167–9

OLIVIA. *Viola.* The honourable Lady of the house, which is she?
OLIVIA. Speak to me, I shall answer for her: your will?

41B   III 120, pencil | I v 286–8

VIOLA. Love makes his heart of flint, that you shall love,
  And let your fervour, likc my Master's, be
  Plac'd in contempt![1]

42   III 121 | I v 300–2

OLIVIA. Run after that same peevish messenger,
  The Duke's man; he left this ring behind him,/\
  Would I, or not: tell him, I'll none of it.

Him, the Duke's Man—

43   III 125 | II iii 22–5

SIR ANDREW. . . . Insooth, thou wast in very gracious fooling last night,
  when thou spok'st of *Pigrogromitus*, of the *Vapians* passing the
  equinoctial of *Queubus*: 'twas very good, i' faith:(6) I sent thee sixpence for thy Leman, had'st it?

[Theobald note (6): . . . I have restored, *leman*, i.e. I sent thee sixpence to
spend on thy mistress.]

A note explanatory on Pigrogromitus &c would have been more acceptable.[1]

44   III 126 | II iii 58–9

SIR TOBY. . . . Shall we rouze the night-owl in a catch, that will draw three
  souls out of one weaver? shall we do that?

[Warburton laboriously explains the "three souls" from "the *peripatetic*
philosophy (the learning then in vogue,) which very liberally gave
to every man three souls, the *vegetative* or *plastic*, the *animal*, and the
rational".]

O genuine, inimitable (at least I hope so) Warburton! one in 5 Millions
would be half a one too much.   *S. T. C.*

41B[1] C's mistake: the verb is optative,
not assertive.
43[1] Eighteenth-century editors saw no
need to explain these names; modern editors describe them as "extravagant invented
names": *Sh* (Arden).

44A   I 127, pencil | II iii 95–7

MALVOLIO. Sir *Toby*, I must be round with you. My Lady bade me tell
you, that tho' she harbours you as her uncle, she's nothing ally'd to
your disorders.[1]

45   I 128, pencil | II iii 104–7

CLOWN. *His eyes do shew, his days are almost done.*
MALVOLIO. Is't even so?
SIR TOBY. But I will never die.
CLOWN. Sir *Toby*, there you lye.

(*singing*)[1]

46   III 131, pencil, overtraced | II iv 22–7

DUKE. Thou doest speak masterly.
    My life upon't, young tho' thou art, thine eye
    Hath staid upon some favour that it loves:
    Hath it not, boy?
VIOLA.   A little, by your favour.*
DUKE. What kind of woman is't?
VIOLA.   Of your complexion.
DUKE. She is not worth thee then. . . .

* and yet Viola was to be presented to Orsino as a Eunuch—Either she
forgot this, or Viola had altered her Plan.

47   III 134, pencil, overtraced | II iv 109–12

DUKE.   And what's her history?
VIOLA. A blank, my Lord: she never told her love, !—*
    But let concealment, like a worm i' th' bud,
    Feed on her damask cheek . . .

* After the first line (of which the last 5 words should be spoken with &
drop down in, a deep Sigh) the Speaker should make a pause & then start
afresh, from the activity of thought born of suppressed Feelings, which
thoughts had accumulated during the brief interval, as vital Heat under
the skin during a dip in cold water.[1]

44A[1] C is simply correcting a typographical error.
45[1] C wrote his note twice, against lines 3 and 4 of textus. The lines are based on a popular song, and modern editors concur with C in adding stage directions.
47[1] C may be recalling Dora Jordan's performance of these lines, which he more

48   III 136, pencil, overtraced | II v 63–4

FABIAN. Tho' our silence be drawn from us with <u>cares</u>,* yet, peace.

*   "Cares?"—perhaps *"Cables"*.[1]

48A   III 137, marked in the margin in pencil | II v 86–9

MALVOLIO. By my life, this is my Lady's hand: thesc be her very *C*'s, her *U*'s, and her *T*'s, and thus makes she her great *P*'s. It is, in contempt of question, her hand.
SIR ANDREW. Her *C*'s, her *U*'s, and her *T*'s: why that?

49   III 141 | III i 11–13

CLOWN. . . . A sentence is but a chev'ril glove to a good wit; how quickly the wrong side may be turned outward?

[Theobald's note:] . . . I never heard yet of any *glove* or *leather* made of a *cockrel*'s skin . . . . The etymology is therefore to be disputed. I shew'd in my SHAKESPEARE *restor'd*, that *cheveril* leather is made of the skin of a *kid*, or goat . . .

Theobald's Etymō[1] is doubtless right; but he is mistaken in supposing that there are no such things as Gloves of Chicken Skin/ They were at one time a main article in Chirocosmetic.[2]

50   III 142, pencil, overtraced | III i 67–8

VIOLA. . . . For folly, that he wisely shews, is fit;
   But wise men's, folly fall'n, quite taints their wit.*

*   I can scarcely construe this Linc[1]

---

than once refers to with rapture: *SW & F* (*CC*) 290, *TT* (*CC*) I 78 and n 7.

48[1] The Folio reads "cars"; Johnson suggested "carts" and Tyrwhitt "cables": *Sh* (Reed).

49[1] I.e. "etymon". Although *OED* records for "cheveral" the secondary meaning of "cockerel", none of Shakespeare's editors appears ever to have made the mistake Theobald suggested: all gloss it as "kid-leather".

49[2] *OED* gives "chirocosmetics" ("the art of adorning the hands") but not C's

meaning, which has to do with caring for them by oiling and softening them. If Mary Morgan was not actually the source of C's domestic information (as in **10**), she would at least have been interested in it.

50[1] The wording, punctuation, and meaning of this line had already been much discussed. *Sh* (Reed) prints "But wise men, folly-fallen, quite taint their wit" (which is also the *Sh*—Arden—reading), and notes paraphrases by Tyrwhitt ("Fallen into folly") and Johnson ("the folly of wise men, when it *falls* or *happens* . . .").

51   iii 144 | iii i 111–13

OLIVIA.   . . . I did send,
After the last enchantment, you did <u>hear</u>,*
A ring in chase of you . . .

here[a] * After the last enchantment, which you worked in this place.[1]—
Cæsario perceived it, saw it—not merely heard of it.—

52   iii 169–70, pencil, overtraced | v i 20–3

CLOWN. . . . and by my friends I am abused: so that, conclusion to be
asked, is, if your four negatives make your two affirmatives, why, then
the worse for my friends, and the better for my foes.

[Warburton's note on the original reading:] *So that conclusions to be* as
kisses,—* . . . what monstrous absurdity have we here? . . . the *Clown* is
affecting to argue seriously and in form. I imagine, the Poet wrote;
    So that, conclusion to be asked, is
i.e. So that the conclusion I have to demand of you is this . . .

Surely, Warburton could never have wooed by kisses & won, or he would
not have flounder-flatted[1] so just & humorous an Image, nor less pleasing than humorous, into so profound a Nihility!—In the name of Love
and Wonder do not four kisses make a double affirmative? The Humor
lies in the whispered "No", the inviting "Don't", with which the Maiden's
kisses are accompanied, and thence compared to Negatives, which by
repetition constitute an affirmative.—[2]

53   iii [243–4] | *Winter's Tale* (fly-title and Dramatis Personae)

Altho' on the whole exquisitely respondent to its Title, and ever[a] in the
fault, I am about to mention, still a Winter's Tale;[1] yet it seems a mere
Indolence of the great Bard not to have in the Oracle provided some
ground for Hermione's seeming Death & 15 years concealment, volun-

---

51[a] The first word is written in the margin against the line in question, the remainder at
the foot of the page
53[a] Perhaps a slip for "even"

51[1] The Folio reading was "heare";
commentators are virtually unanimous in
the view that this was a variant spelling for
"here".
52[1] I.e. made as flat as a flounder: cf
BEAUMONT & FLETCHER COPY A **11**.
52[2] This is the opinion of most commentators before and after C, defending the
original text.
53[1] Proverbially, an old tale told to
while away a winter evening. In the play itself, we hear, "A sad tale's best for winter"
(ii i 25). On the significance of Shakespeare's titles see also **5** and n 1 above.

tary Concealment. This might have been easily effected by some obscure sentence of the Oracle, as ex. gr. ["]Nor shall he ever recover an heir, if he have a Wife before that recovery." S. T. C.

54 III 248 | I ii 40–2

HERMIONE. . . . I'll give him my commission,
To let him there a month, behind the gest (2)
Prefix'd for's parting . . .

[Theobald's note (2):] . . . I have suspected, that the poet wrote:
—*behind the* just
Prescrib'd for's parting.

(2) More probably, the syllable "lon" had slipped out in the press-form of the first Edition.
—behind the longest
Prefix'd &c.[1]

55 II 285 | III ii 185–7

PAULINA. That thou betray'dst *Polixenes*, 'twas nothing;(15)
That did but shew thee of a soul inconstant,
And damnable ingrateful . . .

[Theobald suggests *fool* for *Soul* in his note (15):] . . . It is certainly too gross and blunt in *Paulina* . . . to call him [the King] downright a fool. And it is much more pardonable in her to arraign his morals, and the qualities of his mind, than rudely to call him *ideot* to his face.

(15) I think the original to be Shakespear's—1. My ear feels it Shakespearian—2. the involved grammar is Shakespearian—i.e. shews thee, being a fool naturally, to have improved your folly by inconstancy &c. 3 the alteration is most flat & *unshakespearian*. as to grossness, "gross & foolish" follow[1]

56 III 296–7, pencil, overtraced | IV iii 24–30

AUTOLICUS. . . . My father nam'd me *Autolicus*, being litter'd under *Mercury*; who, as I am, was likewise a snapper-up of unconsider'd trifles: with die and drab, I purchas'd this caparison, and my revenue is the

54[1] Warburton had already supplied the definitive explanation, "*gest* is right, and signifies a stage or journey" (especially in a royal progress): *Sh* (Reed).

55[1] In the same speech, III ii 197 following: "That could conceive a gross and foolish Sire".

silly cheat. Gallows, and knock, are too powerful on the high-way; beating and hanging are terrors to me: <u>for the life to come, I sleep out the thought of it.</u>—*

* Fine as this is, and delicately characteristic of one who had lived & been reared in the best society, & had been precipitated from it by "Die & Drab"; yet still it strikes against my feelings as a note out of time & as not co-alescing with that *pastoral* TINT*ᵃ* which gives such a charm to this IV*th* Act. It is too Macbeth-like in the "Snapper-up of unconsidered trifles".

57   III 302–3, pencil, overtraced | IV iii 116–20

PERDITA.   . . . O *Proserpina,*
    For the flowrs now, that, frighted, thou let'st fall
    From *Dis*'s waggon! ∧ daffadils,
    That come before the swallow dares, and take
    The winds of *March* with beauty; violets dim . . .

∧ an epithet is wanting here not merely or chiefly for the Metre, but for the *Balance*, for the *æsthetic* Logic. Perhaps "*golden*", or "*brighter*" which would set off the "violets dim."*

    * "brightest" would, (tho' to my ear not unpleasingly) jingle with "frighted"; "glorious" was perhaps the word dropt out.[1]   S: T: C:

58   III 302, pencil, overtraced | IV iii 122–5

PERDITA.   . . . pale primroses,*
    That die unmarried, ere they can behold
    Bright *Phoebus* in his strength; (a malady
    Most incident to maids;) . . .

* "and the rathe Primrose that forsaken dies"—MILTON.[1]

59   III 312–13, pencil, overtraced; marked with a pencil line in the margin | IV iii 441–50

PERDITA.   Even here undone:
    I was not much afraid; for once or twice
    I was about to speak, and tell him plainly,

56*ᵃ* Small caps (double underlining) not in overtracing

57[1] This line has been accepted as it   58[1] Milton *Lycidas* line 142.
stands by other commentators.

The self-same sun, that shines upon his court,
Hides not his visage from our cottage, but
Looks on alike. Wilt please you, Sir, be gone? [*To* Flor.
I told you, what would come of this. 'Beseech you,
Of your own state take care: this dream of mine,
Being now awake, I'll queen it no inch farther,
But milk my ewes, and weep.

O how more than exquisitly is this whole Speech & that profound Nature
of noble Pride & Grief venting themselves in a momentary peevishness
of Resentment toward Florizel "wilt please you Sir be gone"[a]

60   III 316, pencil, overtraced | IV iii 565–8

CAMILLO.   A course more promising
    Than a wild dedication of yourselves
   *To unpath'd waters, undream'd/ shores, most certain,
    To miseries enough . . .

* I suspect some corruption in this Line. As Theobald punctuates it, it is
neither metre nor meaning.[1]

61   III 320, pencil, overtraced | IV iii 722–6

AUTOLICUS. A lye; you are rough and hairy; let me have no lying; it becomes none but tradesmen, and they often give us soldiers the lye; but
we pay them for it with stamped coin, not stabbing steel, therefore they
do not *give* us the lye.*

* As we *pay* them, they therefore do not *give* it us[1]

62   III 322, pencil, overtraced | IV iii 787–90

AUTOLICUS. . . . . then raw as he is . . . shall he be set against a brick-wall,
the sun looking with a southward eye upon death.*

I cannot avoid suspecting the word "death". I should prefer the simple
"him"; but at all events it should be, [a]meâ quidem sententiâ,[b1] "upon *his*
Death."[2]   S. T. C.—

59[a] Three or four further words in pencil have been erased   **62**[a–b] Not overtraced

60[1] Apparently a typo peculiar to this
edition. The line should read, "To unpath'd
waters, undream'd shores; most certain . . .".
61[1] This was Johnson's explanation too,
widely accepted: "The meaning is, they are

paid for lying, therefore they do not *give* us
the lie, they *sell* it us" (*Sh*—Reed).
62[1] "In my opinion at least".
62[2] Other editions read "him" without
comment.

62A   III 328, pencil | v i 139–41

FLORIZEL.   . . . and from him
   Give you all greetings, that a King, (at̸s friend)
   Can send his brother . . .

63   III 337, pencil | v iii 14–18

PAULINA.   As she lived peerless,
   So her dead likeness, I do well believe
   Excels whatever yet you look'd upon,
   Or hand of man hath done; therefore I keep it
   Lovely, apart.

perhaps, n for v. i.e. *lonely*[1]

64   III 346, pencil, overtraced | *King John* I i 35–6

ELINOR. . . . This might have been prevented, and ∧
   With very easy arguments of love . . .

∧ Should we not add some such phrase as "that too" Not that a foot is
wanting; but that the 8 syllable line make[a] no metre.[1]

65   III 353–5, part in pencil, overtraced | I i 230–1

PHILIP. *James Gurney*, wilt thou give us leave awhile?
GURNEY. Good leave, good *Philip*.
PHILIP.   *Philip!*—spare me, *James* . . .

[Warburton had suggested "spare me" for the original "sparrow";
Theobald incorporates his emendation.]

O true Warburton! and the sancta Simplicitas[1] of honest dull Theobald's
Faith in him!—Nothing can be more lively or characteristic than Philip?
Sparrow! [a]Had Warburton read old Skelton's "Phillip Sparrow["], an ex-

---

64[a] For "makes": perhaps an error in the overtracing only
65[a] Continuing in pencil, overtraced

63[1] The Folio reads "Louely"; Hanmer appears to have been the first to see the likelihood of the press error that C notices. *Sh* (Reed) and *Sh* (Arden) both give "Lonely".

64[1] A typo in C's copy. The line should read ". . . prevented, and made whole".

65[1] "Holy Simplicity". This phrase has been used in many contexts, the most appropriate here perhaps being the apocryphal attribution to John Huss at the stake commenting on the innocent faith of an old man who came with his contribution of faggots to feed the flames.

quisite & original Poem, & no doubt popular in Shakespears time, even Warburton would scarcely have made so deep a plunge into the Bathetic as to have deathified *Sparrow* into *Spare* me.[2]

66   III 361 | II i 185–90

CONSTANCE. But God hath made her sin and her the plague
  On this removed issue, plagu'd for her,
  And with her plague her sin; his injury,
  Her injury, the beadle to her sin,
  All punish'd in the person of this child,
  And all for her, a plague upon her!

This cannot but be a corrupt Text.[1]

67   III 376, pencil | III i 104–5

CONSTANCE. The grapling vigour, and rough frown of war,
  Is <u>cold</u> in amity and painted peace . . .

Qu? coil'd?[1]

68   III 377–9, pencil, marked with pencil lines in the margins

AUSTRIA. Methinks, that *Richard*'s pride and *Richard*'s fall
  Should be a precedent to fright you, Sir.
FALCONBRIDGE. What words are these? how do my sinews shake!
  My father's foe clad in my father's spoil!
  How doth *Alecto* whisper in mine ears,
  "Delay not, *Richard*, kill the villain straight;
  "Disrobe him of the matchless monument,
  "Thy father's triumph o'er the savages—["]
  Now by his soul I swear, my father's soul,
  Twice will I not review the morning's rise,

65[2] "Philip" was apparently a popular name for pet sparrows, and Shakespeare's 18th-century editors came to his defence by explaining that the name represents the sparrow's call "phip, phip", and by producing contemporary parallels such as the one C cites, John Skelton's *Phyllyp Sparowe* (1542), a mock elegy for a sparrow killed by Gib the cat.
66[1] C returns to this passage in COPY B 7. Editors agree that the text is difficult, but they differ about ways of dealing with it, generally choosing paraphrase (in notes) over emendation. Cf *Sh* (Arden): "The sense of these intentionally obscure lines is that Arthur is punished for Eleanor's sins and by her person."
67[1] Hanmer had found the metaphor confusing, and proposed changing "cold" to "cool'd", but later editors have not usually considered it necessary to alter the line.

Till I have torn that trophy from thy back;
And split thy heart, for wearing it so long.

omit[a1]

69 III 386, pencil, overtraced | III ii 1–3

FALCONBRIDGE. Now, by my life, this day grows wond'rous hot;
Some fiery devil hovers in the sky,
And pours down mischief.

[Theobald accepts Warburton's alteration of "airy" to "fiery"]

I prefer "airy"; the word "Devil" implies "fiery".[a] One need only read the Line, laying a full & strong emphasis on *Devil* to perceive the uselessness & tastelessness of W's alteration. Some airy DEVIL hovers in the Sky[1]

70 IV [3] | *Richard II* (fly-title)

From the Length of the Speeches, the number of long Speeches, and that (with one exception) the events are all *historical*, presented in their *results* not produced by acts seen, ~~on the Stage~~ or that take place before the audience, this Tragedy is ill-suited to our present large Theatres—But in itself, and for the Closet I feel no hesitation in placing it the first and most admirable of all Shakespear's *purely* historical Plays.[1] For the two parts of Henry the IVth form a species of themselves, which may be named the *mixt* drama.—The distinction does not depend on the quantity of historical events compared with the fictions, for there is as much *History* in Macbeth as in Richard, but in the relation of the History to the Plot—in the purely historical plays the History ~~dir~~ *informs* the plot, in the mixt it *directs* it—in the rest, as Macbeth, Hamlet, Cymbeline, Lear, it subserves it.

71 IV 6–7, marked with a line in the margin | I i 41–6

BOLINGBROKE. . . . . Since, the more fair and crystal is the sky,
The uglier seem the clouds, that in it fly.

68[a] The text spreading over 3 pp, C has written "omit" three times
69[a] Here C has written "*" and continued the note in the foot-margin with "*"

68[1] These lines are not Shakespeare's; they were taken from an earlier *King John* and interpolated into Shakespeare's text by Pope, to the resounding disapproval of later editors: *Sh* (Reed) prints the passage in a footnote.

69[1] Warburton's emendation was disregarded by later editors.

70[1] In COPY D **40**, C refers to this as "the purest Historic Play" of all of Shakespeare's works.

Once more, the more to aggravate the note,
With a foul traitor's name stuff I thy throat:
And wish, so please my Sov'reign, ere I move,
What my tongue speaks, my right-drawn sword may prove.

These six Lines are suspicious. At all events they are out of place[1]

72   IV 92, pencil, overtraced | *1 Henry IV* I i 5–6

KING. . . . No more the thirsty entrance of this soil
   Shall damp her lips with her own children's blood . . .

[Theobald's note:] . . . The expression is very obscure; but I take this to
be the meaning: That the *thirsty* earth, *chapt* and *flaw'd* with *drought*,
shall no more *damp* or *moisten* her lips, or surface, with her own children's blood.

It is a most obscure passage; but I think Theob's interpretation right, vizt.
that thirsty entrance means the dry penetrability ~~of~~ or bibulous drought
of the Soil. The obscurity of the passage is of the Shakespearean sort.

73   IV 96–7, pencil, erased, largely illegible | I ii 23–9

FALSTAFF. Marry then, sweet wag, when thou art King, let not us that are
   squires of the night's body, be call'd thieves of the day's booty. Let us
   be *Diana*'s foresters, gentlemen of the shade, minions of the moon; and
   let men say, we be men of good government, being governed as the sea
   is, by our noble and chaste mistress the moon . . .

[Theobald's note defends his substitution of "booty" for the usual reading "beauty":] . . . and this I take to be the meaning. Let us not be called
thieves, the purloiners of that *booty*, which, to the proprietors, was the
purchase of honest labour and industry by day.

I cannot explain the phrase but Beauty & [. . . . .] rogue, in both Beauty
and [. . . . .][1]

74   IV 213 | *2 Henry IV* II ii 166

PRINCE HENRY. Fare ye well: Go. This *Dol Tear-Sheet* should be some
   road.*

* This passage might suggest a *Quere*, whether Shakespear did not name

71[1] C seems to be alone in objecting to
these lines.
73[1] C himself proposes "booty" as an
emendation in COPY B 8, and notes a parallel text to support that reading in JONSON
32.

this Street-walker Dol Tear-street—*Terere viam.*[1] Else what means the some Road?[2]

75 IV 229 | III i 30–1

KING HENRY. . . . then happy low! lie down;
    Uneasy lies the head, that wears a crown.

[Theobald's note:] Though I have not disturb'd the text, Mr. *Warburton* thinks, *Shakespeare* would not have used so poor a repetition as *lie down* and *uneasy lies.**

* I know no arguments by which to persuade any one of my opinion or rather of my feeling; but yet I cannot help *feeling* that Happy *low—lie—down!* is either a proverbial expression or the burthen of some old Song—& means, Happy the man who lays himself down on his Straw-bed or Chaff-pallat on the ground or floor.[1]

76 IV 239 | III ii 278–86

SHALLOW. He is not his craft-master, he doth not do it right. I remember at Mile-End-Green, when I lay at *Clement's-Inn*,(24) I was then Sir *Dagonet* in *Arthur*'s show;(25) there was a little quiver fellow, and he would manage you his piece thus; and he would about, and about, and come you in, and come you in: Rah, tah, tah, would he say; bounce, would he say, and away again would he go, and again would he come: I shall never see such a fellow.

[Theobald's notes:] (24) . . . The only intelligence I have glean'd of this worthy wight, Sir *Dagonet*, is from *Beaumont* and *Fletcher* in their *Knight* of the *Burning Pestle*.

Boy. Besides, it will show ill favouredly to have a *Grocer's prentice to court a King's daughter.*

Cit. Will it so, Sir? you are well read in histories! I pray you, what was Sir *Dagonet*? was not he *prentice* to a *Grocer* in *London*? read the play of the *Four Prentices* of *London*, where they toss their pikes so: &c.
(25) . . . This extreme fine sketch of nature and humour . . . seems, in my

74[1] "To tread a road": *terere* in this sense is cognate with *terere* meaning "to rub", "to wear out", etc, hence C's "tear". C repeats this speculation in COPY B 12, COPY D 57. Steevens had earlier proposed—and found analogues for—"a tearer of sheets", which is a more obvious explanation of the name: *Sh* (Reed).

74[2] Prostitutes were vulgarly likened to much-travelled streets and common highways, as both *Sh* (Reed) and *Sh* (Arden) indicate.

75[1] C appears to be alone in this speculation.

opinion, invidiously enough sneer'd at in the *Burning Pestle* above quoted.

That B. and F. have more than once been guilty of sneering at their great master, cannot I fear be denied;[1] but the passage here quoted is ⟨an⟩ *imitation*. If it be chargeable with any fault, it is with Plagiary not with Sarcasm.[2]

77   IV 243 | IV i 93–4

YORK. My brother general, the commonwealth,
    To brother born an houshold cruelty,
    I make my quarrel in particular.

[Theobald's note:] From the same corrected old *quarto* I retriev'd the intermediate line now added to the text; and which, as Mr. *Warburton* observ'd to me, is a very sensible and very necessary line. "The sense is this; (says my ingenious friend;) my brother general the commonwealth, which ought to be the nursing father of us all, equally distributing its benefits, is become an houshold enemy even to those of his own house, to *brothers born*; by disinheriting some who have an equal title to the patrimony with others, to whom it gives all: And this I make my quarrel. . . ."

Spite of Mr W. there is surely either a corruption here, or an omission of a line, or this line is interpolated. Perhaps, a single 's to commonwealth might give a sense.—
                    the Commonwealth's
    (To brother born an *household*) Cruelty &c.[1]

78   IV 294–7 | *Henry V* I ii 125–7

WESTMORLAND. They know, your Grace hath cause, and means, and might,(6)
    So hath your Highness; never King of *England*
    Had nobles richer, and more loyal subjects . . .

76[1] The suggestion is that in *The Knight of the Burning Pestle* (pub 1613), Beaumont and Fletcher were making fun of the figure of Shallow in *2 Henry IV*. C comments on their "base and silly Sneers at Shakespear" also in JONSON **31**.

76[2] C comments on their imitation of Shakespeare likewise in BEAUMONT & FLETCHER COPY A **4**, COPY B **58**; and on a "parody" in COPY A **2**.

77[1] The second line does not appear in the Folio; commentators agree that even without it, the passage is obscure. Several attempts had been made to explain or emend the passage before C's, but his suggestion was new.

[Theobald note (6):]

> *They know your Grace hath cause, and means and might;*
> *So hath your Highness, never King of England*
> *Had nobles richer,—*

Thus has this speech hitherto been most stupidly pointed, without any regard to common sense.

Does "Grace" mean the King's own peculiar Domains, & legal revenue, & "Highness" his feudal rights in the military services of his nobles?—I have sometimes thought it possible, that the words "Grace" and "cause" might have been transposed in the copying, or printing—[1]

> They know, your Cause hath grace, &c.

What T. meant, I cannot guess. To me his pointing makes the passage still more obscure. I should recite the Lines dramatically—

> They know, your Grace hath cause & means & might:—
> So hath your Highness—Never K. of E.
> HAD nobles richer or more loyal subjects.

viz. a break off from ~~the~~ grammar & natural order from earnestness—in order to give the meaning more passionately.

79 IV 295 | I ii 174–5

EXETER. It follows then, the cat must stay at home,
   Yet that is but a *'scus'd* necessity . . .

[Theobald's note mentions two alternative readings, "curs'd" and "crush'd".]

either crash for *crass*, from crassus, = clumsy: or curt, defective, imperfect—cur'd would be better than *scus'd*.[1]

80 IV 296 | **79** textus continued I ii 176–83

   Since we have locks to safeguard necessaries,
   [a]And pretty traps to catch the petty thieves.
   While that the armed hand doth fight abroad,
   Th' advised head defends itself at home:

80[a] From here to the end of textus marked with an ink line in the margin

78[1] This line has been variously explained, and occasionally repunctuated or emended (Warburton had suggested reading "race" for "grace"), but not as C proposes.

79[1] The Quarto reading is "curs'd", the Folio "crush'd". Warburton had suggested "'scused", Hanmer "o' course", Johnson "crude"; Steevens defended "curs'd": *Sh* (Reed).

For government, though high, and low, and lower,
Put into parts, doth keep in one consent;
Congreeing in a full and natural close,
Like musick.

—This Speech belongs, I doubt not, to Cant. not Ex. and altered for & by the Actors.[1]

81   IV 359–61 | IV v 1–6

CONSTABLE. *O Diable!*
ORLEANS. *O Signieur! le jour est perdu, tout est perdu.*
DAUPHIN. *Mort de ma vie!* all is confounded, all!
Reproach and everlasting shame
Sits mocking in our plumes.
O meschante fortune!—do not run away.

Ludicrous as these introductory Scraps of French appear, so instantly followed by good nervous mother-english, yet they are judicious, & produce the impression, *Sh.* intended—a sudden *feeling* struck at once, on the ears as well as eyes of the Audience, that here come the *French*—the baffled *French* Braggards!—And this will appear still more judicious, when we reflect on the scanty apparatus of distinguishing Dresses in Shakespear's Tyring-room.[1]   *S. T. C.*

82   VI ⁻5–⁻2 | *King Lear*

It is well worthy notice, that Lear is the only serious performance of Shakespear, the interest & situation of which are derived from the assumption of a gross Improbability[;][a] whereas Beaumont & Fletcher's Tragedies are, almost all, founded on some out-of-the-way Accident or Exception to the general Experience of Mankind.[1]—But observe the matchless Judgement of Shakespear!—First, improbable as the Conduct of Lear is, in the first Scene, yet it was an old Story, rooted in the popular Faith—a thing taken for granted already, & consequently, without any

82[a] Punctuation mark lost in remounting the flyleaf

80[1] There does not appear to be any precedent for this proposal.

81[1] References to costume are rare in C's commentary on Shakespeare, though he uses the Prologue to *Henry V* as evidence of the scanty physical resources of Shakespeare's theatre in lectures of 1811–12 and 1813: *Lects 1808–1819 (CC)* I 228 and n

32, 519 and n 26.

82[1] For C's regular use of Beaumont and Fletcher as foils to Shakespeare, see e.g. BEAUMONT & FLETCHER COPY A 9, COPY B 20, 21, 41, 49, 57, 65; also *Lects 1808–1819 (CC)* II 145–52, *TT (CC)* I 401, 464, 467–8.

of the *effects* of Improbability.[2] 2ndly—It is merely the canvass to the Characters & Passions, a mere *occasion*—not (as in B. & F.) perpetually recurring, as the cause & sine quâ non of the Incidents & Emotions.—Let the first Scene of Lear have been lost, & let it be only understood that a fond Father had been duped by ~~th~~ hypocritical professions of Love & Duty on the part of two Daughters to disinherit a third, previously, & deservedly, more dear to him/ & all the rest of the Tragedy would retain its ~~whol~~ interest, undiminished, & be perfectly intelligible. The *Accidental* is no where the ground-work of the Passions; but the καθολον,[3] that which in all Ages has been & ever will be close & native to the heart of Man—Parental Anguish from filial Ingratitude, the genuineness of worth, tho' coffered in bluntness, the vileness of smooth Iniquity—Perhaps, I ought to have added the Merchant of Venice; but here too the same remarks apply.[4] It was an old Tale: & substitute any other danger, than that of the Pound of Flesh, (the circumstance in which the improbability lies) yet all the situations & the emotions ap~~propriate~~pertaining to them remain equally excellent & appropriate.—Whereas take away from "the Mad Lover" the fantastic hypothesis of his engagement to cut out his own Heart, & have it presented to his Mistress, & all the main Scenes must go with it.[5]

Kotzebue is the German B. & F., without their poetic powers & without their vis comica.[6] But like them he always deduces his situations & passions from marvellous Accidents, & the trick of bringing one part of our moral nature to counteract another—as our pity for misfortune & admiration of generosity ⟨& Courage⟩ to combat our Condemnation of Guilt, as in Adultery, Robbery &c: & like them too, he excels in his mode of telling a story clearly, & interestingly, in a series of dramatic Dialogues. Only the trick of making Tragedy-Heroes & Heroines out of

82² C gave an extended analysis of the first scene in his lecture of 28 Jan 1819: COPY D **75**, *Lects 1808–1819* (*CC*) II 322–9.

82³ The "universal", incorrect as in BEAUMONT & FLETCHER COPY A **5** (and n 2) and elsewhere.

82⁴ C makes the same point about improbability, linking *Lear* with *The Merchant of Venice*, in the lectures of 28 Oct 1813 and 28 Jan 1819: *Lects 1808–1819* (*CC*) I 520, II 326 (COPY D **75**). For a context in earlier critics' complaints about Shakespeare's plots, see *Lects 1808–1819*

(*CC*) I 117 and n 13.

82⁵ There is a single note (not addressing this point) on *The Mad Lover* in C's copy: BEAUMONT & FLETCHER COPY B **40**.

82⁶ "Comic power". C repeats this point, referring to "*Beaumont* and *Fletcher*, the *Kotzebues* of his day" in the 1813 lecture cited in n 4; cf a more extended comparison in *TT* (*CC*) II 325, and remarks on the superiority of the two English dramatists to the school of Kotzebue in *BL* ch 23 (*CC*) II 212.

Shopkeepers & Barmaids was too low for the age, & too unpoetic for the genius, of Beaumont & Fletcher, infcrior in every respect as they are to their great Predecessor & Contemporary! *How* inferior would ~~he~~ they have appeared, had not Shakespear existed for them to *imitate*?—which in every play, more or less, they do—& in their Tragedies most glaringly—and yet (o Shame! Shame!) miss no opportunity of sneering at the divine Man & subdetracting from his Merits!!—   S. T. Coleridge
    1 Jany 1813.   71, Berners' St, Oxford Street.

83 vi 15–17 | i ii 9–14

EDMUND.   . . . why brand they us
    With base? with baseness? bastardy? base, base?
    Who, in the lusty stealth of nature, take
    More composition and fierce quality;
    Than doth, within a dull, stale, tired bed,
    Go to the creating a whole tribe of fops . . .

[Warburton cites these lines as characteristic of Edmund's atheism and quotes the wish of the atheist Vanini that he might have been born out of wedlock, for reasons similar to those given by Edmund in defence of his own birth.]

Poor Vanini! Any one but Warburton would have thought the Quotation more characteristic of Mr Shandy than of Atheism![1] If the Fact really were so, (which it not only is not, but almost contrary) I do not see, why the most confirmed Theist might not very rationally utter the same Wish. But it is proverbial, that the youngest Son in a large Family is commonly the man of the greatest Talents of the Family, et incalescere in venerem ardentiùs, spei Sobolis injuriosum.[2]   *S. T. C.*

84 vi 104–5 | v i 24–7

ALBANY.   . . . 'fore this business,
    It toucheth us, as *France* invades our land,
    (Not holds the King, with others, whom, I fear,
    Most just and heavy causes make oppose,)—

83[1] C thought of Tristram's father Walter Shandy—in Sterne's *Tristram Shandy*—perhaps partly as a devotee of ingenious or paradoxical arguments, and certainly as a fictional representative of "dull, stale, tired" marriages.

83[2] C switches to Latin presumably to spare the blushes of the Morgan women. Tr "and to be heated too violently in love is detrimental to the hope of offspring".

[Theobald gives the "old quarto" text:]
—for *this business,*
It touches us, as France *invades our land,*
Not holds the King, with others whom I fear
Most just and heavy causes make oppose . . .

Evidently the old reading is the right one. As to this business, however, I do feel myself honestly engaged, I mean, as far as we are resisting *Invasion*, not in relation to the good King & other justly provoked opponents, of our own Countrymen. *S. T. C.*

85 VI 126–8 | *Timon of Athens* I i 128–31

TIMON. The man is honest.
OLD ATHENIAN. Therefore he will be, *Timon.*
His honesty rewards him in itself,
It must not bear my daughter.

[Warburton paraphrases:] "If the man be honest, my Lord, for that reason he will be so in this; and not endeavour at the injustice of gaining my daughter without my consent."

Like all W's comments, ingenious in Blunder—he can never see any other Writer's Thoughts for the mist-making Swarm of his own. The meaning of the first Line the Poet himself explains or rather unfolds in the second. "The man is honest./—True! and for that very cause, & with no additional or extrinsic motive, he will be so. No man can be justly called honest, who is not so for honesty's sake, itself including its own reward.["][1]

Mem: that Honesty in S's age retained much of its old dignity, & that contra-distinction of the Honestum from the Utile, in which its very Essence & Definition consisted.[2] If it be *honestum*, it can not depend on the Utile.— *S. T. C.*

86 VI 129–31 | I i 247–51

*APEMANTUS. So, so! aches contract, and starve your supple joints! that there should be small love amongst these sweet knaves, and all this courtesy! the strain of man's bred out into baboon and monkey.

85[1] C's paraphrase is in harmony with the predominant interpretation: cf Malone in *Sh* (Reed), and *Sh* (Arden).

85[2] I.e. of the "honourable" or "morally right" from the "useful" or "profitable". The whole of bk 3 of Cicero *De officiis* is devoted to the subject: C refers to this work specifically in *CN* IV 4939.

* As Morgan allows me thus to spoil his Book, I will remark here the fineness of Shakespear's sense of musical period, which would almost have of itself suggested (if the hundred positive proofs had not been extant) that the word "aches" was then a dissyllable = aitches.[1] For read it "akes", in this sentence, & I would challenge you to find any period in Shakespear's writings with the same musical, or rather dissonant, notation.—Try the one and then the other, by your ear, reading the sentence aloud, first with aches as a dissyllable & then as a monosyllable, & you will feel what I mean—N.B. This is not meant to palliate, much less justify, Kemble's insufferable Coxcombry.[2]

87   vi 134 | i ii 125–7

CUPID. . . . . Th' ear, taste, touch, and smell, pleas'd from thy table rise,
   These only now come but to feast thine eyes.

[Theobald's note praises Warburton's "incomparable emendation" of the original: "There taste, touch, all, pleas'd from thy table rise: / They only now . . . "]

This *is* an excellent Emendation.   S. T. C.

88   vi 138 | i ii 230–1

APEMANTUS.   What a coil's here,
   Serving of becks and jutting out of bums!

[Theobald's note:] I have not ventur'd to alter this phrase, tho' I confess freely, I don't understand it. It may be made intelligible two ways, with very slight alteration. Mr. *Warburton* acutely propos'd to me,
   Serring *of becks,*—
from the *French* word *serrer,* to join close together, to lock one within another; by a *metaphor* taken from the *billing of pigeons,* who intersert their bills into one another.—Or, we might read,
   Serving of backs, *and jutting out of bums!* For *Apemantus* is observing

---

86[1] C is correct on this point, which does not appear to have been commented on by his predecessors.

86[2] The *DNB* notes that "Kemble's affectations of speech were the subject of much satire", and mentions his pronunciation of "aches" as "aitches" as one of the few such affectations that could be justified.

According to a report of one of the 1813 lectures, C said of his first-hand experience of John Philip Kemble's Macbeth and his sister Sarah Siddons's Lady Macbeth that "these might be the Macbeths of the Kembles, but they were not the Macbeths of Shakespear": *Lects 1808–1819* (*CC*) i 563.

on the ridiculous *congees*, and complimental motions of the flattering guests in taking their leave. Both conjectures are submitted to judgment.

—The latter is probable, & requirita[1] as thesis for the antithesis.[2]

89   vi 140–1 | ii i 17–19

SENATOR.   . . . nor then silenc'd with
   Commend me to your master—and the cap*
   Plays in the right hand, thus . . .

* either, methinks, "Plays" should be "play'd", or "and" should be changed to "while". I can certainly understand it as a parenthesis, an interadditive of Scorn; but it does not sound to my ear as in Shakespear's manner—[1]

90   vi 141 | ii ii 4–6

FLAVIUS.   . . . and resumes no care
   Of what is to continue: never mind
   Was to be so unwise, to be so kind.*

I suspect the first "*to be*" in this Line[1]

91   vi 145–7 | ii ii 129–32

TIMON. . . . . Perchance some single vantages you took,
   When my indisposition put you back:
   And that unaptness made your? minister*
   Thus to excuse yourself.

* at least, I cannot otherwise understand the Line—you took,—& made my chance indisposition & ⟨occasional⟩ unaptness your minister (i.e. the ground on which you now) excuse yourself. Or perhaps no correction is necessary, if we construe "made you" as "~~you~~ did you make"—and that unaptness did you make help you Thus to excuse yourself. But the former seems more in Shakespear's manner, & is less liable to be misunderstood.[1]

88[1] "Required".
88[2] The phrase "serving of becks" is usually explained, without emendation, as referring to greeting with a nod—in Johnson's gloss reported in *Sh* (Reed), "a salutation made with the head".
89[1] Other commentators do not appear to have been troubled by these lines.

90[1] Although the line has been thought obscure, editors from the 18th century onwards have dealt with it by explanation rather than by emendation.
91[1] The First Folio reads "your", the Second "you", as Johnson had pointed out, himself preferring "your": *Sh* (Reed).

92   vi 154–5 | iii iii 31–4

SERVILIUS. . . . How fairly this Lord strives to appear foul? takes virtuous copies to be wicked: <u>like those that under hot, ardent, zeal would set whole realms on fire. Of such a nature is his politick love.</u>

This I grievously suspect to have been an addition of the Players, which had *hit*, & being constantly applauded procured a settled occupancy in the Prompter's Copy.[1] Not that Shakespear does not elsewhere sneer at the Puritans; but ⟨here⟩ it is introduced so nolente volente,[2] by head & shoulders—& is besides so much more likely to have been conceived in the age of Charles the first/.

93   vi 168–73 | iv iii 9

TIMON. . . . Raise me this beggar, and denude that Lord . . .

[Warburton has introduced "denude" in place of "deny't".]

I cannot see the necessity of this alteration.[1] The Editors are all of them ready enough to cry out against Shakespear's laxities & licences of Style, forgetting that he is not merely a Poet but a *dramatic* Poet—that when the Head & Heart are swelling with fullness, a man does not ask himself whether he has grammatically *arranged*, but only whether (context taken in) he has *conveyed*, his meaning. "Deny" is here clearly equal to "withhold"—& the "it" quite in the genius of vehement conversation (which a Syntaxist explains by ellipses & *subauditurs*[2] in a Greek or Latin Classic as yet triumphs over, as ignorance, in a Contemporary) refers to accidental & artificial Rank or Elevation, implied in the verb "Raise".

S. T. C.

? Does the word *"denude"* occur in any Writer before or of Shak[r's] Age?[3]

92[1] C made the same conjecture in 1818, according to Collier, alluding to "the clumsy 'clap-trap' blow at the Puritans in Act iii. sc. 3, as an interpolation by the actor of the part of Timon's servant": *Lects 1808–1819 (CC)* II 247. The interpretation of the lines as a satire against the Puritans dates back to Warburton, who did not, however, question their being of Shakespeare's composition. The continuation of the note here shows that C meant that he thought the lines a very late addition, possibly dating from the Restoration.

92[2] From *nolens volens*, i.e. dragged in "willy-nilly" or "by hook or by crook".

93[1] It had the support of Malone and Steevens (*Sh*—Reed), but later editors agree with C: *Sh* (Arden).

93[2] That which is not spoken, but understood: C uses the term also in J. SEDGWICK **19** at n 3.

93[3] In the sense of "make naked or bare", all the illustrations for "denude" in the *OED* postdate Shakespeare.

94 VI 206–8 | *Titus Andronicus*

[Theobald's note on VI 205 argues against admitting *Titus Andronicus* into the Shakespeare canon on the grounds that it was already "on the stage" before Shakespeare came to London:] . . . Ben Johnson in the induction to his *Bartholomew-Fair*, (which made its first appearance in the year 1614) couples *Jeronymo* and *Andronicus* in reputation, and speaks of them as plays of twenty-five or thirty years standing. Consequently, *Andronicus* must have been on the stage, before *Shakespeare* left *Warwickshire* to come and reside in *London:* and I never heard it so much as intimated, that he [Shakespeare] had turned his genius to stage-writing, before he associated with the players, and became one of their body.

That Sh. never "turned his genius to Stage-writing" (as T. Theobaldicè[1] phrases it) is an assertion of about as much authority as the precious Story that he left Stratford for Deer-stealing, and lived by holding Gentlemen's Horses at the Doors of the Theatre & other trash of that Arch-gossip, old Aubrey.[2]—The metre is an argument against its being Shakespear's worth a score such chronological Surmises. Yet I incline to think that both in this and in Jeronymo Shakespear wrote some passages, and that they are the earliest of his Compositions—[3]

95 VI 271 | v ii 21–59, marked with a line in the margin

TITUS. I am not mad; I know thee well enough;
 Witness this wretched stump, these crimson lines,

94[1] "T[heobald] Theobaldishly".

94[2] John Aubrey (1626–97) was the source of several legends about Shakespeare—namely, that he was the son of a Stratford butcher; that he spent some time as a country schoolmaster; and that he fathered William Davenant—but not of the deer-stealing or horse-holding stories that C mentions specifically: see S. Schoenbaum *Shakespeare's Lives* (Oxford 1970) 100–1, 106–7, 116–17. The "Minutes of Lives" that Aubrey recorded for Anthony Wood's *Athenae Oxonienses* (1690) were first published as *Letters Written by Eminent Persons in the Seventeenth and Eighteenth Centuries* in 1813, and C may have read what is now known as *Brief Lives* or seen reviews of it then. He was reading Aubrey's *Miscellanies* in 1818 (*CN* III 4390, 4393 and nn), but much earlier (c 1807) references to Aubrey's "gossiping Testimony"

in ANDERSON COPY B 3 show that C had been aware of Aubrey, at least by reputation, for a long time.

94[3] By "Jeronymo" C and Theobald mean Thomas Kyd's *Spanish Tragedy*; C consistently maintained, at least from 1809 on, that some scenes in it, the mad scenes, were part of Shakespeare's earlier dramatic work: *Friend* (*CC*) II 495, *Lects 1808–1819* (*CC*) II 373 and n 4. The extent of Shakespeare's responsibility for *Titus Andronicus* was and still is a matter of debate among scholars: though C himself evidently entertained doubts occasionally, in Lect 2 of the 1813 series he referred to it as "admitted not to have been Shakespear's" and in Lect 2 of the 1818–19 series—as here—he used the "rhythmless Metre" of the play as evidence against it: *Lects 1808–1819* (*CC*) I 527 and n 3, II 284, 301 and n 25; COPY D 35, **151**.

Witness these trenches, made by grief and care,
Witness the tiring day and heavy night;
Witness all sorrow, that I know thee well
For our proud Empress, mighty *Tamora:*
Is not thy coming for my other hand?

TAMORA. Know thou, sad man, I am not *Tamora:*
She is thy enemy, and I am thy friend;
I am Revenge, sent from th'infernal kingdom,
To ease the gnawing vulture of thy mind,
By working wreakful vengeance on thy foes.
Come down, and welcome me to this world's light;
Confer with me of murder and of death;
There's not a hollow cave, nor lurking place,
No vast obscurity, or misty vale,
Where bloody murder or detested rape
Can couch for fear, but I will find them out;
And in their ears tell them my dreadful name,
Revenge,/! ~~which makes the foul offender quake.~~

TITUS. ~~Art thou~~ Revenge? and art thou sent to me,
To be a torment to mine enemies?

TAMORA. I am; therefore come down, and welcome me.

TITUS. Do me some service, ere I come to thee:
Lo, by thy side where Rape and Murder stand;
Now give some surance that thou art Revenge,
Stab them, or tear them on thy chariot-wheels;
And then I'll come and be thy waggoner,
And whirl along with thee about the globes:
Provide two proper palfries black as jet,
To hale thy vengeful waggon swift away,
And find out murders in their guilty caves.
And when thy car is loaden with their heads,
I will dismount, and by thy waggon wheel
Trot like a servile foot-man all day long;
Even from *Hyperion*'s rising in the east,
Until his very downfal in the sea.
And day by day I'll do this heavy task,
So thou destroy Rapine and Murder there.

These Lines, I think it not improbable, were written by Shakespear, in his earliest period.—[1]

95[1] See **94** n 3.

96   VI 295 | *Macbeth* I iii 137–8

MACBETH.   . . . present feats
    Are less than horrible imaginings.

[Theobald follows Warburton in emending "fears" to "feats".]

Mercy on this most wilful Ingenuity of Blundering, which was the very
Warburton of Warburton—his Being!—*Fears* here are *present* fear-
striking Objects—Terribilia adstantia—[1]

97   VI 297 | I iv 22–5

MACBETH. The service and the loyalty I owe,
    In doing it, pays itself. Your Highness' part
    Is to receive our duties; and our duties
    Are to your throne, and state, children and servants . . .

reasoning/ instead of Joy!! effort, stammering Rep. of "Duties—"

98   VI 297 | I iv 31–5

KING.   . . . let me enfold thee,
    And hold thee to my heart.
BANQUO.   There if I grow,
    The harvest is your own.
KING. —————   My plenteous joys,
    Wanton in fulness, seek to hide themselves
    In drops of sorrow. . . .

Compare with vulgar Dramatists, whose characters seem to have made
their speeches as Actors learn them/

99   VI 298 | I iv 37–42

KING. . . . We will establish our Estate upon
    Our eldest *Malcolm*, whom we name hereafter
    The Prince of *Cumberland:* which honour must,
    Not unaccompanied, invest him only;
    But signs of Nobleness, like stars, shall shine
    On all deservers.—

Messiah = Satan/[1]

96[1] C translates his English phrase into
Latin: "Terrible things standing close by".
Warburton's substitution of "feats" for
"fears" has found few supporters.

99[1] C's cryptic note is written next to
textus lines 3–4. If this is indeed the correct
textus, C may be noticing that Malcolm
combines features associated with the Son

100 VI 298 | I iv 44

MACBETH. The rest is labour, which is not us'd for you . . .

Hollow Hyperb.

101 VI 299 | I v 40–3

LADY MACBETH. . . . Come, all you spirits
    That tend on mortal thoughts, unsex me here;
    And fill me, from the crown to th' toe, top-full
    Of direst cruelty . . .

one who had habitually familiarized her Imag[1] to dreadful Conceptions, & is now trying to do it still more/

102 VI 300–1 | I v 53–4

LADY MACBETH. Nor heav'n peep through the <u>blanket</u> of the dark,*
    To cry, hold, hold!

* Height is often spelt in our oldest Manuscripts, *Het*. I suspect, that Shakespear wrote—"Nor Heaven peep thro' the blank Height of the Dark—To cry, Hold! Hold!"[1] The Classical Reader will recollect the [? proud] Image in Lucretius of Superstition looking down from the dark Heaven.—[2]   S. T. C.—

103 VI 300 | I v 56–8

LADY MACBETH. . . . Thy letters have transported me beyond
    This ign'rant present time, and I feel now
    The future in the instant.

No woman's Life, no joyous Terrors, at the thought of his past Dangers— but all Future/

---

of God and Satan in *Paradise Lost*, where God presents his Son to the angels (III 274–343) and where Satan, the Prince of Darkness, Lucifer, is likened to the morning star (X 426).
101[1] I.e. imagination.
102[1] Johnson thought the image of the blanket too mean or low in this context (*Rambler* 168), but other commentators defended it, citing parallel passages from Shakespeare's contemporaries. C's suggestion was rejected as absurd by the 19th-cen-

tury scholar Alexander Dyce: *TT* (*CC*) I 465 n 7.
102[2] Lucretius *De rerum natura* 1.62–5. Tr: "When man's life lay for all to see foully grovelling upon the ground, crushed beneath the weight of Religion, which displayed her head in the regions of heaven, threatening mortals from on high with horrible aspect . . .". C renders *religio* as "Superstition" rather than "Religion", an equally appropriate interpretation that he defends in LEIGHTON COPY B **21**.

104   vi 301 | i v 66–70

LADY MACBETH.   . . . He, that's coming,
   Must be provided for; and you shall put
   This night's great business into my dispatch,
   Which shall to all our nights and days to come
   Give solely sovereign sway and masterdom.

The consummate art of first using herself as incentives what his Conscience would perhaps have used as motives of abhorrence/ so to herself, p. 300.[1]

105   vi 301 | i vi 14–18

LADY MACBETH.   All our service
   (In every point twice done, and then done double,)
   Were poor and single business to contend
   Against those honours deep and broad, wherewith
   Your Majesty loads our house.

still the same—no personal sense—all "Dignities &c"

106   vi 308 | ii ii 24–7

MACBETH. One cry'd, God bless us! and Amen, the other;
   As they had seen me with these hangman's hands.
   Listening their fear, I could not say, Amen,
   When they did say, God bless us.

the Novelty given to the most familiar usages by a new state of feeling—

107   vi 308 | ii ii 32–7

MACBETH. Methought, I heard a voice cry, Sleep no more!
   Macbeth doth murder sleep; the innocent sleep;
   Sleep, that knits up the ravell'd sleeve of care,
   The death of each day's life, sore labour's bath,
   Balm of hurt minds, great nature's second course,
   Chief nourisher in life's feast.—

now Conscience rushes in in her own person—compare this with 302, 303, before the Deed when Cons. hid herself in selfish prudential Fears—[1]

104[1] I.e. Lady Macbeth's earlier speech, i v 41–55, partly commented on in **101–102**.

107[1] "Cons" is "conscience": C alludes to i vii, not annotated in this copy.

108   VI 309 | II ii 65–6

LADY MACBETH.   . . . your constancy
    Hath <u>left</u> you unattended—

a woman of high Rank/[1]

109   VI 310–11 | II iii 1–19

PORTER. Here's a knocking, indeed . . . "I'll devil-porter it no further: I
    had thought to have let in some of all professions, that go the primrose
    way to th' everlasting bonfire." . . .

This low Porter Soliloquy I believe written for the Mob by some other
Hand, perhaps with Shakespear's Consent—& that finding it take, he
with the remaining Ink of a Pen otherwise employed just interpolated it
with the sentence, "I'll devil-porter it no further:" & what follows to
"bonfire." Of the rest not one syllable has the ever-present Being of
Shakespear.[1]

110   VI 330 | III iv 121–5

MACBETH. It will have blood, they say; blood will have blood:
    Stones have been known to move, and trees to speak;
   *Augurs, that understood relations, have
    By mag-pies, and by choughs, and rooks brought forth
    The secret'st man of blood.—

* who by guilt tears himself live-asunder from Nature is himself in a
præternatural State—no wonder therefore, if inclined to all Superstition
& Faith in the Præternatural—

111   VI 342 | IV ii (the murder of Lady Macduff and her son)

This Scene dreadful as it is, is still a relief because a variety, because do-
mestic/ Something in the domestic affections always soothing because
associated with the only real pleasures of life.[1]

108[1] Lady Macbeth is chiding her husband for his inconstancy or vacillation, and
chooses, as C observes, a metaphor appropriate to a woman of her station.

    109[1] C denies Shakespeare's authorship
of this scene likewise in lectures of 2 Nov
1813 and 17 Feb 1818: *Lects 1808–1819*

(*CC*) I 527, II 149; and in COPY C **28**. In retrospect, *Sh* (Arden) describes this opinion
as "an aberration of one of the greatest of
critics" (xxiii).

    111[1] C's notes for the lecture of 2 Nov
1813 also refer to this scene as "a pleasing
relief": *Lects 1808–1819* (*CC*) I 528.

112   VI 398–9 | *Coriolanus* I x 10–24

AUFIDIUS.   . . . By th' elements,
If e'er again I meet him beard to beard,
He's mine, or I am his: mine emulation
Hath not that honour in't, it had; for where
I thought to crush him in an equal force,
True sword to sword; I'll potch at him some way,
Or wrath, or craft may get him.
SOLDIER.   He's the devil.
AUFIDIUS. Bolder, tho' not so subtle: my valour (poison'd,
With only suffering stain by him) for him
Shall fly out of itself: not sleep, nor sanctuary,
Being naked, sick, nor fane, nor capitol,
The prayers of priests, nor times of sacrifice,
Embarkments all of fury, shall lift up
Their rotten privilege and custom 'gainst
My hate to *Marcius*.

I have such deep Faith in Shakespear's *Heart-Lore* (Herzlehre)[1] that I take for granted, this is in nature, & not as a mere anomaly, altho' I cannot ⟨in⟩ myself discover any germ of possible feeling, which could wax & unfold itself into such Sentiment.[2]   *S. T. C.*

113   VI 413 | II ii 109–12

COMINIUS. . . . He was a thing of blood, whose every motion
Was tim'd with dying cries: alone he enter'd
The mortal gate o' th' city, which he <u>painted</u>?
With shunless destiny . . .

What means this?[1]

114   VI 418–19 | II iii 115–16

CORIOLANUS. Why in this <u>woolvish</u> gown should I stand here,
To beg of *Hob* and *Dick* . . .

112[1] "Heart-lore", not in *OED*, is an example of C's fondness for the compounds with "lore" (exactly analogous to the German *-lehre*) that, as he noted in *CN* II 2442, had virtually disappeared from English prose usage. Fichte's *Wissenschaftslehre* he translated as a "*Lore* of Ultimate Science":

BL ch 9 (*CC*) I 157 and n 3.
   112[2] C comments further on this speech, but from a political rather than a psychological point of view, in COPY D **59**.
   113[1] *Sh* (Reed) does not gloss the word. *Sh* (Arden) suggests "stained with the blood that was inescapably to flow".

? That the Gown of the Candidate was ⱥ of whitened Wool, we know—
and it is natural for Coriolanus to call it a "wool-wash'd" Gown; but why
wolfish? and (if it means not this) what does "woolvish" mean?—[1]

115 vi 467 | iv vii 28–57, Aufidius's speech "All places yield to him ere he sits
down"

I have always thought this in itself so beautiful Specch the least explicable from the mood & full Intention of the Speaker, of any in the whole
works of Shakespear. I cherish the Hope, that I am mistaken; & becoming wiser shall discover some profound excellence, in what I now appear
to myself to detect an imperfection.   *S. T. C.*

116 vi [+1]

[1]1. Drawn from the fontal faculties of the Human Mind, the Idea always
a priori, tho' incarnated by Observation a posteriori et ab extra—[2]
2. No appeals to appetites; but to the Passions.
3. In the high road of nature.
4. The only Poet, except Milton's Eve,[3] who drew women as they are in
their uncorrupted Nature—
5. The only modern English Poet who was both a poet & at the same time
a dramatic Poet—[4]
6. The only one who supplied all the beauties of the observant Chorus
without its defects ⟨&⟩ limitations, first by the exquisite Lyric Intermix-
tures, & 2—by making general Truths the outbursts of Passion—[5]
7. Reverence for all the Professions & established Ranks & Usages of
Society—Friar—Physician—&c[6]

114[1] *Sh* (Reed) records various suggestions, ranging from Johnson's *"rough hir-
sute* gown" to Ritson's reminder of the wolf
in sheep's clothing and Malone's similarly-
based "false or deceitful"; modern editors,
as represented by *Sh* (Arden), combined
their ideas: "the 'napless vesture of humility' (II.i.232) worn by Coriolanus as the fa-
bled wolf wears sheep's clothing."

116[1] This note is published as perhaps
having some connection with Lect 11 of the
1812–13 series, in *Lects 1808–1819 (CC)* II
430–1.

116[2] "From the outside".

116[3] I.e. with the exception of Milton in
his portrayal of Eve. C makes the same

point in Lect 7 of the 1811–12 series, speaking of *Romeo and Juliet: Lects 1808–1819*
(*CC*) I 313.

116[4] Lect 4 of the 1808 series outlines "a
dramatic poet's characteristics" and the
psychology underlying them: *Lects 1808–
1819 (CC)* I 85.

116[5] According to HCR, C made a similar point about Shakespeare's way of substituting for the Chorus in a lecture of 1808:
Lects 1808–1819 (CC) I 117.

116[6] C makes the same point ("no jokes
on professions"), referring back to his notes
on *Romeo and Juliet*, in memoranda for a
lecture of 28 Oct 1813: *Lects 1808–1819*
(*CC*) I 511–12.

8.—In very few Instances mere Monsters introduced, as in Gonerill—& then with what Judgement—[7]
9. Moral & prudential Wisdom.
10. Comparative Purity[8]

117 VII ¯1

In the notes + means "added to"
= "equal to, or the same as"—
− less by
⋇ in opposition to or in contrast with.[1]

118 VII 6 | *Julius Caesar* I i 15–18

FLAVIUS. What trade, thou knave? thou naughty knave, what trade?
COBLER. Nay, I beseech you, Sir, be not out with me: yet if you be out, Sir, I can mend you.
~~FLAVIUS.~~ *Mar.* What mean'st ~~thou~~ by that? mend me, thou saucy fellow? . . .

Flavius and Marullus speak thro'out in verse—
What trade, what trade? Thou naughty knave, what Trade?
—What mean'st by that? *Mend* me, thou saucy fellow?[1]

119 VII 6 | **118** textus, and note as follows

[Folios give the first speech to Flavius, the second to Marullus. Theobald's note:] As the *Cobler*, in the preceding speech, replies to *Flavius*, not to *Marullus*; 'tis plain, I think, this speech must be given to Flavius.

Aye! Theobald *thinks*! But Sh. thought far better & gave it to Marullus,

---

116[7] Cf C's resistance to the facile labelling of Shakespeare's characters as monsters, with regard to Lady Macbeth and the Second Murderer in *Macbeth* (COPY C **26**, **34**) and Edmund in *King Lear* (COPY D **75**). "The Monster, Goneril", is admitted as one of the rare exceptions in COPY D **83**; cf COPY C **26**.

116[8] In reaction against critics who complained about the coarseness of Shakespeare's plays, C habitually emphasised their decency relative to other plays of the same period, e.g. BEAUMONT & FLETCHER COPY B **49**, JONSON **1**.

117[1] C repeats this set of shorthand symbols, a subset of his usual system (as in JOANNES **4**) in COPY D **2**.

118[1] There are two issues here: how the lines ought to be assigned, and whether the Tribunes' lines are verse or prose. The Folio gave the first line to Flavius and the last to Marullus (as he is named in this ed); Capell thought both should be Marullus's, and this is the solution adopted in both *Sh* (Reed) and *Sh* (Arden). It was Steevens who pointed out that the Tribunes' lines should be set as verse, as they now usually are. C reiterates this latter point in **120** below and in COPY D **61**.

even as before Flavius had intervened for him. This is nature "mend me" is an echo, not = mend *me*.[1]

120   VII 6 | I i 27–8

FLAVIUS. But wherefore art not in thy shop to-day? / Why dost thou lead
 these men about the streets? /

Two verses.[1]

121   VII 10–11 | I ii 85–9

BRUTUS. . . . If it be aught toward the general good,
 Set Honour in one eye, and Death i' th' other,
Both And I will look on Death indifferently:
 For, let the Gods so speed me, as I love
 The name of honour, more than I fear death.

[Warburton's note, defending the substitution of "Death" for "both":] . . .
Honour thus is but in equal balance to Death, which is not speaking at all
like *Brutus*: for, in a soldier of any ordinary pretension, it should always
preponderate. We must certainly read,
 And I will look on *Death* indifferently.*

* I prefer the old reading.[1] There are 3 things here, the Public Good—
the Individual Brutus's Honor—& his Death. The 2 latter so balanced
each other that he could decide for the ~~former~~ first by equipoise. Nay—
(the thought *growing*) Honor had more weight than Death. That Cassius
understood it as Warb. is the Beauty of Cass. ⅋ Brutus.[2]

122   VII 13–14 | I ii 203–4

CAESAR.   . . . He loves no Plays,
 As thou dost, *Antony*; he hears no musick . . .

[Theobald's note:] This is not a trivial observation, nor does our poet
mean barely by it, that *Cassius* was not a merry, sprightly man; but that

119[1] I.e. C indicates by putting the emphasis on "mend" (in **118**) rather than on "me" how the line might be spoken by Marullus.

120[1] See **118** n 1.

121[1] *Sh* (Reed) and *Sh* (Arden) print the original (Folio) reading "both". Johnson defended it in a note that closely resembles C's explanation: "When Brutus first names *honour* and *death*, he calmly declares them *indifferent*; but as the image kindles in his mind, he sets *honour* above *life*. Is not this natural?": *Sh* (Reed).

121[2] The conspirator Cassius "as opposed to" Brutus would think of honour (as Warburton does) as certainly more important than life, not as even conceivably of equal value. In his next speech he says, "Well, honour is the subject of my story." According to reports of later lectures, C described Cassius as a figure representing envy, and yet with many fine qualities besides: *Lects 1808–1819 (CC)* II 501.

he had not a due temperament of harmony in his composition; and that therefore natures, so uncorrected, are dangerous.

O Theobald! what a Commentator wast thou, when thou would'st affect to *understand* Shakespear!—instead of collating his Text. The meaning here was too deep for a Line 10 fold thye Length of thine to fathom!—

123   VII 17 | I iii

Thunder and Lightning. Enter Casca, *his sword drawn; and* Cicero, *meeting him.*

I suspect, that for want of Actors the part of some other Conspirator was thrown into Casca's. However neglectful of Time Shakespear never outrages—Casca had but quitted the Stage—& he re-appears, his Language & Tone quite altered.[1]

124   VII 36–7 | II ii 75–8

CAESAR. . . . *Calphurnia* here, my wife, stays me at home:
    She dreamt last night, she saw my Statue,*
    Which, like a fountain, with an hundred spouts,
    Did run pure blood . . .

A modern Tragic Poet would have written:
    "Last night she dreamt, that she my statue saw" &c—
but Sh. never avails himself of the supposed Licence of transposition merely for the metre. There is always some Logic either of Thought or Passion to justify it. In the present Line we must read Statue "Stătŭā[":]: as in the same age they pronounced Heroes more often Hēroĕs, than Hērōse.[1]

125   VII 47–9 | III i 204–8

ANTONY. . . . Pardon me, *Julius*—here wast thou bay'd, brave hart;
    Here didst thou fall, and here thy hunters stand
    Sign'd in thy spoil, and crimson'd in thy death.
  ⎛ O world! thou wast the forest to this hart,   ⎞
  ⎝ And this, indeed, O world, the heart of thee. ⎠

123[1] No inconsistency is complained of by other commentators.

124[1] Shakespearean scholarship agrees, *Sh* (Reed) printing "statua" in the text and justifying it in the notes, *Sh* (Arden) printing "statue" but observing that it must be pronounced as a trisyllable, and that the spelling "statua" would have been an acceptable variant.

I doubt these Lines:[1] not because they are vile; but first on account of the Rhythm which is not Shakespearian but just the very *Tune* of some old Play, from which the Actor might have interpolated them: and 2ndly because it they interrupts not only the sense and connection, but likewise the flow both of the Passion, & (what is with me still more decisive) the Shakespearian Link of Association.[2] As with the Parenthesis or Gloss slipt into the Text concerning Jonah in the Gospel, we have only to read the passage without it, to see that it never was in it.[3] I venture to say, there is no instance in Shakespear fairly like it. Conceits he has; but they not rise out of some *word* in the Lines before, but they *lead* to the Thought in the Lines following. Here it is a mere alien: Ant. forgets an image—when he is even touching it; & then recollects it when the Thought last in his mind must have led him away from it.

126 VII 64–5 | IV iii 21–4

BRUTUS.   . . . what, shall one of us,
  That struck the foremost man of all this world,
  But for supporting robbers; shall we now *
  Contaminate our fingers with base bribes?

* This seemingly strange Assertion of Brutus is unhappily verified in the present Day. What are an immense Army, in whom the Lust of Plunder has quenched all the duties of the Citizen, other than Robbers, or differenced only as Fiends from reprobate men?—Cæsar supported & was supported by, those—even as Napoleon in our days.   S. T. C.

127 VII 66–7 | IV iii (the quarrel between Brutus and Cassius)

I know no part of Shakespear that more impresses on me the Belief of his Genius being superhuman, than this Scene. In the Gnostic Heresy it might have been credited with less absurdity than most of their dogmas, that the Supreme had employed him to *create* previously to his function of representing.[1]   S. T. C.—

125[1] C's predecessors did not doubt these lines; *Sh* (Arden) quotes C's comment but considers it unsubstantiated.
125[2] Cf "Shakespear's manner of connection by unmarked influences of association from some preceding metaphor" in **37** above.
125[3] Matt 12.40: "For as Jonas was three days and three nights in the whale's belly; so shall the Son of man be three days

and three nights in the heart of the earth." This verse glosses the phrase "the sign of the prophet Jonas" in Matt 12.39, but does not reappear when the phrase does, in Matt 16.4, Luke 11.29–30. C concludes that it was interpolated by a commentator. Cf his scornful remark about "the pious Dullman" who was responsible for "the Jonas Text in Matthew", in a note of 1825–6: *CN* IV 5297.
127[1] C had a lifelong interest in Gnosti-

128 VII 67 | IV iii 88

BRUTUS. I do not, 'till you practise them on me.

[Warburton's note:] i.e. "I deny the charge; and must tell you further, that this charge is an addition to your faults."

Nonsense!

129 VI [87] | *Antony and Cleopatra* (fly-title)

Shakespear can be complimented only by comparison with himself: all other eulogies are either heterogeneous, (ex. gr. in relation to Milton, Spencer, &c) or flat truisms (ex. gr. to prefer him to Racine, Corneille, or even his own immediate Successors, Fletcher, Massinger &c.) The highest praise or rather form of Praise, of this Play, ⟨which I can offer in my own mind,⟩ is the Doubt which its ⟨perusal⟩ always occasions in me, whether it is not in all exhibitions of a giant power in its ~~force~~ strength and vigor of maturity a formidable Rival of the Macbeth, Lear, Othello, and Hamlet. Feliciter audax[1] is the motto for its style comparatively with his other works, even as it is the general motto of all his works compared with those of other Poets. Be it remembered too, that this happy Valiancy of Style is but the representative & result of all the material excellencies so exprest.—

130 VII [89] | I i 6–8

PHILO.   . . . His captain's heart,
    Which in the scuffles of great fights hath burst
    The buckles on his breast, reneges all temper* . . .

* should be spelt reneagues, or renigues; as leagues from ligare, fatigues &c—or reniegues.[1]

---

cism, his remarks about it being sometimes admiring and sometimes scornful: see e.g. *Lects 1795* (*CC*) 195–202, CHILLING-WORTH COPY B **1** and n 2, FLEURY **32–37** and nn, *TT* (*CC*) I 35–6 (and nn 28–30), 158 and n 11. Here he alludes particularly to a version of Gnostic doctrine in which the Creator was separate from the Supreme Being but not hostile or evil; C's note further separates creation from representation.

129[1] "Successfully daring": proverbial in this form. Cf Horace *Epistles* 2.1.166, where the Roman imitator of Greek tragedy

"dares successfully"; and Quintilian *Institutio oratoria* 10.1.96, where Horace himself is said to have been "most successfully daring with words".

130[1] C suggests changing the spelling and pronunciation for the sake of the scansion. "League" is indeed derived from *ligare*, "fatigue" from *fatigare*, and "renege"—in its various spellings—from the late Latin *renegare*. C's point is supported by some other critics, both earlier and later, as summarised in *Sh* (Arden).

131   vii 90–1 | i i 11–13

PHILO. Take but good note, and you shall see in him
    The triple pillar of the world transform'd
    Into a Strumpet's fool.

[Warburton suggests:] . . . *Into a Strumpet's* stool.* Alluding to the common custom of strumpets sitting on the laps of their lovers. By this correction the metaphor is admirably well preserved, (for both stool and pillar are things for support) and the contrast in this image is beautiful.

* This is an ingeni⟨o⟩us conjecture, & would be a probable reading, if the Scene opening had discovered Antony with Cleopatra on his Lap. But entering as they do, and Antony flattering & jesting with her, Fool must be the word.[1] Warburton's Objection is shallow, and implies that he confounded the dramatic with the Epic Style—/[2] The Pillar of a State is so common a metaphor, as to have lost the image in the thing meant—

132   vii 98–9 | i ii 192–4

ANTONY.   . . . Much is breeding:
    Which, like the Courser's hair, hath yet but life,
    And not a serpent's poison.

[Theobald's note:] This alludes to an old opinion, which obtain'd among the vulgar . . . that the hair of a horse in corrupted water would take life, and become an animal.

This is however so far true, that a Horse-hair thus treated will become the supporter of apparently one, worm, tho' probably of an immense number, of small slimy water-lice. The Hair will twirl round a finger, and sensibly compress it. It is a common experiment with the School-boys in Cumberland and Westmoreland.—[1]

133   vii 117 | ii ii 120–2

CAESAR.   Say not so, *Agrippa*;
    If *Cleopatra* heard you, your approof
    Were well deserv'd of rashness.

131[1] Shakespearean scholarship almost unanimously agrees.
131[2] On the relationship between epic and drama, see also COPY D **33, 151** and nn.
132[1] HC (b 1796) and DC (b 1800) were, or had recently been, "School-boys in Cumberland", and C's observation gives the impression of first-hand experience supporting popular belief. A letter written by RS in 1813 records his and WW's amazement on being shown such horsehairs by a schoolboy in the Lake District: *Life and Correspondence* ed C. C. Southey (6 vols 1850) iv 34–5. They were also a matter of scientific interest, e.g. in *Phil Trans RS* vii (1672) 4064–6.

[Theobald defends "approof" as meaning "allowance, admitting".]

It seems plain, that approof is either reproof, or else the treatment, that would follow, your reception from her would be more than your rashness merited.[1]

134   VII 120–1, partly in pencil, overtraced | II ii 206–9

ENOBARBUS. Her Gentlewomen, like the *Nereids*,
   *So many Mermaids, tended her i' th' eyes,
   And made their Bends adornings. At the helm,
   A seeming Mermaid steers . . .

*   Some as Sea-Graces?—or—So many Graces?

   [a]* I strongly suspect that Shakespear wrote either Sea-Queens, or rather *Sea-brides/* He never, I think, would have so weakened by useless anticipation the fine Image immediately following. At the Helm a seeming Mermaid—[b] The epithet "seeming" becomes so extremely improper, after the whole number had been positively called so. Submarine Graces?[1]

135   VII 142–3 | III ii 27–33

CAESAR.   . . . Most noble *Antony*,
   (33) Let not the piece of virtue, which is set
   Betwixt us, as the cement of our love,   cross-beam? or crossment?
   To keep it builded, be the ram to batter
   The fortress of it: for better might we   else far? or for far
   Have lov'd without this mean, if on both parts
   This be not cherisht.

[Theobald's note (33):] There is no consonance of metaphor preserv'd in the close of this sentence . . .

(33) I conjecture that the whole passage is somehow or other corrupted.

134[a–b] Pencil, overtraced, then continuing in ink

133[1] The Folio reads "your proofe"; the general consensus of scholars favours "your reproof" as either a compositor's error or an error in transcription through mishearing: *Sh* (Reed), *Sh* (Arden).

   134[1] C questions this text also in COPY C **9**, objecting to the repetition of the mermaid figure; and in COPY B **20**, where he proposes "sea-queens" as an alternative faithful to—though not actually appearing in—Shakespeare's source, North's translation of Plutarch (a passage printed as a footnote in *Sh*—Reed—and other editions of C's period). In the latter note, and again in *TT* (*CC*) I 464–5, he considers the first "Mermaids" as a typical compositor's error.

I suspect both "cement" and "builded".[1] At least I recollect no instance in Shakespear of such an unrepresentable Eye-image, as—a *Piece* of—*set* betwixt—as *cement*—turned to a *Battering-ram*. Let not that which is the mortar of the wall, be turned to a ram! Both the Image and Shakespear's manner require a Beam, or buttress-tree, or slant-column.

136　VII 217–19 | *Cymbeline* I i 1–3

I GENTLEMAN. You do not meet a man, but frowns: our bloods
　　No more obey the heavens than our courtiers;
　　Still seem, as does the King's.*

* Mispointed. Our Bloods
　　Not more obey the Heavens, than our Courtiers
　　Still seem as does the King's.—i.e. The Circulation of men's blood in general does not more depend on the Stars (as was almost universally believed in Shakesp's time) than our Courtiers' Blood seems to sympathize with the King's—But I should greatly prefer the following:—
　　　　　　　　　　　Our Bloods
　　Not more obey the Heavens, than our Courtiers
　　Still seem as does the King.—i.e. The Motion of our Blood is not more dependent on the motion of the Heavens, than the appearance of our Courtiers' Faces depends on that of the King's./[1]

137　VII 221 | I i 86–8

IMOGEN. . . . . I something fear my father's wrath, but nothing
　　(Always reserv'd my holy duty) what
　　His rage can do[a] on me.

the emphasis on the word "~~do~~" "me": *rage* is the mere repetition of *wrath*.—

138　VII 222 | I i 131–3

CYMBELINE.　　　　　　　　　O disloyal thing,
　　That should'st repair my youth, thou heap'st
　　A yare age on me.*

137[a]　C first underlined "do", deleted the underlining, and underlined "me"

135[1] Other commentators appear to have been untroubled by the image.
136[1] These lines have always puzzled the editors, who have generally tried to make sense of them by slight alterations in the punctuation along the lines C indicates.

C's changing "no" to "not" in the second line is unconventional, but the emendation of "king" for the Folio reading "Kings"—originally proposed by Tyrwhitt—has been widely accepted. C returns to this passage in COPY B **20–21** and COPY D **73**.

[Theobald remarks upon the weakness of the earlier text "a year's age" and defends Warburton's emendation to "yare age" as "i.e. a sudden, precipitate old age".]

* But the *unshakespearian* defect in the metre, & what in Sh. is the same, in the harmony with the sense & feeling—Some word or words have slipped out after "youth"—possibly *"and see."*

Thou should'st repair my youth: and see! thou heap'st.[1]

139 VII 226 | I iii 8–12

PISANIO.   . . . for so long
    As he could make me with this eye, or ear,
    Distinguish him from others, he did keep
    The deck, with glove, or hat, or handkerchief,
    Still waving . . .

[Warburton suggests "this eye" for "his eye" of the Folios.]

this, spite of the δεικτικῶς,[1] is awkward—either "or" or "the" was Sh's word.—

    As he could make me or with eye or ~~eye~~ ear

140 VII 237 | I vi 32–6

IACHIMO.   . . . hath nature given them eyes
    To see this vaulted arch, and the rich crop
    Of sea and land, which can distinguish 'twixt
    The fiery orbs above, (10)and the twinn'd stones
    Upon th' unnumber'd beach?

[Theobald's note (10):] I have no idea, in what sense the beach, or shore, should be call'd *number'd*. I have ventur'd, against all the copies to substitute
    Upon th' unnumber'd *beach.*

I prefer umber'd (darkened, antithetic to fiery) or cumber'd.[1]

138[1] The second line of the textus is metrically incomplete; other editors had suggested other ways of filling it out.

139[1] "Demonstratively" or "pointingly" —part of Warburton's argument being that the "expression is δεικτικῶς, as the Greeks term it: the party speaking points to the part spoken of". Warburton's emendation is generally accepted.

140[1] Johnson glossed the original reading "number'd" simply as "numerous", and his opinion has prevailed against various attempts at emendation, including Warburton's "humbled" and Malone's "unnumber'd". C returns to this passage in COPY D **74**, where he discovers that "umber'd" had

(10) But what is the meaning of *twinn'd* stones? For number'd read humbled ⟨(or umber'd or cumber'd.—)⟩ May not twinned Stones be a bold catachresis for Shells, as muscles, Cockles, & other empty shells with hinges. These are truly twinn'd?[2]

---

141   VII 339 | v v 435–49

SOOTHSAYER. [Reads]. *When as a lion's whelp shall, to himself unknown, without seeking find, and be embraced by a piece of tender air . . . then shall* Posthumus *end his miseries,* Britaine *be fortunate, and flourish in peace and plenty.*

Thou, *Leonatus,* art the lion's whelp;
The fit and apt construction of thy name,
Being *Leonatus,* doth import so much:
The piece of tender air, thy virtuous daughter   [*To* Cymbeline.
Which we call *Mollis Aer*; and *Mollis Aer*
We term it *Mulier:* which *Mulier,* I divine,
Is this most constant wife . . .

It is not easy to conjecture why Shakespear should have introduced this ludicrous Scroll, ~~with the~~ which answers no one purpose, either propulsive or explicatory, unless as a Joke on etymology.

141A VII 363 | *Troilus and Cressida* I iii 78

ULYSSES. . . . . The specialjty of rule hath been neglected . . .[1]

---

142   VII 363, pencil | I iii 105

ULYSSES. . . . . *Peaceful commerce from dividable shores,

$$- \cup\ |\ \cup\ -|\ \cup\ -\ \cup\ \cup|\ \cup\ -\ .^a$$

* Here the effect from the polysyllable compensates for the loss of one ⌣ in the number of Times.

142[a] The marks of scansion are written in the margin, the note in the foot-margin

---

been proposed by an earlier critic, Farmer, but in the sense of "shaded" (which appears to be C's meaning here) whereas C by that time took it to refer to the colour of umber, "a dingy yellow-brown Soil".

140[2] "Twinn'd" has also been much debated. Johnson suggested "*Twinn'd shells,* or *pairs of shells*": *Sh* (Reed). C proposes an even bolder alternative in COPY D **74**. *Sh* (Arden) pours scorn on the shells idea and says "that is, stones which are exactly alike".

141A[1] C corrects a typographical error.

143   VIII 83–5 | *Romeo and Juliet* IV v (the discovery of Juliet "dead" in her chamber)

As the *Audience* know that Juliet is not dead, this Scene is, perhaps, excusable—at all events, it is a strong Warning to minor Dramatists not to introduce at one time many different characters agitated by one and the same Circumstance. It is difficult to understand what *effect*, whether that of pity or laughter, Shakespear meant to produce/ The occasion & the characteristic Speeches are so little in harmony: ex. gratiâ, what the Nurse says, is excellently suited to the Nurse's Character, but grotesquely unsuited to the occasion—[1]

144   VIII 145 | *Hamlet* II ii 86

[Warburton's note on Polonius's speech, beginning "My Liege, and Madam, to expostulate":] . . . It is so just a satire on impertinent oratory, (especially, of that then in vogue) which was of the formal cut, and proceeded by definition, division, and subdivision, that I think, every body must be charm'd with it. Then as to the *jingles*, and *play* on words, let us but look into the sermons of Dr. *Donne*, (the wittiest man of that age) and we shall find them full of this vein: only, there they are to be admired, here to be laugh'd at.

I have (and that most carefully) read Dr Donne's Sermons—and find none of these Jingles. The great art of an Orator, to make whatever he talks of appear of importance, this indeed Donne has effected with consummate Skill.[1]

145   VIII 149, pencil | II ii 210–11

POLONIUS. . . . Which <u>sanctity</u> and reason could not be
     So prosp'rously deliver'd of.

Sanity[1]

146   VIII 165 | III i 78–9

HAMLET. . . . (That undiscover'd country, from whose bourne
     No traveller returns)

143[1] E.g. IV v 49–54, in C's copy thus:
O woe! oh woful, woful, woful day!
Most lamentable day! most woful day!
That ever, ever, I did yet behold.
Oh day! oh day! oh day! oh hateful day!
Never was seen so black a day as this:
Oh woful day, oh woful day!
144[1] C annotated at least two copies of

Donne's sermons, one about 1809–10 and the other about 1831–2: DONNE *Sermons* COPY A, COPY B. In one of the early notes, COPY A 7, he remarks on "an excellent Paragraph grounded on a mere *Pun*!—Suc[h] was the taste of the Age".
     145[1] C corrects a typographical error.

[Theobald's note:] As some superficial critics have . . . accused the Poet of *forgetfulness* and *self contradiction* from this passage; seeing that in this very play he introduces a character from the other world, the *ghost* of *Hamlet*'s father: I have thought this circumstance worthy of a justification . . .

O miserable Defender! If it be necessary to remove the apparent Contradiction; if it be not rather a great Beauty; surely, it were easy to say, that no Traveller returns home, as to his Home, or *abiding-place*.

147   VIII 166–7 | III i 99–102

OPHELIA.   . . . for to the noble mind
   Rich gifts wax poor, when givers prove unkind.
   There, my Lord.
HAMLET. Ha, ha! are you honest?*

* Here, it is evident, that the penetrating Hamlet perceived, from the strange & forced manner of Ophelia, that the sweet girl was not acting a part of her own—in short, saw into the Stratagem—& his after Speeches are not directed for Ophelia, but to the Listeners & Spies.—

148   VIII 181–2 | III ii 335–6

ROSENCRANZ. My lord, you once did love me.
*HAMLET. So I do still, by these pickers and stealers.

* I never heard an Actor give this word its proper emphasis.—Shakespear's meaning is—Lov'd *you?—Hem!*
So—I do still, &c—There has been no *change* in my opinion. Else Hamlet tells an ignoble Falsehood, & a useless one—as the last speech to him *Why, look you now*—proves.[1]

149   VIII 108 | IV v 102–7

MESSENGER. . . . young *Laertes*, in a riotous head,
   O'er-bears your officers; the rabble call him Lord;*
  [a]And as the world were now but to begin,
   Antiquity forgot, custom not known,
   The ratifiers and props of every Ward;[b]
   They cry, "Chuse we *Laertes* for our King."

      149[a–b] Passage marked in the margin with an ink line

148[1] III ii 363–72, Hamlet's speech (as printed in this edition): "Why, look you now, how unworthy a thing you make of me; you would play upon me, you would seem to know my stops; you would pluck out the heart of my mystery . . . . call me what instrument you will, though you can fret me, you cannot play upon me."

[Warburton's note:] . . . The messenger is complaining, that the riotous head had over-born the King's officers; and then subjoins, that antiquity and custom were forgot, which were the ratifiers of every *ward* . . . . All this is rational and consequential.

* Fearful and self-suspicious as I always feel when I seem to see an error of judgement in Shak^e, yet I cannot reconcile the cool "rational & consequential" reflection in these 3 lines with the anonymousness or the alarm of the Messenger.

150 VIII 209 | IV v 132

LAERTES. . . . To hell, allegiance! vows, to the blackest devil!

[Warburton's note:] *Laertes* is a <u>good</u>* character; but he is here in actual rebellion.

* Mercy on Warburton's notions of goodness—see p. 219, especially after the King's description of Hamlet—["]He being remiss, most generous & free from all contriving."—[1]

151 VIII 218–19 | IV vii 117–23

KING. . . . For goodness growing to a pleurisy,
  Dies in his own too much; what we would do,
  We should do when we would; for this *would* changes,
  And hath abatements and delays as many
  As there are tongues, are hands, are accidents;
  And then this *should* is like a spend-thrift sigh
  That hurts by easing . . .

[Warburton suggested "plethory" for "pleurisy", and Theobald observes:] . . . the *pleurisy* is an inflammation of the membrane which covers the whole *thorax*; and is generally occasioned by a stagnation of the blood; but a *plethora*, is when the vessels are fuller of humours than is agreeable to a natural state, or health . . .

I rather think, that Sh. meant Pluerisy[a], but involving in it the thought of Plethora, as supposing Pleurisy to arise from too much Blood: else I can not explain the 5th line after "And then this *Should*" &c—/ For a *Stitch*

151[a] A slip for "Pleurisy" which is correctly spelled two lines below

150[1] C refers to the scene (IV vii) in which the King and Laertes connive to kill Hamlet, and Laertes proposes to poison the tip of his sword.

in the Side every one must have heaved a sigh, that hurt by easing. S. T. C. I was right—in the old Medical Dictionaries Pleurisy is often called a Plethory.[1]

152   VIII 230 | v i 275–6

HAMLET. . . . Woo't weep? woo't fight? woo't fast? woo't tear thyself?
   Woo't drink up Eisel, eat a crocodile?

[Theobald has changed the reading *Esill* or *Esile* to *Eisel*, i.e. vinegar.]

Eisel, I suppose, *is* the word; but I suspect, that Hamlet alluded to the Cup of Anguish at the Cross, & that it should be—th' Eisel—i.e. would'st drink it *up*? Christ simply tasted it.[1] Theobald does not explain the "drink *up!*" We do not say drink up Vinegar, but drink Vinegar.

153   VIII 243 | v ii 369–74

AMBASSADOR. . . . The ears are senseless, that should give us hearing;
   To tell him his commandment is fulfill'd,
   That *Rosencrantz* and *Guildenstern* are dead:
   Where should we have his thanks?
HORATIO.   Not from his mouth,
   Had it th'ability of life to thank you:
   He never gave commandment for their death.

[Theobald's note:] We must either believe, the Poet had forgot himself with regard to the circumstance of *Rosencrantz* and *Guildenstern*'s death;* or we must understand . . . that he [Hamlet] no otherways gave a command for their deaths, than . . . warding off the fatal sentence from his own head.

* why, surely "He" means the king, & not Hamlet.—The King's, not Hamlet's, signature was forged by Hamlet.—

151[1] This is a famous crux, and both 18th-century and recent editors support the "pleurisy" reading by reference to works—esp dramatic works—of Shakespeare's period that make the mistake C suspects, i.e. by mistaken etymology suppose that a "pleurisy" arises from having "too much" of something: see also *OED*. The older English medical dictionaries to which C is known to have had access, however, never confuse pleurisy with plethora; perhaps he was thinking of a medical *treatise* or textbook, such as "Mascal's Treatise on Cattle, 1662" which is given in evidence by Tollet in *Sh* (Reed).

152[1] Matt 27.48, Mark 15.36, Luke 23.36, John 19.29 and 30.

154　VIII 250 | *Othello* I i 8–10

IAGO.　　　　. . . Three great ones of the city,
　　In personal suit to make me his lieutenant,
　　Off capp'd to him . . .

[Theobald's note, preferring "off-capp'd" to the earlier reading "oft-capt":] . . . *off-capt*; i.e. stood cap in hand, soliciting him.

More probably & more in Sh's style, Off'd Cap to Him—(the imitative action expected from the Player being the comment & preventing any possible equivoque.)[1]

155　VIII 251–3 | I i 20–1

IAGO. . . . One *Michael Cassio*;—("the *Florentine*'s
　　A fellow almost damn'd in a fair wife;") . . .

[Theobald suggests that Iago, not Cassio, is a Florentine; that his reading should be accepted in place of "a Florentine"; and that the passage should be in quotation marks as a report of the words of Othello.]

Absurd ingenuity! Who says, that Cassio was not a Florentine? But that being so, Iago should use it to Roderigo, a "young Venetian" to excite the contempt that follows national rivalry, is quite exquisite & Shakespearian. The following Line has been since corrected beyond all doubt, but "wife" is a misprint for "Life"[1]—alluding to the Text—"Cursed are you when all men speak well of you"[2]—likewise an allusion quite & as the Saints say, too much in Shakespear's manner.[3]　　　　　　S. T. C.

156　VIII 259–61 | I ii 22–4

OTHELLO.　　　　　　　　　. . . and my demerits
　　May speak, and bonnetted, to as proud a fortune
　　As this that I have reach'd.

154[1] The Quarto reads "Oft capp'd", the Folio "Off-capt". Editors have defended both readings and indeed the meaning is fundamentally the same; C's emendation is therefore unnecessary.

155[1] There is no textual basis for the "life" reading, which was proposed by Tyrwhitt with the explanation C goes on to record. C confirms his preference for "life" in COPY D **185**, where the text provides both the emendation and the explanation that follows here: *Lects 1808–1819 (CC)* II 313–14 and n 3.

155[2] "Woe unto you, when all men shall speak well of you!": Luke 6.26.

155[3] "Saint" is a term used ironically to refer to goody-goodies, particularly the Evangelicals in the C of E: cf *Lects 1808–1819 (CC)* I 133 and n 26.

[Theobald cites *Lear* III i 14 "unbonnetted he runs" in support of his own preference of "and bonnetted" to "speak unbonnetted." He also defends his own suggestion in favour of Pope's emendation of the same line to "May speak unbonnetting", i.e. without pulling off the bonnet.]

The argument here proceeds on the assumption, that Shakespear could not use the same word differently in different places—whereas I should conclude, that as in the Quotation from Lear the word is employed in its direct meaning, so here it is used metaphorically: and this is confirmed by what has escaped the Editors, that it is ⟨not⟩ "I" but "my Demerits" that may speak, unbonnetted—i.e. without the aid of the Cap. There is a passage in Coriolanus which gives additional probability to this as well as to Pope's "unbonneting"—but the "ing" would better suit "I", the "ed" "my Demerits".[1]

157   VIII 351 | IV iii 80–2

AEMILIA. Why, the wrong is but a wrong i' th' world; and having the world for your labour, 'tis a wrong in your own world, and you might quickly make it right.

[Warburton's note interprets this as showing Shakespeare's intention . . .] to ridicule the opinion of those philosophers, who hold, that *right* and *wrong* are of so arbitrary natures, that *God*, consistently with his attributes, may authorize *injustice*. For, because it becomes *injustice* only by his *will*, it ceases to be so when that will is alter'd.

What any other man, who had learning enough, ~~would~~ might have quoted as a playful and witty illustration of his remarks against this Calvinistic Thesis, Warburton gravely attributes to Shakespear as intentional! & this too with mouth of Lady's Woman.

158   VIII 368–70 | V ii 346–8

OTHELLO.   . . . of one, whose hand,
   Like the base *Judian*, threw a pearl away
   Richer than all his tribe . . .

[Theobald follows in part a suggestion of Warburton's in giving the Quarto reading "Iudean" rather than the Folio "Indian":] . . . I am satis-

---

156[1] C is probably thinking of *Corio-lanus* II ii 26–7, "having been supple and courteous to the people, bonneted", a paral- lel passage cited by *Sh* (Arden) but not by C's predecessors.

fied, in his *Judian*, he is alluding to *Herod*; who in a fit of blind jealousy, threw away such a jewel of a wife as *Mariamne* was to him.

Thus it is for no-poets to comment on the greatest of Poets!—To make Othello say, that he who had killed his wife was like Herod, who had killed his!—O how many beauties in this one Line were impenetrable by the *thought*-swarming ever *idea*less Warburton! Othello wishes to excuse himself on the score of ignorance; & yet not to excuse himself—to excuse himself by accusing. This struggle of feeling is finely conveyed in the word "*base*" which is applied to the *rude* Indian not in his own character, but as the momentary representative of Othello's. Indian means *American* or *Caribb*: a Savage, in genere.—[1]

Annex

C has marked the following passages in *As You Like It* (in Vol ii, between **23** and **34**) with an enclosing line in pencil, apparently for omission.

A   ii 273 | i ii 48–56

ROSALIND. Indeed, there is fortune too hard for nature; when fortune makes nature's natural the cutter off of nature's wit.
CELIA. Peradventure, this is not fortune's work neither, but nature's; who, perceiving our natural wits too dull to reason of such goddesses, hath sent this natural for our whetstone: for always the dulness of the fool is the whetstone of the wits. How now, wit, whither wander you?

B   ii 274 | i ii 81–9

CELIA. Pr'ythee, who is that thou mean'st?
CLOWN. One that old *Frederick* your father loves.
CELIA. My father's love is enough to honour him enough; speak no more of him, you'll be whipt for taxation one of these days.
CLOWN. The more pity, that fools may not speak wisely what wise men do foolishly.
CELIA. By my troth, thou say'st true; for since the little wit that fools have was silenc'd, the little foolery that wise men have makes a great show . . .

C   ii 275 | i ii 107–8

CLOWN. Nay, if I keep not my rank,—
ROSALIND. Thou losest thy old smell.

158[1] "In kind", i.e. it is a generic term for "savage". Most of the commentators before C supported the "Judean" reading, and Malone, who is almost alone in preferring "Indian", takes it to refer to "a people of the East", where there are pearls: *Sh* (Reed).

D II 276 | I ii 141–3

ROSALIND. But is there any else longs to see this broken musick in his sides? is there yet another dotes upon rib-breaking?

E II 278 | I ii 211–15

CELIA. I would I were invisible, to catch the strong fellow by the leg!
ROSALIND. O excellent young man!
CELIA. If I had a thunderbolt in mine eye, I can tell who should down.

F II 281 | I iii 5–9

CELIA. . . . Come, lame me with reasons.
ROSALIND. Then there were two cousins laid up; when the one should be lam'd with reasons, and the other mad without any.

G II 292 | II iv 60–3

ROSALIND. Jove! Jove! this shepherd's passion is much upon my fashion.
CLOWN. And mine, but it grows something stale with me.

H II 305 | III ii 117–22

ROSALIND. I'll graff it with you, and then I shall graff it with a medler; then it will be the earliest fruit i' th' country; for you'll be rotten ere you be half ripe, and that's the right virtue of the medler.
CLOWN. You have said; but whether wisely or no, let the forest judge.

I II 306 | III ii 167–71

CELIA. That's no matter: the feet might bear the verses.
ROSALIND. Ay, but the feet were lame, and could not bear themselves without the verse, and therefore stood lamely in the verse.

J II 307 | III ii 176–8

ROSALIND. . . . I was never so be-rhymed since *Pythagoras*'s time, that I was an *Irish* rat, which I can hardly remember.

K II 307–8 | III ii 197–205

ROSALIND. . . . I pr'ythee, tell me, who is it; quickly, and speak apace; I would thou could'st stammer, that thou might'st pour this concealed man out of thy mouth, as wine comes out of a narrow-mouth'd bottle; either too much at once, or none at all. I pr'ythee, take the cork out of thy mouth, that I may drink thy tidings.
CELIA. So you may put a man in your belly.
ROSALIND. Is he of God's making? . . .

L II 308 | III ii 214–15

ROSALIND. . . . speak, sad brow, and true maid.

M   II 308 | III ii 242–5

ROSALIND. Though it be pity to see such a sight, it well becomes the ground.
CELIA. Cry holla! to thy tongue, I pr'ythee; it curves unseasonably. . . .

N   II 311 | III ii 322–4

ROSALIND. . . . the one lacking the burden of lean and wasteful learning; the other knowing no burden of heavy tedious penury. . . .

O   II 311 | III ii 338–40

ORLANDO. Are you native of this place?
ROSALIND. As the cony, that you see dwell where she is kindled.

P   II 316–17 | III iv 7–17

ROSALIND. His very hair is of the dissembling colour.
CELIA. Something browner than *Judas*'s: marry, his kisses are *Judas*'s own children.
ROSALIND. I' faith, his hair is of a good colour.
CELIA. An excellent colour: your chestnut was ever the only colour.
ROSALIND. And his kissing is as full of sanctity, as the touch of holy beard.
CELIA. He hath bought a pair of cast lips of *Diana*: a nun of winter's sisterhood kisses not more religiously; the very ice of chastity is in them.

Q   II 317 | III iv 21–5

ROSALIND. Do you think so?
CELIA. Yes; I think, he is not a pick-purse, nor a horse-stealer; but for his verity in love, I do think him as concave as a cover'd goblet, or a worm-eaten nut.

R   II 317 | III iv 42–5

CELIA. . . . quite travers athwart the heart of his lover; as a puisny tilter, that spurs his horse but on one side, breaks his staff like a noble goose . . .

S   II 320 | III v 54–6

ROSALIND. . . . 'Tis not her glass, but you, that flatter her;
    And out of you she sees herself more proper,
    Than any of her lineaments can show her.

T   II 320 | III v 66–71

ROSALIND. He's fallen in love with your foulness, and she'll fall in love with my anger. If it be so, as fast as she answers thee with frowning looks, I'll sauce her with bitter words: why look you so upon me?
PHEBE. For no ill will I bear you.

U   II 322–3 | IV i 1–38

JAQUES. I pr'ythee, pretty youth, let me be better acquainted with thee.
ROSALIND. They say, you are a melancholy fellow.

JAQUES. I am so; I do love it better than laughing.

ROSALIND. Those, that are in extremity of either, are abominable fellows; and betray themselves to every modern censure, worse than drunkards.

JAQUES. Why, 'tis good to be sad, and say nothing.

ROSALIND. Why then, 'tis good to be a post.

JAQUES. I have neither the scholar's melancholy, which is emulation; nor the musician's, which is fantastical; nor the courtier's, which is proud; nor the soldier's, which is ambitious; nor the lawyer's, which is politick; nor the lady's, which is nice; nor the lover's, which is all these: but it is a melancholy of mine own, compounded of many simples, extracted from many objects, and indeed the sundry contemplation of my travels, in which my often rumination wraps me in a most humorous sadness.

ROSALIND. A traveller! by my faith, you have great reason to be sad: I fear, you have sold your own lands, to see other mens; then, to have seen much, and to have nothing, is to have rich eyes and poor hands.

JAQUES. Yes, I have gain'd my experience.

Enter Orlando

ROSALIND. And your experience makes you sad: I had rather have a fool to make me merry, than experience to make me sad, and to travel for it too.

ORLANDO. Good-day and happiness, dear *Rosalind!*

JAQUES. Nay, then, God b'w'y you, an you talk in blank verse.

Exit.

ROSALIND. Farewel, monsieur traveller; look, you lisp, and wear strange suits; disable all the benefits of your own country; be out of love with your nativity, and almost chide God for making you that countenance you are; or I will scarce think, you have swam in a gondola.

V   II 323–4 | IV i 51–67

ROSALIND. Nay, an you be so tardy, come no more in my sight; I had as lief be woo'd of a snail.

ORLANDO. Of a snail?

ROSALIND. Ay of a snail; for tho' he comes slowly, he carries his house on his head: a better jointure, I think, than you make a woman; besides, he brings his destiny with him.

ORLANDO. What's that?

ROSALIND. Why, horns; which such as you fain to be beholden to your wives for; for he comes armed in his fortune, and prevents the slander of his wife.

ORLANDO. Virtue is no horn-maker; and my *Rosalind* is virtuous.

ROSALIND. And I am your *Rosalind.*

CELIA. It pleases him to call you so; but he hath a *Rosalind* of a better leer than you.

W   II 324 | IV i 81–8

ORLANDO. Who could be out, being before his beloved mistress?

ROSALIND. Marry, that should you, if I were your mistress? or I should think my honesty ranker than my wit.

ORLANDO. What, of my suit?

ROSALIND. Not out of your apparel, and yet out of your suit.

X II 324–5 | IV i 100–6

ROSALIND. . . . *Leander*, he would have liv'd many a fair year, tho' *Hero* had turn'd nun, if it had not been for a hot midsummer night; for, good youth, he went but forth to wash in the *Hellespont*, and, being taken with the cramp, was drown'd; and the foolish chroniclers of that age found it was,—*Hero* of *Sestos*. But these are all lies . . .

Y II 325 | IV i 138–42

ROSALIND. I might ask you for your commission, but I do take thee *Orlando* for my husband: there's a girl goes before the priest, and certainly a woman's thought runs before her actions.
ORLANDO. So do all thoughts; they are wing'd.

Z II 325 | IV i 165–73

ORLANDO. A man that had a wife with such a wit, he might say, wit, whither wilt?
ROSALIND. Nay, you might keep that check for it, 'till you met your wife's wit going to your neighbour's bed.
ORLANDO. And what wit could wit have to excuse that?
ROSALIND. Marry, to say she came to seek you there: you shall never take her without her answer, unless you take her without her tongue.

AA II 325 | IV i 182–7

ROSALIND. Ay, go your ways, go your ways; I knew what you would prove, my friends told me as much, and I thought no less; that flattering tongue of yours won me; 'tis but one cast away, and so come death: Two o' th' clock is your hour!
ORLANDO. Ay, sweet *Rosalind*.

BB II 327 | IV i 202–4

CELIA. . . . We must have your doublet and hose pluck'd over your head, and show the world what the bird hath done to her own nest.

CC II 328 | IV iii 1–5

ROSALIND. How say you now, is it not past two o'clock? I wonder much, *Orlando* is not here.
CELIA. I warrant you, with pure love and troubled brain, he hath ta'en his bow and arrows, and is gone forth to sleep: Look, who comes here.

DD II 329 | IV iii 22–30

ROSALIND.   Come, come, you're a fool,
    And turn'd into th' extremity of love.
    I saw her hand, she has a leathern hand,
    A free-stone coloured hand; I verily did think,
    That her old gloves were on, but 'twas her hands;
    She has a huswife's hand; but that's no matter;

I say, she never did invent this letter;
This is a man's invention and his hand.
SILVIUS. Sure, it is hers.

EE II 329 | IV iii 32–6

ROSALIND. . . . A stile for challengers; why, she defies me,
Like *Turk* to Christian; woman's gentle brain
Could not drop forth such giant rude invention;
Such *Ethiop* words, blacker in their effect
Than in their countenance; will you hear the letter?

FF II 336 | v ii 30–2

ROSALIND. . . . There was never any thing so sudden, but the fight of two rams,
and *Caesar*'s thrasonical brag of I *came, saw,* and *overcame* . . .

GG II 336 | v ii 38–40

ROSALIND. . . . which they will climb incontinent, or else be incontinent before
marriage; they are in the very wrath of love, and they will together . . .

HH II 336 | v ii 52–9

ROSALIND. . . . for now I speak to some purpose, that I know, you are a gentleman of good conceit. I speak not this, that you should bear a good opinion of
my knowledge; insomuch, I say, I know what you are; neither do I labour for
a greater esteem than may in some little measure draw a belief from you to do
yourself good, and not to grace me. Believe then, if you please . . .

II II 338 | v ii 103–8

PHEBE. If this be so, why blame you me to love you?
SILVIUS. If this be so, why blame you me to love you?
ORLANDO. If this be so, why blame you me to love you?
ROSALIND. Who do you speak to, why blame you me to love you?
ORLANDO. To her that is not here, nor doth not hear?

JJ II 345 | Epilogue 1–3, 7–9

ROSALIND. It is not the fashion to see the Lady the epilogue; but it is no more un-
handsome, than to see the Lord the prologue. . . . What a case am I in then, that
am neither a good epilogue, nor can insinuate with you in the behalf of a good
play?

Copy B

Stockdale's Edition of Shakespeare: including, in one volume, the whole of his dramatic works; with explanatory notes compiled from various commentators. Embellished with a striking likeness of the author, &c. London 1784. 8°.

Harvard University (Houghton Library)

Inscribed on the title-page: "Miss Holm from her affectionate friend A. Gillman"; and on p ‾3: "Ellen Holm given to her by her dear friend Mrs Gillman", and above this the cancelled name "James Harding." There are short strokes in pencil or ink against the titles of most of the plays in the Table of Contents; these do not appear to have been C's work.

CONTENTS. Sig A2–[A2ᵛ] Preface; sig A3–A4 [x] Rowe's *Life* and Shakespeare's Will; 1–22 *Tempest*; 23–44 *Two Gentlemen*; 45–73 *Merry Wives*; 75–102 *Measure for Measure*; 103–20 *Comedy of Errors*; 121–46 *Much Ado*; 147–74 *Love's Labour's Lost*; 175–96 *Midsummer Night's Dream*; 197–222 *Merchant of Venice*; 223–50 *As You Like It*; 251–76 *Taming of the Shrew*; 277–305 *All's Well*; 307–32 *Twelfth Night*; 333–62 *Winter's Tale*; 363–86 *Macbeth*; 387–411 *King John*; 413–40 *Richard II*; 441–72 *1 Henry IV*; 473–507 *2 Henry IV*; 509–41 *Henry V*; 543–70 *1 Henry VI*; 572–602 *2 Henry VI*; 603–32 *3 Henry VI*; 633–69 *Richard III*; 671–702 *Henry VIII*; 703–39 *Coriolanus*; 741–65 *Julius Caesar*; 767–802 *Antony and Cleopatra*; 803–29 *Timon of Athens*; 831–55 *Titus Andronicus*; 857–91 *Troilus and Cressida*; 893–928 *Cymbeline*; 929–65 *Lear*; 967–98 *Romeo and Juliet*; 999–1041 *Hamlet*; 1043–79 *Othello*.

DATE. Probably between Apr 1816 and 1818, but possibly earlier. The name "James Harding" on p ‾3 ties the vol to the Gillman family: Anne Gillman's maiden name was Harding, and both her father and her brother were named James. It is possible that C gave or bequeathed his own Shakespeare to the brother, a notary with whom he was on cordial terms (*CL* v 132), but more likely that this copy had belonged to the father, and that C found it in the house when he moved in in Apr 1816. C does not appear to have used this copy in the preparation of any of the lectures on Shakespeare.

1   pp 45–6 | *Merry Wives* I i 22–3

SLENDER. All his successors, gone before him, have done't; and all his ancestors, that come after him, may: they may give the dozen white luces in their coat.

SHALLOW. It is an old coat.

EVANS. The dozen white louses do become an old coat well; it agrees
well, passant: it is a familiar beast to man, and signifies—love.*

SHALLOW. The luce is the fresh fish,/. Eva. t/The salt fish is an old coat.

[Editor's note:] The luce is a pike or jack. This passage is also supposed
to point at Sir Thomas Lucy, who was the cause of Shakspeare's leaving
Stratford.

* The jest in this passage has not been understood, from two speeches
having been printed as one, & both given to Shallow—whereas the words
"The salt fish is an old coat." belongs to the Welshman. Shallow no
soon⟨er⟩ corrects one mistake of Sir Hugh's, namely, Louse for Luce i.e.
Pike, the honest Welshman falls into another, namely, Cod (which he pronounces Cot) for Coat. The Luce is a fresh Fish, quoth Shallow—Aye!
aye! quoth Sir Hugh—you are right. The *fresh* Fish is a Luce, it is an old
Cod (Baccalà) that is the *salt* fish.[1]

2   p 177, pencil | *Midsummer Night's Dream* I i 214–19

HERMIA. And in the wood, where often you and I
Upon faint primrose-beds were wont to lye,
Emptying our bosoms of their counsels ~~swell'd~~ sweet;
There my Lysander and myself shall meet:
And thence, from Athens, turn away our eyes,
To seek new friends and strange compani~~ons~~es.

* The whole of the three speeches being in rhyme there is evidently a
mistake of swell'd for sweet, and strange companions for stranger Companies.[1]

2A   p 179, pencil | II i 32–4

FAIRY. ~~Either~~ Or I mistake your shape and making quite,[1]
Or else you are that shrewd and knavish sprite,
Call'd Robin Goodfellow . . .

3   p 283 | *All's Well* II i 12–15

KING.   . . . let higher Italy
(Those '~~bated,~~ that inherit but the fall

1[1] See COPY A **10** and nn. The point is
reiterated in COPY D **4**.

2[1] C comes back to this point in COPY D
7. The Quarto text read "sweld" and
"strange companions". Theobald pointed
out that these words violated the rhyme
scheme, and "restored" the lines as C indicates. *Sh* (Arden) also accepts Theobald's
emendations.

2A[1] C objects to the extra syllable in the
line, but appears to be alone in doing so.

Of the last monarchy) see, that you come
Not to woo honour, but to wed it . . .

bastards[1]

4 p 310, pencil | *Twelfth Night* I iii 129–31

SIR TOBY. . . . My very walk should be a jig; I would not so much as make
water, but in a sink-a-pace.

[Editor's note:] * That is, a *cinque-pace*; the name of a dance, the measures whereof are regulated by the number five.

* Evidently, a Pun: & one quite worthy of Sir Toby Belch. Sink of
p——.[1]

5 p 312, pencil | I v 174–6

VIOLA. . . . Good beauties, let me sustain no scorn; I am very comptible,
even to the least sinister usage.

[Editor's note on "comptible":] That is, very *submissive.

* sensible[1]

6 p 316 | II iii 164–9

SIR TOBY. He shall think, by the letters that thou wilt drop, that they come
from my niece, and that she is in love with him.
MARIA. My purpose is, indeed, a horse of that colour.
SIR ANDREW. And your horse now would make him an ass.

Sir To.[1]

7 pp 392–3, cropped | *King John* II i 187–90

CONSTANCE.   I have but this to say,—
That he's not only plagued for her sin,

3[1] See COPY A **37** and n 1.

4[1] C this time is not challenging the editor's explanation (which continues to be standard), but adding another dimension to it: in keeping with the heroic scale of all his actions, Sir Toby would make water in a "Sink of Piss". C makes the point again in COPY D **12**.

5[1] That is, in 20th-century usage, sensitive. C repeats this gloss—an improvement on his predecessors' efforts—in COPY D **14**.

6[1] Others have noted that this line is rather quick-witted for Sir Andrew; Tyrwhitt and others suggested that it might be reassigned to Sir Toby.

But God hath made her sin and her the plague
On this removed issue, plagu'd for her,
And with her. (1) Plague her son; his injury,
Her injury, the beadle to her sin,
All punish'd in the person of this child,
And all for her (2); A plague upon her!*

[Editor quotes Johnson's notes:] at (1) "He is not only made miserable by vengeance for her *sin* or *crime*; but her *sin*, her *offspring*, and she, are made the instruments of that vengeance, on this descendant; who, though of the second generation, is *plagued for her and with her*; to whom she is not only the cause but the instrument of evil"; and at (2) "Instead of inflicting vengeance on this innocent and remote descendant, *punish her son*, her immediate offspring: then the affliction will fall where it is deserved; *his injury* will be *her injury*, and the misery of her *sin*; her son will be a *beadle*, or chastiser, to her *crimes*, which are now *all punished in the person of this child*."

* Dr Johnson's [e]xplanation reminds me of the School-boy's Construing [o]f his Guy Vulpes, calidus, frigidus, [p]ostquam [o]mnia [c]œpit, Attamen inventus ille recepit eum; Guy Vulpes, Guy Faux, calidus, a hot-headed Fanatic, frigidus, a cool deliberate villain, postquam [o]mnia cœpit, after he had stowed all the barrels of Gun-powder in the Cellar under the Parliament House, Attamen inventus, Never the less having been found out, ille he recepit eum took him into custody.[1] [. . . . .]^a Ille, [? boy]?—Ille is the Constable. This passage is evidently corrupted & mispointed—it should be thus: And with her plagued: her Sin (i.e. John) his Injury (⟨i.e. and his⟩ injurious act, and conduct), Her injury (⟨&⟩ her own cruelty to her Grandchild) the beadle (i.e. abettor and executor) to her Sin (i.e. her Son, John) All punish'd &c[2]

7^a A few words lost in cropping

7[1] C recorded this elaborate joke—apparently his own invention—on at least three occasions, once in a notebook entry assigned to 1808 (*CN* III 3313); once in this marginal note; and once in a letter (*CL* III 512, 29 Jun 1814). It will appear as an entry in *PW* (*CC*). The imaginary situation is that of a schoolboy who has composed a bad Latin elegiac couplet and is then asked to construe it. A literal and as nearly as possible word-for-word translation of the Latin text might run: "Guy Fawkes, hot, cold, after he began everything, but nevertheless having been discovered, *he* received him." With *ille*, the subject suddenly changes, producing an obscurity. What Johnson's explanation had in common with the school-boy's construing, to C's mind, was perhaps not only an obscurity in pronoun reference but also the function or identity of the imaginary law-officer, Johnson's "*beadle*".

7[2] See COPY A **66** and n 1.

8　p 443 | *1 Henry IV* I ii 23–5

FALSTAFF. Marry, then, sweet wag, when thou art king, let not us, that
　are squires of the night's body, be call'd thieves of the day's beauty . . .

[Editor's note:] Mr. Steevens is of opinion, that our poet, by the expression *thieves of the day's beauty*, meant only, "*Let not us who are body
squires to the night*, i.e. adorn the night, *be called a disgrace to the day*."

? *booty*[1]

9　p 457 | III i 13–23

GLENDOWER. I cannot blame him: at my nativity,
　　The front of heaven was full of fiery shapes,
　　Of burning cressets/-lights; and, at my birth,
　　The frame and the foundation of the earth
　　Shak'd like a coward.
HOTSPUR. Why, so it would have done,
　　At the same season, if your mother's cat
　　*Had ~~but~~ kitten'd, though yourself had ne'er been born.
GLENDOWER. I say, the earth did shake when I was born.
HOTSPUR. And I̲ say, that the earth was not of m̲y̲ mind,
　　If you suppose, as fearing you it shook.

* or—had your Mother's Cat
But kitten'd, tho' &c[1]

10　pp 459–60, cropped | III i 209–11

*GLENDOWER. Nay, if you melt, then will she run mad.
　　　　　[*The Lady speaks again in Welsh.*
MORTIMER. O, I am ignorance itself in this.
†GLENDOWER. She bids you,
　　Upon the wanton rushes lay you down . . .

* Even this "*Nay*" so *be-dwelt on* in the Speaking as to be equivalent to
a dissyllable – ᴗ, is characteristic of the old solemn Glendower; but † the
imperfect—She bids you—is one of those fine Hair-lines of exquisite
Judgement peculiar to Shakespear—thus detaching the Lady's speech &
giving it the individuality and entireness of a little Poem, while he draws
attention to it.

8[1]　See COPY A **73** and n 1.
9[1]　In each of the three changes C pro-　poses to this passage, he is concerned with
the metre of the lines.

11   p 481, cropped | *2 Henry IV* II ii 23–4

PRINCE HENRY. . . . and God knows, whether those that bawl out $\wedge$ the ruins of thy linen, shall inherit his kingdom . . .

$\wedge$ of—i.e. his Bastar[ds][1]

12   p 482 | II ii 151–3

PRINCE HENRY. Sup any women with him?
PAGE. None, my lord, but old mistress Quickly, and mistress Doll Tear-sheet.*

* I am disposed to think that this respectable young Lady's name is a very old corruption, & that Shakespear wrote Doll Tear-street, *terere viam*—i.e. Street-walker. Indeed, the Prince's observation proves it. This Doll Tear-*street* should be some *road*?[1]

13   p [542] | *1 Henry VI*

Read aloud any two or three passages in blank verse even from Sh's earliest Dramas, as Love's Labour lost & Romeo and Juliet: and then read in the same way the introductory Speech of Hen. VI. I. with especial attention to the *Metre*: & if you not[a] feel the impossibility of the latter having been written by Shakespear—all I dare suggest, is, that you may have Ears: for so have Asses! But *an Ear* you can not have, judice[1]

S. T. C.

14   p 641 | *Richard III* I iii 323–5

GLOUCESTER. I do the wrong, and first begin to brawl.
    The secret mischiefs that I set abroach,
    I lay unto the grievous charge of others.*

* the ordinary trick of bad poets, how gloriously appropriate here

15   p 644 | II i

Hardihood *in boasting* [? of] to himself of villainy, while others are present to feed his pride of Superiority—

13[a] Presumably in error for "do not"

11[1] C gives the customary explanation. Other critics have not thought it necessary to add "of" to the line.
12[1] See COPY A **74** and n 1.

13[1] "In the opinion of". This opinion is not supported by Shakespearean scholarship.

16   p 652 | III iv

[Richard, as Lord Protector, interrupts a council that is setting a date for the Coronation, appearing to be in a good humour though actually plotting the death of Hastings—a member of the council—for treason.]

presence of *mind*

16A   p 667 | v iii 201–3

KING RICHARD. . . . . And, if I die, no soul shall pity me:—
Nay, wherefore should they? since that I myself
Find in myself no pity to myself.*

17   p 705 | *Coriolanus* I i 179–82

MARCIUS.   . . . He that depends
Upon your favours, swims with fins of lead,
*And hews down oaks with rushes. Hang ye! Trust ye?
With every minute you do change a mind . . .

* I suspect that Sh. wrote—*Trust* ye? HANG ye!—
With every &c.[1]

18   p 768 | *Antony and Cleopatra* I ii 38–9

CHARMIAN. Then, belike, my children shall have no names: Pr'ythee, how many boys and wenches must I have?
SOOTHSAYER. If every of your wishes had a womb,
And fortel every wish, a million.

[Editor's note:] The meaning is, If you had as many wombs as you will have wishes, and *I should* foretel all those wishes, I should foretel a million of children. It is an ellipsis very frequent in conversation;—I should shame you, and tell all; that is, *and if I should* tell all. *And is* for *and if*, which was anciently, and is still provincially used for *if*.

It may be so, certainly: & therefore I would not alter the text. Still however I hold it most probable, that foretel is a mistake for fertile. And the more so because fer*tile* is so frequent an adjective to Womb, elsewhere.[1]

---

[17][1] This line does not appear to have been questioned by other commentators.

[18][1] The Folio reading is "foretell". Johnson thought it defensible, but Malone said that the emendation to "fertile" was "absolutely necessary" to make sense of the lines, and Steevens supported him by pointing out a parallel use of "fertile" as an epithet to "womb" in *Timon of Athens*: all these statements are included in *Sh* (Reed). "Fertile" is accepted by *Sh* (Arden). C returns to this passage in COPY D **69**.

19   p [827] | *Timon of Athens* v i 179–81

TIMON.   . . . for myself,
  There's not a whittle in the unruly camp,
  But I do prize it at my love, before
  The reverend'st throat in Athens.

[Editor's note:] A *whittle* is still in the midland counties the common name for a pocket clasp knife, such as children use.

4.[1] ~~or~~ "whittle" has here the same double meaning as Degen in German, and *Blade* in English—the sword & the swordsman, *an honest blade* &c.[2]

20   p 892 | *Cymbeline* I i 1–3

I GENTLEMAN. You do not meet a man, but frowns: our bloods
  No more obey the heavens, than our courtiers',
  Still seem, as does the king's.

[Editor's note:] * Dr Johnson observes, that this passage is so difficult, that commentators may differ concerning it without animosity or shame;—that the lines stand as they were originally written, and that a paraphrase, such as the licentious and abrupt expressions of our author too frequently require, will make emendation unnecessary. *We do not meet a man but frowns; our bloods*—our countenances, which, in popular speech, are said to be regulated by the temper of the blood,—*no more obey* the laws of *heaven,*—which direct us to appear what we really are,—*than our courtiers*; that is, than the *bloods of our courtiers*; but our bloods, like theirs,—*still seem, as doth the king's.*

  You do not meet a man but frowns: our *Bloods*
  Not more obey the Heavens, than our Count'nances
  Still seem, as does the King's.—
See my Mss Note.[1] The word "You" is an additional Confirmation of the *our* being used in this place for *men* generally and indefinitely: just as "*You* do not meet" is the same as "*One* does not meet."
  Of the Erratum by Anticipation or Fore-glance of the Printer's Eye, there is a striking Instance in Ant. and Cleopatra, where "Mermaids" still stands instead of "Sea-queens," the word demanded by the Poetry & the word in North's Plutarch from which the whole Speech is borrowed.[2] To have called Cleopatra's Ladies of Honour Mermaids collectively, & then

---

19[1] The number refers to the editorial note number.
  19[2] *Degen* is indeed used with the same double meaning.
  20[1] I.e. **21** below.
  20[2] See COPY A **134** n 1.

to describe *one* of them as "a seeming Mermaid" is the very last fault that can with any minimum of probability be attributed to Shakespear.—

21   pp 893–5,[a] cropped | **20** textus

* One of the commonest errors of Compositors in setting the types is that of anticipation, the eye having glanced on some word in the Mss beginning with the same Syllable or perhaps only the same letter:—as the Text stands, it is capable of a good sense by omitting the comma after Courtiers, & a break after King's—when the 2[nd.] Gent. [. . . . .] interrupts the Speaker.—But yet I strongly suspect, that Shakespear first expresses *generally* the same thought that he lower down repeats with a particular application to the persons meant—a common use of the pronoun, *we*; where the Speaker does not really mean to include himself—& that the original word was "Count'nances"/ Johnson's assertion that Bloods means Countenances is false both in thought conveyed (for it was never a popular belief that the Stars governed men's Countenances) and in the usage which requires an antithesis of Blood (i.e. the Temperament of the four *Humors*, Choler, Melancholy, Phlegm, and the red globules, or sanguine portion) which was supposed not to be in our own power, but dependent on the influence of the heavenly bodies, & the Countenances which are in our power really, tho' from flattery we bring them into ~~the~~ no less apparent dependence on the Sovereign's than the form⟨er⟩ are in actual dependence [on] the Constellations[1]

22   pp 1012–13, cropped | *Hamlet* II ii 178–82

HAMLET. Ay, sir, to be honest, as this world goes,
     Is to be one man pick'd out of ten thousand.
POLONIUS. That's very true, my lord.
HAMLET. For if the sun breeds maggots in a dead dog,
     Being a god, kissing carrion,—

[Editor's note quotes Warburton's gloss:] . . . *For if the sun breed maggots in a dead dog, which though a god, yet shedding its heat and influence upon carrion—*

1.[1] It *is* a *very* ingenious comment; but yet its validity is by no means clear to me. I rather think that the train of Thought in Hamlet's mind is sim-

---

21[a] Written before **20**

21[1] See COPY A **136** and n.   note number.
22[1] The number refers to the editorial

ply—If the Sun being a god breeds maggots in a dead Dog, we need not marvel that ~~the~~ an ungodly *world* (which is the opposite of heavenly) breeds Scoundrels out of such carrion as Human [. . . . .][2] the Objection of Libertines had intervened, between "as the world goes" and the Sun &c, Shakespere would have given some hint, tho' but in a single word, even tho' hidden in a corner of a metaphor. Absolute Chasms I find no where in his writings. By the bye, there is a difficulty in Hamlet's answer to Ros: Then are our Beggars Bodies[3]

22[2] C returns to this much controverted passage, with a different explanation, in COPY D **147**; and in COPY D **149**. In the last line of textus, "god" is an emendation proposed for the original reading "good" by Hanmer and Warburton; C is following the general line of Warburton's reasoning.

22[3] I.e. in the dialogue between Hamlet and Rosencrantz in II ii 261–4, where Rosencrantz says (the text follows this edition), "Truly, and I hold ambition of so airy and light a quality, that it is but a shadow's shadow", to which Hamlet replies, "Then are our beggars, bodies; and our monarchs, and out-stretch'd heroes, the beggars' shadows . . .". The "difficulty" that struck other editors was not in the text but in the train of thought, which C continued to find obscure: he returns to this passage in COPY D **150**. *Sh* (Reed) offers Johnson's comment: the passage "is a ridicule of those declamations against wealth and greatness, that seem to make happiness consist in poverty". *Sh* (Arden) paraphrases: "Since ambition is 'a shadow's shadow', the only substantial beings must be those with no ambition, i.e. beggars, and the ambitious . . . must be shadows of them."

Copy C

The Dramatic Works of Shakspeare, in six volumes; with notes by Joseph Rann, A.M. Vicar of St. Trinity, in Coventry. 6 vols. Oxford 1786–[94]. 8°.

Folger Shakespeare Library

On v 343, below **10**, is written in pencil in an unidentified hand: "Notes by Coleridge. I. E.—." The same hand, again in pencil, has written "2 leaves misplaced" on IV 693—mysteriously, since there is nothing wrong with the collation of the volume. Perhaps two leaves of notes had once been inserted there. There are light pencil-marks in the text of *The Tempest* that do not seem to be connected with C: I 12, 14, 18, 61, 68, 71, 76, 78, 79. Pencilled notations by librarians or bookdealers appear in all vols.

CONTENTS. I [1]–83 *Tempest*; [85]–164 *Two Gentlemen*; [165]–263 *Merry Wives*; [265]–368 *Measure for Measure*; [369]–434 *Comedy of Errors*; [435]–527 *Much Ado*; [529]–628 *Love's Labour's Lost*; II [1]–79 *Midsummer-Night's Dream*; [81]–174 *Merchant of Venice*; [175]–269 *As You Like It*; [271]–364 *Taming of the Shrew*; [365]–470 *All's Well*; [471]–561 *Twelfth Night*; [563]–676 *Winter's Tale*; III [1]–130 *Troilus and Cressida*; [131]–265 *Cymbeline*; [267]–361 *King John*; [363]–461 *Richard II*; [463]–572 *1 Henry IV*; [573]–690 *2 Henry IV*; IV [1]–120 *Henry V*; [121]–221 *1 Henry VI*; [223]–336 *2 Henry VI*; [337]–446 *3 Henry VI*; [447]–580 *Richard III*; [581]–699 *Henry VIII*; V [1]–141 *Coriolanus*; [143]–237 *Julius Caesar*; [239]–382 *Antony and Cleopatra*; [383]–485 *Timon of Athens*; [487]–607 *Romeo and Juliet*; VI [1]–141 *King Lear*; [143]–243 *Macbeth*; [245]–410 *Hamlet*; [411]–549 *Othello*.

DATE. Oct–Nov 1813, intensively, and probably other times as well. Notes for the Bristol lectures of this period include page references to this edition (*Lects 1808–1819—CC*—I 503, 525, 549); **25** appears to be a lecturer's direction to himself; and several notes overlap with the content of the Bristol lectures, as indicated in footnotes below.

1   I 7, lightly cropped | *Tempest* I ii 16–20

PROSPERO. . . . I have done nothing but in care of thee,
(Of thee, my dear one! thee, my daughter!) who
Art ignorant of what thou art, nought knowing
Of whence I am; nor that I am more better(r)[a]
Than Prospero . . .

1[a] Here and in subsequent entries, Rann's footnote indicators, superscript in the original, have been set in parentheses to avoid confusion with editorial matter

[Rann's note (*r*):] Such ungrammatical expressions, as *double comparatives* and *superlatives*, occur so frequently in our author, and the generality of old dramatic writers, that it would be endless to remark them all, and impertinent to correct them.*

* Yet, tho' I admit there is no necessity for alteratio[n] here, I incline to think that the Line as written by Shakes[p.] stood "Of whence I am; nor that I'm more or better Than &c"—

2   I 11, lightly cropped | I ii 118–20

MIRANDA.   I should sin
     To think but nobly of my grandmother:
     Good wombs have borne bad sons.*

* This half-line evidently belongs to Prospero. In the innocent recluse, Miranda, it is inappropriate & unnatural.——["]grandmother."—You do rightly, answers Prospero. "Good wom[bs] have borne bad Sons."[1]

3   II ⁻2, referring to II 91 | *Merchant of Venice* I ii 68–72

PORTIA. . . . he understands not me, nor I him: he hath neither Latin, French, nor Italian; and you will come into the court and swear that I have a poor pennyworth in the English.

How boldly Sh. outstares the absurd system of cold-blooded Probability, (i.e. fac simile of real Life) in the Drama, i.e. the Imitation, ergo, *not* the Copy or Fac Simile of it, may be instanced among a 1000 others in p. 91, last three lines[1]—in which he makes Portia in English disdain her knowlege of English.

4   II 92 | I ii 79–83

PORTIA. That he hath a neighbourly charity in him; for he borrow'd a box of the ear of the Englishman, and swore he would pay him again, when he was able: I think the Frenchman became his surety, and (*q*)seal'd under for another.

[Rann's note (*q*):] bound himself to give the *Englishman* another;—alluding to the frequent assistance, and constant promises given by the *French* to the *Scots*, during their contests with the *English*.

2[1] See COPY A **2** and n 1.
3[1] The distinction between imitation and copy is a staple of C's criticism; see QUAR- TERLY JOURNAL **3** and n 10 above, and COPY D **3** below (where C once again cites these lines from *The Merchant of Venice*).

No!—likewise received a box of the Ear for his Interference, & like his Ally, the Scotchman, bound himself to return it at a fit time.[1]—This Play must, therefore, have been written under Elizabeth. Sʰ.ʳᵉ was too wise to have hazarded this *just* sarcasm under "the minion-kissing Scot," James I.[2]   S. T. C.

5   II 133, cropped | III ii 115–18

BASSANIO.   . . . What demy-god
    Hath come so near creation? Move these eyes?
    Or whether, riding on the balls of mine,
    Seem they in motion?*

Beautiful Illustration of the true cause of pleasure derived from [? ~~pain~~] fine painting—CAUSATUM, i.e., transfert IN REM CAUSANTEM[1]—the Picture moves, [. . .] O! ανηρ [. . .][2]

6   I 13 | *Coriolanus* I i 270–2

SICINUS.   Besides, if things go well,
    Opinion, that so sticks on Marcius, shall
    Of his (*f*)demerits rob Cominius . . .

[Rann's note (*f*):] *demerits*]—formerly the same as *merits*.

due merits?[1]

7   v 20 | I iv 13–15

MARCIUS. . . . . Tullus Aufidius, is he within your walls?
I SENATOR. No, nor a man (*r*)~~but~~ fears you less than he,
    That's lesser than a little.

4¹ C is right, but his explanation is not incompatible with Rann's (which is based on Warburton's).

4² C's respect for the learning of James I was always balanced against his nationality and his notorious favouritism towards handsome young men: see e.g. HACKET *Scrinia reserata* **14, 32, 35**. In the last of these notes he uses the word "minionism"; but no direct source has been traced for the phrase in quotation marks, and it may not, in fact, be a quotation.

5¹ I.e. "*the thing caused* carries over *into the thing causing*". C was to pursue this idea in a lecture on the fine arts on 10 Mar

1818 when he discussed "the effect produced by the congruity of the animal impression with the reflective Powers of the mind—so that not the Thing presented, but that which is *re*-presented, by the Thing, is the source of the Pleasure": *Lects 1808–1819* (*CC*) II 218.

5² The missing word here was almost certainly μυριόνους "myriad-minded"—an epithet C used frequently for Shakespeare: see COPY A **23** n 1.

6¹ *Sh* (Reed) cites Steevens and Malone to the effect that "*Merits* and *Demerits* had anciently the same meaning"; *Sh* (Arden) concurs.

[Rann's note (*r*):]—*that fears you less*; *fears you more*.

evidently, "*that*": "*but*" would imply that Aufidius did fear Marcius a little, which never could be the Senator's meaning.[1]

---

8   v 31, cropped | I ix 45–6

MARCIUS.   . . . When steel grows
   Soft as the parasite's silk, (*u*)let him be made
   A coverture for the wars!—

(*u*) *corrupt* but I can propose no amendmen[t.*]

   * those who are familiar with the manuscripts of the age of Elizabeth & James, will not recoil, as others would naturally do, at the conjectural reading: "*be thimbles made.*"[1] The b is often confounded with the l, & the initial of one word made the last letter of the preceding, while the last syllable of common words is expressed by abridgement, as *thimb* for thimbles & the[a]

---

9   v 276, cropped | *Antony and Cleopatra* II ii 206–7

ENOBARBUS. Her gentlewomen, like the Nereides,
   So many <u>mermaids,</u> tended her i' the eyes . . .

An evident [cor]ruption. [Wh]at to [su]bstitute, [is] not so [c]lear.—[1]

---

10   v 343 | IV vii 7–8

SCARUS. I had a wound here that was like a T,
   But now 'tis made an H.

β—ergo, he must have received two other wounds, α and β:

8[a] The remainder of the note is cut away

7[1] The Folio reading is "that"; Johnson's emendation to "but" has been generally ignored.

8[1] The speech in which these lines appear is the most disputed passage in the play, but no other commentator appears to have suggested or approved of C's conjectured "thimbles". Rann at n (*u*) proposes "let that silk be wrought into armour instead of *steel*".

9[1] See COPY A **134** and n 1.

$\underset{\alpha}{\vrule} \vdash \beta$—but besides there is a Pun here—his wound growing cold began to ache, which was then pronounced "aitch"—[1]*

* By the bye, what is the origin of the phrase, "to a T": as, "it fits me to a T."? Why, was the Letter chosen?—*Perhaps*, T. might usually stand in accounts & for a Thousandth part, as M. does now for a million; but this is indeed a mere *"Perhaps."*—[2]

11   VI ⁻2, referring to VI 5 | *King Lear* I i 55

This Edition, and half a score others of this, & other great Poets, by their own Countrymen, furnish by their notes & explanations a good ground of analogy for the faith, we ought to *pin upon* the old Scholiasts of the old Greek Poets. Ex. gr./p. 5. "wield the matter"—vide note—*"describe, express."*[1] What a fine notion a foreigner would gather of the meaning of the plain English word, "wield", from this gloss!!—And how unfathomably *bathetic* the Line of the Poet would become!!—This once for all: for all the explanations are of the same Character, obsolete words excepted.—   S. T. C.—

12   VI 3, cropped | I i 3–7

GLOUCESTER. . . . now, in the division of the kingdom, it appears not which of the dukes he values most; for (*a*)equalities are so weigh'd, that curiosity in neither can make choice of either's moiety.

[Rann's note (*a*):]—the <u>qualities</u> are so exactly balanced, that the severest scrutiny, the most scrupulous or capricious disposition, cannot give one portion the preference to the other.

! The sens[e] is evidently[:] the *shares, intended* to be equal, are, indee[d,] so equal that the most minute & scrupulous Care ⟨(*curiositas*)⟩ could find *no* ground for choosing one rather than another. This Sh. calls *"Equalities"* i.e. shares perfectly equal.[1]   S. T. C.

10[1] C makes the same point about the pronunciation of "ache" in COPY A **86**.

10[2] According to *OED*, the original sense of "T" in this phrase is obscure: various suggestions are reported, the idea that "T" stood for the initial of a particular word (as in C's proposal)—but particularly that that word may have been "tittle" ("to a tittle")—seeming the most plausible explanation.

11[1] When Goneril assures her father, "Sir, I love you more than words can wield the matter," Rann produces only the gloss quoted (in full) by C.

12[1] As earlier editors had pointed out, the Quarto reading is "equalities", the Folio "qualities": *Sh* (Reed).

12A VI 5 | I i 37–8

LEAR. The map there.—Know, that we have ∧ divided,
　In three, our kingdom . . .[1]

12B VI 6 | I i 69–70

REGAN. I am made of that self metal as my sister,
　(*l*)And prize me at her worth. . . .

[Rann's note (*l*):] And, as such, conceive myself equally entitled to your regard—*And prize you*—set the same high value upon you that she does.!!!

13 VI 8 | I i 127–8

LEAR.　　　　　　　　　　. . . Cornwall, and Albany,
　With my two daughters' dowers (*b*)digest this third:

[Rann's note (*b*):] *digest*]—possess, enjoy.!!*

* digerere, i.e. bear off between you, or blend into your former portions this third. The metaphor is taken from pharmacy.[1]

14 VI 152, pencil | *Macbeth* I iii 51–61

BANQUO. Good sir, why do you start; and seem to fear
　Things that do sound so fair?—I' the name of truth,
　Are ye fantastical, or that indeed
　Which outwardly ye shew? My noble partner
　You greet with present grace, and great prediction
　Of noble having, and of royal hope,
　That he seems rapt withal; to me you speak not:
　If you can look into the seeds of time,
　And say, which grain will grow, and which will not;
　Speak then to me, who neither beg, nor fear,
　Your favours, nor your hate.

12A[1] C suggests that a word may be missing, but does not attempt to fill in the gap. The line is complete without it, and neither Quarto nor Folio includes another word at this point.

13[1] For his first suggestion, C typically goes back to the root meaning of the compound verb. The prefix *di-* stands in this case for *dis-* "apart" or "in different directions", and *gerere* is "bear", "carry", etc. In favour of his second, *OED* gives examples of the pharmaceutical sense—"digest" (vb) 10, "digestion" (sb) 5, both denominating a process of dissolving by gentle heat.

Strict moral feeling of Sh./ those only are tempted who have tempted the Tempter by [? false/former] Thoughts[1]

15 VI 155, pencil, cropped | I iii 130–7

MACBETH. . . . This supernatural soliciting
    Cannot be ill; cannot be good:—If ill,
    Why hath it given me earnest of success,
    Commencing in a truth? I am thane of Cawdor:
    If good, why do I yield to that suggestion
    Whose horrid image doth unfix my hair,
    And make my seated heart knock at my ribs,
    Against the use of nature?

First Struggl[e] of Conscience[,] his disobedien[ce] to which is to destroy him b[y] the very pang[s] of Compuncti[on]. *"Remorse."*[1]

16 VI 155, pencil, cropped | I iii 143–4

MACBETH. If chance will have me king, why, chance may crown me,
    Without my stir.

Superstit[ion]

17 VI 156, pencil, cropped | I iii 149–52

MACBETH.   . . . my dull brain was wrought
    With things forgotten. Kind gentlemen, your pains
    Are register'd where every day I turn
    The leaf to read them.—Let us toward the king.—

already [? temporizing—*Publicola*][1]

18 VI 157, pencil | I iv 15–20

KING. . . . The sin of my ingratitude even now
    Was heavy on me: Thou art so far before,

14[1] Cf a report of the lecture of 2 Nov 1813 (*Lects 1808–1819—CC*—I 531): "Mr. COLERIDGE proceeded to show how Macbeth became early a tempter to himself".

15[1] I.e. a similar psychological process is represented in C's tragedy *Remorse*, which had had a successful run of 20 nights at Drury Lane Jan–Feb 1813 and had gone through three editions in the same year.

17[1] Otherwise unlike Macbeth, and not especially noted for "temporizing", Publius Valerius Publicola (subject of Plutarch's *Life of Publicola*) was known as "friend of the people" or "cultivator of the people" for his unassuming behaviour.

That swiftest wing of recompence is slow
To overtake thee. 'Would thou hadst less deserv'd;
That the proportion both of thanks and payment
Might have been mine!

Contrast between the honest King—and the already scheming Macbeth

19 VI 159, pencil, cropped | I v 18–20

LADY MACBETH. . . . Thou would'st be great;
Art not without ambition; but without
The illness should attend it.

Proof, th[at] ambitiou[s] schemes had been talked over betwe[en] them

20 VI 160, pencil, cropped | I v 38–54

[Lady Macbeth's soliloquy "The raven himself is hoarse".]

Here [. . . . .]*[a]* [C]haracter of L.M. bullying her own feelings, with the [B]ravado of Cowardice—desperate reprobate Villains talk no such Language—

21 VI 161, pencil, cropped | I v 63–70

[Lady Macbeth's greeting to her husband: "To beguile the time, Look like the time".]

no possibl[e] medium between fleeing fro[m] the one only without[1] Ghost (the Conscience) & *running* to it [—] both [? inward]

22 VI 162, pencil | I v 71

MACBETH. We will speak further.

another proof of prior Consult[?ation]

23 VI 164, pencil, cropped | I vii 1–28

[Macbeth's soliloquy "If it were done, when 'tis done".]

[2][nd] [s]truggle/ [Co]ntrast [th]is with [p.] 172.[1]

20[a] Four or five words too rubbed to read

21[1] Meaning, presumably, "outward".   **23**[1] I.e. **27**.

24 VI 166, pencil, cropped | I vii 54–9

LADY MACBETH. . . . I have given suck; and know
How tender 'tis, to love the babe that milks me:
I would, while it was smiling in my face,
Have pluck'd my nipple from his boneless gums,
And dash'd the brains out, had I so sworn
As you have done to this.

[S]till [bu]llying[1]

25 VI 169, pencil, cropped | II i 31–2

MACBETH. Go, bid thy mistress, when my drink is ready,
She strike upon the bell. Get thee to bed.

This explai[n] as the Genius of the momen[t] perm[its][1]

26 VI 171, pencil, cropped | II ii 11–13

LADY MACBETH. . . . I laid their daggers ready,
He could not miss them.—Had he not resembled
My father as he slept, I had don't.—

Confirmati[on] that S. never means L. M. more than Macbeth himself for
moral Monster, like Gonerill/[1]

27 VI 172, pencil, cropped | II ii 13

[Macbeth enters after the murder.]

3. Now comes the [r]esult,/ [C]ompare with p. 164[1]

28 VI 175, pencil, cropped | II iii 1–21

[Speech of the Porter: "Here's a knocking indeed!"]

Not Shakesp[eare][1]

24[1] A report of C's lecture on *Macbeth* at Bristol on 2 Nov 1813 quotes a phrase from C's analysis of Lady Macbeth, in which he declared her effort "if the expression may be forgiven, to *bully* conscience": *Lects 1808–1819 (CC)* I 532 and n 22.

25[1] This note looks like a lecturer's instruction to himself; unfortunately none of the records of the 1813 lecture indicates how he *did* explain it.

26[1] Cf *Lects 1808–1819 (CC)* I 532 (and n 21): "The lecturer alluded to the prejudiced idea of *Lady Macbeth* as a Monster". On Shakespeare's representation of "monstrosity" in evil, see also COPY A **116** at n 7 and COPY D **75**.

27[1] I.e. **23** above.

28[1] See COPY A **109** n 1.

29 VI 177, pencil, cropped | II iii 50–3

MACBETH. The labour we delight in, physicks pain.
    That is the door.
MACDUFF.   I'll make so bold to call,
    For 'tis my limited service. [*Exit Macduff.*
LENOX. Goes the king hence to-day?
MACBETH. He does: he did appoint so.

Wonderf[ul] assimila[tion] of feel[ing] homogenei[ty in] order to unity
of Impr[ession]

30 VI 180, pencil | II iii 108–12

MACBETH. Who can be wise, amaz'd, temperate, and furious,
    Loyal and neutral in a moment? No man:
    The expedition of my violent love
    Out-ran the pauser reason.—Here lay Duncan,
    His silver skin lac'd with his golden blood . . .

Contrast this forced Hurry of Talkativeness with—"And so do I."[1]

31 VI 182, pencil | II iv 1–10

OLD MAN. Threescore and ten I can remember well:
    Within the volume of which time, I have seen
    Hours dreadful, and things strange; but this sore night
    Hath trifled former knowings.
ROSSE.   Ah, good father,
    Thou seest, the heavens, as troubled with man's act,
    Threaten this bloody stage: by the clock, 'tis day,
    And yet dark night strangles the travelling lamp:
    Is it night's predominance, or the day's shame,
    That darkness does the face of earth intomb,
    When living light should kiss it?

Homogeneity of feeling & Imagination/

32 VI 185, pencil, cropped | III i 40–3

MACBETH. . . . . Let every man be master of his time
    Till seven at night; to make society

30[1] Macduff's line later in the same scene, II iii 132.

The sweeter welcome, we will keep ourself
Till supper-time alone: while then, God be with you.

Even in this the insupportab[le] anxiety that drives him from faces, he cannot bear, to his own Heart, still more dreadful—

33   VI 186, pencil, cropped | III i 48–53

MACBETH.   . . . Our fears in Banquo
   Stick deep; and in his royalty of nature
   Reigns that, which would be fear'd: 'Tis much he dares;
   And, to that dauntless temper of his mind,
   He hath a wisdom that doth guide his valour
   To act in safety.

One [c]rime leading to [a]nother, even [b]y the [v]ery virtues of the agent/ as by Macbeth's generous confession of Banquo's excellences—

34   VI 188, pencil, overtraced in ink by another hand | III i 107–10

2 MURDERER.   I am one, my liege,
   Whom the vile blows and buffets of the world
   Have so incens'd, that I am reckless what
   I do, to spite the world.

Even an assassin, *in this play*, S. will not let be a perfect monster/[a][1]

35   VI 190, pencil, cropped | III ii 13–15

MACBETH. We have scotch'd the snake, not kill'd it,
   She'll close, and be herself; whilst our poor malice
   Remains in danger of her former tooth.

Terror [fro]m crimes [? i/co]mpelling to crimes, that increase terror, & involve other crimes/

36   VI 192, pencil | III ii 55

MACBETH. . . . Things bad begun make strong themselves by ill . . .

N.B.

[34][a] The commas, underlining (italics) and solidus are not overtraced

[34][1] Cf **26** and n 1.

37   vi 195, pencil, cropped | iii iv 27–30

[Murderer reports that he has killed Banquo.]

MACBETH.   Thanks for that:—
    There the grown serpent lies; the worm, that's fled,
    Hath nature that in time will venom breed,
    No teeth for the present.—

Dwell o[n] the immedi[acy] of this Conversat[ion] with the Assassin, &
the Ghost of Banquo in Macbeth's dreadfully agitated State of Mind &
Body—Now he at once appeals to & avails himself of popular supersti-
tion/[1]

38   vi 197, pencil | iii iv 36–72

Controversy, whether the Ghost ought to *appe[ar]* to the Audience?—
Depends on the overbalance of the Educated to Uneducated/

39   vi 198, pencil, overtraced in ink in another hand, cropped | iii iv 92–5

MACBETH. Avaunt! and quit my sight! Let the earth hide thee!
    Thy bones are marrowless, thy blood is cold;
    Thou hast no speculation in those eyes
    Which thou dost glare with!

[F]ine Assertion [of] the [? firmness of] bodily spirit & Courage/
                                                    ⟨S. T. C⟩[a]

40   vi 200, pencil, cropped | iii iv 133–5

MACBETH.   . . . for now I am bent to know,
    By the worst means, the worst: for mine own good,
    All causes shall give way

All the [?m]eannesses [?ba]llance [ou]t of [te]rror

41   vi 211, pencil, cropped | iv i 144–8

MACBETH. Time, thou anticipat'st my dread exploits:
    The flighty purpose never is o'er-took,
    Unless the deed go with it: From this moment,

39[a] The initials may not have been part of the original note; only the inked version shows

37[1] This note, again, seems a lecturer's self-directed memorandum.

The very firstlings of my heart shall be
The firstlings of my hand.

Still desperate from Terr[or] of the ma[n] who ha[d] a 100 t[imes] laughe[d] at Deat[h] while he was doing his Duty—[1]

42　VI 219, pencil, cropped, referring to the first part of IV iii

[Dialogue between Malcolm and Macduff: the note begins beside lines 65–6, "Better Macbeth / Than such an one to reign."]

Even this scene tho' less pleasing is yet a fine picture of the Evil prod[uced] even in good men by public Insecurity[.] The point itself is most instructive/

43　VI 227, pencil, cropped | v i

[Lady Macbeth, watched by a Doctor of Physic and a waiting Gentlewoman, walks in her sleep.]

pro[of] of m[y] Asser[tion] respec[ting] L. M.['s] drea[m]-wa[king] & wake-dreaming Character/[1]

44　VI 236–7, pencil, cropped | v v 16–18

SEYTON. The Queen, my lord, is dead.
MACBETH. She should have dy'd hereafter;
　　There would have been a time for such a word.—

Not as Schlegel supposes because L. M. was wickeder, does she die/ suicide & [. . .] Death of [. . .];[1] but because she was the more visionary, did actual Life & its [? impassive] habit—　　　　　　　　　　S. T. C.

41[1] C's notes for the lecture of 2 Nov 1813 show that he intended to quote this speech: *Lects 1808–1819 (CC)* I 529.

43[1] Cf the report of C's 1813 lecture in *Lects 1808–1819 (CC)* I 532: "she was a woman of a visionary and day-dreaming turn of mind". "Visionary" is an epithet applied to her again in **44**, and "day-dreamer" in COPY D **17** at n 28.

44[1] A. W. Schlegel remarks on the discrimination with which retribution is visited on various characters, Lady Macbeth as the most guilty party dying "unlamented by her husband, with all the symptoms of reprobation", whereas "Macbeth is still found worthy of dying the death of a hero on the field of battle": *A Course of Lectures on Dramatic Art and Literature* tr John Black (2 vols 1815) II 202. C's notes for the lecture of 2 Nov 1813 show that he was responding to points made by Schlegel about the play, though this one is not specifically mentioned: *Lects 1808–1819 (CC)* I 524, 528.

45   VI 448 | *Othello* II i 120–3

DESDEMONA. Come on, assay:—*There's one gone to the harbour?
IAGO. Ay, madam.
DESDEMONA. I am not merry; but I do beguile
   The thing I am, by seeming otherwise.—

* The sweet attempt in a lovely & good woman to at once perform the
duties of Decorum to those present—/ yet shew the predominance of affection of to her indeed Duties.   S. T. C.

46   VI 452 | II i 224

[Iago falsely tells Roderigo that Cassio and Desdemona are in love.]

IAGO. . . . And will she love him still for prating? . . .

all[1]

47   VI 452, cropped | II i 226–42, continuing Iago's speech to Roderigo

IAGO. . . . When the blood is made dull with the act of sport, there should
   be,—again to inflame it, and to give satiety a fresh appetite,—loveli-
   ness in favour; sympathy in years, manners, and beauties; all which the
   Moor is defective in: Now, for want of these requir'd conveniences,
   her delicate tenderness will find itself abus'd, begin to heave the gorge,
   disrelish and abhor the Moor; very nature will instruct her in it, and
   compel her to some second choice. Now, sir, this granted, (as it is a
   most pregnant and unforc'd position) who stands so eminently in the
   degree of this fortune, as Cassio does? a knave very voluble; no farther
   conscionable, than in putting on the mere form of civil and humane
   seeming, for the better compassing of his salt and most hidden loose
   affections: A slippery and subtle knave; a finder out of occasions . . .

[Wi]ckedness [app]eals to [the] Base, & [Se]lfish of—[? Nature/Fortune]

46[1] I.e. C proposes substituting "all"
(meaning "only" or "entirely" or "exclusively") for "still". This is not a point taken
up by other commentators.

Copy D

The Dramatic Works of William Shakspeare: with explanatory notes. To which is added, a copious index to the remarkable passages and words, by Samuel Ayscough. 2 vols. London 1807. 8°.

"Printed for John Stockdale" and therefore sometimes misleadingly (given the actual title of COPY B) referred to as the "Stockdale edition". This copy is interleaved with writing paper.

British Library C 61 h 7

Bookplate of James Gillman on I ⁻6 (original p-d) and II ⁻1 (original p-d); and below both in pencil, the inscription: "Uncle from Raby Howard 1877". On I ⁻2 Richard Garnett, the Keeper of Printed Books, has written a note dated 26 Apr 1897: ". . . At the sale of the effects of Mʳ Gillman's son, the Rev. James Gillman, it was bought by his daughter Mʳˢ Howard, and presented to Dʳ S. B. Watson, editor of Coleridge's Theory of Life, who bequeathed it to the British Museum." On II ⁻1, in pencil, above the bookplate: "S. B. Watson D. M. from S Howard née Gillman"; and below this the name Watson is glossed—"Editor of 'The Theory of Life' by S. T. C."

Since the margins of the printed pages are of unusually limited extent, C has written most of his notes on the interleaved sheets; in the following transcript only those notes marked (p) after the page number are written directly on the printed pages, the remainder appearing on the facing interleaved pages. In many of his notes, C refers to specific parts of the text by using α or β for the first and second columns on the page, and the line numbers provided in the edition.

CONTENTS. The two vols are paginated continuously. I Sigs a3–b2 Prefaces, Rowe's "Life", and Shakespeare's will; I 1–22 *Tempest*; 23–44 *Two Gentlemen*; 45–74 *Merry Wives*; 75–102 *Measure for Measure*; 103–20 *Comedy of Errors*; 121–46 *Much Ado*; 147–74 *Love's Labour's Lost*; 175–96 *Midsummer Night's Dream*; 197–222 *Merchant of Venice*; 223–50 *As You Like It*; 251–76 *Taming of the Shrew*; 277–306 *All's Well*; 307–32 *Twelfth Night*; 333–62 *Winter's Tale*; 363–86 *Macbeth*; 387–412 *King John*; 413–40 *Richard II*; 441–72 *1 Henry IV*; 473–508 *2 Henry IV*; 509–42 *Henry V*; II 543–70 *1 Henry VI*; 571–602 *2 Henry VI*; 603–32 *3 Henry VI*; 633–70 *Richard III*; 671–702 *Henry VIII*; 703–40 *Coriolanus*; 741–66 *Julius Caesar*; 767–802 *Antony and Cleopatra*; 803–30 *Timon of Athens*; 831–56 *Titus Andronicus*; 857–92 *Troilus and Cressida*; 893–928 *Cymbeline*; 929–66 *King Lear*; 967–98 *Romeo and Juliet*; 999–1042 *Hamlet*; 1043–79 *Othello*.

DATE. 1817–19: one note dated 7 Jan 1819 (**127**). C took these vols into the lecture-room with him when he gave two series of lectures on Shakespeare in

1818–19; as R. A. Foakes says, he "developed his lectures from these notes": *Lects 1808–1819 (CC)* II 257.

1   I ‾4, pencil

In Shakspear and Cervantes it is wit so precious that it becomes wit even to quote or allude to it. Thus Sterne is a secondary Wit of this order—and how many a Stern-tertiaries, quartaries &c?

2   I ‾4

Observe

+ means in addition to
− without, or subtracted from
= the same as, equal to
⚹ contrasted with, in opposition to[1]

3   I sig b5ʳ, b4ᵛ, b5ᵛᵃ | *Tempest*

[1]⟨We commence with the Tempest, as a specimen of the Romantic Drama. But⟩ ~~With~~ Whatever Play of Shakespere's we had ~~begun~~ selected, ~~for the subject of our commencement,~~ there is one preliminary point to be first settled, as the indispensable Condition not only of just and genial criticism, but of all consistenɟcy ~~judgement~~ in our opinions.—This point is contained in the words, probable, natural. We are all in the habit of praising Shakespear, or of hearing him extolled for his fidelity to Nature. Now what are we to understand by these words, in their application to the Drama? Assuredly, not the ordinary meaning of them. Farquhar ⟨the⟩ most ably and if we except a few sentences in one of Dryden's Prefaces (written for a partic. purp. and in contrad. to the opinions elsewhere supported by him) ~~the most~~ first exposed the ludicrous absurdities involved in the supposition, and demolished as with the single sweep of a careless hand the whole Edifice of French Criticism respecting the so called Unities of Time and Place.[2]—But a moment's reflection suffices to make

---

3ᵃ Three blank leaves before *The Tempest*; C has numbered sig b5ʳ as "1" and sig b4ᵛ as "2"

2[1] C uses the same system of notation in COPY A **117**.

3[1] This note is published as part of C's lecture-material for 17 Dec 1818 in *Lects 1808–1819 (CC)* II 264–6 along with its continuation from BM MS 2800 ff 26–7 (II 266–8).

3[2] Dryden was generally a supporter of the unities, but on occasion described them as excessively strict: *Lects 1808–1819 (CC)* II 264, glossing this note of C's, cites Dryden's 1695 Preface to C. A. du Fresnoy's *Art of Painting* and his 1697 address to the Earl of Mulgrave, prefixed to Dry-

every man conscious of what every man must have before felt, that the
Drama is an *imitation* of reality not a *Copy*—and that Imitation is contra-
distinguished from Copy by this, that a certain quantum of Difference is
essential to the former, and ~~both~~ an indispensable condition and cause of
the pleasure, we derive from it; while in a Copy it is a defect, contravening its name and purpose.[3] If illustration were needed, it would be sufficient to ask—why we prefer a Fruit View of Vanhuysen's to a marble
Peach on a mantle piece—or why we prefer an historical picture of
West's to Mrs Salmon's Wax-figure Gallery.[4] Not only that we ought, but
that we actually do, all of us judge of the Drama[b] under this impression,
we need no other proof than the impassive~~ness~~ Slumber of our Sense of
Probability when we hear an Actor announce himself a Greek, Roman,
Venetian or Persian in good Mother English. And how little our great
Dramatist feared awakening on it, we have a lively instance in proof in
Portia's Answer to Neæra's question, What say you then to Falconbridge,
the young Baron of England?—to which she replies—You know, I say
nothing to him: for he understands not me nor I him. He hath neither
Latin, French or Italian: and you will come into the Court and swear that
I have a poor Penny-worth in the English.[5]

Still, however, there is a sort of Improb^y with which we are shocked in
~~the~~ dramatic repres^n no less than in the narration of real Life—Consequently, there must be Rules respecting it, and as Rules are nothing but
Means to an end previously ascertained (the inattention to which simple
truth has been the occasion of all the pedantry of the French School) we
must first ascertain what the immediate End or Object of the Drama is—
Here I find two extremes in critical decision—The French, which evidently presupposes that a perfect Delusion is to be aimed at—an Opinion
which now needs no fresh confutation—The opposite, supported by D^r

---

[3][b] Here C has written "(read from the Top of the page opposite)" and continued the note
with "(continued from the bottom of the page opposite)"

---

den's translation of Virgil. If these passing
references are overlooked, C says, the playwright George Farquhar was the first to deal
decisively with the unities, in *A Discourse
upon Comedy* (1702).

[3][3] For the distinction between imitation
and copy see QUARTERLY JOURNAL **3** n 10
above.

[3][4] C's audience would have been familiar at least in a general way with the still-life
paintings of the Dutch artist Jan van Huy-
sum (1682–1749), the large-scale paintings

of historical subjects by the American Benjamin West (1738–1820), and the famous
waxwork gallery established by Mr Salmon
at the end of the 17th century and carried on
at first actually by his widow (d 1760) and,
later, in her name. There are full notes on
these artists in *Lects 1808–1819* (*CC*) II
265 nn 4–5.

[3][5] See COPY c **3** and n 1 above, where
the same lines are cited in a similar context.
"Neæra" is a slip for "Nerissa".

Johnson, supposes the auditors throughout as in the full ~~possession of~~ and positive reflective knowlege of the contrary. In evincing the impossibility of Delusion he makes no sufficient Allowance for an intermediate State, which we distinguish by the term, Illusion. In what this consists, I cannot better explain, than by referring you to the highest degree of it, namely, Dreaming.[6] It is laxly said, that during Sleep we take our Dreams for Realities; but this is ~~improbable~~ irreconcilable with the nature of Sleep, which consists in a suspension of the voluntary and therefore of the comparative power. The fact is, that we pass no judgement either way—we ~~neither~~ simply do *not* judge them to be ⟨un⟩real—in conseq. of which the Images act on our minds, as far as they act at all, by their own ~~foree~~orce as images. Our state while we are dreaming differs from that in which we are in the perusal of a deeply interesting Novel, in the degree rather than in the Kind, and from three causes—First, from the exclusion of all outward impressions on our senses the images in Sleep become proportionally more vivid, than they can be when the organs of ~~self~~ Sense are in their active state. Secondly, in sleep the Sensations, and with these the Emotions & Passions which they counterfeit, are the causes of our Dream-images, ~~and~~ while in our waking hours our emotions are the effects of the Images presented to us—(*apparitions so detectible*) Lastly, in sleep we pass at once by a sudden collapse into this suspension of Will and the Comparative power: whereas in an interesting Play, read or ~~pr~~represented, we are brought up to this point, as far as it is requisite or desirable gradually, by the Art of the Poet and the Actors, and with the consent and positive Aidance of our own will. We *chuse* to be deceived.—The rule therefore may be easily inferred. What ever tends to prevent the mind from placing it or from being gradually placed, in this state in which the Images have a negative~~ly~~ reality,[7]

4 | 1 45 (p) and interleaf, pencil | *Merry Wives* 1 i 16–22

SLENDER. . . . they may give the dozen white luces in their coat.
SHALLOW. It is an old coat.

[3][6] C had also discussed the relationship between dramatic illusion and the dreaming state in notes that were probably prepared for the lectures of 1808: *Lects 1808–1819* (*CC*) 1 135–6. For further explorations of dream psychology see *TT* (*CC*) 1 151 n 9. What Samuel Johnson said, in his Preface to Shakespeare, was, "The truth is, that the spectators are always in their senses, and know, from the first act to the last, that the stage is only a stage, and that the players are only players. . . . It will be asked, how the drama moves, if it is not credited. It is credited with all the credit due to a drama": *Johnson on Shakespeare* ed Arthur Sherbo in *Works* (New Haven & London 1958–) VII 77–8.

[3][7] This note was continued on separate sheets of paper, pub *Lects 1808–1819* (*CC*) II 266–8.

EVANS. The dozen white louses do become an old coat well; it agrees well, passant: it is a familiar beast to man, and signifies—love.
SHALLOW. The luce is the fresh fish; the salt fish is an old coat.*

[Editor's note:] The luce is a pike or jack. This passage is also supposed to point at Sir Thomas Lucy, who was the cause of Shakspeare's leaving Stratford.

* I do not understand this; but I suspect a double corruption, first, in the words "the salt fish", and 2nd, in the Speaker—who should, I suspect, be Sir H. Evans.[1]

a* "The salt fish is an old coat."—. I suspect that the passage should be thus restored:
SHALLOW. The Luce is the fresh-Fish: the salt fish—
Sir H. Evans.—is an old Cot or Coat—i.e. an old Cod, Cambricè,[2] Cot or Coat. As it now stands the passage has no sense at all.

5   I 49, pencil | I iii 52–5

FALSTAFF. Now, the report goes, she has all the rule of her husband's purse; she hath a legion of angels.
PISTOL. As many devils entertain; and *To her, boy*, say I.

—Qy? *As* many Devils enter swine (or, enter'd swine)—and "to her, boy" say I—[1]
a somewhat profane but not unshaksperian allusion to the "We are Legion" in Luke's Gospel.[2]

6   I 147 (interleaf facing the opening of the play) | *Love's Labour's Lost*

[1] According to internal evidence the earliest of Shakspear's dramas, probably prior to the V. and A.[2] and sketched out before he left Stratford.—

4[a] The rest of the note is written on the interleaf

4[1] This is the explanation proposed also in COPY A **10** and COPY B **1**.
4[2] I.e. "in Welsh".
5[1] C's proposed emendation, not one that has attracted other commentators, is explained in the next sentence.
5[2] Luke 8.30, 33, of the man possessed by devils, and the Gadarene swine: "And Jesus asked him, saying, What is thy name? And he said, Legion: because many devils were entered into him. . . . Then went the devils out of the man, and entered into the swine: and the herd ran violently down a steep place into the lake, and were choked." C offers a biblical allusion to cap the one ("legions of angels", Matt 26.53) in the previous line.
6[1] This note is published as part of C's lecture-material for 25 Feb 1819 in *Lects 1808–1819 (CC)* II 375–6; the editor's note there points out that it summarises what C had said about the play in earlier lectures in 1811–12.
6[2] I.e. *Venus and Adonis*. The point about the date of composition is one that C made consistently: he was convinced that

Characters either impersonated out of his own multiformity, by imaginative Self-position, or of such as a Country Town and a School-boys Observation might supply—the Curate, School-master, the Armado[3] (which even in my time was not extinct in the cheaper Inns of N. Wales)—the Satire too on follies of *Words*—Add too that the characters of Byron and Rosaline are evidently the pre-existent state of his Beatrice and Benedict—.[4] Add too the number of the rhymes, and the sweetness as well as smoothness of the metre—and the number of acute and fancifully illustrated Aphorisms. Just as it ought to be. True Genius begins by generalizing, and condensing;—it ends in realizing, and expanding—It first collects the seeds—

Yet if this juvenile Drama had been the only one extant of our Shakspeare, and we possessed the tradition only of his riper works or from Writers who had not even mentioned the Love's Labor Lost—how many of S's characteristic Features might we not discover, tho' as in a portrait taken of him in his Boyhood.—

---

7   I 177 | *Midsummer Night's Dream* I i 214–19

HERMIA. And in the wood, where often you and I
   Upon faint primrose-beds were wont to lye,
   Emptying our bosoms of their counsels swell'd;
   There my Lysander and myself shall meet:
   And thence, from Athens, turn away our eyes,
   To seek new friends and strange companions.

Column 2. l. 9. for swell'd read sweet.
      l. 12. r. stranger companies.[1]

---

8   I 225, pencil | *As You Like It* I i 163–73

OLIVER. Farewell, good Charles.—Now will I stir this gamester: I hope, I shall see an end of him; for my soul, yet I know not why, hates nothing more than he. Yet he's gentle; never school'd, and yet learn'd; full of noble device; of all sorts enchantingly beloved; and, indeed, so much in the heart of the world, and especially of my own people, who

---

Love's Labour's Lost was the earliest of Shakespeare's plays. (That it was *one* of the earliest has never been contested.) Putting the emphasis on internal evidence for the dating of the plays was C's response to what he appears to have considered the unsuitable and unsuccessful efforts of scholars such as Malone: *Lects 1808–1819 (CC)* II

371.
   6[3] Don Armado, a figure of "absurd Coxcombry", as C remarked in a lecture of 2 Dec 1811: *Lects 1808–1819 (CC)* I 266.
   6[4] C had made the same point in 1811: *Lects 1808–1819 (CC)* I 276.
   7[1] See COPY B 2.

best know him, that I am altogether misprised: but it shall not be so long; this wrestler shall clear all: nothing remains, but that I kindle the boy thither, which now I'll go about.

It is too venturous to charge a speech in Shakespear with want of truth to Nature. And yet at first sight this speech of Oliver's *expresses* truths which it almost seems impossible that any mind should ~~have~~ so distinctly and so livelily have voluntarily presented to itself in connection with feelings and intentions so malignant and so contrary tḥo those which the qualities expressed ~~were~~ould naturally have called forth.—But I dare not say, that this *unnaturalness* is not in the nature of an abused *Wilfulness* when united with a strong intellect. In such Characters there is sometimes a gloomy self-gratification in making the *absoluteness* of the Will (sit pro ratione Voluntas!)[1] evident to themselves by setting the Reason & Conscience in full array against it.[2]

9   I 227, pencil | I ii 243–5

CELIA. . . . . If you do keep your promises in love,
But justly as you have exceeded <u>all</u> promise,
Your mistress shall be happy.

l. 29.—the word "all" is beyond doubt an interpolation.—It not only destroys the metre but it changes & deforms the sense.—
If you do keep your promises*ᵃ* in LOVE
But justly as you have exceeded *promise*.
The adjunct "all" is senseless.[1]

10   I 283, pencil | *All's Well* II i 12–15

KING.   . . . let higher Italy
(Those 'bated, that inherit but the fall
Of the last monarchy) see that you come
Not to woo honour, but to wed it . . .

[Editor's footnote:] The epithet *higher* is here to be understood as referring to situation rather than to dignity.

9*ᵃ* Word first underlined, then the underlining cancelled with a scribbled stroke

8[1] "Let Will take the place of reason": Juvenal *Satires* 6.223.
8[2] This note expands upon C's comment on the same speech in COPY A **23**.

9[1] This defect had been noted before, and some editions dropped the "all" of the Folio: *Sh* (Reed).

—let hired Italy,
Those bastards, that inherit but the fall
Of the last Monarchy—[1]

11   I 286 (p) and interleaf, pencil | II iii 71–2

HELENA. . . . *Let the white death sit on thy cheek for ever,*
   We'll ne'er come there again.

[Editor's note on "white death":] Meaning, perhaps, the *chlorosis.*∧

∧ !! The Devil! I would gladly give a Crown to see the rare Fellow, that
fathered this Gloss!!—Dr Slop?[1] *a*or a young Apothecary, fond of the
muses?—"*Meaning, perhaps*——the *chlorosis!*"[2] The innocenc∉y of it!
Oh 'tis rich.

12   I 310, pencil | *Twelfth Night* I iii 130–1

SIR TOBY. . . . I would not so much as make water but in a sink-a-pace.

[Editor's note:] That is, a *cinque-pace*; the name of a dance, the measures
whereof are regulated by the number five.

⟨Line⟩ 1 ⟨Col.⟩ α sink-a-pace *puni*cè for a Sink of πισς.[1]

12A   I 310, pencil | I iv 11

VIOLA. On your attendance, ⌈my lord;⌉ ⌊here.⌋

13   I 311, pencil | I v 51–3

CLOWN. . . . As there is no true cuckold but calamity, so beauty's a
   flower: the lady bade take away the fool; therefore, I say again, take
   her away.

⟨Line⟩ 6 ⟨Column⟩ α Was any meaning intended in this adage, No true
Cuckold but Calamity?[1]

> 11^*a*   The rest of the note is written on the interleaf

10[1] See COPY A **37** and nn.
11[1] Dr Slop is the bumbling man-midwife in Sterne's *Tristram Shandy.*
11[2] "Chlorosis" or "green-sickness" was supposed to afflict young women; the symptoms included anaemia; the cure was marriage. This gloss was originally Johnson's, more firmly expressed, "The *white death* is the *chlorosis*": *Sh* (Reed). If C means to imply some further and more shameful significance, e.g. venereal disease, it has not occurred to the commentators.
12[1] See COPY B **4**. Here C puts the word "piss" into letters of the Greek alphabet.
13[1] *Sh* (Reed) contains no comment on this line, for which there seems to be even now no fully satisfactory explanation.

14 ɪ 312 (p), pencil | ɪ v 175–6

VIOLA. . . . I am very compatible, even to the least sinister usage.

[Editor's note on "compatible":] That is, very submissive.*

* No!—first, ɨ̸ the word is comptible, and secondly, it means, susceptible, sensitive, alive to—[1]

15 ɪ 314 (p), pencil | ɪɪ ii 31–2

VIOLA. Alas, our frailty is the cause, not we;
    For, such as we are made, if such we be.*

* Corrupt Text. Probably
    For such as we are made of, such we be
or   Such as we are, we are made: if such we be.[1]

16 ɪ 349 (p), pencil | *Winter's Tale* ɪv iv 3–5

FLORIZEL. . . . This your sheep-shearing
    Is as a meeting of the petty gods,
    And you the queen on't.

Ī s, | ăs ă mēe|tĭng | ŏf thĕ pētty̆ Gōds[1]

17 ɪ 363–6ᵃ | *Macbeth* ɪ i–iii

[1]The opening of Macbeth contrasted with that of Hamlet—. In the latter
the gradual ascent from the simplest forms of conversation to the language of impassioned Intellect, yet still the Intellect remaining the *seat*
of Passion—in the Macbeth the invocation is made at once to the Imagination, and the emotions connected therewith. ~~The~~ A Superstition in both;
yet in each not merely different but opposite. The Wierd Sisters, as true
a *Creation* of Shakspear's as his Ariel and Caliban—the Fates, the
Furies, and the *materializing* Witches being the elements.—

17ᵃ Beginning on the interleaf facing the opening of the play (ɪ 363), and continued on
both sides of the interleaves to end on ɪ 366, the note is written in paragraphs as a summary
of reading

14[1] See COPY B 5. Besides explaining
the meaning of the phrase, C corrects the
reading of this edition, reverting to the
"comptible" of COPY B.

15[1] The emendation that C proposes in
his first attempt (from "if" to "of"), which
had been suggested by Tyrwhitt before him,

has been generally accepted.

16[1] The omission is merely a typographical error in this edition.

17[1] Most of the notes on *Macbeth* in
COPY D are published as part of C's lecture-
material for 14 Jan 1819 in *Lects
1808–1819* (*CC*) ɪɪ 305–10.

The II Scene illustrated by reference to the Play in Hamlet, in which the Epic is substituted for the Tragic in order to make the latter be felt as the *real-Life* Diction.[2]

Scene III. That I have assigned the true reason for the first appearance of the Weird Sisters, as the Key-note of the character of the whole Play is proved by the re-entrance of the Sisters—after such an order of the King's as establishes their supernatural *powers of information.

The wish that in Macbeth the attempt might be made to introduce the flexile character-mask of the Ancient Pantomime—that a Flaxman might contribute his Genius to the embodying of Shakspear's.[3]

King hereafter[4] was still contingent—still in Macbeth's moral will—tho' if he yielded to the temptation & thus forfeited his free-agency, then the link of *cause* and *effect more physico*[5] would commence—& thus the prophetic Visions afterwards. I surely need not say, that the *general* Idea is all that can be required from the Poet—not a scholastic logical consistency in all the parts so as to meet metaphysical Objections.

But O how truly Shakspearian is the opening of Macbeth's Character given in the *unpossessedness*[6] of Banquo's mind, wholly present to the present Object—an unsullied un-scarified Mirror—& in strict truth of Nature that he and not Macbeth himself directs our notice to the effect produced on ~~his~~ Macbeth's Mind, rendered *temptible* by ⟨previous⟩ dalliance of the Fancy with ambitious Thoughts. (See Wallenstein's Soliloquy, Part I.)[7]

> Good Sir, why do you start?—and seem to fear
> Things that do sound so fair?[8]

And then again, still unintröitive,[9] addresses the appearances—The ques-

17[2] Cf the counterpart to this note, C's remark about the "substitution of the Epic for the Dramatic" in the Players' scene in *Hamlet*, **151** below.

17[3] C may be remembering A. W. Schlegel's suggestion, in Lecture 3 of *Ueber dramatische Kunst und Litteratur* (3 vols Heidelberg 1809–11) I 98, that the theatrical masks of the ancients might have been like those recently produced at the Roman carnival, which were capable of imitating the very movements of life. The tribute to the sculptor John Flaxman (1755–1826) is unusual for C, though Flaxman was a celebrity and there were significant personal links between him and C—both had enjoyed the patronage of the Wedgwoods, and both were friends of HCR.

17[4] *Macbeth* I iii 50.

17[5] "In a physical manner".

17[6] *OED* attributes this nonce-word to C, on the basis of this note as pub in *LR*.

17[7] C alludes to his own translation of Schiller's *Wallenstein* IV iv 3–5 (*PW—EHC*—II 690): "I / Must do the deed, because I thought of it, / And fed this heart here with a dream?" On the temptibility of Macbeth, and the contrast between him and Banquo in this scene, see the report of C's lecture of 2 Nov 1813 in *Lects 1808–1819* (*CC*) I 531.

17[8] Banquo's question to Macbeth, I iii 51–2. C proceeds with his running commentary, quoting intermittently from the text.

17[9] Not going into himself; unreflective or unintrospective. Cf "extroitive" in COPY A **5**, and BÖHME **143** and n 1 for a related

tions of Banquo those of natural Curiosity—such as a Girl would make after she had heard a Gypsey tell her School-fellow's Fortune—all perfectly general—or rather *planless*. But Macbeth, lost in thought, rouses himself to Speech only by their being about to depart—STAY, you imperfect Speakers[10]—and all that follows is reasoning on a problem already discussed in his mind—on a hope which he welcomes, and the doubts concerning its attainment he wishes to have cleared up—. His eagerness—the eager eye with which he had pursued their evanition, compared with the easily satisfied mind of the self-uninterested Banquo

The Earth hath bubbles—

Whither are they vanished?

M. Into the Air—and what seem'd corporal melted

As Breath into the wind—WOULD THEY HAD STAY'D![11]

Is it too minute to notice the appropriateness of the Simile "As Breath" in a cold Climate?

Still again Banquo's wonder that of any Spectator "Were such things here["][12]—and Macbeth's recurrence to the *self-concerning*—Your Children shall be Kings—.[13] So ~~as~~ truly is the guilt in its Germ anterior to the supposed cause & immediate temptation—. Before he can cool, the *confirmation* of the tempting half of the Prophecy—and the *catenating* tendency fostered by the sudden coincidence.

Glamis and Thane of Cawdor—The greatest is behind[14]— ⚹ Banquo's what can the Devil speak true—[15]

I doubt whether *enkindle* has not another sense than that of *stimulating*—whether the Kind, & Kin—as in Rabbits *kindle*[16]—However, Macbeth hears no more *ab extra*.[17] "Two truths &c["][18] And (p. 365) the necessity of recollecting himself—I thank you, Gentlemen!—in the third line of his speech.[19]—30–45, Col. β.[20]—confirm. of the remark on the birth-date of guilt.—And then the warning of the Conscience—& the mode of lulling it—If chance will have me King, why &c[21]—and the sus-

---

family of words. *OED* gives this passage as its only illustration of "unintroitive".

[17][10] I iii 70.

[17][11] I iii 79–82 var.

[17][12] I iii 83.

[17][13] I iii 86.

[17][14] I iii 116–17.

[17][15] I iii 107; C's symbol means "as opposed to".

[17][16] Banquo says (I iii 120–2), "That, trusted home, / Might yet enkindle you unto the crown, / Besides the Thane of Cawdor." The editor's gloss (still the conventional

one) is "*Enkindle*, for to stimulate you to seek"; C proposes an alternative or additional meaning, "kindle" being, as his example shows, a term used of animals giving birth.

[17][17] "From without".

[17][18] I iii 127.

[17][19] I iii 129.

[17][20] I iii 127–42, Macbeth's speech from "Two truths are told" to ". . . nothing is / But what is not."

[17][21] I iii 143, noted also in COPY C **16**.

picion that others might see what was passing in his mind, all prospective, by the LIE—wrought with Things *forgotten*[22]—and instantly the *promising Courtesyies* of a Usurper in intention.—

And O the affecting beauty of the Death of Cawdor, and the King's presentimental remark, interrupted by the "Worthiest Cousin"! on the entrance of the deeper Traitor to whom Cawdor had made way[23]—and here in contrast with Duncan's "plenteous Joys"[24] Macbeth has nothing but the common-places of Loyalty, in which he hides himself in the "our".[25]—and in the same language of *effort* "The REST is Labor &c["][26]—at the moment that a new difficulty suggests a new crime. This, however, seems the first distinct notion, as to the *plan* of realizing his wishes—and here therefore with great propriety Macbeth's Cowardice of his own Conscience discloses itself.

Macbeth described by Lady M. so as at the same time to describe her own character[27]—intellectually considered, he is powerful in all, but has strength in none.—morally, *selfish* ~~but~~ i.e. as far as his weakness will permit him. Could he have every thing, he wanted, he would *rather* have it innocently—ignorant, as alas! how many are! that he who wishes a temporal end for itself does in truth will the *means*—hence the danger of indulging fancies—

"Lady Macbeth = with the valor of my Tongue." Day-dreamer's valiance.[28]

* yet still information/

18   I 367 | I v 40–71

LADY MACBETH.   . . . Come, you spirits
That tend on mortal thoughts, unsex me here;
And fill me, from the crown to the toe, top-full
Of direst cruelty! make thick my blood,
Stop up the access and passage to remorse;
That no compunctious visitings of nature
Shake my fell purpose, nor keep pace between
The effect, and it; Come to my woman's breasts,
And take my milk for gall, you murd'ring ministers,

17[22] I iii 150, noted also in COPY C 17.
17[23] I iv 14.
17[24] I iv 33, marked in COPY A 98.
17[25] I iv 23–5: "Your Highness' part / Is to receive our duties; and our duties / Are to your throne".

17[26] I iv 44, noted as "Hollow Hyperb[ole]" in COPY A 100.
17[27] C summarises the speech of Lady Macbeth in I v 15–30.
17[28] I v 27; for Lady Macbeth as a day-dreamer, see also COPY C 43 and n 1.

Wherever in your sightless substances
You wait on nature's mischief! Come, thick night,
And pall thee in the dunnest smoke of hell!
That my keen knife see not the wound it makes;
Nor heaven peep through the blanket of the dark,
To cry, *Hold, hold*! Great Glamis! worthy Cawdor!
     Enter Macbeth
Greater than both, by the all-hail hereafter
Thy letters have transported me beyond
This ignorant present time, and I feel now
The future in the instant.
MACBETH.   My dearest love,
 Duncan comes here to-night.
LADY MACBETH.   And when goes hence?
MACBETH. To-morrow, as he purposes.
LADY MACBETH.   Oh, never
 Shall sun that morrow see!
 Your face, my thane, is as a book, where men
 May read strange matters:—To beguile the time,
 Look like the time; bear welcome in your eye,
 Your hand, your tongue: look like the innocent flower,
 But be the serpent under it. He that's coming
 Must be provided for: and you shall put
 This night's great business into my dispatch;
 Which shall to all our nights and days to come
 Give solely sovereign sway and masterdom.
MACBETH. We shall speak further.

All the false efforts of a mind accustomed only to the Shadows of the Imagination, vivid enough to throw the every day realities into shadows but not yet compared with their own correspondent realities.

 No womanly, no wifely Joy at the return of her Husband—no retrospection on the dangers, he had escaped—⟨⚹ Macbeth's⟩[1] My dearest Love—and his shrinking from the boldness with which she presents his own thoughts to him—We shall speak further—

19 I 367 | I vi 14–20

LADY MACBETH.   All our service
 In every point twice done, and then done double,
 Were poor and single business, to contend

18[1] "As opposed to Macbeth's".

Against those honours deep and broad, wherewith
Your majesty loads our house: for those of old,
And the late dignities heap'd up to them,
We rest your hermits.

25 β.[1] The very rhythm expresses the conscience over-much in Lady M.'s
Answer to the King.

20   ɪ 368 | ɪ vii 1–28: Macbeth's soliloquy "If it were done"

The inward pangs & warnings of Conscience interpreted into *prudential*
reasonings.—

21   ɪ 369 | ɪɪ i 4–9

BANQUO. Hold, take my sword:—there's husbandry in heaven,
        Their candles are all out.—Take thee that too.
        A heavy summons lies like lead upon me,
        And yet I would not sleep: Merciful powers!
        Restrain in me the cursed thoughts, that nature
        Gives way to in repose! . . .

10. α[1]
    The disturbance of an innocent soul by painful suspicions of another's
guilty intentions & wishes—and fear of the *cursed thoughts*.

22   ɪ 369 | ɪɪ ii 8–11

MACBETH. (Within.)^*a*   Who's there?—what, ho!
LADY MACBETH. Alack! I am afraid they have awak'd,
        And 'tis not done:—the attempt, and not the deed,
        Confounds us:—

40. β.[1]—The very first reality, L. M. shrinks.

23   ɪ 370 | ɪɪ ii 70–1

MACBETH. To know my deed,—'Twere best not know myself.
        Wake Duncan with thy knocking! I would, thou couldst!

Need I say, contrast with Soliloquy, p. 368.[1]

22^*a* Square brackets of original are printed as parentheses

19[1] The line reference is to the very be-   **21**[1] Line 1 of textus.
ginning of ɪɪ i, but "Lady M.'s Answer to   **22**[1] Line 2 of textus.
the King" designates rather the earlier lines   **23**[1] I.e. **20** above.
given as textus.

24   I 373 | III i 72 ff (Macbeth with the two Murderers)

The Mistake of Schiller in his Wallenstein respecting the Assassins—[1]

25   I 374 | III ii 26–35

LADY MACBETH.   Come on; Gentle my lord,
    Sleek o'er your rugged looks; be bright and jovial
    Among your guests to-night.
MACBETH.   So shall I, love;
    And so, I pray, be you: Let your remembrance
    Apply to Banquo; present him eminence, both
    With eye and tongue . . .
    And make our faces vizards to our hearts,
    Disguising what they are.

Ever & ever mistaking the anguish of Conscience for Fears of Selfishness, and thus as a punishment of that Selfishness, plunging deeper in guilt & ruin.

26   I 374 | III ii 40–6

MACBETH.   . . . Ere the bat hath flown
    His cloister'd flight; ere, to black Hecat's summons,
    The shard-borne beetle, with his drowsy hums,
    Hath rung night's yawning peal, there shall be done
    A deed of dreadful note.
LADY MACBETH.   What's to be done?
MACBETH. Be innocent of the knowledge, dearest chuck,
    'Till thou applaud the deed.

Sympathy with his own state of feelings—& mistaking his Wife's opposite state—

27   I 376 | III iv 36 (the appearance of the Ghost)

Tell the story of the *Portrait* that frightened every one—[1]

24[1] C compared Schiller's *Wallenstein* to *Macbeth* in **17** above at n 7. His objection to Schiller's treatment of a parallel situation here is that Schiller tried to make the assassins semi-comical figures ("The assassins talk ludicrously"), whereas in *Macbeth* "They are fearful and almost pitiable Beings—not loathsome, ludicrous miscre- ants": *Lects 1808–1819* (*CC*) II 309 n 36, *PW* (EHC) II 599.

27[1] This is almost certainly the story recorded by John Taylor Coleridge and pub *TT* (*CC*) I 18–19. An Italian painter who had murdered his former patron was so haunted by him that he painted a portrait of "the phantom as it looked at him" and then

28   I 379 | IV i 141–53

LENNOX. 'Tis two or three, my lord, that bring you word,
  Macduff is fled to England,/—
MACBETH.   Fled to England?
LENNOX. Ay, my good lord.
MACBETH. Time, thou anticipat'st my dread exploits:
  The flighty purpose never is o'er-took,
  Unless the deed go with it: From this moment,
  The very firstlings of my hearts shall be
  The firstlings of my hand. And even now
  To crown my thoughts with acts, be it thought and done:
  The castle of Macduff I will surprise;
  Seize upon Fife; give to the edge o' the sword
  His wife, his babes, and all unfortunate souls,
  That trace him in his line.

Acme of the avenging Conscience—

29   I 381 | IV iii

[Malcolm tests Macduff by representing himself as even more vicious than Macbeth, and drives Macduff to reject him as a suitable king for Scotland before revealing the deceit.]

Moral—of the dreadful effects even on the best minds by the soul-sickening sense of Insecurity—

30   I 382 | IV iii 211–19

MACDUFF. My children too?
ROSSE.   Wife, children, servants, all
  That could be found.
MACDUFF.   And I must be from thence!
  My wife kill'd too?
ROSSE.   I have said.
MALCOLM.   Be comforted:
  Let's make us med'cines of our great revenge,
  To cure this deadly grief.

---

surrendered himself to justice. He gave the portrait to a merchant who had befriended him; the merchant's guests, however, who tried to sleep in the room in which the portrait was hung, found it so disturbing that it had to be removed.

MACDUFF. He has no children—All my pretty ones?
Did you say, all?—Oh, hell-kite!—All?
What, all my pretty chickens, and their dam,
At one fell swoop?

The manliness of the Pathos in harmony with the Play—it rends, not dissolves the heart—"the tune goes manly".[1]

31 I 384 | The end of v iii

Now all is *inward*—no more prudential prospective reasonings—

32 I 385 | v v 9–17

MACBETH. I have almost forgot the taste of fears:
The time has been, my senses would have cool'd
To hear a night-shriek; and my fell of hair
Would at a dismal treatise rouse, and stir
As life were in't: I have supt full with horrors;
Direness, familiar to my slaught'rous thoughts,
Cannot once start me.—Wherefore was that cry?
SEYTON. The queen, my lord, is dead.
MACBETH. She should have dy'd hereafter . . .

Despondency the final wretched Heart-armour—

33 I [413] | *Richard II*

[1]The transitional state between the Epic and the Drama is the Historic Drama. In the Epic a pre-announced Fate gradually adjusts and employs the will and the ~~Events~~ Incidents as its instruments—επομαι sequor:[2] while the Drama places Fate & Will in opposition, then most perfect when the victory of fate is obtained in consequence of imperfections in the opposing Will, so as to leave the final impression, that the Fate itself is but a higher and more intelligent Will.[3]

30[1] "This tune goes manly" is Malcolm's approving comment to Macduff when Macduff turns his grief to a resolution to confront Macbeth in battle, *Macbeth* IV iii 235.

33[1] All the notes on *Richard II* in COPY D are published as part of C's lecture-material for 31 Dec 1818 in *Lects 1808–1819* (CC) II 283–7.

33[2] C refers to the then accepted etymo-

logical connection between the Greek *epos*, which means "epic" as well as "word", and *hepomai* (Greek) and *sequor* (Latin), meaning "follow".

33[3] The view of *Richard II* as "the conversion of the Epic into the Dramatic"—an idea for which C may have been indebted to Schlegel—is a theme of Lect 5 of the 1813 series: *Lects 1808–1819* (CC) I 559 and n 1.

34   I [413], pencil

But this Richard the IInd—O God forbid that however unsuited for the Stage yet even there it should fall dead on the hearts of Jacobinized Englishmen—then indeed Præteriit gloria mundi[1]—The Spirit of patriotic reminiscence is the all-permeating Spirit of this Drama.

35   I [413] | I i 1–6

KING RICHARD. Old John of Gaunt, time-honour'd Lancaster,
    Hast thou, according to thy oath and band,
    Brought hither Henry Hereford thy bold son;
    Here to make good the boisterous late appeal,
    Which then our leisure would not let us hear,
    Against the duke of Norfolk, Thomas Mowbray?

The six opening Lines of this Play, each closing at the tenth syllable, to be compared with the rhythmless Metre of the verse in Henry 6th and Titus Andronicus—in order, that the difference, yea, heterogenëity, may be felt, etiam in simillimis primâ superficie.[1] Here the weight of each *word* supplies all the relief afforded by intercurrent verse: while the whole represents the *Mood.*

36   I [413] | I i 8

KING RICHARD. Tell me moreover, hast thou sounded him . . .

L. 14. Compare with 1. 31, 2nd Col. p. 2. of the Tempest[1]—"Twelve years since, Miranda! twelve years since["]—examp. of the involved instructions to the actors how to pronounce the line.

37   I 414 | I i 30–46

BOLINGBROKE. First (heaven be the record to my speech!)
    In the devotion of a subject's love . . .
    Come I appellant to this princely presence.— . . .
    Thou [Mowbray] art a traitor, and a miscreant;
    Too good to be so, and too bad to live;
    Since, the more fair and crystal is the sky,
    The uglier seem the clouds that in it fly.

34[1] "The glory of the world has passed away"—a variant of the proverbial *sic transit gloria mundi* "Thus passes away the glory of the world".

35[1] "Even in those most alike on the surface".

36[1] *Tempest* I ii 53 (not commented on in any of the extant annotated editions). C's page references are to this edition.

Once more, the more to aggravate the note,
With a foul traitor's name stuff I thy throat;
And wish (so please my sovereign) ere I move,
What my tongue speaks, my right-drawn sword may prove.

10.[1] I remember even in the Sophoclean Drama no more striking example of (the) το πρεπον, και σεμνον.[2] Yea, the rhymes in the 6 last lines well express the *preconcertedness* of Bolingbrook's Scheme—so beautifully contrasted with the vehemence and sincere irritation of Mowbray.

38　ɪ 414, footnote in pencil | ɪ i 39–46, the last 7 lines of **37** textus

19.[1] The passion that carries off its excess by play on words as naturally and therefore as appropriately to drama as by gesticulations, looks or tones. This belonging to human nature as *human*, independent of associations and habits from any particular rank of Life or mode of employment—and in this consists Sh.'s vulgarisms, as in Macbeth, (The Devil damn thee black, thou ~~pale~~ cream faced Loon! &c)[2] it is (to plays on Dante's words) in truth the *Nobile* volgare eloquenza[3]*.—

*Defer this to p. 420, interview with old Gaunt/[4]

39　ɪ 414 | ɪ i 104–18

BOLINGBROKE [accusing Mowbray of murdering the Duke of
　Gloucester].
　　. . . Which blood, like sacrificing Abel's, cries,
　　Even from the tongueless caverns of the earth,
　　To me, for justice, and rough chastisement;
　　And, by the glorious worth of my descent,
　　This arm shall do it, or this life be spent.
KING RICHARD. How high a pitch his resolution soars!—
　　Thomas of Norfolk, what say'st thou to this?

37[1] Line 1 of textus.
37[2] "Appropriate and dignified". For a conjunction of the same pair of epithets in a different context, see RHENFERD **17** at n 3.
38[1] Actually line 1 of **37** textus.
38[2] *Macbeth* v iii 11, not commented on in any of the extant annotated copies.
38[3] "The *noble* common speech", C alluding to the Italian title of Dante's unfinished Latin treatise on language *De vulgari eloquentia*, which was indeed published in an Italian translation as *De la volgare elo-*

quenza (freely translated as *Literature in the Vernacular*) in 1529. Dante's concern is to identify the highest level of the vernacular idiom, suitable for the most demanding poetry. C refers to this work using the variant title he gives it here—with "nobile"—in *BL* ch 16 (*CC*) ɪɪ 30 and n 2, where a similar phrase, *illustre vulgare*, is translated "the Illustrious Vulgar Tongue"; he quotes from it in SOUTHEY *Joan of Arc* **1**.
38[4] I.e. **51** below.

MOWBRAY. O, let my sovereign turn away his face,
    And bid his ears a little while be deaf,
    'Till I have told this slander of his blood,
    How God, and good men, hate so foul a liar.
KING RICHARD. Mowbray, impartial are our eyes, and ears:
    Were he my brother's, nay, my kingdom's heir,
    (As he is but my father's brother's son)
    Now by my sceptre's awe I make a vow . . .

26.[1]—The δεινον[2] "*to me*["], & so felt by Richard—"How *high* a pitch
&c.["]—and the *effect*—As he is but my Father's Brother's Son—

40 I 415, completed in pencil | I i 148–51

MOWBRAY [challenging Bolingbroke].
    . . . To prove myself a loyal gentleman
    Even in the best blood chamber'd in his bosom;
    In haste whereof, most heartily I pray
    Your highness to assign our trial-day.

10.[1] Q.y The occasional interspersion of rhymes and the more frequent
winding up of a Speech therewith—what purpose was this to answer? In
the earnest Drama, I mean.—Deliberateness? An attempt as in Mowbray
to collect himself and *be cool* at the close? I can see that in the following
Speeches the rhyme answers the purposes of the Greek Chorus, and distinguish[a] the *general* truths from the passions of the Dialogue—but this
is not exactly to *justify* the practice which is unfrequent in proportion to
the excellence of Sh's Plays—. One thing, however, is to be observed—
they are *historical, known,* & so far *formal* Characters, the reality of
which is already a *fact.*—[b]*This dwelt upon* as predominant in Richard,
the purest Historic Play—indeed, John & Henry VIIIth excepted, the only
pure[c]

41 I 415 | I ii 37–41

GAUNT. Heaven's is the quarrel; for heaven's substitute,
    His deputy anointed in his sight,
    Hath caus'd his death: the which if wrongfully,

40[a] A slip for "distinguishes"   40[b] Afterthought in pencil
            40[c] The note remains incomplete

39[1] Line 4 of textus, "To me" etc.   to Aristotle *Poetics* 14.6–9 (1453b).
39[2] "Terrible". The deliberate use of the   40[1] Last line of textus.
Greek term may signify a specific allusion

Let heaven revenge; for I may never lift
An angry arm against his minister.

55.[1] Without the hollow extravagance of Beaum. and Fletch's Ultra-royalism,[2] how carefully does Shakspear acknowlege and reverence the eternal distinction between the mere Individual, and the Symbolic or representative: on which all genial Law no less than Patriotism depends!

42   I 416 | I ii

This second Scene quite commencing and anticipative of, the tone and character of the Play at large.

43   I 416 | I iii

Scene III, compared with any of Shakespear's fictitious dramas, or those found in a History as unknown to his Auditors generally as Fiction: & no where this violent violation of the succession of Time.—Proof that the pure *historic* Drama had its own laws.

44   I 416 | I iii 69–73

BOLINGBROKE. . . . Oh thou, the earthly author of my blood,—
    Whose youthful spirit, in me regenerate,
    Doth with a two-fold vigour lift me up
    To reach at victory above my head,—
    Add proof unto mine armour with thy prayers . . .

55.[1] Boling's Ambition.

45   I 417 | I iii 144–73

BOLINGBROKE. Your will be done: This must my comfort be,—
    That sun, that warms you here, shall shine on me;
    And these his golden beams, to you here lent,
    Shall point on me and gild my banishment. . . .
MOWBRAY. . . . A dearer merit, not so deep a maim
    As to be cast forth in the common air,
    Have I deserved at your highness' hand. . . .
    I am too old to fawn upon a nurse,
    Too far in years to be a pupil now;

41[1] Line 2 of textus.
41[2] The plays of Beaumont and Fletcher are constant foils to Shakespeare in C's commentary: see COPY A **82** and n 1. C

comments on their politics esp in BEAUMONT & FLETCHER COPY B **20, 41**.
44[1] Line 1 of textus.

What is thy sentence then but speechless death,
Which robs my tongue from breathing native breath?

20.[1] Bolingbroke's ambitious hope, not yet shaped into definite plan, beautifully contrasted with Mowbray's desolation

46   I 417 | I iii 156 (in **45** textus)

31 "A dearer *Merit*" Shakespear's *instinctive* propriety in the choice of Words.

47   I 418 | I iii 183–90

KING RICHARD. . . . . You never shall (so help you truth and heaven!)
Embrace each other's love in banishment;
Nor ever look upon each other's face;
Nor ever write, regret, nor reconcile
This lowering tempest of your home-bred hate;
Nor never by advised purpose meet,
To plot, contrive, or complot any ill,
'Gainst us, our state, our subjects, or our land.

5.[1] Already the selfish Weakness of Richard's character opens. Nothing which such minds so readily embrace, as indirect ways softened down to their quasi Consciences by *Policy*, expedience &c—

48   I 418 | I iii 206–7

MOWBRAY.   . . . Now no way can I stray;
Save back to England, all the world's my way.

25.[1] "The world was all before them" Milton.[2]

49   I 418 | I iii 211–15

KING RICHARD.   . . . Six frozen winters spent,
Return with welcome home from banishment.
BOLINGBROKE. How long a time lies in one little word!
Four lagging winters, and four wanton springs,
End in a word: Such is the breath of kings.

31–35.[1] admirable anticipation.

45[1] Line 2 of textus.
47[1] Line 6 of textus.
48[1] Line 2 of textus.
48[2] Milton *Paradise Lost* XII 646, referring to Adam and Eve cast out from the Garden.
49[1] Line 31 corresponds to line 2 of textus.

49A I 419 (p) | I iv 29–30

KING RICHARD. . . . And patient underbearing of his fortune,
  As 'twere, to banish their ẹaffects with him.[1]

50 I 419, pencil | I iv 54–64

BUSHY. Old John of Gaunt is grievous sick, my lord;
  Suddenly taken; and hath sent post-haste,
  To intreat your majesty to visit him.
KING RICHARD. Where lies he?
BUSHY. At Ely-house.
KING RICHARD. Now put it, heaven, in his physician's mind,
  To help him to his grave immediately!
  The lining of his coffers shall make coats
  To deck our soldiers for these Irish wars.—
  Come, gentlemen, let's all go visit him:
  Pray heaven, we may make haste, and come too late!

A striking conclusion of a first Act—letting the reader into the secret—
⟨having before⟩ impressinged the dignified & kingly manners of Richard,
yet by well managed anticipations, leading to the full gratification of the
Auditor's pleasure in his own penetration—

51 I 420, pencil | II i 73–84

GAUNT. Oh, how that name befits my composition!
  Old Gaunt, indeed; and gaunt in being old:
  Within me grief hath kept a tedious fast;
  And who abstains from meat that is not gaunt?
  For sleeping England long time have I watch'd;
  Watching breeds leanness, leanness is all gaunt:
  The pleasure that some fathers feed upon,
  Is my strict fast, I mean my children's looks;
  And therein fasting, thou hast made me gaunt:
  Gaunt am I for the grave, gaunt as a grave,
  Whose hollow womb inherits nought but bones.
KING RICHARD. Can sick men play so nicely with their names?

Turn back to p. 414 (blank Mss page)—and here the death-bed feeling in
which all things appear but as *puns* and equivocations—[1]

49A[1] C corrects a typographical error.
51[1] I.e. **38** above. In Lect 12 of the 1811–12 series, and again in Lect 5 of the 1813 series, C gave a psychological analysis of the appropriateness of the punning in this speech: *Lects 1808–1819 (CC)* I 379–81, 564.

52   I 421, pencil | II i 141–6

YORK. 'Beseech your majesty, impute his [Gaunt's] words
    To wayward sickliness and age in him:
    He loves you, on my life, and holds you dear
    As Harry duke of Hereford, were he here.
KING RICHARD. Right; you say true: as Hereford's love, so his;
    As theirs, so mine; and all be as it is.

35. The depth of this—compared with the first scene, 414.[1] "How high a pitch".

53   I 422, pencil | II ii 5–13

QUEEN. To please the king I did; to please myself,
    I cannot do it; yet I know no cause
    Why I should welcome such a guest as grief,
    Save bidding farewel to so sweet a guest
    As my sweet Richard: Yet again, methinks,
    Some unborn sorrow, ripe in fortune's womb,
    Is coming toward me; and my inward soul
    With nothing trembles: at something it grieves,
    More than with parting from my lord the king.

It is clear, that Sh. never meant to represent Richard II[d] as a vulgar Debauchee/ but merely a wantonness in feminine shew, feminine *friendism*,[1] intensely ~~fem~~ Woman-like love of those immediately about him—mistaking the delight of being loved by him for a love for him—[2]

54   I 423, pencil | II ii 20–4

BUSHY.   . . . so your sweet majesty,
    Looking awry upon your lord's departure,
    Find shapes of grief, more than himself, to wail;
    Which, look'd on as it is, is nought but shadows
    Of what it is not.

Tender Superstition encouraged by S.—Terra incognita of the Human Mind—

52[1] Line 35 in C's copy corresponds to the last line of textus; "414" alludes to **39** above.
53[1] C's coinage, so attributed by *OED*.

53[2] C further expounds on the "weak and womanish" character of Richard in *Lects 1808–1819* (*CC*) I 381.

55   I 439, pencil | v v 76–92

GROOM. . . . O, how it yearn'd my heart, when I beheld,
   In London streets, that coronation day,
   When Bolingbroke rode on roan Barbary!
   That horse, that thou so often hath bestrid;
   That horse, that I so carefully have dress'd!
KING RICHARD. Rode he on Barbary? Tell me, gentle friend,
   How went he under him?
GROOM. So proudly, as if he disdain'd the ground.
KING RICHARD. So proud, that Bolingbroke was on his back!
   That jade hath eat bread from my royal hand;
   This hand hath made him proud with clapping him;
   Would he not stumble? Would he not fall down,
   (Since pride must have a fall) and break the neck
   Of that proud man, that did usurp his back?
   Forgiveness, horse! why do I rail on thee,
   Since thou, created to be aw'd by man,
   Wast born to bear?

The affecting Incident of the very Horse, as *realizing*

56   I 448 | *1 Henry IV* II i 19–21

2 CARRIER. Why, they will allow us ne'er a jourden, and then we leak in
   your chimney; and your chamber-lie breeds fleas like a loach.

[Editor's footnote on "loach":] Warburton explains this by a scotch word
loch, a lake: while Mr. Steevens thinks that the carrier means to say—
fleas as big as a *loach*, i.e. resembling the fish so called, in size.

27.[1] I rather take it for a misprint or perhaps a provincial pronunciation
for Leɖech.—i.e. blood-suckers.[2] Had it been Gnats, instead of Fleas,
there might have been some sense tho' small probability in Warburton's
suggestion of the Scottish, Loch. But possibly loach, or lutch, may be
some lost word for Dove-cote, or Poultry-lodge, notorious for breeding
Fleas. In Steevens' and in my Reading it should have been Loaches, or
Leeches, in the plural—tho' I do n't know, either. I think, I have heard
anglers speak of Trouts like *a* Salmon.

   56[1] Last line of Shakespeare's text in   fer explanation to emendation. *Sh* (Reed)
textus.   and *Sh* (Arden) both record the ancient the-
   56[2] This is not an idea that had occurred   ory that some fish bred fleas.
to C's predecessors, who on the whole pre-

57   I 482 | *2 Henry IV* II ii 151–3, 166–8

PRINCE HENRY. Sup any women with him?
PAGE. None, my lord, but old mistress Quickly, and mistress Doll Tear-
   sheet. . . .
PRINCE HENRY. . . . This Doll Tear-sheet should be some road.
POINS. I warrant you, as common as the way between St. Alban's and
   London.

Strange that the so evident misreading of Tear-sheet instead of Tear-
street, i.e. Street-walker, terere *stratam* (viam), should have escaped the
Editors—To what other word could Prince Henry's remark apply—this
Doll Tear-street should be some *road*—Several of our roads are called
Streets to this day.[1]

58   I 531 | *Henry V* IV iii 34–9

KING HENRY. . . . Rather proclaim it, Westmoreland, through my host,
   That he which hath no stomach to this fight,
   Let him depart; his passport shall be made,
   And crowns for convoy put into his purse:
   We would not die in that man's company,
   That fears his fellowship to die with us.

Q? We would not *live* in that man's company—?[1]

59   II 705, referring to II 711 | *Coriolanus* I x 7–27

AUFIDIUS.   . . . Five times, Marcius,
   I have fought thee; so often hast thou beat me;
   And would'st do so, I think, should we encounter
   As often as we eat.—By the elements,
   If e'er again I meet him beard to beard,
   He is mine, or I am his: Mine emulation
   Hath not that honour in't, it had; for where
   I thought to crush him in an equal force,
   True sword to sword, I'll potch at him some way;
   Or wrath, or craft, may get him.
SOLDIER.   He's the devil.
AUFIDIUS. Bolder, though not so subtle: My valour's poison'd
   With only suffering stain by him; for him

57[1] See COPY A **74** and n 1.   emendation but rejects it as unnecessary.
58[1] *Sh* (Arden) records C's proposed

Shall flie out of itself: nor sleep nor sanctuary,
Being naked, sick; nor fane, nor capitol,
The prayers of priests, nor times of sacrifice,
Embarquements all of fury, shall lift up
Their rotten privilege and custom 'gainst
My hate to Marcius: where I find him, were it
At home, upon my brother's guard, even there,
Against the hospitable canon, would I
Wash my fierce hand in his heart.

Look at 711. for a fine prevention of a Shock in Aufidius's Character—
The wonderful philos. impartiality in Shaks: Politics—His own Country's History had furnished him with no *matter* but what was too recent—
& he devoted it to *Patriotism*—Besides, the dispassionate Instruction of
ancient Hist—This most remarkable in Julius Cæsar—In all this good-
humored Laugh at Mobs, collate with Sir T. Brown/[1]

60   II 713 | II i 116–18

MENENIUS. . . . the most sovereign prescription in Galen is but empyric
qutique, and, to this preservative, of no better report than a horse-
drench . . .

An old Question. Was it without or in contempt of Historical Information
that Shakespear made the Contemporaries of Coriolanus quote Cato and
Galen?[1]—What the Blunder of the Press after "empiric" stands for, I cannot recollect.[2]

60A   II 713 (p) | II i 163–5

HERALD.   . . . where he hath won,
     With fame, a name to Caius Marcius: these
     In honour follow̧eth, Coriolanus.[1]

59[1] According to notes published by
HNC, C was to make similar points about
Shakespeare's impartiality and about his
"good nature" in treating "a mob" in Lect 1
of the 1818–19 series: *Lects 1808–1819*
(*CC*) II 272–3. About 1817–18, C copied
out an extract having to do with "the Multitude, that numerous piece of monstrosity,
which taken asunder seem men and the reasonable creatures of God" from Sir Thomas
Browne *Religio Medici* pt 2 § 1 (1659) ii 23;
he also at some point remarked upon the excellence of this passage in SH's copy of

Browne's *Works*: *CN* III 4366 and n,
BROWNE *Works* 44 and n.

60[1] For C's general dismissal of complaints about anachronisms in Shakespeare
see also *Lects 1808–1819* (*CC*) II 245, 268,
338. C alludes to this reference to Galen in
a note of 1821–2: *CN* IV 4839 f 121.

60[2] The text should read "empirickqu-
tique" (one word). It is not strictly a "Blunder of the Press" but an adjective made up
from "empiric" and meaning "quackery", as
Ritson first pointed out: *Sh* (Reed).

60A[1] "Follows" is the correct reading.

61 II 741 | *Julius Caesar* I i 12–21

MARULLUS. But what trade art thou? answer directly.

COBLER. A trade, sir, that, I hope, I may use with a safe conscience; which is, indeed, sir, a mender of bad soals.

FLAVIUS. What trade, thou knave? thou naughty knave, what trade?

COBLER. Nay, I beseech you, sir, be not out with me: Yet, if you be out, sir, I can mend you.

MARULLUS. What meanst thou by that? Mend me, thou saucy fellow?

COBLER. Why, sir, cobble you.

FLAVIUS. Thou art a cobbler, art thou?

COBLER. Truly, sir, all that I live by is, with the awl . . .

The Speeches of Flavius and Marullus are in Blank Verse.[1] Whenever regular metre can be rendered truly imitative of character, passion or personal rank, Shakspeare seldom, if ever, neglects it. Hence, l. 26, Column α, should be printed

What mean'st by that? Mend *me*, thou saucy fellow?

N.B. I say, *regular* metre: for even the prose ~~is~~ has in the highest and lowest Dram. Pers., a Cobler or a Hamlet, ~~a mov~~ a rhythm so felicitous and so severally appropriate, as to be a virtual metre.

62 II 741 | I i 30–2

COBLER. . . . we make holiday, to see Caesar, and to rejoice in his triumph.

MARULLUS. Wherefore rejoice? What conquest brings he home?

15, Col. β.[1] for "conquests" I would read "triumphs".[2]

63 II 742 | I ii 19

BRUTUS. A soothsayer bids you beware the ides of March.

Column β, l. 2. If my ear does not deceive me, the metre of this line was meant to express that sort of mild philosophic contempt, characterizing Brutus even in his first casual speech—. The line is a ~~Tetra~~ Trimeter, each foot containing two accented and two unaccented syllables, but variously arranged—

$$\cup - - \cup \, | - \cup \cup - | \cup - \cup - | .$$

61[1] See COPY A **118** n 1.
62[1] Line 2 of textus.

62[2] Other commentators accept "conquest".

64   II 741, referring to II 744 | I ii 215–300

See 744 compared with Ant. & Cleop 777[1]

The power of interesting never more strongly manifested than in these plays—why, they really are flesh & blood Individuals. More true Pathos in Brutus & Cassius Quarrel—[2]

65   II 746 (p), pencil | I iii 116–20

CASCA. You speak to Casca; and to such a man
　　That is no flearing tell-tale. Hold my hand:
　　Be factious for redress of all these griefs;
　　And I will set this foot of mine as far,
　　As who goes farthest.

[Footnote 2:] *Factious* seems here to mean *active*.

2. You have *spoken* as a Conspirator; be so *in fact*—& I will join you. *Act* on what your principles:[a] and *realize* them in a *fact*.[1]

66   II 747 | II i 10–21

BRUTUS. It must be by his death; and, for my part,
　　I know no personal cause to spurn at him,
　　But for the general. He would be crown'd:—
　　How that might change his nature, there's the question.
　　It is the bright day, that brings forth the adder;
　　And that craves wary walking. Crown him? That;—
　　And then, I grant, we put a sting in him,
　　That at his will he may do danger with.
　　The abuse of greatness is, when it disjoins
　　Remorse from power: And, to speak truth of Caesar,
　　I have not known when his affections sway'd
　　More than his reason. . . .

This is singular—at least, I do not at present see into Shakspear's motive, the rationale—or in what point he meant Brutus's character to appear. For

65[a]   Verb—"are"?—omitted in error

64[1] These page numbers refer to *Julius Caesar* I ii 215–300 (the dialogue of Brutus and Cassius and Casca) and to *Antony and Cleopatra* II v 23–106 (the scene in which a messenger comes to Cleopatra with the news that Antony has married Octavia).

64[2] C probably refers to the quarrel and reconciliation in *Julius Caesar* IV iii 1–123.

65[1] "Active" had been Johnson's suggestion, but the gloss of Malone, as recorded in *Sh* (Reed), namely, "embody a party or faction", has been more generally adopted.

surely (this I mean is what I say to myself, in my present quantum of Insight, only modified by my experience in how many instances I have ripened into a perception of Beauties where I had before descried faults)—surely, nothing can seem more discordant with our historical pre-conceptions of Brutus, or more *lowering* to the intellect of this Stoico-platonic Tyrannicide, than the Tenets here attributed to him, to *him*, the stern Roman Republican—viz.—that he would have no Objection to a King, or to Cæsar, a Monarch in Rome, would Cæsar be as good a Monarch as he now seems disposed to be—. How too could Brutus say, he finds no personal cause/ i.e. none in Cæsar's past conduct as a man? Had he not passed the Rubicon? Entered Rome as a Conqueror? Placed his Gauls in the Senate?—Shakespear (it may be said) has not brought these things forward. True! and this is just the Ground of my perplexity. What character does Sh. mean *his* Brutus to be?—[1]

67   II 747 | II i 83–5

BRUTUS. . . . For if thou path, thy native semblance on,
    Not Erebus itself were dim enough
    To hide thee from prevention.

[Footnote on "path":] i.e. If thou *walk* in thy true form.

747. 2nd Col. l. 20. Surely there need be no scruple in treating this path as a mere misprint or mis-script for put. In what place does Shakes., where does any other Writer of the same age, use path as a verb for walk?[1]

68   II 767 | *Antony and Cleopatra*

[1]But of all perhaps of Shakspeare's Plays the most wonderful is the Antony & Cleopatra—scarcely any in which he has followed history more minutely, and yet ~~perhap~~ few even of his own in which he impresses the notion of giant strength, so much, perhaps none in which he impresses it more strongly.—This owing to the manner in which it is sustained throughout—that he *lives* in & through the Play—to the numerous mo-

66[1] In C's experience, "our historical pre-conceptions of Brutus" all tended to make him an heroic figure: so in *Friend* (*CC*) I 320–4 C defends the assassination of Caesar and refers to "the fervent admiration felt by the good and wise in all ages when they mention the name of Brutus" (323).

67[1] Editors have tended to stay with the Folio reading "path". *Sh* (Arden) notes *OED* evidence of the use of the word as a verb in Shakespeare's period.

68[1] This note is published as part of C's lecture-material for 18 Feb 1819 in *Lects 1808–1819* (*CC*) II 368.

mentary flashes of Nature counteracting the historic abstraction—in short take as a specimen the 801 ad finem.—[2]

69   II 768 (p), pencil | I ii 35–9

CHARMIAN. Then, belike, my children shall have no names: Pry'thee, how many boys and wenches must I have?
SOOTHSAYER. If every of your wishes had a womb, And foretell every wish, a million.

[Footnote:] The meaning is, If you had as many wombs as you will have wishes, and *I should* foretell all those wishes, I should foretell a million of children.

Strange! the word is plainly, fruitful—fertile.[1]

70   II 857–856[a] | *Troilus and Cressida*

[Footnote to title:] Mr. Pope (after Dryden) informs us, that the story of Troïlus and Cressida was originally the work of one Lollius, a Lombard: but Dryden goes yet further; he declares it to have been written in Latin verse, and that Chaucer translated it.—Lollius was a historiographer of Urbino in Italy.—Shakspeare received the greatest part of his materials for the structure of this play from the *Troy Boke* of Lydgate, printed in 1513.— . . .

"Lollius was an historiographer of ⟨Urbino in⟩ Italy"—So affirms the *Notary* to whom the ~~Seur~~ Sieur Stockdale committed the Disfacciamento of Ayscough's excellent edition of Shakspear: which or in defect of the first an unalte⟨re⟩d Re-print of the same suffer not to pass by you, tho' at double the price.[1]—L. an H. of I!! Pity that the researchful Notary had not either told us in what century, ~~and in what part of Italy~~ and of what History he was the O'Grapher, or been content to depone, that Lollius if a writer of that name existed at all was a somewhat somewhere.[2]—I have

70[a] The note runs from II 857 interleaf verso (marked "P. 3 = 1: that is, the Note begins here.") to II 856 interleaf verso ("Page I—but continued from page 3.rd") and finally to II 857 interleaf recto ("Page 2.nd: but the third of the Notes to Tr. & Cress.")

68[2] The last two pages of the play in this edition, beginning at v ii 216—but essentially, the death-scene of Cleopatra.
69[1] See COPY B 18 and n.
70[1] By "excellent edition" C must mean the one-vol *Stockdale's Edition* of 1784 (COPY B); it is not certain, however, that Ayscough was the editor of that edition, his

name first appearing as the contributor of an index to the 3-vol 1790 ed. "Disfacciamento", meaning "unmaking", not in *OED*, is one of C's group of words based on the Italian *facimento*: cf MORE *Theological Works* 14 and n 2.
70[2] The edition C was using perpetuates a now-celebrated error. In his own *Troilus*

never seen Lydgate's *Troy Boke*, printed 1513; but deeply regret, that M^r
A. Chalmers had not substituted the whole of Lydgate's Works from the
Mss extant, for the almost worthless Gower.[3]
[4]The Troil: and Cressida of Sh. can scarcely be classed with his Gr.
and Rom. *History* Dramas; but it forms an intermediate Link between the
fictitious ⟨G. & R.⟩ Histories, which we may call Legendary Dramas and
the proper ancient Histories: ex. gr. between the Pericles or Tit. Andron.
and the Coriolanus, Julius Cæsar &c. Cymbeline is congener with Pericles—distinguished from Lear by not having any declared prominent Object. But where shall we class the Timon of Athens? Immediately, below
Lear. It is a Lear of the satirical Drama, a Lear of domestic or ordinary
Life—a local Eddy of ~~nar~~ Passion on the High Road of Society while all
around is the week-day Goings on of Wind and Weather—a Lear therefore without its soul-scorching flashes, its ear-cleaving Thunder Claps,
its meteoric splendors, without the contagion & fearful sympathies of Nature, the Fates, the Furies[b] the frenzied Elements dance in ~~or~~ and out, now
breaking thro' and scattering, now hand in hand, with the ~~group of Human~~
fierce or fantastic Group of Human Passions, Crimes and Anguishes,
~~whirling~~ reeling ⟨on the unsteady ground⟩ in a wild harmony to the Swell
and Sink of the Earthquake.—But my present Subject was Troilus &
Cressida: and I suppose that scarcely knowing what to say of it I by a cunning of instinct ran to off[c] to Subjects on which I should find it difficult
not to say too much, tho' certain after all I should still leave the better part
unsaid, and the gleaning for others richer than my own harvest. Indeed,
there is none of Sh's Plays harder to characterize. The name & the re-

70[b] Here C has written "(turn *back* to p. 1 = 2.)"
70[c] C probably meant to omit the first "to"

and Criseyde, Chaucer says he is retelling a story told by Lollius, who wrote an old book about Troy in Latin; and in *The House of Fame* he introduces him as an actual histor-ical figure, but "There is no such historian, ancient or modern, known to the world under that name" (Gilbert Highet *The Classical Tradition*—Oxford 1949—96), and it appears that Chaucer himself mistook a playful reference to "Maximus Lollius" in Horace *Epistles* 1.2.1–2 for a specific au-thor, rather than for the addressee of the let-ter itself. Between Chaucer's time and C's, generations of scholars muddied the waters by confusing the nonexistent Lollius with Lollius Urbicus, a third-century figure said

to have written a history of his own time; and *Urbicus* being mistaken for *Urbinas* ("of Urbino") this real but shadowy figure acquired a birthplace. See G. L. Kittredge "Chaucer's Lollius" *Harvard Studies in Classical Philology* XXVIII (1917) 47–133, esp 83–5.
70[3] In *Works of the English Poets, from Chaucer to Cowper* (21 vols 1810), a col-lection C annotated (CHALMERS), although very few of his notes have been preserved and there is no comment on Gower.
70[4] The remainder of this note, and **71** following, are published as part of the lec-ture-material for 25 Feb 1819 in *Lects 1808–1819 (CC)* II 376–8.

membrances connected with it, prepare us for the representation of attachment no less faithful than fervent on the side of the youth, and of sudden and shameless inconstancy on the part of the Lady. And this indeed is the ~m~ gold thread on which the scenes are strung, tho' often kept out of sight and out of mind by gems of greater value than itself. But as Sh. ~takes no subject~ calls-forth nothing from the Mausoleum of Hist. or the Catacombs of Tradition without giving ~it calling~ or eliciting some permanent and general interest, brings forward no subject which he does not moralize or intellectualize, so here he has ~contrasted the~ drawn in Cressida the Portrait of a vehement *Passion* that ha~s~ving its true origin and proper cause in warmth of temperament ~and~ fastens on, rather than fixes to, some one Object by *Liking* and temporary Preference/ ⟨881, 40, β.[5] This he has contrasted⟩ with the profound Affection represented in Troilus, and alone worthy the name of Love, Affection, passionate indeed, ~and~ swoln from the confluence of youthful ~ardor~ instincts and youthful Fancy, glowing in the radiance of Hope newly risen, in short enlarged by the collective sympathies of Nature; but still having a depth of calmer element, ~and a channel in of the rock of a single and entire~ in a Will, stronger than Desire, more ~total~ entire than Choice, and which gives permanence to its own act by converting it into Faith and Duty.—Hence with ~more than ju~ excellent Judgement and with an excellence higher than mere Judgement can give, at the close of the Play, when Cressida has sunk into infamy below retrieval and beneath a hope, the same Will, ~acting with that same energy, of which,~ which had been the substance and the basis of his Love, while the restless Pleasures and Passionate Longings, like Sea-waves, had tossed but on its surface, the same moral energy ~preserves him~ snatches him ⟨aloof⟩ from all neighbourhood ~of~ with her Dishonor, from all lingering Fondness and languishing Regrets while it rushes with him into ~a new Channel of~ other and nobler Duties, and deepens the Channel, which his heroic Brother's Death had left empty for its collected Flood.—Yet another, ~an~ secondary and subordinate purpose he has inwoven with the two characters, that of opposing the inferior ~refinement~ civilization but purer morals of the Trojans to the refine~d~ments, deep policy, but duplicity and sensual corruptions of the Greeks.

To all this, however, there is so little comparative projection given, nay, the ~characters of~ masterly Group of Agamemnon, Nestor, Ulysses, and still more in advance, of Achilles, Ajax, and Thersites so manifestly occupy the foreground ~of this Albert Durer-like History Painting~,, that

---

70[5] *Troilus and Cressida* IV v 54–9, **72** textus.

the subservience and vassalage of Strength and animal Courage to Intellect and Policy seem to be the ~~moral impression Purpose~~ Lesson most often in our Poet's View, and which he has taken little pains to connect with the former more interesting ~~Lesson~~ Moral impersonated in the titular Hero & Heroine of the Drama. But I am half inclined to believe, that Shakspeare's ~~moving~~ main object, or shall I rather say that his ruling impulse was to translate the ⟨poetic⟩ Heroïces ~~Age of~~ Paganism into the not less rude but more intellectually vigorous, more *featurely*[6] Warriors of Christian Chivalry, to substantiate the distinct and graceful Profiles or Outlines of the Homeric Epic into the flesh and blood of the Romantic Drama—in short, to give a grand History-piece in the robust style of Albert Durer.—[7]

71 II 858

The character of Thersites well deserves a more particular attention— ~~but~~ as the Caliban of ~~the Real~~ Life[a] Demagogues/—the admirable Portrait of intellectual power ~~strugg~~ deserted by all grace, all moral principle, all not momentary purpose, ~~a slave by tenure of his own baseness, made to growl, and be beaten,~~ just wise enough to detect the weak~~ness with~~ head and fool enough to provoke the ~~strong hand~~ armed fist of his Betters, whom Malcontent Achilles can ~~can~~ inveigle from ~~the care of~~ Malcontent Ajax, under the condition, that he ~~may be~~ shall be called on to do nothing but to abuse and slander and that he shall be allowed to abuse as much and as [? pour] purulently as he likes—that is, a[b] can—in short, a ~~rebel that flings up from asinine instinct~~ mule, ⟨~~malignant~~ quarrelsome by the original discord of its Nature,⟩ a slave by tenure of his own baseness made to ~~growl~~ bray and be ~~beaten~~ brayed,[1] to despise and be despicable—

Aye, Sir! but say what you will, he is a devilish clever fellow; tho'— the best friends will fall out; but there was a time when Ajax thought, he ~~oug~~ deserved to have a statue of Gold erected to him, and ~~tha~~ handsome

> 71[a] "Life" should have been included in the deletion
> 71[b] A slip or archaism for "he"?

70[6] I.e. having strongly marked features. This passage is the first illustration of the word given in *OED*.

70[7] A sentence in a notebook entry of about 1821–2 clarifies this very rare reference to Albrecht Dürer (1471–1528). C there uses as an analogy for historical detail in symbolic narrative "the Costume and Drapery in . . . Albert Durer's grand Scripture-history Pictures": *CN* IV 4839 f 121

and n, where the editor gives several examples of Dürer's paintings from scripture-history. C's friend Charles Aders, who collected German and Netherlandish paintings, owned at least one Dürer, according to the report of an exhibition of 1832: *G Mag* CII (Feb 1832) 153–4.

71[1] Surely an allusion to Prov 27.22, "Though thou shouldest bray a fool in a mortar . . .".

Achilles, ⟨at⟩ the head of the Myrmidons, gave no little credit to his "friend["], Thersites.[2]

72   II 881 | IV v 54–9

ULYSSES.   Fie, fie, upon her!
    There's language in her eye, her cheek, her lip,
    Nay, her foot speaks; her wanton spirits look out
    At every joint and motive of her body.
    O, these encounters, so glib of tongue,
    That give a coasting welcome ere it comes . . .

[Footnote on "coasting":] i.e. an amorous address; a courtship.

45, β. Q[y] *Accosting?*[1] See the Twelfth Night, "Accost her, knight! accost."[2]—Yet there *sounds* a something so Shakspearish in the phrase, ~~That~~ "*give* a *coasting* welcome", taking coasting as the epithet and adjective to Welcome, that had the following been "ere *they* land" instead of "ere *it* comes", I should have preferred the interpretation. The sense now is, that give welcome to a Salute ere it comes.

73   II 893 | *Cymbeline* I i 1–3

I GENTLEMAN. You do not meet a man, but frowns: our bloods
    No more obey the heavens, than our courtiers'
    Still seem, as does the King's.

[Footnote:] Dr. Johnson observes, that this passage is so difficult, that commentators may differ concerning it without animosity or shame. . . . Mr. Tyrwhitt proposes to make the passage clear by a very slight alteration, only leaving out the last letter; ". . . our bloods no more obey the heavens than our courtiers still seem as does the *king:*—That is, *Still look as the king does.*"

There can be no doubt of M[r] Tyrwhitt's emendation, as to the sense—only it is not impossible that Shakespear's dramatic language may permit of the word, brows or faces, being understood after the word

---

71[2] The word "friend" is much bandied about in this play, notably in III i, though not particularly in connection with Thersites, who had passed from the company of Ajax to that of Achilles.

72[1] This was the emendation proposed by Mason; but "coasting" has prevailed,

Steevens putting editors onto a nautical track by pointing out that "a coasting salute" was a phrase used of ships that did not intend to stop or land.

72[2] *Twelfth Night* I iii 49, 56–7: "Accost, Sir Andrew, accost. . . . 'accost' is front her, board her, woo her, assail her."

"courtiers'["], which might then remain in the Gen. Case Plural. But the Nom. Plural makes excellent sense & is sufficiently elegant and sounds to my ear Shakspearian.[1]

[a]More probably, the word Courtiers' is a misprint from an anticipation of the Compositor's eye (l. 20) for Count'nances: the mss r is easily and often ~~mis~~ confounded with the mss n. The Compositor read the first syllable *Court*, and his eye catching at the same time the word "courtier" at the end of a line (the 20th) he completed the word without reconsulting the Copy.[2]

74   II 899 | I vi 32–8

IACHIMO. . . . What! are men mad? Hath nature given them eyes
    To see this vaulted arch, and the rich crop
    Of sea and land, which can distinguish 'twixt
    The fiery orbs above, and the twinn'd stones
    Upon the number'd beach? and can we not
    Partition make with spectacles so precious
    'Twixt fair and foul?

[Footnotes on "crop" and "number'd beach":] *The crop of sea and land* means the productions of either element. . . . Dr. Johnson says, he knows not well how to regulate this passage. *Number'd* is perhaps *numerous.—Twinn'd stones* he does not understand. *"Twinn'd shells*, or *pairs of shells*, are very common."—Mr. Steevens adds, that the pebbles on the sea-shore are so much of the same size and shape, that *twinn'd* may mean as like as *twins.*—Dr. Farmer thinks we may read the *umbered*, the *shaded* beach.

41, α–46. For "crop" I do not hesitate to read "cope"[1]—and the following lines thus—
            which can distinguish twixt
    The fiery orbs above, and the grimed stones
    Upon an umber'd Beach/
I have found grind in an old Mss so written as that I mistook it for twind, and here the origin of the Printer's erratum is evident, from the "*tw*ixt" above and below. But tho' I take D[r] Farmer's "umber'd" which I had proposed before I ever saw or heard of its having been already suggested, I

73[a]   Change of pen, and possibly a note made on a later reading

73[1] See COPY A **136** and n 1.
73[2] See COPY B **21**.
74[1] This emendation was proposed by

Warburton, but "crop" (in the sense of "harvest") has prevailed.

do not adopt his interpretation of the word, which I doubt not is derived not from Umbra, a shade, but from umber, a dingy yellow-brown Soil, which most frequently forms the mass of the Sludge on the Sea Shore and on the Banks of Tide-rivers at Low Water.[2]—One other *possible* interpretation of this sentence had occurred to me—just barely worth mentioning—the twinn'd stones = the *augrim* (alogarithm) stones upon the number'd Beech = the astronomical Tables of Beech-wood—[3]

75　II 928–32, including 929 (p)[a] | *King Lear* I i, esp 1–7

KENT. I thought, the king had more affected the duke of Albany, than Cornwall.
GLOUCESTER. It did always seem so to us: but now, in the division of the kingdom, it appears not which of the dukes he values most; for equalities are so weighed, that curiosity in neither can make choice of either's moiety.

[1]~~Page~~ ⟨Line.⟩ 5–10 ⟨Column.⟩ α.—It was without forethought,[b] and it is not without its due significance, that the triple division is stated here as already determin'd, and in all its particulars, previously to the Trial of Professions, as the relative rewards of which the Daughters were to be made to consider their several portions. The strange yet by no means unnatural, mixture of Selfishness, Sensibility, and Habit of Feeling derived from & fostered by the particular rank and usages of the Individual—the intense desire to be intensely beloved, selfish and yet characteristic of the Selfishness of a loving and kindly nature— ~~the weak Soul within itself unblest~~ a feeble Selfishness, self-supportless and Leaning for all pleasure on another's Breast—the selfish Craving after a sympathy ~~in~~ with a prodigal Disinterestedness, contradicted by its own Ostentation and the mode and nature of its Claims—the anxiety, ~~and~~ the distrust, the jealousy, which more or less accompany all selfish Affections, and are among the surest contradiction of mere fondness from Love, and which originate Lear's eager wish to⌀ enjoy his Daughter's violent Professions, while the

75[a] The note runs from II 929 interleaf, facing the opening of the play and marked "LEAR, 1.ˢᵗ page of the Notes.", with an insert at the foot of II 929 (p), through II 928 interleaf ("LEAR Notes on. 2ⁿᵈ page, continued from over-leaf"), II 930 interleaf ("LEAR: Notes on, p. 3.ʳᵈ"), and II 931 interleaf, to II 932 interleaf
75[b] This appears to be a slip for "not without forethought"

74[2] See COPY A **140** and n 1.
74[3] C means augrim or "algorism" stones—a much more far-fetched suggestion than his earlier gloss in COPY A **140** (and see n 2).

75[1] All the notes on *Lear*—i.e. **75–98** in this copy—are published as part of C's lecture-material for 28 Jan 1819 in *Lects 1808–1819* (*CC*) II 325–34.

inveterate habits of Sovereignty convert the wish into claim and positive Right, and the incompliance with it into crime and treason—these facts, these passions, these moral verities, on which the whole Tragedy is founded, ⟨are⟩ all prepared for, and will to the retrospect be found implied in, these first 4 or 5 lines of the Play.—They let us know that the Trial is but a Trick—and that the grossness of the old King's rage ~~results~~ is in part the natural result of a silly Trick suddenly and most unexpectedly baffled, and disappointed.[c] ⟨*Here* notice the improbability and nursery-tale character of the tale./ prefixed as the *Porch* of the Edifice, not laid as its foundation—So Shylock's Lb of Flesh—item, an old popular Ballad—with how great judgment which still remains is [? combatable])[2] This having been provided in the fewest words, in a natural reply to as natural[d] question, which yet answers a secondary purpose[e] of attracting our attention to the difference or diversity between the characters of Cornwall and Albany, ~~Shakspear instantly passes to the second Agent Character second in importance in the conduct of the Plot, and introduce[f] Edmund to our notice with similar felicity and judgment of preparation. Lear indeed is rather the great *Subject*-matter of the Drama, the Centre to which all converges—he is the Patient (persona passtiens) of the Tragedy, his Passions the Actors in it, while Edmund is the Main Agent, whose Will plans and conducts the movement and circumstances.~~ the premises and *Data*, as it were, having been thus afforded for ~~the Character~~ our after-insight into the mind and mood of the Person, whose character, passions and sufferings are the main *subject-matter* of the Play—from Lear, the Persona PATIENS[3] of his Drama Shaksp. passes without delay to the second in importance, to the Main *Agent*, ~~who~~ and prime Mover—introduces Edmund to our acquaintance, and with the same felicity of Judgement in the same easy, natural, ~~and seemingly casual~~ way prepares us for his character in the seemingly casual communication of its origin and occasion.— ~~Gifted~~ From the first drawing up of the Curtain he has stood

75[c] Here C has written "*∧" and marked the insert, at the foot of II 930 (p), with "*∧"
75[d] A slip for "a natural" or "as natural a"?
75[e] Here C has written "(overleaf, backwards.)"—i.e. 928 interleaf, the recto of 929 interleaf
75[f] A slip for "introduces"

75[2] C had made this connection between *King Lear* and *The Merchant of Venice* before: see COPY A **82** and n 4. The reference to the ballad is explained in *Lects 1808–1819* (CC) II 326 n 1, the ballad—*Gernutus the Jew of Venice*—having been identified as a source for Shakespeare by Joseph Warton (*Observations on the Faerie Queene of Spenser*—1754) and pub by Thomas Percy in *Reliques of Ancient English Poetry* (3 vols 1765) I 189.

75[3] The "person who suffers", C as usual emphasising the difference between *patior* ("I feel" or "I suffer"), the verb that is the root of both "passive" and "passion", and *ago* "I act" or "I do".

before us in the united strength and beauty of ~~youthful~~ earliest Manhood. Our eyes have been questioning him. Gifted thus with high advantages of *person*, and further endowed by Nature with a powerful intellect and a strong energetic Will, even without any concurrence of circumstances and accident, Pride will be the Sin that most easily besets him/. But he is the known, and acknowleged Son of the princely Gloster—Edmund therefore has both the germ ⟨of Pride⟩ and the conditions best fitted to evolve and ripen it into a predominant feeling. Yet hitherto no reason appears why it should be other than the not unusual pride of Person, Talent and Birth, a pride auxiliary if not akin to many Virtues, and the natural ally of honorable[g] But, alas! in his own presence his own father ~~no~~ takes shame to himself for ~~his~~ the frank avowal—that he is his Father—has blushed so often to acknowlege him that he is now braz'd to it. He hears his Mother and the circumstances of his Birth spoken of with a most degrading and licentious Levity—described as a Wanton by her own Paramour, and the remembrance of the animal sting, ~~of~~ the low criminal gratifications connected with her Wantonness and prostituted Beauty assigned as the reason, why "the Whoreson must be acknowleged."[4]—This and the consciousness of its notoriety—the gnawing conviction that every shew of respect is an effort of courtesy which ~~represses~~calls while it represses a contrary feeling—this is the ever-trickling flow of Wormwood and Gall into the wounds of Pride—the corrosive Virus which inoculates Pride with a venom not its own, with Envy, Hatred, a lust of that Power which in its blaze of radiance would hide the dark spots on his disk[5]—pangs of shame, personally undeserved, and therefore felt as wrongs—and a blind ferment of vindictive workings towards the occasions and causes, especially towards a Brother whose stainless Birth and lawful Honors were the constant remembrancers of *his* debasement, and were ever in the way to prevent all chance of its being unknown or ~~forgotten~~ overlooked—&—forgotten.[h] Add to this that with excellent Judgement, and provident for the claims of the moral sense, for that which relatively to the Drama is called Poetic Justice; and as the fittest means for reconciling the feelings of the Spectators to the horrors of Gloster's after Sufferings—at least, of rendering them somewhat less unendurable—(for I will not disguise my conviction, that in this ~~poi~~ one point the Tragic has been urged beyond the outermost Mark and Ne plus Ultra of the Dramatic)—Shakspeare has precluded all excuse and palliation of the guilt

75[g] Noun—"impulses"? "actions"?—omitted by oversight at the end of the page
75[h] Here C has written "+", perhaps introducing what follows as an afterthought; there is no corresponding footnote

75[4] *King Lear* I i 24.   75[5] The analogy is to sun-spots.

incurred by both the Parents of the base-born Edmund by Gloster's confession, that he was at the time a married man and already blest with a lawful Heir of his fortunes. The mournful alienation of brotherly Love occasioned by Primogeniture in noble families, or rather by the unnecessary distinctions engrafted thereon, and this in Children of the same Stock, is still almost proverbial on the Continent—especially as I know from my own observation in the South of Europe, and ~~we~~ appears to have been scarcely less common in our own Island, before the Revolution of 1688, if we may judge from the ~~writers~~ characters and sentiments so frequent in our elder Comedies—the Younger Brother, for instance, in B. and F's Scornful Lady, on one side, and the Oliver in Sh's own As you like it, on the other.[6] Need it be said how heavy an aggravation the stain of Bastardy must have been—were it only, that the younger Brother was liable to hear his own dishonor and his Mother's infamy related by his Father with an excusing shrug of the shoulders, and in a tone betwixt waggery and Shame.

By the circumstances here enumerated, as [? ~~so~~] so many predisposing causes, Edmund's Character might well be deem'd already sufficiently explained and prepared for. But in this Tragedy the story or fable constrained Shakespear to introduce wickedness in an outrageous form, in Regan and Gonerill. He had read Nature too heedfully not to know, that Courage, Intellect, and strength of Character were the most impressive Forms of Power: and that to Power in itself, without reference to any moral end, an inevitable Admiration & Complacency appertains, whether it be displayed in the conquests of a Napoleon or Tamurlane, or in the foam and thunder of a Cataract. But in the display of such a character it was of the highest importance to prevent the guilt from passing into utter *monstrosity*—which again depends on the presence or absence of causes and temptations sufficient to *account* for the wickedness, without the necessity of recurring to a thorough fiendishness of nature for its origination—For such are the appointed relations of intellectual Power to Truth, and of Truth to Goodness, that it becomes both morally and poetic[i] unsafe to present what is admirable—what our nature compels to admire—in the mind, and what is most detestable in the Heart, as co-existing in the same individual without any apparent connection, or any modification of

75[i] A slip for "poetically"

75[6] To illustrate both sides of the "mournful alienation of brotherly love" occasioned by the system of primogeniture, C cites the reckless younger brother, Young Loveless, in Beaumont and Fletcher's play *The Scornful Lady*, and Oliver, the cruel elder brother in *As You Like It*. C wrote a few notes on the former play: BEAUMONT & FLETCHER COPY B 22–26.

the one by the other. That Shakespeare has in one instance, that of Iago, approached to this, and that he has done it successfully, is perhaps the most astonishing proof of his genius, and the opulence of its resources.— But in the present Tragedy, in which he compelled[j] to present a Goneril & Regan, it was most carefully to be avoided—and therefore the one only conceivable addition to the inauspicious influences on the preformation of Edmund's character is given in the information, that all the kindly counteractions to the mischievous feelings of Shame that might have been derived from co-domestication with Edgar & their common father, had been cut off by an absence from home ~~and~~ and a foreign education from Boyhood to the present time—and the prospect of its continuance, as if to preclude all risk of his interference with the Father's ~~view~~ Views for the elder and legitimate Son. "He hath been out nine years, and away he shall again"—[7]

76   II 932, referring to II 930 | I i 85–93

LEAR.   . . . what can you say, to draw
    A third, more opulent than your sisters? Speak.
CORDELIA. Nothing, my lord.
LEAR. Nothing.
CORDELIA. Nothing.
LEAR. Nothing can come of nothing: speak again.
CORDELIA. Unhappy that I am, I cannot heave
    My heart into my mouth: I love your majesty
    According to my bond; nor more, nor less.

P. 930. l. 45, α.[1]—Something of Disgust at the ruthless hypocrisy of her Sisters, some little faulty admixture of pride and sullenness in Cordelia's—Nothing. well contrived to lessen the glaring absurdity of Lear—but the surest plan that of forcing away the attention from the nursery-tale the moment, it has answered its purpose that of supplying the canvas to paint on. This done by Kent—and displaying ~~the~~ Lear's *moral* incapability of resigning the Sovereign power in the very moment of disposing of it.

77   II 932, referring to II 931 | I i 155–7

KENT. My life I never held but as a pawn
    To wage against thine enemies; nor fear to lose it,
    Thy safety being the motive.

                    75[j] For "was" or "felt" compelled?

75[7] *King Lear* I i 32–3.   **76**[1] Line 2 of textus.

931. . α.[1]—KENT—the nearest to perfect goodness of all Sh's Characters—and yet the most *individualized/* his passionate affection & fidelity to LEAR acts on our feelings in Lear's own favor—Virtue itself seems to be in company with him—

78   II 933 | I ii 103–33

GLOUCESTER. These late eclipses in the sun and moon portend no good to us . . .

EDMUND. This is the excellent foppery of the world! that, when we are sick in fortune, (often the surfeit of our own behaviour) we make guilty of our disasters the sun, the moon and the stars . . . . Tut, I should have been that I am, had the maidenliest star in the firmament twinkled on my bastardizing.

933, 30, β–934, 7 α.[1]—Scorn and misanthropy often the anticipations and mouth-pieces of Wisdom in the detection of superstitions. Both individuals and Nations may be free from superstition by being below it as well as by rising above it.

79   II 934 | I iii 7–11

GONERIL. . . . When he returns from hunting,
    I will not speak with him: Say, I am sick:
    If you come slack of former services,
    You shall do well; the fault of it I'll answer.
STEWARD. He's coming, madam; I hear him.

934. 20, β.[1]—The Steward (⚵ Kent)[2] the only character of utter unredeemable *Basness*[a] in Shakespear—even in this the judgment & invention. What could the willing Tool of a Goneril be/ Not a vice but this of Baseness was left open for him—

80   II 935 | I iv

Old age, like Infancy, is itself a character—in Lear the natural imperfections increased by life-long habits of being promptly obeyed—. Any addition of Individuality unnecessary & painful—The relations of others to

---

79[a] A slip for "Baseness", correctly given later in this note

77[1] The column designated by C begins with Kent's rebuke to Lear and continues to his exit and beyond.

78[1] The first line of textus corresponds to β 31.

79[1] Last line of textus.

79[2] I.e. "as opposed to" Kent—C's habitual symbol.

him, of wondrous fidelity and frightful ingratitude, sufficiently distinguish him— ~~and~~ thus he is the open and ample Play-Room of *Nature's* Passions.

81   II 935 | I iv 73–4

KNIGHT. Since my young lady's going into France, sir, the fool hath much pin'd away.

935. 15, β. The Fool no comic Buffoon to make the groundlings laugh, no forced condescension of Shakspeare's Genius to the taste of his Audiences. Accordingly, he is *prepared* for—brought into living connection with the pathos of the play, with the sufferings.—Since my young Lady's &c—

82   II 935 | I iv 94 (the entrance of the Fool)

40, β.—THE FOOL as wonderful a creation as the Caliban—an inspired Ideot—

83   II 937 | I iv 188 ff (Goneril's quarrel with Lear)

937

The Monster, Goneril, performs what is *necessary*—while the character of Albany renders a still more madning grievance possible, viz— Regan & Cornwall in perfect Sympathy of Monstrosity.—Not a sentiment, not an image, that can give pleasure on its own account, admitted—Pure Horror when they are introduced—& brought forward as little as possible.

84   II 937 | I iv 259–61

LEAR.   . . . Ingratitude! thou marble-hearted fiend,
    More hideous, when thou shew'st thee in a child
    Than the sea-monster!

5, β.[1]—The *one* general sentiment, as the main spring of his Feelings throughout, in Lear's first speeches—in the early stage the outward Object is the Pressure—not yet sufficiently familiarized with the anguish ~~to~~ for the imagination to work upon it.[2]

84[1] Last line of textus.
84[2] Cf C's remark in the lecture of 1 Apr 1808, ". . . we find undoubted proof in his mind of Imagination or the power by which

one image or feeling is made to modify many others, & by a sort of *fusion to force many into one*—that which after shewed itself in such might & energy in Lear, where

85 II 938 | I iv 310–13

GONERIL. Do you mark that, my lord?
ALBANY. I cannot be so partial, Goneril,
To the great love I bear you.
GONERIL. Pray you, content.—

938, 8, α.[1] the baffled endeavor of Goneril to act on the fears of Albany—and yet his passiveness, inertia—not convinced, yet afraid of looking into the thing. Such characters yield to those who will take the trouble of governing them or for them. Σιρ τ. β. + Σ. Γ. Β.[2]—The influence of a Princess whose choice of him had so royalized his state, some little excuse for Albany.

86 II 938 | I v 46–7

LEAR. O, let me not be mad, not mad, sweet heaven! Keep me in temper; I would not be mad!—

50. β.—The mind's own anticipation of madness—

87 II 939[a] | II i 64–70, 83–5

EDMUND. When I dissuaded him from his intent,
And found him pight to do it, with curst speech
I threaten'd to discover him: He replied,
"Thou unpossessing bastard! dost thou think,
If I would stand against thee, could the reposal
Of any trust, virtue, or worth in thee
Make thy words faith'd? . . ."

87[a] C has written "939" at the head of the interleaf

---

the deep anguish of a Father spreads the feeling of Ingratitude & Cruelty over the very Elements of Heaven—": *Lects 1808–1819* (*CC*) I 81. The refinement here appears to be the idea that Lear's own language will become increasingly imaginative as the play progresses, "marble-hearted fiend" in this early scene being a relatively commonplace metaphor.

85[1] The line reference is to a stage direction immediately preceding textus.

85[2] The Greek letters are used as a code for the initials of two contemporaries, "Sir

T. B. and S. G. B."—identified in *Lects 1808–1819* (*CC*) II 331 n 9 as Sir Thomas Bernard (1750–1818) and Sir George Beaumont (1753–1827), both at one time patrons and supporters of C's. Bernard, both a philanthropist and a connoisseur, was a founder of the British Institution, with Beaumont on the board of directors. C implies that both of them tended to give way to people less well equipped to make decisions—something he says of the British Institution also in a notebook entry: *P Lects* Lect 2 (1949) 95n.

GLOUCESTER. . . . And of my land,
Loyal and natural boy, I'll work the means
To make thee capable.

31, β. *Thou unpossessing Bastard* = the secret poison in Edmund's own heart—and then poor Gloster's
50, β. Loyal and *natural* Boy, as if praising the *crime* of his Birth!—

88 II 940ᵃ | II i 88–93

REGAN. If it be true, all vengeance comes too short,
Which can pursue the offender. How does my lord?
GLOUCESTER. O, madam, my old heart is crack'd, is crack'd!
REGAN. What, did my father's godson seek your life?
He whom my father named? your Edgar?
GLOUCESTER. O, lady, lady, shame would have it hid!

6, α.—Incomparable!—What, did *my father's* &c—compared with the unfeminine violence of the "all vengeance comes too short["]—& yet no reference to the guilt but to the accident &c

89 II 941 | II ii 95–100

CORNWALL. This is some fellow,
Who, having been prais'd for bluntness, doth affect
A saucy roughness; and constrains the garb,
Quite from his nature: He cannot flatter, he!
An honest mind, and plain,—he must speak truth:
An they will take it, so; if not, he's plain.

10, β.¹—In thus placing these profound general Truths in such mouths, as Cornwalls, Edmunds, Iagos &c. Sh. at once gives them & yet shews how indefinite their application.

90 II 942 | II iii (Edgar resolves to disguise himself as a "Bedlam beggar")

Edgar's false Madness taking off part of the Shock from the true, as well as displaying the profound difference—Modern Light-headedness—in Otway &c¹

88ᵃ C has written "940" at the head of the interleaf

89¹ Line 1 of textus.
90¹ C had already used lines from Shakespeare and Otway to suggest the dif- ference in kind between mania and delirium and imagination and fancy respectively, quoting from *King Lear* III iv 63 "What!

91 II 943 | II iv 101–5

LEAR. The king would speak with Cornwall; the dear father
     Would with his daughter speak; commands her service:
     Are they inform'd of this?—My breath and blood!
     Fiery? the fiery duke? Tell the hot duke, that—
     No, but not yet:—may be he is not well . . .

40, β[1] The strong interest now felt by Lear to try to find excuses for his Daughter—most pathetic.

92 II 944 | II iv 133–40, 146–52

LEAR.   . . . Beloved Regan,
     Thy sister's naught; O Regan, she hath tied
     Sharp-tooth'd unkindness, like a vulture, here . . . .
REGAN. I pray you, sir, take patience; I have hope,
     You less know how to value her desert,
     Than she to scant her duty. . . .
LEAR. My curses on her!
REGAN.   O, Sir, you are old;
     Nature in you stands on the very verge
     Of her confine; you should be rul'd, and led
     By some discretion, that discerns your state
     Better than you yourself: Therefore, I pray you,
     That to our sister you do make return;
     Say you have wrong'd her, sir.

30, α.[1] Nothing so heart-cutting as a cold unexpected defence &c of a cruelty complained of passionately—or so expressive of—hearard-heartedness—

     And the horror of—O Sir, you are old—and then drawing from that universal object of reverence and indulgence the reason for—Say, you have wronged her.

     All Lear's faults increase our pity—we refuse to know them otherwise than as means and aggravations of his Sufferings & his Daughters' ingratitude—

---

have his daughters brought him to this pass?" and from Otway's *Venice Preserv'd* v 369 "Lutes, laurels, seas of milk, and ships of amber", in *BL* ch 4 (*CC*) I 84–5 (with "lobsters" for "laurels"); and he is presumably thinking of the same example here.
 91[1] Line 1 of textus.
 92[1] Line 5 of textus.

93 II 945 | II iv 264–86

LEAR. O, reason not the need: our basest beggars
  Are in the poorest thing superfluous:
  Allow not nature more than nature needs,
  Man's life is cheap as beast's: thou art a lady;
  If only to go warm were gorgeous,
  Why, nature needs not what thou gorgeous wear'st,
  Which scarcely keeps thee warm.—But for the true need,—
  You heavens, give me that patience, patience I need!
  You see me here, you gods, a poor old man,
  As full of grief as age: wretched in both!
  If it be you that stir these daughters' hearts
  Against their father, fool me not so much
  To bear it tamely; touch me with noble anger!
  O, let not women's weapons, water-drops,
  Stain my man's cheeks!—No, you unnatural hags,
  I will have such revenges on you both,
  That all the world shall,—I will do such things,—
  What they are, yet I know not; but they shall be
  The terrors of the earth. You think, I'll weep;
  No, I'll not weep:—
  I have full cause of weeping; but this heart
  Shall break into a hundred thousand flaws,
  Or ere I'll weep:—O fool, I shall go mad!

10–35, β.[1]—The tranquillity from the first *stun* permitting Lear to REA-SON—recite this—

94 II 948 | III iv (Lear, Kent, and the Fool encounter Edgar, as Poor Tom, outside the hovel on the heath)

915.[a] What a World's *Convention* of Agonies—surely, never was such a scene conceived before or since—Take it but as a picture, for the eye only, it is more terrific than any a Michael Angelo inspired by a Dante could have conceived, and which none but a Michael Angelo could have executed[1]—or let it have been uttered to the Blind, the howlings of ⟨convulsed⟩ Nature would seem concentered in ⟨f⟩ the voice of conscious Humanity—

94[a] A slip for "948", which is indistinctly printed (II 915 is in *Cymbeline*)

93[1] Line 35 is the last line of textus.
94[1] C also links Dante to Michelangelo,
but through the medium of Giotto, in *TT*
(*CC*) I 168–9.

95 II 949 | III iv

Scene V.[1]

The scene ends with the first symptoms of positive derangement—here how judiciously interrupted in order to allow an interval for Lear in full madness to appear.

96 II 951, afterthought in pencil | III vii 27–34 (the blinding of Gloster)

CORNWALL. . . . Who's there? The traitor?
　　　　　Enter Gloster, brought in by servants
REGAN. Ingrateful fox! 'tis he.
CORNWALL. Bind fast his corky arms.
GLOSTER. What mean your graces?—Good my friends, consider
　　You are my guests: do me no foul play, friends.
CORNWALL. Bind him, I say.　　　　　　　*[They bind him.*
REGAN.　　　　　　　　Hard, hard:—O filthy traitor!
GLOSTER. Unmerciful lady as you are, I am none.
CORNWALL. To this chair bind him . . .

Scene VII 25. β.[1]—What can I say of this scene? My reluctance to think Sh. wrong—and yet—[a]necessary to harmonize their cruelty to their father[2]

97 II 957 | IV vi

The Thunder recurs, but still at a greater distance from our feelings[1]

98 II 960 | IV vii 51–3

LEAR. Where have I been? Where am I?—Fair day-light?—
　　I am mightily abus'd.—I should even die with pity,
　　To see another thus.—I know not what to say.— . . .

The affecting return of Lear ~~and~~ to reason, and the mild pathos preparing the mind for the last sad yet sweet consolation of his Death—

96[a] Remainder in pencil

95[1] C means Scene iv: the running head to this page is "Act 3. Scene 5." because Scene v begins towards the end of the page.
　96[1] Line 1 of textus.
　96[2] Of this notorious scene Johnson had remarked that it represented "an act too horrid to be endured in dramatick exhibition"

(*Sh*—Reed—XVII 612); he supposed, however, that Shakespeare knew what would please the audience of his day.
　97[1] C is probably referring to that part of the scene in which Lear, "fantastically drest up with flowers", encounters Gloucester.

99 II [966], afterthought in pencil | *Romeo and Juliet*

[1]Memoranda on Pathos—introductory to Romeo and Juliet.
The Gamester, Fatal Marriage, liable to the same Objections, as Novels[2]—[a](transcribe from the marble leaf of Mrs Milne's Sh V. VIII.)[3]

100 II [966]–[7][a]

Romeo and Juliet

We have had occasion to speak at large on the subject of the three Unities, Time, Place, and Action, as applied to the Drama in abstract, and to the particular stage for which Shakspeare wrote as far as he can be said to have written for any stage but that of the universal Mind. We succeeded in demonstrating that the two former, instead of being ~~Principles~~ Rules were mere inconveniences attached to the local peculiarities of the Athenian Drama; that the last alone deserved the name of a Principle, and that in this Shakspear stood pre-eminent.[1]

Yet instead of Unity of Action I should great[b] prefer ~~somewhat the phrase, Harmony as more~~ the more appropriate tho' scholastic and uncouth words—Homogeneity, proportionateness and totality of Interest.—The distinction or rather the essential difference betwixt the Shaping skill of mechanical Talent, and the creative productive Life-power of inspired Genius.[2] In the former each part separately conceived and then by a succeeding Act put together—not as Watches are made for wholesale—for here each part supposes a preconception of the Whole in *some* mind—but as the Pictures on a motley Screen.[3] (N.b. I must seek for a happier illustration.)

99[a] Written in pencil to the end of the note
100[a] I.e. interleaf II [966]/[967], recto and verso   **100[b]** A slip for "greatly"

99[1] All the notes in this copy of *Romeo and Juliet* are published as part of C's lecture-material for 18 Feb 1819: *Lects 1808–1819 (CC)* II 361–8.

99[2] As far as pathos is concerned, sentimental novels and popular domestic tragedies such as Edward Moore's *Gamester* (1753) and Thomas Southerne's *Fatal Marriage* (1694) were alike vulnerable to the objection that they allowed audiences to indulge in tears without leading to any moral improvement or social reform. Cf C's analyses of this phenomenon in "Satyrane's Letters" in the 1809 *Friend (CC)* II 216–20 and again in *BL (CC)* II 184–9; and *BL* ch 23 *(CC)* II 210–12.

99[3] C wrote to request the loan of "a small sized tolerably *pocketable* Edition of Shakspere" from the Gillmans' Highgate neighbours Mr and Mrs Milne about 15 Dec 1818: *CL* IV 898. This he evidently wrote some notes in, but it is not known to have survived. It may have been the edition by George Steevens in 8 vols (1811): see SHAKESPEARE COPY F.

100[1] C may be referring particularly to his lecture of 21 Jan 1819, based on notes on *Othello* in this copy: *Lects 1808–1819 (CC)* II 312–19, esp 312, 316–17 (and 316 n 10, where "unity of interest" is shown to be derived from Schlegel).

100[2] A favourite distinction, developed esp in *BL* ch 2 *(CC)* I 31 (and see n 5).

100[3] C probably means pictures pinned

Whence the Harmony that strikes us in the wildest natural landscapes? In the relative shapes of rocks, the harmony of colors in the Heath, Ferns, and Lichens, the Leaves of the Beech, and Oak, the stems and rich chocate-brown[c] [? ~~Tr~~] Branches of the Birch, and other mountain Trees, varying from varying Autumn to returning Spring—compared with the visual effect from the greater number of artificial Plantations?—The former are effected by a single energy, modified ab intra[4] in each component part—. Now as this is the particular excellence of the Shakespearian Dramas generally, so is it especially characteristic of the Romeo and Juliet.—First, the groundwork of the Tale is altogether in family Life, and the events of the Play have their first origin in family-feuds— ~~Dim and~~ Filmy as are the eyes of Party-spirit, at once dim and [? ~~frat~~] truculent, still there is commonly some real or supposed Object in view, or Principle to be maintained—and tho but = the twisted Wires on a/ the Plate of rosin in the preparation for electrical pictures, it is still a guide in some degree, an assimilation to an Outline;[5] but in family quarrels, which have proved scarcely less injurious to States, wilfulness, and precipitancy and passion from the mere habit and custom can alone be expected—With his accustomed Judgement Shak. has begun by placing before us a lively picture of all the impulses of the Play, like a prelude/ and human folly ~~has~~ ever presents two sides, one for Heraclitus & one for Democritus,[6] he has first given the laughable absurdity of the Evil in the contagion of the Servants—The domestic Tale begins with ~~the~~ Domestics that have so little to do that they are under the necessity of letting the superfluity of sensorial power fly off thro' the escape-valve of J Wit-combats and Quarreling with Weapons of sharper edge—all in humble imitation of their Masters—Yet there is a sort of unhired fidelity, an *our* ishness[7] about it that makes it rest pleasant on one's feelings—and all that follows to p. 968, 55, β[8]—is a motley dance of all ranks and ages to one Tune, as if the Horn of Huon had been playing—[9]

100[c] A slip for "chocolate-brown"

---

up to decorate a folding screen—a fashionable way of demonstrating good taste, but an obviously fragmented process.

100[4] "From within".

100[5] The foundation, then, is purposeful; it guides and governs the result. Examples of the experimental "electrical pictures" of the early nineteenth century, achieved by passing an electrical current through wires on a resinous plate, are documented in *Lects 1808–1819* (*CC*) II 362n–3n.

100[6] Traditionally "the weeping philo-

sopher" and "the laughing philosopher", representing opposite reactions to the absurdities of human life.

100[7] I.e. the quarreling of the servants is nevertheless a proof of their loyalty to the houses they serve. *OED* cites the word as C's coinage, quoting this note.

100[8] From Tybalt's entrance to Lady Montague's line at I i 117 "Right glad I am, he was not at this fray."

100[9] One of the properties of the magic horn given by Oberon, king of the fairies, to Huon of Bordeaux, in the French romance

101   II 968 | I i 118–23

BENVOLIO. Madam, an hour before the worshipp'd sun
   Peer'd forth the golden window of the east,
   A troubled mind drave me to walk abroad;
   Where—underneath the grove of sycamour,
   That westward rooteth from the city's side—
   So early walking did I see your son . . .

56, β.[1] This but far more strikingly the following speech of old Montague,[2] first, proves that Sh. meant it to approach to a Poem—which and its early date proved likewise by the multitude of rhyming Couplets—[3]

102   II 969 | I i 160–8

BENVOLIO. Good morrow, cousin.
ROMEO.   Is the day so young?
BENVOLIO. But new struck nine.
ROMEO.   Ay me! sad hours seem long.
   Was that my father that went hence so fast?
BENVOLIO. It was:—What sadness lengthens Romeo's hours?
ROMEO. Not having that, which, having, makes them short.
BENVOLIO. In love?
ROMEO. Out—
BENVOLIO. Of love?
ROMEO. Out of her favour where I am in love.

If, as I believe from the internal evidence, this was one of Sh. early Dramas,[1] it marks strongly the fineness of his insight into the nature of the Passions, that Romeo is introduced already love-bewildered—The necessity of loving creating an Object for itself &c—and yet a difference there is, tho' to be known only by the perception—. The difference in this respect between Men & Women—it would have displeased us that Juliet had been in love or fancied herself so—
   R. running away from his Rosaline to woods & Nature, in which she

---

of that title, was that whoever heard it, however poor or feeble or ill, should feel such joy that he would sing and dance.

101[1] Line 1 of textus.

101[2] I i 131–42.

101[3] C's attempt to formulate a chronology of Shakespeare's plays based largely on internal evidence—that is, on a pattern of artistic development—produced varying results, but *Romeo and Juliet* always appears early in his lists, as indeed it is generally agreed it should: cf *Lects 1808–1819* (*CC*) I 240, 244, 253, 257; II 371 and, for the chronology closest to the date of the writing of these notes, II 374.

102[1] See **101** n 3.

indeed alone existed, as the name for his yearning—contrast this with his Rushing to Juliet—

103   II 970 | I ii 86–93

BENVOLIO. . . . Compare her face with some that I shall show,
   And I will make thee think thy swan a crow.
ROMEO. When the devout religion of mine eye
   Maintains such falsehood, then turn tears to fires!
   And these,—who, often drown'd, could never die,—
   Transparent hereticks, be burnt for liars!
   One fairer than my love! the all-seeing sun
   Ne'er saw her match, since first the world begun.

The POSITIVENESS of Romeo in a Love of his own making—and the boastfulness, never shewn of what's near the heart—again shewn 45, β.[1]

104   II 971 | I iii

The character of the Nurse, the nearest of any thing in Shakespear to borrowing Observation[1]—the reason is, that as in infancy & childhood the individual in Nature is a representative—Like Larch Trees, in describing one you generalize a grove—the garrulity of ǫ ʂ Age strengthened by the long-trusted Servant, whose sympathy with the Mother's affections gives her privileges & rank in the House—the mode of connecting by accidents of Time & Place and the ƚ childlike fondness of repetition in her child age—and that happy ~~ser~~ humble ducking under yet resurgence against the check, Yes, Madam!—*yet I cannot choose but laugh.*[a2]

105   II 972 | I iv

Scene IV introduces Mercutio to us—O how shall I describe that exquisite ebullience and overflow of youthful Life, wafted on over the laughing Wavelets of Pleasure & Prosperity, Waves of the Sea like a wanton Beauty that distorted a face on which she saw her lover gazing ~~enam~~rap-

---

104[a] About ¾ inch below the note C has written "55": the corresponding line in the first column is the Nurse's "'Thou wilt fall backward, when thou hast more wit . . .'" and in the second Juliet's "But no more deep will I endart mine eye"

103[1] I.e. line 1 of textus.
104[1] The analysis of the character of the Nurse was one of C's set-pieces, and he usually insisted, in opposition to critics who marvelled at Shakespeare's observation of life in the portrayal of this character, that although observation was an important factor, meditation and self-awareness were more important: *Lects 1808–1819* (*CC*) I 225, 231, 307–9. Here the emphasis is shifted in the other direction.
104[2] The Nurse's line, I iii 50.

tured, had wrinkled her surface in the Triumph of its smoothness—Wit, ⟨Fane ever wakeful, Fancy ⟨busy &⟩ procreative as Insects,⟩ Courage, an easy mind that without cares of its own was at once disposed to laugh at away those of others & yet be interested in them/ these and all congenial qualities, melting into the common copula of all, the man of quality and the Gentleman, with all its excellencies & all its foibles—/

106   II 974 | I v 75–83

TYBALT. It fits, when such a villain is a guest;
    I'll not endure him.
I CAPULET.   He shall be endur'd;
    What, goodman boy!—I say, he shall:—Go to;—
    Am I the master here, or you? go to.
    You'll not endure him!—God shall mend my soul—
    You'll make a mutiny among my guests!
    You will set cock-a-hoop! you'll be the man!
TYBALT. Why, uncle, 'tis a shame.
I CAPULET.   Go to, go to;
    You are a saucy boy . . .

15, α^1—the old man's impetuosity at once contrasting with, yet harmonized with, the young Tybalt's/ but this it would be endless to repeat.— Every leaf is different on an Oak: but still we can only say, our Tongues defrauding our Eyes, this is another Oak Leaf—

107   II 975 | II ii (the balcony scene)

The contrast with Romeo's former boastful positiveness—.[1] Skill in justifying Romeo from inconstancy by making us feel the difference of the passion/—

    Yet this too is a Love in, tho not merely of, the Imagination: as in R. & J.'s Language

108   II 976 | II ii 62–5

JULIET. How cam'st thou hither, tell me; and wherefore?
    The orchard walls are high, and hard to climb;
    And the place death, considering who thou art,
    If any of my kinsmen find thee here.

With Love, pure Love, the anxiety for the safety of the Object—the dis-

106[1] Line 4 of textus.   **107**[1] Noted in **103**.

interestedness by which it is distinguished from the counterfeits of its name—

109   II 976 | II ii 85–92

JULIET. Thou know'st, the mask of night is on my face;
    Else would a maiden blush bepaint my cheek,
    For that which thou hast heard me speak to-night.
    Fain would I dwell on form, fain fain deny
    What I have spoke; But farewell compliment!
    Dost thou love me? I know, thou wilt say—Ay;
    And I will take thy word: yet if thou swear'st,
    Thou may'st prove false . . .

40, α^1
Compared with Miranda & Ferdinand[2]—how fine the variety on the same Air/
and the truly sweet girlish Lingering & *Bus*yness

110   II 977 | II iii (the scene between Friar Lawrence and Romeo)

The reverend Character of the Friar as always in Sh.[1] & yet no digression but carrying on the Plot—

111   II 978 | II iv 49–60

ROMEO. Pardon, good Mercutio, my business was great; and, in such a
    case as mine, a man may strain courtesy.
MERCUTIO. That's as much as to say—such a case as yours constrains a
    man to bow in the hams.
ROMEO. Meaning—to curt'sy.
MERCUTIO. Thou hast most kindly hit it.
ROMEO. A most courteous exposition.
MERCUTIO. Nay, I am the very pink of courtesy.
ROMEO. Pink for flower.
MERCUTIO. Right.
ROMEO. Why, then is my pump well flower'd.

Romeo's half-exerted, half real ease of mind—here again compared with Rosaline—his Will had come to the clenching point—

109[1] Line 1 of textus.
109[2] I.e. with the love scene in *The Tempest* (III i), not commented on in any of C's

notes.
110[1] See COPY A **116** and n 6.

112   II 981 | II vi 6–14

ROMEO. . . . Do thou but close our hands with holy words,
    Then love-devouring death do what he dare,
    It is enough I may but call her mine.
FRIAR. These violent delights have violent ends,
    And in their triumph die; like fire, and powder,
    Which, as they kiss, consume: The sweetest honey
    Is loathsome in his own deliciousness,
    And in the taste confounds the appetite;
    Therefore, love moderately . . .

5, β.[1]—The precipitation which is the character of the Play, so well marked in both the Speakers—

113   II 982 | III i 95–100

ROMEO. Courage, man; the hurt cannot be much.
MERCUTIO. No, 'tis not so deep as a well, nor so wide as a church-door;
    but 'tis enough; 'twill serve: ask for me to-morrow, and you shall find
    me a grave man. I am pepper'd, I warrant, for this world.—A plague
    o' both your houses! . . .

The wit and raillery habitual to Mercutio struggling with the pain giving so fine an effect to Romeo's Speech, & the whole so completely justifying him—

114   II 983 | III i 152–9

BENVOLIO. Tybalt, here slain, whom Romeo's hand did slay;
    Romeo that spoke him fair, bid him bethink
    How nice the quarrel was, and urg'd withal
    Your high displeasure: all this—utter'd
    With gentle breath, calm look, knees humbly bow'd,—
    Could not take truce with the unruly spleen
    Of Tybalt deaf to peace, but that he tilts
    With piercing steel at bold Mercutio's breast . . .

The *small* portion of untruth in Benvolio's Narration finely conceived—"*but that he tilts*["] &c

---

112[1] Line 1 of textus.

115 II 983 | III ii 17–19

JULIET. . . . Come, night!—Come, Romeo! come, thou day in night!
For thou wilt lie upon the wings of night
Whiter than new snow on a raven's back.—

50, β.[1]—The imaginative sustained to the highest—what an effe⟨c⟩t on
the *purity* of the mind—think what Dryden & W. of C. II. would have
made—[2]

116 II 984 | III ii 83–92

JULIET. . . . Was ever book, containing such vile matter,
So fairly bound? O, that deceit should dwell
In such a gorgeous palace!
NURSE.   There's no trust,
No faith, no honesty in men; all perjur'd,
All forsworn, all nought, all dissemblers.—
Shame come to Romeo!
JULIET.   Blister'd be thy tongue,
For such a wish! he was not born to shame:
Upon his brow shame is asham'd to sit . . .

The Nurse's mistake of the minds audible struggles with *itself* for its decision in toto—

117 II 985 | III iii 24–33

FRIAR. O deadly sin! O rude unthankfulness!
Thy fault our law calls death; but the kind prince,
Taking thy part, hath rush'd aside the law,
And turn'd that black word death to banishment:
This is dear mercy, and thou seest it not.
ROMEO. 'Tis torture, and not mercy: heaven is here,
Where Juliet lives; and every cat, and dog,
And little mouse, every unworthy thing,

115[1] Line 2 of textus.
115[2] Perhaps "Dryden and Wycherley",
or perhaps "Dryden and [the] Wits" of [the
reign of] Charles II. C liked to stress the relative decency of Shakespeare's language in
comparison with his contemporaries and
later playwrights: cf COPY A **116** and n 8.
Here he points out that they would hardly
have let go an opportunity to turn Romeo's
lying on the wings of night into sexual
innuendo.

Live here in heaven, and may look on her,
But Romeo may not.

All deep Passions a sort of Atheists, that believe no Future—

118   II 988 | III v (Juliet resists her parents' attempts to make her accept Paris)

A noble scene—Don't I see it? with my own eyes? Yes! but not with
Juliet's.—

119   II 989 | III v 176–8

CAPULET. God's bread! it makes me mad: Day, night, late, early,
    At home, abroad, alone, in company,
    Waking, or sleeping, still my care hath been
    To have her match'd . . .

and the mistake as if Love's causes were generalizable—

120   II 991 | IV iii 55–8

JULIET. . . . O, look! methinks I see my cousin's ghost
    Seeking out Romeo, that did spit his body
    Upon a rapier's point:—Stay, Tybalt, stay!—
    Romeo, I come! this do I drink to thee.

The taking the poison in a fit of fright! how S. provides for the finest de-
cencies!—A Girl of 15—too bold for her but for—

121   II 992 | IV v (Juliet discovered "dead" by her family)

~~What~~ Something I must say on this scene—yet without it the Pathos
would have been anticipated—[1]

122   II 993 | v i 1–2

ROMEO. If I may trust the flattering truth of sleep,
    My dreams presage some joyful news at hand . . .

Fondness for presentiments and as if aware—yet reconciling with the superstition all-reconciling of opposites—of any thing unusual as unlucky/

---

[1] **121** C recorded his uneasiness about this scene also in COPY A **143**.

123   II 994 | v i 34–8

ROMEO. . . . Well, Juliet, I will lie with thee to-night.
Let's see for means:—O, mischief! thou art swift
To enter in the thoughts of desperate men!
I do remember an apothecary,—
And hereabouts he dwells . . .

30, α¹
So beautiful as to have been self-justified—yet what a fine preparation
for the Tomb scene—

124   II 995 | v iii 59–63

ROMEO. Good gentle youth, tempt not a desperate man,
Fly hence and leave me;—think upon these gone;
Let them affright thee.—I beseech thee, youth,
Pull not another sin upon my head,
By urging me to fury . . .

The gentleness of Romeo shewn before as softened by Love; but now by
Love & Sorrow & the Awe of the Place—

125   II 995 | v iii 88–96

ROMEO. . . . How oft when men are at the point of death
Have they been merry? which their keepers call
A lightning before death: O, how may I
Call this a lightning?—O, my love! my wife!
Death, that hath suck'd the honey of thy breath,
Hath had no power yet upon thy beauty:
Thou art not conquer'd; beauty's ensign yet
Is crimson in thy lips, and in thy cheeks,
And death's pale flag is not advanced there.—

45, β.¹
Here, here, is the master-example how Beauty can at once increase &
modify Passion—like the subtle net of Vulcan— ~~which Apollo only~~²

123¹ Line 2 of textus.
125¹ Line 2 of textus.
125² Vulcan's "subtle net" must be the
invisible but inescapable one in which he
trapped his wife Venus with her lover Mars,

having been alerted to their affair by Apollo
(*Odyssey* 8.265 ff); C's point is perhaps that
beauty in a similar way imperceptibly im-
prisons you. Cf a similar analogy in *CN* III
3708 f11ᵛ.

126　ii 997 | v iii 208 ff

a beautiful Close—*poetic* Justice indeed! all are punished!—
　The Spring & Winter meet, & Winter assumes the character of Spring,
Spring the sadness of Winter—[1]

127　ii [999] | *Hamlet*

[1]Hamlet was the Play, or rather Hamlet himself was the Character, in the intuition and exposition of which I first made my turn for philosophical criticism, and especially for insight into the genius of Shakespear, *noticed*,[2] first among my ~~Friends~~ Acquaintances, as Sir G. Beaumont will bear witness,[3] and as Mr Wordsworth knows, tho' from motives which I do not know or impulses which I *cannot* know, he has thought proper to assert that Schlegel and the German Critics [? ~~were~~] *first* taught Englishmen to admire their own great Countryman intelligently[4]—and secondly, long before Schlegel had given at Vienna the Lectures on Shakespear which he afterwards published, I had given eighteen Lectures on the same subject, *substantially* the same, proceeding from the same, the *very* same, point of view, and deducing the same conclusions, as far as I either then or now agree with him/ I gave them at the Royal Institution, before from six to seven hundred Auditors of rank and eminence, in the spring of the same year in which Sir H. Davy, a fellow-lecturer, made his great revolutionary Discoveries in Chemistry.[5] Even in detail the coincidence

126[1] Cf a remark about the general tone of the play, in a lecture of 1813 (*Lects 1808–1819—CC*—i 519): "A *unity of feeling* pervades the whole of his plays. In *Romeo and Juliet* all is Youth and Spring . . .".

127[1] Several of the notes in this copy between **127** and **154** are published as part of C's lecture-material for 7 Jan 1819 in *Lects 1808–1819 (CC)* ii 293–302.

127[2] As the editor of the lectures points out, C in this note is responding defensively on the day of his third lecture to newspaper comments, in a report of the first, about the relationship of his criticism to Schlegel's. The *Morning Chronicle* concluded that Schlegel had been the first to publish (in 1801) a defence of Shakespeare's judgment, and that therefore while C might not actually be indebted to Schlegel, he could not claim "the title of a *discoverer*": *Lects 1808–1819 (CC)* ii 278–80, 290. See also n 5 below.

127[3] Sir George and Lady Beaumont had attended C's lectures at the Royal Institution in 1808: *Lects 1808–1819 (CC)* i 13.

127[4] WW "Essay, Supplementary to the Preface" pub with *Poems* (1815) observes that among the English, Shakespeare is still regarded as a wild and irregular genius, and that "The Germans only, of foreign nations, are approaching towards a knowledge and feeling of what he is." This remark would have been all the more galling to C in that a footnote in the following paragraph commends C's Royal Institution lectures of 1808 for their position on Shakespeare's sonnets: *W Prose* iii 69.

127[5] Perhaps ten of C's lectures at the Royal Institution in 1808 were on Shakespeare; unfortunately, no record of those particular lectures in the series survive. There is no doubt that C made use of Schlegel's criticism of Shakespeare from the time of his being given a copy of Schlegel's lectures in Dec 1811, but his de-of Schlegel with my Lectures was so extra-ordinary, that all ⟨at a later period⟩ who heard the same *words* (taken from my Royal Instit. Notes) concluded a borrowing on my part from Schlegel.—Mʳ Hazlitt, whose hatred of me is in such an inverse ratio to my zealous Kindness toward him as to be defended by his warmest Admirer, C. Lamb (⟨ who (besides his characteristic obstinacy of adherence to old friends, as long at least as they are at all down in the World,) is linked as by a charm to Hazlitt's conversation, only under the epithet of *"frantic"*⁶—Mʳ Hazlitt himself replied to an assertion of my plagiarism from Schlegel in these words— "That is a Lie; for I myself heard the very same character of Hamlet from Coleridge before he went to Germany and when he had neither read or could read a page of German." Now Hazlitt was on a visit to my Cottage at Nether Stowey, Somerset, in the summer of the year 1798, in the September of which (as see my Literary Life) I first was out of sight of the Shores of Great Britain.—⁷

Recorded by me, S. T. Coleridge, Janʸ 7, 1819. Highgate.⁸

128   II 1000

Compare the easy language of common life, in which this Drama opens, with the wild wayward Lyric of the opening of Macbeth.¹ The Language is familiar: no poetic descriptions of Night, no elaborate information conveyed by one speaker to another of what both had before their immedi-

fence of Shakespeare's judgment in 1808 was almost certainly arrived at independently. See *Lects 1808–1819 (CC)* I liii–lxiv (esp lx–lxiv), 19–21, 172–5, where the editor's conclusion is that "No convincing evidence that Coleridge knew Schlegel's lectures before December 1811 has been found" (I 175). HD, who had been instrumental in obtaining for C the invitation to lecture at the Royal Institution and was himself a regular lecturer there, had announced the isolation of sodium and potassium in a lecture given before the Royal Society in Nov 1807.

127⁶ This is not a word used by CL in any published comment, but it is consistent with his attitude towards both C and Hazlitt: he could deplore Hazlitt's cruelty as a reviewer while continuing to be fond of him as an old friend. As he said in a letter to WW on 23 Sept 1816, apropos of Hazlitt's severities towards himself and WW as well as to C, "in spite of all, there is something tough

in my attachment to H—— which these violent strainings cannot quite dislocate or sever asunder": *LL* (M) III 225.

127⁷ We have only C's authority for Hazlitt's supposed statement, and the date of Hazlitt's visit to Nether Stowey, though accurate, seems beside the point. C describes his departure for Germany in Sept 1798 in "Satyrane's Letters" in *BL (CC)* II 160.

127⁸ In the atmosphere of charge and counter-charge generated by the issue of C's plagiarism, it is worth noting that the report of C's lecture on *Hamlet* of this date, carried in Thelwall's *Champion* for 10 Jan 1819, insinuated that C might have borrowed some ideas from Hazlitt's own recent lectures on Shakespeare (which had pointedly ignored C): *Lects 1808–1819 (CC)* II 302 and nn.

128¹ C introduced his analysis of *Macbeth* with a similar comparison in **17** above.

ate perceptions (such as the first Distich in Addison's Cato, which is a ~~po-etical~~ translation into poetry of Past 4 °clock, and a damp morning)[2]—yet nothing bordering on the comic on the one hand, and no striving of the Intellect on the other. It is the language of *sensation* among Men who feared no charge of effeminacy for ~~noticing~~ feeling what they felt no want of resolution to bear.—Yet the armour, the dead silence, ~~broken by the~~ the watchfulness that first interrupts it, the welcome relief of guard, the Cold—the broken expressions as if a man's compelled attention to bodily feelings allowed no man, all excellently accord with and prepare for the after gradual rise into Tragedy—but above all into a Tragedy the interest of which is emiently[a] ad et apud *intra*—as Macbeth e contra is ad extra.[3]

129   II 1000 | I i 23–39

MARCELLUS. Horatio says, 'tis but our phantasy;
    And will not let belief take hold of him,
    Touching this dreaded sight, twice seen of us:
    Therefore I have entreated him, along
    With us to watch the minutes of this night;
    That, if again this apparition come,
    He may approve our eyes, and speak to it.
HORATIO. Tush! tush! 'twill not appear. . . .
BERNARDO. Last night of all,
    When yon same star, that's westward from the pole,
    Had made his course to illume that part of heaven
    Where now it burns, Marcellus, and myself,
    The bell then beating one . . .

1000.—Tush, tush! twill not appear.—Then the shivery feeling, at such a time, with two eye-witnesses, of sitting down to hear a story of a Ghost—and this too a ghost that had appeared two nights before about this very time—the effort of the narrator to master his own imaginative terrors —the consequent elevation of the style, itself a continuation of this effort—the turning off to an *outward* Object "yon same Star"—O heaven!—words are wasted to those that feel and to those who do not feel the exquisite Judgement of Sh.

128[a] A slip for "eminently"

128[2] Joseph Addison's tragedy *Cato* (1712) opens with the lines, "The dawn is overcast, the morning lowers, / And heavily in clouds brings on the day . . .".

128[3] I.e. "towards and in the *inward*" as *Macbeth* "on the other hand is [directed] towards the outward".

130 II 1000 | I i 40–55, continuing **129** textus

MARCELLUS. Peace, break thee off; look where it comes again!
>   *Enter Ghost.*
BERNARDO. In the same figure, like the king that's dead.
MARCELLUS. Thou art a scholar, speak to it, Horatio.
BERNARDO. Looks it not like the king? mark it, Horatio. . . .
HORATIO. Stay; speak; I charge thee, speak.
>   *Exit Ghost.*
MARCELLUS. 'Tis gone, and will not answer.
BERNARDO. How now, Horatio? you tremble, and look pale:
> Is not this something more than phantasy?
> What think you of it?

20.[1] The preparation *informative* of the Audience, just as much as was precisely necessary—how gradual first, and with the uncertainty appertaining to a question, What? has *this* THING appeared *again* to night? (even the word *again* has its *credibilizing* effect[)].—Then the representative of the ignorance of the Audience, Horatio (not himself but ~~Bernar~~ Marcellus to Bernardo) anticipates the common solution—"tis but our phantasy["][2]—but Marc. rises 2[ndly] into dreaded Sight—Then this "thing" becomes at once an APPARITION, and that too an intelligent Spirit that is to be *spoken* to.—

131 II 1001, referring to II 1000 | I i 56–8

HORATIO. Before my God, I might not this believe,
> Without the sensible and true avouch
> Of mine own eyes.

1000. 35–40.[1] "of mine own eyes."—Hume & himself could not but have faith in *this* Ghost dramatically, let his anti-ghostism be as strong as Samson against Ghosts less powerfully raised—[2]

130[1] Line 4 of textus, "Looks it not like the king?" etc.

130[2] Marcellus's earlier line at I i 23, in **129** textus.

131[1] Line 35 in C's edition is I i 54, "Is not this something more than phantasy?" (in **130** textus).

131[2] Hume stands here for all sceptics, but C may be thinking of passages such as the following, from the famous essay on miracles that C knew well: "When any one tells me, that he saw a dead man restored to life, I immediately consider with myself, whether it be more probable, that this person should either deceive or be deceived, or that the fact, which he relates, should really have happened"—*Essays Moral, Political and Literary* ed T. H. Green and T. H. Grose (2 vols 1889) II 94.

132   II 1001, referring to II 1000 | I i 70–2

MARCELLUS. Good now, sit down, and tell me, he that knows,
　　Why this same strict and most observant watch
　　So nightly toils the subject of the land? . . .

55. α.[1] The exquisitely natural transit into the narration retrospective.

133   II 1001 | I i 139–46

HORATIO.　. . . stay, and speak.—Stop it, Marcellus.
MARCELLUS. Shall I strike at it with my partizan?
HORATIO. Do, if it will not stand.
BERNARDO.　　　　　　　　'Tis here!
HORATIO.　　　　　　　　　　'Tis here!
MARCELLUS. 'Tis gone!　　　　[*Exit Ghost.*
　　We do it wrong, being so majestical,
　　To offer it the show of violence;
　　For it is, as the air, invulnerable,
　　And our vain blows malicious mockery.

1001. α. Horatio's increased Courage from having translated the late individual Spectum[1] into Thought & past experience. And Marcellus' & Bernardo's Sympathy with it, in daring to strike—while yet the former feeling returns in "We do it wrong &c."

134   II 1001 | I i 149–61

HORATIO.　　　　　　. . . I have heard,
　　The cock, that is the trumpet to the morn,
　　Doth with his lofty and shrill-sounding throat
　　Awake the god of day . . .
MARCELLUS. It faded on the crowing of the cock.
　　Some say, that ever 'gainst that season comes
　　Wherein our Saviour's birth is celebrated,
　　This bird of dawning singeth all night long:
　　And then, they say, no spirit dares stir abroad . . .

30–45. α.[1] No Addison more careful to be poetical in diction than Shake-

---

132[1] Line 2 of textus.

133[1] Either C has coined the word *spectum* "thing seen" to express Horatio's experience of the situation as a whole, or this is a slip for "spectrum" in the sense of apparition or phantom or spectre.

134[1] Line 30 corresponds to line 3 of textus.

spear in providing the grounds and sources of its propriety.[2]—But *how* to elevate a thing almost mean by its familiarity, young Poets may learn in the Cock-crow.

135 II 1001 | I i 169–71

HORATIO. . . . Let us impart what we have seen to-night
 Unto young Hamlet; for, upon my life,
 This spirit, dumb to us, will speak to him . . .

50 α.[1] the unobtrusive and yet fully ₫ adequate mode of introducing the main Character, *Young* Hamlet, upon whom transfers itself all the interest excited for the acts & concerns of the King, his Father.

136 II 1001 | I ii

5. β.[1] Relief by change of Scene to the Royal Court—this on any occasion; but how judicious that Hamlet should not have to take up the Leavings of Exhaustion.—The set pedantically antithetic form of the King's Speech—yet tho' in the concerns that galled the heels of Conscience, rhetorical below a King, yet in what follows not without Majesty. Was he not a Royal Brother?

137 II 1001 | I ii 42–3

KING. . . . And now, Laertes, what's the news with you?
 You told us of some suit; what is't, Laertes?

50. β.[1]—Shakespear's art in introduce[a] a most important but still subordinate character first—Milton's Beelzebub[2]—So Laertes—who is yet thus graciously treated from the assistance given to the election of the King's Brother instead of Son by Polonius—

137[a] A slip for "introducing"

134[2] C is probably alluding again to the example of Addison's *Cato*, as in **128**; but he may also have in mind precepts about poetic diction in *Spectator* 618 (though this issue was not in fact written by Addison): "But let our Poet, while he writes Epistles, though never so familiar, still remember that he writes in Verse, and must for that reason have a more than ordinary care not to fall into Prose, and a vulgar Diction, excepting where the Nature and Humour of the Thing does necessarily require it"—

Spectator ed Donald F. Bond (5 vols Oxford 1965) v 113.
 135[1] Line 3 of textus.
 136[1] Stage directions at the beginning of the scene.
 137[1] Line 1 of textus.
 137[2] In *Paradise Lost* I Beelzebub is indeed introduced by name before Satan, but C's example is not a strong one, since Satan's torment has been described beforehand, and Satan is actually the first speaker in the poem.

138 II 1002 | I ii 65–7

HAMLET. A little more than kin, and less than kind.   [*Aside.*]
KING. How is it that the clouds still hang on you?
HAMLET. Not so, my lord; I am too much i' the sun.

[Footnote:] Mr. Farmer questions whether a quibble between *sun* and *son* be not here intended.

1002.

22 α. A little more than kin yet less than kind—Play on words[1]—either to[a] 1. exuberant activity of mind, as in Shakespear's higher Comedy. 2. Imitation of it as a fashion which has this to say for it—why is not this now better than groaning?[2]—or 3 contemptuous Exultation in minds vulgarized and overset by their success—Milton's Devils[3]—Or 4 as the language of resentment, in order to express Contempt—most common among the lower orders, & origin of Nick-names—or lastly as the language of suppressed passion, especially of hardly smothered dislike.—3 of these combine in the present instance.—and doubtless Farmer is right in supposing the equivocation carried on into too much in the *Son*.

139 II 1002 | I ii 72–5

QUEEN.   . . . all, that live, must die,
    Passing through nature to eternity.
HAMLET. Ay, madam, it is common.
QUEEN.   If it be,
    Why seems it so particular with thee?

35 α.[1] Suppression prepares for overflow—

140 II 1002 | I ii 115–20

KING. . . . And, we beseech you, bend you to remain
    Here, in the chear and comfort of our eye,
    Our chiefest courtier, cousin, and our son.

138[a] A word is missing here: perhaps "due either to" was intended

138[1] Himself a keen punster for appreciative friends, C defended Shakespeare's much-criticised use of puns on several occasions, notably in *Lects 1808–1819 (CC)* I 311–12, 379–80; and cf **38** above.

138[2] C quotes from Mercutio's approval of Romeo's word-play in *Romeo and Juliet* II iv 88–9, "Why, is not this better now than groaning for love?"

138[3] In *Paradise Lost* VI 607–27, Satan and Belial indulge in word-play as they exult over the apparent success of their artillery in the war in heaven. C also cites this passage as an example of punning that arises from "scornful Triumph exulting and insulting" in OMNIANA 3.

139[1] Line 4 of textus.

QUEEN. Let not thy mother lose her prayers, Hamlet;
I pray thee, stay with us, go not to Wittenberg.
HAMLET. I shall in all my best obey you, madam.

33. β[1] Hamlet's Silence to the long Speech of the King, & general answer to his Mother.

141 II 1002 | I ii 129–32

HAMLET. O, that this too too solid flesh would melt,
Thaw, and resolve itself into a dew!
Or that the Everlasting had not fix'd
His canon 'gainst self-slaughter!

45 β.[1] See & transcribe from MSS*. & in M[rs] Milne's Vol.[2]

142 II 1005 | I iii 107–9

POLONIUS. . . . Tender yourselves more dearly;
Or (not to crack the wind of the poor phrase)
Wronging it thus, you'll tender me a fool.

[Footnote on "wronging":] That is, if you continue to go on thus wrong.

1005. 1. 48.[1]—I suspect that "wronging" is here used much in the same sense as "wringing" or "wrenching": and that the parenthesis should ~~end~~ be extended to "thus"

Or (not to crack the wind of the poor phrase,
Wringing it thus) you'll tender me a fool.[2]

143 II 1005–6 | I iii 115–20

POLONIUS. Ay, springes to catch woodcocks. I do know,
When the blood burns, how prodigal the soul
Lends the tongue vows: These blazes, daughter,
Giving more the light than heat,—extinct in both,
Even in their promise, as it is a making,—
You must not take for fire . . .

140[1] Last line of textus.
141[1] Line 2 of textus.
141[2] For "M[rs] Milne's Vol." see **99** n 3 above. The editor of the lectures suggests that what C meant to copy here was a note written for Lect 3 of the 1813 series at Bristol: *Lects 1808–1819 (CC)* II 298 n 17.

142[1] Line 3 of textus.
142[2] The Quarto reading is "Wrong", the Folio "Roaming"; "Wronging" was Pope's proposed solution, and "Wringing" Warburton's. *Sh* (Arden) emends to "Running". The lines have usually been punctuated as C suggests.

Line 7. 2nd Column/[1]—a Spondee has, I doubt not, dropt out of the text. After "vows": insert either Gō tō! or—"Mārk yōu!["] If the latter be preferred, it might end the line.

"Lends the tongue vows.—Go to!—these Blazes, Daughter["]

or

Lends the tongue vows.—These Blazes, Daughter—mark you—[2]

N.B. Shakespear never introduces a catalectic line without intending an equivalent to the foot omitted in the pauses, or the dwelling emphasis, or the diffused retardation. I do not, however, deny, that a good actor might by employing the last mentioned, viz. the retardation or ~~draw~~ solemn knowing drawl, supply the missing Spondee with good effect. But I do not believe, that in this or the foregoing Speeches Shakespear meant to bring out the senility or weakness of Polonius's mind. In the great ever-recurring dangers and duties of Life, where ⟨to distinguish⟩ the fit objects for the application of the maxims collected ~~during~~ by the experience of a long life requires no fineness of tact—as in the admonitions to his Son and Daughter, Polonius is always made respectable—But if the Actor were capable of catching these shades in the character, the Pit and Gallery would be malcontent.—

144 II 1006 | I iv 8–12 (and continuing to line 57)

HAMLET. The king doth wake to-night, and takes his rouse,
   Keeps wassel, and the swaggering up-spring reels:
   And, as he drains his draughts of Rhenish down,
   The kettle-drum, and trumpet, thus bray out
   The triumph of his pledge.

1006.—In addition to the other excellencies of Hamlet's Speech concerning the *Wassel* Music, so finely revealing the predominant idealism, ⟨the ratiocinative meditativeness,⟩ of his character, it has the advantage of giving nature and probability to the impassioned continuity of the Speech instantly directed to the Ghost. The momentum had been given to ~~the~~ his mental Activity—the full current of the thoughts & words had set in—and the very forgetfulness, in the fervor of his Argumentation, of the purpose for which he was there, aided in preventing the Appearance from benumming the mind—Consequently, it acted as a new impulse, a sudden Stroke which increased the velocity of the body already in motion while it altered the direction.—The co-presence of Horatio, Marcel-

143[1] Line 3 of textus.
143[2] As *Sh* (Arden) observes, "The metrical deficiency of this line has given rise to many suggestions for supplying a supposed omission"—none of them ultimately satisfactory.

lus and Bernardo is most judiciously contrived—for it renders the courage of Hamlet and his impetuous eloquence perfectly intelligible/. The knowlege, the *unthought-of* consciousness, the *Sensation*, of human Auditors, of Flesh and Blood Sympathists,[1] ~~as~~ acts as a support, a stimulation *a tergo*,[2] while the *front* of the Mind, the whole Consciousness of the Speaker, is filled by the solemn Apparition. Add too, that the Apparition itself has by its frequent previous appearances been brought nearer to a Thing of this World. This accrescence[3] of Objectivity in a Ghost that yet retains all its ghostly attributes & fearful Subjectivity, is truly wonderful.

145 II 1007 | I v 92–109

HAMLET. O all you host of heaven! O earth! What else?
And shall I couple hell?—O fie!—Hold, hold, my heart:
And you, my sinews, grow not instant old,
But bear me stiffly up! Remember thee?
Ay, thou poor ghost, while memory holds a seat
In this distracted globe. Remember thee?
Yea, from the table of my memory
I'll wipe away all trivial fond records,
All saws of books, all forms, all pressures past,
That youth and observation copied there;
And thy commandment all alone shall live
Within the book and volume of my brain,
Unmix'd with baser matter: yes, by heaven.
O most pernicious woman!
O villain, villain, smiling, damned villain!
My tables,—meet it is, I set it down,
That one may smile, and smile, and be a villain:
At least, I am sure, it may be so in Denmark . . .

1007.—O all you Host of Heaven!—&c
    I remember nothing equal to this burst unless it be the first speech of Prometheus, after the exit of Vulcan & the two Afrites, in Eschylus.[1] But

---

144[1] I.e. sympathisers. *OED* attributes this coinage to C in this note.

144[2] "From behind".

144[3] Although *OED* cites C in *SM* as first using this word in the sense of "continuous growth", it also quotes this note, not as its first example, to illustrate another meaning, "something which grows on a thing

from without; an accretion".

145[1] I.e. Aeschylus *Prometheus Bound* lines 87–159, after Prometheus has been chained to the rock by order of Zeus, who has newly become ruler of heaven by patricide and usurpation. Prometheus calls on sky, winds, streams, ocean, and earth to witness his undeserved suffering. "Afrite" or

Shakespear alone could have produced the Vow of Hamlet to make his memory a blank of all maxims and generalized truths, that Observation had copied there, followed by the immediate noting down the generalized fact, that one may smile and smile and be a villain.

146 II 1009 | II i

In all things dependant on or rather made up of fine Address, the *manner* is no more or otherwise rememberable than the light motions, steps, and gestures of Youth and Health.—But this is almost every thing—no wonder therefore, if that which can be *put down by rule* in the memory should appear mere poring, maudlin-eyed Cunning, slyness blinking thro' the watry eye of superannuation. So in this admirable Scene. Polonius, who is throughout the Skeleton of his own former Skill and State-craft, hunts the trail of policy at a dead scent, supplied by the weak fever-smell in his own nostrils.—

147 II 1011 | II ii 173–82

POLONIUS. Do you know me, my lord?
HAMLET. Excellent well;
    You are a fishmonger.
POLONIUS. Not I, my lord.
HAMLET. Then I would you were so honest a man.
POLONIUS. Honest, my lord?
HAMLET. Ay, sir; to be honest, as this world goes,
    Is to be one man pick'd out of ten thousand.
POLONIUS. That's very true, my lord.
HAMLET. For if the sun breed maggots in a dead dog,
    Being a god, kissing carrion,—Have you a daughter?

50. β.[1]—i.e. You are sent to *fish* out the secret./ This is Hamlet's meaning. The purposely obscure lines—For if the Sun &c. I rather think refers to some thought in Hamlet's mannind contrasting the lovely daughter with such a tedious old fool, her Father: as *he* represents Polonius to himself.—"Why, fool as he is, he is some degrees in rank above a dead dog's carcase—and if the Sun, being a God that kisses carrion can raise life out

---

"afreet" or "efreet", meaning "evil spirit" or "demon", is a word derived from Arabic and familiarised by translations of the *Arabian Nights*: C refers to the assistants of

Hephaestos ("Vulcan") who have executed the orders of Zeus.
147[1] Textus line 3.

of a dead Dog, why may*ᵃ* good fortune, that favors fools, have raised a lovely Girl out of this dead-alive old fool.["]—²

148   II 1011, referring to 1012 | II ii 213–17

POLONIUS. . . . I will most humbly take my leave of you.

HAMLET. You cannot, sir, take from me any thing that I will more willingly part withal; except my life, except my life, except my life.

1012.40, α. The repetition of *"except my life"* is most admirable—

149   II 1012 | II ii 181–2 (in **147** textus)

HAMLET. For if the sun breeds maggots in a dead dog,
  Being a god, kissing carrion,—Have you a daughter?

[Footnote to "carrion":] Dr. Warburton's comment (which Dr. Johnson says almost sets the critic on a level with the author) on this passage is as follows: "The illative particle ["for"] shows the speaker to have been reasoning from something he had said before . . . . But this wonderful man had an art not only of acquainting the audience with what his characters *say*, but with what they *think*. The sentiment too is altogether in character; for Hamlet is perpetually moralizing, and his circumstances make this reflection very natural."

⟨1012⟩ 1, α.¹ Warburton is often led astray in his interpretations by his attention to general positions without the due Shakspearian reference to what is probably passing in the mind of his speaker, characteristic and expository of his particular character and present mood. In confirmation of my preceding note, see 1014, l. 7, β.—O Jephta, judge of Israel! what a treasure hadst thou &c²

150   II 1013 | II ii 263–5

HAMLET. Then are our beggars, bodies; and our monarchs, and outstretch'd heroes, the beggars' shadows:—Shall we to the court? for, by my fay, I cannot reason.

147*ᵃ* Negative omitted, "why may not"?

147² See COPY B **22** and n 1, and **149** below.
149¹ Line 2 of textus.
149² By "preceding note" C means **147**; his page reference leads to a later part of the same scene that confirms the sense of contrast in Hamlet's mind, registered in **147**, between "the lovely daughter" and the "tedious old fool" her father: *Hamlet* II ii 403.

7, α.[1] I do not understand this—and S. seems to have ⟨intended the⟩ meaning it not to be more than snatched at—By my fay! I cannot reason.

151   II 1015 | II ii 468–97 (the recitation of Aeneas' speech about Priam)

10, α to 22, β.

This admirable substitution of the Epic for the Dramatic, giving such a *reality* to the impassioned Dramatic Diction of Shakspear's own Dialogue, and authorized too by the actual style of the Tragedies before Shakspeare (Porrex and Ferrex, Titus Andronicus &c) is worthy of notice.[1] The fancy, that a Burlesque was intended, sinks below criticism. The lines, as *epic* narrative, are superb.[2]

152   II 1015 | II ii 502–4

I PLAYER. *But who, ah woe! had seen the mobled queen—*
HAMLET. The mobled queen?
POLONIUS. That's good; mobled queen is good.

[Footnotes on "mobled":] According to Warburton, . . . *veiled*; according to Dr. Johnson, . . . *huddled, grossly covered.*—Mr. Steevens says, . . . *led astray by a will o' the whisp*, or *ignis fatuus.*—Mr. Tollet adds, that . . . the rabble that attended the earl of Shaftesbury's partisans was first called *mobile vulgus*, and afterwards, by contraction, the *mob*; and ever since, the word *mob* has been proper English.

5, β. A mob-cap is still a word in common use for a morning cap, which conceals the whole head of hair and passes under the chin—.[1] It is nearly the same as the Night-cap—i.e. an imitation of it so as to answer the pur-

---

150[1] Textus line 1. See COPY B **22** n 3.

151[1] On the relationship between epic and dramatic, see also **33**. *Ferrex and Porrex, or Gorboduc* (1562) is by Thomas Sackville and Thomas Norton; C along with previous and contemporary scholars thought *Titus Andronicus* was for the most part not by Shakespeare (cf COPY A **94–95**).

151[2] In an earlier note (**17**, at n 2) C observes that the temporary substitution of the Player's epic mode makes the dominant tragic mode of the play to be "felt as the *real-Life* Diction". In the perpetual debate

as to whether or not the speech is a burlesque, C is a strong supporter of its seriousness.

152[1] Malone was of the opinion that the word should be "mabled" (meaning "in a slovenly head-dress"; from "mabble" or "mable", "to wrap or muffle the head"— *OED*), and Steevens noted that in Essex and Middlesex "this morning cap has always been called—a *mob*, and not a *mab*": *Sh* (Reed). *Sh* (Arden) derives it from a related verb, "mobble" or "moble" ("to muffle one's head or face"—*OED*).

pose ("I am not drest for company") and yet reconciling it with neatness and perfect purity.

Q^y etymologically connected with *Mop*?—[2]

153 II 1015 | II ii 550–62

HAMLET. . . . . O, what a rogue and peasant slave am I!
    Is it not monstrous, that this player here,
    But in a fiction, in a dream of passion,
    Could force his soul so to his own conceit,
    That, from her working, all his visage warm'd;
    Tears in his eyes, distraction in's aspect,
    A broken voice, and his whole function suiting
    With forms to his conceit? And all for nothing!
    For Hecuba!
    What's Hecuba to him, or he to Hecuba,
    That he should weep for her? What would he do,
    Had he the motive and the cue for passion,
    That I have?

55, β.[1] Here after the recapit. and charact. of Hamlet recommence the particular Criticism—as these lines contain Sh's own attestation of the truth of the Idea, I have started.—

154 II 1016 | **153** textus

5, α.[1] Turn likewise to 1028, as Ham.'s Ch. self-attested.[2]

155 II 1016 | II ii 598–603

HAMLET.   . . . The spirit, that I have seen,
    May be a devil: and the devil hath power
    To assume a pleasing shape; yea, and, perhaps,
    Out of my weakness, and my melancholy,
    (As he is very potent with such spirits)
    Abuses me to damn me . . .

25, β.[1]—Sir T. Brown These apparitions and ghosts of departed persons are not the wandering souls of men but the unquiet walks of Devils,

---

152[2] *OED* does not indicate any connection between them.
153[1] Line 1 of textus.
154[1] Line 6 of **153** textus.

154[2] I.e. Hamlet's "Ch[aracter]" is self-attested in IV iv 32 ff, "How all occasions do inform against me", etc.
155[1] Line 4 of textus.

prompting and suggesting us unto mischief, blood and villainy &c. Relig. Medici: Sect. 37 ad finem.[2]

156   II 1017 | III i 46–9

POLONIUS. . . . 'Tis too much prov'd,—that, with devotion's visage,
And pious action, we do sugar o'er
The devil himself.
KING.   O, 'tis too true! how smart
A lash that speech doth give my conscience!

22, α.[1] The O here is to be so pronounced as to be equal in effect of sound to a spondee or at least an iambic dissyllable: and the metre to be thus restored—

The devil himself. Ōh̆! it is too true!
How smart a lash, that speech doth give my Conscience.

157   II 1017 | III i 55–9

HAMLET. To be, or not to be, that is the question:—
Whether 'tis nobler in the mind to suffer
The slings and arrows of outrageous fortune;
Or to take arms against a sea of troubles,
And, by opposing, end them?

[1]33, α.

Of such universal interest, and yet ~~in~~ to which of all Shakspear's other characters could it have[a] *appropriately* given but to Hamlet? For Jaques it would have been too deep: for Iago too habitual a communion with the *heart*, that belongs or ought to belong, to all mankind.[2]

157[a] A slip for "have been"?

155[2] C quotes from Sir Thomas Browne *Religio Medici* i § 37 (6th ed 1669) 82–3—the passage not annotated, however, in BROWNE *Religio Medici* or in BROWNE *Works*: "I believe . . . that the souls of the faithful, as they leave Earth, take possession of Heaven; that those apparitions and ghosts of departed persons are not the wandring souls of men, but the unquiet walks of Devils, prompting and suggesting us unto mischief, blood, and villany, instilling, and stealing into our hearts; that the blessed spirits are not at rest in their graves, but wander sollicitous of the affairs of the world; but that those phantasms appear often, and do frequent Coemeteries, Charnel-houses, and Churches, it is because those are the dormitories of the dead, where the Devil like an insolent Champion beholds with pride the spoils and Trophies of his Victory in *Adam*."

156[1] Line 3 of textus.

157[1] Most of the notes **157–183** are published as part of C's lecture-material for 11 Feb 1819 in *Lects 1808–1819 (CC)* II 351–6.

157[2] I.e. for the melancholy Jaques in *As You Like It*, or for Iago in *Othello*.

158 II 1017 | III i 102–14

HAMLET. Ha, ha! are you honest?

OPHELIA. My lord?

HAMLET. Are you fair?

OPHELIA. What means your lordship?

HAMLET. That, if you be honest, and fair, you should admit no discourse to your beauty.

OPHELIA. Could beauty, my lord, have better commerce than with honesty?

HAMLET. Ay, truly; for the power of beauty will sooner transform honesty from what it is to a bawd, than the force of honesty can translate beauty into its likeness: this was some time a paradox, but now the time gives it proof. I did love you once.

27, β.[1]—Hamlet here discovers that he is watched, and Ophelia a Decoy.—Even this in a mood so anxious and irritable accounts for a certain harshness in him; and yet a wild upworking of Love sporting with opposites with a wilful self-tormenting Irony is perceptible throughout—ex. gr. I *did* love you—& the faults of the sex from which Oph. is so charact. free, that the freedom therefrom constitutes her Character.—Here again Shakespear's Charm of constituting female character by absences of characters, = outjuttings—[2]

159 II 1018 | III i 128–49

HAMLET. . . . Go thy ways to a nunnery. Where's your father?

OPHELIA. At home, my lord.

HAMLET. Let the doors be shut upon him . . . . If thou dost marry, I'll give thee this plague for thy dowry; Be thou as chaste as ice, as pure as snow, thou shalt not escape calumny. Get thee to a nunnery; farewell: Or, if thou wilt needs marry, marry a fool; for wise men know well enough, what monsters you make of them. . . . I say, we will have no more marriages: those that are married already, all but one, shall live; the rest shall keep as they are. To a nunnery, go.

1–25, α.[1] The dallying with the inward purpose that of one who had not brought his mind to the steady acting point—would fain *sting* the Uncle's Mind, but—to stab the body!—

158[1] Line 1 of textus.

158[2] As the editor of the lectures points out, C had anticipated this observation about Shakespeare's characterisation of women in Lect 6 of the 1813 series and in Lect 1 of the 1818–19 series: *Lects 1808–1819 (CC)* I 573, II 270 (on "the want of prominence" in women), 351 n 3.

159[1] Line 25 corresponds to the last line of textus.

160   II 1018 | III i 150–61 (Ophelia's soliloquy "O what a noble mind is here o'erthrown!")

The soliloquy of Ophelia is the perfection of Love/ so exquisitely unselfish.

161   II 1018 | III ii (Hamlet with the Players)

Scene II. one and among the happiest of Shaks' power of diversifying the scene while he is carrying on the plot.

162   II 1019 | III ii 98–106

HAMLET. . . . My lord, you play'd once i' the university, you say?
POLONIUS. That did I, my lord: and was accounted a good actor.
HAMLET. And what did you enact?
POLONIUS. I did enact Julius Caesar: I was kill'd i' the Capitol; Brutus kill'd me.
HAMLET. It was a brute part of him, to kill so capital a calf there.—

β. in any direct form to have kept Hamlet's Love for Ophelia before the Audience, would have made a breach in the unity of the interest; but yet to the thoughtful reader it is suggested by *his* spite to poor Polonius whom he cannot let rest.

163   II 1019 (p) | III ii 112–19

HAMLET. Lady, shall I lie in your lap?
OPHELIA. No, my lord.
HAMLET. I mean, my head upon your lap?
OPHELIA. Ay, my lord.
HAMLET. Do you think I meant country matters?
OPHELIA. I think nothing, my lord.
HAMLET. That's a fair thought to lie between maids' legs.

[Footnote:] Dr. Johnson thinks we must read, *Do you think I meant country* manners?*   Do you imagine that I meant to sit in your lap, with such rough gallantry as clowns use to their lasses?

* I am afraid that a painfully gross play on syllables was intended.[1]

163[1]   Both *Sh* (Reed) and *Sh* (Arden) approach "cunt" obliquely, Malone in the former saying, "What Shakespeare meant to allude to, must be too obvious to every reader, to require any explanation".

164   II 1020 | III ii 177–80

PLAYER QUEEN.   O, confound the rest!
Such love must needs be treason in my breast:
In second husband let me be accurst!
None wed the second, but who kill'd the first.

As in the first interview with the Players by *epic* verse, so here by rhyme.[1]

165   II 1022 | III ii 335–6

ROSENCRANTZ. My lord, you once did love me.
HAMLET. And do still, by these pickers and stealers.

[Footnote:] i.e. by these hands.

9, α.[1] I believe, it should be: And do *so* still—i.e. as well as I ever did.—[2]

166   II 1022, pencil | III ii 350–60

HAMLET. . . . Will you play upon this pipe? 'Tis as easy as lying: govern these ventages with your finger and thumb, give it breath with your mouth, and it will discourse most eloquent music. Look you, these are the stops.

The perfect equal to any call of the moment in Hamlet, let it only not be for a Future[1]

167   II 1022 | III ii 388–92

HAMLET.   . . . 'Tis now the very witching time of night;
When church-yards yawn, and hell itself breathes out
Contagion to this world: Now could I drink hot blood,
And do such business as the bitter day
Would quake to look on.

10, β.[1] The Utmost Hamlet arrives to, is a disposition, a mood, to do

---

164[1] Cf **151** above.
165[1] Line 2 of textus.
165[2] Cf C's comment on this line in COPY A **148**.

166[1] C's point is that Hamlet is perfectly capable of acting on the spur of the moment, but that he cannot be counted on to act according to a plan. The textus here is doubt-ful, the note being on one of the interleaved pages without a clear attachment to Column α or Column β—but this seems the more likely.

167[1] Actually the line preceding textus: "By and by is easily said. Leave me, friends."

something. What is still left undecided—while every word, he utters, tends to betray his disguise.

168 II 1022 | III iii 11–15

ROSENCRANTZ. The single and peculiar life is bound,
   With all the strength and armour of the mind,
   To keep itself from 'noyance; but much more,
   That spirit, upon whose weal depends and rest,
   The lives of many . . .

40, β.[1]—To bring all possible good out of evil, yet how characteristically is this just sentiment placed in the mouth of Rosencrantz.

169 II 1023 | III iii 27–9

POLONIUS. My lord, he's going to his mother's closet;
   Behind the arras I'll convey myself,
   To hear the process . . .

Polonius's volunteer obtrusion of himself into this business while it is appropriate to his character still letching after former importance removes all likelihood that Hamlet should suspect his presence, and prevents us from making his death injure Hamlet in our opinion.

170 II 1023 | III iii 36–72

KING. O, my offence is rank, it smells to heaven;
   It hath the primal eldest curse upon 't,
   A brother's murder! . . . What then? what rests?
   Try what repentance can: What can it not?
   O wretched state! O bosom, black as death!
   O limed soul; that, struggling to be free,
   Art more engag'd! Help, angels, make assay!
   Bow, stubborn knees! and, heart, with strings of steel,
   Be soft as sinews of the new-born babe;
   All may be well!

The King's Speech well marks the difference between Crime and Guilt of Habit. The Conscience is still admitted to Audience. Nay, even as an audible soliloquy, it is far less improbable than is supposed by such as

---

168[1] Again, the line preceding textus, the end of a speech by Guildenstern.

have watched men only in the beaten road of their feelings.—But it deserves to be dwelt on, that final "All may be well"!—a degree of Merit attributed by the self-flattering Soul to its own struggle, tho' baffled—and to the indefinite half-promise, half-command, to persevere in religious Duties. The divine Medium of the Christian Doctrine of Expiation—in the—Not what you have done, but what you *are*, must determine—Metanoia[1]

171   II 1023 | III iii 73–98

HAMLET. Now might I do it, pat, now he is praying;
And now I'll do't;—And so he goes to heaven:
And so am I reveng'd? . . .
                    And am I then reveng'd,
To take him in the purging of his soul,
When he is fit and season'd for his passage?
No . . .
                    [*The King rises*
KING. My words fly up, my thoughts remain below:
Words, without thoughts, never to heaven go.

55, α.[1] Dr Johnson's mistaking of the marks of reluctance & procrastination for impetuous horror-striking fiendishness![2] Of such importance is it to understand the *Germ* of a character. But the interval taken up by Hamlet's Speech is truly aweful! And then—"My words fly up"—O what a lesson concerning the essential difference between Wishing & Willing:[3] and the folly of all motive-mongering, while the individual Self remains.

172   II 1024 | III iv 25–30

POLONIUS. O, I am slain.
QUEEN.   O me, what hast thou done?
HAMLET. Nay, I know not:
    Is it the king?

170[1] The Greek term for "repentance" or—as C translates it in *AR* (*CC*) 132 "*the Passing into a new mind*" or "*Transmentation*". C wrote eloquently on this theme, sometimes using this word, e.g. LACUNZA **88**, LEIGHTON COPY B **32**, and *AR* as cited.
171[1] Line 3 of textus.
171[2] Johnson commented on this pas-

sage very severely, taking Hamlet to be not content with murder but wishing also to "contrive damnation" for his victim.
171[3] This distinction is closely related to the distinction between regret and remorse elsewhere, e.g. SCHELLING *Philosophische Schriften* **54**, J. SEDGWICK **57**.

QUEEN. O, what a rash and bloody deed is this!
HAMLET. A bloody deed;—almost as bad, good mother,
    As kill a king, and marry with his brother.
QUEEN. As kill a king?
HAMLET.   Ay, lady, 'twas my word.—

I confess, that Sh. has left the character of the Queen in an unpleasant perplexity—was she or was she not conscious of the fratricide.

173   II 1026 | IV ii 14–21

ROSENCRANTZ. Take you me for a spunge, my lord?
HAMLET. Ay, sir; that soaks up the king's countenance, his rewards, his
    authorities. But such officers do the king best service in the end: He
    keeps them, like an ape, in the corner of his jaw; first mouth'd, to be
    last swallow'd: When he needs what you have glean'd, it is but squeez-
    ing you, and, spunge, you shall be dry again.

Hamlet's madness is made to consist in the full utterance of all the thoughts that had past thro' his mind before—in telling home truths.—

174   II 1028 | IV v 21 ff (Ophelia's song)

The conjunction here of these two thoughts that had never subsisted in disjunction, the Love for Hamlet and her filial Love, and the guiless[a] floating on the surface of her pure imagination of the cautions so lately expressed and the fears not too delicately avowed by her Father and Brother concerning the danger to which her honor lay exposed.—. Thought and Affliction, Passion, Murder itself She turns to favor and to prettiness.[1]—This play of association is sweetly instanced in the close. "My brother shall know of it: and I thank you for your good COUNSEL."[2]

175   II 1029 | IV v 124–6

KING. . . . There's such divinity doth hedge a king,
    That treason can but peep to what it would,
    Acts little of his will . . .

25, β.[1] Proof, as indeed all else is, that Sh. never intended us to see

---

174[a] A slip for "guileless"

174[1] C quotes Laertes' observation on Ophelia's madness (IV v 188–9), substituting "Murder" for "hell".

174[2] One of Ophelia's parting lines earlier in the scene, IV v 70–1.

175[1] Line 1 of textus.

the King with Hamlet's Eyes—tho' I suspect, the Managers have long done so.

176   II 1030 | IV v 155–9

Enter Ophelia, fantastically dress'd with straws and flowers.
LAERTES. O heat, dry up my brains! tears, seven times salt,
    Burn out the sense and virtue of mine eye!—
    By heaven, thy madness shall be pay'd with weight,
    'Till our scale turn the beam. O rose of May!
    Dear maid, kind sister, sweet Ophelia!—

Shakespeare evidently wishes as much as possible to spare the character of Laertes, to break the extreme turpitude of his consent to become an Agent and Accomplice of the King's treacherous[a]—and to this end works the re-introduction of Ophelia—

177   II 1031 | IV vi 13–20

[Hamlet's letter:] *HORATIO, when thou shall have overlook'd this, give these fellows some means to the king; they have letters for him. Ere we were two days old at sea, a pirate of very warlike appointment gave us chace . . . in the grapple I boarded them: on the instant, they got clear of our ship; so I alone became their prisoner . . .*

Almost the only play of Shakespeare, in which mere accidents independent of all will form an essential part of the plot; but here how judiciously in keeping with the Character of the over-meditative Hamlet ever at last determined by accident or by a fit of passion—

178   II 1032 | IV vii 81–105

KING.   . . . Two months since,
    Here was a gentleman of Normandy,—
    I have seen myself, and serv'd against, the French,
    And they can well on horseback: but this gallant
    Had witchcraft in 't; he grew unto his seat;
    And to such wondrous doing brought his horse,
    As he had been incorps'd and demi-natur'd
    With the brave beast . . .
    He made confession of you;
    And gave you such a masterly report,

176[a] A slip for "treacherousness" or "treachery"

For art and exercise in your defence,
And for your rapier most especial,
That he cried out, 'Twould be a sight indeed,
If one could match you . . .
                              Sir, this report of his
Did Hamlet so envenom with his envy,
That he could nothing do, but wish and beg
Your sudden coming o'er, to play with him . . .

15, α¹

First awakens Laertes' Vanity by the praises of the Report—then gratifies it by the report itself—and then. "Did Hamlet so envenom with his envy.—["]

179   II 1033 | End of Act IV

And that Laertes might be excused in some degree for not cooling the Act concluding with the affecting Death of Ophelia—who does not seem like a little projection of Land into a Lake or Stream, covered with spring-flowers lay quietly reflected in the great waters but at length undermined and loosened becomes a floating Faery Isle, and after a brief vagrancy sinks almost without an eddy.

180   II 1033 | v i

The contrast between the Clowns and Hamlet as two extremes—the mockery of Logic, the traditional wit valued like [? truth] for its Antiquity, and treasured up like a Tune for use—

181   II 1035 | v i 226–42

PRIEST. Her obsequies have been as far enlarg'd
    As we have warranty: Her death was doubtful;
    And, but that great command o'ersways the order,
    She should in ground unsanctify'd have lodg'd
    'Till the last trumpet . . . .
LAERTES. Must there no more be done?
PRIEST.   No more be done;
    We should profane the service of the dead,

178¹ Line 2 of textus.

To sing a *requiem*, and such rest to her
As to peace-parted souls.
LAERTES.   Lay her i' the earth;—
And from her fair and unpolluted flesh
May violets spring!—I tell thee, churlish priest,
A ministering angel shall my sister be,
When thou liest howling.

Shall I tell the story of the fierce Methodist & my Answer?[1]

182 II 1036 | v i

Sh. seems to mean *all Hamlet's* character to be brought together before his final disappearance from the scene—his med.[1] excess in the grave-digging—his yielding to passion—his Love for Ophelia blazing out—his tendency to generalize on all occasions in the dialogue with Horatio—his fine gentlemanly manners with Osrick—

183 I 1039 | v ii 212–20

HAMLET. . . . But thou would'st not think, how ill all's here about my heart: but it is no matter.
HORATIO. Nay, good my lord,—
HAMLET. It is but foolery; but it is such a kind of gain-giving, as would, perhaps, trouble a woman.
HORATIO. If your mind dislike any thing, obey it: I will forestall their re-pair hither, and say you are not fit.
HAMLET. Not a whit, we defy augury; there is a special providence in the fall of a sparrow.

and his & Shakespear's fondness for presentiment[1]—O my prophetic Soul[2]—and his "Most generous and free from all contriving"[3] in his D Fencing-Duel—and all at last done by [? shock] & accident at the conclusion.

181[1] This is almost certainly the story C planned to use in a lecture, possibly in 1808. In the context of Methodist disapproval of the theatre, he mentions a reviewer who "pronounces it a Sin even to doubt, that Shakespear is in Hell"; to which his retort is to quote a variant of Laertes's last lines: "Churlish Priest! / A blessed angel will our sweet Shakespear be / When thou liest howling!"—*Lects 1808–1819* (*CC*) I

132–3. C used these lines again, in a similar context, in OMNIANA **28**.
182[1] For "meditative", presumably.
183[1] C comments on this quality with reference to *Romeo and Juliet* in **122** above.
183[2] Hamlet's line at I v 40, when he learns the identity of his father's murderer.
183[3] Claudius's description of Hamlet as he and Laertes plot his death: IV vii 135.

184   II [1042] (blank), and interleaf 1042, 1043 | *Othello* I i 1–7

RODERIGO. Never tell me:—I take it much unkindly,
   That thou, Iago,—who hast had my purse,
   As if the strings were thine,—should'st know of this.
IAGO. But you'll not hear me:
   If ever I did dream of such a matter, abhor me.
RODERIGO. Thou told'st me, thou didst hold him in thy hate.
IAGO. Despise me if I do not . . .

[1]Othello. Act I. Scene I.

The admirable preparation, so characteristic of Shakspeare—/ in the introduction of Roderigo as the Dupe on whom Iago first exercises his art, and in so doing displays his own character.—Roderigo, already fitted & predisposed by his own passions—without any fixed principle or strength of character,/ (The want of character and the power of the passions, like the wind loudest in empty houses, forms his character) but yet not without the moral notions and sympathies with honor, which his rank, connections had hung upon him. The very 3 first lines happily state the nature and foundation of the friendship—the purse—as well the contrast of R's intemperance of mind with Iago's coolness, the coolness of a pre-conceiving *Experimenter*.—The mere language of protestation in "If ever—abhor me.["] which fixing the associative link that ~~produces~~ determines Roderigo's continuation of complaint—in thy hate—elicits a true feeling of Iago's—the dread of contempt fatal to those who encourage in themselves & have their keenest pleasure in the feeling & expression of contempt in others.—His high self-opinion—& how a wicked man employs his real feelings & as well as assumes those most alien from his own, as instruments of his purposes.—

   The necessity of Tyrwhytt's alteration of "wife" into life[2]—as contempt for whatever did not display power, & that intellectual—What follows, let the Reader *feel*—how by & thro' the glass of ~~one~~ two passions, disappointed Passion & Envy, the very vices, he is complaining of, are made to act upon him as so many excellences—& the more appropriately, because Cunning is always admired & wished for by minds conscious of inward weakness—and yet it is but *half*—it acts like music on an inattentive auditor, *swelling* the thoughts which prevented him from listening to it. Roderigo—turns off to Othello—& here comes the one if not

184[1] The notes from **184** to **202** are all published as part of C's lecture-material for 21 Jan 1819 in *Lects 1808–1819 (CC)* II 313–19.

184[2] *Othello* I i 21 reads "A fellow almost damn'd in a fair wife", but a footnote in this edition proposes Tyrwhitt's emendation of "wife" to "life" with the rationale recorded by C in his discussion of this line in COPY A **155**.

the only justification of the Blackamoor Othello, namely as a Negro—who is not a *Moor* at all—.³ Even if we supposed this an uninterrupted Tradition of the Theatre, and that Sh. himself from want of scenes & the experience that nothing could be made too *marked* for the senses of his Audience—would this prove aught concerning his own intentions as a Poet for all ages?—Can we suppose him so utterly ignorant as to make a barbarous *Negro* plead Royal Birth—Were Negros then known but as Slaves—on the contrary were not the Moors the Warriors &c— ⸰

Iago's Speech to Brabantio implies merely that he was *a Moor*—i.e. black.⁴ Tho' I think the rivalry of Roderigo sufficient to account for his wilful confusion of Moor & Negro—yet tho' compelled to give this up, I should yet think it only adapted for the then *Acting*—& should complain of an enormity built only on one single word—in direct contradiction to Iago's "*Barbary* horse"⁵—If we can in good earnest believe Sh. ignorant of the distinction, still why take one against 10—as Oth. cannot be *both*—?—

"This accident is not unlike my dream"⁶—the old *careful* Senator who caught careless transfers his *Caution* to his *Dreaming* Power at least—

The forced praise of Othello—followed by the bitter hatred— — Iago—

and Brabantio's recurrence to philtres, so prepared by the Dream—& both so prepared for the carrying on of the Plot by the arraignment of Othello on *this ground*—/

185   II [1042] | I ii

Scene II

" 'Tis better as it is.—" "not easily wrought"¹ above all low passions—"unbonnetted" without the symbol of a petitioning inferior.²—*By Janus*—In Iago's mouth—³

184³ C had made a point of this distinction before, in 1813, when according to a newspaper report of his lecture, "Mr. C. ridiculed the idea of making Othello a negro, he was a gallant Moor, of royal blood, combining a high sense of Spanish and Italian feeling . . .": *Lects 1808–1819* (*CC*) I 555 and n 25. The "one if not the only justification of the Blackamoor Othello", as far as C is concerned, is Roderigo's remark at I i 66–7, referring to Othello, "What a full fortune does the thick-lips owe, / If he can carry 't thus!"

184⁴ Iago crudely tells Brabantio that "an old black ram / Is tupping your white

ewe" (I i 88–9).

184⁵ *Othello* I i 111–12, "you'll have your daughter covered with a Barbary horse"—i.e. an Arab (or Berber) horse.

184⁶ Brabantio's line at I i 142.

185¹ I.e. Othello's mild response in I ii 6, " 'Tis better as it is", shows him "not easily wrought" (C abridging *Othello* v ii 345, "Of one not easily jealous, but, being wrought . . .").

185² C discusses "unbonnetted" also in COPY A **156** (and see n 1).

185³ Janus is the two-faced god, ironically appropriate for Iago.

186　ii 1050 | i iii 292–5

BRABANTIO. Look to her, Moor; have a quick eye to see;
　　She has deceiv'd her father, and may thee.
OTHELLO. My life upon her faith.—Honest Iago,
　　My Desdemona must I leave to thee . . .

30, α.[1] In real life how do we look back to little speeches, either as pre-sentimental or most contrasted with an affecting Event. Shak. as secure of being read over and over, of becoming a family friend, how he provides this for *his readers*—& leaves it to them.

187　ii 1050 | i iii 319–26, 334–5

IAGO. Virtue? a fig! 'tis in ourselves, that we are thus, or thus. Our bodies are our gardens; to the which, our wills are gardeners: so that if we will plant nettles, or sow lettuce; set hyssop, and weed up thyme; supply it with one gender of herbs, or distract it with many; either have it sterile with idleness, or manur'd with industry; why, the power and corrigible authority of this lies in our wills. . . . [Love] is merely a lust of the blood, and a permission of the will.

5, β.[1]—Iago's passionless character, all *will* in Intellect—therefore a bold partizan here of a truth, but yet of a truth converted into falsehood by absence of all the modifications by the frail nature of man—and the LAST SENTIMENT—there lies the Iago-ism of how many! And the repetition, Go, make money![2]—a pride in it, of an anticipated Dupe stronger than the love of Lucre—

188　ii 1050–1 | i iii 381–3

IAGO. Go to; farewell; put money enough in your purse.
　　Thus do I ever make my fool my purse . . .

12, α.[1] The triumph! Again, *put money* after the effect has been fully produced.—The last Speech, the motive-hunting of motiveless Malignity—how awful! In itself fiendish—while yet he was allowed to bear the divine image, too fiendish for his own steady View.—A being next to Devil—only *not* quite Devil—& this Shakespear has attempted—executed—without disgust, without Scandal!—[a]

188[a] Here C has written "(Here turn back to the blank fronting the first page)—": that is, ii 1044 and **189** following

186[1] Line 30 in C's text is the *exeunt* stage direction preceding the textus.
187[1] From a point near the beginning of textus, "the which . . . if we".

187[2] I.e. **189** textus, in Iago's next speech.
188[1] Line 1 of textus.

189   II 1043–4, referring to II 1051 | End of Act I

(After the first act)

Dʳ Johnson has remarked that little or nothing is wanted to render the Othello a regular Tragedy but to have opened the play with the arrival of Othello in Cyprus, and to have thrown the preceding Act into the form of narration.[1] Here then is the place to determine, whether such a change would or would not be an improvement, nay (to throw down the glove with a full challenge) whether or not the Tragedy would by such an arrangement become *more regular*, i.e. more consonant with the rules dictated by universal reason or the true Common Sense of mankind in its application to the particular case. *ᵃ*For surely we may safely leave ~~to~~ it to Common sense ~~the~~ whether to reply to or laugh at such a remark—as for instance—Suppose a man ~~were~~ had described a rhomboid or parallelogram, and a Critic were with great gravity to observe—if the lines had only been in true right-angles, or if the horizontal parallels had been but of the same length as the two perpendicular parallels that form the sides, the diagram would have been according to the strictest rules of Geometry.*ᵇ* For ⟨in all acts of judgement⟩ it never*ᶜ* be too often recollected and scarcely too often repeated, that rules are means to ends, consequently, that the End must be determined and understood before it can be known what the rules are or ought to be. Now ~~in~~ from a certain species of Drama, proposing to itself the accomplishment of certain Ends, these partly arising from the Idea of the Species itself but in part likewise forced upon the Dramatist by accidental circumstances beyond his power to remove or controll three rules have been abstracted—in other words, the means most conducive to the attainment of the proposed ends have been generalized and prescribed under the names of the three Unities, the unity of Time, the unity of Place, and the unity of Action, which last would perhaps have been appropriately as well as more intelligibly entitled the Unity of Interest.[2] With this the present Question has no immediate concern. ⟨In fact ~~the~~ its conjunction with the two former is a mere delusion of *words*.⟩ It is not properly *a rule*; but in itself the great End, not only of

189[a–b] C has drawn a wiggly line in the margin beside this passage, and written beside it, vertically: "N.B. *Very awkwardly expressed.*"

189[c] Perhaps a slip for "can never" or "never can"

189[1] This well-known comment is not included in the notes to this edition or in the other editions annotated by C, but it is included in *Sh* (Reed) among the general notes at the end of the play (XIX 527) and in other editions of the period.

189[2] The related issues of dramatic illusion and the status of the unities had been staples of 18th-century criticism of Shakespeare. C had himself tackled the unities in earlier lectures in 1811, 1813, and 1818: *Lects 1808–1819* (*CC*) I 226–7, 518, II 265–7; and cf "unity of interest" in his notes on *Romeo and Juliet* in **100** above.

the Drama but of the Epic, Lyric, even to the Candle-flame Cone of an Epigram—not only of Poetry but of Poesy in general, as the proper generic term inclusive of all the fine Arts, as its Species. But of the unities of Time and Place which alone are entitled to the name of Rules, the history of their origin will be their best criterion.—Chorus—you may take people to a place, but only by a palpable equivoque can you bring Birnam Wood to Macbeth at Dunsinane.[3] The same in a less degree as to the unity of Time—the positive fact, not for a moment removed from the Senses, the presence, of I mean, of the very same persons is a continued measure of Time—and tho' the imagination may supersede perception, yet it must be granted an imperfection (tho' even here how easily do we not tolerate it?) to place the two in broad contradiction to each other./ Yet—dark scenes—*asides*—&c.—.[4] But in truth it is a mere accident of Terms in the first place—(the Trilogy = Acts)[5]—and notwithstanding this, the strange contrivances as to place, as in THE FROGS[6]—and there is no lack of instances in the Greek Tragedies—the allowance extorted of 24 hours—as if perception once violated, it was more difficult to imagine 3 hours 3 years, or a whole day & night.—Fine instance in Eschylus—Agamemnon.[7]

The danger of introducing into a situation of great interest one for whom you had no previous Interest— φρςφρρ Ιωαν.[8]

189[3] This rather cryptic point was treated more expansively in a lecture of 1811, where C as here compares Shakespearean plays to classical Greek drama (*Lects 1808–1819—CC*—I 226): "As the Chorus was always on the stage, there was no dropping of curtains—the same men could not be at the same time at Thebes & at Rome." Bringing "Birnam Wood to . . . Dunsinane" is an allusion to *Macbeth* V v 30–7.

189[4] These are examples of other artificial conventions of the theatre that audiences accept without question.

189[5] Cf the expansion of this point in *Lects 1808–1819* (*CC*) I 518–19, where C represents the Greek trilogies ("three plays . . . performed in one day") as equivalent to a modern tragedy, and imagines the *Oresteia* as divided into acts.

189[6] Aristophanes' play *The Frogs* involves travel between this world and the underworld, violating the supposed rule of unity of place.

189[7] I.e. if an action occupying a single day were considered acceptable with regard to unity of time (as it was generally agreed to be, and as the action of *Othello* would be but for the events of the first act, in Venice), then any time-scheme other than the strict duration of the performance should be just as acceptable. In the *Agamemnon*, the first play in the Oresteian trilogy, Agamemnon arrives on stage shortly after a watchman reports sighting the beacon, on the opposite shore, that announces the fall of Troy. As C says, using the same illustration in 1813, "he must have passed over from Troy in less than 15 minutes": *Lects 1808–1819* (*CC*) I 518.

189[8] The Greek may be transliterated "phrsphrr Jōan" or "phrstphrr Jōan". The second word is the Greek for "John" as in NT, but the first, not a Greek word but a cipher, is unexplained: *Lects 1808-1819* (*CC*) II 317 speculates that C might mean John Thelwall. For "Philosopher John"?

190   II 1051

Act II.

Confirmation of my reason—in how many ways is not Othello made, first, our acquaintance—then friend—then object of anxiety—before the deep interest is to be approached—so the storm &c—

191   II 1052 | II i 60–5

MONTANO. But, good lieutenant, is your general wiv'd?
CASSIO. Most fortunately: he hath atchiev'd a maid
    That paragons description, and wild fame;
    One that excels the quirks of blazoning pens,
    And, in the essential vesture of creation,
    Does bear all excellency.

15, α.[1] Cassio's warm-hearted yet perfectly disengaged praise of Desdemona—& sympathy with the "most fortunately" wived Othello—& yet an enthusiastic *Admirer*, almost Worshipper, of Desdemona.—Again, I must touch the detestable code that excellence can not be loved in *any* form/ ~~but~~ that because it is female, it must needs be selfish—. The Venus de Medici/—[2]

192   II 1052 | II i 74–7

CASSIO. She that I spake of, our great captain's captain,
    Left in the conduct of the bold Iago;
    Whose footing here anticipates our thoughts,
    A se'nnight's speed . . .

30, α.[1] (N.b. It is Othello's *honest*,[2] Cassio's *bold* Iago—& Cassio's full-guiless[a]-hearted Wishes!—But again the exquisite Circumstance of kissing Iago's Wife—as if ~~la.~~ it ought to be impossible that the dullest Auditor should not feel Cassio's religious Awe of Desdemona's purity—

192[a] For "guileless", as in **174** above

191[1] Line 5 of textus.
191[2] C may have more in mind, in citing the example of a famous statue representing an ideal of female beauty, than the possibility of separating admiration from lust. He used the same example in the 1814 "Essays on Genial Criticism" to suggest the possi-

bility of an absolute standard independent of all individual circumstances of time or place: *SW & F (CC)* 364.
192[1] Line 2 of textus.
192[2] Othello's habitual epithet for Iago, as in **196** textus.

Say, something a fair moral Critic ought to do on the sneers which a proud bad intellect feels towards woman, & expresses to a wife—[3]

The struggle of courtesy in Desdemona to abstract her attention—

193   II 1053 | II i 167–70

IAGO. He takes her by the palm: Ay, well said, whisper: with as little a web as this, will I ensnare as great a fly as Cassio. Ay, smile upon her, do; I will gyve thee in thine own courtship . . .

25, α.[1] O excellent. The importance given to fertile trifles, made fertile by the villainy of the observer—

194   II 1053 | II i 221–45

IAGO. Lay thy finger—thus, and let thy soul be instructed. Mark me with what violence she first lov'd the Moor, but for bragging, and telling her fantastical lies: And will she love him still for prating? let not thy discreet heart think it. Her eye must be fed . . . . Now, sir, this granted . . . who stand so eminently in the degree of this fortune, as Cassio does? . . . Why, none; why, none: A slippery and subtle knave; a finder out of occasions; that has an eye can stamp and counterfeit advantages, though true advantage never present itself: A devilish knave!

30–55—Iago's Ɒ rehearsing on the Dupe Roderigo his intentions on Othello—

195   II 1054 | II i 291–9

IAGO.   . . . Now I do love her too;
    Not out of absolute lust, (though, peradventure,
    I stand accountant for as great a sin)
    But partly led to diet my revenge,
    For that I do suspect the lusty Moor
    Hath leap'd into my seat: The thought whereof
    Doth, like a poisonous mineral, gnaw my inwards:
    And nothing can or shall content my soul,
    'Till I am even with him, wife for wife . . .

192[3] Iago speaks insultingly of his wife to her face, later in this scene (II i 100 ff). In the 1813 lectures C had noted with reference to this speech, "Surely a high compliment to Women that all the sarcasms on them Shakespear has put in the mouth of villains, like Iago": *Lects 1808–1819 (CC)* I 553.

193[1] Just after the beginning of the textus, "well said . . . as this"—i.e. C draws attention to the image of the web.

50, α.[1] The thought at first by his own confession a mere suspicion—now ripening—Tho' perhaps Shak. *compromised*

196   II 1054 | II iii 4–6

CASSIO. Iago hath direction what to do;
But notwithstanding, with my personal eye
Will I look to't.
OTHELLO.   Iago is most honest . . .

Oth. Iago is most honest—/ here perhaps the time for ~~Iago's~~ Othello's *not* jealous character—& the proofs—[1]

197   II 1057 | II iii 246–9

OTHELLO.   I know, Iago,
Thy honesty and love doth mince this matter,
Making it light to Cassio:—Cassio, I love thee;
But never more be officer of mine.—

Thy *Honesty* & Love—

198   II 1058 | II iii 336–9

IAGO. And what's he then, that says—I play the villain?
When this advice is free I give, and honest,
Probal to thinking, and (indeed) the course
To win the Moor again?

15.[1] Not absolute fiend—at least, he wishes to think himself so[2]

199   II 1059 | III iii 19–23

DESDEMONA. Do not doubt that; before Aemilia here,
I give thee warrant of thy place: assure thee,
If I do vow a friendship, I'll perform it
To the last article: my lord shall never rest;
I'll watch him tame, and talk him out of patience . . .

20, β.[1]
The overzeal of Innocence in Desdemona

195[1] Line 4 of textus.
196[1] This was the paradox C repeated over the years in his lectures about *Othello*, as e.g. in 1812, when he was reported as having said that Othello was "of too noble a nature to be jealous; and that he was deceived by a man of profound wisdom, but of the deepest subtlety and of the most malignant disposition": *Lects 1808–1819 (CC)* I 471, cf I 554.
198[1] Line 3 of textus.
198[2] I.e. wishes to think himself "not absolute fiend".
199[1] Line 2 of textus.

200   II 1061 | III iii 213–17

OTHELLO.   I am bound to thee forever.
IAGO. I see, this hath a little dash'd your spirits.
OTHELLO. Not a jot, not a jot.
IAGO.   Trust me, I fear it has.
  I hope, you will consider, what is spoke
  Comes from my love . . .

Not a jot, not a jot

201   II 1062 | III iii 277–81

OTHELLO.   . . . Desdemona comes:
  If she be false, O, then heaven mocks itself!—
  I'll not believe it.
DESDEMONA.   How now, my dear Othello?
  Your dinner, and the generous islanders
  By you invited, do attend your presence.

20, β¹
  Divine! the effect of innocence & the better genius

202   II 1076 | v ii 20–8

OTHELLO.   . . . I must weep,
  But they are cruel tears: This sorrow's heavenly;
  It strikes, where it doth love.—She wakes—
DESDEMONA. Who's there? Othello?
OTHELLO.   Ay, Desdemona.
DESDEMONA. Will you come to bed, my lord?
OTHELLO. Have you pray'd to-night, Desdemona?
DESDEMONA.   Ay, my lord.
OTHELLO. If you bethink yourself of any crime,
  Unreconcil'd as yet to heaven and grace,
  Solicit for it straight.

Is this Jealousy?¹

201¹ This line (omitted from textus) is   Desdemona.
the stage direction for the entrance of   **202**¹ See **196** n 1.

Copy E

Lost Book

The Plays of William Shakespeare, from the correct edition of Isaac Reed, Esq. 12 vols. London 1809. 8°.

Not located; marginalia not recorded. In *CN* III 4486, C appears to refer to an annotated copy of this edition, in which he read *Pericles* (not included in the 1807 edition, COPY D, which is also referred to in the notebook entry). Cf *Lects 1808–1819 (CC)* II 373 and n 3.

CONTENTS. I 1–24 Rowe's "Life" of Shakespeare; 25–88 Johnson's "Preface"; 89–152 Farmer's "Essay on the Learning of Shakespeare"; [1]–[81] *Tempest*; [82]–163 *Two Gentlemen*; II [1]–79 *Midsummer-Night's Dream*; [81]–181 *Merry Wives*; [183]–272 *Twelfth Night*; [273]–366 *Much Ado*; III [1]–99 *Measure for Measure*; [101]–98 *Love's Labour's Lost*; [199]–293 *Merchant of Venice*; IV [1]–96 *As You Like It*; [97]–199 *All's Well*; [201]–99 *Taming of the Shrew*; V [1]–116 *Winter's Tale*; [117]–208 *Macbeth*; [209]–302 *King John*; VI [1]–100 *Richard II*; [101]–207 *1 Henry IV*; [209]–323 *2 Henry IV*; VII [1]–116 *Henry V*; [117]–216 *1 Henry VI*; [217]–332 *2 Henry VI*; VIII [1]–110 *3 Henry VI*; [111]–242 *Richard III*; [243]–[358] *Henry VIII*; IX [1]–126 *Troilus and Cressida*; [127]–258 *Coriolanus*; [259]–351 *Julius Caesar*; X [1]–127 *Antony and Cleopatra*; [129]–251 *King Lear*; [253]–391 *Hamlet*; XI [1]–128 *Cymbeline*; [129]–218 *Timon of Athens*; [219]–342 *Othello*; XII [1]–114 *Romeo and Juliet*; [115]–181 *Comedy of Errors*; [183]–277 *Titus Andronicus*; [279]–373 *Pericles*.

Copy F

Lost Book

The Plays of William Shakspeare, accurately printed from the text of the corrected copy left by the late George Steevens, Esq. With glossarial notes, and a sketch of the life of Shakspeare. 8 vols. London 1811. [*Probably* this edition, in which Vol VIII contains *Lear, Romeo and Juliet, Hamlet*, and *Othello*.] 12°.

Not located; marginalia not recorded. "Mrs Milne's" Shakespeare referred to in COPY D **99** and n 3, **141** and n 2.

CONTENTS. I v–xv "Sketch of the Life of Shakspeare"; [1]–74 *Tempest*; [75]–147 *Two Gentlemen*; [149]–243 *Merry Wives*; [245]–328 *Twelfth Night*; [329]–422 *Measure for Measure*; II [1]–86 *Much Ado*; [87]–157 *Midsummer-Night's Dream*; [159]–249 *Love's Labour's Lost*; [251]–335 *Merchant of Venice*; [337]–426 *As You Like It*; III [1]–101 *All's Well*; [103]–93 *Taming of the Shrew*; [195]–299 *Winter's Tale*; [301]–63 *Comedy of Errors*; [365]–451 *Macbeth*; IV [1]–88 *King John*; [89]–184 *Richard II*; [185]–286 *1 Henry IV*; [287]–398 *2 Henry IV*; [399]–509 *Henry V*; V [1]–98 *1 Henry VI*; [99]–208 *2 Henry VI*; [209]–317 *3 Henry VI*; [319]–444 *Richard III*; VI [1]–109 *Henry VIII*; [111]–228 *Troilus and Cressida*; [229]–315 *Timon of Athens*; [317]–441 *Coriolanus*; VII [1]–87 *Julius Caesar*; [89]–211 *Antony and Cleopatra*; [213]–334 *Cymbeline*; [335]–419 *Titus Andronicus*; [421]–504 *Pericles*; VIII [1]–124 *King Lear*; [125]–232 *Romeo and Juliet*; [233]–367 *Hamlet*; [369]–486 *Othello*.